The Comparative Constitutional Foundations of Private-Public Arbitration

The Comparative Constitutional Foundations of Private-Public Arbitration

Edited by
STEPHAN W. SCHILL
Professor of International and Economic Law and Governance, University of Amsterdam, The Netherlands

OXFORD
UNIVERSITY PRESS

OXFORD
UNIVERSITY PRESS

Great Clarendon Street, Oxford, OX2 6DP,
United Kingdom

Oxford University Press is a department of the University of Oxford.
It furthers the University's objective of excellence in research, scholarship,
and education by publishing worldwide. Oxford is a registered trade mark of
Oxford University Press in the UK and in certain other countries.

Published in the United States of America by Oxford University Press
198 Madison Avenue, New York, NY 10016, United States of America.

British Library Cataloguing in Publication Data
Data available

Library of Congress Control Number: 2024951960

ISBN 9780198876687

DOI: 10.1093/9780191987960.001.0001

Printed and bound by
CPI Group (UK) Ltd., Croydon, CR0 4YY

MIX
Paper | Supporting
responsible forestry
FSC® C013604
FSC
www.fsc.org

The manufacturer's authorised representative in the EU for product safety is Oxford University Press España S.A. of El Parque Empresarial San Fernando de Henares, Avenida de Castilla, 2 – 28830 Madrid (www.oup.es/en or product.safety@oup.com). OUP España S.A. also acts as importer into Spain of products made by the manufacturer.

Preface and Acknowledgements

The present book engages with the increasingly important phenomenon of arbitrations between private and public actors and puts the concerns center stage that this mode of settling private-public disputes outside of domestic courts raises for the protection of public interests and core principles of constitutional law—specifically the principles of democracy, the rule of law, and the protection of fundamental rights. These concerns are all the more important as private-public arbitration, as a structure, is not limited to settling individual disputes, but increasingly functions as part of a system of transnational governance, in which arbitrators exercise significant authority in reviewing the legality of conduct of private and public actors and in contributing, with transnational legal effects, to the further development of the law governing private-public relations.

The book approaches the analysis of private-public arbitration and the concerns this phenomenon raises for the protection of the public interest and core constitutional principles from a comparative law angle, featuring 20 chapters that deal with almost 40 jurisdictions from different corners of the world. These chapters, which have been guided by a questionnaire reproduced in the book's annex, explore how domestic legal systems approach the involvement of public entities as parties to arbitration agreements and arbitration proceedings, to which extent the constitutional legal frameworks involved problematize private-public arbitration as a constitutional concern, and how domestic legal systems ensure that private-public arbitration develops in line with, and does not undermine, the public interest.

This approach provides a basis for developing and distilling what the book calls the comparative constitutional foundations of private-public arbitration, that is, the idea that a cross-jurisdictional analysis can provide insights into the constitutional contours that are able to legitimize, but also provide limits for, the use of private-public arbitration. These foundations help conceptualize the tensions the operation of private-public arbitration raises with core principles of constitutional law and offer guidance on how domestic legal systems can ensure that the public interest and principles of constitutional governance are not compromised when the settlement of private-public disputes moves from domestic courts to arbitral tribunals.

The project has been of unusually long gestation. It started with an authors' workshop held on 21 and 22 November 2014 at the Max Planck Institute for Comparative Public Law and International Law in Heidelberg, where several of the chapters now published have been presented in draft form. The length it took for this book to see the light of day after that initial workshop was mainly due to the project's original ambitions, which went much beyond what is now published. Originally, chapters on a much larger number of jurisdictions had been commissioned, including Brazil, Canada, Chile, Colombia, Ecuador, Venezuela, Egypt, Nigeria, the Organisation for the Harmonisation of Corporate Law in Africa (OHADA, for its acronym of the

French Organisation pour l'harmonisation en Afrique du droit des affaires), Italy, the Russian Federation, Sweden, Switzerland, Turkey, India, Japan, and the countries of the Association of Southeast Asian Nations (ASEAN). For various reasons, these chapters, while they ultimately did not materialize, required adjustments of the project and caused considerable delay. This notwithstanding, the comparative basis of what now appears in this book goes much beyond any previous publication on the topic and will, it is hoped, stimulate further comparative research on private-public arbitration and enrich the discussions about practical questions in, as well as the legitimacy of, the field.

Against this background, I am grateful to all authors who have continued to believe in the successful outcome of this book project, who have been incredibly patient, and who, partly, have engaged in repeated updates of their chapters. I am equally grateful to a number of people whose support I was able to rely on during the book's genesis, both at the Max Planck Institute for Comparative Public Law and International Law, and later at the University of Amsterdam. Thanks are due to Katrine R. Tvede and Devin Bray who supported the editorial process during the first years by commenting on and editing a large number of draft chapters. Nadine Berger proved indispensable in finalizing the manuscript; she brought the reference systems in the chapters into shape and prepared the book's tables.

Funding for this book and the work it involved came from a European Research Council-funded Starting Grant on "Transnational Private-Public Arbitration as Global Regulatory Governance: Charting and Codifying the Lex Mercatoria Publica" (*LexMercPub*, Grant agreement no. 313355), whose support I gratefully acknowledge.

Finally, my thanks are due to those involved on the side of the publisher in the process. At Oxford University Press, Merel Alstein, Emma Endean-Mills, James Baird, Nicole Leyland, Jack McNichol, Luise F. Wilde, Charlotte Holloway, and Mirza Rizwaan Ahmad accompanied the book at different stages of the process with unfailing professionalism and patience. Reyman Joseph of Newgen KnowledgeWorks and Alan O'Dowd did an excellent job at copy-editing and funneling the book through production.

Stephan W. Schill
January 2025

Contents

List of Contributors xi
Table of Cases xiii
Table of Treaties, Legislation, and Related Instruments xxxix

INTRODUCTION

1. The Comparative Constitutional Foundations of Private-Public Arbitration: An Introduction 3
Stephan W. Schill

PART I. PRIVATE-PUBLIC ARBITRATION IN EUROPE

2. Private-Public Arbitration in English Law: The Splendid Isolation of Arbitration from Public Law 37
Stavros Brekoulakis and Margaret Devaney

3. The Private-Public Divide and Its Influence over French Arbitration Law: Tradition and Transition 67
Florian Grisel

4. Eroding the Rule of Law through Private-Public Arbitration? Constitutionalization of Private-Public Arbitration in the German Legal System 92
Stephan W. Schill and Nadine Berger

5. Private-Public Arbitration in Spain: Legislative Timidity in the Shadow of the Constitution 131
Victor Ferreres Comella and Pol Fontboté Pradilla

6. Private-Public Arbitration under Greek Law: A (Nearly Complete) Public Law Paradigm 158
Nikolaos Askotiris

7. Can a State Swim against the Tide? Hungarian Perspectives on Public-Private Arbitration 184
Csongor István Nagy

8. Protection of the Public Interest in Private-Public Arbitration in the Baltic States 203
Eglė Zemlytė, Tadas Varapnickas, Inga Kačevska, Aleksandrs Fillers, Karin Sein, and Pirkka-Marja Põldvere

PART II. PRIVATE-PUBLIC ARBITRATION IN THE AMERICAS

9. Whither Leviathan? The Seepage of Constitutional Law into Public-Private Arbitration in the United States 233
Peter B. Rutledge

10. The Extrinsic Factors of World Trade that Galvanized Mexican Public-Private Arbitration during the Pre-NAFTA Years and the Evolution of Safeguards for the Public Interest 252
Orlando Federico Cabrera Colorado and Andrea Orta González Sicilia

11. Reconciling Arbitral and Constitutional Governance: The Critical Role of the (Caribbean) Courts 287
Conway Blake

12. The Legitimacy of Private-Public Arbitration in Argentina and Its Slight, but Yet Strong Differences with Private-Private Arbitration 320
Diego P. Fernández Arroyo, Francisco A. Amallo, and Ezequiel H. Vetulli

PART III. PRIVATE-PUBLIC ARBITRATION IN ASIA, AFRICA, AND AUSTRALIA

13. Public-Private Arbitration in the Iranian Legal System: The Intersection of Preferential Rights and Constitutional Constraints on Arbitration 355
Jamal Seifi and Kamal Javadi

14. The Attorney General as Guardian of the Public Interest and the Evolution of Private-Public Arbitration in Israel 391
Tamar Meshel

15. Living on the Edge of Judicial Review: The Law and Practice of Private-Public Arbitration in Pakistan 415
Ahmad Ghouri

16. China's Bifurcated Attitudes towards Private-Public Arbitration 450
Manjiao Chi

17. Public Policy Dimensions of Public-Private Arbitration: Recent Development and New Systemic Awareness in Korea 467
Jaemin Lee

18. The Constitutional and Public Interest Foundations of Public-Private Arbitration in Ghana 495
Dominic Npoanlari Dagbanja

19. The Dichotomy of Arbitration with the State in South Africa 529
Engela C. Schlemmer

20. Private-Public Arbitration in Australia: Public Law Concerns, Private Law Responses 562
Caroline Henckels

Annex: Author Questionnaire 585

Contributors

Francisco A. Amallo is Partner, Martínez de Hoz & Rueda, Buenos Aires, Argentina

Nikolaos Askotiris is Partner, Karatzas and Partners, Athens, Greece

Nadine Berger is PhD Candidate, Amsterdam Center for International Law, University of Amsterdam, Netherlands

Conway Blake is Partner, International Dispute Resolution, Debevoise & Plimpton LLP, London, United Kingdom

Stavros Brekoulakis is Michael & Laura Hwang Professor in International Arbitration, National University of Singapore, Singapore

Manjiao Chi is Professor, School of Law, University of International Business and Economics, Beijing, China

Dominic Npoanlari Dagbanja is Associate Professor of International Economic Law, Curtin University Law School, Perth, Australia; and Research Fellow, African Procurement Law Unit, Department of Mercantile Law, Stellenbosch University, South Africa

Orlando Federico Cabrera Colorado is Senior Associate, Hogan Lovells, Mexico City, Mexico

Margaret Devaney is Manager, Policy and Legal Department, Financial Services Regulatory Authority, Abu Dhabi Global Market, Abu Dhabi, United Arab Emirates

Diego P. Fernández Arroyo is Full Professor and Director of the LLM in Transnational Arbitration and Dispute Settlement, Sciences Po, Paris, France

Victor Ferreres Comella is Professor of Constitutional Law, Pompeu Fabra University, Spain

Aleksandrs Fillers is Associate Professor, Riga Graduate School of Law, Riga, Latvia, and Affiliated Member, Faculty of Law, University of Antwerp, Antwerp, Belgium

Pol Fontboté Pradilla is Part-time Lecturer of Constitutional Law, Universitat Pompeu Fabra, Barcelona, Spain

Ahmad Ghouri is Associate Professor in Commercial Law, School of Law, Politics and Sociology, University of Sussex, United Kingdom

Florian Grisel is Associate Research Professor, Université de Strasbourg, CNRS, SAGE UMR 7363, Strasbourg, France

Caroline Henckels is Associate Professor, Faculty of Law, Monash University, Australia

Kamal Javadi is Legal Adviser, Iran-United States Claims Tribunal, The Hague, Netherlands

Inga Kačevska is Associate Professor, Faculty of Law, University of Latvia, Riga, Latvia, and Partner, Law Office of Inga Kačevska, Riga, Latvia

Jaemin Lee is Professor of Law, School of Law, Seoul National University, Seoul, Republic of Korea

Tamar Meshel is Associate Professor and CN Professor of International Trade, University of Alberta Faculty of Law, Canada

Csongor István Nagy is Professor of Law, University of Galway, Ireland and University of Szeged, Hungary; and Research Professor, HUN-REN Center for Social Sciences, Hungary

Andrea Orta González Sicilia is Founding Partner, Orta Gonzalez Sicilia Abogados, SC, Mexico

Pirkka-Marja Põldvere is Partner, LEADELL Pilv Law Office, Tallinn, Estonia

Peter B. Rutledge is Dean and Talmadge Professor of Law, University of Georgia School of Law, Athens, United States

Stephan W. Schill is Professor of International and Economic Law and Governance, University of Amsterdam, Amsterdam, Netherlands

Engela C. Schlemmer is Professor of Law, University of the Witwatersrand, Johannesburg, South Africa

Jamal Seifi is Judge, Iran-United States Claims Tribunal, The Hague, Netherlands

Karin Sein is Professor of Civil Law, University of Tartu, School of Law, Tartu, Estonia

Tadas Varapnickas is Senior Lecturer, Faculty of Law, Department of Private Law, Vilnius University, Vilnius, Lithuania

Ezequiel H. Vetulli is an International Arbitration Practitioner, New York City, New York, United States

Eglė Zemlytė is Assistant Professor, Faculty of Law, Department of Private Law, Vilnius University, Vilnius, Lithuania

Table of Cases

I. INTERNATIONAL COURTS

Permanent Court of International Justice

The Losinger & Co Case (Switzerland v Yugoslavia) (Preliminary Objection), Order, 27 June 1936, PCIJ Series A/B, No 67 .... 373n.65, 374
Treatment of Polish Nationals and Other Persons of Polish Origin or Speech in the Danzig Territory, Advisory Opinion, 4 February 1932, PCIJ Series A/B, No 44 .... 520n.114

International Court of Justice

Case of Certain Norwegian Loans (France v Norway), Separate Opinion of Judge Lauterpacht, 6 July 1957, ICJ Reports 1957, 34 .... 520n.114
Land and Maritime Boundary Between Cameroon and Nigeria (Cameroon v Nigeria; Equatorial Guinea intervening), Judgment, 10 October 2002, ICJ Reports 2002, 303 .... 520n.116
Reservations to the Convention on the Prevention and Punishment of the Crime of Genocide, Advisory Opinion, 28 May 1951, ICJ Reports 1951, 15............ 387n.123

European Court of Human Rights

Rumpf v Germany, Judgment, 2 September 2010, Application No 46344/06.......... 108n.76

Inter-American Court of Human Rights

Claude-Reyes et al v Chile Merits, Reparations and Costs, Judgment, 19 September 2006, IACtHR Series C, No 151................................ 334n.67

II. SUPRANATIONAL COURTS

Court of Justice of the European Union

Case C-284/16, *Slovak Republic v Achmea BV*, Judgment, 6 March 2018, EU:C:2018:158...............13n.40, 196n.60, 196n.61, 197, 197n.64, 198n.66, 198n.67, 198n.69, 199n.71, 199n.73, 199, 200, 222n.71
Case C-591/17, *Austria v Germany*, Judgment, 18 June 2019, ECLI:EU:C:2019:504 ....95n.14
Case C-741/19, *Republic of Moldova v Komstroy LLC*, Judgment, 2 September 2021, ECLI:EU:C:2021:655.......................................13n.40
Case C-109/20, *Republiken Polen v PL Holdings Sàrl*, Judgment, 26 October 2021, ECLI:EU:C:2021:875 ....13n.40
Opinion 1/17, *CETA*, Opinion, 30 April 2019, EU:C:2019:341.........................13n.40

Caribbean Court of Justice

Attorney General et al v Jeffrey Joseph and Lennox Ricardo Boyce [2006] CCJ 1 (AJ) 291n.16, 291n.17, 291n.22, 296n.53, 296n.55, 296n.56
BCB Holdings Limited and Belize Bank Limited v Attorney General of Belize [2013] CCJ 5 (AJ)........................... 295n.47, 295n.50, 297, 297n.58, 297n.61, 303–4, 307–8, 312n.127, 313n.131

Belize Bank Limited v Attorney General of Belize [2017] CCJ 18 (AJ) 306n.93
Belize Natural Energy Limited v Maranco Limited [2015] CCJ 2 (AJ).................297n.59
British Caribbean Bank v Government of Belize [2013]
CCJ 4 (AJ) 296n.52, 308, 309n.108, 309n.112, 311n.122, 312, 313n.130

Eastern Caribbean Supreme Court

Dantzler Inc v Galloway Hardware & Building Materials Limited, Claim No
MNIHCV2014/0024, Judgment, 3 December 2014.............................297n.61
Ennio Zanotti v Interlog Finance Corp et al, Claim No BVIHCV 2009/0394,
Judgment, 8 February 2010 ....307n.97
Hualon Corporation (M) SDN BHD (in receivership) v Marty Limited,
Claim No BVIHC (COM) 2014/0090, Judgment, 8 April 2018..................298n.65
IPOC International Growth Fund Limited v LV Finance Group Limited, Civil
Appeal No 30 of 2006, Judgment, 18 June 2007 ....298n.64, 307n.98

III. INTERNATIONAL ARBITRAL AWARDS

ICC arbitrations

Corporación Mexicana de Mantenimiento Integral, S de RL de CV v Pemex Exploración y Producción, ICC Case No 13613/CCO/JRF, Final Award,
16 December 2009 .... 277, 277n.154
Framatome v Atomic Energy Organization of Iran, ICC Case 3986,
Decision on Jurisdiction, 30 April 1982, VIII Yearbook Commercial
Arbitration 106 ....371–72, 374n.68, 375
The Ministry of Defence and Support for Armed Forces of the Islamic Republic of Iran v Westinghouse Electric Corporation, ICC Case No 7375/CK,
Preliminary Award, 5 June 1996 .... 380–84, 382n.96
Waterville Holdings (BVI) Limited v Republic of Ghana, ICC Case No 205.61/TO,
Partial Award on Jurisdiction, 20 March 2017 .... 522n.119, 526

ICSID arbitrations

Accession Mezzanine Capital LP & Danubius Kereskedöház Vagyonkezelö Zrt v Hungary, ICSID Case No ARB/12/3 ....189n.16
Decision on Respondent's Objection under Arbitration Rule 41(5), 8 August 2013.....189n.17
Award, 17 April 2015 ....189n.16
AES Summit Generation Limited and AES-Tisza Erömü Kft v Hungary,
ICSID Case No ARB/07/22, Decision of the ad hoc Committee on the
Application for Annulment, 29 June 2012....................................190n.21
Aguas del Tunari SA v Republic of Bolivia, ICSID Case No ARB/02/3, Decision on
Respondent's Objections to Jurisdiction, 21 October 2005.........................5n.8
Ansung Housing Co, Ltd v People's Republic of China, ICSID Case No ARB/14/25,
Award, 9 March 2017...459n.46, 461n.58
Ambiente Ufficio SpA and others v Argentine Republic, ICSID Case No ARB/08/9,
Decision on Jurisdiction and Admissibility, 8 February 2013....................515n.78
ATA Construction, Industrial and Trading Company v Hashemite Kingdom of Jordan, ICSID Case No ARB/08/2, Award, 18 May 2010......................474n.47
Azienda Elettrica Ticinese v Federal Republic of Germany,
ICSID Case No ARB/23/47 ....97n.30
Azurix Corporation v Argentine Republic, ICSID Case No ARB/01/12,
Decision on Jurisdiction, 8 December 2003 ....309n.111

Beijing Urban Construction Group Co Ltd v Republic of Yemen, ICSID Case No ARB/14/30, Decision on Jurisdiction, 31 May 2017 .... 459n.46
Biwater Gauff (Tanzania) Limited v United Republic of Tanzania, ICSID Case No ARB/05/22, Award, 24 July 2008 ....5n.8, 44n.37
Bureau Veritas, Inspection, Valuation, Assessment and Control, BIVAC BV v Republic of Paraguay, ICSID Case No ARB/07/9, Decision of the Tribunal on Objections to Jurisdiction, 29 May 2009........................361n.22, 361, 361n.24, 362, 367n.41, 387n.124, 388n.125
Compañia de Aguas del Aconqija SA and Vivendi Universal SA v Argentine Republic, ICSID Case No ARB/97/3, Award, 21 November 2000....................5n.8, 44n.37
Continental Casualty Co v Argentine Republic, ICSID Case No ARB/03/9, Decision on Argentina's Application for a Stay of Enforcement of the Award, 23 October 2009 .... 341n.90
Cyprus Popular Bank Public Co Limited v Hellenic Republic, ICSID Case No ARB/14/16, registered 16 July 2014........................ 180n.108
Dan Cake (Portugal) SA v Hungary, ICSID Case No ARB/12/9, Decision on Jurisdiction and Liability, 24 August 2015 .... 192n.36
Desert Line Projects LLC v Republic of Yemen, ICSID Case No ARB/05/17, Award, 6 February 2008 .... 474n.47
Eiser Infrastructure Limited and Energía Solar Luxembourg Sàrl v Kingdom of Spain, ICSID Case No ARB/13/36, Award, 4 May 2017..................... 144n.58
Ekran Berhad v People's Republic of China, ICSID Case No ARB/11/15...... 459n.46, 461n.58
Electrabel SA v Hungary, ICSID Case No ARB/07/19, Award, 25 November 2015..... 191n.28
Emilio Agustín Maffezini v Kingdom of Spain, ICSID Case No ARB/97/7, Award, 13 November 2000.. 144n.57
Espiritu Santo Holdings, LP and L1bre Holding, LLC v United Mexican States, ICSID Case No ARB/20/13 .... 258n.35
Fengzhen Min v Republic of Korea, ICSID Case No ARB/20/26, registered 3 August 2020 .... 477n.68
Gustav FW Hamester GmbH & Co KG v Republic of Ghana, ICSID Case No ARB/07/24, Award, 18 June 2010.. 497n.12
Hanocal Holding BV and IPIC International BV v Republic of Korea, ICSID Case No ARB/15/17... 475n.51
Jan de Nul NV and Dredging International NV v Arab Republic of Egypt, ICSID Case No ARB/04/13, Award, 6 November 2008 .... 474n.49
Joy Mining Machinery Limited v Arab Republic of Egypt, ICSID Case No ARB/03/11, Decision on Jurisdiction, 30 July 2004 .... 474n.48
Karkey Karadeniz Elektrik Uretim AS v Islamic Republic of Pakistan, ICSID Case No ARB/13/1, Award, 22 August 2017 .... 419n.32
Klesch Group Holdings Limited & Raffinerie Heide GmbH v Federal Republic of Germany, ICSID Case No ARB/23/49 ....98n.31
Legacy Vulcan, LLC v United Mexican States, ICSID Case No ARB/19/1............. 258n.35
Lighthouse Corporation Pty Ltd and Lighthouse Corporation Ltd, IBC v Democratic Republic of Timor-Leste, ICSID Case No ARB/15/2, Award, 22 December 2017 .... 474n.46
LSF-KEB Holdings SCA and others v Republic of Korea, ICSID Case No ARB/12/37... 475n.50
Mainstream Renewable Power Ltd and others v Federal Republic of Germany, ICSID Case No ARB/21/26 ....97n.28
Masdar Solar & Wind Cooperatief UA v Kingdom of Spain, ICSID Case No ARB/14/1, Award, 16 May 2018 .... 198n.66
Mobil Corporation, Venezuela Holdings, BV and others v Bolivarian Republic of Venezuela, ICSID Case No ARB/07/27, Decision on Jurisdiction, 10 June 2010 ....18n.54

MOL Hungarian Oil and Gas Company Plc v Republic of Croatia, ICSID Case No ARB/13/32 . . . . . 199n.72
Ping An Life Insurance Company of China, Limited and Ping An Insurance (Group) Company of China, Ltd v Kingdom of Belgium, ICSID Case No ARB/12/29, Award, 30 April 2015 . . . . . 459n.46
Poštová banka AS and ISTROKAPITAL SE v Hellenic Republic, ICSID Case No ARB/13/8 Award, 9 April 2015 . . . . . 180n.107
Decision on Poštová Banka's Application for Partial Annulment of the Award, 29 September 2016 . . . . . 180n.107
Qatar National Bank (QPSC) v Republic of South Sudan and Bank of South Sudan, ICSID Case No ARB/20/40 . . . . . 6n.16
RREEF Infrastructure (GP) Limited and RREEF Pan-European Infrastructure Two Lux Sàrl v Kingdom of Spain, ICSID Case No ARB/13/30, Award, 30 November 2018 . . . . . 144n.58
RWE AG and RWE Eemshaven Holding II BV v Kingdom of the Netherlands, ICSID Case No ARB/21/4, Request for Arbitration, 20 January 2021 . . . . . 5–6n.14
Saipem SpA v People's Republic of Bangladesh, ICSID Case No ARB/05/7, Award, 30 June 2009 . . . . . 474n.47
Salini Costruttori SpA et Italstrade SpA v Royaume du Maroc, ICSID Case No ARB/00/4, Decision on Jurisdiction, 23 July 2001 . . . . . 309n.111, 474n.49
Sempra Energy International v Argentine Republic, ICSID Case No ARB/02/16 . . . . . 341n.91, 474n.48
Decision on the Argentine Republic's Request for a Continued Stay of Enforcement of the Award (Rule 54), 5 March 2009 . . . . . 341n.91
Decision on Annulment, 29 June 2010 . . . . . 474n.48
SGS Société Générale de Surveillance SA v Islamic Republic of Pakistan, ICSID Case No ARB/01/13 . . . . . 311n.120
Procedural Order No 2, 16 October 2002, 8 ICSID Review–FILJ 293 . . . . . 310–11, 311n.120
Decision on Jurisdiction, 3 August 2003 . . . . . 474n.48
SGS Société Générale de Surveillance SA v Republic of Paraguay, ICSID Case No ARB/07/29, Decision on Jurisdiction, 12 February 2010 . . . . . 361n.23
SGS Société Générale de Surveillance SA v The Philippines, ICSID Case No ARB/02/6, Decision of the Tribunal on Objections to Jurisdiction, 29 January 2004 . . . . . 361n.23, 474n.48
Standard Chartered Bank (Hong Kong) Limited v Tanzania, ICSID Case No ARB/15/41, Award, 11 October 2019 . . . . . 474n.46
Strabag SE, Erste Nordsee-Offshore Holding GmbH and Zweite Nordsee-Offshore Holding GmbH v Federal Republic of Germany, ICSID Case No ARB/19/29 . . . . . 97n.28
Suez, Sociedad General de Aguas de Barcelona SA, and Vivendi Universal SA v Argentine Republic, ICSID Case No ARB/03/19 . . . . . 5n.8
Telenor Mobile Communications SA v Hungary, ICSID Case No ARB/04/15, Award, 13 September 2006 . . . . . 188n.8, 189n.11, 189n.15
Tethyan Copper Company Pty Limited v Islamic Republic of Pakistan, ICSID Case No ARB/12/1, Award, 12 July 2019 . . . . . 4–5n.6, 419n.31, 419n.32, 424n.72, 424–25, 433
Total SA v Argentine Republic, ICSID Case No ARB/04/1, Decision on Liability, 27 December 2010 . . . . . 18n.54
Toto Costruzioni Generali SpA v Lebanese Republic, ICSID Case No ARB/07/12, Decision on Jurisdiction, 11 September 2009 . . . . . 474n.48
Tza Yap Shum v Republic of Peru, ICSID Case No ARB/07/6, Decision on Jurisdiction and Competence, 20 January 2017 . . . . . 459n.46, 459n.48, 459–60

Uniper SE, Uniper Benelux Holding BV and Uniper Benelux NV v Kingdom of the Netherlands, ICSID Case No ARB/21/22, Order of the Tribunal Taking Note of the Discontinuance of the Proceedings and Decision on Costs, 17 March 2023 .... 5–6n.14
Vattenfall AB, Vattenfall Europe AG, Vattenfall Europe Generation AG & Co KG v Federal Republic of Germany, ICSID Case No ARB/09/6
Request for Arbitration, 30 March 2009 .... 5n.11
Award, 11 March 2011 .... 96n.22
Vattenfall AB and others v Federal Republic of Germany, ICSID Case No ARB/12/12, Order of the Tribunal Taking Note of the Discontinuance of the Proceeding, 9 November 2021 .... 5–6n.14, 96n.23
Vigotop Limited v Hungary, ICSID Case No ARB/11/22, Award, 1 October 2014 .... 191n.32, 192

ICSID (Additional Facility) arbitrations

Abengoa SA and Cofides SA v United Mexican States, ICSID Case No ARB(AF)/09/2, Award, 18 April 2013 .... 258n.35
Cemusa – Corporación Europea de Mobiliario Urbano, SA and Corporación Americana de Equipamientos Urbanos, SL v United Mexican States, ICSID Case No ARB(AF)/13/2 .... 258n.35
Foresti, de Carli and others v Republic of South Africa, ICSID Case No ARB(AF)/07/1, Award, 4 August 2010 .... 5n.9, 44n.38, 548n.127, 549n.129
Gemplus SA and others v United Mexican States, ICSID Case No ARB(AF)/04/3, Award, 16 June 2010 .... 258n.35, 259n.39
Gold Reserve Inc v Bolivarian Republic of Venezuela, ICSID Case No ARB(AF)/09/1, Award, 22 September 2014 .... 18n.54
Metalclad Corporationv United Mexican States, ICSID Case No ARB(AF)/97/1, Award, 30 August 2000, 16 ICSID Review–FILJ 168; 40 ILM 36; 119 ILR 618; 5 ICSID Reports 212 .... 5n.11, 258n.35
Robert Azinian and others v United Mexican States, ICSID Case No ARB(AF)/97/2, Award, 1 November 1999, 14 ICSID Review–FILJ 538; 39 ILM 537; 121 ILR 2; 5 ICSID Reports 272 .... 258n.35
Técnicas Medioambientales Tecmed, SA v United Mexican States, ICSID Case No ARB(AF)/00/2, Award, 29 May 2003 .... 258n.35
Telefónica SA v United Mexican States, ICSID Case No ARB(AF)/12/4 .... 258n.35
The Loewen Group, Inc and Raymond L Loewen v United States of America, ICSID Case No ARB(AF)/98/3, Decision on Hearing of Respondent's Objection to Competence and Jurisdiction, 5 January 2001; Award, 26 June 2003 .... 515n.78
Waste Management, Inc v United Mexican States, ICSID Case No ARB(AF)/00/3, Award, 30 April 2004 .... 258n.35

SCC arbitrations

Charanne and Construction Investments v Kingdom of Spain, SCC Case No V062/2012, Final Award, 21 January 2016 .... 144n.58
Foresight Luxembourg Solar 1 Sàrl, et al v Kingdom of Spain, SCC Case No 2015/150, Award, 14 November 2018 .... 144n.58
Isolux Netherlands, BV v Kingdom of Spain, SCC Case No V2013/153, Award, 17 July 2016 .... 144n.58
Novenergia II – Energy & Environment (SCA) (Grand Duchy of Luxembourg), SICAR v Kingdom of Spain, SCC Case No 2015/063, Award, 15 February 2018 .... 144n.58, 198n.69, 199n.73

UAB Vilniaus Energija and Veolia Environnement SA v SP AB Vilniaus Šilumos Tinklai and Vilnius City Municipality, SCC Case No V2016/183, Final Award, 30 November 2023 .... 5–6n.14

UNCITRAL arbitrations

Alicia Grace and others v United Mexican States, ICSID Case No UNCT/18/4 (UNCITRAL) 258n.35

AWG Group v Argentine Republic, UNCITRAL, Decision on Liability, 30 July 2010 .... 5n.8

Balkan Energy Limited (Ghana) v The Republic of Ghana, PCA Case No 2010-7 (UNCITRAL)
Interim Award, 22 December 2010........ 12, 367n.39, 378n.83, 380n.89, 516–17, 526
Award on the Merits, 1 April 2014 .... 12, 517–18, 519, 526

Bankswitch Ghana Limited (Ghana) v The Republic of Ghana, PCA Case No 118294 (UNCITRAL), Award Save as to Costs, 11 April 2014........ 12n.36, 300n.73, 379n.84, 379n.85, 379n.88, 519n.106, 521n.118, 521, 526

Cairn Energy PLC and Cairn UK Holdings Limited v Republic of India, PCA Case No 2016-7 (UNCITRAL), Award, 21 December 2020 .... 18n.54

Chemtura Corporation (formerly Crompton Corporation) v Government of Canada, UNCITRAL, Award, 2 August 2010........ 5n.10

Chevron Corporation v Republic of Ecuador, PCA Case No 2009-23 (UNCITRAL), Fourth Interim Award on Interim Measures, 7 February 2013........ 515n.78

China Heilongjiang International Economic & Technical Cooperative Corp, Beijing Shougang Mining Investment Company Ltd and Qinhuangdaoshi Qinlong International Industrial Co Ltd v Mongolia, PCA Case No 2010-20 (UNCITRAL), Award, 30 June 2017 .... 459n.46

Dow AgroSciences LLC v Government of Canada, UNCITRAL 5n.10

Elliott Associates, LP v Republic of Korea, PCA Case No 2018-51 (UNCITRAL), registered 12 July 2018........ 475n.53

EnCana Corporation v Republic of Ecuador, LCIA Case No UN3481 (UNCITRAL), Award, 3 February 2006 .... 307n.103

Hulley Enterprises Limited (Cyprus) v The Russian Federation, CA Case No AA 226 (UNCITRAL), Final Award, 18 July 2014 .... 4–5n.6

Jin-Hye Seo v Government of the Republic of Korea, HKIAC Case No 18117 (UNCITRAL), Final Award, 24 September 2019 .... 475n.57, 476n.59

KBR, Inc v United Mexican States, ICSID Case No UNCT/14/1 (UNCITRAL), Award, 30 April 2015........ 258n.35

Lone Pine Resources Inc v Government of Canada, ICSID Case No UNCT/15/2 (UNCITRAL), Final Award, 21 November 2022........ 5n.11

Mason Capital LP and Mason Management LLC v Republic of Korea, PCA Case No 2018-55 (UNCITRAL)........ 475n.55

Mesa Power Group, LLC v Government of Canada, PCA Case No 2012-17 (UNCITRAL), Award, 24 March 2016 .... 5n.13

Methanex Corporation v United States of America, UNCITRAL, Final Award, 3 August 2005 .... 5n.10, 45n.39

Mohammad Reza Dayyani and others v The Republic of Korea, PCA Case No 2015-38 (UNCITRAL), Award, 6 June 2018 .... 474n.49, 475n.52

Occidental Exploration and Production Company v Republic of Ecuador, LCIA Case No UN3467 (UNCITRAL), Final Award, 1 July 2004........ 307n.102

Odyssey Marine Exploration, Inc v United Mexican States, ICSID Case No UNCT/20/1 (UNCITRAL) 258n.35
Philip Morris Asia Ltd v Commonwealth of Australia, PCA Case No 2012-12 (UNCITRAL), Award on Jurisdiction and Admissibility, 17 December 2015 .... 562n.1, 563n.8
Sancheti v Germany, UNCITRAL, Award, 6 June 2001 .... 96n.20
Sanum Investments Ltd v Lao People's Democratic Republic, PCA Case No 2013-13 (UNCITRAL), Award, 6 August 2019 .... 459n.46
Tennant Energy, LLC v Government of Canada, PCA Case No 2018-54 (UNCITRAL), Final Award, 25 October 2022 .... 5n.13
Schindler Holding AG v Republic of Korea, PCA Case No 2019-44 (UNCITRAL) 476n.62
Veteran Petroleum Limited (Cyprus) v The Russian Federation, PCA Case No AA 228 (UNCITRAL), Final Award, 18 July 2014 .... 4–5n.6
White Industries Australia Limited v Republic of India, UNCITRAL, Final Award, 30 November 2011 .... 474n.47
William Ralph Clayton, William Richard Clayton, Douglas Clayton, Daniel Clayton and Bilcon of Delaware, Inc v Government of Canada, PCA Case No 2009-04 (UNCITRAL), Award on Jurisdiction and Liability, 17 March 2015 .... 5n.11
Yukos Universal Limited (Isle of Man) v The Russian Federation, PCA Case No AA 227 (UNCITRAL), Final Award, 18 July 2014 .... 4–5n.6
Zeph Investments Pte. Ltd v The Commonwealth of Australia, PCA Case No 2023-40 (UNCITRAL) 562n.2

Other arbitrations

Aero-lukss v Latvijas finieris [2002] 206n.17
Arbitral Award rendered on 7 July 2008 in the dispute between CDR Créances, Consortium de Réalisation and Selafa MJA, Me Didier Courtoux, Mr Bernard Tapie, Ms Bernard Tapie <www.lexinter.net/JPTXT4/JP2005/tapie.pdf> 82n.75, 82
Benteler et al v Belgian State, Award, 18 November 1983, (1984) 1(2) J Int'l Arb 184 .... 11n.30, 212n.40, 366–67, 371–72, 375–76, 376n.75, 377, 379–80
Berjaya Land Berhad v Republic of Korea, Notice of Intent, 10 July 2019 .... 476n.66
Bundesrepublik Deutschland v Daimler Financial Services AG, Deutsche Telekom AG and Toll Collect GbR 94n.10
Elf Aquitaine Iran v National Iranian Oil Company, Preliminary Award, 14 January 1982, XI Yearbook Commercial Arbitration 97 .... 371–72, 372n.60
Gale Investments Company LLC v Republic of Korea, Notice of Intent to Submit a Dispute to Arbitration, 9 June 2019 .... 476n.60
Greenland Minerals A/S (GMAS) v Government of Greenland and the Government of the Kingdom of Denmark 6n.15
Partial Award, 16 August 1982, (1984) 16 Entscheidungen des Oberverwaltungsgerichts Berlin 256 .... 93n.5
Process and Industrial Developments Ltd v The Ministry of Petroleum Resources of the Federal Republic of Nigeria, ad hoc, Final Award, 31 January 2017 .... 4–5n.6
Sapphire International Petroleums Limited v National Iranian Oil Company, Arbitral Award, 15 March 1963, (1967) 35 ILR 136 .... 176n.89
Saudi Arabia v Arabian American Oil Company (Aramco), Award, 23 August 1958, (1962) 27 ILR 117 .... 360n.16
Texaco Overseas Petroleum Company and California Asiatic Oil Company v Libya, Award on the Merits, 19 January 1977, (1978) 17 ILM 1 .... 360n.18

IV. NATIONAL COURTS

Argentina

Algavi SA v Esso SRL [2013] CNCom-C, LL AR/JUR/49967/2013 .... 330n.52
Bear Service SA v Cervecería Modelo SA [2005] CSJN, LL Online 35001744.......... 325n.31
Cacchione, Ricardo Constantino c Urbaser Argentina SA [2006] CSJN Fallos 329:3399 .... 336n.80
Cayetano Paino [1956] CSJN Fallos 235:940............................ 327n.35, 327n.38
CCI - Compañía de Concesiones de Infraestructura SA v pedido de quiebra (por República de Perú) [2015] CNCom-A, LL AR/JUR/33122/2015 .... 341n.92
Cerámica San Lorenzo [1985] CSJN, [1986] LL A-179 .... 344n.100
Cía Ítalo Argentina de Electricidad [1937] CSJN Fallos 178:293............. 327n.35, 327n.37
Compañía Argentina de Navegación 'Nicolás Mihanovich Ltda' [1931] CSJN Fallos 160:133 .... 327n.38
CRI Holding Inc Sucursal Argentina v Compañía Argentina de Comodoro Rivadavia Explotación de Petróleo SA [2010] CNCom-C, [2011] LL A-555 .... 330n.53
Deutsche Ruckversicherung AG v Caja Nacional de Ahorro y Seguro en liquidación [2014] CNCivComFed-III; [2019] CSJN (CCF 6461/2009/CS1).... 338n.83
Don Gerardo Pagano [1920] CSJN Fallos 133:61................................ 327n.35
Estado Nacional – Procuración del Tesoro Nacional c (nulidad del laudo del 20-III-2009) [2018] CSJN Fallos 341:1485 .... 327n.35, 327n.38, 336n.80
Estado Nacional - Procuración del Tesoro v Tribunal Arbitral [2006] CNCAF-II, [2012] LL C-35 .... 332n.60
Francisco Ctibor SACI Y F V Wall-Mart Argentina SRL [2016] CNCom-D............ 330n.53
Galli, Elena v Kairuz, Alfredo F [2003] CNCiv-F, [2004] LL D-1034................. 343n.97
Gardebled Hermanos SA [2007] CSJN Fallos 330:3565 .... 330n.54
Giroldi, Horacio David [1995] CSJN, [1995] LL D-462........................... 349n.106
Giustiniani, Rubén Héctor v YPF SA [2015] CSJN, [2015] ED 25/11/15-12 ... 334n.68, 334n.70
Guido Simonini [1942] CSJN Fallos 194:155 .... 327n.35
Honda Motor Argentina SA v Cinter SRL [2014] CNCom-B 349n.107
José Cartellone Construcciones Civiles SA c/Hidroeléctrica Norpatagónica SA o Hidronor SA [2004] CSJN Fallos 327:1881 .... 336n.78, 336, 341n.89
KCK Tissue SA y otros v Citibank NA Nassau et al [2005] CNCom-A................ 343n.98
La Nación SA v La Razón SA [1988] CSJN, [1989] LL B-476............... 325n.23, 325n.24
Milantic Trans SA v Ministerio de la Producción (Astilleros Río Santiago y otro) [2016] SCJPBA, LL AR/JUR/12408/2016 .... 339n.84
Milantic Trans SA v Ministerio de la Producción (Astilleros Río Santiago y otro) [2021] CSJ 1460/2016/CS1 .... 339n.85
Mobil Argentina SA v Gasnor SA [2007] CNCom-D 330n.53
Nidera SA v Rodríguez Alvarez de Canale, Elena [1988] CSJN, [1990] LL A-419 .... 325n.23, 325n.24
Oscar A Diez SAI y C v SEGBA [2000] CACCF-III................................ 338n.83
Otondo, César A y otro v Cortina Beruatto SA et al [2003] JNCom No 10, [2003] Rev JA, vol IV-73 .... 330n.53, 343n.98
Pan American Energy LLC (Sucursal Argentina) c Metrogas SA (Chile) s/organismos externos [2017] CNCom-D [2018] LL A-494................. 323–24n.19
Pérez Aznar, Facundo Pablo v Procuración del Tesoro de La Nación [2018] Federal Court of Appeals of La Plata, Sala II, 27 December 2019............... 334n.71
Pestarino de Alfani, Mónica Amalia c Urbaser Argentina SA [2008] CSJN 336n.80
Ricardo Agustín López c Gemabiotech SA [2017] CSJN Fallos 340:1226.............. 336n.80
Smit International Argentina SA v Puerto Mariel SA, [2011] CNACCF-I, [2011] LL D-645 .... 325n.30

Sociedad Anónima Puerto del Rosario [1926] CSJN Fallos 146:373 .... 327n.35
Sociedad Anónima Puerto del Rosario [1928] CSJN Fallos 152:347 .... 327n.35
Szwarc, Rubén Mario and others v Estado Nacional [2013]
CNCom-A, LL E-522 .... 332n.62
Techint Compañía Técnica Internacional SACE e I[2007]
CSJN Fallos 330:2215 .... 327n.35, 327n.38
Vago, Jorge A v Ediciones La Urraca SA [1991] CSJN, [1992] LL B-367 .... 326n.33
*Wilbers SS, Enrique C v Extraktionstechnik Gesellschaft Fur Anlagenbau
MBM* [1988] CNCom-E, [1989] LL E-302 .... 325n.30
Yacimientos Petrolíferos Fiscales [1974] CSJN Fallos 290:458 .... 327n.37, 327n.38
YPF SA v AES Uruguaiana Emprendimientos SA et al, Federal Court of Appeals in
Administrative Matters, Chamber No IV, Case No 41.255/2013/CA1,
Decision, 7 October 2014 .... 328–29n.48

Australia

Castel Electronics Pty Ltd v TCL Air Conditioner (Zhongshan) Co Ltd (No 2)
[2012] FCA 1214 .... 63n.158, 63n.160
Comandate Marine Corp v Pan Australia Shipping Pty Ltd [2006] FCAFC 192 .... 570n.58
Combet v Commonwealth (2005) 224 CLR 494 .... 573n.80
*Construction, Forestry, Mining and Energy Union v Australian Industrial Relations
Commission* (2001) 203 CLR 645 .... 577n.106
*Ebner v Official Trustee in Bankruptcy, Clenae Pty Ltd v Australia and
New Zealand Banking Group Ltd* (2000) 205 CLR 337 .... 567n.28
Emerald Grain Australia Pty Ltd v Agrocorp International Pte Ltd
[2014] FCA 414 .... 63n.166
Esso Australia Resources Ltd v Plowman (1995) 183 CLR 10 .... 568n.38
*Gas & Fuel Corporation of Victoria v Wood Hall Ltd & Leonard Pipeline
Contractors Ltd* [1978] VR 385 .... 63n.159
Griffith University v Tang (2005) 221 CLR 99 .... 574n.88
Kable v Director of Public Prosecutions for New South Wales (1996) 189 CLR 51 ...... 576n.99
Larkden Pty Ltd v Lloyd Energy Systems Pty Ltd (2011) 279 ALR 772 .... 570n.51
Neat Domestic Trading Pty Ltd v AWB Ltd (2003) 216 CLR 277 .... 574n.88
Plaintiff M61/2010E v Commonwealth (2010) 243 CLR 319 .... 575n.91
Plaintiff M68/2015 v Minister for Immigration (2016) 257 CLR 42 .... 575n.96
R v Kirby; Ex parte Boilermakers' Society of Australia (1956)
94 CLR 254 .... 577n.103, 577n.104
Tanning Research Laboratories Inc v O'Brien (1990) 169 CLR 332 .... 570n.59
*TCL Air Conditioner (Zhongshan) Co Ltd v Castel Electronics Pty Ltd
[2014] FCAFC 83*, (2014) 311 ALR 387 .... 63n.163, 64n.167, 571n.65
*TCL Air Conditioner (Zhongshan) Co Ltd v The Judges of the
Federal Court of Australia* [2013] HCA 5 .... 302n.81, 577n.105, 577n.107,
578, 579n.114
Webb v The Queen (1994) 181 CLR 41 .... 567n.29
Williams v Commonwealth of Australia[2012] HCA 23,
(2012) 248 CLR 156 .... 573n.77, 580n.121
Williams v Commonwealth of Australia (No 2) [2014] HCA 23,
(2014) 252 CLR 416 .... 573n.78, 573–74, 579–80

Barbados

Auto-Guadeloupe Investissement SAS v Alvarez & Ors (2014)
84 West Indian Reports 49 (High Court) 299n.70, 301–2, 313n.129

Belize

Attorney General of Belize v Carlisle Holdings Limited, Supreme Court, Action No 15 of 2005, Decision, 21 February 2005 (Conteh CJ) 297n.60, 298n.62
BCB Holdings Limited and the Belize Bank Limited v the Attorney General of Belize, ClaimNo. 743 of 2009 (unreported, decision of the Supreme Court of Belize, delivered on22 December 2010) 307n.101
Belize Telemedia et al v Attorney General of Belize, Supreme Court, Claim No 464 of 2008, Decision, 28 October 2008 (Conteh CJ) 297n.60, 298n.62

Canada

The Honourable Paul Helleyer, PC et al v Justin Trudeau et al, Case No T-1789-16, registered 21 October 2016, discontinued 13 June 2017 .... 13n.40

China

Bureau of Land and Resource of Yazhou District of Jining Municipality v Jiangsu Nuoya Investment Development Co Ltd, Intermediate People's Court of Ji'nan Municipality, Judgment, Doc No (2014) Ji Zhong Li Chu Zi Di 31 Hao 457n.36
Democratic Republic of the Congo and others v FG Hemisphere Associates LLC [2009] 1 HKLRD 410 (Court of First Instance);[2010] 2 HKLRD 66 (Court of Appeal);FACV 5, 6 & 7/2010 (Court of Final Appeal) 463n.69

Colombia

Constitutional Court, Judgment C-252/19, 6 June 2019 .... 13n.40

Ecuador

Constitutional Court, Judgment Case No 2-23-TI, 28 July 2023 .... 13n.40

Estonia

Avaldaja Vene Föderatsiooni äriühing OF v D OÜ [2016] Supreme Court, Civ 3-2-1-186-15 .... 216n.54
Constitutional Judgment [2008] Supreme Court, Civ 3-4-1-1-08 .... 210n.33
JKKI v JMUDI[2018] Supreme Court, Civ 2-17-5977 .... 210n.32, 210n.35
Parties unknown [2018] Supreme Court, Civ 2-16-15675 .... 217n.55
Parties unknown [2018] Supreme Court, Civ 2-18-4731 .... 216n.53

France

Conseil constitutionnel, Decision No 2004-506 DC, 2 December 2004 .... 75n.48
Conseil constitutionnel, Decision No 2017-749 DC, 31 July 2017 .... 13n.40
Conseil d'État, *Evèque de Moulin*, 23 December 1887 .... 74n.44
Conseil d'État, *Héritiers Guérard v le Trésor*, 19 February 1825 .... 74n.44, 75
Conseil d'État, No 352750, 19 April 2013 .... 87n.101
Conseil d'État, Opinion No 339710, 6 March 1986, EDCE 1987, No 38 .... 75n.47
Cour de cassation, Nos 15/13755, 15/13904 and 15/14145, 30 June 2016, ECLI:FR:CCASS:2016:C100932 .... 82n.78, 83n.83
Cour de cassation, *Trésor Public v Galakis*, 2 May 1966, Bull Civ 1966, I, No 199 .... 86, 367–68, 376, 377n.77, 381n.94, 381, 383n.101
Cour de cassation, *Syndicat mixte des Aéroports de Charente (SMAC) v Ryanair*, No 13-25846, 8 July 2015, Bull Civ 1 2016, No 834 .... 86–88, 88n.104

Paris Cour d'Appel, CDR Créances SAS et CDR-Consortium de Réalisation SA c/Selafa MJA et autres, No 13/13278, 17 February 2015 ....82n.77
Paris Cour d'Appel, *République Hellenique c/Bombardier*, No 14/07043, 14 April 2015 ....85n.94
Paris Cour d'Appel, *Société Gatoil International Inc v National Iranian Oil Company*, 17 December 1991, (1993) Rev Arb 281.....................381n.93, 381–82
Paris Cour d'Appel, *Syndicat Mixte des Aéroports de Charente (SMAC) c/Airport Marketing Services (AMS) et Ryanair Limited*, No 12/11596, 10 September 2013..84, 87n.102, 88n.103, 88
Paris Cour d'Appel, *Thalès SA et Thalès Underwater System SAS c/la Marine de la République de Chine*, No 09/10252, 11 May 2010 .... 80n.66, 80n.67
Paris Cour d'Appel, *Thalès SA et Thalès Underwater System SAS c/la Marine de la République de Chine (Taïwan)*, No 10/11853, 9 June 2011.... 80n.66, 80n.67
Tribunal des Conflits, No A4043, 11 April 2016................................. 86n.100
Tribunal des Conflits, No C3754, 17 May 2010 ....84–86, 85n.93, 87, 88
Tribunal des Conflits, No C4075, 24 April 2017................................. 88n.107
Tribunal des Conflits, *Société Myrtoon Steamship*, 19 May 1958 .... 83n.80, 83

Germany

Administrative Court Berlin, Case No 4 K 403.09, Order, 11 February 2010, (2010) 8(2) Zeitschrift für Schiedsverfahren 107 ....103n.51, 124–25
Federal Administrative Court, Case No VII C 97/57, Judgment, 5 June 1959, (1959) 12(44) Neue Juristische Wochenschrift 1985......................... 102n.50
Federal Administrative Court, Case No 5 C 22/88, Judgment, 20 February 1992, (1993) 46(9) Neue Zeitschrift für Verwaltungsrecht 584............... 100n.40, 102n.48
Federal Administrative Court, Case Nos 7 B 18/13, 7 B 19/13, Order, 20 December 2013 ....97n.25
Federal Constitutional Court, Case No 1 BvR 46/66, Order, 1 March 1967, BVerfGE 21, 207 .... 109n.81
Federal Constitutional Court, Case No BvL 52/71, Order, 29 May 1974, BVerfGE 37, 271 .... 112n.89, 112n.91
Federal Constitutional Court, Case No 2 BvR 134 and 268/76, Order, 15 February 1978, BVerfGE 47, 253 .... 116n.107
Federal Constitutional Court, Case No 2 BvR 1107/77, Order, 23 June 1981, BVerfGE 58, 1 ....112n.89, 112n.91, 115n.104
Federal Constitutional Court, Case No 2 BvR 1058/79, Order, 10 November 1981, BVerfGE 59, 63 .... 115n.104
Federal Constitutional Court, Case No 2 BvE 13/83, Judgment, 18 December 1984, BVerfGE 68, 1 .... 112n.89
Federal Constitutional Court, Case No 2 BvR 197/83, Order, 22 October 1986, BVerfGE 73, 339 .... 112n.89, 115n.104
Federal Constitutional Court, Case No 2 BvR 1178, 1179 and 1191/86, Order, 1 October 1987, BVerfGE 77, 1 .... 116n.107
Federal Constitutional Court, Case No 2 BvR 624/83, Order, 29 October 1987, BVerfGE 77, 170 .... 113n.94
Federal Constitutional Court, Case No 2 BvF 3/89, Judgment, 31 October 1990, BVerfGE 83, 60 .... 116n.107
Federal Constitutional Court, Case No 2 BvR 2134/92, Judgment, 12 October 1993, BVerfGE 89, 155 .... 112n.92
Federal Constitutional Court, Case No 2 BvF 1/92, Order, 24 May 1995, BVerfGE 93, 37 .... 116n.107

Federal Constitutional Court, Case No 1 BvR 2623/95, Judgment, 7 November 2000, BVerfGE 103, 44 .... 120n.120
Federal Constitutional Court, Case No 2 BvL 5 and 6/98, Order, 5 December 2002, BVerfGE 107, 59 .... 116n.107
Federal Constitutional Court, Case No 2 BvE 2/08, Judgment, 30 June 2009, BVerfGE 123, 267 .... 112n.90, 112n.92, 113n.94
Federal Constitutional Court, Case No 1 BvR 1916/09, Order, 19 July 2011, BVerfGE 129, 78 .... 109n.81
Federal Constitutional Court, Case No 2 BvR 987/10, Judgment, 7 September 2011, BVerfGE 129, 124 .... 112n.92
Federal Constitutional Court, Case No 2 BvR 133/10, Judgment, 18 January 2012, BVerfGE 130, 76 .... 116n.108, 124n.131
Federal Constitutional Court, Case No 2 BvR 2728/13 .... 112n.90
Request for Preliminary Ruling, 14 January 2014, BVerfGE 134, 366 .... 112n.90
Judgment, 21 June 2016, BVerfGE 142, 123 .... 112n.90, 112n.92, 112n.93
Federal Constitutional Court, Case No 2 BvR 1390/12, Judgment, 18 March 2014, BVerfGE 135, 317 .... 112n.92
Federal Constitutional Court, Case No 2 BvE 5/11, Judgment, 21 October 2014, BVerfGE 137, 185 .... 124n.131
Federal Constitutional Court, Case No 2 BvL 1/12, Order, 15 December 2015, BVerfGE 141, 1 .... 104n.58
Federal Constitutional Court, Case No 2 BvR 2735/14, Order, 15 December 2015, BVerfGE 140, 317 .... 112n.90, 112n.91, 112n.93
Federal Constitutional Court, Case No 2 BvR 1368/16, Judgment, 13 October 2016, BVerfGE 143, 65 .... 13n.40, 110n.86, 112n.88
Federal Constitutional Court, Case No 1 BvR 2821/11, Judgment, 6 December 2016, BVerfGE 143, 246 .... 97n.25
Federal Constitutional Court, Case No 2 BvR 1444/16, Order, 7 December 2016, BVerfGE 144, 1 .... 13n.40, 110n.86
Federal Constitutional Court, Case No 2 BvL 6/13, Order, 13 April 2017, BVerfGE 145, 171 .... 97n.25
Federal Constitutional Court, Case No 2 BvR 859/15 .... 112n.90
Request for Preliminary Ruling, 18 July 2017, BVerfGE 146, 216 .... 112n.90
Judgment, 5 May 2020, BVerfGE 154, 17 .... 112n.90, 112n.92, 112n.93
Federal Constitutional Court, Case No 2 BvE 2/11, Judgment, 7 November 2017, BVerfGE 147, 50 .... 124n.131, 124n.133
Federal Constitutional Court, Case No 2 BvR 1961/09, Order, 24 July 2018, BVerfGE 149, 346 .... 115n.104, 115n.105
Federal Constitutional Court, Case No 2 BvR 1685/14, Judgment, 30 July 2019, BVerfGE 151, 202 .... 112n.90, 112n.92
Federal Constitutional Court, Case No 2 BvR 966/19, Order, 28 October 2019, ECLI:DE:BVerfG:2019:rk20191028.2bvr096619 .... 110n.86, 112n.88
Federal Constitutional Court, Case No 2 BvR 882/19, Order, 7 November 2019, ECLI:DE:BVerfG:2019:rk20191107.2bvr088219 .... 110n.86, 112n.88
Federal Constitutional Court, Case No 1 BvR 1679/17, Order, 30 June 2020, BVerfGE 155, 238 .... 97n.29
Federal Constitutional Court, Case No 2 BvR 2047/16, Order, 14 September 2020, ECLI:DE:BVerfG:2020:rk20200914.2bvr204716 .... 110n.86
Federal Constitutional Court, Case No 1 BvR 1550/19, Order, 29 September 2020, BVerfGE 155, 378 .... 97n.26
Federal Constitutional Court, Case No 2 BvR 1845/18, Order, 1 December 2020, BVerfGE 156, 182 .... 112n.91

Federal Constitutional Court, Case No 2 BvE 4/16, Judgment, 2 March 2021, BVerfGE 157, 1 . . . . . 110n.86, 112n.88, 124n.131
Federal Constitutional Court, Case Nos 2 BvR 1368/16, 2 BvR 1444/16 and others, Order, 9 February 2022, ECLI:DE:BVerfG:2022: rs20220209.2bvr136816 . . . . . 13n.40, 110n.86, 111n.87, 112n.88
Federal Constitutional Court, Case No 1 BvR 2103/16, Order, 3 June 2022, ECLI:DE:BVerfG:2022:rk20220603.1bvr210316 . . . . . 26n.103, 106n.67, 113n.96, 114n.100, 115n.106, 117n.110, 118n.114, 120n.120, 120n.122, 125n.134
Federal Constitutional Court, Case No 2 BvR 557/19, Order, 23 July 2024, ECLI:DE:BVerfG :2024:rk20240723.2bvr055719 . . . . . 112n.88
Federal Court of Justice, Case No VI ZR 214/65, Judgment, 6 June 1967, (1967) 20(41) Neue Juristische Wochenschrift 1911 . . . . . 100n.41
Federal Court of Justice, Case No II ZR 373/98, Judgment, 3 April 2000, (2000) 53(23) Neue Juristische Wochenschrift 1713 . . . . . 114n.99
Federal Court of Justice, Case No XII ZR 165/06, Judgment, 29 October 2008, (2009) 22(8) NVwZ-Rechtsprechungsreport 317 . . . . . 94n.8
Federal Court of Justice, Case No V ZB 86/12, Order, 19 September 2012, (2013) 32(1-2) Neue Zeitschrift für Verwaltungsrecht 96 . . . . . 100n.41
Higher Administrative Court Kassel, Case No 6 C 824/11.T, Judgment, 27 February 2013 . . . . . 97n.25
Joint Senate of the Federal Supreme Courts (*Gemeinsamer Senat der obersten Gerichtshöfe des Bundes*), Order, 10 April 1986, (1986) 39(38) Neue Juristische Wochenschrift 2359 . . . . . 100n.41

Ghana

Amidu v The Attorney-General, Writ No JI/15/2012, Judgment, 14 June 2013 . . . . . 513n.70
Dey v The Republic [1997-1998] 2 GLR 919 . . . . . 510n.55
The Attorney-General v Balkan Energy Ghana Ltd & Ors, Writ No J6/1/2012, Judgment, 16 May 2012 . . . . . 517n.89, 519n.104, 520
The Attorney-General v Faroe Atlantic Co Ltd [2005-2006] SCGLR 271 . . . . . 518n.94, 520, 521n.117
The Republic v High Court: Ex Parte; Attorney-General, Case No J5/10/2013, Judgment, 20 June 2013 . . . . . 514n.72, 514n.75

Greece

Administrative Court of Appeals of Athens, Judgment No 1553/2011 . . . . . 170n.60
Council of State, Judgment No 1395/1954 . . . . . 163n.21
Council of State, Judgment Nos 433–37/1983 (Plenary Session) 167n.45
Council of State, Judgment No 2080/1987 (1988) 39 Epitheorisi Emporikou Dikaiou 38 . . . . . 158–59n.3
Council of State, Judgment Nos 3439–3442/1988 (1989) 27 Dioikitiki Dikaiosyni 505 . . . . . 168n.46
Council of State, Judgment No 3131/1989 (1989) 25 To Syntagma 702 . . . . . 168n.49
Council of State, Judgment No 3132/1989 (Plenary Session) 164n.31
Council of State, Judgment No 1792/1991 (1992) 40 Nomiko Vima 779 . . . . . 168n.51
Council of State, Judgment No 1793/1991 (1991) 35 Epitherorisi Dimosiou Dioikotikou Dikaiou 404 . . . . . 168n.51
Council of State, Judgment No 889/1994 . . . . . 172n.70
Council of State, Judgment No 1472/1994 . . . . . 169n.59

Council of State, Judgment No 1749/1995 .... 172n.72
Council of State, Judgment No 976/1998 .... 170n.60
Council of State, Judgment No 977/1998 .... 170n.60
Council of State, Judgment No 978/1998 .... 170n.60
Council of State, Judgment No 979/1998 .... 170n.60
Council of State, Judgment No 980/1998 .... 170n.60
Council of State, Judgment No 238/1999 .... 170n.62
Council of State, Judgment No 105/2000 .... 172n.74
Council of State, Judgment No 3291/2002 .... 172n.71, 172n.75, 173n.76
Council of State, Judgment No 3312/2002 .... 172n.74
Council of State, Judgment No 3335/2002 .... 172n.70
Council of State, Judgment No 1197/2005 .... 172n.72
Council of State, Judgment No 1199/2005 (2006) 47 Elliniki Dikaiosyni 1309 .... 169n.59, 172n.75
Council of State, Judgment No 1069/2013 .... 169n.59
Council of State, Judgment No 2624/2013 (2013) 57 Epitheorisi Dimosiou Dioikitikou Dikaiou 1110 .... 169n.59, 172n.72, 172n.73
Council of State, Judgment No 3248/2014 .... 172n.74
Council of State, Judgment No 3873/2014 .... 158–59n.3
Council of State, Judgment No 21/2019 .... 171n.66
Special Highest Court, Judgment No 24/1993 (1984) 20 To Syntagma 171 .... 169n.56, 172n.69, 173n.76
Supreme Civil and Criminal Court of Greece (*Areios Pagos*), Judgment No 438/1932 .... 162n.17
Supreme Civil and Criminal Court of Greece (*Areios Pagos*), Judgment No 981/1982 (1984) 20 To Syntagma 178 .... 168n.48, 169n.53
Supreme Civil and Criminal Court of Greece (*Areios Pagos*), Judgment No 1684/1986 (1987) 54 Efimeris Ellinon Nomikon 615 .... 168n.46, 172n.68
Supreme Civil and Criminal Court of Greece (*Areios Pagos*), Judgment No 356/1991 (1993) MD Epitherorisi Emporikou Dikaiou 386 164n.28, 168n.48, 172n.68, 173n.78
Supreme Civil and Criminal Court of Greece (*Areios Pagos*), Judgment No 159/1996 .... 169n.59
Supreme Civil and Criminal Court of Greece (*Areios Pagos*), Judgment No 1952/2013 (2014) 62 Nomiko Vima 914 .... 169n.59, 170n.62
Supreme Civil and Criminal Court of Greece (*Areios Pagos*), Judgment No 1791/2014 .... 173n.81
Supreme Civil and Criminal Court of Greece (*Areios Pagos*), Judgment No 66/2016 .... 172n.68, 173n.79

Hungary

Constitutional Court, Case II/03736/2012, Decision No 14/2013, 17 June 2013 .... 193n.46, 194n.53, 195n.56
Constitutional Court, Case IV/01263/2016, Decision No 3265/2017, 10 October 2017 .... 186n.3

Iran

Court of Administrative Justice, Case No 376-90/654, Judgment of the Full Court, 11 June 2012 .... 369n.49
Jahan Profil Pars Company v Ascotec Steel Trading GmbH, Tehran Court of Appeal, Chamber 15, Judgment No 9209970221401544, 5 June 2013 .... 367n.42

Tehran Court of Appeal, Chamber 12, Case No 600/12/88, Judgment No 221200948, 14 September 2009 .... 369n.54
Tehran Court of Appeal, Chamber 12, Judgment No 232, 21 June 2003 .... 370n.57
Tehran General Court, Chamber 19, Case No 633/87-109/19/88, Judgment No 880559, 11 October 2009 .... 369n.52
Tehran General Court, Chamber 27, Case No 1341/27/86, Judgment No 102, 3 May 2009 .... 369n.55

Ireland

Costello v Government of Ireland and others [2021] IEHC 600 .... 13n.40

Israel

Abed-Alla Balum et al v the Israel Land Administration et al, Supreme Court of Israel 570/66, 31 January 1967 .... 393n.18
Afula Municipality et al v Mekorot Water Company Ltd, Tel-Aviv District Court 4330/08, 5 May 2008 .... 403n.91
Alsint Ltd v the State of Israel, Supreme Court of Israel 569/80, 30 July 1981 .... 394n.27, 403n.86
Amidar the National Housing Company in Israel Ltd v Zohar Hai, Supreme Court of Israel 10487/07, 5 May 2010 .... 408n.113
Avner Yifat v Israel Land Administration, High Court of Justice 692/88, 14 August 1989 .... 403n.86
Beemuna Trust and Property Management Company Ltd v the Rabbinical Courts Administration– the State of Israel, Supreme Court of Israel 1877/04, 19 June 2005 .... 404n.92
Dead Sea Factories Ltd v the State of Israel-Ministry of Finance, Supreme Court of Israel 37987-01-13, 15 July 2013 .... 396n.41, 410n.130
Dead Sea Factories Ltd v the State of Israel Ministry of Finance, Supreme Court of Israel (sitting as an Administrative Court of Appeal) 6634/13, 19 February 2014 .... 411n.133
Dead Sea Factories Ltd v the State of Israel-the Government of Israel, Jerusalem District Court 49394-04-14, 1 October 2014 .... 395n.35
Efraim Shuali Construction and Investments Ltd v Local Council Tel-Mond, Supreme Court of Israel 2237/03, 10 January 2005 .... 403n.90
Eliyahu Aminof v Shmuel Altalef, High Court of Justice 816/98, 23 June 1998 .... 394n.28
Fast Lane Ltd v Trans Israel Highway Ltd, District Court of Jerusalem 16864-03-14, 4 May 2014 .... 396n.41
Fast Lane Ltd v Trans Israel Highway Ltd, District Court of Jerusalem 49820-09-12, 12 June 2014 .... 396n.41
Hertzelia City Parents Association v Hertzelia City Hall, Tel-Aviv District Court 156/97, 10 March 2004 .... 394n.27, 403n.86
Ilan Levi v Hagoshrim Cooperative Agricultural Society, Tel-Aviv District Court 58/10, 12 October 2010 .... 395n.34
Israel Land Administration v Han Manuli Ltd, Supreme Court of Israel 5114/05, 23 August 2005 .... 404n.93
Israeli Labor Party v The New General Histadrut Labor Federation, Tel-Aviv District Court 107/02, 10 February 2002 .... 395n.34
Karmel Desalination Ltd v the State or Israel Ministry of Finance, Jerusalem District Court 5094/06, 16 December 2007 .... 397n.46
Karmel Desalination Ltd v the State or Israel-Ministry of Finance, Supreme Court of Israel 470/08, 4 March 2010 .... 397n.47

Karmel Ulpinim Ltd v Electrochemical Industries Ltd (in liquidation), Supreme Court of Israel 9567/08, 5 January 2011 .... 393n.20
Kfar Vradim Development Company Ltd v Israel Land Administration – Northern District, District Court of Jerusalem 60876-05-12, 24 September 2013 .... 401n.80
Lahav Independents Bureau in Israel v Yaakov Verker, Supreme Court of Israel 6187/93, 24 March 1994 .... 393n.9
Levi Eliezer v the Israeli Electric Company Ltd, Tel-Aviv District Court 11288/01, 24 December 2001 .... 396n.39
M Adler Engineering Ltd v Yechezkel Katan, Supreme Court of Israel 1242/15, 12 April 2016 .... 407n.102
Metrodan Beer-Sheva Ltd v the State of Israel Ministry of Transportation, Tel-Aviv District Court 6532/06, 15 June 2006 .... 404n.94
Moshe Fichtenbaum v The Land Registrar, Supreme Court of Israel 258/88, 19 April 1990 .... 393n.18
Ottman – Bir el Maksur Election Officer, Election Appeal 3971/93 .... 395n.34
State of Israel v Boaz Raiter (late), Central District Court 56572-06-18, 5 November 2018 .... 393n.10
State of Israel v Pikali, Supreme Court of Israel 4123/19, 1 July 2019 .... 399n.62
State of Israel – Desalination Administration v H2ID Ltd, Supreme Court of Israel 2279/16, 1 May 2016 .... 395n.30
The State of Israel v Margalit SA Auto Ltd, Central District Court 40903-04-10, 6 January 2013 .... 411n.134
The State of Israel v Yaakov Levy, Supreme Court of Israel 141/75, 22 March 1976 .... 394n.21
The State of Israel v Yaakov Shimshon Shapira, Tel-Aviv District Court 6056/75, 1 January 1976 .... 399n.59, 403n.85
The State of Israel-Ministry of Defense v Jon Doe, Supreme Court of Israel 4826/12, 7 August 2012 .... 393n.19
The State of Israel-Ministry of Housing v Apropim Housing and Development (1991) Ltd, Supreme Court of Israel 5985/03, 3 November 2003 .... 393n.17
The State of Israel Ministry of Transportation v Metrodan Beer-Sheva Ltd, Supreme Court of Israel 7146/06, 15 January 2007 .... 404n.94
The Union of Engineers, Architects and Academics in Technological Professions v The New General Histadrut Labor Federation, Supreme Court of Israel 9048/05, 20 October 2009 .... 395n.32
Veinman, Rabbi, Arbitrator v National Inspector, National Assessment Unit Department of Income and Property Tax, Beer-Sheva District Court 1065/96, 21 July 1997 .... 396n.40
Yessod Ha'maala Local Municipality v Uri Miloslavsky, Supreme Court of Israel 449/73, 9 January 1974 .... 394n.26
YM Einy Bakrey Ltd v Bank Leumi Le Israel, Supreme Court of Israel 4781/12, 6 March 2013 .... 396n.38

Jamaica

Attorney General v Construction Developers Associates Ltd, Claim No HCV 2428 of 2004(Supreme Court) 293n.32
Revere Jamaica Alumina Limited v Attorney General (1977) 26 West Indian Reports 486 (Supreme Court) 296n.51

Korea

Constitutional Court, 6-1 KCCR 38, 92Hun-Ka15, etc, 24 February 1994 .... 487n.112
Seoul Administrative Court, Case 2008 Guhab 43805, 10 March 2009 .... 482n.96

Seoul Administrative Court, Case 2012GuHap15029, 30 May 2013 .... 473n.33
Supreme Court, Decision 95Da11436, 26 April 1996 .... 477n.72
Supreme Court, Decision 2001Da33604, 11 December 2001 .... 477n.72
Supreme Court, Decision 2003Da318, 22 August 2003 .... 480n.83
Supreme Court, Decision 2009Da16766, 13 December 2011 .... 490n.128
Supreme Court, Decision 2015Da215526, 9 November 2017 .... 478n.73
Supreme Court, Judgment 98Da60422, 22 August 2000 .... 487n.112
Supreme Court, Judgment 2012Da15696, 27 December 2012 .... 486n.108
Supreme Court, Judgment 2012Du22911, 23 July 2015 .... 488–89n.121

Latvia

Ģenerālprokuratūras Personu un valsts tiesību aizsardzības departamenta virsprokurora v AS 'Latvijas valsts meži' [2013] Supreme Court, Civ SPC-46/2013 .... 211n.38
On Compliance of Para 2361 'Use of Territory and Construction Rules' of Binding Regulation No 8 of 24 March 2016 by Jūrmala City Council 'On Approving the Graphic Part, Regulation on the Use of Territory and Construction in the Spatial Plan of Jūrmala City' with Article 115 of the Satversme of the Republic of Latvia [2017] Constitutional Court 2016-24-03 .... 218n.58
On Compliance of Para 55 and Para 56 of the Riga City Council Binding Regulation of 18 June 2013 No 221 'The Binding Regulation on the Use of and Construction in the Territory of Culture and Recreation Park "Mežaparks", as well its Annex No 1 "The Planned (Permitted) Use of the Territory", Insofar They Apply to the Planned (Permitted) Use of the Immovable Property at 10 Pāvu Street, Riga (Cadastre No 0100 095 0003) with Article 105 of the Satversme of the Republic of Latvia [2014] Constitutional Court 2014-04-03 .... 218n.58
On Compliance of Section 3, 5, 6, 7 and 9 of the Law On Solidarity Tax with the First Sentence of Article 91 and Article 109 of the Satversme [2017] Constitutional Court 2016-14-01 .... 217n.57
On Compliance of Section 27(4) and the Text of Section 28(2) 'for the Time Period until the Age of 65 Years' of Law on Institutions of Higher Education and Section 29(5) of Law On Scientific Activity with Articles 91 and 106 of the Satversme of the Republic of Latvia [2003] Constitutional Court 2002-21-01 ..... 218n.59
On Compliance of Section 495(1) of the Civil Procedure Law with the first sentence in Article 92 of the Constitution of the Republic of Latvia [2014] Constitutional Court 2014-09-01 .... 218n.60
On Compliance of Section 534, 5341, 535, 536 and 537 with the first sentence of Article 92 of the Satversme of the Republic of Latvia, Constitutional Court 2022-03-01, pending 203n.*, 226n.81

Lithuania

Belaja Rus v Westintorg Corp, Supreme Court, Case No 3K-3-443/2008, Judgment, 30 September 2008 .... 220n.68
Interperformances Inc v RJ, Supreme Court, Case No e3K-3-483-421/2015, Judgment, 25 September 2015 .... 220n.68
LB v Valstybės įmonė Valstybės turto fondas, Supreme Court, Case No 3K-3-363/2014, Judgment, 27 June 2014 .... 220n.70
Limited Liability Company 'Kutter' v UAB 'Abipa Logistics', Supreme Court, Case No 3K-7-181/2013, Judgment, 28 June 2013 .... 220n.69
NVK et al v UAB 'Luksora', Supreme Court, Case No 3K-3-353/2012, Judgment, 26 June 2012 .... 213n.41

On a Decree of the President of the Republic, Constitutional Court, Case No 40/03, Judgment, 30 December 2003 .... 219n.63
On Drawing Up and Announcing the Reasoning of Court Decisions, on the Institute of a Decision Adopted in Absentia and on Appeals, Constitutional Court, Case No 35/03-11/06, Judgment, 21 September 2006 .... 220n.66
On Private Accusations and on the Right of the Person, Against Whom the Institution of a Criminal Case is Refused, to Lodge a Complaint Against the Decision of the Prosecutor, Constitutional Court, Case No 7/03-41/03-40/04-46/04-5/05-7/05-17/05, Judgment, 16 January 2006 .... 219n.63
On the Compensation for Damage Inflicted by Unlawful Actions of Interrogatory and Investigatory Bodies, the Prosecutor's Office, and a Court, Constitutional Court, Case No 23/04, Judgment, 19 August 2006 .... 219n.62
On the Law on Hunting, Constitutional Court, Case No 14/02, Judgment, 13 May 2005 .... 220n.64
On the Law on Presidential Elections, Constitutional Court, Case No 24/04, Judgment, 25 May 2004 .... 219n.62
On the Lawfulness of the Establishment of a National Investor, Constitutional Court, Case No 28/08, Judgment, 2 March 2009 .... 225n.79
On the Ownership Rights of Functionaries, Constitutional Court, Case No 13/96, Judgment, 6 May 1997 .... 220n.64
On the Prevention of Organised Crime, Constitutional Court, Case No 8/02-16/02-25/02-9/03-10/03-11/03-36/03-37/03-06/04-09/04-20/04-26/04-30/04-31/04-32/04-34/04-41/04, Judgment, 29 December 2004 .... 219n.63
On the State Service, Constitutional Court, Case No 51/01-26/02-19/03-22/03-26/03-27/03, Judgment, 13 December 2004 .... 219n.63
Suraleb, INC v Atviroji akcinė bendrovė Minsko traktorių gamykla, Supreme Court, Case No 3K-3-267-611/2017, Judgment, 15 June 2017 .... 220n.68
UAB 'Giedra' v Šiaulių miesto savivaldybės administracija, Court of Appeal of Lithuania, Case No 2A-149/2008, Judgment, 22 January 2008 .... 214n.46
UAB 'Kauno vandenys' and Aplinkos projektų valdymo agentūra v 'WTE Wassertechnik GmbH' and AB 'Požeminiai darbai', Supreme Court, Case No 3K-7-304/2011, Judgment, 17 October 2011 .... 213n.42
VĮ Klaipėdos valstybinio jūrų uosto direkcija v 'Hydro Soil Services NV', Supreme Court, Case No 3K-3-62/2007, Judgment, 5 March 2007 .... 214n.46
VilniusLux, UAB, Gemmo SpA VSLS OU v Vilniaus miesto savivaldybės administracija, Court of Appeal of Lithuania, Case No e2A-644-370/2017, Judgment, 4 December 2017 .... 214n.46

Mexico

Acceso a los Mecanismos Alternativos de Solución de Controversias, como Derecho Humano. Goza de la misma dignidad que el acceso a la jurisdicción del Estado [2012] 2nd Collegiate Court in Civil Matters 3rd Cr., SJFG, XXV, III.2°.C.6 K(10ª) 1723 (2004620) 266n.79
Arbitraje. Cuando el accionante Ocurra ante el Juez a Presentar su Demanda y el Reo dé Contestación a Ésta o Reconvenga, quedará Extinguido el Compromiso Arbitral, Siempre que no se oponga la Excepción de Incompetencia [2007] 5th Collegiate Court in Civil Matters 3rd Cr., SJFG, XXV, III.5o.C.115 C, 1660 (172829) 265n.69
Arbitraje. Implicaciones normativas derivadas de su constitucionalización a partir de la reforma de junio de 2008[2017] First Chamber, SJFG, I, 1a. XXXVI/2017, 438 (2014010) 265n.78

Arbitraje Comercial. Los Artículos 1415 A 1463 del Código de Comercio, No Violan el Artículo 13 de la Constitución Federal [2005] First Chamber, SJFG, XXI, 1a.CLXXVI/2004, 411 (179667)........................... 264n.66
Autoridades [1924] SCJN, XV, 250 (810781)........................... 271n.115
Autoridades, Facultades de las [1934] SCJN, XLI, 944 (336190)........................... 271n.115
Autoridades Administrativas, Facultades De Las. Limite [1988] 4 Collegiate Court in Administrative Matter 1st Cr, I, 144 (231059)........................... 271n.117
Case [2011] First Chamber, Amparo en Revisión 527/2011........................... 264n.65
Case [2012] First Chamber, Amparo en Revisión 755/2011........................... 264n.65
Case [2016] First Chamber, Amparo Directo 71/2014............. 264n.64, 265n.77, 266n.84
Competencia. Deriva de la Ley no de un Contrato de Obra Pública [2008] RTFJFA, 378/08-03-01-2........................... 272n.121
Competencia. Solo Deriva de la Ley no de un Contrato [1989] 3rd Collegiate Court in Administrative Matter 1st Cr, III, 991 (229439)........................... 272n.121
Consorcio de Aguas Bilbao Bizkaia Bilbao Bizkaia Ur Partzuergoa y otro v En- M Hacienda s/ Proceso de ejecución [2021] Juzgado Contencioso Administrativo Federal 3, case 20642/2021........................... 342n.93
Contradicción de Tesis 422/2009 [2010] Second Chamber, SJFG, XXXI, 1977 (22066)........................... 270n.111
Contrato administrativo y contrato civil o mercantile. Diferencias [2001] 6th Cr, SJFG, XIV, VI.3o.A.50 A 1103 (188644)........................... 270n.106
Contratos Administrativos. Se distinguen por su finalidad de orden público y por el régimen exorbitante del Derecho Civil a que están sujetos [2001] SCt, SJFG, XIII, P.IX/2001, 324 (189995)........................... 270n.107
Finiquito de obra pública por el incumplimiento de la persona moral, emitido por Caminos y Puentes Federales de Ingresos y Servicios Conexos. Constituye un acto definitivo impugnable mediante juicio de nulidad ante el Tribunal Federal de Justicia Fiscal y Administrativa [2010] 1st Collegiate Court in Administrative Matter 6 Cr, SJFG, XXXI, VI.1o.A.282 A, 2122 (165549)........................... 271n.114, 273n.133
Justicia alternativa. Constituye un derecho humano de rango constitucional [2019] 3rd Collegiate Court in Civil Matters, 1st Cr, GSJF, I.3o.C.3 CS (10a.) (2020851)........................... 266n.83
Laudos Arbitrales. Estándar de Revisión Judicial para Determinar la Validez de la Decisión de un Tribunal Arbitral sobre su Propia Competencia [2017] First Chamber, SJFG, 40, I, 1a.XXXVII/2017, 445 (2014012)........................... 256n.15
Pacto comisorio expreso. Opera de pleno derecho, sin que sea necesario que la autoridad judicial determine la procedencia o improcedencia de la rescisión del contrato [2001] 1st Chamber of the SCt, SJFG, XIII, 2001, 1ª./J. 23/2001, 165 (189425)........................... 273n.129
Pemex-Exploracion y Producción v Corporacion Mexicana De Mantenimiento Integral, S De RL De CV [2010] Fifth District Court, juicio de nulidad de laudo 207/2010-II........................... 279n.157
Pemex-Exploracion y Producción v Fifth District Court [2010] Tenth District Court, amparo indirecto 604/2010-IV........................... 279n.159
Pemex-Exploracion y Producción v Tenth District Court [2010] Eleventh Collegiate Court, amparo en revision 358/2010........................... 279n.160
Rescisión Administrativa de contratos de adquisiciones o de obra pública. Contra dicha determinación debe agotarse el juicio contencioso administrativo federal [2012] 2nd Collegiate Court in Administrative Matter 3rd Cr, SJFG, IV, 5, III.2º.A.253 A (9ª), 4600 (160355)........ 271n.114, 273n.133

Rescisión Administrativa de contratos de obras públicas y servicios relacionados con las mismas, y de adquisiciones, arrendamientos y servicios del sector público, decretada por las dependencias y entidades de la administración pública federal. Es impugnable en el juicio contencioso administrativo ante el Tribunal Federal de Justicia Fiscal y Administrativa [2010] Second Chamber, SJFG, XXXI, 2ª./J.4/2010, 312 (165410) 271n.114, 273n.133
Rescisión administrativa de contratos de obras públicas y servicios relacionados con las mismas y su cumplimiento. Son impugnables mediante el juicio contencioso administrativo federal [2018] 1st Cr, SJFG, 58, I.4o.A.132 A (10ª.) 2510 (2018019). 270n.106
Resolución recaída a la solicitud de modificación de pena convencional derivada de un contrato celebrado con base en la Ley de Adquisiciones, Arrendamientos y Servicios del Sector Público. Se surte la competencia material del Tribunal Federal de Justicia Fiscal y Administrativa [2008] RTFJFA, I, 2, 43 (50215) 271n.114, 273n.133

The Netherlands

Defence Industries Organisation of the Ministry of Defence and Support for Armed Forces of the Islamic Republic of Iran v International Military Services Ltd, Supreme Court, NJ 2006/469, Judgment, 28 January 2005, ECLI:NL: HR:2005:AR3645. . . . . 371–72, 377–80, 377n.79, 378n.83, 379n.84, 379n.85

New Zealand

Downer-Hill Joint Venture v Government of Fiji [2005] 1 NZLR 554 (HC) 62–63n.157
Ironsands Investments Ltd v Toward Industries Ltd[2011] NZHC 870 . . . . 62–63n.157

Pakistan

A Meredith Jones & Co v Usman Textile Mills Ltd, 2002 CLD (Karachi) 1121 . . . . 443n.191
Abdullah v CNAN Group SPA through Chief Executive/Managing Director, 2014 PLD (Karachi) 349. . . . . 418n.24, 438n.163, 438n.165
Alleged Corruption in Rental Power Plants; Fraud in Payment of Rental Power Plants Detected by NEPRA, 2012 SCMR 273 . . . . 419n.30
Anjuman-e-Ahmadlya Sergodha v Deputy Commissioner, Sargodha, 1966 PLD (Supreme Court) 639 . . . . 429n.100
Capital Development Authority v Muhammad Ahsan, 2009 MLD 451 . . . . 423n.66
Capital Development Authority v RM Gulistan Engineers and Contractors (Pvt) Ltd, 2015 CLC 734. . . . . 423n.66
Ch Qaiser Mehmood v Province of Punjab through Secretary, Government Communication and Works, 2012 SCMR 1606 . . . . 435n.132, 438n.155
Dar Okaz Printing and Publishing Ltd v Printing Corporation of Pakistan (Pvt) Ltd, 2003 PLD (Supreme Court) 808 . . . . 443n.190
Fal Oil Company Ltd v Pakistan State Oil Company Ltd, 2014 PLD (Karachi) 427. . . . . 418n.24, 438n.163
Government of Balochistan v Enterprise and Development Consulting (Pvt) Ltd, 2015 CLD 1743 . . . . 434n.130
Haji Abdul Rashid Arif v Aziz Rehman and others, 2010 CLC 1014 . . . . 434n.129
Haji Naimatullah v Federation of Pakistan Through Secretary Ministry of Defense, 2013 PLD (Sindh) 406. . . . . 436n.139, 440n.171
Hajj Corruption Case, 2014 SCMR 484 . . . . .415n.5

Islamic Republic of Pakistan v Messrs Sabah Shipyard (Pakistan) Ltd, 2009 CLD 999 .... 439n.167
Karachi Dock Labour Board v Quality Builders LTD, 2016 PLD (Supreme Court) 12 .... 437n.146
Khawaja Muhammad Usaf v North-West Frontier Province, 1955 PLD (Peshawar) 72 .... 421n.49, 428n.94, 433n.119
Lakhra Power Generation Company Limited (LPGCL) v Karadeniz Powership Kaya Bey, 2014 CLD (Karachi) 337 .... 418n.25, 419n.30, 419n.33, 424n.71, 433, 434n.131, 438n.164, 441n.179
Maulana Abdul Haque Baloch v Government of Balochistan, 2013 PLD (Supreme Court) 641 and 2012 SCMR 402 .... 419n.31, 424n.72, 438n.166
Messrs Airport Support Services v The Airport Manager, Civil Aviation Authority, Karachi, 1997 CLC (Karachi) 1212 .... 428n.97
Messrs Airport Support Services v The Airport Manager, Quaid-E-Azam International Airport, Karachi, 1998 SCMR 2268 .... 427n.90, 429n.99, 430, 431–32, 433n.116
Messrs Inpaktech Industries (Pvt) Ltd v Government of Punjab, 1998 MLD 1383 .... 429n.102, 430, 431–32
Messrs M Esmailjee & Sons v The Federation of Pakistan, 1959 PLD (Karachi) 87 .... 428n.95, 433n.120
Messrs Pharmax Pakistan (Pvt) Ltd v Government of Pakistan through Secretary, Ministry of Health, 2000 CLC 628 .... 431n.107, 431–33, 433n.121
Messrs Wak Orient Power and Light Ltd v Government of Pakistan, Ministry of Water and Power, 1998 CLC 1178 .... 430n.104, 430, 431–32, 433n.117
Muhammad Ashraf Ali v Muhammad Naseer, 1986 SCMR 1096 .... 429n.100
Nan Fung Textiles Ltd v Nichimen & Co (Pakistan), 1999 YLR 2226 .... 443n.192
Orient Power Company (Private) Limited v Sui Northern Gas Pipelines Limited, 2019 PLD (Lahore) 607 .... 425n.75, 425, 425n.80, 426n.83, 442n.185, 443n.193
Pakistan Steel Mills Corporation Ltd v Messrs Mustafa Sons (Pvt) Ltd, 2003 YLR 1560 .... 439n.170
Province of Punjab v Shafsal Enterprises, Government Contractor, 1994 SCMR 1993 .... 440n.171
Province of Punjab v Sh M Riaz Shahid, 2005 SCMR 1435 .... 439n.168
Retex Global (Pvt) Ltd v Export Processing Zones Authority, 2009 CLD 814 .... 438n.165
Société Générale de Surveillance SA v Pakistan, 2002 SCMR 1694 .... 419n.28, 424n.72, 424–25, 433n.122
Suo Motu Case No 18 of 2010, 2014 SCMR 585 .... 443n.194
The Hub Power Company Ltd (Hubco) v Pakistan WAPDA, 2000 PLD (Supreme Court) 841 .... 424n.72, 424n.73, 438n.154, 443n.191
Toyota Frontier Motors (Pvt) Ltd v Government of Khyber Pakhtunkhwa through Chief Secretary, KPK, 2016 YLR (Peshawar) 1631 .... 432n.114

South Africa

Afrox Healthcare Bpk v Strydom, 2002 (6) SA 21 (SCA) 542n.81
Airports Company South Africa Ltd v ISO Leisure OR Tambi (Pty) Ltd, 2011 (4) SA 642 (GSJ) 538n.56
AllPay Consolidated Investment Holdings (Pty) Ltd v CEO, South African Social Security Agency, 2014 (4) SA 179 (CC) 538n.52, 559n.178
Barkhuizen v Napier, 2007 (5) SA 323 (CC) 542n.82
Brisley v Drotsky, 2002 (4) SA 1 (SCA) 542n.80

Cape Metro Council v Metro Inspection Services (Western Cape) CC, 2001 (3) SA 1013 (SCA) 536n.42
Glenister v President of the RSA, 2011 (3) SA 347 (CC)............................ 549n.130
Goodman Brothers (Pty) Ltd v Transnet Ltd, 1998 (4) SA 989 (W) 532n.16, 532n.19
Gray Moodliar Inc v Nelson Mandela Bay Metropolitan Municipality and Another, 2019 (10) BLLR 1163................................ 545n.98, 546n.103
Helen Suzman Foundation v President of the RSA, 2015 (2) SA 1 (CC).............. 549n.130
Indwe Aviation (Pty) Ltd v Petroleum Oil and Gas Corporation of South Africa (Pty) Ltd (No 1), 2012 (6) SA 96 (WCC) 547n.107
Logbro Properties CC v Bedderson NO, 2003 (2) SA 460 (SCA) 535n.38, 535n.39
Lufuno Mphaphuli & Associates (Pty) Ltd v Andrews, 2009 (4) SA 529 (CC) 542n.74, 542n.76, 556n.167, 556n.168
Minister for Justice and Constitutional Development v Nyathi, 2010 (4) SA 567 (CC) 543n.83
Minister of Home Affairs v Scalabrini Centre, 2013 (6) SA 421 (SCA)............... 549n.130
MV Alina II, Transnet Ltd v MV Alina II, 2013 (6) SA 556 (WCC).................. 555n.159
Ntshangase v MEC for Finance, Kwazulu-Natal, 2010 (3) SA 201 (SCA) 547n.107
Pharmaceutical Manufacturers Association of SA: In re Ex parte President of the RSA, 2000 (2) SA 674 (CC) 559n.177
President of the Republic of South Africa v South African Rugby Football Union, 2000 1 SA 1 (CC) 549n.130
Replication Technology Group v Gallo Africa Ltd, 2009 (5) SA 531 (GSJ)...554n.157, 554n.158, 555n.159
South African National Parks v MTO Foresty (Pty) Ltd, 2018 (5) SA 177 (SCA) 535n.39, 535n.40, 535–36, 536n.43
Steenkamp NO v Provincial Tender Board, Eastern Cape, 2007 (3) SA 121 (CC) 538, 538n.53
Telcordia Technologies Inc v Telkom SA Ltd, 2007 (3) SA 266 (SCA) 541n.71, 542n.73, 556n.165
Transnet Ltd v Goodman Brothers (Pty) Ltd, 2001 (1) SA 853 (SCA) 559n.177
Waenhuiskrans Arniston Ratepayers Association v Verreweide Eiendomsontwikkeling (Edms) Bpk, 2011 (3) SA 434 (WCC).................. 547n.107

Spain

Consejo de Estado, Dictamen 214/1992 (21 May 1992)........................... 135n.23
Consejo de Estado, Dictamen 4464/1998 (22 December 1998) 135n.23
Consejo de Estado, Dictamen 490/2008 (3 April 2008) 144n.56
Tribunal Supremo, Sala 1ª, Sentencia de 6 de marzo de 1987 ....132n.3
Tribunal Supremo, Sala 1ª, Sentencia de 18 de abril de 1998........................ 142n.50
Tribunal Supremo, Sala 3ª, Sentencia de 28 de junio de 1994, App No 7105/1992 ..... 137n.29
Tribunal Supremo, Sala 3ª, Sentencia de 16 de diciembre de 2000, App No 2360/2008... 138n.34
Tribunal Supremo, Sala 3ª, Sentencia de 20 de diciembre de 2017, App No 1715/2015... 132n.4, 150n.87
Tribunal Supremo, Sala 3ª, Sentencia de 18 de julio de 2018, App No 2438/2016...... 138n.34
Tribunal Supremo, Sala 3ª, Sentencia de 21 de diciembre de 2018, App no 5720/2017 .... 138n.34
Tribunal Supremo, Sala 3ª, Sentencia de 31 de enero de 2019, App No 1306/2016..... 138n.34
Tribunal Constitucional, ATC 259/1993, 20 July 1993 .... 139n.38
Tribunal Constitucional, STC 73/1983, 30 July 1983 .... 137n.29
Tribunal Constitucional, STC 22/1984, 17 February 1984 .... 138n.36
Tribunal Constitucional, STC 66/1984, 6 June 1984............................. 138n.36

Tribunal Constitucional, STC 62/1991, 22 March 1991 .... 135n.22
Tribunal Constitucional, STC 294/1994, 7 November 1994 .... 137n.29
Tribunal Constitucional, STC 174/1995, 23 November 1995 .... 140n.45
Tribunal Constitucional, STC 176/1996, 11 November 1996 .... 140n.41, 142n.51
Tribunal Constitucional, STC 140/2016, 21 July 2016 .... 135n.21
Tribunal Constitucional, STC 1/2018, 11 January 2018 .... 140n.46

Sweden

Finants Collect v Heino Kumpula, Swedish Supreme Court, Case No Ö 4842-14, Judgment, 17 June 2015 .... 207n.19
Kingdom of Spain v Novenergia II – Energy & Environment (SCA), SICAR, B 124550, Svea Court of Appeal, Case No T 4658-18, Decision, 19 May 2020 .... 198n.69

Trinidad and Tobago

Collymore and Abraham v Attorney General (1967) 12 West Indian Reports 5, CA; (1970) 15 West Indian Reports 229, PC 291n.19, 291n.20, 312n.126
High Court, Claim Number CV2008-04881, Judgment, 21 October 2009 .... 293n.37

United Kingdom

AIG Capital Partners, Inc and ors v Republic of Kazakhstan [2005] EWHC 2239 (Comm) 48n.59
Anisminic Ltd v Foreign Compensation Commission [1969] 2 AC 147 .... 58n.131
Associated Provincial Picture Houses v Wednesbury Corporation [1947] EWCA Civ 1 .... 59n.138, 62n.150
Atkins Ltd v The Secretary of State for Trnsport [2013] EWHC 139 (TCC) 46n.47
Bremer Vulkan Schiffbau und Maschinenfabrik v South India Shipping Corporation Ltd [1981] 2 WLR 141 .... 60n.144
Buttes Gas and Oil Co v Hammer (No 3) [1982] AC 888 .... 48n.55
Czech Republic v European Media Ventures SA [2008] 1 Lloyd's Rep 186 .... 48n.58
Dallah Real Estate and Tourism Holding Company v The Ministry of Religious Affairs, Government of Pakistan [2010] UKSC 46 .... 54n.101, 415nn.3–5
Dardana v Yukos [2002] 2 Lloyd's Rep 326 .... 54n.100
Davy v Spelthorne BC [1984] AC 262 .... 53n.96
Demco Investments & Commercial SA v SE Banken Forsakring Holding AB [2005] EWHC 1398 (Comm) 47n.50
Department of Economic Policy and Development of the City of Moscow v Bankers Trust Co [2004] EWCA Civ 314 .... 56n.114
Fulham Football Club (1987) Ltd v Sir David Richards, The Football Association Premier League Ltd [2011] EWCA Civ 855 .... 56n.112, 308n.105
Gatoil International Incorporated v National Iranian Oil Company, Judgment, 22 February 1990, 1990 WL 10622722 .... 380–84, 380n.90
Guangzhou Dockyards Co Ltd v ENE Aegiali I [2010] EWHC 2826 (Comm) 46n.44
Holman v Johnson (1775) 1 Cowp 341 .... 57n.123
Irvani v Irvani [2000] CLC 477 .... 54n.101
JH Raymer (Mincing Lane) Ltd v Department of Trade and Industry [1990] 2 AC 418 .... 48n.55
John Forster Emmott v Michael Wilson & Partners Ltd [2008] EWCA Civ 184 .... 57n.116
Kanoria v Guinness [2006] EWCA Civ 222 .... 54n.101
Keydon Estates Ltd v Western Power Distribution (South Wales) Ltd [2004] EWHC 996 (Ch) 47n.50
Law v National Greyhound Racing Club [1983] 1 WLR 1302 .... 60n.143
Minister of Home Affairs & Ors v Fisher [1979] AC 319 .... 290n.12

Occidental Exploration & Production Company v Republic of Ecuador[2005] EWCA Civ 1116; [2007] 2 CLC 16 47–48
Padfield v Minister of Agriculture [1968] AC 997 . . . . . 59n.135
Petroships Pte Ltd of Singapore v Petec Trading and Investment Corporation of Vietnam and Others (the Petro Ranger) (2001) 2 Lloyd's Rep 348 . . . . . 56n.108
R v Criminal Injuries Compensation Board, ex p Lain [1967] 2 QB 864. . . . . 60n.143
R v Deputy Industrial Injuries Commissioner, Ex parte Moore [1965] 1 QB 456. . . . . 63n.159
R v Disciplinary Committee of the Jockey Club, ex parte Aga Khan [1993] 2 All ER 853 . . . . . 60n.143
R v Industrial Court, ex p ASSET [1964] 1 QB 456 . . . . . 60n.144
R v Jockey Club Disciplinary Committee, ex parte Aga Khan [1993] 2 All ER 853 . . . . . 575n.95, 576
R v Lord President of the Privy Council, ex p Page [1993] 2 AC 682. . . . . 58n.132
R v National Joint Council for the Craft of Dental Technicians, ex p Neate [1953] 1 QB 704. . . . . 60n.144
R v Panel on Take-overs and Mergers; ex parte Datafin plc [1986] EWCA Civ 8; [1987] QB 815 . . . . . 575n.93
Re Kirkpatrick's Application [2003] NIQB 49 . . . . . 58n.129
Re McBride's Application[1999] NI 299 . . . . . 58, 58n.129
Re Racal Communications Ltd [1981] AC 374. . . . . 58n.132
Richardson v Mellish (1824) 2 Bing 229 . . . . . 57n.122
Soleimany v Soleimany[1998] EWCA Civ 285 . . . . . 57n.120, 57n.126
The Secretary of State for the Home Department v Raytheon Systems Ltd[2014] EWHC 4375 (TCC); [2015] EWHC 311 (TCC). 43–44, 56
The Federal Republic of Nigeria v Process & Industrial Developments Ltd [2023] EWHC 2638 (Comm) 7n.19, 14n.41, 29n.121
Vinava Shipping Co Ltd v Finelvet AG (The 'Chrysalis') [1983] 1 Lloyd's Rep 503. . . . . 46n.44
Westacre Investments Inc v Jugoimport-SDPR Holding Co Ltd [1999] EWCA Civ 1401 . . . . . 57n.126
YL v Birmingham City Council [2007] UKHL 27; [2008] 1 AC 95 . . . . . 58n.129
Zermalt Holdings SA v Nu-Life Upholstery Repairs Limited [1985] 2 EGLR 14 . . . . . 56n.108

United States of America

Allied Bruce Terminix, Co v Dobson, 513 US 265 (1995). 236n.10
Am Spring Wire Corp v United States, 8 CIT 20, 590 F Supp 1273 (Ct Int'l Trade 1984) 482n.97
AT&T Mobility, LLC v Concepcion, 563 US 333 (2011). 239n.24
BCB Holdings Limited v Government of Belize, 110 F Supp 3d 233 (DDC 2015) 306n.94
BG Group plc v Republic of Argentina, 134 SCt 1198 (2014). 235n.5
Block v Cmty Nutrition Inst, 467 US 340 (1984) 244n.36
Bowen v Amoco Pipeline Co, 254 F3d 925 (10th Cir 2001) 238n.17, 240–41n.26
Cable Connection, Inc, v Directv, 190 P 3d 586 (Cal 2008) 240–41n.26
CFTC v Schor, 478 US 833 (1986) 237n.15, 237, 243–44
Citizens Bank v Alfabco, Inc, 539 US 52 (2003) (per curiam). 236n.10
CompuCredit Corp v Greenwood, 565 US 95 (2012) 236n.11
Corporacion Mexicana De Mantenimiento Integral, S De RL De CV v Pemex-Exploracion y Producción, Case No 10 Civ 206 (AKH) (SDNY, 27 August 2013). 280n.162
Corporacion Mexicana De Mantenimiento Integral, S De RL De CV v Pemex-Exploracion y Producción, Docket No 13-4022 (2d Cir 2016). 280n.163
Cremin v Merrill Lynch, Pierce, Fenner & Smith, 957 F Supp 1460 (ND Ill 1997). 237n.16

Delaware Coalition for Open Government, Inc v Strine, 733 F3d 510 (3rd Cir 2013) 240n.25, 247n.48
Doctor's Associates, Inc v Casarotto, 517 US 681 (1996) 236n.11, 239n.23
First Options of Chicago, Inc v Kaplan, 514 US 938 (1995) 239n.21
Hall Street Assocs LLC v Mattel Inc, 552 US 576 (2007) 240–41n.26
Hoeft v MVL Group, Inc, 343 F3d 57 (2d Cir 2003) 240–41n.26
Johnson v Robinson, 415 US 361 (1974) 244n.36
Katz v Cellco P'ship [2013] WL 6621022 (SDNY, 12 December 2013) 237n.14
NAFTA Traders, Inc v Quinn, 399 SW3d 84 (TX 2011) 240–41n.26
MACTEC, Inc v Gorelick, 427 F3d 821 (10th Cir 2005) 240–41n.26
Marbury v Madison, 5 US 137 (1803) 291n.18
Marmet Health Care Center, Inc v Brown, 132 SCt 1201 (2012) 239n.22
Mobil Cerro Negro Ltd v Venezuela, 863 F3d 96 (2d Cir 2017) 243n.34
Medellin v Texas, 525 US 491 (2008) 245n.38
Mitsubishi Motors Corporation v Soler Chrysler-Plymouth Inc, 473 50 US 614 (1985) 542
Morris v Gressette, 432 US 491 (1977) 244n.36
New York Times Co v Sullivan (No 39), 376 US 254 (1964) 326n.32
Novenergia II – Energy & Environment (SCA) v Kingdom of Spain, Case No 1:18-cv-1148 (DDC, 7 December2018) 199n.73
Parsons & Whittemore Overseas Co, Inc v Societe Generale de L'Industrie du Papier (RAKTA), 508 F2d 969 (2d Cir 1974) 241n.28
Siegel v Prudential Ins Co, 67 Cal App 4th 1270 (Cal Ct App 1998) 238n.19
Southland Corp v Keating, 465 US 1 (1984) 238n.18, 248
The Paquette Habana, 175 US 677 (1900) 244n.35
Thomas v Union Carbide Agricultural Products Co, 473 US 568 (1985) 236n.12, 237, 243–44
Webster v Doe, 486 US 592 (1988) 244n.36
Zernicek v Brown & Root, Inc, 826 F2d 415 (5th Cir 1987) 256n.16
Zernicek v Petroleos Mexicanos (Pemex), 614 F Supp 407 (SD Tex 1985) 256n.16

Table of Treaties, Legislation, and Related Instruments

I. MULTILATERAL TREATIES

Additional Protocol to the Framework Agreement of the Pacific Alliance, signed 10 February 2012, entered into force 1 May 2016
- Ch 10 . . . . 259n.37

Agreement among the Government of Japan, the Government of the Republic of Korea and the Government of the People's Republic of China for the Promotion, Facilitation and Protection of Investment (China–Japan–Korea Trilateral Investment Agreement), signed 13 May 2012, entered into force 17 May 2014
- Art 15 . . . . 458n.43

Agreement between the United States of America, the United Mexican States, and Canada (USMCA), signed 30 November 2018, entered into force 1 July 2020 . . . . 243n.30
- Ch 14 . . . . 259n.37

Agreement Establishing the Caribbean Court of Justice, adopted 14 February 2001, entered into force 23 July 2002, 2255 UNTS 319 . . . . 292n.24

Agreement for the Termination of Bilateral Investment Treaties between the Member States of the European Union [2020] OJ L 169/1 221–22

Agreement on Reciprocal Promotion and Protection of Investments between States of the Economic Cooperation Organization, adopted 7 July 2005, not yet in force
- Art 9 384–85
- Art 10 384–85
- Art 17 384–85
- Art 17(1) 384–85

Agreement on Promotion, Protection and Guarantee of Investments amongst the Member States of the Organization of the Islamic Conference, adopted 5 June 1981, entered into force February 1988 . . . . 384n.105
- Art 17 384

Comprehensive and Progressive Agreement for Trans-Pacific Partnership (CPTPP), signed 8 March 2018, entered into force 30 December 2018
- Ch 9 . . . . 259n.37
- Art 2 . . . . 259n.38
- Annex 9- L 259n.38

Comprehensive Economic and Trade Agreement (CETA), signed 30 October 2016, in parts provisionally in force since 21 September 2017, [2017] OJ L 11/23 . . . . 13n.40, 109–11

Convention on the Execution of Foreign Arbitral Awards, adopted 26 September 1927, entered into force 25 July 1929, 92 LNTS 301 . . . . 418, 438n.161

Convention on the Recognition and Enforcement of Foreign Arbitral Awards (New York Convention), adopted 10 June 1958, entered into force 7 June 1959, 330 UNTS 3 . . . 9n.25, 10n.27, 23, 48, 54, 81, 88, 105, 118, 193, 194, 205, 215–16, 217n.56, 218, 222, 223*t*, 235n.5, 242, 256, 287–88, 294, 305–6, 307n.98, 313–15, 337, 380–81, 418, 424, 454–55, 458, 460, 461–62, 502, 513, 514–15, 526–27, 566n.25

Art I(1) 81, 105, 222–23
Art I(3) 356–57
Art II(1) 195, 440n.173
Art II(2) 440n.173
Art II(3) 418, 426, 513–14
Art III 242–44, 462n.63
Art V 241n.27, 243, 336–37, 338, 426, 440n.173, 442–43, 502
Art V(1)(b). 241, 248n.50
Art V(2)(a). 222–23, 383–84, 388
Art V(2)(b). 215n.48, 306, 314, 339, 383–84, 388, 442n.184, 513–14
Art VII. 443n.189

Convention on the Settlement of Investment Disputes between States and Nationals of Other States (ICSID Convention), adopted 18 March 1965, entered into force 14 October 1966, 575 UNTS 159. . . . . . . 10n.26, 23, 48, 60, 77–78, 105n.64, 113, 132, 193n.45, 194, 203–4, 221–23, 225, 235n.5, 242, 243, 244, 259–60, 287–88, 321n.1, 340, 418–19, 424, 438, 458, 460, 461, 462, 501n.23, 501, 544, 566n.25, 571–72
Preamble, para 3 . . . . 501n.25
Art 14. . . . . .119n.118
Art 25. 195
Art 25(1). 474n.46
Art 25(3). 195
Art 25(4). 195
Art 26. 105
Arts 38–40 . . . . 119n.118
Art42 . . . . 190n.20
Art 44. . . . . 119n.118
Art 48(3). 119n.118
Art 52(1). 222n.73
Art 52(1)(a)–(e) 119n.119
Art 52(1)(d). 119, 119n.118
Art 52(1)(e) 119n.118
Art 53. . . . . .119, 340, 341
Arts 53–54 . . . . 243n.34
Art 53(1). 105
Art 54. . . . . 340, 341–42
Art 54(1). 105, 119, 222, 461, 461n.53
Art 55. . . . . 462n.62
Art57 . . . . 119n.118
Art 69. . . . . 461n.54

Energy Charter Treaty (ECT), adopted 17 December 1994, entered into force 16 April 1998, 2080 UNTS 95 . . . . . . 96–98, 99, 104, 126–27, 184–85, 196, 198–99, 200, 221–22
Art 26. 98
Art 47(3). 99n.37

European Convention on International Commercial Arbitration, adopted 21 April 1961, entered into force 7 January 1964, 484 UNTS 349. . . . . . . .11, 23, 81n.71, 193n.43, 194, 205, 256, 376–77
Art I(1) 203–4n.2
Art II(1) 11n.31, 81, 105, 194–95, 203–4n.2, 211–12, 376–77
Art II(2) 194–95, 211n.39
Art X(9). 195

Free Trade Agreement between the United Mexican States and the Republics of Costa Rica, El Salvador, Guatemala, Honduras and Nicaragua (Central America–Mexico FTA), signed 22 November 2011, entered into force 1 July 2013
Ch XI. 259n.37
Art 17.22. . . . . . 260n.42, 261n.46, 262n.53, 265n.76

Inter-American Convention on International Commercial Arbitration (Panama Convention), adopted 30 January 1975, entered into force 16 June 1976, 1438 UNTS 245 . . . . .22n.75, 235n.5, 243, 337n.82
Art V 280–81

Investment Protection Agreement between the European Union and Its Member States, of the One Part, and the Republic of Singapore, of the Other Part, signed 19 October 2018, not yet in force, COM(2018) 194 final, Annex 1, ch 3, s A 110n.85, 110n.86

Investment Protection Agreement between the European Union and Its Member States, of the One Part, and the Socialist Republic of Viet

Nam, of the Other Part, signed 30 June 2019, not yet in force, COM(2018) 694 final,
Annex, arts 3.38 ff. 110n.85
North American Free Trade Agreement (NAFTA), signed 17 December 1992, entered into force 1 January 1994, 32 ILM 289 and 605. . . . . . 23, 243, 244–46, 252, 260–61, 264
Art 2022 . . . . . . 260n.42, 261n.45, 262n.53, 265n.76
Protocol on Arbitration Clauses, signed 24 September 1923, entered into force 28 July 1924, 27 LNTS 157 . . . . 418, 438
Treaty of the Southern African Development Community, adopted 17 August 1992, entered into force 30 September 1993. . . 540n.62
Art 22. . . . . 540n.62
Treaty on Free Trade between the Republic of Colombia, the Republic of Venezuela and the United Mexican States, signed 13 June 1994, entered into force 1 January 1995. 262–63
Ch XVII 259n.37
Art 19.19 . . . . . . 260n.42, 261n.46, 262n.53, 265n.76
United Nations Convention on Jurisdictional Immunities of States and Their Property, adopted 2 December 2004, not yet in force, UN Doc A/RES/59/38, Annex. 463
United Nations Convention on Transparency in Treaty-based Investor-State Arbitration, adopted 10 December 2014, entered into force 18 October 2017, UNTC Reg No 54749 . . . . 29n.118, 49n.64, 124n.132, 344–45
Annex 556n.161
Vienna Convention on the Law of Treaties (VCLT), adopted 22 May 1969, entered into force 27 January 1980, 1155 UNTS 331 . . . . 386–87, 513–15, 526–27
Art 19(a). 384–85
Art46 514
Art 46(1). 520–21

II. BILATERAL TREATIES

Agreement between Japan and the United Mexican States for the Strengthening of the Economic Partnership, signed 17 September 2004, entered into force 1 April 2005
Ch 7. . . . . 259n.37
Agreement Between the Government of Canada and the Government of the People's Republic of China for the Promotion and Reciprocal Protection of Investments, signed 9 September 2012, entered into force 1 October 2014
Art 20. . . . . 458n.42
Art21 . . . . 458n.42
Agreement between the Government of the French Republic and the Government of the United Arab Emirates relating to the Universal Museum in Abu Dhabi, signed 6 March 2007 77
Agreement between the Government of the Islamic Republic of Iran and the Government of the Republic of Yemen on the Reciprocal Promotion and Protection of Investments, signed 29 February 1996, entered into force 16 October 2000 . . . . 385n.113
Agreement between the Government of the Kingdom of Denmark and the Government of the Republic of Ghana Concerning the Promotion and Protection of Investments, signed 13 January 1992, entered into force 6 January 1995
Art 10. . . . . .504–5n.36
Art 10(1). 505n.38
Agreement between the Government of the Kingdom of Norway and the Government of the Republic of Hungary on the Promotion and Reciprocal Protection of Investments, signed 8 April 1991, entered into force 4 December 1992. . . . . 189n.14

Agreement between the Government of the Kingdom of Thailand and the Government of the People's Republic of China for the Promotion and Protection of Investments, signed 12 March 1985, entered into force 12 December 1985. . . . . 458n.39
Agreement between the Government of the People's Republic of China and the Government of Romania Concerning the Encouragement and Reciprocal Protection of Investments, signed 12 July 1994, entered into force 1 September 1995. . . . . 458n.39
Agreement between the Government of the People's Republic of China and the Government of the Republic of Ghana Concerning the Encouragement and Reciprocal Protection of Investments, signed 12 October 1989, entered into force on 22 November 1991
Art 10. . . . . .504–5n.36
Art 10(1). 505n.37
Agreement between the Government of the People's Republic of China and the Government of Turkmenistan on Encouraging and Mutual Protection of Investments, signed 21 November 1992, entered into force 4 June 1994. . . . . 458n.39
Agreement between the Government of the Republic of Ghana and the Government of Malaysia for the Promotion and Protection of Investments, signed on 8 November 1996, entered into force18 April 1997
Art 7. . . . . .504–5n.36
Art 7(1). 505n.38
Agreement between the Government of the Republic of Peru and the Government of the People's Republic of China Concerning the Encouragement and Reciprocal Protection of Investments, signed 9 June 1994, entered into force 1 February 1995. 459
Art 8.3 . . . . 459n.47
Agreement between the Government of the United Kingdom of Great Britain and Northern Ireland and the Government of the Republic of Ghana for the Promotion and Protection of Investments, signed 22 March 1989, entered into force 25 October 1991
Art 10. . . . . .504–5n.36
Art 10(1). 505n.38
Agreement on Encouragement and Reciprocal Protection of Investments between the Kingdom of the Netherlands and the Republic of Ghana, signed 31 March 1989, entered into force 1 July 1991
Art 9. . . . . .504–5n.36
Art 9(1) 505n.38
Agreement on Reciprocal Promotion and Protection of Investments between the Government of the Italian Republic and the Government of the Islamic Republic of Iran, signed 10 March 1999, entered into force 8 August 2003
Art 8(2). 385n.114
Agreement on Reciprocal Promotion and Protection of Investments between the Government of the Republic of Armenia and the Government of the Islamic Republic of Iran, signed 6 May 1995, entered into force 26 February 1997. . . . . 385n.112
Free Trade Agreement between Australia and the United States of America, signed 18 May 2004, entered into force 1 January 2005. 579–80
Annex 2- C. 563n.7
Free Trade Agreement between Chile and Mexico, signed 17 April 1998, entered into force 1August 1999
Ch 9. . . . . 259n.37
Art 18.19. . . . . 260n.42, 261n.46, 262n.53, 265n.76
Free Trade Agreement between the Government of Australia and the Government of the People's

Republic of China, signed 17 June 2015, entered into force 20 December 2015 .... 574n.82
Free Trade Agreement between the United Mexican States and the Republic of Panama, signed 3 April 2014, entered into force 1 July 2015
Ch X 259n.37
Art 18.21 ...... 260n.42, 261n.46, 262n.53, 265n.76
Free Trade Agreement between the United Mexican States and the Republic of Peru, signed 6 April 2011, entered into force 1 February 2012
Ch XI 259n.37
Free Trade Agreement between the United Mexican States and the Oriental Republic of Uruguay, signed 15 November 2003, entered into force 15 July 2004
Ch XIII 259n.37
Free Trade Agreement between the United States of America and the Republic of Korea (KORUS FTA), signed 30 June 2007, entered into force 15 March 2012 475–76
Art 7.6 .... 491n.132
Treaty between the United Kingdom of Great Britain and Northern Ireland and the French Republic Concerning the Construction and Operation by Private Concessionaires of a Channel Fixed Link, signed 12 February 1986, entered into force 29 July 1987, 1497 UNTS 325
Art 19 .... 77n.59

III. OTHER INTERNATIONAL INSTRUMENTS AND MODEL TREATIES

Greek Model BIT 2001 .... 179n.105
ICSID Administrative and Financial Regulations, amended 2006, ICSID/15 (April 2006), 51
Art 22(1) 491n.130
United Nations Commission on International Trade Law (UNCITRAL), Model Law on International Commercial Arbitration, adopted 21 June 1985, amended 7 July 2006, UNGA Res 40/72 and 61/33, UN GAOR 40th Sess, Supp No 17, UN Doc A/40/17, Annex I and UN GAOR 61st Sess, Supp No 17, UN Doc A/61/17, Annex I 17, 23, 46, 55–56, 62n.153, 101n.43, 118, 140–41, 161, 203n.*, 204, 205, 215–16, 252, 260–61, 262, 278, 313n.133, 314–15, 325, 336–37, 356–57, 391–92, 478, 551, 558, 566
Art 1(3) 160n.9
Art 1(5) 479
Art 5 .... 294n.40, 313
Art 7 .... 565n.20
Art 11 .... 565n.21
Art 12 .... 118n.117, 567n.26
Art 16 .... 566n.22
Art16(3) 161
Art 18 .... 118n.117
Art 26 .... 256n.22
Art 31(2) 118n.117
Art 34(2) 203n.*, 215n.50
Art 34(2)(b)(i) 383n.103, 569n.50
Art 34(2)(b)(ii) 383n.103, 570n.61
Art 36 .... 256n.22, 572n.69
United Nations Commission on International Trade Law (UNCITRAL), Rules on Transparency in Treaty-based Investor-State Arbitration, effective 1 April 2014 .... 29n.116, 124n.132, 179–81, 247, 344–45, 555–56
Preamble 246n.43, 249n.51
Art 1(1)–(3) 247n.47
Arts 2–3 .... 247n.44
Art 3(1) 491n.131
Arts 4–5 .... 247n.45
Art6 .... 247n.44
Art 8 .... 247n.46

IV. ARBITRATION RULES

Arbitration Rules of the Arbitration Institute of the Stockholm Chamber of Commerce 2017
Art 18 .... 118n.116
Art23(2) 118n.116
Art42(1) 118n.116
Arbitration Rules of the International Chamber of Commerce 2012 165
Art 34.6 .... 47n.49

Arbitration Rules of the International Chamber of Commerce 2021....... 378
Art 11(1)..................... 118n.116
Art22(4) 118n.116
Art32(2) 118n.116
Arbitration Rules of the London Court of International Arbitration 2014
Art 26.8......................... 47n.49
Arbitration Rules of the London Court of International Arbitration 2020............. 297n.61
Art5.3 .... 118n.116
Art14.1 .... 118n.116
Art 26.2....................... 118n.116
ICSID Arbitration Rules 2022
r 3(2).......................... 119n.118
r13(2)–(4) 119n.118
r 59(1)(g)–(j) 119n.118
rr 62–68 .... 29n.117
United Nations Commission on International Trade Law (UNCITRAL), Arbitration Rules as revised in 2010, UNGA Res 65/22, UN GAOR 65th Sess, Supp No 17, UN Doc A/65/17, Annex I 118, 179n.105, 275
Arts 11–13 .... 118n.116
Art 17(1)...................... 118n.116
Art34(3) 118n.116

V. NATIONAL LAWS

Antigua and Barbuda

Arbitration Act 1975 (Cap 33) 293n.34
Constitution of Antigua and Barbuda 1981
s 2............................ 290n.13

Argentina

Argentine Constitution 1853, reinstated 1983, revised 1994 ....322–23, 334, 342–43, 344, 345
Art 14*bis* 322n.4
Art 18....................... 322, 322n.6
Art 27...........................340–41
Art 75(12)..................... 323n.11
Art75(13) 323n.11
Art 75(22)............. 321, 340–41, 349
Art 76........................ 345n.104
Art 116 .... 322, 326–27, 331n.58, 340–41, 343n.96
Art 120 .... 334n.72
Art 121 .... 323n.12
Art126......................... 323n.11
Federal Civil and Commercial Code (Law 26,994) 2015 ....323, 325, 329
Art 3............................... 326
Art 959 349
Art 1644 329
Art 1649 .... 323n.16, 329
Art 1651 .... 323n.16, 328, 329
Art 2600 329–30
Art 2605 .... 323n.18, 328
Art 2609(a)..................... 328n.43
Art 2651 344
Federal Civil and Commercial Procedural Code (Law 17,454) 1976........ 323, 325n.25, 329, 330, 338
Art 1............... 323n.18, 327n.40, 328
Art 17.......................... 347, 348
Art 36(6)....................... 335n.76
Art 125(1)..................... 345n.105
Art 164 .... 345n.105
Art 166(2)...................... 335n.76
Art 198 332
Art 202 332
Art 302 344
Art 303 344
Arts 499–516 337–38
Art 499 337–38
Art 506 339
Arts 517–19 338
Art 519*bis* 338, 341
Art 736 .... 322, 329, 329n.49
Art 737 .... 322n.10, 329, 329n.49
Art 743 347–48
Art 746 347
Art 758 335
Art 759 335
Art 760 .... 335, 336, 337, 348
Art 760(2)...................... 336n.77
Art 761 335
Art 763 335–36
Art 765 347–48
Art 766 348–49
International Commercial Arbitration Law (Law 27,449) 2018....... 323, 324, 325, 328, 329, 335, 337–38, 339
Art 5............................... 329
Art 6........................... 323n.17
Art 18.............................. 348
Art 27.............................. 346
Art 28.................... 346–47, 348

Art 79 344
Art 81 348–49
Art 93 337
Art 98 336–37
Art 99 .... 336–37, 348
Art 99(A)(III) 337
Art 100 337
Art 101 337
Art 104 338
Law on Consulting Services (Law 22,460) 1981 330–31
Law on Performance of Works, by Concession to Individuals, Joint Stock Companies or Public Entities (Law 17,520) 1976 330–31
Art 12 328
New Public Works Regime (Law 13,064) 1947 336
Art 55 330–31

Australia

Administrative Decisions (Judicial Review) Act 1977 (Cth)
s 3 .... 574n.87
s 5 .... 574n.87
s 6 .... 574n.87
s 12 .... 568n.41
Commercial Arbitration Act 2010 (NSW) 566n.24
s 7 .... 565n.20
s 11 .... 565n.21
s 12 .... 567n.26
s 26G 568n.36
ss 27E–27I 568n.35
ss 27H–27I 568n.37
s 34(2)(b)(i) 569n.50
s 34(2)(b)(ii) 570n.61
s 34A 569n.45, 569n.48
s 35 .... 572n.68
s 36(b) 572n.68
s 40 .... 566n.23
Commercial Arbitration Act 2011 (SA) 566n.24
Commercial Arbitration Act 2011 (Tas) 566n.24
Commercial Arbitration Act 2011 (VIC) 566n.24
Commercial Arbitration Act 2012 (WA) 566n.24
Commercial Arbitration Act 2013 (Qld) 566n.24
Commercial Arbitration (National Uniform Legislation) Act 2011 (NT) 566n.24
Commonwealth of Australia Constitution Act (The Constitution) (Cth) 302n.81
ChIII 577
s 71 .... 577n.102
s 75(iii) 575n.90
s 75(v) 575n.90
Human Rights Commission Act 1986 (Cth)
s 46PV(1)(a) 568n.43
International Arbitration Act 1974 (Cth) 62–63, 566
s 2B 566n.23
s 8 .... 572n.68
s 16 .... 569n.50, 570n.61
s 19 .... 62n.154, 571n.62
ss 23C– 23D 568n.35
s 23E 568n.36
s 23F 568n.37
s 23G 568n.37
s 35 .... 571n.67
s 39(2) 572n.68
Judiciary Act 1903 (Cth)
s 39B 575n.90
s 78A 568n.42

Bahamas

Arbitration Act 42/2009 .... 294n.43
Arbitration (Foreign Arbitral Awards) Act 43/2009 .... 294n.43
Constitution of the Commonwealth of The Bahamas 1973
s 2 290–91

Barbados

International Commercial Arbitration Act 2007 .... 294–95, 302
s 1(5) 294n.42
s 2(7) 294n.41
s 18(8) 302n.80
s 53 .... 295n.45
Constitution of Barbados 1966
s 1 290–91

Belgium

Belgian Judicial Code
Art 1676 376–77
Art 1676(2) 11, 376

Civil Code
Art 2060 376

Belize

Arbitration (Amendment) Ordinance 1980 . . . . . 292n.29
s 16 . . . . . 294n.44, 294–95
Constitution of Belize 1981
Art 2 290–91
Art 17 308–9
Supreme Court of Judicature Amendment Act 2011 . . . . . 308n.107

Brazil

Decree No 10.025 of 20 September 2019 . . . . . 253n.3
Law No 13.129 of 26 May 2015
Art 1 . . . . . 253n.5

China

Administrative Litigation Law 1989, amended 2014
Art 2 455
Art 3 457
Art 12 . . . . . 455n.32, 456n.33
Art 13 . . . . . 455n.32, 457n.34
Arbitration Law 1994 . . . . . 451, 462–63
Art 2 . . . . . 452–53, 454–55
Art 62 . . . . . 462n.60
Civil Procedural Law 462–63
Ch 16 . . . . . 461n.55
Art 283 . . . . . 462n.61
Company Law 1993, amended 2013 453
Art 2 . . . . . 453n.19
Constitution of the People's Republic of China1982, revised 2018 452–53
Preamble 452n.15
Art 7 . . . . . 454n.24
Art 33 . . . . . 452n.16
General Principles of Civil Law 1986 452
Ch III 452n.11
Art 36 . . . . . 452n.12
Law of Immunity of Assets of Foreign Central Banks 2005 462–63
Art 1 . . . . . 463n.66

Colombia

Arbitration Statute, Law 1563 of 2012
Art 8 . . . . . 253n.8
Art 16 . . . . . 253n.8
Art46 . . . . . 253n.8
Political Constitution 1991
Art 116 . . . . . 26n.101

Dominica

Constitution of the Commonwealth of Dominica 1987
s 117 290–91

Dominican Republic

Law No 489-08 on Commercial Arbitration 2008
Art 2 . . . . . 253n.6

Ecuador

Constitution 2008
Art422 . . . . . 26n.102

Estonia

Code of Civil Procedure 2005 205–6
Arts 712– 57 . . . . . 205n.8
Art 718 209
Art 718(3) 209–10
Implementation Act of the Constitution of the Republic of Estonia 1992 . . . 225–26
Statutes of Arbitration
Art 1 . . . . . 204n.3

France

Civil Code 79, 325
Art 3 78–79
Art 2059 . . . . . 75, 75n.45
Art 2060 . . . . . 75–77, 78, 83, 86
Art 2060(1) 75, 76, 84
Art 2060(2) 76
Art 2060 al 1 . . . . . 75n.46
Code of Administrative Justice
Art L 311-6 76
Code of Civil Procedure 20–21, 72, 73, 75, 79
Title II 79
Art 83 . . . . . 73, 78–79
Art 595 . . . . . 82n.76
Art 1003 . . . . . 72, 72n.36
Art 1004 . . . . . 72, 73, 74, 78–79
Art 1464(4) 79
Art 1505 85
Constitution of 3 September 1791 . . . . 71, 140
Title III, Ch V, Art 5 . . . . . 26n.101, 71n.25, 140n.44

Constitution of 24 June 1793 . . . . 71, 234
Art 86. . . . . 234n.2
Arts 86 ff 71n.26
Art 91. . . . . 71n.26
Art 94. . . . . 71n.26
Art 95. . . . . 71n.26
Constitution of 22 August 1795 . . . . . . 71, 140
Art 210 . . . . 26n.101, 140n.44
Arts 210 ff. 71n.27
Constitution of 13 December 1799 71
Arts 60 ff 71n.27
Constitution of 4 August 1802 72
Constitution of 4 November 1848
Art 89. . . . . 68n.10
Decree No 2002-56,
8 January 2002. . . . . 76n.51
Decree No 2008-879,
1 September 2008
Art 18. . . . . 77n.60
Decree No 2011-48 of
13 January 2011. 79
Decree of 6/7 September 1790 . . . . 70n.21
Decree of 11 June 1793. 72
s I, Art 1(3). 71n.29
s V, Art 1(3) 71n.30
s V, Art 1(4) 71n.30
Decree of 2 October 1793
Art 2. . . . . 72n.31
Art 4. . . . . 72n.31
Art 5. . . . . 72n.31
Art 8. . . . . 72n.31
Law No 86-972 of 19 August 1986
laying down various
provisions relating to
local authorities 21n.61, 77n.55
Ordonnance No 2004-559,
17 June 2004, repealed
Art 11(1). 76–77
Ordonnance No 2015-899,
23 July 2015
Art 102 . . . . 76n.53
Statute of 16/24 August 1790. 49–50,
67–68, 70, 71
Art 1. 70–71
Art 2. 71
Art 10. . . . . 68n.8
Art 13. . . . . 68n.7
Statute of 9 June 1796. . . . . . .71–72, 72n.34

Germany

Gesetzüber die schiedsgerichtliche
ErledigungprivatrechtlicherStreitigkeiten des Reiches und der
Länder (1933) (Law on Arbitration
of Private Law Disputes ofthe
German Reich and the
German States) 101n.46
Grundgesetz (GG) (Basic Law –
German Constitution) 92, 107,
108–9, 110–11, 113,
116–18, 120–21,
123, 125
Art 1. 111–12
Art 2(1). 108n.79, 117
Art 3. 108–9
Art 3(1) 109n.80
Art 12(1). 107–9
Art 14. 107–9
Art 14(3). 113, 115
Art 19(3). 108–9
Art 19(4). 107–8, 113, 115
Art 20. 111–12
Art 20(1). 116
Art 20(2). 116
Art 20(3). 99n.38, 107–8, 113,
117, 122–23
Art 24(3). 116
Art 59(2). 104n.58
Art 79(3). 111–12, 113
Art 92. 114–15
Art93 . . . . 26n.104, 114
Art 93(1). 114n.98, 116
Arts 94–96 114
Art 100(1). 114n.98
Art 101 107–8
Art 101(1). 114–15
Art 103(1). 107–8
Art 106 131–32
Lebensmittel-, Bedarfsgegenstände-
und Futtermittelgesetzbuch
(Food Code)
s 45. . . . . 102n.50
Verpackungsgesetz (German
Packaging Act)
s 23(8)–(9) 114n.99
Verwaltungsgerichtsordnung (VwGO)
(Code of Administrative Court
Procedure). 99–100
s 40(1) 101n.44
s 40(1), first sentence 100n.39
s 40(2), first sentence 100n.39
s 168(1) No 5 103
s 173. . . . . 100–1, 126
s 173, third sentence. 101–2

Verwaltungsverfahrensgesetz (VwVfG) (Administrative Procedures Act) 99–100
s 54, first sentence. 102n.50
s 54, second sentence 102
s 59. . . . . 102n.50
Zivilprozessordnung (ZPO) (Code of Civil Procedure) 478
Ch 10. 100–1
ss 1025 ff. 118n.114
s 1025(1). 100n.42
s 1030(1). 102
s 1032(1). 102
s 1034(2). 102
s 1035(3)–(5). 102
s 1036. 118
s 1037(3). 102
s 1041(2). 102
s 1042(1). 118
s 1042(2). 118
s 1042(3). 103
s 1042(4). 126n.135
s 1042(4)(1). 103
s 1050, first sentence. 102
s 1053(a). 443n.188
s 1055. 103
s 1059. . . . . .103, 118
s1059(2)(b) 443n.188
s 1060. 118
s 1061. 118
s 1063. 103

Ghana

Alternative Dispute Resolution Act 2010 (Act 798). 496, 497, 498, 499n.16, 503, 526
s 1. . . . . 503, 508–10
s 2(1) 505n.39
s 2(2) 505
s 3. 523–24
s 5. 503–4
ss 6–7. . . . . 497n.11
s 14. . . . . 504n.35
s 24. 510
s 25(1) 510
s 26. . . . . .497n.11, 510
s 26(4) 510n.58
s 39. . . . . 497n.11
s 40. 510–11
s 40(1) 510n.59
s 40(2) 511n.60
s 40(3) 511n.61
s 52. 511–12
s 54(2). 511
s 57(1). 512n.63
s 57(2). 512n.64
s 58. . . . . 497n.11
s 58(1). 512
s 58(2). 512n.66
s 58(3). 512n.66
s 59(1). 512n.68
s 59(1)(a) 512n.67
s 114. 503–4
s 115. 503–4
s 116. 508–9
s 135. . . . . .503, 510n.57
Arbitration Act 1961 (Act 38). 499n.15, 501–2, 503
s 5. 502
s 5(1) 502
s 5(2) 502
s 39. 502
Arbitration Ordinance 1928 (Cap 16) 501–2
Arbitration (Foreign Awards) Ordinance 1928 (Cap 17). 501–2
Constitution of the Republic of Ghana 1992 . . . . 496, 498, 499, 506, 507, 514–15, 526–27
Art 1(1). 498, 507–8, 515
Art 2. 525
Art 11(1). 497
Art 11(2). 497
Art 33. 508–9
Art 36(2)(b). 506n.42, 507
Art 36(2)(c) 506, 506n.42
Art 36(4). 507–8
Art 75. . . . . .498, 514
Art 125(1). 516
Art 125(2). 516
Art 125(5). 516
Art 127(1). 516
Art 129(1). 516
Art 130 . . . . 508–9, 524
Art 130(1). 516, 525
Art 130(1)(a) 26n.104, 497–98, 503
Art 133 516
Art 181 . . . . .12, 523
Art 181(1). 517–18, 519–20
Art 181(2). 517–18, 519–20
Art 181(5). 295n.49, 300, 371–72, 379–80, 513, 516–18, 519–20, 522
Art 295(1). 509n.54

Ghana Investment Promotion Centre Act 2013 (Act 865) . . . 498
s 3(a) . . . 507–8
s 33(1) . . . 504
s 33(2) . . . 504
s 33(3) . . . 504, 505

Greece

Act 4171/1961 on the Adoption of General Measures to Foster the Economic Development of the Country . . . 168n.50, 175, 176, 177
Art 1 . . . 176n.92
Art 1(1) . . . 176
Art 1(2) . . . 176n.91
Art 1(8) . . . 177n.93
Art 4 . . . 176n.92
Art 4(2) . . . 176
Art 5(1) . . . 176n.91
Art 5(2) . . . 176
Act 159/1975
Art 5(1) . . . 176n.91
Act 849/1978 on the Provision of Incentives to Reinforce the Regional and Economic Development of the Country
Art 6(5) . . . 175n.84
Act 1406/1983 . . . 168n.52
Act 2289/1995 on Prospecting, Exploration and Exploitation of Hydrocarbons
Art 2 . . . 158–59n.3
Art 10(13) . . . 159n.6
Act 2779/1999
Art 2 . . . 175
Act 3389/2005 on Public-Private Partnerships
Art 31(1) . . . 178
Art 31(2) . . . 178
Art 31(3) . . . 178
Act 3614/2007 on Cofinanced Construction Projects
Art 25A . . . 178
Art 25A(4) . . . 178–79
Art 25A(7) . . . 179
Art 25A(8) . . . 179
Art 25A(9) . . . 179
Act 3669/2008 . . . 177–78
Art 78 . . . 177n.94
Act 4001/2011
Art 162(5) . . . 159n.6
Act 4281/2014 . . . 177–78
Art 194 . . . 177
Act 4403/2016
Art 57 . . . 177n.95
Act 4412/2016 on Public Works, Procurement and Services Contracts . . . 180–81
Art 176 . . . 178
Art 176(4) . . . 178
Art 176(5) . . . 178
Art 377(1)(31) . . . 177n.94
Act 4413/2016 on the Award and Execution of Concession Contracts – Harmonisation with Directive 2014/23/EU . . . 159–60, 177–78, 180–81
Art 65(1) . . . 177–78
Art 65(2) . . . 177–78
Art 65(5) . . . 177–78
Act 4362/2016 . . . 179–80
Art 10 . . . 179–80
Art 10(4) . . . 179–80
Art 14 . . . 179n.104
Code of Civil Procedure . . . 159n.4, 160, 167, 177–78
Art 867 . . . 166, 167n.43, 168n.46
Arts 867 ff . . . 160
Art 897 . . . 160n.13, 179
Art 900 . . . 173
Art 901 . . . 160n.12
Constitution of the Hellenic Republic 1974 . . . 161, 165–66, 167
Art 1(2) . . . 169n.56
Art 1(3) . . . 169n.56
Art 5(1) . . . 166
Art 8(1) . . . 166–67
Art 20(1) . . . 161, 171–72, 173
Art 25(1) . . . 172n.67
Art 28(1) . . . 179
Art 78(4) . . . 169
Art 94(1) . . . 161, 168, 169–70, 172
Art 95(1)(a) . . . 172
Art 107(1) . . . 161, 164–65, 168n.49
Art 100 . . . 169
Art 110 . . . 164–65
Constitution of the Kingdom of Greece 1952 . . . 164
Art 112 . . . 162–63, 168n.49
International Arbitration Act (Act 2735/1999) . . . 160, 161
Introductory Act to the Code of Civil Procedure . . . 177–78

Art 49(1) 159n.4
Legislative Decree 2687/1953 on the Investment and Protection of Foreign Capital 26n.101, 161–66, 167–68, 172, 175–76
Art 1 162–63
Art 2 162–63
Art 2(2) 162–63
Art 3(3) 163n.24
Art 11(1) 163n.24
Art 12 162–63
Art 13(1) 162–63
Art 13(2) 163n.24
Legislative Decree 736/1970
Art 8(1) 159n.4
Legislative Decree 916/1971
Art 1(8) 177n.93
Statute on the Legal Council of the State (Act 3086/2002)
Art 6(3A) 159–60n.7

Grenada

Constitution of Grenada 1973
s 106 290–91

Guyana

Arbitration Act 1931 295
Constitution of the Cooperative Republic of Guyana 1980
Art 8 290–91
Investment Act 2004 295
s 28(2)(d) 295n.46

Hungary

Act I of 1988 on Public Traffic 187–88
s 9/D(8) 188n.6
Act LXXI of 1994
s 4 193
Act CLI of 2011 on the Constitutional Court
s 42 .... 194n.55
Act CXCVI of 2011 on National Property 193n.49
s 1(2) 193n.42
s 17 193
s 17(1) 194
s 17(3) 194
Act LXV of 2012
s 2 .... 194n.51
s 4 .... 194n.52
Act VII of 2015 on the Investment Related to the Maintenance of the Capacity of the Nuclear Plant of Paks 197n.63
Act CXXX of 2016 on Civil Procedure
Pt VII 185
Act I of 2017 on Administrative Court Procedure 185, 186, 187–88
s 4(2)–(3) 188n.7
s 4(7)2 .... 187n.5
Act LX of 2017 on Arbitration
s 1(3) 185, 188
s 3(1)(1) 185
s 3(1)(7) 185
s 4 .... 195, 197
s 17(3) 197
Fundamental Law of Hungary 2011
Art 24(2)(f) 194n.54
Art 38(1) 193n.42
Art Q 193n.47, 194n.54

India

Arbitration and Conciliation Act (XXVI of 1996)
s 34 .... 443n.188
s 47 .... 443n.188
s 57 .... 443n.188

Iran

Civil Procedure Code of 2000
Art 457 370
Constitution of the Islamic Republic of Iran 1979
Art 55 370
Art 77 386
Art 94 .... 384n.107
Art 98 .... 366n.37
Art 139 ...... 24n.88, 355, 355n.2, 356–57, 362, 364–65, 366–67, 368–70, 371–72, 373, 374–76, 377–78, 379, 380–85, 386, 387–89
Art 173 363
Council of State Act 1960 362–63
Art 2 362–63
Law Concerning the Accession of Iran to the 1958 New York Convention on the Recognition and Enforcement of Foreign Arbitral Awards 2001 .... 357n.6
Single Article Act authorizing the Ministry of Defence to refer the

dispute with the Italian company Agusta to arbitration 1988 ..... 369n.50
Single Article Acts ratifying the Iran-Luxemburg BIT 2019 386
Single Article Acts ratifying the Iran-Singapore BIT 2019 386

Israel

Arbitration Law 1968, last amended 2018 392–93
Art 1 .... 394n.24
Art 3 .... 394n.28
Art 5 .... 393n.11
Art 21a 397n.48
Art 24 .... 396n.42
Art 24(10) 397n.49
Art 26(a) 397n.43
Art 26(b) 397n.45
Art 29(b) 394n.21
Art 36 .... 393n.13
Art 39 .... 394n.23
Sch 2 .... 397n.50
Civil Procedure Amendment Law (The State as a Party) 1958 393–94
Art 1 .... 393n.15
Art 2 .... 393n.15
Art 4 .... 398n.58
Art 8 .... 393n.15
Art 11 .... 393n.16
Evidence Ordinance [New Version] 1971
Ch 3 .... 395n.36
Regulations for Procedure in Matters of Arbitration 1968 392–93

Jamaica

Arbitration Act 2017 .... 294n.43
Constitution of Jamaica 1962 303
s 2 290–91
s 13(1)(C) 303n.84

Korea

Act on Contracts to Which the State is a Party 487
Art 7 .... 487n.111
Art 13 .... 487n.111
Art 27 .... 487n.111
Act on Public-Private Partnerships in Infrastructure 2017
Art 47 472
Administrative Procedures Act 483
Art 1 .... 483n.98
Art 2(2) 483n.99
Art 2(3) 483n.100
Art 3 483
Art 8(2) 488
Arbitration Act 478, 480, 481, 484
Art 1 479
Art 2 479
Art 2(1) 478n.79
Art 2(2) 478, 479
Art 3 480
Art 3(1) 479–80
Art 20 .... 481n.87, 485n.101
Art 36 479
Art 36(2) 479
Judicial Conciliation of Civil Procedure Act
Art 1 .... 488n.115
State Contract Act 2012 477–78
Art 2 .... 477n.71

Latvia

Civil Procedure Law 1998 225–26
Ch D 206
Art 536 .... 219n.61
Art 1489(3) 211n.36
Constitution 218
Preamble 217
Art 105 217–18
Law on Arbitrations 2015 ...... 206, 219n.61
Art 5(1)(2) 211
Art 32(4) 207n.23
Law on European Convention on International Commercial Arbitration 2003 .... 205n.5
Law on Municipalities 1994
Art 77(5) 211
Law on State Administration
Art1(3) 211

Lithuania

Code of Civil Procedure of 1964
Art 28 .... 204n.3
Art 36(2) 213
Art 620(1)(1) 216n.51
Art 751(1) 216
Art 751(2)(2) 215n.49, 216
Constitution of the Republic of Lithuania 1992 .... 216, 219–20

Law on Amending Article 11 of the Law on Commercial Arbitration 2001 .... 214n.44
Law on Commercial Arbitration 1996, amended in 2012 205
Art 3(5) 213, 214
Art 12(1) 213
Art 12(2) 213
Art 12(3) 213, 214, 215
Art 12(4) 213, 214
Art 50(3)(6) 215n.49

Mexico

Acquisitions Law and Works Law 1993, repealed
Art 2 .... 253n.1
Art13 .... 253n.1
Art 15 .... 263n.59
Art 32 .... 257n.27
Art 98 .... 255n.11
Acquisitions Law 2000 .... 257–58, 259, 263–64, 271, 276, 277
Art 2 .... 253n.1, 268n.93, 268n.94
Art 11 .... 253n.1, 268n.93, 268n.96
Art 13 .... 271n.119
Arts 15–16 .... 274n.135, 274n.135
Art 15 .... 264n.60, 269n.105, 271n.119, 272n.125
Arts 26–55 .... 271n.119
Art 26 .... 269n.103
Art 30 .... 257n.27
Art 41 .... 256n.23
Art 41.IV 269n.104
Art42 .... 256n.23
Art 54 .... 273n.130, 273n.131
Art 80 .... 255n.11, 272n.124, 273n.132, 278n.156
Art 85 .... 274n.134
Administrative Federal Court of Justice Organic Law 2016
Art 3.VIII 270n.106
Amparo Law 2013
Art 81.I.e 275n.146
Commerce Code 1889 268
Art 1415 .... 255n.13
Art 1417 .... 261n.48
Art 1417(II) 255n.12
Art 1419 .... 261n.49
Art 1423 .... 261n.50
Arts 1427–28 .... 255n.14
Art 1432 .... 256n.15
Art 1457 .... 256n.22
Art1462 .... 256n.22
Commercial Code
Arts 1415–80 .... 255n.11
Dispute Resolution Manual 2016
Art 3.2.6 .... 276n.149
Art 3.5 .... 276n.150
Decretoporel que se reforman y adicionandiversasdisposiciones de la ConstituciónPolítica de losEstados Unidos Mexicanos, 18 June 2008
Art 17 .... 26n.101, 264n.63, 265n.70
Art 25 .... 263n.58
Art 27 .... 263n.58
Art 28 .... 263n.58
Decreto que reforma, adiciona y derogadisposiciones de diversasleyesrelacionadas con elTratado de Libre Comercio de América del Norte, 22 December 1993
Arts 7–8 .... 263n.56
Electric Power Industry Law 2014 .... 257–58, 276
Art 5 .... 253n.1
Art 96 .... 275n.148
Federal Civil Code 1928 268
Art 6 279
Art 1949 .... 273n.128
Federal Code of Civil Procedure 1943
Art 4 .... 256n.19
Art 568.III 275n.143
Art 598 .... 258n.34
Federal Constitution 1917
Art 6 .... 257n.28
Art 13 264–65
Art 14 .... 264–65, 278
Art 16 .... 270n.110, 278
Art 17 .... 265–66, 267, 278
Art 28 .... 271n.118
Art 134 269
Federal Electricity Commission (Comisión Federal de Electricidad – CFE) Law 2014 276
Art 3 .... 253n.1, 268n.93, 268n.100
Art 7 .... 253n.1, 268n.93, 268n.100
Art 45.I 272n.123
Art 82 .... 253n.1, 268n.93, 268n.100
Art 118 ..... 255n.11, 272n.124, 276n.151
Federal Judicial Power Organic Law 1995
Art 52.I 270n.106

Federal Law on Administrative Procedure 1994
Art 3(I) 271n.113
Art 3(V) 271n.113, 273n.131
Arts 5–6. . . . . 273n.131
Art 51(I) 271n.113
Art 51(II) 271n.113
Art 60. . . . . 273n.131
Federal Transparency Law 2016
Art 4. . . . . 257n.29
Art 67. . . . . 257n.30
General Law on Administrative Liabilities 2016
Art 7. . . . . 257n.26
Art 7.1 . . . . . 272n.120
Art49 . . . . . 257n.26, 272n.120
Art50 . . . . . 257n.26, 272n.120
Hydrocarbons Law 2014 . . . . . 259, 268, 271, 275, 276, 277
Arts 11–31 . . . . . 271n.119
Art 20. . . . . 273n.130
Art 21. . . . . 255n.11, 272n.124, 275n.147
Art 22. . . . . 253n.1, 268n.93, 268n.98
Energy Regulatory Coordinated Bodies Law 2014
Art 27. . . . . 275n.145
Law on Public Works and Related Services 2000 (Works Law) 259, 263–64, 271, 276, 277, 280
Art 2. . . . . 268n.93, 268n.95
Art 13. . . . . 268n.93, 268n.96
Arts 15–16 . . . . . 274n.135
Art 15. . . . . 264–65, 269n.105, 271n.119, 272n.125
Arts 27–69 . . . . . 271n.119
Art 42.6 . . . . . 269n.104
Art 61. . . . . 273n.131
Art 62. . . . . 270n.109, 272n.126, 273n.130
Art 98. . . . . 272n.124, 273n.132, 278n.156
Art 103 . . . . . 274n.134
Organic Law of the Federal Administrative Justice Court 2016
Art 3.VIII 273n.133
Organic Statute of the Federal Electricity Commission (CFE) 2017
Art 32. . . . . 256n.25, 257n.26
Art 51. . . . . 256n.25
Organic Statute of Pemex (2015)
Art 19. . . . . 256n.24
Organic Statute of PetróleosMexicanos (PEMEX)2017 . . . . . 276, 277
Art 3. . . . . 268n.100
Art 14. 263
Art 46.I 272n.123
Art 115 . . . . . 255n.11, 272n.124, 276n.151
PEMEX Law 2014
Art 3. . . . . 253n.1, 268n.93
Art 80. . . . . 253n.1, 268n.93, 268n.100
Public-Private Partnership Law 2012 . . . . . 259, 268, 271, 276, 277
Art 2. . . . . 274n.139
Art 3(VI) 274n.137
Art 8. . . . . 253n.1, 268n.93, 268n.97
Art 44. . . . . 257n.27
Art 46. . . . . 269n.103
Arts 38–66 . . . . . 271n.119
Arts 91–111 . . . . . 271n.119
Art 122 . . . . . 271n.119, 275n.141
Arts 134–43 . . . . . 271n.119
Art 138 . . . . . 272n.124
Art 139 . . . . . 274n.140
Tax and Administrative Federal Court of Justice Organic Law 2007, repealed. 271n.114

Netherlands

Arbitration Act 1986, revised 2014 . . . 379–80

New Zealand

Arbitration Act 1996
Sch 1, Art 34(6) 62n.155
Sch 1, Art36(3) 62n.155

Pakistan

Arbitration Act (X of 1940) 416, 417, 423–24, 433–36, 443, 444–45
ss 3–19. . . . . 434n.126
s 3. . . . . 435n.133, 435n.134, 436n.140, 437n.147
s 4. . . . . 435n.135
s 5. . . . . 435n.137
ss 8–12. . . . . 437n.149
s 8. . . . . 435n.136
s 13. . . . . 436n.142
s 15. . . . . 437n.150
s 17. . . . . 437n.151
s 18. . . . . 437n.152
s 19. . . . . 437n.153
s 20. . . . . 434n.127
ss 21–25 . . . . . 434n.128
s 27. . . . . 436n.144

s 30 .... 437n.153
Sch 1, item 1 435n.133, 435n.134, 436n.140
Sch 1, item 6 .... 437n.147
Arbitration (International Investment Disputes) Act (IX of 2011) 418–19
Arbitration (Protocol and Convention) Act (VI of 1937) 418, 438n.159
Capital Development Authority (Abatement of Arbitration Proceedings) Act (XXVII of 1975) 423
Companies Act (XIX of 2017) 423–24
s 278 .... 423n.68
s 278(3) 423n.69
s 356(3)(b) 423n.70
Contract Act (IX of 1872)
s 28 417
s 74 425–26
Constitution of the Islamic Republic of Pakistan 1973 .... 417–18, 420, 424
Art 16 .... 420n.47
Art 17 .... 420n.47
Art18 .... 26n.103, 420
Art 19 .... 420n.47
Art 89 .... 438n.158
Art 146(3) 420n.43
Art 152 .... 420n.44
Art 159(4) 420n.45
Art 199 .... 427, 428–29
Art 184(3) 427, 429, 434n.131
Art 268 417–18
Sch 4, Pt I, item 32 .... 417n.16
Indian Independence Act (10 & 11 geo 6, ch 30 of 1947)
s 18 .... 417n.9
Partnership Act (IX of 1932) 423–24
s 19(2)(a) 423n.67
Public Procurement Regulatory Authority Ordinance (XXII of 2002) 421n.54
s 26 421
s 27 421
Recognition and Enforcement (Arbitration Agreements and Foreign Arbitral Awards) Act (XVII of 2011) 418
s 4(2) 418
Regulation of Mines and Oilfields and Mineral Development (Government Control) Act (XXIV of 1948) 421–22
s 2 .... 422n.60
Special Economic Zones Act (XX of 2012) 421, 432, 433–34
s 21(2)(iii) 421n.51
s39 .... 421n.51
The Constitution (Eighteenth Amendment) Act (X of 2010) 417n.14

Panama

Political Constitution of the Republic of Panama 1972
Art 202 .... 322n.3, 322n.9

Peru

Law No 30225 on Public Procurement, amended by Legislative Decree No 1341
Art 45.1 .... 253n.7
Legislative Decree No 1071 on Arbitration (2008), amended by Emergency Decree No 020-2020
Art 56 .... 253n.7
Political Constitution of Peru 1993
Art 139 .... 322n.3, 322n.9

Saint Christopher and Nevis

Constitution of the Federation of Saint Christopher and Nevis 1983
s 2 .... 290n.13

Saint Vincent and the Grenadines

Constitution of Saint Vincent and the Grenadines 1979
s 101 .... 290n.13

Singapore

International Arbitration Act (Cap 143A, 2002 Rev Ed)
s 24 .... 62n.155

South Africa

Arbitration Act 42 of 1965 .... 539–40, 543n.88, 558–59
s 2 543
s 39 .... 529n.4, 543n.84
s 34 556–57
s 42 .... 539n.58
s 55(2) 557
Broad-Based Black Economic Empowerment Act 53 of 2003 .... 534n.30

Cape Arbitration Act 29 of 1898 (repealed)....................539n.58
Constitution of the Republic of South Africa 1996................539
s 2..............................531n.13
s 25...........................550n.137
s 32............................534n.32
s 32(1)............................532
s 33....................530–31, 532, 537
s 33(3)............535n.36, 537, 537n.47
s 34...............................542
s 35(3)(c) 543n.84
s 42............................531n.14
s 55(2)................531n.12, 531n.15
s 167(6)(a) 537n.47
s 170...........................538n.54
s 172...........................538n.55
s 217..............................532
s 217(2)........................532n.21
Expropriation Act 63 of 1975
s 14............................547–48
Extension of Security of Tenure Act 62 of 1997
s 22............................547–48
Insurance Act 27 of 1943
s 63...........................547n.109
s 63(1)........................547n.110
International Commercial Arbitration Act 15 of 2017 ....530, 544, 551, 553–55, 558–59
s 1............................551n.149
s 4.............................543n.84
s 5........... 529n.3, 551n.146, 552n.150
s 7.........................530n.7, 551
s 7(1).............................544
s 11........................530n.5, 555
Labour Relations Act 66 of 1995
s 33............................541n.68
Local Government: Municipal Finance Management Act 56 of 2003.... 532n.22
Local Government: Municipal Systems Act 32 of 2000..........547–48
s 109..........................546n.102
s 109(2).......................548n.122
Long-term Insurance Act 52 of 1998..... 547
Mineral and Petroleum Development Act 28 of 2002
s 1............................550n.136
Natal Arbitration Act 24 of 1898 (repealed)....................539n.58
National Environmental Management Act 107 of 1998 547–48
s 19...........................547n.118
Nuclear Energy Act 46 of 1999.......547–48
s 44...........................548n.121
Patent Act 57 of 1978 547
s 18(1)........................547n.108
Preferential Procurement Policy Framework Act 5 of 2000 ...... 532n.21
Promotion of Access to Information Act 2 of 2000 557
s 42...........................557n.175
Promotion of Administrative Justice Act 3 of 2000 ....537, 543n.86
s 1............533n.28, 537n.46, 537n.47
s 5(3).............................545
s 6....................535n.36, 537n.47
s 7(4)..........................538–39
Protection of Investment Act 22 of 2015 .....550–51, 553–54, 558
s 1.......................550n.140, 552
s 2......................... 550–51, 552
s 2(2)(e) 550n.141
s 10...........................550n.137
s 13............................551–52
s 13(1)........................552n.152
s 13(1)–(3)....................551n.142
s 13(3)(d).....................552n.152
s 13(4)........................551n.143
s 13(5)........................551n.145
s 15...........................552n.150
s 15(2).............................551
Public Finance Management Act 1 of 1999 ....532n.22, 545
s 76(4)(g)......................545n.99
Sch 3A..........................545n.99
Sch3B 545n.99
Sch3C 545n.99
Sch3D 545n.99
Public Protector Act 23 of 1994
Preamble 557n.172
Short-term Insurance Act 53 of 1998 547
s 55...............................547
Water Services Act 108 of 1997
s 21............................547–48

Spain

Constitution of 1812...............140n.43
Art 280 ....26n.101, 140
Constitution of 1978.......... 133, 136, 137, 143, 154–55
Art 1...........................139–40
Arts 14–30(2)...................... 155

Art 24. . . . . 133, 139–40, 145
Art 86. 149–50
Art 94. 144
Art 103 141–44
Art 103(1). 138, 141
Art 106 145–46
Art 106(1). 136, 137, 145–46
Art 117 . . . . 137n.28
Art 117(3). 139
Art 117(5). 136–37
Art 149(1). 135
Art 153 . . . . 145n.62
Ley 10/ 2012, de 20 de noviembre 135n.19
Ley 11/1977, de 4 de enero, General Presupuestaria. 147
Art 39. . . . . 149n.78
Ley 29/1998, de 13 de Julio, Reguladora de la JurisdicciónContencioso-Administrativa 134n.16
Art 25. . . . . 134n.13
Art 46. . . . . 134n.13
Art 70. . . . . 138n.32
Art 88. . . . . 134n.12
Arts 129–36 . . . . 134n.15
Ley 33/2003, de 3 de noviembre, del Patrimonio de las AdministracionesPúblicas (Law on the Estate of the Public Administration) 150
Art 31. 150
Ley 47/2003, de 26 de noviembre, General Presupuestaria(General Law on the State Budget). 149n.76, 149, 150
Art 7(3) 149
Ley 60/2003, de 23 de diciembre, de Arbitraje 132n.2, 140n.47, 147n.69, 151
Art 2(1) 141
Art 41(1). 143n.52
Ley 39/2015, de 1 de octubre, del Procedimiento Administrativo Común de las AdministracionesPúblicas 147n.70
Art 112(2). 147–48
Ley 9/2017, de 8 de noviembre, de Contratos del Sector Público (Law on Contracts of the Public Sector) 151n.88
Ley de Administración y Contabilidad de la Hacienda Pública, de 1 de julio de 1911
Art 6. . . . . 149n.79
Ley Orgánica 6/1985, de 1 de julio, del Poder Judicial
Arts 53–103 . . . . 136n.26
Ley Organica 7/ 2015, de 21 de julio 134n.12

Trinidad and Tobago

Arbitration Act 1939
Ch 5:01 . . . . 292n.28
s 35. . . . . 294n.44
Constitution of the Republic of Trinidad and Tobago 1976
s 2. . . . . 290n.13

United Kingdom (including British Overseas Territories)

Arbitration (International Investment Disputes) Act 1966. . . . . 48n.59
Arbitration (Scotland) Act 2010. . . . . . 45n.43
British Virgin Islands Arbitration Act 2013 . . . . 294n.43
Cayman Islands Arbitration Law 2012 . . . . 294n.43
Civil Procedure Rules
Pt 54. . . . . 50n.66, 60
r 62.10(3)(b) 56n.114
English Arbitration Act 1996 . . . . .45, 56, 523
s 4(1) 46n.48
s 7. 523–24
s 24. . . . . 56n.107
s 45. 55–56, 56n.114
ss 67–69 . . . . .46n.44, 48, 56, 62
s 67. 46–48
s 68. 46–48
s 68(2) 46
s 69. 46–47, 56n.114
s 69(3) 46–47
ss 80–91 . . . . 45n.43
s 81. . . . . 56n.110
s 81(1)(c) 57n.120
ss 100–4 . . . . 57n.120
s 101. . . . . 54n.100
s 103(3). 54n.99, 443n.188
Sch 1 . . . . 46n.48
Human Rights Act 1998. 58–59

Montserrat Arbitration Act 1907 .... 292n.28
Scotland Act 1998 .... 45n.43

United States of America

Articles of Confederation 1781
Art IX. 234n.3
Constitution of the United States of America 1789..... 233, 234–36, 239–40, 245, 325, 326
Art I, s 8. .... 235n.4
Art III 236n.9, 237–38
Art VI 244n.35
Federal Arbitration Act 1925, 9 USC § 1 et seq. 235
s 2. .... .238, 239, 248
s 10. .... .235, 236, 240–41n.26, 243
s 10(a)(4) 238, 240–41n.26
Foreign Sovereign Immunities Act 1976 243

Venezuela

Constitution of the Bolivarian Republic of Venezuela 1999
Art 253 .... 322n.3, 322n.9

INTRODUCTION

1

The Comparative Constitutional Foundations of Private-Public Arbitration

An Introduction

Stephan W. Schill

I. Rise of Private-Public Arbitration

Arbitrations between private and public actors are on the rise, not only under international investment treaties, but also under different instruments of domestic law, including domestic foreign investment legislation, and contractual arrangements, such as concession agreements, public-private partnerships, or procurement contracts.[1] The rise in private-public arbitration is precipitated by several factors: the turn towards more private-public cooperation to achieve and finance public policy goals, whether in respect of energy, infrastructure, education, health, or transport;[2] the interest of, and need for, states to integrate into global markets and global supply chains, including through attracting foreign private investment;[3] and the need to

[1] While comprehensive empirical studies are missing, the following provide some indicators of the rise of private-public arbitration. As of 31 July 2023, there were 1,303 known treaty-based investor-state dispute settlement (ISDS) cases: see United Nations Conference on Trade and Development (UNCTAD), 'Investment Dispute Settlement Navigator' (2023) <https://investmentpolicy.unctad.org/investment-dispute-settlement> accessed 22 January 2025. At the International Centre for Settlement of Investment Disputes (ICSID), 967 investor-state dispute settlement proceedings had been registered as of 31 December 2023, 78% of which were based on treaties, 15% on contracts, and 7% on domestic investment laws: see ICSID, 'The ICSID Caseload – Statistics, Issue 2024-1' (2024) pdf pp 4, 11 <https://icsid.worldbank.org/resources/publications/icsid-caseload-statistics> accessed 22 January 2025. On private-public arbitration based on domestic legislation, see also Jarrod Hepburn, 'Domestic Investment Statutes in International Law' (2018) 112 AJIL 658, 659 (counting, at the time of writing, at least 61 claims based on investment laws that were brought before ICSID and other arbitral forums). At the International Chamber of Commerce, approximately 10% of all arbitrations administered by the institution include public entities as disputing parties. See International Chamber of Commerce, *ICC Commission Report: States, State Entities and ICC Arbitration* (International Chamber of Commerce 2012) para 7.

[2] See Ian Harden, *The Contracting State* (Open University Press 1992); Jody Freeman, 'The Contracting State' (2000) 28 Fla St U L Rev 155; Karl-Heinz Ladeur, 'The Changing Role of the Private in Public Governance – The Erosion of Hierarchy and the Rise of a New Administrative Law of Cooperation: A Comparative Approach' EUI Working Paper No 2002/9 (2002) <https://hdl.handle.net/1814/187> accessed 22 January 2025. This development is in line with the increasing importance of contractual tools as ordering instruments in modern societies: see Peter Zumbansen, 'The Law of Society: Governance Through Contract' (2007) 14 Indiana J Global Legal Studies 191.

[3] Zachary Elkins, Andrew T Guzman, and Beth A Simmons, 'Competing for Capital: The Diffusion of Bilateral Investment Treaties, 1960–2000' (2006) 60 Int Organ 811. On the importance of investment, including foreign investment, for (sustainable) development see already, with regard to the 2000 Millennium

Stephan W. Schill, *The Comparative Constitutional Foundations of Private-Public Arbitration* In: *The Comparative Constitutional Foundations of Private-Public Arbitration*. Edited by: Stephan W. Schill, Oxford University Press.
 DOI: 10.1093/9780191987960.003.0001

accommodate the preference of private actors for arbitration in order to facilitate private-public cooperation and address (real or perceived) shortcomings in many jurisdictions in terms of judicial independence, impartiality, and neutrality in the adjudication of disputes resulting from private-public cooperation by domestic courts.[4]

As a result, in an increasing number of cases, arbitrators, instead of domestic courts, are called to settle a wide array of private-public disputes, ranging from simple breaches of contractual obligations in procurement contracts to complex controversies about the limits of statutory or regulatory powers. Depending on the applicable law, these disputes, and their resolution, can raise a variety of issues of private or public law. While some have little importance beyond the specific dispute—think of the non-delivery of low-value office supplies[5]—others have a clear impact on the public interest, either because of their budgetary implications, with disputes at times going into the billions of USD in compensation,[6] or because they go to the heart of

Development Goals, United Nations Development Program, *Investing in Development: A Practical Plan to Achieve the Millennium Development Goals* (Earthscan 2005) 46–50, 239 ff; and regarding the subsequent Sustainable Development Goals, UNCTAD, *World Investment Report 2014: Investing in the SDGs – An Action Plan* (United Nations 2014) 135 ff. See also David Gaukrodger, 'The Future of Investment Treaties: Possible Directions' OECD Working Papers on International Investment 2021/03 (2021) 10 <https://dx.doi.org/10.1787/946c3970-en> accessed 22 January 2025 (stating that '[l]iberalisation for foreign investment and in particular FDI appears likely to play a greater role in the future of investment treaties. Through the elimination of regulatory barriers to investment based on nationality, it generates more potential investment primarily based on market considerations. Increased potential investment ... is essential to addressing the sustainable development goals.').

4 For discussion of concerns with domestic courts in the specific context of settling foreign-investment-related disputes, see Jonathan Bonnitcha, Lauge N Skovgaard Poulsen, and Michael Waibel, *The Political Economy of the Investment Treaty Regime* (OUP 2017) 86–91. For general corporate attitudes towards the choice of arbitration versus the choice of dispute settlement in court, see Christian Bühring-Uhle, 'A Survey on Arbitration and Settlement in International Business Disputes' in Christopher R Drahozal and Richard W Naimark (eds), *Towards a Science of International Arbitration: Collected Empirical Research* (Kluwer 2005) 25; Queen Mary University of London, School of International Arbitration, '2020 QMUL-CCIAG Survey: Investors' Perceptions of ISDS' (May 2020) 7 ff <https://www.qmul.ac.uk/arbitration/media/arbitration/docs/QM-CCIAG-Survey-ISDS-2020.pdf> accessed 22 January 2025. More generally on the functional logic behind the rise of private-public arbitration as a way for states to make credible commitments and to reduce transaction costs in transborder public-private cooperation in light of weaknesses of domestic institutions in the public actors' home jurisdiction, see the contributions in Richard P Appelbaum, William LF Felstiner, and Volkmar Gessner (eds), *Rules and Networks: The Legal Culture of Global Business Transactions* (Hart 2001); A Claire Cutler, *Private Power and Global Authority: Transnational Merchant Law in the Global Political Economy* (CUP 2003); Douglass C North, *Institutions, Institutional Change, and Economic Performance* (CUP 1990); Walter Mattli, 'Private Justice in a Global Economy: From Litigation to Arbitration' (2001) 55 Int Org 919; Alec Stone Sweet, 'The New *Lex Mercatoria* and Transnational Governance' (2006) 13 JEPP 627.

5 See eg Naizak Mohamed, 'Ventilator Case: Company Instructed to Pay MVR 34 Million to Maldivian Govt' (*Sun Siyam Media*, 26 February 2024) <https://en.sun.mv/87827> accessed 22 January 2025 (concerning an arbitration proceeding under the auspices of the Maldives International Arbitration Centre for the payment of damages in the amount of approximately USD 2 million for the non-delivery of ventilators ordered by the Maldives Ministry of Health from a Dubai-based company).

6 See eg the three awards rendered in the *Yukos* arbitrations against the Russian Federation, resulting cumulatively in an awarded sum of more than USD 50 billion in damages: *Hulley Enterprises Limited (Cyprus) v The Russian Federation*, PCA Case No AA 226 (UNCITRAL), Final Award (18 July 2014); *Yukos Universal Limited (Isle of Man) v The Russian Federation*, PCA Case No AA 227 (UNCITRAL), Final Award (18 July 2014); *Veteran Petroleum Limited (Cyprus) v The Russian Federation*, PCA Case No AA 228 (UNCITRAL), Final Award (18 July 2014). For further examples, see *Process and Industrial Developments Ltd v The Ministry of Petroleum Resources of the Federal Republic of Nigeria*, ad hoc, Final Award (31 January 2017) (ordering the payment of more than USD 6.5 billion in compensation plus interest); *Tethyan*

how private interests relate to public concerns and public policy, such as environmental protection, labour rights, public health, or climate change.

Examples of public interest-related private-public disputes that nowadays are settled through arbitration are abundant, in particular in the investment treaty field, where public information is more widely available than in the non-treaty-based context. Illustrative examples of disputes involving issues of public interest in the treaty context include private-public arbitrations that have involved or arisen from: Argentina's legislative response to its economic and financial crisis in 2001/02;[7] water concessions in Bolivia, Argentina, and Tanzania;[8] an affirmative action programme that aimed at remedying injustices of apartheid in South Africa;[9] the ban of harmful substances in the United States and Canada;[10] measures for the protection of the environment in Germany, Canada, or Mexico;[11] anti-tobacco legislation in Uruguay and Australia;[12] the reregulation of tariffs for renewable energy production in Spain, Italy, the Czech Republic, or Canada;[13] and the phase-out of nuclear power in Germany or of coal power in the Netherlands.[14] But also contract-based private-public arbitration

Copper Company Pty Limited v Islamic Republic of Pakistan, ICSID Case No ARB/12/1, Award (12 July 2019) (ordering the payment of more than USD 4 billion in compensation plus interest). For discussion of the concerns the awarding of such sums raises, see Martins Paparinskis, 'Crippling Compensation in the International Law Commission and Investor–State Arbitration' (2022) 11 ICSID Rev-FILJ 289.

[7] See Paola Di Rosa, 'The Recent Wave of Arbitrations Against Argentina under Bilateral Investment Treaties: Background and Principal Legal Issues' (2004) 36 U Miami Intern-Am L Rev 41.

[8] See eg *Compañía de Aguas del Aconquija SA and Vivendi Universal SA (formerly Compañía de Aguas del Aconquija, SA and Compagnie Générale des Eaux) v Argentine Republic*, ICSID Case No ARB/97/3, Award (21 November 2000); *Biwater Gauff (Tanzania) Ltd v United Republic of Tanzania*, ICSID Case No ARB/05/22, Award (24 July 2004); *Aguas del Tunari SA v Republic of Bolivia*, ICSID Case No ARB/02/3, Decision on Respondent's Objections to Jurisdiction (21 October 2005); *Suez, Sociedad General de Aguas de Barcelona SA, and Vivendi Universal SA v Argentine Republic*, ICSID Case No ARB/03/19 and *AWG Group v Argentine Republic*, UNCITRAL, Decision on Liability (30 July 2010).

[9] *Piero Foresti, Laura de Carli and others v Republic of South Africa*, ICSID Case No ARB(AF)/07/1, Award (4 August 2010).

[10] See eg *Methanex Corporation v United States*, UNCITRAL, Final Award of the Tribunal on Jurisdiction and Merits (3 August 2005); *Chemtura Corporation (formerly Crompton Corporation) v Government of Canada*, UNCITRAL, Award (2 August 2010). See also *Dow AgroSciences LLC v Government of Canada*, UNCITRAL (registered 31 March 2009, settled 25 May 2011).

[11] *Vattenfall AB, Vattenfall Europe AG, Vattenfall Europe Generation AG & Co KG v Federal Republic of Germany*, ICSID Case No ARB/09/6, Request for Arbitration (30 March 2009); *Metalclad Corporation v The United Mexican States*, ICSID Case No ARB(AF)/97/1, Award (30 August 2000); *William Ralph Clayton, William Richard Clayton, Douglas Clayton, Daniel Clayton and Bilcon of Delaware, Inc v Government of Canada*, PCA Case No 2009-04 (UNCITRAL), Award on Jurisdiction and Liability (17 March 2015); *Lone Pine Resources Inc v Government of Canada*, ICSID Case No UNCT/15/2, Final Award (21 November 2022).

[12] See Tania Voon and Andrew Mitchell, 'Time to Quit? Assessing International Investment Claims Against Plain Tobacco Packaging in Australia' (2011) 14 JIEL 515.

[13] For an overview of the cases in Europe, see Yulia S Selivanova, 'Changes in Renewables Support Policy and Investment Protection under the Energy Charter Treaty: Analysis of Jurisprudence and Outlook for the Current Arbitration Cases' (2018) 33(2) ICSID Review 433; Norah Gallagher, 'ECT and Renewable Energy Disputes' in Maxi Scherer (ed), *International Arbitration in the Energy Sector* (OUP 2018) 250. For cases involving Canada, see *Mesa Power Group, LLC v Government of Canada*, PCA Case No 2012-17 (UNCITRAL), Award (24 March 2016); *Tennant Energy, LLC v Government of Canada*, PCA Case No 2018-54 (UNCITRAL), Final Award (25 October 2022).

[14] *Vattenfall AB and others v Federal Republic of Germany*, ICSID Case No ARB/12/12, Order of the Tribunal Taking Note of the Discontinuance of the Proceeding (9 November 2021); *RWE AG and RWE Eemshaven Holding II BV v Kingdom of the Netherlands*, ICSID Case No ARB/21/4, Request for Arbitration

provides examples of disputes that touch on public interest-sensitive matters, such as a ban on uranium mining in Greenland,[15] central bank measures affecting the functioning of the banking system in South Sudan,[16] or disputes involving allegations of corruption in the conclusion of private-public contracts in key industry sectors for host states.[17]

All of these examples show that arbitral tribunals deciding on private-public disputes can have manifest implications on how states operate, both in fiscal and regulatory matters, thereby affecting not just the actors that are party to the concrete dispute settlement proceedings but the general public at large. This observation, coupled with the hunch that arbitral tribunals may decide the underlying disputes differently from how an otherwise competent court would—because the applicable law, the epistemic context, and the individuals making decisions differ—is the present book's starting point for analysing and evaluating the use of arbitration to settle private-public disputes and its interaction with public interest concerns.

Approaching the topic from a comparative perspective, the book is motivated by providing answers to a number of questions: how are arbitrators in private-public dispute settlement proceedings legitimized? What powers do and should arbitrators in such proceedings have? What is the proper role of arbitrators when reviewing government conduct? What is the appropriate normative framework governing the activity of arbitrators in private-public arbitration? And how does private-public arbitration interact with the legal and constitutional frameworks and institutions at state level that normally ensure the protection and promotion of the public interest and provide the legitimating framework for settling private-public disputes.

II. Emerging Constitutional Concerns: Private-Public Arbitration as Transnational Governance

The book's comparative approach is owed not least to the fact that the extent to which public entities are legally allowed to submit to arbitrating disputes with private actors is a matter of each state's sovereign decision. Yet, making such decisions is not just a matter of political or economic expedience; instead, core principles of constitutional law—democracy, separation of powers, rule of law, and the protection of competing fundamental and human rights—may channel that decision, impact the extent to which private-public arbitration is permissible, or require certain safeguards for its

(20 January 2021); *Uniper SE, Uniper Benelux Holding BV and Uniper Benelux NV v Kingdom of the Netherlands*, ICSID Case No ARB/21/22, Order of the Tribunal Taking Note of the Discontinuance of the Proceedings and Decision on Costs (17 March 2023).

[15] *Greenland Minerals A/S (GMAS) v Government of Greenland and the Government of the Kingdom of Denmark*, ad hoc (initiated 22 March 2022, pending).

[16] *Qatar National Bank (QPSC) v Republic of South Sudan and Bank of South Sudan*, ICSID Case No ARB/20/40 (registered 7 October 2020, pending).

[17] See eg *UAB Vilniaus Energija and Veolia Environnement SA v SP AB Vilniaus Šilumos Tinklai and Vilnius City Municipality*, SCC Case No V2016/183, Final Award (30 November 2023) paras 312–426.

operation.[18] After all, the operation of the principle of the separation of powers or the principle of democratic accountability may be negatively affected as the control of government conduct and the determination of its legal and budgetary implications is undertaken not by democratically legitimized domestic courts, but by party-appointed one-off arbitral tribunals.

The shift in settling private-public disputes from courts to arbitral tribunals is significant as, even if tribunals apply the same governing law, they may not only strike the balance between private rights and public interests, as well as the relationship between rights of private economic actors and competing fundamental and human rights of the host state's population, differently from domestic courts; they may also review the legality of conduct of the disputing parties less rigorously, and at the expense of the public interest, than domestic courts would, for example in respect of allegations of misconduct by either the private or public actors involved, or both—think of bribery, corruption, or fraud.[19] Furthermore, the one-off nature of private-public arbitration tribunals may lead to inconsistent, contradictory, and unpredictable arbitral decisions, casting core rule-of-law values into question.

The risks to democratic and rule-of-law accountability in private-public arbitration are compounded by the fact that tribunals in private-public arbitration operate under a legal framework that often follows the same rules as those applicable to private-private arbitration; is based on private law rationales, such as party autonomy and confidentiality of proceedings; is adjudicated by individuals that have a background in commercial arbitration; and is subject only to limited control (mostly for compliance with procedural rights and due process) by the supervisory courts at the arbitral seat and the courts involved in enforcement proceedings.[20] Most significantly, the

[18] For an analysis of how arbitration and constitutional law interrelate from the perspective of constitutional theory rather than positive constitutional law, see Victor Ferreres Comella, *The Constitution of Arbitration* (CUP 2021) 1. For an analysis of how investment treaty arbitration creates friction with core constitutional principles, see Stephan W Schill, 'Reforming Investor–State Dispute Settlement: A (Comparative and International) Constitutional Law Framework' (2017) 20 JIEL 649, 652–57. For further analysis and critique of investment treaty arbitration from the perspective of constitutional law values, see eg David Schneiderman, *Constitutionalizing Economic Globalization—International Investment Law and Democracy's Promise* (CUP 2008); Gus Van Harten, 'Investment Treaty Arbitration, Procedural Fairness, and the Rule of Law' in Stephan W Schill (ed), *International Investment Law and Comparative Public Law* (OUP 2010) 627; Alfred-Maurice de Zayas, 'Report of the Independent Expert on the Promotion of a Democratic and Equitable International Order' (14 July 2015) UN Doc A/HRC/30/44 and 'Report of the Independent Expert on the Promotion of a Democratic and Equitable International Order' (5 August 2015) UN Doc A/70/285; Andreas Kulick, 'International Investment Arbitration, Treaty Interpretation, and Democracy' (2015) 4 CILJ 441; Lorenzo Cotula, 'Democracy and International Investment Law' (2017) 30 LJIL 351; August Reinisch and Stephan W Schill (eds), *Investment Protection Standards and the Rule of Law* (OUP 2023) 235; David R Boyd, 'Report of the Special Rapporteur on the Issue of Human Rights Obligations Relating to the Enjoyment of a Safe, Clean, Healthy and Sustainable Environment' (13 July 2023) UN Doc A/78/168.

[19] For an example of such concerns, which have only been remedied in set-aside proceedings, and which have given rise to criticism by the supervisory court of the approach taken by arbitral tribunals to private-public arbitration more generally, see *The Federal Republic of Nigeria v Process & Industrial Developments Ltd* [2023] EWHC 2638 (Comm) paras 578–95.

[20] For comprehensive discussion of the framework applicable to commercial arbitration, including from a comparative perspective, see Stefan Kröll, Andrea K Bjorklund, and Franco Ferrari (eds), *Cambridge Compendium of International Commercial and Investment Arbitration* (CUP 2023); Stephan Balthasar (ed), *International Commercial Arbitration: International Conventions, Country Reports and Comparative Analysis – A Handbook* (2nd edn, Hart/Beck/Nomos 2021); Gary B Born, *International Commercial Arbitration* (3rd edn, Wolters Kluwer 2020); Jean-François Poudret and Sébastian Besson, *Comparative*

legal framework applicable to the conduct of private-public arbitration proceedings lacks the safeguards usually in place for the adjudication of private-public disputes in domestic courts, such as openness and transparency of proceedings, possibilities for third-party participation, limitations on damages as public law remedies, the need for specific expertise of adjudicators in the law governing the activity of the state party, and the availability of appeals procedures.[21] All of this leads to a very limited control and accountability of how arbitral tribunals settle private-public disputes, and correspondingly a considerable degree of autonomy and authority of the tribunals in reviewing the legality of the conduct of both government and private parties involved.

Differences in how arbitral tribunals, as compared with domestic courts, settle private-public disputes can ultimately come at the expense of government accountability under the rule of law in individual cases. But it may also lead to a more general shift in standards for reviewing the legality of private and public conduct. This is so because the design of control mechanisms for private-public arbitration not only grants arbitrators considerable powers in deciding concrete private-public disputes in a binding manner; it also gives arbitrators the power to shape the behaviour of private and public actors more generally by interpreting, applying, and further developing the legal standards applicable to private-public arbitration.

To the extent arbitrators in private-public disputes are able to do so independently of concrete domestic legal orders, they can function, just as domestic courts would otherwise, as a mechanism of governance. In reviewing the legality of the conduct of disputing parties, arbitrators not only assess past conduct of private and public actors; they also steer, by resolving the disputes and interpreting the law applicable to the underlying social relations, how governments and private actors will behave in the future. In addition, by providing legal reasons for deciding individual disputes, arbitrators also contribute to the further development of the law applicable to private-public relations. All of these elements are fostered as arbitration becomes the default mechanism for dispute settlement in certain areas of private-public cooperation and, in particular, to the extent that arbitral decisions become public and start influencing subsequent arbitral decision-making as precedent.

Investment treaty arbitration, as one form of private-public arbitration, but also international commercial arbitration more generally, have morphed into functioning

Law of International Arbitration (2nd edn, Sweet & Maxwell 2007); Julian DM Lew, Loukas A Mistelis, and Stefan M Kröll, *Comparative International Commercial Arbitration* (Kluwer Law International 2003).

21 See eg on the criticism and potential shortcomings of international arbitration, Charles N Brower, Charles H Brower II, and Jeremy K Sharpe, 'The Coming Crisis in the Global Adjudication System' (2003) 19 Arb Int'l 415; Jan Paulsson, *The Idea of Arbitration* (OUP 2013) 147–73; for criticism specifically with regard to ISDS, see Ari Afilalo, 'Towards a Common Law of International Investment: How NAFTA Chapter 11 Panels Should Solve Their Legitimacy Crisis' (2004) 17 Geo Int'l Envtl L Rev 51; Susan D Franck, 'The Legitimacy Crisis in Investment Treaty Arbitration: Privatizing Public International Law Through Inconsistent Decisions' (2005) 73 Fordham L Rev 1521; Charles N Brower and Stephan W Schill, 'Is Arbitration a Threat or a Boon to the Legitimacy of International Investment Law?' (2009) 9 Chicago JIL 471; Louis T Wells, 'Backlash to Investment Arbitration: Three Causes' in Michael Waibel and others (eds), *The Backlash against Investment Arbitration: Perceptions and Reality* (Kluwer Law International 2010) 341; International Bar Association, Subcommittee on Investment Treaty Arbitration, 'Consistency, Efficiency and Transparency in Investment Treaty Arbitration' (2018) 3 ff <https://uncitral.un.org/sites/uncitral.un.org/files/investment_treaty_report_2018_full.pdf> accessed 22 January 2025.

as governance systems over the course of the past decades. Investment treaty arbitration, which has only emerged in practice since the early 1990s, is a field that, once it had left its infancy, became heavily focused on the operation of precedent generated by earlier investment treaty tribunals.[22] International commercial arbitration, in turn, has been put center stage in forming and further developing the *lex mercatoria*, a concept used to designate the emergence of a transnational body of law governing international commercial relations.[23] Both fields of legal practice—investment treaty arbitration and international commercial arbitration—thus already function as mechanisms of governance, not just as instruments to settle individual disputes, and are increasingly analysed as such.[24] It is difficult to see why similar developments should not also take place, if they have not already emerged, in respect of private-public arbitrations based on domestic legislation or private-public contracts.

Notably, the governance effects connected to a rise in private-public arbitration will hardly be confined to playing out within the respective bounds of each domestic legal order. Instead, governance effects of private-public arbitration will unfold in a transnational context in which individual domestic legal orders and their institutions have difficulties in exercising controlling influence to protect the public interest at stake, both in respect of private-public disputes that take place in a transborder context and those that are purely domestic. This is the case for a number of reasons:

- First, the law applicable to (transborder as well as purely domestic) private-public arbitration is a transnational amalgam of national and international, private and public law sources. It includes national arbitration legislation, international treaties (including, above all, the New York Convention,[25] as well as the

[22] The literature on the use of precedent in investment treaty arbitration is vast. See eg Jeffery P Commission, 'Precedent in Investment Treaty Arbitration: A Citation Analysis of a Developing Jurisprudence' (2007) 24 J Int'l Arb 129; Ole K Fauchald, 'The Legal Reasoning of ICSID Tribunals' (2008) 19 EJIL 301, 333–43; Stephan W Schill, *The Multilateralization of International Investment Law* (CUP 2009) 321–57; Frédéric G Sourgens, *A Nascent Common Law: The Process of Decisionmaking in International Legal Disputes Between States and Foreign Investors* (Brill 2015); Patrick M Norton, 'The Role of Precedent in the Development of International Investment Law' (2018) 33 ICSID Rev-FILJ 280; Richard C Chen, 'Precedent and Dialogue in Investment Treaty Arbitration' (2019) 60 Harv ILJ 47.

[23] See Thomas E Carbonneau (ed), *Lex Mercatoria and Arbitration: A Discussion of the New Law Merchant* (2nd edn, Juris 1998); Klaus Peter Berger, *The Creeping Codification of the New Lex Mercatoria* (2nd edn, Kluwer Law International 2010); Dolores Bentolila, *Arbitrators as Lawmakers: The Creation of General Rules Through Consistent Decision Making in International Commercial and Investment Arbitration* (Kluwer Law International 2017).

[24] For an account placing international commercial arbitration and investor-state arbitration into a transnational or global governance context, see Alec Stone Sweet and Florian Grisel, *The Evolution of International Arbitration: Judicialization, Governance, Legitimacy* (OUP 2017). For analysis focused specifically on international commercial arbitration as transnational or global governance, see Christopher A Whytock, 'Private-Public Interaction in Global Governance: The Case of Transnational Arbitration' (2010) 12(3) Bus Politics, Article 10; Walter Mattli and Thomas Dietz (eds), *International Arbitration and Global Governance – Contending Theories and Evidence* (OUP 2014). Specifically on understanding investment treaty arbitration as a form of global governance, see Benedict Kingsbury and Stephan W Schill, 'Investor-State Arbitration as Governance: Fair and Equitable Treatment, Proportionality and the Emerging Global Administrative Law' in Albert J van den Berg (ed), *50 Years of the New York Convention: ICCA International Arbitration Conference* (Kluwer Law International 2009) 5; Stephan W Schill, 'International Investment Law and Comparative Public Law: An Introduction' in Schill, *International Investment Law and Comparative Public Law* (n 18) 3, 17–23.

[25] Convention on the Recognition and Enforcement of Foreign Arbitral Awards (adopted 10 June 1958, entered into force 7 June 1959) 330 UNTS 3.

Washington (or ICSID) Convention),[26] private-public contracts governed partly by private (domestic or foreign) and partly by public law, as well as administrative legislation and other public law principles; all of these layers of rules have not developed in strict isolation from each other but, rather, interact and influence each other and cross-fertilize across jurisdictions and national legal traditions.[27]

- Second, the amalgam of legal rules and principles is generally applied by a community of arbitration specialists with a transnational outlook and *esprit de corps* who have not been socialized under a common domestic legal order, and who endorse comparative law and transnational legal reasoning as characteristic approaches to dispute settlement, independently of whether a concrete dispute transcends jurisdictional boundaries or remains limited to one jurisdiction.[28]
- And third, the authority of domestic courts, both those supervising private-public arbitration at the seat and those involved in proceedings concerning the recognition and enforcement of arbitral awards, is limited to the state territory in which they operate; consequently, even if arbitral awards have been set aside at the seat of the arbitration, they can turn out to be enforceable in other jurisdictions.[29]

[26] Convention on the Settlement of Investment Disputes between States and Nationals of Other States (adopted 18 March 1965, entered into force 14 October 1966) 575 UNTS 159.

[27] For the corresponding observation in respect of international commercial arbitration in the words of a leading commentator and arbitrator, see Julian DM Lew, 'Foreword' in Lew, Mistelis, and Kröll (n 20) v, vi ('International arbitration has become independent from national laws and courts in practice and legally. Parties and arbitrators do, in the main, conduct proceedings in a rarefied non-national or international legal environment. Whilst there may, in some cases, be influences from national law on the procedure, this can be controlled by the parties, the arbitrators and international practice. Experienced arbitration lawyers and the major international arbitration institutions have recognized national procedural laws are generally irrelevant and inapplicable. These international practices are acknowledged and upheld by arbitration awards being recognized and enforced under the New York Convention.'). For an analysis of the different legal layers, processes, and actors connected to transnationalization, using the field of public contracts as an example, see Mathias Audit and Stephan W Schill (eds), *The Transnational Law of Public Contracts* (Bruylant 2015).

[28] For a sociological analysis of the arbitration community and their operation within a transnational context, see Yves Dezalay and Bryant G Garth, *Dealing in Virtue: International Commercial Arbitration and the Construction of a Transnational Legal Order* (Chicago University Press 1996); see also Emmanuel Gaillard, 'Sociology of International Arbitration' in David D Caron and others (eds), *Practising Virtue: Inside International Arbitration* (OUP 2015) 187. For accounts that focus on the transnational legal aspects in international arbitration, see Emmanuel Gaillard, *Legal Theory of International Arbitration* (Martinus Nijhoff 2010) 35 ff; Thomas Schultz, *Transnational Legality: Stateless Law and International Arbitration* (OUP 2014); Paulsson (n 21). See also Joshua Karton, *The Culture of International Arbitration and the Evolution of Contract Law* (OUP 2013) 23 ('In many ways, international arbitrators have more in common than the body of legal practitioners within any one country . . . [t]herefore, it actually makes more sense to speak of an ICA [ie international commercial arbitration] community than to speak of a legal community within a country.').

[29] See especially Gaillard, *Legal Theory* (n 28) 135–44 (showing how the authority of arbitral awards cannot be grounded in either the domestic legal order of the seat or in the legal orders of enforcement jurisdictions, but rather in a transnational legal order that is autonomous); Julian DM Lew, 'Achieving the Dream: Autonomous Arbitration' (2006) 22 Arb Int'l 179; Jan Paulsson, 'Enforcing Arbitral Awards Notwithstanding Local Standard Annulments' (1998) 6(2) APLR 1. See further on the enforcement of annulled awards, Christopher Koch, 'The Enforcement of Awards Annulled in their Place of Origin: The French and US Experience' (2009) 26(2) J Int'l Arb 267; and more generally on the effects of post-award decisions by national courts including set-aside judgments, Maxi Scherer, 'Effects of Foreign Judgments Relating to International Arbitral Awards: Is the "Judgment Route" the Wrong Road?' (2013) 4 JIDS 587, 590–604.

All of these factors together lead to a considerable autonomy of private-public arbitration tribunals, especially in relation to domestic law and institutions, and accordingly have the potential to evade domestic law strictures. Several examples from the field of contract-based private-public arbitration illustrate the autonomy private-public arbitration enjoys, and the difficulties individual domestic legal orders and their institutions face in controlling it effectively.

In *Benteler v Belgium*, for example, an arbitral tribunal found that it had jurisdiction over a dispute between Belgium and two German claimants based on an arbitration clause in a contract between the parties, even though Article 1676(2) of the Belgian Judicial Code at the time provided that public entities were not permitted to enter into arbitration agreements except by means of an international treaty.[30] In reaching this conclusion, the tribunal considered it relevant that both Belgium and Germany were parties to the 1961 European Convention on International Commercial Arbitration, which specifically provided that public entities were able validly to agree to submit disputes to arbitration rather than domestic courts.[31] But the decision in *Benteler*, and its underlying rationale, indicate the existence of a broader principle at play. As stated by Jan Paulsson, a highly influential arbitration practitioner and academic:

> *Benteler v. Belgium* ... provides guidance for the situation in which a State invokes its internal law as a bar to arbitral jurisdiction, but – unlike the case of Belgium – is not bound by a contrary treaty obligation. Although its discussion on this point is *obiter dictum*, the Award clearly approves the rule against recognition of such national bars to international arbitration.[32]

Another example is the decision of the arbitral tribunal in *Balkan Energy Limited (Ghana) v The Republic of Ghana*, which was seated in the Netherlands.[33] The Tribunal accepted the claimant's claim for breach of a power purchase agreement (PPA) between a foreign-owned company and the state, even though the Supreme Court in Ghana had determined that the agreement lacked the parliamentary approval that Article 181 of the Constitution of Ghana required for 'international business transaction'. In the Tribunal's view, its jurisdiction had to be determined by applying Dutch

[30] *Benteler v Belgium*, Award (18 November 1983) (1984) 1(2) J Int'l Arb 184.

[31] ibid (relying on European Convention on International Commercial Arbitration (adopted 21 April 1961, entered into force 7 January 1964) 484 UNTS 349, art II(1), which provides that 'legal persons considered by the law which is applicable to them as "legal persons of public law" have the right to conclude valid arbitration agreements').

[32] Jan Paulsson, 'May a State Invoke Its Internal Law to Repudiate Consent to International Commercial Arbitration?' (1986) 2 Arb Int'l 90, 97–98. For discussion of further examples where limitations to private-public arbitration under domestic constitutional law were not recognized by arbitral tribunals as well as domestic courts, see Jamal Seifi and Kamal Javadi, 'Public-Private Arbitration in the Iranian Legal System: The Intersection of Preferential Rights and Constitutional Constraints on Arbitration' (in this volume) 355, 371–383.

[33] *Balkan Energy Limited (Ghana) v Republic of Ghana*, PCA Case No 2010-7 (UNCITRAL), Interim Award (22 December 2010) and ibid, Award on the Merits (1 April 2014). For discussion of the Tribunal's decisions, and the decisions in the courts in Ghana, see Dominic Npoanlari Dagbanja, 'The Constitutional and Public Interest Foundations of Public-Private Arbitration in Ghana' (in this volume) 495, 516–517.

law, being the law of the seat. Non-compliance of the PPA with Ghana's constitutional law was therefore only relevant insofar as this violated Dutch public policy. This, the Tribunal found, was not the case, as otherwise, 'any arbitration agreement or contract which encounters an argument of constitutional nature in a foreign country would be excluded from the jurisdiction of an arbitration tribunal to decide upon'.[34] Similarly, the Tribunal found that, in spite of the Supreme Court's finding, the PPA could not be treated as being *void ab initio*; instead, the Tribunal found, 'the Claimant had reasonable expectation that the Respondent had accepted the validity of the Agreement and was, therefore, entitled to rely on the PPA and to expect that the Respondent would fulfil the obligations that it had assumed thereunder'.[35]

Finally, in *Bankswitch Ghana Ltd (Ghana) v The Republic of Ghana*, an arbitral tribunal reached a similar conclusion, finding that the state was estopped from invoking the lack of parliamentary approval required under Article 181 of the Constitution of Ghana as a defence to the validity and enforceability of an agreement for the provision of price evaluation software and an electronic data interchange system for the state's customs administration.[36] The Tribunal determined that the validity of the agreement not only had to be measured against domestic law, but also 'against international standards and . . . principles of customary international law'.[37] On this basis, the Tribunal concluded that Ghana 'cannot rely on its own Constitution to avoid the customary international law rule that a host State must act in good faith and in a manner that is consistent with international law principles when dealing with a foreign investor'.[38]

These examples show that using arbitration to settle private-public disputes facilitates cross-jurisdictional manoeuvering and enables private and public actors to circumvent limitations contained in domestic law. For example, parties to private-public disputes may agree to submit their relations to a governing law other than the law of the public entity's home jurisdiction, either from the start in a contract governing their relations, or subsequently once a dispute arises, and arbitral tribunals may accept the parties' choices even if they contravene domestic law. Similarly, parties to private-public relations can agree on the seat of the arbitration, which may impact on the governing law, as arbitral tribunals may determine the applicable law differently from how a domestic court of the public entity's home state would. In both situations, arbitration agreements or the parties' choice of law may be enforced by arbitral tribunals, and resulting arbitral awards may subsequently be enforced as well, even if the parties' agreements contravene domestic law rules in the public entity's home jurisdiction. This indicates a significant degree of autonomy of arbitral tribunals from the domestic law of the public entity's state in determining their jurisdiction over private-public disputes, as well as the validity and enforceability of agreements concluded between private and public actors.

[34] *Balkan Energy*, Interim Award (n 33) para 144.
[35] ibid para 397.
[36] *Bankswitch Ghana Ltd (Ghana) v The Republic of Ghana*, PCA Case No 118294 (UNCITRAL), Award Save as to Costs (11 April 2014).
[37] ibid para 11.57.
[38] ibid para 11.59.

All of these developments illustrate that private-public arbitration is functioning as part of a transnational system of governance, in which arbitral tribunals dispose of considerable authority to decide private-public disputes, have significant impact on shaping the law applicable to private-public relations rather independently of domestic law, are able to influence the future behaviour of disputing and non-disputing parties, and bear the burden of ensuring accountability of both private and public actors in cases that may involve substantial amounts of public money or other public interest-related matters. This, in turn, compounds the constitutional concerns private-public arbitration raises for the public interest and for core constitutional principles that protect it, such as democracy, the rule of law, and fundamental and human rights.

III. Comparative Constitutional Analysis of Private-Public Arbitration

Concrete constitutional concerns have already arisen in respect of investment treaty arbitration[39] and have reached the constitutional courts in a number of jurisdictions.[40] But related, if not identical, concerns are likely to arise in a similar manner in respect of any private-public arbitration that functions, like investment treaty arbitration, as a transnational governance system. And, indeed, some domestic courts are starting to query, without yet placing the issues in a constitutional context, or using the language of constitutional law and constitutional values, whether arbitral tribunals are able to ensure accountability and compliance with the law applicable to the conduct of private and public actors in settings of private-public cooperation, in particular when tribunals approach private-public disputes in the same way they approach private-to-private disputes in international commercial arbitration.

The English High Court, for example, when setting aside an award in *The Federal Republic of Nigeria v Process & Industrial Developments Ltd*, which had ordered the respondent state to pay compensation to a private party in excess of USD 6.5 billion for breach of a contract in the area of natural gas processing, because the contract had

[39] See the contributions in Stephan W Schill and Christian J Tams (eds), *International Investment Protection and Constitutional Law* (Edward Elgar Publishing 2022). See also the references in n 18 above.

[40] See eg Constitutional Chamber of the Supreme Court of Costa Rica, Resolution No 2007-09469 (3 July 2007) (on the Central America Free Trade Agreement); Constitutional Court of Colombia, Judgment C-252/19 (6 June 2019) (on the 2014 France-Colombia BIT) and Judgment C-254/19 (6 June 2019) (on the 2013 Israel-Colombia Free Trade Agreement); Constitutional Court of Ecuador, Judgment Case No 2-23-TI (28 July 2023) (on the Ecuador-Costa Rica Trade Association Agreement). The Comprehensive Economic and Trade Agreement (CETA) concluded between Canada and the European Union (EU) has occupied several national courts, see eg German Constitutional Court, Case No 2 BvR 1368/16, 2 BvR 1444/16, 2 BvR 1482/16, 2 BvR 1823/16, 2 BvE 3/16, Judgment (13 October 2016), Case No 2 BvR 1444/16, 2 BvR 1482/16, 2 BvR 1823/16, 2 BvE 3/16-, Order (7 December 2016) (both concerning provisional measures), Case No BvR 1368/16, 2 BvR 1444/16, 2 BvR 1482/16, 2 BvR 1823/16, 2 BvE 3/16, Order (9 February 2022); Conseil constitutionnel (France), Decision No 2017-749 DC (31 July 2017); High Court of Ireland, *Costello v Government of Ireland and others* [2021] IEHC 600; Federal Court of Canada, *The Honourable Paul Helleyer, PC et al v Justin Trudeau et al*, Case No T-1789-16 (registered 21 October 2016, discontinued 13 June 2017). For cases concerning the constitutional limits established by European Union (EU) law, see Case C-284/16, *Slovak Republic v Achmea BV*, Judgment (6 March 2018) ECLI:EU:C:2018:158; Case C-741/19, *Republic of Moldova v Komstroy LLC*, Judgment (2 September 2021) ECLI:EU:C:2021:655; Case C-109/20, *Republiken Polen v PL Holdings Sàrl*, Judgment (26 October 2021) ECLI:EU:C:2021:875, Opinion 1/17, *CETA*, Opinion (30 April 2019) EU:C:2019:341.

been procured through bribes, acknowledged that the tribunal's 'very traditional approach', in particular its hands-off and insufficiently interventionist attitude towards the taking of evidence, had contributed to bringing about an award whose defects had almost escaped the safety net of the domestic courts' supervisory jurisdiction.[41] Cases such as this, the Court suggested, should lead to

> debate and reflection among the arbitration community, and also among state users of arbitration, and among other courts with responsibility to supervise or oversee arbitration [and] provide an opportunity to consider whether the arbitration process, which is of outstanding importance and value in the world, needs further attention where the value involved is so large and where a state is involved.[42]

However, broader engagement about, and analyses of, how private-public arbitrations interact with the legal and, above all, constitutional framework for promoting and protecting public interests beyond a purely national context are still limited.[43] Describing the status quo in a study bringing together arbitration and constitutional theory, Victor Ferreres Comella has aptly observed:

> It is striking . . . that most constitutional scholars have neglected arbitration in their studies. They have tended to treat arbitration as a marginal institution, a small piece in the grand scheme of things constitutional. Experts in arbitration, in turn, have failed to link their analyses to a broader constitutional discourse. In spite of the brilliance and sophistication they have often displayed in their academic work, such experts have generally forgotten about the constitution.[44]

Apart from private-public arbitrations often being confidential, the generally limited interaction between constitutional law and private-public arbitration is due not least to the topic falling into a curious disciplinary gap: from an international law perspective, private-public arbitrations based on contract or legislation are matters for domestic law to address; from a commercial arbitration perspective, public entities are viewed just as any other disputing party, so that private-public arbitrations are but a subset of commercial arbitration whose purpose is the settlement of individual disputes; and, from a public (administrative and constitutional) law perspective, the issue is often relegated to the realm of private law, with little sensitivity to the possibility of public entities being involved in disputes other than before the state's own courts.[45] In short, as Bo Rutledge has

[41] See *Nigeria v Process & Industrial Developments* (n 19) (quote at para 588).

[42] ibid para 582.

[43] This is certainly true outside the context of investment treaty arbitrations, where the involvement of constitutional courts in addressing the constitutional limits of private-public arbitration has sparked some interest. For the constitutional court cases in question, see the references in n 40 above.

[44] Ferreres Comella (n 18) 1.

[45] The unease of combining arbitration and constitutional law is compounded by the fact that matters concerning arbitration themselves fall into different legal disciplines at the domestic level. Depending on the respective national epistemic communities, arbitration is treated as part of civil procedure, as is the case in Germany, Austria, Italy, and Greece; as part of private international law or conflicts of law, as in France or

poignantly put it, constitutional law and arbitration are generally seen as 'strange bedfellows'.[46]

Rather than discussing in the abstract how constitutional theory and abstract constitutional values and principles impact private-public arbitration, the present book seeks to bridge the divide between arbitration and constitutional analysis in respect of private-public arbitration, and address the constitutional concerns private-public arbitration raises, by approaching the topic from a comparative perspective. Featuring nineteen substantive chapters dealing with almost forty jurisdictions from different corners of the world, the book examines how domestic legal systems and legal practice approach the involvement of public entities as parties in arbitration proceedings, to what extent the constitutional legal frameworks involved problematize private-public arbitration as a constitutional concern, and how different domestic legal systems ensure that private-public arbitration conforms to, and does not undermine, the public interest. The method for developing such a framework and grounding the demands for protecting the public interest in private-public arbitration that result from such a comparative approach is what the book designates as the comparative constitutional foundations of private-public arbitration. These comparative foundations allow an analysis of the impact private-public arbitration has, as a governance system, on constitutional values and principles and provide a framework for legitimizing, but also for limiting, the use of private-public arbitration in a transnational context.

To lay the groundwork for the comparative constitutional foundations of private-public arbitration, the book takes a functional approach.[47] It contains chapters that look towards domestic law to determine issues such as: whether private-public arbitration is treated differently from private-private commercial arbitration, whether differences are made between treaty-based and non-treaty-based arbitration of private-public disputes; to what extent private-public arbitration is permitted; what regulatory framework is put in place; and what control mechanisms exist. The goal is to determine what the requirements are that domestic law, including in particular domestic constitutional law, establishes for the involvement of public actors in settling disputes with private actors through arbitration, rather than in domestic courts, and how it ensures that the public interest remains protected. This focus on the domestic level is important, as the definition of what qualifies as a public interest and the protection afforded to such interests are, first and foremost, matters of domestic (constitutional) law. Furthermore, it is domestic law that determines, within the normative space provided by the respective constitutional framework, which private-public disputes can lawfully be submitted to arbitration; what arbitral procedures, remedies, and arbitral powers public entities can consent to; what control mechanisms must

Switzerland; or as part of ordinary contract law, as in the common law tradition. See Stavros L Brekoulakis, 'International Arbitration Scholarship and the Concept of Arbitration Law' (2013) 36 Fordham ILJ 745, 763–64.

[46] Peter B Rutledge, *Arbitration and the Constitution* (CUP 2013) 1.

[47] For a detailed discussion of the functionalist method and its functions in comparative law, see Ralf Michaels, 'The Functional Method of Comparative Law' in Mathias Reimann and Reinhard Zimmermann (eds), *The Oxford Handbook of Comparative Law* (2nd edn, OUP 2019) 345.

exist; and under which circumstances decisions by arbitral tribunals in private-public disputes can lawfully be enforced at the domestic level.

The chapters on the approaches to private-public arbitration under domestic law in the jurisdictions covered can then be used as a basis to explore differences, but also commonalities of the constitutional foundations of private-public arbitrations. This allows not only a better understanding of the operation of a concrete domestic system, but also provides insight into whether a baseline, best practices, or comparable models for the treatment of private-public arbitration exist, and for how cross-cutting constitutional concerns can be addressed. Comparison, in other words, will allow the determination of whether common constitutional approaches exist that legitimize but also limit the use of arbitration to settle private-public disputes, and that can ensure the protection of the public interest and core constitutional values, such as democracy, the rule of law, separation of powers, access to justice, and the protection of human rights and other public concerns.

Such a comparative analysis of how different domestic legal systems approach private-public arbitration, including from a constitutional perspective, is not only beneficial for a better understanding of a specific domestic legal system. It is also crucial for grappling with the transnational aspects of private-public arbitration and its impact on the public interest when taking into account the possibilities the use of arbitration offers for cross-jurisdictional manoeuvering and for avoiding domestic law strictures, such as the restrictions on arbitrability under the domestic laws of Ghana and Belgium discussed above show.[48] Only a comparative approach provides insight into the extent to which parties to arbitration agreements and arbitration proceedings in private-public disputes can exploit differences in the regulation of private-public arbitration among different domestic legal systems, and into whether and how private and public actors can contract out of one, and into another, domestic legal system, and engage in forum shopping in deciding on the seat of an arbitration proceeding or when enforcing arbitral awards across various domestic legal orders. Similarly, only efforts at developing and implementing common constitutional foundations cooperatively across jurisdictions will ensure that domestic law strictures are not eroded by transnational manoeuvering, and that domestic law and institutions maintain a certain degree of control in protecting the public interest.

Comparatively developed standards are likely to resound well in the field of private-public arbitration, as they do in respect of international arbitration generally. Thus, in the legislative processes for preparing and passing domestic arbitration statutes, comparative studies that canvas the approaches to arbitration in other jurisdictions, as well as international model legislation, namely the UNCITRAL Model Law

[48] Notably, the transnational dimensions are increasingly recognized, not only in the context of private-private transborder transactions, but also in the context of comparative administrative and comparative constitutional law. See eg John S Bell, 'Comparative Administrative Law' in Reimann and Zimmermann (n 47) 1250, 1257–59; Mariana Mota Prado, 'Diffusion, Reception, and Transplantation' in Peter Cane and others (eds), *The Oxford Handbook of Comparative Administrative Law* (OUP 2021) 255; Peer Zumbansen, 'Carving Out Typologies and Accounting for Differences Across Systems: Towards a Methodology of Transnational Constitutionalism' in Michel Rosenfeld and András Sajó (eds), *The Oxford Handbook of Comparative Constitutional Law* (OUP 2012) 75.

on International Commercial Arbitration,[49] are widespread.[50] The results of these developments, as noted by Poudret and Besson, are 'similarities [that] are due both to the inspiration taken from other laws and the solutions imposed by the identical needs in international arbitration'.[51] Similar observations concerning the influence of developments in comparative and international law can also be made in respect of private-public arbitration.[52]

Comparative approaches also fall on futile grounds within the arbitration community, both in respect of the administration of disputes by arbitration institutions and in the decision-making of arbitral tribunals in private-public arbitrations. As Joshua Karton explains:

> comparativism is pervasive in international arbitrations. Comparative law methods are employed at every stage, even where the circumstances do not require a comparative analysis or assessment. Comparative law goes beyond merely a method of deriving rules; it constitutes an ethos of the field, a core aspect of its professional culture. That is, comparative law is not just something that is *used* in international commercial arbitrations; it is an essential constituent of the field.[53]

Thinking about the constitutional foundations of private-public arbitration in a comparative perspective, and engaging in a quest for the development of certain minimum standards, therefore holds significant potential in being drawn on by all actors that engage with private-public arbitration, whether in a legislative, administrative, or adjudicatory function. Such an approach has also already been successful in respect of investment treaty arbitration, as one subfield of private-public arbitration. In that respect, comparative analyses have been used not only to concretize the meaning and application of open-ended substantive standards of treatment of foreign investors, such as fair and equitable treatment, national treatment, or the concept of indirect expropriation, but also as guidance on questions relating to the conduct of arbitral

[49] UNCITRAL Model Law on International Commercial Arbitration (adopted 21 June 1985, amended 7 July 2006) UN Doc A/40/17, Annex I and UN Doc A/61/17, Annex I.

[50] For a recent example showing the importance of comparative approaches, see the discussions on the reform of arbitration legislation in Germany, where the approaches in other jurisdictions and developments in model legislation are named among the reasons for legislative reform. See Bundesministerium der Justiz (Ministry of Justice), 'Eckpunkte des Bundesministeriums der Justiz zur Modernisierung des deutschen Schiedsverfahrensrechts' (18 April 2023) <https://www.bmj.de/SharedDocs/Downloads/DE/Gesetzgebung/Eckpunkte/Eckpunkte_Schiedsverfahrensrecht.pdf?__blob=publicationFile&v=2> accessed 22 January 2025. For discussion of the impact of the Model Law on domestic arbitration legislation, see eg Pieter Sanders, 'Unity and Diversity in the Adoption of the Model Law' (1995) 11 Arb Int'l 1. See also Gilles Cuniberti, *The UNCITRAL Model Law on International Commercial Arbitration: A Commentary* (Elgar 2022); Ilias Bantekas and others, *The UNCITRAL Model Law on International Commercial Arbitration: A Commentary* (CUP 2020).

[51] Poudret and Besson (n 20) para 971.

[52] A particularly clear example of the external influences that have shaped the law governing private-public arbitration is the situation in Mexico, as discussed in Orlando Federico Cabrera Colorado and Andrea Orta González Sicilia, 'The Extrinsic Factors of World Trade that Galvanized Mexican Public-Private Arbitration during the Pre-NAFTA Years and the Evolution of Safeguards for the Public Interest' (in this volume) 252.

[53] Joshua Karton, 'International Arbitration as Comparative Law in Action' [2020] J Disp Resol 293, 295 (emphasis in the original).

procedure, including in respect of applicable procedural maxims on governing the gathering of evidence, determining the content of the applicable law, transparency, third-party participation, or applicable standards of review.[54]

The choice of the legal orders for comparison is, of course, an important matter for any comparative project, in particular if one intends to determine common approaches and distil minimum standards adopted across jurisdictions. After all, one has to avoid that comparative legal analysis becomes 'manipulable according to subjective preferences'[55] or that it produces insufficiently representative, selective, and, as is too often the case, Western-centric results.[56] In an ideal world with unlimited resources, a comparative analysis would be comprehensive and encompass the legal approach to private-public arbitration of all jurisdictions worldwide. Since such an approach is not feasible within the bounds of the present book, certain limitations have to be made.[57] While covering the classic legal systems addressed in comparative studies, namely the English and United States common law, as well as the legal systems of France, Germany, and Spain, the present book takes a broader approach and encompasses a wider array of domestic legal orders, including from jurisdictions in Latin America and the Caribbean, Africa, the Middle East, East Asia, Australia, and Eastern and Southeastern Europe.

Contributors to the present volume were guided in their preparation by a comprehensive questionnaire setting out the questions that are necessary for developing an in-depth comparative analysis of the constitutional foundations of private-public arbitration. The questionnaire is reproduced in the Annex to the present volume. It is organized in three parts: 1. Context; 2. Arbitration as Dispute Resolution; and 3. Arbitration as Governance:

- Part 1 of the questionnaire covers questions on the context in which private-public arbitration takes place in the jurisdiction in question, including the practical importance of private-public arbitration, the frequency of arbitration agreements being included in private-public contracts and the amount of dispute settlement practice, the contours of the statutory and constitutional framework,

[54] See the contributions in Schill, *International Investment Law and Comparative Public Law* (n 18). See also Valentina Vadi, *Analogies in International Investment Law and Arbitration* (CUP 2016); Daniel Peat, *Comparative Reasoning in International Courts and Tribunals* (CUP 2019). A comparative approach has also been adopted in a number of arbitral awards in investor-state arbitration, particularly in respect of the interpretation and application of substantive standards of treatment. See eg *Total SA v Argentine Republic*, ICSID Case No ARB/04/1, Decision on Liability (27 December 2010) para 111; *Gold Reserve Inc v Bolivarian Republic of Venezuela*, ICSID Case No ARB(AF)/09/1, Award (22 September 2014) para 576; *Cairn Energy PLC and Cairn UK Holdings Limited v Republic of India*, PCA Case No 2016-7 (UNCITRAL), Award (21 December 2020) paras 1715–817; *Mobil Corporation, Venezuela Holdings, BV and others v Bolivarian Republic of Venezuela*, ICSID Case No ARB/07/27, Decision on Jurisdiction (10 June 2010), paras 169–85.

[55] M Sornarajah, *The International Law on Foreign Investment* (5th edn, CUP 2021) 533.

[56] José E Alvarez, '"Beware: Boundary Crossings" – A Critical Appraisal of Public Law Approaches to International Investment Law' (2016) 17 JWIT 171; Jaye Ellis, 'General Principles and Comparative Law' (2011) 22 EJIL 949, 955–58, 968.

[57] Note that even the Handbook of International Commercial Arbitration, published under the auspices of the International Council for Commercial Arbitration (ICCA) and the Permanent Court of Arbitration (PCA), does not cover the legislative frameworks on arbitration in all jurisdictions worldwide, but 'only' those of 85 jurisdictions.

and the theoretical and academic context in which the law governing private-public arbitration is set.

- Part 2 of the questionnaire then turns to the technical rules and principles relating to private-public arbitration as a dispute settlement mechanism. It is structured along the lines of the key issues dealt with in relation to any arbitration proceeding, starting from the agreement to arbitrate, the constitution of arbitral tribunals, the principles governing the conduct of arbitration proceedings, including the powers of arbitral tribunals, confidentiality versus transparency, and the rules concerning the control of arbitral proceedings by courts and the enforcement of arbitral awards. Part 2 asks contributors specifically to consider possible differences in domestic regulation between private-private and private-public arbitration, and to engage with the question how the legal system in question ensures that the public interest is not negatively affected by recourse to private-public arbitrations.
- Part 3, finally, focuses on the assessment of private-public arbitration from the perspective of the constitutional principles of democracy, the protection of fundamental and human rights, and government under the rule of law, if private-public arbitration is not only seen as a means to settle individual disputes, but also has a governance function in increasingly replacing domestic courts in settling disputes and controlling the other branches of government, and in actively crafting and further developing the law governing private-public relations.

The use of a questionnaire notwithstanding, contributors were not asked to deliver country reports that stick slavishly to the questions asked, but rather to develop chapters that forward a thesis about how the domestic legal system or systems in question approach private-public arbitration, both in respect of the technicalities of arbitration law and practice and in respect of the constitutional framework in place. The outcome is chapters that each constitute in-depth intellectual endeavours probing the relationship between arbitration and constitutional law and values.

The original concept had been even broader, and encompassed the commissioning of chapters on further important jurisdictions, including Brazil, Canada, Colombia, Ecuador, Venezuela, Egypt, Nigeria, the Organisation for the Harmonisation of Corporate Law in Africa (OHADA, for its acronym of the French Organisation pour l'harmonisation en Afrique du droit des affaires), Italy, the Russian Federation, Sweden, Switzerland, Turkey, India, Japan, and the countries of the Association of Southeast Asian Nations (ASEAN). Chapters on these jurisdictions, unfortunately, did not materialize, leaving the present book with the analysis of the approach to private-public arbitration of some 40 jurisdictions. While important gaps and concomitant limitations remain from such a study, in particular as concerns jurisdictions that reign over large populations and whose conceptual ideas radiate, either regionally, or globally, and hence attract considerable attention in the analysis of the law of arbitration in scholarship and legal practice, such as Brazil, Egypt, India, Japan, Nigeria, the Russian Federation, Sweden, Switzerland, or Turkey, the breadth of comparative chapters presented here outbalances previous comparative approaches to private-public arbitration. These limitations notwithstanding, the chapters in the present volume, it is hoped, will be a valuable contribution and help in getting a clearer picture about how different domestic legal orders approach private-public arbitration, to what extent they see it as a constitutional concern, and how they ensure that arbitrating private-public disputes does not undermine, but rather helps, the public interest thrive.

IV. Findings

Because of the limitations in the scope of the comparative exercise undertaken in the nineteen substantive chapters in the present book, the findings are necessarily tentative and no more than a first chart of the comparative constitutional foundations of private-public arbitration. They also necessarily need to abstract from specific domestic legal systems and specific constitutional approaches. This notwithstanding, they are meaningful in conceptualizing private-public arbitration, structuring its interaction with constitutional law and values, and devising approaches to ensure that the use of private-public arbitration does not undermine the public interest.

First, as an empirical observation, the contributions to the present volume illustrate that private-public arbitration is a reality, and is practiced, albeit to different degrees, in all jurisdictions addressed. This is, of course, the case for jurisdictions that take the English approach of treating private-public arbitration rather indistinctly from private-private arbitration and subjecting it to identical rules on arbitrability, set aside, and enforcement.[58] But even in jurisdictions that take a generally restrictive approach, an absolute prohibition on using arbitration to settle private-public disputes is nowhere to be found. The developments in France are a case in point: while its Code of Civil Procedure has, since 1806, prohibited public entities from agreeing to arbitrate disputes, numerous exceptions have been introduced since the 1970s, including for commercial activities performed by public entities, private-public partnerships, disputes arising from international trade relations, and arbitrations based on international treaties.[59] Concluding that private-public arbitration is per se incompatible with the public interest, as is occasionally suggested in debates about investment treaty arbitration,[60] is therefore hardly sustainable from a comparative perspective.

On the contrary, the widespread use of private-public arbitration points to the exact opposite, namely that there are circumstances in which arbitrating private-public disputes is itself in the public interest, because insisting on recourse to domestic courts may prove detrimental to private-public cooperation and the public interest thus pursued. Legislation in France permitting arbitration between foreign companies

[58] See Stavros Brekoulakis and Margaret Devaney, 'Private-Public Arbitration in English Law: The Splendid Isolation of Arbitration from Public Law' (in this volume) 37.

[59] See Florian Grisel, 'The Private-Public Divide and Its Influence over French Arbitration Law' (in this volume) 67.

[60] See eg Gus Van Harten, 'Investment Treaty Arbitration, Procedural Fairness, and the Rule of Law' in Schill, *International Investment Law and Comparative Public Law* (n 18) 627 (criticizing investment treaty arbitration for its failure to provide adequate assurances of judicial independence and, unlike court-based adjudication, being problematic for the settlement of public law disputes because of the appearances of bias caused by investment treaty arbitration's 'unique combination of arbitration and public law, its asymmetrical claims structure, its reliance on executive officials to make case-by-case appointments, and its attenuation of judicial oversight' (ibid 629–30)).

and French public entities 'for the implementation of operations of general interest',[61] which was passed because Disney had conditioned establishing Euro Disney Paris on including arbitration clauses in its contracts with various French public entities, illustrates this vividly.[62] Similarly, in Ghana, arbitration, including for private-public disputes, is promoted in order to meet the public interest in development and contribute to stimulating private enterprise and private-public cooperation in fulfilment of the state's constitutional duty to work towards a healthy economy.[63] Ghana, just like Iran, has also set up public institutions that are mandated to administer arbitrations of private-public disputes.[64] Germany, but also Switzerland, in turn, provide examples where arbitration is used to settle disputes between constituent sub-entities in a federal state.[65] In Argentina, arbitral tribunals are even institutionally understood to form part of the judicial branch of government.[66] All of this suggests that recourse to private-public arbitration can serve the public interest.

Second, despite differences in the regulatory approaches towards private-public arbitration, there is considerable convergence towards a common core of practices relating to private-public arbitration, in particular in respect of the circumstances in which private-public arbitration is considered acceptable. For example, when looking at England and France, as two polar opposites in their approach to private-public arbitration—the former equally broadly permissive of private-public as of private-private arbitration, the latter departing from a general prohibition of private-public arbitration with numerous targeted exceptions—private-public arbitration is made use of in practice in similar circumstances, in particular in relation to disputes resulting from cross-border transactions between public entities and foreign companies; by contrast, in purely domestic contexts, the permissibility of private-public arbitration is often more restricted.[67] Similarly, many jurisdictions are more restrictive in permitting recourse to private-public arbitration when disputes are governed by administrative law, rather than private law.[68] A somewhat curious distinction is drawn in South

[61] France, Loi No 86-972 (19 August 1986).

[62] See Grisel (n 59) 77.

[63] See Dagbanja (n 33) 498, 505–508.

[64] ibid 503–504 (discussing the Alternative Dispute Resolution Centre, which is a 'public institution' through which the state is 'directly involved in the administration and facilitation of arbitration'). For the situation in Iran, see Seifi and Javadi (n 32) 364–65 (discussing the establishment of the High Technical Council, 'a public body composed of adjudicators specializing in public contracts' which functions as 'a separate arbitral body with a built-in mechanism to protect the public interest in conducting public-private arbitration').

[65] See Eleanor McGregor, 'Le recours à l'arbitrage pour la résolution de différends de droit public' (2018) 137:I Zeitschrift für Schweizerisches Recht 443, 446, 454, 457–58; Stephan W Schill and Nadine Berger, 'Eroding the Rule of Law through Private-Public Arbitration? Constitutionalization of Private-Public Arbitration in the German Legal System' (in this volume) 92, 93.

[66] See Diego Fernández Arroyo, Francisco Amallo, and Ezquiel H Vetulli, 'The Legitimacy of Private-Public Arbitration in Argentina and Its Slight, but Yet Strong Differences with Private-Public Arbitration' (in this volume) 320, 324–25.

[67] For examples of jurisdictions which permit transborder disputes to be settled through arbitration, while excluding arbitration for domestic private-public disputes, see Jaemin Lee, 'Public Policy of Public-Private Arbitration – Recent Developments and New Awareness in Korea' (in this volume) 462; McGregor (n 65) 458; Peter B Rutledge, 'Whither Leviathan: The Seepage of Constitutional Law into Private-Public Arbitration in the United States' (in this volume) 233, 244–46.

[68] The distinction between arbitration being permissible in respect of disputes governed by private law, while not being permissible at all, or only subject to greater restrictions, in respect of disputes governed by public law, is present in many legal orders. See eg Csongor István Nagy, 'Can a State Swim Against the

Africa, where domestic and international investment-related disputes cannot be submitted to arbitration, whereas commercial private-public disputes can, independently of whether they are international or domestic.[69]

Third, the reasons why recourse to arbitration, rather than to domestic courts, is considered in the public interest by domestic legislation, treaty networks, or general policy, converge. Arbitration is seen as a tool to manage and minimize political risk in helping to attract and facilitate cooperation with private parties and respond to certain shortcomings in neutrality and efficiency of the domestic courts that are normally competent to decide disputes. This is particularly true in relation to foreign parties. Greece, to pick one example, permitted recourse to private-public arbitration in domestic legislation based on a specific constitutional authorization already in the early 1950s—and hence before the first international investment treaties started being concluded—in order to enhance the credibility of government commitments and attract foreign investment that was much needed for rebuilding the country's war-wrecked economy and infrastructure.[70] Relatedly, allowing recourse to arbitration particularly in respect of disputes with foreign actors corresponds, in some jurisdictions, to tangible differences in treatment under domestic, including constitutional, law. In Germany, for example, foreigners and foreign companies receive less protection under constitutional law than their German counterparts: they face limitations in coverage under certain fundamental rights, in access to the constitutional court, and broad possibilities of the legislator to differentiate between foreign and domestic actors, and, as in most other systems, have no rights of democratic participation.[71] However, the management of political risk is also a factor in entirely domestic contexts: in Spain, for example, the slowness of domestic court proceedings is one of the main reasons for promoting private-public arbitration.[72]

Moreover, it is notable that transnational processes themselves influence countries' increasing acceptance of private-public arbitration, with international organizations and agencies (such as the International Centre for Settlement of Investment Disputes (ICSID), the Permanent Court of Arbitration (PCA), or the United Nations Commission on International Trade Law (UNCITRAL)), international treaty regimes (such as the ICSID Convention,[73] the New York Convention,[74] the Panama Convention,[75] or the European Convention on International Commercial

Tide? Hungarian Perspectives on Public-Private Arbitration' (in this volume) 184; Tamar Meshel, 'The Attorney General as Guardian of the Public Interest and the Evolution of Private-Public Arbitration in Israel' (in this volume) 391; Fernández Arroyo, Amallo, and Vetulli (n 66) 326–27; Engela C Schlemmer, 'The Dichotomy of Arbitration with the State in South Africa' (in this volume) 529; Manjiao Chi, 'China's Bifurcated Attitudes towards Private-Public Arbitration' (in this volume) 450; Lee (n 67).

[69] Schlemmer (n 68) 558–59.

[70] See Nikolaos Askotiris, 'Private-Public Arbitration under Greek Law: A (Nearly Complete) Public Law Paradigm' (in this volume) 158, 161–65.

[71] See Schill and Berger (n 65) 108–109.

[72] See Victor Ferreres Comella and Pol Fontboté Pradilla, 'Private-Public Arbitration in Spain: Legislative Timidity in the Shadow of the Constitution' (in this volume) 131, 133–35.

[73] See n 26 above.

[74] See n 25 above.

[75] Inter-American Convention on International Commercial Arbitration (adopted 30 January 1975, entered into force 16 June 1976) 1438 UNTS 245.

Arbitration,[76] as well as bilateral and multilateral investment treaties), and international soft law instruments (such as the UNCITRAL Model Law),[77] promoting international arbitration. For example, closer integration into the global economy, and participation in international treaty regimes that promote trade and investment, specifically the North American Free Trade Agreement (NAFTA), was the key driver for Mexico to liberalize its formerly restrictive approach towards private-public arbitration.[78] Conversely, states individually have difficulties opposing the trend towards increasing acceptance of private-public arbitration, as illustrated by Hungary's rather short-lived attempt to restrict the arbitrability of private-public disputes relating to 'national assets'.[79]

Fourth, the large majority of legal systems—with England being perhaps a striking exception, as it fully equates private-public with private-private arbitration[80]—recognize that the privatization of justice connected to a rise in private-public arbitration can raise concerns, or even threats, for the public interest. Consequently, most jurisdictions provide for safeguards to ensure that the use of private-public arbitration does not undermine the public interest and circumvent statutory or even constitutional limitations that exist to protect it.

Three models or approaches for such safeguards can be distilled from the comparative analysis presented in the book:

- In order to protect the public interest, some jurisdictions emphasize front-end or *ex ante* controls that focus on the conditions under which private-public disputes can be submitted to arbitration. This entails making restrictions on subjective arbitrability, that is, the ability of public entities to agree to arbitrate disputes, ranging from prohibitions in principle (as in France or Latvia),[81] via exclusions of disputes about certain government acts, such as regulatory powers or constitutional matters (as in Israel)[82] or the termination of administrative contracts for overriding public interests (as in Mexico),[83] to limiting arbitration to disputes that are tied to the ability of private and public actors to contract on the subject matter in question (as in Australia, Germany, or Switzerland).[84]

[76] European Convention on International Commercial Arbitration (n 31).

[77] UNCITRAL Model Law (n 49).

[78] See Cabrera Colorado and Orta González Sicilia (n 52) 260–64. For similar developments, see also Eglė Zemlytė and others, 'Protection of the Public Interest in Private-Public Arbitration in the Baltic States' (in this volume) 203–204.

[79] See Nagy (n 68) 192–97 (describing how the Hungarian Parliament, in 2011/12, passed legislation to exclude the possibility to use arbitration for the settlement of disputes concerning (Hungarian) national property, which embraced virtually all government-owned assets, such as real estate, shares in companies held by the state, intellectual property rights, bonds, and debentures, and in 2015 revoked the provisions in question because of the conclusion of an agreement on the expansion of a nuclear energy plant in Hungary).

[80] See Brekoulakis and Devaney (n 58) 49–53 (explaining that England's divergence from most other jurisdictions in this respect results from the absence of a developed administrative law system for much of England's history and a century-old and well-developed practice of commercial arbitration, which in combination had the effect for private-public arbitration that 'the resolution of disputes involving public law and public entities was effectively shoehorned into a dispute resolution framework which had been operating as an entirely private mode of dispute resolution for a very long time' (quote at ibid 53)).

[81] See Grisel (n 59) 72–74; Zemlytė and others (n 78) 211–212.

[82] See Meshel (n 68) 395.

[83] See Cabrera Colorado and Orta González Sicilia (n 52) 272–74.

[84] See Caroline Henckels, 'Private-Public Arbitration in Australia: Public Law Concerns, Private Law Responses' (in this volume) 562, 572–74 (explaining that one of the main limits on private-public arbitration

Other jurisdictions require specific statutory authorization for public entities to enter into arbitration agreements, either as an exception to a general prohibition of subjective arbitrability (as in France),[85] or as a general prerequisite for public entities for agreeing to an otherwise arbitrable dispute (as in Argentina, Australia, Greece, Mexico, or Pakistan).[86] Again, other jurisdictions provide for specific institutional mechanisms as part of *ex ante* controls, for example by requiring specific approvals, at times by entities with constitutional rank, for public entities to agree to arbitrate private-public disputes. In Israel, for example, the Attorney General's authorization of a private-public arbitration agreement is required.[87] In Iran, the Council of Ministers has to approve the agreement to arbitrate disputes concerning public and state property; where foreigners are involved as a party, and for some other important domestic disputes, parliamentary approval must be sought.[88] In Spain, the Council of Ministers, after advice from the Council of State, must authorize agreements to arbitrate disputes that affect the economic rights of the central government's treasury.[89]

- In other jurisdictions, back-end or *ex post* controls are entrusted to bear the brunt of ensuring that recourse to private-public arbitration does not undermine the public interest. This involves, in particular, protecting public interests through the need for arbitral awards to comply with public policy at the arbitral tribunal's seat and in enforcement action. In Pakistan, for example, domestic courts adopt a particularly vigilant attitude in reviewing private-public arbitration awards in set-aside and enforcement actions, inter alia in order to ensure that corruption in the underlying dealings between private and public actors is detected and sanctioned.[90] The courts in the Commonwealth Caribbean, while having inherited, and partly kept to this day, English laws, including on arbitration, have indicated that they would review arbitral awards in private-public disputes for compliance with fundamental individual rights and core constitutional principles.[91] China, in turn, protects the public interest in private-public arbitration through very broad rules on enforcement immunity that allow public

stems from restrictions that lie on the government's power to contract); Schill and Berger (n 65) 102 (explaining that the extent to which public actors can contract with private actors is a key factor for determining the scope of arbitrability); McGregor (n 65) 458–59 (explaining that, in Switzerland, the ability to dispose of rights has led courts to uphold the arbitrability of disputes in areas of expropriation, public transport, servitudes, concessions, and competition law, while they have rejected it for disputes about tax matters, public employment, money laundering, water supply, urban planning, and social health insurance).

[85] See Grisel (n 59) 75–79.

[86] See Fernández Arroyo, Amallo, and Vetulli (n 66) 327–28; Henckels (n 84) 572–74; Askotiris (n 70) 170–71; Cabrera Colorado and Orta González Sicilia (n 52) 270–72; Ahmad Ghouri, 'Living on the Edge of Judicial Review: The Law and Practice of Private-Public Arbitration in Pakistan' (in this volume) 415, 421–24.

[87] See Meshel (n 68) 392, 401–402 (discussing the directives issued by the Attorney General that concretize scope and conditions of his or her authorization of agreements to arbitrate disputes involving the government).

[88] See Seifi and Javadi (n 32) 365–70 (discussing Article 139 of the Iran Constitution as the basis for these specific approval requirements).

[89] See Ferreres Comella and Fontboté Pradilla (n 72) 149.

[90] See Ghouri (n 86) 424–25, 430, 434, 438.

[91] See Conway Blake, 'Reconciling Arbitral and Constitutional Governance: The Critical Role of the (Caribbean) Courts' (in this volume) 290, 301–307.

entities to resist enforcement of arbitral awards.[92] Specific concerns for ensuring the protection of public interests through back-end controls are likely also the reason why certain jurisdictions, such as France and Germany, grant the competence to set aside and enforce (certain) private-public awards to their administrative, rather than civil, courts.[93]

- A third approach to controlling that private-public arbitration does not undermine the public interest is process-oriented and involves domestic jurisdictions requiring that the arbitral proceedings in private-public arbitration provide procedural and organizational safeguards. In Germany, for example, while not distinguishing between private-private and private-public disputes in this respect, arbitration is only acceptable, and arbitration agreements and awards will only be enforced, if the tribunal's independence and impartiality is ensured and due process in arbitral proceedings is complied with.[94] In Greece and in the United States, limitations on what remedies tribunals can order in private-public arbitrations, notably excluding the annulment of administrative acts, is another process-oriented way to ensure that private-public arbitrations protect the public interest.[95] Finally, transparency for the conduct of private-public arbitration is an emerging requirement for ensuring the protection of public interests.[96]

In practice, these three models or approaches are hardly ever pure, and many jurisdictions combine different approaches to ensure that private-public arbitration does not undermine the public interest. Also, it is too early to tell which of these approaches, or which combination thereof, is best able to ensure that the public interest is not undermined, while also remaining open towards the benefits that can flow from recourse to private-public arbitration. What is clear, by contrast, is that the absence of any control mechanism would be detrimental for the protection of the public interest.[97]

Fifth, the concerns that exist with respect to the impact of using arbitration to settle private-public disputes on the public interest, and the safeguards put in place to protect it, are not disconnected from constitutional analysis, values, and principles, as suggested by the metaphor of arbitration and constitutional law being 'strange bedfellows'.[98] Instead, in many jurisdictions, arbitration generally, and private-public

[92] See Chi (n 68) 462–63.

[93] See Grisel (n 59) 84–88; Schill and Berger (n 65) 101–102, 126.

[94] See Schill and Berger (n 65) 117–19.

[95] See Askotiris (n 70) 170; Rutledge (n 67) 244–46.

[96] See Schill and Berger (n 65) 119–20, 123–24 . Notably, in some jurisdictions, freedom of information legislation is being applied, albeit to different degrees, to access information and material concerning private-public arbitration. For examples, see Meshel (n 68) 410–11; Fernández Arroyo, Amallo, and Vetulli (n 66) 333–34, 345; McGregor (n 65) 464–67.

[97] For an example of a domestic arbitration system that lacks even the basic control mechanisms, notably the possibility to provide for a set-aside mechanism for arbitral awards, see the situation in Latvia discussed by Zemlytė and others (n 78) 206–08, 212 (giving examples of fictitious arbitration proceedings and so-called 'pocket arbitrations'; that is, arbitrations 'in which an arbitration institution established by one of the parties to an agreement (or its affiliated entity) administers a resolution of disputes which arise from an agreement, negatively affecting the neutrality and fair treatment of a dispute', quoting Maija Tipaine and Līga Fjodorova, 'Arbitration in Latvia: Was a Restart a Failure?' (*Kluwer Arbitration Blog*, 25 January 2016).

[98] Rutledge (n 46) 1.

arbitration in particular, are subject to constitutional analysis, either in constitutional law doctrine or the decision-making of constitutional courts; this analysis in turn translates into regulations of, and control mechanisms for, private-public arbitration. For example, in Germany, Greece, Mexico, Spain, the United States, and the European Union (EU), there is a sizeable amount of scholarship that addresses the import of constitutional law for the law and practice of arbitration, both private-to-private and private-to-public, including but not limited to investment treaty arbitration.[99] In addition, constitutional courts, inter alia in Colombia, Costa Rica, Ecuador, France, Germany, and Ireland, as well as the Court of Justice of the European Union (CJEU) as the EU's constitutional court, are increasingly involved in pronouncing on the demands constitutional law makes of, and the limits it imposes on, private-public arbitration, including, but not limited to, investment treaty arbitration.[100]

Certainly, the constitutional starting points differ. Some constitutions expressly address arbitration, either by granting it constitutional status and protection, including at times by recognizing an individual right to access to arbitration,[101] or by laying down limits to the use of arbitration (at least in some form or fora).[102] By contrast, most constitutions are silent on arbitration and instead look at it through general constitutional principles. This may include, in some cases, grounding a right to arbitrate as part of the constitutionally protected freedom to contract.[103] More commonly, it involves deriving limitations for, and requiring regulation of, the use of private-public arbitration based on constitutionally grounded judicial monopolies,[104] or structural

[99] See Schill and Berger (n 65) 109–11; Askotiris (n 70) 166–67; Cabrera Colorado and Orta González Sicilia (n 52) 254; Ferreres Comella and Fontboté Pradilla (n 72) 133–36; Rutledge (n 67) 233. On the limits EU constitutional law imposes on investment treaty arbitration, see eg Angelos Dimopoulos, 'The Constitutional Fundamentals of EU Investment Policy' in Schill and Tams (n 39) 180; Hannes Lenk, 'Constraints on Intra-EU BITs in the Union Legal Order' (ibid 221).

[100] See the references to decisions of constitutional courts listed in n 40 above.

[101] For historical examples, see Spanish Constitution (1812), art 280 (referenced in Ferreres Comella and Fontboté Pradilla (n 72) 140); French Constitution (1791), title III, ch V, art 5, and French Constitution (1795), art 210 (discussed in Grisel (n 59) 71). Modern examples include Article 17 of the Mexican Constitution, which was introduced in 2008 and requires that legislation has to offer mechanisms for alternative dispute resolution, which includes private-public arbitration; see Cabrera Colorado and Orta González Sicilia (n 52) 265. In Greece, Legislative Decree 2687/1953 on the Investment and Protection of Foreign Capital, which gives foreign investors access to private-public arbitration, has constitutional rank: see Askotiris (n 70) 164. Article 116 of the Colombian Political Constitution (1991) states that '[i]ndividuals may be entrusted temporarily with the function of administering justice . . . as arbitrators, thus conferring arbitration constitutional status'.

[102] See eg Article 422 of Ecuador's Constitution (2008), which prohibits certain private-public arbitration in which the state 'yields its sovereign jurisdiction to international arbitration entities in disputes involving contracts or trade between the State and natural persons or legal entities', but exempts 'regional arbitration entities' from that prohibition. Similarly, in disputes involving foreign debt, arbitration remains a possible mechanism for dispute resolution.

[103] For example, Article 18 of Pakistan's Constitution, which grants freedom of trade, business, or profession, arguably covers the freedom to conclude arbitration agreements, including in private-public arbitration; see Ghouri (n 86) 420. In Germany, the right to agree to arbitrate, at least in private-private disputes, is covered by the constitutionally protected freedom to contract: see German Federal Constitutional Court, Case No 1 BvR 2103/16, Decision (3 June 2022) para 39 – *Pechstein*. In several Caribbean states, the government's power to agree to arbitrate in the context of commercial cases is part of the constitutionally protected prerogatives of the executive's power to contract: see Blake (n 91) 295.

[104] For example, in Germany, the competence of the Federal Constitutional Court in proceedings that Article 93 Grundgesetz (the German Constitution) allocates to it cannot be relegated to arbitration; see Schill and Berger (n 65) 114. In Ghana, Article 130(1)(a) of the Constitution reserves matters of constitutional interpretation to the Supreme Court: see Dagbanja (n 33) 503.

constitutional principles that are shared across constitutional systems, namely principles connected to the rule of law, the principle of democracy, and the protection of fundamental and human rights. It is against the background of these principles that constitutional law in several jurisdictions covered by the present book analyses the concerns with private-public arbitration sketched out above,[105] and develops control mechanisms to ensure that the public interest remains respected. Control mechanisms and safeguards that correspond to the above-mentioned approaches result from constitutionally grounded concerns to ensure that: (i) the process of private-public arbitration proceedings is rule-of-law compatible (including in respect of access to justice, independence and impartiality of adjudicators, and due process of law);[106] (ii) recourse to private-public arbitration does not reduce government accountability under domestic law, including in particular in respect of limits on the exercise of government powers, rules on the use of public funds, fair competition, anti-corruption, etc;[107] and (iii) private-public arbitration respects democratic principles of openness, transparency, and participation of affected actors and constituencies.[108]

Sixth, when comparing how domestic legal orders translate constitutional principles into regulatory frameworks for private-public arbitration, a number of observations can be made:

- To start with, it is notable that none of the jurisdictions analysed in the present book subject private-public arbitration to a general constitutional ban, or otherwise view it as unconstitutional as a matter of course. On the contrary, independently of whether arbitration is mentioned in constitutional texts, whether permissibly or prohibitively, or is to be measured against general constitutional principles, constitutional law leaves room for private-public arbitration. It does so, however, to different degrees. One important constitutional limit in this respect is provided by constitutionally grounded, but in practice generally very limited, judicial monopolies that often translate into limits on the arbitrability of disputes.[109]
- Moreover, with respect to the public entity involved in a dispute, consent without an underlying legal basis that authorizes the public entity to give it is often an insufficient basis for private-public arbitration. This reflects the fact

[105] See the discussion in section II above.

[106] For analysis of such rule-of-law-based principles as part of the framework limiting and guiding private-public arbitration, see, inter alia, the analysis in the chapters on Australia (Henckels (n 84) 566–67, 569–72), Germany (Schill and Berger (n 65) 113–19), Greece (Askotiris (n 70) 171–72), Spain (Ferreres Comella and Fontboté Pradilla (n 72) 133–38, 145–46, 153–55), and the United States (Rutledge (n 67) 240–41).

[107] Concerns for the accountability of government are noticeable in particular in Australia (see Henckels (n 84) 572–76, 580–81), Israel (see Meshel (n 68) 392, 400, 405, 413), Pakistan (see Ghouri (n 86) 416, 427, 428–33, 444), and South Africa (see Schlemmer (n 68) 554–57). In Iran, limitations on international arbitration, namely the need to seek parliamentary approval for some agreements to arbitrate, are geared to safeguard against external influences that could pressure government to agree to contractual arrangements that harm the public interest (see Seifi and Javadi (n 32) 356, 368).

[108] Confidentiality versus transparency in private-public arbitration is an increasingly important concern in several domestic legal systems. See eg the discussion in Argentina (Fernández Arroyo, Amallo, and Vetulli (n 66) 333–34), Australia (Henckels (n 84) 567–69), Germany (Schill and Berger (n 65) 119–20), Israel (Meshel (n 68) 395–96, 403, 405, 408–11), Mexico (Cabrera Colorado and Orta González Sicilia (n 52) 257–58), and South Africa (Schlemmer (n 68) 554–57).

[109] See eg the discussion on the situation in Ghana in Dagbanja (n 33) 508–09.

that the public entity is constitutionally bound to, and has to comply with, its own domestic law, and cannot usurp the power to agree to arbitrate. Such a grant of competence does not necessarily have to be highly specific, as sometimes is the case in domestic legislation,[110] but it has to follow with sufficient clarity from domestic law that the public entity has the authority to arbitrate disputes with private actors. Conceptually and philosophically, private-public arbitration therefore has to be grounded in the public law principle of legality rather than party autonomy.[111]

- By contrast, comparative constitutional law often presupposes that the private party must voluntarily accept and consent to arbitrate private-public disputes, based on the idea that access to justice presupposes the possibility for private actors to have recourse to domestic courts to review government conduct.[112] It is only under limited circumstances that a few jurisdictions make use of so-called mandatory arbitration, where disputes have to be settled through arbitration rather than in domestic courts, for example to provide access to justice when the court system is majorly clogged or where judges lack necessary knowledge and expertise to settle disputes efficiently and fairly.[113]
- A comparative constitutional analysis also provides support for the idea that the arbitration proceedings themselves must conform to constitutionally grounded minimum procedural standards. This includes the requirement that the arbitration proceedings respect the equality of the parties, their due process rights, and their right to be heard, and that the arbitral tribunal has a duty to give reasons; in addition, arbitrators must be independent and impartial and mechanisms must exist to challenge the lack thereof.[114] Similarly, in order to ensure that arbitration does not undermine the public interest in private-public disputes, it is necessary that control mechanisms in set-aside and enforcement proceedings are available for the disputing parties, either before domestic courts or independent supervisory bodies, such as ICSID annulment committees; by contrast, the possibility to opt out of any right to have awards reviewed would sit squarely with

[110] For examples, see the situation in France (Grisel (n 59) 75–79) or Spain (Ferreres Comella and Fontboté Pradilla (n 72) 147–51), where permissions to private-public arbitration are generally highly specific in terms of sector or type of contract and are contained in subject-matter-specific regulations or legislation.

[111] This does not necessarily mean, however, that any violation of domestic rules would, or should, be recognized by arbitral tribunals and other domestic legal orders, which are tasked to exercise supervisory jurisdiction over arbitral tribunals or decide on the enforcement of arbitral awards, and who may determine the limits to private-public arbitration differently from the legal order of the public entity involved. See on the diverging perspectives on these issues in a transnational context, nn 29–38 above and accompanying text.

[112] See eg the situation in Australia (Henckels (n 84) 572–74), Germany (Schill and Berger (n 65) 114–15), and Spain (Ferreres Comella and Fontboté Pradilla (n 72) 140, 153–54). See also the jurisprudence of the Italian Constitutional Court, declaring mandatory arbitration to be unconstitutional, referenced in Tony Cole, Pietro Ortolani, and Barbara Warwas, 'Arbitration in Southern Europe: Insights from a Large-Scale Empirical Study' (2015) 26 Am Rev Int'l Arb 187, 234 fn 132.

[113] See eg the situation in Pakistan (Ghouri (n 86) 421–22, 432) and South Africa (Schlemmer (n 68) 547–58), which know mandatory arbitration, including in private-public disputes for a narrow set of sectors and disputes. Similarly, Malta, as discussed in Cole, Ortolani, and Warwas (n 112) 234 fn 132, seems to mandate arbitration for certain, but seemingly limited, private-private disputes.

[114] See, inter alia, the analysis in the chapters on Australia (Henckels (n 84) 566–67, 569, 572), Germany (Schill and Berger (n 65) 113–19), Greece (Askotiris (n 70) 171–72, 173–74), Spain (Ferreres Comella and Fontboté Pradilla (n 72) 146), and the United States (Rutledge (n 67) 240–41).

the need to ensure that private-public arbitration does not undermine the public interest or be used to circumvent important legal strictures that are binding on the disputing parties.[115]

- Finally, it is notable that constitutional law analysis is not static and evolves as private-public arbitration develops towards a transnational governance system. In this context, transparency and third-party participation constitute an emerging procedural principle. It is pushed for in the realm of investment treaty arbitrations, with the UNCITRAL Rules on Transparency,[116] the ICSID and ICSID Additional Facility Arbitration Rules,[117] and the Mauritius Convention on Transparency[118] all providing for increased transparency and allow third-party participation.[119] But also various domestic constitutional orders are becoming increasingly sensitized to the need to enhance transparency and third-party participation in private-public arbitration in order to account for the public interest involved.[120] This is even the case in jurisdictions, such as England, that traditionally do not make differences between private-private and private-public arbitrations.[121] These developments notwithstanding, in contract-based private-public arbitrations confidentiality is still prevalent, and the perception that change is needed to ensure the accountability of both the public party involved and arbitral tribunals themselves is only starting to take root.

Taken together, there is considerable convergence not only in the analysis of the constitutional concerns private-public arbitration raises, but also in respect of how the underlying constitutional principles and values translate into legal and institutional safeguards that ensure that private-public arbitration works in line with, and does not undermine, the public interest.

Finally, while supporting the importance of safeguard mechanisms for private-public arbitration, a comparative analysis also shows the limitations with which constitutional analysis has so far operated. Most importantly, most domestic legal systems, and their constitutional analyses, conceptualize private-public arbitration only as a mechanism for resolving individual disputes, and do not grasp sufficiently

[115] This is supported also by the concern that, without such supervisory mechanisms, there is a tangible risk of reducing government accountability, including, but not limited to, issues of corruption. See in particular Ghouri (n 86) 424–25, 430, 434, 438, discussing the position from the perspective of Pakistan's legal system. See also the discussion at nn 41–42 above and accompanying text. See also n 97 above for discussion of the example of Latvia, which is missing any such control mechanism.

[116] UNCITRAL Rules on Transparency in Treaty-based Investor-State Arbitration, in Report of the United Nations Commission on International Trade Law, Forty-Sixth Session (8–26 July 2013), General Assembly, Official Records, Sixty-eighth session, Supplement No. 17, UN Doc No A/68/17, Annex I.

[117] ICSID, Rules of Procedure for Arbitration Proceedings (Arbitration Rules) (1 July 2022) ICSID/15/Rev. 3, Rules 62–68; ICSID, Additional Facility Arbitration Rules (1 July 2022) ICSID/11/Rev. 3, Rules 73–78.

[118] United Nations Convention on Transparency in Treaty-based Investor-State Arbitration (signed 10 December 2014, entered into force 18 October 2017) 3208 UNTS 54749.

[119] For discussion and further references, see Stephan W. Schill, 'United Nations Convention on Transparency in Treaty-based Investor-State Arbitration' in Hélène Ruiz-Fabri (ed), *Max Planck Encyclopedia of International Procedural Law* (OUP, online edition) (January 2019).

[120] See eg the discussion in Argentina (Fernández Arroyo, Amallo, and Vetulli (n 66) 333–34), Australia (Henckels (n 84) 567–68), Germany (Schill and Berger (n 65) 119–20), Israel (Meshel (n 68) 395–401, 403, 405, 408–11), Mexico (Cabrera Colorado and Orta González Sicilia (n 52) 257–58), and South Africa (Schlemmer (n 68) 554–57).

[121] See *Nigeria v Process & Industrial Developments* (n 19) paras 589–91.

its functioning as a transnational governance system. These deficits are likely going to become increasingly obvious, and constitutional law analysis in many jurisdictions will need to develop apace. Drawing on the insights that follow from the comparative approach developed in the present book may help in that endeavour and contribute to private-public arbitration and constitutional law functioning as complementary systems that do not enter into conflict with each other, but instead pursue the same foundational values, namely the rule of law, democracy, and the protection of fundamental and human rights.

V. Outlook

The rise of private-public arbitration towards a transnational system of governance poses novel challenges, both for the law and practice of arbitration and for constitutional law. With disputes between private and public actors that have manifest impact on the public interest being resolved by arbitrators instead of domestic courts, constitutional values and principles become directly affected, including principles of state organization, access to justice, separation of powers, the rule of law, democracy, the right to regulate, and the protection of public interests and competing fundamental and human rights. This requires constitutional law and the law and practice of arbitration to engage with each other and determine under which conditions constitutional law does and should give room to private-public arbitration, and to what extent constitutional law and values should affect the practice of private-public arbitration. While both legal fields have been, for a long time, at a maximum distance from each other, private-public arbitration requires a rapprochement that will be difficult to resolve through traditional claims for supremacy of constitutional law, because private-public arbitration functions as a transnational governance system that can evade constitutional law's claims for supremacy; conversely, domestic legal systems will have difficulties avoiding private-public arbitration altogether as efficient transborder private-public cooperation sees the resolution of private-public disputes through arbitration as an established building block of the global economy. At the same time, private-public arbitration cannot ignore constitutional principles that are the founding values of any legal system, whether domestic, international, or transnational. Constructive engagement of constitutional law and arbitration are therefore much needed to bring an era where both are qualified as 'strange bedfellows'[122] to an end.

[122] Rutledge (n 46) 1. One may, however, legitimately doubt whether arbitration and constitutional law have always been 'strange bedfellows', considering that choices on arbitration, including private-public arbitration, in many jurisdictions appear to have had constitutional dimensions all along. Independently of whether constitutional texts address arbitration, and what stance constitutions take, the regulation of (private-public) arbitration is often deeply constitutional and reflects constitutional experiences, positions, and arrangements going to the relationship between the state and the economy, the value and role of individual rights as compared with common interests, and forms of state and political organization. That arbitration has such larger constitutional dimensions can well be illustrated by looking at the historical developments in France, where, after the French Revolution in the late eighteenth century, the right to arbitrate was laid down in several constitutions because the revolutionaries had a deep-seated distrust of the courts, which were seen as emanations of the *Ancien Régime*, whereas at a later stage private-public

While constitutional law and practice will have to make their own efforts at understanding the rationale for, and the internal logics of, arbitration proceedings, most constitutional court cases that have dealt with private-public arbitration[123] have operated in a mode of accommodation. Equal efforts at understanding and accommodating constitutional demands have to be made in the field of arbitration. The field, however, is not necessarily well-equipped to grasp the constitutional concerns raised by private-public arbitration, as the predominant frame of thinking is based on party autonomy and party consent as the key legitimizing pillars of arbitration, as if private-public arbitration was a pure creature of contract. Yet, as the comparative analysis in the present book shows, the legitimacy of private-public arbitration can hardly be thought of simply in terms of the disputing parties' consent. It requires a broader justification of the authority of arbitral tribunals, and of the functioning of private-public arbitration, in terms of compliance with the principle of legality, and consideration of its impact on the public interest and the constitutional principles that define and protect it. One way of doing so, which the present book promotes, is to look, in a comparative perspective, at how different domestic legal systems and their constitutional underpinnings approach and regulate private-public arbitration and ensure that the resulting practice does not undermine, but instead protects, the public interest and democratic government under the rule of law.

Despite limitations in scope, the contributions to the present volume show how promising comparative approaches to private-public arbitration, and the possibility to distil common principles or constitutional minimum standards, are in providing a jurisdiction-overarching, transnational normative framework to ensure that private-public arbitration does not undermine core constitutional principles and the public interest. In this context, comparative constitutional analysis can provide guidance on the extent to which domestic legal orders should permit and limit private-public arbitration; how constitutional courts review domestic legislative and regulatory frameworks governing private-public arbitration; how domestic courts in set-aside and enforcement proceedings should control tribunals deciding private-public disputes; how arbitration institutions act in administering private-public arbitrations; and how arbitral tribunals conduct arbitration proceedings in private-public disputes. Moreover, it appears important that control mechanisms focus not only on the arbitration process as such, but also consider mechanisms to ensure accountability in government contracting, including contract negotiation, contract management, conflicts prevention and mitigation, and dispute management.

Rather than presenting final results and discussing all details of how private-public arbitration and constitutional law interact, the book is but a start to rethinking private-public arbitration from a comparative constitutional law perspective, to make the concerns this burgeoning form of transborder dispute settlement raises visible, and to illustrate the promise this transnational governance regime holds if it is practiced with sensitivity for the constitutional concerns it raises. If there is one main takeaway from

arbitration was prohibited in the early nineteenth century as adverse to the Napoleonic project of centralization. For discussion of these developments in France, see Grisel (n 59) 69–74.

[123] See the references in n 40 above.

the study presented here, it is that private-public arbitration should not be viewed as a subdiscipline of international commercial arbitration, but as a form of dispute settlement in which the presence of a public actor imposes specific public interest-related demands on the applicable framework and the conduct of the arbitration process. The comparative exercise promoted here overcomes the traditional divide between arbitration and constitutional law analysis and helps unveil what the book calls the comparative constitutional foundations of private-public arbitration. These foundations help to sensitize all those involved in private-public arbitration for the constitutional concerns the system raises but also intend to help the transnational governance system that is put in place through recourse to arbitration in private-public disputes to enter into fruitful interaction with constitutional law analysis and actively contribute to, live by, and foster core principles of constitutional governance. That way, grounding private-public arbitration in comparative constitutional analysis should help constitutional law and arbitration to work in a complementary fashion and bring core constitutional values, including, in particular, democracy, the rule of law, and the protection of fundamental and human rights, to bear in a transnational legal environment.

Select Bibliography

Audit, Mathias and Stephan W Schill (eds), *The Transnational Law of Public Contracts* (Bruylant 2015)

Bentolila, Dolores, *Arbitrators as Lawmakers: The Creation of General Rules Through Consistent Decision Making in International Commercial and Investment Arbitration* (Kluwer Law International 2017)

Berger, Klaus Peter, *The Creeping Codification of the New Lex Mercatoria* (2nd edn, Kluwer Law International 2010)

Bonnitcha, Jonathan, Lauge N Skovgaard Poulsen, and Michael Waibel, *The Political Economy of the Investment Treaty Regime* (OUP 2017)

Born, Gary B, *International Commercial Arbitration* (3rd edn, Wolters Kluwer 2020)

Brower, Charles N and Stephan W Schill, 'Is Arbitration a Threat or a Boon to the Legitimacy of International Investment Law?' (2009) 9 Chicago JIL 471

Cane, Peter and others (eds), *The Oxford Handbook of Comparative Administrative Law* (OUP 2021)

Carbonneau, Thomas E (ed), *Lex Mercatoria and Arbitration: A Discussion of the New Law Merchant* (2nd edn. Juris 1998)

Caron, David D and others (eds), *Practising Virtue: Inside International Arbitration* (OUP 2015)

Cotula, Lorenzo, 'Democracy and International Investment Law' (2017) 30 LJIL 351

Cutler, A Claire, *Private Power and Global Authority: Transnational Merchant Law in the Global Political Economy* (CUP 2003)

Dezalay, Yves and Bryant G Garth, *Dealing in Virtue: International Commercial Arbitration and the Construction of a Transnational Legal Order* (Chicago University Press 1996)

Ferreres Comella, Victor, *The Constitution of Arbitration* (CUP 2021)

Franck, Susan D, 'The Legitimacy Crisis in Investment Treaty Arbitration: Privatizing Public International Law Through Inconsistent Decisions' (2005) 73 Fordham L Rev 1521
Freeman, Jody, 'The Contracting State' (2000) 28 Fla St U L Rev 155
Gaillard, Emmanuel, *Legal Theory of International Arbitration* (Martinus Nijhoff 2010)
Harden, Ian, *The Contracting State* (Open University Press 1992)
Hepburn, Jarrod, 'Domestic Investment Statutes in International Law' (2018) 112 AJIL 658
International Chamber of Commerce, *ICC Commission Report: States, State Entities and ICC Arbitration* (International Chamber of Commerce 2012)
Karton, Joshua, *The Culture of International Arbitration and the Evolution of Contract Law* (OUP 2013)
Karton, Joshua, 'International Arbitration as Comparative Law in Action' [2020] J Disp Resol 293
Kröll, Stefan, Andrea K Bjorklund, and Franco Ferrari (eds), *Cambridge Compendium of International Commercial and Investment Arbitration* (CUP 2023)
Kulick, Andreas, 'International Investment Arbitration, Treaty Interpretation, and Democracy' (2015) 4 CILJ 441
Ladeur, Karl-Heinz, 'The Changing Role of the Private in Public Governance – The Erosion of Hierarchy and the Rise of a New Administrative Law of Cooperation: A Comparative Approach' EUI Working Paper No 2002/9 (2002) <https://hdl.handle.net/1814/187> accessed 22 January 2025
Lew, Julian DM, Loukas A Mistelis and Stefan M Kröll, *Comparative International Commercial Arbitration* (Kluwer Law International 2003)
Mattli, Walter, 'Private Justice in a Global Economy: From Litigation to Arbitration' (2001) 55 Intl Org 919
Mattli, Walter and Thomas Dietz (eds), *International Arbitration and Global Governance – Contending Theories and Evidence* (OUP 2014)
Paulsson, Jan, *The Idea of Arbitration* (OUP 2013)
Poudret, Jean-François and Sébastian Besson, *Comparative Law of International Arbitration* (2nd edn, Sweet & Maxwell 2007)
Reimannm Mathias and Reinhard Zimmermann (eds), *The Oxford Handbook of Comparative Law* (2nd edn, OUP 2019)
Reinisch, August and Stephan W Schill (eds), *Investment Protection Standards and the Rule of Law* (OUP 2023)
Rosenfeld, Michel and András Sajó (eds), *The Oxford Handbook of Comparative Constitutional Law* (OUP 2012)
Rutledge, Peter B, *Arbitration and the Constitution* (CUP 2013)
Schill, Stephan W (ed), *International Investment Law and Comparative Public Law* (OUP 2010)
Schill, Stephan W, 'Reforming Investor–State Dispute Settlement: A (Comparative and International) Constitutional Law Framework' (2017) 20 JIEL 649
Schill, Stephan W and Christian J Tams (eds), *International Investment Protection and Constitutional Law* (Edward Elgar Publishing 2022)
Schultz, Thomas, *Transnational Legality: Stateless Law and International Arbitration* (OUP 2014)

Schneiderman, David, *Constitutionalizing Economic Globalization—International Investment Law and Democracy's Promise* (CUP 2008)

Sourgens, Frédéric G, *A Nascent Common Law: The Process of Decisionmaking in International Legal Disputes Between States and Foreign Investors* (Brill 2015)

Stone Sweet, Alec and Florian Grisel, *The Evolution of International Arbitration: Judicialization, Governance, Legitimacy* (OUP 2017)

Whytock, Christopher A, 'Private-Public Interaction in Global Governance: The Case of Transnational Arbitration' (2010) 12(3) Bus Politics, Article 10

Zumbansen, Peter, 'The Law of Society: Governance Through Contract' (2007) 14 Indiana J Global Legal Studies 191

PART I
PRIVATE-PUBLIC ARBITRATION IN EUROPE

2

Private-Public Arbitration in English Law

The Splendid Isolation of Arbitration from Public Law

Stavros Brekoulakis and Margaret Devaney[*]

I. Introduction

The last forty years have witnessed an increased number of disputes between public entities, including states, and private actors. The growth in private-public disputes can be attributed to two main reasons. First, most of the over 2,500 international investment treaties now in force have adopted international arbitration as the preferred model for the resolution of disputes between states and investors, and at least 600 foreign investors have submitted such treaty-based investment claims to arbitration to date.

Second, there has been a growing interaction between public and private sectors and increased reliance on private actors to perform public functions in a wide range of areas, which in turn has led to a dramatic increase in the number of private-public contracts, many of which favour arbitration and other private forms of dispute resolution. As a result, a number of significant arbitrations between public and private entities arising out of contractual disputes have recently arisen, with the most prominent example in England being the *e-Borders* arbitration between the Secretary of State for the Home Department and the US defence company Raytheon Systems Limited, in respect of a 2007 contract for the design, development, and delivery of a multimillion pound technology system (e-Borders) which would reform UK border controls by establishing an electronic system to vet travellers leaving and entering the UK. Although, like a typical commercial arbitration between private parties, such private-public disputes are contractual in nature, the crucial point of distinction is the public interest implications associated with the latter, and it is these implications that make these private-public arbitrations important to examine.

This chapter aims to clarify the concept of private-public arbitration and to offer a critique of the way in which private-public arbitration is treated under English arbitration law. The main thesis of this chapter is that the private law paradigm upon which English arbitration law is based leaves the public interest both unaccounted for and unprotected, in respect of private-public arbitrations.

The chapter proceeds as follows: section II offers an account of the rise of private-public arbitration, including both disputes under private-public contracts and investment treaty arbitration, and examines the extent to which the phenomenon of

* The content of the chapter was last updated in January 2019.

Stavros Brekoulakis and Margaret Devaney, *Private-Public Arbitration in English Law* In: *The Comparative Constitutional Foundations of Private-Public Arbitration*. Edited by: Stephan W. Schill, Oxford University Press.
 DOI: 10.1093/9780191987960.003.0002

private-public arbitration has been considered in existing literature. It concludes by noting that the rise of arbitration under private-public contracts and its legal treatment has remained largely uncharted and that, while extensively discussed in an international law context, the public-private distinctions which underlie the investment treaty regime remain unexplored under English law. Section III examines the concept of public interest and, in taking a unitary and normative approach to the concept of public interest, argues that private-public arbitration merits consideration because it typically concerns matters that affect the economic welfare of the public, including the expenditure of public monies and the allocation of public resources, and because it can affect the exercise and implementation of governmental policies in sectors that are sensitive for the public, such as immigration and security, health, and public infrastructure.

Section IV examines the treatment of private-public arbitration under English law. As is demonstrated, unlike the law of other jurisdictions, English law draws no meaningful distinction between purely private arbitrations and private-public arbitrations. Similarly, section IV examines how the English courts have treated investment treaty arbitration awards and notes that, while investment treaty arbitration has been conceptualized as forming part of public international law by the English courts, this has, in practice, not led to a significant distinction between international commercial arbitration and investment treaty arbitration vis-à-vis the role of the English courts in reviewing such awards.

The lack of a distinct legal and conceptual framework for private-public arbitration in England raises two important questions. The first is why such a framework is lacking. The second, and possibly more important, question is whether the existing private law arbitration paradigm on which English arbitration law is based can adequately account for, and protect, the public interest in arbitrations involving public entities in England. Section V addresses the first question and provides two explanations as to why private-public arbitration has developed as an entirely private mode of dispute resolution. The first is that, in England, in contrast to Continental European jurisdictions, there is a lack of a developed administrative law sphere and of a separate body of administrative courts which would claim interest in the regulation of private-public arbitrations. The second reason is that arbitration in England has traditionally been embedded in private law and developed as an exclusively private mode of dispute resolution.

Section VI then proceeds to examine the question of whether English arbitration law adequately accounts for the public interest in arbitrations involving public entities. In relation to investment treaty arbitrations, the circumscribed nature of the review undertaken of investment treaty arbitration awards by English courts can be seen as problematic when viewed from a traditional public international law perspective. Equally, however, the role of investment treaty tribunals is consistent with the emergence of a significant number of a new style of international adjudicative bodies in recent years which have the power to review the validity of administrative decisions and assess compliance of states with international law and to which non-state actors can submit disputes. In any event, any attempt to reform the investor-state dispute settlement system must take place at an international level. Therefore, English law can only hope to address contractual disputes under private-public arbitrations.

However, as is submitted in section VI, the private law paradigm on which English arbitration law is currently based leaves the public interest both unaccounted for and unprotected in respect of such private-public arbitrations. In light of this conclusion, section VII offers some preliminary suggestions as to how this void in respect of how the public interest is accounted for, and protected, in relation to arbitrations under private-public contracts may be filled.

II. The Rise of Private-Public Arbitration

Traditionally, arbitration has been the predominant mode of dispute resolution for contractual disputes between two private parties, typically corporations. However, in the past forty years, with the collapse of the non-arbitrability doctrine, the scope of arbitration has greatly expanded. For example, in the area of commercial arbitration, it is now accepted that tribunals have authority to determine not only claims pertaining to the formation, interpretation, and performance of commercial contracts but also statutory claims that may have crucial social implications,[1] such as antitrust claims, tax claims, or claims arising out of securities transactions.[2] Similarly, the majority of international investment treaties have adopted arbitration as the preferred model of dispute resolution. Accordingly, although investment treaty arbitration really only came into its own in the 1990s,[3] international arbitration tribunals now regularly review investor claims concerning government measures, including financial and environmental measures, which concern the regulatory sovereignty of the host nation and would normally fall within the exclusive jurisdiction of national courts.[4]

Concurrent with this development, a combination of economic and ideological factors has led to increased interaction between public and private sectors and increased reliance on private actors to perform public functions in virtually every industrialized state.[5] In the UK, the transfer of government powers to the private sector gathered pace during the 1980s and was driven by a belief that provision of services by the private sector would be more efficient and more responsive to consumers.[6] Such outsourcing arrangements can take various forms, including entrusting private partners with the legal responsibility to provide such services ('contracting out') and collaborating with private entities for the purpose of achieving a public function, albeit

[1] Thomas Carbonneau, 'Cartesian Logic and Frontier Politics: French and American Concepts of Arbitrability' (1994) 2 Tul J Intl & Comp L 196.

[2] See Karim Youssef, 'The Death of Inarbitrability' in Loukas Mistelis and Stavros Brekoulakis (eds), *Arbitrability: International and Comparative Perspectives* (Kluwer 2009) 47. For a more general overview see Loukas Mistelis and Stavros Brekoulakis (eds), *Arbitrability: International and Comparative Perspectives* (Kluwer 2009).

[3] Campbell McLachlan, Laurence Shore, and Matthew Weiniger, *Investment Treaty Arbitration: Substantive Principles* (OUP 2007) 5.

[4] In 2014, 42 new investor-state dispute settlement cases were initiated, bringing the total number of known treaty-based claims to 608 and the total number of concluded cases to 405: UNCTAD, *World Investment Report 2015: Reforming International Investment Governance* (United Nations 2015) xi.

[5] Jody Freeman, 'The Private Role in Public Governance' (2000) 75 NYU L Rev 543; Jean-Bernard Auby, 'Contracting Out and "Public Values": A Theoretical and Comparative Approach' in Susan Rose Ackerman and Peter L Lindseth (eds), *Comparative Administrative Law* (Edward Elgar Publishing 2013) 512.

[6] Anne Davies, *Accountability: A Public Law Analysis of Government by Contract* (OUP 2001) 3.

that ultimate legal responsibility to the public remains with the public body.[7] These developments, in turn, have led to a dramatic increase in the number of private-public contracts (ie contracts entered into by public bodies with private entities) as a means of documenting and structuring these arrangements.[8] Crucially, many of these private-public contracts include an agreement to arbitrate. For example, the Model Terms and Conditions of Contracts for Goods issued by the UK Office of Government Commerce provide for a multi-tiered dispute resolution process which ends in arbitration in the event that informal negotiation and mediation are unsuccessful,[9] and similar dispute resolution provisions are also common in standard forms of international construction contracts, typically adopted for procurement of public works.[10]

Thus, the combination of these two developments—the expansion of arbitration's domain (in particular in respect of investor-state disputes) and the rise of the '*contracting state*'—has led to a marked increase in recent years in private-public arbitrations. The term 'private-public arbitration' is used, for the purposes of this chapter, to encompass both investment treaty arbitration (ie an international arbitration between a public entity and a private entity arising under an international investment treaty) and arbitrations between a public entity and a private entity, arising out of a contractual dispute, which implicate the public interest. While there are important differences between these two types of arbitrations, notably in the way in which the state entity agrees to submit to arbitration, the applicable law, and the source of authority of the arbitral tribunal, both forms of arbitration have public interest implications. Furthermore, although investment treaty arbitration has been the subject of extensive academic and popular discourse,[11] the concept of private-public arbitration as a whole remains under-theorized, especially in respect of contractual disputes between public entities and private entities.[12] As a result, the question of whether private-public arbitration should be viewed through a private law or a public law lens has not been extensively examined under domestic law, and certainly not under English law.[13]

Thus, while a number of authors have recognized that international commercial arbitration does not fit neatly into the category of 'private' governance, this analysis has not extended to analysing the rise of private-public arbitration. For example, Whytock recognizes that both rule-making and enforcement in the international

[7] ibid 1–2.

[8] Jean-Bernard Auby, 'Comparative Approaches to the Rise of Contract in the Public Sphere' [2007] PL 40, 41.

[9] See Office of Government Commerce (OGC), 'Model Terms and Conditions of Contracts for Services' (2009) cl I2.

[10] For example, such clauses are found in standard forms of contract, including the FIDIC Red, Yellow, and Silver Books and the World Bank's Standard Bidding Document Procurement of Works.

[11] See eg Gus Van Harten, *Investment Treaty Arbitration and Public Law* (OUP 2007); Stephan W Schill (ed), *International Investment Law and Comparative Public Law* (OUP 2010). For an example of popular discourse on the topic see Claire Provost and Matt Kennard, 'The Obscure Legal System that Lets Corporations Sue Countries' *The Guardian* (London, 10 June 2015).

[12] Notably, Stephan Schill's *Lex Mercatoria Publica* project aims to address this deficit: see Stephan Schill, 'Transnational Private-Public Arbitration as Global Regulatory Governance: Charting and Codifying the Lex Mercatoria Publica' <www.mpil.de/en/pub/research/archive/erc-project.cfm> accessed 18 January 2025.

[13] There has been some debate on this topic in relation to other jurisdictions, see eg David Renders, Pierre Delvolvé, and Thierry Tanquerel (eds), *L'arbitrage en droit public* (Bruylant 2010); Mathias Audit (ed), *Contrats publics et arbitrage international* (Bruylant 2011).

commercial arbitration system depend to a large extent on interactions between public and private actors and thus conceptualizes the international commercial arbitration system as a hybrid private-public form of governance.[14] However, Whytock's analysis does not consider the role of public actors as participants in arbitrations, nor does it consider how arbitrations involving such actors that have public interest implications should be conceptualized.

Similarly, the question of whether investment treaty arbitration should be viewed through a public or private law lens has been extensively discussed, with some commentators characterizing international investment law as an aspect of the bilateral relationship between particular states and international investment treaties as 'private', quasi-contractual, agreements between individual states,[15] with others taking the view that international investment law constitutes a form of public law.[16] However, the emphasis of this discussion has been on the characterization of investment treaty arbitration as a matter of international law, and the question of its characterization from a national law perspective (and, in particular, an English law perspective) has not been focused upon.

Finally, a considerable body of literature has developed which describes the rise of the 'contracting state' and of '*government by contract*', particularly in the UK and other common law jurisdictions. This literature highlights the tensions that arise between this contractualization process and public law and argues that the public law framework needs to adapt to take account of this development.[17] However, in doing so, it does not consider the implications of the use of arbitration, as a private dispute resolution mechanism, in respect of disputes under such contracts, or the question of whether, due to the nature of such contracts, the arbitration process should be subject to public law values.

Therefore, while it has been recognized that contracts with public bodies are not purely creatures of private law and also that international commercial arbitration depends on interactions between public and private actors, the rise of private-public arbitration and its legal treatment, which essentially combines both of these elements, has remained largely uncharted. Similarly, the divide between public and private in international investment arbitration remains unexplored under national laws and English law in particular.

[14] Christopher A Whytock, 'Private-Public Interaction in Global Governance: The Case of Transnational Commercial Arbitration' (2010) 12 Business & Politics, Article 10. See also Alec Stone Sweet, 'The New Lex Mercatoria and Transnational Governance' (2006) 13 J Eur Public Policy 627, 627; Thomas Hale, 'The Rule of Law in the Global Economy: Explaining Intergovernmental Backing for Private Commercial Tribunals' (2015) 21 Eur J Intl Rel 483.

[15] Bernard Kishoiyian, 'The Utility of Bilateral Investment Treaties in the Formulation of Customary International Law' (1994) 14 Nw J Intl L & Bus 327, 373; Andrew T Guzman, 'Why LDCs Sign Treaties that Hurt Them: Explaining the Popularity of Bilateral Investment Treaties' (1997–1998) 38 Va J Intl L 640; Benedikt Pirker, *Proportionality Analysis and Models of Judicial Review* (Europa Law Pub 2013) ch 8.

[16] See eg Andreas F Lowenfeld, 'Investment Agreements and International Law' (2003) 42 Colum J Transnational L 123; Gus Van Harten and Martin Loughlin, 'Investment Treaty Arbitration as a Species of Global Administrative Law' (2006) 17 EJIL 121.

[17] See eg Gillian S Morris and Sandra Fredman, 'The Costs of Exclusivity: Public and Private Re-examined' [1994] PL 69; Mark R Freedland, 'Government by Contract and Public Law' [1994] PL 86; Peter Vincent-Jones, 'The Regulation of Contractualisation in Quasi-Markets for Public Services' [1999] PL 304; Davies (n 6).

III. Why Should Private-Public Arbitration Be Examined?

It is the public interest implications associated with both investment treaty arbitration and arbitration between public and private entities that make private-public arbitration important to examine. As the concept of public interest lies at the heart of private-public arbitration and informs the approach taken and proposals made in this chapter, it is necessary to take a closer look into its meaning. Defining what is meant by the public interest is notoriously difficult,[18] as the term carries a variety of meanings depending on the context in which is it used: for example, the term 'public interest' may have a different meaning in constitutional discourse than it has in discourse relating to economics, sociology, political theory, or regulation.[19] Further, the meaning of public interest can vary significantly depending on the methodological approach adopted.

As Held's seminal work demonstrated, there are three types of approaches to public interest: preponderance theories, common interest theories, and unitary conceptions.[20] Common interest theories are based on the hypothetical of the existence of interests common to all members of society, while preponderance theories look to a majority of interests. Thus, preponderance and common interest theories tend to conceptualize public interest on a majoritarian basis, that is, a consensus of a large portion of the electorate mainly identified quantitatively. On the other hand, the unitary conception takes a normative approach and places emphasis on what ought to be in the public interest on a social welfare basis.[21]

While a crude conception of democracy would favour a majoritarian approach to public interest, the present authors submit that, in a system displaying constitutional features, the public interest can, and should, be directed towards serving fundamental constitutional values, including values reflecting the interests of minority sectors of a society.[22] Therefore, taking a normative approach, we subscribe to an inclusive definition of public interest as a set of interests reflecting the minimal value structure underpinning society, as these values are shaped by constitutional and administrative law principles, and democratic institutions and traditions.[23] Such a normative approach allows us to identify a core meaning of public interest in considering disputes under private-public contracts and under investment treaties which involve both economic and social considerations. While economic considerations include considerations such as 'value for money' (which arise in relation to procurement contracts, for example), economic welfare, and the development of important infrastructure needed for the operation of an economy (eg airports, highways, power supplies),[24]

[18] For an overview see Stephen M King, Bradley S Chilton, and Gary E Roberts, 'Reflections on Defining the Public Interest' (2010) 41 Administration & Society 954.

[19] ibid 966.

[20] Virginia Held, *The Public Interest and Individual Interests* (Basic Books 1970).

[21] Mike Feintuck, *The Public Interest in Regulation* (OUP 2014) 11.

[22] Andreas Kulick, *Global Public Interest in International Investment Law* (CUP 2012) 151–52. See also Ian O'Flynn, 'Deliberating About the Public Interest' (2010) 16 Res Publica 299, 313.

[23] King, Chilton, and Roberts (n 18) 958.

[24] See Gerhart Niemeyer, 'Public Interest and Private Utility' in Carl J Friedrich (ed), *Nomos V: The Public Interest* (Atherton Press 1962).

the latter include considerations such as social welfare and governmental policies, including policies concerning health, education, and security.[25] In accordance with this analysis, private-public arbitration implicates the public interest because it typically concerns matters that affect the public's economic welfare, including the expenditure of public monies and the allocation of public resources, and because it can affect the exercise and implementation of governmental policies in sectors that are sensitive for the public, such as immigration and security, health, and public infrastructure.

This working definition of public interest allows us to identify two potential threats to the public interest which may arise from the exercise of public authority under private-public contracts. One possible threat is associated with the manner in which private entities exercise public power through private-public contracts. For example, public interest issues may arise as to whether the manner in which a private entity is performing its obligations under a private-public contract meets certain social requirements, particularly in relation to the provision of an essential public service.[26] On the other hand, public interest concerns may arise when a government abuses its authority and discriminates against an investor, expropriates an investor's property, or fails to adhere to due process in dealing with an investor.[27] Where a host state acts in this manner, the host state may be required to pay a substantial quantum of damages to the claimant investor under an international investment treaty, which is likely to have implications for the host state's ability to fund public services. Where (as is quite often the case)[28] the dispute relates to the provision of essential public services such as water, gas, or electricity supply or waste management services, the public interest implications of the dispute are heightened. For similar reasons, where public authorities make decisions that adversely affect the position of a private entity under a private-public contract, given the repercussions for taxpayers and for the implementation of important governmental policies, it is in the interest of the public that the public authority and its responsible officers are held accountable for these decisions.

To illustrate this, a recent example of a private-public arbitration concerned a dispute between the Secretary of State for the Home Department and the US defence company Raytheon Systems Limited, in respect of a 2007 contract for the design, development, and delivery of a multimillion pound technology system (e-Borders) which would reform UK border controls by establishing an electronic system to vet travellers leaving and entering the UK. When the Home Office terminated the contract in 2010 for significant delays in the progress of the works, the US defence company commenced arbitration proceedings, claiming substantial damages for unlawful termination. The arbitration proceedings under the rules of the London Court of International Arbitration were confidential. The arbitrators decided that the Home

[25] Feintuck (n 21) 23.

[26] An essential public service can be defined as one that is burdened with carrying out an activity necessary for the furtherance of a 'public interest' or for pursuing public policy objectives: see Antenor Hallo de Wolf, 'Human Rights and the Regulation of Privatised Essential Services' (2013) 60 NILR 165, 172.

[27] Andrea Bjorklund, 'The Public Interest(s) in Investment Arbitration' (Paper presented at the Workshop 'Empirical Perspectives on the Legitimacy of International Investment Tribunals', Oslo, August 2015).

[28] ICSID, 'The ICSID Case Load: Statistics (Issue 2014-2)' (2014) 12 <https://documents.worldbank.org/en/publication/documents-reports/documentdetail/646011468142790944/the-icsid-caseload-statistics-issue-2014-2> accessed 18 January 2025.

Office had unlawfully terminated the contract and awarded damages to the US defence company of the amount of approximately £190 million plus £38 million in respect of interest and the claimant's costs. The *e-Borders* award raised serious concerns in the British government and attracted intensive media and public interest, with the focus being on the impact of the award on the public finances and the security of the UK borders.[29] While the award was challenged by the Home Office and was subsequently set aside by the High Court for serious irregularity,[30] the High Court ultimately determined that the dispute should be referred back to arbitration before a different panel of arbitrators.[31] Following the issuance of the High Court judgment referring the dispute back to arbitration in February 2015, Keith Vaz, the chairman of the Commons Home Affairs Select Committee, observed that the e-Borders dispute had 'cost the British taxpayer millions of pounds. We still do not have an e-Borders programme, nor do we have information that can help us determine what went wrong with the Raytheon contract.'[32] Despite the Home Office's success in challenging the arbitral award, the Home Office continued to negotiate with Raytheon and, in March 2015, announced that, 'to protect the best interests of the taxpayer, including from further litigation costs', it had reached a negotiated resolution with Raytheon and was to pay £150 million to Raytheon in full and final settlement of the dispute.[33]

The *e-Borders* case exemplifies why, although private-public arbitrations arise out of contractual disputes, they may affect the allocation of public resources and the ability of public sector bodies to implement government policies. Similarly, while there have been virtually no instances of investors seeking relief against the UK pursuant to investment treaties,[34] investment treaty disputes involving other states have undoubtedly touched on delicate policy issues relating to the ability of the state to legislate in the public interest.[35] These disputes include the more than forty arbitrations concerning the lawfulness of Argentina's legislative response to its economic crisis and sovereign default of 2000 to 2002;[36] arbitrations involving water concessions;[37] an arbitration challenging an affirmative action programme that aimed at remedying the injustices of apartheid in South Africa;[38] arbitrations challenging the ban of

[29] See Ben Quinn, 'UK Taxpayer Faces £220m Bill Over E-Borders Contract Termination' *The Guardian* (London, 19 August 2014).

[30] *The Secretary of State for the Home Department v Raytheon Systems Limited* [2014] EWHC 4375 (TCC).

[31] *The Secretary of State for the Home Department v Raytheon Systems Limited* [2015] EWHC 311 (TCC).

[32] Quoted in Alan Travis, 'Award for Cancellation of E-Borders Contract is Set Aside by Court' *The Guardian* (London, 17 February 2015).

[33] Home Secretary Letter on e-Borders Settlement (27 March 2015) <www.gov.uk/government/news/home-secretary-letter-on-e-borders-settlement> accessed 18 January 2025.

[34] Alejandro Escobar and Kate Hill, 'Multilateral and Bilateral Investment Treaties and the United Kingdom' in Julian DM Lew and others (eds), *Arbitration in England, with Chapters on Scotland and Ireland* (Kluwer Law International 2013) 267, 288.

[35] William Burke-White and Andreas von Staden, 'The Need for Public Law Standards of Review in Investor-State Arbitrations' in Schill (n 11) 691–92.

[36] William W Burke-White, 'The Argentine Financial Crisis: State Liability under BITs and the Legitimacy of the ICSID System' in Michael Waibel and others (eds), *The Backlash against Investment Arbitration: Perceptions and Reality* (Kluwer 2010) 407.

[37] See eg *Biwater Gauff (Tanzania) Ltd v Tanzania*, ICSID Case No ARB/05/22; *Compañia de Aguas del Aconqija SA and Vivendi Universal SA v Argentina*, ICSID Case No ARB/97/3.

[38] *Foresti, de Carli and others v Republic of South Africa*, ICSID Case No ARB(AF)/07/1, Award (4 August 2010).

harmful substances;[39] and arbitrations challenging anti-tobacco legislation.[40] Thus, the public interest implications associated with private-public arbitration make it important to analyse how English law views private-public arbitration and, in particular, to examine how the public interest is accounted for, and protected, under English arbitration law.

IV. The Approach of English Arbitration Law to Private-Public Arbitration

While the use of arbitration to resolve disputes between a public body and a private party has become more common globally,[41] the English law of arbitration does not draw any meaningful distinction between purely private arbitrations and private-public arbitrations. The next subsections of this chapter will describe how the English legal system treats private-public arbitration, both on the domestic and the international level.

A. Domestic Private-Public Arbitration

Having developed around the private law paradigm of a commercial dispute involving private actors,[42] English arbitration law has adopted the principle of party autonomy as its cardinal principle. In accordance with this principle, the process of submitting a dispute to arbitration is conceptualized as a process whereby the parties choose to contract out of the system of public justice and submit their disputes to a private dispute resolution mechanism. Therefore, the Arbitration Act 1996 (the 1996 Act)[43] requires the English courts to adopt a non-interventionist approach in respect of the review of arbitration awards. This means that the role of the courts up to the point at which the arbitral award is made does not vary depending on whether or not the arbitration involves a public actor.

Further, English law does not differentiate between private-public arbitrations and private arbitrations in considering whether a particular dispute may be submitted to arbitration or whether public bodies can submit to arbitration. This lack of differentiation also extends to the conduct of the proceedings, including the appointment of arbitrators, the qualifications which arbitrators are required to have, the presentation of evidence, the grounds for intervention by third parties (including members of the

[39] See eg *Methanex Corporation v United States of America*, UNCITRAL, Final Award (3 August 2005).

[40] Tania S Voon and Andrew D Mitchell, 'Time to Quit? Assessing International Investment Claims Against Plain Tobacco Packaging in Australia' (2011) 14 JIEL 515.

[41] See Arnoldo Wald and Jean Kalicki, 'The Settlement of Disputes between the Public Administration and Private Companies by Arbitration under Brazilian Law' (2009) 26 J Intl Arb 557, 559.

[42] See generally Julian DM Lew and Melissa Holm, 'Development of the Arbitral System in England' in Lew and others (n 34) 1.

[43] Technically, the Arbitration Act 1996 is a UK statute (Scotland did not acquire a separate parliament until after the enactment and implementation of the Scotland Act 1998). However, while only ss 80–91 of the 1996 Act apply in Scotland, the Arbitration (Scotland) Act 2010 is quite similar to the 1996 Act (albeit with some differences in detail).

general public), and, significantly, whether the arbitration proceedings will be confidential and private.

Similarly, after the arbitration is concluded, the scope of review of arbitral awards by English courts does not depend on whether or not the arbitration involves a public entity or implicates the public interest. Once the arbitration tribunal has rendered its award, a party may generally only[44] challenge the award on the basis that the tribunal lacked substantive jurisdiction (under section 67 of the 1996 Act) or on the basis that there was a serious irregularity affecting the tribunal, proceedings, or award (under section 68 of the 1996 Act). An appeal on a question of law (under section 69 of the 1996 Act) is also permitted in certain limited circumstances. However, while, in retaining the right for a losing party to appeal an award on a question of law, the 1996 Act deviated from approach taken in those jurisdictions that adopted the UNCITRAL Model Law,[45] it remains difficult to successfully challenge an arbitral award under English law, as the grounds for review are narrowly construed and fall short of providing for a review of the award on the merits, including an error in law.[46] Thus, as noted by Akenhead J in a private-public arbitration involving Atkins Limited, a construction company appointed as managing agent and contractor in respect of the maintenance of the highways network in East Anglia, and the Secretary of State for Transport:

> 'Serious irregularity' within the meaning of Section 68 does not mean in itself an error of fact or law on the part of the arbitrator, perhaps on the basis that 'to err is human'. It is important that the parties do not consciously or sub-consciously dress up challenges to the factual findings or legal reasoning or conclusions of an arbitrator as 'serious irregularity'. Whilst such errors may well be present when there are other genuine serious irregularities subject to the Court's intervention under Section 68, that is or may be coincidental.[47]

Therefore, under section 68, the challenging party must demonstrate conduct amounting to a serious irregularity which falls within the exhaustive list of categories in section 68(2) and that one or more of the irregularities identified caused, or will cause, the party substantial injustice.

Similarly, because, unlike sections 67 and 68, section 69 of the 1996 Act is not mandatory in nature,[48] parties typically agree in advance that an arbitral award will be

[44] There is case law to the effect that the parties cannot agree to extend the scope of review of arbitral awards by English courts beyond the grounds specified in ss 67–69 of the 1996 Act: see *The Chrysalis* [1983] 1 Lloyd's Rep 503; *Guangzhou Dockyards Co Ltd v ENE Aegiali I* [2010] EWHC 2826 (Comm).

[45] Lord Steyn, 'England's Response to the UNCITRAL Model Law of Arbitration' (1994) 10 Arb Intl 1; Wendy Miles and Justin Li, 'Do England's Expansive Grounds for Recourse Increase Delay and Interference in Arbitration?' (2014) 80 Arbitration 35.

[46] See Kate Davies, 'In Defence of Section 69 of the English Arbitration Act' (*Kluwer Arbitration Blog*, 1 November 2010) <https://arbitrationblog.kluwerarbitration.com/2010/11/01/in-defence-of-section-69-of-the-english-arbitration-act/> accessed 18 January 2025 (observing that the case law under s 69 suggests that a s 69 appeal would only be successful if the error of law is clear on the face of the award).

[47] *Atkins Ltd v The Secretary of State for Transport* [2013] EWHC 139 (TCC) para 25.

[48] See s 4(1) and sch 1 of the 1996 Act.

final and binding and cannot be appealed.[49] Furthermore, even in those cases in which the possibility of an appeal under section 69 has not been excluded by the parties' prior agreement, the right to bring such an appeal is subject to stringent conditions. In particular, unless all other parties to the proceedings agree to such appeal, leave of the court must be sought to bring the appeal and leave will only be granted if certain circumstances specified in section 69(3) of the 1996 Act apply. For example, one of these circumstances is that, on the basis of the findings of fact in the award, the question is one of general public importance and the decision of the tribunal is at least open to serious doubt. However, it has been held that the fact that an appeal relates to a matter of public interest will not necessarily be sufficient, but rather the court will also consider whether the particular question is likely to arise on other occasions.[50] For these reasons, leave to appeal on a point of law is rarely granted by English courts and successful section 69 applications are rare.[51] Overall, therefore, the grounds for challenge of arbitral awards under English law are quite restrictive and do not differentiate as between private-public and private arbitrations.

To date, therefore, the rise of private-public arbitration has left undisturbed the private law paradigm which underlies English arbitration law. This means that arbitration and public law have been regarded as occupying separate legal spheres under English law and neither area of law has substantially influenced the design or practice of the other.

In adopting this approach, English law differs from the approach taken in a number of other jurisdictions such as France and Brazil, in which the potential for overlap between the law of arbitration and public law has been recognized.[52]

B. International Private-Public Arbitration

Turning to investment treaty arbitration, while, in England, international commercial arbitration is considered to form part of private international law (even where a public entity is involved),[53] investment treaty arbitration has been conceptualized as forming part of public international law. However, the English courts have also recognized features of investment treaty arbitration that deviate from the traditional terrain of public international law. While the dispute in *Republic of Ecuador v Occidental Exploration and Production Co* did not involve the UK government, and therefore

[49] See eg art 26.8 of the LCIA Arbitration Rules 2014; art 34.6 of the ICC Arbitration Rules 2012. cf Taner Dedezade, 'Are You In? Or Are You Out? An Analysis of Section 69 of the English Arbitration Act 1996 – Appeals on a Question of Law' (2006) 9 Intl Arb L Rev 56, 56.

[50] *Keydon Estates Ltd v Western Power Distribution (South Wales) Ltd* [2004] EWHC 996 (Ch), paras 21, 24; *Demco Investments & Commercial SA v SE Banken Forsakring Holding AB* [2005] EWHC 1398 (Comm) para 52.

[51] See Matt Marshall, 'Section 69 Almost 20 Years on . . .' (*Kluwer Arbitration Blog*, 24 June 2015) <https://arbitrationblog.kluwerarbitration.com/2015/06/24/section-69-almost-20-years-on/> accessed 18 January 2025.

[52] See Arnoldo Wald and Jean Kalicki, 'The Settlement of Disputes between the Public Administration and Private Companies by Arbitration under Brazilian Law' (2009) 26 J Intl Arb 557, 559–63.

[53] All of the major private international law textbooks and reference works include a chapter on commercial arbitration. See eg Paul Torremans and others (eds), *Cheshire, North and Fawcett: Private International Law* (14th edn, OUP 2008) ch 17.

did not implicate the public interest in the UK, it is a good example to illustrate how the English courts view investment treaty arbitration. Specifically, in *Occidental* a Californian corporation brought an arbitration claim against the Government of Ecuador before an UNCITRAL arbitral tribunal under the bilateral investment treaty (BIT) between Ecuador and the US.[54] The place of arbitration was London and Ecuador applied to the English courts seeking to set the award aside under sections 67 and 68 of the 1996 Act. This was the first time that an arbitration award rendered pursuant to a BIT had been brought before the English courts. Occidental challenged the jurisdiction of English courts to review the award under section 67 on the basis of the doctrine of non-justiciability. Thus, Occidental argued that an English court should not embark upon an examination of a treaty between two other countries, as the matters submitted to arbitration could involve a decision upon the scope of rights enforceable not just by Occidental but necessarily also by the United States, and could have international implications.[55]

However, both the High Court and the Court of Appeal rejected Occidental's arguments. The Court of Appeal acknowledged that, while investment arbitration disputes are predominantly creatures of public international law, BITs deviate from traditional public international law treaties by giving investors a direct standing to pursue the state of the investment in respect of any investment dispute, without their home state's involvement or even consent.[56] Equally, the Court of Appeal relied on the fact that the BIT provided for direct rights in favour of investors to reject Occidental's argument.[57]

Therefore, while ICSID awards are, under the Washington Convention, not reviewable by English courts (or by any national court), non-ICSID investment treaty awards are, under sections 67 to 69 of the 1996 Act, subject to the same grounds of review as commercial arbitration awards.[58] This approach has, in practice, narrowed the gap between international commercial arbitration and investment treaty arbitration in relation to the role of the English courts in reviewing such awards. Similarly, while enforcement of an ICSID award can only be refused by domestic courts on grounds of state immunity,[59] the grounds for refusing recognition and enforcement of foreign awards which fall under the scope of the New York Convention on the Recognition and Enforcement of Foreign Arbitral Awards 1958 (the New York Convention) apply equally to commercial awards and non-ICSID investment treaty awards.

This lack of differentiation between commercial and investment treaty awards under English law can be contrasted with the discourse in the international law literature, which emphasizes the public law character of international investment disputes. Thus, some international law scholars have emphasized the constitutional

[54] [2005] EWCA Civ 1116; [2007] 2 CLC 16.

[55] There was English precedent in support of Occidental's submissions: see *JH Raymer (Mincing Lane) Ltd v Department of Trade and Industry* [1990] 2 AC 418 and the wider principle of 'judicial restraint or abstention' stated by Lord Wilberforce in *Buttes Gas and Oil Co v Hammer* (No 3) [1982] AC 888.

[56] [2005] EWCA Civ 1116, para 7.

[57] ibid paras 37–41.

[58] See also *Czech Republic v European Media Ventures SA* [2008] 1 Lloyd's Rep 186.

[59] Under the Arbitration (International Investment Disputes) Act 1966, an ICSID award may be registered in the High Court, and it has the same effect as a judgment of the court. See also *AIG Capital Partners, Inc and ors v Republic of Kazakhstan* [2005] EWHC 2239 (Comm).

character of the system of international investment law and arbitration.[60] Similarly, drawing on Kingsbury's seminal work on global administrative law,[61] Kingsbury and Schill emphasize that investment tribunals are part of a global governance structure, by shaping standards of administrative conduct and helping to crystallize general principles of global administrative law.[62] Thus, to enable states to recapture political control of international investment law, these scholars have called for international investment law and arbitration to be subject to a regime that is distinct from that applicable to international commercial arbitration through, for example, the introduction of principles of public law adjudication, such as consistency, transparency, and accountability.[63] This movement has gained momentum in recent years and, although the investment treaty arbitration adjudication model fundamentally remains rooted in the international commercial arbitration model, steps have been taken towards addressing, in particular, the lack of transparency surrounding the investment treaty arbitration process and the lack of public participation. For example, UNCITRAL has issued a set of transparency rules which require disclosure of information submitted to, and issued by, arbitral tribunals throughout proceedings, as well as mandating open hearings, and expressly allowing for participation by non-parties to a dispute.[64]

However, despite this discourse on an international level, private-public arbitration, including international investment arbitration, has not been captured by a public law discourse in England, nor has English arbitration practice evolved in any way to take account of its specific nature. In the next section, we consider the underlying reasons for this.

V. Reasons Underlying the English Approach to Private-Public Arbitration

There are two reasons that can explain the lack of a distinct legal and conceptual framework for private-public arbitration in England. The first is the lack of a developed

[60] David Schneiderman, *Constitutionalizing Economic Globalization: Investment Rules and Democracy's Promise* (CUP 2008). See also Alec Stone Sweet, 'Judicialization and the Construction of Governance' (1991) 31 Comp Political Stud 147.

[61] Benedict Kingsbury, Nico Krisch, and Richard B Stewart, 'The Emergence of Global Administrative Law' (2005) 68 Law & Contemp Probs 15.

[62] Benedict Kingsbury and Stephan W Schill, 'Investor-State Arbitration as Governance: Fair and Equitable Treatment, Proportionality and the Emerging Global Administrative Law' in Albert Jan van den Berg (ed), *50 Years of the New York Convention: ICCA International Arbitration Conference* (Kluwer 2009) 5. See also Gus Van Harten and Martin Loughlin, 'Investment Treaty Arbitration as a Species of Global Administrative Law' (2006) 17 EJIL 121.

[63] Alec Stone Sweet and Florian Grisel, 'Transnational Investment Arbitration: From Delegation to Constitutionalization?' in Pierre-Marie Dupuy, Ernst-Ulrich Petersmann, and Francesco Francioni (eds), *Human Rights in International Investment Law and Arbitration* (OUP 2009) 118; Ernst-Ulrich Petersmann, 'Constitutional Theories of International Economic Adjudication and Investor-State Arbitration' (ibid 137); Cornel Marian, 'Balancing Transparency: The Value of Administrative Law and Mathews–Balancing to Investment Treaty Arbitrations' (2010) 10 Pepperdine Dispute Resolution LJ 275.

[64] UNCITRAL, 'Rules on Transparency in Treaty-based Investor-State Arbitration' (effective date 1 April 2014) <https://uncitral.un.org/sites/uncitral.un.org/files/media-documents/uncitral/en/rules-on-transparency-e.pdf> accessed 18 January 2025.

administrative law sphere,[65] and of a separate body of administrative courts tasked with safeguarding the public interest which would claim interest in the regulation of private-public arbitrations. In England, disputes involving public bodies with public interest implications have traditionally been submitted to the same ordinary courts as disputes between two private entities, and largely made subject to the same procedures.[66] The absence of a distinct body of administrative law rules in England can be contrasted with the emergence of administrative power and the strict separation between administration and justice in Continental Europe. In this regard, it is generally accepted that the French Revolution of 1789 was the catalyst for the emergence of *administration publique*.[67] While previously the space between the state and the citizen was occupied by monarchy and a corporate society (the *Ancien Régime*),[68] after the French Revolution this space came to be occupied by the state, which developed its own institutional capacities, in order to pursue the interests of the public. This was the point that marked the birth of administration in a Continental European sense and the separation between justice and administration. Therefore, under the law of 16/24 August 1790, the ordinary courts in France were prohibited from reviewing administrative acts. With the development of this separate system of administrative courts (with the Conseil d'État at its apex)[69] came the development of a distinct body of administrative law, whereby the activities of the state were subjected to legal principles and norms.[70] The French model of administration and administrative law then effectively emerged as the prevailing system of administration in the European continent.[71]

Like France, Germany also has a long tradition of administrative law, albeit that the emergence of administrative law in the Germanic tradition was the result of evolution rather than revolution.[72] Thus, during the nineteenth century, German liberals strove to establish legal structures which would limit the unfettered exercise of state power by the monarchs of the various German states.[73] The idea of *Rechtsstaat* was therefore constructed in order to reconcile the freedom of action of the state with the rights of the citizen, and it gave birth to administrative law having the task of setting

[65] While there are different definitions of administrative law, the form of administrative law focused on here is the law relating to the control of government power, the main object of which is to protect individual rights: see Paul P Craig, *Administrative Law* (4th edn, Sweet & Maxwell 1999) 3.

[66] Notably, however, in judicial review actions, different procedural rules apply: see Civil Procedure Rules, Part 54.

[67] Bernando Sordi, 'Révolution, Rechtsstaat and the Rule of Law: Historical Reflections on the Emergence of Administrative Law in Europe' in Ackerman and Lindseth (eds) (n 5) 25. cf Albert Venn Dicey, 'Droit Administratif in Modern French Law' (1901) 17 LQR 302, 307.

[68] C Sumner Lobingier, 'Administrative Law and Droit Administratif: A Comparative Study with an Instructive Model' (1942) U Penn L Rev 36, 37–39 (on the position in France prior to the Revolution).

[69] On the particular role of the Conseil d'État see ibid 39–45. The Conseil d'État has the dual functions of advising government and arbitrating disputes about executive power.

[70] Leon Duguit, 'The French Administrative Courts' (1914) 29(3) Polit Sci Q 385, 407.

[71] Sordi (n 67) 28.

[72] ibid. However, German administrative legal development still drew heavily on French experience: see Hellmut Wollmann, 'Comparing Institutional Development in Britain and Germany' in Hellmutt Wollmann and Eckhard Schröter (eds), *Comparing Public Sector Reform in Britain and Germany* (Ashgate 2000) 7.

[73] Georg Nolte, 'General Principles of German and European Administrative Law – A Comparison in Historical Perspective' (1994) 57 MLR 191, 198.

legal boundaries to central administration.[74] This development was 'perfected' by the creation of a separate system of administrative law courts.[75]

Thus, in France and Germany (and in much of Continental Europe), review of administrative action, for various reasons, came to be placed within the purview of administrative courts, and this institutional structure eventually gave rise to a self-conscious divide between public and private law. The emergence of public administration and of an independent body of administrative law in Continental Europe also resulted in a new manner of conceptualizing the public interest. In particular, in France, service of the public interest or *service d'intérêt général* is regarded as the foundational principle of administrative law and the litmus test for defining the ultimate purpose of the public administration, and for delimiting its permissible scope of action.[76] This means that, in France, administrative action and entities in charge of a *service public* are generally governed by specific provisions which are different from private law, regardless of whether the body which provides the service is a public or private body.[77] This focus on the public interest as the core principle of administrative law has also prevailed in those administrative law systems influenced by French law, such as Belgium, Greece, Luxembourg, Italy, Portugal, Spain, and Turkey,[78] and, within such systems, the task of safeguarding the public interest has also been entrusted to the administrative courts.[79]

The development of the English administrative law model diverged from the Continental model. In particular, it was only during the course of the twentieth century, and because of the growth of a more centralized government, that a distinct discipline of civil service and administrative law started to emerge.[80] Until well into the nineteenth century, the English administrative apparatus had developed on a case-by-case basis focusing on certain aspects of public life, such as regulation of work, railways, health, public education, and poor relief.[81] While the emergence of a more centralized form of government in England resulted in the creation of independent tribunals to hear appeals from decisions of certain administrative bodies and governmental departments, the adjudication of a large number of disputes involving public bodies still remained within the purview of the ordinary courts. In addition, while admittedly the advent of tribunals led to the review of certain administrative conduct being excluded from the jurisdiction of the ordinary courts,[82] the function of such

[74] Ricardo Gosalbo-Bono, 'The Significance of the Rule of Law and its Implications for the European Union and the United States' (2010) 72 U Pittsburgh L Rev 229, 241.

[75] Kenneth F Ledford, 'Formalising the Rule of Law in Prussia: The Supreme Administrative Law Court 1876–1914' (2004) 37 Central European History 203, 204.

[76] Guillaume Merland, 'L'intérêt général, instrument efficace de protection des droits fondamentaux?' (2004) 16 Les Cahiers du Conseil constitutionnel 155, 155.

[77] Bernard Schwartz, *French Administrative Law and the Common-Law World* (New York UP 1954) 68.

[78] John Bell, 'Mechanisms for Cross-Fertilisation of Administrative Law in Europe' in Jack Beatson and Takis Tridimas (eds), *New Directions in European Public Law* (Hart 1998) 149; Esin Örücü, 'Conseil D'Etat: The French Layer of Turkish Administrative Law' (2000) 49 ICLQ 679.

[79] ibid.

[80] Albert Venn Dicey, 'The Development of Administrative Law in England' (1915) 31 LQR 148, 149.

[81] Sordi (n 67) 31.

[82] Peter L Lindseth, 'Reconciling with the Past: John Willis and the Question of Judicial Review in Inter-War and Post-War England' (2005) 55 U Toronto L J 657, 665.

tribunals has been confirmed to be essentially judicial (as opposed to administrative) in nature.[83]

This absence of a distinct system of adjudicative bodies claiming interest in disputes involving public authorities has meant that public law has traditionally not been conceived of as an autonomous branch of English law.[84] This conflation between public and private law spheres has, for example, resulted in the application of the same principles of contractual and tortious liability to both public bodies and private bodies, whereas, in French law, specific procedural rules and principles of liability have developed to take account of the public setting of disputes.[85]

The distinct approach taken under English law to the private-public law divide has also been significantly influenced by the lack of a written British constitution.[86] Thus, due to the unwritten[87] and evolutionary (rather than revolutionary) nature of the British constitution, rather than setting out governing principles in a clear manner, British constitutional law instead 'offers an account of how the country has come to be governed; and, importantly, in doing so it confers legitimacy on the arrangements it describes'.[88] This loose, largely convention-based, system of constitutional law, which has influenced, in different ways, the constitutions of all Commonwealth jurisdictions,[89] has undoubtedly made it difficult for English administrative law to develop in a coherent manner.[90] In addition, the primacy of the rule of law within the British constitutional system has served to shape the views of those (such as Albert Venn Dicey) who have argued that English law does not require a distinction to be drawn between private and public law. Indeed, the influence of Dicey's views is such that his views can be considered to constitute a separate factor contributing to the view that a private-public law distinction does not form part of English law.[91] Dicey was suspicious of the very concept of administrative or public law and argued that English law, in general, subjects citizens and officials to the same rules of ordinary common law as developed by the ordinary courts. Dicey argued that the rule of law, which he regarded as a private law concept from which the UK's unwritten constitution was derived,[92] was sufficient to keep in check administrative power and governmental discretion. In Dicey's view, therefore, the idea of a separate body of administrative law

[83] *Report of the Committee on Administrative Tribunals and Enquiries* (Cmnd 218, 1957) para 40; Report of the Review of Tribunals by Sir Andrew Leggatt, *Tribunals for Users: One System, One Service* (TSO 2001). See also Janina Boughey, 'Administrative Law: The Next Frontier for Comparative Law' (2013) 67 ICLQ 55, 67.

[84] Carol Harlow, '"Public" and "Private" Law: Definition Without Distinction' (1980) 43 MLR 241.

[85] AW Bradley, KW Ewing, and CJS Knight, *Constitutional & Administrative Law* (16th edn, Pearson 2014) 573.

[86] See generally Eric Barendt, 'Is There a United Kingdom Constitution?' (1997) 17 OJLS 137.

[87] The UK constitution can be said to be comprised of a variety of written and unwritten sources, including statutes, case law, and established patterns of political behaviour ('constitutional conventions').

[88] Stephen Sedley, 'The Sound of Silence: Constitutional Law without a Constitution' (1994) 110 LQR 270, 270.

[89] See Stephen Gardbaum, 'The New Commonwealth Model of Constitutionalism' (2001) 49 Am J Comp L 707.

[90] Mark R Freedland, 'Government by Contract and Public Law' [1994] PL 86, 95.

[91] Harlow (n 84); Jack Beatson, '"Public" and "Private" in English Administrative Law' (1987) 103 LQR 34.

[92] Albert Venn Dicey, *Introduction to the Study of the Law of the Constitution* (8th edn, Macmillan 1915) 107–22 and 202–3.

(such as the French *droit administratif*) rested on ideas which are 'absolutely foreign to English law'.[93]

Admittedly, the distinction between public and private law (and the concept of administrative law in particular) has become increasingly significant in English law in recent times, a development which can largely be attributed to the rapid development since the 1960s of judicial review of administrative action.[94] Fundamentally, however, the common law principle of the rule of law and the requirements of natural justice,[95] safeguarded by the ordinary courts, have remained the main legal construction under English law for dealing with disputes involving public bodies and the public interest more generally, and the idea of an autonomous body of public law rules extraneous to the common law remains a 'cuckoo in the nest'.[96]

The second, related, reason to which the underdeveloped conception of private-public arbitration in England can be attributed is that arbitration in England has traditionally been embedded in private law and developed as an exclusively private mode of dispute resolution. Thus, English merchants and guilds have been using arbitration since as early as the Middle Ages, mainly because the royal courts were deemed ill-suited to deal with trade disputes due to their lack of familiarity with trade rules and customs.[97] Arbitration in England was therefore conceived, designed, and developed over the course of more than four centuries to accommodate contractual disputes between private parties, typically disputes arising out of maritime and sales of goods transactions or construction projects.[98] By the time public entities started to enter into contracts including arbitration clauses in the late twentieth century, the private character of the arbitration law and process was well crystallized. Accordingly, the resolution of disputes involving public law and public entities was effectively shoehorned into a dispute resolution framework which had been operating as an entirely private mode of dispute resolution for a very long time.

Thus, having considered the reasons underlying the lack of differentiation between private arbitration and private-public arbitration under English law, it is necessary to consider the question of whether English arbitration law can, nonetheless, adequately account for the public interest in private-public arbitrations.

VI. Does English Arbitration Law Adequately Account for the Public Interest in Private-Public Arbitrations?

In considering the question of whether English arbitration law adequately accounts for the public interest, investment treaty arbitration needs to be considered separately to other private-public arbitrations under English law, due to the differences in the

[93] Albert Venn Dicey, 'Droit Administratif' (n 67) 304.
[94] Beatson (n 91) 34–40.
[95] Natural justice is a term of art that denotes specific procedural rights in the English system. Natural justice includes two fundamental principles: the rule against bias and the right to a fair hearing.
[96] See *Davy v Spelthorne BC* [1984] AC 262, 276. See also Harlow (n 84) 241.
[97] Lew and Holm (n 42) para 1.01.
[98] ibid. See also Gary B Born, *International Commercial Arbitration* (2nd edn, Kluwer Law International 2014) 34–38.

way in which the state entity agrees to submit to arbitration, in the applicable law, and in the source of authority of the arbitral tribunal. We address these two cases in turn.

A. International Investment Arbitration

The answer to the question of whether English arbitration law adequately accounts for the public interest in international investment arbitrations is somewhat complex. This is the case since, as mentioned above, in relation to ICSID awards at least, there is less opportunity for review of arbitral awards by courts than exists in domestic legal systems. While, in relation to non-ICSID investment treaty awards, as is the case with domestic arbitration awards, an English court may refuse to recognize or enforce an international arbitral award where it would be contrary to English public policy to do so,[99] as is discussed below in the context of domestic arbitration awards, the public policy ground has generally been narrowly construed. In addition, in relation to foreign awards, the scope of the public policy ground can be considered to be further restricted by the pro-enforcement bias displayed by the English courts.[100] This tendency to favour enforcement is also evident in respect of the other grounds for refusing recognition and enforcement and, therefore, the English courts have only rarely refused enforcement of a New York Convention award, whether of a private-private or private-public nature.[101]

The circumscribed nature of the review undertaken of investment treaty arbitration awards by English courts can be seen as problematic (or at least unusual) when viewed from a traditional public international law perspective, which would hold that governmental conduct may not be reviewed other than by the state itself or by state courts. However, this belies the reality of the large number of international courts and tribunals that have been established over the last twenty-five years or so, which play an important role in making international law effective and, importantly, to which states have delegated authority, for example, in the context of investment treaty arbitration, by entering into bilateral or multilateral investment treaties. These international adjudicative bodies have far-reaching powers, including the power to review the validity of administrative decisions and assess state compliance with international law. In addition, these international courts and tribunals are not used only by states, but, crucially, also by a wide range of non-state actors, including international commissions, institutional actors, and private litigants. As a measure of the strength of this phenomenon, these international courts and tribunals have collectively issued over 37,000 binding decisions, more than 90 per cent of which were issued in the last

[99] Although English courts will usually have regard to the public policy provisions in both the New York Convention and the 1996 Act (s 103(3)), the rules which English courts will primarily consider and apply are common law rules on public policy.

[100] See eg *Dardana v Yukos* [2002] 2 Lloyd's Rep 326, per Mance LJ noting that an award creditor seeking to enforce a New York Convention award in England under s 101 'has a prima facie right to recognition and enforcement'.

[101] See Craig Tevendale and Andrew Cannon, 'Enforcement of Awards' in Lew and others (n 34) 563. See also *Irvani v Irvani* [2000] CLC 477; *Kanoria v Guinness* [2006] EWCA Civ 222; *Dallah v Pakistan* [2010] UKSC 46.

twenty-five years, and only a few of which concern traditional inter-state disputes.[102] This can be viewed as part of a more general movement towards a less state-driven form of international law and a greater role for private market forces in shaping its contours.

As mentioned above, a number of international law scholars have argued that the body of law generated by such bodies should be viewed as global administrative law. This perspective would require that all global actors, including states, be subject to fundamental administrative law standards, such as transparency, participation, and accountability,[103] with the task of conducting such administrative review entrusted to a number of international courts and tribunals, including investment treaty arbitration tribunals.

Thus, while the increase in the number and adjudicative scope of these new international courts and tribunals seems to conflict with traditional conceptions of national sovereignty, and with the principle of democratic legitimization, it may also reflect the realization that in today's strongly interdependent world, national isolation is not a viable political choice.[104] In such context, the crucial issue is not whether international tribunals should review governmental conduct per se, but rather the permissible scope and standard of that review and the safeguards that are required to ensure that the public interest is protected. This is an issue that all state parties to investment treaties, including the UK, must confront over the coming years.[105]

B. Arbitration Between Public Entities and Private Entities Under English law

Turning from the case of international investment arbitration to arbitration between public entities and private entities under English law, the picture becomes clearer. Here, we submit that the private law paradigm upon which English arbitration law is based leaves the public interest both unaccounted for, and unprotected, in private-public arbitrations. Specifically, the primacy afforded to the principle of party autonomy will typically prevent the English courts from intervening in private-public arbitrations, even when issues of public interest may arise in such arbitrations. For example, while, unlike under the arbitration legislation of most jurisdictions, including jurisdictions which have adopted the UNCITRAL Model Law, an application may be brought by a party to the courts under section 45 of the 1996 Act for the determination of 'any question of law arising in the course of proceedings', and while such applications may bring points of law of general interest before the courts,[106] such points

[102] Karen J Alter, *The New Terrain of International Law* (Princeton 2014) 68.

[103] Kingsbury, Krisch, and Stewart (n 61).

[104] Alter (n 102) 339.

[105] See as an example of engagement with the topic of investor-state dispute settlement in the UK, House of Lords, European Union Committee, 14th Report of Session 2013–14, 'The Transatlantic Trade and Investment Partnership' (TSO 2014) paras 156–70 <www.publications.parliament.uk/pa/ld201314/ldselect/ldeucom/179/17902.htm> accessed 18 January 2025.

[106] Departmental Advisory Committee on Arbitration Law, '1996 Report on the Arbitration Bill' (Chairman The Rt Hon Lord Justice Saville) (1996) 13 Arb Intl 275, para 218.

may only be brought before the court at a party's initiative and the parties may agree in advance not to bring such applications.[107] Absent an application from one or both of the parties, therefore, the English courts do not have the power to intervene in arbitration proceedings, even where a matter of public interest is implicated.

Similarly, while the possibility for court review of the arbitral process under sections 67 to 69 of 1996 Act is intended to act as a public policy safeguard to some extent, the threshold for court intervention is set at a high level.[108] Furthermore, the 1996 Act does not reference in any guise the concept of public interest as a possible ground for challenging an award and, even in cases such as the *e-Borders* case with public interest implications, the jurisprudence typically does not allude to the public interest but rather confines itself to the specific (and rather narrow) grounds for challenge enumerated under sections 67 to 69, while emphasizing the deference that should be afforded to the principle of party autonomy.[109]

In addition, while certain elements of the law of arbitration are not encompassed within the parameters of the 1996 Act and are subject to common law principles,[110] jurisprudence in those areas has, thus far, failed to develop a coherent account of how the public interest may interact with the arbitral process. For example, the question of whether or not a particular dispute is arbitrable is left to the courts to determine and, under English law, there are few prescriptive rules as to the scope and application of the concept of arbitrability.[111] Thus, the English courts have approached this issue on a case-by-case basis, considering whether: 'the matters in dispute . . . engage third party rights or represent an attempt to delegate to the arbitrators what is a matter of public interest which cannot be determined within the limitations of a private contractual process'.[112] However, Longmore LJ's judgment in the *Fulham Football Club* case confirmed that what is considered a matter of public interest in this context will be narrow in scope: '[t]o the extent therefore that public policy has a part to play it can only be a "safeguard . . . necessary in the public interest". This is a demanding test'.[113] Therefore, the test for arbitrability is narrowly construed and there are no separate principles governing the range of subject matters which are arbitrable in arbitrations with a public actor.

Similarly, the common law recognizes that the parties' desire for confidentiality and privacy generally outweighs the public interest in a public hearing.[114] This general

[107] See also s 24 of the 1996 Act.

[108] See *Zermalt Holdings SA v Nu-Life Upholstery Repairs Limited* [1985] 2 EGLR 14. See also *Petroships Pte Ltd of Singapore v Petec Trading and Investment Corporation of Vietnam and Others (the Petro Ranger)* (2001) 2 Lloyd's Rep 348.

[109] See eg *The Secretary of State for the Home Department v Raytheon Systems Limited* [2014] EWHC 4375 (TCC).

[110] See s 81 of the 1996 Act.

[111] See generally Julian DM Lew and Oliver Marsden, 'Arbitrability' in Lew and others (n 34) 399.

[112] *Fulham Football Club (1987) Ltd v Richards* [2011] EWCA Civ 855, para 40.

[113] ibid paras 98–99.

[114] *Department of Economic Policy and Development of the City of Moscow v Bankers Trust Co* [2004] EWCA Civ 314. See also Civil Procedure Rule 62.10(3)(b), which provides that, subject to the power of the court to order that an arbitration claim may be heard in public or in private, all arbitration claims will be heard in private (except the determination of a preliminary point of law under s 45 of the 1996 Act or an appeal under s 69 of the 1996 Act on a question of law arising out of an award).

principle of confidentiality is qualified by a number of exceptions,[115] including where disclosure is required in the interests of justice and (perhaps) where disclosure is required in the public interest.[116] However, while these exceptions could potentially be of particular relevance in the context of private-public arbitration, the public interest-based exception is not well-established under English law[117] and there is no consensus as to whether the interest-of-justice exception constitutes an exception in itself, or whether it is part of a wider public interest exception.[118] Furthermore, in delineating the scope of such exceptions, the English courts have not distinguished between private-public arbitrations and purely private arbitrations. This means that, even in respect of private-public disputes such as the *e-Borders* case with clear public interest implications, confidentiality remains the default rule.[119]

Finally, it is often argued that any public interest concerns with regard to arbitral awards can be addressed at the conclusion of the arbitral process when English courts may refuse to recognize or enforce a domestic or international arbitral award where it would be contrary to English public policy to do so.[120] However, the public policy ground under English arbitration law has considerable limitations.[121] Specifically, while the general concept of public policy can be considered closely connected to that of the public interest,[122] the legal concept of public policy in English law has been developed by the courts as a set of narrow and clearly defined legal rules applicable in certain areas of law, such as the *ex turpi causa non oritur actio* rule[123] and the doctrine of restraint of trade.[124] Similarly, in arbitration, the public policy rule has been afforded a narrow scope.[125] For example, the Court of Appeal has stated that, in order for enforcement of an award to be contrary to public policy, there would have to be some element of illegality or the underlying contract or activity would have to violate principles of public policy which are 'of the greatest importance'.[126] Finally, while the public policy ground has, to date, largely been considered in the context of purely private disputes, there is no indication that the English courts would expand its scope where private-public arbitrations are concerned, despite the public interest implications associated with such arbitrations.

[115] See generally Hew R Dundas, 'Confidentiality in English Arbitration: The Final Word? *Emmott v Michael Wilson & Partners Ltd*' (2008) 74 Arbitration 458.

[116] See *John Forster Emmott v Michael Wilson & Partners Ltd* [2008] EWCA Civ 184, para 107.

[117] Andrew Tweeddale, 'Confidentiality in Arbitration and the Public Interest Exception' (2005) 21 Arb Intl 61.

[118] ibid.

[119] See Departmental Advisory Committee on Arbitration Law (n 106) paras 13–16.

[120] In respect of domestic awards, this ground for refusing recognition or enforcement is not included in the 1996 Act, but has been recognized by case law: see *Soleimany v Soleimany* [1998] EWCA Civ 285 and s 81(1)(c) of the 1996 Act. In respect of international awards, see ss 100 to 104 of the 1996 Act.

[121] See generally Tevendale and Cannon (n 101).

[122] *Richardson v Mellish* (1824) 2 Bing 229, 252.

[123] See Lord Mansfield's well-known dictum in *Holman v Johnson* (1775) 1 Cowp 341, 343: 'The principle of public policy is this; *ex dolo malo non oritur actio*. No court will lend its aid to a man who founds his cause of action upon an immoral or an illegal act.'

[124] See John Bell, *Policy Arguments in Judicial Decisions* (OUP 1983) 157 ff.

[125] See generally Audley Sheppard and Stavros Brekoulakis, *Public Policy in English Arbitration Law* (OUP 2016).

[126] *Westacre Investments Inc v Jugoimport-SDPR Holding Co Ltd* [1999] EWCA Civ 1401. See also *Soleimany v Soleimany* [1998] EWCA Civ 285.

Therefore, there is little indication that the public interest concerns that arise in the context of private-public arbitration are capable of being addressed under English law, including the law of arbitration. This exclusively private law approach, endorsed by the legislature and judiciary, is reinforced by the manner in which arbitrators perceive their role. Thus, while the function and training of national judges is directed at serving the interests of the public, and while judges are, particularly in public law cases, required to have regard to the broader societal implications of their judgments,[127] arbitrators (who are typically private lawyers) perceive their role and function as more akin to a service provider whose mandate comes from a private contract, and who is responsible for resolving the dispute between the parties.[128]

These factors have all contributed to a conceptual and legal disconnect as between the private law sphere of arbitration and the public law sphere of administrative law. This disconnect exists despite the close connection that has been established in other contexts between matters of public interest and the scope of public law. For example, in *Re McBride's Application*, Kerr J stated as follows:

> an issue is one of public law where it involves a matter of public interest in the sense that it has an impact on the public generally and not merely on an individual or group. That is not to say that an issue becomes one of public law simply because it generates interest or concern in the minds of the public. It must affect the public rather than merely engage its interest to qualify as a public law issue.[129]

Notwithstanding this recognition of the connection between the public interest and public law, however, the conceptual schism between arbitration and public law remains. This precludes (or at least severely restricts) the possibility of arbitration law being informed by rules of domestic administrative law which are directed at protecting the public interest.

This disconnect is best illustrated by contrasting the typically narrow scope of review of arbitral awards by English courts with the approach taken by the English courts in respect of the judicial review of administrative action. Thus, while initially the scope of judicial review was restricted to issues of jurisdiction and only errors of law which were deemed to be 'jurisdictional' in nature were reviewed by the courts,[130] since the House of Lords' decision in *Anisminic Ltd v Foreign Compensation Commission*[131] the scope of judicial review has been significantly broadened so that virtually all errors of law, including jurisdictional and non-jurisdictional ones, are reviewable.[132] Crucially, the concept of error of law is broader than a mistake in the interpretation of a statute as, typically, the English courts tend to characterize all inferences from primary facts

[127] See Abram Chayes, 'The Role of the Judge in Public Law Litigation' (1975–1976) 89 Harv L Rev 1281.

[128] See Paula Hodges and Joanne Greenaway, 'Duties of Arbitrators' in Lew and others (n 34) 293, paras 15.49–15.52.

[129] [1999] NI 299, 310. See also *Re Kirkpatrick's Application* [2003] NIQB 49; *YL v Birmingham City Council* [2007] UKHL 27, [2008] 1 AC 95, Baroness Hale dissenting, paras 65–67.

[130] Paul Craig, 'Judicial Review of Questions of Law: A Comparative Perspective' in Ackerman and Lindseth (eds) (n 5) 449 ff.

[131] [1969] 2 AC 147.

[132] *Re Racal Communications Ltd* [1981] AC 374, 383; *R v Lord President of the Privy Council, ex p Page* [1993] 2 AC 682. See also B Gould, 'Anisminic and Judicial Review' [1970] PL 358, 365.

as questions of law.[133] Thus, a public body will commit an error of law if it acts where there is no evidence to support the action or where it comes to a conclusion to which it could not reasonably have come on the evidence.[134] Similarly, while public bodies are accorded discretionary powers when choosing between several decisions or courses of action, each of which may be lawful, courts will supervise a decision in terms of whether the public body has, intentionally or inadvertently, unlawfully exercised its discretion, albeit the court will not substitute its own decision for the decision made by the public body.[135] Finally, and significantly, the introduction of the Human Rights Act 1998 has had broad implications for administrative law, including the introduction of new rules of statutory interpretation, and the requirement that public authorities act consistently with Convention rights, which has to some extent expanded the scope of judicial review, not least through the introduction of proportionality as the test of substantive view where Convention rights are at issue.[136] Thus, while the low-intensity irrationality review,[137] which applies under the well-established *Wednesbury* test,[138] ensures that courts do not interfere lightly with the substance of administrative decisions, judicial review is nonetheless notably broader than the review of arbitral awards by English courts.

While, in respect of arbitrations involving private parties, the existing arbitral framework is unproblematic, the resolution of private-public disputes involving public projects and governmental policies within a private law framework wholly removed from the ambit of public law seems incompatible with fundamental public law values, such as rationality, openness, and accountability.[139] Therefore, the existing arbitral framework, with its emphasis on party autonomy, is not necessarily adequate to account for the public interest in private-public arbitrations. As a result, important disputes arising under private-public contracts can escape public law scrutiny by being reconfigured in terms which have traditionally been viewed as exclusively falling within the domain of private law.[140] Accordingly, it becomes clear that there is a conceptual and legal void in respect of how public interest is accounted for, and protected, in arbitrations involving public entities under English law. The next section makes some preliminary suggestions as to how that void may be filled.

[133] Jack Beatson, 'The Scope of Judicial Review for Error of Law' (1983) 4 Oxford J Legal Studies 21, 39–44. See also Dedezade (n 49) 66 on how the concept of error of law is construed in cases under s 69 of the 1996 Act.

[134] Beatson (n 133) 30.

[135] *Padfield v Minister of Agriculture* [1968] AC 997, 1030. See also Bradley, Ewing, and Knight (n 85) 636.

[136] Bradley, Ewing, and Knight (n 85) 579; Thomas Poole, 'The Reformation of English Administrative Law' (2009) 68 CLJ 142, 144–48.

[137] See generally Eric C Ip, 'Taking a "Hard Look" at "Irrationality": Substantive Review of Administrative Discretion in the US and UK Supreme Courts' (2014) 34 OJLS 481.

[138] *Associated Provincial Picture Houses v Wednesbury Corporation* [1947] EWCA Civ 1.

[139] As noted above, this point has been extensively discussed in the field of investment treaty arbitration and has led to calls for reform of the investor-state dispute settlement system and for international investment arbitration to be made subject to general principles of global administrative law. It has also been raised in the context of the 'contracting out' of public functions: see eg Sir Gordon Borrie, 'The Regulation of Public and Private Power' [1989] PL 552.

[140] Morris and Fredman (n 17).

VII. Preliminary Suggestions for 'Filling the Void'

While our definition of private-public arbitration encompasses both contractual arbitrations between public and private entities with public interest implications and investment treaty arbitrations, the suggestions made in this section focus on the former. This is the case as, unless (perhaps) the UK is the respondent state in the investment treaty arbitration, there is no obvious reason why English courts should review and purport to safeguard the public interest of another sovereign state. In any event, due to the self-contained nature of the Washington Convention system, domestic courts are effectively precluded from reviewing ICSID awards. Thus, in order to address the conceptual and legal void in terms of how the public interest is accounted for in investment treaty arbitration, change can come only on an international level, whether such reform relates to the scope of the standards of review under investment treaties or to the application of public law safeguards in resolving investor-state disputes.[141]

Thus, turning to contractual private-public arbitrations under English law, the conceptual and legal void in respect of how the public interest is accounted for, and protected, could potentially be addressed in at least two possible ways. One suggestion is that private-public arbitrations and awards become subject to administrative law standards and to judicial review.[142] However, it is questionable whether such a proposition could be doctrinally supported. Despite the decision in *Datafin*, the current position of the English courts is that the decision of a private tribunal is excluded from the scope of judicial review, on the basis that its authority is based on the consent of the parties and is derived solely from contract,[143] and this analysis has been applied to the field of arbitration.[144] Although this reasoning has been criticized for leading to arbitrary results,[145] it is safe to say that there is no current doctrinal basis under English law for judicial review of arbitral awards under Part 54 of the Civil Procedure Rules.

Perhaps more significantly, subjecting the decisions of arbitration tribunals to judicial review would not be desirable either. This is the case as the decision-making power exercised by arbitration tribunals is of a markedly different nature to that exercised by administrative authorities: in particular, arbitration tribunals have no discretionary powers (at least in substantive terms) and their decisions are strictly made on the basis of legal rules, as embodied in the text of the law, rather than on the basis of what is politically expedient.[146] Unless an arbitration tribunal is expressly authorized by the parties to decide as *amiable compositeurs*, which very rarely happens in

[141] As an example of such initiative see UNCTAD, *Investment Policy Framework for Sustainable Development* (United Nations 2012).

[142] On a related point see Morris and Fredman (n 17). See also Fraser P Davidson, 'The Relationship between Arbitration and the Courts in Scotland and England' (1993) CJQ 372, 372–78 on the (historic) availability of judicial review under Scots law in respect of arbitration awards.

[143] See Lord Parker in *R v Criminal Injuries Compensation Board, ex p Lain* [1967] 2 QB 864, 882. See also *Law v National Greyhound Racing Club* [1983] 1 WLR 1302; *R v Disciplinary Committee of the Jockey Club, ex parte Aga Khan* [1993] 2 All ER 853.

[144] *R v National Joint Council for the Craft of Dental Technicians, ex p Neate* [1953] 1 QB 704, 707; *R v Industrial Court, ex p ASSET* [1964] 1 QB 456; *Bremer Vulkan Schiffbau und Maschinenfabrik v South India Shipping Corporation Ltd* [1981] 2 WLR 141, 148.

[145] See generally Morris and Fredman (n 17).

[146] Dedezade (n 49) 62.

practice, arbitral legal reasoning is typically constrained by legal doctrine.[147] In contrast, while administrative authorities and statutory tribunals cannot exceed their statutory or prerogative powers, they engage in the implementation of public policy and have considerable decision-making discretion when choosing between several decisions or courses of action. Therefore, it is submitted that bringing private-public arbitrations wholly into the domain of administrative law would be unwarranted and could lead to a problematic coalescence of the grounds for judicial review and the existing grounds of review of arbitration awards.

Thus, instead of introducing arbitration law into an unfamiliar domain, it would seem preferable for English arbitration law to evolve from within to take account of the rise of private-public arbitration by, first, allowing public law values to inform the approach taken in respect of private-public arbitrations and, secondly, by applying a form of public interest scrutiny in respect of private-public arbitration awards, albeit outside the judicial review framework. It is submitted that such an evolution may not necessarily require legislative reform but would require the judiciary to reconceptualize private-public arbitration and to embed it in a public law narrative. Admittedly, such a development would require a willingness to question the private law paradigm upon which arbitration law is currently based. However, there is no reason why this could not occur.

Turning to some specific examples of what this evolution may entail, it is submitted that the confidentiality principle and the extent of review of arbitral awards by the courts need to be re-evaluated. While currently private-public arbitrations remain confidential by default (and it is far from certain that the ill-defined public interest-related exception will apply), where a private-public dispute has repercussions for the public interest, it is submitted that the English courts should develop a jurisprudence which promotes openness and accountability,[148] and which provides that private-public arbitrations and claims relating to private-public arbitrations that come before the courts are excluded from the general principle of confidentiality.[149] Such openness would allow for accountability to be attributed to either the public body (in which case political accountability should ensue) or to the private party (in which case civil liability should follow), thereby avoiding the scenario which arose in the *e-Borders* case whereby, as noted by Keith Vaz, the confidentiality of the arbitration proceedings effectively precluded any consideration of 'what went wrong' in the multimillion pound contract for the design, development, and delivery of the technology system which would reform UK border controls and implement a sensitive governmental policy on safety.

[147] See generally William W Park, 'The Predictability Paradox: Arbitrators and Applicable Law' in Fabio Bortolotti and Pierre Mayer (eds), *The Application of Substantive Law by International Arbitrators* (ICC 2014) 60.

[148] On the importance of openness and accountability where a public body 'contracts out' public functions see Jody Freeman, 'The Contracting State' (2000–2001) 28 Fla St U L Rev 155, 156.

[149] This could be achieved either through introduction of a new rule whereby it is deemed to be an implied term of private-public arbitrations that there is a public interest in a public hearing or through further defining (and possibly expanding) the scope of the current 'public interest'-based exception to the general principle of confidentiality.

Secondly, English courts could and should engage in a more rigorous review of awards in private-public arbitrations. This may require English courts to develop a special public policy rule in respect of private-public arbitration which is aligned with the wider scope of public interest, and which expands the public policy review beyond the issue of illegality of the underlying contract. One possibility in this regard is expansion of the public policy ground to encompass a low-intensity irrationality review, similar to that propounded in *Wednesbury*, which would allow review of whether the authority came to a conclusion 'so unreasonable that it might almost be described as being done in bad faith' or 'so unreasonable that no reasonable authority could ever have come to it'.[150] While this review could be considered to supplement the grounds for challenging an arbitral award under sections 67 to 69 of the 1996 Act and so could prove controversial, given the effect which the decision of the arbitration tribunal may have on the parties to the dispute and, more importantly, on the public interest, it would seem eminently reasonable to require the arbitration tribunal to meet a minimum standard of rationality and fairness in its decision-making.[151]

Alternatively, English courts could potentially expand the public policy test to encompass review of the award's compliance with requirements of natural justice in respect of private-public arbitration awards. Australian law, which remains heavily influenced by English law, and which in recent years has influenced the development of English law,[152] provides precedent for such an approach to the public policy ground, even in respect of private arbitrations.[153] Admittedly in Australia, the International Arbitration Act 1974 (the 1974 Act) expressly provides that an award will be in conflict with public policy where a 'breach of the rules of natural justice' has occurred[154] and similar wording is also used in the legislation of other common law jurisdictions, such as New Zealand and Singapore.[155] However, given the centrality of the rules of natural justice to any system of adjudication forming part of a legal system based on the rule of law, it is submitted that an express legislative mandate is not required to expand the public policy ground in this manner.[156]

The more difficult question is, however, the appropriate level of scrutiny that should be applied by the courts under a natural justice review. The Australian courts (as well as those in New Zealand and Singapore) have come to somewhat variable conclusions on this point.[157] For example, in *Castel Electronics Pty Ltd v TCL Air Conditioner*

[150] *Wednesbury* (n 138).

[151] See Dawn Oliver, 'Common Values in Public and Private Law and the Public/Private Divide' (1997) PL 630, 633 ff.

[152] See Michal Bobek, *Comparative Reasoning in European Supreme Courts* (OUP 2013), ch 5 noting that, since severing the judicial links with London, the amount of citation of Australian, New Zealand, and Canadian decisions in the English courts has been growing.

[153] Other jurisdictions that have adopted the UNCITRAL Model Law have, on occasion, also used the public policy ground to allow a review on the merits of an arbitral decision: see Peter Binder, *International Commercial Arbitration in UNCITRAL Model Law Jurisdictions* (Sweet & Maxwell 2010) 387–88.

[154] Act No 136 of 1974, s 19.

[155] New Zealand Arbitration Act 1996, sch 1, arts 34(6) and 36(3); International Arbitration Act (Cap 143A, 2002 Rev Ed) (Sing), s 24.

[156] See Julian Sher and Nicholas Kazaz, 'When Even Fraud Is Not Nearly Enough. Recourse Against Arbitral Awards and Public Policy Considerations: An Anglo-Australian Perspective' (2014) 80(2) Arbitration 124, 132.

[157] In relation to New Zealand, see *Downer-Hill Joint Venture v Government of Fiji* [2005] 1 NZLR 554 and *Ironsands Investments Ltd v Toward Industries Ltd* CIV-2010-404-004879 (8 July 2011). In relation to

(Zhongshan) Co Ltd (No 2),[158] Murphy J favoured a more intensive review of the arbitral process. Relying on administrative law concepts, including the 'error of law doctrine', he found that the rules of natural justice mandated a close examination of the evidence submitted in the arbitration to enable the reviewing court to determine whether the 'no evidence rule' and the 'hearing rule' were breached in the arbitration. The 'no evidence rule' requires the court to review whether there was rationally probative evidence in support of the findings of the tribunal,[159] while the 'hearing rule' requires the court to review whether the tribunal made its findings based upon its own opinions and ideas which were not the reasonable outcomes of the arguments submitted by the parties.[160] While this level of scrutiny of a tribunal's decision does not go as far as reviewing the facts of the case *de novo*,[161] it does require a close examination of both the dispositive part and, crucially, the reasoning of the award in light of the evidence submitted by the parties.[162] However, on appeal, the Full Court of the Federal Court of Australia[163] took a more restrictive approach and ruled that an international commercial arbitration award should not be set aside or denied recognition or enforcement under the 1974 Act for breach of the rules of natural justice, unless there is demonstrated 'real unfairness or real practical injustice' in how the international dispute resolution was conducted or resolved.[164] It therefore cautioned against a conclusion that any wrong factual conclusion that may be seen to lack probative evidence (and so amount to legal error) should necessarily be characterized as a breach of the rules of natural justice.[165] The Full Federal Court also noted that judicial review of arbitral awards should not be 'used (or hijacked) to undertake, in substance, a rehearing of factual or legal reasoning under the guise of a complaint about a breach of the rules of natural justice based on the "no evidence rule".'[166]

Therefore, in considering whether the rules of natural justice have been breached, the courts must thread what may, at times, be a fine line between reviewing the reasoning adopted by the tribunal to ensure that the applicant has not suffered a fundamental lack of fairness in the arbitral proceedings and, in effect, engaging in a full rehearing of the merits of the case. Significantly, however, the Australian courts have repeatedly emphasized that the content of the rules of natural justice vary according to the circumstances, and have indicated that, while a high threshold must be met in order to prove breach of such rules in the context of an international commercial

Singapore, see Khushboo Hashu Shahdadpuri, 'The Natural Justice Fallability in Singapore Arbitration Proceedings' (2014) 26 SAcLJ 562.

[158] [2012] FCA 1214.
[159] See *R v Deputy Industrial Injuries Commissioner, Ex parte Moore* [1965] 1 QB 456, 488. However, it has been questioned whether the no evidence rule forms part of the rules of natural justice as recognised by Australian law, see *Gas & Fuel Corporation of Victoria v Wood Hall Ltd & Leonard Pipeline Contractors Ltd* [1978] VR 385.
[160] *Castel* (n 158), paras 157–58.
[161] ibid para 53.
[162] ibid para 64.
[163] *TCL Air Conditioner (Zhongshan) Co Ltd v Castel Electronics Pty Ltd* [2014] FCAFC 83.
[164] ibid para 55.
[165] ibid para 83.
[166] ibid para 113. See also *Emerald Grain Australia Pty Ltd v Agrocorp International Pte Ltd* [2014] FCA 414.

arbitration, the content of such rules differ in an administrative law context. For example, the Full Federal Court in the *Castel Electronics* case distinguished between how the rules of natural justice should be construed when dealing with the exercise of public or state power in the context of administrative law as opposed to the exercise of private power in the context of international commercial arbitration.[167] This would suggest that, in the context of domestic private-public arbitration, a different approach to what is meant by the term 'rules of natural justice' would be justified. It is submitted therefore that the malleable nature of the rules of natural justice is such that expanding the public policy ground to encompass such rules and developing a jurisprudence to elaborate on the content of such rules could allow the public policy ground to act as a powerful safeguard of the public interest in respect of private-public arbitrations.

The suggested proposal for English arbitration law to evolve from within to take account of the rise of private-public arbitration by applying public law values in private-public arbitrations, and a form of public interest scrutiny in private-public arbitration awards, can fill the conceptual and legal void left by the divide between public (administrative) law and private (arbitration) law and provide an adequate legal framework to account for, and protect, the public interest in private-public arbitrations.

VIII. Conclusion

English arbitration law has been characterized as a mature and highly sophisticated body of law. However, while this is certainly the case in relation to commercial disputes between private parties, in respect of either contractual arbitrations between public and private entities with public interest implications or investment treaty arbitrations, this is not necessarily the case. In relation to the former, the existing arbitral framework, with its emphasis on party autonomy, does not adequately account for, or protect, the public interest in private-public arbitration and precludes (or at least severely restricts) the possibility of arbitration law being influenced by public law. Similarly, along with the wide-ranging nature of the standards of review under investment treaties, the borrowing of the main elements of the international commercial arbitration model to resolve investor-state disputes has garnered much criticism. However, due to the narrow scope of review afforded to national courts, reform on an international level is required to ensure that investor-state disputes can be resolved in a manner that accounts for, and protects, the public interest. Therefore, while acknowledging the parallels between domestic private-public arbitration and investment treaty arbitration, this chapter recognizes that English law and the English courts can only hope to safeguard the public interest in relation to the former. Subject to that limitation, this chapter argues that there is a need to reconceptualize private-public arbitration and to subject it to public law values. While engaging with this reconceptualization process would require a willingness to depart from existing practices and principles, fundamentally this reconceptualization is necessary to ensure

[167] *Castel Electronics* (n 163) paras 74–76 and 105–12.

that the rise of private-public arbitration does not lead to the inappropriate subjugation of the public interest to the hallowed arbitral principle of party autonomy.

Select Materials

Bibliography

Ackerman, Susan Rose and Peter L Lindseth (eds), *Comparative Administrative Law* (Edward Elgar Publishing 2013)
Beatson, Jack, '"Public" and "Private" in English Administrative Law' (1987) 103 LQR 34
Bradley, Anthony W, Keith W Ewing, and Christopher J S Knight, *Constitutional & Administrative Law* (16th edn, Pearson 2014)
Craig, Paul, *Administrative Law* (7th edn, Sweet & Maxwell 2012)
Davies, Anne, *Accountability: A Public Law Analysis of Government by Contract* (OUP 2001)
Dicey, Albert Venn, *Introduction to the Study of the Law of the Constitution* (8th edn, London, 1915; reprint ed, Indianapolis, 1982; 1st edn, London, 1885)
Dicey, Albert Venn, 'The Development of Administrative Law in England' (1915) 31 LQR 148
Dupuy, Pierre-Marie, Ernst- Ulrich Petersmann, and Francesco Francioni (eds), *Human Rights in International Investment Law and Arbitration* (OUP 2009)
Feintuck, Mike, *The Public Interest in Regulation* (OUP 2014)
Freedland, Mark R, 'Government by Contract and Public Law' [1994] PL 86
Freeman, Jody, 'The Private Role in Public Governance' (2000) 75 NYU L Rev 543
Harlow, Carol, '"Public" and "Private" Law: Definition Without Distinction' (1980) 43 MLR 241
Held, Virginia, *The Public Interest and Individual Interests* (Basic Books 1970)
Kulick, Andreas, *Global Public Interest in International Investment Law* (CUP 2012)
Lew, Julian DM and others (eds), *Arbitration in England, with Chapters on Scotland and Ireland* (Kluwer Law International 2013)
McLachlan, Campbell, Laurence Shore, and Matthew Weiniger, *Investment Treaty Arbitration: Substantive Principles* (OUP 2007)
Mistelis, Loukas and Stavros Brekoulakis (eds), *Arbitrability: International and Comparative Perspectives* (Kluwer 2009)
Morris, Gillian S and Sandra Fredman, 'The Costs of Exclusivity: Public and Private Re-Examined' [1994] PL 69
Oliver, Dawn, 'Common Values in Public and Private Law and the Public/Private Divide' (1997) PL 630
Poole, Thomas, 'The Reformation of English Administrative Law' (2009) 68 CLJ 142
Schill, Stephan W (ed), *International Investment Law and Comparative Public Law* (OUP 2010)
Sheppard, Audley and Stavros Brekoulakis, *Public Policy in English Arbitration Law* (OUP 2016)
Van Harten, Gus, *Investment Treaty Arbitration and Public Law* (OUP 2007)
Whytock, Christopher A, 'Private-Public Interaction in Global Governance: The Case of Transnational Commercial Arbitration' (2010) 12 Business & Politics, Article 10

Legislation

Arbitration Act 1996 (c 23)
Arbitration (International Investment Disputes) Act 1966 (c 41)

Cases

Associated Provincial Picture Houses v Wednesbury Corporation [1947] EWCA Civ 1
Atkins Ltd v The Secretary of State for Transport [2013] EWHC 139 (TCC)
Fulham Football Club (1987) Ltd v Richards [2011] EWCA Civ 855
Guangzhou Dockyards Co Ltd v ENE Aegiali I [2010] EWHC 2826 (Comm)
John Forster Emmott v Michael Wilson & Partners Ltd [2008] EWCA Civ 184
Keydon Estates Ltd v Western Power Distribution (South Wales) Ltd [2004] EWHC 996 (Ch)
Padfield v Minister of Agriculture [1968] AC 997
R v Criminal Injuries Compensation Board, ex p Lain [1967] 2 QB 864
Re Racal Communications Ltd [1981] AC 374, 383
Soleimany v Soleimany [1998] EWCA Civ 285
TCL Air Conditioner (Zhongshan) Co Ltd v Castel Electronics Pty Ltd [2014] FCAFC 83
The Chrysalis [1983] 1 Lloyd's Rep 503
The Secretary of State for the Home Department v Raytheon Systems Limited [2014] EWHC 4375 (TCC)
The Secretary of State for the Home Department v Raytheon Systems Limited [2015] EWHC 311 (TCC)
Westacre Investments Inc v Jugoimport-SDPR Holding Co Ltd [1999] EWCA Civ 1401

Reports

Departmental Advisory Committee on Arbitration Law, '1996 Report on the Arbitration Bill' (Chairman The Rt Hon Lord Justice Saville) (1996) 13 Arb Intl 275

3

The Private-Public Divide and Its Influence over French Arbitration Law

Tradition and Transition

*Florian Grisel**

I. Introduction

The private-public divide is a distinguishing feature of French law.[1] This divide echoes an ancient distinction between legal relationships among 'equals' (regulated by private law) and legal relationships among 'unequals' (regulated by public law).[2] It also mirrors another distinction of a jurisdictional nature between 'civil' courts and 'administrative' courts, which was inherited from the French Revolution. Indeed, the Revolutionaries nurtured a solid distrust for courts, caused by the abuses of the royal courts (called '*parlements*'), which acted as appellate courts and local legislators before the Revolution.[3] These '*parlements*' were accused of overstepping into the realm of the executive branch by creating local customs and norms through so-called '*arrêts de règlements*' (regulatory judgments),[4] and by interfering with the royal administration.[5] As pointed out by Merryman and Perez-Perdomo, the courts were 'targets of the Revolution'.[6] In order to limit the powers of judges, the Revolutionaries tried to strictly separate the executive from the judicial branch. Specifically, the Statute of 16/24 August 1790 insulated 'judicial' from 'administrative' functions. It forbade courts from 'troubling, in any way whatsoever, the operations of administrative bodies, or

* The author thanks the organisers of the Lex Mercatoria Publica Workshop held in Heidelberg on 21–22 November 2014 for their useful comments on earlier drafts of this chapter. The content of this chapter was last updated in September 2022.

[1] See René David, *Le droit français – Tome I : Les données fondamentales du droit français* (LGDJ 1960) 85–93.

[2] ibid; Alan Watson, *The Making of the Civil Law* (Harvard University Press 1981) 144 ff.

[3] On the '*parlements*', see Harold J Berman, *Law and Revolution – The Formation of the Western Legal Tradition* (Harvard UP 1983) 465–77, in particular 465: 'The emergence of such a court took place in the thirteenth century. At first, periodic judicial sessions of the curia regis, called *parlements* (meaning "discussions" or "deliberations") were held several times a year. Eventually, after about 1250, the Parlement of Paris sat as a permanent judicial body, with full-time professional judges presiding regularly over civil and criminal cases, sometimes in first instance but mostly on appeal from courts of bailiff or, less frequently, from courts of dukes, counts and other lords. Eventually the king participated in person only rarely and finally not at all. The Parlement of Paris survived as the supreme royal court of France until the French Revolution.'

[4] See Mirjan R Damaska, *The Faces of Justice and State Authority – A Comparative Approach to the Legal Process* (Yale UP 1986) 34–38.

[5] See John M Merryman and Rogelio Perez-Perdomo, *The Civil Law Tradition – An Introduction to the Legal Systems of Europe and Latin America* (3rd edn, Stanford UP 2007) 17.

[6] ibid.

Florian Grisel, *The Private-Public Divide and Its Influence over French Arbitration Law* In: *The Comparative Constitutional Foundations of Private-Public Arbitration*. Edited by: Stephan W. Schill, Oxford University Press.
 DOI: 10.1093/9780191987960.003.0003

citing before them administrators in connection with their functions'.[7] The executive branch was therefore insulated from judicial review, and the judicial branch was deprived of the power to interfere with the activities of the former branch. This insulation of the judiciary reflected a strict conception of the separation of powers inherited from Montesquieu, which also led to a prohibition for courts to 'take part directly or indirectly in the exercise of the legislative power'.[8]

Despite this strict separation of powers, which should have prevented courts from controlling decisions made by the executive branch, administrative courts (with the Conseil d'Etat at their apex) progressively gained the possibility to review decisions emanating from the executive branch and to decide upon the liability of public entities.[9] The Conseil d'Etat started heading a system of administrative courts which have created and applied a set of 'administrative' or public laws, separate from 'civil' courts (with the Cour de cassation at their apex) that apply a set of 'private' or 'civil' laws. A Tribunal des Conflits, equally composed of members of the Conseil d'Etat and the Cour de cassation,[10] is in charge of delimiting the jurisdiction of each set of courts (civil and administrative). As a result, the private-public divide has structured the French legal system: this divide separates the judges, the courts, the law itself, but also law students and scholars (who claim their identity as either '*privatistes*' or '*publicistes*').

Another related aspect of French law is its strong favour for arbitration. It is, in fact, a great paradox for a highly centralized legal system, such as that of France, to strongly favour a private system of dispute settlement. This apparent paradox finds an explanation in the Revolutionaries' distrust for courts: because they distrusted courts, the Revolutionaries were eager to develop alternative methods of dispute settlement, while building a strong executive branch. The Revolutionaries' unwillingness to see the judiciary rein in the executive can also explain why the right to arbitrate only concerned arbitration between private entities, while the settlement of disputes involving public entities through arbitration (or private-public arbitration) was prohibited.[11] A brief historical background will further highlight the choices that led to the prohibition of private-public arbitration under French law (section II). The present chapter will then explain how the growing involvement of French public entities in international trade led to various exceptions being carved out from the prohibition of private-public arbitration (section III). As private-public arbitration cases grew in number, so did the debates concerning the ways in which to preserve the public

[7] Statute of 16/24 August 1790, title II, art 13.

[8] ibid, title II, art 10.

[9] See Merryman and Perez-Perdomo (n 5) 88–89.

[10] See Constitution of 4 November 1848, art 89.

[11] A private-public arbitration (also referred to in this chapter as a 'public' arbitration) is an arbitration between a private actor and a public actor. Public actors encompass the state itself; state organs; sub-state entities, such as regions or municipalities; instrumentalities of the state, including state enterprises, to the extent they are organized in accordance with public law; as well as entities organized under private law to the extent they exercise public authority or public functions. The legal basis of the dispute—that is, whether it is based on a treaty or contract, whether it involves a purely commercial relationship between private and public actors, or whether the relationship is one subjected to public law—is irrelevant for purposes of the research envisioned here. Equally, it does not matter whether the arbitration is between a public actor and a foreign private entity.

interest in these cases. A string of recent cases has taken up these debates and created a new competence for administrative courts in the annulment and enforcement of awards rendered in private-public arbitration (section IV).

II. The Arbitration of Public Disputes in France: A Brief Historical Background

The perception of private-public arbitration in France has oscillated between enthusiastic fervour and utter distrust. These varying perceptions have generally been associated with debates concerning arbitration as a mode of dispute settlement, which have revolved around the following question: should private tribunals be allowed to exercise governance functions normally associated with state courts? The answer has evolved over the centuries depending on the relationship between the executive and the judicial branch, particularly the degree of independence of courts towards the executive branch.[12]

In particular, the executive branch has either favoured arbitration as a way to weaken the judicial branch or curtailed its powers due to fear that it would compete with public courts. In the context of the French Revolution, arbitration first benefited from the general distrust for public courts, leading to a short-lived experimentation with public arbitration between 1793 and 1796 (A). This popularity faded away with the reorganization of state justice under Napoleon Bonaparte, which led to the prohibition of private-public arbitration in 1806 (B).

A. A Failed Experimentation with Public Arbitration during the French Revolution

In the pre-Revolutionary context, arbitration benefited from a general distrust for state courts. As briefly explained in the Introduction, the courts (also called '*parlements*') were generally deemed to be arbitrary and unpredictable, as they had discretion to create their own customary rules through so-called '*arrêts de règlement*' (regulatory judgments). As an old saying went, 'God saves us from the equity of the Parliaments'.[13] These customs could vary across different provinces, thereby undermining the legal certainty across the kingdom. In addition, the '*parlements*' occasionally threatened the executive power by challenging the authority of the King. As a result of its insubordination, for instance, Chancellor Maupéou dissolved the Parliament of Paris between 1771 and 1774.[14] By contrast, arbitration was seen as a more predictable system of dispute settlement (and one that was more respectful of executive powers).

[12] See Carine Jallamion, 'Arbitrage et pouvoir politique en France du XVIIe au XIXe siècle' (2005) 1 Rev l'arb 3.

[13] Cited in André Tunc, 'The Grand Outlines of the Code' in Bernard Schwartz (ed), *The Code Napoleon and the Common Law World* (New York UP 1956) 19 (*'Dieu nous garde de l'équité des Parlements.'*).

[14] See François Furet, *The French Revolution 1770–1814* (Antonia Nevill tr, Blackwell 1988) 17–18.

In addition, many philosophers during the Enlightenment greatly valued arbitration as a mode of dispute settlement that was more democratic than public courts. For instance, Voltaire praised the recourse to arbitration in the Netherlands as 'the best law, the most excellent and useful usage that I have ever seen'.[15] Montesquieu, in a famous extract of *The Spirit of the Laws*, argued that adjudicative powers should never be granted to a permanent body, but to ad hoc tribunals composed of 'persons drawn from the people'.[16] Montesquieu believed that such a system would better preserve the separation of powers by limiting the authority of the judiciary. Another relevant example is Diderot, who commented under the alias of Guillaume Raynal on William Penn's devolution of land in the American colonies and his setting up of arbitral tribunals to settle disputes arising therefrom.[17] Diderot praised a system in which arbitrators worked gratuitously for the adjudication of land property rights.[18]

It is in this historical and philosophical context that the Revolutionaries reorganized the French judiciary after 1789. Their distrust for state courts was obvious. For instance, Thouret (a prominent lawyer and President of the Constituent Assembly between 1789 and 1791) blamed state courts for continuously breaching the separation of powers and interfering with the executive branch.[19] At stake was the complex relationships between the King and the '*parlements*' (and the autonomy gained by these courts vis-à-vis the executive branch).[20] The Revolutionaries intended to reassert the authority of the executive branch by making it independent from a judiciary that was held responsible for the failures of the *Ancien Régime*. The main step in this process was the Statute of 16/24 August 1790, which strengthened the separation of powers and reorganized the judiciary in its entirety. In September 1790, the '*parlements*' were permanently dissolved and replaced by elected judges.[21]

A key aspect of this judicial reorganization concerned arbitration. In line with the ideals of the Enlightenment, the Revolutionaries placed arbitration at the heart of the French legal system and constitutionalized the right to arbitrate in Article 1 of the Statute of 16/24 August 1790, which provides as follows:[22] 'Arbitration being the most reasonable way to end disputes between citizens, legislatures shall not make any

[15] Voltaire, *Fragments d'une lettre sur un usage très utile etabli en Hollande* (1758).

[16] Montesquieu, *De l'Esprit des Lois* (1784) book XI, ch VI.

[17] Guillaume-Thomas Raynal, *Histoire Philosophique et Politique des Etablissements et du Commerce des Européens dans les Deux Indes* (1770) vol 9, 18–19.

[18] ibid.

[19] Jacques-Guillaume Thouret, 'Discours sur la réorganisation du pouvoir judiciaire' (24 March 1790). This speech can be found at <https://www.justice.gc.ca/fra/pr-rp/sjc-csj/pji-ilp/rev4/rev4.pdf> accessed 10 January 2025.

[20] On the birth of the royal courts and their relationship to the King of France, see Michel Foucault, *Théories et Institutions Pénales – Cours au Collège de France 1971–1972* (EHESS Gallimard Seuil 2015).

[21] Decree of 6/7 September 1790 (Décret relatif à la forme de procéder devant les autorités administratives et judiciaires, en matière de contributions, de travaux publics, et de commerce, et à la suppression des cours, tribunaux et juridictions d'ancienne création) in Jean-Baptiste Duvergier, *Collection complète des lois, décrets, ordonnances, règlements et avis du Conseil d'Etat* (A Guyot et Sribe, L Larose et JB Sirey 1824) vol 1, 406.

[22] The constitutional nature of this right arose out of the constituent nature of the assembly that issued the statute. See Bruno de Loynes de Fumichon, 'La passion de la Révolution française pour l'arbitrage' (2014) 1 Rev l'arb 3, 35. As anecdotal evidence of this favour for arbitration, the fishers of Marseille compared their medieval court (the Prud'homie de Pêche) to an arbitral tribunal in order to (successfully) maintain its powers. They argued that their judges were 'true arbitrators elected by the general trust and

acts that would tend to diminish, either the favour for, or the efficiency of arbitration agreements.'[23]

However, this favour for arbitration found some limitations. Article 2 of the Statute narrowed the scope of arbitration to the settlement of 'private interests', which arguably excluded the settlement of claims involving public entities. This language reflected the position adopted by some French courts before the Revolution, which limited arbitration to the settlement of disputes between persons 'having the free exercise of their rights'.[24]

Subsequent texts confirmed the constitutional right to arbitrate disputes (without drawing a distinction, however, between 'private' and 'public' arbitration). For instance, the Constitution of 1791 stated the citizens' constitutional right to settle their disputes through arbitration.[25] The Constitution of 1793 distinguished between 'private' and 'public' arbitrators, but with a different meaning than the one implied by the Statute of 16/24 August 1790 (public arbitrators being in charge of solving disputes that had not been completely 'extinguished' by private arbitrators).[26] Similarly, the Constitutions of 1795 and 1799 referred to the parties' right to have recourse to arbitration.[27] As will be seen further below, this reference to arbitration disappeared from the Constitution in 1802. Arbitration (whether private or public) progressively fell into disfavour at the turn of the eighteenth century, which coincided with two events: an ill-fated experience with public arbitration during the Great Terror,[28] and the reorganization of the French judiciary by Napoleon Bonaparte.

Indeed, during the Great Terror, the Revolutionaries experimented with public arbitration. In 1793, public lands were distributed to inhabitants of municipalities in order to favour the emergence of a middle class of landowners.[29] The decree allowing the land distribution also provided for the settlement of disputes through arbitration (between municipalities or between private individuals and municipalities).[30] Another decree specified certain aspects of the arbitral procedure: the number of arbitrators should not exceed three, challenges were allowed against arbitrators on

the free will [of the fishers]'. See Florian Grisel, *The Limits of Private Governance: Norms and Rules in a Mediterranean Fishery* (Hart Publishing 2021) 113.

[23] Statute of 16/24 August 1790, art 1.

[24] See Jean-Guillaume Locré, *Esprit du Code de procédure civile, ou Conférence du Code de procédure avec les discussions du Conseil, les observations du Tribunat, les exposés des motifs, les discours des orateurs du Tribunat* (P Didot l'Aîné 1816) vol 4, 348.

[25] Constitution of 3 September 1791, art 5.

[26] Constitution of 24 June 1793, arts 86 ff. Unlike private arbitrators, public arbitrators were appointed through yearly elections, deliberated in public, and had a duty to support their judgment with reasons (Constitution of 24 June 1793, arts 91, 94 and 95).

[27] Constitution of 22 August 1795, arts 210 ff; Constitution of 13 December 1799, arts 60 ff.

[28] The Great Terror (1793–94) was a campaign of political violence during the French Revolution which gave rise to conflicts between two political factions (the Girondins and the Jacobins) and mass executions.

[29] Decree of 11 June 1793 (Décret concernant le mode de partage des biens communaux) s I, art 1(3) in Duvergier (n 21) vol 5, 403: '*Tous les biens appartenant aux communes, soit communaux, soit patrimoniaux, de quelque nature qu'ils puissent être, pourront être partagés, s'ils sont susceptibles de partage, dans les formes et d'après les règles ci-après prescrites, et sauf les exceptions qui seront prononcées.*'

[30] Decree of 11 June 1793 (Décret concernant le mode de partage des biens communaux), s V, arts 1(3) and 1(4) in Duvergier (n 21) vol 5, 410.

certain grounds, and the awards were to be reasoned.[31] The disputes submitted to arbitration primarily concerned claims from individuals or local communities (the '*communes*') over lands that had been expropriated or confiscated prior to the Revolution.[32] Hundreds of claims were reportedly submitted to arbitral tribunals.[33] However, the recourse to arbitration appears to have been unpopular as the balancing of property rights with the public interest raised difficulties, as reflected in a Statute of 1796 that put a halt to this experimentation:

> the examination of all the difficulties that this law [ie the Decree of 1793] has caused, and the measures that shall be adopted to balance the preservation of private properties with the public interest, the examination resulting from a greater number of land clearings and the improvement of agriculture, will demand a long discussion.[34]

This failed experience weighed negatively on the fate of arbitration. The Constitution of 4 August 1802—adopted after the arrival of Napoleon Bonaparte to power as First Consul—did not refer to arbitration and, consequently, the recourse to arbitration ceased to have constitutional value. In addition, Napoleon Bonaparte launched a deep overhaul of France's judicial institutions, leading to the reorganization of state courts and the limitation of the scope of arbitration.

B. The Reorganization of the French Judicial System and the Prohibition of Private-Public Arbitration after the Revolution

When he came to power, Napoleon Bonaparte planned to reorganize and centralize state powers. His plan concerned the three branches of state authority, including the judicial one. For instance, Bonaparte promoted the professionalization of the judiciary by suppressing the election of judges and by limiting the power of juries to criminal matters.[35] As part of a large codification plan, Napoleon Bonaparte famously unified French law in a series of codes. This codification process, which led, inter alia, to the adoption of the Code of Civil Procedure ('Code de procédure civile') in 1806, constrained the possibility to have recourse to arbitration and prohibited public arbitration. Articles 1003 and 1004 of the Code of Civil Procedure provided as follows:

> Anyone can enter into an arbitration agreement pertaining to rights of which they freely dispose.[36]

[31] Decree of 2 October 1793 (Décret qui ordonne que les procès de communes, à raison des biens communaux, seront jugés par la voie de l'arbitrage) arts 2, 4, 5, and 8 in Duvergier (n 21) vol 6, 251.

[32] Gérard Béaur, 'Révolution et redistribution des richesses dans les campagnes: mythe ou réalité' (2008) 2 Annales historiques de la Révolution française 209, 217.

[33] ibid.

[34] Statute of 9 June 1796 (Loi portant qu'il sera provisoirement sursis aux poursuites résultant de l'exécution de la loi du 10 juin 1793, sur le partage des biens communaux) in Duvergier (n 21) vol 9, 127. It is not clear what were the 'difficulties' referred to in the Statute of 1796.

[35] See Furet (n 14) 229.

[36] Code of Civil Procedure (1806), art 1003.

> One cannot enter into an arbitration agreement pertaining to gifts and bequeathal of food, housing and clothes; to the separations between husbands and wives, divorces, questions of state, nor *to any disputes that shall be communicated to the public prosecutor*.[37]

Originally, the prohibition against public arbitration arose out of these italicized words. Article 83 of the Code of Civil Procedure defines the wording 'disputes that shall be communicated to the public prosecutor' as matters pertaining to public policy or involving a public entity: "The following matters shall be communicated to the public prosecutor: 1. Those that relate to public policy, the State, the public domain, municipalities."[38]

A review of the *travaux préparatoires* of the Code of Civil Procedure indicates the reasons underlying the above prohibition.[39] The drafters of the Code of Civil Procedure deemed arbitration as a contractual tool that was ill-placed to adjudicate public matters with the same authority and independence as courts. Indeed, the *travaux préparatoires* of the Code of Civil Procedure stated as follows:

> We shall find in our laws, and we see in our draft a formal prohibition to enter into arbitration agreements on questions that relate more or less to public policy. The reason for this prohibition flows from the very nature of arbitration agreements. Only interests that are purely private can be subject to a contract: no one can insert any provision that would touch upon public policy. . . . These issues [ie the issues that shall be communicated to the public prosecutor] are too closely related to public policy for the decision to be given up to arbitrators, who, no matter how instructed and wise they may be, never offer to society the same guarantee, the same independence as judges instituted by law, and invested by the Chief of State of his authority.[40]

This extract from the *travaux préparatoires* also suggests that the true reason for the demise of public arbitration may have been the growing centralization of power under Napoleon Bonaparte and the fear that arbitral tribunals might interfere with public affairs. As a matter of fact, the broadness of the terms 'disputes that shall be communicated to the public prosecutor' under Article 1004 prompted debates before the adoption of the Code of Civil Procedure in 1806, with some of its drafters expressing fear that any disputes would likely be communicated to the public prosecutor (thus emptying the right to arbitrate of its substance).[41]

[37] ibid, art 1004 (emphasis added).

[38] Code of Civil Procedure (1806), art 83.

[39] This prohibition also concerned the arbitration of disputes between private entities that would touch upon public policy. As a consequence, all disputes between private entities that touched upon public policy were deemed inarbitrable until the 1950s. See Emmanuel Gaillard and John Savage (eds), *Fouchard Gaillard Goldman On International Commercial Arbitration* (Kluwer Law International 1999) para 565.

[40] Locré (n 24) vol 4, 359–60. See also one of the first commentaries of the Code of Civil Procedure: Boitard (published by Gustave de Linage), *Leçons sur le code de procédure civile* (4th edn, Gustave Thorel 1847) vol 2, 447–54.

[41] Locré (n 24) 355–56.

These concerns turned out to be well-founded, as French courts strictly applied the prohibition for public entities to enter into arbitration agreements, even after the fall of Napoleon Bonaparte. For instance, a decision rendered by the Conseil d'Etat in the case of *Guérard v le Trésor* in 1825 illustrates the strict application of Article 1004 of the Code of Civil Procedure. In that case, Mr Guérard entered into a contractual agreement with the French state for the import and export of goods overseas. This contract contained an arbitration clause. After the death of Mr Guérard, his heirs sought the reimbursement of contractual debts owed by the French state, which submitted the dispute to the Court of Finances ('Cour des comptes'). The heirs subsequently challenged the jurisdiction of this state court based on the arbitration clause contained in the contract. However, the Conseil d'Etat affirmed the jurisdiction of the Court of Finances, on the basis that Mr Guérard (and his heirs) 'could no longer rely on the arbitration clause' pursuant to Article 1004 of the Code of Civil Procedure.[42]

A factor that may have contributed to the strict application of Article 1004 of the Code of Civil Procedure by French courts was the growing powers of administrative courts throughout the nineteenth century. Administrative courts, with the Conseil d'Etat at their forefront, were wary of any interference from competing authorities. In particular, the Conseil d'Etat progressively affirmed through its case law the right to review executive decisions and to decide upon the liability of public entities. In this context, the Conseil d'Etat may have sought to protect its jurisdictional turf from the intervention of arbitral tribunals by giving a strict interpretation to Article 1004 of the Code of Civil Procedure. For instance, Edouard Laferrière, a prominent member of the Conseil d'Etat (and its vice president between 1886 and 1898), argued in his seminal treatise of administrative law that the 'jurisdiction of administrative courts is mandatory' and therefore invalidates an arbitration agreement when a public entity is involved.[43] In a case decided in 1887, the Conseil d'Etat held that the Ministry of Public Instruction could not 'delegate powers to arbitrators [through an arbitration agreement] and give authority to decide to a jurisdiction other than those established by law'.[44]

At the turn of the twentieth century, the prohibition for public entities to enter into arbitration agreements was solidly grounded in the French legal system. However, numerous exceptions to this prohibition were subsequently carved out because of the growing involvement of French public entities in international trade in the twentieth century. These exceptions have blurred the lines between 'private' and 'public' arbitration and have prompted vibrant discussions as to how state courts can safeguard the public interest in private-public arbitration.

[42] CE *Héritiers Guérard v le Trésor* (19 February 1825) in *Recueil des arrêts du Conseil, ou ordonnances royales rendues en Conseil d'Etat sur toutes les matières du contentieux de l'administration* (Delhomme 1823) 103.

[43] Edouard Laferrière, *Traité de la juridiction administrative et des recours contentieux* (Berger-Levrault et Cie 1896) vol 2, 152–53.

[44] CE *Evèque de Moulin* (23 December 1887).

III. A Recent Evolution: Bridging the Gap between Private and Public Arbitration

The distinction between public and private arbitration progressively lost its relevance in the second half of the twentieth century, as French public entities became increasingly involved in international trade (as illustrated, for instance, by the above-cited case of *Guérard v le Trésor*). Consequently, French law introduced numerous exceptions to the prohibition against private-public arbitration, allowing public entities to take part in arbitration proceedings (A). In procedural terms, these exceptions have led to an alignment of private and public arbitration, except for a few specificities that will be set out below (B).

A. Exceptions Made to the Prohibition against Private-Public Arbitration

As seen above, the prohibition for public entities to enter into arbitration agreements was first laid out in the Code of Civil Procedure of 1806. The two relevant provisions of the Code of Civil Procedure were incorporated in Articles 2059 and 2060(1) of the Civil Code in 1972, stating as follows:

> Anyone can enter into an arbitration agreement pertaining to rights of which they freely dispose.[45]
>
> One cannot enter into an arbitration agreement pertaining to questions of status or personal capacity, to those relating to divorce or separation or to the disputes involving public entities and organizations and more generally in any field that touches upon public policy.[46]

The prohibition of public arbitration contained in these articles is now considered to be a general principle of public law, with 'legislative' rank.[47] However, the Conseil constitutionnel held in a Decision of 2 December 2004 that the prohibition of public arbitration does not have 'constitutional' rank under French law.[48] At stake in that case was the constitutionality of the Executive Order of 27 June 2004, specifically of its provision allowing private-public arbitration in the case of disputes arising from private-public partnerships. In that case, the Conseil constitutionnel decided, without detailing its reasons, that the 'principle of the prohibition of the recourse to arbitration by public persons' has 'legislative and not constitutional value'.[49] As a

[45] Civil Code (2015), art 2059.
[46] ibid art 2060 al 1.
[47] CE (Avis) No 339710 (6 March 1986) (this opinion of the Conseil d'Etat concerned the legality of the draft contract for the creation of Euro Disney, between the French State, the Ile-de-France region, and the public entity for the urban planning of the city of Marne-la-Vallée, on the one hand, and the Walt Disney Productions corporation on the other hand, which contained an arbitration clause, particularly in light of the prohibition of public arbitration under Article 2060 of the Civil Code).
[48] Conseil constitutionnel, Décision No 2004-506 DC (2 December 2004) paras 31–32.
[49] ibid.

consequence, the constitutional court implied that legislators can carve out exceptions to the prohibition contained in Article 2060 of the Civil Code.

In fact, several exceptions were carved out by means of statute (1) or treaty (2). In addition, French civil courts have interpreted the prohibition set out under Article 2060(1) of the Civil Code restrictively, leading to another general exception in circumstances where public entities operate as 'actors of international trade' (3).

1 Statutory Exceptions

The main exception to the prohibition contained under Article 2060(1) of the French Civil Code has been carved out under Statute No 75-596 of 9 July 1975. The following provision was added to Article 2060 pursuant to this statute: "However, categories of public entities of an industrial and commercial character (*Etablissements publics à caractère industriel et commercial*) may be authorized by decree to enter into arbitration agreements."

Pursuant to Article 2060(2) of the Civil Code, the executive branch is authorized to issue decrees allowing a specific category of public entities (called '*établissements publics à caractère industriel et commercial*'—EPICs) to enter into arbitration agreements after a dispute has arisen (and not before the dispute arises).[50] EPICs are public law organizations that undertake missions of public service (in addition to industrial and commercial activities). Relevant examples include transportation companies (for instance, the company operating the subway system in Paris, the RATP) or cultural institutions (such as the Paris Opera or the Comédie Française). All these legal entities routinely enter into commercial contracts and often face the need to include arbitration clauses in these contracts. Pursuant to Article 260(2) of the Civil Code, for instance, the government passed a decree in 2002 to authorize EPICs operating in the energy sector to enter into arbitration agreements after a dispute has arisen.[51]

Other exceptions have been laid out by statutes allowing specific legal entities to enter into arbitration agreements. These entities are listed in Article L 311-6 of the Code of Administrative Justice and include, inter alia, the railroad companies (SNCF and RFF) and the postal services (La Poste).

Finally, some exceptions have been carved out in connection with specific types of contracts or business activities. For instance, an executive order of 2004 allowed the recourse to arbitration for the settlement of disputes arising from private-public partnerships.[52] This executive order mentions the possibility for private-public partnerships to contain arbitration clauses providing for 'the application of French law'.[53] The

[50] The French original makes this temporal limitation clear, as the word '*compromettre*', used in Article 2060(2) of the Civil Code, refers to agreements to arbitrate concluded after a dispute has arisen.

[51] Décret No 2002-56 (8 January 2002).

[52] Ordonnance No 2004-559 (17 June 2004).

[53] Ordonnance No 2004-559 (17 June 2004) art 11(1). This provision was abrogated as of 1 April 2016 and replaced by a similar provision through a new Ordonnance No 2015-899 (23 July 2015) art 102 (which also referred to the possibility for disputes arising from private-public partnerships to be settled through arbitration).

goal was to encourage private companies to enter into private-public partnerships and promote the collaboration between private and public entities for various infrastructure projects (hospitals, prisons, roads, etc).[54] More importantly, another exception was made for contracts between public entities and foreign companies 'for the implementation of operations of general interest'.[55] This legislative exception arose out of the negotiations between the French government and Disney for the creation of a leisure park in France (Euro Disney).[56] Disney insisted on including an arbitration clause in their contracts with various public entities (the state, the Ile-de-France region, and the public entity in charge of urban planning for the city of Marne-la-Vallée). However, in a legal opinion to the French government,[57] the Conseil d'Etat deemed this arbitration clause invalid under Article 2060 of the Civil Code.[58] In order to circumvent the prohibition contained under Article 2060 (and attract Disney to the French territory), the government passed a special law pursuant to which public entities can enter into arbitration agreements with foreign companies in contracts that implement operations of general interest, thereby creating another exception to the general prohibition.

In sum, many of the statutory exceptions to the prohibition against private-public arbitration arose out of the need to increase the attractiveness of France. The same rationale applies to most treaty exceptions.

2 Treaty Exceptions

Other exceptions to the prohibition against private-public arbitration are contained in treaties signed by France. The Treaty of Canterbury of 12 February 1986 provides, for instance, that disputes between the Governments of France and/or the United Kingdom, on the one hand, and the private concessionaires in charge of the construction and operation of the Channel Tunnel, on the other hand, should be settled through arbitration.[59] Another treaty exception is contained in the Agreement between the Governments of France and the United Arab Emirates concerning the construction and operation of the Louvre Abu Dhabi museum.[60]

Another exception that raised controversies relates to the Convention on the Settlement of Investment Disputes between States and Nationals of Other States (Washington or ICSID Convention) (to which France has been a party since 1967). In its legal opinion rendered on 6 March 1986 (on the draft contractual agreement

[54] See for instance 'Exposé Général' in Projet de loi relatif aux contrats de partenariat, French Senate <http://www.senat.fr/rap/l07-239/l07-2391.html> accessed 10 January 2025.

[55] Loi No 86-972 (19 August 1986).

[56] Some aspects of these negotiations are described in James B Stewart, *Disney War: The Battle for the Magic Kingdom* (Pocket Books 2006) 81–84.

[57] The Conseil d'Etat acts as legal advisor to the French government (in addition to its adjudicative functions).

[58] CE (Avis) No 339710 (6 March 1986).

[59] Treaty between the United Kingdom of Great Britain and Northern Ireland and the French Republic concerning the Construction and Operation by Private Concessionaires of a Channel Fixed Link with Exchanges of Notes (12 February 1986) art 19.

[60] Décret No 2008-879 (1 September 2008) publishing the Agreement between the Government of the French Republic and the Government of the United Arab Emirates relating to the Universal Museum in Abu Dhabi, signed in Abu Dhabi on 6 March 2007, art 18.

between French public entities and Disney), the Conseil d'Etat gave the following interpretation of the Washington Convention:

> the Washington Convention 'for the settlement of investment disputes between States and nationals of other States' . . . *which is limited to organizing the modalities for the settlement of disputes* that parties to a dispute have decided to submit to the 'international centre for settlement of investment disputes', *does not bear any consequences regarding the possibility for a French public person to enter into an arbitration agreement.*[61]

The Conseil d'Etat implied that the ICSID Convention does not create an exception to the prohibition against private-public arbitration under French law (providing instead a procedural framework for arbitration between foreign investors and states). Relying on this opinion, the French government (or French public entities) could seek to renege on their promise to arbitrate before the International Centre for Settlement of Investment Disputes (ICSID) on the basis of the prohibition contained under Article 2060 of the French Civil Code.[62] As will be seen further below, French public entities have sought to derail arbitration proceedings based on this very argument.

3 Exception Laid Out by the Cour de cassation

Civil courts (specifically the Cour de cassation) have created a general exception to the prohibition for public entities to enter into arbitration agreements when these entities are involved in international trade. This exception has placed public entities involved in international trade on an equal footing with private entities when it comes to the arbitration of their disputes.

The leading case arose out of a dispute between the French Treasury and Mr Galakis, the Greek owner of a ship chartered by the French government for the transportation of goods from West Africa in April 1940.[63] The charter party provided for arbitration proceedings to be held in London. After a dispute arose between the parties, the French government refused to participate in the arbitral proceedings and were subsequently held liable to pay contractual damages to Mr Galakis. The Court of the Seine refused to grant exequatur to the award in a judgment that was subsequently reversed by the Paris Court of Appeal. The French Treasury then challenged the appellate decision before the Cour de cassation on the basis that the arbitral proceedings (and the resulting award) breached the prohibition for public entities to enter into arbitration agreements under French law.

When deciding upon the appeal, the Cour de cassation construed this prohibition under French law in a very restrictive manner:

> the invalidity required by Articles 83 and 1004 of the Code of Civil Procedure does not raise any question of capacity within the meaning of Article 3 of the Civil Code . . . the primary duty of the Court of Appeal was to decide whether the rule, enacted for internal

[61] CE (Avis) No 339710 (6 March 1986) (emphases added).

[62] This issue could arise when the arbitration clause is contained in a state contract signed by a French public entity.

[63] Cass 2 May 1966, 1966 Bull Civ I 199.

> contracts, should also apply to international contracts entered into for the purposes and in accordance with the usages of maritime commerce . . . the judgment under attack rightly holds that the rule denying validity does not apply to such a contract.[64]

The *Galakis* case laid out a general exception to the prohibition for public entities to enter into arbitration agreements. In short, the Cour de cassation validated an arbitration agreement contained in an international commercial contract to which a public entity was a party, notwithstanding the prohibition contained in the Civil Code. While leaving out 'public' or 'administrative' contracts (ie contracts entered without a commercial purpose and/or for the performance of a public service), the decision created an important exception through which cases involving a public entity could be submitted to arbitration, namely when they relate to international trade.

To conclude, the prohibition for public entities to consent to arbitration agreements in their contracts has been subject to an increasing number of exceptions under French law. The general trend under French law has been to treat public entities as any other actors engaged in international trade and broaden the possibility for them to enter into arbitration agreements. This trend arose out of the growing involvement of French public entities in international trade and the need for the French legal system to encourage this involvement. As will be shown below, the progressive recognition of private-public arbitration also concerns the law pertaining to the arbitral procedure.

B. The Conduct of Arbitral Proceedings Involving Public Entities

The procedure for arbitral proceedings under French law is essentially the same whether these proceedings involve private or public entities. The rules governing this procedure are set out under Book 4, Title II of the Code of Civil Procedure and do not contain any distinction based on the nature of the parties involved in the proceedings.

However, the growing importance of private-public arbitration influenced the reform of the French arbitration law in 2011 (codified in the Code of Civil Procedure), particularly with respect to confidentiality matters (1). In addition, relying on the special nature of private-public arbitration, disputing parties sometimes seek to exclude evidence in these types of proceedings (2).

1. Confidentiality Matters

French arbitration law sets out two distinct procedural regimes for domestic and international arbitration. Although these procedural regimes are close in substance, they differ with respect to specific procedural issues. One important difference was introduced by Decree No 2011-48 of 13 January 2011, which created an overarching confidentiality duty in domestic arbitration (but not in international arbitration), as reflected under Article 1464(4) of the Code of Civil Procedure: 'Subject to legal obligations and unless the parties decide otherwise, the arbitral procedure is subject to the principle of confidentiality.'

[64] ibid. On this case, see the comments from Henri Batiffol, 'Arbitration Clauses Concluded between French Government-Owned Enterprises and Foreign Private Parties' (1968) 7 Col J Transnat'l L 32.

When distinguishing between domestic and international arbitration, the drafters were keen to accommodate the rise of private-public arbitration in international proceedings: in their eyes, the growing involvement of public entities in international arbitration and the need to preserve transparency in private-public arbitration justified the lack of confidentiality obligation in these proceedings.[65]

2. Evidentiary Matters

Another subject where the public/private divide bears significance relates to evidentiary matters. Parties sometimes rely on the 'public' character of their disputes in order to seek the exclusion of evidence from the arbitration. It should be noted, however, that arbitral tribunals and French courts have been reluctant to follow this course, thereby refusing to distinguish between private and public arbitration when it comes to evidentiary matters.

One relevant example is the arbitration brought by the Republic of China Navy (ROCN) against Thales SA (formerly Thomson-CSF, a state-owned corporation) in the so-called '*Frigates* case'. In this arbitration case, the ROCN claimed damages corresponding to commission payments made by Thomson-CSF in connection with a military procurement contract for the sale of frigates to Taiwan in the early 1990s.[66] In the course of the arbitration, the French party (Thales SA) raised the argument that the classified character of the evidence rendered the dispute non-arbitrable (as the rules on military classification are mandatory under French law) and justified the exclusion of this evidence from the records.

The arbitral tribunal dismissed Thales' arguments in two awards that were upheld by the Paris Court of Appeals.[67] Although the French party—a formerly state-owned company—relied on public policy rules (military classification) to obtain the dismissal of the case, the arbitrators and French courts rejected these arguments and treated this case as a 'regular' commercial case. The case led to the condemnation of Thales SA to pay damages amounting to USD 875 million, two-thirds of which were paid by the French state.[68] This case illustrates some of the procedural questions raised by the involvement of French public entities in arbitration proceedings.

IV. The Return of the Repressed: The Creeping Involvement of Administrative Courts in the Annulment and Enforcement of Private-Public Awards

The growing involvement of public entities in arbitration cases has prompted debates concerning the potential effects and limitations of private-public arbitration (A). In the context of these debates, administrative courts have asserted jurisdiction over the

[65] Emmanuel Gaillard and Pierre de Lapasse, 'Commentaire analytique du décret du 13 janvier 2011 portant réforme du droit français de l'arbitrage' (2011) 2 Cah l'arb 263, para 106.

[66] See CA Paris No 09/10252 (11 May 2010); CA Paris No 10/11853 (9 June 2011).

[67] CA Paris No 09/10252 (11 May 2010); CA Paris No 10/11853 (9 June 2011).

[68] Alison Ross, 'The End of the Frigates Affair' (*Global Arbitration Review*, 14 July 2011) <https://globalarbitrationreview.com/article/1030466/the-end-of-the-frigates-affair> accessed 10 January 2025.

annulment and enforcement of a category of private-public awards, thus putting an end to the monopoly of French civil courts over arbitration matters (B).

A. A Growing Debate on the Public-Private Divide in International Arbitration

Private-public arbitration has come to the forefront of French legal news in the past decades, prompting debates as to how to preserve the public interest in these proceedings (1). As part of this discussion, the French government appointed a working group in charge of exploring how the French legal system should accommodate these concerns (2).

1 The Rise of Private-Public Arbitration

Specialists in international arbitration long anticipated the rise of private-public arbitration. For instance, the text of the New York Convention on the Recognition and Enforcement of Foreign Arbitral Awards of 10 June 1958 foresaw the involvement of public entities in international arbitration.[69] Its Article I(1) refers to 'differences between persons, whether physical or legal', which was broadly construed in the course of the treaty negotiations as including public entities.[70] Even more explicitly, the European Convention on International Commercial Arbitration of 21 April 1961 refers at its Article 2(1) to 'legal persons of public law'.[71] Their anticipation turned out to be correct.

For instance, the caseload of ICSID has grown quickly in the 2000s, resulting in the registration of 66 arbitration cases against public entities (states and state instrumentalities) in 2021 alone.[72] In the same period, the International Chamber of Commerce (ICC) saw a significant increase in the involvement of public entities in its arbitration proceedings: between 2012 and 2013, the number of ICC cases involving a public entity rose from seventy-five to eighty-six (out of 767 new cases).[73] For 2017, the ICC reported the registration of 150 cases involving states or state entities, emphasizing that this 'number has grown by 50% in the past five years and has doubled in ten years'.[74]

[69] New York Convention on the Recognition and Enforcement of Foreign Arbitral Awards (signed 10 June 1958, entered into force 7 June 1959) 330 UNTS 38.

[70] See UN ECOSOC, 'Report of the Committee on the Enforcement of International Arbitral Awards' UN Doc E/AC.42/4/Rev.1 (28 March 1955) para 24: 'Article I provides that the Convention would apply to arbitral awards arising out of differences "between persons, whether physical or legal". The Representative of Belgium has proposed that the article should expressly provide that public enterprises and public utilities should be deemed to be legal persons for purposes of this article if their activities were governed by private law. The Committee was of the opinion that such a provision would be superfluous and that a reference in the present report would suffice.' See also UN Conference on International Commercial Arbitration, 'Summary Record of the Seventh Meeting' UN Doc E/CONF.26/SR.7 (12 September 1958) 3.

[71] European Convention on International Commercial Arbitration (signed 21 April 1961, entered into force 7 January 1964) 484 UNTS 349.

[72] See ICSID Case Database at <https://icsid.worldbank.org/cases/case-database> accessed 10 January 2025.

[73] See 'ICC 2013 Statistical Report' (2014) 25/1 ICC International Court of Arbitration Bulletin 5.

[74] See 'ICC 2017 Statistical Report' (2018) 2 ICC International Court of Arbitration Bulletin 55.

Even more significant for fuelling the debates on private-public arbitration in France is the dispute between a high-profile businessman and former politician, Bernard Tapie, and the Consortium de Réalisation, a public entity in charge of liquidating the assets of a state-owned bank (Crédit Lyonnais) on the verge of bankruptcy in 1993.[75] These assets included an 80 per cent participation in Adidas, the German sport manufacturer, which Crédit Lyonnais had bought from Bernard Tapie in 1992 and sold shortly thereafter. Tapie argued that he had been defrauded by Crédit Lyonnais in the sale of Adidas. After years of litigation before French courts, the parties agreed to solve their dispute through arbitration. A three-member arbitral tribunal decided in 2008 that the Consortium de Réalisation had breached its duty of loyalty towards Tapie and condemned it to the payment of damages in the amount of 285 million euros (plus interest).

Shortly after payment of these damages, several allegations of arbitral misconduct surfaced, particularly with respect to the arbitrator appointed by Tapie (Mr Pierre Estoup). These allegations prompted civil and criminal proceedings that led, inter alia, to the revision of the 2008 arbitral award.[76] In February 2015, the Paris Court of Appeals declared admissible the request for the revision of the award rendered in 2008, on the basis that Mr Estoup had breached his duty of impartiality by 'deliberately and systematically' relaying the position of his party within the arbitral tribunal and had fraudulently influenced its final decision.[77] The Cour de cassation confirmed the judgment of the Paris Court of Appeals in June 2016[78] and the Paris Court of Appeals subsequently 'revised' the arbitral award by overturning the case on the merits.[79]

The *Tapie* case has deeply undermined the credibility of arbitration as a mode of dispute settlement in the eyes of the French public, particularly when a state entity is involved in the proceedings. Although debates concerning private-public arbitration have a wider scope than the *Tapie* case, this case undoubtedly fed the belief that private-public disputes should be treated with caution, particularly when the public interest is at stake.

2 The Growing Influence of French Public Law over International Arbitration

The numerous exceptions to the prohibition against private-public arbitration, coupled with the many cases that arose in this field, ran against a traditional pillar of French law: the exclusive jurisdiction of civil courts (as opposed to administrative courts) over private law matters, which include the annulment and enforcement of arbitral awards. The jurisdiction of civil courts over arbitration cases seemed justified as long as these cases did not involve state entities and/or public interests. As private-public arbitration grew in importance, however, debates concerning the jurisdiction

[75] See Arbitral Award rendered on 7 July 2008 in the dispute between CDR Créances, Consortium de Réalisation and Selafa MJA, Me Didier Courtoux, Mr Bernard Tapie, Ms Bernard Tapie.

[76] The revision is an 'extraordinary' *de novo* review of a case that has initially been decided through arbitration (or litigation), when evidence of fraud surfaces after the award has been rendered (art 595 of the Code of Civil Procedure).

[77] CA Paris No 13/13278 (17 February 2015).

[78] Cass Civ 1, Nos 15/13755, 15/13904, and 15/14145 (30 June 2016) ECLI:FR:CCASS:2016:C100932.

[79] See 'Tapie: The End of the End of the Affair?' (*Global Arbitration Review*, 20 May 2017) <https://globalarbitrationreview.com/article/1141869/tapie-the-end-of-the-end-of-the-affair> accessed 10 January 2025.

of these courts arose. These debates have directly challenged the monopoly held by civil courts over arbitration cases, and introduced the idea that administrative courts should exercise at least some jurisdiction when these cases involve public entities or public matters.

Pre-existing signs of this evolution already existed for quite some time. For instance, in the case of *Myrtoon Steamship* (1958), the Tribunal des Conflits decided that civil courts have jurisdiction where a charter party involves 'for the ship-owner, no participation to the implementation of a public service and no provision outside the scope of ordinary law *[stipulation exorbitante du droit commun]*'.[80] The Tribunal des Conflits concluded that it 'belongs only to the civil authority to appreciate the validity of an arbitration clause that is contained under [the charter party]'.[81] One could surmise, *a contrario*, that civil courts lack jurisdiction when an entity, whether public or private, participates in the implementation of a public service or when the underlying contract contains a provision exceeding the scope of 'ordinary' law.

Long after the *Myrtoon Steamship* case, the French Ministry of Justice mandated the Conseil d'Etat to gather a 'working group' in order to explore the 'hypothesis and conditions under which moral persons of public law could have recourse to arbitration for the settlement of their disputes, except for those related to the disputes arising from unilateral administrative acts'.[82] The task of this working group was to analyse and simplify the numerous exceptions made to the prohibition contained under Article 2060 of the Civil Code. The working group, headed by Daniel Labetoulle,[83] issued its final report in March 2007 (the so-called 'Labetoulle Report') and recommended to end the prohibition for public entities to enter into arbitration agreements.[84] The working group advised that only claims of a contractual nature could be submitted to arbitration,[85] and that administrative law should apply to private-public arbitration (except for disputes involving EPICs).[86] In addition, according to the working group, administrative courts should gain jurisdiction over claims related to private-public arbitration proceedings (for instance, the annulment and enforcement of awards rendered in these proceedings).[87] The working group also argued that hearings and arbitral awards should be made public, while the instruction and deliberations of arbitral tribunals remain confidential.[88]

The Labetoulle Report prompted academic debates[89] and also raised significant interest among administrative judges. For instance, at a colloquium held in 2009, the vice president of the Conseil d'Etat (the de facto head of administrative courts)

[80] TC *Société Myrtoon Steamship* (19 May 1958).
[81] ibid.
[82] Daniel Labetoulle, 'Rapport du Groupe de travail sur l'arbitrage' (13 March 2007) 1 <https://www.justice.gouv.fr/arbitrage-litiges-interessants-personnes-publiques> accessed 10 January 2025.
[83] Daniel Labetoulle is a Senior Member of the Conseil d'Etat. He was the rapporteur of the Conseil d'Etat in CE (Avis) No 339710 (6 March 1986).
[84] Labetoulle (n 82) para 1.2.1.
[85] ibid paras 1.2.2 and 1.3.
[86] ibid para. 2.1.
[87] ibid.
[88] ibid paras. 3.3.1–3.3.4.
[89] See, for instance, Sophie Lemaire, 'La libéralisation de l'arbitrage international en droit administratif – Approche critique du projet de réforme du 13 mars 2007' (2007) 3 Rev l'arb 403.

expressed his wish that administrative courts expand their jurisdiction over the regulation of private-public arbitration in order to safeguard 'fundamental principles' of public law, such as equality, legal certainty, and transparency.[90] Most importantly, the Labetoulle Report planted the seeds of a court decision that gave jurisdiction to administrative courts over the annulment and enforcement of private-public awards.

B. The Jurisdiction of French Administrative Courts over Private-Public Arbitration

In the case of *Inserm v Fondation Letten F Saugstad* (2010), the Tribunal des Conflits granted jurisdiction to administrative courts over the annulment of awards rendered in private-public arbitration, thus putting an end to the exclusive jurisdiction of civil courts over these matters (1). This solution was extended to the enforcement of the same type of awards in the case of *Syndicat mixte des Aéroports de Charente v Ryanair* (2013) (2).

1 The Jurisdiction of Administrative Courts over the Annulment of Awards: The *Inserm v Fondation Letten F Saugstad* Case

Inserm v Fondation Letten F Saugstad is arguably the most important case of the past few decades in French arbitration law. In this case, a dispute arose out of the performance of a contract between the Letten Saugstad Foundation, based in Norway, and INSERM, the French biomedical and public health institution, in connection with the construction of a research institute in Marseille specializing in neuroscience. INSERM initiated proceedings before the First Instance Court in Paris (Tribunal de grande instance), which condemned the Letten Saugstad Foundation to the payment of damages. The Paris Court of Appeal subsequently annulled the judgment of the First Instance Court, based on an arbitration clause contained in the contract. Following the initiation of arbitral proceedings, a sole arbitrator seated in Paris rejected the claims from INSERM and found in favour of the Letten Saugstad Foundation. INSERM subsequently sought the annulment of the arbitral award, concurrently before the Paris Court of Appeal and the Marseille Court of Administrative Appeal, claiming that the arbitration agreement was invalid based on the prohibition contained under Article 2060(1) of the French Civil Code.

Because civil and administrative courts deemed themselves equally competent, the Tribunal des Conflits was asked to decide upon this 'conflict of jurisdiction'. General Advocate Guyomar defended a split of jurisdiction between the civil and administrative courts over the annulment of arbitral awards.[91] In particular, the General Advocate argued that arbitrators should apply mandatory rules of French public law (such as general principles applicable to public procurements arising out of public supply, contracts for the delegation of public service and private-public partnerships,

[90] See Jean-Marc Sauvé, 'L'arbitrage et les personnes morales de droit public' (30 September 2009) <https://www.conseil-etat.fr/publications-colloques/discours-et-interventions/l-arbitrage-et-les-personnes-morales-de-droit-public> accessed 10 January 2025.

[91] 'Conclusions du Commissaire du Gouvernement M. Matthias Guyomar' (2010) 3 Rev l'arb 275.

and mandatory substantive rules pertaining to the public domain or the enforcement of the public service).[92] The Tribunal des Conflits followed the reasoning of the General Advocate, deciding that the jurisdiction over the annulment of awards should be distributed among civil and administrative courts. The relevant extract of the Tribunal's decision is reproduced below:

> the recourse initiated against an arbitral award rendered in France, on the basis of an arbitration agreement, in a dispute arising from the enforcement or the breach of a contract concluded between a moral person of French public law and a person of foreign law, implemented on the French territory, involving the interests of international trade, irrespective of whether it is administrative according to the criteria of French domestic law, is brought before the [civil] Court of Appeals in the territory of which the award was rendered, in accordance with Article 1505 of the Code of Civil Procedure, this recourse bringing no harm to the principle of the separation of administrative and civil authorities; that it goes otherwise, however, when the recourse, brought against an award rendered in the same conditions, necessitates a control of the compliance of the award with mandatory rules of French public law regarding the occupation of the public domain or to those governing public procurements and applicable to public supply, partnership contracts and contracts for the delegation of public service; that because those contracts fall under a mandatory administrative regime, the recourse against an arbitral award rendered in a dispute arising from the enforcement or breach of such a contract, falls under the jurisdiction of the administrative judge.[93]

The Tribunal des Conflits thus decided to maintain the jurisdiction of civil courts over the annulment of most arbitral awards, including awards rendered in private-public arbitration when they involve 'the interests of international trade'. As an exception, however, the Tribunal decided to grant jurisdiction to administrative courts over the annulment of international awards rendered in private-public arbitration when the underlying contract is implemented on the French territory *and* when the annulment proceedings involve 'mandatory rules of French public law regarding the occupation of the public domain or to those governing public procurements and applicable to public supply, partnership contracts and contracts for the delegation of public service'.

It should be noted that the jurisdiction of administrative courts over the annulment of awards does not apply—as made clear by the above-cited reasoning of the Tribunal des Conflits—when the arbitral proceedings involve a foreign public entity (as was the case in annulment proceedings brought by the Greek state before the Paris Court of Appeals in 2015).[94]

[92] ibid 287–88.
[93] TC No C3754 (17 May 2010).
[94] CA Paris No 14/07043 (14 April 2015). In that case, the Paris Court of Appeals refused to consider whether the foreign public law applicable to the dispute (Greek law) barred the arbitrators from deeming the contractual agreement null and void.

Arbitration practitioners reacted very strongly against the decision of the Tribunal des Conflits. For instance, Emmanuel Gaillard claimed that this decision 'torpedo[ed] French arbitration law'.[95] In addition, the French Committee on Arbitration (Comité français de l'arbitrage) harshly criticized the decision in a public statement.[96] In substance, arbitration specialists blamed the decision for confusing the law, and feared that parties might become reluctant to choose Paris as a place of arbitration.

Following this outcry within the arbitral community, the Ministry of Finance and the Ministry of Justice jointly appointed a committee headed by Michel Prada,[97] in order to explore solutions to the issues raised by private-public arbitration in the wake of the *Inserm v Fondation Letten F Saugstad* decision.[98] The Prada Report made three main recommendations with respect to private-public arbitration: codifying the *Galakis* decision, which allowed public entities to enter into arbitration agreements when they are involved in international trade, in Article 2060 of the Civil Code; prohibiting the breach of certain mandatory rules of French public law in international arbitration; and giving exclusive jurisdiction to the civil courts over disputes arising in international arbitration (whether public or private).[99]

Notwithstanding these recommendations, the Tribunal des Conflits subsequently confirmed this split of jurisdiction,[100] which it extended to the enforcement of arbitral awards in the case of *Syndicat mixte des Aéroports de Charente v Ryanair*, discussed below.

2 The Jurisdiction of Administrative Courts over the Enforcement of Awards: The *Ryanair* case

The case of *Syndicat mixte des Aéroports de Charente (SMAC) v Ryanair* concerns a dispute over the performance of two contractual agreements concluded between a French public entity (SMAC) and a low-cost airline (Ryanair) for the operation of a regular line between London and Angoulême. Both agreements contained an arbitration clause.

After SMAC initiated proceedings before an administrative court (Tribunal administratif de Nantes), Ryanair initiated arbitral proceedings before a sole arbitrator seated in London, who rendered an award on 22 July 2011 retaining his jurisdiction over the case (the Award on Jurisdiction) and another award on 18 June 2012 dismissing SMAC's claims against Ryanair (the Final Award). SMAC

[95] Emmanuel Gaillard, 'Le tribunal des conflits torpille le droit français de l'arbitrage' (2010) 21 Semaine juridique 1096.

[96] 'Avis du Comité français de l'arbitrage dans l'affaire INSERM c/ Fondation Letten F. Saugstad' (2010) 2 Rev l'arb 401.

[97] Michel Prada is a member of the Inspection of Finances (Inspection des Finances), a special unit within the French Ministry of Finance that is often said to compete for political influence with the Conseil d'Etat. The government's goal might have been to counterbalance the Conseil d'Etat's influence over the regulation of private-public arbitration.

[98] Michel Prada, 'Rapport sur certains facteurs de renforcement de la compétitivité juridique de la place de Paris' (March 2011) <http://www.textes.justice.gouv.fr/art_pix/1_Rapport_prada_20110413.pdf> accessed 10 January 2025.

[99] ibid 17.

[100] TC No A4043 (11 April 2016).

initiated annulment proceedings against the Final Award before the Conseil d'Etat. In parallel, Ryanair obtained an order for the exequatur of the Award on Jurisdiction from the President of the Court of First Instance of Paris (who has jurisdiction over the exequatur of arbitral awards) on 21 May 2012. SMAC appealed this order before the Paris Court of Appeals. In short, the disputing parties initiated parallel proceedings before administrative and civil courts regarding, respectively, the annulment of the Final Award and the enforcement of the Award on Jurisdiction.

In a decision dated 19 April 2013, the Conseil d'Etat held that French courts lacked jurisdiction to hear a request for the annulment of an award rendered abroad (which is non-controversial).[101] On this sole basis, the Conseil d'Etat could have rejected SMAC's request for the annulment of the final award. However, the Conseil d'Etat also added, by way of *obiter dictum*, that it would have jurisdiction to hear a request for the enforcement of an award rendered in a case involving 'mandatory rules of French public law', thus referring directly to the decision of the Tribunal des Conflits in *INSERM v Fondation Letten F Saugstad* and extending its reasoning to enforcement cases. In other words, according to the Conseil d'Etat, administrative courts have jurisdiction over the enforcement of arbitral awards (which had been under the exclusive jurisdiction of civil courts until then), when these awards fall under the category of proceedings defined in the above-cited extract of *INSERM v Fondation Letten F Saugstad.*

The Paris Court of Appeals referred even more directly to *INSERM v Fondation Letten F Saugstad* in its decision of 20 September 2013. In this decision, the Court reversed the order for the exequatur of the Award on Jurisdiction from the President of the Paris Court of First Instance on two grounds: it first cited the decision of the Tribunal des Conflits in *Inserm v Fondation Letten F Saugstad* and then specified that the split of jurisdiction decided by the Tribunal des Conflits should extend to the enforcement of arbitral awards. The Paris Court of Appeals held that:

> the dismissal of the recognition or exequatur of an award rendered abroad falls under the same substantive conditions as the annulment of an award rendered in France in the field of international arbitration . . . therefore, the rules set out above [citation from the Tribunal des Conflits] apply to international awards, irrespective of the seat of the arbitration.[102]

The Paris Court of Appeals further held that, in the case at hand, the contractual agreements concerned 'a public supply of services in accordance with Article 1 of the Code of Public Supply'. As such, these contractual agreements fell within the exception set out by the Tribunal des Conflits. The Paris Court of Appeals accordingly dismissed its own jurisdiction to hear the case:

> the present Court, which is not entitled to determine the ways by which the tribunals of the administrative order are likely to be seized of a request for the exequatur of an

[101] CE No 352750 (19 April 2013).
[102] CA Paris No 12/11596 (10 September 2013).

> award rendered abroad, shall declare the lack of jurisdiction of the judicial jurisdictions with respect to the case at hand and annul the order [from the President of the Paris Court of First Instance].[103]

In a surprising turn of events, the Cour de cassation subsequently reversed the decision of the Paris Court of Appeals, arguing that the New York Convention of 1958 prohibited the distinction between the enforcement of domestic awards (over which civil courts have plain jurisdiction) and that of international awards (which would be subject to the split of jurisdiction between civil and administrative courts).[104] The Cour de cassation also mentioned the prohibition of the substantive review of arbitral awards under the New York Convention, thus implying that administrative courts were more likely (than civil courts) to review the substance of awards.[105]

Following this controversial decision, the highest civil and administrative courts held contrary views as to which courts have jurisdiction over the enforcement of arbitral awards.[106] This 'conflict of jurisdiction' ended when the Tribunal des Conflits sided with the Conseil d'Etat and the Paris Court of Appeals in 2017 and decided that administrative courts have jurisdiction over the enforcement of awards when these awards fall under the category of proceedings defined in *INSERM v Fondation Letten F Saugstad*.[107] Consequently, administrative courts now have jurisdiction over the annulment *and* the enforcement of arbitral awards falling under this narrow category.

V. Conclusion

The court decisions in *INSERM v Fondation Letten F Saugstad* and *Syndicat mixte des Aéroports de Charente v Ryanair* are the latest developments in a long-standing debate concerning the prohibition of private-public arbitration under French law. Many exceptions to this prohibition were carved out throughout the second half of the twentieth century and, under French law, arbitrators have been progressively allowed to decide private-public disputes.

In an interesting turn of events, administrative courts have progressively showed interest in controlling the ways in which arbitrators decide private-public disputes. Consequently, these courts have gained jurisdiction over the annulment and the enforcement of a limited category of private-public awards. This evolution is not surprising considering the growing importance of private-public arbitration and

[103] CA Paris No 12/11596 (10 September 2013).
[104] Cass civ (1) No 13-25846 (8 July 2015) Bull Civ 1 2016, No 834.
[105] ibid.
[106] See Edern Coënt and Florian Grisel, 'When Two Are Too Many? Jurisdictional Skirmishes over the Enforcement of Arbitral Awards in France' (2016) 3 Paris J Int Arbitr 661.
[107] TC No C4075 (24 April 2017).

the complex challenges it raises in terms of legitimacy and public interest. However, this evolution should not undermine the long-standing favour that French law has given, for complex historical reasons, to the resolution of disputes through arbitration. For this reason, the ways in which administrative courts exercise their new area of competence will be particularly scrutinized in the coming years.

Select Materials

Bibliography

Batiffol, Henri, 'Arbitration Clauses Concluded between French Government-Owned Enterprises and Foreign Private Parties' (1968) 7 Colum J Transnat'l L 32

Coënt, Edern and Florian Grisel, 'When Two Are Too Many? Jurisdictional Skirmishes over the Enforcement of Arbitral Awards in France' (2016) 3 Paris J Int Arbitr 661

Damaska, Mirjan R, *The Faces of Justice and State Authority – A Comparative Approach to the Legal Process* (Yale University Press 1986)

David, René, *Le droit français – Tome I : Les données fondamentales du droit français* (LGDJ 1960)

Furet, François, *The French Revolution 1770–1814* (Antonia Nevill tr, Blackwell 1988)

Jallamion, Carine, 'Arbitrage et pouvoir politique en France du XVIIe au XIXe siècle'' (2005) 1 Rev l'arb 3

de Loynes de Fumichon, Bruno, 'La passion de la Révolution française pour l'arbitrage' (2014) 1 Rev l'arb 3

Gaillard, Emmanuel and Pierre de Lapasse, 'Commentaire analytique du décret du 13 janvier 2011 portant réforme du droit français de l'arbitrage' (2011) 2 Cah l'arb 263

Laferrière, Edouard, *Traité de la juridiction administrative et des recours contentieux,* (Berger-Levrault et Cie 1896) vol 2

Lemaire, Sophie, 'La libéralisation de l'arbitrage international en droit administratif – Approche critique du projet de réforme du 13 mars 2007' (2007) 3 Rev de l'arb 403

Locré, Jean-Guillaume, *Esprit du Code de procédure civile, ou Conférence du Code de procédure avec les discussions du Conseil, les observations du Tribunat, les exposés des motifs, les discours des orateurs du Tribunat* (P Didot l'Aîné 1816) vol 4

Merryman, John M and Rogelio Perez-Perdomo, *The Civil Law Tradition – An Introduction to the Legal Systems of Europe and Latin America* (3rd ed, Stanford University Press 2007)

Tunc, André, 'The Grand Outlines of the Code' in Bernard Schwartz (ed), *The Code Napoleon and the Common Law World* (New York University Press 1956)

Legal Instruments

Statute of 16/24 August 1790
Decree of 6/7 September 1790
Constitution of 3 September 1791

Constitution of 24 June 1793
Decree of 2 October 1793
Constitution of 22 August 1795
Treaty between the United Kingdom of Great Britain and Northern Ireland and the French Republic concerning the Construction and Operation by Private Concessionaires of a Channel Fixed Link with Exchanges of Notes (12 February 1986)
Loi No 86-972, 19 August 1986
Décret No 2002-56, 8 January 2002
Ordonnance No 2004-559, 17 June 2004
Décret No. 2008-879, 1 September 2008 publishing the Agreement between the Government of the French Republic and the Government of the United Arab Emirates relating to the Universal Museum in Abu Dhabi, signed in Abu Dhabi on 6 March 2007
Civil Code: Art. 2059, 2060

Cases

Conseil constitutionnel

Decision No. 2004-506 DC of 2 December 2004

Conseil d'Etat

19 February 1825, *Héritiers Guérard v. le Trésor*
23 December 1887, *Evèque de Moulin*
6 March 1986 (*Avis*)
19 April 2013, *Syndicat mixte des Aéroports de Charente (SMAC) v. Ryanair*

Cour de cassation

2 May 1966, *Galakis*
8 July 2015, *Syndicat mixte des Aéroports de Charente (SMAC) v. Ryanair*

Tribunal des Conflits

19 May 1958, *Société Myrtoon Steamship*
17 May 2010, *Inserm v. Fondation Letten F. Saugstad*
11 April 2016, No. A4043
24 April 2017, *Syndicat mixte des Aéroports de Charente (SMAC) v. Ryanair*

Reports

'Avis du Comité français de l'arbitrage dans l'affaire INSERM c/ Fondation Letten F. Saugstad' (2010) 2 Rev l'Arb 401

'Conclusions du Commissaire du Gouvernement M. Mattias Guyomar' (2010) 3 Rev l'arb 275
Labetoulle, Daniel, 'Rapport du Groupe de travail sur l'arbitrage' (13 March 2007)
Prada, Michel, 'Rapport sur certains facteurs de renforcement de la compétitivité juridique de la place de Paris' (March 2011)

4

Eroding the Rule of Law through Private-Public Arbitration?

Constitutionalization of Private-Public Arbitration in the German Legal System

Stephan W. Schill and Nadine Berger

Public law is not only an instrument for managing economic, technical, and social risks through regulation. Public law itself can pose a risk to cooperation between private and public actors, in particular when it requires change that economic actors have difficulties in coping with, imposes unreasonable, disproportionate, and unpredictable costs on economic actors, or goes contrary to protected rights and interests. Usually, disputes about the resulting 'political risk', such as the legality of government action, the limits of regulatory powers, and possible entitlements to compensation, are settled before domestic courts. They ensure compliance with the applicable administrative and constitutional law, as well as contractual undertakings made under private-public contracts.

More recently, however, arbitration has increasingly been used to settle private-public disputes about political risk. Germany is no exception in this respect, with mounting instances of private-public arbitrations, in particular in high-stakes disputes both under private-public contracts and international investment agreements (IIAs). While Germany is party to many IIAs and has, for a long time already, had a permissive statutory framework for contract-based private-public arbitrations, private-public arbitration has remained an under-studied subject in German legal scholarship. This is gradually changing, however, as criticism of private-public arbitration, the loss of state-centred dispute settlement it comes with, and the risks this development poses for an erosion of the rule of law in private-public relations, are mounting. Notably, criticism of private-public arbitration is formulated in terms of the limits Germany's Constitution, the Grundgesetz (GG), sets for private-public arbitration, and has resulted in cases before Germany's Federal Constitutional Court, the Bundesverfassungsgericht. As with other fields of law in Germany, all of this leads the way towards constitutionalizing private-public arbitration, that is, conceptualizing the field, its foundations, possibilities, and limits from the perspective of constitutional law rather than political or economic expediency.

The present chapter zooms in on the following points. First, it discusses the recent surge in private-public arbitration in Germany (section I). Second, the chapter discusses Germany's (generally permissive) statutory framework and treaty network

Stephan W. Schill and Nadine Berger, *Eroding the Rule of Law through Private-Public Arbitration?* In: *The Comparative Constitutional Foundations of Private-Public Arbitration*. Edited by: Stephan W. Schill, Oxford University Press. © Stephan W. Schill 2025. DOI: 10.1093/9780191987960.003.0004

governing private-public arbitration and their effect on limiting control by domestic courts over private-public disputes (section II). Third, the chapter focuses on how the German Constitution enables, but also limits, the participation of German public entities in (domestic and international) private-public arbitration, suggesting that private-public arbitration is in the process of constitutionalization in the shadow of litigation before the German Federal Constitutional Court (section III). Section IV concludes the chapter.

I. Private-Public Arbitration in Practice

Getting an empirically accurate picture of the actual use of arbitration for settling disputes involving German public actors faces considerable hurdles given the sparsity of publicly available information; confidentiality, after all, has been a revered principle of arbitration.[1] It is therefore no surprise that private-public arbitration has attracted relatively little attention in German legal scholarship.[2] The lack of academic interest is amplified by the fact that private-public arbitration falls into a disciplinary gap, as both public law and private law scholars and practitioners tend to see it as alien to the core of their respective fields, and generally focus on court-administered legal orders.

Yet, agreements to arbitrate involving German public actors are not as infrequent as one might assume from the scant scholarly treatment. They exist across all levels of German law, including for disputes under constitutional and administrative law, involving public actors only as well as private-public disputes.[3] For example, the 1950 Treaty between the German States of Bavaria, Württemberg-Baden, and Hessen concerning the Water Police on the Rivers Rhine, Main, and Neckar relegated disputes on the validity of that treaty, and hence a question of constitutional law, to an arbitral tribunal.[4] The Treaty on the Northern German Broadcasting Station concluded between several German States, in turn, provides for arbitration to settle disputes under the treaty that are non-constitutional in nature.[5] Agreements to arbitrate public law disputes also exist in the relations between Germany and the Christian churches (which in Germany are organized under public law).[6] Furthermore, arbitration is

[1] For comprehensive background, see Gary B Born, *International Commercial Arbitration* (3rd edn, Kluwer 2021) vol 2, 3001 ff (with further references on literature).

[2] In the last 30 years, only a handful of monographs have addressed arbitrations involving public actors. See Michel Schenk, *Schiedsfreiheit und staatliche Schutzpflichten* (Springer 2019) 189 ff; René Rosenau, *Die öffentliche Hand als Partei in verwaltungs- und zivilrechtlichen Schiedsverfahren* (Peter Lang 2018); Kaspar Henrik Möller, *Echte Schiedsgerichtsbarkeit im Verwaltungsrecht. Eine Studie zu Rechtsrahmen und Kontrolle nichtstaatlicher Streitentscheidung im Verwaltungsrecht* (Duncker & Humblot 2014); Christoph A Stumpf, *Alternative Streitbeilegung im Verwaltungsrecht* (Mohr Siebeck 2006). Older monographs include Richard Woltereck, 'Die Erledigung verwaltungsrechtlicher Streitigkeiten durch Schiedsgerichte' (doctoral thesis, University of Hamburg 1965); Helmut Weidemann, 'Schiedsgerichtsbarkeit in verwaltungsrechtlichen Streitsachen' (doctoral thesis, University of Marburg 1968); Christa Loos, 'Die Schiedsgerichtsbarkeit in der Verwaltungsgerichtsbarkeit' (doctoral thesis, University of Kiel 1984).

[3] See in detail Weidemann (n 2) 13 ff, 58 ff.

[4] ibid 15–16.

[5] ibid 15. For an example of a related arbitration, see Partial Award (16 August 1982), reported in (1984) 16 Entscheidungen des Oberverwaltungsgerichts Berlin 256.

[6] Weidemann (n 2) 17 ff.

a possible method of settling disputes in several specialized areas of public law, including under the law governing the status of civil servants; social security law; the law governing relations between public health insurances and doctors; the law concerning administrative aspects of regulating the economy; the law relating to public traffic; water law and fisheries; and the law governing public insurances.[7]

These examples notwithstanding, it is only the more recent surge in arbitration proceedings in high-stakes private-public disputes that has brought arbitration involving public bodies into the limelight. In the subsections below, we canvas that practice, which regularly addresses the core question of public law that traditionally comes before Germany's domestic courts—namely how public authority should be exercised—in respect of both contract-based (A) and IIA-based arbitrations (B). Moreover, attention to private-public arbitration is rising also in respect of a nascent backlash against treaty-based arbitrations which manifests itself in the inclusion of contractual waivers of foreign investor recourse to, and the withdrawal from treaties providing for, private-public arbitration (C).

A. Contract-Based Private-Public Arbitrations

Focusing only on the level of central government,[8] the Federal Republic of Germany has recently been involved in a number of high-stakes contract-based private-public arbitrations, both as claimant and respondent.[9] Two sets of arbitrations concerning the introduction of toll systems on German highways exemplify some of the issues involved.

The first set of contract-based arbitrations involved the delayed introduction of a highway toll system for trucks in the early 2000s. In 2004, Germany initiated, on the basis of an arbitration clause in a concession agreement, an arbitration against the operating consortium, claiming losses of more than 5 billion euros due to the system's late start.[10] The operators, in turn, brought a counterclaim alleging breach

[7] ibid 58 ff.

[8] Private–public arbitration may also involve public entities at the state or local level. For an example, see German Federal Court of Justice, Case No XII ZR 165/06, Judgment (29 October 2008) (2009) 22(8) NVwZ-Rechtsprechungsreport 317 (involving an arbitration agreement in a lease agreement between a municipality and a private party).

[9] Contract-based private-public arbitrations reflect the increasing use of contracts in private-public co-operation, including through privatizations, public-private partnerships, and similar arrangements. While no statistical data is available, anecdotal evidence suggests that the conclusion of arbitration agreements in private-public contracts in Germany is substantial. See eg the privatization agreement concerning Berlin's water supply services (Konsortialvertrag (18 June 1999) s 44.2 and Annex 44.2 <www.berlin.de/sen/finanzen/vermoegen/downloads/artikel.7166.php> accessed 22 January 2025). See also Johanna Wolff, 'Grenze der Heimlichkeit – Nicht-öffentliche Schiedsverfahren mit Beteiligung der öffentlichen Hand am Maßstab des Verfassungsrechts' (2012) 31 Neue Zeitschrift für Verwaltungsrecht 205, 205–06 (sharing the view that arbitration clauses are frequently included in agreements involving German public entities). For a comparative perspective, see Arnaldo Wald and Jean Kalicki, 'The Settlement of Disputes between the Public Administration and Private Companies by Arbitration under Brazilian Law' (2009) 26 J Int'l Arb 557, 559 ff (discussing the situation in Argentina, Belgium, Colombia, the Dominican Republic, France, Iran, Lebanon, Peru, Spain, the United States, and Venezuela).

[10] *Bundesrepublik Deutschland v Daimler Financial Services AG, Deutsche Telekom AG and Toll Collect GbR* (not public).

of contract by Germany with regard to the agreed remuneration. The strict confidentiality of both the proceedings and the underlying concession agreement, even for Members of Parliament, attracted countrywide criticism.[11] In 2018, the parties reached a settlement providing for the payment of 3.2 billion euros in damages to the German state.[12] It was only then—fourteen years after the proceedings had started—that the government released some further information, for example on the costs of the proceedings.[13]

The second set of contract-based arbitrations followed a similar pattern, this time concerning the failed introduction of a highway toll system for passenger vehicles that was to be implemented by a German–Austrian consortium. After the Court of Justice of the European Union (CJEU) had declared that system to be incompatible with EU law,[14] Germany terminated the agreements with the consortium. Shortly thereafter, the consortium instituted arbitration proceedings under the agreements, claiming damages of 560 million euros; Germany, in turn, counterclaimed for breach of contract by the consortium.[15] In March 2022, the arbitral tribunal reportedly found Germany liable for damages, without yet determining the amount due.[16] In July 2023, the parties reportedly settled, with Germany agreeing to pay 243 million euros to the consortium.[17] The dispute again attracted significant political debate, not least in respect of the budgetary implications of the proceedings.[18]

Both proceedings highlight the increased demand for transparency and government accountability in arbitration proceedings involving public actors with significant budgetary consequences. The proceedings also illustrate how the widespread use of confidentiality in contract-based private-public arbitrations is at odds with that demand.[19]

B. Treaty-Based Private-Public Arbitrations

Arbitrations against Germany based on one of the many IIAs to which Germany is party are also on the rise. After a first small-scale arbitration under the Germany–India

[11] See Frank Schorkopf, 'Transparenz im „Toll-Haus“ – Anmerkungen zur Vertraulichkeit des Maut-Konzessionsvertrages aus staatsrechtlicher Perspektive' (2003) 22 Neue Zeitschrift für Verwaltungsrecht 1471.

[12] See Lacey Yong, 'German Dispute No Longer Takes Its Toll' (*Global Arbitration Review*, 17 May 2018).

[13] See *Bundestagsdrucksache* (Parliament Document) 19/2488 (31 May 2018) (providing, inter alia, that the overall procedural costs incurred by Germany up until 2018 amounted to 253.6 million euros (ibid 5)). Parliamentary documents, including *Bundestagsdrucksachen*, are available through the Documentation and Information System for Parliamentary Material at <https://dip.bundestag.de> accessed 22 January 2025 (in German).

[14] Case C-591/17 *Austria v Germany* (Judgment, 18 June 2019) ECLI:EU:C:2019:504.

[15] Lisa Bohmer, 'Failed Vehicle Toll Project Leads to Contract-Based Arbitration Proceedings Against Germany' (*IAReporter*, 26 July 2020).

[16] Lisa Bohmer, 'Tribunal Holds Germany Liable for Unilateral Termination of Passenger Vehicle Toll Agreement; Arbitration Proceeds to Quantum Phase' (*IAReporter*, 29 March 2022).

[17] Lisa Bohmer, 'Germany Agrees to Pay 243 Million EUR for Settlement of Passenger-Vehicle Toll Arbitration' (*IAReporter*, 6 July 2023).

[18] See *Bundestagsdrucksachen* (Parliament Documents) 19/24949 (7 December 2020) and 19/27609 (17 March 2021).

[19] See further Wolff (n 9) 206–09.

Bilateral Investment Treaty (BIT), governed by the United Nations Commission on International Trade Law (UNCITRAL) Arbitration Rules, and about which little is publicly known,[20] Germany has been hit with a number of arbitrations brought by foreign investors in the energy sector.

The first large-scale arbitration, initiated in 2009, concerned a claim for damages in the amount of 1.4 billion euros brought by the Swedish energy company Vattenfall against Germany for breach of the Energy Charter Treaty (ECT)[21] before the International Centre for Settlement of Investment Disputes (ICSID).[22] The dispute resulted from the imposition of environmental conditions for a coal-fired power plant in the City of Hamburg that allegedly contravened representations made by the then mayor of Hamburg as the investor was granted a preliminary permission to start construction. Local elections subsequently brought about a change in government, which, in turn, imposed stricter environmental conditions when issuing a final operating licence. Vattenfall claimed that these conditions thwarted the economic viability of the project and breached the standards of protection under the ECT. In parallel, Vattenfall initiated proceedings before domestic administrative courts, challenging the legality of the environmental conditions under German administrative law. Although the dispute was ultimately settled, it highlights how issues that domestically are of an administrative law nature, and even elicit proceedings before administrative courts, are being brought in private-public arbitrations, where they may find a solution that decidedly differs from that of domestic law. After all, a German court applying German administrative law would likely have found that oral promises made before a final operating licence was issued cannot bind the City, and therefore do not give rise to claims for compensation.

A second ICSID arbitration, also brought by Vattenfall, concerned the assessment of the different aspects of Germany's 2011 nuclear power phase-out under the ECT.[23] Apart from raising issues because of the long-time confidential nature of the arbitration proceedings,[24] the dispute provided an example of issues of a constitutional law nature being brought to private-public arbitration, considering that it concerned, from a domestic perspective, limits to legislative action. In addition, the dispute provided another example of the relations of parallel proceedings before arbitral tribunals and domestic courts: Vattenfall had not only brought an ECT claim before ICSID, but also challenged the nuclear power phase-out before the German Federal Constitutional Court. The Constitutional Court ultimately found the nuclear power phase-out to be constitutional, but required compensation which was to

[20] *Sancheti v Germany*, UNCITRAL, Award (6 June 2001) (terminating the proceedings because claimant failed to pay advances on costs).

[21] Energy Charter Treaty (adopted 17 December 1994, entered into force 16 April 1998) 2080 UNTS 95 (ECT).

[22] *Vattenfall AB, Vattenfall Europe AG, Vattenfall Europe Generation AG & Co KG v Federal Republic of Germany*, ICSID Case No ARB/09/6, Award (11 March 2011).

[23] *Vattenfall AB and others v Federal Republic of Germany*, ICSID Case No ARB/12/12 (discontinued 9 November 2021 following settlement).

[24] This included information on the amount of compensation claimed (4.38 billion euros, excluding interest), and on Germany's legal costs: see *Bundestagsdrucksache* (Parliament Document) 19/22571 (16 September 2020). The disputing parties later agreed to open the hearings on jurisdiction, liability, and quantum to the public.

be determined by the legislator.[25] After a further constitutional challenge regarding the amount of compensation set by parliament,[26] the parties settled their claims, including those in the ICSID proceedings, as part of an agreement between the German government and the country's major energy companies, in which the latter undertook to withdraw all pending legal action and waived any claims or legal remedies against the agreed-upon compensation scheme.[27] Accordingly, the ICSID proceeding was discontinued in late 2021 before the tribunal could issue an award.

By the end of 2023, Germany faced four further ECT claims before ICSID. Two of these concern offshore wind energy projects in the North Sea and revolve around legislative changes in the offshore renewable energy sector.[28] Here, too, legislative changes not only sparked proceedings before ICSID, but also before German courts. Thus, prior to lodging its investment claim, the claimant in one of the proceedings, Austrian investor Strabag, through one of its German holdings, had already successfully challenged parts of the new legislation before the German Federal Constitutional Court.[29] This is yet another illustration that matters of constitutional relevance are being brought before arbitral tribunals, and of the close relationship between domestic court proceedings and treaty-based arbitration. Legislative measures are also at the origin of the two other disputes pending under the ECT before ICSID, one relating to the consequences of Germany's coal phase-out,[30] and the other to the implementation of an EU regulation that resulted in the levy of a windfall tax on profits

[25] German Federal Constitutional Court, Case No 1 BvR 2821/11, Judgment (6 December 2016) BVerfGE 143, 246. See also on other (tax-related and administrative law-related) aspects of the nuclear phase-out, German Federal Constitutional Court, Case No 2 BvL 6/13, Order (13 April 2017) BVerfGE 145, 171 (concerning the nuclear fuel tax); Higher Administrative Court Kassel, Case No 6 C 824/11.T, Judgment (27 February 2013) and Federal Administrative Court, Case Nos 7 B 18/13, 7 B 19/13, Order (20 December 2013) (concerning the moratorium for nuclear power plants). English translations of much of the German Federal Constitutional Court's case law, including the aforementioned decisions, are available via the Court's website at <www.bundesverfassungsgericht.de> accessed 22 January 2025. Unless indicated otherwise, this chapter uses translations provided on that website.

[26] See German Federal Constitutional Court, Case No 1 BvR 1550/19, Order (29 September 2020) BVerfGE 155, 378.

[27] Öffentlich-rechtlicher Vertrag zwischen der Bundesrepublik Deutschland sowie der E.ON SE, der Vattenfall GmbH, der RWE AG, der EnBW Energie Baden-Württemberg AG, der Vattenfall AB, der Vattenfall Europe Nuclear Energy GmbH and others (signed 25 March 2021). The German text is available at the website of the Federal Ministry for the Environment, Nature Conservation, Nuclear Safety and Consumer Protection at <www.bmuv.de/DL2682> accessed 22 January 2025.

[28] *Strabag SE, Erste Nordsee-Offshore Holding GmbH and Zweite Nordsee-Offshore Holding GmbH v Federal Republic of Germany*, ICSID Case No ARB/19/29, Award (18 December 2024) (see Lisa Bohmer, '[Updated] Austrian Investors Are Awarded Damages in ICSID/ECT Offshore Wind Dispute with Germany' (IAReporter, 19 December 2024)); *Mainstream Renewable Power Ltd and others v Federal Republic of Germany*, ICSID Case No ARB/21/26 (registered 13 May 2021).

[29] See German Federal Constitutional Court, Case No 1 BvR 1679/17, Order (30 June 2020) BVerfGE 155, 238 (ruling that the legislation creating a new framework for the establishment of offshore wind farms by introducing a public tender process for the approval and development of such projects, and a resulting termination of processes that had been initiated under the pre-existing legislative framework, was not fully compatible with the constitutional principle of protection of legitimate expectations *(allgemeines Vertrauensschutzgebot)*, entitling developers whose projects had been started under the pre-existing legislation, but which were terminated as a result of the new legislation, to compensation for incurred costs for planning and site investigation).

[30] *Azienda Elettrica Ticinese v Federal Republic of Germany*, ICSID Case No ARB/23/47 (registered 20 October 2023).

made by certain energy companies following the steep increase in energy prices in the wake of the Russia–Ukraine conflict.[31]

All in all, the high-stakes arbitration proceedings against Germany discussed above illustrate that private-public arbitrations, be they contract- or treaty-based, often pertain not simply to compliance or non-compliance with quid pro quo bargains, but to the legality of the exercise of public authority. They regularly address, in other words, core issues of domestic public (administrative and constitutional) law. This contrasts starkly with the widespread recourse to confidentiality in private-public arbitrations, both in contract- and treaty-based arbitration proceedings. Finally, the cases highlight that domestic courts are no longer the exclusive arbiters of legality of public actor conduct in cases involving subject matters that are of an administrative or even constitutional law nature.

C. Backlash Against Treaty-Based Arbitrations

Finally, it is not only actual disputes that illustrate the increasing importance of private-public arbitration in Germany, but also a newly emerging dispute avoidance technique by which the German government contractually tries to preclude foreign investors from having recourse to treaty-based investment arbitration. For instance, in the context of Germany's recently decided coal phase-out, the contract on the 'Gradual Reduction and Eventual Termination of Lignite-Based Power Generation in Germany' concluded between the German government and the country's major energy producers in February 2021 provides that the latter:

> waive their right to seek investment protection remedies before international arbitral tribunals or to initiate corresponding arbitration proceedings against the Federal Republic of Germany arising from and in connection with the rights and obligations under this public contract and/or the [underlying statutory law]. This obligation extends in particular to arbitration proceedings arising from and in connection with claims under the Energy Charter Treaty, the rights of the Companies and their dependent companies under Article 26 of the Energy Charter Treaty and to any rights under other bilateral or multilateral investment protection agreements.[32]

The agreement on financial compensation following Germany's nuclear power phase-out contains a similar clause.[33] Irrespective of whether such a waiver is valid,[34] it becomes

[31] *Klesch Group Holdings Limited & Raffinerie Heide GmbH v Federal Republic of Germany*, ICSID Case No ARB/23/49 (registered 24 October 2023).

[32] See s 24(2) of the draft contract 'Öffentlich-rechtlicher Vertrag zur Reduzierung und Beendigung der Braunkohleverstromung in Deutschland' published in *Bundestagsdrucksache* (Parliament Document) 19/25494 (5 January 2021) 3 ff for approval by the German Bundestag pursuant to section 49 of the Act to Reduce and End Coal-Fired Power Generation (translation by the authors). The Bundestag granted approval on 13 January 2021, see 'Vertrag zum Braunkohleausstieg mit Koalitionsmehrheit zugestimmt' <www.bundestag.de/dokumente/textarchiv/2021/kw02-de-braunkohleverstromung-816476> accessed 22 January 2025.

[33] See Öffentlich-rechtlicher Vertrag (n 27) s 10(2).

[34] See further on this issue Ole Spiermann, 'Individual Rights, State Interests and the Power to Waive ICSID Jurisdiction under Bilateral Investment Treaties' (2004) 20(2) Arb Int'l 179.

apparent that Germany is taking efforts to limit recourse to treaty-based investment arbitration in respect of measures involving the country's major energy transition.

Moreover, in the autumn of 2022, Germany's then governing coalition, consisting of the Social Democrats, the Greens, and the Liberal Democrats, reached agreement to exit the ECT, which is perceived to be 'a giant roadblock to greater climate protection . . . as illustrated by the many claims worth billions'.[35] In December 2022, Germany notified the ECT's depositary of its decision to withdraw from the ECT, which took effect on 20 December 2023.[36] Although the ECT's provisions will continue to apply for another twenty years to existing investments,[37] the envisaged withdrawal highlights the increasingly critical stance of the German government towards treaty-based investment arbitration. Still, all these attempts to limit or even preclude investor recourse to treaty-based arbitrations illustrate both the importance private-public arbitration has gained in Germany over the past two decades and the concerns for public law and governance this development raises.

II. Statutory Framework and Treaty Network Applying to Private-Public Arbitration

The rising concerns about private-public arbitration in Germany contrast with a legal framework which, even if little used to settle disputes until recently, has long been rather permissive regarding the involvement of public entities in arbitration. This holds true for both Germany's statutory framework governing arbitrations that involve German public entities (A) as well as the large network of international treaties Germany has concluded that allow and/or facilitate private-public arbitration (B).

A. Statutory Framework

To start with, Germany's statutory framework has long recognized that the participation of German public entities in arbitration agreements and proceedings is legally possible. Following the constitutional principle that public entities require, as a matter of substantive law, a legal basis for their action,[38] German legislation permits public entities to agree to arbitrate a broad set of disputes both in public and private

[35] See 'Konkrete Weiterentwicklung der Ampel-Handelsagenda' (press release, 11 November 2022) <www.fdpbt.de/koehleraudretschhubertz-konkrete-weiterentwicklung-ampel-handelsagenda> accessed 22 January 2025 (translation by the authors). See also Lisa Bohmer, 'Germany's Governing Coalition Reaches Agreement on Trade Issues – Including Withdrawal from the ECT, Ratification of CETA, and Initiating Negotiations with the USA for a Free Trade Agreement' (*IAReporter*, 11 November 2022).

[36] See International Energy Charter Secretariat, 'Written Notifications of Withdrawal from the Energy Charter Treaty' (news item, 22 March 2023) <www.energycharter.org/media/news/article/written-notifications-of-withdrawal-from-the-energy-charter-treaty/> accessed 22 January 2025.

[37] See the so-called sunset clause in ECT (n 21) art 47(3).

[38] This principle is enshrined in Article 20(3) GG, which provides: 'The legislature shall be bound by the constitutional order, the executive and the judiciary by law and justice.' English translations of German constitutional and most statutory law cited in this chapter are available via the website of the German Federal Ministry of Justice at <www.gesetze-im-internet.de/Teilliste_translations.html> accessed 22 January 2025.

law matters. In addition, the law governing access to, and the procedures before, the different branches of Germany's judiciary broadly permit arbitration as an alternative means of settling disputes involving public entities. Notably, this encompasses arbitration as an alternative to dispute settlement before Germany's administrative courts, which are, roughly speaking, competent for public law disputes (other than those concerning taxation and social security), and before the ordinary (civil) courts, which are, again roughly speaking, competent for private law disputes, but also for certain state liability claims.[39] Thus, in public law matters, both the German Administrative Procedures Act (Verwaltungsverfahrensgesetz—VwVfG) and the German Code of Administrative Court Procedure (Verwaltungsgerichtsordnung—VwGO) permit private-public arbitration to a considerable extent.[40] Similarly, German public entities can agree to arbitrate under contracts governed by private law—including, most notably, contracts entered into by the state for the procurement of goods and services, the acquisition and disposal of property, etc—as well as for the state liability claims that are within the competence of ordinary (civil) courts, in the same way, and following the same rules, as private actors.[41]

In all those cases—that is, public and private law matters—the statutory framework applicable to the arbitration of private-public disputes in Germany is the framework governing commercial arbitration between private parties set out in Chapter 10 of the German Code of Civil Procedure (Zivilprozessordnung—ZPO).[42] Having been reformed in 1997 and now following, with a few exceptions, the UNCITRAL Model

[39] The German judiciary consists of the ordinary (civil) courts and several specialized jurisdictions for administrative law matters, taxation, labour relations, social security, and constitutional disputes. For the purposes of the present chapter, we limited ourselves to the practically most relevant private-public disputes that come to arbitration, namely those that would otherwise come before ordinary (civil) and administrative courts. Administrative courts are competent, pursuant to s 40(1), first sentence, VwGO, 'in all public-law disputes of a non-constitutional nature insofar as the disputes are not explicitly allocated to another court by a federal statute'. Ordinary (civil) courts are competent in all private law disputes, including those involving public entities as parties, as well as for certain categories of state liability claims, namely 'property claims from sacrifice for the public good and from public-law deposit, as well as for compensation claims from the violation of public-law obligations which are not based on a public-law contract', as provided for in s 40(2), first sentence, VwGO. The possibilities for arbitrating private-public disputes concerning taxation, social security, and labour relations are very limited.

[40] See German Federal Administrative Court, Case No 5 C 22/88, Judgment (20 February 1992) (1993) 46(9) Neue Zeitschrift für Verwaltungsrecht 584, 585; Claus Meissner and Christine Steinbeiß-Winkelmann, '§ 173 VwGO' in Friedrich Schoch and Jens-Peter Schneider (eds), *Verwaltungsrecht VwGO: Kommentar* (looseleaf, CH Beck 2022) para 316 (with further references). cf also Woltereck (n 2) 81 ff (with references to discussions on this topic in the past).

[41] On the capacity of German public entities to enter into contracts governed by private law, especially in the case of so-called fiscal auxiliary transactions *(fiskalische Hilfsgeschäfte)*, see German Federal Court of Justice, Case No VI ZR 214/65, Judgment (6 June 1967) (1967) 20(41) Neue Juristische Wochenschrift 1911; Joint Senate of the Federal Supreme Courts (*Gemeinsamer Senat der obersten Gerichtshöfe des Bundes*), Order (10 April 1986) (1986) 39(38) Neue Juristische Wochenschrift 2359; German Federal Court of Justice, Case No V ZB 86/12, Order (19 September 2012) (2013) 32(1–2) Neue Zeitschrift für Verwaltungsrecht 96.

[42] German arbitration law, in principle, applies whenever the seat of arbitration is in Germany (s 1025(1) ZPO). This would leave the possibility for German public entities to opt out of German arbitration law by agreeing to a seat of arbitration abroad. This possibility exists and seems to be an accepted option in private-public disputes governed by private law, at least when the private party involved is foreign. See Karl-Heinz Böckstiegel, *Der Staat als Vertragspartner ausländischer Privatunternehmer* (Athenaeum 1971) 91–92. In private-public disputes governed by public law such a possibility would require—in application of the principle of legality—a sufficient legal basis, which will regularly be missing. cf Möller (n 2) 175.

Law,[43] Chapter 10 of the ZPO applies directly to all claims falling under the jurisdiction of the ordinary (civil) courts, that is, whenever the underlying dispute, including those involving a public entity, is of a private law nature or involves specific state liability claims. If the dispute involves public law matters that are subject to the jurisdiction of administrative courts,[44] the rules in Chapter 10 of the ZPO apply via a general reference in section 173 VwGO, which provides in the relevant part that, '[u]nless this Act contains provisions with regard to the proceedings ... the Code of Civil procedure ... shall apply *mutatis mutandis* if the fundamental differences between the two types of procedure do not rule this out.'

This reference in section 173 VwGO has been consistently considered to include Chapter 10 of the ZPO, without any visible discussion as to whether fundamental differences exist between judicial recourse in public law and private law disputes that would merit an exclusion of ZPO's Chapter 10.[45] In addition, (substantive) administrative law does not contain further specificities as regards the participation of public actors in arbitration. In fact, the requirement that certain administrative law bodies had to obtain the consent of their supervisory agency to enter into arbitration agreements was repealed with the 1997 reform of German arbitration law, therefore subjecting public actors to the same arbitration regime that is also applicable to private actors.[46] This is in line with the paradigm of Germany's arbitration statute that arbitration is a dispute settlement mechanism that is fully equivalent to litigation before domestic courts, be they civil or administrative courts.[47]

Consequently, all questions concerning the law applicable to arbitration, such as questions of arbitrability, powers of arbitrators, and standards of review by controlling courts, are governed by an overarching framework that does not distinguish as to whether the parties to a proceeding are private actors or public entities. Similarly, there is no difference in Germany in the applicable legal framework to an arbitral proceeding depending on whether the dispute in question is governed by private or public law. The only relevant difference concerns the issue of which courts are competent to hear requests relating to concrete arbitral proceedings (such as set-aside or enforcement action, court involvement needed to obtain evidence, or decisions on challenges against arbitrators): these depend on whether the underlying dispute would, absent an agreement to arbitrate, fall under the jurisdiction of the ordinary (civil) courts or that of the administrative courts. In the former case, the ordinary

[43] UNCITRAL Model Law on International Commercial Arbitration (adopted 21 June 1985, amended 7 July 2006) UN Doc A/40/17, Annex I and UN Doc A/61/17, Annex I.

[44] Pursuant to s 40(1) VwGO, this applies to 'all public-law disputes of a non-constitutional nature insofar as the disputes are not explicitly allocated to another court by a federal statute'. See n 39 above.

[45] See Meissner and Steinbeiß-Winkelmann (n 40) paras 316–17. In this sense, see Partial Award (n 5) 258 (arbitral tribunal comprising the President of the Higher Administrative Court Berlin as presiding arbitrator and two honorary judges of the same court).

[46] The 1933 Law on Arbitration of Private Law Disputes of the Reich and the Länder (Gesetz über die schiedsgerichtliche Erledigung privatrechtlicher Streitigkeiten des Reiches und der Länder) stipulated the need for certain administrative law bodies to obtain the consent of their supervisory agency, eg the Federal Ministry of Finance. It was suggested in the preparatory works to the 1997 law reforming the German arbitration framework that this outdated remnant of Nazi legislation should be scrapped: see *Bundestagsdrucksache* (Parliament Document) 13/5274 (12 July 1996) 36 and 66.

[47] See further on this paradigm, ibid 34, 36, and 46.

(civil) courts decide on the issue; in the latter case, it is the administrative courts (see section 173, third sentence, VwGO).

That said, Germany's statutory framework governing private-public arbitration has the following core characteristics, which it largely shares with private-private arbitration:

- First, a valid agreement to arbitrate constitutes an objection to the jurisdiction of the otherwise competent domestic courts, including in cases of public law disputes, which normally would be before the administrative courts (section 1032(1) ZPO).[48]
- Second, only pecuniary obligations and non-pecuniary obligations that the parties can dispose of, and that can form part of a settlement agreement, are arbitrable (section 1030(1) ZPO);[49] this is not limited to claims in private-public arbitrations governed by private law, but also applies to a wide variety of claims under public law, including claims connected to the unilateral exercise of public authority, as German public law allows administrative agencies and private actors to conclude public contracts not only to coordinate (ie establish, amend, or repeal) a legal relationship under equals governed by public law, but also to use contracts as a substitute for a sovereign act an administrative agency is entitled to take (so-called 'subordination contracts' governed by section 54, second sentence, VwVfG), or in order to settle a disagreement between the administration and a private party; consequently, it is widely accepted that even the review of a sovereign act of an administrative agency can form the subject matter of an arbitration proceeding.[50]
- Third, the role of domestic courts during a pending arbitration is limited to a *numerus clausus* of admissible actions (section 1032(1) ZPO), which includes

[48] See German Federal Administrative Court (n 40) 585; Dirk Ehlers and Jens-Peter Schneider, '§ 40 VwGO' in Friedrich Schoch and Jens-Peter Schneider (eds), *Verwaltungsrecht VwGO: Kommentar* (looseleaf, CH Beck 2022) para 717; Holger Wöckel, '§ 40 VwGO' in Erich Eyermann (ed), *Verwaltungsgerichtsordnung: Kommentar* (16th edn, CH Beck 2022) para 161. Parts of the literature even assume that an agreement to arbitrate must be observed by a domestic court *ex officio*: see Helmuth von Nicolai, '§ 40 VwGO' in Konrad Redeker and Hans-Joachim von Oertzen (fdrs), *Verwaltungsgerichtsordnung* (17th edn, Kohlhammer 2022) para 79; Hanswerner Müller, 'Entscheidung verwaltungsgerichtlicher Streitigkeiten durch Schiedsgerichte' (1963) 16(7) Neue Juristische Wochenschrift 282, 285 (with references to older case law from before the entry into force of the VwGO).

[49] s 1030(1) ZPO provides: 'Any claim involving property rights *("vermögensrechtlicher Anspruch")* may become the subject matter of an arbitration agreement. An arbitration agreement regarding claims not involving property rights has legal effect insofar as the parties are entitled to settle regarding the object of the dispute.'

[50] Stumpf (n 2) 112 ff, 116 ff. One example where legislation expressly provides for arbitration as a possible form of reviewing sovereign acts is s 45 of the German Food Code (*Lebensmittel-, Bedarfsgegenstände- und Futtermittelgesetzbuch*). Limits to arbitrability exist, however, whenever a statutory provision prohibits contractual action by an administrative body (see ss 54, first sentence, and 59 VwVfG). For the now antiquated position that disputes involving the review of sovereign acts of administrative agencies could not be arbitrated under German law, see Woltereck (n 2) 100 ff; Stumpf (n 2) 28 (in particular fn 100). See also, on the legal situation prior to the entry into force of the VwGO, German Federal Administrative Court, Case No VII C 97/57, Judgment (5 June 1959) (1959) 12(44) Neue Juristische Wochenschrift 1985, 1986 (agreeing, in principle, that arbitration agreements may also concern public law disputes, yet only insofar as the parties may enter into a settlement agreement, and where the subject matter of the dispute does not concern sovereign acts, eg tax claims of the state).

measures that are aimed at safeguarding the effectiveness of the arbitration proceeding, such as involvement in the appointment of arbitrators (sections 1034(2), 1035(3)–(5) ZPO), decisions on challenges to arbitrators (section 1037(3) ZPO),[51] decisions on requests for provisional measures (section 1041(2) ZPO), and decisions concerning the taking of evidence in the event that this requires the exercise of public powers (section 1050, first sentence, ZPO).[52]

- Fourth, private-public arbitrations, under both private and public law, in principle follow a private-law-inspired paradigm as regards questions of procedure, subjecting their determination to party autonomy (section 1042(3) ZPO), and only in the absence of such an agreement to the arbitral tribunal's discretion (section 1042(4)(1) ZPO); in practice, this mostly results in the maxims of civil procedure, rather than those governing administrative court proceedings, being applied by arbitral tribunals, not least because those sitting as arbitrators and practising as counsel tend to have a background in private-private, rather than private-public, arbitration;[53] in addition, private-public arbitrations usually do not take place in public, but are often confidential, as illustrated by several of the arbitrations discussed in section I above.[54]
- Fifth, an arbitral award in private-public arbitrations has the same effect between the parties as a final and binding judgment by a domestic court (section 1055 ZPO) and can also be enforced like a domestic court judgment, including in cases that would otherwise be before the administrative courts (see section 168(1) No 5 VwGO).
- Sixth, control of the arbitral proceeding in private-public disputes by domestic courts may only take place *ex post* and is limited to two types of procedures:[55] (1) set-aside proceedings, in which only breaches of the rules on arbitral jurisdiction and procedure, as well as breaches of the *ordre public*, may be invoked (section 1059 ZPO); and (2) recognition and enforcement proceedings in which a domestic court declares an arbitral award enforceable, in which case compliance with the *ordre public* and the arbitrability of the dispute are verified by the competent court *ex officio* (section 1063 ZPO); by contrast, the misapplication of German law—whether private or public—or the issue whether public interests were correctly taken into account, that is, without breach of fundamental

[51] See eg Administrative Court Berlin, Case No 4 K 403.09, Order (11 February 2010) (2010) 8(2) Zeitschrift für Schiedsverfahren 107 (challenge against arbitrator – *Toll Collect*).

[52] cf Stumpf (n 2) 103 ff.

[53] See ibid 138–39. Yet, several voices in the German literature demand that arbitral tribunals in private-public disputes should take the principles governing court proceedings under administrative law, such as the principle that adjudicators must investigate and determine evidence, as a point of reference when determining the procedural rules to apply under s 1042(4)(1) ZPO. See Meissner and Steinbeiß-Winkelmann (n 40) para 317; Jan Albers, '§ 1042 ZPO' in Adolf Baumbach and others, *Zivilprozessordnung* (64th edn, CH Beck 2006) para 18 (both relying on Partial Award (n 5) 260); Woltereck (n 2) 123 ff.

[54] See Born (n 1). Non-publicness of an arbitration designates the fact that third parties cannot participate in the hearings, cannot make submissions to the tribunal, and do not have access to the decisions of the tribunal; confidentiality designates the agreement to keep information about the very existence of an arbitration unknown to anybody but the parties to the proceedings.

[55] Stumpf (n 2) 105–06.

constitutional rights or other principles forming part of the *ordre public*, neither constitute a ground for a set-aside, nor hinder the award's enforcement.[56]

In sum, at the level of legal rules, Germany's statutory framework treats private-public arbitration like private-private arbitration. It presents itself as a dispute settlement mechanism that is, as expressed by the preparatory works of the law reforming German arbitration law in 1997, equivalent to litigation before domestic courts.[57] As with private-private disputes, the statutory framework governing private-public arbitration not only excludes recourse to domestic courts to settle the underlying dispute, but also reduces the courts' involvement to limited *ex post* controls for compliance of the award with fundamental legal principles *(ordre public)*, and tends to level procedural differences between how private law and public law disputes are settled in German civil and administrative courts in favour of the maxims and mindset governing civil, rather than administrative, court procedure.

B. Treaty Network

Germany's permissive statutory framework governing arbitration is accompanied by a large network of international treaties that permits and supports private-public arbitration involving German public actors.[58] Following its first investment treaty, with Pakistan in 1959, Germany has entered into 147 BITs, of which 113 are in force.[59] These treaties allow covered investors to initiate private-public arbitrations to settle disputes that are of a genuinely public law nature because they involve the question whether (sovereign as well as non-sovereign) action taken by the government vis-à-vis a foreign investor is in accordance with the applicable legal standards (ie depending on the wording of the arbitration clause at issue, domestic and international law, or international law only). In addition, Germany is party to a number of other treaties with investment provisions, which permit private-public arbitration, and continues to be bound by the ECT under its sunset clause even after Germany's withdrawal in 2023.[60] As discussed in section I, some of these treaties have given rise to arbitration proceedings against Germany.

[56] On the applicable standards of review, see Stephan Wilske and Lars Markert, '1059 ZPO' in Volkert Vorwerk and Christian Wolf (eds), *Beck'scher Online-Kommentar ZPO* (46th edn, CH Beck 2022) paras 27 ff.

[57] *Bundestagsdrucksache* (Parliament Document) 13/5274 (n 46) 34, 36, and 46.

[58] These treaties, which require the consent of Parliament in the form of a federal law pursuant to Article 59(2) GG, have the status of federal statutory law. See German Federal Constitutional Court, Case No 2 BvL 1/12, Order (15 December 2015) BVerfGE 141, 1, 31 – *Treaty Override*.

[59] See German Federal Ministry for Economic Affairs and Climate Action, 'Investitionsschutzverträge' (2025) <www.bmwk.de/Navigation/DE/Service/Investitionsschutzvertraege/investitionsschutzvertraege.html> accessed 22 January 2025. On investment treaties and their content more generally, see August Reinisch and Christoph Schreuer, *International Protection of Investments: The Substantive Principles* (CUP 2020); Rudolf Dolzer, Ursula Kriebaum, and Christoph Schreuer, *Principles of International Investment Law* (3rd edn, OUP 2022). Specifically on German investment treaty practice, see Joachim Karl, 'The Promotion and Protection of German Foreign Investment Abroad' (1996) 11 ICSID Review–FILJ 1; Matthias Füracker, 'Relevance and Structure of Bilateral Investment Treaties – The German Approach' (2006) 4(5) Zeitschrift für Schiedsverfahren 236.

[60] Note Germany's recent withdrawal from the ECT. See nn 35–37 above and accompanying text.

Furthermore, Germany is party to several multilateral treaties that govern arbitration proceedings, including those involving public entities. In 1961, Germany ratified the 1958 New York Convention, which provides for the obligation to recognize a written agreement to arbitrate as well as to recognize and enforce foreign arbitral awards.[61] According to Article I(1) of the New York Convention, it applies to arbitral awards 'arising out of differences between persons, whether physical or legal', which is broadly understood to include public law entities,[62] and thus to cover private-public disputes that are commercial in nature, both on the basis of contracts and treaties. In 1964, Germany ratified the European Convention on International Commercial Arbitration,[63] which specifically recognizes in Article II(1) that 'legal persons considered by the law which is applicable to them as "legal persons of public law" have the right to conclude valid arbitration agreements'. Finally, Germany is also party to the ICSID Convention,[64] which opens the possibility for ICSID-administered contract- and treaty-based investment arbitrations under a distinct set of rules. Most importantly in the present context, the ICSID Convention limits recourse to domestic courts and other dispute settlement mechanisms to settle disputes covered by the disputing parties' consent (Art 26 ICSID Convention), excludes remedies before domestic courts against ICSID awards (Art 53(1) ICSID Convention), and requires Contracting States to recognize and enforce ICSID awards (Art 54(1) ICSID Convention). Taken together, the obligations stemming from these international instruments emphasize Germany's general openness towards private-public arbitration in contract- and treaty-based disputes.

C. Summary

All in all, Germany's statutory framework, as well as its international treaty obligations, show a broad acceptance of the participation of public actors in private-public arbitration. At the same time, the legal framework provides for limits, inter alia in the form of the rules on arbitrability, and of certain control mechanisms to ensure compliance of arbitral proceedings with basic standards of justice, mostly in the form of proceedings before domestic courts in non-ICSID arbitrations, and before annulment committees in ICSID proceedings. However, to what extent these limits are sufficient to protect the public interest has been little discussed. It is only due to the increasing reality, recently, that private-public disputes are settled in arbitration rather than, as before, in domestic courts, that this question is becoming critical. Interestingly, the question is not principally formulated as one of

[61] Convention on the Recognition and Enforcement of Foreign Arbitral Awards (adopted 10 June 1958, entered into force 7 June 1959) 330 UNTS 3 (New York Convention).

[62] International Council for Commercial Arbitration (ICCA), *ICCA's Guide to the Interpretation of the 1958 New York Convention: A Handbook for Judges* (ICCA 2011) 85.

[63] European Convention on International Commercial Arbitration (adopted 21 April 1961, entered into force 7 January 1964) 484 UNTS 349.

[64] Convention on the Settlement of Investment Disputes between States and Nationals of Other States (adopted 18 March 1965, entered into force 14 October 1966) 575 UNTS 159 (ICSID Convention).

political, administrative, or economic expediency, but as one that goes to tensions between private-public arbitration and a number of core principles of German constitutional law. These tensions will be addressed next.

III. Constitutional Foundations of Private-Public Arbitration in Germany

Arbitration has been heralded for certain advantages as compared with settling disputes in domestic courts, including the expertise of arbitrators in highly specialized disputes, reducing costs and duration of proceedings, and helping to unclog the overburdened dockets of courts.[65] These advantages have also been invoked in Germany in respect of private-public arbitration: arbitration would relieve the mounting caseload of domestic courts and reduce public expenditure for the judiciary.[66] Furthermore, the possibility for recourse to arbitration has also been bolstered from the perspective of constitutional law. Thus, in the context of private-private arbitration, the German Federal Constitutional Court held that the freedom to contract, which it recognized as protected under the German Constitution, encompasses the disputing parties' right to arbitrate, rather than litigate, their disputes.[67]

While the analogy with private-private arbitration has limits in respect of private-public arbitration, not least because public entities are not entitled to the protection of fundamental constitutional rights,[68] various considerations of constitutional law provide, at least in parts, a justification for private-public arbitration in Germany. At the same time, the loss of control over dispute settlement by domestic courts gives rise to constitutional concerns, in particular in respect of private-public arbitration, and has led to litigation before the German Federal Constitutional Court, namely with regard to treaty-based private-public arbitration. Although the Court has so far declined to rule on the matter, the proceedings reflect how private-public arbitration in Germany is subject to a process of constitutionalization, that is, conceptualizing the foundations and limits of private-public arbitration from the perspective of constitutional law rather than political or economic expediency. Against this background, this section first looks at the constitutional justifications for private-public arbitration (A) before turning to constitutional tensions and limits (B).

[65] See, on the general advantages of arbitration, Born (n 1) vol 1, 71–91 (with an emphasis on the parties' point of view).

[66] cf Stumpf (n 2) 1. Similarly, Woltereck (n 2) 20. See also *Bundestagsdrucksache* (Parliament Document) 13/5274 (n 46) 1 (stressing that arbitration may help relieve demand for, and work pressure in, domestic courts).

[67] See German Federal Constitutional Court, Case No 1 BvR 2103/16, Order (3 June 2022) para 39 – *Pechstein* (with further references to German literature). For a comparative view, see Victor Ferreres Comella, *The Constitution of Arbitration* (CUP 2021) 31–40.

[68] Claus Dieter Classen, 'Art 92' in Hermann von Mangoldt, Friedrich Klein, and Christian Starck (eds), *Grundgesetz: Kommentar* (7th edn, CH Beck 2018) vol 3, para 43a.

A. Constitutional Justification for Private-Public Arbitration

Opening up arbitration for the settlement of private-public disputes, as is the case with Germany's permissive statutory framework and network of international treaties, is not only a matter of political expediency or economic efficiency. It connects to, reflects, and runs parallel to a number of core values enshrined in the German Constitution. In fact, private-public arbitration can be understood as an instrument to address political risk that is not only compatible with, but reflects, the German constitutional model of democratic government under the rule of law.

Political risk differs from commercial risk found in respect of private-private co-operation and refers to risk factors that are specific to the relationship between private and public actors. Political risk, in other words, results from the presence of the state itself. The state possesses sovereign powers over the law applicable to private-public relations and, at the extreme, can unilaterally change it.[69] At the same time, the mechanisms to ensure government's accountability and compliance with its own law, and to settle any disputes that may derive from private-public relations, come in the form of the state's own courts, which, despite the constitutional guarantees of independence and impartiality of the judiciary, are ultimately subject to the state's control.[70] This is an additional risk factor not present in relation to private-private interactions.

The response the German Constitution gives to political risk is the principle of the rule of law (*Rechtsstaat*) enshrined in Article 20(3) GG, which provides: 'The legislature shall be bound by the constitutional order, the executive and the judiciary by law and justice.' In this model, the legislature is bound to respect constitutional rights and guarantees, the executive is bound to the limits set by legislation, and independent and impartial domestic courts[71] control compliance of the legislative and executive powers with the applicable legal framework and settle resulting disputes. The Constitution complements this institutional guarantee of the rule of law with a number of fundamental rights that private actors are entitled to, including the right to property (Art 14 GG),[72] freedom of enterprise (Art 12(1) GG),[73] and access to domestic courts to request review of government compliance with the rule of law (Art 19(4) GG),[74] as well as a number of other procedural guarantees in those

[69] cf from the perspective of customary international law, FA Mann, 'State Contracts and State Responsibility' (1960) 54 AJIL 572, 581.

[70] cf Pierre Mayer, 'La neutralisation du pouvoir normatif de l'Etat en matière de contrats d'Etat' (1986) 113 JDI 5.

[71] See further, on the German court system, n 39 above.

[72] Article 14 GG reads: '(1) Property and the right of inheritance shall be guaranteed. Their content and limits shall be defined by the laws. (2) Property entails obligations. Its use shall also serve the public good. (3) Expropriation shall only be permissible for the public good. It may only be ordered by or pursuant to a law that determines the nature and extent of compensation. Such compensation shall be determined by establishing an equitable balance between the public interest and the interests of those affected. In case of dispute concerning the amount of compensation, recourse may be had to the ordinary courts.'

[73] Article 12(1) GG provides: 'All Germans shall have the right freely to choose their occupation or profession, their place of work and their place of training. The practice of an occupation or profession may be regulated by or pursuant to a law.'

[74] Article 19(4) GG reads, in the relevant part: 'Should any person's rights be violated by public authority, he may have recourse to the courts. If no other jurisdiction has been established, recourse shall be to the ordinary courts.'

courts, including, in particular, due process (Arts 101 and 103(1) GG).[75] The constitutional principle of the rule of law and accompanying fundamental rights, in other words, function to address and minimize political risk stemming from the state and its entities.

From a structural/conceptual perspective, German constitutional law, the statutory framework passed on its basis, and domestic institutions, in particular the courts, adequately address political risk. There are, however, problems of a practical nature, notably the lack of efficiency of domestic courts in settling private-public disputes. As the European Court of Human Rights has found recurrently, Germany has a systemic deficit in providing efficient dispute settlement procedures, in particular in its administrative courts, thus breaching its obligation to ensure access to justice and fair trial under the European Convention on Human Rights.[76] It is not least against this background that some scholars understand private-public arbitration as taking pressure off Germany's court system[77] by offering a form of access to justice. Provided, of course, that arbitrators are themselves independent and impartial, and arbitral proceedings efficient and compliant with due process, the institution of private-public arbitration would represent an embodiment of the German Constitution's rule-of-law principle.

Private-public arbitrations involving foreign private actors can rely on additional constitutional arguments for justification. Not only is it more difficult to instill foreigners' confidence in the ability of domestic law and domestic courts to control government and contain political risk—after all, it is the state's own courts that are involved—but the German Constitution also contains significant gaps in the legal protection of foreigners.[78] Although German legislation only rarely makes differences in legal protection between foreign and domestic actors, the German Constitution limits the application of a number of fundamental rights to German nationals. For example, while the right to property under Article 14 GG is afforded to anyone, foreigners are not covered by the freedom of enterprise under Article 12(1) GG, which protects, inter alia, against certain restrictions of market access.[79] Similarly, the equal protection clause in Article 3 GG, while prohibiting discrimination, inter alia, on the basis of 'homeland and origin', does not rule out different treatment based on nationality alone. Instead, as confirmed by the German Federal Constitutional Court, the legislator enjoys considerable policy space to differentiate between foreigners and nationals based on considerations of economic policy, including measures with a

[75] Article 101 GG provides: '(1) Extraordinary courts shall not be allowed. No one may be removed from the jurisdiction of his lawful judge. (2) Courts for particular fields of law may be established only by a law.' Article 103(1) GG stipulates: 'In the courts every person shall be entitled to a hearing in accordance with law.'

[76] *Rumpf v Germany* App no 46344/06 (ECHR, 2 September 2010).

[77] See eg the references cited in n 66 above.

[78] See, on this and the following, Stephan W Schill, 'Der Schutz von Auslandsinvestitionen in Deutschland im Mehrebenensystem: deutsches, europäisches und internationales Recht' (2010) 35 Archiv des öffentlichen Rechts 498, 503 ff.

[79] In the context of these 'Germans-only' rights, foreigners are relegated to the much weaker protections found in the general personal freedom, or 'freedom of action', laid down in Article 2(1) GG, which provides: 'Every person shall have the right to free development of his personality insofar as he does not violate the rights of others or offend against the constitutional order or the moral law.'

protectionist purpose.[80] Even more drastic in limiting fundamental rights protection of foreigners is the effect of Article 19(3) GG, which provides that '[t]he basic rights shall also apply to domestic juridical persons to the extent that the nature of such rights permits.' This provision constitutes a wholesale exclusion of foreign companies from the protection of the Constitution's fundamental rights and, consequently, from bringing complaints for their violation to the German Federal Constitutional Court.[81] Substantive protection and access to private-public arbitration under IIAs, or private-public contracts, close this constitutional gap and substitute for the Constitution's shortcomings in protecting foreigners against various forms of political risk.

In sum, both purely domestic private-public arbitrations and those involving foreign actors can rely on constitutional values and principles for justification, namely the constitutional principle of the rule of law. While not addressed anywhere in the Constitution, the institution of private-public arbitration and its operation is thus not merely a matter permitted under Germany's statutory framework and network of international treaties; it is grounded on, and reflects values that are inherent in, Germany's constitutional model of democratic government under the rule of law.

B. Constitutional Tensions and Limits

Although private-public arbitration finds justification in the structural principles of German constitutional law, in particular the concept of the rule of law, it also raises tensions with constitutional principles. These tensions have been particularly brought to the fore—both in academic debates[82] and general public

[80] Uwe Kischel, 'Art 3 GG' in Volker Epping and Christian Hillgruber (eds), *Beck'scher Online-Kommentar Grundgesetz* (CH Beck 2018) paras 55, 65, 135. Article 3(1) GG stipulates: 'All persons shall be equal before the law.'

[81] See already German Federal Constitutional Court, BVerfGE 21, 207, 208–09 (concerning the constitutional complaint of a Delaware-incorporated company with its seat in New York): 'Under Art 19(3) of the Basic Law, the basic rights granted to natural persons are also granted to legal persons, insofar as they are essentially applicable to them. However, this extension of the basic rights only relates to domestic legal persons by means of explicit constitutional provisions. Wording and rationale prohibit any extensive interpretation with respect to foreign legal persons' (translation by the authors). The only exception to this general rule is made with respect to corporate entities of EU Member States, which must be afforded equal protection due to the non-discrimination provisions and the freedom of establishment under EU law. See German Federal Constitutional Court, Case No 1 BvR 1916/09, Order (19 July 2011) BVerfGE 129, 78, paras 68–82.

[82] See Claus Dieter Classen, 'Die Unterwerfung demokratischer Hoheitsgewalt unter eine Schiedsgerichtsbarkeit' (2014) 25(16) Europäische Zeitschrift für Wirtschaftsrecht 611; Christoph Ohler, 'Die Vereinbarkeit von Investor-Staat-Schiedsverfahren mit deutschem und europäischem Verfassungsrecht' (2015) 70 Juristenzeitung 337; Axel Flessner, 'Investitionsschutz durch völkerrechtliche Verträge wie TTIP und CETA – ein Fall für das Verfassungsrecht!' (2015) 51(3) Recht und Politik 149; Siegfried Broß, 'Freihandelsabkommen, einige Anmerkungen zur Problematik der privaten Schiedsgerichtsbarkeit', Hans-Böckler-Stiftung Report No 4/2015 (January 2015) <www.boeckler.de/de/faust-detail.htm?sync_id=7241>; Kathrin Groh and Daniel-Erasmus Khan, 'Rechtsgutachten' (9 March 2015) <www.abgeordnetenwatch.de/system/files/qa-files/gutachten_ttip_groh_khan_09032015.pdf> both accessed 22 January 2025; Christian Tietje, 'Investitionsschutzgerichtsbarkeit in CETA und anderen Freihandelsabkommen der EU: Völkerrecht als Verfassungsverstoß?' (2016) 19(4) Zeitschrift für Europarechtliche Studien 421; Kathrin Groh, 'Endstation Karlsruhe! – Schiedsgerichtsbarkeit in Freihandelsverträgen' (2016) 19(4) Zeitschrift für Europarechtliche Studien 433; Claus Dieter Classen, 'Die Unterwerfung unter völkerrechtliche (Schieds-)Gerichte: kein Verfassungsverstoß!' (2016) 19(4) Zeitschrift für Europarechtliche Studien 449; Bernd Grzeszick, 'CETA als Präzedenzfall

discourse[83]—as constitutional limits to private-public arbitration in the context of the negotiation of the Comprehensive Economic and Trade Agreement (CETA) between the European Union (EU) and Canada, which was signed in 2016,[84] and the Transatlantic Trade and Investment Partnership (TTIP) between the EU and United States, which was put on ice. Both agreements initially foresaw arbitration to settle investor-state disputes under the agreements. CETA, as well as other EU investment agreements,[85] later replaced investor-state arbitration with the so-called Investment Court System, a model that relies on arbitration rules for purposes of dispute settlement and enforcement procedures, but draws on a standing body of adjudicators appointed by the Contracting Parties.

CETA led to the lodging of several applications before the German Federal Constitutional Court.[86] These constitutional complaints alleged, amongst other points of concern, the unconstitutionality of the investor-state dispute settlement mechanisms included in CETA. Three sets of constitutional limits were claimed in this respect: (1) that the German Constitution mandates a judicial/state monopoly

für die demokratischen Anforderungen an völkerrechtliche Verträge' (2016) 35(24) Neue Zeitschrift für Verwaltungsrecht 1753; Björn Schiffbauer, 'Investitionsschutz und Grundgesetz: Bilaterale Investitionsschutzabkommen („BITs") aus verfassungsrechtlicher Perspektive' (2016) 7(2) Kölner Schrift zum Wirtschaftsrecht 145; Armin Steinbach, 'Investor-Staat-Schiedsverfahren und Verfassungsrecht' (2016) 80 Rabels Zeitschrift für ausländisches und internationales Privatrecht 1; Peter-Tobias Stoll, Till Patrick Holterhus, and Henner Gött, *Investitionsschutz und Verfassung* (Mohr Siebeck 2017); Markus Ludwigs and Oliver Remien (eds), *Investitionsschutz, Schiedsgerichtsbarkeit und Rechtsstaat in der EU* (Nomos 2018).

[83] See eg 'Hundreds of Thousands Protest in Berlin Against EU-US Trade Deal (*Reuters*, 10 October 2015) <www.reuters.com/article/us-trade-germany-ttip-protests-idUSKCN0S40L720151010>; 'Germans Stage Anti-TTIP, CETA Rallies' (*Deutsche Welle*, 17 September 2016) <https://p.dw.com/p/1K456> both accessed 22 January 2025.

[84] Comprehensive Economic and Trade Agreement (signed 30 October 2016, in parts provisionally in force since 21 September 2017) [2017] OJ L 11/23 (CETA).

[85] These include the EU–Singapore Investment Protection Agreement (signed 19 October 2018, not yet in force) COM(2018) 194 final, Annex 1, ch 3, s A; EU–Vietnam Investment Protection Agreement (signed 30 June 2019, not yet in force) COM(2018) 694 final, Annex, arts 3.38 ff. See also EU–Mexico Agreement in Principle (text as of 21 April 2018) s 19 ('Resolution of Investment Disputes'); EU–India Investment Protection Draft Agreement, EU Textual Proposal (15 July 2022) arts 3.9 ff, texts available at <https://policy.trade.ec.europa.eu/eu-trade-relationships-country-and-region/negotiations-and-agreements_en> accessed 22 January 2025.

[86] For the constitutional complaints and applications in *Organstreit* proceedings (disputes between constitutional organs) against CETA, see German Federal Constitutional Court, Case No 2 BvR 1368/16, Judgment (13 October 2016) BVerfGE 143, 65 (preliminary measures); German Federal Constitutional Court, Case No 2 BvR 1444/16, Order (7 December 2016) BVerfGE 144, 1 (preliminary measures); German Federal Constitutional Court, Case No 2 BvR 2047/16, Order (14 September 2020) ECLI:DE:BVerfG:2020:rk20200914.2bvr204716; German Federal Constitutional Court, Case No 2 BvE 4/16, Judgment (2 March 2021) BVerfGE 157, 1; German Federal Constitutional Court, Case Nos 2 BvR 1368/16, 2 BvR 1444/16 and others, Order (9 February 2022) ECLI:DE:BVerfG:2022:rs20220209.2bvr136816 (merits). See also the constitutional complaints lodged against the EU–Singapore Free Trade Agreement: German Federal Constitutional Court, Case No 2 BvR 966/19, Order (28 October 2019) ECLI:DE:BVerfG:2019:rk20191028.2bvr096619 (preliminary measures); German Federal Constitutional Court, Case No 2 BvR 882/19, Order (7 November 2019) ECLI:DE:BVerfG:2019:rk20191107.2bvr088219 (preliminary measures). Generally, on the role of constitutional courts with respect to the EU's common trade policy, see Alexander Proelß, 'Die Rolle nationaler Verfassungsgerichte bei der Kontrolle der Gemeinsamen Handelspolitik' in Christoph Herrmann (ed), *Europarecht: Beiheft 2/2020* (Nomos 2020) 127.

for the settlement of (certain or all) private-public disputes, thus excluding private-public arbitration; (2) that the Constitution's model of democratic government under the rule of law limits private-public arbitration by requiring specific safeguards for how arbitrators settle private-public disputes so as to comply with the rule of law and the principle of democratic legitimacy; and (3) that the possible governance effects of private-public arbitration, that is, impacts beyond the settlement of individual disputes, restrict domestic law and policy space and are hence constitutionally problematic. Unfortunately, the decisions rendered by the German Federal Constitutional Court left most of these issues unresolved. Still, the proceedings help crystallize the constitutional tensions and contribute to the constitutionalization of private-public arbitration in the German debate.

In this section, we first address the limited outcome of the litigation before the German Federal Constitutional Court relating to investor-state dispute settlement provisions in the EU's new generation of trade and investment agreements (1). We then review the different constitutional limits discussed in the related constitutional challenges, namely arguments about a constitutionally enshrined judicial monopoly that recourse to private-public arbitration would violate (2), the need for procedural and organizational safeguards for how arbitrators settle individual disputes under the principle of democratic government under the rule of law (3), and, finally, systemic impacts of private-public arbitration that pose a risk to the constitutional separation-of-powers framework which ensures both compliance with the rule of law and the principle of democracy (4).

1 Constitutional Litigation Related to Treaty-Based Private-Public Arbitration

Although targeting the Investment Court System included in the EU's free trade and investment agreements, the constitutional complaints against CETA promised insight into the limits the German Constitution sets for private-public arbitration more generally. The German Federal Constitutional Court, however, dismissed the complaints and only provided minimal guidance on the limits the German Constitution imposes on private-public arbitration. The Court ultimately found that the rules on investment protection and investment dispute settlement included in CETA were constitutionally innocent, as these rules were not subject to provisional application and no decision had yet been taken for CETA to enter fully into force.[87]

The German Federal Constitutional Court did clarify, however, what standard of review applies to private-public arbitration based on an international treaty, as compared with private-public arbitration in a purely domestic context. While public-private arbitrations not based on treaty are subject to the full set of constitutional disciplines, public-private arbitrations based on treaty must only comply with a more limited constitutional standard, namely the constitutional principles that form part of Article 79(3) GG, the Constitution's so-called 'eternity clause', whose content is immune to, and cannot be modified by, constitutional amendments. Article 79(3) GG provides that '[a]mendments to this Basic Law affecting the division of the Federation into *Länder*, their participation in principle in the legislative process, or the principles

[87] See the German Federal Constitutional Court's decision on the merits in Order (9 February 2022) (n 86) paras 169 ff.

laid down in Articles 1 and 20 shall be inadmissible.' It is this standard that the Court has used consistently as a yardstick to assess whether CETA, including its investor-state dispute settlement mechanism, as well as other EU trade agreements, comply with the German Constitution.[88] This standard is applicable not only to determine whether EU acts comply with the German Constitution, or more precisely the constitutionality of Germany's participation in the EU; the Court uses the same standard in respect of any other international treaty arrangement that Germany is party to.[89]

Article 79(3) GG, in the reading of the German Federal Constitutional Court, requires in particular that acts based on the international treaty in question, whether EU or otherwise, remain within the limits of powers ceded to the international level, but also that they are in line with Germany's so-called 'constitutional identity', a notion the Constitutional Court uses to refer to the constitutional principles covered by the eternity clause in Article 79(3) GG, both when the treaty in question is concluded but also as it is applied and develops further.[90] Compliance with Germany's constitutional identity requires, amongst others, that treaty-based conferrals of powers comply, as expressly mentioned in Article 79(3) GG, with the core of the principles laid down in Articles 1 and 20 of Germany's Constitution, namely respect for human dignity and other fundamental or human rights,[91] the principle of democracy,[92] and government under the rule of law.[93]

[88] See, in the context of CETA, German Federal Constitutional Court, Judgment (13 October 2016) (n 86) paras 50 ff; German Federal Constitutional Court, Order (9 February 2022) (n 86) para 139; German Federal Constitutional Court, Judgment (2 March 2021) (n 86) para 69; and in the context of the EU–Singapore Free Trade Agreement, German Federal Constitutional Court, Order (28 October 2019) (n 86) paras 12, 14–17; German Federal Constitutional Court, Order (7 November 2019) (n 86) paras 21 ff. cf also German Federal Constitutional Court, Case No 2 BvR 557/19, Order (23 July 2024) ECLI:DE:BVerfG :2024:rk20240723.2bvr055719 – *Achmea*, para 61.

[89] See already German Federal Constitutional Court, Case No BvL 52/71, Order (29 May 1974) BVerfGE 37, 271, 279 – *Solange I*; German Federal Constitutional Court, Case No 2 BvR 1107/77, Order (23 June 1981) BVerfGE 58, 1, 40 – *Eurocontrol I*; German Federal Constitutional Court, Case No 2 BvE 13/83, Judgment (18 December 1984) BVerfGE 68, 1, 96 – *Nuclear Weapons Stationing*; German Federal Constitutional Court, Case No 2 BvR 197/83, Order (22 October 1986) BVerfGE 73, 339, 375–76 – *Solange II*.

[90] See fundamentally German Federal Constitutional Court, Case No 2 BvE 2/08, Judgment (30 June 2009) BVerfGE 123, 267, 340 ff – *Lissabon*; German Federal Constitutional Court, Case No 2 BvR 2735/14, Order (15 December 2015) BVerfGE 140, 317, 336 ff – *European Arrest Warrant II*; German Federal Constitutional Court, Case No 2 BvR 2728/13, Request for Preliminary Ruling (14 January 2014) BVerfGE 134, 366, 382 ff and Judgment (21 June 2016) BVerfGE 142, 123, 186 ff – *Outright Monetary Transactions (OMT)*; German Federal Constitutional Court, Case No 2 BvR 1685/14, Judgment (30 July 2019) BVerfGE 151, 202, 287 ff – *European Banking Union*; German Federal Constitutional Court, Case No 2 BvR 859/15, Request for Preliminary Ruling (18 July 2017) BVerfGE 146, 216, 252 ff and Judgment (5 May 2020) BVerfGE 154, 17, 85 ff – *Public Sector Asset Purchase Programme*.

[91] See *Solange I* (n 89) 279–80; *Eurocontrol I* (n 89) 40; *European Arrest Warrant II* (n 90) 341; German Federal Constitutional Court, Case No. 2 BvR 1845/18, Order (1 December 2020) BVerfGE 156, 182, para 58 – *European Arrest Warrant III*.

[92] See German Federal Constitutional Court, Case No 2 BvR 2134/92, Judgment (12 October 1993) BVerfGE 89, 155, 182 ff – *Maastricht*; *Lissabon* (n 90) 341 ff; German Federal Constitutional Court, Case No 2 BvR 987/10, Judgment (7 September 2011) BVerfGE 129, 124, 177 ff – *European Financial Stability Facility*; German Federal Constitutional Court, Case No 2 BvR 1390/12, Judgment (18 March 2014) BVerfGE 135, 317, 399 ff – *European Stability Mechanism*; *OMT* (n 90) 188 ff; *European Banking Union* (n 90) 286 ff; *Public Sector Asset Purchase Programme*, BVerfGE 154, 17 (n 90) 86 ff.

[93] See eg *European Arrest Warrant II* (n 90) 341; *OMT* (n 90) 195; *Public Sector Asset Purchase Programme*, BVerfGE 154, 17 (n 90) 93–94.

Applied to private-public arbitration, this means that the constitutionality of treaty-based systems, such as those based on IIAs and the ICSID Convention, cannot be measured against the norms of 'ordinary' constitutional law; instead, their constitutionality is only at issue if the system established, or decisions produced, violate the structural constitutional principles protected under the Constitution's eternity clause in Article 79(3) GG. Only if, in other words, treaty-based private-public arbitration is contrary to the core of the principles of democracy or the rule of law, or is at odds with the central tenets of other fundamental or human rights, does a constitutional conflict arise. The participation of German public actors in private-public arbitration solely based on domestic law, by contrast, can be measured against all norms of constitutional law, including norms of 'ordinary' constitutional law. This difference in standard is only logical, considering that the government, as compared with purely domestic settings, requires more policy space to act on the international plane and enter into agreements with foreign states, including, if needed, on issues of private-public arbitration.[94] It is with these different constitutional standards in mind that arguments about the constitutional limits of private-public arbitration must be assessed.

2 Judicial Monopoly of State Courts and Private-Public Arbitration

The German Constitution contains several provisions that guarantee the independence of the judiciary, lay down the courts' competence for resolving disputes and exercising judicial reviews, and ensure access to justice. All of these are discussed as sources of a judicial monopoly for the resolution of private-public disputes and hence as possible constitutional limits to private-public arbitration.[95]

Access to justice is protected under the German Constitution as an unwritten constitutional entitlement (so-called *allgemeiner Justizgewährleistungsanspruch*). It finds its constitutional foundations in the principle of the rule of law, as enshrined in Article 20(3) GG, and entails the right of access to domestic courts, the right to a comprehensive factual and legal examination of the grievances brought, and the right to a binding court decision.[96] The German Constitution also provides expressly for the right to access to justice for specific instances: Article 19(4) GG ensures a person's fundamental right to judicial review of sovereign acts before domestic courts;[97] Article 14(3) GG, fourth sentence, stipulates that, '[i]n case of dispute concerning the amount of compensation [following expropriation], recourse may be had to the ordinary courts.'

[94] For reflections of this idea in the Court's jurisprudence, see German Federal Constitutional Court, Case No 2 BvR 624/83, Order (29 October 1987) BVerfGE 77, 170, 231 – *Chemical Weapons Stationing*; *Lissabon* (n 90) 345.

[95] Weidemann (n 2) 43 ff, 102 ff; Stumpf (n 2) 28 ff. cf also the discussion in the context of non-judicial forms of alternative dispute settlement in administrative law in Markus Kaltenborn, *Streitvermeidung und Streitbeilegung im Verwaltungsrecht* (Nomos 2007) 124 ff. Arguments that the German Constitution provides for a judicial monopoly that excludes private-public arbitration, or at least certain forms of it, are prominent particularly in the debates in Germany on the constitutionality of international investment arbitration. For support regarding the existence of a judicial monopoly, see eg Groh and Khan (n 82) 4–6; Groh (n 82) 435–39; and, with regard to CETA, the constitutional complaints by Andreas Fischer-Lescano in the name and on behalf of 63 plaintiffs (15 July 2016) 38 and Bernhard Kempen in the name and on behalf of 125,047 plaintiffs (29 August 2016) 61–66, both available at <www.ceta-verfassungsbeschwerde.de> accessed 22 January 2025 (in German).

[96] *Pechstein* (n 67) para 38 (with further references to the Court's case law).

[97] For the text of Article 19(4) GG, see n 74 above.

In addition, the German Constitution contains provisions on the organization and independence of the judiciary. To this end, Article 92 GG provides that '[t]he judicial power shall be vested in the judges; it shall be exercised by the Federal Constitutional Court, by the federal courts provided for in this Basic Law and by the courts of the Länder.' Articles 94–96 GG contain rules on the composition of the Federal Constitutional Court and the establishment of the federal supreme courts for the different branches of the judiciary as well as other federal courts. Article 101(1) GG, in turn, prohibits the establishment of 'extraordinary courts' and ensures that '[n]o one may be removed from the jurisdiction of his lawful judge.' What the German Constitution does not contain, however, is a provision that lays down specific competences of the different courts, with the exception of Article 93 GG, which lists the matters the German Federal Constitutional Court is competent to decide on.[98]

Several of the above-mentioned provisions of the German Constitution would indeed be violated if recourse to arbitration was made mandatory for the resolution of disputes, whether between private actors or between private and public parties.[99] With the exception of Article 93 GG, none of these provisions, however, can be read as establishing a monopoly of domestic courts that would prevent private actors and German public entities from agreeing voluntarily to settle disputes by recourse to private-public arbitration.

As regards the guarantee in Article 92 GG that judicial power is vested in the judges, as well as the general constitutional right of access to justice, the German Federal Constitutional Court has recently confirmed in the *Pechstein* case that neither of those constitutional norms can be read as establishing a judicial monopoly for the resolution of private-private disputes.[100] The same must hold true for private-public disputes. To start with, there is nothing in the wording of Article 92 GG nor in the very concept of access to justice that would suggest that private-public disputes are to be treated differently from private-private disputes. Furthermore, Article 92 GG is not concerned with the role of judges in relation to disputing parties, but addresses

[98] These matters include, amongst others, disputes between the main state organs about their constitutional rights and duties; requests for the determination of constitutionality of federal and state law initiated by the main state organs; disputes between the Federation and the *Länder* and between different *Länder*; constitutional complaints by private parties, political parties, and municipalities (see art 93(1) GG); and proceedings concerning the review of unconstitutionality of legislation requested by domestic courts (see art 100(1) GG).

[99] See Christian Hillgruber, 'Art 92 GG' in Roman Herzog and others (eds), *Grundgesetz: Kommentar* (looseleaf, CH Beck 2021) vol 6, para 91; Classen (n 68) para 41. See also, on the requirement of voluntary consent to arbitration, German Federal Court of Justice, Case No II ZR 373/98, Judgment (3 April 2000) (2000) 53(23) Neue Juristische Wochenschrift 1713. Against this background, the 2019 reform of the German Packaging Act, which introduced mandatory arbitration for disputes concerning the tendering process for waste disposal services to the exclusion of access to the ordinary courts (see Gesetz zur Fortentwicklung der haushaltsnahen Getrennterfassung von wertstoffhaltigen Abfällen (Verpackungsgesetz) [2017] 1 BGBl 2234, s 23(8)–(9)) is highly problematic and widely considered to be unconstitutional. In this sense, see Karl von Hase, Franz-Rudolf Groß, and Ulf-Dieter Pape, 'Primärrechtsschutz durch zwingende Schiedsgerichtsbarkeit im Ausschreibungsverfahren nach § 23 VerpackungsG: Gut gemeint, aber verfassungswidrig' (2019) 17(6) Zeitschrift für Schiedsverfahren 324, 325; Markus Köhler and Stephan Hudetz, 'Gesetzliche Anordnung eines Schiedsverfahrens? Zur Verfassungsmäßigkeit von § 23 Abs 8 und 9 VerpackG' (2020) 18(2) Zeitschrift für Schiedsverfahren 68; Wolfgang Voit, '§ 1025 ZPO' in Hans-Joachim Musielak and Wolfgang Voit (eds), *Zivilprozessordnung mit Gerichtsverfassungsgesetz: Kommentar* (18th edn, Vahlen 2021) para 1.

[100] *Pechstein* (n 67) para 39.

an issue concerning the separation of powers between the judiciary, the legislature, and the executive: it prevents the latter two branches of government from exercising judicial functions,[101] but cannot be understood as preventing disputing parties from voluntarily having recourse to arbitration or arbitrators from exercising functions that would otherwise be vested in the courts.[102] Similarly, the prohibition in Article 101(1) GG of 'extraordinary courts' and of removing anybody from 'the jurisdiction of [one's] lawful judge' are directed at unilateral interferences by the state with the organization of, and case distribution in, the judiciary, but do not establish a judicial monopoly that would limit disputing parties from agreeing to arbitration.[103]

The same must hold true with respect to the specific rights of access to justice laid down in Articles 19(4) and 14(3) GG. While these ensure access to justice with respect to specific matters, and would prevent unilateral government measures limiting the right of an affected private actor to domestic courts, there is no indication that these provisions limit disputing parties in voluntarily dispensing with their right to recourse to domestic courts, either in the form of contractual agreements to arbitrate disputes or by accepting the state's offer to arbitrate private-public disputes in an IIA. While the German Federal Constitutional Court has not made a specific decision on whether Articles 19(4) and 14(3) GG have any impact on private-public arbitration on the matters covered by each provision, it has decided that Article 19(4) GG is not violated if the state confers powers to an international organization that permit the exercise of public authority vis-à-vis private actors, and at the same time excludes recourse to its own courts by affected individuals seeking judicial review of the exercise of that authority, provided that effective alternatives of judicial review are available at the international level before an instance that itself complies with the requirements of independence and impartiality and ensures due process and a fair trial.[104] In that context, the Court held that Article 19(4) GG does not give rise to a constitutionally protected right of access to German courts.[105] The same considerations arguably apply *mutatis mutandis* in respect of private-public arbitration, so that neither Article 19(4) GG, nor for that matter Article 14(3) GG, can be understood as creating a judicial monopoly of German courts that would exclude the possibility of parties to agree to arbitrate private-public disputes.[106]

[101] Dieter Wilke, '§ 112: Die rechtsprechende Gewalt' in Josef Isensee and Paul Kirchhof (eds), *Handbuch des Staatsrechts der Bundesrepublik Deutschland* (3rd edn, CF Müller 2007) vol 5, 633, paras 24 and 90.

[102] Classen (n 68) paras 41–43a; Steffen Detterbeck, 'Art 92' in Michael Sachs (ed), *Grundgesetz: Kommentar* (9th edn, CH Beck 2021) para 28; Helmuth Schulze-Fielitz, 'Art 92' in Horst Dreier (ed), *Grundgesetz: Kommentar* (3rd edn, Mohr Siebeck 2018) vol 3, para 50 (with further references); Stoll, Holterhus, and Gött (n 82) 141 and 150. Similarly Hillgruber (n 99) paras 7, 90 (limiting this finding, however, to private-private arbitration in civil matters).

[103] Ohler (n 82) 344.

[104] *Eurocontrol I* (n 89) 26–30, 40 ff; German Federal Constitutional Court, Case No 2 BvR 1058/79, Order (10 November 1981) BVerfGE 59, 63, 85 ff – *Eurocontrol II*; *Solange II* (n 89) 376; German Federal Constitutional Court, Case No 2 BvR 1961/09, Order (24 July 2018) BVerfGE 149, 346, 363 ff – *European Schools*.

[105] *European Schools* (n 104) 366, para 43.

[106] cf *Pechstein* (n 67) para 46 (clarifying that Article 19(4) GG is but a special case of the general right of access to justice, which the Court in the *Pechstein* case held not to create a judicial monopoly that would exclude private-private arbitration).

Finally, the idea of a judicial monopoly that would exclude or limit the use of private-public arbitration can also not be based on the principle of democratic governance as enshrined in Article 20(1) and (2) of the German Constitution. While the principle of democracy does require that all public authority, whether legislative, executive, or judicial, is derived from the people and legitimized by them through elections and other votes,[107] it does not mandate a specific organizational structure for how certain public functions are to be fulfilled.[108] Applied to the context of dispute resolution, the principle of democracy thus does not require that disputes, including private-public disputes, are necessarily settled by state courts rather than through arbitration. What the democratic principle does require, however, is that the public actor's agreement to arbitrate is democratically legitimized and, therefore, based on a legal framework that provides for the conditions and limits of private-public arbitration, such as the one described in section II above.[109]

That the idea of a judicial monopoly for the settlement of certain disputes, with the exception of those that have to come before the German Federal Constitutional Court pursuant to Article 93(1) GG, is alien to the German Constitution is further confirmed by Article 24(3) GG, which provides: 'For the settlement of disputes between states, the Federation shall accede to agreements providing for general, comprehensive and compulsory international arbitration.' While referring expressly to arbitration of disputes in inter-state relations, the provision not only covers disputes governed by international law, but would also encompass disputes governed by domestic law, including German law—just imagine a dispute arising out of an agreement for the lease of a German government-owned building in Germany to a foreign state, which would be governed by German law. Yet, Article 24(3) GG is not formulated as an exception to an otherwise existing judicial monopoly of domestic courts, but even as an encouragement to make use of arbitration.

In sum, the German Constitution does not lend support to the idea, as some voices in the literature argue, of a judicial monopoly of state courts that excludes or limits private-public arbitration, whether in a purely domestic or an international context. The different provisions and constitutional principles discussed simply cannot be construed in that way. This does not mean, however, that German constitutional law

[107] See German Federal Constitutional Court, Case No 2 BvR 134 and 268/76, Order (15 February 1978) BVerfGE 47, 253, 272–73; German Federal Constitutional Court, Case No 2 BvR 1178, 1179 and 1191/86, Order (1 October 1987) BVerfGE 77, 1, 40; German Federal Constitutional Court, Case No 2 BvF 3/89, Judgment (31 October 1990) BVerfGE 83, 60, 73; German Federal Constitutional Court, Case No 2 BvF 1/92, Order (24 May 1995) BVerfGE 93, 37, 68; German Federal Constitutional Court, Case No 2 BvL 5 and 6/98, Order (5 December 2002) BVerfGE 107, 59, 87.

[108] Friedrich Schoch, 'Privatisierung von Verwaltungsaufgaben' (1994) 109(17) Deutsches Verwaltungsblatt 962, 969–70. The delegation of sovereign functions to private actors is therefore compatible with the principle of democracy provided that it is founded on a legal basis and that the state meets its responsibility to ensure that the private actors fulfil their functions properly, which includes a corresponding monitoring obligation that also applies to parliament; see German Federal Constitutional Court, Case No 2 BvR 133/10, Judgment (18 January 2012) BVerfGE 130, 76, 123 – *Forensic Psychiatric Services.*

[109] The arbitral tribunal itself does not exercise state authority in the sense of Article 20(2) GG, as its jurisdiction is solely based on party consent. This also appears to be the majority view in German literature, although the legal consequences of this finding remain disputed, especially in the context of international investment arbitration, as some scholars nevertheless require sufficient democratic legitimation of the tribunal: see eg Ohler (n 82) 344; Classen, 'Die Unterwerfung unter völkerrechtliche (Schieds-)Gerichte' (n 82) 451–52; Steinbach (n 82) 10–13.

is irrelevant for private-public arbitration. On the contrary, as discussed in the next section, it provides a framework that guides how private-public arbitrations involving German public entities are to be conducted, what safeguards must be in place, and what limits must be observed.

3 Procedural and Organizational Safeguards for Private-Public Arbitration Proceedings

While the German Constitution does not provide for a judicial monopoly for the resolution of private-public disputes and therefore is open to such disputes being settled through arbitrations, provided an enabling statutory framework is in place, Germany's constitutional model of democratic government under the rule of law has an impact on what that framework must look like in terms of procedural and organizational safeguards so that private-public arbitrations comply with the rule of law and the principle of democracy. To start with, as the German Federal Constitutional Court has held in the context of private-private arbitration, upholding agreements to arbitrate and excluding access to domestic courts for the resolution of the underlying dispute is only acceptable from the perspective of the rule of law, and the entitlement to access to justice that forms part of it, if the arbitration proceedings themselves meet certain constitutional minimum standards and comply with the different facets flowing from the rule of law. In the Court's words:

> In order for the state to recognise arbitration decisions, and enforce them in the exercise of its public authority, it must ensure that the arbitration procedure guarantees effective legal protection and meets the minimum standards of the rule of law. When interpreting and applying the statutory provisions on the recognition and enforcement of arbitration procedures and the validity of arbitration agreements, the specific guarantees of the general right of access to justice under Art. 2(1) in conjunction with Art. 20(3) GG must be taken into account.[110]

Consequently, any arbitration proceeding under the German Constitution's remit, be it national or international, must ensure the independence and impartiality of arbitrators in order to comply with the minimum requirements under the rule of law,[111] and ensure due process including, in particular, the parties' right to be heard.[112] Moreover, mechanisms must be put in place that allow for review of whether arbitration proceedings comply with minimum rule-of-law requirements, for example in the course

[110] *Pechstein* (n 67) para 40.

[111] ibid para 53 (stating that both national and international arbitral proceedings must ensure that arbitrators are impartial and independent, exercising neutrality and distance vis-à-vis all parties to the proceedings).

[112] ibid para 44 (linking the guarantee of public proceedings, which was at issue in the present case, to due process and the rule of law by stressing that, in principle, '[t]he guarantee of public proceedings serves to protect those involved in a hearing against a secret judiciary that is not subject to public scrutiny. . . . The rule-of-law dimension of public proceedings aims to ensure adherence to formal and substantive law. It is intended to strengthen procedural fairness in the sense of a procedural safeguard for the parties involved'). See also Classen, 'Art 92' (n 68) para 44; Hillgruber (n 99) para 91. See further on the constitutional requirements for the conduct of arbitral proceedings, Bianka Brach, *Die Verfassung als Grundlage und Grenze der Schiedsgerichtsbarkeit* (Logos 2013) 129 ff.

of proceedings concerning requests for set-aside, recognition, and enforcement.[113] This holds true not only for private-private arbitration, but must equally apply to private-public arbitration.

The German statutory framework governing arbitration, as presented above in section II, ensures the observance of these constitutional requirements for both private-private and private-public arbitration. It requires, amongst others, that arbitrators are independent and impartial (section 1036 ZPO), and that the arbitral tribunal affords due process and allows parties to involve counsel (section 1042(1) and (2) ZPO). Moreover, the German statutory framework also provides for remedies against an arbitral award in the context of set-aside proceedings before domestic courts (section 1059 ZPO), as well as in proceedings concerning the recognition and enforcement of arbitral awards (sections 1060 and 1061 ZPO). Arbitration proceedings involving German public entities to which the German statutory arbitration framework applies should therefore not raise concerns from the perspective of constitutional law, as they live up to the minimum requirements under the rule of law.[114]

The German Constitution's minimum requirements under the rule of law are not only met with respect to private-public arbitration that is subject to domestic legislation, but also in respect of those subject to other—including foreign—arbitration frameworks.[115] For instance, the UNCITRAL Arbitration Rules, as well as those of all major arbitration institutions, contain identical minimum rule-of-law requirements providing for the independence and impartiality of arbitrators, the parties' right to be heard, and the duty to give reasoned decisions.[116] The same applies to most arbitration laws worldwide, including, but not limited to, those based on the UNCITRAL Model Law for International Commercial Arbitration.[117] Domestic arbitration laws, as exemplified by the Model Law, also provide for possibilities of recourse to domestic courts in set-aside and enforcement proceedings that are comparable to Germany's statutory framework. Moreover, the New York Convention upholds the possibility for refusing recognition and enforcement of foreign arbitral awards for violation of public policy in the case that minimum requirements under the rule of law have not been complied with in an arbitration proceeding. Consequently, having private-public disputes involving German public entities settled through arbitration, and subjecting that arbitration to a foreign statutory arbitration framework, should comply with the minimum requirements under the rule of law required under German constitutional law.

[113] Classen (n 68) para 44.

[114] But see Detterbeck (n 102) para 29 (deeming ss 1025 ff ZPO to be 'constitutionally doubtful' – translation by the authors). Of note, in *Pechstein* (n 67) paras 34–49, the German Federal Constitutional Court took issue not with the legal framework in place, but with its interpretation and application in the concrete case, which it found to have fallen short of the requirements of German constitutional law.

[115] In the same vein, see Stoll, Holterhus, and Gött (n 82) 158. For views in the literature arguing for the opposite position, see Groh and Khan (n 82) 9–12; Groh (n 82) 439–40; Kempen (n 95) 67 ff.

[116] See UNCITRAL Arbitration Rules (as revised in 2010) arts 11–13, 17(1), 34(3); Arbitration Rules of the International Chamber of Commerce (2021) arts 11(1), 22(4), 32(2); Arbitration Rules of the London Court of International Arbitration (2020) arts 5.3, 14.1, 26.2; Arbitration Rules of the Arbitration Institute of the Stockholm Chamber of Commerce (2017) arts 18, 23(2), 42(1).

[117] See UNCITRAL Model Law (n 43) arts 12, 18, 31(2). For detailed analysis of the arbitration laws of more than 85 jurisdictions, see Lise Bosman (ed), *ICCA International Handbook on Commercial Arbitration* (ICCA & Kluwer Law International 2020).

The same holds true with respect to delocalized private-public arbitrations governed by the ICSID Convention. The ICSID Convention and the ICSID Arbitration Rules guarantee the observation of fundamental rules of procedure, such as the parties' right to be heard and the duty to provide reasoned decisions, as well as the impartiality and independence of arbitrators.[118] Moreover, even though domestic courts cannot be approached with requests to set aside ICSID awards or to resist their recognition and enforcement (see Arts 53, 54(1) ICSID Convention), the ICSID Convention itself provides for mechanisms to ensure that violations of the minimum requirements under the rule of law can be effectively remedied. In the case of ICSID arbitration, the annulment committee performs the review tasks of the otherwise competent national courts, examining, inter alia, whether 'there has been a serious departure from a fundamental rule of procedure' (Art 52(1)(d) ICSID Convention). There is no ground to believe that an ICSID annulment committee, which is fully independent of the original arbitral tribunal, is any less equipped to do so than a domestic court. The review mechanism under ICSID therefore sufficiently ensures the required minimum level of access to justice as mandated by the German Constitution.[119]

Mechanisms that ensure that arbitrators are independent and impartial and observe due process and other rule-of-law requirements in conducting arbitration proceedings are, however, not the only procedural safeguards required under German constitutional law. In addition, transparency in private-public arbitration proceedings is an important constitutional demand. It flows from both the principle of democracy and the rule of law, as acknowledged by the German Federal Constitutional Court in the context of a private-private arbitration:

> The public nature of oral hearings is an essential part of the principle of the rule of law and its importance goes far beyond individual procedural rules. It is also linked to the general principle of the public nature of democracy. The guarantee of public proceedings serves to protect those involved in a hearing against a secret judiciary that is not subject to public scrutiny. Given that the legal design of an arbitration procedure must ensure equally effective legal protection that satisfies minimum standards of the rule of law, it must then be recognised that the rule of law includes the principle of public proceedings . . . The rule-of-law dimension of public proceedings

[118] ICSID Arbitration Rules (2022) rr 3(2), 13(2)–(4), 59(1)(g)–(j). See also ICSID Convention (n 64) arts 14, 38–40, 57 (concerning independence and impartiality); arts 44 and 52(1)(d) (concerning the need to observe fundamental rules of procedure); arts 48(3) and 52(1)(e) (concerning the duty to provide reasons).

[119] As a final resort, if a violation of the German Constitution persists after an ICSID annulment proceeding has concluded, compliance with an ICSID award could be refused within Germany's internal legal order, as in the internal hierarchy of norms the ICSID Convention has the status of ordinary legislation that not only has to comply with the Constitution's superior norms, but can also be validly overridden by later legislation. See, on international treaties and their normative rank within the German legal order, as well as on the possibility, from the perspective of German constitutional law, of a so-called treaty override, *Treaty Override* (n 58) 28 ff. This possibility, however, is highly unlikely, as it is difficult to imagine outcomes that contravene the German Constitution's minimum requirements under the rule of law without at the same time constituting grounds for annulment under ICSID Convention (n 64) art 52(1)(a)–(e). Besides, such a refusal to comply with an ICSID award would also expose Germany to international responsibility for breach of the ICSID Convention.

> aims to ensure adherence to formal and substantive law. It is intended to strengthen procedural fairness in the sense of a procedural safeguard for the parties involved.[120]

The Court therefore recognizes that, in principle, there is a constitutional entitlement of disputing parties to transparent arbitration proceedings. The Court also recognizes, however, that 'the public can be partially or completely excluded from proceedings for compelling reasons of the common good even in cases where public proceedings are in principle required by the Constitution'.[121] What is required, in other words, is a justification that must pass a high threshold ('compelling reasons') for excluding the public from arbitration proceedings. Such compelling reasons would be present, for example, in the context of private-private arbitrations to protect confidential business information or trade secrets, but they were not present, the Court held, in respect of the sports arbitration before the Court of Arbitration for Sport in the *Pechstein* case.[122] However, the considerations presented by the German Federal Constitutional Court cannot be limited to private-private arbitration, but must also apply to private-public arbitration. In this context as well, transparent proceedings protect the disputing parties against secret justice and ensure the arbitral tribunal's adherence to the substantive and procedural law that has been made democratically in the interest of the general public.

In conclusion, while the German Constitution generally permits private-public arbitration, it also requires a legal framework for these arbitrations to ensure that certain procedural and organizational safeguards flowing from the principles of the rule of law and of democracy are respected, independently of whether the basis for private-public arbitration is in contract or treaty. The safeguards that are constitutionally required encompass the need for arbitral tribunals to be independent and impartial, to respect due process in conducting proceedings, and to abide by the principle of transparency; in addition, complaint mechanisms against the decisions of arbitral tribunals in private-public disputes must be available, either before domestic courts or another instance that provides for equivalent legal protections.

4 Systemic Impacts of Private-Public Arbitration as a Constitutional Challenge

The shift away from settling private-public disputes before domestic courts, and towards arbitration, raises constitutional concerns not only with respect to the resolution of individual disputes; it also involves broader implications that require attention from the perspective of constitutional law. Systemically, an increase in private-public arbitration, especially if it reflects a general pattern for certain disputes, is accompanied by a decrease in court-based settlement of the (types of) disputes in question. Such a development can have negative implications for how the legislator, executive, and judiciary interact with each other in the constitutionally established separation-of-powers framework, because the functions exercised by domestic courts

[120] *Pechstein* (n 67) para 44 (relying on the Court's previous statements on the guarantee of public proceedings, including its constitutional foundations and limits, in BVerfGE 103, 44, 63 f, which concerned the admissibility of television recordings during court hearings).
[121] ibid.
[122] ibid para 32.

in that system shift to arbitral tribunals, or risk getting lost altogether. This poses a challenge for Germany's constitutional model of democratic governance under the rule of law, because in that separation-of-powers framework courts take up two functions: (1) ensuring, with respect to individual cases, that the executive complies with the law enacted by the legislator, thereby upholding the rule of law; and (2) ensuring the consistent, coherent, and predictable application of democratically enacted laws, for example by concretizing their meaning for concrete classes of cases, or by further developing the law in case of lacunae, under the continued scrutiny of the legislator who can step in by adapting the applicable law in the case of unwanted developments. A loss of these functions of domestic courts threatens the constitutionally established separation-of-powers framework within the German Constitution's system of democratic governance under the rule of law and risks eroding the law governing private-public relations as it has hitherto developed.

Three, partly overlapping, partly independent, concerns can be identified in this context. The first arises when private-public dispute resolution systematically shifts from domestic courts to a private-public arbitration system whose proceedings take place behind closed doors and whose outcomes remain confidential. This is widely the case in contract-based private-public arbitrations, as shown above in section I, but also still occurs, despite existing developments towards enhanced transparency, in respect of treaty-based private-public arbitrations. Such a development is not only problematic for ensuring that arbitrators apply the applicable law correctly in individual disputes and remain accountable;[123] a systematic shift of dispute settlement to confidential private-public arbitration also reduces, or even excludes, the generation of jurisprudence/precedent both by domestic courts (which will no longer have the necessary caseload to apply, concretize, and further develop the applicable law) and arbitral tribunals (whose decisions will remain confidential and therefore cannot provide guidance about the applicable law beyond the disputing parties). Such a loss in precedent would take away an important public good that allows private as well as public actors that are not parties to a concrete dispute to understand how the law governing their relations is applied in dispute settlement proceedings, what consequences follow from it, and how they should behave in order to comply with the governing law. Such a development has already taken place in German commercial law, for example as regards the sale and purchase of companies, where there is virtually no more Supreme Court jurisprudence that could provide guidance to the parties engaged in such transactions as well as to arbitral tribunals that hear the respective disputes,[124] and is equally conceivable in respect of the law governing private-public relations, especially if private-public arbitration gradually substitutes dispute settlement before domestic courts. This would upset the constitutionally established separation-of-powers framework and risk eroding the law governing private-public relations.[125]

[123] See the discussion above at nn 120 ff and accompanying text.

[124] Christian Duve and Moritz Keller, 'Privatisierung der Justiz – bleibt die Rechtsfortbildung auf der Strecke?' (2005) 3(4) Zeitschrift für Schiedsverfahren 169, 172–73.

[125] After all, one important function of the law is to stabilize normative expectations of private and public actors who are duty-bound by the law. On this function of law, see Niklas Luhmann, *Das Recht der Gesellschaft* (Suhrkamp 1993) 124 ff.

The second concern consists of arbitral tribunals interpreting and applying the law governing private-public relations in an inconsistent, incoherent, and unpredictable manner. The resulting loss of legal certainty, which is a discrete element of the constitutional principle of the rule of law, not only makes it difficult for both private and public actors to adapt their conduct so as to comply with the legal framework governing private-public relations;[126] inconsistencies are also problematic under the constitutionally established separation-of-powers framework because they undermine the democratic principle that, in applying the law to concrete cases, and thereby implementing the legislator's intentions, like cases should be treated alike.[127] The concern for inconsistencies in the resolution of private-public arbitrations results from the structure of the system of arbitration, which is characterized by a lack of hierarchy among arbitral tribunals, the inexistence of centralized control mechanisms, and the absence of a rule of *stare decisis*, and has already surfaced prominently in the practice of international investment arbitration, where rules and principles of general international law, core standards of treatment under international investment treaties, and rules governing arbitration procedures have at times received incompatible interpretations and applications.[128] By contrast, domestic court systems contain numerous features to minimize, if not avoid, comparable inconsistencies in the interpretation of the law governing private-public relations, such as a hierarchical court structure with appellate and supreme courts, and, additionally in the case of Germany, the German Federal Constitutional Court as a court in which questions of constitutional law are centralized, as well as the Joint Senate of the Federal Supreme Courts, which ensures consistency in general legal matters across Germany's functionally differentiated domestic court system.

Even if arbitral decisions were to become public and arbitral tribunals capable of creating consistent and coherent case law, the shift away from dispute settlement before domestic courts towards private-public arbitration raises a final concern, which relates to the impact arbitral tribunals have on the governing law more generally. In such a scenario, it is not unlikely that arbitral tribunals will in fact take up similar functions as domestic courts through their dispute resolution activities, that is, contribute to concretizing the governing law beyond its application to individual cases, or even further develop it. While such governance effects have not been noticed in respect of domestic private-public arbitration in Germany, they have come to the fore in the context of international investment arbitration and, to a lesser degree, also in

[126] On the issue of inconsistency in international investment law and arbitration from the perspective of the rule of law, see Julian Arato, 'Two Moralities of Consistency' in August Reinisch and Stephan W Schill (eds), *Investment Protection Standards and the Rule of Law* (OUP 2023) 235.

[127] See Stephan W Schill, 'Reforming Investor–State Dispute Settlement: A (Comparative and International) Constitutional Law Framework' (2017) 20 JIEL 649, 652–57. See also Susan D Franck, 'The Nature and Enforcement of Investor Rights Under Investment Treaties: Do Investment Treaties Have a Bright Future?' (2005) 12 UC Davis J Int'l L & Pol'y 47, 65–66.

[128] See Susan D Franck, 'The Legitimacy Crisis in Investment Treaty Arbitration: Privatizing Public International Law Through Inconsistent Decisions' (2005) 73 Fordham LR 1521; Stephan W Schill, *The Multilateralization of International Investment Law* (CUP 2009) 285 ff, 339 ff; Irene M Ten Cate, 'The Costs of Consistency: Precedent in Investment Treaty Arbitration' (2013) 51 Columbia Journal of Transnational Law 418; Julian Arato, Chester Brown, and Federico Ortino, 'Parsing and Managing Inconsistency in Investor-State Dispute Settlement' (2020) 21(2–3) JWIT 336, 337–38 and 348 ff.

international commercial arbitration. In these fields, there is little doubt that arbitral tribunals, rather than domestic courts, do not just settle individual disputes, but concretize and at times even actively develop arbitral precedent that shapes and further develops the understanding of the governing law.[129] Such a development entails risks for the constitutionally established separation-of-powers framework as arbitral tribunals lack the direct democratic legitimacy for such governance activities and may concretize or further develop the law governing private-public relations quite differently from domestic courts. For example, different biases may come in when arbitral tribunals resolve private-public disputes or when balancing private and public interests. This risks watering down the principle of legality as it could reduce the accountability of both the executive and arbitral tribunals vis-à-vis the legislator, contrary to what is provided for in Article 20(3) GG.[130] The accountability of the executive to the law enacted by the legislator could, for example, be reduced if arbitral tribunals were to systematically review the legality of executive action less strictly than domestic courts would. Conversely, if arbitral tribunals were to interpret the law overly strictly, they would hamper the executive's constitutional duty to implement the law enacted by the legislator.

At least for now, the systemic impacts presented above remain largely in the sphere of future possibilities and have not (yet) materialized in respect of private-public arbitration involving German public entities. This notwithstanding, a shift in the settlement of private-public disputes from domestic courts to arbitral tribunals poses challenges to the constitutionally established separation-of-powers framework that plays a central role for Germany's constitutional model of democratic government under the rule of law. Although the risks involved do not, per se, make private-public arbitration unconstitutional, they call for vigilance in order to avoid future developments in private-public arbitration that undermine the functioning of the separation-of-powers framework as well as its importance for the principles of rule of law and democracy, thereby potentially violating the German Constitution.

In this context, transparency in private-public arbitration appears as a core constitutional demand. It not only increases arbitral tribunals' accountability for how they apply the law governing private-public relations in the settlement of individual disputes, but also helps avoid that the systemic impacts of private-public arbitration undermine core constitutional principles. For one, the publicity of the arbitral proceeding and its outcome would ensure sufficient compensation for the diminished role of domestic courts in interpreting, concretizing, and further developing the law applicable to private-public relations, which would be taken up by arbitral tribunals instead. Secondly, transparency of private-public arbitration would not only increase

[129] For the governance role of arbitral tribunals in investment treaty arbitrations, see Stephan W Schill, *The Multilateralization of International Investment Law* (CUP 2009); Frédéric Gilles Sourgens, *A Nascent Common Law: The Process of Decisionmaking in International Legal Disputes between States and Foreign Investors* (Brill Nijhoff 2015); Renè Urueña, 'Of Precedents and Ideology: Lawmaking by Investment Arbitration Tribunals' in Prabhakar Singh and Benoît Mayer (eds), *Critical International Law: Postrealism, Postcolonialism, and Transnationalism* (OUP 2014) 276. For a discussion of the exercise of governance functions by arbitral tribunals in the context of international commercial and investment arbitration, see Dolores Bentolila, *Arbitrators as Lawmakers: The Creation of General Rules Through Consistent Decision Making in International Commercial and Investment Arbitration* (Kluwer Law International 2017).

[130] For the text of Article 20(3) GG, see n 38 above.

the arbitral tribunals' accountability, but also that of the executive. Not only would the conduct of the disputing parties be subject to broader public scrutiny; transparency is also a prerequisite to allow sufficient parliamentary oversight over both executive conduct in private-public relations and of how arbitral tribunals settle private-public disputes, not only with respect to legality, but also in regard to expediency and political desirability. As emphasized by the German Federal Constitutional Court in a context unrelated to private-public arbitration, 'parliamentary oversight is also a manifestation of the Federal Government's accountability to Parliament, which is derived from the principle of democracy'.[131] Therefore, both the concept of the rule of law and the principle of democracy require that the conduct of public actors be sufficiently transparent to ensure effective parliamentary oversight over the Executive Branch in private-public relations as well as over the way resulting disputes are settled in arbitration proceedings, and to allow the legislator, if needed, to intervene by adapting the legal framework governing private-public arbitration.

Yet, the fact that many private-public arbitration proceedings at both the domestic and international level are, despite positive developments, particularly in the context of investment treaty arbitrations,[132] often still confidential and non-transparent severely restricts the exercise of parliamentary control in a constitutionally relevant manner. Above all, the legislator must be able to form an opinion on how private-public arbitration operates and what effects it has on the balance between private and public rights, and on public interests more generally. This is particularly important in high-profile cases that have a considerable impact on the public purse, such as the *Toll Collect* case, or that have an important impact on society as a whole, as was the case with the *Vattenfall II* proceeding concerning Germany's nuclear power phase-out, but it holds true also in less emblematic cases, as legality of government conduct, and of the settlement of private-public disputes through arbitration, are key concerns for Germany's constitutional model of democratic government under the rule of law. To ensure effective democratic control of private-public arbitration and its compliance with the principle of the rule of law, it is necessary that the existence of arbitration clauses and of arbitral proceedings—that is, their initiation, conduct, and outcome—are, in principle, public,[133] subject only to exceptions based

[131] German Federal Constitutional Court, Case No 2 BvE 2/11, Judgment (7 November 2017) BVerfGE 147, 50, 127 – *Parliamentary Right to Information* (on parliament's right to receive information vis-à-vis the German government and its constitutional limits, here with respect to several queries regarding discussions and agreements between the Federal Government and a legal entity fully controlled by the state, as well as questions regarding regulatory measures of other state agencies). Parliamentary oversight over the executive has also been confirmed in areas of foreign policy: see eg German Federal Constitutional Court, Case No 2 BvE 5/11, Judgment (21 October 2014) BVerfGE 137, 185, 231 ff – *Arms Exports*; and, recently in the context of CETA, German Federal Constitutional Court, Judgment (2 March 2021) (n 86) para 76. See also, on the importance of parliamentary oversight in the case of a delegation of sovereign functions to private entities, *Forensic Psychiatric Services* (n 108).

[132] See especially the United Nations Convention on Transparency in Treaty-based Investor-State Arbitration (adopted 10 December 2014, entered into force 18 October 2017), as well as the UNCITRAL Rules on Transparency in Treaty-based Investor-State Arbitration (effective 1 April 2014).

[133] In this sense, see also Rosenau (n 2) 227–28; Wolff (n 9) 207–09 (who argues that arbitral clauses providing for the exclusion of the public during arbitral proceedings are null and void). Examples of competing concerns that constitute exceptions to transparency are the protection of business interests and of fundamental rights of the private actors. cf *Parliamentary Right to Information* (n 131) 129 ff.

on 'compelling reasons of the common good'.[134] Only transparency permits the control of the public body that is party to the arbitration, as well as of how arbitral tribunals control the conduct of the public entities involved, by parliament, supervisory government agencies, and the general public. It is such oversight, in turn, that can translate into political decisions about whether to maintain, reform, or discontinue participation of German public entities in otherwise constitutionally permissible private-public arbitrations.

C. Summary

All in all, as with any other field of German law and legal practice, constitutional law provides an important benchmark for the analysis of the statutory framework and treaty network governing private-public arbitration in Germany. Although the German Federal Constitutional Court has not pronounced itself expressly on the matter, constitutional law can be seen as both providing a justification for Germany's liberal approach to private-public arbitration and as setting out its limits. The principle of the rule of law can, on the one hand, be used to justify the availability of recourse to private-public arbitration, particularly when seen as a form of access to justice that provides adjudicatory means for resolving disputes in private-public relations, thereby ensuring the protection of both private interests and government powers. On the other hand, the constitutional rule-of-law principle also shapes the practices and procedures of private-public arbitration and the institutional safeguards that must be available so that private-public arbitration involving German public entities qualifies as a dispute settlement mechanism that conforms to the German Constitution. These include the need to ensure that arbitrators are independent and impartial and extend due process to the disputing parties, the availability of legal recourses against arbitral awards, and transparency of the proceedings (subject to exceptions to protect certain competing legitimate interests). In addition, the principle of democracy, the rule of law, and the constitutionally established separation-of-powers framework are the basis for formulating specific constitutional law demands that private-public arbitration must conform to in light of the systemic impacts and governance effects that a more frequent use of arbitration entails. Here again, transparency, as a prerequisite for parliamentary oversight over how private-public arbitration is practised, appears as the central constitutional demand that private-public arbitration must live up to, but in practice largely still falls short of. Finally, transparency of private-public arbitration will also ensure that constitutional law can continuously function as the ultimate normative and legal yardstick that the dynamic process of private-public arbitration involving German public interests must conform to in order to avoid a potential erosion of the law governing private-public relations.

[134] *Pechstein* (n 67) para 44.

IV. Conclusion

Already, for a considerable amount of time, the German legal system has taken a rather liberal approach towards private-public arbitration. Germany's statutory framework, as well as its international treaty commitments, allow for the participation of public entities in arbitration proceedings with private actors in a broad range of disputes. Most administrative law disputes, except for taxation and social security-related matters, as well as private law disputes and disputes concerning state liability, are arbitrable and can be submitted, with the disputing parties' agreement, to resolution by arbitration. Once within the range of arbitrable disputes, the law governing arbitration proceedings, and the role it prescribes for domestic courts, is formally identical to that governing commercial arbitrations, with the exception that administrative courts act as supervisory courts in matters of administrative law (see the reference in section 173 VwGO). Hence, the attention given to the protection of public interests in private-public arbitrations is, from a formal standpoint, no different from that accorded to the protection of public interests involved in private-private arbitrations.

At the same time, the German statutory arbitration framework also acknowledges that there are differences between private-public and private-private disputes. For one, the reference in section 173 VwGO to the rules on civil procedure only applies 'if the fundamental differences between the two types of procedures do not rule this out'. Furthermore, the statutory arbitration framework currently in place in Germany is sufficiently open to adapt private-public arbitrations, as well as connected proceedings before supervisory courts, to the specific needs arising out of the participation of public actors as disputing parties and the public interest issues typically involved in private-public relations. For instance, if the circumstances of the case so warrant, the statutory framework allows arbitrators in private-public disputes to take recourse to procedural principles governing judicial review in administrative courts, including *suo motu* powers, the principle of *iura novit curia*, and participation of affected non-parties.[135] Similarly, in order to ensure the correct application of the law governing private-public relations, arbitrators with the requisite expertise can be appointed. In addition, in set-aside or enforcement proceedings before domestic courts, existing possibilities for scrutiny under Germany's *ordre public* could be tailored so as to ensure that the public interest is not compromised by parties agreeing to arbitrate private-public disputes rather than litigating them before domestic courts.

Despite Germany's liberal approach to private-public arbitration, practical experience with it is still rather limited when compared with other legal systems. This somewhat reduces the extent to which one can learn from Germany's experience with private-public arbitration, particularly its impact on the protection of public interests and the evaluation of the mechanisms German law provides for safeguarding them.

[135] On constitutionally mandated modifications to the statutory arbitration framework in private-public arbitrations, see Möller (n 2) 137–81 and, especially with regard to the arbitral procedure, ibid 171 ff. See also the references cited in n 53 above. Notably, in the absence of party agreement, the arbitral tribunal already has discretion to determine questions of procedure by itself pursuant to s 1042(4) ZPO: see eg Partial Award (n 5) 260.

What is notable, however, is that the debate in Germany has taken a specific turn in recent years, driven mostly by the reaction to several high-profile disputes that involved the German state under both contracts and, more prominently, under IIAs to which Germany is party, most notably the ECT. This rise in case law has not just sparked increased criticism of private-public arbitration; instead, the debate has placed questions of constitutional law center stage by focusing on the constitutional foundations of, and potential limits to, private-public arbitration. This phenomenon induced what can be understood as a constitutionalization of the field of private-public arbitration. In that debate, concerns about private-public arbitration are framed as interferences of private-public arbitration with, or threats to, specific constitutional values, particularly the protection of the rule of law and the principle of democracy. At the same time, constitutional values, notably the idea of access to justice and government under the rule of law, are also used to provide justifications for allowing recourse to private-public arbitration, in particular under IIAs, where constitutional protections to foreigners are more limited than in purely domestic settings.

This turn of the debate towards the constitutionalization of private-public arbitration in Germany is likely of broader interest, also beyond the borders of Germany, as the constitutional analysis of private-public arbitration in Germany does not involve scrutiny of specific, or even idiosyncratic, constitutional rules, but concerns the impact of broadly formulated general principles of constitutional law, such as the insurance of the independence of the judiciary, the right of access to justice, the concept of the rule of law, the principle of democracy, or the constitutionally established separation-of-powers framework. What the debate in Germany about the constitutionalization of private-public arbitration shows is that neither general constitutional principles, such as the rule of law or democracy, nor the arguments about a constitutionally grounded monopoly for domestic courts provide a basis for fundamental constitutional opposition to consent-based private-public arbitration. Similarly, calls for withdrawing from private-public arbitration can hardly be founded on constitutional demands. While constitutional law in Germany does not require the legislator to permit private-public arbitration, the conscious choice for private-public arbitration complies with core constitutional values of the rule of law and democracy. Still, the German debate also shows that private-public arbitration is not entirely free of constitutional concern either, but entails potential risks for constitutionally enshrined values. Thus, once permitted, arbitration proceedings must live up to constitutional standards, including due process and the independence and impartiality of arbitrators; in addition, the framework governing private-public arbitration must provide for certain recourses against arbitral awards in order to ensure tribunals' compliance with basic rule-of-law standards.

Finally, the German case is instructive for grounding the need for transparency in private-public arbitration in constitutional law, that is, as a constitutionally mandated safeguard to ensure that arbitrators adhere to the rule of law in resolving individual disputes, but also to guarantee parliamentary supervision over the system of private-public arbitration and its impact on the law governing private-public relations more generally, thereby allowing the legislator to make the necessary changes to ensure that private-public arbitration continues to further, and not create risks for, the public interest. All of this shows how the constitutionalization of private-public arbitration witnessed in the German debate can leave its mark in evaluating the benefits that private-public arbitration brings, as well as the risks it entails, for the rule of law in private-public relations, and in designing the rules, institutions, and procedures needed to ensure that private-public arbitration enhances democratic government under the rule of law instead of undermining it.

Select Materials

Bibliography

Böckstiegel, Karl-Heinz, *Der Staat als Vertragspartner ausländischer Privatunternehmer* (Athenaeum 1971)

Brach, Bianka, *Die Verfassung als Grundlage und Grenze der Schiedsgerichtsbarkeit* (Logos 2013)

Classen, Claus Dieter, 'Die Unterwerfung demokratischer Hoheitsgewalt unter eine Schiedsgerichtsbarkeit' (2014) 25(16) Europäische Zeitschrift für Wirtschaftsrecht 611

Classen, Claus Dieter, 'Die Unterwerfung unter völkerrechtliche (Schieds-)Gerichte: kein Verfassungsverstoß!' (2016) 19(4) Zeitschrift für Europarechtliche Studien 449

Groh, Kathrin, 'Endstation Karlsruhe! – Schiedsgerichtsbarkeit in Freihandelsverträgen' (2016) 19(4) Zeitschrift für Europarechtliche Studien 433

Groh, Kathrin and Daniel-Erasmus Khan, 'Rechtsgutachten' (9 March 2015) <www.abgeordnetenwatch.de/system/files/qa-files/gutachten_ttip_groh_khan_09032015.pdf> accessed 22 January 2025

Grzeszick, Bernd, 'CETA als Präzedenzfall für die demokratischen Anforderungen an völkerrechtliche Verträge' (2016) 35(24) Neue Zeitschrift für Verwaltungsrecht 1753

Duve, Christian and Moritz Keller, 'Privatisierung der Justiz – bleibt die Rechtsfortbildung auf der Strecke?' (2005) 3(4) Zeitschrift für Schiedsverfahren 169

Kaltenborn, Markus, *Streitvermeidung und Streitbeilegung im Verwaltungsrecht* (Nomos 2007)

Köhler, Markus and Stephan Hudetz, 'Gesetzliche Anordnung eines Schiedsverfahrens? Zur Verfassungsmäßigkeit von § 23 Abs 8 und 9 VerpackG' (2020) 18(2) Zeitschrift für Schiedsverfahren 68

Loos, Christa, *Die Schiedsgerichtsbarkeit in der Verwaltungsgerichtsbarkeit* (doctoral thesis, University of Kiel 1984)

Ludwigs, Markus and Oliver Remien (eds), *Investitionsschutz, Schiedsgerichtsbarkeit und Rechtsstaat in der EU* (Nomos 2018)

Meissner, Claus and Christine Steinbeiß-Winkelmann, '§ 173 VwGO' in Friedrich Schoch and Jens-Peter Schneider (eds), *Verwaltungsrecht VwGO: Kommentar* (looseleaf, CH Beck 2022)

Möller, Kaspar Henrik, *Echte Schiedsgerichtsbarkeit im Verwaltungsrecht. Eine Studie zu Rechtsrahmen und Kontrolle nichtstaatlicher Streitentscheidung im Verwaltungsrecht* (Duncker & Humblot 2014)

Müller, Hanswerner, 'Entscheidung verwaltungsgerichtlicher Streitigkeiten durch Schiedsgerichte' (1963) 16(7) Neue Juristische Wochenschrift 282

Ohler, Christoph, 'Die Vereinbarkeit von Investor-Staat-Schiedsverfahren mit deutschem und europäischem Verfassungsrecht' (2015) 70 Juristenzeitung 337

Rosenau, René, *Die öffentliche Hand als Partei in verwaltungs- und zivilrechtlichen Schiedsverfahren* (Peter Lang 2018)
Schenk, Michel, *Schiedsfreiheit und staatliche Schutzpflichten* (Springer 2019)
Schiffbauer, Björn, 'Investitionsschutz und Grundgesetz: Bilaterale Investitionsschutzabkommen („BITs") aus verfassungsrechtlicher Perspektive' (2016) 7(2) Kölner Schrift zum Wirtschaftsrecht 145
Schill, Stephan W, 'Der Schutz von Auslandsinvestitionen in Deutschland im Mehrebenensystem: deutsches, europäisches und internationales Recht' (2010) 35 Archiv des öffentlichen Rechts 498
Steinbach, Armin, 'Investor-Staat-Schiedsverfahren und Verfassungsrecht' (2016) 80 Rabels Zeitschrift für ausländisches und internationales Privatrecht 1
Stoll, Peter-Tobias, Till Patrick Holterhus, and Henner Gött, *Investitionsschutz und Verfassung* (Mohr Siebeck 2017)
Stumpf, Christoph A, *Alternative Streitbeilegung im Verwaltungsrecht* (Mohr Siebeck 2006)
Tietje, Christian, 'Investitionsschutzgerichtsbarkeit in CETA und anderen Freihandelsabkommen der EU: Völkerrecht als Verfassungsverstoß?' (2016) 19(4) Zeitschrift für Europarechtliche Studien 421
von Hase, Karl, Franz-Rudolf Groß, and Ulf-Dieter Pape, 'Primärrechtsschutz durch zwingende Schiedsgerichtsbarkeit im Ausschreibungsverfahren nach § 23 VerpackungsG: Gut gemeint, aber verfassungswidrig' (2019) 17(6) Zeitschrift für Schiedsverfahren 324
Weidemann, Helmut, 'Schiedsgerichtsbarkeit in verwaltungsrechtlichen Streitsachen' (doctoral thesis, University of Marburg 1968)
Wolff, Johanna, 'Grenze der Heimlichkeit – Nicht-öffentliche Schiedsverfahren mit Beteiligung der öffentlichen Hand am Maßstab des Verfassungsrechts' (2012) 31 Neue Zeitschrift für Verwaltungsrecht 205
Woltereck, Richard, *Die Erledigung verwaltungsrechtlicher Streitigkeiten durch Schiedsgerichte* (doctoral thesis, University of Hamburg 1965)

Legislation

Gesetz über die schiedsgerichtliche Erledigung privatrechtlicher Streitigkeiten des Reiches und der Länder (1933) (Law on Arbitration of Private Law Disputes of the German Reich and the German States)
Grundgesetz (GG) (German Constitution), arts 19, 20, 24(3), 92, 93, 101, 103(1)
Lebensmittel-, Bedarfsgegenstände- und Futtermittelgesetzbuch (Food Code), § 45
Verpackungsgesetz (German Packaging Act), § 23(8)–(9)
Verwaltungsgerichtsordnung (VwGO) (Code of Administrative Court Procedure), §§ 40, 173
Verwaltungsverfahrensgesetz (VwVfG) (Administrative Procedures Act), §§ 54–62
Zivilprozessordnung (ZPO) (Code of Civil Procedure), §§ 1025–1066

Cases

Arbitral tribunal

Partial Award (16 August 1982), reported in (1984) 16 Entscheidungen des Oberverwaltungsgerichts Berlin 256

Bundesverfassungsgericht (German Federal Constitutional Court)

Case No 2 BvR 133/10, Judgment (18 January 2012) BVerfGE 130, 76, 123 – *Forensic Psychiatric Services*

Case No 2 BvE 5/11, Judgment (21 October 2014) BVerfGE 137, 185, 231 ff – *Arms Exports*

Case No 2 BvE 2/11, Judgment (7 November 2017) BVerfGE 147, 50, 127 – *Parliamentary Right to Information*

Case No 2 BvE 4/16, Judgment (2 March 2021) BVerfGE 157, 1 – *CETA*

Case No 1 BvR 2103/16, Order (3 June 2022) – *Pechstein*

Case No 2 BvR 557/19, Decision (23 July 2024) ECLI:DE:BVerfG:2024:rk20240723.2 bvr055719 – *Achmea*

Bundesverwaltungsgericht (German Federal Administrative Court)

Case No VII C 97/57, Judgment (5 June 1959) (1959) 12(44) Neue Juristische Wochenschrift 1985

Case No 5 C 22/88, Judgment (20 February 1992) (1993) 46(9) Neue Zeitschrift für Verwaltungsrecht 584

Other courts

Administrative Court Berlin, Case No 4 K 403.09, Order (11 February 2010) (2010) 8(2) Zeitschrift für Schiedsverfahren 107

5
Private-Public Arbitration in Spain
Legislative Timidity in the Shadow of the Constitution

Victor Ferreres Comella and Pol Fontboté Pradilla[*]

I. Introduction

If we ask the question whether it is possible in Spain for private individuals or entities to refer their disputes with public authorities to arbitration, when such disputes are governed by public law, the answer is 'we do not know'. There is, indeed, profound legal uncertainty on this issue. On the one hand, no legal provision in Spain categorically prohibits private-public arbitration; instead, this kind of arbitration is mentioned in some pieces of legislation. On the other hand, no statute has been enacted to lay down a comprehensive and systematic regulation of private-public arbitration which addresses the many institutional and procedural matters that need to be regulated for this type of arbitration to be workable in practice.

Indeed, the legislator has been remarkably shy. To a significant extent, this timidity can be explained by the existence of doubts concerning the constitutionality of private-public arbitration in Spain. A number of scholars have argued that the Spanish Constitution includes certain rules and principles that would make it unconstitutional for public authorities to use arbitration to resolve disputes with private actors. In particular, those scholars contend that arbitration is only possible when the interests at stake can be disposed of by the parties to the dispute. Since Article 103 of the Constitution establishes that the public administration 'shall serve with objectivity the general interests', it is argued that the administration cannot freely dispose of public interests and cannot, therefore, submit to arbitration private-public disputes.

Another argument advanced to challenge the constitutionality of private-public arbitration rests on Article 106(1) of the Constitution, which provides that 'courts shall check the power to issue regulations and shall ensure that the rule of law prevails in administrative action'. This provision is read by those considering private-public arbitration to be unconstitutional as entailing the consequence that only courts, but not arbitral tribunals, can pass judgment on the legality of the actions of the public administration. The practical consequence of these constitutional doubts is that arbitration is not used in Spain to resolve differences between public authorities and private actors as far as public law matters are concerned. Instead, public law disputes, in particular when they involve the control of legality of administrative action, are settled

[*] This contribution was last updated on 1 April 2019.

Victor Ferreres Comella and Pol Fontboté Pradilla, *Private-Public Arbitration in Spain* In: *The Comparative Constitutional Foundations of Private-Public Arbitration*. Edited by: Stephan W. Schill, Oxford University Press.
 DOI: 10.1093/9780191987960.003.0005

through internal administrative procedures or before external 'administrative courts', which are part of the ordinary judicial branch.

It is critical to note, however, that the administration sometimes acts in its private law capacity. It does so – albeit rarely – when it enters into some types of contracts governed by private law (such as in the field of financial services). The administration may also acquire a dominant shareholding position in a commercial company that is generally subject to private law. The administration, moreover, owns some assets that are partially subject to private law. In addition, an entity may be created within the public sector to provide services under a regime partially based on private law.[1] In all these contexts, arbitration may be employed, insofar as private law governs the underlying dispute. The general statute that regulates arbitration in the private sphere is then applicable.[2] The Spanish Supreme Court so held in a number of cases. For example, in a 1987 case, it declared that a state company may arbitrate disputes that are connected to its commercial activity. The case involved a company (Hispano-Alemana de Construcciones) that had been expropriated by the government.[3] In a more recent case, the Supreme Court has held that disputes that affect public assets governed by private law can be arbitrated.[4]

It is also important to observe, by way of exception, that private-public arbitration exists in Spain in the field of investment treaty law. In particular, foreign investors are protected by a large number of international investment treaties ratified by Spain.[5] Arbitration clauses are often included in such treaties, so that foreign investors can institute arbitral proceedings. Spain also became party to the Convention on the Settlement of Investment Disputes between States and Nationals of Other States (ICSID Convention)[6] on 17 September 1994. Interestingly, no questions have been raised so far about the constitutionality of investment treaty arbitration. This is in contrast to the debates that have developed concerning the constitutionality of other—that is, non-treaty based—private-public arbitration.

In what follows, we will first describe the academic interest that private-public arbitration has generated among Spanish scholars, and the timidity with which the legislator has approached this mechanism for dispute settlement (section II). We will then turn to the constitutional issues that private-public arbitration poses in Spain. After describing the general constitutional framework that applies to the public administration (section III), we will identify the main arguments advanced by some scholars to question the constitutionality of private-public arbitration, and will offer our objections to such arguments (section IV). We will then discuss the various pieces of Spanish legislation that are relevant in this field and show that the current law is fragmentary and uncertain. The consequence is that private-public arbitration has

[1] Examples of such bodies include Sociedad Estatal de Correos y Telégrafos, which is the Spanish universal postal service provider, and Renfe-Operadora, which is in charge of railroad transportation services.

[2] Ley 60/2003, de 23 de diciembre, de Arbitraje.

[3] Tribunal Supremo, Sala 1ª, Sentencia de 6 de marzo de 1987.

[4] Tribunal Supremo, Sala 3ª, Sentencia de 20 de diciembre de 2017, App No 1715/2015.

[5] For a list of bilateral investment treaties and treaties with investment provisions signed by Spain, see <https://investmentpolicy.unctad.org/international-investment-agreements/countries/197/inftrees> accessed 22 January 2025.

[6] 575 UNTS 159.

not, in practice, got off the ground (section V). For this to happen, a statute that systematically regulates private-public arbitration would be needed (section VI).

II. Academic Interest in Private-Public Arbitration, and Legislative Timidity

In spite of the practical absence of private-public arbitration in Spain, some scholars working in the field of administrative law have exhibited a special interest in it. Especially in the 1990s and 2000s, several books and articles were published that explored the possibilities of using arbitration as an alternative dispute resolution mechanism.[7] These works set the stage for contemporary discussions on the matter. In part, the publication in France, in 1993, of the report by the Conseil d´État, *Régler autrement les conflits: conciliation, transaction, arbitrage en matière administrative*, attracted the interest of Spanish scholars, who have always been influenced by developments in French public law.[8]

The main concern animating this scholarly literature was connected to the fact that Spanish administrative courts usually took a long time to adjudicate disputes. To a large extent, this resulted from the expansion of public law litigation. In any modern society, private individuals often interact with the administration, and conflicts are likely to arise. The Spanish Constitution of 1978, moreover, brought about a significant change to Spain's legal system, for it recognized fundamental rights that citizens could invoke vis-à-vis public authorities. Inter alia, a right of access to courts was established in Article 24 of the Constitution, so the judiciary was expected to play a key role in protecting the interests of private individuals. As citizens became aware of their rights, they were eager to litigate, thus causing a dramatic increase of judicial workload.[9] In this context, promoting arbitration struck some experts, starting from the mid-1990s, as a promising way to reduce backlogs in judicial dockets.[10]

Indeed, some commentators suggested that a better division of labour should be established between the judicial process and other methods to bring legal disputes to an end.[11] They argued that courts should focus on cases raising new legal issues that needed to be clarified through judicial pronouncements. More routine cases, by contrast, ought to be settled outside the courts—by means of arbitration, for example. This proposal was in keeping with a general theory several authors had put forward

[7] Juan Rosa Moreno, *El arbitraje administrativo* (McGraw-Hill 1998); Alejandro Huergo Lora, *La resolución extrajudicial de conflictos en Derecho Administrativo* (Publicaciones del Real Colegio de España 2000); Roberto O Bustillo Bolado, *Convenios y Contratos Administrativos: Transacción, Arbitraje y Terminación Convencional del Procedimiento* (Aranzadi-Thomson Reuters 2010); Marta García Pérez, *Arbitraje y Derecho Administrativo* (Aranzadi-Thomson Reuters 2011).

[8] Joaquín Tornos Mas, 'Medios complementarios a la resolución jurisdiccional de los conflictos administrativos' (1995) 136 Revista de Administración Pública 149 (citing Conseil d'État, *Régler autrement les conflits: conciliation, transaction, arbitrage en matière administrative* (Documentation Française 1993)) is representative of the academic literature in the field.

[9] Rosa Moreno (n 7) 6; Tornos Mas (n 8) 151.

[10] Rosa Moreno (n 7) 10–12; Tornos Mas (n 8) 151; Bustillo Bolado (n 7) 458; Juan Manuel Trayter Jiménez, 'El arbitraje de Derecho Administrativo' (1997) 143 Revista de Administración Pública 75, 75–76.

[11] Rosa Moreno (n 7) 12; Huergo Lora (n 7) 15–28.

in recent decades, emphasizing the need for courts in general, and the Supreme Court in particular, to contribute to the development of the law. According to this theory, the settlement of disputes was not the only mission of the judiciary. Courts should also produce legal doctrines to help clarify and develop the law, thus bringing legal certainty to the legal system as a whole.[12]

It bears emphasizing that public authorities in Spain occupy a comfortable position when private parties litigate against them. Private parties usually have the burden of first bringing an administration-internal complaint to the administration, whenever they question the legality its decisions.[13] In most cases, therefore, they cannot go directly to the courts to litigate the dispute. Moreover, the administration tends to insist on the legality of its decisions, even when the contending private party is clearly right and the courts will eventually so declare.[14]

In the past, the situation was particularly bad, since courts were reluctant to decree interim measures requested by litigants to safeguard their rights before the adoption of the decisions on the merits. A new law on administrative courts was enacted in 1998, however, that facilitated the issuance of such measures, and significant progress has been made over the years.[15] According to the new law, interim measures were no longer to be considered exceptional.

The arguments in favour of arbitration offered by scholars in the 1990s and 2000s have not lost their force today. There are still unreasonable delays in the administration of justice. It is true that the situation improved with the passage in 1998 of the new law on administrative courts,[16] which created new first-instance tribunals (Juzgados de lo contencioso-administrativo) and introduced an expedited type of procedure.[17] The burden that courts have to bear in terms of caseload, however, is still very heavy.[18]

[12] On the debate concerning the relevance of judicial case law, see Víctor Ferreres and Juan Antonio Xiol, *El carácter vinculante de la jurisprudencia* (Fundación Coloquio Jurídico Europeo 2009). It bears mentioning that a recent law (Ley Orgánica 7/2015, de 21 de julio) has redefined the role of the third chamber of the Supreme Court, which is the chamber that specializes in administrative law matters. Under the new regime, the Supreme Court will only examine cases posing legal issues that raise an objective interest for the development of case law and doctrine. The Court has been granted wide discretion in this regard. See the new Article 88, Ley 29/1998, de 13 de julio, Reguladora de la Jurisdicción Contencioso-Administrativa (enumerating the admissibility criteria). This is quite a radical change in the architecture of the Supreme Court, as commentators have noted, since the Supreme Court had no discretion in the past in this regard. See Eduardo García de Enterría and Tomás-Ramón Fernández, *Curso de Derecho Administrativo* (Aranzadi-Thomson Reuters 2015) vol II, 710–16.

[13] Ley 29/1998, de 13 de Julio, Reguladora de la Jurisdicción Contencioso-Administrativa, arts 25 and 46.

[14] See García de Enterría and Fernández (n 12) 547–52.

[15] Ley 29/1998, de 13 de Julio, Reguladora de la Jurisdicción Contencioso-Administrativa, arts 129–36. For a discussion of the legislative reforms on interim measures, see Mariano Bacigalupo, *La nueva tutela cautelar en el contencioso-administrativo* (Marcial Pons 1999). One of the most prestigious professors of administrative law in Spain, Eduardo García de Enterría, wrote extensively on the need to improve the existing laws and judicial practices in this area. See eg Eduardo García de Enterría, *La batalla por las medidas cautelares. Derecho comunitario europeo y proceso contencioso-administrativo español* (Aranzadi-Thomson Reuters 2006).

[16] Ley 29/1998, de 13 de julio, Reguladora de la Jurisdicción Contencioso-Administrativa.

[17] Bustillo Bolado (n 7) 450.

[18] A report issued by the Consejo General del Poder Judicial (General Council of the Judiciary) indicates that, in 2014, it took an average of 14.9, 12.5, and 14.3 months for first-instance courts, courts of appeal, and the Supreme Court, respectively, to decide cases in the field of administrative law. See Consejo General del Poder Judicial, 'Memoria sobre el estado, funcionamiento y actividades del Consejo General del Poder

It therefore seems reasonable to alleviate that burden through the introduction and promotion of extrajudicial dispute settlement mechanisms.

Promoting alternative dispute resolution in private-public relations is certainly a better alternative than the path the government took some years ago, when it introduced a new set of laws imposing rather high fees for litigants seeking access to the courts.[19] This reform produced a chilling effect on potential plaintiffs.[20] The number of proceedings that were instituted against the administration diminished, of course. The government's approach, however, attracted widespread criticism from many different quarters. Most importantly, the Constitutional Court, which was finally asked to rule on the matter, invalidated the heart of the fees system on the grounds that it restricted the right of access to courts in a disproportionate manner.[21] So the strategy that the government pursued to reduce judicial overload ultimately failed. As a result, the arguments developed by scholars in the 1990s to promote private-public arbitration are still plausible today.

The political branches, however, have been reluctant to enact a comprehensive regulation of private-public arbitration. (It should be noted that it is for the central state, and not the regions, to enact laws on arbitration).[22] The central government, in particular, has not been eager to propose a law on the matter, even though the Council of State (Consejo de Estado), which is the institution that advises the government on legal matters, has expressed several times a positive view of private-public arbitration, especially in the field of public contracts.[23] The Council has viewed arbitration as a good means to reduce litigation involving public contracts, particularly when the amounts at stake are small. The government has nevertheless failed to produce a legislative proposal on private-public arbitration.

The only important institutional gesture in this field took place on 21 December 2001, when the government circulated a draft of a legislative proposal (Borrador de Anteproyecto de Ley) regulating private-public arbitration in a systematic manner.[24] The draft addressed important legal issues, such as the matters that could be arbitrated, the constitution of arbitral tribunals, the procedures arbitrators had to follow, and the grounds for judicial review of awards. Some months earlier, on 12 September 2001, a member of the Cabinet, the minister of public administration, had announced in Congress that he expected the pertinent bill to be submitted to Congress by the end

Judicial y de los juzgados y tribunales en al año 2014' (2015) 489 < https://www.poderjudicial.es/cgpj/es/Poder-Judicial/Consejo-General-del-Poder-Judicial/Actividad-del-CGPJ/Memorias/Memoria-anual-2015--correspondiente-al-ejercicio-2014-> accessed 22 January 2025.

[19] This strategy started with Ley 10/2012, de 20 de noviembre.

[20] For a discussion of the impact of this reform, see César Cierco Seira, *Tasas judiciales y justicia administrativa* (Marcial Pons 2014).

[21] STC 140/2016 (21 July 2016). For a critical comment on the Court's decision, see Gabriel Doménech Pascual, 'Las tasas judiciales a juicio' [2017] 1 InDret <www.indret.com/pdf/1276.pdf> accessed 22 January 2025.

[22] The Constitutional Court has so held on the basis of Article 149(1) of the Spanish Constitution. See STC 62/1991 (22 March 1991).

[23] See eg Consejo de Estado, Dictamen 214/1992 (21 May 1992); Consejo de Estado, Dictamen 4464/1998 (22 December 1998).

[24] Document on file with authors; no official reference could be located.

of the parliamentary period.[25] The bill was part of a larger plan to modernize the administration. The proposal, however, was never adopted. No public justification was given for the failure, and no other legislative project has been considered since.

Why has the Spanish government failed to produce a comprehensive law in this area? To a significant extent, the reasons have to do with the Constitution. As we will discuss in the next section, while some scholars have been supportive of private-public arbitration, others have contended that the Constitution establishes certain principles that make it unlawful for disputes between private persons and public authorities to be referred to arbitrators. In the light of these constitutional concerns, the government has been reluctant to send a legislative proposal to parliament containing a systematic regulation of private-public arbitration, as the risk exists that the Constitutional Court will end up declaring such a regulation to be at unconstitutional, at least in part.

III. The Constitutional Framework: The Relationship between Public Authorities and Courts

To understand the constitutional debates in Spain about the possibility and limits of private-public arbitration, it is first necessary to offer some background information about the constitutional principles governing the relationships between administrative authorities and courts.

A key provision is Article 106(1) of the Spanish Constitution, which establishes that 'courts shall check the power to issue regulations and shall ensure that the rule of law prevails in administrative action and that the latter is subordinated to the ends that justify it'. Therefore, the administration is under the legal control of the judiciary. Regardless of whether the administration acts in its public law capacity or in its private law capacity, courts are empowered to verify that the administration's actions comply with the applicable law.

Article 106(1) of the Constitution has been understood to entail two important consequences. The first concerns the type of bodies that are tasked with checking the legality of administrative decisions. As per Article 106(1), 'courts' are in charge. Ordinary legislation, in turn, has designed a set of specialized courts to deal with controversies involving public authorities acting under administrative law (in contradistinction to private law).[26] Judges who serve on those tribunals are experts in the specific branch of public law that governs the actions of the administration. Such tribunals make up the so-called *jurisdicción contencioso-administrativa*.

A specific constitutional provision supports the idea that these specialized administrative courts must be part of the ordinary judicial branch. Article 117(5) of the Constitution proclaims that 'the principle of jurisdictional unity is the basis of the organization and operation of courts'. This means that all courts must be part of a single judicial structure. The rationale for this principle is linked to judicial independence.

[25] Diario de sesiones del Congreso de los Diputados, Año 2001, VII Legislatura, Núm 101, 12 de septiembre de 2001, 4924.

[26] See Ley Orgánica 6/1985, de 1 de julio, del Poder Judicial, arts 53–103.

The courts in charge of controlling the executive branch must be protected from the pressures coming from the latter as the rest of courts are. All judges must belong to the same institutional branch, governed by the same organizational principles. Although the rules of procedure may differ from one jurisdiction to another, the basic organizational principles must be the same.

In this respect, Spanish constitutional law deviates from the French legal model, which was otherwise so influential in the construction of the modern administration in Spain.[27] Whereas administrative courts in France are (relatively) detached from the ordinary judiciary, such a separation is not possible in Spain.[28] Instead, administrative courts in Spain must be subject to the same legal standards that apply to the judiciary as a whole.

The second important consequence that has been drawn from Article 106(1) of the Constitution is the idea that there are no spaces or spheres where administrative action is exempt from judicial review. The Constitutional Court insisted on this proposition soon after the Constitution was enacted in 1978, reading the Constitution as repudiating any authoritarian legal practices that immunized 'political acts' and 'administrative inactivity' against judicial control.[29] During Franco's dictatorship (1936–75), in particular, the 'political acts doctrine' was often invoked to block judicial checks on the government. The Constitutional Court interpreted the Constitution as dismantling that doctrine.[30]

Public authorities, of course, enjoy different degrees of discretion when exercising their powers. Sometimes the law specifies very clearly the content of the decision the administration must adopt in a given case. In other instances, by contrast, the law grants the administration a fair amount of discretion, either because more than one decision can be regarded as legally correct, or because the administration is accorded wide powers of appreciation in order to identify the single legally correct decision. The important point, however, is that discretionary powers are not shielded from judicial review.[31]

[27] On the parallel evolution of French and Spanish administrative justice, see Santiago Muñoz Machado, *La reserva de jurisdicción* (La Ley 1989) 82–134.

[28] Luis María Díez-Picazo, *Régimen constitucional del Poder Judicial* (Civitas 1991) 36. See also Ignacio Díez-Picazo Giménez, commenting on Article 117 of the Spanish Constitution, in Miguel Rodríguez-Piñero y Bravo-Ferrer and María Emilia Casas Baamonde (eds), *Comentarios a la Constitución Española* (Wolters Kluwer 2018) vol II, 668–69.

[29] Tribunal Supremo, Sala 3ª, Sentencia de 28 de junio de 1994, App no 7105/1992; STC 73/1983 (30 July 1983); STC 294/1994 (7 November 1994).

[30] On this evolution, see Eduardo García de Enterría, *La lucha contra las inmunidades del poder* (Civitas-Thomson Reuters 2016) and Santiago Muñoz Machado, *Tratado de Derecho Administrativo y Derecho Público General* (Agencia Estatal Boletín Oficial del Estado 2015) vol III, 304–13 (also available at <https://www.boe.es/biblioteca_juridica/publicacion.php?id=PUB-PB-2015-66&tipo=L&modo=2> accessed 22 January 2025).

[31] For a description of the various tools that judges can use when reviewing discretionary decisions, see Eduardo García de Enterría and Tomás-Ramón Fernández, *Curso de Derecho Administrativo* (Aranzadi-Thomson Reuters 2017) vol I, 499–532. In the 1990s, at the same time that private-public arbitration generated academic interest, a vibrant debate developed among Spanish scholars about the form and degree of judicial control over discretionary administrative decisions. For a good account of the debate, see Mariano Bacigalupo, *La discrecionalidad administrativa* (Marcial Pons 1997), and Muñoz Machado (n 30) 217–321.

Indeed, there are procedural as well as substantive limits that the administration must observe when exercising discretionary powers, and courts are empowered to control these.[32] The margin of administrative discretion must be exercised in light of general public interests. And the restrictions that the administration imposes on private parties must be proportional, taking into account the weight of the legitimate goals it pursues.[33] Public authorities, moreover, must justify their decisions: they must provide reasons to support them—reasons whose legitimacy the courts can assess. The factual considerations the authorities adduce to justify their decisions must be true, of course. And it is the burden of public authorities to bring the appropriate evidence to prove the relevant facts. The Supreme Court has clarified the meaning and scope of all these legal requirements through its case law.[34]

All this does not mean that courts are insensitive to the fact that the administration is a special entity, for it acts in pursuance of public interests. The presence of such interests justifies the special treatment that public authorities are accorded in some respects. In particular, the administration is endowed with the so-called 'privilege of *autotutela*', according to which it is empowered to enforce its own decisions without having to go to the courts to get authorization. A judicial warrant may be required only in some circumstances, for example when the fundamental right to the privacy of one's home is at stake. As a general rule, however, the administration can directly execute its own decisions. Private parties, by contrast, need to resort to the courts to force another party to comply with any legal obligation.[35]

The Constitutional Court has held that the administration's privilege of *autotutela* is not contrary to the Constitution, provided that a system is set up empowering judges to review the legality of such decisions and adopt interim measures.[36] The Constitutional Court has linked the privilege of *autotutela* to the principle of 'administrative effectiveness' mentioned in Article 103(1) of the Constitution. Since the administration serves public interests, it must have at its disposal effective instruments to implement its decisions; the administration's decisions may be challenged in court, but there is no need for the prior intervention of the judiciary to licence the use of force by the administration.

With this background in mind, we now turn to the discussion about the constitutional legitimacy of private-public arbitration.

[32] See Ley 29/1998, de 13 de julio, Reguladora de la Jurisdicción Contencioso-Administrativa, art 70, providing that courts can uphold a challenge against the administration if the latter has committed 'any infraction of the legal order'.

[33] On the importance of the principle of proportionality in administrative law, see Daniel Sarmiento Ramírez-Escudero, *El control de proporcionalidad de la actividad administrativa* (Tirant lo Blanch 2004).

[34] See, among others, Tribunal Supremo, Sala 3ª, Sentencia de 18 de julio de 2018, App no 2438/2016 (setting aside administrative decisions for lack of appropriate justification); Tribunal Supremo, Sala 3ª, Sentencia de 31 de enero de 2019, App no 1306/2016 (control of 'technical administrative discretion' regarding the appointment of civil servants); Tribunal Supremo, Sala 3ª, Sentencia de 21 de diciembre de 2018, App no 5720/2017 (control of technical assessments made by a regulatory agency); Tribunal Supremo, Sala 3ª, de 16 de diciembre de 2000, App no 2360/2008 (control of administrative discretion regarding urban planning).

[35] For a discussion of the different dimensions of the *autotutela* privilege in Spanish administrative law, see García de Enterría and Fernández (n 12) vol I, 555–80 and Muñoz Machado (n 30) 321–55.

[36] STC 22/1984 (17 February 1984) and STC 66/1984 (6 June 1984).

IV. The Constitutional Problem

Scholars in Spain have discussed extensively the foundational question of whether private-public arbitration is constitutionally acceptable.[37] In order to contextualize this discussion, it is first necessary to briefly explain the Constitutional Court's jurisprudence on the constitutionality of arbitration involving private parties. It is against this background that we can then proceed to assess the constitutionality of arbitration in the field of public law.

A. The Constitutionality of Arbitration in the Sphere of Private Law

Two constitutional provisions have sometimes been invoked to cast doubt on the constitutionality of arbitration in the private law domain. One provision is Article 117(3) of the Constitution, which establishes that 'the jurisdictional power in any type of proceeding, by which controversies are resolved and judgments are enforced, is vested exclusively in the courts laid down by the law, in accordance with the rules of jurisdiction and procedure established therein'.

According to this provision, the power to resolve disputes through a binding decision is reserved to the courts. Does it follow that arbitration is unconstitutional on the grounds that it undermines the principle of judicial exclusivity?

The Constitutional Court has answered in the negative.[38] It has explained that arbitration is different from judicial adjudication. Whereas arbitration is based on the joint consent of the disputing parties, adjudication by courts amounts to an exercise of power. While arbitrators carry out a task that the parties have agreed to entrust to them, courts do not base their jurisdictional power on the parties' agreement. Arbitrators, moreover, cannot enforce their own decisions—the parties need to use courts to secure enforcement. The Court has thus concluded that there is no violation of judicial exclusivity, since the arbitrators do not hold the power that courts are constitutionally endowed with.[39]

Some scholars have added to the Court's argument the consideration that what Article 117(3) of the Constitution really establishes is that, within the institutional machinery of the state, only courts are conferred the power to adjudicate disputes.[40] In other words, this constitutional provision is to be understood as part and parcel of the doctrine of separation of powers, under which it is for courts, and not for parliament or the executive branch, to adjudicate controversies. This constitutional clause therefore says nothing about the division of labour between public courts and arbitral tribunals set up by private parties.

The other constitutional provision that has sometimes been appealed to in order to contest the constitutionality of arbitration is Article 24 of the Constitution, which

[37] For the relevant literature, see the references in n 7 above.
[38] ATC 259/1993 (20 July 1993).
[39] ibid FJ 1.
[40] Juan Montero Aroca, Juan Luis Gómez Colomer, and Silvia Barona Vilar, *Derecho Jurisdiccional* (Tirant lo Blanch 2013) vol I, 85–87.

establishes that 'every person has the right to obtain the effective protection of the judges and the courts in the exercise of his or her legitimate rights and interests'. The Constitutional Court has reasoned that when private parties choose to refer their disputes to arbitration, they are exercising their liberty to arrange their private affairs as they see fit. Arbitration, the Court has said, is linked to the 'superior value' of liberty announced in Article 1 of the Constitution.[41] When private actors agree to use arbitration, they are waiving, with respect to a specific case, their fundamental right to go to court. This waiver is perfectly valid, to the extent that it expresses a free choice. Liberty, the Court has held, is 'the foundation and the engine' of arbitration.[42]

It is interesting to note, in this context, that Article 280 of the Constitution of 1812, the first constitutional charter that Spain adopted in its modern history, explicitly recognized the right of individuals to submit their disputes to arbitration.[43] The Constitution of 1812, which was the product of liberalism, was committed to the idea that private parties should have a legally protected freedom to organize their own affairs. The right to resort to arbitration was in keeping with this liberal notion. In this regard, the Constitution was influenced by the French Constitutions of 1791 and 1795, which explicitly guaranteed a fundamental right to arbitration.[44]

Given this liberal tradition, it is not surprising that the Spanish Constitutional Court has insisted that arbitration flows from private autonomy. Arbitration cannot be imposed by the law. The Court once struck down a statute that established that arbitration under a special administrative body (Juntas Arbitrales del Transporte) would be available to adjudicate certain disputes regarding transport contracts unless both parties agreed otherwise in the contract. Thus, if one party wanted arbitration, while the other preferred to go to court, arbitration was forced on the latter party. The Court held that this arrangement was contrary to the constitutional foundation of arbitration, which is tied to individual liberty, and breached the right of access to courts enshrined in Article 24 of the Constitution.[45] More recently, the Court invalidated a law that mandated arbitration for certain types of insurance contracts, if the insured party opted for arbitration. The Court insisted on its understanding that arbitration stems from private autonomy, and that both parties must agree to it.[46]

The Court, however, has not specified the due process standards arbitration must meet to be constitutionally legitimate. It is an open question what procedural constraints the Constitution must be read to impose on arbitration. It is widely believed, however, that the Spanish Arbitration Act,[47] which is patterned after the United

[41] STC 176/1996 (11 November 1996).

[42] ibid FJ 4.

[43] On this feature of the Constitution of 1812, see José Fernando Merino Merchán, 'La Constitución de 1812 y el arbitraje' (2012) 14 Revista del Club Español del Arbitraje 33–44.

[44] See French Constitution of 1791, title III, ch V, art 5, and Constitution of 1795, art 210. On this French constitutional tradition, see Florian Grisel, 'The Private-Public Divide and Its Influence over French Arbitration Law: Tradition and Transition' (in this volume) 67, 69–72.

[45] STC 174/1995 (23 November 1995). This decision by the Constitutional Court was rendered in the context of a constitutional question raised by an ordinary court. The latter doubted that it was constitutionally possible for a law to force arbitration on a party that had not consented to it.

[46] STC 1/2018 (11 January 2018).

[47] Ley 60/2003, de 23 de diciembre, de Arbitraje.

Nations Commission on International Trade Law (UNCITRAL) Model Law, requires fair procedures that arguably live up to constitutional due process requirements.

With all this in mind, let us now explore the arguments that scholars have made concerning the constitutionality of arbitration in the realm of administrative law.

B. The Constitutionality of Arbitration in the Sphere of Administrative Law

The Constitutional Court has rendered no decision dealing with the question whether arbitration is constitutionally permitted when one of the contending parties is the administration (whether acting in its public law or its private law capacity). Some commentators have argued against the constitutionality of private-public arbitration. As we will see, plausible counter-arguments can be offered to undermine their arguments so that private-public arbitration can be saved from constitutional objections.

1 First Argument: The Administration Cannot Freely Dispose of General Public Interests (Article 103 of the Constitution)

The first argument to question the constitutionality of private-public arbitration relies on Article 103(1) of the Constitution, which provides that 'the Administration shall serve with objectivity the general interests'. This provision has traditionally been understood to mean that the powers exercised by the administration have a 'vicarial' nature: they are granted to the administration in order to serve the public interests of the community.[48]

The consequence of this provision, it has been asserted, is that when it comes to concluding settlements or submitting disputes to arbitration, the administration does not have the freedom that private individuals have. While individuals are at liberty to decide what to do with their own interests, the administration is not, for it is under the constitutional duty to serve the general interests. Because of this constraint, it is argued, the administration is not able to freely dispose of public interests, and therefore cannot subject administrative law disputes to the arbitral process.[49]

As we can see, this argument relies on a strong conceptual connection between three ideas: (1) free disposition of interests; (2) settlements; and (3) arbitration. Actually, Spanish law appears to reflect this understanding in relation to arbitration in the private law domain, as Article 2(1) of the Spanish Arbitration Act provides that 'all disputes relating to matters within the free disposition of the parties according to law are capable of arbitration'. Furthermore, as already noted, the Constitutional Court has linked arbitration to liberty, which would suggest that arbitration is only legally acceptable when the interests at stake are interests the parties can freely dispose of.

[48] See García de Enterría and Fernández (n 12) 490–93; Luciano Parejo Alfonso, 'Algunas reflexiones sobre el "arbitraje administrativo", a propósito de la adecuación al nuevo procedimiento administrativo común del ordenamiento de la Comunidad de Madrid' (1999) 1 Asamblea. Revista Parlamentaria de la Asamblea de Madrid 11, 20–21.

[49] Huergo Lora (n 7) 201.

This argument against private-public arbitration, however, is not persuasive. To begin with, it is not clear why the fact that the administration cannot dispose of general interests in the same way as private individuals can dispose of their own interests should have the consequence that the administration is not empowered to make decisions as to how best to pursue general interests. After all, the administration is entrusted by the community to realize the general interests, including through settling disputes about how private and public interests relate to each other in individual cases. Also, in private law, a person (principal) can appoint another person (agent) to take care of his or her interests. When this happens, it is perfectly possible for the agent to enter into settlement agreements on behalf of the principal, for example, if the latter has allowed the agent to do so.

More importantly, there are good reasons to cast doubt on the centrality of the principle of free disposition of interests as the normative foundation of all sorts of arbitration. Consider, first, arbitration in the realm of private law. It is often the case that contracts must comply with norms that the parties cannot derogate from (so-called mandatory norms). The law assumes that public interests, or the interests of third parties, are affected in such a way that contracting parties are not allowed to conclude certain types of agreements. In addition, the law sometimes establishes that the interests of the weaker party to a contract (the consumer, for example) needs to be especially protected, and chooses not to permit those interests to be waived by means of the contract. Now, the fact that a particular dispute is subject to mandatory law does not make it legally impossible for such dispute to be settled through arbitration. Actually, in Spain, as is true in many other jurisdictions, cases involving the violation of mandatory laws may be arbitrated.[50]

This suggests that the principle of free disposition of interests is not central to the demarcation of the scope of arbitrability. If arbitration can be employed when mandatory laws apply, it follows that arbitration is not simply one of the ways in which private parties can dispose of their interests. Arbitration must be understood differently, as an institution possessing certain features that make it a reliable mechanism for the resolution of disputes in accordance with the law. Indeed, if arbitration is not to be excluded when the interests at stake in a given case are covered by mandatory laws, arbitration cannot merely rest on the principle of free disposition of interests. In this regard, the Spanish Constitutional Court's theory of arbitration, which links arbitration to private autonomy,[51] makes sense only insofar as the interests at stake in the specific dispute are interests the parties can waive ex ante. But if the legislator has chosen to go further by allowing arbitration to encompass cases governed by mandatory laws, the principle of free disposition of interests no longer serves as a sufficient justification for the possibility to have recourse to arbitration. It is necessary to embrace the additional

[50] For a general comparative law overview of this issue, see George A Bermann and Loukas A Mistelis (eds), *Mandatory Rules and International Arbitration* (Juris 2011). On the arbitrability of mandatory law in Spain, and its links to the notion of public policy, see Juan Cadarso Palau, 'Article 41' in Julio González Soria (coord), *Comentarios a la nueva Ley de Arbitraje* (Aranzadi-Thomson Reuters 2011) 553, 577–91. The Spanish Supreme Court has confirmed the arbitrability of mandatory law: see Tribunal Supremo, Sala 1ª, Sentencia de 18 de abril de 1998.

[51] STC 176/1996 (11 November 1996).

assumption that arbitration is a reliable mechanism to enforce the law. Otherwise we cannot justify the wide scope of arbitrability under current laws.

The assumption that arbitration is a reliable method for the application of the law to settle disputes does not mean, of course, that no judicial checks on arbitral decisions should be established. In Spain, like in many other jurisdictions, arbitral awards can be reviewed on the ground that they breach public policy *(orden público)*.[52] Courts can thus control whether arbitrators have properly applied the mandatory laws that shape public policy.[53]

All this is relevant to the question of whether it is constitutionally possible for a statute to establish the arbitrability of the general interests the public administration serves. If we break the connection between the principle of free disposition of interests, on the one hand, and arbitrability, on the other, the idea cannot be excluded that the administration may be empowered by the law to submit to arbitration controversies implicating general interests. Indeed, the fact that the administration must serve the general interests, as the Constitution requires, and the fact that such interests are not 'owned' by the administration, as scholars have always emphasized, should not be a bar to arbitration. If arbitration is designed in the right manner, there is no risk that it will detract from the general interests protected by the law. Arbitrators may err in particular cases, of course, but so may judges. There is no structural reason to believe that arbitration is biased in the direction of under-enforcement of the laws that safeguard relevant public interests. If properly conceived, arbitration can be a good adjudicative mechanism to employ in specific fields of administrative action. A pragmatic argument needs to be made, then, about the desirability of arbitration in particular domains. The important point is that there is no a priori constitutional objection against arbitration in the sphere of administrative law, even if it is true that the administration cannot freely dispose of public interests.[54]

Furthermore, we need to assume that arbitration is not confined to the area where the principle of free disposition applies, if we want to understand why arbitration has been generally accepted in certain important contexts. At the international level, for example, two states may submit a boundary dispute to arbitration. If the constitutions of the countries involved require the respective governments to serve the general public interests (ie interests that the governments are not free to dispose of), why is it that it is not problematic for those governments to agree to arbitrate such a dispute? The answer, basically, is that arbitration is regarded as a trustworthy method to resolve such differences in accordance with the relevant principles of international law.

Similarly, many states have signed international investment treaties according foreign investors certain substantive rights and procedural guarantees. The governments have to serve the general interests, but this has not been taken to be a reason why investor-state arbitration should be banned in the name of the constitution. The debate on investor-state arbitration centres on its reliability as a mechanism to interpret

[52] See Ley 60/2003, de 23 de diciembre, de Arbitraje, art 41(1).

[53] On the notion of public policy, see Silvia Barona Vilar, 'Artículo 41' in Silvia Barona Vilar (ed), *Comentarios a la Ley de Arbitraje* (Civitas-Thomson Reuters 2011) 1659, 1739–61.

[54] For a similar thesis, which breaks the link between free disposition, settlement, and arbitration, see Francisco López Menudo, 'Arbitraje y Derecho Público' (1999) 2 Justicia administrativa. Revista de derecho administrativo 5, 19.

and apply investment law correctly, which largely depends on the impartiality and objectivity of arbitral tribunals and the arbitral system as a whole.[55] It is an open question whether this modality of arbitration is ultimately legitimate. No one can seriously argue, however, that the fact that the government is not free to dispose of general interests is automatically a reason to exclude investor-state arbitration.

The Spanish Constitutional Court has not had the opportunity to pass judgment on international treaties providing for investor-state arbitration, but the Council of State has. The Council has held that, in accordance with Article 94 of the Spanish Constitution, the government needs to get parliament's authorization to enter into such treaties.[56] Article 94 provides that the prior authorization of parliament is required for Spain to give its consent to international treaties 'which involve amendment or repeal of some law or require legislative measures for their execution'. The Council of State has reasoned that arbitration clauses in investment treaties entail a derogation of the statutes that confer on Spanish courts the authority to check the legality of administrative decisions. The Council of State has not questioned, however, that it is consistent with the Constitution for a treaty to grant an international arbitral body the authority to test administrative decisions against substantive norms protecting foreign investors. Consequently, the principle that the administration cannot freely dispose of public interests has not been regarded as a constitutional obstacle in this connection.

Overall, there has not been much debate in Spain regarding the legitimacy of investor-state arbitration. Things may change in the future, however. In the past, the arbitral cases the Spanish government lost were of relatively minor importance.[57] In recent years, in contrast, dozens of cases have been brought against Spain by foreign investors claiming large amounts of damages caused by the legal reforms adopted in Spain concerning renewable energies.[58] If the investors finally prevail in a large number of instances, controversy will most probably erupt in many quarters over the legitimacy of this form of dispute settlement.

In any event, if treaty-based investor-state arbitration is understood to be constitutionally acceptable, even when public interests are at stake, there is no powerful reason to invoke Article 103 of the Spanish Constitution to question the legitimacy of private-public arbitration more generally.

[55] See Gus Van Harten, *Investment Treaty Arbitration and Public Law* (OUP 2007) 167–75.

[56] See eg Consejo de Estado, Dictamen 490/2008 (3 April 2008) concerning the Bilateral Investment Treaty between Spain and Bahrain. On the Council of State's doctrine on this matter, see Alejandro Huergo Lora, 'La transacción y el arbitraje' in Carmen Chinchilla Marín (ed), *Comentarios a la Ley 33/2003, del Patrimonio de las Administraciones Públicas* (Civitas 2004) 247, 289–90.

[57] See, for instance, *Emilio Agustín Maffezini v The Kingdom of Spain*, ICSID Case No ARB/97/7, Award (13 November 2000).

[58] Two arbitral awards issued in this context were favourable to the Spanish government. See *Charanne and Construction Investments v Spain*, SCC Case No V062/2012, Award (21 January 2016); *Isolux Netherlands, BV v Kingdom of Spain*, SCC Case V2013/153, Award (17 July 2016). In later cases, by contrast, the government lost. See *Eiser Infrastructure Limited and Energía Solar Luxembourg S.à.r.l v Kingdom of Spain*, ICSID Case No ARB/13/36, Award (4 May 2017); *Novenergia II – Energy & Environment (SCA) (Grand Duchy of Luxembourg), SICAR v The Kingdom of Spain*, SCC Case No 2015/063, Award (15 February 2018); *Foresight Luxembourg Solar 1 Sàrl, et al v Kingdom of Spain*, SCC Case No 2015/150, Award (14 November 2018); *RREEF Infrastructure (GP) Limited and RREEF Pan-European Infrastructure Two Lux Sàrl v Kingdom of Spain*, ICSID Case No ARB/13/30, Award (30 November 2018).

2 Second Argument: The Administration Can Only Be Checked by (Administrative) Courts (Article 106 of the Spanish Constitution)

A different strand of arguments to challenge the constitutionality of arbitration in the terrain of administrative law relies on Article 106(1) of the Constitution, which provides, as already noted, that 'courts shall check the power to issue regulations and shall ensure that the rule of law prevails in administrative action'. According to this provision, the judiciary must control the legality of administrative decisions. This clause has been read by some experts to mean that 'only courts' can.[59]

It is important to observe that the argument that relies on Article 106(1) of the Constitution need not question the theory developed by the Constitutional Court regarding private law arbitration. As we saw, the Court has held that private parties are free to choose arbitration, thereby waiving (in the particular case) their fundamental right to go to court, enshrined in Article 24 of the Constitution. This doctrine is irrelevant when it comes to arbitration in the administrative domain, however. The reason is this: if Article 106(1) of the Constitution is taken to mean that only courts can check the validity of administrative decisions, there is no room for arbitration here, since this objective reservation cannot be waived by the parties.[60] Hence, the question is whether reading 'courts' as 'only courts' is a plausible interpretation of Article 106(1) of the Constitution.

Some commentators have even gone so far as to claim that it is not 'courts' in general, but 'administrative courts' in particular, that the Constitution wants to be in the business of checking the actions of the administration.[61] This is a questionable thesis, however. It is true that Spain has traditionally entrusted specialized administrative courts with the task of scrutinizing the legality of decisions adopted by public authorities. But it does not follow that it would be unconstitutional for the legislator to depart from such tradition and move towards a model under which non-specialized courts would be empowered to carry out that task, as is typically the case in common law countries.[62] Thus, let us focus on the more plausible thesis that 'courts' in Article 106(1) of the Constitution (not necessarily administrative courts) are the only institutions that can adjudicate controversies involving public authorities.

The thesis that only courts can be tasked with the adjudication of controversies involving public authorities can be rebutted. As was explained before, Article 106(1) of the Constitution repudiated authoritarian practices that shielded the administration against external checks.[63] In the past, certain bodies that were part of the administration, or which were not sufficiently detached from it, were sometimes given the

[59] José Ramón Parada Vázquez, 'Arbitraje y Derecho Administrativo. La actividad arbitral de la Administración' (1999) 23 Revista Galega de Administración Pública 13, 15.

[60] López Menudo (n 54) 12.

[61] Parada Vázquez (n 59) 15.

[62] Admittedly, there is a provision in the Constitution that explicitly mentions administrative courts: Article 153 refers to the *jurisdicción contencioso-administrativa* for purposes of controlling the administration that operates at the regional level. This is too fragile a foundation, however, for the argument that such a specialized judiciary must exist and that only that judiciary can control the administration in the context of Article 106(1) of the Constitution. The Constitution is silent in the title that really matters in this connection, that is, the one devoted to the structure of the judiciary (Title VI).

[63] See nn 27–32 above and accompanying text.

power to resolve disputes to the exclusion of courts. At other times, the courts were authorized to intervene, but many administrative decisions were exempt from judicial review on the grounds that they amounted to 'political acts'. What Article 106(1) of the Constitution does is to reject those past practices and insist on the need to subject the administration to full review by external adjudicative institutions. No areas of administrative activity should be immune from such control.

If this is the point of Article 106(1) of the Constitution, arbitration should not be automatically excluded as a mechanism to settle disputes involving public authorities. Arbitral tribunals can be set up as external and independent adjudicative bodies with the power to subject the administration to legal review.[64] Actually, if private-public arbitration is cast in the right manner, it may turn out to be easier for private parties to challenge administrative decisions if they initiate arbitral procedures than if they litigate cases in court, due to lower costs and speedier proceedings, for example. If this were so, the goal of Article 106(1) of the Constitution would be better realized by offering arbitration as an option.[65] Moreover, the fact that arbitral awards can be scrutinized by courts in set-aside and enforcement proceedings helps reinforce the case for the constitutionality of private-public arbitration.[66]

Other scholars have argued that, although Article 106(1) of the Constitution does not generally permit private-public arbitration, exceptions could be justified regarding controversies involving large investments, especially those of an international nature.[67] In such cases contractors enjoy a superior bargaining power over public authorities; they are thus in a position to require the inclusion of arbitration clauses in their agreements with public entities. In such circumstances, it is contended, an exception to the constitutional rule that bars private-public arbitration should be acceptable. This argument, however, is not persuasive. If the starting point is the assumption that the Constitution does not permit arbitration in the domain of public law, it is hard to see how an exception should be introduced on the grounds that the administration is not strong enough to resist the pressures of large investors. It is precisely in such circumstances that one would think the Constitution might play a significant role to shield the administration from unacceptable pressures.

In sum, the better argument to support private-public arbitration against objections based on Article 106(1) of the Constitution is to insist that the point of this constitutional clause is to ensure that the administration is subject to external checks by independent adjudicative bodies. Courts must be available to operate as checks, but arbitral bodies may be given a part to play as well. If arbitrators are conferred an adjudicative role, however, it is probably necessary for courts to have the power of judicial review of arbitral awards, to better secure private-public arbitration against constitutional challenges.

[64] For an argument along these lines, see López Menudo (n 54) 12–14; García Pérez (n 7) 40.
[65] Bustillo Bolado (n 7) 458–59.
[66] Parejo Alfonso (n 48) 26.
[67] Huergo Lora (n 7) 204–06.

V. Legislative References to Private-Public Arbitration

In the previous section, we described the main constitutional arguments developed by a number of scholars to contest the constitutionality of private-public arbitration, and we offered the objections that can be articulated in response. In our view, there is constitutional room for the legislator to adopt a comprehensive law on private-public arbitration.

No such law has been enacted, however. As already noted, no statute specifies the types of controversies that may be arbitrated in the field of public law, the manner in which arbitrators are to be appointed or the procedures to be conducted, the kinds of review that judges may be asked to exercise over arbitral awards, the organs that are in charge of enforcing the awards, etc. Without such a law, private-public arbitration cannot exist in practice.[68]

At the same time, there is no legislative provision that categorically excludes private-public arbitration in the area of public law.[69] On the contrary, there are scattered references to it in different pieces of legislation, as we will see in this section. But these references are utterly insufficient to compensate for the absence of a systematic regulation. References to private-public arbitration appear in four different laws: the Law on Administrative Procedure, the General Law on the State Budget, the Law on the Estate of the Public Administration, and the Law on Contracts of the Public Sector.

A. The Law on Administrative Procedure

A reference to 'arbitration' in the domain of public law appears in Article 112(2) of the Law on Administrative Procedure, which mentions the possibility of establishing 'arbitral procedures' to settle disputes between private parties and public authorities.[70] This provision was first introduced in 1992, intensifying the academic discussion on the potential advantages of using mechanisms of alternative dispute resolution in administrative law.[71] There is ambiguity, however, as to what the legislator had in mind when it enacted this provision.

Article 112(2) of the Law on Administrative Procedure contemplates the establishment of procedures to deal with complaints brought by private actors. Such procedures are to be conducted by institutions that are not subject to administrative instructions and are thus 'independent'. The provision, however, does not regulate in

[68] López Menudo (n 54) 7.

[69] As already noted, when the administration acts in its private law capacity, the general statute that regulates arbitration in the private sphere—Ley 60/2003, de 23 de diciembre, de Arbitraje—can be applied. The administration is then treated like any other private actor. See Rosa Moreno (n 7) 106–07.

[70] Ley 39/2015, de 1 de octubre, del Procedimiento Administrativo Común de las Administraciones Públicas. Article 112(2) of this recent law reproduces Article 107(2) of the previous law, Ley 30/1992, de 26 de noviembre, de Régimen Jurídico de las Administraciones Públicas y del Procedimiento Administrativo Común.

[71] For the academic discussion, see the literature cited in n 7 above.

any detail how these procedures are to work. Instead, it defers this task to future laws governing specific matters.

Commentators are basically in agreement that the institutions referred to in Article 112(2) of the Law on Administrative Procedure cannot be characterized as truly 'arbitral'.[72] First, such institutions intervene at the internal administrative stage. Their decisions do not settle the controversy between private parties and the administration in a final and binding manner, since courts retain their full authority to adjudicate the cases at a later stage. Second, private parties are required to submit their complaints to those institutions, if they want to preserve their right to go to court afterwards. This is in contrast with the voluntary character of arbitration. For these reasons, legal experts have concluded that the legislative reference to 'arbitral procedures' that figures in Article 112(2) of the Law on Administrative Procedure is misleading, for the procedures alluded to are not really of an arbitral nature.[73]

One of the most surprising aspects, however, is that the legislative draft on private-public arbitration the government adopted on 21 December 2001, which was mentioned earlier,[74] invoked Article 112(2) of the Law on Administrative Procedure as the basis for the establishment of a mechanism to resolve private-public disputes through genuine arbitration.[75] As the 21 December 2001 draft never made it to parliament, it is hard to speculate as to the kinds of debates the proposal would have triggered. It is remarkable, however, that the proposal was clearly at odds with the scholarly consensus concerning the meaning of Article 112(2) of the Law on Administrative Procedure. The proposal would have introduced a true arbitral mechanism for private-public disputes, and presented itself as a mere development of Article 112(2) of the Law on Administrative Procedure, in spite of all the weight of academic opinion that had concluded that the latter provision had nothing to do with arbitration properly understood. Perhaps the government thought it was safer to link its quite novel proposal to the rather modest framework of Article 112(2) of the Law on Administrative Procedure, in order to mask the radical character of the proposal. Once again, we can see the extent to which the Spanish legislator has been shy when dealing with private-public arbitration.

[72] For a good summary of the reasons adduced by most scholars, see Victor Escartín Escudé, 'El arbitraje y otros medios alternativos de resolución de conflictos en el Derecho Administrativo' (2012) 39–40 Revista Aragonesa de Administración Pública 101, 133–40.

[73] Huergo Lora (n 7) 153–58, 166–68; Bustillo Bolado (n 7) 475; Rosa Moreno (n 7) 99; Tornos Mas (n 8) 173–74.

[74] See n 24 above and accompanying text.

[75] There is no doubt that the procedure designed in the 2001 draft was truly arbitral. First of all, the decisions made by the adjudicative bodies that were to be created (Juntas Arbitrales) would effectively settle the disputes. Courts would not review their decisions, except for very limited reasons, as is typically the case for arbitration in the sphere of private law. Secondly, the procedure was optional: private parties were given the liberty to choose it but were not forced to do so. They could instead resort to the ordinary administrative procedures and then go to court. As to the composition of the tribunal, the legislative draft established a system under which arbitrators would be selected by lot from a list drawn by the administration. In an earlier draft (dated 5 September 2001), the system that was to be set up was different: each party to the controversy was entitled to pick an arbitrator.

B. The General Law on the State Budget

A second reference to private-public arbitration appears in the General Law on the State Budget, enacted in 2003.[76] It regulates in a comprehensive way budgetary matters concerning the central government. Article 7(3) of this law provides that, when it comes to disputes that affect the economic rights of the public treasury, the administration cannot enter into a settlement, nor can it consent to arbitration, unless the Council of Ministers (that is to say, the Cabinet, which is made up of the prime minister and the ministers) grants an authorization by decree, after having obtained an advisory opinion (non-binding) from the Council of State (Consejo de Estado). This provision does not distinguish between disputes governed by public law and those governed by private law. In practice, however, since no general statute has been enacted to regulate public law arbitration, Article 7(3) of the General Law on the State Budget can only be applied when the dispute to be arbitrated is subject to private law.[77]

It is worthy of note that the General Law on the State Budget imposes onerous procedural conditions on the administration before it can refer a dispute that affects the economic rights of the treasury to arbitration. It is not easy to get the Council of Ministers to consider a specific case and give the green light to arbitration through a decree. The additional step of first obtaining the report of the Council of State introduces a further element of complexity and causes delay. These procedural conditions are therefore hard to satisfy. Their existence illustrates the legislator's reluctance to accept private-public arbitration. This reluctance is deeply rooted in the Spanish legal tradition. The provision under examination reproduces the same terms of another provision that was contained in an earlier 1977 law on the budget.[78] Before the 1977 law, the legal regime was even more restrictive: arbitration that concerned the economic rights of the public treasury needed to be expressly authorized in each case by a specific ad hoc statute.[79]

The Spanish government invoked this legal provision in 1988, when it adopted a decree authorizing the inclusion of arbitration clauses in the contract signed by the government to borrow, from Favorita Trustees Limited, the Thyssen-Bornemisza artistic collection.[80] Favorita Trustees Limited was a foreign entity that insisted on subjecting the contract to English law and on inserting an arbitration clause into the contract.[81] The parties to the agreement later decided to conclude a sales contract regarding the collection. There was some controversy in the Spanish parliament about the relevant contractual terms. The government issued an emergency law-decree *(decreto-ley)* to expedite the purchase.[82] Congress had to intervene pursuant

[76] Ley 47/2003, de 26 de noviembre, General Presupuestaria. Because of the quasi-federal nature of the Spanish constitutional order, regional and local governments are governed by other statutes, but these statutes are similar in this regard.

[77] See Huergo Lora (n 7) 172.

[78] Ley 11/1977, de 4 de enero, General Presupuestaria, art 39.

[79] Ley de Administración y Contabilidad de la Hacienda Pública, de 1 de julio de 1911, art 6.

[80] Real Decreto 1525/1988, de 16 de diciembre, por el que se autoriza el sometimiento a legislación extranjera y a arbitraje internacional de los contratos relativos a la colección Thyssen-Bornemisza.

[81] On the legal issues the contract raised, see Mercedes Cabrera, *El arte del Derecho. Una biografía de Rodrigo Uría Meruéndano* (Debate 2019) 165–80.

[82] Real Decreto-ley 11/1993, de 18 de junio, sobre medidas reguladoras del contrato de adquisición de la colección Thyssen-Bornemisza.

to Article 86 of the Constitution to ratify the law-decree. During the parliamentary debate, some members of Congress objected to a contractual agreement that avoided Spanish law. The majority, however, finally voted in favour.[83]

C. The Law on the Estate of the Public Administration

Arbitration is also referred to in the 2003 Law on the Estate of the Public Administration, which regulates the different types of assets that belong to the public administration.[84] This law distinguishes between two types of assets: those that belong to the 'public domain' (eg beaches, the territorial sea, the continental shelf, buildings that are used to provide public services), and those that belong to the 'private domain' (eg the shares of a company that the administration owns).

Similar to the General Law on the State Budget, Article 31 of the Law on the Estate of the Public Administration provides that a decree of the Council of Ministers is required to enable the administration to reach a settlement on rights and goods that belong to the state, or to submit to arbitration any dispute that affects such rights or goods. As with the General Law on the State Budget, the Council of Ministers must first obtain the (non-binding) opinion of the Council of State. The predecessor of the Law on the Estate of the Public Administration was even more restrictive, since it required the passage of a specific statute authorizing arbitration in each individual case.[85]

It is noteworthy that Article 31 of the Law on the Estate of the Public Administration, when it refers to settlements and arbitrations involving state assets, does not explicitly exclude property that belongs to the 'public domain'. Some scholars have contended, however, that an implicit restriction must be read into this legal provision.[86] Because the property that falls within the 'public domain' cannot be transferred to private actors, it is not possible, they argue, for the administration to reach a settlement on disputes that affect that property, nor is it possible to submit such disputes to arbitration. The Supreme Court has recently endorsed this position.[87] According to the Supreme Court, only controversies concerning assets that fall outside the public domain can be arbitrated. However, for the reasons given earlier, the present authors do not agree with the argument made by the Court, since we do not share the view that arbitration can only operate when the interests at stake can be freely disposed of.

[83] See Andrés Fernández Rubio, 'El Congreso aprueba la compra de la colección Thyssen tras un duro debate' *El País* (Madrid, 24 June 1993) <https://elpais.com/diario/1993/06/24/cultura/740872811_850215.html> accessed 22 January 2025.

[84] Ley 33/2003, de 3 de noviembre, del Patrimonio de las Administraciones Públicas. A similar body of law applies to regional and local administrations.

[85] Decreto 1022/1964, de 15 de abril, por el que se aprueba el Texto Articulado de la Ley de Patrimonio del Estado, art 41.

[86] García Pérez (n 7) 53; Huergo Lora (n 56) 252–53.

[87] Tribunal Supremo, Sala 3º, Sentencia de 20 de diciembre de 2017, App No 1715/2015.

D. The Law on Contracts of the Public Sector

Another reference to arbitration is found in the 2017 statute that governs contracts concluded by the administration and other public sector entities.[88] This statute regulates both contracts subject to administrative law and contracts subject to private law. The law contains a special provision that applies when the contracts signed by the public administration are formalized outside Spain and are to be performed outside Spain.[89] According to this provision, if the other contracting party is a Spanish company, the contract must provide for the submission of disputes to Spanish courts. If the other party is a foreign company, the administration must first seek to include clauses submitting disputes to Spanish courts. Should that not be feasible, the administration must then try to include an arbitral clause in the contract. In this context, arbitration is regarded as a better alternative than adjudication by foreign courts.

It is important to observe that this law facilitates arbitration, in that the inclusion of arbitration clauses in contracts signed by the administration and foreign companies does not need the authorization of the Council of Ministers (or of the relevant organ of the regional government). Interestingly, such authorization is needed, in contrast, in order to reach a settlement, as provided by the statute that governs contracts involving the administration and other public sector entities. Arbitration, under the present circumstances, is treated more favourably than settlement.

VI. Jurisdictional and Procedural Aspects: Arbitrability, Submission to Arbitration, Arbitral Procedure, and Judicial Review

As we have seen in the previous section, the references to private-public arbitration in Spanish legislation are fragmentary. There is no statute that regulates this type of arbitration in a systematic fashion. Many details concerning arbitrability, procedures, and judicial review need to be worked out. Private-public arbitration, therefore, has not been able to get off the ground in practice. The existing Spanish Arbitration Act of 2003, which applies to private law controversies, cannot simply be extended to disputes that involve public entities (unless the latter operate in their private law capacity). The legislative draft of 21 December 2001 would have filled in the gap, but it was never submitted to parliament. If a statute were enacted in the future to govern private-public arbitration, the question arises of what it should say about jurisdiction and the conduct of arbitration procedures. In this section, we will discuss different features that are relevant to protect the public interest. We will refer to the 2001 draft to structure our discussion.

[88] Ley 9/2017, de 8 de noviembre, de Contratos del Sector Público.
[89] See Disposición adicional primera, Ley 9/2017, de 8 de noviembre de 2017.

A. Arbitrability

The first issue such a statute would have to clarify concerns arbitrability. The 2001 legislative draft specified in Article 3 the matters that could be arbitrated. This provision mentioned controversies regarding the performance and interpretation of administrative contracts, the amount of damages arising from non-contractual liability, and the compensation to be paid in the event of a taking of private property. It also included a general clause which would have permitted arbitration involving matters that are open to a settlement according to the law.

When thinking about what a future statute regulating arbitrability should say, some experts have suggested drawing general categories to define arbitrability. They have argued, for example, that disputes should be arbitrable in those cases where the public administration enjoys discretion—that is, where the applicable law does not specify the contents of the decision that the authority should adopt in a given situation.[90] This theory is not plausible, however.

First, it equates 'discretion' with 'free choice' and therefore seems to rely on the idea that arbitrability depends on the principle of free disposition. But we already saw that this principle cannot be extended to the public administration, since the latter serves the general interests of the community, not its own interests.

Second, the theory is based on a distinction that is ultimately a matter of degree, not of kind. As was explained earlier, the law limits the administration in a number of ways when the latter adopts decisions of a discretionary nature.[91] There is no sharp distinction to be drawn, therefore, between discretionary and non-discretionary acts. The gradual character of the contrast makes it difficult to use this criterion in order to define the boundaries of arbitrability.

Third, insofar as this difference in degree matters, it is not obvious why it should matter in the direction advocated by this theory. The task of controlling the administration is complicated when the latter enjoys ample discretion. Checking whether the authorities have made a reasonable decision comporting with the principle of proportionality, for example, is a more delicate function to carry out than verifying whether a very precise legal rule has been properly applied to the facts. It is thus counter-intuitive to propose that arbitration should be allowed when a complex adjudicative performance is needed, while it is to be excluded when a more mechanical adjudicative function is involved.

This is connected to a fourth consideration, relating to democratic legitimacy. When public authorities make decisions within the area of discretion that the law carves out for them, they can often claim some measure of democratic legitimacy to defend their choices. Those institutions are politically accountable to the citizenry. Judicial review is problematic when the decisions under scrutiny are linked to democratic political processes, even if indirectly. It would be surprising, therefore, to maintain that arbitrability ought to be circumscribed to controversies concerning such discretionary acts, as to which judicial review raises the most serious concerns from a democratic perspective. It is interesting to recall that, in the field of investor-state

[90] See, for instance, Rosa Moreno (n 7) 75–79 and 107–11.

[91] See section III above.

arbitration, it is precisely the very open-ended nature of the principles that figure in international investment treaties that has sparked controversy about the democratic legitimacy of arbitration.[92]

Thus, instead of stipulating a general distinction between discretionary and non-discretionary administrative acts, it is more plausible to work out a more specific list of areas where it makes pragmatic sense for the law to permit private-public arbitration, as Article 3 of the 2001 legislative draft did. Some scholars have suggested, for example, that the law should permit arbitration to resolve disputes concerning: (1) the property of the administration (except for inalienable goods, perhaps), (2) the economic aspects of takings of private property or of state liability for damages, (3) public contracts, and (4) civil servants.[93] Whether this particular list is the right one remains an open question, of course, but there is much to be said for a pragmatic approach along these lines.

B. Consent to Arbitration

It seems clear that a statute regulating private-public arbitration should not impose arbitration on private parties but should instead offer it as an option. Given the Constitutional Court's case law mentioned earlier, in section IV, it would be unconstitutional for a law to force arbitration on private parties. Individuals have a fundamental right of access to regular courts. They can freely waive this right, but no law can force them to forego it.[94]

The public authority whose decisions are being challenged, in contrast, should be required by the law to arbitrate the controversy, if the private party opts for it. After all, forcing the administration to arbitrate is not objectionable on liberty grounds. The administration cannot have a will that differs from the will of the law.[95] The reason why public authorities should be required to arbitrate is straightforward: if their specific consent were necessary in each particular case, they would often refuse to give it. Recall that the administration has the power to enforce its own decisions, and courts may take a long time to decide a case. Arbitration offers the private party an expeditious mechanism to resolve the controversy, but the public authority whose decision is at stake may not be especially interested in a speedy procedure.[96]

The system should be similar, therefore, to the investor-state arbitration regime that has been designed at the international level, under which foreign investors are accorded the right to use an arbitral mechanism to settle disputes with the host state. The latter cannot refuse to submit the dispute to arbitration, since the relevant treaty forces the government to do so, if the investor elects arbitration.

The legislative draft that the government circulated in December 2001 shaped the arbitral process along these lines. Article 4 of that draft established that the will of the

[92] See, for instance, Van Harten (n 55) 122–24.
[93] García Pérez (n 7) 52–55; Bustillo Bolado (n 7) 469; Trayter (n 10) 95–102.
[94] Tornos Mas (n 8) 176–77.
[95] Joaquim Ferret Jacas, 'Límites del arbitraje administrativo' (1999) 35 Revista Andaluza de Administración Pública 11, 17.
[96] García Pérez (n 7) 66–67; López Menudo (n 54) 16–17.

interested party to refer to arbitration the settlement of an administrative controversy would bind the relevant public authority. The consent of the latter was not required. In our view, this was a reasonable arrangement.

C. Composition of the Arbitral Tribunal, and Arbitral Procedure

The legislative draft of December 2001 deviated from the private law model of arbitration in an important respect: it provided that the administration would be in charge of administering the arbitration process. Among other things, the administration would draw and update the list of persons empowered to act as arbitrators. The candidates were required to have professional experience of at least five years in the field of public law. Only individuals included in the list could be serve as arbitrators.[97] The 2001 legislative proposal did not confer any appointment power to the disputing parties. Instead, three arbitrators were to be chosen by lot from a pre-established list. These arbitrators would serve on the list for two years and would adjudicate the controversies the parties referred to them.[98]

One of the difficult issues private-public arbitration raises is related to the fact that a plurality of interests is often at stake in a given dispute. The administration is supposed to take care of the general interests, but there is often more than one private individual whose particular interest is engaged.[99] The 2001 draft legislation established that if several 'interested' persons were affected in a given dispute, the explicit consent of all of them would be necessary for a dispute to be sent to arbitration.[100] It is not clear how arbitrators and courts would have dealt with this provision, if it had been enacted into law. The more extensively the notion of 'interested' persons were interpreted, the harder it would be for private-public arbitration to develop, since it would be more likely for someone to claim an interest in a given case and veto the arbitral process by refusing to give consent.

Interestingly, the 2001 legislative draft did not require the publication of arbitral awards. Some scholars, however, have suggested that publication should be mandatory. Because a public authority is involved in the controversy, the arbitral decision should be made available to the political community for its public scrutiny.[101] After all, it is the general interests of the community, and not its own interests, that the administration must serve.

D. Judicial Review of Arbitral Awards

The 2001 draft legislation provided that arbitrators should apply the law when resolving a dispute; arbitration *ex aequo et bono* was not admissible.[102] This requirement

[97] See art 7 of the draft.
[98] See art 8 of the draft.
[99] Escartín Escudé (n 72) 124.
[100] See art 12 of the draft.
[101] Bustillo Bolado (n 7) 466.
[102] See art 1(3) of the draft.

was fully justified. As we have seen, the Spanish Constitution provides that the administration is bound by the law and must serve the general interests as defined by the law (Article 103.1). For arbitration to be constitutionally legitimate in this domain, therefore, it is necessary to ensure that arbitrators will adjudicate the cases in accordance with the law.

The 2001 draft legislation also regulated the grounds upon which arbitral awards could be reviewed by administrative courts. Presumably, the draft considered it necessary for administrative courts to be in charge of reviewing the arbitral awards in order to protect the public interest. The grounds for review were not exactly the same as those operating in the sphere of private-private arbitration. In addition to issues of procedure and competence, Article 23 of the draft included as a ground for review the violation of 'fundamental rights'. Not all fundamental rights listed in the Constitution were encompassed, however. The only rights that were mentioned were those that can be protected by the Constitutional Court through a special procedure called '*amparo*', namely the rights enumerated in Articles 14 through 30.2 of the Spanish Constitution. These include the right to equality, the right to life and to physical integrity, religious freedom, personal liberty, privacy, freedom of movement, freedom of speech, the right to assembly, the right of association, the right to political participation, the right to judicial protection, the principle of legality in criminal law, the right to education, the right to strike and to unionize, and the right to petition the government. The rights to private property and to free enterprise, by contrast, were not included in that list. This would mean, for instance, that an arbitral award resolving an expropriation controversy could not be challenged on the grounds that constitutional norms protecting private property had been breached.

The scope of this ground for review of arbitral awards—breach of fundamental rights—was thus more limited than the ground of review for violation of 'public policy' (*orden público*), which is available in private law arbitration. This limitation is not warranted, however. There is no good reason for judicial review to be more circumscribed in the field of administrative law than in the field of private law. Safeguarding public policy norms through courts is necessary in all branches of the law. Actually, it is especially necessary in the domain of administrative law, where the range of public policy norms is even wider than in the domain of private law.

VII. Conclusion

The absence of a systematic regulation of private-public arbitration in Spain has made it virtually impossible for this type of dispute resolution mechanism to be used in practice. The Thyssen-Bornemisza agreements that were mentioned earlier proved to be rather exceptional, and a special law-decree had to be approved by Congress concerning the final purchase. The scattered references to private-public arbitration in various pieces of legislation have been insufficient to generate the necessary legal infrastructure for such arbitration. To a large extent, this legislative failure is to be attributed to the constitutional objections launched by legal scholars. Persuasive arguments can be given, however, to counter those objections. Once the constitutional obstacles are eliminated, there is room for the development of a pragmatic approach concerning the types of disputes than could be submitted to arbitration. If the legislator overcame its traditional timidity in this area, a system could be designed to check the legality of administrative actions through arbitration. The introduction of a well-designed mechanism of private-public arbitration could be a step towards a better institutional guarantee of the rule of law, securing a more effective protection of private rights. Its success, of course, would depend on the details of the institutional arrangements to be created.

Select Materials

Bibliography

Barona Vilar, Silvia (ed), *Comentarios a la Ley de Arbitraje: Ley 60/2003, de 23 de Diciembre, tras la reforma de la Ley 11/2011, de 20 de mayo de 2011* (2nd edn, Civitas Thomson Reuters 2011)

Bustillo Bolado, Roberto, *Convenios y contratos administrativos: transacción, arbitraje y terminación convencional del procedimiento* (3rd edn, Aranzadi-Thomson Reuters 2010)

Cordón Moreno, Faustino, *Arbitraje y jurisdicción: algunas cuestiones polémicas* (Civitas Thomson Reuters 2010)

Escartín Escudé, Víctor, 'El arbitraje y otros medios alternativos de resolución de conflictos en el Derecho administrativo' (2012) 39–40 Revista Aragonesa de Administración Pública 101–64

Fernández Montalvo, Rafael and others, *El arbitraje: ensayo de alternativa limitada al recurso contencioso-administrativo* (Consejo General del Poder Judicial, Centro de Documentación Judicial 2004)

Ferret i Jacas, Joaquim, 'Límites del arbitraje administrativo' (1999) 35 Administración de Andalucía: revista andaluza de administración pública 11–19

García Pérez, Marta, *Arbitraje y derecho administrativo* (Aranzadi-Thomson Reuters 2011)

Huergo Lora, Alejandro, *La resolución extrajudicial de conflictos en Derecho Administrativo* (Publicaciones del Real Colegio de España 2000)

López Menudo, Francisco, 'Arbitraje y Derecho Público' (1999) Justicia Administrativa: Revista de derecho administrativo 5–22

Rosa Moreno, Juan, *El arbitraje administrativo* (McGraw-Hill 1998)

Tornos Mas, Joaquín, 'Medios Complementarios a La Resolución Jurisdiccional de Los Conflictos Administrativos' (1995) 136 Revista de Administración Pública 149–77

Trayter Jiménez, Juan Manuel, 'El Arbitraje de Derecho Administrativo' (1997) 143 Revista de Administracion Pública 75–106

Legislation

Ley 60/2003, de 23 de diciembre, de Arbitraje

Ley Orgánica 6/1985, de 1 de julio, del Poder Judicial

Ley 29/1998, de 13 de Julio, Reguladora de la Jurisdicción Contencioso-Administrativa

Ley 39/2015, de 1 de octubre, del Procedimiento Administrativo Común de las Administraciones Públicas
Ley 47/2003, de 26 de noviembre, General Presupuestaria
Ley 33/2003, de 3 de noviembre, del Patrimonio de las Administraciones Públicas
Ley 9/2017, de 8 de noviembre, de Contratos del Sector Público

Cases

Tribunal Constitucional (Constitutional Court)

STC 62/1991 (22 March 1991)
STC 176/1996 (11 November 1996)
STC 174/1995 (23 November 1995)
STC 1/2018 (11 January 2018)

Tribunal Supremo (Supreme Court)

Tribunal Supremo, Sala 1ª, Sentencia (6 March 1987)
Tribunal Supremo, Sala 3ª, App No 1715/2015, Sentencia (20 December 2017)

Consejo de Estado (Council of State)

Consejo de Estado, Dictamen 214/1992 (21 May 1992)
Consejo de Estado, Dictamen 4464/1998 (22 December 1998)
Consejo de Estado, Dictamen 490/2008 (3 April 2008)

6

Private-Public Arbitration under Greek Law

A (Nearly Complete) Public Law Paradigm

Nikolaos Askotiris[*]

I. Introduction

Arbitration between the government and private economic actors has been well known in Greece since the beginning of the twentieth century, and has taken several forms, with perhaps the most emblematic among them being investor-state arbitration under domestic statutes called 'Economic Development Acts', adopted in the 1950s and 1960s. Greek law currently allows for several forms of arbitration involving private actors, on the one hand, and the Greek government, a separate public entity, or a private entity authorised to exercise a public function (collectively referred to as public entities), on the other, in relation to both private and public law disputes (collectively referred to as private-public arbitration).

Arbitration clauses related to private law disputes can be found in private law agreements which are concluded between private and public entities. In relation to public law disputes, the main legal instruments containing arbitration clauses are administrative contracts[1] or unilateral authorizations (administrative acts), which are regarded in this context as quasi-administrative contracts.[2] Furthermore, it should be noted that, apart from the executive and public agencies, an entity established under private law that is authorized to exercise public authority is also able to adopt administrative acts and conclude administrative contracts within the scope of its (limited) authority.[3]

[*] Unless indicated otherwise, cited judgments are available at <www.dsanet.gr>. Any reference to the text of the Greek Constitution is based on the translation published by the Hellenic Parliament. All other texts cited herein, which have been originally drafted in Greek, have been translated in English by the author of this chapter. The content of this chapter has been updated in October 2019 and reflects Greek law provisions and case law that were relevant at that time.

[1] Greek public law, and particularly administrative law, forms part of the French public law tradition. This is to be attributed to two major historical events: the adoption of Napoleonic institutions in the 1830s, as well as the establishment of the Greek Council of State (CoS) in 1929, which is modelled after the French Conseil d'Etat, in the context of the state reforms launched by the reformist Prime Minister Eleftherios Venizelos.

[2] An agreement can be characterized as an administrative contract when three criteria are met: (1) one of the contracting parties is a public law entity; (2) a public service is involved or a public purpose is sought; and (3) a clause entitling the public entity to unilaterally interfere with the agreement *(clause exorbitante de droit commun)* has been included. See Epameinondas P Spiliotopoulos, *Εγχειρίδιο Διοικητικού Δικαίου (Administrative Law Handbook)* (15th edn, Nomiki Vivliothiki 2017) vol I, 75 ff; Velissarios Karakostas and Sophia Pavlaki, *Κώδικας Διοικητικής Διαδικασίας (Code of Administrative Procedure)* (Nomiki Vivliothiki 2009) 558.

[3] This situation follows the so-called theory of persons with a dual legal nature. See, for instance, *CoS 2080/1987* (1988) 39 Epitheorisi Emporikou Dikaiou 38. An illustrative example of such a person with a

Nikolaos Askotiris, *Private-Public Arbitration under Greek Law* In: *The Comparative Constitutional Foundations of Private-Public Arbitration*. Edited by: Stephan W. Schill, Oxford University Press. © Stephan W. Schill 2025.
DOI: 10.1093/9780191987960.003.0006

As the arbitrability of private law disputes between a public and a private entity is expressly recognized in law,[4] and most of the relevant issues discussed in case law and doctrine concern the arbitration of public law disputes, this chapter concentrates on private-public arbitration in relation to public law disputes. After a brief introduction into the general legal framework on private-public arbitration (II), the chapter deals with the pertinent constitutional law issues, notably the scope of arbitrability[5] of private-public disputes and possible procedural safeguards setting limits to party autonomy (III). Moreover, it is necessary to examine specific regimes of arbitration under Greek law, particularly in the context of legislative Acts on investment protection and public procurement (IV). For the sake of completeness, light will also be shed on investment treaty arbitration (V). The chapter concludes that the Greek law on private-public arbitration represents a nearly complete public law paradigm (VI). Although numerous legal provisions and court rulings reflect, by and large, a public law paradigm considering the possible impact of such arbitrations on the general welfare, private-public arbitration is only treated as an alternative dispute resolution method. Its potential functioning as a governance mechanism, by contrast, is neglected; there seems to be no sufficient guarantee for the transparency of the proceedings, making it difficult for civil society to be informed and potentially involved in the making of arbitral awards in private-public arbitration.

II. General Framework

Individual legal provisions applying to private-public arbitration can be found in statutes regulating certain types of administrative contracts (such as the Act on Prospecting, Exploration and Exploitation of Hydrocarbons[6] or Act 4413/2016 regulating concession agreements), or even in more general statutes.[7] However, there is

dual legal nature is the Hellenic Hydrocarbon Resources Management SA, which has the power to grant mining concessions (Article 2 of the Act 2289/1995, as amended). However, Greek courts seem to be reluctant to uphold that a private entity qualifies as a person with a dual legal nature: for instance, it has been ruled that an entity seeking to privatize formerly government-owned assets did not exercise sovereign power in concluding an agreement extending for 10 years a concessionaire's exclusive right to organize games of chance (*CoS 3873/2014*).

[4] Article 49(1) of the Introductory Act to the Code of Civil Procedure (IACCP) contains an explicit acknowledgement, by stipulating that the Greek government may enter into a written arbitration agreement for the purposes of the Code of Civil Procedure (CCP) and appoint arbitrators on the basis of a joint decision of the minister of finance and the competent minister, after having received an opinion from the Legal Council of the State (LCS)—a public body providing legal support and representing the Greek government before courts—adopted at a plenary session. It is noted that, pursuant to Article 8(1) of the Legislative Decree 736/1970, Article 49(1) IACCP applies only to arbitration with Greek nationals. See also Theodoros Fortsakis, *Διαιτησία και Διοικητικές Διαφορές (Arbitration and Administrative Disputes)* (P N Sakkoulas 1998) 149 ff.

[5] Throughout this chapter, arbitrability refers to objective arbitrability, that is, the 'capab[ility] of resolution by arbitration', as defined by Yves Fortier, 'Arbitrability of Disputes' in Gerald Aksen and others (eds), *Global Reflections on International Law, Commerce and Dispute Resolution: Liber Amicorum in Honour of Robert Briner* (ICC Publishing 2005) 269, 270.

[6] Article 10(13) of Act 2289/1995, as amended by Article 162(5) of Act 4001/2011.

[7] For instance, Article 6(3A) of the Statute on the LCS (Act 3086/2002) sets forth an exhaustive list of professionals that could be appointed as arbitrators by a public entity: chief justices, chief LCS officers,

no general code on private-public arbitration setting out procedural rules tailored to private-public disputes, the Greek commercial arbitration legislation being the only relevant source of law.[8]

The Greek commercial arbitration regime has been designed for the resolution of private law disputes, but in practice arbitral tribunals hearing public law cases may apply commercial arbitration rules by analogy or because the relevant arbitration agreement so provides. Greek commercial arbitration law is based on the distinction between domestic and international arbitration; domestic arbitration is governed by the Code of Civil Procedure (CCP), while international arbitration, in the sense of the United Nations Commission on International Trade Law (UNCITRAL) Model Law,[9] is regulated by Act 2735/1999, that is, the International Arbitration Act (IAA).

For domestic arbitrations, Articles 867 ff CCP set out a number of provisions regarding, inter alia, the composition of arbitral tribunals, which (unless otherwise agreed upon by the parties)[10] must include a presiding arbitrator (in Greek, *επιδιαιτητής*), who directs the hearing and has a casting vote, if the votes of all members of the arbitral panel are equally divided;[11] the competence-competence principle; and the relevant powers of the competent court (ie to decide on challenges to arbitrators; to set a time limit for the rendering of the award, where necessary; or even to order interim measures). Given that, historically, the appointment of judges has been a rather common practice in Greece, the CCP provides that judges can be appointed only as sole arbitrators or presiding arbitrators and sets out specific rules for such an appointment. The CCP also specifies the grounds on which an arbitral award should be treated as inexistent,[12] or could be annulled by a court (including for nullity or lapse of the arbitration agreement, inappropriate appointment of arbitrators, violation of the equality of arms principle, excess of power of the arbitral tribunal, or violation of the *ordre public*).[13]

university professors, and lawyers authorized to represent clients before the Greek supreme courts. It bears noting, however, that this provision does not apply whenever later and/or more specific provisions set out different procedural rules.

[8] cf Stelios Kousoulis, *Δίκαιο της Διαιτησίας (Arbitration Law)* (Sakkoulas Publications 2006) 33.

[9] 'An arbitration is international if: a) the parties to an arbitration agreement have, at the time of the conclusion of that agreement, their places of business in different States; or b) one of the following places is situated outside the State in which the parties have their places of business: (i) the place of arbitration as determined in, or pursuant to, the arbitration agreement; (ii) any place where a substantial part of the obligations of the commercial relationship is to be performed or the place with which the subject-matter of the dispute is most closely connected; or c) the parties have expressly agreed that the subject matter of the arbitration agreement relates to more than one country.' See UNCITRAL Model Law on International Commercial Arbitration (1985, with amendments as adopted in 2006) art 1(3) <https://uncitral.un.org/sites/uncitral.un.org/files/media-documents/uncitral/en/19-09955_e_ebook.pdf> accessed 24 January 2025.

[10] The parties are allowed to agree on the appointment of a sole arbitrator or of a multi-member panel without a presiding arbitrator within the meaning of CCP, or even on the appointment of a presiding arbitrator in case of lack of consensus between the members of the arbitral panel.

[11] Where the votes are not equally divided, but a majority is formed, the vote of the presiding arbitrator is equal in weight to the vote of any other arbitrator.

[12] This includes the inarbitrability of the subject matter, failure to conclude an arbitration agreement, and inexistence of the defendant. See CCP, art 901.

[13] CCP, art 897.

The International Arbitration Act (Act 2735/1999) is based on the UNCITRAL Model Law, with only a few peculiarities, such as the exclusion of the possibility to annul a decision on jurisdiction before the award on the merits has been rendered (Article 16(3)). Although not expressly provided for in the text of the CCP or the IAA, both domestic and international arbitrations are confidential under Greek law. The scope of confidentiality depends on the specific terms of an arbitration agreement. However, in the absence of express consent by all parties to an arbitration, third parties cannot have access to the arbitration proceedings and an arbitral award cannot be published—at least to the extent that the identity of the parties is disclosed or can be inferred from the facts exposed in the arbitral award.

III. The Greek Constitutional Framework Governing Private-Public Arbitration

The 1974 Constitution of the Hellenic Republic, as amended in 1986, 2001, and 2008, (Greek Constitution) is generally silent on the issue of whether—and, if so, to what extent—a dispute between a public body, agency, or enterprise exercising a public function, on the one hand, and a private individual or company, on the other, can be validly submitted to arbitration. Only Article 107(1) of the Greek Constitution makes indirect reference to private-public arbitration. It clarifies that the legislation enacted prior to the 1967 *coup d'état* for the protection of foreign capital invested in Greece (the 1953 Code), which contains certain provisions on investor-state arbitration, remains in force (A). However, beyond the reach of Article 107(1) of the Greek Constitution, doubts have been cast as to whether the submission of administrative law disputes to arbitration can be reconciled with a number of constitutional provisions, such as the assignment of administrative law disputes to administrative courts (Article 94(1) of the Greek Constitution) or the principle of effective judicial protection (Article 20(1) of the Greek Constitution) (B). In addition, a number of constitutional law principles apply to private-public arbitration (C).

A. The 1953 Code

The idea that, due to their particular importance for the economic development of the country, foreign investments deserve protection that goes beyond the general framework on the right to property and the freedom of business is reflected in Greek constitutional law.

Following the end of World War II and the Greek Civil War (1946–49), the Greek economy was ravaged, while public infrastructure and utilities were wrecked. The economic development of the country required capital and technical expertise that could only be imported.[14] Initially, the increased need for capital was partially covered

[14] See, for instance, Antonia K Dimolitsa, 'Arbitration Agreements and Foreign Investments: The Greek State Between Contractual Commitment and Sovereign Intervention' (1988) 5 Journal of International Arbitration 17.

through US aid received under the Marshall Plan. As the Marshall Plan was expected to end in the early 1950s, the Greek state, which was part of the Western world and endorsed the market economy model, had to adopt measures encouraging private investors to inject foreign capital into the Greek economy.[15]

Moreover, the devastated shipping industry could not have access to financing from foreign banks unless there were sufficient guarantees that the relevant tax and legal regime in Greece would remain stable. To preserve and increase the number of Greek shipping companies and ships under Greek flag, the Greek state had to adequately guarantee that the operation of ships imported and registered in Greece would not be subject to regulatory changes affecting profitability.[16]

Within this historical context, Article 112 of the 1952 Constitution of the Kingdom of Greece set out that a statute be enacted that would 'once and for all' ensure the 'protection of capital imported from abroad for the purpose of being placed within the country'. The inclusion of this provision in the Constitution was regarded as necessary, given that Greek case law[17] and doctrine[18] relied on the principle that parliament was not prevented from unilaterally modifying the terms of contracts concluded by the government, and the Greek state could not be held liable under Greek law for such an interference. For instance, in a comment on the relevant case law from 1932, Professor Alexandros Svolos, one of the fathers of Greek constitutional law, concluded that the legislator had the power to 'unilaterally alter the subjective rights of a person that has entered into a contract with the Government, by increasing that person's obligations'.[19] Similarly to a bilateral investment treaty (BIT), Article 112 of the 1952 Constitution has been designed to enhance the credibility of government commitments towards foreign investors, by making certain minimum standards, set out in a statute, binding on all branches of the government, and enforceable by means of arbitration.[20]

The 'once-and-for-all' statute would not be subject to political volatility, as any new parliamentary majority would not have the power to repeal or amend it through a

[15] Konstantinos G Mavrias, 'Η Συνταγματική Προστασία των Ξένων Επενδύσεων κατά το Ελληνικό Δίκαιο και τα Διεθνή Πρότυπα Προστασίας (Constitutional Protection of Foreign Investments under Greek Law and International Protection Patterns)' (1975) 1 To Syntagma 41, 47. cf also Nikolaos Davrados, 'Greece' in Wenhua Shan (ed), *The Legal Protection of Foreign Investment: A Comparative Study* (Hart 2012) 395.

[16] See Ioannis D Markianos-Daniolos, 'Νομική Αξιολόγηση των Εγκριτικών Πράξεων Νηολόγησης Πλοίων κατά το Άρθρο 13 του ΝΔ 2687/53 (Legal Assessment of Acts Approving the Registration of Ships under Article 13 of Legislative Decree 2687/53)' (2013) 41 Epitheorisis Nautiliakou Dikaiou 161; cf Peter J Buckley and Patrick Artisien, *North South Direct Investment in the European Communities* (Macmillan Press 1987) 39.

[17] See *Areios Pagos (or AP) 438/1932.*

[18] For instance, Professor Vasileios Oikonomidis had used the emblematic phrase: 'The liability to pay damages presupposes a wrongful act. However, the legislature does no wrong in legislating.' See Vasileios Oikonomidis, *Civil Procedure Manual* (3rd edn, Publishing Company of A Kanariotis and Z Gryparis 1890) 203.

[19] See this citation in an analysis of the relevant work of Alexandros Svolos by Christos Tsaitouridis, 'Other Legal Analyses' in Giorgos Kasimatis and Giorgos Anastasiadis (eds), *Alexandros Svolos, The Constitutional Lawyer, the Politician, the Visionary* (Greek Parliament Foundation 2009) 118, 123, particularly fn 26.

[20] It seems that this was the lesson learnt following the governmental interference with certain public contracts during the first half of the nineteenth century, which had been seen as having a negative impact on the ability of Greece to attract foreign investments; see Markianos-Daniolos (n 16) fn 1.

new statute. Indeed, it has been recognized that Article 112 of the 1952 Constitution empowered and required the legislature to establish a specific regime governing certain investments, which would be ranked higher than mere statutes.[21] Article 112 of the 1952 Constitution has been implemented through Legislative Decree 2687/1953 on the Investment and Protection of Foreign Capital (the '1953 Code'). This Code is applicable to companies and projects financed with 'foreign capital imported from abroad'. Apparently, the purpose of the 1953 Code was to attract not only foreign investors, but also (if not primarily) Greek investors who had significant assets in foreign jurisdictions and therefore disposed of 'foreign capital'. The concept of 'foreign capital' itself is a broad one and encompasses money as well as tangible and intangible assets, including 'machinery and material, inventions, technical methods, as well as trademarks and trade names' (see Article 1),[22] insofar as they are a contribution to a 'productive investment', that is, an investment designed to promote domestic growth or otherwise foster economic development (Article 2(2)).[23] In order to provide an incentive to the import of ships to Greece, Article 13(1) of the 1953 Code makes clear that 'ships of 1,500 tons gross tonnage and above that are to be registered under Greek flag' qualify as 'foreign capital' within the meaning of Articles 1 and 2 of the 1953 Code. However, the 1953 Code does not apply automatically to any person or entity, but only to those who have requested and been granted an authorization (so-called 'act of approval'— in Greek, '*εγκριτική πράξη*') in the form of an irrevocable ministerial decision or—depending on the importance of an investment—royal (now presidential) decree.

Broadly speaking, investment protection afforded under the 1953 Code is comparable with, and in certain instances higher than, that under a typical BIT[24]—an 'act of approval' amounting to the 'guarantee of the Greek State, toward an importer of foreign capital, that such capital will hereinafter be invariably subject to the regime established by [the 1953 Code]'. Importantly, Article 12 of the 1953 Code provides for investor-state arbitration, as follows:

> Disputes arising between the Greek Government and companies submitted to the present legislative decree concerning the interpretation or possible *lacunae* of the act of approval, shall be resolved by means of arbitration, as provided for in the said act of approval, with the appointment of a foreign person, either natural or legal, having

[21] This issue has been determined by the CoS, *Judgment 1395/1954*.

[22] See Norman M Littell, 'The International Investment of Private Capital - Opportunities and Problems: Legal Incentives for Private Investments Abroad' (1954) 40 Virginia Law Review 977, 987.

[23] Pursuant to Article 2(2) of the 1953 Code, '[b]y productive investments are meant those that aim at the development of the national production or otherwise contribute to the economic progress of the country'.

[24] For instance, 'acts of approval' issued under the 1953 Code cannot be modified without the consent of the investor concerned (art 3(3)), while the expropriation of protected assets is precluded (art 11(1)). See Mavrias (n 15) 46; Paul Stephen Dempsey, 'Foreign Investment Incentives in the Developing World: The Legislation of Greece, Egypt, Pakistan, Thailand and the Republic of China' (1979) 11 Case W Res J Int'l L 575, 586; Constantine E Lambadarios, 'Greece' in Wolfgang G Friedmann (ed), *Legal Aspects of Foreign Investment* (Little, Brown and Company 1959) 233, 245 ff. It must also be noted that, pursuant to Article 13(2) of the 1953 Code, read together with Legislative Decree 2928/1954, an 'act of approval' related to the import and registration of a specific vessel in Greece can regulate a number of issues, even by derogation from otherwise generally applicable provisions.

an official status or being a prominent legal authority, as presiding arbitrator being allowed.

It appears that this provision builds upon both the experience of developing countries, including the Greek government, with arbitrations with foreign investors during the interwar period, and the international discussion at the time regarding the usefulness of the arbitral resolution of foreign investment disputes.[25] In fact, the provision can be regarded as a precursor of direct investor-state arbitration on the basis of a standing arbitration offer made by the host government through the standard insertion of investor-state arbitration clauses in international investment agreements (IIAs).[26] However, the arbitration procedure to be followed is not regulated by the 1953 Code, but specified in the text of each 'act of approval', which typically incorporates the arbitration agreement negotiated and concluded by the Greek government and the investor concerned.

Article 107(1) of the current Greek Constitution explicitly affirms that the 1953 Code remains applicable to future investment projects and enjoys 'legal force higher than that of statutes', as it did under the 1952 Constitution.[27] This is a unique feature of the Greek Constitution, as it confers supralegislative rank to a legal instrument on investor protection which provides for the arbitral resolution of investor-state disputes.[28]

The place in the hierarchy attributed to the 1953 Code under Article 107(1) may be lower than that of the Greek Constitution itself.[29] However, essentially there is no practical difference between any constitutional provision and the provisions of the 1953 Code, as both are not subject to judicial review and can only be amended through the time-consuming and complex procedure applicable to the revision of the Greek Constitution (Article 110).[30] That is to say that, unlike common statutes, which are subject to incidental constitutional review whenever a court is called upon to apply them, there is no room for the judicial control of the conformity of the Code's provisions with the Greek Constitution.[31] Moreover, the regime under the 1953

[25] cf Earl Snyder, 'Foreign Investment Protection: A Reasoned Approach' (1963) 61 Mich L Rev 1087, 1098, n 46.

[26] cf Ignacio Suarez Anzorena, 'Consent to Arbitration in Foreign Investment Law' in Mahnoush H Arsajani and Jacob Katz Cogan (eds), *Looking to the Future, Essays on International Law in Honor of W Michael Reisman* (Martinus Nijhoff 2011) 63, 67.

[27] See, for instance, Konstantinos L Georgopoulos, *Constitutional Law* (12th edn, Ant N Sakkoulas 2001) 602; Philippos K Spyropoulos and Theodore Fortsakis, *Constitutional Law in Greece* (Ant N Sakkoulas/Wolters Kluwer 2009) 71–72.

[28] cf *AP 356/1991*, MD (1993) Epitherorisi Emporikou Dikaiou 386, which confirms the 'superior legal force' of the arbitration provisions contained in the 1953 Code.

[29] This view has been taken by Prokopios Pavlopoulos, 'L'arbitrage dans le contentieux administratif' (1992) 4 Revue européenne de droit public 61, 67.

[30] cf Helena Kalyva, *Ausländische Privatinvestitionen in Schwellenländern, Rechtsschutz im Konflikt – Eine Untersuchung am Beispiel des verfassungsrechtlich gewährten Schutzes in Griechenland* (Peter Lang 1987) 80; Davrados (n 15) 401.

[31] cf *CoS 3132/1989* (Plenary Session) para 5 ('[N]o issue could, in any case, be raised, as to whether arbitral tribunals constituted on the basis of the . . . legislative decree 2687/1953 are contrary, in terms of their constitution and function, to other constitutional provisions regarding the organization and function of Courts in Greece.').

Code cannot be repealed or modified unless a qualified majority of three-fifths of all Members of Parliament vote in favour of amending Article 107(1), general elections are held, and the newly elected parliament approves the repeal or amendment by absolute majority of all its members.[32]

Since its entry into force, the 1953 Code has always been the basic legal instrument for the importation and registration of ships, which are typically connected to an 'act of approval' containing an arbitration clause for disputes arising in this connection between the Greek government and the shipowner concerned. Apart from that, the 1953 Code provides an incentive for international investors to participate in privatization projects. As for the arbitration mechanism, a private party and the Greek government are free to agree on specific procedural rules, as well as to opt for institutional arbitration or not. As a more recent example, Article 224 of Act 4389/2016, which ratifies certain concessions for the renovation, management, and operation of a number of regional airports, provides for the application of the 1953 Code to these investments, at the request of the holders of the concessions. On this basis, two 'acts of approval' have been issued, the Presidential Decrees 27/2017 and 28/2017, which specify the scope of protection granted to the concessionaires and provide for the arbitral resolution of disputes between the concessionaires and the Greek government 'in relation to the interpretation or possible *lacunae*' of these presidential decrees. Such disputes are to be resolved by a three-member arbitral panel under the '2012 ICC Arbitration Rules', 'subject to the provisions' of Article 9 of Presidential Decree 27/2017 and of Article 9 of Presidential Decree 28/2017 (the 'Arbitration Clauses').[33] However, the Arbitration Clauses are based on a purely commercial arbitration pattern, whereby the arbitration proceedings are fully confidential and the arbitral award to be rendered cannot be challenged before the Greek courts through set-aside or any other type of proceedings.

B. Arbitrability of Other Public Law Disputes

The Greek Constitution contains no explicit provision regarding the arbitrability, or prohibition thereof, of any type of dispute. Above all, the Constitution has never been an obstacle to the development of alternative dispute resolution methods under Greek law or the submission of private law disputes to arbitration. However, the meaning of the silence of the Greek Constitution regarding the resolution of public law disputes by arbitration outside the scope of application of the 1953 Code is not clear. That is to say, it could be concluded that the Greek Constitution is predominantly 'friendly' to arbitration, regarding disputes between private parties, whereas

[32] Or alternatively, that parliament can, by a supermajority of three-fifths of its members, approve proposals concerning provisions whose amendment had been decided by the absolute majority of all members of the parliament before elections were held.

[33] Inter alia, the Arbitration Clauses provide that any arbitration proceedings will be conducted in Greece, in the Greek language (with any party appointing an arbitrator not fluent in Greek bearing the translation and interpretation costs), and that the arbitral tribunal will decide by majority, applying 'the provisions of the [relevant] presidential decree, of the [1953 Code] as well as the related general and specific Greek law provisions'.

it restricts arbitral proceedings over public law disputes other than those explicitly referred to (*a contrario* argument). Indeed, the arbitrability of public law disputes has consistently been a controversial issue in legal doctrine in Greece (1) and has also been dealt with by Greek courts (2).

1 The Debate in Legal Doctrine

The debate concerning the arbitrability of public law issues reflects the controversy about the nature of arbitration as contractual or jurisdictional. While the defenders of the contractual character of arbitration see significant limits to arbitration in public law disputes, those supporting the essentially judicial role of arbitral tribunals generally accept the arbitrability of such disputes.

On the one hand, the late Professor Kostas Beys, an emeritus professor of civil procedure of the University of Athens and former Secretary General of the Presidency of the Hellenic Republic, has argued that, under Greek law, only those private law claims are arbitrable that the parties can dispose of.[34] In his view, this principle, which is anchored in Article 867 CCP, applies to any type of arbitration. In his opinion, the legal basis of arbitration is contractual freedom and is derived from Article 5(1) of the Greek Constitution, which guarantees economic freedom, subject to third parties' rights and other constitutional provisions.[35] Professor Beys contends that submitting public law issues to arbitration, instead of bringing them before the competent court, impedes the enforcement of the principle of legality.[36] Article 5(1) of the Greek Constitution, therefore, does not cover the possibility of submitting such issues to arbitration.[37] Furthermore, the late professor of administrative law at the University of Thessaloniki, Anastasios Tachos, took the view that a private procedure is, by definition, not apt to give effect to the public interest underlying any legal relationship between the government and private persons under public law.[38]

On the other hand, several leading scholars of Greek public law have taken the view that arbitration is a legitimate method for the resolution of public law disputes. For instance, Professor Prokopios Pavlopoulos, who has served as the President of the Hellenic Republic, notes that the possibility to resort to arbitration flows from the right to a 'natural judge' under Article 8(1) of the Greek Constitution. This article sets out that '[n]o person shall be deprived of the judge assigned to him by law against his will.' Conversely, whoever benefits from that fundamental right may also opt not to resort to court litigation (relying on the so-called negative aspect of the right to a natural judge), but to conclude an arbitration agreement and settle disputes through arbitration proceedings rather than in a domestic court.[39] Moreover, Professor Vassilios

[34] Kostas E Beys, *Civil Procedure, General Principles and Interpretation of the Articles, Arbitration* (Afoi P Sakkoula 1994) 89 ff; Kostas E Beys, 'Οι Δεκτικές Διαιτησίας Διαφορές (Arbitrable Disputes)' in *Αφιέρωμα στον Ανδρέα Α Γαζή (Liber Amicorum Andreas A Gazis)* (Ant N Sakkoulas 1994) 417, 446.

[35] Beys, 'Οι Δεκτικές Διαιτησίας Διαφορές (Arbitrable Disputes)' (n 34) 446.

[36] ibid.

[37] In this connection, see also Panagiotis A Kargados, 'Is the Arbitral Resolution of Tax Law Disputes Possible?' in Kostas E Beys (ed), Δικανικοί Διάλογοι (*Dialogues About Justice*) (Afoi P Sakkoula 1994) vol I, 205; Velissarios Karakostas, 'Διαιτησία και Διοικητικές, Ιδίως Φορολογικές Διαφορές – Έννοιες Ασύμπτωτες (Arbitration and Administrative, Particularly Tax Law Disputes – Irreconcilable Concepts)' in ibid 219, 221.

[38] Anastasios I Tachos, *Ελληνικό Διοικητικό Δίκαιο (Greek Administrative Law)* (Sakkoulas Publications 2008) 788 ff.

[39] Pavlopoulos (n 29) 62; see also Apostolis Gerontas, 'Η διαιτητική επίλυση των διαφορών από τις συγχρηματοδοτούμενες συμβάσεις δημοσίων έργων: Μια πρώτη ερμηνευτική προσέγγιση (The

Skouris, the former President of the Court of Justice of the European Union (CJEU), takes the view that arbitration is not, by its very nature, restricted to commercial dispute resolution,[40] although he stresses that the submission of a public law dispute to arbitration should not render inapplicable mandatory provisions or deprive parties of any legal remedy whatsoever against deficiencies of an arbitral award.[41]

Greek academics and scholars, therefore, are divided. Apparently, a considerable number of scholars are concerned that arbitral tribunals could replace administrative courts, in particular the Council of State (CoS), that is, the Supreme Administrative Court, which has established and specified the fundamental principles of administrative law. However, the arguments advanced against the arbitrability of public law disputes are not convincing. Neither the text nor the spirit of the Greek Constitution seem to preclude arbitration of public law disputes.[42] It can reasonably be assumed that the drafters of the Greek Constitution were aware of arbitral practice in relation to public law disputes preceding the adoption of the Greek Constitution, and that, if they had wished to ban arbitration of public law disputes not subject to the 1953 Code, they could have inserted in the Greek Constitution an explicit clause to this effect. Moreover, the parties' power to dispose of rights underlying the dispute is a requirement under the CCP, which applies only to arbitration proceedings about private law claims;[43] the application of such a requirement to arbitration of public law claims is therefore not a logical necessity, nor can it be derived from any constitutional provision.[44] Consequently, the better arguments militate for accepting that the Greek Constitution does not exclude the arbitrability of public law disputes.

2 Relevant Case Law

The arguments put forward in the above doctrinal debate are not fully reflected in case law. However, Greek courts have on several occasions ruled on the arbitrability of public law disputes outside the scope of the 1953 Code. Until the early 1990s, the main principle underlying Greek case law was that an arbitral tribunal could resolve public law issues and validly determine the lawfulness of government measures, albeit not annul them. In fact, the CoS and the Areios Pagos (AP)—that is, the Supreme Civil and Criminal Court of Greece—had repeatedly affirmed, either tacitly,[45]

Arbitral Dispute Settlement in Cofinanced Public Works Contracts: A First Interpretation Approach)' (2014) 34 Hellenic Rev Eur L 423, 426; Prodromos D Dagtoglou, 'Η Απόφαση του ΑΕΔ για την Συνταγματικότητα της Διαιτητικής Επιλύσεως Διοικητικών Διαφορών (The Judgment of the SHC on the Compatibility with the Constitution of the Arbitral Resolution of Administrative Law Disputes)' in Beys (n 37) 212–13.

[40] Vassilios Skouris, *Διοικητικό Δικονομικό Δίκαιο (Administrative Procedural Law)* (Sakkoulas Publications 1991) 171 ff.

[41] ibid 175.

[42] cf Konstantinos Ir Rigas, 'Διαιτητική επίλυση διοικητικών διαφορών (The Arbitral Resolution of Administrative Law Disputes)' (2011) 59 Nomiko Vima 1190, 1195–96.

[43] For the history of the provision of Article 867 CCP, see Konstantinos F Kalavros, *(Θεμελιώδη Ζητήματα του Δικαίου της Διαιτησίας) Fundamental Issues of Arbitration Law* (Sakkoulas Publications 2011) 91 ff.

[44] Stelios N Kousoulis, *Θεμελιώδη Προβλήματα της Διαιτησίας (Fundamental Arbitration Issues)* (Ant N Sakkoulas 1996) vol B, 68.

[45] So, for instance, *CoS 433-437/1983* (Plenary Session).

or on the basis of an analysis of constitutional law,[46] that the submission of public law disputes to arbitration was not contrary to the Greek Constitution. Interestingly, this seems to be one of the rare instances where Greek courts—particularly the CoS—manifestly departed from the French administrative law tradition, which at the time did not favour the resolution of public law disputes by arbitration.[47] Greek courts did not adopt an ideological but, rather, a pragmatic approach, by repeatedly referring to the advantages of arbitration, particularly in terms of time efficiency. Furthermore, Greek courts recognized the relevance of private-public arbitration to the attraction of foreign capital, and thus to economic development.[48]

Nevertheless, while the AP has consistently confirmed its case law in this regard, in 1989 the CoS took, in an *obiter*, the view that arbitration of public law disputes was only permissible under the 1953 Code.[49] Crucially, in 1991 the CoS ruled, in a case concerning the construction and operation of an oil refinery which had not been authorized under the 1953 Code,[50] that tax law disputes (which in Greece are regarded as administrative law disputes, and are subject to the jurisdiction of administrative courts) could not be submitted to arbitration.[51] Founding its position on Article 94(1) of the Greek Constitution, which at the time stipulated that administrative courts had jurisdiction to hear substantive administrative law claims, the CoS concluded:

> In light of this provision of the Constitution, the legislator may not allow the submission to arbitration of tax law disputes, ie [disputes relating to] the review of legality of tax burden measures adopted in the exercise of sovereign authority.[52]

[46] See, for instance, the most frequently cited judgments *CoS 3439-3442/1988* (1989) 27 Dioikitiki Dikaiosyni 505, stating that the constitutional provisions defining the jurisdiction of Greek administrative courts do not preclude jurisdictional agreements on the submission to arbitration of disputes otherwise subject to the jurisdiction of these Courts; *AP 1684/1986* (1987) 54 Efimeris Ellinon Nomikon 615, confirming inter alia that private-public arbitration is compatible with Article 8(1) of the Greek constitution providing for the fundamental right to a natural judge.

[47] For the situation in France, see Florian Grisel, 'The Private-Public Divide and Its Influence over French Arbitration Law: Tradition and Transition' (in this volume) 67.

[48] See, for instance, *AP 981/1982* (1984) 20 To Syntagma 178; *AP 356/1991* (1993) MD Epitherorisi Emporikou Dikaiou 386.

[49] *CoS 3131/1989* (1989) 25 To Syntagma, 702, para 5: 'In the absence of this specific constitutional provision [ie Article 112 of the 1952 Constitution in connection with Article 107(1) of the Greek Constitution], which allows the statute to be enacted "once and for all" to provide for arbitration, those of the [disputes at issue] that are administrative disputes would, under the Constitution, be within the jurisdiction of the Greek administrative courts.'

[50] The relevant authorization had been based on Act 4171/1961.

[51] *CoS 1792/1991* (1992) 40 Nomiko Vima 779; *CoS 1793/1991* (1991) 35 Epitherorisi Dimosiou Dioikitikou Dikaiou 404.

[52] Substantive administrative law claims before the 'ordinary administrative courts' are distinguished from actions for annulment before the CoS (or, exceptionally, before an administrative court of appeal), in that an administrative court hearing them not only examines certain grounds for annulment, which could lead to the annulment of the contested measure, but can proceed to the full judicial review and, potentially, modify that measure. The legal issues that might give rise to substantive administrative law claims are defined in a number of legal provisions (such as those contained in the Act 1406/1983); they include tax law disputes.

This finding conflicted with the position of the AP on the same issue.[53] The resulting conflict between the AP and CoS on the issue of arbitrability of tax disputes was finally ruled upon by the Special Highest Court (SHC). The SHC is an ad hoc constitutional court whose exceptional jurisdiction under Article 100 of the Greek Constitution mainly covers conflicts between the country's supreme courts,[54] in particular when the conformity of a statute with the Greek Constitution is at stake.[55] The SHC held by majority in Decision 24/1993 that Article 94(1) of the Greek Constitution does not prevent the Greek government and private persons from submitting tax law disputes to the jurisdiction of an arbitral tribunal.[56] It reasoned:

> This provision of the Constitution, according to its true meaning, does not preclude the legislator from allowing the executive and a person subject to tax to submit to arbitration, upon agreement, a specific tax law dispute or tax law disputes arising from a certain legal relationship, since after all the Constitution (Article 78(4)) does not preclude the legislator from providing for a tax exemption or relief.[57]

Prima facie, the SHC based its ruling on the fact that the allocation of taxes falls within the discretion of the legislator. However, the SHC did not suggest that it endorses the conservative approach connecting the arbitrability of a claim to the possibility of its holder disposing of that claim. As the SHC stated, even under such an approach, submitting tax law claims to arbitration would not be contrary to the Greek Constitution. Its main underlying argument was that Article 94(1) of the Greek Constitution has to be read literally, that is, as positively conferring jurisdiction upon the administrative courts, but not as precluding the parties to a public law dispute from waiving the jurisdiction of administrative courts in relation to certain disputes or categories of disputes in favour of arbitration.[58]

The SHC's seminal judgment did not trigger any legislative reaction, nor did it seem to have any major impact on the contractual practice of the Greek government. Yet, since the decisions of the SHC are binding *erga omnes*, Greek courts have consistently recognized the conformity with the Greek Constitution of resolving tax disputes through arbitration.[59] Moreover, in reliance upon the case law of the SHC, Greek courts seem to assume that private-public arbitration agreements in public law matters more generally are fully compatible with the Greek Constitution. For instance, in

[53] The relevant conflicting judgment is the aforementioned *AP 981/1982* (1984) 20 To Syntagma 178.

[54] This encompasses the AP, the CoS, and the Court of Auditors.

[55] The second major field of competence of the SHC covers certain election law disputes.

[56] Indeed, certain members of the Court expressed a dissenting opinion, according to which only 'waivable private claims' can be submitted to arbitration under Greek law. Presumably, this is because assigning the resolution of public law disputes to a private body would amount to establishing a capitulations regime(!), contrary to the principle of popular sovereignty as provided for in Article 1(2) and (3) of the Greek Constitution: *HSC 24/1993* (1984) 20 To Syntagma 171, para 9.

[57] ibid.

[58] cf Prodromos D Dagtoglou, 'Η Συνταγματικότητα της Συμφωνίας περί Διαιτησίας (The Conformity of Arbitration Agreements with the Constitution)' 4 (1992) Dioikitiki Diki 1, 5.

[59] See, inter alia, *CoS 1472/1994*, para 4; *AP 159/1996*; *CoS 1199/2005* (2006) 47 Elliniki Dikaiosyni 1309, para 3; *CoS 1069/2013*; *CoS 2624/2013* (2013) 57 Epitheorisi Dimosiou Dioikitikou Dikaiou 1110, para 6; *AP 1952/2013* (2014) 62 Nomiko Vima 914.

a series of cases concerning construction projects, the CoS ruled, in a dispute between the Greek Army and a private constructor, that 'the arbitral resolution of substantive administrative disputes, such as the disputes that arise from an administrative contract, as for instance a contract for the execution of public works ... is not precluded by paragraph 1 of Article 94 of the Constitution'.[60]

In light of the jurisprudence of Greek courts, it would therefore be very difficult to challenge the arbitrability of public law claims under Greek law. Instead, it is settled case law that private-public disputes which are governed by public law can be validly submitted to arbitration.

A. Fundamental Procedural Guarantees

A number of fundamental procedural guarantees have developed in Greek case law in order to give effect to the public law elements of private-public arbitration. These guarantees primarily concern: (1) the requirement of a statutory authorization of each arbitration agreement entered into by the government; (2) procedural fairness; (3) the exclusive competence of Greek courts to annul state acts; (4) the limits to the res judicata effect of arbitral awards, notably the residual power of Greek courts to review, under any circumstances, arbitral awards and refuse to rely on, or enforce, them where they have been rendered in excess of power; and (5) the limits set by case law to the exclusion of set-aside proceedings by an arbitration clause ratified by a statute.

1 Requirement of a Statutory Authorization

The principle of legality under Greek law is very strict in the sense that the executive cannot take a decision or action unless it is permitted to do so by a provision of a statute or other legal instrument adopted by the executive (eg a presidential decree) on the basis of a statute.[61] This is translated into the principle that no public entity (or private entity exercising public power) may enter into an arbitration agreement unless parliament, or the executive acting on the basis of a parliamentary authorization, has explicitly authorized the relevant entity to conclude an arbitration agreement or to agree with the private parties concerned on the applicable dispute resolution method.[62] As regards public entities, the requirement of a statutory authorization applies to arbitration of both private law and public law disputes;[63] in contrast, private law entities should not be concerned with such authorizations, save for in public law disputes relating to the exercise of sovereign authority on their part.

[60] *CoS* 976/1998, para 9; *CoS* 977/1998; *CoS* 978/1998, *CoS* 979/1998; *CoS* 980/1998. See also *Administrative Court of Appeals of Athens 1553/2011*, para 5, related to arbitration proceedings on the validity of a concession agreement for the operation of a port on the island of Skiathos.

[61] Spiliotopoulos (n 2) 75–76.

[62] See *CoS* 238/1999, para 12; *AP 1952/2013*, 62 (2014) Nomiko Vima 914. See also Fortsakis (n 4) 167.

[63] The principle of legality applies to both sovereign and commercial acts: see, for instance, Legal Opinion of the LCS 197/2016, para 9. See also Article 79 of the Public Accounts Act which provides that no agreement giving rise to an obligation of the Greek state can be concluded unless there is an authorization to enter into the agreement in question.

However, there is no general statutory authorization of the executive to enter into contracts with individuals or companies and to agree to arbitrate disputes arising under such contracts. Although the expert committee that was responsible for the first draft of the 'Greek Code of Administrative Process' proposed the adoption of a provision that would have authorized administrative authorities to include an arbitration clause in public contracts, this idea has never been implemented, as the scope of that Code has been restricted to the codification of certain purely procedural rules.[64] Moreover, no reference is made to arbitration in the Greek Code of Administrative Procedure.

Thus, the needed parliamentary authorization of private-public arbitration can only be found in sector-specific statutes or regulations, for instance on concession agreements. The insertion of arbitration clauses in such instruments is regarded as an incentive for potential bidders to invest. In addition, parliament can also give consent to an arbitration clause negotiated by the relevant public authority *ex post*, by adopting an act incorporating and ratifying the relevant private-public arrangement.[65] Indeed, the ratification of highly important administrative contracts, such as concessions or privatization transactions (eg for the sale and transfer of shares in a utilities company owned by the state), through the incorporation into law (so-called ratification by law) of the relevant agreement is:

> common practice and is required, where a contract either has been concluded through a process other than those provided for in general or specific legal provisions, or contains terms binding on third parties (not privy to the contract), or contains provisions that are contrary to applicable legislation or [sets out] provisions for the settlement of disputes arising out of the execution of the contract by means of arbitration.[66]

The method of ratifying such agreements increases their legitimacy, as it allows discussion on specific contractual arrangements in parliament while precluding any unilateral modification of the contractual terms by the administrative authorities involved.

2 Procedural Fairness

Article 20(1) of the Greek Constitution provides for the right to effective judicial protection. This right is the basis for a number of further procedural guarantees, including the principle *audiatur et altera pars*, independence and impartiality of judges, and the principle of equal and fair treatment of all parties to a judicial proceeding.

[64] Apostolis Gerontas, *Δίκαιο Δημοσίων Έργων, Η Διοικητική Σύμβαση – Ανάθεση – Εκτέλεση – Δικαστική Προστασία (Κατά το Εθνικό και Κοινοτικό Δίκαιο) (Public Works Law, Administrative Contract – Award, Execution – Judicial Protection (Under National and Community Law))* (Sakkoulas Publications 2009) 895.

[65] ibid 896 ff.

[66] This is repeated in several Reports of the Scientific Service of the Parliament on bills for the ratification of administrative contracts: see, for instance, the Report of the Scientific Service of the Parliament on the bill for the ratification of a 'lease agreement' related to the exploration and exploitation of hydrocarbons, dated 30 September 2019, available at <www.hellenicparliament.gr/UserFiles/7b24652e-78eb-4807-9d68-e9a5d4576eff/k-respol-epist.pdf> accessed 24 January 2025; see also *CoS* 21/2019, para 10.

These rights cannot, in principle, be waived by means of an arbitration agreement. Any arbitral tribunal that hears a dispute instead of the competent state court has to respect Article 20(1) of the Greek Constitution, insofar as it exercises a judicial or quasi-judicial function; otherwise, the resort to arbitration would amount to an abusive circumvention of Article 20(1) of the Greek Constitution.[67] On this basis, Greek courts and legal scholars emphasize that the right to a fair hearing before an independent and impartial panel and the closely related principle of equality of arms apply not only to court proceedings, but also to arbitration proceedings.[68]

3 Exclusive Competence of Greek Courts to Annul Administrative Acts

Although the same procedural guarantees govern proceedings before domestic courts and arbitral tribunals, the scope of jurisdiction of arbitral tribunals is not fully equal to that of state courts under Greek law. In Judgment 24/1993, the SHC ruled that administrative courts are the only authority that can annul administrative decisions.[69] In fact, it has been unanimously acknowledged, in both case law and doctrine, that an arbitral tribunal, while being allowed to review the legality of an administrative decision in order to decide on the merits of the claims before it, does not have the power to annul or modify the administrative decision as such.[70] Under Articles 94(1) and 95(1)(a) of the Greek Constitution, this is an exclusive power of the administrative courts and of the CoS. To paraphrase the CoS, only the Greek Constitution can confer such a power on a state organ or other body; its delegation by parliament to an arbitral tribunal (even if it has been constituted under the 1953 Code), through the enactment of a law, is therefore excluded.[71]

4 Limits to the Res Judicata Effect of Arbitral Awards

An arbitral award is final and binding on the executive and the courts, and has res judicata effect.[72] The CoS has pointed out that, apart from set-aside proceedings before the competent civil courts,[73] Greek courts cannot annul a private-public arbitral award or review the issues resolved by an arbitral tribunal, including arbitral rulings on public policy issues, such as the conformity of an administrative contract provision with the Greek Constitution or EU law,[74] even when they are called upon to rule on related issues in the context of a distinct claim.[75]

However, the CoS consistently holds that, even if an award has not been set aside, or if there is no possibility to initiate set-aside proceedings, any Greek court 'has the

[67] cf Article 25(1) of the Greek Constitution, which provides that the fundamental rights granted by the Constitution to private persons 'also apply to the relations between individuals to which they are appropriate'.

[68] *AP* 66/2016; *AP* 356/1991; *AP* 1684/1986; cf Konstantinos Kerameus, *Νομικές Μελέτες (Legal Studies)* (Sakkoulas Publications 1994) vol II, 428.

[69] *HSC 24/1993* (1984) 20 To Syntagma 171, para 9.

[70] ibid; see, also, for instance, *CoS 889/1994*; *CoS 3335/2002*, para 5. See also Pavlopoulos (n 29) 64.

[71] *CoS 3291/2002*, para 3.

[72] There are numerous judgments of the CoS referring to the res judicata effect of awards rendered in the context of private-public arbitration: see eg *CoS 1749/1995*, para 4; *CoS 1197/2005*, para 3; *CoS 2624/2013* (2013) 57 Epitheorisi Dimosiou Dioikitikou Dikaiou 1110, para 6.

[73] CoS 2624/2013 (2013) 57 Epitheorisi Dimosiou Dioikitikou Dikaiou 1110, para 5.

[74] See, inter alia, *CoS 3312/2002*, para 5; *CoS* 105/2000, para 2; *CoS* 3248/2014, para 5 (available at <lawdb.intrasoftnet.com> accessed 24 January 2025).

[75] See, for instance, *CoS 3291/2002*, para 3; *CoS 1199/2005* (2006) 47 Elliniki Dikaiosyni 1309, para 3.

power (and is required) to ignore an arbitral award brought before it where it finds that the arbitral tribunal has exceeded its power'.[76] As a consequence, any Greek court called upon to decide on an issue connected to a private-public dispute which has already been resolved by means of arbitration must therefore examine whether the arbitral tribunal went beyond the scope of its jurisdiction. If it did, the resulting award is to be ignored, even if it cannot be annulled any more.[77]

5 Limits to the Exclusion of Set-Aside Proceedings

Article 900 CCP sets out that the right to bring an action to set aside an arbitral award cannot be waived prior to the rendering of an award. This applies to private-public arbitration proceedings unless otherwise provided for in law. Indeed, in practice numerous statutes have ratified concessions or other private-public agreements providing that any arbitral award is not subject to set-aside or any equivalent proceedings. Greek courts have upheld that, after its ratification by law, a private-public arbitration clause excluding set-aside proceedings supersedes Article 900 CCP as *lex posterior et specialis* and is valid, as it does not infringe the right to a fair trial under Article 20(1) of the Greek Constitution or Article 6 of the European Convention on Human Rights and Fundamental Freedoms, but is a legitimate restriction on the right to be heard by a judicial authority.[78]

Nevertheless, the AP has set clear limits to the interpretation and possible scope of the exclusion of set-aside proceedings through arbitration clauses ratified by law. More specifically, according to the relevant case law, a tacit or implied exclusion of set-aside proceedings is not possible, and the relevant clauses must be interpreted strictly literally and not broadly.[79] For instance, the AP has held that a clause providing that arbitral awards are not subject to any 'appeal' (in Greek, *endiko meso*) cannot be interpreted as referring to an action to set aside an award, which in Greek procedural law does not qualify as 'appeal', but as a 'remedy' (in Greek, *endiko voithima*).[80] Moreover, the AP has made clear that an arbitration clause intending to exclude set-aside proceedings is valid to the extent it concerns a 'violation of substantive or procedural provisions but not with respect to a violation of conditions and breach of restrictions provided for in the ratifying statute itself'. As the AP pointed out in its reasoning:

> [It cannot] be accepted that the specific statute ratifying [a private-public] agreement, which has incorporated provisions and conditions with a view to expediting arbitration proceedings, dispenses even with the requirement that such proceedings comply with the terms and conditions that the ratifying statute defines and contains, eg regarding the composition of the arbitral tribunal or when the arbitral award violates [*ordre public* provisions].[81]

[76] *CoS 3291/2002*, para 3; see also *HSC 24/1993* (1984) 20 To Syntagma 171, para 9.

[77] Aggelos K Foustoukos, 'Διαιτησία διοικητικών και ιδιαίτερα φορολογικών διαφορών (Arbitration of Administrative and Particularly of Tax Law Disputes)' in Beys (n 37) 214, 219 (taking the view that the courts should also be able to control whether an arbitral tribunal has respected the principle of equality of the parties to the proceedings).

[78] *AP 356/1991* (1993) MD Epitherorisi Emporikou Dikaiou 386.

[79] *AP* 66/2016.

[80] ibid.

[81] ibid; see also *AP* 1791/2014.

Thus, Greek constitutional law is based on a comprehensive set of rules and principles which enable private-public arbitration while establishing certain safeguards designed to ensure respect for the constitutional role of parliament, and of the judiciary. However, although the relevant constitutional framework enhances the legitimacy of private-public arbitration, the need for transparency and participation of civil society is not reflected in any constitutional norm.

IV. Statutes Providing for Private-Public Arbitration

Greek statutes referring private-public disputes to arbitration have historically been based on a purely private concept of arbitration. However, more recent statutes give greater consideration to the public law relevance of private-public arbitration, or even the increased need for transparency of private-public arbitration proceedings. At the outset, we present an overview of Acts providing for ad hoc arbitration (A), as well as of investment Acts (usually referred to as 'Economic Development Acts'), containing provisions relating to, or authorizing, private-public arbitration (B). Thereafter, we focus on Greek statutes regulating certain types of administrative contracts, such as public procurement or construction concession agreements, and public-private partnerships, which provide for private-public arbitration proceedings more tailored to the peculiarities of public law disputes arising in relation to them (C).

A. Acts Providing for Ad Hoc Arbitration

Ad hoc arbitration of private-public disputes has been well known in Greece since at least the interwar period. As a matter of fact, at the beginning of the twentieth century, Greece attracted certain foreign investors in the public utilities sector, in particular in public transportation and the production and distribution of electricity. Several concessions granted during this period contained arbitration clauses and gave rise to disputes that were resolved through arbitration,[82] with some of these cases having gained international attention. For instance, J Gillis Wetter and Stephen M Schwebel have analysed a number of arbitral cases related to a 1925 concession, most of which concerned state measures. The measures included staff or safety regulations and the imposition of social contributions, and were perceived by the concessionaire as interferences breaching the government's contractual commitments.[83]

[82] Charles Leben, 'L'évolution du droit international des investissements: Un rapide survol' in Charles Leben (ed), *Le contentieux arbitral transnational relatif à l'investissement: nouveaux développements* (Anthemis 2006) 9, 11.

[83] See J Gillis Wetter and Stephen M Schwebel, 'Some Little-Known Cases on Concessions' (1964) 40 BYBIL 183, 194. The arbitration clause at issue provided that '[a]ny and every dispute, difference or question which may arise . . . touching the construction meaning or effect of this concession . . . or the rights and liabilities of the parties hereunder or otherwise howsoever relating to the premises shall be referred to the arbitration of three arbitrators of whom one shall be nominated by the State and one by [the other party] and the third who shall act as chairman shall be chosen by the other two.'

Ever since that period, ad hoc arbitration clauses have been included in various public contracts. For a more recent example, reference should be made to the arbitration provisions of an agreement relating to the 'exploitation of hydrocarbons in the sea area of the Sea of Thrace' concluded between the Greek government and a private entity on 23 November 1999 and ratified by Article 2 of Act 2779/1999. Article 34 of that agreement sets out that any dispute 'arising under, or in connection with, [its] interpretation and application' is to be resolved by a three-member ad hoc arbitral panel, comprised of two members appointed by the parties and the presiding arbitrator, who is to be appointed by a committee composed of the two eldest vice presidents and the president of the CoS. Interestingly, the agreement provides that the arbitral tribunal 'is not bound by any procedural rule on the conduct of the proceedings', while it has the power to examine witnesses, make on-the-spot inspections, order an expert report to be drawn up, and consider any type of evidence. An arbitral award can be rendered by a majority; it is final and directly enforceable, with annulment proceedings being excluded. However, unless otherwise agreed by the parties, arbitration proceedings under this arbitration clause should be expected to be confidential.

B. Economic Development Acts

Investor-state arbitration in the context of Economic Development Acts appear the most common type of private-public arbitration in Greece. Most relevant in this respect have been (1) the 1953 Code and (2)Act 4171/1961, another economic development Act, since several arbitral proceedings have been conducted in connection with them.[84]

1. The 1953 Code

The 1953 Code does not contain any provision regarding the rules governing arbitration proceedings or the legal effects of arbitral awards. However, 'acts of approval' granted under it typically address issues, such as the seat of arbitration, the law applicable to a dispute, the constitution of arbitral tribunals (always with three members), the applicable arbitration rules, and the enforcement of resulting awards.[85] Furthermore, an 'act of approval' under the 1953 Code might empower arbitral tribunals to determine the procedural rules applicable to arbitration proceedings.[86]

A number of 'acts of approval' granted under the 1953 Code have empowered arbitrators to decide *ex aequo et bono*, taking into account the text of the relevant 'act

[84] An arbitration clause is also contained in Article 6(5) of the Act 849/1978 on the Provision of Incentives to Reinforce the Regional and Economic Development of the Country.

[85] See Ioannis K Dryllerakis, *Επένδυσις και Προστασία Κεφαλαίων Εξωτερικού (Investment and Protection of Foreign Capital)* (I Zacharopoulos 1975) 123 ff.

[86] Antonia K Dimolitsa, 'Διαιτητικές Συμφωνίες και Ξένες Επενδύσεις: Το Ελληνικό Δημόσιο μεταξύ Συμβατικής Δέσμευσης και εξουσιαστικής επέμβασης (Arbitration Agreements and Foreign Investments: The Greek State Between Contractual Commitment and Sovereign Intervention)' (1988) 36 Nomiko Vima 1381, 1404. According to Helena Kalyva, 'Ζητήματα από τις Διαιτητικές Αποφάσεις του ΝΔ 2687/1953 (Issues Regarding Arbitration Agreements under the Legislative Decree 2687/1953)' (1987) 35 Nomiko Vima 9, 16, a typical clause to that effect provides that '[t]he arbitrators are not required to apply the existing procedural . . . provisions, it is up to them to regulate the arbitration proceedings.'

of approval', trade usages, and the principle of good faith.[87] According to Antonia Dimolitsa, a prominent practitioner and commentator, this could be seen as evidence of the parties' intention to functionally 'internationalize' potential disputes by avoiding the reference to any national legal source.[88] Indeed, to a certain extent, parallels could be drawn between such 'acts of approval' and concessions granted during the 1950s to international investors by less developed states, which do not refer to any national legal system and have been construed by international arbitral tribunals as internationalized state contracts, as for instance in *Sapphire v NIOC*.[89]

However, despite the broadness of such clauses, there is no indication that tribunals seized under the 1953 Code attempted to elaborate specific principles applicable to investor-state disputes.[90] The lack of transparency has impeded any interaction among arbitral tribunals that could have led to the development of a set of specific procedural rules for investment disputes.

2. Act 4171/1961

In 1961, Act 4171/1961 on the 'Adoption of General Measures to Foster the Economic Development of the Country' was promulgated with the aim of providing fiscal incentives to potential foreign and national investors in order to make significant[91] investments in Greece.

Similarly to the 1953 Code, Act 4171/1961 applies only to investments approved on the basis of an administrative authorization (Article 1(1)) or included in an administrative contract concluded between an investor and the Greek government (Article 4(2)), while Article 5(2) of Act 4171/1961[92] provides for the arbitral resolution of disputes but does not specify the details of the arbitration procedure to be followed, which are to be agreed upon by the parties and reflected in the arbitration clause included in the relevant authorization or administrative contract. In fact, several investments have been submitted to both the 1953 Code and Act 4171/1961 through a single 'act of approval' incorporating an arbitration clause negotiated and agreed upon between the Greek government and the investor concerned. Arbitration proceedings in relation either to Act 4171/1961 in conjunction with the 1953 Code, or to Act 4171/1961 alone, have always been fully confidential.

[87] Dryllerakis (n 85) 124; see also Dimolitsa (n 86) 1404.

[88] Dimolitsa (n 86) 1384 ff and 1404 ff.

[89] *Sapphire International Petroleums Ltd v National Iranian Oil Company*, Arbitral Award (15 March 1963) (1967) 35 ILR 136, 173.

[90] Dimolitsa (n 86) 1406; cf Aggelos K Foustoukos, 'Διαιτησία διοικητικών και ιδιαίτερα φορολογικών διαφορών (Arbitration of Administrative and Particularly of Tax Law Disputes)' (1994) 25 Dike 590, 594.

[91] The threshold for the eligibility of an investment was initially set at 90m drachmas (art 1(2) of the Act 4171/1961) and subsequently increased and reached the amount of 150m drachmas (art 5(1) of Act 159/1975).

[92] The text reads as follows: '[d]isputes arising between the Government and a person making an investment subject, on the basis of an authorization under Article 1 or a contract under Article 4, to the provisions of this Act, concerning the interpretation or possible *lacunae* of the authorization or contract, shall be resolved by means of arbitration, as provided for in the said authorization or contract, by derogation from the existing provisions on arbitrations to which the Government is a party, with the appointment of a foreign person as arbitrator or presiding arbitrator being allowed.'

Although, since 31 December 1981, it has no longer been possible to request the submission of an investment to the regime of Act 4171/1961,[93] arbitration in relation to investments made on its basis is still possible.

C. Acts Regulating Certain Types of Administrative Contracts

Certain specific Acts regulating administrative contracts, mainly in the sectors of public procurement and construction, aim at providing an alternative to state court litigation. They allow the contracting parties to resort to arbitration, or even set out procedural rules applying to arbitration thereunder.

1 Public Procurement and Concession Agreements

Historically, several Acts regulating administrative contracts in the sectors of public procurement and concessions have conferred upon the government the power to conclude arbitration agreements with private contractors. For instance, Act 3669/2008 (the former 'Public Works Construction Code') allowed the competent ministers to agree with private contractors on the inclusion of an arbitration clause in public works contracts regulated by this Code, 'without being bound by any other provision'.[94] Similarly, Article 194 of Act 4281/2014,[95] which transposed Directive 2004/18/EC and regulated, inter alia, public procurement related to public works, public supply, and public service contracts (as defined in Directive 2004/18/EC), enabled 'by derogation from provisions applicable to arbitrations to which the Government is a party' the inclusion of an arbitration clause specifying the details of the arbitral process in the 'contractual documentation' for projects subject to Act 4281/2014.

The wording of provisions such as Article 194 of Act 4281/2014 seems to provide a carte blanche to the executive for consenting to any type of arbitration, insofar as they enable the 'derogation' from otherwise applicable provisions. Such provisions have accordingly been criticized, including by Professor Skouris,[96] because they can be interpreted as allowing parties to disregard public policy provisions. Clauses of this type, therefore, should be interpreted restrictively, in accordance with the Greek Constitution, in the sense that they merely free the parties from any procedural constraint—where it exists—without affecting the duty of arbitrators to apply *jus cogens*.[97]

However, Act 3669/2008 and Act 4281/2014 have been replaced by Act 4413/2016 on 'the award and execution of concession contracts – harmonisation with Directive 2014/23/EU' and Act 4412/2016 on 'Public Works, Procurement and Services Contracts', which for the first time in Greek history provide for transparency

[93] This is provided for in Article 1(8) of Act 4171/1961, in conjunction with Article 1(8) of legislative decree 916/1971; see also Dimolitsa (n 14) 18.

[94] Article 78 of Act 3669/2008, which has been repealed by Article 377(1)(31) of Act 4412/2016.

[95] This Act came into force in March 2015 and was repealed as of 1 July 2016, by Article 57 of the Act 4403/2016.

[96] Skouris (n 40) 175.

[97] Konstantinos Kalavros, *Δίκαιο της Διαιτησίας, I. Εσωτερική Διαιτησία (Arbitration Law, I. Domestic Arbitration)* (Sakkoulas Publications 2011) vol A, 28.

guarantees in arbitration proceedings related to an administrative contract. More specifically, pursuant to Article 65(1) of Act 4413/2016, the parties to a concession contract may include a clause for the 'arbitral resolution of any dispute arising in relation to the implementation, the interpretation or the validity of a concession contract or ancillary agreements' under the relevant rules of the CCP or the IAA, as the case may be. Article 65(2) of Act 4413/2016 recognizes the right of the parties to define, inter alia, the applicable procedural rules. However, the freedom of the parties is restricted by Article 65(5) of Act 4413/2016, which prescribes that the UNCITRAL Rules on Transparency in Treaty-Based Investor-State Arbitration apply to arbitration proceedings conducted in this context and supersede any agreement between the parties.[98]

In the same vein, Article 176 of Act 4412/2016 allows for the insertion in public procurement contracts regulated by this Act of an arbitration clause determining the applicable rules of procedure 'by derogation from provisions that at the relevant time apply to arbitrations to which the Government is a party'. At the same time, paragraphs 4 and 5 of Article 176 of Act 4412/2016 prescribe the mandatory application of the UNCITRAL Rules on Transparency in Treaty-based Investor-State Arbitration.

2 Act on Public-Private Partnerships

The Greek Act on Public-Private Partnerships allows the contracting parties (ie a private entity, on the one hand, and the Greek government or a public entity or company controlled by the Greek government, on the other) to include an arbitration clause in a public-private partnership agreement (Article 31(1)).[99] Article 31(2) of the Act allows the parties to freely determine the details of the arbitral procedure, such as the appointment of arbitrators, the 'applicable rules of arbitration', the arbitrators' fees, and the language of the arbitration proceedings. However, the parties are not free to choose the law applicable to public-private partnerships, as under Article 31(3) of the Act they are subject to Greek law.

3 'Co-Financed' Construction Projects

A special arbitral procedure is provided for construction contracts where the project owner is a company under the control or substantial influence (for instance, due to holding 'golden shares') of the government, or the project is financed by both EU structural funds and the Greek government (so called 'co-financed' construction projects), under Article 25A of Act 3614/2007, as amended by Act 4155/2013 and Act 4264/2014.[100]

This provision takes into account the public law character of disputes arising under such contracts. The commencement of arbitral proceedings depends on the prior filing of a complaint with the competent authority (Article 25A(4) of the Act). This

[98] Pursuant to Article 65(5) of the Act 4413/2016, the minister of justice will issue a ministerial decision designating the national authority assuming the role of a repository of public information.

[99] Act 3389/2005; see Claire Spirou and Vassiliki Koumpli, 'Public Private Partnerships Under Greek Law' (2010) 63 Revue hellénique de droit international 439, 454–55.

[100] For a detailed analysis, see Eirini Stroggyli, 'Η Νέα Διαδικασία Διαιτησίας στα Συγχρηματοδοτούμενα Δημόσια Έργα (The New Arbitration Procedure in the Field of Cofinanced Public Works)' (2013) 6 Theoria kai Praksi tou Dioikitikou Dikaiou 1071, 1077 ff; and Gerontas (n 39) 426 ff.

rule has apparently been inspired by the procedural steps that need to be taken before bringing an action before an administrative court,[101] but also resembles dispute resolution clauses in IIAs that provide for the resort to negotiations prior to initiating arbitration proceedings.

Furthermore, the president of an arbitral tribunal can only be an independent person who is an expert in Greek administrative law, that is, a CoS judge chosen by the president of the CoS (Article 25A(7) of the Act). Arbitral tribunals have the power to order interim measures (Article 25A(8) of the Act). The arbitral award must be rendered within four months from the date of appointment of the tribunal's president (Article 25A(9) of the Act). Moreover, although awards rendered are directly enforceable, the parties can challenge them on the grounds provided for in Article 897 CCP. However, despite these public law elements, there is no guarantee of transparency of the proceedings.

V. Investment Treaty Arbitration

Greek constitutional law does not contain any specific restrictions regarding the type of claims to be submitted to investment treaty arbitration, the conclusion of arbitration agreements, or the commencement of arbitration proceedings under a BIT. BITs ratified by parliament form an 'integral part of domestic Greek law and shall prevail over any contrary provision of the law' (Article 28(1) of the Greek Constitution). As a result, arbitration clauses in BITs are attributed supralegislative force, albeit that in the event of conflict the Greek Constitution shall prevail, and an arbitral award that is inconsistent with the Constitution risks not being enforceable in Greece.

Greece is party to approximately 40 BITs in force,[102] most of them containing the consent of Greece to arbitration or referring to the possibility of the parties giving their consent to arbitration.[103] For instance, Article 10 of the China–Greece BIT refers to arbitration disputes about the amount of compensation for expropriation, and any other dispute, being submitted to arbitration by 'mutual consent'. By contrast, Article 10 of the United Arab Emirates–Greece BIT (the latest BIT signed and ratified by Greece)[104] is more investor-friendly. It sets out that, where an amicable settlement proves to be impossible within six months, the grieving investor can bring its treaty claims either to a national court or to an international arbitral tribunal.[105] Remarkably, Article 10(4) of that BIT provides for the application to such arbitral

[101] Stroggyli (n 100) 1078–79.

[102] See UNCTAD, 'International Investment Agreements Navigator: Greece' <https://investmentpolicy.unctad.org/international-investment-agreements/countries/81/greece> accessed 24 January 2025.

[103] Davrados (n 15) 410–11; Ioannis Vassardanis, 'National Report for Greece (2012)' in Jan Paulsson and Lise Bosman (eds), *ICCA International Handbook on Commercial Arbitration*, Supplement No 72 (Kluwer Law International 2012) 1, 56.

[104] See Act 4362/2016. However, this BIT is apparently not yet in force, as the governments concerned have not notified each other that the relevant internal procedures have been accomplished, in accordance with Article 14 of the BIT.

[105] Recourse can be had before an ICSID tribunal, an ICSID Additional Facility tribunal, or an ad hoc tribunal constituted under the UNCITRAL Arbitration Rules, as provided for in the dispute resolution clause of the 2001 Greece Model BIT (published in Paulsson and Bosman (n 103)).

proceedings of the UNCITRAL Rules on Transparency in Treaty-based Investor-State Arbitration.

Greece has, to date, been a respondent in a handful of BIT cases,[106] most of them concerning measures taken by the Greek authorities in order to cope with the severe sovereign debt[107] and banking crisis[108] that broke out in the country in the aftermath of the 2008 global financial crisis.

VI. Assessment and Conclusion

Greece has a strong private-public arbitration tradition. Greek law seems to rely on the principle that private-public arbitration is an acceptable alternative to court litigation. Both private and public law disputes are arbitrable. Moreover, Greek constitutional law, as further specified in case law by the CoS and the AP, contains certain safeguards ensuring a minimum of democratic legitimacy and control. For instance, the conclusion of a valid private-public arbitration agreement requires the involvement of parliament, through a prior statutory authorization or *ex post* ratification. Moreover, neither an arbitration agreement nor an arbitral award can affect the monopoly of administrative justice on the annulment of administrative acts or the power of Greek courts to control a possible excess of power by arbitral tribunals, even when set-aside proceedings are for any reason not available.

However, Greek constitutional law, as it currently stands, does not provide for any specific transparency or civil society participation guarantee. So far, any information about private-public arbitration awards is publicly available only from judicial set-aside proceedings. The absolute confidentiality of arbitration proceedings can lead to the 'isolation' of private-public arbitration from existing case law and legal doctrine. Indeed, arbitral tribunals hearing public law disputes in lieu of administrative courts may be able to resolve such disputes in an expedited and efficient manner, but the confidential character of the proceedings might impair their legitimacy and obstruct the development of this field of law, leading to the creation of an 'unexplored area'.[109]

Against this backdrop, the Greek legislator should consider enacting a law regulating the general procedure to be followed by arbitral tribunals in relation to the arbitral resolution of at least certain types of private-public disputes. For instance, this could include a minimum transparency guarantee for arbitration of public law disputes, such as publication of arbitral awards, or the possibility to submit amicus curiae briefs (for instance, in favour of the most representative and relevant non-profit organizations). That said, inflexible solutions that do not consider the peculiarities of Greek private-public arbitration proceedings should be avoided; instead of simply

[106] Greek investors, in turn, have brought several claims on the basis of BITs against foreign host states, including but not limited to neighbouring states of Greece, such as Serbia and Albania.

[107] See *Poštová banka AS and ISTROKAPITAL SE v Hellenic Republic*, ICSID Case No ARB/13/8, Award (9 April 2015). The award has been upheld in annulment proceedings. See Decision on Poštová Banka's Application for Partial Annulment of the Award (29 September 2016).

[108] See *Cyprus Popular Bank Public Co Ltd v Hellenic Republic*, ICSID Case No ARB/14/16 (registered 16 July 2014).

[109] Kalyva (n 86) 10.

referring to the 'UNCITRAL Rules on Transparency in Treaty-based Investor-State Arbitration' in Acts 4412/2016 and 4413/2016 without any refinement or adjustment, it would be more efficient to prepare a new set of rules tailored to the specific needs of the Greek private-public arbitration practice.

Select Materials

Bibliography

in English, French, and German

Davrados, Nikolaos, 'Greece' in Wenhua Shan (ed), *The Legal Protection of Foreign Investment: A Comparative Study* (Hart Publishing 2012) 395

Dempsey, Paul Stephen, 'Foreign Investment Incentives in the Developing World: The Legislation of Greece, Egypt, Pakistan, Thailand and the Republic of China' (1979) 11 Case W Res J Int'l L 575

Dimolitsa, Antonia K, 'Arbitration Agreements and Foreign Investments: The Greek State Between Contractual Commitment and Sovereign Intervention' (1988) 5 J Int'l Arb 17

Kalyva, Helena, *Ausländische Privatinvestitionen in Schwellenländern, Rechtsschutz im Konflikt – Eine Untersuchung am Beispiel des verfassungsrechtlich gewährten Schutzes in Griechenland* (Peter Lang 1987)

Lambadarios, Constantine E, 'Greece' in Wolfgang Friedmann (ed), *Legal Aspects of Foreign Investment* (Little, Brown and Company 1959) 233

Littell, Norman M, 'The International Investment of Private Capital – Opportunities and Problems: Legal Incentives for Private Investments Abroad' (1954) 40 Va Law Rev 977

Pavlopoulos, Prokopios, 'L'arbitrage dans le contentieux administratif' (1992) 4 REDP 61

Spirou, Claire and Vassiliki Koumpli, 'Public Private Partnerships under Greek Law' (2010) 63 Revue hellénique de droit international 439

Spyropoulos, Philippos K and Theodore Fortsakis, *Constitutional Law in Greece* (Ant N Sakkoulas – Wolters Kluwer 2009)

Vassardanis, Ioannis, 'National Report for Greece (2012)' in Jan Paulsson and Lise Bosman (eds), *ICCA International Handbook on Commercial Arbitration*, Supplement No 72 (Kluwer Law International 2012) 1

Wetter, J Gillis and Stephen M Schwebel, 'Some Little-Known Cases on Concessions' (1964) 40 BYBIL 183

in Greek

Beys, Kostas E, 'Οι Δεκτικές Διαιτησίας Διαφορές (Arbitrable Disputes)' in *Αφιέρωμα στον Ανδρέα Α. Γαζή (Liber Amicorum Andreas A Gazis)* (Ant N Sakkoulas, 1994)

Dagtoglou, Prodromos D, 'Η Συνταγματικότητα της Συμφωνίας περί Διαιτησίας (The Conformity of Arbitration Agreements with the Constitution)' 4 (1992) Dioikitiki Diki 1

Dimolitsa, Antonia K, 'Διαιτητικές Συμφωνίες και Ξένες Επενδύσεις: Το Ελληνικό Δημόσιο μεταξύ Συμβατικής Δέσμευσης και εξουσιαστικής επέμβασης (Arbitration

Agreements and Foreign Investments: The Greek State Between Contractual Commitment and Sovereign Intervention)' (1988) 36 Nomiko Vima 1381

Dryllerakis, Ioannis K, *Επένδυσις και Προστασία Κεφαλαίων Εξωτερικού (Investment and Protection of Foreign Capital)* (I Zacharopoulos 1975)

Fortsakis, Theodoros, *Διαιτησία και Διοικητικές Διαφορές (Arbitration and Administrative Disputes)* (P N Sakkoulas 1998)

Foustoukos, Aggelos K, 'Διαιτησία διοικητικών και ιδιαίτερα φορολογικών διαφορών (Arbitration of Administrative and Particularly of Tax Law Disputes)' in Kostas E Beys (ed), *Δικανικοί Διάλογοι (Dialogues About Justice)* (Afoi P Sakkoula 1994) vol I, 214

Gerontas, Apostolis, *Δίκαιο Δημοσίων Έργων, Η Διοικητική Σύμβαση – Ανάθεση – Εκτέλεση – Δικαστική Προστασία (Κατά το Εθνικό και Κοινοτικό Δίκαιο) (Public Works Law, Administrative Contract – Award, Execution – Judicial Protection (Under National and Community Law))* (Sakkoulas Publications 2009)

Gerontas, Apostolis, 'Η διαιτητική επίλυση των διαφορών από τις συγχρηματοδοτούμενες συμβάσεις δημοσίων έργων: Μια πρώτη ερμηνευτική προσέγγιση (The Arbitral Dispute Settlement in Cofinanced Public Works Contracts: A First Interpretation Approach)' (2014) 34 Hellenic Rev Eur L 423

Kalavros, Konstantinos F, *Δίκαιο της Διαιτησίας, I. Εσωτερική Διαιτησία (Arbitration Law, I. Domestic Arbitration)* (Sakkoulas Publications 2011) vol A

Kalavros, Konstantinos F, *Θεμελιώδη Ζητήματα του Δικαίου της Διαιτησίας (Fundamental Issues of Arbitration Law)* (Sakkoulas Publications 2011)

Kalyva, Helena, 'Ζητήματα από τις Διαιτητικές Αποφάσεις του ΝΔ 2687/1953 (Issues Regarding Arbitration Agreements under the Legislative Decree 2687/1953)' (1987) 35 Nomiko Vima 9

Karakostas, Velissarios, 'Διαιτησία και Διοικητικές, Ιδίως Φορολογικές Διαφορές – Έννοιες Ασύμπτωτες (Arbitration and Administrative, Particularly Tax Law Disputes – Irreconcilable Concepts)' in Kostas E Beys (ed), *Δικανικοί Διάλογοι (Dialogues About Justice)* (Afoi P Sakkoula 1994) vol I, 219

Kargados, Panagiotis A, 'Είναι Δυνατή η Διαιτητική Επίλυσις των Φορολογικών Διαφορών (Is the Arbitral Resolution of Tax Law Disputes Possible?)' in Kostas E Beys (ed), *Δικανικοί Διάλογοι (Dialogues About Justice)* (Afoi P Sakkoula 1994) vol I, 205

Kerameus, Konstantinos, *Νομικές Μελέτες (Legal Studies)* (Sakkoulas Publications 1994) vol II

Kousoulis, Stelios N, *Θεμελιώδη Προβλήματα της Διαιτησίας (Fundamental Arbitration Issues)* (Ant N Sakkoulas 1996) vol B

Kousoulis, Stelios, *Δίκαιο της Διαιτησίας (Arbitration Law)* (Sakkoulas Publications 2006)

Markianos-Daniolos, Ioannis D, 'Νομική Αξιολόγηση των Εγκριτικών Πράξεων Νηολόγησης Πλοίων κατά το Άρθρο 13 του ΝΔ 2687/53 (Legal Assessment of Acts Approving the Registration of Ships under Article 13 of Legislative Decree 2687/53)' (2013) 41 Epitheorisis Nautiliakou Dikaiou 161

Mavrias, Konstantinos G, 'Η Συνταγματική Προστασία των Ξένων Επενδύσεων κατά το Ελληνικό Δίκαιο και τα Διεθνή Πρότυπα Προστασίας (Constitutional Protection of Foreign Investments under Greek Law and International Protection Patterns)' (1975) 1 To Syntagma 41

Rigas, Konstantinos Ir, 'Διαιτητική Επίλυση Διοικητικών Διαφορών (The Arbitral Resolution of Administrative Law Disputes' (2011) 59 Nomiko Vima 1190

Skouris, Vassilios, *Διοικητικό Δικονομικό Δίκαιο (Administrative Procedural Law)* (Sakkoulas Publications 1991)
Stroggyli, Eirini, 'Η Νέα Διαδικασία Διαιτησίας στα Συγχρηματοδοτούμενα Δημόσια Έργα (The New Arbitration Procedure in the Field of Cofinanced Public Works)' (2013) 6 Theoria kai Praksi tou Dioikitikou Dikaiou 1071

Legislation and Other Legal Instruments

Legislative Decree 2687/1953 on the Investment and Protection of Foreign Capital
Act 4171/1961 on the Adoption of General Measures to Foster the Economic Development of the Country
Act 2289/1995 on Prospecting, Exploration and Exploitation of Hydrocarbons
Act 3389/2005 on Public-Private Partnerships
Act 3614/2007 on Cofinanced Construction Projects
Act 4413/2016 on the award and execution of concession contracts – harmonisation with Directive 2014/23/EU
Act 4412/2016 on Public Works, Procurement and Services Contracts
2001 Greece Model BIT

Cases

Highest Special Court: 24/1993
Council of State: 1395/1954, 433-437/1983, 3439-3442/1988 3132/1989, 472/1994, 889/1994, 1749/1995, 2346/1996, 976-980/1998, 105/2000, 3291/2002, 3312/2002, 3335/2002, 1199/2005, 751/2008, 1069/2013, 2624/2013, 3248/2014, 582/2015
Administrative Court of Appeals of Athens: 1553/2011
Areios Pagos (Supreme Civil and Criminal Court of Greece): 981/1982, 1684/1986, 356/1991, 159/1996, 1952/2013, 1791/2014, 66/2016

7

Can a State Swim against the Tide?

Hungarian Perspectives on Public-Private Arbitration

*Csongor István Nagy**

I. Introduction

Hungary presents an excellent case for analysing the policy issues surrounding public-private arbitration. On the one hand, Hungarian law has a rather straightforward (binary) approach to arbitrability, where public law disputes are, with the exception of investment arbitration, not arbitrable, while private-public disputes subject to private law are arbitrable and receive no special treatment in comparison to pure civil law matters. In this scheme, public actors' promises as to activities governed by public law may cause tensions that the rigidity of the system cannot handle. On the other hand, Hungary's economic policy, characterized, in general, by relatively intensive regulatory intervention, has given rise to a good number of public-private disputes that ended up before investment treaty tribunals. This chapter presents Hungary's experiences with, and reactions to, public-private arbitration. Its central argument is that, as to public-private arbitration, Hungary has been trying to swim against the tide and, depending on what the country's national interest demanded, this resulted in both anti- and pro-arbitration attitudes.

Section II gives a concise introduction into Hungary's rather straightforward (binary) approach to arbitrability in public-private disputes. Section III gives an account of Hungary's experiences with investor-state arbitration, focusing on cases concerning regulatory autonomy. This section analyses and assesses Hungary's investment protection cases with special emphasis on non-expropriation matters. These, as a possible reason for Hungary's at times relatively hostile approach to public-private arbitration, show investment tribunals' willingness to engage in reviewing national policy decisions and legal proceedings, which, in national constitutional systems, normally come under judicial control. The vast majority of the cases involved no genuine expropriation claims[1] and centred around 'treatment' issues, like fair and equitable treatment and discrimination.

Section IV presents Hungary's legislative efforts to provide special treatment for public-private arbitration cases involving national assets and how these were influenced

* The research for this chapter was supported by the project nr EFOP-3.6.2-16-2017-00007, entitled 'Aspects on the Development of Intelligent, Sustainable and Inclusive Society: Social, Technological, Innovation Networks in Employment and Digital Economy'. The project has been supported by the European Union, co-financed by the European Social Fund and the budget of Hungary.

[1] See Csongor István Nagy, 'Hungarian Cases Before ICSID Tribunals: The Hungarian Experience with Investment Arbitration' (2017) 58(3) Hung J Leg Stud291.

Csongor István Nagy, *Can a State Swim against the Tide?* In: *The Comparative Constitutional Foundations of Private-Public Arbitration*. Edited by: Stephan W. Schill, Oxford University Press. © Stephan W. Schill 2025.
DOI: 10.1093/9780191987960.003.0007

by the idea that public-private arbitration is often not in the national interest. This section analyses and assesses provisions adopted in 2011 and 2012 that excluded arbitration in cases involving national property, as well as the Hungarian Constitutional Court's (CC) judgment on these provisions. By contrast, section V presents two cases where Hungary found arbitration to be in the national interest and made a push for the availability of this mechanism. The first involves Hungary revoking the regime presented in section IV in order to execute a large-scale (project-specific) investment agreement with Russia; the second, Hungary's support for arbitration based on the Energy Charter Treaty (ECT) in intra-EU matters to protect the interests of MOL, a Hungarian 'national champion' in the oil industry. The chapter ends with a summary of the Hungarian conception of, and experiences with, public-private arbitration.

II. Status of Public-Private Arbitration in Hungarian Law

Hungary follows a binary approach to public-private arbitration: private law disputes are arbitrable, while public law disputes are completely inarbitrable. The recent introduction of the concept of administrative law contract somewhat changed this picture by shifting some genuine private law matters to the non-arbitrable zone of public law. The only exception to this binary approach is investment treaty arbitration.

A. Hungary's Binary Approach

Hungarian law follows a rather straightforward approach as to the arbitrability of public-private disputes. The starting point is that only certain civil matters can be subject to arbitration. Hence, public law disputes, which concern the exercise of public authority, are not arbitrable and, although there is no specific judicial practice in this regard, arbitration agreements in public law matters are not legally enforceable.

Section 3(1)(1) of the Hungarian Arbitration Act[2] defines arbitration as a means of solving commercial disputes, while section 3(1)(7) provides that the term 'commercial' embraces all commercial and economic, contractual and non-contractual legal relationships. This implies that, according to the Act, by definition only commercial matters are arbitrable. Section 1(3) of the Act excludes from arbitrability consumer contracts, the special procedures listed in Part VII of Act CXXX of 2016 on civil procedure (which involve a set of matters that are traditionally considered to be non-arbitrable, such as personal status, guardianship, parental responsibility, marriage, parentage, dissolution of adoption, maintenance, personality rights, employment disputes, court enforcement), and matters coming under the scope of Act I of 2017 on administrative court procedure (administrative law matters). In other words, arbitrability is reserved solely for commercial disputes (a circle of matters narrower than private law matters in general) independently of who the parties (private or public) to such commercial relationships are.

[2] Act LX of 2017 on Arbitration (in Hungarian, *2017 évi LX törvény a választottbíráskodásról*).

In line with this binary approach, specifically public-private arbitration has not been a major issue in Hungarian constitutional law. The conformity of the parties' right to opt out of the jurisdiction of state courts with the Hungarian Constitution has been generally accepted.[3] Public law disputes are, in principle, not arbitrable; hence, this subject generated no clash with the Constitution. The only exception to the arbitrability of public law issues is investment treaty arbitration, whose special status is based on international treaties. The conformity of investment treaty arbitration with the Hungarian Constitution has not been questioned.

Although public law disputes, with the exception of investment treaty arbitration, are not arbitrable at all, it has to be noted that public entities normally act under public law only when they exercise public authority, while civil law contracts involving public actors (such as the provision of a public service), notwithstanding any incidental public law issue, come under private law and hence are normally arbitrable. Accordingly, Hungarian law draws no distinction between arbitration in purely civil matters and arbitration in public-private matters. This binary treatment (lack of paying any special consideration to the public interest in public-private arbitration) extends to all aspects of arbitration. Public-private arbitration is governed by the same rules as private arbitration as regards arbitrability, conduct of the proceedings, the arbitrators' qualifications and their appointment, presentation of evidence, status of third parties (eg non-governmental organizations), confidentiality of the proceedings, publication of the arbitral award, and recognition and enforcement of awards.

B. The Concept of Administrative Contracts

The above line between public law and private law matters has been somewhat blurred, however, by the 2017 introduction, in the new Code on Administrative Court Procedure, of the concept of administrative law contract.[4] Until then, public law contracts had been completely unknown to Hungarian law. The inconsistency emerges from the fact that administrative law contracts, which are not arbitrable, embrace certain genuine civil law contracts concluded by public actors. Nonetheless, as will be demonstrated, this law merely changed the borderline between private and public law matters by extending the concept of administrative law contract to certain civil law contracts where the state is a Contracting Party, and did not introduce any special regime for public-private arbitration. While extending the scope of matters which qualify as public law, and are hence inarbitrable, the Code on Administrative Court Procedure did not change in any sense the conceptual approach to determining arbitrability. At the same time, as a matter of practice, it has the tendency to reduce arbitrability in private-public relations by reclassifying matters that previously qualified as private law in nature (eg provision of parking services on public roads).

[3] Hungarian Constitutional Court, Case IV/01263/2016, Decision Nr 3265/2017 (10 October 2017).

[4] Act I of 2017 on administrative court procedure (in Hungarian, *2017. évi I. törvény a közigazgatási perrendtartásról*). See Várhomoki-Molnár Márta, 'A közigazgatás által kötött szerződés, közigazgatási szerződés' (2018) 24(1) Jogi tanulmányok 532.

The Code distinguishes between two cases of administrative law contracts. First, the term 'administrative law contract' embraces agreements concluded between administrative authorities for the purpose of fulfilling their public functions. Second, the Code also provides that a statute or decree of the government may pronounce any other contract as an administrative law contract.[5] The first element of this definition, in principle, does not embrace public-private contracts, as its personal scope is confined to administrative authorities. Accordingly, if one of the parties is an enterprise, the requirements of the definition are not met. Theoretically, it could be conceived that administrative authorities cooperate with the purpose of fulfilling their functions in a matter that is of a private law nature; however, the practical relevance of this scenario is limited.

A more important issue is which matters are designated by other pieces of legislation as 'administrative law contracts'. This gives the possibility to the legislator (and, in fact, signals its intention) to pronounce various public-private agreements that are otherwise of a civil law nature as public law contracts. The authorization of the government to classify any contract as an administrative law contract is a back door that indicates the Hungarian legislator's desire to expand, on a case-by-case basis, the concept of administrative law contract to certain public-private agreements. Although this process is still ongoing, the Hungarian legislator has already pronounced a few agreements which do not necessarily have a public law nature to be administrative contracts. This has reduced the circle of arbitrable matters in public-private relations. If an agreement is classified as an administrative law contract, it no longer comes under the jurisdiction of civil courts and is not arbitrable.

Since the adoption of the Code on Administrative Court Procedure, the Hungarian parliament has designated merely the following agreements as administrative law contracts. Under Act CLXXXV of 2010 on the Media Services and Mass Communication, the Media Council may empower a self-regulatory body to carry out self-management tasks, which do not qualify as an administrative activity and precede the Media Council's administrative procedure. Act C of 2003 on Electronic Communications provides that the authority may provide, in an administrative law contract, access to electronic data for systems providing technical assistance so that they can make this data inaccessible. Settlement planning contracts, regulated by Act LXXVIII of 1997 on the Construction and Protection of the Built Environment, also qualify as 'administrative law contracts'. Under these agreements, an investor carries out or provides financing for certain construction works which would otherwise come under the local self-governing body's remit (for instance, an enterprise renovates a public road leading to its factory), and the local self-governing body (town, municipality) undertakes to carry out the necessary settlement planning procedure (which may be needed to receive administrative approval for the construction works). Under Act I of 1988 on Public Traffic, the manager of public assets may conclude a contract with a public enterprise for the provision of public parking services; it has to be stressed, however, that even though this contract may have a private-public nature, parking services concerning public roads may be provided only by public

[5] s 4(7)2 of Act I of 2017 on administrative court procedure.

enterprises.[6] As these agreements are pronounced to be administrative law contracts, they are not arbitrable.

If a special piece of legislation designates an agreement as an administrative law contract, matters connected to that agreement will qualify as an administrative matter coming under the scope of the Code on Administrative Court Procedure,[7] and matters coming under the scope of this Code are expressly pronounced non-arbitrable by section 1(3) of the Hungarian Arbitration Act.

C. Investment Treaty Arbitration

The only exception to the binary scheme made up of arbitrable private law matters and non-arbitrable public law matters is international investment arbitration, where legal disputes having public law aspects are subjected to arbitration. Even though the reason for this special status is not conceptual, but attributable to the fact that investor-state arbitration is based on international treaty law, which prevails over domestic law, investment arbitration became a battlefield where genuine public law disputes are submitted to arbitration and arbitral tribunals take the power to adjudicate cases that are, at least under Hungarian law, not arbitrable and should not be subject to arbitral proceedings. However, Hungary's experiences with investment arbitration showcasing genuine public-private arbitration cases has been disappointing, and has generated a good deal of public distrust.

III. Hungarian Investment Protection Cases: Experiences and Motivations

Hungary has been a regular target of investment arbitration cases. These have shaped the country's perception about investment arbitration and had an impact on its attitude towards public-private arbitration more generally. Given that, in Hungary, investment arbitration is the only field where genuine public law disputes are submitted to arbitration, these experiences may have contributed to the country's distrust of the ability of arbitrators to handle public law disputes properly. This section presents Hungary's direct experiences in investment arbitration concerning the treatment of regulatory autonomy. The matters discussed below showcase that even though tribunals have been rather deferential in the substantive analysis, they have shown little self-restraint when defining their own jurisdiction. Accordingly, they, reasonably or unreasonably, may have shaped the attitude of the Hungarian government towards arbitration in public-private matters more generally and fuelled the idea that arbitration cannot secure the protection of the public interest.

In *Telenor Mobile Communications*,[8] the claimant demanded damages (for expropriation and for failure to accord fair and equitable treatment and to protect

[6] s 9/D(8) of Act I of 1988 on public traffic.

[7] ss 4(2)–(3) of Act I of 2017 on administrative court procedure.

[8] *Telenor Mobile Communications SA v Hungary*, ICSID Case No ARB/04/15, Award (13 September 2006).

its investment)[9] because of a number of ordinary regulatory measures. One such measure consisted of Hungary's introduction of 'universal service';[10] that is, the duty of telecommunication operators to provide a baseline level of services to every resident in the country irrespective of geographic location and economic considerations. This duty was funded via mandatory contributions from mobile and fixed telecommunications service providers to the Universal Telecommunications Support Fund (UTSF). In the same vein, in order to tackle the problem of market power, Hungary regulated the prices of mobile service providers with significant market power.[11] Furthermore, the Hungarian Competition Office (HCO) fined the claimant's subsidiary for abuse of a dominant position. The HCO's decision was attacked before domestic courts and judicial review was pending at the time arbitral proceedings under the Hungary–Norway BIT (bilateral investment treaty) were started. The arbitral tribunal was quick to discard the expropriation claim, declaring the measures to be a legitimate 'exercise by government of regulatory powers'[12] and concluding that the claimant had 'failed to make out a *prima facie* case of expropriation'.[13] The tribunal had no chance to speak out on the claims based on the BIT's fair and equitable treatment clause due to lack of jurisdiction; the applicable BIT[14] limited the tribunal's jurisdiction to expropriation claims.[15]

In *Accession Mezzanine & Danubius*,[16] the legal dispute emerged from Hungary's rejection of renewal of a nationwide radio broadcasting frequency for Danubius Radio, one of the country's most popular radio channels, which had to close down after twelve years of operation. When the radio's frequency licence expired, Hungary published a call for tenders. Danubius' application was unsuccessful and the frequency licence was awarded to another entity.[17] Even though Hungary's conduct was not impeccable, it was clear that the frequency had originally been given to Danubius for a fixed term without any expectation as to a renewal or prolongation. Nonetheless, the claimants argued that Hungary unlawfully expropriated and impaired their investments in Danubius Radio because Hungary, instead of offering a renewal, decided to carry out a tender procedure that ultimately replaced Danubius with another licensee.[18] As the expropriation claim appeared to be particularly weak, the claimants' arguments principally rested on the BIT's fair and equitable treatment clause and the

[9] ibid para 17.

[10] As to the regulatory concept of universal service, see Csongor István Nagy, 'The Metamorphoses of Universal Service in the European Telecommunications and Energy Sector: A Trans-Sectoral Perspective' (2013) 14(9) German LJ 1731.

[11] *Telenor Mobile Communications* (n 8) paras 23–24.

[12] ibid paras 64–67, 78.

[13] ibid paras 79–80.

[14] Agreement between the Government of the Kingdom of Norway and the Government of the Republic of Hungary on the Promotion and Reciprocal Protection of Investments (signed 8 April 1991, entered into force 4 December 1992).

[15] Although the claimant tried to widen the tribunal's jurisdiction with reference to the BIT's most-favoured-nation (MFN) clause, the tribunal rejected this construction: see *Telenor Mobile Communications* (n 8) paras 91–95, 97, and 101.

[16] *Accession Mezzanine Capital LP & Danubius Kereskedőház Vagyonkezelő Zrt v Hungary*, ICSID Case No ARB/12/3, Award (17 April 2015).

[17] ibid, Decision on Respondent's Objection under Arbitration Rule 41(5) (8 August 2013) para 31.

[18] ibid para 30.

prohibition of unreasonable and discriminatory measures.[19] However, here again, the tribunal had no chance to speak out on these matters, because the BIT confined jurisdiction to expropriation.[20]

In *AES Summit*,[21] the claimants argued that Hungary's reintroduction of regulated prices for electricity amounted to expropriation of their investment and went counter to the requirement of fair and equitable treatment and the prohibition of discrimination. The tribunal was quick to reject the expropriation claim, pointing out that regulated prices had not destroyed the investment's value, even if they may have diminished its profitability.[22] As for fair and equitable treatment, the tribunal established that Hungary 'made no representations/gave no assurances' that could create a legitimate expectation on the side of the claimants that price regulation would not be reintroduced.[23] Given that Hungary had made no specific promise, the claimant could not legitimately expect Hungary to abstain from introducing regulated prices.[24] The tribunal found that Hungary's 'process of introducing the Price Decrees, while sub-optimal, did not fall outside the acceptable range of legislative and regulatory behavior'.[25] The tribunal also dismissed the claim that Hungary had impaired the investment by unreasonable and discriminatory measures, using a fairly deferential standard.[26]

Various investment disputes emerged from the European Commission's decision ordaining that Hungary terminate its long-term power purchase agreements with electricity producers. When privatizing its outdated power plants in the mid-1990s, Hungary guaranteed the purchase of electricity through the Hungarian Electricity Company (MVM), to stimulate investments in the sector. The long-term power purchase agreements turned illegal once Hungary acceded to the EU, as they provided for higher prices than justified under market conditions and hence constituted state

[19] ibid paras 36–37.

[20] To also bring non-expropriation claims into the ambit of the legal dispute, the claimants argued that, as the ICSID Convention, in Article 42, mandates the tribunal to also apply international law, the tribunal has the power to adjudicate all claims emerging from international law as such. However, the tribunal held that, although the interpretation and application of the BIT are, indeed, governed by international law and the concept of expropriation cannot be interpreted 'without considering customary and general principles of international law, as well as any other sources of international law in this area' (ibid para 67), there is no basis 'to expand the tribunal's jurisdiction beyond expropriation and attendant rules of international law'; hence, any international law rules applied by the tribunal would be confined to expropriation (ibid para 70). The tribunal held that customary international law was not 'a distinct and separate basis of potential liability in this case' (since the tribunal's jurisdiction did not extend to such legal bases); customary international law simply intertwined with expropriation law (ibid para 72). Similarly, the tribunal also established that the MFN clause did not create a new legal basis coming under the tribunal's jurisdiction: 'MFN clauses are not and should not be interpreted or applied to create new causes of action beyond those to which consent to arbitrate has been given by the Parties.' (ibid para 73). The MFN clauses can be relied upon only to the extent they are connected to expropriation (ibid para 74).

[21] *AES Summit Generation Limited and AES-Tisza Erömü Kft v Hungary*, ICSID Case No ARB/07/22, Decision of the ad hoc Committee on the Application for Annulment (29 June 2012).

[22] ibid paras 14.3.1–14.3.4.

[23] ibid paras 9.3.8, 9.3.12, 9.3.15, and 9.3.18.

[24] ibid para 9.3.26. Likewise, the tribunal rejected the claims concerning the stable legal and business framework: paras 9.3.27, 9.3.31–9.3.32, and 9.3.35.

[25] ibid para 9.3.73.

[26] ibid paras 10.3.7, 10.3.20, 10.3.23–10.3.24, 10.3.31, 10.3.34, 10.3.36, 10.3.37, 10.3.44, 10.3.45, and 10.3.47.

aid that was contrary to EU law. As ordered by the European Commission,[27] Hungary terminated these agreements through a legislative act. It argued that it should not be held liable, because it terminated the agreements by order of the Commission. Interestingly, arbitral tribunals came to squarely opposing conclusions on this matter. In *Electrabel*,[28] the tribunal accepted that Hungary was not liable because it acted at the Commission's command ('defence of superior orders') and ruled in favour of Hungary.[29] By contrast, in *EDF International*[30] the tribunal rejected the defence of superior orders and awarded the claimant (in ad hoc arbitration proceedings conducted under the UNCITRAL rules) 107 million euros because of the termination of its long-term power purchase agreement.[31] Unfortunately, the latter award is not public, and hence the awards in *Electrabel* and *EDF International* cannot be compared to reveal the details of their inconsistency.

In *Vigotop Limited*,[32] the claimant was awarded a concession to build a casino which it wanted to construct on a plot of land (the Sukoró site) acquired through a transaction that allegedly involved corruption. While the allegations of corruption could not be proven in a criminal investigation, a Hungarian civil court pronounced the acquisition of the Sukoró site to be invalid and ordered the restoration of the initial status. Although the concession agreement listed 133 locations[33] where the claimant could have built the casino, the claimant insisted on the Sukoró site and did not attempt to purchase another site for building the casino. This resulted in Hungary terminating the concession contract. The claim against Hungary was based on the termination of the concession contract. Although the tribunal found that the interpretation of the concession contract was a contractual (commercial) dispute, it held that the termination of a private contract could qualify as an expropriation if it was based on public policy motivations.[34] In the case at hand, it found this to be the case, as the termination was, at least in part, based on the introduction of new public policies relating to the environment and tourism. At the end of the day, the tribunal concluded that Hungary had a solid contractual ground to terminate the concession agreement and had exercised its right to cancel the contract in good faith, as the claimant, instead of securing a suitable plot at one of the other 132 locations listed in the concession, kept on insisting on the Sukoró site.[35]

[27] *State Aid Awarded by Hungary Through Power Purchase Agreements* Commission Decision 2009/609/EC [2009] OJ L225/53.

[28] *Electrabel SA v Hungary*, ICSID Case No ARB/07/19, Award (25 November 2015).

[29] ibid paras 4.169, 4.170, 4.191, 4.196, 6.72, and 6.76.

[30] The award was rendered on 4 December 2014. The tribunal consisted of Karl-Heinz Böckstiegel (chair), Pierre-Marie Dupuy, and Albert Jan van den Berg.

[31] Douglas Thomson, 'EDF Wins Claim Against Hungary' (*Global Arbitration Review*, 11 December 2014) <https://globalarbitrationreview.com/edf-wins-claim-against-hungary> accessed 22 May 2023.

[32] *Vigotop Limited v Hungary*, ICSID Case No ARB/11/22, Award (1 October 2014).

[33] ibid para 145.

[34] The tribunal first analysed whether Hungary had public policy reasons to terminate the contract or whether the decision to terminate was based on purely contractual considerations (ibid paras 328–31).

[35] ibid para 634 ('[T]he Government included in the Contract a list of potential sites (still including Sukoró as one of them) at which the Project could be located. claimant thus had ample options but failed to secure any site other than Sukoró, thereby assuming the risk that it would not have a valid title.').

In *Dan Cake*,[36] Hungary was condemned for a judicial error committed by a Hungarian bankruptcy court. Although the Portuguese parent company of the insolvent Hungarian subsidiary reached an agreement with several creditors, the domestic court, in 'flagrant violation' of the law,[37] refused to convene a 'composition hearing' and thus prevented the execution of a formal compromise with the company's creditors.[38] As a result, the claimant's factory was sold by the court-appointed liquidator. Although the tribunal admitted that '[i]t is impossible . . . to determine whether a composition agreement would have been reached if a composition hearing had been convened',[39] it established that Hungary had violated the BIT's fair and equitable treatment clause in the form of a denial of justice by the court not convening a composition hearing.[40]

All in all, even though most of the above cases resulted in a favourable outcome for Hungary, they impaired the reputation of investment arbitration and public-private arbitration more generally. Although Hungary did prevail in the majority of the cases, the arbitral tribunals were seen as intensely assertive of their jurisdiction: when scrutinizing pure contractual disputes (eg the contractual dispute in *Vigotop Limited*) and genuine regulatory measures, such as the regulation of prices and provision of universal service, arbitral tribunals appeared to have given little evidence of self-restraint.[41] Furthermore, the consistency of arbitral decision-making was called into question when different tribunals came to contradictory decisions in the same matter (long-term power purchase agreements). Arbitral tribunals' willingness to scrutinize apparently legitimate uses of regulatory powers gave rise to the perception that investment arbitration, and public-private arbitration in general, are not susceptible of appreciating and protecting the public interest and tend to view public law disputes through the matrix of quid pro quo. This perception had an effect irrespective of whether it was well-grounded or not.

IV. The 2011/12 Regime Ruling out Arbitration in Relation to National Assets: Is Arbitration Irreconcilable with the National Interest?

Led by the thinking that (private) arbitration does not secure the protection of the public interest, in 2011 and 2012 the Hungarian parliament passed legislation to exclude the possibility to use arbitration for the settlement of disputes concerning (Hungarian) national property, which embraced virtually all government-owned

[36] *Dan Cake (Portugal) SA v Hungary*, ICSID Case No ARB/12/9, Decision on Jurisdiction and Liability (24 August 2015).

[37] ibid para 142 ('It also results from the above analysis of the decision that it was rendered in flagrant violation of the Bankruptcy Act and that it purported to condition the mandatory convening of the hearing upon several requirements, all of which were unnecessary; two of which were in direct violation of Dan Cake's creditor rights; and at least one of which was impossible to satisfy within a reasonable time.').

[38] ibid para 54.

[39] ibid para 142.

[40] ibid para 146.

[41] See András Dániel László, 'Választottbíráskodás nemzeti vagyonnal kapcsolatos ügyekben' (2015) 62(3) Magyar Jog 152; László Kecskés and Péter Tilk, 'A választottbírósági kikötés hazai jog szerinti tilalmának Alaptörvénybe, illetve nemzetközi jogba ütközése' (2012) 12(2) Európai Jog 15.

assets, such as real estate, shares in companies held by the state, intellectual property rights, bonds, and debentures.[42] This, in essence, eliminated the possibility of inserting arbitration clauses in civil law contracts concerning state property. The legislation was the result of Hungary's critical attitude as to arbitration's suitability for handling public law disputes. The consideration behind the law was the perception that arbitrators have a predominantly commercial outlook and are not (or not sufficiently) susceptible to public interest aspects that are eventually involved.

In 2013, the Hungarian Constitutional Court (CC), upon the complaint of the Commissioner for Fundamental Rights (Ombudsman), scrutinized the legislation in question as to whether it complied with Hungary's international obligations, in particular the 1961 Geneva Convention,[43] the 1958 New York Convention,[44] the 1965 Washington Convention,[45] and the BITs signed by Hungary.[46] Under Hungarian constitutional law, norms of domestic law which are contrary to international law may be considered unconstitutional as norms infringing a higher-ranking rule.[47] Ultimately, however, as addressed in section V below, it was not the constitutional and treaty law concerns that led to a revocation of the provisions in question but compelling business considerations.[48]

A. The Provisions Adopted in 2011 and 2012

The regime adopted in 2011 and 2012 rested on two pillars: (1) a prohibition in section 17 of the 2011 Act on National Property on persons (entities), both public and private, having the right to dispose of 'national' property to agree to arbitration (either foreign or Hungarian);[49] and (2) the insertion, in 2012, of a provision into section 4 of the Act on Arbitration declaring contracts concerning national property to be inarbitrable. These rules (jointly the 'provisions of 2011/12') made disputes concerning national property non-arbitrable.[50]

[42] s 1(2) of Act CXCVI of 2011 on National Property. See Fundamental Law of Hungary, art 38(1) ('The property of the State and of local governments shall be national assets. The management and protection of national assets shall aim at serving the *public interest*, meeting common needs and preserving natural resources, as well as at taking into account the needs of future generations.' – emphasis added).

[43] European Convention on International Commercial Arbitration of 1961 (adopted 21 April 1961, entered into force 7 January 1964) 484 UNTS 349 (promulgated in Hungary by Law-Decree 8 of 1964).

[44] Convention on the Recognition and Enforcement of Foreign Arbitral Awards (adopted 10 June 1958, entered into force 7 June 1959) 330 UNTS 3 (promulgated by Law-Decree 25 of 1962).

[45] Convention on the Settlement of Investment Disputes Between States and Nationals of Other States (adopted 18 March 1965, entered into force 14 October 1966) 575 UNTS 159 (promulgated by Law-Decree 27 of 1987).

[46] Constitutional Court of Hungary, Case II/03736/2012, Decision Nr 14/2013 (17 June 2013) <http://public.mkab.hu/dev/dontesek.nsf/0/84BF555A6FE75809C1257AF10020FFD0?OpenDocument> accessed 22 May 2024.

[47] Fundamental Law of Hungary, art Q.

[48] Csongor István Nagy, 'The Lesson of a Short-Lived Mutiny: The Rise and Fall of Hungary's Controversial Arbitration Regime in Cases Involving National Assets' (2016) 27(2) ARIA 239. For an overview of the legislative trajectory, see Ádám Boóc, 'Remarks to the Challenge of Commercial Arbitral Awards Regarding the Breach of Public Policy in Hungarian Law' in Rafal Szczepaniak (ed), *The Constitutionalization of Private Law versus the Europeanization of Private Law* (Brill 2025) 245, 253–55.

[49] Act CXCVI of 2011.

[50] Act LXXI of 1994.

First, persons (entities) having the right of disposition over national property were prohibited from agreeing to include arbitration clauses in any private law contract concerning national assets. Section 17(3) of the Act on National Property provided that, in civil law contracts concerning national property located on the territory of Hungary, the person having the right of disposition over the national property could stipulate only Hungarian language, Hungarian law, and the jurisdiction of Hungarian courts to resolve disputes. This prohibited the use of arbitration for the settlement of the respective legal disputes.

In terms of temporal application, as per section 17(1), the provisions of the Act on National Property did not concern the rights and obligations that were acquired lawfully and in good faith before the Act's entry into force. In other words, the prohibition embedded in section 17(3) had no retrospective effects and thus arbitration agreements concluded prior to the Act's entry into force were not affected.

Second, the 2012 amendment of the Arbitration Act declared legal disputes concerning national property to be inarbitrable.[51] The 2011 amendment, as explained above, instructed entities in charge of national property not to agree to arbitration but did not probibit arbitration agreements explicitly. The 2012 amendment, by contrast, effected such a general legal prohibition, which was applicable to procedures launched after the 2012 amendment's entry into force.[52]

B. Proceedings before the Hungarian Constitutional Court

The Commissioner for Fundamental Rights requested the CC to establish the unconstitutionality of the provisions adopted in 2011 and 2012, alleging that these provisions were contrary to Hungary's international treaty obligations.[53] As noted above, the CC has the competence to examine the compatibility of Hungarian legal rules with international treaties[54] and quash those rules in case of incompatibility.[55] In the Commissioner's view, three international treaties that Hungary was party to had been violated: the 1961 Geneva Convention, the 1958 New York Convention, and the 1965 Washington Convention.

First, the Commissioner advanced that Article II(1) of the 1961 Geneva Convention expressly establishes that public entities shall have the right to enter into arbitration agreements and is irreconcilable with prohibiting entities that manage national assets from agreeing to arbitration. Although Article II(2) of the Convention permits signatory states to make a reservation to limit this right to arbitration, Hungary made no such reservation. It is to be noted that, although Article II(2) does provide for

[51] This was inserted by s 2 of Act LXV of 2012 and entered into force on 13 June 2012.

[52] s 4 of Act LXV of Act 2012.

[53] See Constitutional Court of Hungary, Case II/03736/2012, Decision Nr 14/2013 (17 June 2013) paras 1–12 <http://public.mkab.hu/dev/dontesek.nsf/0/84BF555A6FE75809C1257AF10020FFD0?OpenDocument> accessed 22 May 2024.

[54] art 24(2)(f) of the Fundamental Law of Hungary. With the exception of the 'generally recognized rules of international law', international treaties have to be promulgated and become part of the Hungarian legal order: see art Q of the Fundamental Law of Hungary.

[55] s 42 of Act CLI of 2011 on the Constitutional Court.

the possibility to make a reservation, the exercise of this right is limited in terms of time: signatory states can submit such a reservation only when 'signing, ratifying or acceding' to the Convention.

Second, according to the Commissioner, the violation of Article II(1) of the 1961 Geneva Convention also gave rise to a violation of Article II(I) of the 1958 New York Convention, which provides that Contracting States have to recognize written arbitration agreements covering arbitrable matters. Since arbitration agreements entered into by public entities are arbitrable under Article II(1) of the 1961 Geneva Convention, Article II(I) of the 1958 New York Convention obliges Contracting States to recognize these agreements. Section 4 of the old Arbitration Act violates these rules, as it declares that arbitration agreements concluded by public entities are inarbitrable to the extent they concern national assets.

Finally, according to Article 25 of the 1965 Washington Convention, although the jurisdiction of the International Centre for Settlement of Investment Disputes (ICSID) is not mandatory, once the parties agree to the jurisdiction of ICSID, 'no party may withdraw its consent unilaterally'. To the extent that the provisions of 2011/12 concern investment matters, they may be regarded as a unilateral revocation of this consent.

The CC rejected the complaint of the Commissioner for Fundamental Rights. It found that the exclusion of arbitrability by the legislation in question did not violate treaty law, as the tension between the provisions of 2011/12 and international treaty law could be lifted by Hungary, by way of example, through making a reservation or denouncing the relevant convention.

The CC found that the new provisions did not infringe the 1965 Washington Convention either, since Hungary had various methods to bring Hungarian law in line with the Convention.[56] For instance, according to Article 25(3) of the 1965 Washington Convention, the consent of state entities to the jurisdiction of ICSID could be made dependent on the state's approval. Furthermore, under Article 25(4) of the ICSID Convention, Contracting States could exclude certain classes of disputes from the jurisdiction of ICSID at any time.

The conformity of the provisions of 2011/12 with the 1961 Geneva Convention was more difficult to demonstrate. The CC held that, in case Article II(1) of the 1961 Geneva Convention had to be read as authorizing public entities to enter into arbitration agreements independently of domestic law, it also had to be noted that the Convention ensured the possibility for Hungary to opt out of this rule by making a reservation.[57] The suggestion of the Court is rather odd as the possibility to make a valid reservation to limit the right to arbitration is already time-barred. Thus, what the CC essentially suggested is that Hungary could denounce the Convention on the basis of Article X(9) and then re-enter it, this time with a valid reservation under Article II(2).[58] Such a denunciation would take effect twelve months after the date the Secretary-General of the United Nations received the notification of denunciation.

[56] Constitutional Court of Hungary, Case II/03736/2012, Decision Nr 14/2013 (17 June 2013) paras 55–57.
[57] ibid paras 64–65.
[58] ibid para 75.

The CC's decision was highly criticized as being based on an unreasonable construction of the pertinent treaty provisions.[59] Nonetheless, it demonstrated that the Court was highly reluctant to interfere with the Hungarian legislator's efforts to confine the availability of arbitration in matters involving public actors.

V. The Change of Hungary's Policy Concerning Arbitration: Is Arbitration Still Not in the National Interest?

In the last decade, Hungary has got on the map of international arbitration with two measures: first, the anti-arbitration regime of 2011/12 concerning national assets and its revocation; and, second, a pro-arbitration stance in the current post-*Achmea*[60] debate on intra-EU arbitration. In both cases, the country took a unique position and tried to swim against the tide. These cases also showed that the national interest may sometimes justify an anti-arbitration and sometimes a pro-arbitration policy. While, in 2011/12, Hungary ruled out arbitration in matters involving national assets (see section IV above), in 2015 it stepped back from this position for economic reasons, namely in order to execute an investment deal with Russia that Hungary considered to be in its national interest, but which would have been contrary to the provisions of 2011/12 because Russia insisted on the inclusion of an arbitration clause in the deal. In the same vein, the economic interests of the Hungarian oil company MOL fuelled Hungary's unique stance as to the validity of ECT arbitration: Hungary was the only EU Member State to proclaim that intra-EU ECT arbitration complied with EU law after the ruling of the Court of Justice of the European Union (CJEU) in *Achmea*.[61]

A. The 2015 Revocation of the Ban on Arbitration in Matters Involving National Assets

The regime presented in section IV above did not stand the proof of business reality: in fact, it failed very early, suggesting that arbitration is a 'take it or leave it' matter, even in international economic relations.[62] The legislative provisions in question had to be revoked for business and not for legal reasons. Hungary concluded an inter-state agreement with Russia on the expansion of the nuclear energy plant in Paks (Hungary's only nuclear plant); Russia was not only a contractor to construct a new facility, but also a creditor financing the project. The agreement between

[59] See Gergely Hajdú, 'A nemzeti vagyonról szóló törvény választottbíráskodást érintő rendelkezéseinek alkotmánybírósági tesztje' (2014) 22(10) Gazdaság és Jog 19; Gergely Hajdú, 'A választottbíráskodás kikötési lehetőségének hazai jog szerinti kizárása és annak Alaptörvénnyel való összhangja az Alkotmánybíróság szerint' (2014) 15(3) Jogelméleti Szemle 232–62.

[60] Case C-284/16, *Slovak Republic v Achmea BV*, Judgment (6 March 2018) ECLI:EU:C:2018:158.

[61] Declaration of the Representative of the Government of Hungary, of 16 January on the Legal Consequences of the Judgment of the Court of Justice in *Achmea* and on Investment Protection in the European Union (Brussels, 16 January 2019) <https://finance.ec.europa.eu/document/download/dbdd886c-93bc-4338-bbc6-223573124601_en?filename=190116-bilateral-investment-treaties-hungary_en.pdf> accessed 22 May 2024.

[62] Nagy (n 48).

Hungary and Russia provided for arbitration; however, since it concerned national assets (the power plant was a national asset), it contravened the rules of 2011/12. After the incompatibility of these measures was raised in the parliamentary debate on the promulgation of the inter-state agreement,[63] the provisions of 2011/12 were amended in 2015.

First, the 2015 amendment put an end to the inarbitrability of matters involving national assets under section 4 of the Arbitration Act. Second, the prohibition of arbitration for entities disposing of national assets was considerably softened: it gave international treaty law unquestionable precedence and the right of public actors to agree to arbitration was expressly recognized. The new section 17(3) of the Act on National Property henceforth provided:

> If an international treaty does not provide otherwise, in civil law contracts concerning national property being on the territory delimited by the borders of Hungary, the person having the right of disposition over the national property can stipulate exclusively the application of Hungarian language, Hungarian law, and the jurisdiction of the Hungarian court for any legal dispute. The exclusivity of the jurisdiction of the Hungarian court does not concern the right to stipulate arbitration.

The 2015 revocation of the inarbitrability of the matters involving national property put an end to Hungary's four-year-long mutiny against a dominant precept of international economic relations. At least in this case, public-private arbitration was a prerequisite of the international economic transaction and its disavowal could cause serious difficulties for states that wanted to remain part of the vascular system of international trade.

B. Exclusion of ECT Arbitration from the Ambit of *Achmea*

In 2018, in *Achmea*, the CJEU pronounced an arbitration clause in an intra-EU BIT to fall foul of EU law and thus to be inapplicable:

> Articles 267 and 344 TFEU must be interpreted as precluding a provision in an international agreement concluded between Member States, such as Article 8 of the Agreement on encouragement and reciprocal protection of investments between the Kingdom of the Netherlands and the Czech and Slovak Federative Republic, under which an investor from one of those Member States may, in the event of a dispute concerning investments in the other Member State, bring proceedings against the latter Member State before an arbitral tribunal whose jurisdiction that Member State has undertaken to accept.[64]

[63] Act VII of 2015 on the Investment Related to the Maintenance of the Capacity of the Nuclear Plant of Paks, as well as on the Amendment of Certain Connected Acts (in Hungarian, *2015 évi VII törvény a Paksi Atomerőmű kapacitásának fenntartásával kapcsolatos beruházásról, valamint az ezzel kapcsolatos egyes törvények módosításáról*).

[64] *Achmea* (n 60) para 60.

Although it is generally considered that the ruling signals the end of intra-EU investment arbitration, its scope has raised various questions of interpretation: the CJEU addressed solely the BIT's arbitration clause but not the substantive provisions; the arbitration clause was all-embracing and provided for ad hoc arbitration; and, last but not least, it dealt with a BIT whose parties were two Member States and which had no party from outside the EU.[65] The legal community has remained especially divided as to the implications of the *Achmea* ruling for intra-EU arbitrations under the ECT.[66]

The European Commission, guided by its hostile approach as to intra-EU investment arbitration, took utmost advantage of the *Achmea* ruling and required that the Member States sign a political declaration confirming that intra-EU BITs would be terminated by 6 December 2019 with all sunset and grandfathering clauses being considered inapplicable after this date.[67] While most Member States joined a declaration that *Achmea* prevented all intra-EU treaty-based investment arbitrations, six Member States rejected that conclusion. The major point of dissent among Member States was the application of *Achmea* to intra-EU arbitrations under the ECT. The declaration of the majority of Member States pronounces ECT arbitration to be covered by the *Achmea* ruling and hence to be inapplicable. Five Member States (Finland, Luxembourg, Malta, Slovenia, and Sweden) made a separate joint declaration[68] which considered the issue open, stressing that the *Achmea* ruling was 'silent on the investor-state arbitration clause in the Energy Charter Treaty' and proposing to leave it to the CJEU to decide, in a future case, whether *Achmea* applied to the ECT or not.[69] From the twenty-eight EU Member States, there was a single country, however, that was diametrically opposed to the majority's position: the declaration of Hungary[70]

[65] Csongor István Nagy, 'Intra-EU Bilateral Investment Treaties and EU Law After *Achmea*: Know Well What Leads You Forward and What Holds You Back' (2018) 19(4) German LJ 981.

[66] See *Masdar Solar & Wind Cooperatief UA v Spain*, ICSID Case No ARB/14/1, Award (16 May 2018) paras 678–83 (distinguishing *Achmea* from cases based on the Energy Charter Treaty (ECT)).

[67] Declaration of the Representatives of the Governments of the Member States, of 15 January 2019 on the Legal Consequences of the Judgment of the Court of Justice in *Achmea* and on Investment Protection in the European Union (Brussels, 15 January 2019) <https://ec.europa.eu/info/publications/190117-bilateral-investment-treaties_en> accessed 22 May 2024. For further discussion on the three political declarations concerning *Achmea* and their background, see Csongor Istvan Nagy, 'Intra-EU BITs after *Achmea*: A Cross-Cutting Issue' in Csongor István Nagy (ed), *Investment Arbitration in Central and Eastern Europe: Law and Practice* (Edward Elgar Publishing 2019) 1, 7.

[68] Declaration of the Representatives of the Governments of the Member States, of 16 January 2019 on the Enforcement of the Judgment of the Court of Justice in Achmea and on Investment Protection in the European Union (Brussels, 16 January 2019) <https://www.regeringen.se/contentassets/d759689c0c804a9ea7af6b2de7320128/achmea-declaration.pdf> accessed 22 May 2024.

[69] ibid ('The Member States note that the *Achmea* judgment is silent on the investor-state arbitration clause in the Energy Charter Treaty. A number of international arbitration tribunals post the *Achmea* judgment have concluded that the Energy Charter Treaty contains an investor-State arbitration clause applicable between EU Member States. This interpretation is currently contested before a national court in a Member State. [This is a reference to the annulment proceedings before the Svea Court of Appeal in Case No 4658-18 *Novenergia II – Energy & Environment (SCA) (Grand Duchy of Luxembourg), SICAR v the Kingdom of Spain*, SCC Arbitration Case No 2015/06).] Against this background, the Member States underline the importance of allowing for due process and consider that it would be inappropriate, in the absence of a specific judgment on this matter, to express views as regards the compatibility with Union law of the intra EU application of the Energy Charter Treaty.').

[70] Declaration of the Representative of the Government of Hungary (n 61).

categorically expressed the stance that '[t]he *Achmea* judgment . . . does not concern any pending or prospective arbitration proceedings initiated under the ECT.'[71]

The economic reason for Hungary's firm position was a high-value case pending before ICSID between MOL Hungarian Oil and Gas Company, a regional giant and a 'national champion' of Hungary, and Croatia.[72] The case is based on the ECT and, according to Hungary, it is in the national interest that MOL has the possibility to make use of investor-state arbitration to obtain an effective legal remedy.[73]

Hungary's stance concerning the applicability of the *Achmea* ruling to the ECT reveals how volatile the relationship between public-private arbitration and the public interest is. While generally having been rather distrustful of arbitration in public-private matters, Hungary has also been willing to swim against the opposite tide when it considered investment arbitration to be in the national interest. It seems that, while its operation in individual cases may indeed provoke criticism, public-private arbitration addresses a pressing need for economic constitutionalism.

VI. Conclusions

The approach Hungarian law takes to public-private arbitration is to generally exclude arbitration in public law cases, with the exception of matters based on international investment treaties. Hungarian law conceives the connection between arbitration and the public interest as antagonistic and, apart from investment treaties, rules out arbitration in public law matters in order to ensure that the public interest is not undermined.

Accordingly, Hungary follows a binary approach to public-private arbitration: under Hungarian law, public disputes are not arbitrable, while private (commercial) law disputes involving public actors are arbitrable without enjoying any special treatment in comparison with pure civil law matters. Hungary has been struggling with appropriately accommodating the public law aspects of public-private arbitration cases by ruling out arbitration, first, in matters involving national assets and, after this attempt failed for economic reasons, by starting to expand the recently introduced

[71] ibid ('8. Hungary further declares that in its view, the *Achmea* judgment concerns only the intra-EU bilateral investment treaties. The *Achmea* judgment is silent on the investor-state arbitration clause in the Energy Charter Treaty (hereinafter: "ECT") and it does not concern any pending or prospective arbitration proceedings initiated under the ECT. 9. Against this background, Hungary underlines the importance of allowing for due process and considers that it is inappropriate for a Member State to express its view as regards the compatibility with Union law of the intra-EU application of the ECT. The ongoing and future applicability of the ECT in intra-EU relations requires further discussion and individual agreement amongst the Member States.').

[72] *MOL Hungarian Oil and Gas Company Plc v Croatia*, ICSID Case No ARB/13/32 (registered 5 December 2013).

[73] Not surprisingly, MOL has a strategic interest in shielding ECT arbitration from *Achmea*. See MOL's Motion for Leave to File Amicus Curiae Brief of 12 December 2018 in the US District Court for the District of Columbia in *Novenergia II – Energy & Environment (SCA) v Spain*, Civil Action No 1:18-cv-1148 (TSC) (7 December 2018) <www.italaw.com/sites/default/files/case-documents/italaw10334.pdf> accessed 22 May 2024. This procedure is for the enforcement of the award rendered in *Novenergia II – Energy & Environment (SCA) (Grand Duchy of Luxembourg), SICAR v Spain*, SCC Case No 2015/063, Final Award (15 February 2018).

concept of administrative law contract to certain public-private contracts to pull them out of the scope of arbitrability.

The only case where public law cases can be arbitrated is investor-state arbitration, which is, however, not provided by Hungarian domestic law but by international treaties. The country's experiences with investor-state arbitration, given that this is the only case where genuine public law disputes can be arbitrated, had a significant impact on the country's policy towards public-private arbitration. Even though, in investment matters, tribunals appeared to be highly deferential, one may argue that they showed little self-restraint as to the definition of their jurisdiction.

In the last decade, Hungary's stance on public-private arbitration has been put into the focus of the political and scholarly discourse in the field of international arbitration on two occasions. Ironically, in the first case, Hungary stood out because of its anti-arbitration attitude, while in the second case it did so because of its pro-arbitration approach. Nonetheless, in both cases, Hungary tried to swim against the tide, showcasing that the national interest may at times justify an anti-arbitration policy, while at other times it demands a pro-arbitration policy. Thus, in 2011/12, Hungary ruled out arbitration in matters involving national assets, while in 2015 it stepped back from this position in order to be able to conclude a business deal with Russia which Hungary considered to be in the national interest. In 2019, when all EU Member States adopted joint declarations about the effect of *Achmea*, Hungary was the only Member State pronouncing that ECT arbitration was not governed by the *Achmea* ruling and was compliant with EU law. Although Hungary's acts may seem to have been contradictory, they have in fact been consistent. The stance of Hungary has been the result of its respective positions driven by the national interest, and this national interest has shifted over time, depending on the specific matter at issue. The only consistency is that Hungary has been trying to swim against the tide.

Select Materials

Bibliography

Boóc, Ádám, 'Remarks to the Challenge of Commercial Arbitral Awards Regarding the Breach of Public Policy in Hungarian Law' in Rafał Szczepaniak (ed), *The Constitutionalization of Private Law versus the Europeanization of Private Law* (Brill 2025) 245–70

Hajdú, Gergely, 'A nemzeti vagyonról szóló törvény választottbíráskodást érintő rendelkezéseinek alkotmánybírósági tesztje' (2014) 22(10) Gazdaság és Jog 19–24

Hajdú, Gergely, 'A választottbíráskodás kikötési lehetőségének hazai jog szerinti kizárása és annak Alaptörvénnyel való összhangja az Alkotmánybíróság szerint' (2014) 15(3) Jogelméleti Szemle 232–62

Kecskés, László and Péter Tilk, 'A választottbírósági kikötés hazai jog szerinti tilalmának Alaptörvénybe, illetve nemzetközi jogba ütközése' (2012) 12(2) Európai Jog 15–25

László, András Dániel, 'Választottbíráskodás nemzeti vagyonnal kapcsolatos ügyekben' (2015) 62(3) Magyar Jog 152–60

Mádl, Ferenc and Lajos Vékás, *Nemzetközi magánjog és nemzetközi gazdasági kapcsolatok joga* (ELTE Eötvös Kiadó 2018)
Nagy, Csongor István, 'The Lesson of a Short-Lived Mutiny: The Rise and Fall of Hungary's Controversial Arbitration Regime in Cases Involving National Assets' (2016) 27(2) ARIA 239–46
Nagy, Csongor István, 'Hungarian Cases Before ICSID Tribunals: The Hungarian Experience with Investment Arbitration' (2017) 58(3) Hung J Leg Stud 291–310
Nagy, Csongor István, 'Intra-EU Bilateral Investment Treaties and EU Law after *Achmea*: "Know Well What Leads You Forward and What Holds You Back"' (2018) 19(4) German LJ 981–1016
Várhomoki-Molnár, Márta, 'A közigazgatás által kötött szerződés, közigazgatási szerződés' (2018) 24(1) Jogi tanulmányok 532–41
Víg, Zoltán, 'The Importance of Foreign Direct Investments and Instruments for Their Protection' (2018) 59(4) Acta Juridica Hungarica
Víg, Zoltán, *Taking in International Law* (Patrocinium Kiadó 2019)
Víg, Zoltán and Tamara Gajinov, 'Development of Compensation Theories in International Expropriation Law' (2016) 57(4) Hung J Leg Stud 447–61
Vörös, Imre, *A nemzetközi gazdasági kapcsolatok joga vol I-III* (Krim Bt 2015)

Legislation

Act CLI of 2011 on the Constitutional Court (in Hungarian, *2011. évi CLI. törvény az Alk otmánybíróságról*)
Act CXCVI of 2011 on National Property (in Hungarian, *2011. évi CXCVI. törvény a nemzeti vagyonról*)
Act I of 2017 on administrative court procedure (in Hungarian, *2017. évi I. törvény a közigazgatási perrendtartásról*)
Act LX of 2017 on Arbitration (in Hungarian, *2017 évi LX törvény a választottbíráskodásról*)
Act LX of 2017 on Arbitration (in Hungarian, *2017 évi LX törvény a választottbíráskodásról*)
Act LXXI of 1994 on arbitration (in Hungarian, *1994 évi LXXI törvény a választottbíráskodásról*)
Fundamental Law of Hungary (in Hungarian, *Magyarország Alaptörvénye*)

Arbitral awards

Accession Mezzanine Capital LP & Danubius Kereskedöház Vagyonkezelö Zrt v Hungary, ICSID Case No ARB/12/3, Award (17 April 2015)
AES Summit Generation Limited and AES-Tisza Erömü Kft v The Republic of Hungary, ICSID Case No ARB/07/22, Decision of the ad hoc Committee on the Application for Annulment (29 June 2012)
Dan Cake (Portugal) SA v Hungary, ICSID Case No ARB/12/9, Decision on Jurisdiction and Liability (24 August 2015)
Electrabel SA v Republic of Hungary, ICSID Case No ARB/07/19, Award (25 November 2015)

Masdar Solar & Wind Cooperatief UA v Kingdom of Spain, ICSID Case No ARB/14/1, Award (16 May 2018)

MOL Hungarian Oil and Gas Company Plc v Republic of Croatia, ICSID Case No ARB/13/32

Novenergia II – Energy & Environment (SCA) (Grand Duchy of Luxembourg), SICAR v The Kingdom of Spain, SCC Case No 2015/063, Final Award (15 February 2018)

Telenor Mobile Communications SA v Hungary, ICSID Case No ARB/04/15, Award (13 September 2006)

Vigotop Limited v Hungary, ICSID Case No ARB/11/22, Award (1 October 2014)

8

Protection of the Public Interest in Private-Public Arbitration in the Baltic States

Eglė Zemlytė, Tadas Varapnickas, Inga Kačevska, Aleksandrs Fillers, Karin Sein, and Pirkka-Marja Põldvere[*]

I. Introduction

The end of the twentieth century could be called the golden age of private-public arbitration. Amidst the increase in bilateral investment treaties (BITs) and with the adoption in 1965 of the Convention for the Settlement of Investment Disputes between States and Nationals of Other States (ICSID Convention),[1] arbitration became the preferred method for the resolution of investment disputes. In the area of commercial arbitration, states began to abolish national restrictions on their capacity to enter into arbitration agreements. Moreover, the concept that a state entity is prevented from invoking its own law to contest the arbitrability of a dispute or its capacity to be party to an arbitration has been developed in international commercial arbitration.[2] These developments have put

[*] The content of this chapter reflects the state of law as of 9 September 2022, and any changes or updates made after this date are not reflected. It should be noted, however, that on 23 February 2023, the Constitutional Court of Latvia delivered a judgment in Case No. 2022-03-01, holding that the absence of set-aside proceedings in Latvian law violated the parties' right to a fair trial. Following this judgment, the Latvian Parliament adopted amendments to the Law on Arbitration and the Law of Civil Procedure, introducing set-aside proceedings for arbitral awards. These amendments came into effect on 4 July 2024. The grounds for setting aside mirror those under Article 34(2) of the UNCITRAL Model Law on International Commercial Arbitration. That is, they include the public policy exception, allowing the courts to set aside arbitral awards if they violate public policy. Simultaneously, the Latvian Parliament introduced several other amendments to significantly reduce the gap between Latvian arbitration law and the UNCITRAL Model Law on International Commercial Arbitration. For example, these amendments have rendered ad hoc awards once again enforceable in Latvia. Similarly, new amendments abolished a system where all arbitrators had to be registered in a list of arbitrators at the Commercial Register. Despite these developments not being reflected in the chapter, the chapter remains valuable in illustrating the historical approach and context that preceded these significant legal changes in Latvia.

[1] Convention for the Settlement of Investment Disputes between States and Nationals of Other States (adopted 18 March 1965, entered into force 14 October 1966) 575 UNTS 159 (ICSID Convention).

[2] See art II(1) of the European Convention on International Commercial Arbitration (signed 21 April 1961, entered into force 7 January 1965) 484 UNTS 349 ('In cases referred to in Article I, paragraph 1, of the convention, legal persons considered by the law which is applicable to them as "legal persons of public law" have the right to conclude valid arbitration agreements.'); art 177(2) of the 1987 Swiss Private International Law Act ('A state, or an enterprise held by, or an organization controlled by a state, which is party to an arbitration agreement, cannot invoke its own law in order to contest its capacity to arbitrate or the arbitrability of a dispute covered by the arbitration agreement.'); art 5 of the 1989 International Law Institute Resolution Arbitration between States, State Enterprises, or State Entities, and Foreign Enterprises ((1989) 63(II) Yearbook of the Institute of International Law 324) ('A State, a state enterprise, or a state entity cannot

Eglė Zemlytė, Tadas Varapnickas, Inga Kačevska, Aleksandrs Fillers, Karin Sein, and Pirkka-Marja Põldvere, *Protection of the Public Interest in Private-Public Arbitration in the Baltic States* In: *The Comparative Constitutional Foundations of Private-Public Arbitration*. Edited by: Stephan W. Schill, Oxford University Press.
 DOI: 10.1093/9780191987960.003.0008

arbitral tribunals on an equal footing with state courts. The situation, however, is beginning to change, mainly due to the increased criticism that the public interest is not sufficiently protected and accounted for in cases of public-private arbitration.

The three Baltic States provide an interesting case study in this context. They were part of the Soviet legal system and therefore had very limited powers to adopt their own laws. Both private arbitration and private-public arbitration were treated the same way as for the whole of the Soviet Union and were an unpopular and barely developed dispute resolution method.[3] After the collapse of the Soviet Union, the Baltic States, having regained their independence, adopted market economies and started creating their own legal systems by adopting new laws drawing inspiration from internationally customary models, such as the UNCITRAL Model Law on International Commercial Arbitration (UNCITRAL Model Law), and joined various international conventions, including the ones related to arbitration (both private and private-public).

One might assume that the Baltic States, which are sometimes referred to as 'three Baltic sisters', took the same approach towards arbitration and private-public arbitration specifically. However, there are only few similarities among them: (1) the fact that they did indeed adopt laws to regulate arbitration and joined a number of

invoke incapacity to arbitrate in order to resist arbitration to which it has agreed.'). See also Emmanuel Gaillard and John Savage (eds), *Fouchard, Gaillard, Goldman on International Commercial Arbitration* (Kluwer 1999) 322–29; Fernando Mantilla-Serrano, 'Colombia Enacts a New International Arbitration Law' (2013) Journal Int'l Arb 431; Bernard Hanotiau, 'The Law Applicable to Arbitrability' in Albert Jan van den Berg (ed), *Improving Efficiency of Arbitration Agreements and Awards: 40 Years of Application of the New York Convention. ICCA Congress Series No 9* (Kluwer 1999) 149–53; Gary B Born, *International Commercial Arbitration* (2nd edn, Kluwer 2014) vol I, 727–33.

[3] Arbitration as a dispute settlement mechanism was, in principle, permitted under the law of the Soviet Union, both for domestic and international matters. For example, Article 4 of the Law of the Soviet Union of 8 December 1961 ('On the Approval of the Fundamentals of Civil Procedure of the USSR and Union Republics') provided that civil cases could be solved in arbitration (arbitration in the Soviet Union was called the 'tertiary court' (in Russian, *третейские суды*)). The regulation of the arbitral procedure was left to each of the Soviet Union Republics. For example, in Lithuania, Article 28 of the Code of Civil Procedure of 1964, which was adopted on the basis of the above-mentioned Law of the Soviet Union, set out that, in cases provided for by law or international agreement, disputes arising out of a civil legal relationship on the basis of an agreement between the parties might be referred to 'tertiary courts', the Maritime Arbitration Commission, or the Foreign Trade Arbitration Commission under the All-Union Chamber of Commerce. See Valentinas Mikelėnas, 'Lietuvos Respublikos Komercinio Arbitražo Įstatymo Dvidešimtmetis: Ištakos, Taikymo Patirtis Ir Perspektyvos' (2016) II Arbitražas. Teorija ir praktika. 3, 4–6. The same was also provided for in the Code of Civil Procedure of 1963 in Latvia. See Jānis Rozenbergs and Imants Briģis, *Padomju Civilprocesa tiesības* (Zvaigzne ABC 2010) 93. In Estonia, ad hoc arbitration was allowed in private disputes between 'citizens', except in employment and family relationships. See art 1 of the Statutes of Arbitration, adopted as app 3 of the Code of Civil Procedure of the Estonian Soviet Republic 1964. There were no legal norms addressing private-public arbitration. Domestic arbitration, although regulated in the Soviet Union, had little practical relevance. See Олег Юрьевич Скворцов, *Третейское разбирательство предпринимательских споров в России. Проблемы. Тенденции. Перспективы* (Kluwer 2005) 30. It was different for cases concerning matters of foreign trade, which were conducted as a state monopoly in the Soviet Union. In order to participate in international trade, the Soviet Union had to conform to dispute resolution practices that were customary for cross-border trade. Therefore, in agreements with foreign parties, it was not uncommon to agree to arbitration as a dispute settlement method. See Kazimierz Grzybowski, 'Arbitral Tribunals for Foreign Trade in Socialist Countries' (1972) 37(4) L & CP 592. Moreover, the Soviet Union was a signatory to the New York Convention, while Article 58 of the Law of the Soviet Union of 8 December 1961 ('On the Approval of the Fundamentals of Civil Procedure of the USSR and Union Republics') provided that arbitration awards were to be enforced under the same rules as domestic court decisions.

international treaties providing for arbitration as a dispute resolution method for private-public disputes; and (2) the public interest in private-public arbitration is protected only in two ways, either by excluding private-public arbitration for certain disputes (via arbitrability) or by using public policy to scrutinize arbitral awards for their compliance with fundamental public interests. As there is no widely accepted definition of 'public interest', and this term may have a variety of meanings, it is defined, for the purposes of this chapter, as the set of interests a country is bound to protect in order to ensure the welfare of society.

In section II of this chapter, key features of the approach towards arbitration in general in the Baltic States are analysed. Section III shows how three states that departed from a common starting point at the moment of regaining independence took quite different approaches towards arbitration in general, not least in respect of the arbitrability of private-public disputes. Section IV discusses the protection of the public interest by applying the public policy exception in contractual (commercial) arbitration. Section V compares the protection of the public interest in treaty-based investment arbitration to that in contractual (commercial) arbitration. Section VI concludes the chapter.

II. Key Features of the General Approach towards Arbitration in the Baltic States

After regaining their independence, all three Baltic States joined the Convention on the Recognition and Enforcement of Foreign Arbitral Awards (New York Convention)[4] as well as the ICSID Convention, and Latvia even joined the European Convention on International Commercial Arbitration (European Convention).[5] Still, arbitration was perceived and treated differently in each of the three countries.

Lithuania and Estonia shared the view that the law regulating arbitration should be based on the UNCITRAL Model Law.[6] In Lithuania, the Law on Commercial Arbitration[7] (LCALT), which is based on the UNCITRAL Model Law, was adopted in 1996. Arbitration was perceived as a valuable alternative to litigation, especially for business disputes. It was promoted by legal practitioners and supported by courts and the legislator.

Estonia also based its law on the UNCITRAL Model Law. However, the relevant part of the Estonian Code of Civil Procedure (CCPEST)[8] regulating arbitration took effect only on 1 January 2006. Before that, arbitration was largely unregulated in

[4] Convention on the Recognition and Enforcement of Foreign Arbitral Awards (adopted 10 June 1958, entered into force 7 June 1959) 330 UNTS 38 (New York Convention).

[5] See n 2 above. Law on European Convention on International Commercial Arbitration 2003, Latvijas Vēstnesis No 23 (12 February 2003).

[6] UNCITRAL, Model Law on International Commercial Arbitration (adopted 21 June 1985, amended 7 July 2006) UNGA Res 40/72 and 61/33, UN GAOR 40th Sess, Supp No 17, UN Doc A/40/17, Annex I and UN GAOR 61st Sess, Supp No 17, UN Doc A/61/17, Annex I.

[7] Law on Commercial Arbitration of the Republic of Lithuania 1996. New wording of the LCALT was adopted in 2012.

[8] Effective as of 1 January 2006. Arbitration is regulated by Articles 712–57 of CCPEST, which apply to arbitral proceedings conducted in Estonia except if otherwise provided by law or international agreement.

Estonia.[9] Despite gradual changes in favour of arbitration, in practice it remains a rather unpopular method of dispute resolution in Estonia.

The case of Latvia, compared not only with the remaining Baltic States but also with the rest of the world, is quite unique. Chapter D of the Civil Procedure Law in Latvia regulating arbitration came into force on 1 March 1999. Although the draft law was initially based on the UNCITRAL Model Law, provisions on court assistance in the formation of the arbitral tribunal and during the arbitration process, as well as on the setting aside of the arbitral award, were struck out before the Civil Procedure Law was enacted.[10] To this day, in Latvia, the law does not provide for a setting-aside mechanism at all. Moreover, the establishment of arbitral institutions was not subject to any legal restrictions until the new Law on Arbitration (LALV)[11] was adopted and took effect on 1 January 2015. Before that date, therefore, any legal person was able to establish a permanent arbitral institution.[12] By the end of 2014, there were 214 permanent arbitration institutions in Latvia,[13] a number that dropped to 71 institutions after the LALV introduced more rigorous requirements for arbitrators and for the establishment of permanent arbitration institutions.[14] As one author put it, 'because of the fact that establishing a permanent arbitration institution was so effortless, the whole concept of arbitration became, and still is, a dangerous tool in the hands of the dishonest'.[15]

The liberal regime for setting up permanent arbitration institutions has led to a situation where any company could establish its own arbitration institution where all disputes in connection with goods or services provided by that company are settled.[16] An infamous but stereotypical Latvian arbitration case was the 2002 *Aero-lukss v Latvijas finieris* case.[17] In that case, an arbitration agreement provided that the dispute was to be heard in an arbitration institution that was established by the lawyer of the party involved. The lawyer was also the chairman of the arbitration institution. As a representative of the party, the lawyer submitted the statement of claim. Simultaneously, as the institution's chairman, he appointed himself as the sole arbitrator and rendered an award in favour of his client. Due to the lack of settįng-aside proceedings, the losing party had only one recourse—to file a complaint to the General Prosecutor for having been subjected to unfair proceedings.

[9] Pirkka-Marja Põldvere, 'Kaheksa aastat mudelseadust: kas Eesti vahekohtumenetlus vastab mudelile?' (2014) 1 Juridica 17. The previous CCP included only a few provisions on arbitration, namely the right to agree on solving disputes by arbitration, as well as certain rules on the recognition of arbitral awards. Arbitration was mainly conducted in accordance with the Act of the Republic of Estonia on the Court of Arbitration of the Estonian Chamber of Commerce and Industry, regulating only this one institution. Ad hoc arbitration was not regulated at all and, in general, it was not practised.

[10] Ziedonis Ūdris and Inga Kačevska, 'Arbitration in Latvia: Urgent Need for Statutory Reform' (2004) 21(2) Journal Int'l Arb 211, 212.

[11] Law on Arbitrations of the Republic of Latvia 2015, Latvijas Vēstnesis No 194 (1 October 2014).

[12] Toms Krūmiņš, 'Arbitration in Latvia: A Cautionary Tale?' (2017) 34 Journal Int'l Arb 303, 306.

[13] ibid; Inga Kačevska, 'Ir normāla situācija, un ir Latvijas situācija' (2014) 22 Jurista Vārds 23, 23.

[14] A list of all currently registered permanent arbitration institutions in Latvia is available at <www.ur.gov.lv/lv/registre/organizaciju/skirejtiesa/skirejtiesu-saraksts/> accessed 23 January 2025 (in Latvian).

[15] Krūmiņš (n 12) 307.

[16] Ūdris and Kačevska (n 10) 220.

[17] Reported in ibid.

In Latvia, there have also been numerous 'other reports about fictitious arbitration proceedings taking place for illegal or sometimes criminal purposes'.[18] In some cases, these sham awards were made without properly informing the defendant about the arbitration proceedings. For example, the Supreme Court of Sweden has refused to recognize an award rendered in Latvia against a Swedish party because the latter had never been notified about the proceedings.[19] The use of arbitration in Latvia is also infamous for its involvement in illegal corporate raids when disputes over the ownership of a company are resolved via biased (pocket) arbitration tribunals, rendering awards based on forged documents, etc.[20]

The prevalence of sham awards is what defines the reputation of arbitration in Latvia. As two known Latvian arbitration practitioners wrote:

> [T]he reputation of arbitration in Latvia has been questioned due to 'pocket arbitrations', in which an arbitration institution established by one of the parties to an agreement (or its affiliated entity) administers a resolution of disputes which arise from an agreement, negatively affecting the neutrality and fair treatment of a dispute.[21]

Unsurprisingly, in public opinion (including that of the legal community), arbitration is a tool designed to circumvent justice by one party imposing an arbitration clause upon another party for a permanent arbitration institution that is owned by colleagues, friends, or relatives of the first party or its lawyers, and where the dispute is settled in the most biased way possible. In other words, in Latvia, arbitrators have been known to (often) act in an unethical and biased manner.[22] As a result, arbitration is a synonym for an illegal scheme and a denial of justice.[23]

The mechanism can function in this way not only because there are deficiencies in the legislative framework, but because many members of the legal community have no understanding of conflict of interest in arbitration.[24] This is because principles of legal ethics do not function in arbitration. In many cases it is an unethical environment. At the same time, the legislator has failed to implement any workable mechanisms for the elimination of such conflicts of interest and for ensuring high standards

[18] ibid.

[19] *Finants Collect v Heino Kumpula* [2015] Swedish Supreme Court Ö 4842-14.

[20] Ziedonis Ūdris, 'Uzticību šķīrējtiesām var nodrošināt ar tiesas kontroli pār to nolēmumiem' (2014) 22 Jurista Vārds 21, 23.

[21] Maija Tipaine and Līga Fjodorova, 'Arbitration in Latvia: Was a Restart a Failure?' (*Kluwer Arbitration Blog*, 25 January 2016).

[22] Maija Tipaine, 'Šķīrējtiesu reputāciju grauj neitralitātes trūkums' (2014) 22 Jurista Vārds 20, 21.

[23] We must also note that currently the LALV establishes an 'exotic' system for the qualification of arbitrators. In fact, for a person to be an arbitrator, he/she must be registered in a list of arbitrators at the Commercial Register. First of all, this makes it unclear how internationally recognized arbitration experts can be selected as arbitrators in Latvia. Second, according to Article 32(4) of the LAVL, no person that is or was during the last five years on the list of arbitrators of the particular permanent arbitration institution can act as a legal representative in the said permanent arbitration institution. Moreover, often each permanent arbitration institution has a very limited number of arbitrators on its list, leaving the parties with a very limited choice of arbitrators. This regime, introduced by the LALV, is meant to compensate for the absence of efficient control of conflicts of interests, however it is unlikely that this mechanism will be able to substitute the absence of ethical standards in arbitration.

[24] Kačevska (n 13).

of legal ethics. In fact, the Latvian legislator follows a philosophy of minimal overview of arbitration by the courts (including the lack of setting-aside procedures).[25] This means that ethical standards in arbitration are not only non-existent in practice, but that there is hardly any attempt to introduce them.

The legislator seems to focus on one function of arbitration—to alleviate the caseload for national courts. As any supervision of arbitral tribunals would impose an additional workload on courts, such options are perceived as counterproductive and find no place in the regulatory framework.

Moreover, formally, the legislator has refused to allow the judicial enforcement of awards rendered by ad hoc tribunals on the pretext that the state cannot ensure that those tribunals will respect the rights of the parties.[26] However, this shows that the legislator is unable to grasp the very basics of arbitration law. Disputes are decided by the arbitrators and not the owners or functionaries of the permanent arbitration tribunal, as the legislator thinks. This in itself shows that the whole system of arbitration in Latvia is dysfunctional.[27]

Overall, in many cases in Latvia, due process is not ensured in arbitration, as its main function is to alleviate the caseload of state courts, irrespective of whether the parties to arbitration agreements receive just and unbiased proceedings. As a result, the Latvian arbitration environment has been 'so distorted that arbitration institutions do not operate with the purpose for which they are intended, but to carry out various [illegal] schemes'.[28]

The quite unique situation in Latvia, as well as description of key features of the general approach towards arbitration in Lithuania and Estonia, already suggest that the approach towards private-public arbitration and the protection of public interest in private-public arbitration might be different in these states as well. This is mostly true when it comes to contractual arbitration, but it applies to investment arbitration in a similar fashion. These two types of arbitration are addressed in separate sections: commercial arbitration is discussed in sections III and IV, analysing arbitrability and the application of the public policy exception, which are the only tools working towards protecting the public interest, while investment arbitration is discussed in section V of this chapter.

[25] On different aspects of the legislative leitmotiv, see Agris Repšs, 'Nav pamata neizdot izpildrakstu ad hoc šķīrējtiesu spriedumiem' (2014) 22 Jurista Vārds 18; Kačevska (n 13) 24; Sandris Bērtraitis, 'Valsts nedrīkst pieļaut prettiesisku praksi strīdu alternatīvajā risināšanā' (2014) 22 Jurista Vārds 14, 15.

[26] Ūdris (n 20) 22.

[27] It is worth mentioning that certain experts have claimed that the Latvian legislator decided to make awards rendered by ad hoc tribunals unenforceable, because in the middle of the 2000s it turned out that ad hoc proceedings were cheaper than those rendered by permanent arbitration tribunals. The owners of permanent arbitration tribunals were able to lobby for such prohibition to diminish competition. See Ūdris (n 20) 22. If this is the real motive, then it shows that the legislator cares not about justice but about the interests of lobbyists. If the legislator truly considers that ad hoc arbitration tribunals decide cases differently to permanent arbitration tribunals then it does not understand the basics of arbitration law and thinks it is the arbitration institution that decides the dispute. Taking into account the reputation of permanent arbitration institutions in Latvia, it is hard to imagine how ad hoc tribunals could fare worse. Nevertheless, every explanation of the legislator's motives demonstrates the inadequacy of the environment of arbitration in Latvia and the equally inadequate legislative practice in this area.

[28] Kačevska (n 13). The translation is taken from Krūmiņš (n 12) 304.

III. Arbitrability of Contractual (Commercial) Private-Public Disputes in the Baltic States

Two types of arbitration must be distinguished for the purposes of describing the approach in the Baltic States towards private-public arbitration: contractual (commercial) arbitration and investment (treaty-based) arbitration. This distinction is made not only in the case of the Baltic States but also at the global level due to several differences between these two types.[29]

Contractual arbitration is conducted pursuant to a particular arbitration agreement concluded between the state party and a private person. Investment arbitration is conducted pursuant to an international treaty concluded between two or more states, in which the state consents to arbitration concerning disputes with investors. Such consent of the state is considered a public act of the state, that is, when giving consent to arbitration, the state acts in its sovereign capacity.

Further, contractual arbitration concerns disputes arising from a specific legal relationship between a private party and the state, with the merits generally depending on the terms of the specific contracts and events concerned. While the contract at issue is generally different in each case,[30] such contracts are, in the majority of cases, governed by national substantive law. Investment treaty disputes, on the contrary, are governed by international law and generally involve the same limited range of treaty standards.[31]

Against this background, we now turn to how domestic law in the Baltic States addresses the arbitrability of disputes between state entities and private persons.

A. Estonia

Estonian law, unlike that of the other Baltic countries' legal systems, has no provisions specifically addressing private-public arbitration. Arbitrability is defined in Article 718 of the CCPEST, which provides that the subject matter of an arbitration agreement may be a proprietary claim. An arbitration agreement concerning a non-proprietary claim is valid only if the parties are able to reach a compromise concerning the object of the dispute. An arbitral agreement shall be null and void if the subject matter of the agreement is any of the following: (a) a dispute concerning the validity or cancellation of a residential lease contract, and vacating a dwelling located in Estonia; (b) a dispute concerning the termination of an employment contract; or (c) a dispute arising from a consumer credit contract.

A proprietary claim in public law may be the object of an arbitration agreement if the parties are able to enter into a contract under public law concerning the object

[29] Karl-Heinz Böckstiegel, 'Commercial and Investment Arbitration: How Different Are They Today? The Lalive Lecture 2012' (2012) 28 Arb Int'l 577, 579.

[30] David Gaukrodger, 'Adjudicator Compensation Systems and Investor-State Dispute Settlement' OECD Working Papers on International Investment 2017/05 (2017) 29 <https://doi.org/10.1787/c2890bd5-en> accessed 23 January 2025.

[31] ibid.

of dispute (Article 718(3) of the CCPEST). While the notion of a 'proprietary claim in public law' is little developed, it is generally interpreted rather widely and liberally. The Estonian Supreme Court also stresses party autonomy as the legitimation of an arbitration agreement and emphasizes that non-arbitrability of a private law claim is an exception.[32] For example, when faced with a dispute between the public water supply company and a private textile enterprise, the Constitutional Review Chamber of the Estonian Supreme Court did not question the arbitrability of such a dispute.[33]

In this particular case, the textile enterprise and the company responsible for water supply and waste-water disposal services had signed an arbitration agreement and referred all claims arising out of the water supply agreement to the Arbitration Court of the Estonian Chamber of Commerce. The textile enterprise tried to contest the validity of several acts of the City Council laying down rules and prices for water supply and waste-water disposal services in the city of Narva. Hence, the Constitutional Review Chamber of the Estonian Supreme Court had to deal with the question of whether an arbitration court may submit a petition for constitutional review to the Supreme Court in the same way as ordinary courts do.[34]

The Constitutional Review Chamber of the Estonian Supreme Court denied such a possibility, stating:

> [T]he parties of a civil law relationship enjoy vast discretion to dispose of the relationship and that applies also to the settlement of disputes arising out of that. When submitting themselves to arbitration the parties must necessarily consider that thereby the possibility of constitutional review is excluded to a significant extent. If the arbitration agreement is valid and an arbitration court has jurisdiction, the parties of a civil law relationship have waived their right to settle their dispute in court and thereby at least partly also waived the protection of their fundamental rights in ways that only can be carried out by the court.[35]

Evidently, the Constitutional Review Chamber of the Estonian Supreme Court was not asked to answer the question of whether a dispute between a public body and a private person can be referred to arbitration. Still, the case serves as a good example in showing the approach towards private-public arbitration. Once a dispute between a public body and a private person is arbitrable, it does not matter whether it is related to the public interest or not; it is subject to the same procedure and the same rules as private-public arbitration. The latter means that the only way to protect the public interest in private-public arbitration in Estonia is through the procedures concerning the set-aside and enforcement of arbitral awards, in particular insofar as compliance with public is concerned (see section IV.A of this chapter).

[32] *JKKI v JMUD* [2018] SCE Civ 2-17-5977.

[33] See *Constitutional Judgment* [2008] SCE Civ 3-4-1-1-08.

[34] Under Estonian law, courts of first and second instance are entitled to initiate constitutional review proceedings at the Supreme Court if they deem it necessary in an individual court case. See further Peeter Roosma, 'Constitutional Review under 1992 Constitution' (1998) Juridica Int'l 35, 35–42.

[35] *Constitutional Judgment* [2008] SCE Civ 3-4-1-1-08.

B. Latvia

Latvian law directly regulates the arbitrability of disputes between public bodies and private persons and, so far, has the strictest approach towards arbitrability of state-party disputes among the Baltic States. Article 5(1)(2) of the LALV provides that 'disputes in which even one party is a state or municipal institution, or an arbitration award may affect the rights of a state or municipal institution cannot be settled by means of arbitration'.[36] Also, Article 77(5) of the Law on Municipalities provides that 'property disputes between the State, other legal persons, natural persons and local governments shall be decided in the State court'.[37]

In accordance with Article 1(3) of the Law on State Administration, an 'institution' is an authority which acts on behalf of a public person, is given specified authority in state administration by a legal act, has its own personnel, and is allocated financial resources to implement its activities. Such institutions are, for instance, ministries, the state police, the Competition Council, and the Supreme Court. Conversely, the term 'institution' does not cover capital companies established by the state, as they are treated as commercial entities.[38]

However, this initially highly hesitant approach towards arbitrability of disputes between public bodies and private persons changed in 2013 with Latvia withdrawing a reservation to the application of Article II(1) of the European Convention, which provides that 'legal persons of public law' have the right to conclude valid arbitration agreements.[39] According to the explanatory note to the law withdrawing the reservation, this change in policy reacted to an increase in international transactions in which state institutions participated, and which often provided for the settlement of disputes in neutral foreign arbitration institutions. There was, in other words, a need to allow legal persons under public law to conclude arbitration agreements.

[36] Restrictions for the state and municipalities to be parties to arbitration existed in Latvia long before the LALV. During the interwar period—that is, before the Soviet occupation—Latvian laws regulating arbitration contained a prohibition for state or municipal institutions to be parties to arbitration agreements. These laws were inherited from the Russian Empire. See Vladimirs Bukovskis, *Civīlprocesa mācības grāmata* (Autora izdevums 1933) 570. It must be noted, however, that it was not fully clear from the text of the provision (art 1489(3) of the pre-war Civil Procedure Law) whether the preclusion of a dispute that involved public entities from being arbitrated only concerned matters involving public interests, or whether it encompassed matters involving private interests as well. After Latvia had restored its independence, the new 1999 Civil Procedure Law provided that an arbitral tribunal could not decide disputes where one party was a state or municipality. As of 2005, the Civil Procedure Law also provided that disputes in which an arbitral award might affect the rights of a state or municipal institution could not be settled by means of arbitration. Hence, imposing the same prohibition in the new laws after becoming an independent country can probably be explained by the fact that such prohibitions already existed in Latvia during the interwar period.

[37] Law on Municipalities of the Republic of Latvia 1994 Latvijas Vēstnesis No 61 (24 May 1994).

[38] *Ģenerālprokuratūras Personu un valsts tiesību aizsardzības departamenta virsprokurora v AS 'Latvijas valsts meži'* [2013] SCLV Civ SPC-46/2013. By analogy, the same reasoning applies to capital companies established by municipalities.

[39] When joining the Convention in 2003, Latvia made a declaration under Article II(2) of the Convention that excluded the possibility of arbitration agreements concluded by state and municipal institutions. Article II(2) of the European Convention expressly provided that, when signing, ratifying, and acceding to the Convention, any state shall be entitled to declare such limitations. See Nērika Lizinska, *Valsts kā starptautiska šķīrējtiesas līguma puse* (Latvijas Universitātes Juridiskās fakultātes promocijas darbs 2020) <https://dspace.lu.lv/dspace/handle/7/53367> accessed 23 January 2025.

Latvia's parliament also relied on the *Benteler* award,[40] claiming that the possibility for the state and its institutions to conclude arbitration agreements was fundamental to today's customs in international trade. Revoking the reservation to the European Convention has led to a differentiation in Latvia, as far as the arbitrability of disputes is concerned, between domestic private-public arbitration, where arbitrability is excluded, and international private-public arbitration, where arbitrability is allowed.

It is likely that the prohibition of domestic private-public arbitration in Latvia is mostly caused not by subtle public policy considerations or the influence of foreign legal systems. Instead, the reason why the Latvian legislator opposes the extension of arbitration to the state, and to municipalities, has a lot to do with the reputation of arbitral tribunals in Latvia. After all, the use of arbitration by the state, or by municipalities, would create enormous risks. In Latvia, arbitration could be used by private persons (or crooked officials in collusion with private parties) willing to extort financial or other benefits from the state or municipalities. Any illegal scheme could be confirmed by a biased tribunal. The award would have the power of a judgment and contain a legal assessment of facts and law with very limited means of opposing its enforcement. Such an award would then be used by officials to deny their responsibility for the damage caused to the state or a municipality by their acts. Moreover, arbitration is usually confidential, making these schemes even less transparent.

Certainly, not every arbitrator is biased, nor is every permanent arbitration institution a pocket arbitration. Still, they are generally perceived as such in Latvia, raising suspicion about the idea of private-public arbitration. In this legal environment, it is easy to see why the legislator is reluctant to allow the state or municipalities to submit their disputes to arbitration. Most likely, the legislator also does not trust domestic arbitration. Consequently, the full prohibition of private-public arbitration in Latvia seems self-evident. By contrast, Latvia does allow private arbitration in order to alleviate the workload of courts, and due to the pressure of the arbitration lobbyists and the international tradition to rely on arbitration.

Other than on arbitrability, there are no legal provisions in Latvian law directly addressing the procedure for settling disputes through private-public arbitration. Hence, the public interest, once a dispute is considered arbitrable, can be protected only through procedures in state courts. As already mentioned, and as will be analysed further below (see Section IV.B), since Latvian law does not foresee any setting-aside proceedings, the protection of the public interest is essentially put into the hands of foreign courts, seated outside of Latvia, overseeing arbitrations involving Latvian public bodies.

C. Lithuania

In Lithuania, as in Latvia, the arbitrability of private-public disputes is specifically addressed in the law. However, regulations in Lithuania are rather confusing compared with its Baltic neighbours. The arbitrability of disputes between public bodies and private persons is defined by the provisions regulating both subjective and objective arbitrability.

[40] *Benteler v Belgian State*, Award (18 November 1983) (1984) 1 Journal Int'l Arb 184.

Objective arbitrability is defined in Article 12(2) of the LCALT, which provides:

> Arbitration may not resolve disputes which should be heard under administrative proceedings or hear cases, the examination of which falls within the competence of the Constitutional Court of the Republic of Lithuania. Disputes arising from family legal relationships and disputes regarding the registration of patents, trademarks and design may not be referred to as arbitration. Disputes arising from employment and consumer contracts, except for cases where the arbitration agreement was concluded after the dispute arose, may not be referred to as arbitration.

Although private-public arbitration is not specifically mentioned in this provision, the exclusion of disputes to be heard under administrative proceedings (in administrative courts) may be relevant to private-public arbitration in Lithuania. Pursuant to Article 36(2) of the Code of Civil Procedure of the Republic of Lithuania, the nature of the legal relationship out of which the dispute arose determines whether the dispute falls within the jurisdiction of administrative courts or courts of general jurisdiction. If such a legal relationship is of mixed nature (civil and administrative), the subject-matter jurisdiction is determined by the dominant element. It therefore follows that whenever an arbitration agreement between a private person and a public body concerns a dispute arising out of a contract that would fall within the jurisdiction of the administrative courts, such dispute would not be arbitrable.

Under Article 12(1) of the LCALT, all disputes may be resolved in arbitration, except for cases stipulated in that article. Such wording suggests that the LCALT is the only source regulating arbitrability in Lithuania. Nevertheless, it is established in the case law that other laws might define non-arbitrable disputes as well.[41] Lithuanian courts have rarely expanded the list of non-arbitrable disputes. One such case, however, was directly related to private-public arbitration.

In a dispute between a foreign private company and Lithuanian state entities regarding a change in price under a public procurement contract, the Supreme Court of Lithuania (SCLT) ruled that such disputes are non-arbitrable[42] (which led to the annulment of the arbitral award). The Court based its conclusion, inter alia, on the need to protect the public interest and noted that the purpose of the Law on Public Procurement was to protect the public interest. Therefore, the body resolving public procurement disputes must have the widest possible powers and only courts in Lithuania are vested with such powers.

Subjective arbitrability is regulated in Lithuania by Articles 12(3), 12(4), and 3(5) of the LCALT, and said provisions are those creating the most confusion regarding their purpose and scope of application. Article 12(3) of the LCALT states:

> Disputes to which a state or municipal enterprise or an institution or organisation except for the Bank of Lithuania is a party, may not be referred to arbitration, unless the

[41] For example, the Supreme Court of Lithuania (SCLT) decided that a case regarding the investigation of a legal person's activities was not a commercial dispute and, consequently, the parties could not agree to submit this type of case to arbitration: *NVK et al v UAB 'Luksora'* [2012] SCLT Civ 3K-3-353/2012.

[42] *UAB 'Kauno vandenys' and Aplinkos projektų valdymo agentūra v 'WTE Wassertechnik GmbH' and AB 'Požeminiai darbai'* [2011] SCLT Civ 3K-7-304/2011.

prior consent of the founder of the enterprise, institution or organisation regarding the arbitration agreement has been obtained.

However, at the same time, according to Article 12(4) of the LCALT: 'The Government of the Republic of Lithuania or its authorised state institution may conclude an arbitration agreement in respect of disputes relating to commercial contracts concluded by the Government or its authorised state institution under a general procedure.' In addition, pursuant to Article 3(5) of the LCALT, the state, municipalities, and other public legal entities may also conclude an arbitration agreement.

These provisions make clear that the capacity of public bodies to enter into arbitration agreements with private persons is limited. It is unclear, however, and has not been decided by Lithuanian courts, which public bodies fall within the scope of Article 12(3) of the LCALT. Based on the scarce legal doctrine on this matter, Article 12(3) of the LCALT is interpreted as applying only to those actors whose legal form is expressly mentioned in the LCALT. Accordingly, Article 12(3) of the LCALT is not applicable to private legal persons (eg closed stock companies or the like) even if the state or municipality is a shareholder in such a company.[43]

An exception to the requirement to receive the founder's consent was explicitly made for the Bank of Lithuania by amending the LCALT in 2001.[44] In the explanatory note of this amendment, it was explained that the founder of the Bank of Lithuania was the Parliament of the Republic of Lithuania, and that without such an exception, the Bank of Lithuania would be obliged to ask parliament for consent in order to enter into an arbitration agreement, while parliament is clearly not the institution with the needed expertise and capacity to examine such contracts. Hence, concluding an arbitration agreement should only require the founder's consent where the founder is not parliament, but ministries or municipalities.[45] Nevertheless, the LCALT was never altered by expanding the exception granted to the Bank of Lithuania to other state entities founded by Parliament.

Secondly, public bodies, even if they fall under Article 12(3) of the LCALT, are not prevented from entering into arbitration agreements. Rather, they must only obtain the consent of their founder, that is, another public body. Yet, Lithuanian case law has interpreted the requirement of the founder's consent quite liberally. For example, in relation to the form of the consent, it was established that it is not required to obtain written consent, but that consent must be obtained before entering into an arbitration agreement.[46]

[43] Eglė Zemlytė, *Valstybė kaip arbitražinio susitarimo šalis* (Registrų centras 2015) 118–23.

[44] Law on Amending Article 11 of the Law on Commercial Arbitration of the Republic of Lithuania 2001 Valstybės žinios (30 March 2001) No 28-894.

[45] Explanatory note to the Law on Amending Article 11 of the Law on Commercial Arbitration of the Republic of Lithuania 2000 < https://e-seimas.lrs.lt/portal/legalAct/lt/TAK/TAIS.104732?jfwid=-p5p3uzd1e> accessed 23 January 2025.

[46] *VĮ Klaipėdos valstybinio jūrų uosto direkcija v 'Hydro Soil Services NV'* [2007] SCLT Civ 3K-3-62/2007; *UAB 'Giedra' v Šiaulių miesto savivaldybės administracija* [2008] CAL Civ 2A-149/2008; *VilniusLux, UAB, Gemmo SpA VSLS OU v Vilniaus miesto savivaldybės administracija* [2017] CAL Civ e2A-644-370/2017.

Thirdly, it is unclear to what extent Article 12(3) of the LCALT applies to international commercial arbitration. It is noted in the *travaux préparatoires* of the new wording of the LCALT that international arbitration cases should be treated differently: 'In the case of international commercial arbitration, a public actor assumes particular international obligations (pacta sunt servanda), therefore it is acknowledged that the state is not allowed to rely on domestic law in order to avoid these obligations.'[47]

As regards arbitrability, it is difficult to reach a clear conclusion on the situation in Lithuania. Its approach differs from the one in Latvia since state entities are not prevented from entering into arbitration agreements per se. It differs from the one in Estonia as well, since the arbitrability of a dispute involving a state entity is restricted. Nevertheless, since the application of Article 12(3) of the LCALT has never led to a refusal to enforce an arbitration agreement or arbitral award, nor has it led to the setting aside of an award, it might be said that the Lithuanian approach towards arbitrability of private-public commercial disputes is closer to that of Estonia rather than Latvia. While the scope of arbitrability in private-public arbitrations is therefore subject to uncertainty, it is clear that, as in the case of Latvia and Estonia, once a dispute is considered arbitrable, private-public arbitration is no different from private arbitration. The only way to protect the public interest in such a case is via the public policy exception when reviewing arbitral awards (see section IV.C below).

IV. Protection of Public Interest in Private-Public Contractual (Commercial) Arbitration via the Public Policy Exception in the Baltic States

All three Baltic States are parties to the New York Convention. Hence, if an award falls within the scope of the New York Convention (ie stemming from an arbitration seated abroad), the courts of the Baltic States are entitled *ex officio* to refuse the recognition and enforcement of the award where it would be contrary to the public policy of that country.[48] Further, Lithuania's and Estonia's legal provisions regulating set-aside proceedings,[49] which are a verbatim adoption of the relevant provisions of the UNCITRAL Model Law,[50] permit state courts to set aside arbitral awards issued in those states if such awards violate public policy. Latvia, by contrast, as mentioned above, does not offer that possibility (see section III). To determine to what extent the public policy exception ensures the protection of public interests in private-public

[47] Comments of the Committee of Legal Affairs of the Parliament of the Republic of Lithuania on the Draft Law Amending the Law on Commercial Arbitration 2012 <www3.lrs.lt/pls/inter3/dokpaieska.showdoc_l?p_id=425946> accessed 23 January 2025.

[48] New York Convention (n 4) art V(2)(b) ('Recognition and enforcement of an arbitral award may also be refused if the competent authority in the country where recognition and enforcement is sought finds that . . . the recognition or enforcement of the award would be contrary to the public policy of that country.').

[49] Art 50(3)(6) of the LCALT; art 751(2)(2) of the CCPEST.

[50] UNCITRAL Model Law (n 6) art 34(2) ('An arbitral award may be set aside by the court specified in Article 6 only if . . . the court finds that . . . the award is in conflict with the public policy of this state.').

arbitrations, this section reviews the approaches taken by the three Baltic States in the interpretation of the concept of public policy.

A. Estonia

Estonian legal doctrine or court practice does not provide a clear answer to the question to what extent the public interest in private-public arbitration is protected under the public policy exception. According to Article 751(2)(2) of the CCPEST, the courts are to annul an arbitral award based on the request of a party, or at the initiative of the court, if the court establishes that the award is contrary to Estonian public policy or good morals.

According to the commentaries on the CCPEST, the notion of public policy is an undefined legal term which should likely be interpreted similarly to interpreting the same term in the context of recognition of foreign court judgments. For example, public policy should primarily consist of fundamental rights and obligations known under Estonian law (particularly the Estonian Constitution).[51] It has been further noted that the violation of public policy should be obvious, and that the annulment of an award on this ground should be possible only in truly exceptional cases. In the context of the recognition of foreign awards, it has been emphasized that refusal of recognition shall not be based solely on the fact that the legal relationship regulated in the decision is not recognized in Estonia, or that an Estonian court would have reached a different conclusion. Rather, it has to be the recognition of the decision and not the decision itself that would have the consequence of directly harming Estonian public policy.[52] Furthermore, public policy does not include all the mandatory rules of the law of the recognizing state, but only those provisions which reflect the fundamental values of that state's legal system.[53]

As the Supreme Court of Estonia stated:

> In the assessment of the chamber, the Article 751(2)(2) of the CCPEST covers, in addition to exceptional but in essence material law problems (eg award by which punitive damages are ordered), also the breaches of those important procedural rules, which have not been described in Article 751(1) of the CCPEST. One of these is the requirement that arbitrators shall be neutral. It would be against good morals and Estonian public policy if an award would be made by an arbitrator representing at the same time the interests of one party to the arbitration proceedings.[54]

[51] Villu Kove, Inga Jarvekulg, Jaanus Ots, and Maarja Torga, *Tsiviilkohtumenetluse seadustik III. Kommenteeritud väljanne* (Juura 2018) 1523 (with reference to the explanatory note of the CCPEST) and 934 (commenting on Article 620(1)1, which stipulates that a court decision in a civil matter made by a foreign state is subject to recognition in the Republic of Estonia, except in the case where recognition of the decision would be clearly contrary to the essential principles of Estonian law (public order) and, above all, the fundamental rights and freedoms of persons).

[52] ibid 934.

[53] *Parties unknown* [2018] SCE Civ 2-18-4731.

[54] *Avaldaja Vene Föderatsiooni äriühing OF v D OÜ* [2016] SCE Civ 3-2-1-186-15 (translation by the author).

To date, a violation of public policy has never been successfully invoked to hinder the recognition of foreign awards in Estonia. In a case from 2018, upon assessing whether there was a ground for refusing enforcement of a foreign (Latvian) arbitral award, the Supreme Court concluded that the mere fact that the respondent was deemed to have been duly notified of the arbitral proceedings did not contradict the general principles of Estonian public policy (the defendants remained passive upon reception of documents, which were sent to their registered and economically active address).[55] The Court explained that the fact that one cannot, unlike in Estonia, request the annulment of an award in Latvia does not make the recognition of such an award contravene Estonia's public policy. The Supreme Court also noted that the recognition of an award is not in breach of public policy just because the internal procedural law of the recognizing country might not have been followed.[56] However, the Court stressed that there might be a ground for non-recognition, for example if the subject matter would not be arbitrable according to Estonian law.

The Estonian Supreme Court has, thus far, not relied on the notion of public interest (within the meaning of interest of the state or society as a whole) as a ground for the non-recognition of arbitral awards. The few decisions dealing with non-recognition of foreign awards apply the classical concept of public policy and concentrate on the questions of fundamental procedural rights and freedoms. Estonia seems to follow a liberal understanding of the state, treating public bodies as equal parties in the arbitral proceedings and subjecting them to the same rules and principles as any other party.

B. Latvia

Similarly to Estonia, to what extent the notion of public policy encompasses protection of the public interest is also Hardly discussed in Latvia. On the one hand, the notions of 'public interest' and 'social good', which are usually used interchangeably, seem to have a rather specific meaning in Latvia's legal system. Thus, the notion of 'social good' is mentioned in the Latvian Constitution's preamble, which states that '[e]ach individual takes care of oneself, one's relatives and the common good of society by acting responsibly toward other people, future generations, the environment and nature.' The Constitutional Court has referred to this notion of common good, stating that it implies the existence of solidarity between the individual and the society.[57]

The notion of public interest is also found in the Constitution. Article 105 of the Constitution states that '[e]veryone has the right to own property. Property shall not be used contrary to the interests of the public. Property rights may be restricted only

[55] *Parties unknown* [2018] SCE Civ 2-16-15675.

[56] It was argued that the delivery of documents did not meet the requirements of the CCPEST for state courts. The Supreme Court found that the delivery of documents should follow the rules applicable to the arbitration and not the procedural law of the recognizing state. As it was not proven that one of the parties was a consumer, the court did not analyze whether this fact might be relevant for the outcome. In applying the grounds of New York Convention, the courts made reference to the UNCITRAL Secretariat Guide on the Convention on the Recognition and Enforcement of Foreign Arbitral Awards, 2016 Edition.

[57] *On Compliance of Section 3, 5, 6, 7 and 9 of the Law On Solidarity Tax with the First Sentence of Article 91 and Article 109 of the Satversme* [2017] Constitutional Court of the Republic of Latvia 2016-14-01.

in accordance with the law. Expropriation of property for public purposes shall be allowed only in exceptional cases on the basis of a specific law and in return for fair compensation.' The provision tries to balance the rights of property owners with those of society. For example, the Constitutional Court has ruled that the use of territorial planning is a means of balancing the rights of the owner and public interests.[58]

But also beyond the context of expropriation, the Constitutional Court uses the so-called constitutionality test for virtually all restrictions of human rights. According to this test, any restriction of human rights protected under the Latvian Constitution must: (1) be introduced by law; (2) serve a legitimate objective; and (3) be proportionate to that legitimate objective.[59] The legitimate objective must lie in the protection of public interests.

As the public policy exception in reviewing arbitral awards is not developed in Latvia, and the interpretation of public interest seems to have nothing to do with arbitration, both notions (public policy and public interest) have never been analysed together. It is also difficult to compare the definitions of those two notions and impossible to make any firm conclusions as to what fundamental principles of the Latvian legal system are encompassed by public policy. However, as in the case of Estonia, one cannot exclude that those two notions somehow overlap.

Nevertheless, the absence of a direct link between the notions of public policy and public interest is not the only issue regarding the protection of public interest in private-public arbitration. Latvian law does not provide for a setting-aside mechanism at all (irrespective of whether arbitration is private or private-public), that is, public policy plays a role only when recognition and enforcement of a foreign arbitral award is sought under the New York Convention.

The Constitutional Court of Latvia has urged the legislator to define the grounds and procedures for contesting an arbitration award by criticizing the legislator's 'rationale' behind the absence of such legal regulation:

> [T]his argument per se cannot serve as a ground for depriving a person substantially of his or her rights ie the aim chosen by the legislator – decreasing the workload of the courts of general jurisdiction, thus speeding up other legal proceedings – may not threaten such fundamental rights of a person that he or she has not voluntarily waived.[60]

[58] *On Compliance of Para 55 and Para 56 of the Riga City Council Binding Regulation of 18 June 2013 No 221 'The Binding Regulation on the Use of and Construction in the Territory of Culture and Recreation Park "Mežaparks"', as well its Annex No 1 'The Planned (Permitted) Use of the Territory', Insofar They Apply to the Planned (Permitted) Use of the Immovable Property at 10 Pāvu Street, Riga (Cadastre No 0100 095 0003) with Article 105 of the Satversme of the Republic of Latvia* [2014] Constitutional Court of the Republic of Latvia 2014-04-03; *On Compliance of Para 2361 'Use of Territory and Construction Rules' of Binding Regulation No 8 of 24 March 2016 by Jūrmala City Council 'On Approving the Graphic Part, Regulation on the Use of Territory and Construction in the Spatial Plan of Jūrmala City' with Article 115 of the Satversme of the Republic of Latvia* [2017] Constitutional Court of the Republic of Latvia 2016-24-03.

[59] *On Compliance of Section 27(4) and the Text of Section 28(2) 'for the Time Period until the Age of 65 Years' of Law on Institutions of Higher Education and Section 29(5) of Law On Scientific Activity with Articles 91 and 106 of the Satversme of the Republic of Latvia* [2003] Constitutional Court of the Republic of Latvia 2002-21-01.

[60] *On Compliance of Section 495(1) of the Civil Procedure Law with the first sentence in Article 92 of the Constitution of the Republic of Latvia* [2014] Constitutional Court of Latvia 2014-09-01.

However, no legislative changes have yet been made. The only remedy against an arbitral award issued in Latvia available to an award debtor is to oppose the issuance of a writ of execution requested by the award creditor. Nevertheless, (1) only an arbitral award issued in institutional arbitration is subject to compulsory judicial enforcement (execution); and (2) even if the losing party opposes the issuance of the writ of execution, the court is not entitled to refuse enforcement of such award based on it being contrary to public policy.[61]

Hence, if the place of institutional arbitration was in Latvia, the award would remain valid and be enforced, even if it is potentially contrary to the public interest. By contrast, awards resulting from ad hoc arbitrations seated in Latvia would not be enforced in any way. Due to this situation, it is difficult to imagine that Latvia would be chosen as a place of arbitration in the case of private-public arbitration and, therefore, the issue has never arisen in practice.

C. Lithuania

As in the case of Latvia, in Lithuania, no direct link between the notions of public policy in the context of arbitration and the public interest as determined by constitutional law exists. Still, when considering the case law it becomes obvious that these concepts do indeed overlap.

The notion of public interest has been developed mainly by the Constitutional Court of the Republic of Lithuania. It has emphasized numerous times that the Constitution considers the state as serving the common good of society,[62] that the purpose of the state as a political organization of society is to safeguard human rights and guarantee the protection of the public interest,[63] and that the implementation of

[61] See art 536 of Latvia's Civil Procedure Law of 1998: '(1) A judge may refuse to issue a writ of execution for the enforcement of a judgment of a permanent arbitration court, if: 1) the particular civil legal dispute may be resolved only by a court; 2) the arbitration court agreement has been entered into by a natural person, who has restricted capacity to act, or by a minor; 3) the arbitration court agreement, in accordance with the law applying thereto, has been revoked or declared null and void; 4) the party was not notified of the arbitration court proceedings in the appropriate manner, or due to other reasons was unable to submit his or her explanations, and this significantly has or could have affected the arbitration court proceedings; 5) the party was not notified of the appointing of an arbitrator in the appropriate manner, and this significantly has or could have affected the arbitration court proceedings; 6) the arbitration judge does not conform to the requirements of the Arbitration Law, the arbitration court was not established or the arbitration court proceedings did not take place in accordance with the provisions of the arbitration court agreement or of Arbitration Law; 7) a judgment of the arbitration court was given on a civil legal dispute not provided for in the arbitration court agreement or which does not conform to the provisions of the arbitration court agreement, or also issues are decided in it as not within the scope of the arbitration court agreement.'

[62] *On the Law on Presidential Elections* [2004] CCRL 24/04; *On the Compensation for Damage Inflicted by Unlawful Actions of Interrogatory and Investigatory Bodies, the Prosecutor's Office, and a Court* [2006] CCRL 23/04.

[63] *On a Decree of the President of the Republic* [2003] CCRL 40/03; *On the State Service* [2004] CCRL 51/01-26/02-19/03-22/03-26/03-27/03; *On the Prevention of Organised Crime* [2004] CCRL 8/02-16/02-25/02-9/03-10/03-11/03-36/03-37/03-06/04-09/04-20/04-26/04-30/04-31/04-32/04-34/04-41/04; *On Private Accusations and on the Right of the Person, Against Whom the Institution of a Criminal Case is Refused, to Lodge a Complaint Against the Decision of the Prosecutor* [2006] CCRL 7/03-41/03-40/04-46/04-5/05-7/05-17/05.

the public interest is one of the most important preconditions for the existence and evolution of society.[64]

In the jurisprudence of the Constitutional Court, public interest is defined mostly by quantitative and subject-matter criteria, namely the number of addressees whose interests are protected or the nature of the protected interest.[65] Thus, the Constitutional Court has defined the term 'public interest' as follows: 'The public interest is the common interest of the state, society or part of society which expresses the fundamental values of society enshrined in and protected by the Constitution.'[66] At the same time, the Court has emphasized that a public interest can also be defined as the interest of one person or a group of persons: 'When considering whether a particular interest can be described as the public interest, it must be established that failure to protect particular interests of a person or group of persons would cause a violation of certain values enshrined in and protected by the Constitution.'[67]

The relationship between the notions of public interest and public policy as regards arbitration has never been addressed by the Constitutional Court, or by ordinary courts deciding requests for setting aside or enforcing arbitral awards. Nevertheless, the case law of the SCLT suggests that those two notions have a strong connection and, in fact, overlap. For example, the SCLT has emphasized that the enforcement or recognition of an arbitral award may violate public policy if it contradicts internationally recognized fundamental legal principles enshrined in the Constitution of the Republic of Lithuania.[68]

At the same time, it is also clear from the case law developed by the SCLT that the notion of public policy is to be understood and interpreted narrowly, that is, as international public policy.[69] This is also the case in private-public arbitrations, as is confirmed by a 2014 ruling of the SCLT that concerned the enforcement of an investment treaty award rendered under UNCITRAL Arbitration Rules against Lithuania.[70] In that ruling, the SCLT overturned a decision of the Court of Appeal that had refused enforcement of an award obtained by an Italian investor under the Italy–Lithuania BIT. While the Court of Appeal found that enforcement of the award violated public policy because the investor had committed an abuse of process by initiating arbitration proceedings based on a claim that had already been adjudicated in the Lithuanian courts, the SCLT overturned the Court of Appeal's ruling based on an extensive analysis of the public policy exception.

The SCLT relied on the case law of the courts of other countries, as well as on the legal doctrine on the interpretation of the public policy exception, and concluded that

[64] *On the Ownership Rights of Functionaries* [1997] CCRL 13/96; *On the Law on Hunting* [2005] CCRL 14/02.

[65] Lina Bieliūnienė and others, *Viešojo intereso atpažinimo problema Lietuvos teisėje: kriterijai ir prioritetai* (Eugrimas 2016) 88.

[66] *On Drawing Up and Announcing the Reasoning of Court Decisions, on the Institute of a Decision Adopted in Absentia and on Appeals* [2006] CCRL 35/03-11/06.

[67] Bieliūnienė and others (n 65) 88–89.

[68] *Belaja Rus v Westintorg Corp* [2008] SCLT Civ 3K-3-443/2008; *Interperformances Inc v RJ* [2015] SCLT Civ e3K-3-483-421/2015; *Suraleb, INC v Atviroji akcinė bendrovė Minsko traktorių gamykla* [2017] SCLT Civ 3K-3-267-611/2017.

[69] *Limited Liability Company 'Kutter' v UAB 'Abipa Logistics'* [2013] SCLT Civ 3K-7-181/2013.

[70] *LB v Valstybės įmonė Valstybės turto fondas* [2014] SCLT Civ 3K-3-363/2014.

the case did not fall within the scope of the public policy exception as understood in Lithuania. The SCLT stated that the investor was entitled to rely on the state's consent to arbitration under the BIT, and that the arbitral tribunal had already rejected Lithuania's objection that the arbitration constituted an abuse of process. This conclusion of the arbitration tribunal, the SCLT held, had to be respected. This notwithstanding, the SCLT admitted that a violation of the principle of good faith, on which the prohibition of an abuse of process is based, could be considered as falling within the public policy exception, but only when such a violation is completely evident and not open to doubt, which was not, in the SCLT's opinion, the case in the case at hand.

Although the SCLT's analysis does not suggest how the notions of public policy and public interest relate to each other, the decision makes clear that public policy is to be interpreted narrowly, including in the context of private-public arbitration. It also confirms, however, that the notion of public policy would be how the public interest could be protected in set-aside and enforcement proceedings in private-public arbitrations. Hence, Lithuania shares Estonia's approach towards the notion of public policy: in both jurisdictions the notion is not sufficiently developed to conclude that it would help ensure the protection of the public interest, but there is nothing to suggest the contrary either.

Latvia, on the other hand, due to the absence of set-aside proceedings, shares the above approach only partially. The notion of public policy is applicable only in proceedings for the recognition and enforcement of arbitral awards made outside Latvia. However, contractual private-public arbitrations in Latvia are barely possible due to existing restrictions for public bodies to enter into arbitration agreements (see section III.B above). Thus, the approach towards the protection of the public interest in contractual private-public arbitrations in all three Baltic States is quite inconsistent and fragmented. On the one hand, some efforts are made in Latvia and Lithuania to prevent contractual private-public arbitrations in general (see sections III.B and III.C). On the other hand, if not impeded, contractual private-public arbitrations in Estonia and Lithuania are not subject to any additional safeguards except for *ex post* judicial review on the ground of public policy. Latvia, the jurisdiction with the strictest approach towards arbitrability of private-public disputes, ends up as the jurisdiction with the narrowest scope of *ex post* judicial review, if any at all.

V. Protection of the Public Interest in Treaty-Based Private-Public Arbitration in the Baltic States

All three Baltic States are parties to the ICSID Convention. They have also entered into a number of BITs and joined the Energy Charter Treaty, which provide for state consent to submit investment disputes to arbitration. As such consent is considered a public act of state *(acta jure imperii)* and subject to international law, national legal provisions restricting the arbitrability of private-public disputes do not apply. According to publicly available information, none of the Baltic States have ever contested the arbitrability of a private-public dispute based on national law, let alone objected to the resolution of investment disputes through arbitration in general. However, Latvia and Estonia, along with other EU Member States, supported Slovakia's arguments in the CJEU *Achmea* case,[71] that intra-EU BITs that provide for consent to arbitration were incompatible with EU law. On 5 May 2020, all three signed the Agreement for the Termination of Bilateral Investment Treaties between the Member States of the European Union.[72]

As for the protection of the public interest during set-aside and enforcement proceedings, one must differentiate. For awards rendered in an ICSID arbitration, no state court review via annulment or appeal proceedings is permitted, and the enforcement of ICSID awards is not subject to the New York Convention. Under Article 54(1) of the ICSID Convention, each Contracting State shall recognize an award rendered pursuant to the Convention as binding, and enforce the pecuniary obligations imposed by that award within its territories as if it were the final judgment of a court in that state. Annulment of the arbitral award by the ICSID ad hoc annulment committee is possible, however, only on procedural grounds.[73] These rigorous finality provisions, and the lack of a public policy exception to enforcement, distinguish the ICSID Convention from other international commercial arbitration regimes.[74] This does not mean that ICSID arbitrations shield awards that violate the public interest of a particular state; it only means that the protection of the public interest lies solely in the hands of ICSID tribunals and ICSID annulment committees.

The differences in the application of the public policy exception in treaty-based private-public arbitration in the Baltic States can be summarized in Table 8.1 below:[75] As for non-ICSID awards, foreign arbitral awards are, in all three Baltic States, enforced under the New York Convention. Hence, in ad hoc investment arbitrations or institutional arbitrations other than under the ICSID Convention, the protection of the public interest can be granted by refusing enforcement based on Article V(2)(a) of the New York Convention (public policy exception, see section IV above). However, the New York Convention applies only to awards out of an arbitration seated in a country other than the one where enforcement is sought (Article 1(1) of the New York Convention). If the place of arbitration is in Lithuania or Estonia, the protection of public interest may be ensured only via setting-aside proceedings. In the case of

[71] Case C–284/16, *Slowakische Republik v Achmea BV*, Judgment (6 March 2018) ECLI:EU:C:2018:158.

[72] Agreement for the Termination of Bilateral Investment Treaties between the Member States of the European Union [2020] OJ L169/1.

[73] ICSID Convention (n 1) art 52(1) provides:

'Either party may request annulment of the award by an application in writing addressed to the Secretary-General on one or more of the following grounds:

(a) that the Tribunal was not properly constituted;
(b) that the Tribunal has manifestly exceeded its powers;
(c) that there was corruption on the part of a member of the Tribunal;
(d) that there has been a serious departure from a fundamental rule of procedure; or
(e) that the award has failed to state the reasons on which it is based.'

[74] Lucy Reed, Jan Paulsson, and Nigel Blackaby, *Guide to ICSID Arbitration* (Kluwer 2004) 97.

[75] The comparison would also apply to contractual private-public arbitration under the ICSID Convention.

Table 8.1 Differences in the application of the public policy exception in treaty-based private-public arbitration in the Baltic States

	Lithuania	Latvia	Estonia
Application of public policy exception in setting-aside or enforcement proceedings of ICSID arbitration awards.	No.	No.	No.
Application of public policy exception in enforcement proceedings of foreign arbitral awards.	Yes, under the New York Convention.	Yes, under the New York Convention.	Yes, under the New York Convention.
Application of public policy exception in setting-aside proceedings of domestic awards.	Yes, under national arbitration law.	No (no setting-aside proceedings for arbitration awards at all).	Yes, under national arbitration law.
Enforcement of domestic awards resulting from ad hoc arbitration.	Yes, under the national rules of civil procedure.	No (writs of compulsory judicial execution can be issued only with respect to institutional arbitration awards).	Yes, under the national rules of civil procedure.

arbitral awards issued in Latvia, the protection of the public interest cannot be ensured at all in arbitration proceedings seated in Latvia, as Latvia's law does not provide for a setting-aside mechanism.

In any event, the exposure of the Baltic States to investment treaty arbitration has not given rise to much debate. According to public data from ICSID, eleven claims have been filed at ICSID against the Baltic States (four against Estonia, four against Latvia, and three against Lithuania).[76] Two of these cases are still pending (one against Latvia, and one against Lithuania). From the nine cases that are now closed, the Baltic countries succeeded in three (Lithuania, Latvia, and Estonia in one case each), lost in two (one case each against Estonia and Latvia), and entered into a settlement agreement in one case (against Estonia). In two remaining cases the proceedings were discontinued. A similar picture of limited exposure also emerges from the data collected by UNCTAD, which also includes non-ICSID arbitrations (see Table 8.2 below).[77] The data also confirms that the Baltic States are more often involved in investment treaty disputes as respondents rather than their investors acting as claimants.

These numbers show that Latvia could be considered the least successful of the Baltic States in investment arbitrations. Still, the number of cases is, overall, too small

[76] See ICSID's Cases Database at <https://icsid.worldbank.org/cases/case-database> accessed 23 January 2025.

[77] See UNCTAD, 'Investment Dispute Settlement Navigator' (2022) <https://investmentpolicy.unctad.org/investment-dispute-settlement> accessed 23 January 2025.

Table 8.2 Publicly available data on the treaty-based private-public arbitrations involving the Baltic States

State	Cases as Respondent State	Result of the Cases as Respondent State	Cases of Home State of claimant
Estonia	5	Won – 2 Lost – 1 Settled – 1 Pending – 1	3
Latvia	9	Won – 1 Lost – 3 Discontinued – 3 Settled – 1 Pending – 1	4
Lithuania	7	Won – 2 Lost – 0 Discontinued – 2 Decided in favour of neither party – 1 Pending – 2	6

to trigger any willingness for changes in policy or legislation, or even significant scientific discussions.

VI. Conclusion

The analysis of existing regulations on private-public arbitration suggests that each of the Baltic States follows its own approach in terms of protecting the public interest. Although they have an almost uniform approach towards treaty-based investment arbitration, which is no different from the rest of the world, regulations differ considerably when it comes to domestic arbitration. Although in all Baltic States, the rules applicable to private-public arbitration, once recourse to this means of dispute settlement is possible, are no different from those applicable to private-private arbitration, the Baltic jurisdictions differ in respect of arbitrability, which is given in Estonia and Lithuania, but rather limited in Latvia.

Similarly, in respect of the review of arbitral awards in set-aside proceedings, the three Baltic States differ, with Estonia and Lithuania permitting review for compliance with public policy, whereas Latvia generally excludes such review. However, because in all three states, the notions of public interest and public policy are not developed enough, it is impossible to draw clear conclusions as to the extent to which the public policy exception ensures the protection of public interests in private-public arbitration. As for Lithuania and Estonia, nothing suggests that public policy could not serve as a legal ground for the protection of public interests in private-public arbitration. The case of Latvia is different. If the place of arbitration is in Latvia, there is no possibility of applying the public policy exception, as there are no setting-aside proceedings foreseen in Latvian law. This makes Latvia's approach subject to two extremes: either private-public arbitration is not allowed at all, or when it is allowed, the protection of the public interest lies solely in the hands of arbitral tribunals.

Overall, the lowest level of protection exists in investment treaty arbitration, especially in arbitrations conducted under the ICISD Convention. Treaty-based arbitration usually involves the application of public law and an evaluation of the state's *acta iure imperii*, including legislative acts. Consequently, ICSID arbitration is a rather clear instance of the state's retreat from adjudication, because it replaces courts with a private model of adjudication in matters of public law.[78] While it may be said that investment treaty arbitration therefore requires a higher level of protection of the public interest, the national law of the Baltic States (except for Estonia) imposes restrictions on arbitrability only for contractual disputes involving public entities, even though the disputes often only concern purely commercial interests. In such cases, the Baltic States have much stricter safeguards to protect the public interest than in investment treaty cases.

Yet, the question to what extent private-public arbitration might be in tension with certain constitutional principles has never been raised, either on the theoretical level or in practice. It has never even been considered that the state's consent to arbitration could constitute an undue retreat from state-sponsored adjudication, or whether it is compatible with the principle of the rule of law to confer jurisdiction over public law disputes to private adjudicators.

In the case of Lithuania, the possibility for the state to consent to arbitration was only once cast into question, in the dissenting opinion of a judge at the Constitutional Court who raised the question whether the state was entitled to choose a national investor without a public tender or consent to arbitration under the arbitration rules of the Stockholm Chamber of Commerce Arbitration Institute in the agreement with this investor. However, it was only a very brief remark without any elaboration on which constitutional principles were considered to be at stake or what the constitutional implications were.[79] Similarly, commentaries on the Estonian Constitution do not see any conflict in conferring jurisdiction on private adjudicators either, and stress only the importance of state supervision, which is guaranteed by the possibility of setting aside an arbitral award.[80] In Latvia, the legislator is still not convinced that constitutional principles would require introducing judicial review of any kind of arbitral awards, let alone those rendered in private-public arbitrations. However,

[78] Gus Van Harten, 'The Public-Private Distinction in the International Arbitration of Individuals' Claims Against the State' (2007) 56 ICLQ 371, 372.

[79] Separate Opinion to the Ruling of the Constitutional Court of the Republic of Lithuania, *On the Lawfulness of the Establishment of a National Investor* [2009] CCRL 28/08 ('Whether the State, under the Constitution which has acquired a dimension of Europeanisation, is a commercial entity entitled to enjoy the freedom of contract restricted by the concept of national security . . . ie whether it is entitled to act at its discretion not only on the basis of constitutional powers and restrictions but also on the basis of "private initiative" established in the Law on Nuclear Power Plant, ie without applying any procedures necessary for transparency or fair competition for the purpose of "national security" to choose a private partner from a sole national economic sector . . . to agree that disputes between the state and private entity from the same jurisdiction will be decided by arbitration in Sweden and so on.').

[80] Ülle Madise and others, *Eesti Vabariigi Põhiseadus. Kommenteeritud väljaanne* (Juura 2012) 793.

at the time of the preparation of the present chapter, a case is pending before the Constitutional Court of the Republic of Latvia concerning the constitutionality of the Civil Procedure Law's lack of provisions on the possibility for having awards set aside.[81] Considering this lack of engagement with private-public arbitration from the perspective of constitutional law, all three Baltic States would appear well-advised to revisit their approach towards private-public arbitration and to ensure that it does not compromise the public interests. At the same time, they should bear in mind the purpose of arbitration and the role it plays for the growth of the global economy. It is a difficult balancing exercise to complete.

Select Materials

1. Lithuania

Bibliography

Bieliūnienė, Lina and others, *Viešojo intereso atpažinimo problema Lietuvos teisėje: kriterijai ir prioritetai* (Eugrimas 2016)

Mikelėnas, Valentinas, 'Lietuvos Respublikos Komercinio Arbitražo Įstatymo Dvidešimtmetis: Ištakos, Taikymo Patirtis Ir Perspektyvos' (2016) II Arbitražas. Teorija ir praktika 3

Zemlytė, Eglė, *Valstybė kaip arbitražinio susitarimo šalis* (Registrų centras 2015)

Legislation

Law of the Republic of Lithuania, Re. Provisional Basic Law of the Republic of Lithuania, 1990

Constitution of the Republic of Lithuania 1992

Law on Amending Article 11 of the Law on Commercial Arbitration of the Republic of Lithuania 2001

Law on Commercial arbitration of the Republic of Lithuania 1996 (amended in 2012)

Cases

On the ownership rights of functionaries [1997] CCRL 13/96

On a decree of the President of the Republic [2003] CCRL 40/03

On the state service [2004] CCRL 51/01-26/02-19/03-22/03-26/03-27/03

On the Law on Presidential Elections [2004] CCRL 24/04

[81] *On Compliance of Section 534, 5341, 535, 536 and 537 with the first sentence of Article 92 of the Satversme of the Republic of Latvia*, Constitutional Court of the Republic of Latvia 2022-03-01 (pending).

On the prevention of organised crime [2004] CCRL 8/02-16/02-25/02-9/03-10/03-11/03-36/03-37/03-06/04-09/04-20/04-26/04-30/04-31/04-32/04-34/04-41/0

On the Law on Hunting [2005] CCRL 14/02

On drawing up and announcing the reasoning of court decisions, on the institute of a decision adopted in absentia and on appeals [2006] CCRL 35/03-11/06

On the compensation for damage inflicted by unlawful actions of interrogatory and investigatory bodies, the prosecutor's office, and a court [2006] CCRL 23/04

On private accusations and on the right of the person, against whom the institution of a criminal case is refused, to lodge a complaint against the decision of the prosecutor [2006] CCRL 7/03-41/03-40/04-46/04-5/05-7/05-17/05

VĮ Klaipėdos valstybinio jūrų uosto direkcija v 'Hydro Soil Services NV' [2007] SCLT Civ 3K-3-62/2007

UAB 'Giedra' v Šiaulių miesto savivaldybės administracija [2008] CAL Civ 2A-149/2008

Belaja Rus v Westintorg Corp. [2008] SCLT Civ 3K-3-443/2008

Separate opinion to the Ruling of the Constitutional Court of the Republic of Lithuania *On the lawfulness of the establishment of a national investor* [2009] CCRL 28/08

UAB 'Kauno vandenys' and Aplinkos projektų valdymo agentūra v 'WTE Wassertechnik GmbH' and AB 'Požeminiai darbai' [2011] SCLT Civ 3K-7-304/2011

NVK et al v UAB 'Luksora' [2012] SCLT Civ 3K-3-353/2012

Limited liability company 'Kutter' v UAB 'Abipa Logistics' [2013] SCLT Civ 3K-7-181/2013

LB v Valstybės įmonė Valstybės turto fondas [2014] SCLT Civ 3K-3-363/2014

Interperformances Inc v RJ [2015] SCLT Civ e3K-3-483-421/2015

VilniusLux, UAB, Gemmo S.p.A, VSLS OU v Vilniaus miesto savivaldybės administracija [2017] CAL Civ e2A-644-370/2017

Suraleb, INC v Atviroji akcinė bendrovė Minsko traktorių gamykla [2017] SCLT Civ 3K-3-267-611/2017

Other documents

Explanatory note to the Law on Amending Article 11 of the Law on Commercial Arbitration of the Republic of Lithuania 2000

Comments of the Committee of Legal Affairs of the Parliament of the Republic of Lithuania on the Draft Law Amending the Law on Commercial Arbitration 2012 <http://www3.lrs.lt/pls/inter3/dokpaieska.showdoc_l?p_id=425946> accessed 23 January 2025

2. Estonia

Bibliography

Madise, Ülle and others, *Eesti Vabariigi Põhiseadus. Kommenteeritud väljaanne* (Juura 2012)

Põldvere, Pirkka-Marja, 'Kaheksa aastat mudelseadust: kas Eesti vahekohtumenetlus vastab mudelile?' (2014) 1 Juridica 17

Kove, Villu and others, *Tsiviilkohtumenetluse seadustik III. Kommenteeritud väljanne* (Juura 2018)

Legislation

Implementation Act of the Constitution of the Republic of Estonia 1992
Code of Civil Procedure of the Republic of Estonia 2005

Cases

Constitutional Judgment [2008] SCE Civ 3-4-1-1-08
Avaldaja Vene Föderatsiooni äriühing OF v D OÜ [2016] SCE Civ 3-2-1-186-15
Parties unknown [2018] SCE Civ 2-16-15675

3. Latvia

Bibliography

Bērtraitis, Sandris, 'Valsts nedrīkst pieļaut prettiesisku praksi strīdu alternatīvajā risināšanā, (2014) 22 Jurista Vārds 14
Bukovskis, Vladimirs, *Civīlprocesa mācības grāmata* (Autora izdevums 1933)
Kačevska, Inga, 'Ir normāla situācija, un ir Latvijas situācija' (2014) 22 Jurista Vārds 23
Krūmiņš, Toms, 'Arbitration in Latvia: A Cautionary Tale?' (2017) 34 J Int'l Arb 303
Lizinska, Nērika, *Valsts kā starptautiska šķīrējtiesas līguma puse* (Latvijas Universitātes Juridiskās fakultātes promocijas darbs 2020) <https://dspace.lu.lv/dspace/handle/7/53367> accessed 23 January 2025
Repšs, Agris, 'Nav pamata neizdot izpildrakstu ad hoc šķīrējtiesu spriedumiem' (2014) Jurista Vārds 18
Rozenbergs, Jānis and Imants Briģis, *Padomju Civilprocesa tiesības* (Zvaigzne ABC 2010)
Tipaine, Maija, 'Šķīrējtiesu reputāciju grauj neitralitātes trūkums' (2014) 22 Jurista Vārds 20
Tipaine, Maija and Līga Fjodorova, 'Arbitration in Latvia: Was a Restart a Failure?' (*Kluwer Arbitration Blog*, 25 January 2016)
Ūdris, Ziedonis, 'Uzticību šķīrējtiesām var nodrošināt ar tiesas kontroli pār to nolēmumiem' [2014] 22 Jurista Vārds 21
Ūdris, Ziedonis and Inga Kačevska, 'Arbitration in Latvia: Urgent Need for Statutory Reform' (2004) 21(2) J Int'l Arb 211

Legislation

Law on Municipalities of the Republic of Latvia 1994
Civil Procedure Law of the Republic of Latvia 1999
Law 'On International Treaties of the Republic of Latvia' 2004
Law On Arbitrations of the Republic of Latvia 2015

Cases

On Compliance of Section 27 (4) and the Text of Section 28 (2) 'for the Time Period until the Age of 65 Years' of Law on Institutions of Higher Education and Section 29 (5) of Law On Scientific Activity with Articles 91 and 106 of the Satversme of the Republic of Latvia [2003] Constitutional Court of the Republic of Latvia 2002-21-01

Ģenerālprokuratūras Personu un valsts tiesību aizsardzības departamenta virsprokurora v AS 'Latvijas valsts meži' [2013] SCLV Civ SPC-46/2013

On Compliance of Section 495(1) of the Civil procedure Law with the first sentence in Article 92 of the Constitution of the Republic of Latvia [2014] Constitutional Court of Latvia 2014-09-01

On Compliance of Para 55 and Para 56 of the Riga City Council Binding Regulation of 18 June 2013 No. 221 'The Binding Regulation on the Use of and Construction in the Territory of Culture and Recreation Park "Mežaparks"', as well its Annex No. 1 'The Planned (Permitted) Use of the Territory', Insofar They Apply to the Planned (Permitted) Use of the Immovable Property at 10 Pāvu Street, Riga (Cadastre No 0100 095 0003) with Article 105 of the Satversme of the Republic of Latvia [2014] Constitutional Court of the Republic of Latvia 2014-04-03

On Compliance of Para 2361 'Use of Territory and Construction Rules' of Binding Regulation No 8 of 24 March 2016 by Jūrmala City Council 'On Approving the Graphic Part, Regulation on the Use of Territory and Construction in the Spatial Plan of Jūrmala City' with Article 115 of the Satversme of the Republic of Latvia [2017] Constitutional Court of the Republic of Latvia 2016-24-03

On Compliance of Section 3, 5, 6, 7 and 9 of the Law On Solidarity Tax with the First Sentence of Article 91 and Article 109 of the Satversme [2017] Constitutional Court of the Republic of Latvia 2016-14-01

PART II
PRIVATE-PUBLIC ARBITRATION IN THE AMERICAS

9

Whither Leviathan?

The Seepage of Constitutional Law into Public-Private Arbitration in the United States

Peter B. Rutledge[*]

In *Arbitration and the Constitution*, I sought to undertake the first sustained treatment of the relationship between arbitration law and United States (US) constitutional law.[1] The central theme of the book was that, as arbitration grew in popularity in the US during the second half of the twentieth century, fissures formed in the wall that historically had separated those two fields. As a result of these fissures, doctrines from the two fields began to intermix. Critically, though, this blending of doctrines rarely occurred at the level of express constitutional law. Instead, the underpinning constitutional norms seeped into arbitration law in other ways—through the design of treaties, the interpretation of statutes, and the development of privately enforced norms, just to name a few examples.

The book focused primarily on commercial arbitration (both domestic and international) and offered only sporadic consideration of arbitrations involving states or state-owned entities. This chapter picks up where the book left off and strives to offer a systematic treatment of the issue. While this chapter (as the book did) focuses primarily on US constitutional law, its architecture can be easily adapted to an analysis of other constitutional regimes or, indeed, supply a template for a comparative undertaking.

My central thesis is that constitutional law exerts a powerful influence on arbitration law, though not in the manner that the casual observer would expect. Rarely does a US court hold that a particular arbitration or arbitration law directly transgressed the Constitution. Instead, constitutional norms are more likely to influence arbitration at a subconstitutional level. These means of influence may include, for example, statutory interpretation doctrines, treaty design, and the development of private protocols reflecting constitutional norms. This pattern of influence manifests itself in public arbitration (ie arbitration involving states or state-owned entities) just as it does in private arbitration.

* Dean and Herman E Talmadge Chair of Law, University of Georgia School of Law. The author served as part of the delegation for the American Arbitration Association to the UNCITRAL Arbitration Working Group II during the development of the Transparency Rules. The views expressed in this chapter, however, are entirely his own and do not reflect the views of any institution with which he may be, or has been, affiliated.

[1] Peter B Rutledge, *Arbitration and the Constitution* (CUP 2013).

Peter B. Rutledge, *Whither Leviathan?* In: *The Comparative Constitutional Foundations of Private-Public Arbitration*. Edited by: Stephan W. Schill, Oxford University Press.
DOI: 10.1093/9780191987960.003.0009

The chapter unfolds in three sections. Section I lays out a general theoretical framework for analysing the relationship between arbitration law and constitutional law. Section II applies this theoretical framework to the particular case of arbitrations involving states or state-owned entities (whether in the context of investment arbitration, trade arbitration, or garden-variety commercial arbitration stemming from an agreement with such an entity). Section III examines the implications of the thesis for the broader project and offers a road map for future research in the area, particularly its implications for the ongoing project on the relationship between public-private arbitration and transnational regulatory governance.

I. Architecture

At first glance, constitutional law and arbitration law might seem like strange bedfellows. In many (but certainly not all) instances, constitutions regulate either relationships between the state and private parties (individuals or entities) or relationships among various arms of the state. Constitutions generally have little to say about purely private relationships. By contrast, arbitrations typically involve efforts by private parties to opt out from the state's system of dispute resolution and, instead, have their dispute resolved before neutral private referees whose decisions presumptively bind the parties. (Arbitrations involving states or state-owned entities supply an exception to this general construct, and section II examines this scenario systematically.)

Despite the chasm that would appear to separate constitutional law and arbitration law, this has not historically always been the case. Some early constitutional documents expressly addressed the subject of arbitration. Some documents addressed arbitration involving purely private parties. For example, the French Constitution of 1793 guaranteed that '[t]he right of the citizens finally to resolve their disputes through arbitrators of their choice cannot in any respect be decreased by law.'[2] Other documents addressed arbitration involving state entities. For example, the Articles of Confederation (the organic document governing the US immediately following the American Revolution), specified that disputes among the states shall be resolved by 'five commissioners or judges' who may be subject to peremptory strikes by the parties.[3]

In contrast to these historical examples (both of which, curiously, come from the late eighteenth century), most modern constitutions do not explicitly address the right to arbitration (whether among purely private parties, as in the French Constitution, or involving public entities, as in the Articles of Confederation). One might suppose, then, that the two fields simply have nothing to say to each other—that they are, indeed, strange bedfellows. Or, if they share the same bed, a thick wall separates them.

Such a view would, however, be wrong or, at best, incomplete. Notwithstanding the lack of express textual command, constitutional doctrine exerts important influences on arbitration law at several levels. This section examines that influence at three different levels: horizontal separation of powers, vertical separation of powers, and

[2] French Constitution of the Year (1793) art 86.
[3] Articles of Confederation (1781) art IX.

individual rights. A central theme that cuts across all three areas is that the influence generally does not occur at the level of express constitutional doctrine. Pre-emption, a topic I explore below, supplies an exception to this general principle. Indeed, virtually nothing in the modern jurisprudence of the Supreme Court of the United States suggests that the Constitution mandates issues not to be resolved by arbitration, although, as noted below, the Constitution may mandate that certain issues be resolved by federal courts. Instead, the underlying constitutional norms influence what might be termed subconstitutional behaviour, whether by courts (through their interpretation of statutes or treaties), by lawmakers (through their design of such documents), or by private parties (through their design of dispute resolution systems).

A. Horizontal Separation of Powers

As noted in the Introduction, constitutions ordinarily regulate the distribution of power among different branches of the national government. The US Constitution is no exception. It vests the US Congress with various law-making powers, including, among others, the power '[t]o regulate Commerce with foreign Nations, and among the several States, and with the Indian Tribes.'[4] Pursuant to this commerce-regulating power, Congress enacted the Federal Arbitration Act (FAA), the principal law regulating commercial arbitration in the US.[5] The FAA, like most national arbitration laws, sets forth a presumptive obligation to enforce both executory arbitration agreements and arbitral awards.[6] Under the FAA, a court 'must grant' an order to confirm an arbitral award unless, inter alia, it vacates the award pursuant to section 10.[7] Section 10, again like most national arbitral laws, sets forth limited grounds for vacatur, such as fraud, bias, or misconduct.[8]

The Constitution also vests the federal judiciary (ie the national court system, as opposed to the court systems of the individual states) with jurisdiction over a limited class of cases. This judicial power is vested 'in one Supreme Court, and in such inferior courts as the Congress may from time to time ordain and establish' and extends to various classes of cases or controversies, including 'all cases, in law and equity, arising under this Constitution, the laws of the United States, and treaties made, or which

[4] US Constitution, art I, s 8.

[5] Unlike the laws of many countries, the US does not have a free-standing international arbitration law. Instead, international proceedings often are governed by the provisions of the Federal Arbitration Act (FAA) that govern domestic arbitration. Indeed, the implementing legislation for the New York Convention and the Panama Convention presumptively require application of the domestic chapter of the FAA to the extent that chapter is not inconsistent with the implementing legislation. This general overlap often causes federal courts, including the Supreme Court of the US, to draw on domestic arbitral jurisprudence to inform the resolution of legal questions surrounding an international case. See eg *BG Group plc v Republic of Argentina* (2014) 134 S Ct 1198. The domestic analogy, however, has its limits. Specifically, chs 2 and 3 contain some provisions distinct from the domestic FAA. Moreover, the implementing legislation for the Convention on the Settlement of Investment Disputes between States and Nationals of Other States (ICSID Convention) (adopted 18 March 1965, entered into force 14 October 1966, 575 UNTS 159) expressly provides that the FAA does not apply. See 22 USC §1650a.

[6] 9 USC 2, 9, 10.

[7] 9 USC 9.

[8] 9 USC 10.

shall be made, under their authority'.[9] Pursuant to this judicial power, the Supreme Court and lower federal courts interpret federal laws and assess their compatibility with the Constitution.

Arbitration sets up a potential collision between these two constitutional rules. The FAA enables binding arbitration of disputes, including those involving federal laws (such as the employment or consumer laws). It is justified as an exercise of Congress' power to regulate interstate commerce.[10] That same statute, though, obligates federal courts (with limited exceptions set forth in section 10) to enforce awards rendered in such arbitrations—that is, to give those awards the same effect as if they were court-rendered judgments. This obligation arguably intrudes upon the vesting of the judicial power to resolve cases or controversies in the federal courts.[11]

The Supreme Court has twice rendered decisions that potentially bear on this apparent collision. The first, *Thomas v Union Carbide Agricultural Products Co*, involved a constitutional challenge to an arbitration scheme, albeit an unusual one.[12] *Thomas* involved a scheme for obtaining regulatory approval of pesticides and required registrants to submit data illustrating a product's health, safety, and environmental effects. The agency could consider 'follow-on data' (ie relevant data submitted by a prior applicant) only if the new applicant had offered to compensate the prior applicant for use of the data. In the event that a dispute arose over compensation, the scheme provided for binding arbitration, and the resulting award was judicially reviewable only for 'fraud, misrepresentation, or other misconduct'. Prior applicants challenged the constitutionality of that arbitration scheme, but the Court disagreed. It reasoned that the right at issue (the right to use another registrant's data) qualified as a 'public right' and did not require *de novo* judicial review of the arbitrator's award. The meaning of 'public right' was somewhat unclear—historically, this had been understood as a claim against the state (such as a claim for government benefits), but *Thomas* extended it to encompass statutorily created rights (as opposed to ones that historically existed at common law).[13] This capacious definition of 'public rights'

[9] US Constitution, art III.

[10] *Citizens Bank v Alfabco, Inc* (2003) 539 US 52 (per curiam); *Allied Bruce Terminix, Co v Dobson* (1995) 513 US 265.

[11] At one point, the non-arbitrability doctrine effectively served to reduce the tension between these two systems. The robust non-arbitrability doctrine that prevailed in the US for the first half-century following the FAA's enactment preserved for federal courts a robust 'law-making' (or at least 'law-elaborating') function as to the meaning of federal law. See Rutledge (n 1) 4, 16. Since the mid 1970s, the US Supreme Court has slowly chipped away at the doctrine. The jurisprudential principles were initially developed in the international setting and then slowly incorporated into the domestic arbitration jurisprudence. At present, the trend in US law favours a robust arbitrability jurisprudence absent clear language in a congressional statute precluding arbitration of particular statutory claims. See eg *CompuCredit Corp v Greenwood* (2012) 565 US 95. Moreover, that same jurisprudence has stripped states of any authority to declare claims non-arbitrable except in truly intra-state cases that fall outside the FAA's ambit. See eg *Doctor's Associates, Inc v Casarotto* (1996) 517 US 681.

[12] *Thomas v Union Carbide Agricultural Products Co* (1985) 473 US 568.

[13] For non-American observers, especially ones from civil law traditions, the public rights jurisprudence is puzzling. The implication is that statutorily created rights—where the law-making body has indicated some public interest in their creation—are less entitled to judicial resolution than ones historically rooted in the common law. While this doctrine has been stretched in its modern form, the original form of the doctrine finds its roots in principles of sovereign immunity. Originally, public rights tended to be statutorily created claims against the government (over matters such as customs duties or government benefits). The starting point for the analysis is that a sovereign is generally immune from suit in its own courts (or in the

enabled courts, after *Thomas*, to reject constitutional challenges to arbitration, particularly where the arbitration concerned statutory claims.[14]

The second, *CFTC v Schor*, did not involve arbitration but, instead, an administrative agency adjudicating common law counterclaims that otherwise would have fallen within the jurisdiction of the federal courts.[15] Rejecting a constitutional challenge to this scheme, the Court reasoned that the objecting party had waived any right to a federal judicial forum by consenting to have his counterclaim heard before the agency (he objected to the agency's jurisdiction only after it ruled against him). Based on this waiver theory, other federal courts routinely rejected constitutional challenges to arbitration and reasoned that, by analogy, parties to an arbitration had waived any right to have their dispute heard in a federal forum.[16]

In *Arbitration and the Constitution*, I explain how neither of these theories supplies a completely satisfactory answer to this puzzle. The 'public rights' theory articulated by *Thomas* suffered from at least two shortcomings. First, its definition of 'public rights' went far beyond the historical understanding of the term. Second, however public rights were defined, the decision neither explained whether Congress could eliminate judicial review entirely nor whether a more expansive review (beyond the standard set forth in the statute at issue in *Thomas*) was required for claims that clearly qualified private rights.

Moreover, the consent theory articulated by *Schor* was equally problematic. It failed to explain how a structural guarantee could be waived by individual conduct (by analogy, one could not say that an individual can 'waive' a separation-of-powers challenge to a statutory scheme). Perhaps in recognition of this shortcoming, *Schor* admitted that there was a 'non-waivable' component to Article III of the Constitution, yet nowhere did it clearly demarcate the scope of that 'non-waivable' component or explore its implications for other schemes (such as arbitration). Put another way, *Schor* left open the possibility, however remote, that an arbitral scheme might survive constitutional muster even if Congress eliminated entirely any room for judicial review and simply required federal courts to enforce automatically any arbitral award.

To remedy the shortcomings of these prevailing theories, *Arbitration and the Constitution* articulated an alternative theory. Drawing on the work of Richard Fallon, the book explained how a theory of modified appellate arbitral review can salvage most arbitrations from constitutional challenge. The scope of constitutionally mandated review necessarily had to be calibrated to the nature of the claim. On one end,

courts of another sovereign). Consequently, if the sovereign affirmatively chooses to surrender that immunity (either by waiver or, under the restrictive theory, by engaging in certain non-sovereign activities), the sovereign can subject its amenability to suit to any conditions that it wishes. Thus, the argument concludes, the greater power to immunize the sovereign from suit entirely necessarily includes the lesser power to condition the terms upon which the sovereign can be sued (including the scope of judicial review by the sovereign's courts). While modern jurisprudence has stretched the doctrine beyond its original underpinnings to include statutory claims (irrespective of whether those claims are advanced against a sovereign), the doctrine in its original form continues to have significant explanatory value for arbitration of claims involving states or state-owned entities where sovereign immunity considerations would still be relevant.

[14] See eg *Katz v Cellco P'ship* (SDNY, 12 December 2013) [2013] WL 6621022.
[15] *CFTC v Schor* (1986) 478 US 833.
[16] See eg *Cremin v Merrill Lynch, Pierce, Fenner & Smith* (1997) 957 F Supp 1460.

in cases where the voluntariness of the arbitration agreement was unquestioned and the dispute involved quintessential public rights (ie claims against the sovereign), the need for Article III review was at its nadir. On the other end, in cases where the voluntariness of the agreement was questionable and the dispute involved quintessential private rights (at a minimum, historically common law claims between private parties), the need for Article III review was at its zenith.

Accordingly, where the need for judicial review was relatively greater, other doctrines served to avoid the constitutional conflict. In this regard, the hotly debated manifest disregard of the law doctrine (or, perhaps since the Court's decision in *Stolt Nielsen*, the 'exceeding powers' ground under section 10(a)(4) of the FAA) served a potentially important function. It reserved (at least theoretically) for the courts a 'second look' at the merits of the arbitrator's decision. Such review doctrines (much like the 'public policy' ground found in other arbitral systems) preserved the judiciary's role in the system of checks and balances and helped to avoid the constitutional collision.[17] Here, then, we see our first example of constitutional norms—horizontal separation of powers—operating at a subconstitutional level in the form of judicially created standards for reviewing awards.

B. Vertical Separation of Powers

Federalist systems such as the US raise distinct questions about the distribution of power between national and local sovereigns. Questions about this distribution arise along at least two axes. First, such systems confront questions of prescriptive jurisdiction—that is, the distribution of power between national and local law-making bodies to enact substantive rules regulating conduct. Second, such systems confront questions of judicial jurisdiction, that is, the distribution of power between national and local courts to resolve controversies. Underlying choice-of-law issues thread through both sets of questions—to wit, (1) to what extent do prescriptions by the national law-making body displace those of the local entity (ie pre-emption)? And (2) to what extent are courts in one system (national or local) obliged to apply the substantive rules adopted by the legislative entity in the other system (ie conflict of laws)?

These questions permeate arbitration law in the US, and represent one of the few areas in which constitutional law and arbitration law intermix at an express doctrinal level. As to both sets of questions, the doctrinal boundaries are especially murky. The answer to the conflict-of-laws question is relatively clearer. At a minimum, section 2 of the FAA (governing the enforceability of executory arbitration agreements) applies in state court proceedings.[18] Whether other sections of the FAA (as in the provisions governing judicial review of awards) also apply in state court remains an open, and much more nettlesome, question.[19]

[17] Consistent with this view of the manifest disregard of the law doctrine (or s 10(a)(4) of the FAA), federal courts have resisted efforts to narrow by contract the vacatur grounds available under federal law. See eg *Bowen v Amoco Pipeline Co* (2001) 254 F3d 925 (10th Cir).

[18] *Southland Corp v Keating* (1984) 465 US 1.

[19] See eg *Siegel v Prudential Ins Co* (1998) 67 Cal App 4th 1270 (California Court of Appeal).

The answer to the pre-emption question is even more complex. Section 2 of the Federal Arbitration Act provides that arbitration agreements generally are enforceable 'save upon such grounds as exist at law or in equity for the revocation of any contract'.[20] The Supreme Court has interpreted this provision to require the testing of the arbitration clause against generally applicable state contract law principles.[21] States may not 'single out' arbitration either by declaring certain categories of disputes 'non-arbitrable' or creating unique burdens to arbitration agreements.[22] Courts may, however, refuse to enforce arbitration agreements where they are invalid under a doctrine that would apply to contracts generally (such as fraud, incapacity, or duress).[23]

The answers to these two questions—the conflict of law question and the pre-emption question—have important effects on both the vertical and horizontal distribution of power within a federalist system. Applying the federal standard in state court, but then tying it to the generally applicable state contract law, has the effect of shifting regulation of arbitration agreements to state court judges, who may be more politically unaccountable than their legislative counterparts (depending, of course, on the manner in which those judges are selected). A legislature could not declare a class of arbitration agreements unenforceable, but a court might achieve the same result by finding that the agreement violated public policy (and also finding that public policy constituted a generally applicable defence under that state's contract law).

A brief example elucidates the point. A state court hostile to arbitration could not directly declare an arbitration clause unenforceable. However, it could, under the guise of applying generally applicable contract defences, declare that 'public policy' supplied one such defence (ie contracts contrary to 'public policy' were unenforceable). It would then discern a 'public policy' (such as a public policy favouring access to courts or protection of consumers in its state jurisprudence). Invalidation of the arbitration agreement would follow, then, as a straightforward application of this generally applicable contract defence.

Such was the state of affairs until a few years ago, when the Supreme Court began to show a greater willingness to police state courts' application of their generally applicable contract defences. Beginning with its decision in *AT&T Mobility, LLC v Concepcion*, the Court peered behind those doctrines (like unconscionability) to examine whether state courts were allowing an anti-arbitration jurisprudence to masquerade as the anodyne application of contract doctrines.[24] This had the consequence of vertically wresting some of that authority away from the states entirely and depositing it with Congress, which could declare (and at times has declared) categories of claims non-arbitrable, effectively making these matters of federal law.

FAA pre-emption jurisprudence represents the rare instance in which constitutional law operates directly on arbitration. Through the Constitution's pre-emption provision, federal law applies in state court and, to a degree, displaces state law. That equilibrium has shifted over time, from one that vested state courts with great power

[20] 9 USC 2.
[21] See *First Options of Chicago, Inc v Kaplan* (1995) 514 US 938.
[22] See *Marmet Health Care Center, Inc v Brown* (2012) 132 S Ct 1201.
[23] See *Doctor's Assocs, Inc v Casarotto* (1996) 517 US 681, 682.
[24] *AT&T Mobility, LLC v Concepcion* (2011) 563 US 333.

(indeed, far more than state legislatures enjoyed) to one that has largely vested that power once again in the national political branches.

C. Individual Rights

As noted in the Introduction, one core function of most constitutions is to regulate the relationship between the state and private parties. This typically comes in the form of 'rights' which operate as bulwarks against state action that otherwise might deprive citizens of some liberty (whether it be freedom of speech, freedom of assembly, or something else). A critical right central to dispute resolution generally is the right of 'due process'. While the meaning of that term has been hotly debated for centuries, if not millennia, at its core the concept appears to require some combination of notice, an opportunity to be heard, and a fair (but certainly not flawless) system of procedures for resolving disputes. This right unquestionably constrains dispute resolution systems (such as civil litigation) in which the state's coercive power is invoked.

But does it also constrain private systems, like arbitration, where the state's coercive power may never be invoked (except, perhaps, to enforce an arbitration agreement or award)? As a formal matter, under US constitutional law, the answer would appear to be no. This is because due process, like almost all federal constitutional rights, requires an element of state action.[25] Consequently, many courts have found that arbitration, unlike civil litigation, is not subject to the formal requirements of 'procedural due process' because it does not constitute state action.[26]

[25] The Third Circuit's decision in *Strine* provides a rare case where a court relied on individual rights jurisprudence to invalidate an arbitral system. See *Delaware Coalition for Open Government, Inc v Strine* (2013) 733 F3d 510 (3d Cir). Notably, in *Strine*, sitting judges were serving as arbitrators. This unique feature enabled the Third Circuit to fold the case within the fabric of state action governing most constitutional rights jurisprudence. In most cases, whether commercial arbitrations or public/private arbitrations, that distinctive feature would be lacking.

[26] See Rutledge (n 1) 130 fn 8 (collecting cases). Of course, it could be argued that state action occurs when a court enforces an award rendered by (or compels arbitration in) a system that lacks the ordinary requirements of procedural due process. As I explain in my book, this 'state action by enforcement' argument generally has not carried sway either in the specific context of arbitration law or the more general context of American constitutional law. See Rutledge (n 1) 131 ff. Judicial refusals to enforce racially restrictive covenants on real property stand as a notable exception to this general trend. As to the converse proposition, courts in the US (at least federal ones) generally have been sceptical of party-initiated efforts to cabin the scope of judicial review. The Supreme Court has affirmatively rejected efforts to expand judicial review, though those efforts have found some greater solicitude among state courts. Compare *Hall Street Assocs LLC v Mattel Inc*, 552 US 576 (SCt) with *NAFTA Traders, Inc v Quinn*, 399 SW3d 84 (Tex 2011). In *Hall Street Assocs LLC*, the Supreme Court held that ss 10 and 11 of the FAA provide exclusive grounds for expedited vacatur and modification, precluding parties from contracting to expand the grounds available for vacating and modifying arbitration awards. The Court reasoned that a limited judicial review of an arbitrator's decision was necessary to maintain arbitration's essential value of resolving disputes quickly and efficiently. The decision, however, does not address whether an agreement providing for expanded review may be enforced through utilization of other authorities, such as state statutory authority or common law. Specifically, questions remain as to whether expanded review may be utilized in state court, be obtained using §10(a)(4) of the FAA by directing the arbitrators to follow the law or deny arbitrators authority to make legal or other errors, or under state arbitration law. It is likely that expanded review provisions will be enforceable in state court rather than in federal court. See Christopher R Drahozal, 'Contracting Around Hall Street' (2010) 14 Lewis & Clark L Rev 905. Recent decisions indicate that state courts have been willing to respect the parties' explicit agreement in limiting the arbitrator's authority through contract. In *Cable Connection, Inc v Directv* (Cal 2008), 190 P 3d 586, the California Supreme Court held that the

While that view may be formally accurate, it is woefully incomplete. Despite the absence of express engrafting of procedural due process onto arbitration, many of the same underlying norms have been incorporated into private dispute resolution systems through other means. Major arbitral associations, such as the American Arbitration Association, have required that certain disputes (for instance, those involving employment, consumer, or health care claims) be administered in compliance with their 'due process protocols'. Those protocols, developed by means of a collaborative undertaking with stakeholders in such disputes, contain many of the protections that one would normally associate with the procedural due process constraints on public litigation systems and, in some respects, address matters unaddressed by those systems.

As in the doctrines discussed at the end of subsection A, the due process protocols supply another example of how constitutional norms seep into arbitration jurisprudence through means other than express constitutional doctrine. By contrast, though, those norms develop in a very different fashion. Instead of being designed by a coordinate branch of government, they are assembled through private actors. This raises important questions about not only the *means* whereby constitutional norms infiltrate arbitration but, just as importantly, the *institutions* whereby those norms are developed.

Beyond private norms, due process principles seep into arbitral jurisprudence by another means, namely treaty interpretation. Various international treaties, including the New York Convention, set forth grounds for refusing enforcement of awards.[27] For example, Article (V)(1)(b) of the New York Convention provides that a court may refuse enforcement when the losing party lacked notice of the proceedings was unable to present its case. Notably, this provision does not refer to the constitutional law of the enforcement jurisdiction or, for that matter, even identify the law applicable to this defence. Nonetheless, US courts consistently have held that this ground 'essentially sanctions application of the forum state's standards of due process'.[28] This judicial interpretation helps to embed constitutional principles within international arbitration jurisprudence without expressly 'constitutionalizing' the field as a doctrinal matter.

FAA provisions were not controlling on appellate review of an arbitration award conducted in state court, and that FAA provisions do not pre-empt state law grounds for expanded review. The court reasoned that the FAA did not prevent the enforcement of agreements to arbitrate under different rules, and therefore parties may specify, by contract, the rules under which arbitration will be conducted, including expanded review. Similarly, in *NAFTA Traders, Inc* the Texas Supreme Court, applying s 10(a)(4) of the FAA, held that state law did not preclude parties from agreeing to expanded review provisions, and that the FAA did not pre-empt enforcement of the agreement. As to efforts to contract that review (analogous to Belgium's international arbitration law), the few reported decisions have reached conflicting conclusions. Compare *Hoeft v MVL Group, Inc* (2d Cir 2003) 343 F 3d 57 (overruled in part) and *Bowen v Amoco Pipeline Co* (10th Cir 2001) 254 F3d 925 (requiring the agreement to comply with the standards set forth in s 10 of the FAA) with *MACTEC, Inc v Gorelick* (10th Cir 2005) 427 F3d 821, though the jurisprudence might be reconciled on the standard that any contractual contraction of judicial review must be clear and unequivocal. See generally Patrick Gill, 'No Do-overs for Parties Who Agree to Limit Review of an Arbitrator's Decision' [2006] J Disp Resol 643.

[27] See eg United Nations Convention on the Recognition and Enforcement of Arbitral Awards (adopted 10 June 1958, entered into force 7 June 1959) 330 UNTS 3 (New York Convention) art V.

[28] *Parsons & Whittemore Overseas Co, Inc v Societe Generale de L'Industrie du Papier (RAKTA)* (1974) 508 F2d 969, 975 (2d Cir).

II. The Case of Public Entities

The preceding section articulated a framework by which to evaluate how constitutional law and arbitration law intermix. The upshot was that rarely (with the exception of pre-emption doctrine) does constitutional law expressly constrain arbitration. Instead, the underlying constitutional norms (whether separation of powers, federalism, or individual liberty) influence arbitration law through subconstitutional means. These may include statutory interpretation, the articulation of common law doctrines, or the development of private norms. This section applies that framework to the discrete area of arbitration involving states or state-owned entities.[29] It considers three topics: (A) judicial review, (B) executive power, and (C) transparency. In each of these areas, one can begin to see an answer to the question posed at the end of the last section—how governmental institutions facilitate the seepage of constitutional norms into arbitration, even absent express constitutional command.

A. Judicial Review

As scholars of arbitration repeatedly have noted, limited judicial review of arbitral awards is a near-universal feature of most countries' legal regimes. This limited judicial review manifests itself both in vacatur actions (generally governed by the law of the arbitral forum) and in enforcement actions (often governed by the applicable treaty, such as the New York Convention of 1958 or the Washington Convention of 1965). The precise contours of the legal regime will vary with the country, depending on the sweep of its arbitral law (in vacatur actions) and/or the treaties to which it is a party (in enforcement actions).

Against this general backdrop, trade and investment arbitration presents a unique set of challenges. Unlike purely private commercial arbitration between private parties, arbitrations involving states or state-owned entities raise questions about the sovereign's amenability to suit. Historically, as a matter of international law, sovereigns were absolutely immune from suit. Until the twentieth century, that international norm prevailed in the US as a matter of federal common law (subject to certain exceptions such as waiver of the sovereign's immunity). Consequently, most claims involving foreign sovereigns were resolved through means such as espousal, state-to-state arbitration, or claims settlement mechanisms.

This history helps to frame our understanding of the law governing states or state-owned entities. Any relaxation of the sovereign's absolute immunity from suit often resulted from some action by the legislative and/or executive branches. It followed, then, that if those branches could trim the immunity blanket, they likewise (especially in the case of the legislative branch) could control the scope of judicial review of any decisions in cases involving sovereigns. Review might be plenary or, more likely,

[29] On some of the salient distinctions between commercial and investment arbitration in the context of the development of governance norms, see Stephan W Schill, 'The Sixth Path: Reforming Investment Law from Within' in Jean E Kalicki and Anna Joubin-Bret (eds), *Reshaping the Investor-State Dispute Settlement System: Journeys for the 21st Century* (Brill 2015) 621.

quite limited. Indeed, one hallmark of arbitral awards involving states or state-owned entities is that review is far more limited than the review that might otherwise be available in cases involving purely private parties. But if that is the case, why precisely does this not run afoul of Article III and the vesting of the judicial power in one Supreme Court and the lower federal courts that Congress may establish?

Before further unpacking the answer, it is important to differentiate between two different types of cases. One type of case would be a garden-variety commercial arbitration involving a state (or, more likely, a state-owned entity). The second type of case would be a trade or investment arbitration against a state pursuant to a trade treaty (like the recently replaced North American Free Trade Agreement (NAFTA)) or a bilateral investment treaty.[30]

Differentiating between these two cases is important because the awards are subject to two radically different regimes. Private commercial arbitration involving a state or state-owned entity would generally be subject to federal jurisdiction under the Foreign Sovereign Immunities Act.[31] In arbitrations sited in the US, section 10 of the FAA would generally govern any vacatur actions. In arbitration sited elsewhere, Article V of the New York Convention (or the virtually identical provisions of the Panama Convention) would govern any enforcement actions in the US. This is largely the view articulated by the recent Restatement (Third) of the United States Law of International Commercial Arbitration.[32]

Trade and investment arbitration involving foreign states are subject to very different regimes. In the case of trade arbitration, the relevant trade treaties set forth the scope of judicial review of the award. For example, under the NAFTA, a party's only recourse following an adverse decision by an extraordinary challenge committee (or if such a committee is not convened, a binational panel) is to file a constitutional challenge in federal court.[33] In a case of investment arbitration, section 10 of the FAA again would generally govern any vacatur actions. Depending on the nature of the dispute (and the identity of the states), either the Washington Convention of 1965 or one of the aforementioned commercial arbitration conventions would set forth the standard governing enforceability of the award. In contrast to the New York and Panama Conventions, the Washington Convention provides that the award shall not be subject to any appeal (except annulment by an ICSID annulment committee panel) and obligates signatory states to recognize an ICSID award as if it were a final judgment of that state.[34]

The exceptional limits on judicial review raise potential concerns under Article III. Treaties (at least in cases where they are self-executing or are accompanied by

[30] Since the chapter was originally drafted, the US, Canada, and Mexico have agreed to replace NAFTA with the United States–Mexico–Canada Agreement (USMCA). At present, the effective date of the USMCA is not known. While the USMCA dispute resolution provisions differ in some respects from NAFTA's, those differences do not bear directly on the theoretical argument advanced here. See generally David Gantz, 'The United States-Mexico-Canada Agreement: Settlement of Disputes' (2019) BIPP.

[31] 28 USC § 1605(a).

[32] Restatement (Third) US Law of Int'l Comm Arb ch 5 (Proposed Final Draft, 24 April 2019).

[33] See NAFTA implementing legislation. An example, albeit a rather far-fetched hypothetical, might be a situation where the extraordinary challenge committee resolved a matter on the basis of a party's race.

[34] ICSID Convention (n 5) arts 53–54. See 22 USC §1650a. See also *Mobil Cerro Negro Ltd v Venezuela* (2017) 863 F3d 96 (2d Cir) (discussing the ICSID Convention and implementing legislation).

implementing legislation) form part of the 'laws of the United States'.[35] To the extent those treaties give rise to substantive rights, Article III extends to the federal courts the power to resolve cases or controversies arising under those laws. Arbitration under these schemes, accompanied by limited judicial review, constrains that role. Compared to the schemes at issue in *Thomas* or *Schor*, the scope of judicial review is far more attenuated. Moreover, to the extent these sorts of arbitration do not involve privity between the parties, the dubious but helpful consent rationale employed by *Schor* lacks much explanatory punch.

To escape this dilemma, most commentators (and the governments defending these schemes) typically invoke the public rights doctrine. In these cases, by contrast to *Thomas*, the public rights argument carries more powerful explanatory value. Modern trade and investment arbitration involve the core of public rights—that is, state-created claims against a sovereign government. As to this core of cases, it has been the consistent view of the Supreme Court that Congress is not obligated to provide for any judicial review (in an important, but little-known, line of cases, the Court has actually upheld certain administrative schemes (such as certain claims for government benefits) that provide for no Article III review whatsoever).[36] In other words, not only does the NAFTA scheme survive constitutional scrutiny, but the Washington Convention of 1965 (which has never been subject to constitutional challenge in the US) would do so as well.[37]

Yet, despite the apparent outer constitutional limits of judicial review schemes involving arbitration against states, the political branches have not always chosen to test them. NAFTA's implementing legislation, as already noted, preserved for litigants the ability to bring constitutional challenges to the NAFTA system (whether facially or as applied). Seen in this light, the NAFTA scheme can be understood as an example of a case where constitutional norms influence treaty architecture (or, more accurately, the architecture of treaty implementing legislation). Rather than test the constitutional limit (as the US arguably did in the Washington Convention), NAFTA supplied a safety valve for certain constitutional norms by preserving a right of access to Article III courts.

B. Executive Power

A unique feature of arbitration involving states or state-owned entities is that the arbitrators may require the sovereign party to undertake some act. This may come in the

[35] US Constitution art VI; see also *The Paquette Habana* (1900) 175 US 677.

[36] See *Webster v Doe* (1988) 486 US 592 (holding CIA director's decision to discharge employee was not subject to judicial review); *Block v Cmty Nutrition Inst* (1984) 467 US 340 (holding that consumers of dairy products could not obtain judicial review of milk market orders); *Morris v Gressette* (1977) 432 US 491 (finding that the Attorney General's failure to make timely objection under the Voting Rights Act of 1965 is not subject to judicial review); *Johnson v Robinson* (1974) 415 US 361 (precluding judicial review of certain Veterans Administration determinations).

[37] For an alternative view of this framework—one that conceptualizes it as a form of judicial review of public law disputes where the tribunal itself advances the separation-of-powers value—see Stephan W Schill, 'Deference in Investment Treaty Arbitration: Reconceptualizing the Standard of Review Through Comparative Public Law' (2012) 3 JIDS 577.

form of an interim procedural order (such as an order on a disclosure request). It also may come in the form of the final award. While awards in commercial or investment arbitrations typically will involve an obligation to pay sums of money, awards in trade arbitrations (like NAFTA arbitrations) may involve commands that a Member State cease some practice contrary to the treaty's substantive requirements.

The well-known *Canadian Softwood Lumber* litigation illustrates just how far the remedial powers of an arbitral tribunal might extend. That case began in 2001 when an association of US lumber producers petitioned the US Department of Commerce to impose anti-dumping and countervailing duties on Canadian softwood lumber imports. Following an investigation, the Commerce Department found that the Canadian government had been subsidizing the softwood lumber industry, and the International Trade Commission determined that these subsidies threatened the US lumber industry with material injury. Following these determinations, the Commerce Department imposed anti-dumping and countervailing duties on Canadian imports. In response, the Canadian government and other Canadian parties invoked provisions of Canada's free trade agreements with the US entitling them to review of the Commerce Department decision by a binational panel of arbitrators. During the course of the arbitration, the tribunal issued several orders that, in effect, remanded the case to the US International Trade Commission with express instructions to find that the record did not support a finding of injury to the American producers.

The tribunal's orders in the *Canadian Softwood Lumber* litigation raised profound questions about the interplay between constitutional law and arbitration law. The Constitution vests the Executive Branch with the power to 'take care' that the laws be faithfully executed. It also vests the President with the power to appoint 'Officers of the United States' subject to the advice and consent of the Senate. In light of those provisions, how could a scheme like NAFTA's be constitutional when it enabled a tribunal of private arbitrators (some of whom were appointed by a foreign government) to order a branch of the US government to enforce American trade law in a certain manner?[38]

That was a central question posed to the US Court of Appeals for the District of Columbia when the American lumber producers, following the tribunal's orders, challenged the constitutionality of this arbitral scheme. Though a settlement pretermitted the issue, the case provides a valuable lens into how these constitutional issues might be viewed. Critical in this regard is the so-called fallback mechanism in the NAFTA implementing legislation. According to that mechanism, in the event that NAFTA's dispute resolution mechanisms were declared unconstitutional, the President still would accept a decision by a binational panel (or extraordinary challenge committee) 'as a whole'. The President would then, by executive order, order the relevant cabinet agency to implement the decision of the tribunal (or committee).

[38] Similar issues would not arise in cases of an order from an Article III Court. Insofar as the federal courts are the ultimate expositors of the meaning of federal law (constitutional or otherwise), the Executive Branch's compliance with a court order (as opposed to an arbitral panel's award) discharges its 'take care' duty. The constitutional issues here are not unique to international arbitration but could arise in other contexts involving international tribunals. The Executive Branch's response to the judgment by the International Court of Justice in the *Avena* decision supplies another example. See *Medellin v Texas* (2008) 525 US 491.

Since NAFTA's adoption, Presidents routinely have indicated, by executive order, their intent to implement this option in the event it became necessary.[39]

Here, as with the examples discussed in section I, constitutional values influence development at a sub-doctrinal level. Concerns about the risk of invalidity of NAFTA's dispute resolution mechanism influenced development of the implementing legislation's architecture, leading to the creation of the fallback mechanism. That mechanism enabled the US to send a credible signal to its trading partners that it would honour its treaty obligations, as a matter of international law, even if the bi-national panel system were found to be incompatible with its domestic constitutional framework.

These constitutional values exert a similar influence in the other main field of arbitration involving states or state-owned entities, that is, private commercial arbitration. Although the nature of the disputes and the remedial schemes differ, similar questions arise about the compatibility of this system with the above-described constitutional norms. Here, notwithstanding the absence of an express judicial decision on point, the US has sought to stave off any constitutional questions through executive order. Specifically, a 1991 executive order directs that litigation counsel for the US 'shall neither seek nor agree to the use of binding arbitration or any other equivalent ADR technique'.[40] This order reflected the long-standing position of the US Justice Department that 'the Government cannot enter into agreements to participate in binding arbitration'.[41]

C. Transparency

As numerous scholars have observed, investment arbitration raises important and distinct issues of political accountability.[42] Protecting foreign investors by means of a bilateral investment treaty may supply an important inducement to attract foreign capital. But in the event that investment goes sour and gives rise to a claim by the investor, it presents a conundrum for the capital-importing state. Fighting the investor may score political points back home but risks chilling future foreign investment. Acceding to the investor's claims may placate the investment community but at the expense of the domestic fisc, where the local population may bear the ultimate financial burden.

These political dynamics for several years sparked calls for greater transparency in the investment arbitration process. Following revision to the Model Arbitration Rules (which had often served as the operative rules for investment arbitrations), UNCITRAL took up the task of developing a set of transparency rules to govern investment arbitration.[43] An overarching goal of the rules is to provide some modicum of openness, transparency, and public access to investment arbitration so that the

[39] Executive Orders 12662 and 12889. See generally Yong K Kim, 'The Beginnings of the Rule of Law in the International Trade System Despite U.S. Constitutional Constraints' (1996) 17 Mich JIL 967, 982–83.

[40] Executive Order 12778 (23 October 1991).

[41] Guidance on the Use of Alternative Dispute Resolution for Litigation in the Federal Courts (August 1992) 4.

[42] For a recent discussion of some of these criticisms, see Schill (n 29).

[43] UNCITRAL Rules on Transparency in Treaty-based Investor-State Arbitration (January 2014) Preamble.

affected publics (principally the citizenry of the state party or, perhaps more accurately, their political entrepreneurs) are aware of the details of disputes that might affect their public finances and, more generally, their economies.

The rules focus on a number of norms designed to ensure an adequate degree of publicity about and public participation in the arbitration. For example, the rules contain provisions governing the publication of information about the proceedings, the publication of documents produced in the proceedings, and public access to the proceedings themselves.[44] They also provide for submissions by third parties and non-parties with an interest in the arbitration (a nod to non-governmental organizations concerned about the effect of investment arbitration on matters of public interest).[45] Finally, the rules designate the United Nations (or an entity chosen by UNCITRAL) as the repository for documents published pursuant to the rules.[46]

In this regard, the UNCITRAL Transparency Rules function much like the Due Process Protocols described in section I above. Rather than assuming the form of hard law adopted explicitly by states, they function more like a set of norms to which parties can opt in (at least when the dispute arises from a treaty entered into before the effective date of the Transparency Rules; in other instances, state parties to a new bilateral treaty may incorporate those rules into the treaty).[47] They are, moreover, developed by an institution (UNCITRAL) through inputs from various stakeholders (the UNCITRAL Member States plus the numerous observers who, notably, include the major arbitral institutions as well as various corporate and other non-governmental organizations). In this fashion, though not constitutionally required under US law, the due process norms underpinning the transparency protocols represent a degree of constitutional influence on the administration of investment arbitration without the express application of constitutional doctrine.[48]

III. Implications and Conclusion

My central thesis has been that constitutional law influences the development of arbitration law, though not in the traditional mode. Rather than doing so through direct doctrinal application of constitutional rules, the norms underpinning those rules have seeped into arbitration law, usually through subconstitutional means. These have included, among others, the interpretation of statutes, the design of treaties, and the development of private norms. In the case of arbitration involving states or state-owned

[44] ibid arts 2–3, 6.
[45] ibid arts 4–5.
[46] ibid art 8.
[47] UNCITRAL Transparency Rules (n 43) art I(1)–(3).
[48] Recent litigation in the State of Delaware raised important questions about issues of transparency in arbitration. See *Delaware Coalition for Open Government v Strine* (2013) 733 F3d 510. There, a federal appellate court held that the constitutional right of access to open courts barred Delaware chancery judges from conducting confidential business arbitrations. While this case represents a rare instance of a court explicitly weighing a collision of constitutional norms and arbitration norms, it only sheds limited light on the issues explored here. The crux of the court's decision turned on the propriety of sitting judges serving as arbitrators in non-public proceedings. The decision does not govern how privately appointed arbitrators should be viewed in a comparable setting.

entities, that basic mode of application is the same, though the underlying norms—or the extent of their application—may differ. This thesis carries several implications, both for the study of constitutional law and for the study of arbitration law, including implications for the ongoing study of the relationship between public-private arbitration and transnational regulatory governance.[49]

First, for the study of constitutional law, it calls forth the need to understand why precisely certain constitutional norms seep into arbitration in certain ways. Due process norms seem most amenable to development by means of private or quasi-private activity. This may be due to the robust state action requirement under US constitutional law that effectively serves as a gatekeeper to the direct incorporation of due process (and other norms) on to private conduct. By contrast, norms involving executive power seem more likely to be addressed in treaty architecture or statutory design. Federalism norms remain the one outlier where constitutional law operates in a direct fashion. This might be explained by reference to the preemption clause, but this explanation only works because of the Supreme Court's decision in *Southland* directly applying section 2 of the FAA in federal court, a decision that sparked controversy for some time but presently appears to be accepted by at least eight of the justices. Finally, judicial power norms are most likely incorporated through norms of statutory interpretation, although this perhaps is most easily explained by reference to self-interested efforts by the judiciary to preserve their role in the separation of powers.

Second, once some theoretical framework can be constructed to explain the pattern of constitutional norm and the mode of incorporation, this theory could easily be tested across systems. That is to say, do other countries display a similar pattern in the relationship between arbitration law and constitutional law? Is there a distinct pattern among federalist systems as opposed to non-federalist ones? For states that lack a robust state action requirement does one see a greater incidence of direct incorporation of due process norms on to arbitration? Finally, do a system's treatment of the implications of state arbitration for executive or judicial power correlate at all with the design of its Executive Branch or the form of its judiciary?

Third, the thesis carries several implications for the study of transnational regulatory governance. For one thing, the constitutional principles that influence the design of dispute resolution systems within treaties or the drafting of treaty-implementing legislation will influence the operation of those treaties and, thereby, have both a direct effect on the procedural law and, potentially, an indirect effect on the development of substantive norms.

For another thing, the mode of incorporating constitutional norms through treaty interpretation can also influence the evolution of a system of transnational regulatory governance. Sometimes, treaties will set forth their own transnational substantive standards but leave the applicable law unaddressed.[50] In those instances, national courts of signatory states may interpret that treaty standard by

[49] See eg Benedict Kingsbury and Stephan W Schill, 'Investor-State Arbitration as Governance: Fair and Equitable Treatment, Proportionality and the Emerging Global Administrative Law' in Albert Jan van den Berg (ed), *50 Years of the New York Convention* (ICCA Congress Series No 14) (Wolters Kluwer 2009) 5.

[50] See eg New York Convention (n 27) art V(1)(b).

reference to their own national standard that may be informed by their constitutional norms on a matter such as notice and the opportunity to be heard. When doing so, courts in the US often also observe that they aspire to interpret the treaty in a manner harmonious with how courts in other signatory states have done so. To the extent they hold true to this practice, this mode of treaty interpretation supplies another opportunity whereby courts, through a form of transnational judicial cooperation, might develop a set of constitutional norms governing arbitrations under a particular treaty regime.

Finally, in other cases, sovereign states attempt to achieve this sort of soft constitutional harmonization but by means of different actors. The UNCITRAL Transparency Rules supply a good example in this regard. An express purpose of those rules was to create a 'harmonized legal framework for a fair and efficient settlement of international investment disputes, increase transparency and accountability and promote good governance'.[51] Yet, the drafters of the rules encountered an obvious problem about how to make them effective to disputes arising out of treaties adopted before their enactment, a particularly nettlesome problem in light of the general decline in the rate of new treaty formation in recent years.[52] Drafters of the transparency rules overcame this problem by relying on private conduct (at least as to the investor) to embed these transnational, constitutionally rooted norms in their dispute. This resembles, though is not identical to, how arbitration organizations in the US successfully sought to embed private due process norms into their domestic arbitrations (there the method was by refusing, as private actors, to administer arbitrations if the arbitral procedures did not comply with these norms).

In sum, the ongoing study of the relationship between constitutional law and arbitration law has important lessons for the parallel study of transnational regulatory governance. It teaches us that we must look beyond formal doctrinal forms to understand the seepage of constitutional principles into architecture and practice of arbitration involving states and state-owned entities. It also teaches us that private actors, as much as states, play a critical role in the development and implementation of those norms.

Select Materials

Bibliography

Drahozal, Christopher R, 'Contracting Around Hall Street' (2010) 14 Lewis & Clark L Rev 905

Gantz, David, 'The United States-Mexico-Canada Agreement: Settlement of Disputes' (2019) Baker Institute for Public Policy

[51] UNCITRAL Transparency Rules (n 43) Preamble.

[52] See UNCTAD, *World Investment Report 2013: Global Value Chains: Investment and Trade for Development* (United Nations 2013).

Gill, Patrick, 'No Do-Overs for Parties Who Agree to Limit Review of an Arbitrator's Decision' [2006] J Disp Resol 643

Kim, Yong K, 'The Beginnings of the Rule of Law in the International Trade System Despite U.S. Constitutional Constraints' (1996) 17 Mich JIL 967

Kingsbury, Benedict and Stephan W Schill, 'Investor-State Arbitration as Governance: Fair and Equitable Treatment, Proportionality and the Emerging Global Administrative Law' in Albert Jan van den Berg (ed), *50 Years of the New York Convention* (ICCA Congress Series No 14) (Wolters Kluwer 2009) 5

Rutledge, Peter B, *Arbitration and the Constitution* (CUP 2013)

Schill, Stephan W, 'Deference in Investment Treaty Arbitration: Reconceptualizing the Standard of Review Through Comparative Public Law' (2012) 3 JIDS 577

Schill, Stephan W, 'The Sixth Path: Reforming Investment Law from Within' in Jean E Kalicki and Anna Joubin-Bret (eds), *Reshaping the Investor-State Dispute Settlement System: Journeys for the 21st Century* (Brill 2015) 621

Legislation and Other Legal Instruments

Articles of Confederation (1781)

Federal Arbitration Act (9 USC)

Foreign Sovereign Immunities Act (28 USC §1605)

Exec Order No 12662 54 FR 785 (31 December 1988)

Exec Order No 12778 57 FR 3640 (23 October 1991)

Exec Order No 12889 58 FR 249 (27 December 1993)

Guidance on the Use of Alternative Dispute Resolution for Litigation in the Federal Courts 4 (Aug 1992)

Restatement (Third) US Law of Int'l Comm Arb Ch 5 (Proposed Final Draft, 24 April 2019)

US Constitution

Cases

Allied Bruce Terminix, Co v Dobson, 513 US 265 (1995)

AT&T Mobility, LLC v Concepcion, 563 US 333 (2011)

BG Group plc v Republic of Argentina, 134 S Ct 1198 (2014)

Bowen v Amoco Pipeline Co, 254 F3d 925 (10th Cir 2001)

Cable Connection Inc v Directv, Inc, 190 P 3d 586 (Cal 2008)

CFTC v Schor, 478 US 833 (1986)

Citizens Bank v Alfabco, Inc, 539 US 52 (2003) (per curiam)

CompuCredit Corp v Greenwood, 565 U S 95 (2012)

Cremin v Merill Lynch, Pierce, Fenner & Smith, 957 F Supp 1460 (ND Ill 1997)

Delaware Coalition for Open Government, Inc v Strine, 733 F3d 510 (3rd Cir 2013)

Doctor's Associates, Inc v Casarotto, 517 US 681 (1996)

First Options of Chicago, Inc v Kaplan, 514 US 938 (1995)

Hall Street Assoc, LLC v Mattel, Inc, 552 US 576 (2007)

Katz v Celico P'ship, 2013 WL 6621022 (SDNY Dec 12 2013)
Marmet Health Care Center, Inc v Brown, 132 S Ct 1201 (2012)
Medellin v Texas, 525 US 491 (2008)
Mobil Cerro Negro Ltd v Venezuela, 836 F3d 96 (2d Cir 2017)
NAFTA Traders, Inc v Quinn, 339 SW 3d 184 (TX 2011)
The Paquette Habana, 175 US 677 (1900)
Parsons & Whittemore Overseas Co, Inc v Societe Generale de L'Industrie du Papier (RAKTA), 508 F2d 969 (2 Cir 1974)
Siegel v Prudential Ins Co, 67 Cal App 4th 1270 (Cal Ct App 1998)
Southland Corp v Keating, 465 US 1 (1984)
Thomas v Union Carbide Agricultural Products Co, 473 US 568 (1985)

10

The Extrinsic Factors of World Trade that Galvanized Mexican Public-Private Arbitration during the Pre-NAFTA Years and the Evolution of Safeguards for the Public Interest

*Orlando Federico Cabrera Colorado and Andrea Orta González Sicilia**

I. Introduction

For the last two decades, Mexico's journey towards public-private arbitration (PPA) has been triggered by extrinsic factors. In anticipation of the North American Free Trade Agreement (NAFTA) coming into effect, Mexico's Congress enacted drastic reforms in several fields. These reforms were aimed at enabling world trade, supporting trade liberalization, and, more specifically, preparing Mexico for NAFTA's entry into force.

Notably, Mexico adopted the United Nations Commission on International Trade Law (UNCITRAL) Model Law on International Commercial Arbitration and authorized PPAs with state-owned enterprises (SOEs) and state agencies. These changes were deemed constitutional, and shortly thereafter, Mexico incorporated general provisions for alternative means of dispute resolution (ADR) in the federal Constitution. These provisions grant SOEs and state agencies sufficient leeway to agree to arbitrate. Additionally, the judiciary has been supportive of arbitration and PPAs as trustworthy ADR in state contracts for both private contractors and state agencies.

PPA legislation in Mexico has evolved since the pre-NAFTA years as a patchwork. Mexico has enacted a complex legal framework that varies across agencies, SOEs, and sectors as an immediate response to past experiences and the political and economic needs of the government. No general framework or law safeguards the public interest in PPA across all contracts or industries. Nevertheless, constitutional principles govern all public and private contracts. The principle of legality requires Mexican public entities to agree to arbitration only when a law expressly authorizes them to do

* This chapter was initially prepared in 2015 and updated through early 2020. Significant legal and jurisprudential developments have occurred since then, notably the constitutional amendment of 31 October 2024, which designated PEMEX and CFE as "companies of the state." Implementation legislation for this constitutional reform is pending. As a result, PEMEX and CFE will no longer be "productive companies of the state," and a new legal regime is expected.

Orlando Federico Cabrera Colorado and Andrea Orta González Sicilia, *The Extrinsic Factors of World Trade that Galvanized Mexican Public-Private Arbitration during the Pre-NAFTA Years and the Evolution of Safeguards for the Public Interest* In: *The Comparative Constitutional Foundations of Private-Public Arbitration*. Edited by: Stephan W. Schill, Oxford University Press. © Stephan W. Schill 2025. DOI: 10.1093/9780191987960.003.0010

so. Moreover, the safeguards of the public interest in PPA vary depending on the type of contract.

Accordingly, we identify a dual system composed of two types of contracts: (1) public contracts executed with state agencies; and (2) contracts of a private nature executed with SOEs and state agencies in the electric power industry. In this dual system, the public interest safeguards in PPA vary depending on the nature of the contract. First, for public contracts, the safeguards identified include the doctrine of administrative contracts and the exclusion of certain acts of public authority from arbitration. Second, this legal regime does not, however, apply to contracts executed with SOEs and to acts executed in the electric industry, which have a commercial nature.[1]

This complex legal framework of varied safeguards is unique in Latin America. The exact same Mexican safeguards do not appear in Brazil, Bolivia, Chile, Colombia, Costa Rica, Cuba, Dominican Republic, Ecuador, Panama, Peru, or Venezuela.[2] To illustrate the point, we cite a couple of examples. Brazil requires the Federal Attorney's Office to previously approve the arbitral institution.[3] Bernal observes that Bolivia has an unclear framework that allows two interpretations: (1) PPA is possible arising out of contracts executed between agencies and foreign companies without a domicile in Bolivia; (2) alternatively, SOEs can include arbitration clauses in administrative contracts while they migrate to another legal regime.[4] In Brazil and the Dominican Republic, the law expressly allows parties to agree to arbitration in state contracts but limited to freely transferable property rights *(direito patrimonias disponíveis)*[5] or freely transferable matters *(materias de libre disposición)*.[6] In Peru, the agency's approval of additional works is not subject to arbitration, and arbitrators are not allowed to order administrative fines or costs other than the costs allowed of arbitration in PPA.[7] Other Latin American countries have even more intricate systems. Colombia includes procedural safeguards for the appointment of arbitrators and adds a special conflicts of interest list. In Colombia, the administrative court has jurisdiction to set aside an award where an agency is involved. For all other matters, the Colombian civil chamber has jurisdiction to vacate awards.[8] Procedural safeguards to conduct

[1] See section IV.D below. See also Acquisitions Law, arts 2, 11; Works Law, arts 2, 13; PPP Law, art 8; Hydrocarbons Law, art 22; PEMEX Law (2014) arts 3, 80; CFE Law (2014) arts 3, 7, 82; Electric Industry Law, art 5.

[2] See Orlando Cabrera, 'La arbitrabilidad de los contratos administrativos en Latinoamérica' (2016–2017) 7 Lima Arbitration 272.

[3] See Decree No 10.025 of 20 September 2019 <www.planalto.gov.br/ccivil_03/_Ato2019-2022/2019/Decreto/D10025.htm> accessed 22 January 2025. See also Orlando Cabrera, 'Brazil Allows Arbitration in Public Contract in the Port, Road, Rail, Waterway and Airport Sectors' (*Kluwer Arbitration Blog*, 12 October 2019) < https://arbitrationblog.kluwerarbitration.com/2019/10/12/brazil-allows-arbitration-in-public-contracts-in-the-port-road-rail-waterway-and-airport-sectors/ > accessed 22 January 2025.

[4] José C Bernal Rivera, 'Can Bolivian State-Owned Companies Submit to International Arbitration? Analyzing Bolivia's Intricate Legal Framework on Foreign Investment' (*Investment Treaty News*, 13 March 2017).

[5] See art 1 of Brazilian Law No 13.129 of 26 May 2015 ('Those who are capable of entering into contracts may make use of arbitration to resolve conflicts regarding freely transferable property rights.').

[6] Dominican Law No 489-08 sobre Arbitraje Comercial No 1502 (30 December 2008) art 2.

[7] See art 45.1 of Peru's Law No 30225 as amended by Legislative Decree No 1341; art 56 of Emergency Decree No 020-2020. See also Orlando Cabrera, 'How Peru Embraced Transparency in Arbitration' (*Law 360*, 5 February 2020) <https://www.law360.com/articles/1240899> accessed on 22 January 2025.

[8] See arts 8, 16, and 46 of Law 1563 of 2012.

arbitration remain unknown in Mexico. Arbitrators conduct PPAs like any other arbitral proceeding because the Mexican arbitration law applies equally to private and public arbitrations, as well as to international and domestic arbitrations. Under the Mexican arbitration law, no distinction exists between Mexican PPAs and any other arbitration.

A governance system involving Mexican public actors, where arbitrators contribute to the Mexican lawmaking function, seems unlikely to thrive soon. PPAs are uncommon and dissimilar. They tend to be highly sophisticated, full of technicalities and regulated by different laws. For instance, an award deciding the liability of a construction company in a twenty-year public-private partnership for the development of a hospital may not easily serve for a dispute concerning the construction of an offshore oil platform or a high-speed train or a highway or a gas pipeline.

Arbitration practitioners[9] in Mexico have devoted substantial attention to explaining the complexity and nature of PPAs. However, Mexican administrative and constitutional scholars and practitioners have not shown equal interest, and consequently academic treatises on the field are limited. This chapter intends to contribute to the academic gap by elaborating on whether laws governing arbitration apply differently when dealing with a private or public arbitration and what the impact of constitutional and administrative law is on PPA in order to safeguard the public interest.

This chapter will first address the development of arbitration in Mexico, since arbitration is the most used ADR for resolving disputes with SOEs and state agencies. The chapter discusses the status of arbitration in Mexico to explain the context in which PPA is used. Despite the safeguards in place for the public interest, PPA is conducted like any other commercial arbitration, with some nuances in interim measures and the attachment of assets. Subsequently, this chapter examines the role of democracy and transparency and will comment on the heightened protection offered by investment treaties to foreign investors and their investments compared with Mexican law. Second, this chapter will deal with the history of PPA in Mexico prior to NAFTA's

[9] Bernardo Cortés Araujo, 'Nueva Ley de Petróleos Mexicanos – Implicaciones en el Arbitraje Comercial' [2014] Boletín CAIC 1; Diego A Andrade-Max, 'Las personas morales de derecho público como partes en el arbitraje comercial internacional' (1993) 22 Jurídica Ibero 431; Francisco González de Cossío, 'Arbitraje y Contratación Gubernamental' [2012] 15/2012 SAR España 121; Francisco González de Cossío, 'El arbitraje como solución al dilema de las obras de infraestructura' (2013) 4 Revista de Derecho Privado 441; Julieta Ovalle Piedra, 'Contratos Administrativos y Arbitraje en México' [2013] Boletín CAIC <https://gc.scalahed.com/recursos/files/r161r/w24174w/S11_contratos_administrativos_arbitraje.pdf> accessed 22 January 2025; Herfried Wöss, 'Arbitraje, Medios Alternativos de Solución de Controversias y Compras del Sector Público en México' [2009] Revista Latinoamericana de Mediación y Arbitraje 124, 131–32; Herfried Wöss, 'Arbitration, Alternative Dispute Resolution and Public Procurement in Mexico' [2010] 7 Revista del Club Español del Arbitraje 19, 23; Herfried Wöss, 'Solución de Controversias al amparo de la Nueva Ley Mexicana de Asociaciones Público-Privadas' (2012–2013) 5 Lima Arbitration 185; Herfried Wöss, Dante Figueroa, and Jennifer Cabrera, 'El contrato administrativo, inarbitrabilidad y el reconocimeinto de laudos anulados en el país de origen. El Caso *Commisa*' (2014) 6 Lima Arbitration 77; Herfried Wöss, 'Arbitration under the Mexican Energy Reform: The Lessons of Commisa v PEMEX' (*Kluwer Arbitration Blog*, 7 November 2014); Jennifer Cabrera, Dante Figueroa, and Herfried Wöss, 'The Administrative Contract, Non-Arbitrability, and the Recognition and Execution of Awards Annulled in the Country of Origin: The Case of *Commisa v Pemex*' (2016) 32 Arb Int'l 125; Herfried Wöss and Devin Bray, 'Investment Protection and Mexican Energy Reform' (2018) 12 DRI 41; Orlando F Cabrera Colorado and Eduardo Silva da Silva, 'Law and Arbitration of Oil and Gas Disputes in Brazil and Mexico' (2011) 9(2) OGEL 1; Rafael Martínez Rosas, 'Arbitraje, contratación pública y juicio de amparo' (2013) 15(171) El Mundo del Abogado 34.

entry into force, describing how external forces impacted on the legal framework and discussing the judiciaries' most relevant decisions supporting PPA. Third, this chapter spells out the dual system of state contracts and the existing safeguards in public and private contracts. Finally, it will explain cases in which complications arose due to the patchwork of laws that have been approved in Mexico and the interpretation by US courts of this patchwork and the safeguards of public interest in the field of PPA.

II. The Development of Arbitration in Mexico

Disputes originating from PPA are normally solved through arbitration and not other ADR, given the fear of the sanctions that the Federal Superior Audit Office may impose for deficient work or breaches of the law. These disputes are conducted like any other commercial arbitration, with some nuances regarding interim measures and the attachment of assets. Thus, it is necessary to put forward these distinctive features of arbitration in Mexico, and its evolution. In this section, we also explore the role of democracy in PPA, but we anticipate that an arbitration governance system seems unlikely to thrive soon, even though information concerning arbitrations is available. Irrespective of the complex legal framework of safeguards in place, investment arbitration provides aggrieved investors with an additional avenue to find relief, as they can claim treaty breaches caused by acts of public authority.

A. Arbitration and PPA in Mexico

Mexico has been friendly to commercial arbitration.[10] Concerning PPA matters, an arbitral tribunal may conduct proceedings like any other commercial arbitration, under the Mexican arbitration law[11] or an institution's rules.[12] Mexico used to prefer the rules of arbitration of the International Chamber of Commerce (ICC), but this Mexican tradition of only including ICC clauses has changed, and now Mexico includes UNCITRAL arbitration clauses in contracts for the exploration and extraction of hydrocarbons; ad hoc arbitration in public-private partnership (PPP) projects; and arbitration under the rules of the London Court of International Arbitration (LCIA) in contracts concluded with the Comisión Federal de Electricidad (CFE), the electric power SOE. The Mexican arbitration law applies to both national and international arbitrations seated in Mexico, and to tribunals seated overseas whenever parties require the assistance of Mexican courts.[13] Parties can freely appoint arbitrators provided they comply with the independence and impartiality requirements under Mexican arbitration law[14] or the applicable arbitration rules. Arbitrators do not

[10] José María Abascal, 'Mexico' in JH Carter (ed), *The International Arbitration Review* (5th edn, Law Business Research 2014) 386.

[11] Mexican arbitration law is contained in the Mexican Commercial Code (arts 1415–80); Acquisitions Law, art 80; Works Law, art 98; PPP Law, art 138; Hydrocarbons Law, art 21; CFE Law, art 118; PEMEX Law, art 115.

[12] Commerce Code, art 1417(II).

[13] ibid art 1415.

[14] ibid arts 1427–28.

need to be experts in arbitration or qualified in a certain matter. Petróleos Mexicanos (PEMEX), the oil SOE, and CFE have both recently appointed as arbitrators tax attorneys, trade and tariffs academics, and other lawyers without an arbitration background or arbitration experience. Any arbitral tribunal may rule on its jurisdiction, even in a PPA.[15] To date, no case law has dealt with a waiver of challenge under any laws, nor a state immunity defence advanced by the Mexican state or an SOE in Mexico. However, PEMEX has availed itself of the sovereign immunity doctrine before US courts to dismiss actions.[16] Nonetheless, various state contracts governed by Mexican law contain a waiver of immunity clause, probably because these contracts are translated from US model contracts[17] or executed under foreign law.[18]

There exists no difference when Mexican courts deal with interim measures and award enforcement or annulment deriving from a PPA or from a commercial arbitration. Nevertheless, Mexican courts will not order the attachment of state assets.[19] Mexico is a party to the Convention on the Recognition and Enforcement of Foreign Arbitral Awards (New York Convention)[20] and the Inter-American Convention on International Commercial Arbitration (Panama Convention).[21] Under Mexican arbitration law, the grounds to set aside an award and for refusing recognition are identical to the grounds under the UNCITRAL Model Law.[22] These grounds apply in the same manner to private parties and SOEs.

Depending on the budget and the expertise of in-house counsel, agencies and SOEs may contract outside counsel. External lawyers and experts acting in arbitration proceedings need to comply with both the contracting procedure set by the Acquisitions Law[23] and public procurement principles for their hiring as counsel or experts of SOEs. External lawyers were more common before, but CFE and PEMEX have for some time now been handling arbitrations internally. For this purpose, in 2015, PEMEX created the 'Arbitration and Special Affairs Unit'.[24] CFE's General Counsel has the mandate to represent CFE in arbitral proceedings[25] and CFE's in-house counsel handle arbitrations too.

[15] ibid art 1432; Laudos Arbitrales. Estándar de Revisión Judicial para Determinar la Validez de la Decisión de un Tribunal Arbitral sobre su Propia Competencia [2017] First Chamber, SJFG, 40, I, 1a.XXXVII/2017, 445 (2014012).

[16] *Zernicek v Petroleos Mexicanos (Pemex)*, 614 F Supp 407 (SD Tex 1985) ('[T]he [District] Court concludes that Pemex enjoys sovereign immunity as a matter of law, which immunity bars this action as to it. Accordingly, defendant Pemex's motion to dismiss is granted.'). See also *Zernicek v Brown & Root, Inc*, 826 F2d 415 (5th Cir 1987). The US Court of Appeals affirmed the District Court's decision to dismiss the case.

[17] Modelo de Contrato de APP para la Construcción, Equipamiento Museográfico, Operación y Mantenimiento del Museo Internacional del Barroco [2014] cl 22.3; Comisión Nacional de Hidrocarburos, Bases de Licitación para la Selección de un Socio para PEMEX Licitación CNH-A3-Cárdenas Mora/2017 [2017] cl 18.4.

[18] Convenio de Apertura de Crédito entre CFE y BNP Paribas [2000] art 21.1–4. French law governs this contract except for governmental authorizations that will be governed by Mexican law.

[19] Federal Code of Civil Procedure, art 4.

[20] Convention on the Recognition and Enforcement of Foreign Arbitral Awards (adopted 10 June 1958, entered into force 7 June 1959) 330 UNTS 3.

[21] Inter-American Convention on International Commercial Arbitration (adopted 30 January 1975, entered into force 16 June 1976) 1438 UNTS 245.

[22] Commerce Code, arts 1457, 1462; Model Law, arts 26, 36.

[23] Acquisitions Law, arts 41, 42.

[24] Organic Statute of Pemex (2015) art 19.

[25] Organic Statute of CFE, arts 32, 51.

PEMEX and CFE in-house counsel tend to be litigious. The Federal Superior Audit Office reviews the work of these in-house counsel because they are public officers. This Audit Office may find responsibility and sanction these in-house counsel if it considers that their work was deficient and breached the law. For instance, the Audit Office may consider as a deficiency that the counsel could have elaborated an argument but failed to do so during the arbitration. To prevent sanctions, counsel prefer to err on the side of caution and litigate all aspects of a case, even if they have few chances to win an argument. Their fear of the Audit Office also discourages settlements by negotiation and conciliation.[26]

B. The Role of Democracy in Mexico in PPA

To discuss the role of democracy, we address three aspects. First, the way in which people can find out information about arbitration matters; second, the absence of a system in which arbitrators contribute to the lawmaking function; and third, the absence of participation of third parties in arbitration.

To start with, Mexico deals well with transparency matters. There are three ways to find information about arbitration matters. First, agencies must upload all tendering procedures regarding all contracts to the public procurement website (CompraNet).[27] The present authors downloaded several public-private partnership contracts and verified the existence of arbitration clauses. Second, the Constitution protects access to information as a fundamental right. Everyone has the right of free access to timely information.[28] The General Law on Transparency and Access to Public Information applies to an arbitration where a public entity is a party. Agencies do not automatically disclose the information, but citizens can request it. The agency may provide edited versions of documents or deny information, based on public interest or national security concerns.[29] We requested information from PEMEX, CFE, and the Ministry of Communications and Transportation (SCT). They declined to provide information on pending arbitrations, quoting public interest concerns. However, they provided information and copies of the awards on concluded cases. Third, the Federal Judiciary must publish court proceedings and all judgments.[30] Any person can download edited versions of decisions from the judiciary's website.[31]

Second, despite the availability of information concerning PPA in Mexico, the authors could not identify a system in which arbitrators contribute to lawmaking. Two aspects explain why this system is absent in Mexico. First, even though an award is final, the loser often seeks to set it aside. Second, these projects tend to be unique, capital-intensive, highly sophisticated, full of technicality, and governed by distinct laws that evolve over time, sometimes in a patchwork manner. Distinct laws govern

[26] General Law on Administrative Liabilities, arts 7, 49, and 50; Organic Statute of CFE, art 32.

[27] See Acquisitions Law, art 30; Works Law, art 32; PPP Law, art 44. The website is accessible via <https://compranet.hacienda.gob.mx/web/login.html> accessed 22 January 2025.

[28] Federal Constitution, art 6.

[29] Federal Transparency Law, art 4.

[30] ibid art 67.

[31] See <www.cjf.gob.mx/> accessed 22 January 2025.

distinct projects. Hence, an award interpreting the Hydrocarbons Law may not help another case interpreting the Acquisitions Law or the Electric Power Industry Law. Moreover, PPA arises out of major infrastructure projects, like the La Yesca hydroelectric power plant (the second-highest structure of its type in the world), the licence agreements for the exploration and extraction of hydrocarbons (each field requires approximately USD 4.4 billion of investment during the contract's life),[32] and the Red Compartida, a gigantic PPP telecommunications project (investment sum of USD 10 billion over ten years).[33] Thus, PPAs, like these projects, are uncommon. From our inquiries, PEMEX reported two new arbitrations in 2015; the Ministry of Communications and Transportation, responsible for roads and bridges, reported one case. The possibility of having two similar arbitrations dealing with the same issues, facts, and law is low. Nevertheless, general issues dealing with the liability of the parties or procedural aspects like the competence of arbitral tribunals can help develop a governance system where arbitrators contribute to lawmaking. All other issues dealing with the technicalities of the dispute, like the quality of gas, or the construction of an offshore oil platform, by contrast, may not serve as precedent for a telecommunications dispute.

Lastly, no regulation allows third parties to participate in arbitral proceedings. Amicus curiae filings in arbitration are unknown. In fact, under Mexican law, amicus curiae filings in courts were unknown prior to 2011.[34]

C. Investment Arbitration

Despite the complex framework governing state contracts, and the safeguards of public interest excluding certain acts of public authority from arbitration, foreign investors frequently challenge acts of public authority and find relief in investment arbitration. In fact, of all known cases as of December 2020, claimants have brought thirty-five cases against Mexico, out of which thirteen are related to state contracts.[35] These claims are possible given that Mexico has an important network of treaties protecting foreign investors, including those executing state contracts. Mexico has

[32] Adam Williams, 'Mexico Sees $44 Billion in Investment for Deep Water Oil Fields' (*Bloomberg*, 17 December 2015) <http://www.bloomberg.com/news/articles/2015-12-17/mexico-sees-44-billion-in-investment-for-deep-water-oil-fields> accessed 22 January 2025.

[33] 'Gobierno Federal Iniciará proceso para red compartida' (*Expansión*, 10 March 2015) <http://expansion.mx/economia/2015/03/10/el-gobierno-federal-inicia-proceso-para-red-compartida> accessed 22 January 2025.

[34] In 2011, the Federal Code of Civil Procedure included class actions and amicus curiae filings in these proceedings: see Federal Code of Civil Procedure, art 598.

[35] UNCTAD, 'Investment Dispute Settlement Navigator: Mexico. Cases as Respondent State' <https://investmentpolicy.unctad.org/investment-dispute-settlement/country/136/mexico> accessed 23 January 2025. UNCTAD reports that the following cases deal with state contracts: *Abengoa v Mexico*, ICSID Case No ARB(AF)/09/2; *Alicia Grace and others v Mexico*, ICSID Case No UNCT/18/4; *Azinian v Mexico*, ICSID Case No ARB (AF)/97/2; *Cemusa v Mexico*, ICSID Case No ARB(AF)/13/2; *Espiritu Santo Holdings, LP v Mexico*, ICSID Case No ARB/20/13; *Gemplus v Mexico*, ICSID Case No ARB(AF)/04/3; *KBR v Mexico*, ICSID Case No UNCT/14/1; *Legacy Vulcan v Mexico*, ICSID Case No ARB/19/1; *Metalclad v Mexico*, ICSID Case No ARB(AF)/97/1; *Odyssey v Mexico*, ICSID Case No UNCT/20/1; *Telefónica v Mexico*, ICSID Case No ARB(AF)/12/4; *Tecmed v Mexico*, ICSID Case No ARB(AF)/00/2; *Waste Management v Mexico II*, ICSID Case No ARB(AF)/00/3.

twenty-nine bilateral investment treaties (BITs)[36] in force, and ten free trade agreements (FTAs) with an investment chapter.[37]

As such, all these investment treaties provide foreigners with heightened protection compared with PPA under Mexican law. As this chapter will explain later in detail, the Acquisitions, Leases and Public Services Law (Acquisitions Law), the Public Works and Related Services Law (Works Law), the Public-Private Partnerships Law (PPP Law), and the Hydrocarbons Law exclude certain acts of public authority from contract-based arbitration. Investment treaty tribunals, by contrast, have a broader jurisdiction. Treaties in force normally do not exclude acts of public authority like administrative rescission or revocation from the scope of investment arbitration, although some minor exceptions exist.[38] Conversely, administrative rescission, revocation, and other acts of public authority fall within the jurisdiction of an investment treaty tribunal. Investment tribunals frequently analyse treaty breaches caused by some of these acts of public authority. In *Gemplus*,[39] the tribunal examined two requisitions and a concession's revocation. The tribunal found these acts, in the case at hand, to be manifestly irrational, arbitrary, and perverse, and conducted in bad faith towards claimants. It found that Mexico unlawfully expropriated investments, indirectly by the requisition and directly by the concession's revocation. This fully illustrates how investment treaty arbitration offers a far-reaching spectrum of jurisdiction to assess acts of public authority, as compared with PPA under Mexican law.

Despite the fact that these cases represent a major concern for the Secretary of Economy and her team given the high stakes claimed in pending cases, Mexico decided to become a member of the International Centre for Settlement of Investment Disputes (ICSID). In 2018, the Mexican Senate positively discussed investment arbitration during the ratification process of the Convention on the Settlement

[36] Mexico has concluded BITs with Argentina, Austria, Bahrain, Belarus, Belgium–Luxembourg Economic Union, China, Cuba, Czech Republic, Denmark, Finland, France, Germany, Greece, Iceland, Italy, Korea, Kuwait, the Netherlands, Portugal, Singapore, Slovakia, Spain, Sweden, Switzerland, Trinidad and Tobago, Turkey, United Arab Emirates, United Kingdom, and Uruguay. See Mexican Ministry of Economy, 'Comercio Exterior, Países con Tratados y Acuerdos firmados con México' (10 May 2015) <www.gob.mx/se/acciones-y-programas/comercio-exterior-paises-con-tratados-y-acuerdos-firmados-con-mexico> accessed 22 January 2025.

[37] Comprehensive and Progressive Agreement for Trans-Pacific Partnership (signed 8 March 2018, entered into force 30 December 2018) ch 9 (CPTPP); United States–Mexico–Canada Agreement (signed 30 November 2018, entered into force 1 July 2020) ch 14 (USMCA); Central America–Mexico FTA (signed 22 November 2011, entered into force 1 July 2013) ch XI; Mexico–Chile FTA (signed 17 April 1998, entered into force 1 August 1999) ch 9; Colombia–Mexico–Venezuela FTA (signed 13 June 1994, entered into force 1 January 1995) ch XVII; Agreement between Japan and the United Mexican States for the Strengthening of the Economic Partnership (signed 17 September 2004, entered into force 1 April 2005) ch 7; Mexico–Panama FTA (signed 3 April 2014, entered into force 1 July 2015) ch X; Mexico–Peru FTA (signed 6 April 2011, entered into force 1 February 2012) ch XI; Mexico–Uruguay FTA (signed 15 November 2003, entered into force 15 July 2004) ch XIII; Additional Protocol to the Framework Agreement of the Pacific Alliance (signed 10 February 2012, entered into force 1 May 2016) ch 10. All texts available via UNCTAD's International Investment Agreements Navigator at <https://investmentpolicy.unctad.org/international-investment-agreements> accessed 22 January 2025.

[38] NAFTA Note 43 provides: 'Article 1501 (Competition Law): no investor may have recourse to investor-state arbitration under the Investment Chapter for any matter arising under this Article.' In Annex 9-L of the CPTPP, Mexico established some 'limitations of Mexico's consent to arbitration'. However, according to Article 2 of the CPTPP ('Suspension of the Application of Certain Provisions'), the parties suspended the application of this Annex 'until the Parties agree to end suspension of one or more of these provisions'.

[39] *Gemplus SA and others v United Mexican States*, ICSID Case No ARB(AF)/04/3, Award (16 June 2010).

of Investment Disputes between States and Nationals of Other States (ICSID Convention).[40] The Senate reiterated Mexico's commitment to promoting free trade and foreign investment under all its treaties. The Senate referred to the fact that both BITs and FTAs provide for ICSID arbitration as an avenue to settle disputes, but that they could not be settled under ICSID because Mexico was not an ICSID member. The Senate found the need to adhere to the ICSID Convention to reinforce Mexico's position in favour of investment and send a clear signal of certainty to investors. Among other considerations, the Mexican Senate found delight in the opportunity to appoint four arbitrators and four conciliators for ICSID's lists. Also, the Senate noted that Mexican investments abroad can benefit from the ICSID Convention.[41] Certainly, the Senate's ratification of the ICSID Convention encourages and facilitates the use of arbitration and represents another major step to comply with obligations under BITs and FTAs.[42]

This section has demonstrated the advantages of using arbitration not only to solve disputes between private parties but also disputes of SOEs or those arising out of PPP projects. There are several reasons for this: to mention some, in Mexico arbitration applies in the same way to all types of disputes despite the type of parties involved. Likewise, investment arbitration tends to aid in the protection of investment, particularly by having a wider mandate to analyse acts of public authority.

Now this chapter turns to analyse the origins that enabled PPA in Mexico.

III. Extrinsic Factors Triggered PPA, Its Evolution and Acceptance by Constitutional Law and the Judiciary

External forces caused the modern development of arbitration and PPA in Mexico. NAFTA establishes a bright line between: (1) actions preparing Mexico for NAFTA's entry into force that laid out the foundations of modern arbitration and PPAs in Mexico; and (2) post-treaty actions that underpinned those foundations, continued by Congress and the judiciary after NAFTA's entry into force. First, to start with the pre-NAFTA era, we comment on Mexico's economy and its three main legislative efforts to set foundations for PPA. Congress (1) adopted the 1985 UNCITRAL Model Law on International Commercial Arbitration;[43] (2) authorized arbitration with SOEs; and (3) permitted arbitration in public procurement contracts. These efforts prepared Mexico's legal regime for the entry into force of NAFTA and other FTAs. By promoting trade liberalization, these legislative measures also aligned Mexico

[40] Convention on the Settlement of Investment Disputes between States and Nationals of Other States (adopted 18 March 1965, entered into force 14 October 1966) 575 UNTS 159.

[41] Mexican Senate, 'Dictamen por el que se Aprueba el Convenio Sobre Arreglo de Diferencias Relativas a Inversiones' (18 April 2018).

[42] North American Free Trade Agreement (signed 17 December 1992, entered into force 1 January 1994) (1993) ILM 289 and 605 (NAFTA) art 2022; Central America–Mexico FTA (n 37) art 17.22; Colombia–Mexico–Venezuela FTA (n 37) art 19.19; Mexico–Panama FTA (n 37) art 18.21; Mexico–Chile FTA (n 37) art 18.19.

[43] Mexico partially introduced the Model Law in 1989 with substantive amendments to the original text and adopted the full text later. See Leonel Pereznieto Castro and James A Graham, *Tratado de arbitraje comercial internacional mexicano* (2nd edn, Limusa 2013) 24–25.

with the new reality of world trade. Second, after NAFTA, Congress[44] and the judiciary have acted to comply with international obligations agreed to in other FTAs. Constitutional law has accepted PPA and has not set prohibitions or restrictions to PPA. On the contrary, Mexican constitutional law supports arbitration. The judiciary has acted in a similar vein. Three relevant efforts stand out after NAFTA: (1) the modernization of the legal framework for arbitration and the introduction of ADR at the constitutional level; (2) the judicial interpretation of ADR as a human right; and (3) the rendering of some decisions that set a high threshold for an agency seeking to have an award set aside on public policy grounds.

A. External Forces During the Pre-NAFTA-Era-Implemented PPA

An interest in achieving world trade and preparing for the entry into force of international treaties are the main factors that brought about PPAs in Mexico as well as other relevant changes to arbitration. Before 1986, Mexico's economy was closed to foreign trade and the government managed numerous SOEs. The signature of the General Agreement on Tariffs and Trade (GATT) in 1986 represented the first step towards trade liberalization. Mexico later concluded other FTAs. In the following years, the government privatized many companies. The state went from being a producer in several industries to a regulator and a promoter of investment. The most significant event in this line of liberalization occurred on 12 August 1992 when the NAFTA negotiations ended. On 17 December 1992, Canada, Mexico, and the United States signed NAFTA. They agreed to 'encourage and facilitate the use of arbitration and' other ADR 'for the settlement of international commercial disputes between private parties in the free trade area'.[45] Identical provisions emerged in subsequent FTAs executed by Mexico.[46] This effort opened the door to the use of arbitration also for disputes between private parties and public agents. As stated before, arbitration is used in disputes of SOEs and disputes arising out of PPP projects.

On 1 January 1994, before NAFTA's entry into force, Mexico's Federal Congress enacted reforms to the Mexican arbitration law[47] and permitted PPA. Prior to this amendment, the Mexican arbitration law required the arbitrators' names to be stated in the arbitration clause,[48] the arbitration procedure was supposed to last sixty working days,[49] and in the arbitration agreement parties could waive the appeal.[50] The new bill swept away all these outdated provisions.

First, in the bill amending the Mexican arbitration law, the President recognized the need to consolidate Mexico's opening up to international trade. He affirmed that

[44] Luis Omar Guerrero Rodríguez and Ximena Suárez Enríquez, 'La implementación del artículo 2022 del Tratado de Libre Comercio para América del Norte' [2009] 39 Jurídica 57.

[45] NAFTA (n 42) art 2022.

[46] Central America–Mexico FTA (n 37) art 17.22; Colombia–Mexico–Venezuela FTA (n 37) art 19.19; Mexico–Panama FTA (n 37) art 18.21; Mexico–Chile FTA (n 37) art 18.19.

[47] Fernanda Garza Magdaleno, 'El Arbitraje en México' (undated) <http://cdei.itam.mx/sites/default/files/garzaarbitraje_0.pdf> accessed 22 January 2025.

[48] Commerce Code (as amended on 4 January 1989) art 1417.

[49] ibid art 1419.

[50] ibid art 1423.

'increasing interdependence at the regional and global levels'[51] would determine future development. He continued:

> [A]s part of its economic modernization, Mexico now lives an important process of legislative change that facilitates its full incorporation into the world trade flow. We have entered into a stage of *full trade liberalization* that is allowing us to reap the benefits of global markets. *International treaties* entered by this country, and those held in the process, make it *necessary* . . . to proceed also to *update* commercial laws. . . . Indeed, the intense network of commercial relations brings different countries closer and closer, this has given a larger appeal to . . . commercial arbitration as practical and expeditious means of solving commercial disputes that come to fruition in . . . commercial relations.[52]

The President acknowledged the convenience of a modern commercial arbitration law that is universally known and widely accepted. Congress approved the bill. On 22 July 1993, with slight adjustments, the Mexican Commerce Code incorporated the UNCITRAL Model Law on International Commercial Arbitration (1985). The goals of achieving trade liberalization and complying with international obligations, particularly NAFTA, triggered the amendments to the Mexican arbitration law. Even later, in 2011, Congress amended the Mexican arbitration law to include further detailed provisions on judicial assistance and cooperation with arbitration. Given that, under NAFTA and other FTAs, Mexico undertook to 'encourage and facilitate the use of arbitration',[53] we interpret this 2011 amendment as a response to keep complying with international treaty obligations.

Second, Congress continued to prepare the way for the entry into force of FTAs and particularly NAFTA by introducing PPAs in Mexico. On 25 November 1993, the President sent to the House of Representatives a Project of Decree to reform and add provisions of laws concerning NAFTA.[54] In the foreword, the Project of Decree mentioned that the 1989–94 National Development Plan intended to renovate the economy by setting free trade and strengthening competition in the domestic industry. The Project of Decree stressed that two aspects caused free trade: Mexico's economic ties with other countries, on the one hand, and the decrease of tariffs and the removal of other non-tariff barriers on imports and exports of goods, on the other. To provide context, the Project refers to NAFTA's signature and ratification, the imminent conclusion of negotiations of the Mexico–Colombia–Venezuela FTA, and other negotiations with Latin American countries. To achieve modernization, the Project of Decree refers to the amendments of the legal framework that aimed to respond to the new conditions and challenges presented by globalization. The Project emphasizes

[51] Explanatory memorandum, Commerce and Civil Procedure Codes (1 July 1993).
[52] ibid (emphasis added).
[53] NAFTA (n 42) art 2022; Central America–Mexico FTA (n 37) art 17.22; Colombia–Mexico–Venezuela FTA (n 37) art 19.19; Mexico–Panama FTA (n 37) art 18.21; Mexico–Chile FTA (n 37) art 18.19.
[54] Iniciativa de decreto que reforma, adiciona y deroga diversas leyes relacionadas con el Tratado de Libre Comercio de América del Norte (25 November 1993) <http://cronica.diputados.gob.mx/DDebates/55/3er/Ord1/19931125.html> accessed 22 January 2025.

the bills approved on intellectual property, competition law, and foreign trade law, and reforms on commercial arbitration. Most remarkably, it states as follows:

> [T]o advance the consolidation of the regulatory framework and to make compatible our legal regime with the new economic reality of the country and the international commitments made, the Executive branch under my charge has considered convenient to amend and add various laws . . .
>
> Including *arbitration clauses in contracts* between individuals and governmental entities is a common practice, especially in the international arena. To recognize this reality and to ensure better conditions in the negotiations with PEMEX, its subsidiary bodies and Comisión Federal de Electricidad (CFE), it is considered appropriate to amend Article 14 of Organic Law of Petróleos Mexicanos and Subsidiary Entities, and 45 of the Public Service of Electric Power Law, to clarify that these agencies can agree on arbitration clauses. At the same time, this amendment will fulfill the commitments made by Mexico in international arbitration.[55]

In December 1993, these reforms authorised PEMEX (the national oil company) and CFE (the national electric power utility company) to agree to arbitration for the first time. Congress amended: (1) Article 14 of the Organic Law of PEMEX and its Subsidiary Entities to enable PEMEX to agree to arbitration and; (2) Article 45 of the Public Service of Electric Power Law Congress to authorize CFE to agree to arbitration.[56] In 2008, the Statutory Law of the Constitutional Article 27 in the Oil Field also authorized PEMEX to agree to arbitration clauses in works and services contracts.[57] Many political and economic events have changed the Mexican energy sector since the 1990s. Thus, in 2013, a major energy reform gradually replaced all these provisions with a new regime described in the following section.[58]

Third, in 1993, the Services and Government Procurement Law opened the possibility to agree to arbitration clauses in all the acquisitions, leases of property, and services and public works contracts between the Public Administration and public and private persons. Under Article 15 of the Services and Government Procurement Law, the Secretary of the Treasury had to issue a regulation specifying the disputes that were subject to arbitration, but the Secretary never issued that regulation.[59] On 4 January 2000, the Services and Government Procurement Law was replaced by two laws: the Public Acquisitions, Leases, and Services Law (Acquisitions Law) and the Public Works and Related Services Law (Works Law). Both the Acquisitions Law and the Works Law allowed arbitration. Nevertheless, the Secretary of Public Administration had to issue a regulation specifying the disputes that were subject

[55] ibid (translation by the authors).

[56] Decreto que reforma, adiciona y deroga disposiciones de diversas leyes relacionadas con el Tratado de Libre Comercio de América del Norte, published in the Federal Official Gazette on 22 December 1993, arts 7–8. See also Ovalle Piedra (n 9) 9.

[57] Cabrera Colorado and da Silva (n 9) 20.

[58] See Decreto por el que se reforman y adicionan diversas disposiciones de la Constitución Política de los Estados Unidos Mexicanos, en Materia de Energía, published in the Federal Official Gazette on 20 December 2013, arts 25, 27, 28.

[59] Acquisitions and Works Law, art 15; Ovalle Piedra (n 9) 8.

to arbitration.[60] The Secretary of Public Administration failed to issue the rules.[61] Thus, this legislative effort to advance PPA in public procurement contracts faltered due to the Executive Branch's failure to act. These provisions are no longer in force because, in 2009, the Congress approved a reform to amend both the Acquisitions Law and the Works Law. Among the provisions amended in 2009, Congress introduced a general regulation regarding arbitration as ADR that we comment on in detail in section IV.D.1. The foreword of the bill stated that to 'expedite controversy and reduce costs for agencies and entities due to non-performance, which could well be the subject of resolution by ADR, general arbitration regulation is incorporated'.[62]

In sum, adopting NAFTA forced Mexico to modernize its legislation, especially Mexican arbitration law. It also created the basis for CFE and Pemex to become regular users of arbitration.

B. External Forces after NAFTA's Entry into Force Underpinned PPA

We identify three important governmental actions sustaining PPA after NAFTA's entry into force. First, Congress incorporated ADR provisions in the Constitution.[63] Second, the federal judiciary supported these provisions by positively interpreting ADR as a constitutional right.[64] Third, the judiciary established, in some decisions, a high threshold to review petitions by state agencies to set aside an award based on public policy violations.[65]

First, at the outset arbitration was only regulated in the Mexican arbitration law and not in the Constitution. Therefore, some practitioners considered that arbitration was unconstitutional. Some practitioners argued that arbitral tribunals were 'special courts'[66] that breached Article 13 of the Mexican Federal Constitution. This Article establishes that no one may be tried by private laws or special courts.[67] Other practitioners argued that arbitral tribunals were constituted according to the rules of each arbitration; they were courts not previously established by law breaching constitutional Article 14.[68] This Article establishes that no person shall be deprived of life, freedom, property, possessions, or rights without due process of law in a trial before

[60] Works Law, art 15; Acquisitions Law, art 15.

[61] Ovalle Piedra (n 9) 9.

[62] Iniciativa que expide la Ley para agilizar el Ejercicio del Presupuesto y la Inversión Pública, a cargo del Diputado Carlos Rojas Gutiérrez, del Grupo Parlamentario del PRI, y suscrita por integrantes de diversos grupos parlamentarios (18 March 2009) (translation by the authors).

[63] Decreto por el que se reforman y adicionan diversas disposiciones de la Constitución Política de los Estados Unidos Mexicanos, published in the Federal Official Gazette on 18 June 2008, art 17.

[64] Case [2016] First Chamber, Amparo Directo 71/2014.

[65] ibid. See also Case [2011] First Chamber, Amparo en Revisión 527/2011; Case [2012] First Chamber, Amparo en Revisión 755/2011.

[66] Arbitraje Comercial. Los Artículos 1415 A 1463 del Código de Comercio, No Violan el Artículo 13 de la Constitución Federal [2005] First Chamber, SJFG, XXI,1a.CLXXVI/2004, 411 (179667); José Carlos Fernández Rozas, 'La Constitución Mexicana y el Arbitraje Comercial' [2007] 16 Cuestiones Constitucionales 174.

[67] Federal Constitution, art 13.

[68] ibid art 14.

a previously established court. However, arbitration prevailed based on the contractual freedom of the parties to waive their right to have those matters resolved by state courts.[69]

On 6 June 2008, Congress amended Article 17 of the Constitution to expressly state that 'laws shall provide for [ADR]'.[70] Article 17 establishes that no one may take the law into their own hands or resort to violence in the enforcement of their rights. The amendment introducing ADR occurred as part of a new criminal justice system which aimed at resolving criminal disputes and assisting the overworked judiciary.[71] The amendment states the following: 'Laws shall provide for alternative dispute resolution mechanisms. In criminal matters, laws shall govern their application, ensure redress and establish the cases in which judicial supervision is required.'[72] Although it mainly aims at solving criminal matters, the terms of the amended Article 17 are by their nature expressed in such general terms as to lend themselves to guarantee ADR in all other matters, including commercial arbitration and PPA. The Mexican Supreme Court[73] ruled that, before the constitutional amendment, arbitration was an infraconstitutional legal institution; but today ADR has gained constitutional protection. The amendment wipes out any claim questioning the constitutional validity of arbitration.[74] Even though international treaty obligations did not motivate the amendment,[75] this also represents Mexico's response to comply with FTA obligations because Mexico keeps 'facilitat[ing] the use of arbitration and' other ADR 'for the settlement of international commercial disputes between private parties in the free trade area'.[76]

Some practitioners questioned the constitutionality of arbitration based on Article 17 of the Constitution. The First Chamber of the Supreme Court interpreted Article 17 as not to imply that all controversies must be decided by the judiciary, because it allows ADR.[77] Thus, arbitration is a legislative institution with constitutional relevance. Also, arbitration does not imply a waiver of one's right to have certain matters resolved by a court. Instead, arbitration implies the affirmative exercise of constitutional freedoms protected by the judiciary.[78]

Second, the Third Circuit Court has interpreted the amendment by holding that Article 17 of the Federal Constitution 'recognizes, as a human right, the possibility

[69] Arbitraje. Cuando el accionante Ocurra ante el Juez a Presentar su Demanda y el Reo dé Contestación a Ésta o Reconvenga, quedará Extinguido el Compromiso Arbitral, Siempre que no se oponga la Excepción de Incompetencia [2007] 5th Collegiate Court in Civil Matters 3rd Cr, SJFG, XXV, III.5o.C.115 C, 1660 (172829).

[70] Decreto por el que se reforman y adicionan diversas disposiciones de la Constitución Política de los Estados Unidos Mexicanos (n 63) art 17 (translation by the authors).

[71] Secretaría de Servicios Parlamentarios, 'Cuaderno de Apoyo Reforma Constitucional en Materia de Justicia Penal y Seguridad Pública (Proceso Legislativo)' SAD-07-08 (2008) 11 <www.diputados.gob.mx/sedia/biblio/archivo/SAD-07-08.pdf> accessed 22 January 2025.

[72] Federal Constitution, art 17.

[73] Ovalle Piedra (n 9) 9.

[74] Guerrero Rodríguez and Suárez Enríquez (n 44) 71.

[75] ibid 60.

[76] NAFTA (n 42) art 2022; Central America–Mexico FTA (n 37) art 17.22; Colombia–Mexico–Venezuela FTA (n 37) art 19.19; Mexico–Panama FTA (n 37) art 18.21; Mexico–Chile FTA (n 37) art 18.19.

[77] Case [2016] Amparo Directo 71/2014 (n 64) 229.

[78] Arbitraje. Implicaciones normativas derivadas de su constitucionalización a partir de la reforma de junio de 2008 [2017] First Chamber, SJFG, I, 1a. XXXVI/2017, 438 (2014010).

to settle disputes by [ADR] as long as they are prescribed by law'.[79] The Court reasoned that, as for ADR, 'the parties are the owners of their own problem (litigation) and, therefore, they are the ones who must decide how to solve it, so they can opt for a wide catalogue of possibilities, in which the process is one more'.[80] The Third Circuit noted that among the considerations expressed in the explanatory memorandum of the constitutional reform to Article 17, one consideration underscored that ADR mechanisms 'are a guarantee of the population to access to prompt and expeditious justice ... [ADR mechanisms] will allow . . . to change the paradigm of restorative justice, they will promote a more active participation of the population to find other ways to relate to each other'.[81] With this context, the Court concluded that 'both judicial protection and [ADR mechanisms] are established on the same constitutional level and with the same dignity and have the same purpose, which is to resolve disputes between subjects that are under the rule of law in' Mexico.[82] In a similar vein, the First Circuit underscored that 'the importance and significance of [Article 17's] reform is to elevate the human right of access to [ADR mechanisms] of a civil nature to constitutional level'.[83] The Supreme Court, however, has not addressed the issue of whether the right to use ADR constitutes a human right.

Third, the First Chamber of Mexico's Supreme Court established a high threshold to review an agency's or SOE's petition to set aside an award based on public policy *(orden público)*. A dispute arose out of *force majeure* events and contractual breaches of power generation agreements executed between CFE and a private contractor. An ICC tribunal declared the existence of *force majeure* events and CFE's failure to supply gas within certain technical parameters. CFE sought to set aside the arbitral award but the district court denied CFE's petition because CFE did not prove the grounds for annulment. Unsatisfied with the decision, CFE filed an *amparo* action to review the court's decision arguing, inter alia, (1) that the award breached public policy because it frustrated the contract's purpose (to have a power generation plant); and (2) that the enforcement of the award would cause significant degradation of the electric system's reliability and safety in the region.[84]

The First Chamber of Mexico's Supreme Court found CFE's argument meritless. The Chamber noted that CFE was part of the Public Administration, and that the agreement was the result of a public bidding.[85] The Chamber found that it was a matter of CFE's policy *(política pública)* to prepare a public bidding, enter into a contract, and agree to arbitration. This policy from its origin contained the option to have private arbitrators settle contractual disputes and all aspects of

[79] Acceso a los Mecanismos Alternativos de Solución de Controversias, como Derecho Humano. Goza de la misma dignidad que el acceso a la jurisdicción del Estado [2012] 2nd Collegiate Court in Civil Matters 3rd Cr, SJFG, XXV, III.2º.C.6 K(10ª) 1723 (2004620).

[80] ibid.

[81] ibid.

[82] ibid.

[83] Justicia alternativa. Constituye un derecho humano de rango constitucional [2019] 3rd Collegiate Court in Civil Matters, 1st Cr, GSJF, I.3o.C.3 CS (10ª) (2020851).

[84] Case [2016] Amparo Directo 71/2014 (n 64) 41–42, 45–52, 384.

[85] ibid 402–04.

power-generation subject matter of the agreement without the judiciary. By accepting arbitration, the Public Administration could reasonably anticipate that arbitrators would settle semantic indeterminacy and interpret the contract, and that the arbitral award would impact on the electric power generation.[86] The First Chamber held that the public policy *(orden público)* ground for annulment did not allow constitutional courts to assess arbitrators' policy *(política pública)* to decide a dispute over a public contract. Public policy *(orden público)* did not include policy *(política pública)* considerations; public policy *(orden público)* is a narrow concept dealing with objective principles, not with utilitarian considerations related to policy *(política pública)*.[87]

The First Chamber recalled that, as a general rule, courts should not review the merits of the award. Nonetheless, when a petitioner seeks to set aside the award based on public policy *(orden público)*, courts must assess the merits to ascertain whether the arbitrators have ignored fundamental principles of law.[88] The judiciary must assess the type of public interest at issue in the arbitral award, determine its specific weight in the case, and contrast it with the weight of Article 17 of the Constitution to preserve final and binding arbitration without the judiciary's intervention. The court must balance the type of public interest at issue with the arbitral award against the greatest effectiveness of arbitration.[89] The First Chamber held that, 'to preserve arbitration as an expression of individuals' freedom to settle disputes, only clear violations of important normative content justify the annulment of the award'.[90] The principle of promoting arbitration must prevail when minor clashes between the award and the interest protected occur, and 'given that the parties agreed to submit to arbitration, they must accept the arbitrator's decision, including possible interpretative deficiencies of the law incurred, unless it is blatantly unfair or incorrect'.[91] The Chamber concluded that the breach of public interest argued by CFE did not have enough weight to overcome the greater weight that the objective of preserving arbitration has. Further, the Supreme Court stated that it does not have the capacity to assess arguments based on policies or public utility; this analysis pertains to the technical bodies of the Public Administration. In the end, the state has the power to amend, suspend, or terminate the contract if it finds this convenient given the policy considerations made by CFE.[92]

Congress and the judiciary have generally taken positive endeavours to harmonize their activities with the international commitments set by FTAs, but the legal framework safeguarding public interests in PPA is complex. Now, we turn to explore this framework.

[86] ibid 404–05.
[87] ibid 410.
[88] ibid 411–13.
[89] ibid 415–16.
[90] ibid 417.
[91] ibid.
[92] ibid 418, 409.

IV. A Complex Legal Framework of Dual Public and Private Contracts that Varies across Different Industries Ensures Public Interest in PPA

In Mexico, two types of state contracts exist: (1) public contracts executed with agencies; and (2) private contracts executed with SOEs or agencies in the electric power industry.[93] PPA arises out of both private and public contracts.

On the one hand, public law mainly governs contracts entered into by agencies, although with some nuances. First, the Acquisitions Law[94] and Works Law[95] govern public acquisitions, leases, and works. The Federal Civil Code and administrative laws fill the gaps of both laws.[96] Second, the PPP Law governs PPP contracts. The Commerce Code and the Federal Civil Code (private law) fill the gaps of the PPP Law.[97] Third, the Hydrocarbons Law, which is part of public law, governs contracts for the exploration and extraction of hydrocarbons. Private law fills gaps in the Hydrocarbons Law.[98] Manifold administrative laws govern concessions in telecommunications, roads, mining, and air transportation, among other industries.

On the other hand, private contracts exist: (1) with agencies in the electric power industry;[99] and (2) with the Mexican energy SOEs, CFE and PEMEX. Contracts concluded with CFE and PEMEX start with an administrative process, but ultimately have a private nature. First, CFE and PEMEX tender these contracts with an administrative process that ends with the award of a contract. Thus, all the acts of public authority during the tendering procedure will have an administrative nature. Once parties sign the contract, private law governs the contract,[100] ascribing it a private law nature.

Public interest safeguards vary depending on the public or private nature of the contract at issue. The safeguards relating to public contracts include: (1) the doctrine of administrative contracts; and (2) the exclusion of acts of public authority from the scope of arbitration or arbitrability. The acts of public authority excluded from arbitration vary depending on the law or sector. However, the above two safeguards do not apply to PPA arising out of private contracts concluded with SOEs. No uniform framework governs across all public and private contracts or industries. Nonetheless, general principles of constitutional law and FTAs apply to all contracts. We turn to explore these aspects.

[93] See section IV.D below. See also Acquisitions Law, arts 2, 11; Works Law, arts 2, 13; PPP Law, art 8; Hydrocarbons Law, art 22; PEMEX Law (2014) arts 3, 80; CFE Law (2014) arts 3, 7, 82; Electric Industry Law, art 5.

[94] Acquisitions Law, art 2.

[95] Works Law, art 2.

[96] Acquisitions Law, art 11; Works Law, art 13.

[97] PPP Law, art 8.

[98] Hydrocarbons Law, art 22.

[99] Electric Industry Law, art 5.

[100] PEMEX Law (2014) art 80; CFE Law (2014) art 82. Private law fills the gaps of both laws: PEMEX Law, art 3; CFE Law, arts 3, 7.

A. General Principles of Constitutional Law and International Treaties Apply to All State Contracts

The intricate legal regime governing public and private state contracts is composed of the Constitution, FTAs,[101] statutory laws, regulations, guidelines, and many other bodies of law.[102] Given that thirty-two states compose the Mexican Federation, municipal, state, and federal rules govern public procurement. Nevertheless, lawmakers have harmonized this complex system with the public procurement provisions of the Federal Constitution and FTAs. Under Article 134 of the Federal Constitution, the Federation, states, municipalities, and other entities must manage economic resources with efficiency, effectiveness, economy, transparency, and honesty. Additionally, to secure the best conditions of price, quality, finance, and timing, the government must carry out tendering procedures to award all private and public contracts. However, the Constitution does not set forth limits as to when and how the legislator may authorize the use of PPAs or how to grant power to authorities to agree to arbitration or address the way arbitrators must conduct PPAs. Thus, lawmakers may regulate PPA through specific sector or industry laws with sufficient leeway; however, in this legislative task they must take into account the doctrine of administrative contracts, when applicable, and conform to the principle of legality.

B. The Doctrine of Administrative Contracts

The French doctrine of administrative contracts has influenced the Mexican system, and it explains the main safeguards governing PPA. These administrative contracts traditionally depict six characteristics. First, contracting parties include: (a) a state entity and (b) a private or public person. Second, inequality or subordination exists among the contracting parties, that is, the Public Administration and the contractor. On the one hand, the law restrains the private person's will to freely negotiate; the bidding guidelines and the contractual terms are not subject to negotiation.[103] On the other hand, the contracting parties pursue different aims: the contractor pursues a private economic interest while the government pursues the public interest and the satisfaction of a collective public necessity. Third, administrative contracts are flexible. A state entity may seek a third party to continue the contract's performance when the original contractor fails to perform.[104] Fourth, the principle of legality applies to these contracts.[105] Fifth, traditionally, administrative courts resolve disputes

[101] The FTAs concluded with the United States and Canada, Chile, Costa Rica, Guatemala, Honduras, Colombia, the European Union, Israel, Japan, Nicaragua, Iceland, Liechtenstein, Norway, and Switzerland include a government procurement chapter.
[102] These include the National Development Plan, Sector Development Plans, Políticas, Bases y Lineamientos (POBALINES), Manuales de Aplicación, and Programa Anual de Adquisiciones y Servicios o de Obras.
[103] Acquisitions Law, art 26; PPP Law, art 46.
[104] Acquisitions Law, art 41.IV; Works Law, art 42.6.
[105] Acquisitions Law, art 15; Works Law, art 15; Laura Ruiz García, *Contratos Administrativos* (Flores Editor 2010) 266–72; González de Cossío, 'Arbitraje y Contratación Gubernamental' (n 9).

concerning administrative contracts.[106] Nonetheless, PPA and ADR have recently modified this conception.

Lastly, '*cláusulas exorbitantes*' (exorbitant clauses) that may be abusive under private law appear as valid in these contracts because they ensure the constant operation of public services.[107] Exorbitant clauses mean those clauses that go beyond the orbit of ordinary law; that is, clauses that attribute to the Public Administration prerogatives with respect to the contractor that cannot be conferred upon any of the parties in any ordinary contract or that grant the contractor specific powers with respect to third parties which are impossible to confer under private law.[108] For instance, under the Works Law, once the agency notifies the contractor about the contract's early termination or administrative rescission, the agency must immediately take possession of the works and the property.[109] Later, we analyse in further detail how the legislature uses these safeguards of public interest in PPA. However, as commented above, this doctrine seems to be incompatible with the new legal framework provided by the Pemex Law, the CFE Law, and the Electric Industry Law, which ascribe a private nature to the contracts governed by these laws.

C. The Principle of Legality Concerning Acts of Authority and Arbitration

The doctrine of administrative contracts and the principle of legality set a special framework to tender and perform administrative contracts. The principle of legality becomes relevant to this discussion for three reasons. First, it defines the boundaries under which public agencies can act. This principle also applies to the agencies' contractual performance. Second, public officers can only act under the express terms of the law. Third, public agencies may agree to arbitration if a law so permits. Therefore, the principle of legality constitutes a safeguard of public interest in contracts and PPA by restraining the will or scope of manoeuvring of the agency.

First, the Federal Constitution[110] enshrines the principle of legality, which limits the acts of public authorities and safeguards the public interest in PPA by requiring specific provisions in the law enabling the act. Acts of public authority are unilateral acts of public officers based on law that create, modify, or terminate rights and obligations affecting someone else's rights without a court decision or the aggrieved person's will.[111] The competent authority must issue its acts in writing and state legal grounds

[106] Federal Judicial Power Organic Law, art 52.I; Organic Law of the Administrative Federal Court, art 3.VIII; Rescisión administrativa de contratos de obras públicas y servicios relacionados con las mismas y su cumplimiento. Son impugnables mediante el juicio contencioso administrativo federal [2018] 1st Cr, SJFG, 58, I.4o.A.132 A (10ª.) 2510 (2018019); Contrato administrativo y contrato civil o mercantile. Diferencias [2001] 6th Cr, SJFG, XIV, VI.3o.A.50 A 1103 (188644).

[107] Contratos Administrativos. Se distinguen por su finalidad de orden público y por el régimen exorbitante del Derecho Civil a que están sujetos [2001] S.Ct., SJFG, XIII, P.IX/2001, 324 (189995).

[108] Jorge Fernández Ruiz, *Derecho Administrativo* (Secretaría de Gobernación/Secretaría de Cultura/INEHRM/IIJ-UNAM 2016) 167.

[109] Works Law, art 62.

[110] 'No one shall be molested in his person, family, domicile, papers or possessions except by a written order of the competent authority stating the legal grounds and justification for the action taken': see Federal Constitution, art 16 (unofficial translation).

[111] Contradicción de Tesis 422/2009 [2010], Second Chamber, SJFG, XXXI, 1977 (22066).

with sufficient detail and reasoning. The authority must base its reasoning on legal provisions;[112] otherwise, the act is void.[113] An act of public authority must comply with these requirements to be valid. All administrative, legislative, and judicial authorities must respect this principle. It protects individuals and legal entities in their relationships with the state. This includes public agencies acting as contractual parties. An agency's decision to effect an administrative rescission, or to grant a release arising out of administrative contracts under the Acquisitions Law and Works Law, constitute acts of public authority.[114] These acts of authority must comply with the principle of legality.

Second, according to the principle of legality, 'authorities can only do what the law allows them to do'.[115] '[I]n the absence of a specific provision in the law, regulations, decree or order empowering the authority to give, to do or not to do something, then it must be understood that it is forbidden.'[116] Any act of public authority not expressly authorized by law is void.[117] Consequently, the Constitution regulates the exploitation of certain resources, contractual forms, and payments in certain industries.[118] The Acquisitions Law, Works Law, PPP Law, Hydrocarbons Law, and their respective regulations and guidelines, exhaustively control the tendering procedure and its exceptions to the contract's performance, advance payment conditions, payment procedures, amendments, suspensions, administrative rescission, early termination, and dispute resolution mechanisms. Any act or contract against the law is void.[119]

[112] Raúl Pérez Johnston, 'Artículo 16. Actos de molestia' in Eduardo Ferrer Mac-Gregor Poisot and others (eds), *Derechos Humanos en la Constitución: Comentarios de Jurisprudencia Constitucional e Interamericana* (SCJN/UNAM 2013) 1538–39.

[113] Federal Law on Administrative Procedure, arts 3(I) and (V) and 51 (I), (II).

[114] Rescisión Administrativa de contratos de adquisiciones o de obra pública. Contra dicha determinación debe agotarse el juicio contencioso administrativo federal [2012] 2nd Collegiate Court in Administrative Matter 3rd Cr, SJFG, IV, 5, III.2°.A.253 A (9ª), 4600 (160355); Rescisión Administrativa de contratos de obras públicas y servicios relacionados con las mismas, y de adquisiciones, arrendamientos y servicios del sector público, decretada por las dependencias y entidades de la administración pública federal. Es impugnable en el juicio contencioso administrativo ante el Tribunal Federal de Justicia Fiscal y Administrativa [2010] Second Chamber, SJFG, XXXI, 2ª./J.4/2010, 312 (165410); Finiquito de obra pública por el incumplimiento de la persona moral, emitido por Caminos y Puentes Federales de Ingresos y Servicios Conexos. Constituye un acto definitivo impugnable mediante juicio de nulidad ante el Tribunal Federal de Justicia Fiscal y Administrativa [2010] 1st Collegiate Court in Administrative Matter 6 Cr, SJFG, XXXI, VI.1o.A.282 A, 2122 (165549); Resolución recaída a la solicitud de modificación de pena convencional derivada de un contrato celebrado con base en la Ley de Adquisiciones, Arrendamientos y Servicios del Sector Público. Se surte la competencia material del Tribunal Federal de Justicia Fiscal y Administrativa [2008] RTFJFA, I, 2, 43 (50215).

[115] Autoridades [1924] SCJN, XV, 250 (810781); Autoridades, Facultades de las [1934] SCJN, XLI, 944 (336190).

[116] José Ríos Martínez, 'Interpretación en la Dogmática Jurídica como Posibilidad de Ciencia del Derecho' [2007] 3(5) RPD UNAM 147–69 <www.juridicas.unam.mx/publica/librev/rev/posder/cont/5/cnt/cnt8.pdf> accessed 22 January 2025.

[117] Autoridades Administrativas, Facultades De Las. Limite [1988] 4 Collegiate Court in Administrative Matter 1st Cr, I, 144 (231059); Roberto Islas Montes, 'Sobre el principio de legalidad' [2009] XV Anuario de Derecho Constitucional Latinoamericano 101 (citing Karla Pérez Portilla, *Principio de igualdad* (UNAM 2005) 55).

[118] A concession allows exploitation of mines, water resources, broadcasting and telecommunications. Services agreements, licence agreements, and production sharing agreements enable the extraction of oil: Federal Constitution, art 28.

[119] Acquisitions Law, arts 13, 15, 26–55; Works Law, arts 15, 27–69; PPP Law, arts 38–66, 91–111, 122, 134–43; Hydrocarbons Law, arts 11–31.

Thus, authorities must act according to the express terms of the law and the contract's clauses. A contractual clause against the terms of the law is void. Public officers may be held responsible if they act against the law.[120] Consequently, public officers may only agree to arbitration, pay considerations, or effect administrative rescission provided that certain laws allow them to do so and grant them authority to act accordingly.[121] For instance, a Head of the Administrative Office and the General Directors of the Ministry of National Defence are the competent authorities with powers conferred by a decree to administratively rescind or terminate contracts and to execute surety bonds in works, acquisitions, and leases agreements.[122] The PEMEX Law and the CFE Law grant powers to the General Director to agree to arbitration.[123]

Third, the principle of legality safeguards public interests in PPA by requiring an express provision in the law enabling the authority to agree to arbitration. A law must provide for these clauses. An agency may argue that the Mexican arbitration law provides for arbitration, which in turn enables it to consent to arbitration. This interpretation has not been tested yet. In any case, the principle of legality limits agencies' contractual autonomy to agree to arbitration. For that reason, the corresponding laws lay down the possibility to agree to arbitration.[124] Mexican authorities may not freely agree to arbitration if the law does not allow them to do so.[125] Mindful of these safeguards, we analyse federal law permitting arbitration, and protecting the public interest in the following subsection.

D. Laws Enabling Arbitration and Safeguards of Public Interest

The principle of legality safeguards public interests by requiring an express provision in the law allowing agencies to agree to arbitration. Congress complied with FTAs' obligations to encourage and facilitate the use of arbitration and the principle of legality by including arbitration in some laws. Lawmakers have decided to safeguard public interests by limiting the scope of arbitration. Certain acts of public authority—mainly the exorbitant clauses like early termination and administrative rescission—cannot be subject to arbitration. Congress has never explained its decision to exclude these matters from arbitration. Still, public policy reasons may explain that decision. In the event of an early termination or administrative rescission notice, the agency must take immediate possession of the works.[126] As we will discuss later, Wöss observes that the exclusion of arbitrability is limited to administrative rescission and early termination but arbitral tribunals continue to hold jurisdiction to rule on damages and lost profits.

[120] General Law of Administrative Liabilities, arts 7.1, 49, 50.

[121] Competencia. Solo Deriva de la Ley no de un Contrato [1989] 3rd Collegiate Court in Administrative Matter 1st Cr, III, 991 (229439); Competencia. Deriva de la Ley no de un Contrato de Obra Pública [2008] RTFJFA, 378/08-03-01-2, 576.

[122] Acuerdo por el que se delegan diversas facultades en materia contractual a favor del Oficial Mayor y de los Directores Generales de la Secretaría de la Defensa Nacional (9 July 2014) art 1.

[123] PEMEX Law, art 46.I; CFE Law, art 45.I.

[124] Acquisitions Law, art 80; Works Law, art 98; PPP Law, art 138; Hydrocarbons Law, art 21; CFE Law, art 118; PEMEX Law, art 115.

[125] Acquisitions Law, art 15; Works Law, art 15.

[126] Works Law, art 62.

Nonetheless, arbitral tribunals must respect the decision of the judicial authority on the legality of the administrative rescission or early termination, if contested.[127]

To further understand the safeguards, we must explain the concept of administrative rescission. Under private law, a party who has performed the contract can file a complaint or notice of arbitration asking a judge or arbitrator to declare the rescission of a contract in the case of failure to perform by the other party.[128] However, parties can also agree to rescind the contract without an arbitral or judicial decision.[129] Under administrative law, an agency may rescind a contract without going to court, by an administrative procedure that starts with a notice of breach. The contractor may answer the notice with arguments and provide the evidence it deems pertinent within fifteen working days under the Works Law, and five days under the Acquisitions Law. Thereafter, the agency must decide whether to rescind or not within fifteen working days.[130] The statute of limitations bars the agency from rendering a decision exceeding that period. The decision must comply with the principle of legality; otherwise, the contractor can ask an administrative court to set aside the decision.[131]

1 Works Law and Acquisitions Law

The Works Law governs all public works and related services; the Acquisitions Law governs public purchases, leases, and related services. As previously mentioned, these laws originally allowed arbitration but also required an agency to specify the matters subject to arbitration. This regulation was never issued in principle. In 2009, Congress amended both laws to permit arbitration but excluded administrative rescission and early termination from arbitrability.[132] Thus, the Federal Administrative Justice Court has jurisdiction to resolve disputes regarding the validity of the administrative rescission and early termination.[133] An arbitral tribunal may deal with damages and

[127] Wöss, 'Arbitraje' (n 9) 130.

[128] Federal Civil Code, art 1949.

[129] Pacto comisorio expreso. Opera de pleno derecho, sin que sea necesario que la autoridad judicial determine la procedencia o improcedencia de la rescisión del contrato [2001] 1st Chamber of the SCt, SJFG, XIII, 2001, 1ª./J. 23/2001, 165 (189425).

[130] Works Law, art 62; Acquisitions Law, art 54. The Hydrocarbons Law grants the contractor thirty calendar days to answer the notice, and under the National Hydrocarbons Law the decision whether to effect the rescission must be made within ninety calendar days: Hydrocarbons Law, art 20.

[131] Acquisitions Law, art 54; Works Law, art 61; Federal Law on Administrative Procedure, arts 60, 3.V, 5–6.

[132] Works Law, art 98; Acquisitions Law, art 80.

[133] Organic Law of the Federal Administrative Justice Court, art 3.VIII. See also Rescisión Administrativa de contratos de adquisiciones o de obra pública. Contra dicha determinación debe agotarse el juicio contencioso administrativo federal [2012] 2nd Collegiate Court in Administrative Matter 3rd Cr, SJFG, IV, 5, III.2º.A.253 A (9ª), 4600 (160355); Rescisión Administrativa de contratos de obras públicas y servicios relacionados con las mismas, y de adquisiciones, arrendamientos y servicios del sector público, decretada por las dependencias y entidades de la administración pública federal. Es impugnable en el juicio contencioso administrativo ante el Tribunal Federal de Justicia Fiscal y Administrativa [2010] Second Chamber, SJFG, XXXI, 2ª./J.4/2010, 312 (165410); Finiquito de obra pública por el incumplimiento de la persona moral, emitido por Caminos y Puentes Federales de Ingresos y Servicios Conexos. Constituye un acto definitivo impugnable mediante juicio de nulidad ante el Tribunal Federal de Justicia Fiscal y Administrativa [2010] 1st Collegiate Court in Administrative Matter 6 Cr, SJFG, XXXI, VI.1o.A.282 A, 2122 (165549); Resolución recaída a la solicitud de modificación de pena convencional derivada de un contrato celebrado con base en la Ley de Adquisiciones, Arrendamientos y Servicios del Sector Público. Se surte la competencia material del Tribunal Federal de Justicia Fiscal y Administrativa [2008] RTFJFA, I, 2, 43 (50215).

lost profits claims regarding the rescission or early termination since they are not expressly excluded from arbitrability.[134] Preferably, arbitration dealing with damages and lost profits should wait for the Court's decision on the legality of the administrative rescission or early termination, if claimed. Mexican law governs these contracts; foreign law can only govern contracts concluded abroad.[135] Wöss opines that if the performance takes place in Mexico, the contract must be subject to Mexican law and the place of arbitration should be in Mexico. Normally, Mexico City is agreed to as the seat of arbitration.[136]

2 Public-Private Partnerships Law

Federal PPPs have recently appeared in Mexico. Consistent with the patchwork tradition of approving and amending laws, the Acquisitions Law used to govern them,[137] and although the framework was not specifically tailored for PPPs, major infrastructure projects came into existence on its basis. In 2012, a separate PPP Law entered into force, henceforth governing all PPPs. PPP projects establish a long-term relationship between the public and private sectors for the provision of public services. They use infrastructure provided by the private sector with the purpose of increasing social welfare and investment levels in Mexico.[138] The new framework currently governs around sixty projects; the most notable ones include vehicular traffic facilities, hospitals, two viaducts, roads, the Red Compartida (a telecommunications project), a museum, and an aqueduct. These projects are highly technical and require lots of permits. We analysed seven contracts, of which six contained arbitration clauses (three ad hoc arbitration, and three ICC clauses) and one had no arbitration clause.[139]

The PPP Law allows arbitration, but only in the Spanish language and governed by Federal Mexican Law. The PPP Law excludes from arbitration the revocation of concessions, and authorizations; and acts of public authority. Federal courts have exclusive jurisdiction to rule on the validity of administrative acts.[140] Congress did not provide any reason for excluding these matters from arbitration. The arbitral tribunal

[134] Acquisitions Law, art 85; Works Law, art 103; Wöss, 'Arbitraje' (n 9) 131–32; Abascal (n 10) 386.

[135] Works Law, arts 15–16; Acquisitions Law, arts 15–16.

[136] ibid; Wöss, 'Arbitraje' (n 9) 131.

[137] PPP Law, art 3 (VI).

[138] ibid art 2.

[139] Contrato de Asociación Público-Privada que celebran el Organismo Promotor de Inversiones en Telecomunicaciones y Telecomunicaciones México con Altán Redes, SAPI de CV [2017] cl 41.2 (ICC arbitration); Modelo de Contrato Plurianual de Prestación de Servicios para la Conservación del Tramo Carretero Texcoco-Zacatepec [2017] cl 20.2.2.b (ad hoc arbitration); Modelo de Contrato Plurianual de Prestación de Servicios para la Conservación del Tramo Carretero Pirámides, Tulancingo, Pachuca [2017] cl 20.2.2 (ad hoc arbitration); Modelo de Contrato APP para la Autopista Monterrey-Nuevo Laredo Tramo La Gloria-San Fernando [2017] cl 23.2 (ICC arbitration); Modelo de Contrato de APP para la Prestación de Servicios Complementarios a los Servicios Médicos que Presta el IMSS para el Diseño y Construcción, Equipamiento, Operación, Mantenimiento y Prestación de Servicios en el Inmueble Ubicado en Tapachula, Chiapas [2017] cl 23 (federal jurisdiction); Modelo de Contrato de Prestación de Servicios en la Modalidad de APP para el Proyecto de Sustitución del Actual Hospital General Dr. Daniel Gurría Urgell en Centro, Tabasco [2017] cl 23.2.3 (ad hoc arbitration); Modelo de Contrato de APP para la Construcción, Equipamiento Museográfico, Operación y Mantenimiento del Museo Internacional del Barroco [2014] cl 22.2 (ICC arbitration). All available via<https://compranet.funcionpublica.gob.mx/> accessed on 22 January 2025.

[140] PPP Law, art 139.

can decide any other matter beyond the validity of the administrative acts.[141] This division of competences, however, creates problems. First, the judiciary can interpret the concept of 'acts of public authority' in such general terms as to cover any act of the public administration related to the contract. Second, some PPP projects include a concession agreement without an arbitration clause; they tend to have a jurisdictional clause.[142] Hence, courts have jurisdiction to hear disputes related to concession agreements[143] and arbitral tribunals will have jurisdiction to hear disputes related to the PPP contract.[144] Parallel proceedings may arise—arbitration for contractual disputes and litigation for concession disputes—and may create contradictory decisions.

3 The Energy Field

In December 2013, Congress approved a comprehensive energy reform that allowed more participation from the private sector in this field. Congress took a mixed approach to allow PPA and safeguard the public interest in upstream activities, the electric power market, and the energy SOEs. As we navigate the regulation of PPA in the hydrocarbons and electric power sectors, we will confirm that there exists no general framework that safeguards the public interest in PPA across all contracts.

4 Upstream Activities

The Hydrocarbons Law allows arbitration of contracts for the exploration and extraction of hydrocarbons but excludes administrative rescission and termination from arbitration. To challenge the validity of the administrative rescission, an aggrieved party must file an indirect *amparo* action[145] before a district court. Later, the unsatisfied contractor may appeal this decision.[146] In connection with arbitration, this law requires the arbitration to be conducted in Spanish and in accordance with the Mexican arbitration law. Mexican Federal Laws must govern the contract. The award must pay strict adherence to the law.[147] The Model Production-Sharing Agreements for Oil Round 1 contain an arbitration clause under the UNCITRAL Arbitration Rules. The seat of arbitration is The Hague.

5 The Electric Power Market

The electric power market has also accepted arbitration to settle disputes. The Electric Power Industry Law opened the door for arbitration by providing that the Electric Market Regulation (Reglas del Mercado) must establish the mechanisms to settle disputes.[148] Accordingly, the Dispute Resolution Manual, which forms part of the

[141] ibid art 122; Wöss, 'Solución' (n 9) 191.
[142] Título de Concesión para uso comercial que otorga el Instituto Federal de Telecomunicaciones con Carácter de Red Compartida Mayorista de Servicios de Telecomunicaciones, en Favor de Altán Redes, SAPI de CV [2017] cl 22 (cl 22 grants jurisdiction to the Specialised Courts in Competition and Telecommunications Matters).
[143] ibid; Federal Code of Civil Procedure, art 568.III.
[144] Contrato de Asociación Público-Privada que celebran el Organismo Promotor de Inversiones en Telecomunicaciones y Telecomunicaciones México con Altán Redes, SAPI de CV [2017] cl 41.2 (ICC arbitration).
[145] Ley de los Órganos Reguladores Coordinados en Materia Energética, art 27.
[146] Amparo Law, art 81.I.e.
[147] Hydrocarbons Law, art 21.
[148] Electric Power Industry Law, art 96.

Electric Market Regulation, established that, if a resolution of the National Center for Energy Control (CENACE), the Mexican operator of the national electric system, is not satisfactory for the market participants, carriers, or distributors, they may submit the dispute to arbitration, among other dispute resolution options.[149] Arbitration under the rules of the International Centre for Dispute Resolution (ICDR) will proceed, as a default rule, if market participants, carriers, and distributors cannot agree on dispute resolution. Federal Mexican law will govern the merits.[150] No matters are excluded from arbitration.

6 Productive Companies of the State: PEMEX and CFE

The PEMEX Law and the CFE Law govern all acts, agreements, securities, and guarantees entered into by PEMEX or CFE. The PEMEX Law and the CFE Law contain express provisions authorizing ADR, including arbitration. PEMEX, CFE, and their subsidiaries may agree to contracts governed by foreign law when the contracts have effects abroad, as well as to the jurisdiction of foreign courts in commercial matters.[151] But these laws make no reference to administrative rescission or early termination, which is consistent with the new commercial nature ascribed to the contract.[152] Additionally, no matters are excluded from arbitration under these laws. Consequently, these laws improve certainty and predictability by avoiding risks of parallel proceedings and providing an effective avenue for dispute resolution.

E. Conclusion

As we anticipated, there exists no uniform framework safeguarding the public interest across all public and private contracts or industries to which public actors are party. The principle of legality governs across all the laws by demanding them to expressly authorize arbitration in their provisions, but apart from that the legal framework is distinct and convoluted, confirming the existence of a patchwork of laws. The Works Law, Acquisitions Law, PPP Law, and Hydrocarbons Law mainly safeguard the public interest by excluding certain acts of public authority—administrative rescission and termination—from arbitration. This exclusion of acts of public authority lies in the doctrine of administrative contracts. By contrast, the Electric Power Industry Law, Pemex Law, and CFE Law do not contain these safeguards. This approach seems consistent with the new commercial nature ascribed to the contracts by these laws.

Despite the exclusions of certain acts of public authority from arbitration, the application of constitutional principles, and in some cases the doctrine of administrative contracts, arbitral tribunals conduct Mexican PPAs like any other commercial arbitration. Now, we turn to illustrate with one case the effects this legislative patchwork and judicial interpretation can have in practice.

[149] Dispute Resolution Manual, art 3.2.6.
[150] ibid art 3.5.
[151] PEMEX Law, art 115; CFE Law, art 118.
[152] Wöss, 'Arbitration under the Mexican Energy Reform' (n 9).

V. The Effects of a Legislative Patchwork in Practice

As the reader can observe at this point, there have been some advances regarding PPA and arbitration in Mexico; however, there is no uniform framework safeguarding the public interest across all public and private contracts or industries. Mexico has carried out different actions aimed at promoting free trade and foreign investment and modernizing its legislation. However, such efforts have been hindered precisely because lawmakers have passed amendments to the Mexican laws as a patchwork solving the challenges of the political and economic moment, and not by implementing an integral, well-organized, and harmonious system. Not surprisingly, Mexico has a complex legal framework with distinct provisions applicable to different industries. This has caused some practical complications. The authors consider that the *COMMISA* case is a good example for indicating some of these complications. Consequently, in this section the *COMMISA* case will illustrate the problems of Mexico's patchwork approach.

One caveat though: *COMMISA* is unique in many aspects. First, parallel proceedings included commercial and investment arbitration, and litigation, in Mexico, Luxembourg, and the United States. Second, dispute settlement lasted almost fifteen years. Third, during more than a decade, laws and case law evolved in connection with administrative rescission and recourse for challenging the administrative acts. Fourth, nowadays PEMEX contracts have a private nature and the PEMEX Law does not exclude administrative rescission from arbitration. However, *COMMISA*'s precedents serve us to understand other disputes that may arise under the legislative patchwork of the Works Law, Acquisitions Law, PPP Law, and Hydrocarbons Law. The Mexican and US judicial rulings illustrate how one nation's public interest safeguards can result in different interpretations depending on the jurisdiction.

A. Introduction

In 1997, Corporación Mexicana de Mantenimiento Integral, S. de R.L. de C.V. (COMMISA) and Pemex-Exploración y Producción (PEP) concluded a contract for public works (No. PEP-0-129/97) for the execution of engineering, procurement, manufacturing, transportation, installation, interconnection, testing, and starting up of two offshore platforms located in Bahía de Campeche. The contract included, in section 23.3, an arbitration agreement. Pursuant to the contract for public works, COMMISA posted a bond. When COMMISA and PEP entered into this contract, the administrative rescission was not expressly excluded from arbitration.

In 2002, due to disputes between the parties, COMMISA started conciliation proceedings with PEP. The conciliation was not successful, and in 2004[153] PEP notified COMMISA of the administrative rescission of the contract and called the bonds. Therefore, COMMISA started an ICC arbitration.[154] Within the arbitration,

[153] *Oficio* SIDEO/531/04 (16 December 2004).

[154] *Corporación Mexicana de Mantenimiento Integral, S de RL de CV v Pemex Exploración y Producción*, ICC Case No 13613/CCO/JRF.

COMMISA requested the arbitral tribunal to decide whether PEP's decision to rescind the contract was consistent with the law.

While the ICC arbitration was being conducted, and in connection with the administrative rescission of the contract, in 2004 COMMISA filed an indirect *amparo (amparo indirecto)* before the Mexican courts invoking the unconstitutionality of some articles of the Services and Government Procurement Law.[155] COMMISA considered that Articles 14, 16, and 17 of the Mexican Constitution had been breached because certain provisions of the Services and Government Procurement Law did not allow the rescission of an administrative contract to be conducted as a procedure before national courts in which the essential formalities of the procedure were observed. The indirect *amparo* was heard in the Sixth Collegiate Court on Administrative Matters of Mexico (Sixth Collegiate Court). In 2007, this court denied COMMISA's *amparo*.

Based on the Sixth Collegiate Court's ruling, in the arbitration PEP advanced a res judicata defence and requested the arbitral tribunal to terminate the arbitration. In a preliminary award, the tribunal decided that it was competent to resolve the dispute. PEP decided not to challenge this preliminary award and instead, during the arbitration, advanced two new objections to the tribunal's competence: (1) that the *amparo* ruling declared the legality of the administrative rescission; and (2) that the tribunal should not address the validity of the administrative rescission because the *amparo*'s final determination ruled this matter. PEP argued that, if the arbitral tribunal considered the rescission inconsistent with the law, such decision could compromise legal certainty.

In this case, parallel proceedings dealt with the same facts. Both the Sixth Collegiate Court and the arbitral tribunal were analysing the rescission of the contract between COMMISA and PEP. The risk in this case was a potential conflict between the award and the *amparo*'s final judgment. The risk became a fact. In the final award, the tribunal rejected PEP's res judicata arguments. The majority ruled in favour of COMMISA on most counts, although it also granted some of PEP's counterclaims.

The contract between COMMISA and PEP was executed in 1997, a few years after Mexico modernized its legislation due to the entry into force of the NAFTA, and after the adoption of the UNCITRAL Model Law on Arbitration. Considering the date of the contract, one may think that the natural expectation of the parties was that any dispute arising out of the contract would be subject to arbitration, including its rescission; specifically because, at that time, the administrative rescission was not expressly excluded from arbitration. This exclusion was not expressly included in the Works Law until 2009.[156] In fact, the Services and Government Procurement Law governed the contract. The Works Law was not enacted until 2000.

Additionally, it would be natural to think that, even if the legal framework had been subject to amendments after concluding the contract, the applicable rules to the contract would be those in force on the date of the contract, considering that pursuant to Article 14 of the Mexican Constitution no law shall be applied retroactively. The

[155] Specifically, COMMISA argued the unconstitutionality of Articles 40, 72(II), and 92 of the Services and Government Procurement Law, and of Article 52(II) of the Regulation of the Works Law.

[156] Works Law, art 98. See also Acquisitions Law, art 80.

COMMISA case presented some complications that will be set forth in the subsequent sections.

B. Judicial Proceedings in Mexico

In 2010, after COMMISA sought to enforce the award, PEP sought to set aside the award in Mexico City's Fifth District Court.[157] This court decided not to annul the award.[158] Displeased, PEP filed an indirect *amparo*[159] before the Tenth District Court, which declined to annul the award. Later, PEP filed a motion to review. The Eleventh Collegiate Court on Civil Matters[160] determined: (1) that PEP could act as a private entity without imperium, and could enter into agreements with third parties; and (2) PEP could also act as a public entity when the law granted it authority to act without going to court.[161]

Concerning public policy arguments sustained by PEP, the Eleventh Collegiate Court held that an arbitrator could decide on matters not forbidden, and on matters of free disposal that regulate the performance of private entities. A dispute should not be subject to arbitration if mandatory or prohibitive laws govern the matter. This was the limit of private autonomy. An award deciding on acts of public authority was against public policy.

The Eleventh Collegiate Court deemed that PEP entered into an arbitration agreement on an equal level, and not as a sovereign. Afterwards, PEP acted as a public authority in the dispute and its acts of authority were no longer subject to arbitration. Acts of public authority shall be subject to judicial authorities, otherwise the legal system would be transgressed and public policy would be damaged.

Moreover, the Eleventh Collegiate Court stated that authorities could unilaterally terminate a legal or factual situation without going to court. They could not waive these powers; hence, they were not subject to arbitration. Otherwise, this implied an attack on public policy, violating Article 6 of the Federal Civil Code because parties may only waive private rights.

Additionally, regarding res judicata, the Eleventh Collegiate Court concluded that a party could not challenge a res judicata matter. Given that the award ruled that PEP had breached the contract and acted illegally, the arbitral tribunal had disrupted the act of public authority because, in the *amparo* filed by COMMISA where it was seeking to challenge the administrative rescission, the court denied the *amparo*. This implied that PEP effected the administrative rescission as a valid act of public authority.

[157] *Pemex-Exploracion y Producción v Corporacion Mexicana De Mantenimiento Integral, S De RL De CV* [2010] Fifth District Court, juicio de nulidad de laudo 207/2010-II.

[158] ibid.

[159] *Pemex-Exploracion y Producción v Fifth District Court* [2010] Tenth District Court, amparo indirecto 604/2010-IV.

[160] *Pemex-Exploracion y Producción v Tenth District Court* [2010] Eleventh Collegiate Court, amparo en revision 358/2010.

[161] ibid 218–19.

The Eleventh Collegiate Court concluded that: (1) the arbitral tribunal lacked competence to decide on the facts and reasons causing the administrative rescission because they were not subject to arbitration; and (2) that the administrative court, and not the arbitral tribunal, had to deal with the issues related to COMMISA's performance and non-payment.

The Eleventh Collegiate Court indicated that an arbitral tribunal affected public policy if such tribunal ruled, modified, or altered the rescission. The court strengthened its reasoning by highlighting that the Congress amended the Works Law by excluding administrative rescission from arbitration to prevent this situation. The Court stressed that it was not retroactively applying the law but using it as a guiding principle.

The Court held that a federal administrative proceeding provided the proper venue for challenging the res judicata effect of the administrative rescission, which estopped the arbitral tribunal from rendering its award. The Eleventh Collegiate Court revoked the Fifth District Court's judgment, granted PEP's *amparo*, which sought to set aside the judgment, and remanded the case to the Fifth District Court with the instruction to issue a new judgment annulling the award. In 2011, the Fifth District Court set aside the award.

Once again, we can observe a legislative patchwork which caused complications when applying the law. First, the Eleventh Collegiate Court used the provisions of the Works Law, which excluded administrative rescission, to strengthen and guide its decision, even though such provisions were not in force when the contract was concluded. Second, the court's decision that the proper venue to challenge the administrative rescission was before federal administrative courts implied that COMMISA was precluded from challenging the administrative rescission because the forty-five-day statute of limitations had already elapsed.

C. The Award's Confirmation in the United States

In 2010, COMMISA petitioned the US District Court for the Southern District of New York to confirm the award. The District Court confirmed the award notwithstanding the nullification of the award by Mexico's Eleventh Collegiate Court;[162] PEP appealed this decision. The US Second Circuit Court of Appeals[163] held that the Southern District Court had properly exercised its discretion in confirming the award because giving effect to the award's nullification would run counter to US public policy and be 'repugnant to fundamental notions of what is decent and just'[164] in the United States.

In this case, given that the District Court's holding encompassed a denial of comity to a foreign judgment, the Court of Appeals reviewed the underlying conclusions

[162] *Corporacion Mexicana De Mantenimiento Integral, S De RL De CV v Pemex-Exploracion y Producción*, Case No 10 Civ 206 (AKH) (SDNY, 27 August 2013).

[163] *Corporacion Mexicana De Mantenimiento Integral, S De RL De CV v Pemex-Exploracion y Producción*, Docket No 13-4022 (2d Cir 2016).

[164] ibid 5.

of law *de novo* and the underlying findings of fact for clear error.[165] Article V of the Panama Convention limits a court's discretion in enforcing foreign awards. A court may refuse recognition and execution only when the requesting party can prove one of seven defences. On one of those grounds, an annulled award constitutes a ground to refuse confirmation. However, discretion to enforce an annulled arbitral award is constrained by the prudential concern of international comity.

Retroactive legislation that cancels the existing rights of a contract is repugnant under US law.[166] Fairness dictates that individuals should know what the law is and should conform their conduct accordingly, and thus expectations should not be disrupted. The amendment of the Works Law represented a retroactive application of the law.

If the Southern District Court had voided the award, COMMISA would have had no forum to bring its contract claims.[167] Absent confirmation of the award, COMMISA would lose the opportunity to bring its claims before a court because the forty-five-day statute of limitations to bring COMMISA's claims before the Administrative Court had elapsed. It is no conjecture that COMMISA's suit would be dismissed as time-barred; this Administrative Court did precisely that. COMMISA's inability to have its claims heard demonstrates the injustice.

The US court stated that PEP, acting on behalf of the Mexican government, had rescinded the contract. Then, through legislation, Mexico frustrated the possible relief available to COMMISA through arbitration, thus consigning COMMISA to a forum in which relief was foreclosed both by the statute of limitations and res judicata. The enforcement of such Mexican law amounted to a taking of private property without compensation and for the benefit of the government. This reasoning demonstrates the complexity that the application of laws, amended as a patchwork without a well-structured system considering all the consequences, has in practice. Additionally, the exclusion of acts of public authority from arbitration magnifies the problem.

The Court of Appeals affirmed the judgment. In 2017, KBR, COMMISA's parent company, reached a settlement for USD 435 million, which "provides for mutual dismissals and releases of all claims".[168]

VI. Final Comment

Constitutional principles concerning public contracting, especially the principle of legality, safeguard the public interest in all contracts. Concerning public contracts, Congress—without giving any explanation and approving a patchwork of laws—decided to allow arbitration, but has limited its scope by excluding certain matters, including the application of exorbitant clauses (administrative rescission or early

[165] ibid 12.
[166] ibid 30–32.
[167] ibid 36.
[168] See KBR, 'KBR Recovers Almost Half Billion Dollar Judgment, Resolves Lengthy Commercial Dispute' (Press Release, 10 April 2017) <https://seekingalpha.com/filing/3499833> accessed 22 January 2025.

termination) and other acts of public authority. This may create inefficiency when settling disputes because excluding matters from arbitration creates the risk of parallel judicial and arbitral proceedings—just as occurred in the COMMISA case—with delays and uncertainty. Private contracts concluded with SOEs and in the electric power industry do not face these problems. The principle of legality constitutes the main safeguard of the public interest in arbitration arising out of both public and private contracts. In private contracts, Congress, under the new regime, did not exclude from arbitration matters arising out of contracts with PEMEX, CFE, or in the electric industry.

By allowing PPA, the legislative acts comply with the international commitments laid down in Mexico's FTAs. These commitments and the spirit to liberalize the economy and aim to insert Mexico into world trade were the main forces causing PPA to come into existence in the early 1990s. NAFTA's entry into force constituted the most immediate cause for the reforms that allowed PPAs, and has formed Mexican arbitration law.

Select Materials

Bibliography

Andrade-Max, Diego A, 'Las personas morales de derecho público como partes en el arbitraje comercial internacional' (1993) 22 Jurídica Ibero 431

Cabrera, Jennifer, Dante Figueroa, and Herfried Wöss, 'The Administrative Contract, Non-Arbitrability, and the Recognition and Execution of Awards Annulled in the Country of Origin: The Case of *Commisa v Pemex*' (2016) 32 Arb Intl 125

Cabrera, Orlando F and Eduardo Silva da Silva, 'Law and Arbitration of Oil and Gas Disputes in Brazil and Mexico' (2011) 9(2) OGEL 1

Cabrera, Orlando F and Eduardo Silva da Silva, 'La arbitrabilidad de los contratos administrativos en Latinoamérica' (2016–2017) 7 Lima Arbitration 272

Cortés Araujo, Bernardo, 'Nueva Ley de Petróleos Mexicanos – Implicaciones en el Arbitraje Comercial' [2014] Boletín CAIC 1

Fernández Rozas, José Carlos, 'La Constitución Mexicana y el Arbitraje Comercial' [2007] 16 Cuestiones Constitucionales 174

Fernández Ruiz, Jorge, *Derecho Administrativo* (Secretaría de Gobernación/Secretaría de Cultura/INEHRM/IIJ-UNAM 2016)

González de Cossío, Francisco, 'Arbitraje y Contratación Gubernamental' [2012] 15/2012 SAR España 121

González de Cossío, Francisco, 'El arbitraje como solución al dilema de las obras de infraestructura' (2013) 4 Revista de Derecho Privado 1

Guerrero Rodríguez, Luis Omar and Ximena Suárez Enríquez, 'La implementación del Artículo 2022 del TLCAN' [2009] 39 Jurídica 57

Islas Montes, Roberto, 'Sobre el principio de legalidad' [2009] XV Anuario de Derecho Constitucional Latinoamericano 101

Martínez Rosas, Rafael, 'Arbitraje, contratación pública y juicio de amparo' (2013) 15(171) El Mundo del Abogado 34

Ovalle Piedra, Julieta, 'Contratos Administrativos y Arbitraje en México' [2013] Boletín CAIC 1

Pérez Johnston, Raúl, 'Artículo 16. Actos de molestia' in Eduardo Ferrer Mac-Gregor Poisot and others (eds), *Derechos Humanos en la Constitución: Comentarios de Jurisprudencia Constitucional e Interamericana* (SCJN/UNAM 2013) 1538–39

Pereznieto Castro, Leonel and James A Graham, *Tratado de arbitraje comercial internacional mexicano* (2nd edn, Limusa 2013) 24–25

Ríos Martínez, José, 'Interpretación en la Dogmática Jurídica como Posibilidad de Ciencia del Derecho' [2007] 3(5) RPD UNAM 147

Ruiz García, Laura, *Contratos Administrativos* (Flores Editor 2010) 266–72

Secretaría de Servicios Parlamentarios, 'Cuaderno de Apoyo Reforma Constitucional en Materia de Justicia Penal y Seguridad Pública (Proceso Legislativo)' SAD-07-08 (2008)

Wöss, Herfried, 'Arbitraje, Medios Alternativos de Solución de Controversias y Compras del Sector Público en México' [2009] Revista Latinoamericana de Mediación y Arbitraje 124

Wöss, Herfried, 'Arbitration, Alternative Dispute Resolution and Public Procurement in Mexico' [2010] 7 Revista del Club Español del Arbitraje 19

Wöss, Herfried, 'Solución de Controversias al amparo de la Nueva Ley Mexicana de Asociaciones Público-Privadas' (2012–2013) 5 Lima Arbitration 185

Wöss, Herfried, 'Arbitration under the Mexican Energy Reform: The Lessons of Commisa v PEMEX' (*Kluwer Arbitration Blog*, 7 November 2015)

Legislation and Other Legal Instruments

Treaties

Comprehensive and Progressive Agreement for Trans-Pacific Partnership (Tratado Integral y Progresista de Asociación Transpacífico) [2018]

Mexico–Central America Free Trade Agreement (Tratado de Libre Comercio entre los Estados Unidos Mexicanos y las Repúblicas de Costa Rica, El Salvador, Guatemala, Honduras y Nicaragua) [2011]

Mexico–Chile Free Trade Agreement (Tratado de Libre Comercio entre los Estados Unidos Mexicanos y la República de Chile) [1998]

Mexico–Colombia Free Trade Agreement (Tratado de Libre Comercio entre los Estados Unidos Mexicanos y la República de Colombia) [1994]

Mexico–Japan Free Trade Agreement (Acuerdo para el Fortalecimiento de la Asociación Económica entre los Estados Unidos Mexicanos y el Japón, y de su Acuerdo de Implementación) [2004]

Mexico–Panama Free Trade Agreement (Tratado de Libre Comercio entre los Estados Unidos Mexicanos y la República de Panamá) [2014]

Mexico–Peru Free Trade Agreement (Acuerdo de Integración Comercial entre los Estados Unidos Mexicanos y la República del Perú) [2011]

Mexico–Uruguay Free Trade Agreement (Tratado de Libre Comercio entre los Estados Unidos Mexicanos y la República Oriental del Uruguay) [2003]

North American Free Trade Agreement (Tratado de Libre Comercio de América de Norte) [1994]

Statutes and Regulations

Acquisitions and Works Law (Ley de Adquisiciones y Obras Públicas) [1993] (repealed)
Acquisitions Law (Ley de Adquisiciones, Arrendamientos y Servicios del Sector Público) [2000]
Administrative Federal Court of Justice Organic Law (Ley Orgánica del Tribunal Federal de Justicia Administrativa) [2016]
Amparo Law (Ley de Amparo, Reglamentaria de los artículos 103 y 107 de la Constitución Política de los Estados Unidos Mexicanos) [2013]
CFE Law (Ley de la Comisión Federal de Electricidad) [2014]
Commerce Code (Código de Comercio) [1889]
Decreto por el que se reforman y adicionan diversas disposiciones de la Constitución Política de los Estados Unidos Mexicanos [18 June 2008]
Decreto que reforma, adiciona y deroga disposiciones de diversas leyes relacionadas con el Tratado de Libre Comercio de América del Norte [22 December 1993]
Dispute Resolution Manual (Manual de Solución de Controversias) [2016]
Electric Power Industry Law (Ley de la Industria Eléctrica) [2014]
Energy Regulatory Coordinated Bodies Law (Ley de los Órganos Reguladores Coordinados en Materia Energética) [2014]
Federal Civil Code (Código Civil Federal) [1928]
Federal Code of Civil Procedure (Código Federal de Procedimientos Civiles) [1943]
Federal Constitution (Constitución Política de los Estados Unidos Mexicanos) [1917]
Federal Judicial Power Organic Law (Ley Orgánica del Poder Judicial de la Federación) [1995]
Federal Law on Administrative Procedure (Ley Federal de Procedimiento Administrativo) [1994]
Federal Transparency Law (Ley Federal de Transparencia y Acceso a la Información Pública) [2016]
General Law of Administrative Liabilities (Ley General de Responsabilidades Administrativas) [2016]
Hydrocarbons Law (Ley de Hidrocarburos) [2014]
Iniciativa de Decreto que reforma, adiciona y deroga disposiciones de diversas leyes relacionadas con el Tratado de Libre Comercio de América del Norte [presented on 25 November 1993].Organic Law of the Federal Administrative Justice Court (Ley Orgánica del Tribunal Federal de Justicia Administrativa) [2016]
Organic Statute of CFE (Estatuto Orgánico de la Comisión Federal de Electricidad) [2017].
Organic Statute of Pemex (Estatuto Orgánico de Petróleos Mexicanos) [2017]
PEMEX Law (Ley de Petróleos Mexicanos) [2017]
PPP Law (Ley de Asociaciones Público Privadas) [2012]
Tax and Administrative Federal Court of Justice Organic Law (Ley Orgánica del Tribunal Federal de Justicia Fiscal y Administrativa) [2007] (repealed)
Works Law (Ley de Obras Públicas y Servicios Relacionados con las Mismas) [2000]

Cases

Acceso a los Mecanismos Alternativos de Solución de Controversias, como Derecho Humano. Goza de la misma dignidad que el acceso a la jurisdicción del Estado [2012] 2nd Collegiate Court in Civil Matters 3rd Cr, SJFG, XXV, III.2°.C.6 K(10^{a}) 1723 (2004620)

Arbitraje. Cuando el accionante Ocurra ante el Juez a Presentar su Demanda y el Reo dé Contestación a Ésta o Reconvenga, quedará Extinguido el Compromiso Arbitral, Siempre que no se oponga la Excepción de Incompetencia [2007] 5th Collegiate Court in Civil Matters 3rd Cr, SJFG, XXV, III.5o.C.115 C, 1660 (172829)

Arbitraje. Implicaciones normativas derivadas de su constitucionalización a partir de la reforma de junio de 2008 [2017] First Chamber, SJFG, I, 1a. XXXVI/2017, 438 (2014010).

Arbitraje Comercial. Los Artículos 1415 A 1463 del Código de Comercio, No Violan el Artículo 13 de la Constitución Federal [2005] First Chamber, SJFG, XXI,1a.CLXXVI/2004, 411 (179667)

Árbitros privados. No tienen el carácter de autoridades responsables en el juicio de amparo [2015] 8th Collegiate Court in Civil Matters 1st Cr., SJFG, III, I.8°.C.23(10^{a}), 2107 (2009139)

Autoridades [1924] SCJN, XV, 250 (810781)

Autoridades, Facultades de las [1934] SCJN, XLI, 944 (336190)

Autoridades Administrativas, Facultades De Las. Limite [1988] 4 Collegiate Court in Administrative Matter 1st Cr, I, 144 (231059)

Case [2011] First Chamber, Amparo en Revisión 527/2011

Case [2012] First Chamber, Amparo en Revisión 755/2011

Case [2016] First Chamber, Amparo Directo 71/2014

Competencia. Deriva de la Ley no de un Contrato de Obra Pública [2008] RTFJFA, 378/08-03-01-2, 576

Competencia. Solo Deriva de la Ley no de un Contrato [1989] 3rd Collegiate Court in Administrative Matter 1st Cr., III, 991 (229439)

Contradicción de Tesis 422/2009 [2010], Second Chamber, SJFG, XXXI, 1977 (22066)

Contrato administrativo y contrato civil o mercantil. Diferencias [2001] 6th Cr, SJFG, XIV, VI.3o.A.50 A 1103 (188644)

Contratos Administrativos. Se distinguen por su finalidad de orden público y por el régimen exorbitante del Derecho Civil a que están sujetos [2001] SCJN, SJFG, XIII, P.IX/2001, 324 (189995)

Finiquito de obra pública por el incumplimiento de la persona moral, emitido por Caminos y Puentes Federales de Ingresos y Servicios Conexos. Constituye un acto definitivo impugnable mediante juicio de nulidad ante el Tribunal Federal de Justicia Fiscal y Administrativa [2010] 1st Collegiate Court in Administrative Matter 6 Cr, SJFG, XXXI, VI.1o.A.282 A, 2122 (165549)

Justicia alternativa. Constituye un derecho humano de rango constitucional [2019] 3rd Collegiate Court in Civil Matters, 1st Cr., GSJF, I.3o.C.3 CS (10^{a}) (2020851)

Justiciabilidad de los Laudos Arbitrales cuando un sujeto de la Administración Pública afirma que se viola el orden público [2017] First Chamber, SJFG, I, 1a.XXXVIII/2017, 442 (2014011)

Laudos Arbitrales. Estándar de Revisión Judicial para Determinar la Validez de la Decisión de un Tribunal Arbitral sobre su Propia Competencia [2017] First Chamber, SJFG, 40, I, 1a.XXXVII/ 2017, 445 (2014012)

Pemex-Exploracion y Producción v Corporacion Mexicana De Mantenimiento Integral, S De RL De CV [2010] Fifth District Court, juicio de nulidad de laudo 207/2010-II

Pemex-Exploracion y Producción v Fifth District Court [2010] Tenth District Court, amparo indirecto 604/2010-IV

Pemex-Exploracion y Producción v Tenth District Court [2010] Eleventh Collegiate Court, amparo en revision 358/2010

Rescisión Administrativa de contratos de adquisiciones o de obra pública. Contra dicha determinación debe agotarse el juicio contencioso administrativo federal [2012] 2nd Collegiate Court in Administrative Matter 3rd Cr, SJFG, IV, 5, III.2º.A.253 A (9ª), 4600 (160355)

Rescisión administrative de contratos de obras públicas y servicios relacionados con las mismas y su cumplimiento. Son impugnables mediante el juicio contencioso administrativo federal [2018] 1st Cr, SJFG, 58, I.4o.A.132 A (10ª) 2510 (2018019)

Rescisión Administrativa de contratos de obras públicas y servicios relacionados con las mismas, y de adquisiciones, arrendamientos y servicios del sector público, decretada por las dependencias y entidades de la administración pública federal. Es impugnable en el juicio contencioso administrativo ante el Tribunal Federal de Justicia Fiscal y Administrativa [2010] Second Chamber, SJFG, XXXI, 2ª./J.4/2010, 312 (165410)

Resolución recaída a la solicitud de modificación de pena convencional derivada de un contrato celebrado con base en la Ley de Adquisiciones, Arrendamientos y Servicios del Sector Público. Se surte la competencia material del Tribunal Federal de Justicia Fiscal y Administrativa [2008] R.T.F.J.F.A, I, 2, 43 (50215)

11
Reconciling Arbitral and Constitutional Governance
The Critical Role of the (Caribbean) Courts

*Conway Blake**

I. Introduction

As sovereign states become ever more involved in international arbitral disputes, there is growing interplay between the rules and procedures of international arbitration and those within domestic constitutions. That international arbitration between private entities and sovereign states (hereafter 'public-private arbitration') implicates issues of constitutional governance is beyond question. National constitutions and arbitral mechanisms both involve the exertion of legal discipline on the exercise of state power and sovereign authority. Further, public-private arbitral disputes are increasingly addressing traditional 'public law' issues, such as the legitimacy of government policies, states' imposition of emergency measures, and the balancing of private rights against the public interest.[1] In these and other respects, international arbitration and national constitutional regimes often occupy similar or overlapping spheres.

Yet, there has been little theoretical or doctrinal consideration of the relationship between the two regimes. As Professor Rutledge has noted:

> Over the past half-century, constitutional norms increasingly have worked their way into arbitration law and, to a lesser extent, arbitration law has influenced the development of constitutional norms. Tellingly, this seepage between the two disciplines has not occurred with a great deal of systematic thought or deliberation. Instead, it has tended to take place through incremental developments in various fields of arbitration, often occurring in isolation from each other and with little consideration of the broader implications of the growing interconnectivity of these two disciplines.[2]

Not only has there been a failure to address the overlap and complementarities between these bodies of law, but there has also been a failure to address the tensions and conflicts that may arise in this context. The prevailing consensus within the arbitration

* Conway Blake is a partner in the International Dispute Resolution Group at Debevoise & Plimpton LLP in London. The views expressed in this chapter are the author's own and do not express the views of Debevoise & Plimpton LLP.

[1] See Gus Van Harten, *Investment Treaty Arbitration and Public Law* (OUP 2007).

[2] Peter B Rutledge, *Arbitration and the Constitution* (CUP 2013) 5.

Conway Blake, *Reconciling Arbitral and Constitutional Governance* In: *The Comparative Constitutional Foundations of Private-Public Arbitration*. Edited by: Stephan W. Schill, Oxford University Press. © Stephan W. Schill 2025.
DOI: 10.1093/9780191987960.003.0011

community is that sovereign consent to arbitration grounds the authority of arbitral tribunals to adjudicate all disputes properly submitted to them, including those that involve far-reaching questions of public policy.[3] Accordingly, judicial interference in arbitral proceedings, outside the limits of the rules laid down in the Convention on the Recognition and Enforcement of Foreign Arbitral Awards (New York Convention)[4] or the Convention on the Settlement of Investment Disputes between States and Nationals of Other States (ICSID Convention),[5] is deemed an illegitimate incursion on the autonomy of the arbitral process. However, the position may appear radically different when viewed through the lens of constitutional law. From that vantage point, the national constitution is the democratically legitimate framework which exhaustively establishes the conditions for the valid exercise of public authority within the state. On this view, international arbitration cannot, a priori, remove areas of governmental power from constitution controls and scrutiny.

While the dichotomous characterization outlined above may be something of an oversimplification of the position, it nonetheless highlights the difficult questions that arise at the interface between constitutional law and arbitral regimes. How can conflicts between public-private arbitration and domestic constitutional law be properly resolved? What is the role of constitutional law in protecting core politico-legal values of the state in the face of perceived intrusions by arbitral and other transnational legal processes? Given the transnational nature of arbitration, and well-established international and domestic norms regarding judicial non-intervention in arbitral proceedings, what is the legitimate role for constitutional law in regulating arbitral procedures?

This chapter explores the role of domestic constitutional law in the regulation of public-private arbitration, taking as its point of departure the laws and legal systems in the Commonwealth Caribbean. It argues that, in the absence of explicit legislative or constitutional guidance, courts in the Commonwealth Caribbean have played a crucial role in managing the tensions and conflicts which arise between the arbitral and constitutional regimes. When faced with such tensions, the courts have not conceded constitutional impotence but have affirmed their power to exert judicial controls on arbitration proceedings where they threaten fundamental constitutional interests. However, this affirmation of judicial controls has not served as a pretext for the courts to retreat into legal parochialism. Rather, they have sought to strike a balance between fidelity to their constitutional mandate and respect for the autonomy and effectiveness of arbitral processes. In so doing, the courts strive to affirm the complementarity of the two governance regimes rather than their incommensurability.

[3] See eg Emmanuel Gaillard, *Legal Theory of International Arbitration* (Martinus Nijhoff 2010) 35 ('Considering the widespread trend in favor of the recognition of international arbitration as the normal means of settling international disputes, the legitimacy of arbitrators performing this function cannot be disputed.'); Nigel Blackaby and others, *Redfern and Hunter on International Arbitration* (6th edn, OUP 2015) para 2.30 ('Suffice to say for now that, in principle, any dispute should be just as capable of being resolved by a private arbitral tribunal as by the judge of a national court.').

[4] Convention on the Recognition and Enforcement of Foreign Arbitral Awards (adopted 10 June 1958, entered into force 7 June 1959) 330 UNTS 3 (New York Convention).

[5] Convention on the Settlement of Investment Disputes between States and Nationals of Other States (adopted 18 March 1965, entered into force 14 October 1966) 575 UNTS 159 (ICSID Convention).

The rest of this chapter proceeds in five sections. Section II provides a brief overview of the laws and legal systems of the Commonwealth Caribbean. Section III examines the general legal framework governing arbitration in the various jurisdictions in the Commonwealth Caribbean, with particular focus on public-private arbitration. Section IV considers some of the ways in which arbitral regimes implicate and may come into contention with rules and values enshrined in domestic constitutions. Section V uses a study of regional case law to outline how Caribbean courts may employ constitutional law 'controls' to regulate such tensions, and in particular how these controls may apply to regulate arbitral proceedings which threaten or undermine core constitutional values and principles. In light of this case study, section VI concludes by drawing some general observations on the role and limits of national constitutions in regulating the impacts of public-private arbitration on the national constitutional order.

II. Caribbean Constitutions and Legal Systems

Throughout this chapter, the terms 'Caribbean' and 'Commonwealth Caribbean' are used interchangeably to refer to the independent anglophone states within the Caribbean basin, who share similar legal and political traditions by virtue of their common history as former colonies of Great Britain. These states also form the majority of the membership of the regional international organization known as the Caribbean Community (CARICOM).[6] This grouping comprises the states of Jamaica, the Republic of Trinidad and Tobago, the Windward Islands (Dominica, St Lucia, St Vincent and the Grenadines, and Grenada), Barbados, the Leeward Islands (Antigua and Barbuda, St Christopher and Nevis, the British Virgin Islands, Anguilla, and Montserrat), and the so-called Northern Islands (the Bahamas, the Cayman Islands, and the Turks and Caicos Islands). It also encompasses the Central and South American states of Belize and the Republic of Guyana.

The laws and legal systems of the Commonwealth Caribbean emerged out of the experience of imperial rule, during which Britain imposed its law and systems of governance on its erstwhile colonies. On gaining independence from Britain in the second half of the twentieth century, the nations of the Caribbean retained the common law and much of the rules and customs of the English legal system.[7] Accordingly, Caribbean courts today apply the common law and the rules of equity, and often look to the courts in England (as well as the wider common law world) for precedential guidance. Regional legislatures and legislative drafters are also heavily influenced by their counterparts in the United Kingdom. However, as discussed further below, this influence is gradually waning as Caribbean states move to adopt indigenous legislative policies more suited to their particular national circumstances.

[6] See Dennis Byron and Christopher Malcolm, 'Caribbean Community (CARICOM)' in Rüdiger Wolfrum (ed), *Max Planck Encyclopedia of Public International Law* (online edn, July 2009) <http://opil.ouplaw.com/view/10.1093/law:epil/9780199231690/law-9780199231690-e597> accessed 26 January 2025.

[7] Rose-Marie B Antoine, *Commonwealth Caribbean Law and Legal Systems* (Routledge 2008) 3, 18.

The legacy of colonialism meant that the countries of the Commonwealth Caribbean all adopted what have been loosely called 'Westminster Model constitutions'. The appellation 'Westminster Model' is not a technical legal category or term of art.[8] However, it has come to be deployed by courts and scholars as a convenient descriptor for those constitutions adopted throughout the Commonwealth that have been 'modelled on the political system of the UK and . . . derived from the Palace of Westminster where the UK Parliament is seated'.[9]

Issues of legal taxonomy aside, certain key features of Westminster Model constitutions, as adopted in the Caribbean, are now beyond question.[10] First, almost all constitutions in the region establish the state as a constitutional monarchy, with the monarch of the United Kingdom as the ceremonial head of state.[11] Second, the head of government is usually a prime minister, who is the Member of Parliament able to command the support of the majority of the elected members of the legislature. Third, the executive is comprised of a prime minister and a Cabinet of ministers, all of whom are collectively responsible to the government. Fourth, the legislatures are bicameral, with a 'lower house' comprised of elected parliamentarians and a smaller 'upper house' comprised of nominated members. Fifth, Caribbean constitutions all contain enforceable 'bills of rights' which enshrine the fundamental rights of all citizens and, in so doing, define the relationship between the individual and the state. These 'bills of rights', which are largely based on the European Convention on Human Rights and the Universal Declaration of Human Rights,[12] broadly inform the interpretation and application of the whole constitutional document.

In a significant departure from the British constitutional doctrine of parliamentary sovereignty, Caribbean constitutions all enshrine the principle of constitutional supremacy. All regional constitutions expressly declare themselves to be the 'supreme law' of the land and provide that any law inconsistent with the constitution is void to the extent of the inconsistency.[13] In this way, Caribbean constitutions are the 'highest authority in the legal system and an overriding force'[14] and impose procedural and substantive constraints on public authority and governmental power.[15] Caribbean

[8] Stanley A de Smith, *The New Commonwealth and its Constitutions* (Stevens & Sons 1964) 77; AR Carnegie, '*Floreat* the Westminster Model? A Commonwealth Caribbean Perspective' (1996) 6 Carib L Rev 1.

[9] See Arif Bulkan, Tracy Robinson, and Adrian Saunders, *Fundamentals of Caribbean Constitutional Law* (Sweet & Maxwell 2014) 67; de Smith (n 8).

[10] See Derek O'Brien, *The Constitutional Systems of the Commonwealth Caribbean* (Hart 2014) 29.

[11] The exceptions being the Republics of Trinidad and Tobago, Dominica, and Guyana.

[12] *Minister of Home Affairs & Ors v Fisher* [1979] AC 319. Here the Judicial Committee of the Privy Council noted: 'It is known that [the bill of right], as similar portions of other constitutional instruments drafted in the post-colonial period, starting with the Constitution of Nigeria, and including the constitutions of most Caribbean territories, was greatly influenced by the European Convention for the Protection of Human Rights and Fundamental Freedoms. That convention was signed and ratified by the United Kingdom and applied to dependent territories including Bermuda. It was in turn influenced by the United Nations Universal Declaration of Human Rights 1948.'

[13] See eg Constitution of Antigua and Barbuda, s 2; Constitution of the Bahamas, s 2; Constitution of Barbados, s 1; Constitution of Belize, s 2; Constitution of Dominica, s 117; Constitution of Grenada, s 106; Constitution of Guyana, art 8; Constitution of Jamaica, s 2; Constitution of St Kitts and Nevis, s 2; Constitution of St Vincent and the Grenadines, s 101; and Constitution of Trinidad and Tobago, s 2.

[14] Bulkan, Robinson, and Saunders (n 9) 175.

[15] See Dieter Grimm, 'Types of Constitutions in Contemporary History from 18th Century Classic Liberal to Post-Colonial and Post Authoritarian' in Michel Rosenfeld and Andras Sajo (eds), *The Oxford Handbook of Comparative Constitutional Law* (OUP 2012) 98, 109.

states adhere to the doctrine of dualism and, as such, international law (whether under treaty or customary law) has no pre-eminence over domestic law or the constitution.[16] However, international law (including unincorporated treaties) plays a role in the interpretation of domestic enactments and in constitutional adjudication.[17]

In another departure from British constitutional doctrine, the courts in the Caribbean are competent to review laws for their compliance with the constitution and declare those laws null and void to the extent that they are inconsistent with constitutional norms (whether express or implied). While Caribbean constitutions are formally silent on the question of judicial review of legislation, like the United States Supreme Court in *Marbury v Madison*,[18] Caribbean courts have arrogated to themselves the power of judicial review as a necessary incident to constitutional supremacy and to constitutional efficacy.[19] The courts have therefore assumed the role of 'guardians of the constitution'[20]—the function of upholding the integrity of the constitution and maintaining proper limits on governmental power through the tool of judicial review.

Another feature worthy of note is that Commonwealth Caribbean constitutions extend beyond the formal legal documents and include unwritten principles implicit in the structure and informed by the historico-political context of these documents. These unwritten norms include such fundamental principles as the separation of powers, the rule of law, the protection of the law, and the principle of judicial independence.[21] These principles are recognized as justiciable rules and enforced by the courts as if they were explicitly expressed in the constitutional text. Allied to these unwritten constitutional rules are also fundamental constitutional values which inform constitutional interpretation and governance, including the requirements of rationality, reasonableness, and fairness.[22] The courts have embraced the task of articulating and applying these unwritten constitutional principles and values in concrete cases.

Finally, it should be noted that, while Caribbean constitutional law has been fashioned in the image of English law and political institutions, the congruence between these legal systems should not be exaggerated. Caribbean law has made definitive breaks from its colonial antecedent, as legislative reform and judicial activism have moved the law firmly towards a more autochthonous path.[23] One significant effort in

[16] See *The Attorney General et al v Jeffrey Joseph and Lennox Ricardo Boyce*, CCJ Appeal No CV 2 of 2005, per Justice Pollard, para 21, noting that within Commonwealth Caribbean constitutions, '[t]reaties normally have legal incidence only at the international plane. Given that international law and municipal law are ordinarily conceived as two non-convergent normative regimes, municipal courts maintain that unincorporated treaties are incapable of creating legal rights for private entities'.

[17] *The Attorney General et al v Jeffrey Joseph and Lennox Ricardo Boyce*, CCJ Appeal No CV 2 of 2005.

[18] *Marbury v Madison*, 5 US 137 (1803).

[19] See *Collymore and Abraham v Attorney General of Trinidad & Tobago* (1967) 12 WIR 5, CA; (1970) 15 WIR 229, PC.

[20] *Collymore* (n 19) (1967) 12 WIR 5 CA, para 19.

[21] See Tracy Robinson, 'Our Inherent Constitution' in David Berry and Tracy Robinson (eds), *Transitions in Caribbean Law: Law-Making, Constitutionalism and the Convergence of National and International Law* (Ian Randle 2013) 248, 259.

[22] See eg *The Attorney General et al v Jeffrey Joseph and Lennox Ricardo Boyce*, CCJ Appeal No CV 2 of 2005, per Justice Wit, para 20, noting that '[t]he ... concept of the rule of law ... imbues the Constitution with other fundamental requirements such as rationality, reasonableness, fundamental fairness and the duty and ability to refrain from and effectively protect against abuse and arbitrary exercise of power.'

[23] See eg Leighton Jackson, 'Fi We Law: The Emergence of Caribbean Jurisprudence and the Doctrine of Precedence' in Berry and Robinson (n 21) 13.

this respect was the establishment of a regional final appellate court—the Caribbean Court of Justice (CCJ)—established with the aim of, inter alia, 'further[ing] the development of Caribbean Jurisprudence through the judicial process'.[24] Until recently, all final civil and criminal appeals from courts within the Caribbean were determined by the Judicial Committee of the Privy Council (JCPC)—effectively a chamber of the United Kingdom Supreme Court—sitting as the final appellate court for the various Caribbean jurisdictions. This inevitably meant that post-independence Caribbean law remained in the shadow of English law. However, a number of Caribbean states have abolished appeals to the JCPC and transferred appellate jurisdiction to the CCJ.[25] Thus, while the majority of states are subject to the jurisdiction of the JCPC, a growing number are subject to the jurisdiction of the CCJ. In this way, Commonwealth Caribbean legal systems are hybrid systems, and are most accurately described as a post-colonial admixture of inherited and indigenous legal norms and institutions.

III. International Arbitration in the Caribbean

A. The Arbitration Legislative Framework

Like other aspects of Caribbean legal systems, the law on arbitration is heavily influenced by the region's colonial past. Much of the law in this area is based on outdated colonial statutes inherited from the United Kingdom. That being said, a growing number of jurisdictions have revised their laws to embrace a modern approach to international arbitration.[26] Thus, rather than referring to a Caribbean arbitral regime, it is perhaps more accurate to speak of 'regimes' falling into three broad categories.

First, there is the large category of jurisdictions which have retained colonial-era statutes. For example, until recently, arbitration in Jamaica was governed by a statute enacted in 1900, which was based on the even earlier English Arbitration Act of 1889.[27] Similar legislation can be found in Montserrat, Trinidad and Tobago,[28] and Belize.[29] Unsurprisingly, these statutes reflect outdated assumptions about arbitral procedure and the role of the courts in the arbitral process, and make no reference to the particular context of international arbitral disputes.[30] Most of these statutes are skeletal documents containing only sparse provisions dealing with limited aspects of the arbitral process.[31] For example, they contain no provisions relating to the seat of the arbitration, the nature of arbitration agreements, the general conduct of arbitral

[24] See Agreement Establishing the Caribbean Court of Justice (adopted 14 February 2001, entered into force 23 July 2002) 2255 UNTS 319.

[25] At the time of writing, the following countries had acceded to the appellate jurisdiction of the CCJ: Barbados, Belize, Dominica, and Guyana.

[26] See eg Rene Gayle, 'Jamaica Replaces Century-Old Arbitration Act with UNCITRAL Model Law' (2018) 1(6) Lat Am J Int'l Trade L 1.

[27] This statute has now been repealed. See eg ibid.

[28] See eg the Montserrat Arbitration Act (1907); and the Arbitration Act of Trinidad and Tobago, ch 5:01.

[29] Arbitration (Amendment) Ordinance of 1980 (which is based on the English Arbitration Act of 1926).

[30] See Emilia Onyema, 'Modernising the Framework for Arbitration in Jamaica: Some Salient Points' (18 February 2010) (unpublished manuscript) <https://eprints.soas.ac.uk/8252/> accessed 26 January 2025.

[31] For example, the Arbitration Act of Belize has only sixteen provisions.

proceedings, the circumstances in which judicial intervention in arbitral proceedings is justified, or the specific bases on which an award may be set aside. As such, there are real doubts about whether these statutes are compatible with modern arbitral practice and the expectations of users of arbitration.[32]

The second category comprises those jurisdictions in which the laws reflect attempts in the mid twentieth century to modernize arbitration in England. The laws in these jurisdictions are largely based on the English Arbitration Act of 1950, which is in turn substantially based on the English Arbitration Acts of 1889 and 1934.[33] States falling into this category include Dominica, Grenada, St Vincent and the Grenadines, Antigua and Barbuda,[34] and St Kitts and Nevis.[35] While the laws in these jurisdictions represent a modest improvement on the position in the jurisdictions in the first category above, they too fall woefully short of the requirements of a modern international arbitral practice.

It is uncontroversial to note that the English Arbitration Act 1950 does not serve as a particularly adequate legislative model. The criticisms of that 1950 Act are now well rehearsed. The regime under that Act led to protracted and expensive proceedings, and facilitated excessive judicial intervention in the arbitral process.[36] The situation is no different in Caribbean jurisdictions in which the law is modelled on that legislative regime. For example, regional statutes based on that scheme still allow for the outdated 'case stated' procedure by which a party to arbitration may at any time during the proceedings request that the arbitrator seek a judicial ruling from the courts on a point of law. The flaws in this procedure are aptly illustrated by a decision from the High Court of Trinidad and Tobago in which one of the parties in an ICC arbitration seated in Trinidad and Tobago referred twenty-two separate issues from the arbitrator for judicial determination pursuant to this procedure.[37] Statutes in this category also empower the courts to set aside arbitral awards on broad terms, including on the basis of errors of law on the face of the award.[38] In these and other ways, the legislation in these jurisdictions does not comport with modern expectations of confidentiality, autonomy, efficiency, and finality in international arbitration.

The final category comprises jurisdictions that have adopted modern arbitration statutes incorporating international standards and best practice with respect to commercial arbitration. This category is almost exclusively composed of the so-called 'offshore financial jurisdictions', including Barbados, the British Virgin Islands, and the

[32] See eg Claim No HCV 2428 of 2004 (Supreme Court of Jamaica), in which the court tries to reconcile Jamaican arbitral rules with respect to arbitrator appointment with those under the ICC rules.

[33] Maurice J Stoppi, *Commercial Arbitration in the Caribbean: A Practical Guide* (University of the West Indies Press 2001) 1.

[34] The Arbitration Act of Antigua and Barbuda, 1975 (Cap 33).

[35] See Albert Fiadjoe, *Alternative Dispute Resolution: A Developing World Perspective* (Routledge 2004) 76.

[36] Guy Pendell and David Bridge, 'Arbitration in England and Wales' in Torsten Loercher, Guy Pendell and Jeremy Wilson, CMS Guide to Arbitration, vol 1 (4th edn, CMS 2012) 299. The authors note that three broad criticisms were levelled against the 1950 Act: (1) 'it was slow and expensive'; (2) 'the law was inaccessible to laypersons and foreign users'; and (3) the 'courts were too ready to intervene in the arbitral process'.

[37] *In the Matter of the Decision of Dr Robert Gaitskell QC* (Sole Arbitrator under the ICC Rules of Arbitration 1998) Claim Number CV2008-04881, Judgment (21 October 2009).

[38] Roy Goode, 'Arbitration – Should Courts Get Involved?' (2002) 2 IJS Journal 33, 34.

Cayman Islands, which provide corporate and commercial services to non-resident offshore companies, and consequently are regular sites for international commercial disputes. The enactment of these modern statutes can be explained, in part, by the desire of regional offshore centres to bolster their image as facilitators of transborder commercial activity. It is further explained by the aspiration of these jurisdictions to be more fully integrated into the 'arbitration industry' by becoming international arbitral seats and venues.[39]

In line with these aims, the legislation in these jurisdictions reflects, and in some instances improves upon, the principles contained within the United Nations Commission on International Trade Law (UNCITRAL) Model Law.[40] For example, the International Commercial Arbitration Act 2007 of Barbados expressly incorporates 'general principles of arbitration', including the principles of party autonomy, competence-competence, separability, and a limited regime for challenging arbitral awards consistent with the New York Convention.[41] The Act does not merely lay down rules on arbitration, but aims to engender a liberal judicial policy with respect to international arbitration. Thus, for example, the Act mandates that, when interpreting its provisions, 'regard shall be had to its international origin and the need to promote uniformity in its application'.[42] Other statutes based substantially on the UNCITRAL Model Law have been enacted in the Cayman Islands, the British Virgin Islands, the Bahamas, and Jamaica.[43]

B. The Framework for Public-Private Arbitration

The law in the Commonwealth Caribbean draws no clear distinction between the state and private parties in the context of arbitration. The provisions of the various arbitration statutes apply equally to private entities as they do to public bodies. There are usually no provisions addressing the state specifically, save for brief provisions expressly stating that the arbitration legislation applies to 'the Crown'. Thus, for example, section 16 of the Arbitration Act of Belize states that the provisions of that Act 'shall . . . apply to any arbitration to which the Crown is a party'.[44] The position is similar in jurisdictions in which the law is based on the UNCITRAL Model Law.

[39] See eg Peter Goldsmith QC, 'A Brave New World – Can the BVI International Arbitration Centre Knock New York, London and Paris Off Their Perch?' (JS Archibald QC Memorial Lecture, BVI International Arbitration Conference, 20 October 2015).

[40] As is well known, Article 5 of the UNCITRAL Model Law provides that, '[i]n matters governed by this law, no Court shall intervene except where so provided in this law.'

[41] s 2(7), Commercial Arbitration Act 2007.

[42] s 1(5) Commercial Arbitration Act 2007.

[43] See eg the Arbitration Act (42/2009) and the Arbitration (Foreign Arbitral Awards) Act (43/2009), which both came into force on 20 May 2010 in the Commonwealth of the Bahamas; the Cayman Islands Arbitration Law (2012); the British Virgin Islands Arbitration Act (2013); and the Arbitration Act (Jamaica 2017).

[44] See Arbitration (Amendment) Ordinance (1980), s 16. Similarly, s 35 of the Arbitration Act of Trinidad and Tobago provides that, '[t]his Act, except as herein expressly mentioned, applies to any arbitration to which the State or any officer of the Government in respect of any act by him or by his department, is a party.'

Thus, for example, the Barbados International Commercial Arbitration Act states rather tersely, '[t]his Act binds the Crown.'[45]

For the most part, these terse provisions represent the totality of the legislative provisions which address public-private arbitration. Regional statutes provide no guidance on the permissible bases and scope of the state's involvement in international arbitration or on the categories of disputes which may be determined by arbitral tribunals and those which, for reasons of policy, may only be adjudicated by the courts. One notable exception is the Investment Act 2004 of Guyana, which establishes a legislative framework for foreign direct investment, and in that context provides that:

> [I]n the event of disputes . . . between [foreign] investors and the Government with respect to an investment enterprise, the parties to the dispute . . . may . . . submit their dispute . . . under the Arbitration Act; or . . . submit their dispute to the International Centre for the Settlement of Investment Disputes (ICSID).[46]

However, beyond recognition of the possibility of submitting certain investments disputes to international arbitration, this legislation also leaves key legal questions regarding private-public arbitration unanswered.

Caribbean constitutions shed no light on the issue of the states' participation in arbitration. They are all silent on this point. This silence is consistent with the relatively skeletal structure of Westminster Model constitutions. Therefore, whatever rules may govern the states' involvement in arbitration, they are left to be gleaned from general constitutional principles and the pronouncements of the courts.

As it relates to commercial arbitration, the power of Caribbean governments to enter into contracts, and hence conclude agreements to submit to arbitration, falls within the prerogative powers of the executive vested under the constitution.[47] These wide powers ensure that the government is able to contract so as to 'secure objectives and implement policies that it is . . . allowed to pursue'.[48] The power is subject to no express limitation in the constitution. This is in contrast to the position under other Commonwealth constitutions, such as in Ghana, where the constitution provides that parliamentary approval is required in respect of 'international business transactions' to which the state of Ghana is a party.[49]

However, while broad and uncodified, the power to contract is not unfettered. Implicit limitations on the executive's power to contract may be engaged if, for example, contrary to core constitutional principles, the executive were by way of contract to purport to exercise functions vested in the legislative or judicial branches, in breach of the separation of powers.[50] Similar limitations exist, pursuant to the principle of executive necessity, to limit the executive's ability 'when making a private

[45] Barbados International Commercial Arbitration Act (2007), s 53.

[46] See s 28(2)(d).

[47] *BCB Holdings Limited and the Belize Bank Limited v the Attorney General of Belize* [2013] CCJ 5 (AJ), paras 38–41. The Court affirmed the position that 'the Crown at common law had a wide prerogative power to enter into contracts and this power was unfettered by restrictions as to subject matter or persons'.

[48] Mark Elliott and Robert Thomas, *Public Law* (OUP 2011) 158.

[49] Constitution of Ghana, art 181(5).

[50] See eg *BCB v Belize* (n 47).

contract in general terms, to undertake ... to fetter itself in the use of [public] powers, and in the exercise of its discretion'.[51] In this way, constitutional principles impose substantive limits on governments' ability to contract and therefore also have clear implications for states' engagement in arbitration.

As it relates to arbitration under bilateral and multilateral investment treaties, it is the Executive Branch that is constitutionally empowered to conclude treaties on behalf of the state, and thereby commit the state to international arbitration pursuant to such agreements.[52] There are no express constitutional provisions addressing the limitations on the content of treaties negotiated by governments, or the related dispute resolution mechanisms within them. This is due to the 'deafening silence'[53] of Caribbean constitutions on the subject of treaties—a silence due in no small part to the influence of 'Westminster constitutionalism' in the Caribbean.[54] Caribbean courts have noted the stark under-articulation of the foreign relations and treaty powers in Caribbean constitutions, and have commented in this regard:

> Most of the newly created States in the world do have constitutions that elaborately deal with the relationship between their domestic law and international law, the treaty-making power of the State and possible democratic involvement at the ratification stage. Not so in the Commonwealth Caribbean. In their constitutions these issues are simply ignored. Quite surprisingly, notwithstanding the fact that in today's globalising world these subjects have become more important than they already were in the past, even the two recently produced drafts for a new Constitution of the modern Republic of Trinidad and Tobago are silent on them ... [I]t is when wandering through the provisions of the Constitutions one tends to get the impression that beyond the skies of the State no relevant law exists.[55]

The absence of clear rules addressing the state's engagement in investment treaty arbitration is compounded by the fact that Caribbean constitutions adhere to the doctrine of dualism. Accordingly, '[r]atification of a treaty cannot *ipso facto* add to or amend the Constitution and laws of a State because that is a function reserved strictly for the domestic Parliament'.[56] The fact that commitments under investment treaties have no direct effect in domestic law means that legislators and policymakers have largely ignored these treaties and the implications of the obligations and arbitral mechanisms contained within them.[57]

[51] *Revere Jamaica Alumina Ltd v Attorney General* (1977) 26 WIR 486 (Supreme Court of Jamaica).

[52] See *British Caribbean Bank v Government of Belize* [2013] CCJ 4 (AJ).

[53] *The Attorney General et al v Jeffrey Joseph and Lennox Ricardo Boyce*, CCJ Appeal No CV 2 of 2005, para 38.

[54] See Campbell McLachlan, *Foreign Relations Law* (CUP 2014) 114, where Professor McLachlan has noted in relation to the foreign relations powers under Commonwealth Constitutions: 'Traditionally the British constitution concentrated the foreign relations power on the executive, as an exercise of the prerogative power of the Crown. The decision to leave the exercise of the foreign relations power with the King at the time of the Bill of Rights 1688 has proved remarkably durable Grundnorm in the constitutional arrangements of the Anglo-Commonwealth states.'

[55] *Attorney General v Joseph and Boyce* (n 53) para 38.

[56] *Attorney General v Joseph* [2006] CCJ 1 (AJ), para 55.

[57] See eg Jonathan Bonnitcha, Lauge Poulsen, and Michael Waibel, *The Political Economy of the Investment Treaty Regime* (OUP 2017).

C. The Role of the Courts in Arbitration Law

Arbitration law is defined as much by judicial policy and decisions as it is by legislative provisions. Despite the largely outdated arbitration legislation in the region, Caribbean courts have demonstrated broad support for arbitration, including the arbitration of disputes involving the state. For example, the CCJ has issued a number of decisions affirming a strong policy in support of international arbitration. In *British Caribbean Bank v Government of Belize*, the CCJ noted with respect to investment treaty arbitration:

> [I]nvestment treaties form an important feature of the modern economic jurisprudence and . . . they constitute an important developmental option for capital-importing developing countries such as those in the Caribbean. The bilateral investment treaty was developed to remedy the vulnerability of the foreign investor and ameliorate the conditions of their investments and the success of the treaty regime depends upon the acceptance and fulfillment by the host state of the legal obligations imposed by the treaty.[58]

The CCJ has been similarly supportive of commercial arbitration, and has noted, for example:

> [A]rbitration is an increasingly preferred method of resolving complex commercial disputes and . . . it rests on the key principle of party autonomy. Parties to an arbitration agreement make the conscious decision to prefer the prompt, expedient, and final settlement of their disputes through the arbitral process rather than the often protracted process of court adjudication. As it is sometimes put, they choose finality over legality. Conflict resolution by arbitral means assists and encourages modern commercial activity and therefore the finality of arbitral awards is supported by public policy considerations.[59]

Consistent with this policy, regional courts have affirmed that when exercising their jurisdiction in relation to international arbitration, they will act to facilitate arbitral proceedings and not to prevent them.[60]

In addition, regional courts play a central role in the development of arbitration law. This is not least because of the deficiencies in the existing statutory framework in a number of jurisdictions. For example, it is the courts that established the autonomy of the arbitration agreement in Caribbean law[61] and recognized the doctrine

[58] *BCB v Belize* (n 52) para 15.

[59] *Belize Natural Energy Ltd v Maranco Ltd* [2015] CCJ 2 (AJ), para 16.

[60] See *Belize Telemedia v Attorney General of Belize*, Claim No 464 of 2008, paras 9 and 11 (Conteh CJ). See also *Attorney General of Belize v Carlisle Holdings Ltd*, Action No 15 of 2005 (Conteh CJ).

[61] *Dantzler Inc v Galloway Hardware & Building Materials Ltd*, Claim No MNIHCV2014/0024 (3 December 2014) para 42 (Eastern Caribbean Supreme Court); *BCB Holding Limited and Belize Bank v Attorney General of Belize* [2013] CCJ 5 (AJ), para 55. In the latter case, while the Caribbean Court of Justice found that a disputed contract was illegal and contrary to public policy, it nonetheless held that 'the agreement to arbitrate was a free-standing agreement separable from the remainder of the Deed', and bound the parties to pursue arbitration under the London Court of International Arbitration (LCIA) Rules.

of competence-competence.[62] The courts have also shown themselves ready to grant interim measures in support of international arbitral proceedings and to enjoin domestic litigation in conflict with arbitration agreements.[63] Several judicial decisions have also affirmed a clear 'pro-enforcement bias' on the part of the courts with respect to the recognition and enforcement of foreign arbitral awards.[64]

What is striking about these developments is that, for the most part, they have occurred in the absence of proper statutory backing. Caribbean courts have used the flexibility of the common law to engage in substantial gap-filling with respect to arbitration principles, often drawing guidance from foreign courts and international legal sources.[65] The upshot is that, despite the outmoded state of the law in most of the region, the judiciaries' demonstrated commitment to the promotion of a non-interventionist and pro-arbitration policy means that Caribbean jurisdictions have been facilitative of arbitration.

IV. Private-Public Arbitration and Domestic Constitutions—A Clash of Regimes?

The courts' embrace of a pro-arbitration policy comes at a time when states within the Caribbean region are increasingly enmeshed in international arbitral disputes. These private-public disputes have brought into sharp focus the intersection between international arbitration and domestic spheres of constitutional law and governance. As noted earlier, constitutional law and private-public arbitration both operate to regulate and exert legal discipline on the exercise of state power. As such, arbitral and constitutional regimes do not merely have the potential for substantive overlap; they may also come into conflict.

At a general level, private-public arbitration may have 'functional constitutional effects'[66] and thus indirectly implicate issues of constitutional governance. As has been observed:

> The political arrangements for governance inaugurated by Caribbean constitutions at independence have been tested and strained by the new global political economy. The forces of globalization, or the 'cross-border interpenetration of economic life' have generated ... 'a new economy' to which Caribbean public law must respond. This includes changing relationships between the market and the state, public and private, global and local economies. In fact, it is less apt to speak of public versus

[62] *Belize Telemedia v AG of Belize* (n 60) para 9: '[I]t is for the arbitration tribunal to determine its competence, whether any particular dispute falls within the remit of the parties' submission to it.'

[63] See eg *Attorney General of Belize v Carlisle Holdings* (n 60) para 21.

[64] See eg *IPOC International Growth Fund Limited v LV Finance Group Limited*, Civil Appeal No 30 of 2006 (18 June 2007) (Eastern Caribbean Court of Appeal).

[65] Jurisprudence from the English, Hong Kong, and Singaporean courts have had an influence. See eg *Hualon Corporation (M) SDN BHD (in receivership) v Marty Limited*, Claim No BVIHC (COM) 2014/0090 (8 April 2016) (Eastern Caribbean Supreme Court).

[66] See Alfred C Aman, 'Globalization, Democracy, and the Need for a New Administrative Law' (2003) 10 Ind J Global Legal Studies 125.

> private law issues because the contemporary scene is characterized by 'new blends of public and private power'.[67]

The system of arbitration undoubtedly forms part of the confluence of 'public and private power' which may operate to disrupt and call into question traditional notions and assumptions of constitutional governance. It has been observed that international arbitration often involves private adjudicators rather than constitutionally competent judges, effectively interpreting and applying public law and reviewing the exercise of public authority without the usual constitutional safeguards and mechanisms of accountability generally associated with such an exercise of judicial power.[68] The rise of arbitral disputes challenging the legitimacy and reasonableness of governmental actions in such areas as health, environmental regulation, and taxation policy may be noted in this context. The substance of these policy-sensitive disputes often mirrors or implicates questions of constitutional law.[69]

There is also the potential for direct conflict between the two regimes. For example, to the extent that international arbitration agreements and proceedings implicate state action, they have the potential to bear upon substantive provisions of a state's constitution (eg structural rules concerning the proper competencies of government and the distribution of power within government) and rights cognizable thereunder (ie fundamental rights of the individual). For example, remedies granted in a commercial arbitration may affect third parties within the state and thereby engage rights protected under constitutional bills of rights (eg the right to property). This also explains why, on occasion, parties to arbitral proceedings have petitioned courts for relief on the basis that arbitral proceedings threaten their constitutional rights.[70]

Further, public-private arbitrations, whether brought pursuant to contracts or investment treaties, are also increasingly addressing significant 'public law' issues.[71] Such disputes often raise questions concerning the constitutional legitimacy of governmental actions, or may raise concrete questions as to the scope and application of provisions of a state's constitution. The potential for conflict between the domestic and transnational spheres is not improved by what some have argued is a lack of proper regard for constitutional law in the context of international arbitration.[72] Even where arbitral tribunals are tasked with resolving disputes under domestic law, tribunals have invoked legal doctrines and techniques to diminish or negate the application of domestic constitutions. In particular, the much-contested doctrine of 'internationalized contracts' has been employed as a basis to override applicable constitutional law principles, despite the parties' express submission to domestic law and the absence of any agreement regarding the application of international law.

[67] Bulkan, Robinson, and Saunders (n 9) 493.
[68] Van Harten (n 1) 175–76.
[69] See Stacie I Strong, 'Constitutional Conundrums in Arbitration' (2013) 15 Cardozo J Conflict Resol 41.
[70] See eg *Auto-Guadeloupe Investissement SAS v Alvarez & Ors* (2014) 84 WIR 49.
[71] See Van Harten (n 1).
[72] See Dominic Npoanlari Dagbanja, 'Reasserting the Role of Municipal Law in International Trade and Investment Protection Through Choice of Law' (UN Conference on International Trade Law, Vienna, 4–6 July 2017).

This was the case in *Bankswitch Ghana Ltd (Ghana) v The Republic of Ghana*,[73] where an international arbitral tribunal effectively disapplied Article 181(5) of the Ghanaian Constitution which stipulates that state contracts concerning 'international business transactions' are not binding under Ghanaian law unless they have been approved by parliament. While the tribunal acknowledged that the contract in dispute was governed by Ghanaian law, and that Article 181(5) of the Ghanaian Constitution clearly applied to the contract, they ruled that as a matter of international law, Ghana was estopped from relying on the provisions of its constitution. In so doing, the tribunal 'render[ed] otiose the decision of the [Ghanaian] Court[s] that estoppel cannot validate or override an unconstitutional contract or agreement'.[74] The decision to circumvent mandatory provisions of the constitution and enforce an arguably unconstitutional contract may cause further concern because the tribunal proceeded on the basis of a legal theory considered one of 'the most contentious issues in doctrine'[75] and not 'correspond[ing] to the existing law'.[76]

Arbitrators justify the preclusion of constitutional law arguments on the basis that states should not be permitted to induce inward investment from abroad and then subsequently invoke their constitutions to avoid liability for impairment to the foreign investor. The upshot is that arbitral jurisprudence often (though not invariably) elevates considerations of fairness and consistency over objective standards of legality. However, there is an inherent contradiction in this approach, as international law requirements are often 'implied [into contracts by tribunals] by virtue of a commitment to the rule of law, only to be discarded a moment later by virtue of a commitment of fairness'.[77] Unsurprisingly, there has often been divergence between domestic courts and arbitral tribunals when approaching issues of constitutional law.

The ever-growing overlap and interaction between arbitral processes and domestic constitutional law raises many difficult questions, including how conflicts between these spheres can be properly regulated. Courts must grapple with normative and policy conflicts in this context, and their role that they play in protecting core constitutional values in the face of intrusion by transnational arbitral processes. This throws up the question of whether courts can ensure fidelity to their core constitutional mandate while upholding states' legal and policy commitments to respect and promote the autonomy and effectiveness of international arbitration.

[73] *Bankswitch Ghana Ltd (Ghana) v The Republic of Ghana*, PCA Case No 118294, Award Save as to Costs (11 April 2014).

[74] Dominic Npoanlari Dagbanja, 'Constitutionalism and Local Remedies Rule as Limitations on Investor-State Arbitration: Perspectives from Ghana' (2017) 17 OUCLJ 110, 127.

[75] See Patrick Dumberry and Jacob Stone, 'International Law, Whether You Like It or Not: An Analysis of Arbitral Tribunal Practice Regarding the Applicable Law in Deciding State Contracts Disputes under the ICSID Convention in the Twenty First Century' in Andrea K Bjorklund (ed), *Yearbook on International Investment Law and Policy 2012–2013* (OUP 2014) 477; Christopher Thomas and Harpreet Dhillon, 'Applicable Law Under International Investment Treaties' (2014) 26 Sing Ac L J 975, 981.

[76] James Crawford, *Brownlie's Principles of Public International Law* (8th edn, OUP 2012) 628.

[77] Jarrod Hepburn, *Domestic Law in International Investment Arbitration* (OUP 2017) 160.

V. Reconciling Arbitral and Constitutional Governance?

In the face of growing friction between arbitral processes and domestic constitutional law, Caribbean courts have not abdicated their duty as 'guardians of the constitution'. The courts have affirmed their powers to exert controls on arbitral proceedings perceived to threaten fundamental constitutional values and principles. The courts have deployed two main mechanisms of constitutional control in the arbitration context, namely: (a) through the application and enforcement of substantive constitutional norms (ie 'normative controls'); and (b) by issuing relevant procedural orders to relieve impairment of legal rights (ie 'procedural controls'). In so doing, Caribbean courts have sought to balance the competing interests of respecting the autonomy of the arbitration process and, at the same time, exercising sufficient supervision and control in the public interest.[78] A review of the courts' application of these principles is illustrative.

A. Regulation Through 'Normative Controls'

Where arbitral proceedings bear upon fundamental constitutional rights or core constitutional principles, constitutional norms potentially provide a basis for courts to intervene in arbitral proceedings in order to uphold fundamental legal interests. In this way, constitutional principles may operate as a 'normative constraint' on arbitration by limiting the freedom of action of the parties in proceedings. As outlined below, Caribbean courts have indicated that they may invoke: (1) fundamental individual rights; and (2) core/structural constitutional principles, as a means of regulating international arbitral proceedings or the parties thereto.

1 Fundamental Individual Rights

Constitutional bills of rights impose substantive limitations on state power vis-à-vis individuals (natural and juristic) and may therefore, in theory, be engaged in the context of an arbitral dispute involving the state. Parties to international arbitration may therefore invoke constitutional bills of rights as a basis for constraining international arbitrations which threaten constitutional rights. Caribbean courts have not ruled out this possibility. However, they have been astute to limit jurisdictional overreach, and have so far resisted attempts to deploy the bill of rights as a basis to thwart or intervene in arbitral proceedings.

This is illustrated by the decision of the High Court of Barbados in *Auto-Guadeloupe Investissement SAS v Alvarez & Ors*,[79] which involved a constitutional challenge raised in the context of international arbitral proceedings seated in Barbados. The claimant brought constitutional proceedings against the Attorney General seeking a stay of the

[78] Winston Anderson, 'Role of the Domestic Courts in the International Commercial Arbitration Process' (Fourth High Level Meeting on the Role of the Judiciary in International Commercial Arbitration, St Lucia, 23–24 October 2014) 4 <https://www.ccj.org/wp-content/uploads/2021/02/Remarks-at-the-Fourth-High-Level-Meeting-on-the-Role-of-the-Judiciary-in-International-Arbitration-_Justice-Winston-Anderson_20141023.pdf> accessed 26 January 2019.

[79] *Auto-Guadeloupe Investissement SAS v Alvarez & Ors* (n 70).

international arbitration proceedings, pending the determination of its constitutional petition. In the constitutional action, the claimant sought an order that the partial award of the arbitral tribunal be quashed and all proceedings in the arbitration be stayed by reason of the arbitrator's alleged lack of independence and impartiality, purportedly in violation of the claimant's right to a fair hearing guaranteed under the constitution.[80]

The arbitration involved a wholly commercial dispute between private contracting parties, touching no discernible state interest. However, the claimant sought to bring the arbitration within the ambit of the constitution by contending that the arbitrator exercised 'judicial powers' of a 'public nature' due to the fact that international commercial arbitration formed an integral part of the administration of justice by virtue of the statutory scheme under the International Commercial Arbitration Act 2007 of Barbados.

The Court struck out the constitutional claim on the basis that it disclosed no cause of action. The court did not rule on the question of whether the alleged lack of arbitrator impartiality could in fact engage the duty to provide a fair hearing and due process rights under the constitution. Rather, the decision turned on the finding that the arbitration lacked a sufficient 'public law dimension' so as to fall within the purview of constitutional review. This was because the powers exercised by the arbitrators derived directly from the arbitral agreement, not from statute or the law of the seat. Accordingly, the arbitrator's acts were not amenable to constitutional review. In so finding, the Court stressed that arbitration legislation did not operate to control or change the inherent character of private arbitration; it served only to supplement the arbitral agreement made by the parties so as to avoid the process being frustrated. This analysis is consistent with the approach of other Commonwealth courts with regard to the constitutional regulation of international commercial contracts.[81]

It is not clear whether the court's conclusion would have been different if the case had involved public-private arbitration. Traditionally, the courts in the Commonwealth Caribbean have been cautious not to extend the scope of judicial review to the purely contractual sphere.[82] As such, the state's entry into a commercial agreement would not, without more, be sufficient to bring related arbitral proceedings within the ambit of constitutional review. Yet, rigid notions of 'public' and 'private' may not provide a definitive framework for addressing the boundaries of constitutional engagement with international arbitration. Modern governance trends such as the privatization of traditional state functions have blurred the line between the so-called 'public' and

[80] s 18(8) provided: 'Any court or other tribunal prescribed by law for the determination of the existence or extent of any civil right or obligation shall be established by law and shall be independent and impartial; and where proceedings for such a determination are instituted by any person before such court or other tribunal, the case shall be given a fair hearing within a reasonable time.'

[81] See eg the decision of the High Court of Australia in *TCL Air Conditioner (Zhongshan) Co Ltd v The Judges of the Federal Court of Australia* [2013] HCA 5, where the claimant sought to challenge the constitutionality of the Australian Arbitration Act on the basis that it resulted in the 'impermissible vesting of judicial power in arbitral tribunals'. The court emphasized the private nature of the agreement by the parties to submit to arbitration, and concluded that '[t]he determination of a dispute by an arbitrator does not involve the exercise of the sovereign power of the State to determine or decide controversies'.

[82] See Eddy Ventose, *Commonwealth Caribbean Administrative Law* (Routledge 2013) 63.

'private' spheres, and have challenged the traditional forms and ambit of the state and of constitutional law. As Professor Chinkin has noted:

> The dualism between public and private spheres of activity has been identified as a key feature of classical, western liberal thought. Despite its pervasiveness, its normative consequences in domestic law have been much criticized on both practical and theoretical grounds. For example, it has been argued that there is no reliable or constant basis for the distinction. Concepts of public and private are complex, shifting, and reflect political preferences with respect to the level and quality of governmental instruction. Since there is no constant, objective basis for labelling an activity or actor as 'private', the judiciary regularly resorts to this as a device to avoid ruling on political issues. This in turn obscures the ways in which government policy regulates the so-called private sphere.[83]

Such observations prompt the question whether arbitral disputes touching on the functions of the state will (at least in some jurisdictions) become subject to standards and procedures of constitutional accountability. The move towards the application of constitutional review to what has traditionally been deemed the 'private sphere' is already being reflected in the constitutional law of the Caribbean. For example, the fundamental rights provisions of the Jamaican Constitution were recently amended so that they apply horizontally to 'natural or juristic persons', meaning that 'all persons are under a responsibility to respect and uphold the rights of others recognised'[84] in the bill of rights. The horizontal application of the constitution has been justified on the basis that 'private persons and entities often command great resources and exercise far-reaching powers which are capable of having an adverse impact on fundamental rights and freedoms of other persons and entities'.[85] Such developments not only have implications for the general scope of judicial review, but potentially for all aspects of the state's contractual engagement with private actors. That being said, there is presently no indication that Caribbean courts intend to expand the scope of constitutional review in any way that would justify greater intervention in arbitral proceedings.

2 Core/Structural Constitutional Principles

In addition to individual rights, 'core' or 'structural' constitutional principles may also provide a legal basis for the regulation of international arbitral proceedings. In particular, Caribbean courts have noted that the state's engagement in international arbitration may be subject to structural principles which undergird the constitution, including the core principles of parliamentary sovereignty and the separation of power.

The application of these principles in the arbitral context is illustrated by the CCJ's decision in *BCB Holdings Limited and the Belize Bank Limited v the Attorney General*

[83] Christine Chinkin, 'A Critique of the Public/Private Dimension' (1999) 10(2) EJIL 387, 389.

[84] Constitution of Jamaica, s 13(1)(C).

[85] Joint Select Committee, 'Joint Select Committee of Parliament on the Charter of Rights and Freedoms (Constitutional Amendment) Bill 2006' (Jamaica, 25 July 2006) 10.

of Belize.[86] In that case, the claimants and the government of Belize sought to settle a pre-existing legal dispute by entering into a settlement deed which provided favourable tax concessions to the claimants and purported to exempt the claimants from the application of provisions of the tax laws in Belize. The settlement deed was signed by the minister of finance, but was never approved by parliament. Following a change of administration in Belize, the new government refused to honour the settlement deed, and the claimants initiated arbitration at the London Court of International Arbitration against the government under the terms of the deed.

A key issue in the arbitration concerned the government's legal capacity to grant the concessions in the settlement deed. The tribunal found that, as a matter of Belizean law, the minister of finance had the capacity to enter into the agreement and that the government's refusal to honour the tax commitments contravened the agreement. However, at the enforcement stage, the CCJ refused to enforce the award on the basis, inter alia, that its enforcement would contravene public policy. It is the CCJ's reasoning on this point that concerns us here, in particular its reliance on the separation-of-powers principle as a ground for refusing enforcement.

In approaching the claimant's application for enforcement, the CCJ went to great lengths to emphasize the 'pro-enforcement bias' that domestic courts ought to show with regard to international arbitral awards. It also took note of the 'universal consensus' that courts will decline to enforce foreign arbitral awards only in exceptional circumstances. However, the CCJ also noted that requests to enforce international arbitral awards often engaged competing policy concerns and required courts to balance divergent policies and interests.[87]

Having carefully examined the terms and effect of the settlement deed, the CCJ concluded that the state was never bound by the deed because implementation of the same without parliamentary approval violated the country's constitution. Specifically, it found that, because matters of taxation law and policy were reserved to the legislature under the express terms of the constitution, the failure of the Executive Branch to obtain legislative approval for the tax concessions was contrary to the separation-of-powers principle. In this context, the CCJ noted:

> The Deed impacted on a host of filing, administrative and other obligations imposed by Parliament's revenue laws. In essence, the framers of the Deed conceptualised and designed a whole new *tax policy* for the benefit of the Companies. This policy was then embodied in the Deed, executed by the parties and implemented with the objective of overriding all current and any future statutes enacted by the National Assembly.
>
> It is not the Court's function in this case to assess the wisdom of this special tax policy. The Government does of course have the power to settle, and to settle in confidence if it so desires, and on terms it considers prudent, claims made against it. But transforming the policy conceived here, effectively into the status of a Money Bill, necessitated the intervention of the National Assembly so that legislation consistent with the imperatives of the Constitution could be enacted to give force to it.

[86] *BCB v Belize* (n 47).
[87] ibid para 20.

> Prime Ministerial governance, a paucity of checks and balances to restrain an overweening Executive, these are malignant tumours that eat away at democracy. No court can afford to encourage the spread of such cancer. In our judgment, implementation of the provisions of the Deed, without legislative approval and without the intention on the part of its makers to seek such approval, is indeed repugnant to the established legal order of Belize. In a purely domestic setting, we would have regarded as unconstitutional, void and completely contrary to public policy any attempt to implement this Agreement.[88]

While recognizing the importance of restrictively applying the public policy exception, the CCJ found that the grounds for refusing enforcement of the award were 'compelling' because fundamental constitutional principles were engaged. In this context, it held:

> The sovereignty of Parliament subject only to the supremacy of the Constitution is a core constitutional value. So too is the principle of the Separation of Powers the observance of which one is entitled to take for granted. To disregard these values is to attack the foundations upon which the rule of law and democracy are constructed throughout the Caribbean. It is said that public policy amounts to no less than those principles and standards that are so sacrosanct as to require courts to maintain and promote them at all costs and without exception. The Committee on International Commercial Arbitration has endorsed 'tax laws' as an example of an area that might fall within the scope of public policy, the breach of which might justify a State court refusing enforcement of an Award. In our judgment, especially as the underlying agreement was to be performed in Belize, the balance here undoubtedly lies in favour of not enforcing this Award. This is a case where the Court actually has a duty to invoke the public policy exception.[89]

A number of points bear noting about this decision. First, the case is a clear illustration of how national constitutions can play a role in regulating international arbitral proceedings. Not only did the CCJ's decision rest on the fundamental principle of the separation of powers, but the CCJ grounded its reasoning in broader constitutional principles and values such as the requirements of 'the rule of law and democratic governance'.[90] In refusing enforcement on these bases, the CCJ affirmed its constitutional obligation to strike down ultra vires administrative or executive actions and its duty to 'appropriately challenge attempts to undermine the Constitution'.[91]

Second, the decision underscores the delicate balance that courts must strike when seeking to reconcile competing policy considerations in the areas of international arbitration and constitution law. On the one hand, the CCJ was careful to establish that the public policy considerations in this case fell squarely within the scope of 'international public policy' concerns that might justify the non-enforcement of a New York

[88] ibid paras 51–53 (emphasis added).
[89] ibid para 59.
[90] ibid para 42.
[91] ibid para 61.

Convention award. On the other hand, the CCJ sought to assess the scope of public policy with reference to 'the values, aspirations, mores, institutions and conception of cardinal principles of law of the people of Belize'.[92] In this way, the CCJ did not seek to justify its decision on the presumptive dominance of constitutional norms over arbitration principles, but grounded its decision in principles and concepts common to both regimes. Indeed, in subsequent decisions, the CCJ has emphasized that it will not strive to set aside awards against the government on the basis that constitutional requirements have not been met, but will 'conduct a balancing exercise weighing the interest of guaranteeing the finality of the award against the competing interest of ensuring respect for fundamental principles of its legal system such as the rule of law'.[93]

Third, while the case illustrates the capacity of courts to subject arbitral proceedings to constitutional scrutiny, it also exposes the limitations of using national constitutions to regulate what is essentially a transnational legal phenomenon. Indeed, after failing to have the award enforced in the courts of Belize, the claimants filed a petition in the United States (US) District Court for the District of Columbia to confirm the award. In response, the government filed a motion to dismiss the petition, claiming, among other things, that public policy and international comity barred the claimants from enforcement because the CCJ had already issued a final judgment refusing to enforce the award. Ultimately, a US District Court granted enforcement of the award in the US.[94]

The District Court rejected the argument that the CCJ's decision precluded US courts from granting enforcement. It found that, because England was 'the country with primary jurisdiction' (ie the arbitral seat), only an English court could set aside the arbitral award issued by the arbitral tribunal. Thus, although the CCJ decided not to enforce the award, on the basis of public policy, its decision to do so did not bind the US courts. The District Court continued to reject the government's argument that the enforcement of an award which implicated the Government of Belize in actions that were contrary to the Belizean constitution would effectively 'violate the public policy of the United States against government corruption'. The District Court noted that, although the US had a 'strong public policy against corruption abroad', that policy did not reach the threshold required to outweigh the policy in favour of enforcement. In this connection, the Court noted that Article V(2)(b) of the New York Convention 'was not meant to enshrine the vagaries of international politics under the rubric of "public policy"'. It found that the government's invitation to refuse to enforce the award on public policy grounds would invariably 'implicate politics abroad', and therefore declined that invitation.[95]

3 Public Policy and Arbitrability

Constitutional law controls may also assume importance with respect to the arbitrability of certain public-private disputes. Whether a matter is capable of being settled by arbitration is largely a question of public policy to be determined by each

[92] ibid para 23.
[93] See *Belize Bank Limited v Attorney General of Belize* [2017] CCJ 18 (AJ), para 8.
[94] See *BCB Holdings Limited v Government of Belize*, 110 F Supp 3d 233 (DDC 2015).
[95] ibid.

state in line with its legal and political values, as reflected in legislation and expounded by common law judges. To the extent that any question of constitutional law is non-arbitrable, a relevant court could restrain arbitral proceedings or refuse to give effect to an arbitral award on the basis that the subject matter of the dispute is not capable of settlement by arbitration. It is, however, an open question whether issues of constitutional law are arbitrable under Commonwealth Caribbean law.

As noted earlier, constitutional texts and arbitration legislation in the Caribbean provide no guidance as to which categories of public-private disputes (if any) are subject to the exclusive jurisdiction of the courts and may not properly be adjudicated by an arbitral tribunal. Consistent with the trend in other jurisdictions,[96] the nascent regional jurisprudence suggests that Caribbean courts take a liberal approach to arbitrability doctrine, and will be slow to invoke that doctrine to limit the categories of disputes which may be submitted to arbitration.[97]

However, the position with respect to the arbitrability of constitutional law issues is unclear. Regional courts have been prepared to accept that a 'foreign act of state' is non-arbitrable at common law.[98] In this context, 'act of state' presumably engages a government's exercise of certain public law and constitutional powers.[99] However, in *BCB Holdings Limited and the Belize Bank Limited v the Attorney General of Belize*,[100] the first-instance court rejected the argument that matters of income taxation were 'quintessentially territorial' and accordingly non-arbitrable.[101] In so holding, the judge pointed to the fact that in the cases of *Occidental Exploration v Ecuador*[102] and *Encana v Ecuador*,[103] which concerned claims relating to tax measures under the bilateral investment treaty (BIT), United States–Ecuador issues of taxation were resolved by international arbitration. It is not clear, however, why BIT claims brought against Ecuador, governed by rules of public international law, provide an answer to the question whether issues of taxation are arbitrable in the Commonwealth Caribbean. Regrettably, the issue of arbitrability was abandoned when the appeal went before the CCJ, and the CCJ declined to opine on the issue because it was 'unnecessary' to do so at that point in the proceedings.[104] Had the CCJ intervened, not only would it have ruled on the narrow issue of taxation, but also on the wider question of the arbitrability of disputes dealing with the capacity and legal powers of state organs

[96] See Karim Abou Youssef, 'The Death of In-arbitrability' in Loukas A Mistelis and Stavros L Brekoulakis (eds), *Arbitrability: International and Comparative Perspectives* (Kluwer 2009) 47.

[97] See *Ennio Zanotti v Interlog Finance Corp et al*, Claim No BVIHCV 2009/0394 (8 February 2010) (unreported). In the case, the Eastern Caribbean Supreme Court affirmed a pro-arbitration approach to questions of arbitrability, and distinguished a line of English authority, to find that statutory company law claims for 'unfair prejudice' were arbitrable.

[98] See *IPOC International Growth Fund Limited v LV Finance Group Limited* (n 64) para 42. Note, however, that the court held that the doctrine did not apply in the case before it, so as to require the court to refuse enforcement under the New York Convention.

[99] See Lawrence Collins and others (eds), *Dicey, Morris and Collins on the Conflict of Laws* (14th edn, Sweet & Maxwell 2006) para 5R-019.

[100] *BCB v Belize* (n 47).

[101] Claim No 743 of 2009 (unreported, decision of the Supreme Court of Belize, delivered on 22 December 2010); Anderson (n 78) 9.

[102] *Occidental Exploration and Production Company v Republic of Ecuador*, LCIA Case No UN3467 (UNCITRAL).

[103] *EnCana Corporation v Republic of Ecuador*, LCIA Case No UN 3481 (UNCITRAL).

[104] *BCB v Belize* (n 47) para 17.

under the Belizean constitution. Such questions have now been deferred to a later date (perhaps out of considerations of judicial economy). At that point, the courts will hopefully provide clarity on whether substantive issues of constitutional law entail 'a degree of state intervention and public interest such as to make [them] inappropriate for disposal by anything other than judicial process'.[105]

B. Regulation Through 'Procedural Controls'

Finally, the courts may also issue procedural remedies to regulate arbitral proceedings which pose a significant threat to, or undermine, fundamental constitutional principles and values. This may include the institution of stays on proceedings, and more controversially, the imposition of anti-arbitration injunctions. The courts have affirmed that such measures may only be imposed in rare circumstances to restrain arbitral proceedings where, for example, the arbitration is deemed 'abusive' or 'inequitable'.

The approach to anti-arbitration injunctions was addressed by the CCJ in the seminal case of *British Caribbean Bank v Government of Belize*.[106] This case arose out of a long-running battle between British Caribbean Bank (BCB) and the government of Belize over the nationalization of BCB's assets in the telecommunications industry in 2009. BCB was initially successful in challenging the constitutionality of the nationalization in the Belizean courts. However, after the Belizean courts had ruled that the expropriation was unconstitutional, the government renationalized BCB's assets under new legislation in 2011, and took steps to amend the constitution so as to prevent the courts from enquiring into the legality of the renationalization.

Faced with these formidable domestic hurdles and no effective constitutional redress, BCB initiated arbitration under the arbitration rules of the United Nations Commission on International Trade Law (UNCITRAL) against Belize under the United Kingdom–Belize BIT, seeking compensation for the expropriated assets. In response, the government passed legislation[107] which empowered the Belizean courts to enter injunctions against international arbitrations anywhere in the world and impose fines on parties who fail to observe the terms of the injunctions. The government then obtained an interim injunction from the courts in Belize restraining BCB from continuing its BIT arbitration on the basis that the arbitration was 'vexatious and oppressive' because the domestic constitutional courts were properly seised of the question of the constitutionality of the nationalization. BCB ultimately appealed this injunction to the CCJ, asking the Court to discharge the orders and uphold its right to arbitrate under the BIT.

One of the issues at the heart of this dispute was the apparent overlap between ongoing constitutional proceedings and the arbitral proceedings initiated pursuant to the United Kingdom–Belize BIT. BCB had initiated a proceeding challenging the

[105] See *Fulham Football Club (1987) Limited v Sir David Richards, The Football Association Premier League Limited* [2011] EWCA Civ 855.
[106] *BCB v Government of Belize* (n 52).
[107] The Supreme Court of Judicature Amendment Act (2011).

nationalization under Article 17 of the Constitution of Belize, which provides in relevant part:

> No property of any description shall be compulsorily taken possession of and no interest in or right over property of any description shall be compulsorily acquired except by or under a law that . . . prescribes the principles on which and the manner in which reasonable compensation therefor is to be determined and given within a reasonable time.

After the various governmental efforts to amend the constitution and thereby undermine BCB's recourse to the constitutional courts, BCB subsequently initiated arbitration under the United Kingdom–Belize BIT seeking a remedy for the government's breach of the treaty's prohibition on expropriation without compensation. The government sought to maintain the injunction on the basis that BCB's right to arbitrate was subject to the prior determination of the domestic constitutional courts.

The CCJ rejected the government's position regarding the pre-eminence of constitutional proceedings. In this context, the Court held that 'the effectiveness of [investment treaty arbitration] would be undermined if the investor was required to exhaust remedies in domestic courts before proceeding to international arbitration'.[108] The CCJ found that BCB had a legally enforceable right under the BIT that should rightfully be recognized by the domestic courts and concluded that the effect of the BIT was to 'oust the jurisdiction of the domestic courts by agreeing to submit such disputes to the selected international arbitral tribunal'.[109] In so doing, the CCJ found that constitutional remedies for expropriation of property have no presumed pre-eminence over international arbitral remedies under a BIT.

It went on to affirm that the mere fact that a constitutional court was seised of an issue did not mean that the matter could not validly be submitted to international arbitration.[110] It noted that BIT standards are separate and autonomous from constitutional or other legal rights and remedies available as a matter of domestic law, and drew a clear distinction between the vindication of rights under domestic law and claims for breaches of international law.[111] In so doing, it appears that the CCJ conceived of the relationship between arbitration law and constitutional law as distinct and complementary regimes rather than competing governance systems. The CCJ has explained that, while constitutional law and arbitral disputes may arise from the same factual matrix, they do not occupy the same legal sphere. In this context, it has noted, for example, that '[a]n expropriation that is perfectly lawful under the national [constitutional] law could nonetheless trigger a successful investment claim under . . . [an] investment treaty'.[112]

[108] *BCB v Government of Belize* (n 52) para 21.

[109] ibid para 17.

[110] ibid para 41.

[111] In this context, the court endorsed arbitral jurisprudence that has affirmed that domestic court proceedings are not *ipso facto* duplicative or coextensive with proceedings brought pursuant to BITs. See *Salini Costruttori SpA et Italstrade SpA v Royaume du Maroc*, ICSID Case No ARB/00/4, Decision on Jurisdiction (23 July 2001), paras 26 and 27; *Azurix Corp v Argentine Republic*, ICSID Case No ARB/01/12, Decision on Jurisdiction (8 December 2003), para 79.

[112] [2013] CCJ 4 (AJ) para 23.

While the CCJ held that the BIT ousted the courts' jurisdiction, it affirmed that Caribbean courts, like other common law courts, had the ability to restrict or enjoin international arbitral proceedings on the grounds that they are either vexatious, oppressive, inequitable, or an abuse of process.[113] It noted, however, that this power was subject to a high threshold. In this context, the CCJ emphasized that courts should exercise restraint and grant injunctions only in the rarest and most exceptional cases. More specifically, it noted that in cases involving international arbitration proceedings:

> [T]he court must re-double the caution it normally exercises in restraining foreign proceedings because of the importance of recognizing and enforcing the agreement of parties to the mechanism for dispute resolution and the accepted principle of international law that the arbitral tribunal should not be subjected to the control of the domestic courts before it makes an award.[114]

The thrust of the government's claim had been that the multiplicity of proceedings and the risk of conflicting or overlapping orders between the constitutional court and the arbitral tribunal rendered the arbitration process 'vexatious and oppressive'. However, the CCJ rejected this assertion, noting that:

> Proceedings could be vexatious where they are absurd or the litigant seeks some fanciful advantage by suing in two courts at the same time but they would not be so held where there are substantial reasons of benefit to the plaintiff to bring the two sets of proceedings. There is no presumption that a multiplicity of proceedings, or that merely bringing the proceeding in an inconvenient place, is vexatious.[115]

The CCJ found that the arbitration proceedings were a bona fide attempt by BCB to vindicate its rights under international law,[116] not least because of the various hurdles BCB encountered in seeking compensation in Belize. There was no risk of 'double recovery' as BCB had entered an undertaking to offset any compensation obtained in the arbitration against any compensation received in domestic proceedings.[117] Consequently, the CCJ discharged the anti-arbitration injunction.

Regional courts have emphasized that they will restrain arbitration proceedings only in the 'rarest cases' but have left the door open for this remedy where arbitral proceedings are deemed 'vexatious and oppressive, inequitable, or . . . an abuse of legal process'.[118] It is not clear, however, when and how the courts will intervene in this way to regulate arbitral proceedings which threaten constitutional proceedings.

To be sure, the imposition of anti-arbitration injunctions is a most contentious issue in international arbitration. Many have long argued that there are no circumstances in which an anti-arbitration injunction may be warranted. For example, Judge

113 ibid.
114 ibid para 41.
115 ibid para 41.
116 ibid para 47.
117 ibid paras 50–54.
118 ibid para 23.

Schwebel has argued that the issuance of an anti-arbitration injunction by domestic courts 'appear[s] to violate conventional and customary international law, international public policy and the accepted principles of international arbitration'.[119] A similar approach was adopted in the case of *Société Générale de Surveillance SA v Islamic Republic of Pakistan*, where the tribunal disregarded an injunction imposed by the Pakistani courts on the basis that:

> The right to seek access to international adjudication must be respected and cannot be constrained by an order of a national court. Nor can a State plead its internal law in defence of an act that is inconsistent with its international obligations . . . Otherwise, a Contracting State could impede access to ICSID arbitration by operation of its own law.[120]

Domestic courts, on the other hand, are loath to relinquish their constitutionally vested powers. It is presumably for this reason that the CCJ did not hold that the courts lacked any competence to enjoin foreign arbitral proceedings.[121] In so holding, the Court roundly rejected the argument that courts could not restrain a claimant's 'unqualified or indefeasible right to proceed to international arbitration',[122] noting that arbitration did not fall entirely outside the reach of the constitutional supervision because '[t]he exercise by one individual of his or her rights often infringes on the rights of other individuals or the society as a whole and the courts are and must remain the final arbiter of the relative distribution of those rights'.[123] In this way, the CCJ sought to ground its power to enjoin international arbitration proceedings within a broad constitutional duty to uphold public order and the societal interests.

However, the power of the courts to restrain arbitral proceedings suffers from a vagueness problem and 'is somewhat unpredictable and potentially open to abuse'.[124] The test is vague in at least two respects. First, there is no clarity as to what constitutes 'oppressive, vexatious, inequitable' arbitral proceedings. The CCJ made clear that arbitral proceedings which overlap with domestic constitutional proceedings will not, without more, be deemed vexatious or oppressive. However, no further guidance was provided on this point. The second area of vagueness relates to the CCJ's statement that injunctions should only be granted in 'exceptional circumstances'. Here, again,

[119] Stephen Schwebel, 'Anti-Suit Injunctions in International Arbitration: An Overview' in Emmanuel Gaillard (ed), *Anti-Suit Injunctions in International Arbitration* (Juris 2005) 5, 15. See also David Sutton, Judith Gill, and Matthew Gearing, *Russell on Arbitration* (23rd edn, Sweet & Maxwell 2007) para 7-058, noting that the jurisdiction is so exceptional that it is 'virtually impossible to obtain an injunction' against an international arbitration.

[120] *SGS Société Générale de Surveillance SA v Islamic Republic of Pakistan*, ICSID Case No ARB/01/13, Procedural Order No 2 (16 October 2002) (2003) 18 ICSID Review – FILJ 293, 300.

[121] Stacie I Strong, 'Anti-Arbitration Injunctions in Cases Involving Investor-State Arbitration: British Caribbean Bank Ltd. v The Government of Belize' (2014) 15 JWIT 324, 332: '[C]ommon law courts are unlikely to deny themselves the ability to enjoin international arbitration. A court may impose a number of restrictions on itself so as to limit the availability of anti-arbitration injunctions to truly extreme situations, but it is highly unlikely that any court will ever rule that it does not have jurisdiction to order this type of relief in appropriate circumstances.'

[122] *BCB v Government of Belize* (n 52) para 14.

[123] ibid.

[124] Strong (n 121) 332.

the CCJ's statements do little to illuminate when it will intervene in arbitral proceedings. One presumes that the judges deliberately left the test vague in order to allow flexibility for the Court to develop the law as it sees fit and to craft what it deems to be an appropriate response to circumstances it has not, and perhaps could not, have foreseen.

But while anti-arbitration injunctions may be viewed by some as arbitral heresy, courts will no doubt retain this remedy as a tool of last resort for resolving conflicts between international arbitration proceedings and fundamental constitutional principles. This remedy is undoubtedly open to abuse and, as such, should be deployed sparingly. However, misuse will be significantly reduced if national courts and international arbitral tribunals remain committed to principles of comity, mutual respect, and a shared understanding of the complementarity of the judicial and arbitral processes. The decision in *British Caribbean Bank v Government of Belize*[125] is a strong signal that Caribbean courts are striving to strike just such a balance.

VI. Whither the Constitutional Regulation of Public-Private Arbitration?

As discussed above, the jurisprudence from the region demonstrates that the courts endeavour to balance the competing policies and normative imperatives at the interface of public-private arbitration and constitution law. On the one hand, the courts have committed to a judicial policy in support of international arbitration. On the other hand, they have been astute to uphold their function as 'guardians of the constitution',[126] and have been willing to impose constitutional constraints on arbitral proceedings where particular proceedings threaten fundamental constitutional principles and community interests. While the Caribbean courts have, to date, been slow to invoke constitutional law as a basis for intervening in arbitral proceedings, they have indicated a willingness to do so in at least three circumstances.

First, where arbitration implicates or offends fundamental structural constitutional principles or core values, the courts may refuse to enforce such awards on public policy grounds. In one of the few instances in which Caribbean courts have refused enforcement of an arbitral award, the CCJ denied enforcement on the basis that the award concerned an agreement that was repugnant to the constitution and 'attack[ed] the foundations upon which the rule of law and democracy are constructed throughout the Caribbean'.[127] The Court held that the constitutional law principles at stake (in this instance, the separation of powers and democratic accountability) were 'so sacrosanct as to require courts to maintain and promote them at all costs and without exception'.[128]

Second, the courts have not ruled out the possibility of granting constitutional redress in circumstances where a party within their jurisdiction alleges that arbitral

[125] *BCB v Government of Belize* (n 52).
[126] See *Collymore* (n 19).
[127] *BCB v Belize* (n 47) para 59.
[128] ibid.

proceedings have impaired, or threaten to impair, individual constitutional rights.[129] The courts are yet to grant such relief, and it is fair to say that they are likely only to do so in the most compelling circumstances.

Third, the courts have affirmed their competence to restrict or enjoin international arbitral proceedings in favour of local constitutional proceedings, where the arbitration in question is vexatious, oppressive, inequitable, or an abuse of process. This may include circumstances where the initiation of the arbitration is 'absurd' or the litigant 'seeks some fanciful advantage', including (one presumes) where a party brings manifestly abusive or frivolous arbitral claims in order to thwart access to constitutional courts.[130] The courts have emphasized, however, that such measures will only be imposed in the rarest and most exceptional of cases.

However, it should be noted that any such interventions in the arbitral process must overcome the strong imperative of 'judicial non-intervention' enshrined in domestic and international law. As we have seen, Caribbean courts have affirmed a judicial policy in support of international arbitration. The policy has been justified, in part, on the basis of the 'universal consensus' in favour of judicial respect for arbitration, and on the basis that the promotion of arbitration contributes to the fulfilment of the development goals of Caribbean states.[131] Such policy considerations serve as a strong disincentive to courts seeking to intervene in arbitration proceedings, on constitutional grounds or otherwise.

This disincentive will become even greater as Caribbean jurisdictions move apace to enact modern arbitration legislation which mandates judicial support for the arbitral process. As Van Harten has noted:

> [M]ost states have enacted legislation since the 1990s (for the distinct purpose of encouraging agreements to arbitrate in order to stimulate international commerce) that directs their courts to defer to foreign arbitration awards, and since then the trend in the jurisprudence . . . is to show a high level of deference to international arbitrators. In general, domestic courts will overturn an award only where they find a jurisdictional error, procedural impropriety, or serious violation of public policy, and crucially, the courts are typically not authorized to correct errors of law by tribunals in their interpretation of broadly framed investor protection.[132]

The apogee of such legislative policy is found in Article 5 of the UNCITRAL Model Law, which mandates that 'no court shall intervene in matters governed by this law'.[133]

Thus, while litigants may continue to press the Caribbean courts to extend the reach of the constitution into the arbitral sphere, they are likely to be unsuccessful. The courts have shown a strong resolve to resist attempts to use the constitution as a pretext to thwart or otherwise interfere with legitimate arbitral proceedings. While Caribbean courts have affirmed their power to apply constitutional law controls to

[129] *Auto-Guadeloupe Investissement SAS v Alvarez & Ors* (n 70).
[130] *BCB v Government of Belize* (n 52) para 41.
[131] *BCB v Belize* (n 47) para 26.
[132] Van Harten (n 1) 154–56.
[133] UNCITRAL Model Law of International Commercial Arbitration, UN Doc A/40/17, Annex 1.

arbitration, they have so far confined such constitutional interventions to the enforcement stage of arbitration, and within the prism and parameters of the exceptions under the New York Convention and the UNCITRAL Model Law framework (where applicable).

This aligns with prevailing arbitration orthodoxy which holds that judicial interference in arbitral proceedings, outside the terms of the New York Convention and the UNCITRAL Model Law, constitutes an illegitimate incursion on the autonomy of arbitral proceedings.[134] On this view, both instruments serve as the legitimate 'control scheme' or 'control system' for international arbitration and the exclusive scheme governing the relationship between national courts and international arbitral proceedings.[135] Caribbean courts have yet to express a definitive view on this issue. The decided cases suggest that the courts envisage a rather minimal role for constitutional law in the context of international arbitration—one consistent with international law and international arbitral standards. However, the courts' position with respect to anti-arbitration injunctions signals willingness, albeit limited, to depart from existing arbitral consensus in compelling circumstances.

There are sound reasons for confining domestic constitutional norms within the regulatory framework of the New York Convention and the UNCITRAL Model Law. First, the New York Convention is a binding international treaty which represents a consensus of over 156 states with respect to the conduct of international arbitration, including the role of domestic courts in that process. Courts, as organs of the state, ought properly to ensure, as far as possible, that the interpretation and application of national constitutions accord with the international obligations of the state. Second, the public policy exception under Article V(2)(b) of the Convention significantly overlaps with fundamental norms enshrined in many national constitutions. As has been noted, 'the public policy defense [is] permitted . . . when enforcement of an award would result in a violation of the enforcing state's most fundamental notions of morality and justice. This may include a violation of constitutional rights as well as a violation of fundamental principles of civil law.'[136] Similarly, the International Law Association has noted that domestic courts may refuse enforcement under Article V(2)(b) where there is 'a manifest breach of a rule of law regarded as essential in the legal order of the State in which enforcement is sought or of a right recognised as being fundamental within that legal order'.[137]

It may appear suboptimal, from the perspective of constitutional effectiveness, for courts to use the New York Convention and the UNCITRAL Model Law as the only entry points through which to impose constitutional law discipline on arbitral procedures that offend core constitutional principles and values. As scholars like Van Harten point out, 'the grounds for judicial review, as laid out in the ICSID

[134] See eg Pierre Mayer and Audley Sheppard, 'Final ILA Report on Public Policy as a Bar to Enforcement of International Arbitral Awards' (2003) 19(2) Arb Int'l 249, 250.

[135] Michael Reisman, *Systems of Control in International Adjudication and Arbitration* (Duke University Press 1992) 109, 113.

[136] Dirk Otto and Omaia Elwan, 'Article V(2)' in Herbert Kronke and others (eds), *Recognition and Enforcement of Foreign Arbitral Awards: A Global Commentary on the New York Convention* (Kluwer 2010) 345, 366.

[137] See Mayer and Sheppard (n 134) 252.

Convention, the New York Convention, and other instruments, are very limited'.[138] Moreover, confining constitutional scrutiny to the limits of the New York Convention would mean that national constitutions only play a role after arbitral proceedings have been concluded, not before, and even then parties may escape constitutional scrutiny by enforcing the award in foreign jurisdictions. It would also mean that constitutional law would only provide protection or have regulatory bite within the geographical boundaries of the state.

Yet, this approach may represent the best balance between legitimate constitutional concerns and the need for a stable and predictable system of international arbitration. Constitutions are inherently political documents which reflect a particular political settlement struck by particular people, in particular circumstances, and at a particular time in their history. Subjecting international arbitration to the variable political demands of global constitutional texts could pose a formidable threat to the current system of international arbitration. The balance struck in the New York Convention allows courts considerable constitutional latitude, while eschewing overly idiosyncratic or parochial norms that may be used as a basis for unduly interfering with the arbitral processes agreed by the relevant parties.

VII. Conclusion

While Caribbean courts have affirmed a clear commitment to promote arbitration and its processes, they have not abdicated their constitutional role when such processes threaten fundamental constitutional norms and values. They have been astute to assert their function as 'guardians of the constitution' and, in so doing, have affirmed their authority to exert normative and procedural 'controls' on international arbitration where proceedings threaten the public interest. However, the application of these 'controls' has only been addressed in an ad hoc manner in the context of a handful of decided cases.

As Caribbean courts, like other courts, continue to grapple with the many tensions and conflicts at the interface of arbitral and constitutional governance, many important questions remain unanswered. Arbitration orthodoxy urges an approach which confines constitutional regulation of arbitration to the framework of the New York Convention and the existing system of international arbitration. On the other hand, constitutional doctrine points to a less constrained role—one guided by the fundamental political values of the polity in question and the overriding aim of constitutional effectiveness and the rule of law. As the analysis here shows, Caribbean courts have sought to strike a balanced position between these two poles, even if there remains uncertainty as to how the balance is struck in individual cases. Such uncertainty serves to underscore the conundrum faced by courts worldwide as they strive to ensure fidelity to their constitutional mandate while upholding states' international commitments and domestic policy imperatives to respect and promote the autonomy and effectiveness of transnational arbitral processes.

[138] Van Harten (n 1) 154–56.

Select Materials

Bibliography

Aman, Alfred C, 'Globalization, Democracy, and the Need for a New Administrative Law' (2003) 10 Ind J Global Legal Studies 125

Anderson, Winston, 'Role of the Domestic Courts in the International Commercial Arbitration Process' (Fourth High Level Meeting on the Role of the Judiciary in International Commercial Arbitration, St Lucia, 23 October 2014)

Antoine, Rose-Marie B, *Commonwealth Caribbean Law and Legal Systems* (Routledge 2008)

Blackaby, Nigel and others, *Redfern and Hunter on International Arbitration* (6th edn, OUP 2015)

Bonnitcha, Jonathan, Lauge Poulsen, and Michael Waibel, *The Political Economy of the Investment Treaty Regime* (OUP 2017)

Bulkan, Arif, Tracy Robinson, and Adrian Saunders, *Fundamentals of Caribbean Constitutional Law* (Sweet & Maxwell 2014)

Byron, Dennis and Christopher Malcolm, 'Caribbean Community (CARICOM)' in Wolfrum, Rüdiger (ed), *Max Planck Encyclopedia of Public International Law* (online edn, July 2009)

Carnegie, AR, '*Floreat* the Westminster Model? A Commonwealth Caribbean Perspective' (1996) 6 Carib L Rev 1

Chinkin, Christine, 'A Critique of the Public/Private Dimension' (1999) 10 EJIL 387

Crawford, James, *Brownlie's Principles of Public International Law* (8th edn, OUP 2012)

Collins, Lawrence and others (eds), *Dicey, Morris and Collins on the Conflict of Laws* (14th edn, Sweet & Maxwell 2006)

Dagbanja, Dominic Npoanlari, 'Constitutionalism and Local Remedies Rule as Limitations on Investor-State Arbitration: Perspectives from Ghana' (2017) 17 OUCLJ 110

Dagbanja, Dominic Npoanlari, 'Reasserting the Role of Municipal Law in International Trade and Investment Protection Through Choice of Law' (United Nations Conference on International Trade Law: Modernizing International Trade to Support Innovation and Sustainable Development, Vienna, 4–6 July 2017)

de Smith, Stanley A, *The New Commonwealth and Its Constitutions* (Stevens & Sons 1964)

Dumberry, Patrick and Jacob Stone, 'International Law, Whether You Like It or Not: An Analysis of Arbitral Tribunal Practice Regarding the Applicable Law in Deciding State Contracts Disputes under the ICSID Convention in the Twenty First Century' in Andrea K Bjorklund (ed), *Yearbook on International Investment Law and Policy 2012–2013* (OUP 2014) 477

Elliott, Mark and Robert Thomas, *Public Law* (OUP 2011)

Fiadjoe, Albert, *Alternative Dispute Resolution: A Developing World Perspective* (Routledge 2004)

Gaillard, Emmanuel, *Legal Theory of International Arbitration* (Martinus Nijhoff 2010)

Gayle, Rene, 'Jamaica Replaces Century-Old Arbitration Act with UNCITRAL Model Law' (2018) 1(6) Lat Am J Int'l Trade L 1

Goode, Roy, 'Arbitration – Should Courts Get Involved?' (2002) 2 IJS Journal 33
Goldsmith QC, Peter, 'A Brave New World – Can the BVI International Arbitration Centre Knock New York, London and Paris Off Their Perch?' (JS Archibald QC Memorial Lecture, BVI International Arbitration Conference, 20 October 2015)
Grimm, Dieter, 'Types of Constitutions in Contemporary History from 18th Century Classic Liberal to Post-Colonial and Post Authoritarian' in Michel Rosenfeld and Andras Sajo (eds), *The Oxford Handbook of Comparative Constitutional Law* (OUP 2012) 98
Hepburn, Jarrod, *Domestic Law in International Investment Arbitration* (OUP 2017)
Jackson, Leighton, 'Fi We Law: The Emergence of Caribbean Jurisprudence and the Doctrine of Precedence' in David Berry and Tracy Robinson (eds), *Transitions in Caribbean Law: Law Making, Constitutionalism and the Convergence of National and International Law* (Ian Randle 2013) 13
Mayer, Pierre and Audley Sheppard, 'Final ILA Report on Public Policy as a Bar to Enforcement of International Arbitral Awards' (2003) 19(2) Arb Int'l 249
McLachlan, Campbell, *Foreign Relations Law* (CUP 2014)
O'Brien, Derek, *The Constitutional Systems of the Commonwealth Caribbean* (Hart 2014)
Onyema, Emilia, 'Modernising the Framework for Arbitration in Jamaica: Some Salient Points' (unpublished manuscript, 18 February 2010) <https://eprints.soas.ac.uk/8252/> accessed 26 January 2025
Otto, Dirk and Omaia Elwan, 'Article V(2)' in Herbert Kronke and others (eds), *Recognition and Enforcement of Foreign Arbitral Awards: A Global Commentary on the New York Convention* (Kluwer 2010) 345
Reisman, Michael, *Systems of Control in International Adjudication and Arbitration* (Duke University Press 1992)
Robinson, Tracy, 'Our Inherent Constitution' in David Berry and Tracy Robinson (eds), *Transitions in Caribbean Law: Law-Making, Constitutionalism and the Convergence of National and International Law* (Ian Randle 2013) 248
Rutledge, Peter B, *Arbitration and the Constitution* (CUP 2013)
Schwebel, Stephen, 'Anti-Suit Injunctions in International Arbitration: An Overview' in Emmanuel Gaillard (ed), *Anti-Suit Injunctions in International Arbitration* (Juris 2005) 5
Stoppi, Maurice J, *Commercial Arbitration in the Caribbean: A Practical Guide* (University of the West Indies Press 2001)
Strong, Stacie I, 'Constitutional Conundrums in Arbitration' (2013) 15 Cardozo J Conflict Resol 41
Strong, Stacie I, 'Anti-Arbitration Injunctions in Cases Involving Investor-State Arbitration: British Caribbean Bank Ltd v The Government of Belize' (2014) 15 JWIT 324
Sutton, David, Judith Gill, and Matthew Gearing, *Russell on Arbitration* (23rd edn, Sweet & Maxwell 2007)
Thomas, Christopher and Harpreet Dhillon, 'Applicable Law Under International Investment Treaties' (2014) 26 Sing Ac L J 975
Van Harten, Gus, *Investment Treaty Arbitration and Public Law* (OUP 2007)
Ventose, Eddy, *Commonwealth Caribbean Administrative Law* (Routledge 2013)
Youssef, Karim Abou, 'The Death of In-arbitrability' in Loukas A Mistelis and Stavros L Brekoulakis (eds), *Arbitrability: International and Comparative Perspectives* (Kluwer 2009)

Legislation and Other Legal Instruments

Agreement Establishing the Caribbean Court of Justice (2001)
Investment Act 2004 (Guyana)
The Arbitration Act (1975) (Antigua and Barbuda)
The Arbitration Act 1931 (Guyana)
The Arbitration Act 1907 (Montserrat)
The Arbitration Act of Trinidad and Tobago, Ch 5:01
The Arbitration Act 2009 (Bahamas)
The Arbitration Act 2013 (British Virgin Islands)
The Arbitration Act 1900 (Jamaica)
The Arbitration Act 2017 (Jamaica)
The Arbitration (Amendment) Ordinance of 1980 (Belize)
The Arbitration (Foreign Arbitral Awards) Act 2009 (Bahamas)
The Arbitration Law 2012 (Cayman Islands)
The Constitution of Antigua and Barbuda
The Constitution of the Commonwealth of the Bahamas
The Constitution of Barbados
The Constitution of Belize
The Constitution of the Commonwealth of Dominica
The Constitution of the Cooperative Republic of Guyana
The Constitution of Grenada
The Constitution of Jamaica
The Constitution of the Republic of Ghana
The Constitution of the Republic of Trinidad and Tobago
The Constitution of St Kitts and Nevis
The Constitution of St Vincent and the Grenadines
The International Commercial Arbitration Act 2007 (Barbados)
The Supreme Court of Judicature Amendment Act 2011 (Belize)

Cases

Attorney General v Carlisle Holdings – Claim No 15 of 2005 (Supreme Court of Belize)
Auto-Guadeloupe Investissement SAS v Alvarez & Ors (2014) 84 WIR 49
Bankswitch Ghana Ltd (Ghana) v The Republic of Ghana, PCA Case No 118294, Award Save as to Costs (11 April 2014)
BCB Holdings Limited and the Belize Bank Limited v the Attorney General of Belize, Claim No. 743 of 2009 (unreported, decision of the Supreme Court of Belize, delivered on 22 December 2010)
BCB Holdings Limited and the Belize Bank Limited v the Attorney General of Belize [2013] CCJ 5
BCB Holdings Limited v. Government of Belize, Civil Action No 2014-1123 (DC 2015)
Belize Bank Limited v Attorney General of Belize [2017] CCJ 18 (AJ)
Belize Natural Energy Ltd v Maranco Ltd [2015] CCJ 2 (AJ)

Belize Telemedia v Attorney General of Belize No 464 of 2008 (Supreme Court of Belize)
British Caribbean Bank v Government of Belize [2013] CCJ 4 (AJ)
Claim No HCV 2428 of 2004 (Supreme Court of Jamaica)
Collymore v Attorney General (Trinidad & Tobago) (1968) 12 WIR 5 CA; (1970) 15 WIR 229, PC
Dantzler Inc v Galloway Hardware & Building Materials Ltd, Claim No MNIHCV2014/0024 (3 December 2014) (Eastern Caribbean Supreme Court)
Ennio Zanotti v Interlog Finance Corp et al, BVIHCV 2009/0394 (8 February 2010) (Eastern Caribbean Supreme Court)
Fulham Football Club (1987) Limited v Sir David Richards, The Football Association Premier League Limited [2011] EWCA Civ 855
Hualon Corporation (M) SDN BHD (in receivership) v Marty Limited, Claim No. BVIHC (COM) 2014/0090 (8 April 2016) (Eastern Caribbean Supreme Court)
In the Matter of the Decision of Dr Robert Gaitskell QC (Sole Arbitrator of an Arbitrator under the ICC Rules of Arbitration 1998*)* Claim Number CV2008-04881 (21 October 2009)
IPOC International Growth Fund Limited v LV Finance Group Limited, BVI Civil Appeal No 36 of 2006 (18 June 2007) (Eastern Caribbean Court of Appeal)
Joseph and Boyce v Attorney General [2006] CCJ 3
Marbury v Madison, 5 US 137 (1803)
*Minister of Home Affairs & Ors v Fish*er [1979] AC 319
Revere Jamaica Alumina Ltd v Attorney General (1977) 26 WIR 486 (Supreme Court of Jamaica)
TCL Air Conditioner (Zhongshan) Co Ltd v The Judges of the Federal Court of Australia [2013] HCA 5
The Attorney General et al v Jeffrey Joseph and Lennox Ricardo Boyce, CCJ Appeal No CV 2 of 2005

12

The Legitimacy of Private-Public Arbitration in Argentina and Its Slight, but Yet Strong Differences with Private-Private Arbitration

Diego P. Fernández Arroyo, Francisco A. Amallo, and Ezequiel H. Vetulli

I. Introduction

The present chapter analyses arbitration between private economic actors and public law bodies (private-public arbitration), in line with the overarching perspective of this book, as a mechanism of regulatory governance. Thus, the object of this chapter is to assess private-public arbitration in a more general social dimension, as an institution that structures public-private relations, contributing to social and political order.

Domestic law is the primary source that determines the legitimacy of private-public arbitrations. Therefore, to assess the overall legitimacy of such an arbitral system, it is necessary to extract from domestic law general principles of law relating to private-public arbitration. Against this background, the present chapter analyses the conditions under which the Argentine legal system permits private-public arbitrations and assesses different aspects of that type of arbitration.

This chapter is structured in the following way. Section II explains the general context of private-public arbitration in Argentina as a practical and theoretical discipline, its regulatory framework, the origin of concepts related to this discipline, and the extent to which foreign legal systems, as well as international principles, are used as a source to fill gaps in the regulatory framework. Section III explains the understanding of arbitration as a dispute resolution mechanism, including various aspects, such as the submission of disputes to arbitration, the constitution of the arbitral tribunal, its powers and authority, and the control of state courts, as well as the recognition and enforcement of arbitral decisions. Section IV describes arbitration as a tool of governance, addressing issues like democracy and the rule of law, as well as human and fundamental rights, and the interaction of these with private-public arbitration. Section V concludes that, overall, Argentina's approach towards private-public arbitration is not so different from its approach to arbitration between private economic actors (private-private arbitration), but that the existing differences may trigger relevant practical effects.

Diego P. Fernández Arroyo, Francisco A. Amallo, and Ezequiel H. Vetulli, *The Legitimacy of Private-Public Arbitration in Argentina and Its Slight, but Yet Strong Differences with Private-Private Arbitration* In: *The Comparative Constitutional Foundations of Private-Public Arbitration*. Edited by: Stephan W. Schill, Oxford University Press.
 DOI: 10.1093/9780191987960.003.0012

II. General Context of Private-Public Arbitration

Argentina does not have a specific approach towards private-public arbitration, which is not identified as a specific field. While it is not a part of private law, it is mostly governed by private law, just like private-private arbitration.

A. Private-Public Arbitration as a Practical and Theoretical Discipline

In Argentina, private-public arbitration is very important, both from a practical and a theoretical point of view. From a practical point of view, private actors cooperate with the state to provide public goods or services in areas like infrastructure, energy, health, and education, among others. In this sense, state entities are increasingly dependent on private finance and expertise to achieve their public policy goals. Therefore, many large projects, such as public services (eg electricity or gas distribution), are carried out by private entities along with public entities.

By the same token, counting on increased cooperation with the private sector also requires meeting the expectations and interests of private economic actors. This not only generates challenges for public policies and decision-making through legislation and administration but also impacts the adjudication of disputes. In this connection, the relationships between private and public entities are sometimes governed by contracts that include arbitration clauses. When it comes to foreign investors, such relationships may be covered by bilateral investment treaties, which also establish the basis for private-public arbitration.

Due to the practical relevance of private-public arbitration, from a theoretical point of view there is rather extensive body of academic work related to the topic. Given the conceptual nature of private-public arbitration, its study is covered by both private and administrative law disciplines.

B. The Relevant Regulatory Framework for Private-Public Arbitration

Despite its practical importance, private-public arbitration is not expressly conceptualized (or regulated) in Argentina. It is governed by some of the rules governing private-private arbitration. One obvious exception is the field of investment law, governed by international instruments,[1] which pursuant to Article 75(22) of the Federal Constitution enjoy supremacy vis-à-vis domestic statutes.[2] Therefore, throughout this chapter, all references made to laws, rules, and principles are related to arbitration in general terms (and, in principle, are applicable to private-private as well as private-public arbitration) unless otherwise stated.

[1] This encompasses bilateral investment treaties and the Convention on the Settlement of Investment Disputes between States and Nationals of Other States (signed by Argentina on 21 May 1991, entered into force 18 November 1994) 575 UNTS 159 (ICSID Convention).

[2] The relevant part of Article 75(22) of the Argentine Constitution states: 'The treaties and agreements have hierarchy superior to the statutes' (translation by the authors).

1 Regulation in the Federal Constitution

Unlike the constitutions of other countries,[3] the Argentine Federal Constitution does not contain any express mention of arbitration in general,[4] let alone private-public arbitration in particular. However, private-public arbitration may be directly influenced by some constitutional provisions.

For example, Article 116 of the Federal Constitution sets forth that it is for the Federal Supreme Court and the lower national courts to entertain and decide 'matters in which the Nation is a party'. As explained below when dealing with subjective arbitrability,[5] the Federal Supreme Court has considered that the state can submit a dispute to arbitration provided that (i) it does not act exclusively as a person of public law (ie as a sovereign political entity) and (ii) is authorized by law to do so, because any exception to the general rule established in Article 116 of the Federal Constitution should be clearly established.

It could also be argued, though without much success, that arbitration, including private-public arbitration, collides with Article 18 of the Federal Constitution, which provides that nobody can be taken away from the judges designated by law.[6] It is sometimes considered that arbitration constitutes an exception to the judicial jurisdiction (which is considered as 'natural'), alleging some sort of fundamental right to the natural judge, who is identified with the 'state judge'.[7] Although the legal justification for this idea remains a mystery,[8] it still generates concerns in the Argentine arbitration community. In the authors' opinion, the true fundamental right at stake (except in criminal cases, where the notion refers to the pre-established authority of state courts) is not to have a natural judge, but the right to access justice, which can be equally provided by a 'state judge' or an 'arbitral judge'.[9] It is noteworthy that Article 736 of the Federal Code of Civil and Commercial Procedure (Federal Procedural Code) expressly refers to arbitrators as 'arbitral judges'.[10]

2 Regulation in Domestic Laws

In the Federal Constitution, the Argentine provinces delegated to the Federal Congress some prerogatives (eg enacting the substantive codes, regulating commerce

[3] See eg the Constitution of Panama, art 202; the Constitution of Peru, art 139; the Constitution of Venezuela, art 253.

[4] There is a mention in Article 14 *bis* of the Argentine Constitution, however, which grants trade unions access to conciliation and arbitration.

[5] See section III.A.1 below.

[6] The relevant part of Article 18 of the Argentine Constitution states: 'No habitant of the Nation may be . . . judged by special commissions, or taken away from the judges designated by the law prior to the cause' (translation by the authors).

[7] Diego P Fernández Arroyo, 'La evolución del arbitraje en América Latina: de la supuesta hostilidad a la evidente aceptación (una evaluación a mediados de 2014)' in *Arbitraje comercial internacional* (OEA 2015) s I.

[8] ibid.

[9] ibid. In effect, this is acknowledged by several Latin American constitutions, eg the Constitution of Panama, art 202; the Constitution of Peru, art 139; the Constitution of Venezuela, art 253.

[10] The original expression is *'jueces árbitros'*. The provision states: 'Any matter between parties, except those mentioned in Article 737, may be submitted to the decision of arbitral judges' (translation by the authors).

with foreign nations, etc)[11] and reserved all other prerogatives not expressly delegated (eg enacting the procedural codes).[12]

Given that arbitration was originally considered a 'procedural' matter, each province has regulated it in its procedural code, and the Federal Congress has regulated it in the Federal Procedural Code, which is applicable in the Federal Capital (the Autonomous City of Buenos Aires) and is applied by federal courts throughout the country.[13]

However, this situation suffered modifications with the enactment by Federal Congress of the Federal Civil and Commercial Code (CCC), which entered into force in August 2015,[14] and the new International Commercial Arbitration Law (ICA Law), which entered into force in August 2018.[15]

The CCC is a substantive law, where the legislator included a whole chapter on the 'arbitration contract' which regulates the substantive aspects of arbitration (eg the form, validity, and effects of the arbitration contract, its autonomy, etc). The CCC regulates arbitration agreements related to disputes that have arisen, or may arise, in respect of a defined legal relationship of private law and does not apply to disputes with the federal or provincial states.[16]

Although the procedural aspects of domestic arbitration continue to be governed by the procedural codes (at federal and provincial levels), the CCC contains some arbitration procedural rules (eg interim measures, challenges to the award, etc) related, or allegedly related, to the arbitration agreement, which could be considered unconstitutional because, as explained before, Federal Congress is not empowered, as a general rule, to regulate procedural matters.

In turn, Federal Congress enacted the ICA Law based on its prerogative to regulate commerce with foreign nations. Thus, this federal law governs international commercial arbitration throughout the entire country, including both its substantive and procedural aspects. The term 'commercial' is defined widely, as any legal relationship, contractual or non-contractual, of private law or governed predominantly by it under Argentine law.[17]

The ICA Law expressly confines its scope of application to 'international' arbitrations. Conversely, neither the CCC nor the Federal Procedural Code specify whether they apply to international or domestic arbitrations. They only recognize that, in monetary and international cases, the parties can submit their disputes to arbitrations seated abroad.[18] In the absence of a specific regulation distinguishing international and domestic arbitrations, said codes applied to both international and domestic arbitrations before the enactment of the ICA Law.[19]

[11] Federal Constitution, arts 75(12), 75(13), and 126.
[12] ibid, art 121.
[13] An analysis of each procedural code would exceed the scope of this work. Therefore, this chapter focuses only on the Federal Procedural Code.
[14] Approved by Law 26,994.
[15] Approved by Law 27,449.
[16] Federal Civil and Commercial Code (Law 26994), arts 1649 and 1651 *in fine*.
[17] Law 27,449, art 6.
[18] Federal Civil and Commercial Code, art 2605; Federal Procedural Code, art 1.
[19] There is a case, however, in which a court of appeals stated that the Federal Civil and Commercial Code does not apply to international arbitration, but only to domestic arbitration. See *Pan American*

As a result of the enactment of the ICA Law, Argentina now has a legal system in place in which: (1) international 'commercial' arbitration is governed by the ICA Law; (2) domestic 'commercial' arbitration is governed by both the CCC and the applicable procedural code (provincial or federal); and (3) domestic 'commercial' arbitrations in which one of the parties is the federal or a provincial state are governed by the applicable procedural code.

Argentine law does not indicate which set of rules governs international and domestic arbitrations that do not qualify as 'commercial' (ie arbitrations on legal relationships of public law or governed predominantly by it under Argentine law). An Argentine court would likely conclude that these arbitrations are governed by the applicable procedural code, provided the dispute is arbitrable.

Private-public arbitrations are not regulated in said law or codes, and the law applicable to such specific type of arbitration will depend on whether the arbitration qualifies as 'commercial' or not, and as international or domestic, but in any case, it will be a law originally designed to regulate private-private arbitration. Yet, the application of one law or the other can have important consequences because, as explained below, they regulate arbitration differently.

C. Origin of Ideas, Concepts, and Principles Related to Private-Public Arbitration

Private-public arbitration involves the application of ideas, concepts, and principles arising, not only from arbitration law, but also from constitutional and administrative law. Many of these have not been developed autonomously, but with the influence of foreign sources.

1 Arbitration Law

In the case of arbitration law, like many other Latin American countries, part of the inspiration was originally received from Iberian countries, and later from Italy.[20] This is the reason, for instance, why the regulation of arbitration was embodied in the procedural codes.[21] This influence still generates some practical difficulties in the implementation of the *Kompetenz-Kompetenz* principle, as many state courts interpret arbitration agreements restrictively rather than broadly.[22] Another consequence of this influence is the conception of the arbitrator as a member of the domestic jurisdictional organization, which in theory may have the effect that positive conflicts of jurisdiction between a judicial and an arbitral tribunal end up being resolved by a

Energy LLC (Sucursal Argentina) c Metrogas SA (Chile) s/organismos externos [2017] CNCom-D [2018] LL A-494.

[20] Diego P Fernández Arroyo, 'La perspectiva argentina y sudamericana' in Julio César Rivera and Diego P Fernández Arroyo (eds), *Contratos y arbitraje en la era global* (CEDEP 2012) 188.

[21] Fernández Arroyo (n 7).

[22] Diego P Fernández Arroyo and Ezequiel H Vetulli, 'Dogmas frente a sentido común e interpretación correcta de las normas en vigor: una oposición decisiva para la evolución deseable del arbitraje internacional' [2015] Revista de derecho comercial y de las obligaciones 1516.

higher judicial body. This theory became a reality in a famous case in which an arbitral tribunal declared its jurisdiction to entertain a claim and, upon the respondent's request, a state court also declared its competence (based on its competence over the respondent's bankruptcy proceedings).[23] The jurisdictional conflict was submitted to the Federal Supreme Court, which accepted its jurisdiction to resolve it, although it finally upheld the arbitral tribunal's competence.[24]

Fortunately, the Iberian and Italian influence has been left aside in the ICA Law, which is based on the United Nations Commission for International Trade Law (UNCITRAL) Model Law on International Commercial Arbitration (Model Law), and the CCC, which is based on French Law,[25] the Model Law, and the 1994 Quebec Civil Code.[26]

Although not expressly stated by the lawmakers, the reasons for relying on those sources may have been that they embody the most globally accepted principles of the theory and practice of arbitration,[27] such as the doctrines of separability and *Kompetenz-Kompetenz*, which despite being previously recognized by case law, were not expressly codified.

2 Constitutional and Administrative Law

To a great extent, Argentine constitutional law has been inspired by the Constitution of the United States. This is because the text of the Federal Constitution is mainly based on the work of Juan B Alberdi,[28] a renowned jurist of the time, whose work had the US Constitution as one of the primary sources. Argentine administrative law is based on European law, mainly French law.[29]

Although they set some relevant principles that have an impact on arbitration, neither constitutional nor administrative law in Argentina provide specific rules on arbitration, let alone on private-public arbitration.

3 Interpretation and Filling of Gaps

The influence of foreign sources is, however, not limited to the origins of ideas, concepts, and principles relevant to private-public arbitration. When developing new laws, interpreting existing laws, or filling lacunae, it is common practice in Argentina to look for solutions in foreign legal systems as well as international principles.

In the field of arbitration law, this can be seen in cases where international principles (eg the doctrines of separability[30] and *Kompetenz-Kompetenz*)[31] have been

[23] See *La Nación SA v La Razón SA* [1988] CSJN, [1989] LL B-476; *Nidera SA v Rodríguez Alvarez de Canale, Elena* [1988] CSJN, [1990] LL A-419.

[24] *La Nación SA* (n 23); *Nidera SA* (n 23).

[25] Civil Procedural Code in accordance with Decree 2011-48.

[26] The Quebec Civil Code became relevant since it was also influenced by the French legal culture.

[27] See the official text of the basis of the draft of the Federal Civil and Commercial Code, para VI (Third Book, Title IV).

[28] Juan B Alberdi, *Bases y puntos de partida para la organización política de la República Argentina* (1852).

[29] Héctor Mairal, 'El Derecho Administrativo y la Decadencia Argentina' (Conference, Buenos Aires, 22 August 2012) 13, 19–20 <www.ancmyp.org.ar/user/files/15Mairal12.pdf> accessed 8 January 2025.

[30] *Wilbers SS, Enrique C v Extraktionstechnik Gesellschaft Fur Anlagenbau MBM* [1988] CNCom-E, [1989] LL E-302; *Smit International Argentina SA v Puerto Mariel SA*, [2011] CNACCF-I, [2011] LL D-645.

[31] *Bear Service SA v Cervecería Modelo SA* [2005] CSJN, LL Online 35001744.

applied by state courts, despite the absence of express provisions in hard law, recognizing that they constitute principles that are internationally accepted. Those principles, however, relate to arbitration in general. Argentine courts have not relied on external sources to import specific principles or fill specific gaps of private-public arbitration.

In the field of constitutional and administrative law, the Supreme Court has many times relied on the US Constitution and US case law to support its decisions. For example, it relied on the famous case *New York Times Co. v Sullivan*,[32] which established the 'actual malice' doctrine, regarding the freedom of speech.[33]

In general terms, the rationale behind seeking inspiration from foreign legal systems and relevant rules of international law can be found in the duty of state courts to decide every case, which is imposed by Article 3 of the CCC.[34] Thus, even where a court does not count on an express rule providing the solution to a case, it shall manage to find the appropriate answer.

III. Arbitration as a Dispute Resolution Mechanism for Private-Public Disputes

As explained in section II above, there is no specific regulation on private-public arbitration in Argentina. Instead, the same statutes govern both private-private and private-public arbitration. Therefore, it becomes necessary to analyse the different aspects of arbitration in order to identify whether they are different regarding private-public arbitration.

A. Submission to Arbitration

1 Subjective Arbitrability

Article 116 of the Federal Constitution sets forth that it is for the Federal Supreme Court and the lower national tribunals to entertain and decide 'matters in which the Nation is a party'. It has been debated whether this provision establishes an exclusive jurisdiction or not. The Federal Supreme Court has in general recognized the ability of the state to bind itself and, therefore, voluntarily submit its disputes to a different jurisdiction.

Regarding the submission to arbitration, the Federal Supreme Court has historically distinguished between the state acting as a person of private law (ie as a private entity) and as a person of public law (ie as a sovereign political entity): the state can submit a dispute to arbitration provided that (i) it does not act exclusively as a person

[32] *New York Times Co v Sullivan* (No 39) [1964] 376 US 254.
[33] *Vago, Jorge A v Ediciones La Urraca SA* [1991] CSJN, [1992] LL B-367.
[34] Article 3 states: 'The judge must resolve the matters submitted to his jurisdiction through reasonably founded decision.' This obligation was previously enshrined in Article 15 of the Federal Civil Code, in the following terms: 'The judges cannot fail to judge under the pretext of silence, obscurity or insufficiency of the laws' (all translations by the authors).

of public law and (ii) is authorized by law to do so because any exception to the general rule in Article 116 of the Federal Constitution should be clearly established.[35]

Under this approach, it would appear that the state can only submit to arbitration when it enters into private law contracts but not when it enters into administrative law or state contracts. However, it has been noted that, in practice, state contracts have not been clearly distinguished from private law contracts, and that the state, without the need of a legislative authorization, can resort to arbitration to settle disputes that do not affect public policy, the constitutional system, or the sovereignty or authority of the state. Thus, even in the case of a state contract, the state could resort to arbitration to settle technical or monetary disputes.[36]

These two issues are somewhat reflected in the case law of the Federal Supreme Court because several of its judgments deal with contracts that would qualify as administrative law or state contracts (eg public works and concessions), and seem to indicate that, when the state is required to act as a person of private law, what is actually required is that the dispute relates to technical or monetary matters.[37]

The need for legislative authorization is debated and the Federal Supreme Court's case law has not always been consistent in the matter. However, there are several precedents, some of them recent, in which the Federal Supreme Court has recognized the need for legislative authorization.[38]

The Federal Supreme Court's case law is also not clear as to whether the authorization to submit a dispute to arbitration must be contained in a specific law for each transaction or can also be a general legislative authorization. However, it is generally understood that a general legislative authorization is sufficient.

The legislation has changed over time, and the state was not always authorized to submit its disputes to arbitration. For example, on 15 December 1933, the Executive Branch issued a decree with the sole purpose of establishing that national agencies could not enter into contracts with private actors in which arbitration was established as a dispute settlement mechanism.[39] In 1967, the Federal Procedural Code regulated arbitration as a dispute settlement mechanism, but expressly prohibited, in Article 1, choice-of-forum agreements in favour of foreign judges or arbitrators acting outside the country.[40] In 1972, Decree 5720, which regulated the contracting regime of the state, prohibited the inclusion of arbitration clauses in contracts.[41]

[35] *Don Gerardo Pagano* [1920] CSJN *Fallos* 133:61; *Sociedad Anónima Puerto del Rosario* [1926] CSJN *Fallos* 146:373; *Sociedad Anónima Puerto del Rosario* [1928] CSJN *Fallos* 152:347; *Cía Ítalo Argentina de Electricidad* [1937] CSJN *Fallos* 178:293; *Guido Simonini* [1942] CSJN *Fallos* 194:155; *Cayetano Paino* [1956] CSJN *Fallos* 235:940; *Techint Compañía Técnica Internacional* [2007] CSJN *Fallos* 330:2215; *Estado Nacional – Procuración del Tesoro Nacional c (nulidad del laudo del 20-III-2009)* [2018] CSJN *Fallos* 341:1485.

[36] Miguel S Marienhoff, *Tratado de Derecho Administrativo* (4th edn, Abeledo-Perrot 1994) vol III-A, 595–97, 602–04.

[37] *Cía Ítalo Argentina de Electricidad* [1937] CSJN *Fallos* 178:293; *Yacimientos Petrolíferos Fiscales* [1974] CSJN *Fallos* 290:458.

[38] *Compañía Argentina de Navegación 'Nicolás Mihanovich Ltda'* [1931] CSJN *Fallos* 160:133; *Cayetano Paino* [1956] CSJN *Fallos* 235:940; *Yacimientos Petrolíferos Fiscales* [1974] CSJN *Fallos* 290:458; *Techint Compañía Técnica Internacional SACE e I* [2007] CSJN *Fallos* 330:2215; *Estado Nacional – Procuración del Tesoro Nacional c/ (nulidad del laudo del 20-III-2009)* [2018] CSJN *Fallos* 341:1485.

[39] Decree dated 15 December 1993 (44 Jurisprudencia Argentina 56).

[40] Law 17,454, art 1.

[41] Decree 5720/1972, art 61(85).

This hectic approach seems to have ended in 1973. From then on, various laws have authorized the state to submit its disputes to arbitration. For example, Law 20,548 introduced an amendment to Law 11,672, pursuant to which the Executive Branch is authorized to submit disputes with foreigners to arbitral tribunals.[42] In 1976, through Law 21,305, and in 1981, through Law 22,434, Article 1 of the Federal Procedural Code was amended to authorize parties (without making any exception in relation to the state) to submit monetary and international disputes to arbitrators acting outside the country, except in those cases in which the Argentine courts have exclusive jurisdiction or when choice-of-forum agreements are prohibited by law.[43]

Similar authorizations can be found in Article 18 of Law 23,982 on debt consolidation,[44] Article 9 of Law 27,249 on public debt,[45] Article 25 of Law 27,328 on public-private participation contracts,[46] and Article 12 of Law 17,520 on public concessions,[47] among others.

Article 2605 of the CCC also contains a general authorization to arbitrate monetary and international disputes, comparable to the one contained in Article 1 of the Federal Procedural Code. The ICA Law does not expressly mention or exclude arbitration with the state.

The fact that Article 1651 *in fine* of the CCC states that its chapter on arbitration agreements 'is not applicable to controversies in which the National or local State is a party' does not constitute a restriction on arbitrability of such disputes. The provision does not say that the state cannot arbitrate its disputes, but only that the CCC regulation does not apply to such disputes. Therefore, the state may submit disputes to arbitration, but under different rules from those in the CCC.

Until the legislator creates a specific legal framework applicable to arbitrations involving the state, it should be interpreted that domestic 'commercial' arbitrations are governed by the applicable procedural code, and international 'commercial' arbitrations with the state by the ICA Law. International and domestic arbitrations that do not qualify as 'commercial' (ie arbitrations on legal relationships of public law or governed predominantly by it under Argentine law) would also likely be governed by the applicable procedural code, provided the dispute is arbitrable, although there is no statute expressly stating so.

Article 1651 *in fine* of the CCC also does not address the situation of state-owned enterprises and its wording suggests that it should not extend to them, as it refers to the 'State' as a party. However, state-owned companies might invoke this provision and try to avoid the application of the CCC. A similar situation occurs regarding the proper judicial forum to which state-owned enterprises are subjected, as they sometimes invoke their state control to avoid the jurisdiction of civil or commercial courts, in order to be subjected to administrative courts instead.[48]

[42] Law 20,548, art 7.

[43] Law 22,434, art 1. For instance, Article 2609(a) of the CCC states that the Argentine courts have exclusive jurisdiction over in rem rights concerning property located in Argentina.

[44] Law 23,982, art 18.

[45] Law 27,249, art 9.

[46] Law 27,328, art 25.

[47] Law 17,520, art 12, as amended by Law 27,742.

[48] For example, in 2012 the National Government expropriated 51% of the shares of YPF (acronym of Yacimientos Petrolíferos Fiscales), the main Argentinian hydrocarbon company (Law 26,741) and,

2 Objective Arbitrability

In addition to the limitations on arbitrations involving the state as a party (subjective arbitrability), there are also some limitations on objective arbitrability. Although objective arbitrability depends on the applicable law, all paths seem to lead to the same result, because neither the ICA Law, the CCC, nor the Federal Procedural Code contain specific provisions regarding objective arbitrability for private-public arbitration.

The ICA Law does not regulate arbitrability. It only states, in Article 5, that the law does not affect any other law by virtue of which certain disputes may not be arbitrable or may be arbitrable only under certain conditions. Therefore, in this regard, there is a renvoi to other laws.

The Federal Procedural Code contains, in Articles 736 and 737, a general rule that states that any matter, except for those that cannot be the subject of a settlement agreement, can be submitted to arbitration. In turn, Article 1644 of the CCC states that rights in which public policy is at stake, among other matters, cannot be the subject of a settlement agreement.

Article 1649 of the CCC excludes the arbitrability of disputes where public policy is at stake. This article, however, should have no impact on private-public arbitration because, as explained above, Article 1651 *in fine* of the CCC sets forth that the chapter on arbitration agreements does not apply to controversies in which a state is a party. This is relevant because, if that chapter were applicable to private-public arbitration, there would also be other limitations that could have an impact on private-public arbitration (eg Article 1651 excludes the arbitrability of disputes related to adhesion contracts, and it could be reasonably argued that some, if not most, state contracts are adhesion contracts because they are unilaterally drafted by the state and the private party simply accepts their terms without intervening in their drafting).

Despite the non-application of Article 1649 of the CCC, public policy is still a limitation for private-public arbitration under the ICA Law because such a limitation is contained in the Federal Procedural Code, which remains applicable.[49] While the public policy limitation is equally applicable to private-public and private-private arbitrations, it is more likely to affect private-public arbitrations, since these would typically involve issues related to public policy.

However, the meaning of 'public policy', and hence the scope of any exceptions to objective arbitrability, is not clear. Public policy is a concept difficult to define and the existing definitions tend to be vague,[50] so there will always be room for debating its exact scope. Argentine scholars have defined it as the group of fundamental principles upon which the social organization is built.[51] Some legal provisions contain a similar

although it remains a private company, the courts have held that, due to the state's control, it should be subject to administrative and not commercial courts. See the Decision of the Federal Court of Appeals on Administrative Matters, Chamber No IV (7 October 2014) recital no 8 (referring to the decision of the National Court of Appeals on Commercial Matters, Chamber D, dated 23 October 2013, available at <http://fallos.diprargentina.com/2014/10/ypf-c-aes-uruguaiana-emprendimientos-s.html> accessed 8 January 2025).

[49] The limitation in the Federal Procedural Code is due to a renvoi from its Articles 736 and 737 to the settlement agreement provisions of the CCC, which include limitations on public policy grounds.

[50] Horacio H De la Fuente, *Orden público* (Astrea 2003) 1–2.

[51] Jorge J Llambías, *Tratado de Derecho Civil – Parte General* (Abeledo Perrot 2007) vol 1, 149.

definition. For example, Article 2600 of the CCC states that provisions of foreign law shall not apply to an international case when they lead to solutions that are incompatible with the fundamental principles of public policy that inspire the Argentine legal system.

It is known that the concept of public policy cannot be determined like any other strict rule, because it is dynamic and constantly evolving. Instead, it is more appropriate to assess it on a case-by-case basis. An example of how Argentine courts have understood the concept of public policy is one in which the Commercial Court of Appeals annulled an arbitral award that resolved a dispute related to the sanitation of soil contamination because it considered that environmental matters could not be the subject of a settlement agreement and, therefore, could not be submitted to arbitration pursuant to the Federal Procedural Code.[52]

It is noteworthy that Argentine courts have recognized that the fact that the merits of a dispute are governed by public policy rules does not mean that the subject matter is not arbitrable to the extent that the parties can dispose of the rights involved in the case (eg monetary rights). In other words, there may be disputes the resolution of which requires the application of a public policy rule, but which involve mere patrimonial rights which can be waived by the parties and are, consequently, objectively arbitrable.[53]

3 Concrete Examples of Private-Public Arbitration

Arbitration in Argentina is widely used in certain specific areas (eg energy). This may trigger both private-private and private-public arbitrations. It is hard to find a specific area within the Argentine system in which arbitration is the primary means for resolving private-public disputes. This may be the reason for the lack of specific regulation for that type of arbitration.

With regard to public works, in 1947 the Argentine government created the 'Public Works Arbitral Tribunal', which in its beginning had competence to resolve disputes regarding variations of costs.[54] Then, Article 55 of Law 13,064 established that all disputes related to the application and interpretation of public works contracts had to be resolved by the administrative courts, waiving the contractors any right to other jurisdiction. However, said article authorized the parties to submit their disputes to arbitration until the administrative procedure was regulated by the legislator. The Public Works Arbitral Tribunal should have been dissolved once the administrative courts were created and the administrative procedure was regulated. However, it remained in effect through the issuance of successive decrees that expanded its competence

[52] *Algavi SA v Esso SRL* [2013] CNCom-C, LL AR/JUR/49967/2013.

[53] See De la Fuente (n 49) 27–28; *CRI Holding Inc Sucursal Argentina v Compañía Argentina de Comodoro Rivadavia Explotación de Petróleo SA* [2010] CNCom-C, [2011] LL A-555, commented in Julio César Rivera, 'Arbitrabilidad: cuestiones regidas por leyes de orden público' [2011] LL A-555; *Otondo, César A v Cortina Beruatto SA* [2003] CNCom-E, LL F-744; *Mobil Argentina SA v Gasnor SA* [2007] CNCom-D; *Francisco Ctibor SACI Y F V Wall-Mart Argentina SRL* [2016] CNCom-D.

[54] Its name was 'Tribunal Arbitral de Obras Públicas'. See Decrees 11511/47, 1978/64, and 1496/91. For further details on the history and functioning of this arbitral tribunal, see *Gardebled Hermanos SA* [2007] CSJN *Fallos* 330:3565; Susana Vega, 'El tribunal arbitral de obras públicas y la irrevisibilidad judicial de sus laudos. El paso del tiempo y la permanencia del criterio' [2000] LL C-119; Eduardo Mertehikian, 'El Tribunal Arbitral de Obras Públicas y la naturaleza de sus decisions' [1994] LL D-786.

and restricted the judicial review of its awards. Thus, in 1991 the Argentine government extended the competence of said tribunal to entertain matters regulated by Law 13,064 on public works, Law 17,520 on public works concessions, and Law 22,460 on consultancy contracts.[55]

The nature of this 'Public Works Arbitral Tribunal' as a true arbitral jurisdiction had been contested and there are conflicting opinions as to whether it constituted a real arbitral tribunal or, rather, an administrative body. This tribunal was finally dissolved in 2001 by Decree 1349.[56] Therefore, it is now sometimes alleged that, by virtue of the provisions contained in Article 55 of Law 13,064, all disputes related to the application and interpretation of public works contracts can only be settled before the administrative courts, and not through arbitration. It is inconsistent to find this restriction in domestic laws when related disputes could be submitted to investment arbitration under an international investment agreement.

With regard to public-private participation projects, in 2016 the Federal Congress passed Law 27,328, which regulates contracts between the organs and entities of the public sector and private entities related to projects on infrastructure, housing, services, productive investment, and technology research and innovation, among other fields. This legislation provides that disputes arising out of said contracts may be resolved through arbitration.[57] However, it states that if the seat of arbitration is abroad, the arbitration agreement must be approved by the Executive Branch and notified to the Congress.[58]

Another example of private-public arbitration can be found in Article 86 of Law 17,319 on hydrocarbons. Said article states that the Executive Branch can include arbitration clauses in permits and concessions with the purpose of settling disputes related to: (i) the monetary consequences of an administrative declaration of revocation or nullity made by the Executive Branch; and (ii) technical issues. In these cases, the number of arbitrators shall be three. Each party will appoint one arbitrator, and the third arbitrator will be appointed by the parties or, otherwise, by the president of the Federal Supreme Court.

Article 86 of Law 17,319 can be interpreted in two ways. On the one hand, it could be interpreted that the article prohibits submitting to arbitration any matter different from those mentioned therein. On the other hand, it could be interpreted that the article does not limit arbitrability, and that it only contains an authorization in favor of the Executive Branch to submit those matters to arbitration and establishes that, in the cases contemplated therein, the arbitral tribunal shall be constituted in the manner described. The fact that the Argentine government has recently included an arbitration clause in the terms of reference that govern an international public tender for the award of offshore permits and concessions, without limiting the scope of the arbitration clause to the two subject matters mentioned in Article 86,[59] may suggest that it is interpreting the article in the second way. This is reasonable because it is

[55] See Decree 1496/1991.
[56] Decree 1349/2001, art 4.
[57] Law 27,328, art 25.
[58] To be clear, Law 27,328 only gives the legislative authorization required by the Supreme Court on the basis of Article 116 of the Constitution. Therefore, it could not be considered as an independent system.
[59] Resolution SE 65/18.

not clear why a monetary dispute arising from, or related to, a permit or a concession could not be submitted to arbitration.

Article 221 of Law 27,742 also contains an example of private-public arbitration. This article states that any dispute between the state and a private company adhering to the incentive regime for large projects (created by said law) may be submitted to arbitration.

B. Powers, Duties, and Jurisdiction of the Arbitral Tribunal

1 The Conduct of the Arbitral Proceedings

There are no specific requirements for the conduct of private-public arbitrations. Arbitrators in private-public arbitrations do not have any additional or special procedural abilities to steer the proceedings or secure that decisions are made on a sufficiently informed basis. For instance, regarding the taking of evidence, there are no provisions establishing whether arbitrators have *suo motu* powers in requesting evidence or are entirely dependent on the parties' submissions without the power to assume a more active role.[60] Instead, the parties retain the same prerogatives to tailor the procedure as in any other arbitration. The situation is not so different from private-private litigation, where the Argentine courts do not have substantial additional or special procedural abilities to steer the proceedings or secure that decisions are made on a sufficiently informed basis either.

A possible difference between private-private arbitration and private-public arbitration could be the request for precautionary measures against the state. If that request is made before an Argentine court, the judge could apply Law 26,854 on precautionary measures against the state.[61] This law differs in several aspects from the regulation of the precautionary measures contained in the Federal Procedural Code. For example, while Article 198 of the Federal Procedural Code establishes that precautionary measures will be issued *inaudita parte*, Article 4 of the law requires prior notification of the state. Also, while Article 202 of the Federal Procedural Code sets forth that precautionary measures will be in force as long as the circumstances on which they are based continue to exist, Article 5 of the law establishes that the judge must establish a reasonable limit, which may not be greater than six months. However, some courts have considered that Law 26,854 is unconstitutional because it unreasonably limits the power of judges, violates the right to effective judicial protection, the division of powers, and the right to due process.[62]

[60] In relation to this aspect, it is worth mentioning the decision of the *Estado Nacional –Procuración del Tesoro v Tribunal Arbitral* [2006] CNCAF-II, [2012] LL C-35. Basically, in the terms of reference the parties had impliedly agreed on conducting a preliminary hearing to deal with issues related to the taking of evidence. However, the arbitral tribunal decided that there were no contested facts and, therefore, directly rendered its award. The Court considered that this constituted an essential procedural irregularity and set aside the award.

[61] Law 26,854.

[62] *Szwarc, Rubén Mario and others v Estado Nacional* [2013] CNCom-A, LL E-522.

2 Appointing Counsel by the State

The procedure for the appointment of external counsel to represent public entities shall be made through a public tender.[63] Only in exceptional circumstances (eg urgency) may counsel be selected directly without a public tender.[64] These rules are those that apply to the procurement process for any goods or service. In the field of legal services, they are applicable to counsel representing the state in both litigation and arbitration proceedings. The Office of the Attorney General has recently issued some resolutions with the purpose of regulating the procedure for the appointment of external counsel,[65] although it is unusual for the state to appoint external counsel for private-private and private-public arbitrations because it normally represents itself through the Office of the Attorney General.

Regarding the communication between counsel and arbitrators, there are no specific rules, for example rules prohibiting *ex parte* communications.

3 Protection of Public Interests

(a) Transparency and Confidentiality

There are no provisions or principles of domestic law providing for a confidentiality obligation in private-public arbitrations. For instance, there are no provisions or principles of domestic law requiring public hearings or other participatory mechanisms before a public actor can submit a dispute to arbitration.

By the same token, there are no provisions or principles of domestic law regulating transparency in private-public arbitrations, including, for example, as to whether the existence, content, or result of private-public arbitrations must be made accessible to the public. However, the general rules on public information may call for some disclosure.

According to the principle of publicity of information, the acts of government, as well as the information related to its functions, should be public to civil society, so that the society is able to exercise surveillance. That principle is contained in Law 27,275 and Decree 1172/03 on the access to public information, as well as in several international treaties, namely the 1948 American Declaration of the Rights and Duties of Man (Article IV), the International Covenant on Civil and Political Rights (Article 19),[66] and the American Convention on Human Rights (Article 13.1). Regarding Article 13 of the latter, the Inter-American Court of Human Rights held:

> [I]t protects the right of all individuals to request access to State-held information, with the exceptions permitted by the restrictions established in the Convention … The information should be provided without the need to prove direct interest or personal involvement in order to obtain it, except in cases in which a legitimate restriction is applied.
>
> … the State's actions should be governed by the principles of disclosure and transparency in public administration that enable all persons subject to its jurisdiction

[63] Decrees 1023/01 and 893/12.
[64] Decree 1023/01, art 25(d)(5).
[65] Resolutions 106/2017, 34/2018, 51/2018, and 112/2018.
[66] UNGA Res 2200A (XXI) (16 December 1966).

> to exercise the democratic control of those actions, and so that they can question, investigate and consider whether public functions are being performed adequately.[67]

The Federal Supreme Court has endorsed these ideas in a recent ruling, in which it decided that said regulation extends to YPF SA, the main Argentinian hydrocarbon company.[68] Although YPF remains a private company, in 2012 the Argentine government expropriated 51 per cent of its shares.[69] In this context, taking into account that the government exercises substantial control over the company, the Supreme Court held that it is a company under the jurisdiction of the state. It also held that YPF develops an activity of public interest (ie the exploitation of hydrocarbons to achieve energy self-sufficiency). Consequently, it requested YPF to disclose its agreement with a foreign company (Chevron Corporation) regarding an investment project for the joint exploitation of hydrocarbons in the Vaca Muerta basin in the Province of Neuquén.[70]

There is also a recent ruling in which a court of appeals, based on Law 27,275 and international treaties, ordered the Office of the Attorney General to disclose five ICSID arbitral awards as requested by a natural person.[71]

(b) Specific Safeguards

There are no special procedural safeguards securing that the public interest is properly and sufficiently represented during a private-public arbitration. For instance, there are no provisions dealing with the intervention of third parties in private-public arbitrations, so in principle there would be no legal basis to allow such an intervention.

In litigation before domestic courts, by contrast, there are certain procedural safeguards securing that the public interest is properly and sufficiently represented, for example through the intervention of the Public Ministry (Ministerio Público), which can intervene not only in private-public litigation but in any litigation where the public interest is at stake. The Public Ministry is an independent organ created by the Federal Constitution to defend the general interest of the society.[72] Among its duties, the Public Ministry must represent and defend the public interest as well as supervise compliance with the Federal Constitution and statutory laws.[73] Thus, whenever there is an issue that could potentially affect the public interest, state courts must allow an intervention of the Public Ministry. The courts have discretion to determine whether there is such risk.

[67] *Claude-Reyes et al v Chile* IACtHR Series C No 151 (19 September 2006) paras 77 and 86.

[68] *Giustiniani, Rubén Héctor v YPF SA* [2015] CSJN, [2015] ED 25/11/15-12.

[69] Law 26,741.

[70] *Giustiniani v YPF* (n 67).

[71] *Pérez Aznar, Facundo Pablo v Procuración del Tesoro de La Nación* [2018] Federal Court of Appeals of La Plata, Sala II, 27 December 2019.

[72] Federal Constitution, art 120 and Law 24946. Article 120(1) states: 'The Public Ministry is an independent organ with functional autonomy and financial autarchy that has the function of promoting justice in defence of the legality of the general interests of society in coordination with the other authorities of the Republic' (translation by the authors).

[73] Law 24,946, art 25.

In addition, in judicial proceedings there are mechanisms for third-party intervention.[74] The fact that these mechanisms do not apply in arbitration is a departure from the standard safeguard used in litigation, but this does not affect the legitimacy of arbitration under democratic principles. Actually, this has not been an issue of debate in Argentina.

C. Control by Domestic Courts

As in many other aspects, there are no specific rules differentiating the recourse against an arbitral award in private-public and private-private arbitrations. Therefore, the legal framework governing both is the same, namely the applicable procedural code or the ICA Law. However, there are differences between one and the other.

1 The System in the Federal Procedural Code

Under the system of the Federal Procedural Code (which, as already explained, would apply to domestic 'commercial' arbitration in which one of the parties is a state), Article 758 of the Federal Procedural Code states that once the arbitral award has been rendered, the parties may challenge it before state courts, under the same recourses that are available against court judgments.[75] This includes the recourses of appeal, annulment, and clarification. The recourse of appeal entails a full revision of the merits.

According to Articles 760 and 761 of the Federal Procedural Code, the annulment recourse may be based on the following grounds: (i) an essential procedural violation; (ii) issuance of the arbitral award after the deadline; (iii) a decision on matters not submitted to the arbitration (ie matters outside of the scope of the arbitration agreement); or (iv) inconsistent decisions in the dispositive part of the award.

The clarification recourse aims at: (i) correcting material errors; (ii) clarifying obscure concepts; or (iii) completing any omissions regarding any request for relief discussed throughout the proceedings, provided that the modification does not substantially alter the decision.[76]

Article 759 of the Federal Procedural Code states that the recourses must be filed with the arbitral tribunal within five days of the date on which the award was notified to the parties. Unlike the clarification recourse, which is resolved by the arbitral tribunal, the recourses of appeal and annulment are ultimately resolved by judicial courts.

Once the recourses of appeal or annulment have been filed with the arbitral tribunal, the latter must grant or refuse to grant leave. If it grants leave, the recourse must be transferred to the competent court (ie the Court of Appeals). If the arbitral

[74] Regulation 7/13 of the Supreme Court.

[75] Article 758 states: 'The recourses admissible with respect to the decisions of judges will be available against the arbitral decision, to the extent that they were not waived in the arbitration agreement' (translation by the authors).

[76] Federal Procedural Code, arts 36(6) and 166(2).

tribunal refuses to grant leave, the moving party can file a complaint against such refusal with the competent court, and the court has discretion to overturn the arbitral tribunals' decision refusing leave. Article 763 of the Federal Procedural Code states that the parties can agree in the *compromis* to submit these remedies to another arbitral tribunal.

Article 760 of the Federal Procedural Code allows waiving the recourses against the arbitral award, except for the clarification and annulment recourses.[77] Therefore, only the recourse of appeal can be waived.

However, in the famous *Cartellone* case,[78] the Federal Supreme Court held that arbitral awards are subject to judicial review, even if the parties have waived their right to appeal the award, whenever they are unconstitutional, illegal, unreasonable, or violate public policy. Based on this doctrine, the Federal Supreme Court reviewed an award on the merits and partially revoked it, notwithstanding that it had to decide on an application for setting aside the award. The Federal Supreme Court considered that the arbitral tribunal had calculated the interest incorrectly because, instead of using the interest rate agreed in the contract, it used an interest rate that was not applicable and that led to a disproportionate and unreasonable result that, in the Court's view, violated public policy, as it was more than triple that what was agreed in the contract.

This decision was strongly criticized by arbitration experts and its scope remains unclear. The fact that the *Cartellone* case was related to public works and involved a state-owned company has led some scholars to conclude that this precedent is limited to decisions issued by the tribunal created by the Public Works Law 13,064 (see above) and does not extend to commercial arbitrations between private parties.[79]

The Federal Supreme Court never explained the scope of its decision. Although it has subsequently analysed the possible application of the *Cartellone* doctrine to other cases, it has not applied it again. In recent cases, the Federal Supreme Court has acknowledged that, if the parties have waived their right to appeal the award, the only possible judicial review would be an application for setting aside the award.[80]

2 The System in the ICA Law

The ICA Law is based on the UNCITRAL Model Law, so there is no recourse of appeal against arbitral awards. Article 98 of the ICA Law states that recourse to a court may be made only by an application for setting aside. The grounds for annulment contained in Article 99 are almost identical to the grounds for refusal contained in

[77] Article 760(2) states: 'The waiver of the recourses will not affect, however, the admissibility of the clarification and set-aside recourse, based on an essential breach of the procedure, on the issuance of the award after the deadline, or related to issues not submitted to arbitration' (translation by the authors).

[78] *José Cartellone Construcciones Civiles SA c/ Hidroeléctrica Norpatagónica SA o Hidronor SA* [2004] CSJN Fallos 327:1881.

[79] Agustín Gordillo, *Tratado de derecho administrativo y obras selectas*, (FDA, Buenos Aires, 2014) vol 2, 656, fn 5.

[80] *Cacchione, Ricardo Constantino c Urbaser Argentina SA* [2006] CSJN *Fallos* 329:3399; *Pestarino de Alfani, Mónica Amalia c Urbaser Argentina SA* [2008] Corte Suprema de Justicia de la Nación; *Ricardo Agustín López c Gemabiotech SA* [2017] CSJN *Fallos* 340:1226; *Estado Nacional – Procuración del Tesoro Nacional c (nulidad del laudo del 20-III-2009)* [2018] CSJN *Fallos* 341:1485.

Article V of the 1958 New York Convention on the Recognition and Enforcement of Foreign Arbitral Awards.[81]

Article 100 of the ICA Law sets forth that an annulment recourse must be filed within thirty days of the date on which the award was notified to the parties. Unlike the Federal Procedural Code, Article 100 does not specify if the recourse must be filed with the arbitral tribunal or the competent court (ie Court of Appeals). However, Articles 98, 99, and 101 expressly refer to judicial courts, which suggests that the legislator has opted for the recourses to be filed directly with the court.

Article 93 of the ICA Law provides for the possibility of requesting the arbitral tribunal to correct and interpret the award within thirty days of notification to the parties, but, unlike the Federal Procedural Code, it does not regulate this as a recourse.

3 The Scope and Standard of Court Review

The aspects of the arbitral award that may be reviewed by state courts in private-public arbitration are not different from those in private-private arbitration. Article 760 of the Federal Procedural Code states that an arbitral award may be set aside if the award deals with a matter not submitted to arbitration, adding that, if the decisions on matters submitted to arbitration can be separated from those not submitted, only that part of the award may be set aside. The same solution is contained in Article 99(A)(III) of the ICA Law.

Regarding the standard of review to be applied by domestic courts when reviewing arbitral awards, there are no specific provisions, either for private-public or private-private arbitration. There is also no indication as to whether their application should be stricter for private-public arbitration, so this would depend on the courts' discretion.

D. Recognition and Enforcement of Awards

As with other aspects, the regime for the enforcement of arbitral awards is not different when it comes to private-private and private-public arbitrations. Argentina is a Contracting State to the 1958 New York Convention.[82] Given the success of this instrument, with more than 160 Contracting States, it is likely to govern most cases on the recognition and enforcement of foreign arbitral awards. In a case where the New York Convention does not apply, the enforcement of an award will depend on the origin of the award, and whether it was issued in an international or domestic arbitration.

Before the entry into force of the ICA Law, the recognition and enforcement of awards was governed exclusively by procedural codes. The Federal Procedural Code used to regulate the recognition and enforcement of awards differently, depending on

[81] Convention on the Recognition and Enforcement of Foreign Arbitral Awards (adopted 10 June 1958, entered into force 7 June 1959) 330 UNTS 3 (New York Convention).

[82] Ratified in 1988 by Law 23,619. Argentina is also a Contracting State of the 1975 Inter-American Convention on international commercial arbitration, regulating the recognition and enforcement of arbitral awards.

whether the award was issued locally or abroad. The enforcement of domestic arbitral awards was governed by Article 499 of the Federal Procedural Code. According to that article, the enforcement of domestic arbitral awards had to be carried out pursuant to the procedure contained in Articles 499 to 516 for the enforcement of domestic judgments.

In turn, the recognition and enforcement of foreign arbitral awards was governed by Article 519 *bis* of the Federal Procedural Code, according to which the recognition and enforcement of foreign arbitral awards had to be carried out pursuant to the procedure contained in Articles 517 to 519 for the recognition and enforcement of foreign judgments. Article 519 *bis* of the Federal Procedural Code was repealed on 3 August 2018, when the ICA Law entered into force to govern international commercial arbitration exclusively. Hence, the provisions on the recognition and enforcement of arbitral awards of the ICA Law apply to arbitral awards issued in international commercial arbitration, regardless of the seat of arbitration.

In sum, under the current regime, the recognition and enforcement of awards issued in international arbitrations is governed by the ICA Law, and the enforcement of awards issued in local arbitrations is governed by the Federal Procedural Code.

1 Arbitral Awards Issued in International Arbitration

The grounds for refusing the recognition and enforcement of foreign awards are listed in Article 104 of the ICA Law and are virtually identical to those set forth in Article V of the New York Convention. There are only two differences. In addition to 'incapacity', the ICA Law includes 'capacity restriction' as a ground for refusal; and instead of referring to 'public policy', the ICA Law refers to the 'Argentine international public policy'.

Of all the grounds for refusal, public policy is the most controversial everywhere. In Argentina, there is no indication that such concept should be interpreted differently in private-public and private-private arbitrations. As examples, there are cases where arbitral awards rendered against the state have been considered by state courts to be against international public policy because they did not respect the specific rules on calculation and means of payment for public debts established by Law 23,982 on consolidation of public debt. This law basically stipulates that public debts, until a specific date, are to be paid in the form of bonds and the interests of those debts are to be calculated in a specific way. Argentine courts have decided that Law 23,982 has a public policy nature, and therefore its provisions shall apply even if Argentine law is not the applicable law to the merits. Nevertheless, instead of refusing the enforcement of those awards, the courts decided to adapt the amount of compensation to be paid by the state in accordance with said law.[83]

Another example is a case in which a court annulled an award related to a vessel construction contract between a state entity and a Panamanian company. The contract established that it had to be approved by a specific law of the Province of Buenos Aires. Based on the arbitration clause contained in the contract, the Panamanian

[83] *Deutsche Ruckversicherung AG v Caja Nacional de Ahorro y Seguro en liquidación* [2014] CNCivComFed-III, and [2019] Corte Suprema de Justicia de la Nación (CCF 6461/2009/CS1; *Oscar A Diez SAI y C v SEGBA* [2000] CACCF-III.

company initiated arbitration in London and obtained two favourable awards. The company requested the recognition and enforcement of the awards in Argentina. The state entity refused the application, arguing that the contract had not been approved by law. The court of first instance ordered the recognition and enforcement of the awards because it considered that the contract had been approved by Provincial Law 11,837. The state entity appealed the first-instance ruling, but only in relation to the costs.

The Court of Appeals and, ultimately, the Supreme Court of Buenos Aires reversed the ruling and refused the enforcement of the awards because the contract had not been approved by law. The Provincial Supreme Court held that the fact that the state entity had appealed only the decision on costs did not prevent the courts from analysing *ex officio* public policy violations under Article V(2)(b) of the New York Convention. The Supreme Court considered that the conclusion of the contract without the necessary legislative approval violated public policy. In its view, the Provincial Law 11,837 was insufficient because it only authorized the financing of the vessel construction but did not specifically approve the construction contract.[84]

The Federal Supreme Court reversed the Supreme Court of Buenos Aires' ruling. It considered that the ruling violated the principles of congruence and res judicata because the appeal filed by the state entity was aimed exclusively at questioning the decision on costs, not the merits of the dispute.[85]

2 Arbitral Awards Issued in Domestic Arbitration

Awards issued in domestic arbitrations (ie arbitrations that do not qualify as 'international' under the ICA Law) are enforced in the same way as domestic judgments. Once the award has the authority of res judicata, a party can request its enforcement if the other party refuses to comply with it voluntarily.

Article 506 of the Federal Procedural Code sets forth that the only possible defences to resist enforcement are: (i) forgery or falsification of the arbitral award; (ii) expiration of the limitation period to request enforcement; (iii) payment of the award; and (iv) extension of the payment period or total or partial waiver of the right to collect the award by the creditor.

3 Arbitral Awards Issued against the Federal State

Arbitral awards against the Argentine state are not enforced automatically. The party seeking the enforcement must have previously complied with a specific procedure to include the payment of the award in the annual budget.

According to Article 22 of Law 23,982 on the consolidation of public debt and Articles 165 to 170 of the Permanent Complementary Budget Law (Law 11,672), any decision against the Federal State must be paid with reserves included in the relevant budget. If the budget corresponding to the fiscal year in which the decision is to be paid has no reserves, the Executive Branch shall adopt all necessary measures to

[84] *Milantic Trans SA v Ministerio de la Producción (Astilleros Río Santiago y otro)* [2016] SCJPBA, LL AR/JUR/12408/2016.

[85] *Milantic Trans SA v Ministerio de la Producción (Astilleros Río Santiago y otro)* [2021] CSJ 1460/2016/CS1.

include the credit in the next budget. To such end, the existence of the debt must be informed to the Secretariat of Treasury before 31 July of each year.

If no budget reserve is made for the concrete debt in the next budget, the creditor is allowed to seek enforcement of the debt after the legislative period in which such budget law should have been discussed and approved. However, if the budget reserve is made but the funds are insufficient to pay the debt in full, the creditor has a two-year waiting period before seeking enforcement.

4 ICSID Awards

The recognition and enforcement of ICSID awards deserves a separate comment because of the specific regulation in the ICSID Convention and the interpretation that Argentina has made of the Convention.

Article 53 of the ICSID Convention states that ICSID awards are binding on the parties and each party shall abide by and comply with its terms. Article 54 of the Convention also states that each Contracting State shall recognize an award rendered pursuant to the Convention as binding and enforce the pecuniary obligations imposed by that award within its territory as if it were a final judgment of a court in that state, and that the execution of the award shall be governed by the laws concerning the execution of judgments in force in the state where such execution is sought.

In 2003, Horacio Rosatti, the Attorney General of the time, and a current member of the Federal Supreme Court, suggested that Argentine federal courts may review ICSID awards if recognition and enforcement is sought in Argentina. He did so by publishing an article in which he explained that, according to the hierarchy of rules provided for in Article 75(22) of the Federal Constitution,[86] international investment agreements are above the law but below the Constitution. Therefore, pursuant to Articles 116[87] and 27 of the Federal Constitution,[88] Argentine federal courts could

[86] Article 75(22) of the Federal Constitution reads: 'Congress is empowered: . . . To approve or reject treaties concluded with other nations and international organizations, and concordats with the Holy See. Treaties and concordats have a higher hierarchy than laws. The American Declaration of the Rights and Duties of Man; the Universal Declaration of Human Rights; the American Convention on Human Rights; the International Pact on Economic, Social and Cultural Rights; the International Pact on Civil and Political Rights and its empowering Protocol; the Convention on the Prevention and Punishment of Genocide; the International Convention on the Elimination of all Forms of Racial Discrimination; the Convention on the Elimination of all Forms of Discrimination against Woman; the Convention against Torture and other Cruel, Inhuman or Degrading Treatments or Punishments; the Convention on the Rights of the Child; in the full force of their provisions, they have constitutional hierarchy, do not repeal any section of the First Part of this Constitution and are to be understood as complementing the rights and guarantees recognized herein. They shall only be denounced, in such event, by the National Executive Power after the approval of two-thirds of all the members of each House. In order to attain constitutional hierarchy, the other treaties and conventions on human rights shall require the vote of two-thirds of all the members of each House, after their approval by Congress.'

[87] Article 116 of the Federal Constitution provides: 'The Supreme Court and the lower courts of the Nation are empowered to hear and decide all cases arising under the Constitution and the laws of the Nation, with the exception made in Section 75, subsection 12, and under the treaties made with foreign nations; all cases concerning ambassadors, public ministers and foreign consuls; cases related to admiralty and maritime jurisdiction; matters in which the Nation shall be a party; actions arising between two or more provinces, between one province and the inhabitants of another province, between the inhabitants of different provinces, and between one province or the inhabitants thereof against a foreign state or citizen.'

[88] Article 27 of the Federal Constitution stipulates: 'The Federal Government is under the obligation to strengthen its relationships of peace and trade with foreign powers, by means of treaties in accordance with the principles of public law laid down by this Constitution.'

control the content of such agreements to determine if they were in accordance with the principles of public law laid down by the Federal Constitution. In his view, a hermetic and self-sufficient arbitration system, like the one of ICSID, was incompatible with the Argentine legal system, insofar as it prevented content control of investment agreements and prevented national courts from intervening in the enforcement of an arbitral award rendered in a different jurisdiction.[89]

Argentina also argued in ICSID arbitrations that its obligation under the ICSID Convention was to satisfy the requirements of both Article 53 and Article 54, and that to obtain payment of an ICSID award the investor had to follow the formalities applicable to enforcement of final local judgments.[90] Although this interpretation was heavily criticized by scholars and has been disregarded by ICSID ad hoc committees,[91] all these facts created among foreign investors the sensation that they would receive an adverse decision if they tried to enforce an ICSID award in Argentina.

However, there are two cases in which recognition or enforcement of an ICSID award was sought in Argentina. The first case was initiated by a foreign state against an Argentine investor. It is a case in which Peru requested, in the City of Buenos Aires, the bankruptcy of an investor based on an ICSID award ordering the investor to pay the arbitration costs. The Court of First Instance rejected the request. It considered that the award did not represent a due debt because Peru had not initiated recognition or enforcement proceedings under Article 519 *bis* of the Federal Procedural Code. The Court of Appeals reversed the decision, stating that, pursuant to the ICSID Convention, ICSID awards are binding on the parties and do not require the initiation of recognition or enforcement proceedings. Nevertheless, the Court of Appeals stressed that the case was not about the enforcement of an ICSID award against Argentina and that its decision was without prejudice to the courts' power to exercise their controlling functions with respect to violations of public policy principles.[92]

The second case was initiated by a foreign investor against the Argentine state. It is a case in which the foreign investor requested, in the City of Buenos Aires, the execution of an ICSID award ordering the Argentine state to contribute to the payment of the arbitration costs. The state resisted the enforcement on grounds that it was not obliged to voluntarily comply with the award because, under Article 54 of the ICSID Convention, the foreign investor had to request first the recognition and enforcement of the award in accordance to Argentine law. After considering that the state did not resist the award on grounds of public policy or violation of human rights, and that the award did not relate to sovereign decisions of the state as it only referred to costs,

[89] Horacio D Rossati, 'Los tratados bilaterales de inversión, el arbitraje internacional obligatorio y el sistema constitucional argentino' [2003] LL F-1283. Soon after that, coincidentally or not, the Federal Supreme Court issued the *Cartellone* judgment, in which it held that arbitral awards could be reviewed when they were unconstitutional, illegal, unreasonable, or violated public policy. See nn 77–79 above and accompanying text.

[90] See eg *Continental Casualty Co v The Argentine Republic*, ICSID Case No ARB/03/9, Decision on Argentina's Application for a Stay of Enforcement of the Award (23 October 2009), paras 7(e), 12.

[91] ibid para 12. See also eg *Sempra Energy International v The Argentine Republic*, ICSID Case No ARB/02/16, Decision on the Argentine Republic's Request for a Continued Stay of Enforcement of the Award (Rule 54) (5 March 2009), paras 59, 72.

[92] *CCI – Compañía de Concesiones de Infraestructura SA v pedido de quiebra (por República de Perú)* [2015] CNCom-A, LL AR/JUR/33122/2015.

the Court of First Instance concluded that that there was no obligation under the ICSID Convention to initiate recognition or enforcement proceedings, and, therefore, treated the awards a local judgement, ordering the state to include the credit in the budget.[93]

In spite of the above, Argentina has complied with some final ICSID awards by entering into payment agreements, all of which contain a 'haircut' to the total value of the arbitral award.[94]

IV. Arbitration as a Tool of Governance

It could be argued that private-public arbitration is not only a mechanism to settle individual disputes, but that it also has the function of actively crafting and further developing the law governing private-public relations. In other words, where arbitration replaces state courts, it might also have the effect of further developing the governing law.

In Argentina, the constitutional legal system does not set up specific requirements to ensure that arbitration, as a governance mechanism, does not affect the public interest (although the public interest is still protected by other more general rules, such as those limiting the arbitrability of disputes). This section IV deals with the interaction between private-public arbitration and democracy, the rule of law, and human rights.

A. Democracy and Private-Public Arbitration

1 Status and Appointment of Arbitrators

In private-public arbitration, the fact that at least one arbitrator is appointed by a private party, who is not accountable to the public, does not put democracy (as understood by the Argentine Constitution) at stake. While the principle of democracy is clearly embodied in the Argentine Constitution, there is no specific definition of such principle. Even following a crude definition of democracy as the 'government of the people, by the people, for the people',[95] there is no doubt that such democracy is exercised in an indirect manner. The people freely elect and empower their representatives to undertake decision-making functions like passing legislation. Thus, since domestic law is the primary source that determines the legitimacy of private-public arbitrations, when said representatives passed the legislation currently in place in Argentina, which allows, within certain limits, private-public arbitration, and which

[93] *Consorcio de Aguas Bilbao Bizkaia Bilbao Bizkaia Ur Partzuergoa y otro v En-M Hacienda s/ Proceso de ejecución* [2021], Juzgado Contencioso Administrativo Federal 3, case 20642/2021.

[94] See, for instance, 'Argentina Settles Abaclat Sovereign Bond Claim' (*Global Arbitration Review*, 2 February 2016); 'Argentina Pays Out to End Sovereign Debt Claim' (*Global Arbitration Review*, 25 April 2016); 'Argentina to Settle More Treaty Awards' (*Global Arbitration Review*, 16 May 2016); 'Third Parties Collect on Argentina's Treaty Awards' (*Global Arbitration Review*, 26 October 2016); 'Argentina and Total Settle' (*Global Arbitration Review*, 19 July 2017).

[95] President Abraham Lincoln, 'Gettysburg Address' (19 November 1863).

does not conflict with the Federal Constitution, the people indirectly legitimated this kind of arbitration. Hence, there is no democracy problem from the point of view of Argentine constitutional law.

2 Law Application by Arbitrators

If democracy is government for the people, it arguably suggests that the outcome of arbitration must be in conformity with legal standards made by the public or admitted by the public. The fact that arbitrators, who are not public officials, exercise an indirect control over the government's conduct does not constitute a problem either from the point of view of Argentine constitutional law.

3 Constitutional Control

The principle of democracy (as understood in Argentina) also does not require a restriction on the remedies available to arbitral tribunals. State courts have the power and duty to exercise constitutional control, that is, a control over due respect of the Federal Constitution.[96] This control is characterized as 'diffuse', in the sense that, instead of being concentrated in certain courts, it may and must be exercised by every judicial body.[97] For these reasons, it only produces *inter partes* effect and not general effect.

Given this limited effect, it is generally understood that arbitral tribunals can also undertake such constitutional control and declare that certain legislation is unconstitutional, without creating any harm to the legal system as a whole.[98] Another reason for this solution is that arbitrators are viewed in the Argentine legal system as exercising a judicial function, much like domestic courts.

Because of the arbitrators' power to exercise constitutional control, they may declare that a given law violates the Constitution. This was the decision in some of the cases concerning challenges to the emergency legislation before arbitral tribunals, where courts upheld arbitral awards declaring that such legislation was in breach of the Constitution.[99]

4 Different Outcomes for Similar Disputes

Although in any legal system inconsistencies are undesirable, the fact that the outcome of a given arbitral proceeding diverges from the outcome of an identical or essentially similar dispute before another arbitral tribunal or a domestic court does not necessarily create a problem for the principle of democracy and equal treatment (as understood in Argentina). There are several reasons for this.

[96] See Article 116 of the Federal Constitution which states: 'It is for the Supreme Court and the lower national tribunals to entertain and decide all the cases related to aspects governed by the Constitution, and the laws of the Nation' (translation by author).

[97] *Galli, Elena v Kairuz, Alfredo F* [2003] CNCiv-F, [2004] LL D-1034.

[98] Roque J Caivano, 'Planteos de inconstitucionalidad en el arbitraje' [2006] Revista Peruana de Arbitraje 153. See the precedents of Argentine courts cited by the author, for instance *Otondo, César A y otro v Cortina Beruatto SA et al* [2003] JNCom No 10, [2003] Rev JA, vol IV-73; *KCK Tissue SA y otros v Citibank NA Nassau et al* [2005] CNCom-A (not public).

[99] Caivano (n 95).

First, by passing legislation allowing the parties to take their case away from the judicial system and submit it to arbitration, the 'people' have indirectly contemplated the possibility that arbitral tribunals may assess cases in a different fashion and reach different results from domestic courts. Moreover, the 'people' indirectly allow arbitration *ex aequo et bono*, that is, that the arbitrators directly leave aside the law and decide according to their honest knowledge and understanding of justice.

Second, according to Article 2651 of the CCC, the parties to an international contract may agree on the application of a foreign law. Thus, even without the intervention of arbitrators, a state court may face cases calling for the application of different laws, and therefore yielding different results. Article 79 of the ICA Law even authorizes the parties to choose a 'rule of law', instead of a hard law, as the law applicable to the merits.

Third, there is no *stare decisis* rule in the Argentine legal system. Since the Argentine judicial system is not based on a rule of precedent, state courts are not bound by previous decisions taken by their fellow courts in essentially similar cases. Hence, there are situations where there is an established practice in one chamber of a court of appeals which is contrary to the practice in another chamber of the same court.

Consequently, the divergence of outcomes may also occur within the judicial system, although there are a few exceptions. For instance, Articles 302 and 303 of the Federal Procedural Code used to allow all the chambers of a Court of Appeals, in certain circumstances, to make plenary rulings that would be binding upon all lower courts. In 2013, Law 26,853 repealed these provisions and ordered the creation of Courts of Cassation (Cámaras de Casación) for different subject matters; however, these new courts have not yet been created.

In turn, the Federal Supreme Court has held that, although its judgments are not formally binding, lower courts should decide in conformity with them and, in any event, courts should provide sufficient arguments if they depart from those judgments because the Federal Supreme Court is the ultimate interpreter of the Federal Constitution.[100]

5 Arbitrators' Law-Making Activity

Theoretically, the arbitrators' activity may craft and develop the law governing private-public relations. Yet, from a practical point of view, it is not clear that arbitral decisions do impact the conduct of public entities in general.

First, public entities do not necessarily get to know what is decided in an arbitration involving another public entity; therefore, those decisions are not likely to be considered by state entities that have not participated in the proceedings. Second, the public sector is so large that there is not always a fluent interconnection between different public entities. Third, different arbitral tribunals are not necessarily aware of previous decisions taken by other arbitral tribunals either.

Of course, in the field of investment arbitration, the scenario is different since most cases are public (including awards, procedural orders, and sometimes pleadings, and even hearings). This trend is likely to increase with recent developments, like the 2014

[100] *Cerámica San Lorenzo* [1985] CSJN, [1986] LL A-179.

UNCITRAL Transparency Rules[101] and the Mauritius Convention on Transparency in Treaty-based Investor-State Arbitration.[102] Nevertheless, even when arbitral tribunals are aware of previous decisions taken by other arbitral tribunals in similar cases, they are not bound by those decisions.[103]

Following the hypothesis that arbitral tribunals actually conduct some sort of lawmaking activity, this could raise problems regarding the democracy principle since, as a rule, the Federal Constitution does not allow the delegation of legislative powers.[104] However, even assuming that individual arbitral decisions in private-public arbitrations have the effect of shaping the conduct of the state, qualifying that as a lawmaking activity would be too far-fetched, as arbitrators do not enact laws and the effects of their decisions would indeed be very limited. Therefore, the arbitrators' activity in this regard would hardly clash with the constitutional principle to protect democracy. In fact, the practical consequences of an arbitral decision are not different from those of a court judgment.

6 Openness and Transparency

There are no specific rules calling for the openness and transparency of private-public arbitration proceedings. The fact that the arbitral proceedings in private-public arbitrations are usually confidential and not open to the public may affect the accountability as to whether the law is properly applied. However, this is not necessarily a problem from the perspective of the democracy principle (as understood in Argentina).

The existence of certain recourses against the arbitral award, which are always available as the parties cannot waive them, may mitigate the lack of transparency. This is because, if any party challenges the arbitral award, the case will move to the state courts, where, as a rule, proceedings are public.[105] The same would happen if one of the parties to the arbitration seeks assistance from a court (eg a precautionary measure, the enforcement of an award). Conversely, if all parties to a confidential arbitration refrain from appearing before a court seeking assistance or control, the award would not be public. In this scenario, the rules on the publicity of information mentioned before, such as Law 27,275 and Decree 1172/03 on the access to public information, may become relevant.

Differently from the situation before state courts, the intervention of third parties, amicus curiae, is not contemplated in the arbitration regulation. It could be interesting

[101] UNCITRAL Rules on Transparency in Treaty-based Investor-State Arbitration (effective as of 1 April 2014).

[102] UN Convention on Transparency in Treaty-based Investor-State Arbitration (adopted 10 December 2014, entered into force 18 October 2017).

[103] See the analysis of Gabrielle Kaufmann-Kohler, 'Is Consistency a Myth?' in Emmanuel Gaillard and Yas Banifatemi (eds), *Precedent in International Arbitration* (Juris 2008) 137, 146.

[104] Article 76 of the Federal Constitution expressly prohibits the delegation of such powers to the executive power, except in cases of emergency. It states: 'The legislative delegation to the Executive Power is prohibited, except in certain matters of administration or public emergency, with a term fixed for its exercise and within the basis that the Congress establishes for the delegation' (translation by the authors).

[105] For instance, under the Federal Procedural Code, hearings (art 125.1) as well as judgments (art 164) are public.

to see the reaction of arbitral tribunals before a motion for amicus curiae despite the lack of a legal basis, but there is no existing case law on the topic.

B. The Rule of Law and Private-Public Arbitration

Like the principle of democracy, there are different and partly diverging definitions of the concept of 'rule of law'. Notwithstanding these differences, there are core components around which such concept converges. Still, there are differences between what may be called 'thin' versions of the rule of law—that is, notions that have a primarily formal/procedural understanding of the rule of law—and 'thick' versions of the rule of law that encompass a yardstick for measuring the outcome of certain decisions. This thick version is supported, for example, in a report by the United Nations Secretary General, which states:

> [The rule of law] refers to a principle of governance in which all persons, institutions and entities, public and private, including the State itself, are accountable to laws that are publicly promulgated, equally enforced and independently adjudicated, and which are consistent with international human rights norms and standards. It requires, as well, measures to ensure adherence to the principles of supremacy of law, equality before the law, accountability to the law, fairness in the application of the law, separation of powers, participation in decision-making, legal certainty, avoidance of arbitrariness and procedural and legal transparency.

Following that definition, it is worth analysing whether any aspects of private-public arbitration may have an impact on the rule of law.

1 The Rule of Law and the Independence and Impartiality of Arbitrators

The Argentinian legal system imposes certain requirements concerning the independence and impartiality of arbitrators. Article 27 of the ICA Law sets forth that, when a person is approached in connection with a possible appointment as an arbitrator, he or she shall disclose any circumstances likely to give rise to justifiable doubts as to his or her impartiality or independence. An arbitrator, from the time of his or her appointment and throughout the arbitral proceedings, shall without delay disclose any such circumstances to the parties.

Article 28 of the ICA Law also states that an arbitrator may be challenged only if circumstances exist that give rise to justifiable doubts as to his or her impartiality or independence, or if he or she does not possess qualifications agreed by the parties.

These articles are based on the Model Law. However, Article 28 of the ICA Law includes a novel paragraph stating that the participation of the arbitrator (or the members of the law firm, consultancy firm, or equivalent organization to which the arbitrator belongs), (i) in other arbitral or judicial proceedings as attorney of one of the parties, regardless of the subject matter of those proceedings, or (ii) in other arbitral or judicial proceedings with the same object or cause of action, as attorney for a third party, constitutes a ground for challenge. In these cases, the provision makes a non-rebuttable presumption of the lack of impartiality or independence. The problem with this provision is that it does not establish any temporal limit to consider the arbitrator's previous participation as counsel in another case, so the courts will have to specify whether it refers to a simultaneous participation or if it also includes past participations (and if so, up until what time).

In the case of the Federal Procedural Code, its Article 746 indicates that arbitrators appointed by a state court may be challenged on the same grounds as judges. Article 17 of the Federal Procedural Code mentions the following grounds for challenging judges:

(i) the judge has a family relationship, up to the fourth degree, with any of the parties or counsel;
(ii) the judge or his or her relatives, up to the fourth degree, have an interest in the case or in the parties;
(iii) the judge has a pending dispute with the challenging party;
(iv) the judge is creditor, debtor, or guarantor of any of the parties, except for official banks;
(v) the judge has filed a criminal action against the challenging party, or the other way around;
(vi) the challenging party has reported the judge and the Supreme Court has initiated an impeachment procedure;
(vii) the judge has been counsel to any of the parties or has issued an opinion or recommendation on the case, either before or after its beginning;
(viii) the judge has received important benefits from any party;
(ix) the judge has a substantial friendship with any party;
(x) the judge has an enmity or hate against a party, manifested in known facts. Offences to the judge made after he or she started hearing the case are excluded.

2 The Rule of Law and the Arbitral Procedure

The rule of law also encompasses a component of due process as understood in Argentine constitutional law. This due process component calls for the application of several procedural rules to conduct arbitral proceedings. Given that it does not impose specific rules to conduct private-public arbitrations, those arbitrations must be conducted in accordance with the same rules of due process that apply to domestic courts and private-private arbitrations.

3 The Rule of Law and the Separation of Powers

One of the main functions of domestic courts in private-public disputes is to review whether public actors conduct themselves in accordance with the applicable law, thus ensuring accountability and responsibility of public actors. From the perspective of the rule of law, it is not a problem that arbitrators may not fulfil this function in the same way as state courts because neither reaching the same results on the merits nor managing the procedure in the same way is a requirement to maintain the rule of law. As already explained above, state courts may also act differently from each other.

Regarding the qualifications of arbitrators, according to Article 743 of the Federal Procedural Code, any person of legal age who is in full exercise of his or her civil rights may act as an arbitrator. Article 765 of the Federal Procedural Code states that judges and officials of the judiciary cannot accept appointments, except in cases in which the Federal State or a province is party to the dispute.

The rule of law does not require arbitrators to be particularly knowledgeable in the applicable law. In fact, the grounds for challenge to arbitrators contained in Article 17 of the Federal Procedural Code and Article 28 of the ICA Law do not refer to knowledge of the law at all.

The rule of law as understood in Argentina does not mandate specific standards for domestic court supervision of arbitral tribunals regarding the respect of procedural or substantive law. Likewise, the rule of law does not require the application of specific standards concerning recognition and enforcement of arbitral awards.

4 The Rule of Law and Legal Predictability in the Decision-Making Process

It goes without saying that inconsistency or incoherence of adjudicatory decisions is inconvenient in any legal system. A natural consequence of the inconsistency is that, even when knowing about previous decisions on similar cases, the parties do not know how to shape their future conduct in order to avoid potential liabilities. However, inconsistencies may also exist in the realm of state justice. Consequently, inconsistencies between arbitral awards are not necessarily a problem from the perspective of the constitutional principle of the rule of law as understood in Argentina.

C. Fundamental Human Rights and Private-Public Arbitration

From the perspective of Argentine constitutional law, it is also worth assessing whether private-public arbitration could have a negative impact, considering the protection of fundamental human rights.

Due process rights, as the individual rights dimension of procedural rights, impose certain requirements in respect of the procedure applied by arbitral tribunals. Basically, they shall respect the generally known rules of due process. In this sense, Article 18 of the ICA Law states that the parties shall be treated with equality and each party shall be given a full opportunity of presenting its case. Article 99 of the ICA Law, as well as Article 760 of the Federal Procedural Code, also include due process violations as a ground for annulment of the award. In this regard, there are no differences between private-private and private-public arbitrations.

The fact that private-public disputes are submitted to arbitration rather than to state courts does not entail a problem of access to justice under Argentine constitutional law. On the contrary, arbitration is a way of granting such access, since justice may be done either by a 'state judge' or an 'arbitral judge'. Therefore, an agreement to arbitrate does not jeopardize the parties' constitutionally guaranteed right to access justice, but is a form of ensuring it.

Even if arbitral tribunals rebalance competing rights through their lawmaking activities, this does not affect fundamental human rights as understood by Argentine constitutional law either. Although the existence of the *iuria novit curia* principle in arbitration is not settled, balancing competing rights at stake is just part of the arbitrators' decision-making duty. Arbitrators, like judges, cannot refuse to adjudicate a dispute, even if there are equally important competing rights at stake. Consequently, they may be somehow forced to rebalance competing rights and there is no indication in the Argentine legal system that they should not do this. This idea is supported by the fact that Article 81 of the ICA Law and Article 766 of the Federal Procedural Code allow the parties to entrust arbitrators to act as *amiable compositeurs*, whose task is exactly to resolve disputes without considering hard law, without any limitation.

The so-called 'double instance'—that is, the right to appeal a judicial decision to a higher court—constitutes a human right. This right is embodied in Article 8(2)(h) of the International Covenant on Civil and Political Rights, as well as in Article 14(5) of the American Convention on Human Rights, both of which have constitutional hierarchy in Argentina pursuant to Article 75(22) of the Federal Constitution. However, this human right does not require a specific accountability and control mechanism for arbitration. Even considering that the right to appeal may be waived, this would not affect fundamental human rights, since it has been understood that the double instance is only required in criminal cases.[106]

To the eyes of a third party not involved in a private-public arbitration, the approach may be different. A third party who considers themselves to be affected by arbitral proceedings might believe that the procedural principles explained above are not enough to protect their rights. This may be true, but despite the global trend in favour of the participation of third parties, the Argentine legal system does not provide such a tool in the field of arbitration. The general principle, embodied in Article 959 of the CCC, is that contracts are binding upon the parties and the arbitration agreement is a contract. Notwithstanding the foregoing, some courts have mitigated such principle in certain cases.[107]

On another note, the fact that third parties demand to be heard in an arbitration to which they are not a party proves the strength of this dispute resolution method. They may have an independent cause of action before national courts but prefer to argue their case before an international tribunal.

V. Concluding Remarks

In Argentina, private-public arbitration is not regulated as a specific type of arbitration. Therefore, in general terms, private-public arbitration is governed by the same rules that apply to private-private arbitration. However, it is possible (yet not easy) to identify some differences between private-private and private-public arbitration.

The main differences relate to: (1) subjective arbitrability, ie the capacity of the state to submit disputes to arbitration; (2) the concept of public policy (relevant to objective arbitrability, annulment recourses against awards, and the recognition and

[106] Roque J Caivano, 'El control judicial en el arbitraje. Apuntes para una futura reforma de la legislación argentina' [2008] LL D-1274, para 4.3.1; Julio César Rivera, 'El arbitraje en Argentina a través de la jurisprudencia de su Corte Suprema' [2007] Academia Nacional de Derecho August, para I.C; *Giroldi, Horacio David* [1995] CSJN, [1995] LL D-462.

[107] See eg *Honda Motor Argentina SA v Cinter SRL* [2014] CNCom-B. In this case, the Commercial Court of Appeals upheld an award on jurisdiction rendered by an arbitral tribunal with regard to a third party to a construction dispute due to the specific characteristics of construction contracts under the Civil Code of the time.

enforcement of awards), which due to the nature of private-public relationships appears to be broader than in private-private arbitration (eg restrictions imposed by the debt consolidation law); (3) precautionary measures because of Law 26,854, which although declared unconstitutional by some courts is still in force; (4) transparency and confidentiality, because there are some rules on the access to public information that could potentially be applied by courts to confidential arbitrations; and (5) the possibility to enforce the award, specifically ICSID awards. While these are only a few differences, they relate to crucial aspects of arbitration, and therefore may be relevant in practice.

The fact that private-public arbitration is considered as a tool of governance would not constitute a conflict with the Argentinian legal system. Regarding the principle of democracy, it is jeopardized neither by the current rules on the constitution of the arbitral tribunal nor the fact that they may apply the law differently from state courts and achieve different results, nor by the fact that constitutional control is taken away from state courts. In turn, although the rule of law requires the fulfilment of certain minimum standards to resolve disputes, those standards are not affected by private-public arbitration.

Although arbitration is well-established as a dispute resolution mechanism in Argentina, some still raise concerns about it. This is understandable due to the natural public interests involved in private-public arbitration. Therefore, it is also reasonable to find some limitations to private-public arbitration. Nowadays, both in theory and practice, there seems to be a good balance between the use of private-public arbitration and the limits to maintain democracy. However, an excessive application of the limitations to private-public arbitration could create a negative impact on the arbitration system. In this sense, the challenge to find a proper balance between democracy (with its legitimate concerns) and arbitration falls on the arbitration community and the judiciary.

Select Materials

Bibliography

Caivano, Roque J, 'Planteos de inconstitucionalidad en el arbitraje' [2006] Revista Peruana de Arbitraje

César Rivera, Julio, 'El arbitraje en Argentina a través de la jurisprudencia de su Corte Suprema' [2007] Academia Nacional de Derecho, August

De la Fuente, Horacio H, *Orden público* (Astrea 2003)

Marienhoff, Miguel S, *Tratado de Derecho Administrativo*, vol III-A

Legislation

Federal Constitution

Federal Civil and Commercial Procedural Code (Law 17,454)

Federal Civil and Commercial Code (Law 26,994)

International Commercial Arbitration Law (Law 27,449)

Cases

Cayetano Paino [1956] CSJN *Fallos* 235:940
Cía Ítalo Argentina de Electricidad [1937] CSJN *Fallos* 178:293
Compañía Argentina de Navegación 'Nicolás Mihanovich Ltda' [1931] CSJN *Fallos* 160:133
Don Gerardo Pagano [1920] CSJN *Fallos* 133:61
Estado Nacional – Procuración del Tesoro Nacional c/ (nulidad del laudo del 20-III-2009) [2018] CSJN *Fallos* 341:1485
Guido Simonini [1942] CSJN *Fallos* 194:155
José Cartellone Construcciones Civiles S.A. c/ Hidroeléctrica Norpatagónica S.A. o Hidronor S.A. [2004] CSJN *Fallos* 327:1881
Sociedad Anónima Puerto del Rosario [1926] CSJN *Fallos* 146:373
Sociedad Anónima Puerto del Rosario [1928] CSJN *Fallos* 152:347
Techint Compañía Técnica Internacional [2007] CSJN *Fallos* 330:2215
Yacimientos Petrolíferos Fiscales [1974] CSJN *Fallos* 290:458

PART III
PRIVATE-PUBLIC ARBITRATION IN ASIA, AFRICA, AND AUSTRALIA

13
Public-Private Arbitration in the Iranian Legal System
The Intersection of Preferential Rights and Constitutional Constraints on Arbitration

*Jamal Seifi and Kamal Javadi**

I. Introduction

In the Iranian legal system, the rules governing public-private relations are based on the premise that in public-private contracts the two sides of the bargain do not represent interests of equal importance. Thus, in domestic public-private contracts (also known as administrative contracts, as originally developed in the French legal system), the protection of the public interest in the first place is guaranteed by departing from the private law paradigm, namely through a built-in mechanism that recognizes certain preferential rights for public bodies. In this regard, Iranian administrative law scholars have noted that the superior position of public law entities remains a relevant consideration throughout the life of public-private contracts.[1] Furthermore, in addition to this substantive protection mechanism, public-private contracts enjoy another layer of protection under Iranian law in the form of arbitration-limiting constitutional provisions, namely Article 139 of the Iranian Constitution, which provides in relevant part that the submission of disputes concerning public and state property to arbitration:

> shall in each case be subject to approval by the Council of Ministers and must be notified to Parliament. Cases in which one party to the dispute is foreign, as well as important domestic disputes, must also be approved by Parliament [the Majlis]. The law determines the important cases.[2]

Needless to say, in principle the substantive protection accorded to public bodies under administrative contracts may not be transferred to public-private contracts

* The text is current as at 1 April 2021. There have not been any notable developments affecting Iran's approach to private-public arbitration since then.

[1] Manoochehr Tabatabai-Motamani, *Administrative Law* (Samt Publication 2008) 307 (in Persian).

[2] As will be discussed in greater detail in section IV below, Article 139 of the Iranian Constitution provides in relevant part that the submission of disputes concerning public and state property to arbitration 'shall in each case be subject to approval by the Council of Ministers and must be notified to Parliament. Cases in which one party to the dispute is foreign, as well as important domestic disputes, must also be approved by Parliament [the Majlis]. The law determines the important cases.'

Jamal Seifi and Kamal Javadi, *Public-Private Arbitration in the Iranian Legal System* In: *The Comparative Constitutional Foundations of Private-Public Arbitration*. Edited by: Stephan W. Schill, Oxford University Press.
 DOI: 10.1093/9780191987960.003.0013

concluded with foreign companies. This consideration, in turn, would explain the reason why, in respect of those contracts, the arbitration-limiting provisions have been frequently relied upon by Iranian public bodies when contesting the jurisdiction of arbitral tribunals over the claims brought against them.

Although the specific constitutional constraints as contained in Article 139 of the Iranian Constitution constitute the central focus of this chapter, in order to fully understand the context of limitations relating to public-private arbitration under Iranian law it is necessary to discuss the institution of administrative contracts in the Iranian legal system. Traditionally, under Iranian law, public contracts have been heavily regulated both in terms of ensuring preferential rights for public law entities and in respect of their forum selection clauses. In fact, as will be discussed in section II, the preferential rights are normally contractually included in the provisions of public contracts through the General Conditions of Contract, which is a mandatory document incorporated by reference into domestic administrative contracts. In addition, domestic public contracts would normally also contain a forum selection clause providing for the exclusive jurisdiction of Iranian courts. The rationale for this selection may be explained by the fact that the substantive protection accorded to public entities may not fully materialize if disputes were to be resolved by commercial arbitrators.[3] This rationale is further supported by the fact that, as will be discussed in greater detail in section III, the General Conditions of Contract were amended in 1999 in order to introduce a public law arbitration mechanism to be conducted by a public body, the High Technical Council (HTC).

In addition, it is important to note that, unlike in the current debate surrounding international investment arbitration, an excessive resort to public-private arbitration was not the main driving force behind the restrictive stance taken in the post-Revolutionary Iranian Constitution of 1979 and Article 139 thereof. Instead, as established by the drafting history of Article 139 of the Iranian Constitution, the inclusion of the parliamentary approval requirement for foreign arbitrations was intended to shield the exercise of sovereign power against the perceived influence of foreign arbitral institutions. In addition, as will be discussed in section IV, despite the fact that the original language of the draft of Article 139 merely required that parliament be notified, during the final reading the wording was changed to specifically require parliamentary approval where the other party to the dispute is non-Iranian or the subject matter of the dispute is regarded by law as important. The latter consideration clearly points to the concept of parliamentary sovereignty in that it was felt that the Executive Branch must not be accorded the final say as to the referral to arbitration.

At the same time, over the past twenty years, there have been legislative efforts in Iran aiming to create a more arbitration-friendly environment, such as the modernization of the law relating to international arbitration as well as a significant increase in the number of bilateral investment treaties (BITs) that the country has concluded with both developed and developing countries. Thus, in 1997, the Iranian Parliament

[3] For the argument that, due to the public law nature of state contracts, international arbitrators should at least take relevant mandatory public law rules of the host state into consideration, see eg AFM Maniruzzaman, 'International Arbitrator and Mandatory Public Law Rules in the Context of State Contracts: An Overview' (1990) 7(3) J Int'l Arb 53.

enacted the International Commercial Arbitration Act, which is to a considerable extent modelled on the United Nations Commission on International Trade Law (UNCITRAL) Model Law.[4] Moreover, Iran acceded to the New York Convention on 15 October 2001. Iran, as envisaged under Article I(3) of the New York Convention, has made a commercial reservation and a reciprocity reservation.[5] Iran's ratification document also contains a reservation to comply with Article 139 of the Iranian Constitution, stating that the submission of disputes to arbitration must be in accordance with Article 139.[6] As for BITs, by late 2019 Iran had concluded seventy BITs, some of which are yet to be ratified.[7]

With these preliminary observations in mind, this chapter proceeds as follows: section II examines the main features of administrative contracts viewed through the prism of Iranian administrative law. Next, in section III, the structure and operation of administrative courts and public law arbitration in Iran will be discussed. Section IV analyses the constitutional constraints imposed by Article 139 of the Iranian Constitution and their impact on the protection of the public interest in public-private arbitration. In section V, a number of leading cases, mainly from the formative years, which relate to various aspects of the constitutional constraints contained in Article 139 of the Iranian Constitution are reviewed. It will become apparent that, in most instances, international arbitral tribunals dismissed the jurisdictional objections raised on the basis of Article 139 of the Iranian Constitution. Despite being contractual in nature, these cases, coupled with the treatment of arbitration-limiting constitutional provisions by investment arbitration tribunals, inform the manner in which investment arbitration tribunals will interpret the constitutional constraints contained in Article 139 in the future. Section VI briefly discusses the implied or express incorporation of Article 139 reservations in the instruments of ratification of Iran's bilateral and multilateral investment treaties. This section concludes that these reservations may be ineffective because of the bilateral nature of Iran's BITs and the apparent lack of notification of such reservations to the other treaty party. Section VII concludes by assessing the effectiveness of the constitutional constraints contained in Article 139 in commercial and treaty-based arbitrations.

II. Administrative Contracts in the Iranian Legal System

As Iran is among the countries recognizing the institution of administrative contract as originally developed in the French legal system, a brief review of the main features of this legal institution is necessary. Commentators have noted that administrative

[4] See Jamal Seifi, 'The New International Commercial Arbitration Act of Iran: Towards Harmony with the UNCITRAL Model Law' (1998) 15(2) J Int'l Arb 5.

[5] See UNCITRAL, '1958 New York Convention Guide: Iran (Islamic Republic of)' <http://newyorkconvention1958.org/index.php?lvl=cmspage&pageid=11&menu=582&opac_view=-1> accessed 10 December 2024.

[6] See Law Concerning the Accession of Iran to the 1958 New York Convention on the Recognition and Enforcement of Foreign Arbitral Awards (10 April 2001) <https://rc.majlis.ir/fa/law/show/90503> accessed 10 December 2024.

[7] For a review of the Iranian BITs, see Ardeshir Atai, 'Iranian Bilateral Investment Treaties: Substantive Principles and Standards' (2013) 14 JWIT 397.

contracts (or domestic public contracts) contain certain preferential rights for public entities.[8] For instance, one of the defining characteristics of administrative contracts in the Iranian legal system is the public entity's right to terminate the public contract without cause, namely for the convenience of the public entity. In other words, this right to terminate the contract is not fault-based; the public law contracting party may, if public interest considerations so require, terminate the administrative contract simply by notification of such termination to the private contractor. Needless to say, administrative contracts also include a provision dealing with a fault-based right to terminate where, for example, the private party is in breach of the terms of the contract. However, a fault-based right to terminate may equally be found in private law contracts. Thus, it is not a preferential right. A no-cause termination provision, by contrast, is a preferential right, reflecting the fact that the contracting parties' interests in an administrative contract are not accorded equal status.

At the same time, although a serious breach of contract by the public entity (such as failure to pay for the goods and services as scheduled) gives the private contracting party the right to terminate the contract, the private party still has to apply to a court in order to seek an order of termination. In contrast, the public entity does not need a court order either to exercise its fault-based right to terminate the contract or to resort to an administrative termination for convenience; it must only give notice of termination to the private party. The private contracting party may, however, apply to the competent court for a review of the lawfulness of the termination.[9] A typical administrative termination clause thus would state that the public law contracting party has the right, at any time, at its convenience, to terminate the contract without any notice of default or judicial intervention being required, and that such termination shall become effective immediately (or after a specified period of time) after delivery of the termination notice.

With respect to other preferential rights relating to public contracts in Iranian law, as envisaged by Article 29 of the General Conditions of Contract[10]—which is a mandatory document incorporated by reference into domestic administrative contracts in its entirety—in the Iranian legal system, administrative contracts would allow the public contracting party to unilaterally adjust the scope of contractual obligations of the private party under the contract. The exercise of this preferential right, however, must take into account the 25 per cent cap imposed by Article 29 of the General Conditions of Contract in respect of changing the original scope of work. In addition, the private party must be compensated via appropriate price adjustments so that the original financial equilibrium of the contract remains intact. It has been observed that the unilateral right to modify the scope of contractual obligations enjoyed by the administrative contracting party is one of the most important features of administrative contracts, and that this distinctive characteristic of administrative contracts would serve as the main test to distinguish administrative contracts from civil contracts.[11]

[8] Vali Ansari, *Generalities of Administrative Contracts Law* (4th edn, Hoghooghdan Press 2008) 28 (in Persian).

[9] See eg ibid 238–39.

[10] Available at <https://rc.majlis.ir> accessed 10 December 2024.

[11] Ansari (n 8) 197–98 (also mentioning, in this context, the step-in rights *(mise en régie)* accorded to the public contracting party, which enable it to take over the work sites to complete the project if necessary).

The administrative preferential rights in public contracts are not limited to the rights discussed above. The Iranian model, and in particular the administrative privileges contained in the General Conditions of Contract, are heavily influenced by the French model. Foreign scholars have identified similar features under French law:

> The leading decisions of the Conseil d'Etat in France have developed certain principles regarding the mutability of administrative contracts. In the public interest the administration can unilaterally modify administrative contracts concluded with private persons. The administration retains inherent powers of control and may interfere in any way or may adjust the terms of the agreement to the changing needs of the public service. Of course, the exercise of this power is subject to review by the administrative courts and in the last instance by the Conseil d'Etat. The administration is not allowed to restrict, alter or abolish terms granting financial advantages to the contractor; the administration must respect the financial equilibrium or equation of the contract.[12]

Thus, it may be argued that there exists a common law of administrative contracts which recognizes a number of preferential rights enjoyed by the public law party to such a contract. It emanates from the fact that the public law contracting party represents notions such as public interest, public service, and public authority.

At the same time, it is important to recognize that, while in Iranian law the protection of the public interest by means of ensuring preferential rights for public law entities through the administrative contract model is a compulsory mechanism, its use is limited to domestic contracts. In general, as noted by commentators, the conceptual distinction between administrative contracts and state contracts must be maintained:

> In legal systems that, like the French, distinguish between private and public law, contracts for public services and those that include clauses overriding ordinary law are called administrative contracts. In the international sphere, however, a State contract is not necessarily an administrative contract. The mere fact that a State is involved in a contract does not in itself make that contract an administrative contract.[13]

In this regard, from a purely contractual point of view it has been stated that the difference between the two kinds of contracts is that the state, enjoying certain preferential rights, plays a pre-eminent role in an administrative contract, but less so in a state contract.[14] In this context, it is also important to note that the exercise of preferential rights by public law entities must be distinguished from sovereign acts of the state. In other words, a state acting in its sovereign capacity and via legislation may make changes to the regulatory framework relating to an activity which, in turn, may affect

[12] AFM Maniruzzaman, 'State Contracts with Aliens: The Question of Unilateral Change by the State in Contemporary International Law' (1992) 9 J Int'l Arb 141, 152.

[13] Philippe Leboulanger, 'Some Issues in ICC Awards Relating to State Contracts' (2004) 15(2) ICC Int'l Ct Arb Bull 93, 96 (fns omitted).

[14] ibid.

the contractual rights of an investor. Whether or not this factual matrix would amount to the frustration of the investor's legitimate expectations is a different debate from the exercise of preferential rights by a public law entity as a contracting party. The legitimate expectations aspect of the issue, which mainly concerns the implications of subsequent legislation for an already existing investment in the context of assessing compliance with the fair and equitable treatment obligation, became apparent only after the development of investment treaty arbitration. This, in turn, was the result of going beyond the traditional doctrine of privity of contract, and was thus described by some commentators as 'a new territory for international arbitration'.[15]

Traditionally, a number of arbitral tribunals dealing with international disputes relating to oil concessions did not find the characterization of these contracts as administrative contracts persuasive, or at any rate were not willing to acknowledge the recognition of the concept of administrative contracts among the general principles of law. Thus, the *Aramco* tribunal,[16] while considering Saudi Arabian law as the law applicable to the question of characterization, 'dismiss[ed] the public contract characterization on the basis that the Saudi law does not possess a system of administrative law comparable to the French one'.[17]

In particular, in the context of expropriation disputes, including the three Libyan arbitration cases in the 1970s, the theory of administrative contracts was invoked by the host states in the face of specific contractual undertakings to protect the foreign investors' reasonable expectations. For example, in the case of *Texaco v Libya*, in the context of an expropriation dispute, the arbitral tribunal did not find the (envisaged) Libyan argument based on the administrative nature of the concession contracts relevant.[18] There, the two concession contracts for the exploitation of oil contained an identical stabilization clause. In addition, each contract contained a governing law clause, which provided in relevant part as follows:

> This concession shall be governed by and interpreted in accordance with the principles of the law of Libya common to the principles of international law and in the absence of such common principles then by and in accordance with the general principles of law, including such of those principles as may have been applied by international tribunals.[19]

In *Texaco*, the sole arbitrator, Professor Dupuy, developed the concept of internationalization of contracts. First, in articulating an argument based on the administrative nature of the oil concession contracts in order to justify what the sole arbitrator termed as the behaviour of the Libyan government, the sole arbitrator stated that 'the first reason could be based on the nature of the contracts under dispute: if they were

[15] See Jan Paulsson, 'Arbitration Without Privity' (1995) 10(2) ICSID Review–FILJ 232.

[16] *Saudi Arabia v Arabian American Oil Company (Aramco)*, Award (23 August 1958) (1962) 27 ILR 117.

[17] Ahmed S El-Kosheri and Tarek F Riad, 'The Law Governing a New Generation of Petroleum Agreements: Changes in the Arbitration Process' (1986) 1(2) ICSID Review–FILJ 257, 264.

[18] *Texaco Overseas Petroleum Company and California Asiatic Oil Company v Libya*, Award on the Merits (19 January 1977) (1978) 17 ILM 1 (English translation). The award on the merits was delivered in French.

[19] ibid para 36.

administrative contracts, they could give rise, under certain conditions, to amendments or even to abrogation on the part of the contracting State; in relation to concession contracts, the nationalization measures would then be analyzed as being decisions bringing about, at least implicitly, abrogation.'[20] Next, in rejecting the argument set out above based on the administrative nature of the concession contracts, the sole arbitrator reasoned that, even on the assumption that Libyan law applies the theory of administrative contracts, which is of French origin, 'this theory is not known in international law'.[21] It would seem that the tribunal's treatment of the issue was influenced by the fact that the theory of administrative contracts was relied on by the nationalizing host state as a justification to frustrate the protections accorded to the foreign investor under the concession contract.

At the same time, outside the expropriation context, arbitral tribunals have been more readily willing to acknowledge the existence of a common law of administrative contracts, heavily influenced by the French model. In the case of *BIVAC v Paraguay*, the dispute arose out of an agreement to provide pre-shipment inspection and related services, entered into between BIVAC, a company incorporated under the laws of the Netherlands and headquartered in Rotterdam, and Paraguay. The claimant alleged that a number of invoices remained unpaid. Among the jurisdictional objections raised by Paraguay, it was argued that BIVAC had not made an investment in the territory of Paraguay within the meaning of Article 1(a) of the Netherlands–Paraguay BIT. The pre-shipment inspection contract, so argued Paraguay, was to be characterized as an administrative contract and thereby not covered by the treaty.[22]

Thus, the *BIVAC* tribunal examined whether or not the claimant had made a protected investment within the meaning of the BIT.[23] It noted that Article 1(a)(v) of the BIT refers to 'rights granted under public law' among the components of a protected investment. Next, the tribunal acknowledged that a distinguishing feature of a public or administrative contract is the right to unilateral termination:

> We note that in many respects a public (or administrative) contract may not be structurally different from a contract under civil law. This is recognised by Paraguayan law, which provides in Article 8 of Law No. 2.051 on Public Contracts that the Civil Code will be applicable if no special rules govern. However, a distinguishing feature of a public contract is that the State may unilaterally terminate the contract if the public interest requires.[24]

The tribunal went on to ask whether the contract conferred rights to BIVAC under public law. On the facts, the tribunal found that BIVAC was performing acts that

[20] ibid para 53.
[21] ibid para 72.
[22] *Bureau Veritas, Inspection, Valuation, Assessment and Control, BIVAC BV v Paraguay*, ICSID Case No ARB/07/9, Decision of the Tribunal on Objections to Jurisdiction (29 May 2009) para 31.
[23] It will be recalled that this issue was also addressed in *SGS Société Générale de Surveillance SA v The Philippines*, ICSID Case No ARB/02/6, Decision of the Tribunal on Objections to Jurisdiction (29 January 2004) paras 99–112 and *SGS Société Générale de Surveillance SA v Republic of Paraguay*, ICSID Case No ARB/07/29, Decision on Jurisdiction (12 February 2010) paras 74–123, under the BITs that were respectively in issue.
[24] See *BIVAC v Paraguay* (n 22) para 85.

allowed the national custom office to fix the level of import duties, and thus 'BIVAC was entrusted with functions that are commonly reserved to the public authority of the State acting through its customs authorities'.[25] From this, in the tribunal's view, it would follow that BIVAC, under the contract, had obtained rights granted under public law as provided by Article 1(a)(v) of the BIT. Furthermore, in addition to the jurisdictional objection on the basis that BIVAC had not made an investment within the meaning of the BIT, Paraguay also advanced a consent-based objection as follows:

> [Paraguay] claims that the ICSID procedure is 'effectively against the Constitutional and legal order of the Republic of Paraguay'. In support of that proposition it invokes, amongst other texts, Article 49 of the Judicial Organisation Code (Paraguayan Law No. 879/81) which, it is said, proclaims that 'controversies related to the properties of the state and municipalities cannot be submitted to arbitral procedures'.[26]

In rejecting the above jurisdictional objection, the *BIVAC* tribunal noted that Paraguay had expressed its written consent to the ICSID arbitration in Article 9 of the Netherlands–Paraguay BIT, 'without any condition concerning compliance with other Paraguayan constitutional or domestic legal requirements'.[27] Thus, the *BIVAC* tribunal held that there was no room for implying into Article 9 of the BIT additional requirements derived from the legal order of Paraguay.

As will be discussed in section VI, the analysis of the *BIVAC* tribunal in dealing with Paraguay's consent-based objection will be relevant for the treatment of any objections raised by Iran in treaty-based claims on the basis of Article 139 of the Iranian Constitution.

III. The Administrative Courts and Public Law Arbitration in Iran

The idea of creating a specialized body to exercise judicial control over public bodies and public interests, and ensuring that public administrations, agencies, and public authorities operate within the confines of the law, has a long history in Iranian law. However, despite the fact that the legislation aimed at establishing an Iranian Council of State (The Council of State Act of 1960) had been in place almost two decades prior to the Islamic Revolution, the Council of State was never established, thus rendering the exercise of judicial review by the Council, as envisaged in the 1960 Act, moot. At any rate, modelled on the French Conseil d'État, the Iranian Council of State would have the highest administrative jurisdiction. For example, in order to ensure that public bodies and local authorities, including municipalities, act intra vires, Article 2 of the Council of State Act would establish the supervisory jurisdiction of the Council. Thus, Article 2 would allow individual petitions claiming that the above-mentioned entities have acted ultra vires. Other grounds for a judicial review claim mentioned

[25] ibid para 87.
[26] ibid para 69.
[27] ibid para 72.

in Article 2 included illegality (including reviewing by-laws made under delegated authority) as well as failure to act. In short, the Council of State would have created a parallel administrative courts system alongside the ordinary courts. However, the disputes arising out of administrative contracts would not have been covered by the administrative jurisdiction exercised by the Council of State. This point will be taken up below in our discussion of the jurisdiction of the Court of Administrative Justice, which is the current administrative courts mechanism.

As noted above, the early attempts to establish an administrative court system did not come to fruition. However, in the course of drafting a new Constitution in 1979, the idea of creating a specialized body to exercise administrative jurisdiction, thus ensuring that public administrations, agencies, and public authorities would operate within the confines of the law, gained new impetus. Article 173 of the Iranian Constitution of 1979 (as amended in 1989) thus envisaged the establishment of a Supreme Administrative Court. Despite the fact that the new administrative court mechanism borrowed heavily from the provisions of the Council of State Act of 1960, a change in language occurred in that the mechanism was referred to in Article 173 as the Court of Administrative Justice (CAJ):

> In order to investigate the complaints, grievances, and objections of the people against governmental officials, units, and protocols, and in order for the people to restore their rights, a court, named the Court of Administrative Justice, will be established under the supervision of the head of the judiciary. The law shall determine the responsibility and the mode of operation of this court.

This immediate post-Revolutionary structure for creating an administrative jurisdiction was completed by the enactment of the law establishing the CAJ in January 1981. In June 2013, a new law was enacted consolidating and amending the original law establishing the CAJ and its procedural rules.[28]

As with the envisaged Council of State, the CAJ can receive individual petitions claiming that public bodies and local authorities, including municipalities (through issuing city ordinances), have acted ultra vires. There are also special rules on standing (who may bring a claim), amenability to judicial review (against whom a claim may be brought), and whether the court operates as a court of last instance (exercising its supervisory jurisdiction where the initial decision has been taken by various administrative bodies, such as tax authorities or local authorities or administrative disciplinary courts) or as a court of first instance. In addition, an appeal system is also in place (as per Article 65 of the 2011 Act) and a right of appeal is conferred upon the disputing parties.

As far as delegated legislation instruments, ordinances, and by-laws are concerned, they can be challenged on the grounds enumerated in Article 12 of the 2011 Act, which include illegality, excess of power, and failure to act. However, whereas in other cases the CAJ operates in several (first-instance or appeal) chambers, under Article 12 the CAJ operates as the Full Court, thus issuing only one Full Court ruling on

[28] Available at <https://divan-edalat.ir/> accessed 10 December 2024.

the challenged delegated legislation instrument, ordinance, or by-law under review. A successful challenge may result in the annulment of the challenged instrument in its entirety or only a partial annulment. In addition, operating under Article 12, the Full Court may also issue judgments of general applicability. Operating in this capacity presupposes a lower-court (chambers) split on a sufficiently important issue, which is similar to the unifying role played by the Iranian Supreme Court when faced with a lower-court split in civil or criminal cases. Thus, under this narrow ground, the CAJ's Full Court would effectively perform a lawmaking function. As per Article 8 of the 2011 Act, two-thirds of the administrative judges of the CAJ constitute a quorum for the Full Court. The Full Court decisions are made by a simple majority of the administrative judges attending. One Full Court ruling resulting in the annulment of a challenged decision of the Council of Ministers in the area of domestic arbitration (approving a referral to arbitration four years after the insertion of the arbitration clause in a contract in which one party was a public entity) will be discussed in section IV.[29]

It is important to note that, in the Iranian legal system, as a departure from the legal framework relating to administrative contracts, disputes arising out of administrative or public contracts would still fall under the jurisdiction of the ordinary courts.[30] In fact, based on a comparative study of administrative contracts in the French legal system and a number of other legal systems, Dr Ansari, a well-known Iranian administrative law scholar, mentions the jurisdiction of administrative courts in resolving disputes arising out of administrative contracts among the constituting elements of the definition of administrative contracts. At the same time, he goes on to observe that, in the Iranian legal system, despite the existence of administrative courts alongside the ordinary courts system, disputes arising out of administrative contracts still fall within the jurisdiction of the ordinary courts.[31]

Iranian administrative law scholars have supported the rationale behind the exercise of jurisdiction by the ordinary courts over administrative contracts, focusing on the contractual nature of the relationship between the public entity and the private party in this context.[32] At the same time, in dealing with public contracts, the ordinary courts are aware of the fact that the interests represented by the contracting parties are not of equal importance, and thus would apply the preferential rights enjoyed by the public contracting party. In fact, the preferential rights discussed in section II above are normally contractually made part of public contracts, either directly, through the General Conditions of Contract (as amended in 1999) as a mandatory document regulating the rights of the parties, or indirectly, through the insertion of similarly worded terms and conditions to this effect.

Moreover, the amended version of the General Conditions of Contract introduced a public law arbitration mechanism to be conducted by a public body composed of

[29] See n 49 and accompanying text.

[30] Furthermore, challenges relating to the validity of arbitration clauses contained in public contracts (as well as the applications seeking to set the resulting arbitral awards aside) must be submitted to the ordinary courts. Thus, unlike the situation in France, there is no need for the Tribunal des Conflits to determine whether the ordinary or administrative courts have jurisdiction in this regard.

[31] Ansari (n 8) 33.

[32] Tabatabai-Motamani (n 1) 430.

adjudicators specializing in public contracts, namely the HTC. Thus, the 1999 version of the General Conditions of Contract specifically states in Article 53 that disputes arising out of the interpretation or execution of public contracts may be referred to arbitration conducted by the HTC. In other words, the HTC is a separate arbitral body with a built-in mechanism to protect the public interest in conducting public-private arbitrations. The HTC, thus, is not an ordinary arbitral body, in that its three members are appointed by the Council of Ministers. At the same time, as with ordinary arbitral awards, the arbitral awards rendered by the HTC may be challenged before the competent general courts. Commentators have pointed out that, due to the fact that the members of the HTC are appointed by the Council of Ministers, in deciding the disputes relating to public contracts where one party, by definition, has governmental status, the impartiality requirement of the HTC would hardly be satisfied.[33] At any rate, so far the aggrieved private parties in public-private contracts have shown a preference for suing public entities in the ordinary courts.[34] Furthermore, the composition of the HTC is likely to be relevant in applying the constitutional constraints imposed by Article 139 in respect of arbitration. A Council of Ministers Regulation issued in 2003 established a delegated authority mechanism whereby a governmental authority (the President of the Budget and Planning Organization, acting *ex officio*) would be responsible for making decisions relating to the referral of disputes arising out of public contracts to the HTC. It has been remarked that the delegated authority mechanism as described above would not meet the authorization requirement under Article 139 of the Constitution, which requires that in each case the decision as to the referral to arbitration be made by the Council of Ministers.[35] However, it would seem that, due to the composition of the HTC, the delegated authority mechanism would obviate the need for a case-by-case scrutiny by the Council of Ministers, which, as discussed in section IV below, would otherwise be required under Article 139 of the Constitution.

IV. The Constitutional Constraints Imposed by Article 139 of the Iranian Constitution

Having briefly reviewed above the institutions which have the specific competence to deal with public-private arbitrations, it is now appropriate to discuss the substantive requirements and constraints specifically relating to public-private arbitrations, namely those contained in Article 139 of the Iranian Constitution. In the context of the arbitrability debate, scholars have pointed out that public interest considerations may require legislators to impose a limitation on the type of disputes that may be resolved outside of the courts' reach:

[33] Ebrahim Esmaili, 'Arbitration in Construction Contracts [Work and Materials Contracts] Subject to the General Conditions of Contract' in Mohammad Kakavand (ed), *Collection of Articles Dedicated in the Memory of Centennial of Arbitration in Iran* (Shahr-e-Danesh 2011) 382; Mohammad-Kazem Emadzadeh and others, 'Dispute Settlement Through Arbitration in the Iranian Administrative Contracts' (2016) 10 Legal Thinkers 95, 103–04 (both in Persian).

[34] Esmaili (n 33) 384.

[35] ibid 382.

> However, it is precisely because arbitration is a private proceeding with public consequences that some types of dispute are reserved for national courts, whose proceedings are generally in the public domain. It is in this sense that they are not 'capable of settlement by arbitration'.[36]

Public interest considerations may be involved in imposing limitations on both subjective and objective arbitrability. Article 139 of the Iranian Constitution is normally discussed in the context of subjective arbitrability. Article 139 of the Iranian Constitution, imposing, among other things, important constitutional constraints on domestic as well as international arbitration, reads as follows:

> The settlement of disputes concerning public and state property, or the submission of such disputes to arbitration, shall in each case be subject to approval by the Council of Ministers and must be notified to Parliament. Cases in which one party to the dispute is foreign, as well as important domestic disputes, must also be approved by Parliament [the Majlis]. The law determines the important cases.

In an unofficial interpretation of Article 139, the Guardian Council has clarified that 'state property' also includes the property belonging to state corporations; that is, corporations in which the government has an interest equivalent to more than 50 per cent of the shares.[37] The impact of the constitutional constraints imposed by Article 139 of the Iranian Constitution on the subjective arbitrability of disputes involving Iranian public law entities has been confronted by various arbitral tribunals and discussed by arbitration scholars. A number of early arbitral awards dealt with the jurisdictional objections raised by the Iranian state parties on the ground of unenforceability of the arbitration clause for failure to meet the requirements of Article 139; that is, lack of necessary approvals. Likewise, commentators have tried to shape the arbitrability debate relating to Article 139 of the Iranian Constitution as follows:

> Suppose that Iran, or an Iranian state entity, enters into a contract containing an arbitration clause, and subsequently argues that the clause is invalid because of Article 139 of the Iranian Constitution. How would that claim be dealt with under *Benteler*?[38]

It should be noted that, in addition to the Iranian cases relating to Article 139 of the Iranian Constitution, the case of *Benteler v Belgium* is among the leading authorities constituting a consistent line of precedents *(jurisprudence constante)* in arbitral case

[36] Nigel Blackaby and others, *Redfern and Hunter on International Arbitration* (5th edn, OUP 2009) 123–24.

[37] Rabia Eskini, 'Arbitrability of Claims in Iranian Law' in Kakavand (n 33) 38 (in Persian). As per Article 98 of the Iranian Constitution, the Guardian Council has exclusive jurisdiction to interpret the Constitution and to pronounce on the compatibility of ordinary laws with the Constitution and the Islamic Sharia. A specific majority of the members of the Guardian Council is required so that an interpretation of the Iranian Constitution may be qualified as an official interpretation. Article 98 of the Constitution provides: 'The interpretation of the Constitution is the responsibility of the Guardian Council. This is determined with the approval of three-fourths of its members.'

[38] Gary Born, *International Arbitration: Cases and Materials* (Kluwer 2011) 418.

law for the proposition that reliance on limitations imposed by internal law should not be permissible to invalidate an arbitration agreement.[39] The facts of this case will be discussed in section V below.[40]

At the same time, it is worth pointing out that the immediate focus of the limitation in Article 139 of the Iranian Constitution is on the term 'property'. A similar focus on state property may be found in Article 49 of the Judicial Organisation Code of Paraguay (Paraguayan Law No 879/81), stating that 'controversies related to the properties of the state and municipalities cannot be submitted to arbitral procedures'.[41] Although the case law regarding Article 139 is predominantly focused on subjective arbitrability (ie the capacity of public law entities to conclude arbitration agreements), there are instances in which the governmental nature of the property in question would bring the arbitration agreement under the scrutiny of Article 139. For instance, in *Jahan Profil Pars Company v Ascotec Steel Trading GmbH*,[42] the Tehran Court of Appeal (Chamber 15), in granting an action for a declaration of the invalidity of an arbitration clause contained in a contract between an Iranian company (Jahan Profil Pars) and a German company (Ascotec Steel Trading) on the basis of Article 139, based its ruling on the governmental nature of the German company's capital; that is, the fact that the company's capital belonged to the Iranian government. There, the Court of Appeal first noted that the company was organized under the laws of Germany and thus Germany was the national state of the company. It follows that, on that basis, Article 139 would be inapplicable to the company. Nevertheless, the court noted that, on the facts, the company was wholly owned by the government of Iran. The court thus reasoned that the governmental nature of the company's capital would result in the applicability of Article 139.

Besides the subject-matter arbitrability discussed above, commentators have pointed out that the constitutional constraints relating to the entering into of arbitration agreements by public law persons could be motivated by public policy concerns.[43] If these concerns have a personal aspect, the constraints normally relate to the subjective arbitrability of disputes involving public law entities. Significantly, despite the fact that these limitations are modelled on or influenced by French legislation, French jurisprudence has long established a rule whereby subjective arbitrability constraints do not apply to international disputes. In the words of one commentator:

> The restrictions provided in French law with regard to the arbitrability of disputes concerning the state and state entities have for more than forty years been declared inapplicable to international disputes. A material rule of international law has been put forward by the French Supreme Court in the *Galakis* decision of May 2, 1966. The *'Cour de cassation'* approved the Court of appeal to have decided that the

[39] See eg *Balkan Energy Limited v Ghana*, PCA Case No 2010-7, Interim Award (22 December 2010) para 161.
[40] See n 75 and accompanying text.
[41] See *BIVAC v Paraguay* (n 22) para 69.
[42] *Jahan Profil Pars Company v Ascotec Steel Trading GmbH*, Tehran Court of Appeal, Chamber 15, Judgment No 9209970221401544 (5 June 2013).
[43] Bernard Hanotiau, 'The Law Applicable to the Issue of Arbitrability' (1998) 7 Rev Dr Aff Intern/IBLJ 755, 758.

> prohibition was not applicable to an international contract concluded for the needs and according to conditions which are conform to the usages of international trade.[44]

This approach is consistent with the approach reflected in Article 177(2) of the Swiss Law on Private International Law, which in effect provides that the subjective and objective arbitrability limitations imposed by national legislators are not meant to be relied on in an international arbitration setting:

> A state, or an enterprise held by, or an organization controlled by a state, which is party to an arbitration agreement, cannot invoke its own law in order to contest its capacity to arbitrate or the arbitrability of a dispute covered by the arbitration agreement.[45]

In contrast to the above distinction in French practice between domestic and international arbitration, as far as Article 139 of the Iranian Constitution is concerned, the context of its adoption, as well as the statements made in the course of its drafting, point to a different rationale, namely that it was equally important to create a shield against 'international' arbitration. For example, comments made by one of the members of the Assembly of Experts, the body in charge of the drafting of the post-Revolutionary Iranian Constitution, to the effect that limitations must be imposed on the conduct of arbitration by international institutions, were supported by the vice president of the Assembly of Experts.[46] In addition, despite the fact that the original language of the draft Article 139 merely required that parliament be notified, during the final reading the wording was changed to specifically require parliamentary approval where the other party to the dispute is non-Iranian or the subject matter of the dispute is regarded by law as important.[47]

Additionally, as is apparent from the phrase 'shall in each case be subject to approval' in Article 139, case-specific bills must be prepared by the Council of Ministers in order to obtain approval. At the same time, in light of the delay caused by the approval process, commentators have pointed out that this inevitably would encourage public entities to finalize their contracts hoping that a subsequent approval would be forthcoming.[48] As a result, public entities would be forced to ignore obtaining the approval altogether prior to the signing of the contract. Needless to say, this situation would result in further complexities in terms of the representations made by the Iranian public entities to their foreign contractual counterparties.

Of course, the complexities arising out of the approval requirement contained in Article 139 of the Iranian Constitution may equally affect domestic arbitration involving public law entities. In fact, with regard to the time of authorization by the

[44] ibid 758–59.

[45] See Article 177(2) of the Swiss Law on Private International Law, as reproduced in Gary B Born, *International Arbitration: Documentary Supplement 2011–2012* (Wolters Kluwer 2011) 123.

[46] See Statement of Dr Ayat, Member of the Assembly of Experts (suggesting the insertion of the parliamentary approval requirement for non-domestic cases) quoted in Mohammad-Taghi Abedi, 'Judicial Jurisdiction and Arbitral Jurisdiction' (2010) 41 Int'l L Rev 89, 132 (in Persian).

[47] Abedi (n 46).

[48] ibid 137.

Council of Ministers, recent practice in respect of domestic arbitration reveals a tendency towards less flexibility in granting subsequent authorizations. Whereas with foreign arbitrations in many instances the practice has been to obtain authorization to arbitrate from the Council of Ministers and parliament only after the occurrence of a dispute, a ruling by the Full Court of the CAJ in 2012 annulled the Council of Ministers' subsequent authorization of a referral to arbitration four years after the arbitration clause had been inserted in the contract between a public entity (the Kish Free Zone Organization) and an Iranian private company.[49] This rendered the arbitration clause in a contract between the public entity and the Iranian company practically unenforceable.

Despite the CAJ decision, a review, by the present authors, of the practice in domestic arbitrations in respect of public-private contracts reveals that, in many instances, the Council of Ministers has granted authorization under Article 139 of the Iranian Constitution after the conclusion of the contract and mostly at the time of occurrence of the dispute and its referral to arbitration. In these cases, as required by Article 139, the Council of Ministers has subsequently notified parliament of its authorization on a case-by-case basis.[50] As regards international public-private arbitration, the authorizations issued by the Iranian Parliament have come in the form of a Single Article Act which has been enacted after the conclusion of the contract and at the time of occurrence of the dispute and its referral to arbitration.[51] At the same time, a number of lower courts, while dealing with domestic arbitration disputes, have attempted to interpret the authorization requirement under Article 139 of the Constitution with more flexibility. Thus, a few courts have reasoned that the property belonging to a state corporation must not be deemed state property within the meaning of Article 139 of the Iranian Constitution.[52] This argument is based on a strict corporate law analysis, which focuses on the fact that a state corporation is an independent legal person. As already noted, the Guardian Council, in an unofficial interpretation of Article 139, which has persuasive authority, has made it clear that the term 'state property' also includes the property belonging to state corporations.[53] Unsurprisingly, the judgments containing the above-mentioned distinction have been reversed on appeal.[54]

Furthermore, a number of lower courts have tried to limit the scope of the constitutional authorization requirement by distinguishing between governmental activities and trade-related activities carried out by state corporations, reasoning that the scope of application of Article 139 in domestic arbitration referrals should be limited to governmental or sovereign activities.[55] As with the first argument, the argument based on

[49] Court of Administrative Justice, Case No 376-90/654, Judgment of the Full Court (11 June 2012).

[50] See Single Article Act authorizing the Ministry of Defence to refer the dispute with the Italian company Agusta to arbitration (27 November 1988) <www.majlis.ir/fa/content/about_research_center> accessed 10 December 2024.

[51] See ibid.

[52] See eg Tehran General Court, Chamber 19, Case No 633/87-109/19/88, Judgment No 880559 (11 October 2009) (cited in Eskini (n 37) 39–40).

[53] Eskini (n 37) 36.

[54] See eg Tehran Court of Appeal, Chamber 12, Case No 600/12/88, Judgment No 221200948 (14 September 2009) (cited in Eskini (n 37) 40).

[55] See eg Tehran General Court, Chamber 27, Case No 1341/27/86, Judgment No 102 (3 May 2009) (cited in Eskini (n 37) 39).

the nature of the transaction is also unpersuasive. Arbitration scholars have pointed out that, in addition to the general context of the post-Revolutionary Constitution, which points to a broad conception of state property for the purposes of the Article 139 supervision, other Articles of the Iranian Constitution, as well as the broad and sweeping language of Article 139, confirm that a broad supervision as to the fate of state property was intended by the drafters of the Constitution. For example, Article 55 of the Constitution, which details the scope of the supervisory function exercised by the National Accounting Bureau, specifically refers to 'state companies', providing in relevant part that:

> [i]n the manner instituted by law, the Accounting Bureau monitors or audits all the accounts of the Ministries, organizations, state companies, and other bureaus that use the general budget of the country in some way. This is to ensure that no expenditure exceeds its approved allocation and that all sums are spent for their proper purpose.

It has been argued, as is clear from the passage quoted above, that the fact that state companies are under the financial supervision exercised by the National Accounting Bureau provides further support for the proposition that the control envisaged by Article 139 is not limited to governmental activities.[56] At the same time, as to this question, in addition to a number of lower court decisions there is also a ruling by Chamber 12 of the Tehran Court of Appeal confirming that the authorization requirement contained in Article 139 does not apply to the property of the state corporation in question (the Islamic Republic of Iran Shipping Lines), which is involved in commercial activities.[57] At any rate, it would seem that, on this point, arbitration scholars are on both sides of the debate. The significance of this debate, however, is limited to domestic arbitration.

Article 139 of the Iranian Constitution is also echoed in Article 457 of the Civil Procedure Code of 2000 (amending the original Civil Procedural Code of 1939), which is found in the Code's arbitration section. Even though the section predominantly deals with the regulation of domestic arbitration, Article 457 of the Civil Procedure Code is a notable exception in that it primarily aims at regulating foreign arbitration. In sum, it appears that, despite the intended overprotection against public-private arbitration envisaged in drafting Article 139 of the Iranian Constitution, arbitral case law in domestic cases reveals a more realistic and liberal interpretation of Article 139.

[56] Eskini (n 37) 43.

[57] Tehran Court of Appeal, Chamber 12, Judgment No 232 (21 June 2003) (cited in Arbitral Award No 36/86/35/195 (4 June 2008), as reprinted in Mohammad Kakavand (ed), *Selected Arbitral Awards of Arbitration Center of Iran Chamber (2004–2008)* (Shahr Danesh 2010) 360).

V. The Treatment by Arbitral Tribunals of Article 139-based Objections Raised by Iranian Public Entities and Related Issues

The culmination of the Iranian Revolution in February 1979 brought substantial upheaval to projects that were already being implemented, including procured products which were in various stages of production. At the same time, against the backdrop of the problems ensuing from the Iranian Revolution, the introduction of the restrictions contained in Article 139 of the new Iranian Constitution could potentially have been used to insulate Iranian public entities from the scrutiny of international arbitral tribunals.[58] Unsurprisingly, in their reaction to contract-based claims brought by foreign companies, many Iranian public entities invoked the authorization requirement as contained in Article 139 in order to seek to override arbitration clauses. Jurisdictional objections based on this ground, however, were consistently rejected by various arbitral tribunals. As observed elsewhere:

> The Article 139 argument occupied a prominent place in some of the important arbitration cases of past two decades with foreign parties. Iranian or non-Iranian parties relied on Article 139 to avoid arbitration, however, with rare success. Arbitral tribunals sitting in Europe have not interpreted non-compliance with Article 139 requirements as a bar to the valid formation of the arbitral agreement. For similar reasons, international arbitral tribunals have rejected the arguments of the non-Iranian party that wanted to avoid arbitration based on Article 139.[59]

It is worth pointing out that, during the formative years of the treatment of Article 139 by arbitral tribunals, Iranian parties involved in international arbitral proceedings were predominantly from the public sector. This, in turn, was because of the widespread nationalization which had occurred in the immediate post-Revolutionary period. In the following subsections a number of early cases, which shaped and cemented various issues arising from the constitutional constraints contained in Article 139 of the Iranian Constitution, are reviewed. In addition, the cases of *Defence Industries Organisation of the Ministry of Defence and Support for Armed Forces of the Islamic Republic of Iran (DIO) v International Military Services Ltd (IMS)* and *Benteler v Belgium*, which are directly relevant to the context of the debate, are also reviewed. With respect to *Benteler*, a leading Belgian case which was decided in November 1983, its complementary feature is due to the fact that, unlike the two leading Iranian cases discussed below, namely *Elf Aquitaine* and *Framatome*, the *Benteler* tribunal was not dealing with a newly imposed restriction as to the capacity of public law entities

[58] Mr Nobari, the governor of Iran's Central Bank, who was also the chairman of the committee in charge of handling international claims, brought the issue to the attention of the Guardian Council in October 1980. In his letter, he sought guidance as to the manner in which Article 139 might affect the arbitration clauses contained in the agreements concluded prior to the Iranian Revolution. On that occasion, however, the Guardian Council did not find it necessary to intervene: see Mohammad Salehi (ed), *Articles of the Iranian Constitution in Light of the Opinions of the Guardian Council: Article 139* (Guardian Council Research Centre 2017) 53–54 (in Persian).

[59] Jamal Seifi, 'New Trends – New Actors in Iranian Law Relating to Arbitration' (2000) 75 Philippine LJ 47, 54.

to agree to arbitration. Additionally, as will be discussed below, in *DIO v IMS*, Iran's Ministry of Defence was involved and the treatment of the Article 139 objection by the Dutch courts has been used as authority by a number of arbitral tribunals to dismiss the jurisdictional objections raised by Ghana on the basis of the requirement of parliamentary approval under Article 181(5) of the Ghanaian Constitution.

A. *Elf Aquitaine Iran v National Iranian Oil Company*

The first arbitral award dealing with the implications of the limitation imposed by Article 139 of the Iranian Constitution was the award rendered on 14 January 1982 by Professor Bernhard Gomard in the case of *Elf Aquitaine Iran (ELF) v National Iranian Oil Company (NIOC)*.[60] The dispute arose out of an oil exploration and production agreement entered into in 1966. Upon the discovery of two oil fields by ELF, the oil production began in December 1978. However, ELF claimed that the NIOC had refused to sell oil to ELF at the preferential price provided for in the agreement. Subsequently, on 8 January 1980, the Islamic Republic Revolution Council of Iran passed an Act establishing a Special Committee to review oil agreements. Implementing its mandate under the Act, the Special Committee reviewed the 1966 oil exploration and production agreement with ELF. The review resulted in declaring the contract null and void. On 11 August 1980, ELF was informed of the decision. ELF subsequently resorted to arbitration pursuant to the arbitral clause contained in Article 41 of the Agreement. The Iranian public entity refused to appoint its own arbitrator. Professor Gomard, the sole arbitrator appointed by the President of the Danish Supreme Court in accordance with the arbitration clause, decided to hold the arbitration in Copenhagen.

The NIOC objected to the tribunal's jurisdiction on a number of grounds, including the limitation imposed by Article 139 of the Iranian Constitution. In the view of the NIOC, the new constitutional constraints imposed by Article 139 should be applicable *ex post facto*, thus rendering the arbitration agreement unenforceable. On 14 January 1982, the sole arbitrator rendered a preliminary award rejecting the jurisdictional objections raised by the NIOC. He formulated the question relating to Article 139 of the Constitution as follows:

> Is it possible to conduct an arbitration on the basis of an arbitration clause in a contract between parties of different nationality if the national law of one of the parties does not permit its subjects to take part in arbitration?[61]

In addressing this issue, the sole arbitrator, as an initial matter, noted that the arbitration clause had referred to an explicit choice of the *lex contractus*, thus recording the parties' agreement that:

[60] *Elf Aquitaine Iran v National Iranian Oil Company*, Preliminary Award (14 January 1982) (1986) XI YB Comm Arb 97.

[61] ibid 98.

> the Arbitration Board or the sole arbitrator in arriving at the award, shall in no way be restricted by any specific rule of law, but shall have the power to base his award on considerations of equity and generally recognized principles of law and in particular International Law.

Next, he referred to Article 38(1)(c) of the Statute of the International Court of Justice (ICJ), where 'the general principles of law recognized by civilized nations' are mentioned among the sources of law that the Court shall apply. Combining these elements, Professor Gomard went on to observe that:

> [a] state which has itself entered into an international agreement or has permitted companies or institutions controlled by it to enter into such agreement regulated as *lex contractus* by recognized principles of international law, is not free to change that *lex contractus* by subsequent legislation.[62]

He further noted that, in the preamble to the agreement, the parties had expressed their intention to carry out the provisions of the agreement in a spirit of good faith and goodwill, and that the principle of *pacta sunt servanda* must prevail. The sole arbitrator thus held that the issue of competence-competence would be decided on the basis of the principles of international law.[63] In dealing specifically with the question raised in relation to Article 139 of the new Iranian Constitution, the sole arbitrator reasoned that the links between the government of Iran and the board of directors of the NIOC was close and thus the legal position of Iran as detailed above should also be extended to the NIOC. This analysis led the sole arbitrator to resolve the subjective arbitrability point in favour of ELF as follows:

> The Sole Arbitrator has, therefore – in accordance with considerations of equity and generally recognized principles of international law – reached the conclusion that the arbitration clause of the Agreement cannot be set aside by the Islamic Republic of Iran unilaterally and the Single Article Act and the decision made by the Special Committee under that Act has not deprived the arbitration clause of its operability.[64]

In fact, the *Losinger* case,[65] which was brought before the Permanent Court of International Justice (PCIJ) in November 1935 by Switzerland against Yugoslavia as a diplomatic protection claim for the non-observance of the arbitration clause contained in a state contract, was directly relevant to this aspect of the debate. There, the underlying dilemma was related to the implications of the passage of subsequent legislation for an already existing arbitration clause. The *Losinger* case concerned a contract for the construction of a railway entered into in March 1929 between an American company (substituted in 1931 by the Swiss company Losinger & Co) and

[62] ibid 100–01.
[63] ibid 101.
[64] ibid 104.
[65] *The Losinger & Co Case (Switzerland v Yugoslavia)* (Preliminary Objection) PCIJ Rep Series A/B No 67, 15.

the District of Pozarevac (the Kingdom of Yugoslavia). The contract, which had been approved by the Yugoslav Ministry of Finance, contained an arbitration clause, as well as a choice-of-law clause providing that the contract was governed by the laws of Yugoslavia. In 1933, Losinger had submitted a dispute arising out of the execution of the contract to arbitration. At the time, Mr Henri Thelin, the President of the Swiss Federal Court, was appointed as umpire and ultimately rendered the arbitral award in October 1934. However, in 1934 Yugoslavia enacted a law concerning the conduct of state litigation, which came into force on 19 October 1934, providing in Article 24 that '[a]ctions against the State may only be brought before the ordinary courts of the State.'[66]

Subsequently, in November 1934, Losinger once more resorted to arbitration and Mr Thelin was appointed by his successor to act in the capacity of umpire again. For its part, Yugoslavia invoked the newly enacted legislation to derail the arbitral proceedings, arguing that 'the umpire should declare himself to have no jurisdiction to adjudicate upon the dispute.'[67] In response to Yugoslavia's objection as to the continued validity of the arbitration clause, the umpire suspended the arbitral proceedings. This decision, in turn, triggered the filing of the *Losinger* case before the PCIJ, in which Switzerland asked the court to declare that Yugoslavia could not, by the enactment of subsequent legislation, claim release from the arbitration clause contained in the Losinger contract. In any event, on that occasion, after the preliminary objection ruling (whereby the court joined the objection to the merits), the parties reached a settlement and thus the case was removed from the docket. The issue of continued validity of an already existing arbitration clause in the face of legislative changes in the host state, however, resurfaced after the 1979 Iranian Revolution as a result of the limitation imposed by Article 139 of the Iranian Constitution and, as set out above, the arbitrability point was decided in favour of ELF by Professor Gomard.

B. *Framatome v Atomic Energy Organization of Iran (AEOI)*

In the case of *Framatome v AEOI*, which concerned the nationalization of Framatome's contractual rights, despite the fact that the arbitration clause contained in the agreement had been included prior to the Iranian Revolution, the Iranian public law entity argued that the new constitutional constraints imposed by Article 139 should be applicable *ex post facto*, thus rendering the arbitration agreement unenforceable. AEOI based its position as to the applicability of the Article 139 limitation on the fact that the proper law of the contract was Iranian law, thus arguing that it also included 'the evolution of that law'.[68] In rejecting this argument, the tribunal reasoned that, in the absence of an express provision providing for retroactivity, it would be impossible

[66] ibid 20.
[67] ibid 21.
[68] *Framatome v Atomic Energy Organization of Iran*, ICC Case 3986, Decision on Jurisdiction (30 April 1982) (1983) VIII YB Comm Arb 106. This award (originally in French) was translated and published without mentioning the names of the parties and their nationality. However, the award subsequently was made public and the President of the Tribunal, Professor Pierre Lalive, in a book chapter addressed the Article 139 argument made by the AEOI.

to attach this characteristic to a constitutional text such as Article 139 of the Iranian Constitution. The tribunal further noted that the language of Article 139 itself lacked explicit indications as to its application *ratione temporis*.[69]

The tribunal further observed that it was for AEOI to make a showing that it had been the intention of the drafters of the new Constitution to invalidate, a posteriori, the previously made undertakings to submit potential disputes to arbitration without the approval of the Council of Ministers and Parliament. The tribunal noted that such a showing had not been made or even attempted, because that would be contrary to the principle of effectiveness, particularly given the fundamental importance of the commitment to submit any potential dispute to arbitration.[70] The tribunal further observed that, as a matter of both public and private international law, as well as the law of international arbitration, the arbitration agreement would be enforceable:

> It is superfluous to add that a general principle, universally recognized nowadays in both inter-State relations and international private relations (whether this principle is considered as international public policy, as appertaining to international commercial usages or to recognized principles of public international law and the law of international arbitration or *lex mercatoria*) would in any case prohibit the [Iranian] State – even if it had the intention, which is not the case – to repudiate the undertaking to arbitrate which it made itself or which a public organization such as [AEOI] would have made previously.[71]

As is apparent from the passage quoted above, in the final analysis the main consideration for the *Framatome* tribunal was the principle of good faith, and thus the tribunal did not even find it appropriate to put too much weight on a lack-of-capacity argument based on the new Iranian Constitution. The tribunal also rejected the objective arbitrability objection advanced by AEOI based on the nature of the problem submitted to arbitration, which, according to AEOI, concerned 'the national sovereignty' of Iran.[72] In rejecting the objective arbitrability objection, the tribunal noted that it was not pronouncing upon whether or not Iran was entitled to nationalize. Rather, the tribunal's pronouncements were limited to 'the financial consequences of this [sovereign] decision in relation to the disputed Contract'.[73]

C. *Benteler v Belgium*

Benteler v Belgium, although not specifically an Article 139 case, provides the closest analogy with an Article 139 discussion because of the type of arguments raised by the Belgian government. In this case, Belgium entered into a protocol of agreement with two German companies, E Benteler and H Benteler (Benteler), which contained an

[69] ibid 107.
[70] ibid 108.
[71] ibid 108–09.
[72] ibid 111.
[73] ibid 112.

arbitration clause. The protocol, signed in Brussels in February 1980, concerned the steel industry and involved the industrial and financial restructuring of the Belgian company ABC. Article 14 of the protocol contained an arbitration clause covering all disputes that could arise out of the subject agreement. In 1982, a dispute arose out of the protocol, as a result of which Benteler commenced an arbitration proceeding under Article 14 of the protocol.

However, Belgium raised a jurisdictional objection on the basis of the arbitration limitation contained in Article 1676(2) of its Judicial Code. Belgium argued that, under Article 1676(2), public law entities were permitted to agree to arbitration only by means of an international treaty, whereas in the case at hand the arbitration clause was contained in a contract.[74] It is worth noting that, unlike the situation under Article 139 of the Iranian Constitution where an approval as to the referral to arbitration must be obtained from the relevant authorities, Article 1676(2) of the Belgian Judicial Code contained an outright prohibition to conclude an arbitration agreement.

In addition, Belgium argued that, unlike the position under French law, where the limitation under Article 2060 of the Civil Code does not apply to international arbitration cases, its lack of capacity due to the limitation imposed by Article 1676(2) of the Belgian Civil Code was equally applicable to domestic as well as international cases. This point was developed as follows:

> This text, continued the State, has always been interpreted in the sense of a rigorous prohibition, both by civil courts and the *Conseil d'Etat*. It is true that in a famous line of cases, in particular in *Trésor public v. Galakis* . . . the French *Cour de Cassation* considered that the prohibition of submitting to arbitration only applied to domestic legal relations and that it was not a matter of international public order. However, this precedent is not applicable under Belgian law since the prohibition of submitting to arbitration has been maintained in the *Code Judiciaire*, adopted after the *Galakis* case.[75]

Benteler, for its part, countered that both Belgium and Germany had adhered to the 1961 European Convention on International Commercial Arbitration (Geneva Convention),[76] which specifically addresses the issue of capacity of public law entities entering into arbitration agreements in Article II(1) by providing that 'legal persons considered by the law which is applicable to them as "legal persons of public law" have the right to conclude valid arbitration agreements'. As a subsidiary argument, Benteler also argued that Article 1676 of the Belgian Judicial Code did not apply to

[74] See Jan Paulsson, *The Idea of Arbitration* (OUP 2013) 238.

[75] *Benteler v Belgium*, Award (18 November 1983) (1984) 1(2) J Int'l Arb 184, 185. It is worth pointing out that the Law of 19 May 1998 replaced this provision with a more liberal rule, providing that, in the absence of a statutory provision to the contrary, public law entities may 'enter into an arbitration agreement only where the purpose of that agreement is to settle disputes arising out of the preparation or performance of a contract': Emmanuel Gaillard and John Savage (eds), *Fouchard, Gaillard, Goldman on International Commercial Arbitration* (Kluwer 1999) s 534.

[76] European Convention on International Commercial Arbitration (adopted 21 April 1961, entered into force 7 January 1964) 484 UNTS 349.

international arbitration, and that the Belgian case law invoked by Belgium all related to domestic arbitration.

In rejecting the Belgian argument, the arbitral tribunal based its ruling on the fact that both Belgium and Germany had adhered to the 1961 Geneva Convention, and thus Article II(1) of the Convention was applicable. Moreover, it held, in *obiter*, that there were additional grounds confirming the tribunal's reasoning based on the 1961 Geneva Convention. The tribunal discussed these additional grounds under the heading 'The common law of arbitration' and, in particular, confirmed the reasoning of the French Cour de cassation in the *Galakis* case, where it was found that subjective arbitrability constraints under national law only applied to domestic legal relations and not to international disputes,[77] thus distinguishing between the domestic public order (ie public policy) and the international public order. In the words of one commentator:

> *Benteler v Belgium* thus also provides guidance for the situation in which a State invokes its internal law as a bar to arbitral jurisdiction, but – unlike the case of Belgium – is not bound by a contrary treaty obligation. Although its discussion on this point is *obiter dictum*, the Award clearly approves the rule against recognition of such national bars to international arbitration.[78]

At any rate, the seminal award in *Benteler* cemented the principle that a protected public law entity cannot be permitted to evade arbitration by asserting its lack of capacity to have entered into an arbitration agreement in the first place. In particular, the complementary feature of *Benteler* is due to the fact that, unlike the Iranian leading cases in the 1980s, which concerned the new restrictions imposed by the new Iranian Constitution, the *Benteler* tribunal was not dealing with a newly imposed restriction. Nevertheless, it found that reliance on internal law should not be permissible to invalidate an arbitration clause.

D. *DIO v IMS*: The Application of the *Lizardi* Rule by the Dutch Supreme Court

Likewise, in the *DIO v IMS* case,[79] the Dutch Supreme Court resorted to the well-known *Lizardi* rule, which is essentially based on the principle of good faith, to dismiss a challenge on the basis of Article 139 of the Iranian Constitution made by Iran's Ministry of Defence (DIO).[80] The rule was first established in 1861 by the French

[77] *Trésor Public v Galakis*, Cour de cassation, First Civil Chamber, Petition No 61-12.255 (2 May 1966). The decision and an English translation are available in Thomas Clay and Philippe Pinsolle (eds), *French International Arbitration Law Reports: 1963–2007* (Juris 2014) 11. See also n 44 and accompanying text.

[78] Jan Paulsson, 'May a State Invoke Its Internal Law to Repudiate Consent to International Commercial Arbitration?' (1986) 2 Arb Int'l 90, 97–98.

[79] *Defence Industries Organisation of the Ministry of Defence and Support for Armed Forces of the Islamic Republic of Iran v International Military Services Ltd*, Supreme Court of the Netherlands, NJ 2006/469, Judgment (28 January 2005) ECLI:NL:HR:2005:AR3645 (*DIO v IMS*).

[80] The *Lizardi* rule, as reflected for instance in Article 11 of the Rome Convention on the Law Applicable to Contractual Obligations (also included in the Rome I Regulation), entitled 'Incapacity', reads: 'In a contract concluded between persons who are in the same country, a natural person who would have capacity

Supreme Court in the *Lizardi* case in connection with a lack-of-capacity claim by a foreign minor who would be an adult under French law. As with the rationale behind the concept of apparent authority in agency, which means that the principal is estopped from denying that the agent had authority despite a lack of actual authority, the *Lizardi* rule revolves around the concept of apparent capacity (defeating a lack-of-capacity claim) or apparent authority (defeating a lack-of-authority claim on the part of the directors of a company). In other words, in its developed form, the *Lizardi* rule protects the innocent party reasonably relying on the apparent capacity or authority of the other contracting party in entering into a contract in good faith with that party. Commentators thus have observed:

> A judge or an arbitrator could overlook the lack of capacity of one of the parties (determined by reference to specific substantive rules or to the party's personal law) or the absence of power of a party's representative (determined by reference to substantive rules or to the law of the source of that power) if it were established that the other party entered into the contract in circumstances in which it could legitimately have been unaware of the lack of capacity or absence of power.[81]

At any rate, the dispute in *DIO v IMS* arose out of two contracts concluded in the 1970s for the construction of Chieftain tanks and armoured recovery vehicles. The contracts were terminated on 6 February 1979 due to the upheaval prior to the Iranian Revolution, leaving disputes between the parties as to the balances payable. This led to two related arbitrations under the Arbitration Rules of the International Chamber of Commerce (ICC) which were seated in The Hague, one commenced by DIO and the other by IMS. In the course of the proceedings, DIO filed a set-aside petition on the basis of Article 139 of the Iranian Constitution, claiming its lack of capacity to enter into the arbitration agreement. The District Court of The Hague ruled in favour of DIO in August 2000. The Court of Appeal, however, in its judgment of 27 March 2003, reversed the decision made by the first-instance court, reasoning that IMS had entered into the arbitration agreement in good faith.[82] The Court of Appeal reasoned:

> The principle that a state or organisation belonging to a state – such as DIO – would not be entitled to argue that an agreement it enters into providing for international arbitration is invalid under its own internal laws, is by now a broadly supported international principle.[83]

under the law of that country may invoke his incapacity resulting from another law only if the other party to the contract was aware of this incapacity at the time of the conclusion of the contract or was not aware thereof as a result of negligence.'

[81] Gaillard and Savage (n 75) s 470.

[82] There are five Courts of Appeal in the Netherlands: Amsterdam, Arnhem, The Hague, 's-Hertogenbosch, and Leeuwarden: see Marieke van Hooijdonk and Peter Eijsvoogel, *Litigation in the Netherlands: Civil Procedure, Arbitration and Administrative Litigation* (Kluwer 2009) 6.

[83] See *DIO v IMS* (n 79) para 3.3 (quoting para 4.2 of the Court of Appeal's judgment) (cited in *Balkan Energy v Ghana* (n 39) para 161).

Ultimately, the Dutch Supreme Court upheld the decision rendered by the Court of Appeal, and in so doing essentially relied on the *Lizardi* rule in dismissing the constitutional constraints argument (ie lack of parliamentary approval) advanced by DIO:

> According to Dutch private international law (a) the laws of the country in which the legal person was incorporated are applicable to the question regarding the restrictions on the legal person's authority and the question regarding the external enforceability of such restrictions and (b) no restrictions on authority can be invoked against a counterparty that was not aware and could not have been aware of such restrictions. In international legal transactions in principle the party that acted in good faith with regard to its counterparty's authority to act will be protected.[84]

As is apparent from the reference to the principle of good faith, it should not come as a surprise that, if prior to the conclusion of the contract, the foreign party had already been put on notice by the Iranian public law entity as to the requirement of obtaining an authorization, that notice should be taken into account in assessing the availability of protection under the principle of good faith. Thus, the Dutch Supreme Court went on to state that '[a] contracting party cannot rely on protection of the rule as formulated by the court of appeal if it was aware or should have been aware of the restrictions on authority of its counterparty.'[85]

For example, in a contract between an Iranian public law entity (Iranian Alumina Company) and a foreign company, where the arbitration clause had specifically referred to the authorization requirement as stipulated in Article 139 of the Iranian Constitution, the arbitral tribunal, in distinguishing the situation presented in this case from the established case law discussed above, reasoned that, on the facts, the foreign company had already been put on notice by the Iranian entity in respect of the Article 139 authorization requirement.[86]

In fact, when the Dutch government introduced a bill in April 2013 for the modernization of the 1986 Dutch Arbitration Act (DAA), the modern version of the *Lizardi* rule, specifically focusing on the capacity of public entities, was included in the bill. Ultimately, when the revised DAA passed in 2014, the new Arbitration Act included a provision to that effect.[87] Needless to say, this codification of the modernized version of the *Lizardi* rule further highlights the vital importance of the principle of good faith in this context as well as the related principle of consistency which is the rationale behind the doctrine of estoppel.[88] In fact, in *Bankswitch Ghana v Ghana*, the arbitral tribunal dismissed Ghana's reliance on the parliamentary approval requirement contained in Article 181(5) of the Ghanaian Constitution on the basis of the principle of estoppel. Likewise, in the case of *Balkan Energy v Ghana*, the arbitral tribunal referred to *DIO v IMS* and *Benteler v Belgium* in holding that reliance on

[84] *DIO v IMS* (n 79) para 3.6.2 (cited in *Bankswitch Ghana Ltd (Ghana) v Ghana*, Award Save As to Costs (11 April 2014) para 11.90).

[85] *DIO v IMS* (n 79) para 3.7.2 (cited in *Bankswitch v Ghana* (n 84) para 11.91).

[86] Abedi (n 46) 141–43. The Iranian Parliament did not approve the referral to the arbitration.

[87] For an unofficial translation of the 2014 Act as provided by the Netherlands Arbitration Institute, see <www.nai-nl.org/en/documents/dutch_arbitration_act/> accessed 12 December 2024.

[88] See *Bankswitch v Ghana* (n 84) paras 11.71–11.97.

internal law should not be permissible to invalidate an arbitration agreement. There, the arbitral tribunal also relied on the doctrine of the separability of the arbitration clause, and held that, regardless of whether the main agreement requires the parliamentary approval under Article 181(5) of the Ghanaian Constitution, the arbitration clause remains valid.[89]

E. Article 139 Objections Raised by a Private Party: *Gatoil* and *Westinghouse*

Interestingly enough, relying on the authorization requirement contained in Article 139 of the Iranian Constitution to avert arbitration has not been limited to Iranian public entities. For example, in 1987, Gatoil, a Panama-incorporated company, advanced an Article 139 argument to fend off arbitration. In the case of *Gatoil International Incorporated v National Iranian Oil Company*, which concerned an oil purchase agreement concluded in 1982, Gatoil alleged that short delivery of some 44 million barrels of oil had been made, and thus on 17 March 1987 Gatoil issued a writ which was served on the defendants (NIOC). The response of the defendants was to issue a summons which, among other things, advanced the argument to the effect that, as a result of the arbitration clause contained in the agreement, the action should be stayed. The oil purchase agreement contained an arbitration clause in section 8, entitled 'Arbitration', stating in relevant part:

> Any dispute between the parties arising out of this contract shall be settled by arbitration in accordance with the laws of Iran. The party who wants to submit such a dispute to arbitration shall advise the other party in writing stating therein its claim and nominating its arbitror. The other party shall nominate a second arbitror within 30 days after receiving the said advice. The two arbitrors thus appointed shall appoint a third arbitror who shall be the President of the board of arbitration. Should the other party fail to nominate a second arbitror or should the two arbitrors fail to agree on the appointment of a third arbitror within 30 days, the interested party may request the President of the Appeal Court of Tehran, Iran to appoint the second arbitror or the third arbitror as the case may be.[90]

London's High Court granted the stay under the 1975 English Arbitration Act, which was enacted to give effect to the New York Convention. Before the High Court judge, Gatoil's arguments, including its reliance on Article 139, were aimed at establishing that the arbitration clause was inoperative or incapable of being performed. On appeal, counsel for Gatoil again put the authorization requirement under Article 139 of the Iranian Constitution in issue for the proposition that there was no effective

[89] See *Balkan Energy v Ghana* (Interim Award) (n 39) paras 158–68. The tribunal noted that '[s]eparability acquires a particular significance in this context' (para 159). See further Dominic Dagbanja, 'The Constitutional and Public Law Foundations of Public-Private Arbitration in Ghana' (in this volume) 495.

[90] *Gatoil International Incorporated v National Iranian Oil Company*, Court of Appeal, 1990 WL 10622722, Judgment (22 February 1990) 1–2.

agreement to refer the dispute to arbitration. Gatoil's argument based on Article 139 of the Iranian Constitution was summarized by the Court of Appeal as follows:

> Gatoil argue that there is no effective agreement in Iranian law for the reference of this dispute to arbitration because the approval of the Iranian Assembly, and perhaps Council of Ministers, is needed for the referral of the dispute to arbitration in each case, and that approval has not been sought or obtained for referral of this dispute to arbitration and, accordingly, there is no effective agreement to refer this particular dispute.[91]

In addressing the above argument concerning the validity of the arbitration agreement, Lord Bingham observed that the wording of Article 139, as applied to the facts of the instant case, would suggest that the approval of the Assembly to a referral is necessary. However, in dismissing the appeal, he observed that, although it is for the Iranian public entity to obtain the necessary approval, '[t]he first step would be for Gatoil to ask NIOC to seek the approval of the Assembly or Council of Ministers, which has not been done.'[92] Lord Bingham thus concluded that there was a valid and subsisting arbitration agreement.

Similarly, this approach was further confirmed by the Paris Court of Appeal in considering Gatoil's application to set aside the partial award dated 16 June 1989 rendered by an ICC tribunal seated in Paris relating to another contract in the same contractual arrangements.[93] Thus, the Paris Court of Appeal, relying on the rationale of the Cour de cassation in the *Galakis* decision,[94] dismissed Gatoil's objection to the arbitration agreement based on the authorization requirement under Article 139 of the Iranian Constitution:

> The Court of appeal rejected the objection on the basis that 'international public policy prohibits NIOC to prevail itself of the restrictive provisions of its national law to object a posteriori to the arbitration procedure agreed upon between the parties' and that 'Gatoil is not either authorized to base its challenge of the capacity and powers of NIOC on the provisions of Iranian law while international public policy is not interested by the conditions fixed in this area in the domestic order.' The *Gatoil* decision confirmed that the *Galakis* case-law is applicable to all public entities, whether French or foreign.[95]

In any event, the *Gatoil* precedent was also followed by subsequent arbitral tribunals in dealing with an objection raised by a foreign company respondent in a case brought against it by an Iranian public law entity on the basis of the constitutional constraints contained in Article 139 of the Iranian Constitution. Thus, in the case of

[91] ibid 6.
[92] ibid 7.
[93] *Gatoil International Inc v National Iranian Oil Company*, Paris Court of Appeal (17 December 1991). For an English translation, see (July 1992) 7 International Arbitration Reporter B-1, B-2.
[94] See nn 44 and 77 above and accompanying text.
[95] Hanotiau (n 43) 759.

Westinghouse, which concerned a claim brought by the Iranian Ministry of Defence against Westinghouse Electric Corporation in respect of a contract for the sale of certain air-defence radar equipment, Westinghouse invoked Article 139 of the Iranian Constitution to challenge the validity of the institution of arbitral proceedings against it. The arbitration clause contained in the contract provided in relevant part as follows:

> All disputes arising out of or in relation to or in connection with this Agreement including termination for failure to deliver which cannot amicably be sealed by discussion and mutual accord, shall be finally settled by arbitration at Zurich, Switzerland, in accordance with the rules then in effect of the International Chamber of Commerce.[96]

Framing its Article 139-based objection, Westinghouse argued that, under Iranian law, state agencies need the approval of the Iranian Parliament to refer a case to arbitration where the other party to the dispute in question is a foreigner. Westinghouse further pointed out that the requirement contained in Article 139 of the Iranian Constitution had been routinely invoked by the claimant in cases brought by foreign companies against it.[97]

In dismissing Westinghouse's objection, the arbitral tribunal noted that, as established by the treatment of the issue by various arbitral tribunals, and as further reflected in Article 177(2) of the Swiss Law on Private International Law, the Iranian public law entity itself cannot invoke its own law to contest the arbitrability of a dispute or its capacity to enter into a contract containing an arbitration clause. The *Westinghouse* tribunal thus held that the rule codified in Article 177(2) must equally be applicable in the reverse situation:

> Based on this provision, Claimant itself would be estopped from asserting, as a defence, any lack of parliamentary authorization to sign an arbitration clause. If, however, Claimant itself could not rely on Article 139 of the Constitution (if faced with a lawsuit against it instituted by a party such as Defendant), the Tribunal would find it quite inappropriate to allow Defendant, in the reverse situation (which is the situation at hand) to rely – in its own favour – on Article 139 of the Iranian Constitution and to claim to be afforded a protection thereunder which, as is obvious, was not thought to be available to a foreign party such as Claimant.[98]

In sum, it is safe to conclude that, as far as the lack-of-capacity objection is concerned, it is well-established in international arbitration cases dealing with Article 139 of the Iranian Constitution that, in a public-private arbitration, neither a state entity nor the private contracting party may successfully object to the arbitration agreement previously entered into on the basis of the incapacity of the public contracting party. Needless to say, the main focus has been on state entities to prevent them from

[96] *The Ministry of Defence and Support for Armed Forces of the Islamic Republic of Iran v Westinghouse Electric Corporation*, ICC Case No 7375/CK, Preliminary Award (5 June 1996) para 6.

[97] ibid para 45.

[98] ibid para 59.

questioning the validity of arbitration agreements. Writing in 1987, Lord Mustill distilled the following formulation to reflect the case law dealing with this issue:

> A State entity cannot be permitted to evade the enforcement of its obligations by denying its own capacity to make a binding agreement to arbitrate, or by asserting that the agreement is unenforceable for want of procedural formalities to which the entity is subject.[99]

Similarly, on 12 September 1989, the Institute of International Law adopted a resolution entitled 'Arbitration Between States, State Enterprises, or State Entities, and Foreign Enterprises', specifically addressing the foreign arbitration aspect of this issue, providing in Article 5 that '[a] State, a state enterprise, or a state entity cannot invoke incapacity to arbitrate in order to resist arbitration to which it has agreed.'[100] Commentators have pointed out that this important soft law instrument was intended to confirm the principle as originally stated by the French Cour de cassation in the *Galakis* case,[101] and as firmly established by international arbitral practice in the 1980s.[102]

As concerns the subject-matter arbitrability_ie referral to arbitration of state and public property—if the arbitration is seated outside of Iran, it is unlikely that an arbitral tribunal will find an objection based on Article 139 to be relevant. This is because the subject-matter arbitrability of the dispute will not normally be checked against the law of one of the contracting parties but only against the law of the seat of arbitration.[103] Moreover, considerations of international public policy and good faith would equally apply in the case of subject-matter arbitrability. As became apparent in our review of the Iranian leading cases, for similar reasons arbitral tribunals often try to find a way around an Article 139-based argument and avoid its application.

At the same time, it is important to recognize that the enforcement of an international arbitral award made under the above scenario sought in Iran would, of course, pose a different challenge. That is because, in accordance with Article V.2(a) of the New York Convention, the subject-matter arbitrability of the dispute can be checked against the law of Iran at the time of enforcement, not to mention the application of the public policy of Iran as an additional ground for refusing enforcement under Article V.2(b) of the Convention. There are suggestions by some Iranian commentators for modification of Article 139 of the Iranian Constitution. In this context, it has been remarked that Article 139 may be amended so that a straightforward scrutiny by the Council of Ministers and parliament may be introduced.[104] However,

[99] Michael Mustill, 'The New Lex Mercatoria: The First Twenty-five Years' (1988) 4(2) Arb Int'l 86, 112 (fn omitted). This article was reprinted, with minor changes, from Maarten Bos and Ian Brownlie (eds), *Liber Amicorum for Lord Wilberforce* (Clarendon Press 1987) 149.

[100] See Institut de Droit International (IDI), 'Arbitration Between States, State Enterprises, or State Entities, and Foreign Enterprises' (12 September 1989) art 5 <www.idi-iil.org/app/uploads/2017/06/1989_comp_01_en.pdf> accessed 12 December 2024.

[101] See nn 44 and 77 above and accompanying text.

[102] Gaillard and Savage (n 75) s 557.

[103] See eg art 34.2(b)(i) of the 1985 UNCITRAL Model Law, which provides for the application of the law of the seat to the issue of subject-matter arbitrability, and art 34.2(b)(ii), which provides for the application of the public policy of the seat.

[104] Abedi (n 46) 135.

a modification of Article 139 is a huge task, impractical and unrealistic under the present circumstances. In particular, it is highly unlikely that an issue-specific amendment would be considered and the possibility of introducing a general constitutional amendment in the foreseeable future is low. An official interpretation of Article 139 of the Iranian Constitution in line with prevailing international arbitration principles, by the Guardian Council, is a more practical option. However, even this does not seem to be a priority in the present circumstances.

VI. The Implied or Express Incorporation of Article 139 in the Instruments of Ratification of Investment Treaties

In addition to the contract-based practice discussed above, a possible treatment of an Article 139-based argument by investment arbitration tribunals with respect to investment-related treaties deserves some discussion. The practice relating to the implied or express incorporation of an arbitration-related limitation based on Article 139 of the Constitution during the course of ratification, while applied to both multilateral and bilateral investment treaties, poses a greater challenge with respect to the effectiveness of such reservations in relation to bilateral investment treaties for the reasons outlined below.

As to the practice with respect to international investment agreements (IIAs) containing investor-state dispute settlement (ISDS) mechanisms, two examples are worth mentioning. The first example relates to the investment agreement signed by the Member States of the Organisation of the Islamic Conference (OIC Investment Agreement) in June 1981, which was ratified by Iran in June 1994.[105] In the course of Iran's ratification, the introductory sentence of the submittal document included a general 'compliance with the law' condition relating to the ISDS provision (Article 17) of the OIC Investment Agreement.[106] 'Compliance with the law' also signifies compliance with the Iranian Constitution, including Article 139 thereof.

By contrast, the ratification of the investment protection agreement signed by the Member States of the Economic Cooperation Organization (ECO Investment Agreement) was more complicated. The ECO Investment Agreement, signed in June 2005, contained arbitration provisions both in an ISDS context (Article 9) and with respect to inter-state disputes (Article 10). Again, the introductory sentence of the submittal document included a general 'compliance with the law' condition relating to Articles 9 and 10. However, after the Iranian Parliament approved the submittal document, the Guardian Council did not confirm the ratification process.[107] In particular,

[105] Agreement on Promotion, Protection and Guarantee of Investments amongst the Member States of the Organization of the Islamic Conference (adopted 5 June 1981, entered into force February 1988) <www.oic-oci.org/> accessed 12 December 2024.

[106] The submittal document, which transmits a treaty to the Iranian Parliament for ratification, contains the full text of the treaty as well as an opening paragraph prepared by the government.

[107] As per Article 94 of the Iranian Constitution, such approval is necessary. The provision reads: 'All legislation of the Islamic Consultative Assembly must be sent to the Guardian Council, which must evaluate it within ten days to assure its compatibility with the Constitution and the Islamic criteria. The Council must return the legislation to the Assembly for reconsideration if it is incompatible; otherwise, the legislation can be executed.'

the Guardian Council noted that Article 17(1) of the ECO Investment Agreement had provided that '[t]his Agreement may not be signed with reservation nor shall reservations be admitted at the time of ratification.'[108] Pursuant to Article 19(a) of the Vienna Convention on the Law of Treaties (VCLT), reservations which are expressly prohibited by the treaty are impermissible.[109] The Guardian Council therefore opined that Article 17 of the ECO Investment Agreement would make any reservation in the form of a general 'compliance with the law' condition as contained in the submittal document inapplicable.[110] Ultimately, due to the fact that Iran's foreign policy decision was to ratify the ECO Investment Agreement, the Article 139 dilemma was resolved by deleting the reservation relating to Article 139 of the Constitution.[111]

As to BITs, the Iranian practice relating to the implied or express incorporation of the authorization requirement under Article 139 of the Constitution has been far from uniform or consistent, which poses challenges to arbitrability. This is due to the different forms of wording adopted by the Iranian legislator (which includes the Majlis (ie the Iranian Parliament) and the Guardian Council, both for legislation and for treaty ratification purposes) when formulating reservations to arbitrability, which include either a general reference to Iranian laws or a specific reference to Article 139 of the Constitution in a considerable number of Iran's BITs. In this context, the following categories can be identified.

First, of course, there is a category of BITs mostly concluded at an early stage of Iran's foreign investment policy in the 1990s, such as the BITs concluded with Armenia (May 1995)[112] and Yemen (February 1996),[113] where no implied or express reference to Article 139 of the Iranian Constitution exists in the text of the treaty or in the respective instruments of ratification.

Second, in a few BITs, the ISDS provision contains a 'compliance with the law' phrase. For example, the ISDS provision of the Iran–Italy BIT, concluded in 1999, provides in the arbitration section that the investor may submit the dispute to arbitration 'with due regard to the laws and regulations of the host Contracting Party'.[114]

[108] Agreement on Promotion and Protection of Investment among Member States of the Economic Cooperation Organization (adopted 7 July 2005) <https://investmentpolicy.unctad.org/international-investment-agreements/treaties/bit/3217/eco-investment-agreement> accessed 12 December 2024.

[109] See Ian Brownlie, *Principles of Public International Law* (7th edn, OUP 2008) 613.

[110] See *Articles of the Iranian Constitution in Light of the Opinions of the Guardian Council* (n 58) 41 (in Persian).

[111] ibid 42.

[112] See Agreement on Reciprocal Promotion and Protection of Investments between the Government of the Republic of Armenia and the Government of the Islamic Republic of Iran (signed 6 May 1995, entered into force 26 February 1997) <https://investmentpolicy.unctad.org/international-investment-agreements/treaties/bilateral-investment-treaties/179/armenia---iran-islamic-republic-of-bit-1995-> accessed 12 December 2024.

[113] See Agreement between the Government of the Islamic Republic of Iran and the Government of the Republic of Yemen on the Reciprocal Promotion and Protection of Investments (signed 29 February 1996, entered into force 16 October 2000) <https://investmentpolicy.unctad.org/international-investment-agreements/treaties/bilateral-investment-treaties/2056/iran-islamic-republic-of---yemen-bit-1996-> accessed 12 December 2024.

[114] See Agreement on Reciprocal Promotion and Protection of Investments between the Government of the Italian Republic and the Government of the Islamic Republic of Iran (signed 10 March 1999, entered into force 8 August 2003) art 8(2) <https://investmentpolicy.unctad.org/international-investment-agreements/treaties/bilateral-investment-treaties/2021/iran-islamic-republic-of---italy-bit-1999-> accessed 12 December 2024.

This provision, regardless of its meaning, constitutes a jointly envisaged requirement in the text of the treaty by both contracting states.

Third, in a different category of BITs, a general reservation of 'compliance with the law' has been included in Iran's instruments of ratification.[115] The Single Article Acts ratifying the Iran–Germany BIT[116] and the Iran–Afghanistan BIT[117] are examples of this category.

The fourth and final category refers to BITs to which a specific reservation concerning the observance of Article 139 of the Constitution has been formulated by Iran in its instruments of ratification.[118] The Single Article Acts ratifying the Iran–Singapore BIT[119] and the Iran–Luxembourg BIT[120] fall into this category. It would seem that a specific reference to Article 139 of the Iranian Constitution using sweeping language in more recent instruments of ratification is intended to further clarify the operation of Article 139 of the Constitution.

As is apparent from the above discussion, the insertion of an Article 139 reservation into the ratification instruments of Iran's BITs, either made generally or specifically, poses an important and quite different question of arbitrability. It follows that this issue deserves a separate analysis,[121] rather distinct from the ones experienced in the context of domestic or international commercial arbitration during the past decades. It must be noted that there is no separation of authority for approvals under the latter part of Article 139 and for ratification of treaties under Article 77 of the Constitution. Accordingly, in general a ratification, without reservation, of treaties containing an arbitration provision under Article 77 constitutes an approval under Article 139 of the Constitution concerning the referral to arbitration. However, a ratification of bilateral treaties making the arbitration provision contingent upon, or requiring 'due regard' to, Iranian laws and/or Article 139 presents a different question, in connection with which the following points can be raised.

First, in the case of bilateral treaties, a reservation is effectively 'a counter offer which the other party can accept or reject'.[122] In other words, the flexible approach in determining the admissibility of reservations adopted by the VCLT is limited to multilateral treaties, and in the case of bilateral treaties the principle of the integrity

[115] In a number of the BITs falling into the third category, the general reservations were already envisaged in the Iranian government's submittal documents to the Majlis for ratification, but from a legislative/ratification point of view it is the legislator which has finally approved/ratified the reservation.

[116] See the ratification instrument dated 13 January 2004, available at https://rc.majlis.ir/fa accessed 12 December 2024.

[117] See the ratification instrument dated 19 August 2007, available at ibid.

[118] In a number of the BITs falling into the fourth category, the Article 139 reservations were already envisaged in the Iranian government's submittal documents to the Majlis for ratification but from a legislative/ratification point of view it is the legislator which has finally approved/ratified the reservation.

[119] Iranian Official Gazette No 21623, ratification instrument dated 12 June 2019, available at <https://rc.majlis.ir/fa> accessed 12 December 2024. The Note to this Single Article Act provided: 'Reference of disputes to arbitration by the government of I.R. Iran is subject to observance of . . . Article (139) of the Constitution of the I.R. of Iran.'

[120] Official Gazette No 21623, ratification instrument dated 12 June 2019, available at <https://rc.majlis.ir/fa> accessed 12 December 2024.

[121] The issue was the subject of the first author's presentation at the ICC International Conference on Arbitration in Tehran on 26 November 2018.

[122] See DJ Harris, *Cases and Materials on International Law* (6th edn, Sweet & Maxwell 2004) 811.

of the treaty[123] (under which the reserving state must seek new consent) must always prevail. At any rate, any proposed reservation or modification added unilaterally at the ratification stage through the submittal documents must be notified to the other Contracting Party to an Iranian BIT. However, in view of the principle of integrity applying to international treaties, it is seriously doubtful whether even a proper notification of a reservation would be able to modify a bilateral treaty once adopted, unless of course the reservation is accepted by the other party.

Second, it appears that the dual function of the Iranian Parliament, acting both as the ratifying institution for BITs and as the authorizing body under Article 139, would be a relevant consideration for investment tribunals dealing with a jurisdictional objection on the basis of Article 139. The question here is, when weighing the grant of approval generally associated with the ratification process of a BIT, of which the arbitration provision is an integral part, and the exclusion of Article 139 approval at the same time, which of these two acts should carry weight. In light of the principle of integrity of bilateral treaties it would seem that the reservation would be ineffective. This conclusion could be strengthened if it is noted that the arbitration provision of a BIT constitutes a key and an integral part of the BIT and its object and purpose. In particular, as set out above in section II above, the reasoning of the tribunal in *BIVAC v. Paraguay* implies that conditions concerning Paraguayan compliance with other Paraguayan constitutional or domestic legal requirements regarding its consent to arbitration should have been made in the text of the applicable BIT itself rather than only under domestic law.[124]

VII. Conclusion

Bearing in mind the background of suspicion against the resort to private justice as a means of protecting the public interest which prevailed in Iran, and the developing world generally, for the most part of the second half of the twentieth century, it seems that the constitutional constraints contained in Article 139 of the 1979 Iranian Constitution are a reflection of that concern. The drafting of Article 139 was intended to send the message that safeguards are in place to ensure that the public interest is adequately protected in public-private arbitration by providing a control to the state over referral to arbitration of disputes concerning state and public property. However, despite this perceived overprotection of the public interest, the practicality of the provision of Article 139 in serving its purported use and the balancing of its concerns with private rights and the exigencies of international commerce needed to be considered in actual practice.

As time passed, the need for a mutually acceptable dispute settlement mechanism such as arbitration presented itself both at the domestic and international levels. This led to an array of arbitration-friendly interpretations of Article 139 by commentators and by some courts in Iran, many of which provided only partial and provisional

[123] See *Reservations to the Convention on the Prevention and Punishment of the Crime of Genocide* (Advisory Opinion) [1951] ICJ Rep 15, 21.
[124] See *BIVAC v Paraguay* (n 22) paras 69–72.

solutions to the issue of how best to regulate public-private arbitration. Also, along the line of partial and provisional solutions, it became necessary to grant individual authorizations under Article 139, where the government felt that it was compelling to refer the dispute to arbitration.

At any rate, despite the extent of the debate surrounding Article 139 of the Iranian Constitution and the prevailing needs, a comprehensive solution could not come about. The attempt at the level of government—ie the establishment of the HTC as a public law arbitration body—has encountered serious difficulties, from the point of view of independence and impartiality, as well as the free choices and party autonomy which constitute the essence of present-day arbitration.

At the international level, except where the limitations arising from Article 139 were stipulated in the underlying contract, arbitral tribunals dealing with a jurisdictional objection based on Article 139, whether termed as a subjective arbitrability issue or an objective arbitrability issue, have been very rarely convinced of the merits of the objection. In so doing, they have relied on the law applicable to subject-matter arbitrability as well as considerations of international public policy and good faith in accepting the submission of the dispute to arbitration. The enforceability in Iran of an international arbitral award made under the above scenario is still an open issue, taking into account Article V(2)(a) and V(2)(b) of the New York Convention. There is little doubt that Article 139 has a mandatory character and may thus embody the public policy of the state. As set out above, a number of commentators have suggested that Article 139 should be amended so that a simplified and less intrusive scrutiny of the consent of the state or its agencies by the Council of Ministers and parliament may be introduced. However, it would seem that the modification of Article 139 through a constitutional amendment is impractical and unrealistic under the present circumstances. It appears that an official interpretation of Article 139 by the Guardian Council in line with the prevailing international arbitration principles as articulated by arbitral tribunals is a more practical option.

On a different note, it would seem that the insertion of an Article 139 reservation into the ratification instruments of Iran's BITs, either made generally or specifically, poses a different question of arbitrability from the ones experienced in the context of domestic or international commercial arbitration during the past decades. It appears that the dual function of the Iranian legislature, acting both as the ratifying institution for BITs and as the authorizing body under Article 139, would be a relevant consideration for investment tribunals dealing with a jurisdictional objection on the basis of Article 139.

Furthermore, it would seem that the principles of good faith and international public policy outlined in the context of international commercial arbitration cases would find relevance here. As set out in section VI above, the reasoning of the arbitral tribunal in the case of *BIVAC v Paraguay* implies that conditions concerning Paraguayan compliance with other Paraguayan constitutional or domestic legal requirements regarding its consent to arbitration should have been specified in the text of the underlying Netherlands–Paraguay BIT.[125] In other words, the *BIVAC* tribunal

[125] See *BIVAC v Paraguay* (n 22) paras 69–72.

held that there was no room for implying into the ISDS provision of the BIT additional requirements derived from the legal order of Paraguay. The reasoning of the *BIVAC* tribunal is persuasive. However, unlike the contractual case law, the case law relating to the treatment of Article 139 of the Iranian Constitution by investment arbitration tribunals is yet to develop.

Select Materials

Bibliography

Abedi, Mohammad-Taghi, 'Judicial Jurisdiction and Arbitral Jurisdiction' (2010) 41 Int'l L Rev 89 (in Persian)

Ansari, Vali, *Generalities of Administrative Contracts Law* (4th edn, Hoghooghdan Press 2008)

Atai, Ardeshir, 'Iranian Bilateral Investment Treaties: Substantive Principles and Standards' 2013 (14) JWIT 397

Blackaby, Nigel and others, *Redfern and Hunter on International Arbitration* (5th edn, OUP 2009)

Born, Gary, *International Arbitration: Cases and Materials* (Wolters Kluwer 2011)

El-Kosheri, Ahmed S and Tarek F Riad, 'The Law Governing a New Generation of Petroleum Agreements: Changes in the Arbitration Process' (1986) 1(2) ICSID Review 257

Emadzadeh, Mohammad-Kazem and others, 'Dispute Settlement through Arbitration in the Iranian Administrative Contracts' (2016) 10 Legal Thinkers 95 (in Persian)

Eskini, Rabia, 'Arbitrability of Claims in Iranian Law' in Mohammad Kakavand (ed), *Collection of Articles Dedicated in the Memory of Centennial of Arbitration in Iran* (Shahr-e-Danesh 2011) 33 (in Persian)

Esmaili, Ebrahim, 'Arbitration in Construction Contracts [Work and Materials Contracts] Subject to the General Conditions of Contract' in Mohammad Kakavand (ed), *Collection of Articles Dedicated in the Memory of Centennial of Arbitration in Iran* (Shahr-e-Danesh 2011) 373 (in Persian)

Gaillard, Emmanuel and John Savage (eds), *Fouchard, Gaillard, Goldman on International Commercial Arbitration* (Kluwer Law International 1999)

Hanotiau, Bernard, 'The Law Applicable to the Issue of Arbitrability' (1998) 7 IBLJ 755

Harris, David J, *Cases and Materials on International Law* (6th edn, Sweet & Maxwell 2004)

Maniruzzaman, AFM, 'State Contracts with Aliens: The Question of Unilateral Change by the State in Contemporary International Law' (1992) 9 J Int'l Arb 141

Mustill, Michael, 'The New Lex Mercatoria: The First Twenty-five Years' (1988) 4(2) Arb Int'l 86

Paulsson, Jan, 'May a State Invoke Its Internal Law to Repudiate Consent to International Commercial Arbitration?' (1986) 2 Arb Int'l 90

Seifi, Jamal, 'The New International Commercial Arbitration Act of Iran: Towards Harmony with the UNCITRAL Model Law' (1998) 15(2) J Int'l Arb 5

Seifi, Jamal, 'New Trends – New Actors in Iranian Law Relating to Arbitration' (2000) 75 Philippine LJ 47

Tabatabai-Motamani, Manoochehr, *Administrative Law* (Samt Publication 2008) (in Persian)

Cases

Benteler v Belgium, Award, 18 November 1983, reprinted in (1984) 1(2) J Int'l Arb 184–90

Elf Aquitaine Iran v National Iranian Oil Company, Preliminary Award of 14 January 1982, YBCA, vol XI, 1986, 97

Framatome v Atomic Energy Organization of Iran, April 1982, YBCA, vol VIII, 1983, 94

Gatoil International Incorporated v National Iranian Oil Company, Court of Appeal, Judgment of 22 February 1990, 1990 WL 10622722

Jahan Profil Pars Company v Ascotec Steel Trading GmbH, Judgment No 9209970221401544, Tehran Court of Appeal, Chamber 15 (in Persian)

The Ministry of Defence and Support for Armed Forces of the Islamic Republic of Iran v Westinghouse Electric Corporation, ICC Case No. 7375/CK, Preliminary Award (5 June 1996)

14

The Attorney General as Guardian of the Public Interest and the Evolution of Private-Public Arbitration in Israel

*Tamar Meshel**

I. Introduction

Israel is a parliamentary democracy with a unicameral parliament as legislature (the Knesset), an executive government headed by a prime minister, and a powerful and independent judiciary. The Israeli legal system is code-based and legislation passed by the Knesset generally holds the highest normative status. At the same time, the Israeli judiciary enjoys wide power to create case law, and functions in accordance with the principle of *stare decisis*. In addition, while Israel has no written constitution, it does have a set of 'basic laws' that lay down the foundations of the system of government and the rights of individuals, such as the right to life, human dignity, liberty, privacy, and property. The Israeli Supreme Court has ruled that these basic laws are supreme to regular legislation, which must be interpreted in light of them.[1] As a result of the normative and constitutional supremacy of these basic laws and the principle of judicial review adopted by the Supreme Court, Israel is considered to be a constitutional democracy with a formal, albeit limited and incomplete, constitution.[2]

Israel is also considered to be an arbitration-friendly jurisdiction, both domestically and internationally. It has legislation in support of arbitration, has adopted the United Nations Commission on International Trade Law (UNCITRAL) Model Law, and has long been a signatory to the New York and Washington Conventions. Israel presents a particularly interesting case when examining private-public arbitration since, in spite of its well-established pro-arbitration tradition, arbitrations involving the state or state entities are relatively uncommon, are governed by directives issued by the Attorney General (AG) rather than by legislation,[3] and at one point were disallowed as a general rule. Restrictions placed on private-public arbitrations were

* The author is grateful to Talila Devir for her invaluable assistance in researching for this chapter. The chapter is current as of March 2020.

[1] Adam Shinar, 'Accidental Constitutionalism: The Political Foundations and Implications of Constitution – Making in Israel' in Denis J Galligan and Mila Versteeg (eds), *Social and Political Foundations of Constitutions* (CUP 2013) 212, 216; The Knesset <www.knesset.gov.il> accessed 7 January 2025 (in Hebrew).

[2] Suzie Navot, *The Constitution of Israel: A Contextual Analysis* (Hart Publishing 2014) 32, 44.

[3] Smadar Ottolenghi, *The Law of Arbitration in Israel* (Kluwer Law International 2001) 23.

Tamar Meshel, *The Attorney General as Guardian of the Public Interest and the Evolution of Private-Public Arbitration in Israel* In: *The Comparative Constitutional Foundations of Private-Public Arbitration*. Edited by: Stephan W. Schill, Oxford University Press. © Stephan W. Schill 2025. DOI: 10.1093/9780191987960.003.0014

eased somewhat in 2009 after legislative amendments were passed providing for an appeal option of arbitral awards before the courts, amendments which were designed in part to increase the state's participation in arbitration. Nonetheless, the Israeli government remains reluctant to enter into arbitration agreements and to participate in arbitration proceedings, and its ability to do so continues to be subject, at least formally, to the exclusive approval of the AG.

The rest of this chapter sets out to examine the legal framework governing and regulating private-public arbitrations in Israel and to evaluate its constitutional underpinnings.[4] It will commence in section II with a brief review of the fundamental legal principles governing such arbitrations, while section III will focus on the key role played by the Israeli AG, who occupies a unique position as guardian of the rule of law and the public interest,[5] in arbitrations involving the state. Finally, section IV will compare three main periods in the development of private-public arbitration in Israel, namely 1969–2003, 2003–09, and 2009 to the present, and discuss the constitutional rationales underlying the different stages of its evolution. It will argue that the approach taken by the Israeli government and AG towards private-public arbitration has developed in three periods. The first period emphasized its functional-procedural advantages for the state. The second period featured a restrictive public interest-based prohibition on such arbitration. Finally, the third and present period reached a middle-ground approach which allows for arbitrations involving the state for functional reasons in certain circumstances, but discourages them where public interest considerations such as transparency and government accountability for public funds are at stake. While this latest period, commencing in 2009, may be said to reflect a renewed recognition of the advantages of arbitration in the private-public context, the Israeli government appears to remain careful, if not reluctant, to submit disputes to arbitration.

II. Private-Public Arbitration in Israel

A. General

The Israeli Arbitration Law (AL)[6] is the governing statutory framework for arbitration in Israel, accompanied by the Regulations for Procedure in Matters of Arbitration.[7] Prior to the enactment of the AL in 1968 the law governing arbitration in Israel was the 1926 Arbitration Ordinance, which was based on the English Arbitration Law of 1889.[8] The AL is not based on the UNCITRAL Model Law but, rather, reflects an evolution from this former British legislation and an attempt to rectify some the faults of the Arbitration Ordinance, such as the ability of parties to prolong arbitration

[4] Since there have been no investment treaty arbitrations involving Israel to date, investment arbitration is not addressed in this chapter.
[5] Navot (n 2) 167.
[6] חוק הבוררות, תשכ"ט-1968 (Israeli Arbitration Law, 1968) (AL).
[7] תקנות סדרי הדין בעניני בוררות תשכ"ט-1968 (Regulations for Procedure in Matters of Arbitration, 1968).
[8] Ottolenghi (n 4) 3.

proceedings and the need for frequent court intervention.[9] The AL has been amended four times, in 1974, in 2008, and twice in 2018. Parties cannot opt out of the application of the AL once they have agreed to submit a dispute to arbitration, but they also cannot waive their right of access to the courts, since this is viewed as a violation of public interest. Therefore, the Israeli courts have held that even where parties have agreed to arbitration, this agreement merely reflects their preference regarding the judicial forum in which their dispute is to be resolved and they still maintain the right to commence proceedings before the courts.[10] Under the AL, however, the court shall stay such proceedings in favour of arbitration unless it finds that there is a 'special reason' why the dispute should not be referred to arbitration.[11]

Most private-public arbitrations in Israel are not governed by any specific statute and therefore also fall under the AL,[12] which provides that 'the State shall have the same status as any other person, provided that the Civil Procedure Amendment (The State as a Party) Law, 5718–1958, shall apply to an arbitration to which the State is a party'.[13] The Civil Procedure Amendment (The State as a Party) Law[14] provides that, for the purpose of any civil procedure, the state shall be considered as any other person and shall be subject to the same rules and procedures, with the exception that it cannot be required to pay fees or deposits or to provide guarantees or assurances.[15] This law applies to the state and 'State institutions' other than corporations,[16] which has been interpreted by the Israeli courts to include, inter alia, government ministries, the State Comptroller,[17] the Land Registrar and Israel Land Administration,[18] and the Israeli Police and Israeli Defence Forces.[19] On the other hand, the Official Receiver in its capacity as permanent liquidator of a company,[20] and the Israel Land

[9] *להב לשכת העצמאים בישראל נ' יעקב ורקר (Lahav Independents Bureau in Israel v Yaakov Verker)* Supreme Court of Israel 6187/ 93 (24 March 1994); Ottolenghi (n 4) 3; Noam Ebner and others, 'Alternative Dispute Resolution in Israel' in Giuseppe De Palo and Mary B Trevor (eds), *Global Trends in Mediation: The Southern Mediterranean* (Kluwer Law International 2007) vol II, 6.

[10] Smadar Ottolenghi, *בוררות דין ונוהל (Arbitral Law and Procedure)* (4th edn, Bursi Publications 2005) vol A, 15–16 (in Hebrew). See also eg מדינת ישראל נ' בועז רייטר (המנוח) *(State of Israel v Boaz Raiter (late))* Central District Court 56572-06-18 (5 November 2018), where the District Court refused to stay the proceedings in favour of arbitration since the case concerned the exercise of administrative functions relating to illegal land use that were of broader public importance. Accordingly, the court held that the public interest requiring such issues to be resolved publicly by the courts must be given considerable weight.

[11] AL (n 7) art 5.

[12] However, some types of private-public arbitrations are governed by special laws such as those concerning labour relations and cooperative societies: Ottolenghi (n 4) 3.

[13] AL (n 7) art 36.

[14] חוק לתיקון סדרי הדין האזרחי (המדינה כבעל דין), 1958 (Civil Procedure Amendment Law (The State as a Party), 1958) (Civil Procedure Amendment Law).

[15] ibid arts 1, 2, 8.

[16] ibid art 11.

[17] *מדינת ישראל (משרד הבינוי והשיכון)נ' אפרופים שיכון וייזום (1991) בע"מ (The State of Israel – Ministry of Housing v Apropim Housing and Development (1991) Ltd)* Supreme Court of Israel 5985/03 (3 November 2003).

[18] *עבד-אללה בלעום ואח' נ' מינהל מקרקעי ישראל, ו-2 אח' (Abed-Alla Balum et al v the Israel Land Administration et al)* Supreme Court of Israel 570/66 (31 January 1967); *משה פיכטנבוים נ' רשם המקרקעין (Moshe Fichtenbaum v The Land Registrar)* Supreme Court of Israel 258/88 (19 April 1990).

[19] *מדינת ישראל משרד הביטחון נ' פלוני (The State of Israel – Ministry of Defense v Jon Doe)* Supreme Court of Israel 4826/12 (7 August 2012).

[20] *כרמל אולפינים בע"מ נ' תעשיות אלקטרוכימיות 1952בע"מ (בפירוק) (Karmel Ulpinim Ltd v Electrochemical Industries Ltd (in liquidation))* Supreme Court of Israel 9567/08 (5 January 2011).

Administrator in its capacity as representative of the Development Authority (a public corporation),[21] are not considered as acting on behalf of the state and have therefore been excluded from the definition of 'State institutions' by the courts.

B. Commencing Arbitration

The existence of a binding arbitration agreement in private-public disputes, as in private-private disputes, is assessed in accordance with the AL, and, where the AL is silent, in accordance with general rules of contract law. In the case of contradictions between the provisions of the AL and the Contracts (General Part) Law, the former shall prevail.[22] According to the AL, in order to conclude a valid arbitration agreement it must be in writing and the parties must consent to it. With regard to the writing requirement, while the AL does not apply to an arbitration agreement which is not evidenced in writing, such an agreement would still be recognized as a binding contract between the parties and the Contracts Law would apply to it. Accordingly, should one of the parties file a claim in court despite the unwritten arbitration agreement, the other party would not be able to request a stay of proceedings pursuant to the AL but could file a claim for breach of contract.[23] As for the consent requirement, such consent may be evidenced by the parties' signature, but a signature is not required and other factors, such as appearance before the arbitrator, can also evidence consent to arbitrate.[24] One exception to this, however, exists in the case of state entities that are governed by specific legal frameworks setting out the functionaries whose signature is required to bind the entity, such as the Municipalities Ordinance or Local Councils Order.[25] The Israeli Supreme Court has held that, as a general rule, a public authority cannot be obligated to arbitrate where it has not signed the arbitration agreement in the manner prescribed by such *lex specialis*.[26] In addition, where a state entity has not obtained the required governmental authorization to enter into an arbitration agreement, the courts have held that the agreement may be invalid.[27] What such governmental authorization entails will be discussed in the next section.

As for subject matter capable of being submitted to arbitration, the AL provides that an agreement to arbitrate a matter that cannot be the subject of an agreement between the parties is invalid.[28] Subject matters that have been found to be non-arbitrable

[21] *מדינת ישראל נ' יעקב לוי (The State of Israel v Yaakov Levy)* Supreme Court of Israel 141/75 (22 March 1976).

[22] Ottolenghi (n 4) 7–8.

[23] AL (n 7) art 39; Ottolenghi (n 4) 17–18.

[24] AL (n 7) art 1; Ottolenghi (n 4) 22–23, 27.

[25] Ottolenghi (n 4) 26.

[26] *המועצה המקומית "יסוד המעלה" נ' אורי מילוסלבסקי (Yessod Ha'maala Local Municipality v Uri Miloslavsky)* Supreme Court of Israel 449/73 (9 January 1974), although the court in this case ultimately confirmed the arbitral award, finding that it did not cause the state entity any injustice: Ottolenghi (n 4) 27.

[27] See eg *אלסינט בע"מ נ' מדינת ישראל (Alsint Ltd v the State of Israel) Supreme Court of Israel* 569/80 (30 July 1981); *ועד ההורים העירוני בהרצליה נ' עיריית הרצליה (Hertzelia City Parents Association v Hertzelia City Hall)* Tel-Aviv District Court 156/97 (10 March 2004).

[28] AL (n 7) art 3. See also eg *אליהו אמינוף נ' שמואל אלטלף (Eliyahu Aminof v Shmuel Altalef)* High Court of Justice 816/98 (23 June 1998).

include certain illegal matters, matter relating to personal status, rights in rem, certain corporate matters, and some labour issues,[29] matters that violate public policy, those that are addressed in a binding and exclusive manner in a statute, matters that common sense dictates are not arbitrable, matters concerning administrative or regulatory powers,[30] and constitutional matters.[31] With regard to constitutional matters, the Israeli Supreme Court has ruled that, in light of their complexity, significance, and impact on the public at large, they should be resolved by the courts rather than in private proceedings that are detached from substantive and procedural rules, and which lack transparency and judicial oversight.[32] Therefore, such matters should be defined narrowly and be limited to cases where there is a clear public interest justifying their exclusion from arbitration.[33] These would include, inter alia, matters that are directly related to the violation of constitutional basic rights, the legality of actions taken by legal bodies such as associations, and elections.[34] For instance, a dispute concerning relations between the citizen and the state, such as the constitutionality of Knesset legislation, was found to be unsuitable for resolution by arbitration.[35]

C. Confidentiality

Although confidentiality is one of the cornerstones of arbitration, it is not expressly provided for either in the AL or any other statute. However, the Evidence Ordinance includes a chapter on confidential evidence, which applies also to arbitration. The chapter protects privileged evidence and evidence that may damage national security, the state's foreign relations, or an important public interest.[36] The parties may also include a confidentiality provision in their arbitration agreement or the arbitrator may issue an order concerning confidentiality, unless instructed otherwise by the parties ahead of the proceedings. It has also been said that a general duty of confidentiality exists in arbitration in light of the nature of process and the protection afforded by the Israeli Privacy Law, 1981 and Basic Law: Human Dignity and Freedom, which would trump the interests of third parties in information disclosed in arbitration.[37]

[29] Jan Paulsson, 'National Report for Israel' in Jan Paulsson (ed), *International Handbook on Commercial Arbitration* (Kluwer Law International 1984) supp no 76, October 2013; Ottolenghi (n 4) 48–77.

[30] See eg מדינת ישראל נ' מנהלת ההתפלה H2ID בע"מ *(State of Israel – Desalination Administration v H2ID Ltd)* Supreme Court of Israel 2279/16 (1 May 2016), where the Supreme Court noted that had the dispute concerned administrative or regulatory powers it could not have been resolved in arbitration.

[31] Ottolenghi (n 4) 48, 78–79; Ottolenghi (n 11) 14.

[32] *הסתדרות המהנדסים, האדריכלים והאקדמאים במקצועות הטכנולוגיים נ' הסתדרות העובדים הכללית החדשה* (*The Union of Engineers, Architects and Academics in Technological Professions v The New General Histadrut Labor Federation*) Supreme Court of Israel 9048/05 (20 October 2009) paras 44, 46.

[33] ibid para 47.

[34] ibid para 48; *עותמן - פקיד הבחירות לישוב ביר אל מכסור (Ottman – Bir el Maksur Election Officer)* Election Appeal 3971/93 (not published); *מפלגת העבודה הישראלית נ' התסדרות העובדים הכללית החדשה (Israeli Labor Party v The New General Histadrut Labor Federation)* Tel-Aviv District Court 107/02 (10 February 2002), cited in Ottolenghi (n 11) 188; *אילן לוי נ' הגושרים אגודה שיתופית חקלאית (Ilan Levi v Hagoshrim Cooperative Agricultural Society)* Tel-Aviv District Court 58/10 (12 October 2010) (Appeal to the Supreme Court filed 21 October 2014).

[35] *מפעלי ים המלח בע"מ נ' מדינת ישראל – ממשלת ישראל (Dead Sea Factories Ltd v the State of Israel-the Government of Israel)* Jerusalem District Court 49394-04-14 (1 October 2014).

[36] פקודת הראיות [נוסח חדש], תשל"א-1971 (Evidence Ordinance [New Version], 1971) ch 3.

[37] Ottolenghi (n 11) 671–72.

This duty has been upheld by the Israeli courts, finding, for instance, that the confidential nature of arbitration was in line with the basic human right to privacy and that parties to arbitration had a legitimate expectation that it would remain confidential.[38]

However, a duty of confidentiality has also been rejected by the courts in some cases, particularly where an important public interest was involved. For instance, in a class action against the Israeli Electric Company, the courts found that arbitration documents should be disclosed since the matter concerned a hidden charge illegally levied on consumers.[39] Similarly, in a case concerning a request by the national income tax inspector that an arbitrator disclose documents submitted in an arbitration, which the arbitrator refused to do, the courts found that in balancing the parties' interest in the confidentiality of the arbitration and the public interest in determining the correct tax to levy on them, the public interest prevailed.[40] In light of this general approach adopted by the Israeli courts, and since the issue of the confidentiality of arbitrations is not clearly anchored in legislation,[41] it may be particularly limited in private-public arbitrations, as will be discussed further below.

D. Setting Aside and Appeal

The AL allows parties to apply to the court to set aside a domestic arbitral award. The court may, in its discretion, set aside an award on any of the following grounds:[42]

- There was no valid arbitration agreement.
- The award was made by an arbitrator not properly appointed.
- The arbitrator acted without authority or exceeded the authority vested in him or her in the arbitration agreement.
- A party was not given a suitable opportunity to state his or her case or to produce his or her evidence.
- The arbitrator did not decide one of the matters referred to him or her for determination.
- It was stipulated in the arbitration that the arbitrator shall state the reasons for the award and the arbitrator did not do so.

[38] *י.מ עיני קונדיטוריה בע"מ נ' בנק לאומי לישראל בע"מ (YM Einy Bakrey Ltd v Bank Leumi Le Israel)* Supreme Court of Israel 4781/12 (6 March 2013).

[39] *לוי אליעזר נ' חברת החשמל לישראל בע"מ (Levi Eliezer v the Israeli Electric Company Ltd)* Tel-Aviv District Court 11288/01 (24 December 2001), cited in Ottolenghi (n 11) 673–74.

[40] *וינמן, הרב, בורר נ' מפקח ארצי, היחידה הארצית לשומה אגף מס הכנסה ומס רכוש (Veinman, Rabbi, Arbitrator v National Inspector, National Assessment Unit Department of Income and Property Tax)* Beer-Sheva District Court 1065/96 (21 July 1997), cited in Ottolenghi (n 11) 675–76. It should be noted that there is also a statutory requirement of disclosure in the Israeli Income Tax Ordinance.

[41] *מפעלי ים המלח בע"מ נ' מדינת ישראל - משרד האוצר (Dead Sea Factories Ltd v the State of Israel-Ministry of Finance)* Supreme Court of Israel 37987-01-13 (15 July 2013). See also הנתיב המהיר בע"מ נ' כביש חוצה ישראל בע"מ *(Fast Lane Ltd v Trans Israel Highway Ltd)* District Court of Jerusalem 16864-03-14 (4 May 2014); הנתיב המהיר בע"מ נ' כביש חוצה ישראל בע"מ *(Fast Lane Ltd v Trans Israel Highway Ltd)* District Court of Jerusalem 49820-09-12 (12 June 2014).

[42] AL (n 7) art 24.

- It was stipulated in the arbitration agreement that the arbitrator shall decide in accordance with the law and the arbitrator did not do so.
- The award was made after the period for making it had expired.
- The content of the award is contrary to public policy.
- There is a ground on which a court would have set aside a final, non-appealable judgment.

This list is exhaustive, and the court may refuse to set aside an arbitral award even where one or more of the enumerated grounds are proven if it is of the opinion that no miscarriage of justice has occurred.[43] The Israeli courts have also generally interpreted these grounds for setting aside narrowly, and have consistently refused to serve as an appellate court over arbitral awards in setting-aside applications.[44] Moreover, the court shall not set aside the entire arbitral award where it is possible to set it aside in part, supplement it, correct it, or remit it to the arbitrator.[45]

The mere fact that the state is party to an arbitration will not necessarily affect the courts' application of the general principles governing setting aside. For instance, the courts have applied a narrow interpretation of the 'public policy' ground for setting aside also in disputes involving the state. In such disputes, the courts have found that, at least where the dispute is of a purely commercial nature, this ground is satisfied only where the content, rather than the result, of an arbitral award amounts to 'a violation of the interests, principles, and values our society seeks to preserve'.[46] In one such case, both the District Court and Supreme Court found that, since the dispute was financial and 'did not raise questions of values related to our moral or cultural views or fundamental concepts of justice', there was no reason to set aside the award on public policy grounds. The Supreme Court further held that the fact that the monetary amount awarded in the arbitration was high did not constitute a violation of public policy since this did not relate to the content of the award. It should be noted, however, that in this case the amount was awarded in favour of the state rather than against it.[47]

As part of the 2008 amendments to the AL, two appeal options were added, which are subject to the stipulation of the parties in the arbitration agreement. The first option[48] provides for an appeal before the arbitrator, in which case the arbitrator's decision may not be further appealed to the courts, and an application to set aside the award may only be brought on the ground of violation of public policy or 'a ground on which a court would have set aside a final, non-appealable judgment'.[49] Schedule 2 of the AL includes a set of procedures for submitting and conducting such an appeal.[50]

[43] AL (n 7) art 26(a).

[44] Ottolenghi (n 4) 391, 395.

[45] AL (n 7) art 26(b).

[46] *כרמל התפלה בע"מ נ' מדינת ישראל משרד האוצר (Karmel Desalination Ltd v the State or Israel Ministry of Finance)* Jerusalem District Court 5094/06 (16 December 2007).

[47] *כרמל התפלה בע"מ נ' מדינת ישראל - משרד האוצר (Karmel Desalination Ltd v the State or Israel-Ministry of Finance)* Supreme Court of Israel 470/08 (4 March 2010).

[48] AL (n 7) art 21a.

[49] ibid art 24(10).

[50] AL (n 7) sch 2. This schedule was amended in 2018 to streamline the process for an appeal before the arbitrator, הצעת חוק הבוררות (תיקון מס' 3) (ערעור לפני בורר), התשע"ח–2018 (ה"ח הכנסת תשע"ח מס' 758 בעמ' 94 פורסם ביום 5.2.2018) (Amendment No 3 to the Arbitration Act, 2018, 5 March 2018).

The second appeal option provides for an appeal with leave before the court where there is 'a fundamental mistake in applying the law which may cause miscarriage of justice'. Such appeal therefore requires the arbitral award to be based on substantive law. Where an appeal of an award has been submitted to the court, it 'shall not entertain an application for setting aside the award, and in the appeal the parties may raise arguments concerning the setting aside of the award pursuant to any of the grounds as set out in [the AL]'.[51] As will be further discussed below, one of the main rationales for adding this second appeal option was to encourage the state to participate in arbitrations.[52]

III. The Attorney General of Israel—Guardian of the Public Interest

The position of AG in Israel is a powerful and complex one. The institution has been said to 'code symbols of right and wrong, impress ways of behaviour and norms and shape the law',[53] and its scope of responsibility and authority is virtually unparalleled among modern democracies.[54] Although one of the most powerful public posts in Israel, the broad powers of the AG, which are held by a single individual,[55] are not prescribed in a single statute nor mentioned in any constitutional text, and no basic law applies to the office.[56] In addition to its role as Israel's chief prosecutor, the AG also serves as legal advisor to the government and is viewed as the 'authorized interpreter of the law', whose legal opinion is binding on the government, who cannot act contrary to it so long as the courts have not ruled otherwise.[57] Another important function of the AG is as head of the litigation branch of the government, which affords him or her the exclusive right to represent the government in any legal proceedings,[58] including

[51] AL art 29(b).

[52] Setty (n 51). A further amendment to the AL that was proposed in 2011 would grant parties a right of appeal of arbitral awards before the courts without the need to seek leave, according to the same rules and procedures applicable to an appeal of court decisions, הצעת חוק בתי המשפט (בוררות חובה) (הוראת שעה),התשע"א-2011 (Courts Law (Mandatory Arbitration) Bill (Temporary Order), 2011). This bill went through first reading on 12 February 2014 <https://oknesset.org/vote/6896/> accessed 4 August 2015.

[53] Gad Barzilai, 'The Attorney General and the State Prosecutor – Is Institutional Separation Warranted?' The Israel Democracy Institute, Policy Paper 84 (July 2010) (in Hebrew) <www.idi.org.il/media/256770/pp_84.pdf> accessed 4 August 2015.

[54] ibid 47.

[55] This is a result of historical developments and the strong personalities of Israeli AGs over time: Navot (n 2) 169.

[56] ibid 168.

[57] Navot (n 2) 168, 173; Israel Ministry of Foreign Affairs, 'The Attorney General' <http://mfa.gov.il/MFA/AboutIsrael/Spotlight/Pages/The%20Attorney%20General.aspx> accessed 4 August 2015; Ruth Lapidoth, 'National Treaty Law and Practice: Israel' in Duncan Hollis and others (eds), *National Treaty Law and Practice: Dedicated to the Memory of Monroe Leigh* (Martinus Nijhoff 2005) 385; Yoav Dotan, *Lawyering for the Rule of Law* (CUP 2014) 55.

[58] Civil Procedure Amendment Law (n 15) art 4; Dotan (n 59) 57. The AG may appoint external lawyers as their agents; however, such lawyers are subject to the AG directives and must receive the AG's approval in order to refer a case to arbitration: Ministry of Justice, Civil Enforcement and Outsourcing Unit <http://index.justice.gov.il/Units/CivilEnforcementOutsourcingUnit/Pages/WorkRegilations.asp> accessed 4 August 2015 (in Hebrew).

in arbitrations.[59] Some argue that, in exercising this function, the AG not only acts as the government's lawyer, but also 'as the lawyer of the people, as a watchdog over the government',[60] so as to ensure that the government observes the principles of equality before the law, human rights, and fairness and reasonableness in its relations with citizens.[61] Relatedly, the AG is also tasked with protecting public interests and may intervene in court proceedings in order to do so.[62] This latter function not only supports the AG's position as 'the ultimate representative of the public interest and the rule of law' but also enables him or her to attack the government in court whenever the public interest might be threatened.[63] The AG may also refuse to represent the government in court or argue that an action of the government is illegal.[64]

In 1951, the Israeli government exclusively authorized the AG to enter into arbitration agreements on its behalf.[65] Since arbitration was viewed as 'a legal proceeding for all intents and purposes',[66] the matter of arbitrations involving the state or state entities has since been governed by directives issued by the AG, which have subjected the government's consent to, and participation in, arbitration to the AG's approval.[67] These directives, discussed in detail in the next section, reflect the development of the AG's approach to private-public arbitration, from emphasizing its advantages for the state as a party to disputes, to a largely adverse, or at best reluctant, view of its use on public interest grounds. This evolution in the AG's approach to private-public arbitration may have resulted in part from the growing complexity of its role, as described above, between the 1950s and 1990s. While in the 1950s the office of the AG was largely focused on the traditional task of representing the government before the courts, beginning in the 1970s the AG rose in influence and its role as watchdog of the government became more pronounced. During this time, for instance, the AG began initiating criminal proceedings against senior politicians and advising the government in political matters. It thus became 'an organ that had as one of its primary functions to *supervise the government* and to assure that it

[59] *מדינת ישראל נ' יעקב שמשון שפירא (The State of Israel v Yaakov Shimshon Shapira)* Tel-Aviv District Court 6056/75 (1 January 1976).

[60] Dotan (n 59) 57–58.

[61] Yitzhak Zamir, 'The Attorney General: Servant of the Public and not of the Government' (January 1989) 5 Bar Assoc Newsletter 453.

[62] Navot (n 2) 168; Civil Procedure Ordinance (appearance of the Attorney General) [New Formulation] (פקודת סדרי הדין (התייצבות היועץ המשפטי לממשלה) [נוסח חדש]); מדינת ישראל נ' אבי פיקאלי (*State of Israel v Pikali*) Supreme Court of Israel, 4123/19 (July 1, 2019). The AG is also authorized, for instance, to appeal the results of Knesset elections: Amnon Rubinshtein and Barak Medinah, *המשפט החוקתי של מדינת ישראל - עקרונות יסוד (The Constitutional Law of Israel – Basic Principles)* (Schocken Publishing 2005) 1000, fn 28 (in Hebrew); Ruth Gavizon, '*היועץ המשפטי לממשלה:בחינה ביקורתית של מגמות חדשות*' ('The Attorney General: A Critical Examination of New Trends') (September 1996) 5 Plilim 34, 45–47 (in Hebrew).

[63] Dotan (n 59) 60.

[64] Navot (n 2) 174.

[65] Yalkut Pirsumim 143, 22 February 1951 <www.nevo.co.il/law_html/Law10/yalkut-0143.pdf> accessed 4 August 2015 (in Hebrew).

[66] Attorney General Directive No 6.1205, 'יישוב סכסוכים שהמדינה צד להם באמצעות בוררות' ('Resolution of Disputes to Which the State Is a Party by Arbitration') (12 October 2009) <http://index.justice.gov.il/Units/YoezMespati/HanchayotNew/Seven/61205.pdf> accessed 4 August 2015 (in Hebrew) (2009 Directive).

[67] Ottolenghi (n 4) 23.

is acting in accordance with the concept of the rule of law'.[68] By the 1990s, the AG was carrying out its duties while 't[aking] into consideration the public interest as [it] understood it'.[69] The department tasked with representing the government before the Israeli High Court of Justice,[70] in particular, was primarily functioning as a 'supervisory organ that seeks to promote the general values of the rule of law in the government'.[71]

This evolution in the AG's view of its own role, therefore, may have also influenced its approach towards the use of private-public arbitration in light of the broader public interests associated with it, such as transparency, accountability of the government, and the various legal and budgetary implications that go beyond the interests of the parties, of which the AG now perceived itself as guardian. In order to protect such interests and to ensure that the government was not acting illegally, the AG office came to view the supervision of the courts as crucial and therefore discouraged the government from settling or using arbitration to resolve disputes, particularly those involving public law matters.[72] Moreover, the AG office also reportedly came to view 'its accountability towards the court on the institutional and ideological level as no less important than its professional duty toward its client agencies'.[73] Further factors that may have also contributed to the development of the AG's cautious approach towards private-public arbitrations include the absence of accountability in the arbitral process in light of its lack of a right of appeal, at least prior to the 2008 amendments to the AL discussed further below, and the fact that rule-of-law values may be perceived as weaker or entirely missing from a private confidential dispute resolution proceeding that is not necessarily subject to procedural and substantive laws.[74] Ultimately, it seems that the main principle guiding the AG gradually shifted from the representation of government interests to the legality of government conduct, which is in turn based in part on the rule that every administrative decision is subject to judicial review.[75] The next section will examine the three AG directives concerning arbitrations involving the state, issued in 1969, 2003, and 2009, and discuss how they reflect the AG's evolving approach to such arbitrations.

[68] Dotan (n 59) 81 (emphasis in original).

[69] ibid.

[70] This department is in charge of representing almost all government agencies before the Supreme Court of Israel on public law matters (ibid 3–4).

[71] ibid 87.

[72] Ariel Bendor, 'מגמות במשפט ציבורי בישראל:בין משפט לשפיטה' ('Trends in Israeli Public Law: Between Law and Adjudication') (2011–12) 14 Mishpat ve Memshal 388 (in Hebrew).

[73] Dotan (n 59) 87.

[74] Israel Shimoni, *Arbitration Laws: A New Horizon in Arbitration* (2nd edn, Bursi 2014) 626; Daphna Lavie, 'לא על הבוררות לבדה ולא על הגישור לבדו הצעה לאימוצו של הגישבור כמענה המתגבר על חולשותיו של מוסד הבוררות בישראל' ('Not on Arbitration Alone and not on Mediation Alone: A Proposal for the Adoption of Arb-Med as a Response to the Weaknesses of Arbitration in Israel') (2012) 41 Mishpatim 595 (in Hebrew).

[75] Zamir (n 63) 418.

IV. The Evolution of Private-Public Arbitration in Israel

A. 1969–2003

The first AG directive concerning arbitrations involving the state was issued in 1969,[76] and is no longer in force. This directive distinguished between two scenarios. The first was where a government body considered arbitration after a dispute had already arisen,[77] in which case the directive provided that the dispute should generally be resolved by the courts[78] unless:

- the dispute involved a 'public body' or a 'State-owned company';
- issues of national security, foreign relations, secrecy or an unwanted 'public echo' were involved;
- arbitration would produce faster and more efficient results;
- the state was interested in a friendly settlement, particularly where a foreign party was involved;
- the parties were unable to reach a settlement on their own and agreed that the rules of civil procedure and evidentiary rules shall not apply;
- the dispute concerned technical matters;
- resolution by the court might result in a strict general precedent that would be undesirable; and
- the resolution of the dispute was largely dependent on document review for accounting purposes.[79]

The second scenario was where a government body considered including an arbitration clause in a contract, in which case it was required to obtain the AG's prior approval.[80] Additional considerations to be taken into account in this case included whether arbitration was customary in the particular field and whether there was a need to find a compromise between divergent approaches that might arise during the execution of the contract.[81]

The 1969 Directive also distinguished between an arbitration to be conducted in Israel under Israeli law, an arbitration to be conducted abroad under foreign law, and

[76] Attorney General Directive No 80.000, 'בוררויות הממשלה' ('State Arbitrations') (1 December 1969) <http://index.justice.gov.il/Units/YoezMespati/Pages/HanchayotHistory.aspx> accessed 4 August 2015 (in Hebrew) (1969 Directive). During this time period, there was another AG directive in force that prohibited as a general matter the state and state entities from entering into a contract governed by foreign law and from submitting disputes to foreign courts: Attorney General Directive No 64.001, 'חוזים עם גורמי חוץ – תחולת החוק הישראלי' ('State Arbitrations') (1 November 1968). This directive was replaced in March 2019 by the Attorney General Directive No 10.200 (64.001), 'הכפפת המדינה לדין זר, לערכאות זרות ולמנגנונים בין-לאומיים ליישוב סכסוכים בחוזים בין-לאומיים בעלי אופי מסחרי' ('State Arbitrations') (5 March 2019).

[77] 1969 Directive (n 78).

[78] ibid paras A(2), C.

[79] ibid para C.

[80] ibid paras B(2); *החברה לפיתוח כפר ורדים בע"מ נ' מינהל מקרקעי ישראל – מחוז צפון (Kfar Vradim Development Company Ltd v Israel Land Administration – Northern District)* District Court of Jerusalem 60876-05-12 (24 September 2013).

[81] 1969 Directive (n 78) para D(1).

an arbitration to be conducted in Israel under foreign law.[82] Where arbitration was to be conducted under foreign law, whether in Israel or abroad, the directive provided additional factors to be considered by a government body before including an arbitration clause in a contract:[83]

- whether a judicial forum could not be agreed upon or whether the applicable judicial forums were inconvenient;
- whether the arbitration clause would be enforceable in Israel or in other relevant places;
- whether preliminary procedural requirements would have to be satisfied for arbitration to take place;
- what would be the procedure for appointing the arbitrators and conducting the proceedings;
- the degree to which the arbitrators would be independent;
- how the arbitral award would be enforced and the rules governing challenges to the award; and
- the applicable domestic law.

Finally, the directive also set out several rules regarding the drafting of arbitration agreements by a government body:[84]

- such agreements must be in writing;
- the type of arbitration must be included, although the names of the arbitrators were not required;
- the particular dispute to be submitted to arbitration must be specified; agreements in Israel under Israeli law must specify whether the Schedule to the AL was applicable in whole or in part;
- agreements concerning foreign matters must specify the arbitrators' powers, whether these are restricted in some way, and whether the arbitrators were to apply procedural and evidentiary rules or substantive laws; and
- it must be stated that the arbitral award shall be final and binding on the parties.

Overall, it seems that the approach adopted in the 1969 Directive towards private-public arbitration largely emphasized the AG's traditional role as legal representative of the government, favouring arbitration where it was convenient or advantageous for the state to avoid the court system or where functional or procedural considerations justified its use. It did not seem to have much of a constitutional or public interest rationale underlying it. The government did reportedly use arbitration during this time

[82] ibid para A(3).
[83] ibid para D(2).
[84] ibid para F(2).

period,[85] although some of these arbitrations took place without the relevant government body obtaining the AG's prior approval as required in the directive, which resulted in the courts invalidating arbitration agreements or awards in some cases.[86]

B. 2003–09

The second AG directive concerning private-public arbitrations was issued in 2003,[87] and is also no longer in force. The short two-page directive presented a significantly more negative approach to the use of arbitration by the government, which seems in line with the AG's evolving role as guardian of the public interest and watchdog of the government. Unlike its predecessor, the 2003 Directive stated that, as a general rule, the state shall not resolve disputes by arbitration but rather before the courts, and noted that the AG's approach to arbitration was 'extremely restrictive'.[88] It further stated that the AG alone was authorized to agree to arbitrations on behalf of the government, even where an arbitration clause was already included in a contract or in a relevant international convention or agreement. Moreover, the AG was to decide on a case-by-case basis whether arbitration should be allowed and under what conditions,[89] which were not specified in the directive.

In addition to functional reasons underlying the approach adopted in the 2003 Directive, for instance that the state should conduct proceedings according to uniform procedural and evidentiary rules, and that the cost of arbitration could be extremely high, there were also public interest rationales for this approach. These included the need for transparency in proceedings related to state assets, the importance of public funds, the ability to appeal court judgments, and the broader implications of the state being viewed as having 'deep pockets' in a process that was not subject to substantive laws or to appeal.[90] These concerns often translated into a complete prohibition on arbitrations involving state entities. In one instance,[91] the AG advised the National Water Company (whose operations the government partially funded and was substantially involved in) not to engage in arbitration to resolve a dispute since it could have serious implications for the state and the entire water-using public, and was of great public importance. The dispute was also seen as involving complex public law questions both with regard to the regulation of water provision by the company

[85] See eg Baruch Bracha, 'על כוחה של הממשלה להשתחרר מהתחייבות חוזית' ('On the Power of the State to Avoid Contractual Obligations') (1975–76) 30 Hapraklit 34 (in Hebrew); *The State of Israel v Yaakov Shimshon Shapira* (n 61).

[86] See eg *Alsint Ltd v the State of Israel* (n 28); *אבנר יפעת נ' מינהל מקרקעי ישראל* (*Avner Yifat v Israel Land Administration*) High Court of Justice 692/88 (14 August 1989); *Hertzelia City Parents Association v Hertzelia City Hall* (n 28).

[87] Attorney General Directive No 6.1204 (80.000A), 'העברת סכסוך שהמדינה צד לו לבוררות' ('Submission of a Dispute to Which the State Is a Party to Arbitration') (14 September 2003) <www.itroltd.com/WEB/8888/NSF/Web/5328/1204.pdf> accessed 4 August 2015 (in Hebrew) (2003 Directive).

[88] ibid preamble, s B.

[89] ibid ss A, C(3).

[90] ibid s B; *אפרים שועלי בנין והשקעות בע"מ נ' המועצה המקומית תל מונד* (*Efraim Shuali Construction and Investments Ltd v Local Council Tel-Mond*) Supreme Court of Israel 2237/03 (10 January 2005).

[91] *עיריית עפולה ו-34 אח' נ' מקורות חברת המים בע"מ* (*Afula Municipality et al v Mekorot Water Company Ltd*) Tel-Aviv District Court 4330/08 (5 May 2008).

and its funding, and with regard to the potential effect of having significant financial claims brought against a public authority that is responsible for the provision of a vital service. Moreover, the AG advised the company that, in light of the public importance of the dispute, the AG should partake in the proceedings for its resolution and that it would not participate in arbitration.

Some of these public interest concerns underlying the AG's approach to private-public arbitration in the 2003 Directive were also reflected in decisions of the Israeli courts. In one case, the Supreme Court found that a dispute between a private party and the Rabbinical Courts Administration involved 'serious questions concerning the validity of the agreement between the State and a private company that was concluded in violation of administrative rules', and that there was a 'risk that the State will be found liable in an amount that exceeded the annual budget of the relevant governmental office'. Therefore, there was 'public importance in resolving it before the courts'.[92] In another case involving arbitration between the state and a private party during this period,[93] the Supreme Court noted that the use of arbitration was desirable and important in private-private arbitrations for 'the public interest and the private interest of the parties'. This was so since arbitration significantly reduced the workload of the courts and the parties benefited from an alternative dispute resolution mechanism that was 'efficient, fast, and able to provide a just result without necessarily being subject to procedural and evidentiary rules'. With respect to private-public arbitration, however, the court noted that, in accordance with the 2003 Directive, the state generally did not settle disputes by way of arbitration except on rare occasions due to considerations of 'public good' and its 'responsibility for State funds'. The court did not pronounce on the merits of this approach, but noted that it was rooted in the view that disputes concerning public funds and property should be resolved by courts that were subject to substantive laws, procedural and evidentiary rules, and appeal. These public interests, moreover, should be accorded considerable weight when balanced against the public interest of preserving and protecting arbitration as an efficient dispute resolution mechanism between private parties. The court also found that, since the approval of the AG to conduct the arbitration was not obtained in this case, the state's agreement to do so was invalid. Moreover, the damage that would be caused to the state from conducting arbitration proceedings in parallel with court proceedings, in the form of wasted public funds and time, was more significant than the damage that would be caused to the private party from being denied recourse to arbitration.

In a subsequent case, however, the Supreme Court narrowed the circumstances under which an arbitration agreement concluded by the state without the approval of the AG would be considered invalid.[94] In this case, the Ministry of

[92] *באמונה חברה לניהול נאמנות והקדשות בע"מ נ' הנהלת בתי הדין הרבניים – מדינת ישראל (Beemuna Trust and Property Management Company Ltd v the Rabbinical Courts Administration – the State of Israel)* Supreme Court of Israel 1877/04 (19 June 2005).

[93] *מינהל מקרקעי ישראל נ' חאן מנולי בע"מ (Israel Land Administration v Han Manuli Ltd)* Supreme Court of Israel 5114/05 (23 August 2005).

[94] *מטרודן באר-שבע בע"מ נ' מדינת ישראל משרד התחבורה (Metrodan Beer-Sheva Ltd v the State of Israel Ministry of Transportation)* Tel-Aviv District Court 6532/06 (15 June 2006); *מדינת ישראל משרד התחבורה נ' מטרודן באר-שבע בע"מ (The State of Israel Ministry of Transportation v Metrodan Beer- Sheva Ltd)* Supreme Court of Israel 7146/06 (15 January 2007).

Transportation had entered into a contract with a private company that included an arbitration clause. When a dispute arose, the company invoked the arbitration clause. However, the Ministry refused to comply with it, arguing that the AG had prohibited it from doing so. The company applied to the District Court to appoint an arbitrator, while the Ministry objected on grounds of, inter alia, the public significance of the dispute, the limited grounds on which an arbitral award could be challenged, and the considerable cost of arbitration to the state. The District Court followed the standard interpretation rules applicable to private-private arbitration agreements, finding that the dispute should be referred to arbitration. The court acknowledged that there may be instances where there would be a public interest in conducting a public hearing in court concerning a matter that raises constitutional or other publicly important questions and that extends beyond the particular case, and that this interest may outweigh the public interest in upholding the arbitration agreement. The court found, however, that this case concerned a particular and narrow dispute between the parties, and therefore should be submitted to arbitration.

The Ministry then sought leave to appeal this decision to the Supreme Court. In dismissing the application, the Supreme Court recognized that, as a matter of policy, the state was not in the practice of submitting disputes to arbitration due to the nature of arbitral proceedings and their flexibility regarding procedural rules and substantive laws, and that the use of arbitration therefore generally required the approval of the AG, which was rarely granted. At the same time, the court held that, where the state signs an arbitration clause, 'there [i]s a presumption with regard to its relationship with the other party that it was bound to arbitrate in accordance with the regular rules, including the rules governing the interpretation and scope of the arbitration clause'. The court found that the circumstances of the case did not justify the grant of leave to appeal since it did not raise a public matter that called for a judicial resolution despite the existence of an arbitration agreement. Moreover, the court found that the parties had intended to submit all disputes concerning the interpretation or execution of the contract to arbitration, and that the state could not rely on its policy of AG approval in order to evade an arbitration agreement it was a party to. The court added, however, that this was the case only 'so long as the arbitration clause did not expressly include such approval as a prerequisite'. Indeed, as will be discussed in the next section, where the arbitration clause does expressly include this prerequisite, the Israeli courts have generally found that it could not bind the state without the approval of the AG, even if the specific dispute does not concern a public matter.

The 2003 Directive therefore signalled a shift in the AG's approach to private-public arbitration, from support for its use in certain circumstances for functional or procedural reasons to a nearly complete prohibition for public interest reasons, in line with its evolving role from government representative to guardian of the rule of law and the public interest. This more restrictive approach was also largely supported by the Israeli courts during this time period, which often found that disputes involving the state should be resolved in a transparent and accountable public forum on grounds of the 'public good', at least where public matters were involved, such as state funds and property. It is hardly surprising, therefore, that not a single request from a government body to refer a dispute to arbitration was submitted to the AG for approval between 2004 and 2010.[95] However, as the case law discussed above indicates, the government appears to have used arbitration clauses and conducted arbitration proceedings during this time period without obtaining such approval. This was particularly the case in large infrastructure contracts, although the reason for using arbitration was arguably not the state's interest in it but rather the insistence of private companies.[96]

C. 2009–present

The most recent AG directive concerning private-public arbitration was issued in 2009[97] and replaced both the 1969 and the 2003 Directives. While it has been considered by some to constitute a 'revolution' in the AG's approach to arbitrations involving the state,[98] the 2009 Directive seems to have changed little in the actual practice of the AG or the government in this regard.[99] Part of the incentive for the new directive was the growing trend in Israel of resolving private-private disputes outside the court system, which was seen as positive and useful for reducing the workload of the courts, expediting the resolution of disputes, and preserving long-term relationships and continued cooperation between parties. In the private-public context, moreover, the lack of a binding precedent in arbitration, the parties' control over the identity of the arbitrator, and the creativity permitted in designing the arbitral process were again recognized as better able, in certain circumstances, to address the special needs and characteristics of the state as a party to disputes. Finally, since the state

[95] Shani Mizrahi, 'מה הפלא שהציבור חושש מבוררות כשהמדינה לא מעבירה תיקים להליך?' ('Is There Any Wonder That the Public Is Afraid of Arbitration when the State Does not Transfer Cases to the Process?') (*The Marker*, 28 November 2010) <www.themarker.com/law/1.592256> accessed 4 August 2015.

[96] ibid. At least two arbitrations pursuant to such contracts were, or still are, being conducted between the government and private contractors: see State Controller 'דוח ביקורת שנתי 62 לשנת 2011 ולחשבונות שנת הכספים 2010' ('Annual Review Report 62 for 2011 and for accounts fiscal year 2010') <www.mevaker.gov.il/%28X%281%29S%28v2js1z1nvzuwe24hwcbt5te0%29%29/he/Reports/Pages/117.aspx?AspxAutoDetectCookieSupport=1> accessed 4 August 2015 (in Hebrew); and 'משרד התחבורה והבטיחות בדרכים- הפיקוח על הפעלת הרכבת הקלה בירושלים' ('Ministry of Transportation and Road Safety – Oversight of the Operation of the Light Train in Jerusalem'), Annual Report 65A (2014) <www.mevaker.gov.il/he/Reports/Report_266/c527d902-2d0c-4483-816c-56aa39daee1a/212-ver-4.pdf> accessed 4 August 2015 (in Hebrew).

[97] 2009 Directive (n 68). In an additional directive issued in March 2019, the AG recognized the growing number of international agreements involving the state or state entities that are routinely subject to foreign law, foreign courts, or other international dispute resolution mechanisms. Accordingly, the new directive provides that the government entity wishing to enter into such an agreement has the authority to do so, subject to general guidelines contained in the directive and in some cases the AG's approval. Interestingly, the directive further provides that, in complex agreements with high financial exposure, or where there are concerns that a foreign court would be partial towards the other party, international arbitration should be the preferred dispute resolution mechanism: Attorney General Directive No 10.200 (64.001), 'הכפפת המדינה לדין זרלערכאות זרות ולמנגנונים בין-לאומיים ליישוב סכסוכים בחוזים בעלי אופי מסחרי-בין לאומיים' ('State Arbitrations') (5 March 2019). This directive replaced the Attorney General Directive No 64.001, 'חוזים עם גורמי חוץ - תחולת החוק הישראלי' ('State Arbitrations') (1 November 1968), which prohibited the state and state entities from entering into a contract governed by foreign law or submitting disputes to foreign courts.

[98] Mizrahi (n 97), citing former AG Meni Mazoz.

[99] 18th Knesset, Law Committee Protocol No 526 (10 January 2012) <www.knesset.gov.il/> accessed 4 August 2015 (in Hebrew) (Protocol 526).

encouraged private parties to resolve disputes outside the court system, it was argued that it should also do so itself.[100]

Therefore, in January 2008, the AG reportedly decided to abandon the position, reflected in the 2003 Directive, of discouraging arbitration in disputes involving the state across the board, and return to the previous starting point, expressed in the 1969 Directive, that viewed arbitration as a 'legitimate and appropriate tool, in certain circumstances, for the resolution of [such] disputes'.[101] To this end, the AG advanced legislative amendments to the AL that would provide parties with an appeal option of arbitral awards before the courts, so long as the arbitration was governed by substantive law, a protocol of the proceedings was maintained, and a reasoned award was rendered.[102] One of the issues discussed during the preliminary deliberations of these proposed amendments in the Knesset was the wholesale ban on arbitrations involving the state under the 2003 Directive.

On the one hand, it was argued that the ban was unjustly viewed as a 'holy commandment', and that it was inappropriate in light of the size and nature of the government and its vast involvement in legal disputes.[103] It was estimated in this regard that 30 per cent of the cases that came before the Israeli courts involved the state as a party, making it the largest litigator in the country.[104] In addition, it was seen as absurd that judges, who work for the state, encouraged parties to use arbitration but the state itself did not use it.[105] It was argued that an appeal option would prevent this absurdity, since one of the reasons for the ban was the lack of an appeal option of arbitral awards, and should such an option be legislated the state would presumably be more inclined to accept arbitration.[106] Moreover, it was argued that some of the other rationales underlying the ban were not necessarily justified, for instance that arbitration does not have clear procedural and evidentiary rules, as such rules could be devised, and that it is expensive, as litigation in the courts could be even more expensive.[107] On the other hand, it was argued that the general ban and the requirement for prior AG approval were justified in order to prevent arbitration from turning into a 'political tool', by allowing it only in those cases where it was truly in the public interest.[108] Moreover, it was said that the state enjoys certain procedural advantages

[100] 2009 Directive (n 68) preamble.

[101] ibid.

[102] ibid. See also מ. אדלר הנדסה בע"מ נ' יחזקאל קטן *(M Adler Engineering Ltd v Yechezkel Katan)* Supreme Court of Israel 1242/15 (12 April 2016) (where Mazoz J noted that his goal, as AG at the time, in promoting the legislation was to encourage the state to participate in arbitration).

[103] Knesset member Menachem Ben-Sasson of the Kadima party, 17th Knesset, Session No 189 (1 January 2008), first reading of the Second Amendment to the Arbitration Act, 2007, Appeal of an Arbitral Award <www.knesset.gov.il/> accessed 4 August 2015 (in Hebrew) (Session No 189).

[104] 17th Knesset, Law Committee Protocol No 313 (16 October 2007) <www.knesset.gov.il/> accessed 4 August 2015 (in Hebrew).

[105] Judge (Ret) Amnon Strashnov, 17th Knesset, Law Committee Protocol No 382 (18 December 2007) <www.knesset.gov.il/> accessed 4 August 2015 (in Hebrew) (Protocol No 382).

[106] Knesset member Menahem Ben-Sasson of the Kadima party 17th Knesset, Law Committee Protocol No 555 (3 June 2008) <www.knesset.gov.il/> accessed 4 August 2015 (in Hebrew) (Protocol No 555); 17th Knesset, Law Committee Protocol No 470 (24 February 2008) <www.knesset.gov.il/> accessed 4 August 2015 (in Hebrew).

[107] Judge (Ret) Amnon Strashnov, Protocol No 382 (n 107).

[108] Knesset member Reuven Rivlin of the Likud party, Session No 189 (n 105).

when appearing before the courts, including an exemption from paying court fees,[109] and that state lawyers are well versed in public law, judicial review, and the procedures and practices of the courts.[110] It was argued that these practices, which were accompanied by a deep-rooted mistrust of the arbitration system,[111] called for a principled and gradual, rather than a technical and immediate, reform of the AG's approach to private-public arbitration.[112]

As this discussion reveals, the amendment to the AL allowing for optional appeal of arbitral awards was designed, at least in part, to increase the state's participation in arbitration.[113] The amendment was approved by the Knesset in November 2008, following which the 2009 Directive was issued. The stated objective of this new directive was to set out guidelines for the inclusion of arbitration clauses in agreements to which the state is a party and the submission of disputes involving the state to arbitration.[114] It reiterated, however, that the AG alone remains authorized to approve and sign arbitration agreements on behalf of the state, whether for inclusion in a contract or after a dispute has arisen. Therefore, an arbitration agreement entered into without such approval would continue to be viewed as null and void. Moreover, the directive stated that, even where the prior approval of the AG for the inclusion of an arbitration clause in a new or renewed contract is obtained, invoking the clause with regard to a particular dispute must also be approved by the AG representative assigned to the relevant governmental body.[115] Finally, the directive provided that any changes made to an existing arbitration clause must also be approved by the AG.[116]

The decision on whether or not to approve the inclusion of an arbitration clause in a contract to which the state is a party, or to refer an existing dispute to arbitration absent such a clause, is to be made on a case-by-case basis in accordance with the circumstances and after taking into account the legal and public implications that such a decision might entail. In this regard, the 2009 Directive provides that the following considerations would 'generally rule out arbitration':[117]

- the dispute concerns the scope or exercise of a governmental power by the state or a competent authority;[118]
- a fundamental, precedential, or otherwise sensitive legal question which ought to be discussed in a transparent manner and in a public proceeding before the court;[119]

[109] Knesset member Gideon Saar of the Likud party, Protocol No 555 (n 108).
[110] Dotan (n 59) 76.
[111] Judge (Ret) Uri Shtruzman, Protocol No 555 (n 108).
[112] ibid, Dr Peretz Segal, Ministry of Justice.
[113] עמידר החברה הלאומית לשיכון בישראל בע"מ נ' זוהר חי *(Amidar the National Housing Company in Israel Ltd v Zohar Hai)* Supreme Court of Israel 10487/07 (5 May 2010).
[114] 2009 Directive (n 68) preamble.
[115] ibid ss B, E.
[116] ibid s D(2).
[117] ibid s C(1).
[118] See eg decisions regarding enforcement, regulation, imposition of financial sanctions, governmental policy or its exercise (ibid para C(1)(a)).
[119] ibid para C(1)(b).

- the dispute concerns a large section of the public, or its resolution could affect a large or unspecified section of the public;[120]
- setting a precedent by a judicial authority is important;[121] and
- the determination and resolution of the dispute may affect third parties that are not participating in the arbitration proceedings, or it requires their joinder.

On the other hand, the following considerations 'may justify submitting a dispute to arbitration':[122]

- the dispute is of a civil-commercial or professional-technical nature, or its subject matter calls for resolution by way of non-public proceedings;[123]
- the identity and nature of the parties to the dispute;[124]
- efficiency;[125]
- the importance of a quick resolution;
- the scope and financial implications of the dispute; and
- the ability to design the arbitral proceedings and decision-making.

The 2009 Directive expressly noted that, while this list is not exhaustive, the mere existence of one or more of these considerations does not necessarily mean that the dispute is appropriate for resolution by arbitration. Rather, these are only 'general guidelines, which must be examined on a case-by-case basis and in light of the concrete circumstances'.[126] In addition, according to the directive, an arbitration agreement must explicitly state that the submission of a concrete dispute to arbitration remains subject to the AG's approval and must address, inter alia, the following issues:[127]

- the type of arbitration;[128]
- the transparency of the proceedings or the need for confidentiality;
- the definition of the dispute;
- the identity of the arbitrators and, where this is not possible, their required qualifications and experience and the manner in which they shall be appointed;

[120] For example, the interpretation of an agreement that the state has concluded where a large number of parties are involved (ibid para C(1)(d)).
[121] For example, due to a lack of clarity regarding the legal situation or the existence of contradictory case law (ibid para C(1)(c)).
[122] ibid s C(2).
[123] For example, where resolution by a court may result in the disclosure of information that could damage national security or the state's foreign relations (ibid para C(2)(b)).
[124] For example, arbitration may be advantageous where a long-term relationship with the other party exists, as it may facilitate a quick resolution and resumption of normal relations, or where international business entities are involved in the dispute (ibid para C(2)(c)).
[125] For example, where the dispute concerns technical or professional issues and it is advantageous for a person with relevant professional knowledge to resolve it (ibid para C(2)(d)).
[126] ibid s C(2).
[127] ibid s F(3).
[128] As a general rule, arbitrations should be conducted before a sole arbitrator unless there are special reasons to appoint additional arbitrators (ibid s H(3)(a)).

- the fee of the arbitrators and additional payments and the manner in which the expenses shall be divided between the parties;[129]
- the powers of the arbitrators;
- the applicable procedural and evidentiary rules;
- the arbitrators' duty to render a reasoned award and to rule on the basis of substantive law;
- an appeal option pursuant to the AL; and
- the resignation, removal, and replacement of an arbitrator.

Since the 2009 Directive was issued, at least one dispute involving the state has been submitted to arbitration and has recently reached the Jerusalem District Court, which considered some of the public interest concerns associated with private-public arbitration as reflected in the directive.[130] The dispute involved the Israeli Ministry of Finance and a private party, the Dead Sea Factories (DSF), and concerned royalties paid by the latter to the former for the use of the resources of the Dead Sea. During the arbitration proceedings, the Ministry received a request from two non-governmental organizations for the disclosure of information concerning the arbitration pursuant to the Freedom of Information Law (FIL), including the parties' submissions, protocols of hearings, and a list of witnesses. Although DSF objected to any disclosure, the Ministry dismissed its objection and decided that the requested materials could be disclosed subject to an exclusion of DSF's trade secrets. DSF appealed this decision to the District Court. The court dismissed the appeal, finding that the FIL applied in this case, and that there was no reason for it to intervene in the Ministry's decision in the circumstances.[131]

In its decision, the District Court discussed at length the tension between the public interest in or right to information, on the one hand, and the parties' interest in or right to non-public or confidential arbitration proceedings, on the other. The court found that both interests were relative rather than absolute and therefore needed to be balanced against each other, and that in the present case this balance must account for the fact that the dispute involved the state. In such disputes, unlike in a private arbitration, the parties' expectation of a confidential process regardless of its subject matter is less reasonable and legitimate, particularly where the dispute has a clear public aspect. Therefore, 'private' and 'public' arbitration should not be equated and the balance of interests must be struck on a case-by-case basis. The court further noted in this regard that the 2009 Directive set out a list of considerations ruling out arbitration where it was not advantageous to resolve the dispute privately, and required that arbitration agreements address the transparency of the process or the need for confidentiality. Although this directive was not in force at the time the arbitration agreement was concluded in this case, the court noted that it reflected 'the broader considerations of the state when it submits a dispute to arbitration'.

[129] Absent special reasons, a maximum fee for the arbitrator, and for additional expenses, should be set out (ibid H(3)(e)).

[130] *Dead Sea Factories Ltd v the State of Israel Ministry of Finance* (n 42).

[131] However, the court did require the Ministry to revisit its decision since it found that doubt existed with regard to DSF's trade and business secrets, documents it had submitted in confidence, and potential damage to third parties.

In balancing freedom of information with the confidentiality of arbitration, the court found that the starting point in the present case was the FIL, although in other circumstances it could also be the AL. The court held that the FIL applied in this case since the Ministry was a 'public authority' also when participating in arbitrations, and the FIL applied to any 'information' held by the Ministry even when it formed part of arbitration proceedings in which it was a party. Moreover, the court found that the parties did not intend to keep the proceedings confidential since the arbitration agreement was silent in this regard; the subject matter of the arbitration was of significant public importance (the state's natural resources); and, at the time DSF had concluded the arbitration agreement, it was a state-owned entity. The court further found that none of the exceptions to the application of the FIL were satisfied in this case. While, in principle, there could be instances in which disclosure of information concerning an arbitration could amount to a violation of privacy and therefore should not be allowed, this did not apply to DSF as a corporation but rather to witnesses, arbitrators, and other third parties. Moreover, arbitration proceedings were not subject to a disclosure ban by law. Although an interest in their secrecy has been recognized, there is no legal requirement of confidentiality. The protection of trade secrets also did not grant complete confidentiality to arbitration proceedings since this was a relative interest, and in any event DSF had failed to prove the required degree of injury from disclosure. Finally, there was no condition placed on the information when it was provided to the Ministry that would invoke its duty of good faith as a party to an arbitration agreement and as a public authority.[132] While the court recognized that its decision might have a 'chilling effect' on the willingness of private parties to conduct arbitration with the state, it found that this risk did not materialize in this particular case and in any event was outweighed by the public authority's duty of transparency, its status as a trustee of the public, and by the fact that 'a public hearing is one of the cornerstones of justice'. DSF appealed to the Israeli Supreme Court; however, its application was dismissed. In a brief decision,[133] the Supreme Court emphasized that the case concerned an arbitration involving the state, relating to one of the most important national resources in the country, and that DSF was operating under a statutory franchise. The court found that all of these factors suggested that this was a matter of great public importance and that there was no ground for preventing the disclosure of the requested documents as decided by the District Court.

Another case that was recently decided by the Israeli courts[134] concerned an arbitration agreement concluded when the 1969 Directive was still in force, and which expressly required the approval of the AG in order for arbitration to take place. As mentioned above, the Israeli courts have generally found that in such circumstances the state could use a failure to obtain such approval in order to avoid an arbitration

[132] Nonetheless, the Court allowed DSF to file an objection to the Ministry on a specific and narrow basis regarding the disclosure of particular portions of the requested information.

[133] *מפעלי ים המלח בע"מ נ' מדינת ישראל משרד האוצר* *(Dead Sea Factories Ltd v the State of Israel Ministry of Finance)* Supreme Court of Israel (sitting as an Administrative Court of Appeal) 6634/13 (19 February 2014).

[134] *מדינת ישראל נ' מרגלית ש.א. רכב בע"מ* *(The State of Israel v Margalit SA Auto Ltd)* Central District Court 40903-04-10 (6 January 2013), leave to appeal to the Supreme Court filed but erased as per the request of the appellant.

agreement it was party to. After the arbitrator was appointed in this case, the government requested to refer the dispute to the courts, since it had mistakenly neglected to obtain the approval of the AG to conduct the arbitration. Moreover, the government declared that it did not wish to seek such approval at that time, since it was unable to comply with the requirements set out in the new 2009 Directive with regard to the content of the arbitration agreement. Specifically, the government argued that two contradictory interests were involved. On the one hand, the new 2009 Directive required that the arbitration agreement provide for the tribunal to render a reasoned award so that it may be appealed to the courts, while on the other hand, the government did not want a reasoned award in order to avoid potentially broad implications for other proceedings ongoing against it. The District Court accepted the government's arguments and declared the arbitration agreement to be void since it was concluded without authority. The court also accepted the government's refusal to seek the approval of the AG to conduct the arbitration, finding that where the state believes that arbitration is inappropriate in the circumstances and considers it to be against its interest, 'there is obviously no need for it to request the approval of the AG to conduct arbitration'.

In sum, the 2009 Directive incorporated many of the public interest rationales underlying the previous ban on private-public arbitrations under the 2003 Directive and continued to subject the use of such arbitrations by the state to the exclusive approval of the AG, and to detailed procedural requirements. However, it also relaxed this ban to some extent by allowing for a case-by-case consideration of functional and procedural factors that may justify the use of arbitration in certain circumstances where this is in the interest of the state, as in the 1969 Directive. Despite this middle ground, as well as the legislative amendments to the AL allowing for appeal of arbitral awards, the 2009 Directive has arguably failed to revolutionize the private-public arbitration field in Israel as anticipated. As the government has argued before the Israeli courts, its interests may in fact collide with the directive's procedural requirements, and it still does not perceive arbitration as being 'in its interest' and does not 'believe' in it.[135] Moreover, budgetary and bureaucratic constraints, as well as the government's preference for having arbitrators who are retired judges, of whom there are relatively few, have all prevented arbitration from becoming a widespread tool in private-public disputes.[136] The 2009 Directive, therefore, has been declared by some to be a 'dead letter'.[137]

V. Conclusion

Israel remains a largely pro-arbitration jurisdiction, in which both legislation and the courts encourage its use in private-private disputes. However, such support of arbitration has generally not been extended to private-public disputes involving the state.

[135] Protocol No 526 (n 101).

[136] Mizrahi (n 97), citing Adv Gali Miara, the State Attorney for the Tel-Aviv District.

[137] Judge (ret) Amnon Strashnov, 'לפני חוק בוררות חובה' ('Before the Mandatory Arbitration Law') (*Haaretz*, 3 October 2011) <www.haaretz.co.il/opinions/1.1487849> accessed 4 August 2015 (in Hebrew).

Since the country's early days, the use of arbitration in the resolution of such disputes has been subjected to the exclusive approval of the AG, whose function in the Israeli legal system has significantly evolved over the years, and with it its approach to private-public arbitration. When the main task and purpose of the AG was to represent the government before the courts, arbitration was generally viewed as a convenient way for the state to resolve its disputes outside the courtroom when this was in line with its interests. However, as the role of the AG became more complex and took on a public interest dimension that entrusted it with the added responsibility of supervising the government and ensuring its compliance with the rule of law, the approach to the use of arbitration in disputes involving the state changed as well. Such use became largely prohibited, mostly for public interest reasons such as the need for transparent and accountable proceedings where public matters are concerned, and approval for the inclusion of arbitration clauses in contracts, or for conducting arbitration proceedings, became rare. This prohibition on the use of arbitration in disputes involving the state was relaxed somewhat after legislative amendments introducing an appeal option of arbitral awards before the courts were passed, and arbitration was again permitted where functional and procedural considerations justified its use. Still, such use remains subject to the exclusive approval of the AG, at least formally, and public interest considerations continue to guide the decisions of both the AG and the Israeli courts in this regard. In fact, the courts have consistently viewed arbitrations involving the state as 'public' rather than 'private' in nature, particularly where the dispute concerns public funds, a 'public good', or an issue extending beyond the interests of the parties. Moreover, the courts continue to favour the protection of such 'public interests' over the interests of the parties in private-public arbitrations, and while such arbitrations may still take place for functional or procedural reasons, they will likely remain subject to more stringent regulation than private-private arbitrations.

Select Materials

Bibliography

Dotan, Yoav, *Lawyering for the Rule of Law* (CUP 2014)

Navot, Suzie, *The Constitution of Israel: A Contextual Analysis* (Hart Publishing 2014)

Ottolenghi, Smadar, *The Law of Arbitration in Israel* (Kluwer Law International 2001)

Ottolenghi, Smadar, *בוררות דין ונוהל* (*Arbitral Law and Procedure*) (4th edn, Bursi Publications 2005)

Zamir, Yitzhak, 'The Attorney General: Servant of the Public and not of the Government' (January 1989) 5 Bar Assoc Newsletter

Legislation and Other Legal Instruments

חוק הבוררות, תשכ"ט-1968 (Israeli Arbitration Law, 1968

תקנות סדרי הדין בעניני בוררות תשכ"ט-1968 (Regulations for Procedure in Matters of Arbitration, 1968)

Attorney General Directive No 80.000, 'בוררויות הממשלה' ('State Arbitrations') (1 December 1969)
Attorney General Directive No 6.1204 (80.000A), 'סכסוך שהמדינה צד לו לבוררות העברת' ('Submission of a Dispute to Which the State Is a Party to Arbitration') (14 September 2003)
Attorney General Directive No 6.1205, 'יישוב סכסוכים שהמדינה צד להם באמצעות בוררות' ('Resolution of Disputes to Which the State Is a Party by Arbitration') (12 October 2009)
Attorney General Directive No 10.200 (64.001), 'הכפפת המדינה לדין זר, לערכאות זרות ולמנגנונים בין-לאומיים ליישוב סכסוכים בחוזים בין-לאומיים בעלי אופי מסחרי' ('State Arbitrations') (5 March 2019)

Cases

מפעלי ים המלח בע"מ נ' מדינת ישראל משרד האוצר (*Dead Sea Factories Ltd v the State of Israel Ministry of Finance*) Supreme Court of Israel (sitting as an Administrative Court of Appeal) 6634/13 (19 February 2014)
אליהו אמינוף נ' שמואל אלטלף (*Eliyahu Aminof v Shmuel Altalef*) High Court of Justice 816/98 (23 June 1998)
הנתיב המהיר בע"מ נ' כביש חוצה ישראל בע"מ (*Fast Lane Ltd v Trans Israel Highway Ltd*) District Court of Jerusalem 16864-03-14 (4 May 2014)
הנתיב המהיר בע"מ נ' כביש חוצה ישראל בע"מ (*Fast Lane Ltd v Trans Israel Highway Ltd*) District Court of Jerusalem 49820-09-12 (12 June 2014)
מינהל מקרקעי ישראל נ' חאן מנולי בע"מ (*Israel Land Administration v Han Manuli Ltd*) Supreme Court of Israel 5114/05 (23 August 2005)
כרמל התפלה בע"מ נ' מדינת ישראל - משרד האוצר (*Karmel Desalination Ltd v the State or Israel-Ministry of Finance*) Supreme Court of Israel 470/08 (4 March 2010)
מטרודן באר-שבע בע"מ נ' מדינת ישראל משרד התחבורה (*Metrodan Beer-Sheva Ltd v the State of Israel Ministry of Transportation*) Tel-Aviv District Court 6532/06 (15 June 2006)
מדינת ישראל נ מנהלת ההתפלה H2ID בע"מ (*State of Israel – Desalination Administration v H2ID Ltd*) Supreme Court of Israel 2279/16 (1 May 2016)
מדינת ישראל נ' בועז רייטר (המנוח) (*State of Israel v Boaz Raiter (late)*) Central District Court 56572-06-18 (5 November 2018)
בש"א 4123/19 מדינת ישראל נ' אבי פיקאלי (*State of Israel v Pikali*) Supreme Court of Israel 4123/19 (1 July 2019)
מדינת ישראל משרד התחבורה נ' מטרודן באר-שבע בע"מ (*The State of Israel Ministry of Transportation v Metrodan Beer-Sheva Ltd*) Supreme Court of Israel 7146/06 (15 January 2007)

15

Living on the Edge of Judicial Review

The Law and Practice of Private-Public Arbitration in Pakistan

*Ahmad Ghouri**

I. Introduction

Arbitration is widely used to resolve disputes between states, between private commercial entities, and between private entities and public authorities. It has been argued that such varied use of arbitration has transformed it from a private dispute resolution system alternative to the courts to a vibrant social institution.[1] Likewise, the use of arbitration to resolve disputes between private entities and public authorities (private-public arbitration), which potentially involves disputes over the making, implementation, and enforcement of public policy, has assigned arbitration an important role in public governance systems.[2] The well-known *Dallah* case,[3] for example, is a striking illustration of public governance implications of private-public arbitration. In *Dallah*, a Pakistani public entity used a private-public contract containing an arbitration clause to implement an important matter of public policy, namely to provide accommodation for persons attending the Hajj (an annual Muslim pilgrimage to Mecca, Saudi Arabia). The contract ended up in a multi-jurisdictional dispute,[4] including a *suo moto* action by the Supreme Court of Pakistan.[5] The result was years of litigation in various jurisdictions, a strong public backlash, and convictions of several public officials.

The aim of this chapter is to examine the existing law and practice of private-public arbitration in Pakistan and its implications as a public governance system.

* The author would like to thank Prof Stephan W. Schill and Dr Kamala Dawar for their meticulous reading and valuable comments on an earlier draft.

[1] See eg Emmanuel Gaillard, 'Sociology of International Arbitration' in David D Caron and others (eds), *Practising Virtue: Inside International Arbitration* (OUP 2015) 187; Jan Paulsson, 'Arbitration in Three Dimensions' (2011) 60 ICLQ 291, 291.

[2] See eg Harold Bruff, 'Public Programs, Private Deciders: The Constitutionality of Arbitration in Federal Programs' (1989) 67 Texas L Rev 441.

[3] The English side of the *Dallah* case is reported as *Dallah Real Estate and Tourism Holding Company v The Ministry of Religious Affairs, Government of Pakistan* [2010] UKSC 46.

[4] For a detailed description of *Dallah*, see Nassib G Ziadé, 'Introductory Note to the United Kingdom Supreme Court: Dallah Real Estate and Tourism Holding Company v. Ministry of Religious Affairs, Government of Pakistan' (2012) 51 ILM 288.

[5] In Pakistan, *Dallah* is known as the *Hajj Corruption Case* (2014 SCMR 484). The *Hajj Corruption Case* was taken up *suo moto* by a six-member bench of the Supreme Court presided over by the Chief Justice Iftikhar Muhammad Chaudhry.

Ahmad Ghouri, *Living on the Edge of Judicial Review* In: *The Comparative Constitutional Foundations of Private-Public Arbitration*. Edited by: Stephan W. Schill, Oxford University Press. © Stephan W. Schill 2025.
DOI: 10.1093/9780191987960.003.0015

Illuminating the pervasive and varied roles played by private actors in all aspects of public governance in liberal societies, Professor Freeman has eloquently proposed a conception of public governance as a decentralized decision-making process where public and private actors negotiate over the making, implementation, and enforcement of public policy.[6] This chapter adopts Professor Freeman's view to analyse the public governance role of private-public arbitration in Pakistan. In this framework of public governance, the chapter examines how private-public arbitration agreements are carried out in Pakistan while maintaining the protection of constitutional rights and accountability for misuse of public authority.

As there is no specific law on private-public arbitration in Pakistan, this field is governed by the general law of arbitration: the Arbitration Act 1940 (AA 1940).[7] A detailed review of the cases decided by Pakistani courts suggests that there is a substantial practice of using arbitration to resolve private-public disputes. Pakistani courts have decided cases involving arbitration in private-public disputes addressing the questions of abuse of administrative authority and protection of public interests. To analyse the practice and public governance implications of private-public arbitration in Pakistan, this chapter primarily addresses the following questions: how has the practice of private-public arbitration evolved? Are there any constitutional requirements for the use of private-public arbitration? What public interest implications arise from the use of private-public arbitration in Pakistan, and how have Pakistani courts dealt with such implications? What are the challenges posed to private-public arbitration as a system of public governance? And how might those challenges be addressed?

The chapter finds answers to these questions by considering the history of legal developments and the present laws and practices of arbitration in Pakistan. It presents a detailed analysis of cases decided by Pakistani courts under their constitutional jurisdiction to review public authorities' actions, including private-public contracts containing arbitration clauses. The chapter finds that there are considerable challenges to the development of private-public arbitration as a system of public governance in Pakistan. However, Pakistani courts, while dealing with questions related to private-public arbitration, have carefully ensured a balance between the legitimate exercise of public authorities' administrative powers, on the one hand, and the protection of public interests and public goods, on the other. In doing so, the courts have, in appropriate cases, enforced private-public arbitration agreements and awards. In other cases where public interests were negatively affected, the courts have declined to enforce private-public arbitration agreements and awards and have exercised their constitutional mandate to provide remedies to private parties or public authorities.

The chapter is structured as follows: section II gives a broad overview of arbitration law and practice in Pakistan. Section III addresses the question as to how private-public arbitration has come about in Pakistan and how it is perceived theoretically and in practice. Section IV gives an in-depth analysis of Pakistani cases involving judicial review of private-public arbitration and finds that the practice of private-public arbitration in Pakistan is indeed living on the edge of judicial review. The analysis in this section identifies how Pakistani courts have explained the legal nature of

[6] Jody Freeman, 'The Private Role in Public Governance' (2000) 75 NYU L Rev 543, 553.

[7] The Arbitration Act (X of 1940) (AA 1940).

private-public contracts and articulated reasoning to decline or enforce arbitration clauses contained in those contracts. Section V gives an overview of the AA 1940 provisions from various perspectives relevant to private-public arbitration, such as the formation of arbitral tribunals and the enforcement of arbitral awards. Section VI discusses the development of arbitration as a system of governance and elaborates how democracy, rule-of-law, and fundamental rights issues arising from the use of private-public arbitration are addressed in Pakistan. Part VII concludes the chapter.

II. The Development of Arbitration Law and Practice

In the present scheme of Pakistani law, legitimacy is primarily granted to arbitration by section 28 of the Contract Act 1872, which provides that agreements in restraint of legal proceedings are void except those referring a dispute to arbitration.[8] Both the Contract Act 1872 and the AA 1940 are legacies of British India inherited by Pakistan on its independence in 1947.[9] The AA 1940 is widely recognized as an inspiration from the English arbitration law prevalent at the time.[10] The AA 1940 continues to be in force in Pakistan without any substantial change. It prescribes rules for arbitration with or without intervention of a court.[11] Historically, courts in Pakistan have had a degree of hostility towards arbitration as an independent system of dispute resolution, and have not always been willing to enforce arbitration agreements.[12] The AA 1940 also caused a degree of uncertainty regarding the enforcement of foreign arbitration agreements and awards.[13] Both these facets have now been starkly reformed by the recent legislative developments and decided cases.

The Constitution of Pakistan 1973 originally included arbitration in the so-called 'Concurrent Legislative List' in the Fourth Schedule, empowering both the federal and provisional governments to legislate on arbitration. The Eighteenth Constitutional Amendment deleted the Concurrent List,[14] meaning that all provincial governments now have autonomy to make their own arbitration laws.[15] However, specific reference to arbitration is also included in the Federal Legislative List, empowering the federal government to make laws on international treaties, conventions, and agreements, and 'international arbitration'.[16] Item 32 in the Federal Legislative List gives exclusive powers to the federal government to legislate on international arbitration, implying

[8] Contract Act (IX of 1872) s 28.

[9] Indian Independence Act (10 & 11 Geo 6, c 30 of 1947) s 18.

[10] See eg Toby T Landau, 'International Arbitration and Pakistan's State Responsibility: Redefining the Role of the Court' (Speech on 50th year celebration of the Supreme Court of Pakistan, Islamabad, August 2006).

[11] Ahmad Ghouri, *Law and Practice of Foreign Arbitration and Enforcement of Foreign Arbitral Awards in Pakistan* (Springer 2012) 5–6.

[12] ibid.

[13] ibid.

[14] The Constitution (Eighteenth Amendment) Act (X of 2010).

[15] See eg Muhammad Rizwan and others, 'Revitalization of Parliamentary Democracy in Pakistan under 18th Amendment' (2014) 19(2) IOSR-JHSS 149, 151–52; Cyril Almeida, 'Are You Current With the Concurrent List!' (*The Dawn News*, 8 April 2010); Raja M Ali Saleem, 'The Special Parliamentary Committee on Constitutional Reforms and the Concurrent List' (*The Forum for Federations*, January 2010).

[16] The Constitution of Pakistan (1973), 4th sch, pt I, item 32.

that the provincial legislative autonomy is limited to domestic arbitration. The AA 1940 predates the 1973 Constitution. However, it continues to be in force because Article 268 of the Constitution has assigned a blanket validity to all pre-existing laws. None of the provinces has yet enacted arbitration laws, meaning that the AA 1940 continues to govern all domestic arbitration proceedings and the enforcement of domestic arbitration awards.[17]

However, the federal government has enacted two important laws governing international arbitration after the Eighteenth Constitutional Amendment. First, the Recognition and Enforcement (Arbitration Agreements and Foreign Arbitral Awards) Act 2011 (REFA).[18] The REFA implements the New York Convention (NYC)[19] in Pakistan, fifty-three years after signing the NYC. Previously, the enforcement of arbitration agreements and foreign arbitral awards in Pakistan was governed by the Arbitration (Protocol and Convention) Act 1937 (APC).[20] The APC was enacted to implement the 1923 Protocol on Arbitration Clauses[21] and the 1927 Convention on the Execution of Foreign Arbitral Awards.[22] Pakistani courts interpreted the APC provisions in a way that did not favour the enforcement of foreign arbitration agreements and awards on various grounds, including inconvenience, non-severability of arbitration clause from the main agreement, and public policy.[23] The REFA has arguably resolved most of these difficulties regarding the enforcement of international commercial arbitration agreements and awards. The REFA section 4(2) reiterates Article II(3) of the NYC and instructs Pakistani courts to refer all disputes to arbitration where parties have concluded a valid arbitration agreement. Some recent cases decided under the REFA suggest that Pakistani courts are now more readily willing to enforce foreign arbitration agreements between private parties,[24] and between private parties and government entities.[25]

The second important law passed by the federal government is the Arbitration (International Investment Disputes) Act 2011 (AIIDA).[26] The AIIDA implements the Convention on the Settlement of Investment Disputes between States and Nationals of Other States (ICSID Convention).[27] The ICSID Convention was ratified by Pakistan in 1966, and it took Pakistani governments forty-five years to pass the implementing domestic legislation, that is, AIIDA. Prior to the enactment of AIIDA,

[17] Ghouri (n 11) 33.

[18] Recognition and Enforcement (Arbitration Agreements and Foreign Arbitral Awards) Act (XVII of 2011).

[19] Convention on the Recognition and Enforcement of Foreign Arbitral Awards (New York Convention) (adopted 10 June 1958, entered into force 7 June 1959) 330 UNTS 3.

[20] The Arbitration (Protocol and Convention) Act (VI of 1937).

[21] Protocol on Arbitration Clauses (signed 24 September 1923, entered into force 28 July 1924) 27 LNTS 157.

[22] Convention on the Execution of Foreign Arbitral Awards (adopted 26 September 1927, entered into force 25 July 1929) 92 LNTS 301.

[23] Ghouri (n 11) 16–23.

[24] ibid. See also *Fal Oil Company Ltd v Pakistan State Oil Company Ltd* (2014 PLD (Karachi) 427); *Abdullah v CNAN Group SPA through Chief Executive/Managing Director* (2014 PLD (Karachi) 349).

[25] *Lakhra Power Generation Company Limited (LPGCL) v Karadeniz Powership Kaya Bey* (2014 CLD (Karachi) 337).

[26] Arbitration (International Investment Disputes) Act (IX of 2011).

[27] Convention on the Settlement of Investment Disputes between States and Nationals of Other States (adopted 18 March 1965, entered into force 14 October 1966) 575 UNTS 159 (ICSID Convention).

the Pakistani Supreme Court, in *Société Générale de Surveillance (SGS)*, issued a restraining order against a foreign investor from pursuing its claim against the government of Pakistan before an ICSID tribunal.[28] Interestingly, the Supreme Court in *SGS* also declared that several bilateral investment treaties (BITs) signed by Pakistan had no domestic legal effect because they were not incorporated in domestic legislation.[29] The Supreme Court in its subsequent decisions in *Rental Power*[30] and *Tethyan*[31] also directly or indirectly interfered in BITs-based private-public arbitrations, leading to two massive ICSID arbitration awards against Pakistan.[32] Subsequently, the Karachi High Court in *Lakhra* tried to tone down the strict stance taken by the Supreme Court in *SGS*.[33] The Court in *Lakhra* suggested that private parties to a private-public arbitration agreement are free to choose between different options regarding the place of arbitration and can take a dispute to ICSID or any other international arbitration tribunal designated in the agreement.

The domestic arbitration practice is not well organised in Pakistan. There is no government-backed formal arbitration institution in Pakistan. A 2009 proposal for a government-backed arbitration institute was subsequently dropped for no apparent reason.[34] However, an ad hoc arbitration practice is well-established. The Karachi Chamber of Commerce and Industry introduced arbitration in its by-laws and published its arbitration rules in 1973.[35] Likewise, the Federation of Pakistan Chambers of Commerce and Industry (FPCCI) established a commercial arbitral tribunal in 1964, which offers to host domestic and international arbitrations. On average, two cases per year have been referred to FPCCI.[36] The Pakistan Engineering Council (PEC) also enacted its own arbitration rules in 2009;[37] however, there is no record of its decided cases.

In 2009, a private institution called the Alternative Dispute Resolution Centre (ADRC) was established in Lahore, modelled on the London Court of International Arbitration (LCIA). However, the ADRC collapsed due to an extremely poor response from the public and industry.[38] Recently, a few private institutions, such as the Centre for International Investment and Commercial Arbitration (CIICA)[39] and the National Centre for Dispute Resolution (NCDR)[40]—formerly known as the Karachi

[28] *Société Générale de Surveillance SA v Pakistan* (2002 SCMR 1694).

[29] ibid.

[30] *Alleged Corruption in Rental Power Plants; Fraud in Payment of Rental Power Plants Detected by NEPRA* (2012 SCMR 273) (Iftikhar Muhammad Chaudhry and Khilji Arif Hussain, JJ). See also *Lakhra* (n 25) paras 11–13.

[31] *Tethyan* (reported in Pakistan as *Maulana Abdul Haque Baloch v Government of Balochistan* (2013 PLD (Supreme Court) 641) and (2012 SCMR 402)) (Iftikhar Muhammad Chaudhry, Gulzar Ahmed, and Sh Azmat Saeed, JJ).

[32] *Karkey Karadeniz Elektrik Uretim AS v Islamic Republic of Pakistan*, ICSID Case No ARB/13/1, Award (22 August 2017); *Tethyan Copper Company Pty Limited v Islamic Republic of Pakistan*, ICSID Case No ARB/12/1, Award (13 July 2019).

[33] *Lakhra* (n 25) paras 38–42.

[34] See Arbitration Bill 2009, pt V. For some analysis of the Arbitration Bill, see Ghouri (n 11) 3–4.

[35] Mahomed J Jaffer and Sarmad J Osmany, 'National Report – Pakistan' in Pieter Sanders (ed), *Yearbook Commercial Arbitration* (Kluwer Law International 1982) 114.

[36] ibid.

[37] Pakistan Engineering Council's Rules of Conciliation and Arbitration (1st edn, March 2009).

[38] Uzair Karamat Bhandari and others, 'Ch 20 – Pakistan' in Michael J Moser and John Choong (eds), *Asia Arbitration Handbook* (OUP 2011) 911.

[39] <www.ciica.org> accessed 6 January 2025.

[40] <www.ncdr.pk> accessed 6 January 2025.

Centre for Dispute Resolution (KCDR)—have emerged in the commercial hubs of Lahore and Karachi. Both CIICA and NCDR have so far not attracted a significant number of arbitration requests. These institutions follow in the footsteps of arbitration institutions prevalent in developed countries. They have been created primarily to meet the specific needs of their targeted clients, that is, private commercial entities having a more sophisticated degree of legal and formal structures. None of them have so far been reported to have arbitrated a private-public dispute.

III. Private-Public Arbitration as a Practical and Theoretical Discipline

Arbitration can be viewed as an undue restriction on legal rights because it divests disputing parties of access to a court.[41] This has led some countries to include specific provisions in their national constitutions that legitimize arbitration as an alternative to courts.[42] The Constitution of Pakistan 1973 has no specific reference to arbitration as a legitimate means for settlement of private or private-public disputes outside of a court. The only references to arbitration in the 1973 Constitution relate to the settlement of disputes between the provinces and the federal government over administration-related expenses,[43] the terms for acquisition of land by the federal government situated in a province,[44] and the conditions imposed by federal government on a province on broadcasting and telecasting.[45] In all these instances, the 1973 Constitution requires arbitration by an arbitrator appointed by the Chief Justice of the Supreme Court of Pakistan.

However, similar to the contemporary constitutional practice in many other countries,[46] the 1973 Constitution effectively mediates between the private rights and associational interests, on the one hand, and the governmental and regulatory interests, on the other. For example, subject to any conditions imposed by law, the freedom of association, freedom of assembly, and freedom of speech are guaranteed in the Constitution.[47] Instead of providing detailed rules on specific types of freedoms, such as the freedom to conclude private contracts,[48] these provisions broadly balance private rights against regulatory interests. Article 18 of the Constitution allows, subject to any regulatory requirements, the freedom of trade, business, or profession. Article 18 arguably covers the freedom to conclude contracts including arbitration clauses. These fundamental freedoms would apply in relation to private-public arbitration as long as their exercise does not conflict with governmental and regulatory interests.

41 Landau (n 10) 1.
42 Peter B Rutledge, *Arbitration and the Constitution* (CUP 2012) 2.
43 Constitution of Pakistan 1973, art 146(3).
44 ibid art 152.
45 ibid art 159(4).
46 Gary B Born, 'Keynote Address: Arbitration and Freedom to Associate' (2009) 38 Ga J of Int'l & Comp L 7.
47 The Constitution of Pakistan 1973, ch 1, arts 16, 17, and 19.
48 This, however, is not exceptional. See Rutledge (n 42) 2.

A. Legal Framework for Private-Public Arbitration

Arbitration has always been present in the public regulatory and governance space in Pakistan since its independence. There is a consistent practice to include arbitration clauses in private-public contracts.[49] An overview of the existing legal framework reveals a three-layered practice of private-public arbitration in Pakistan: (1) as a mandatory requirement included in an Act of Parliament (primary legislation), ie when a statute passed by parliament itself requires the inclusion of arbitration clauses in private-public contracts; (2) as a mandatory provision included in the implementing rules or statutory instruments made by a public authority exercising its powers delegated by an Act of Parliament (primary legislation), ie when such rules or instruments give the public authority's general consent to arbitration to settle disputes over matters falling within the wider scope of the public authority's competence; and (3) as a clause in specific private-public contracts as a matter of general policy.

The most recent example of arbitration in primary legislation is the Special Economic Zones Act 2012 (SEZA).[50] The SEZA requires the inclusion of an arbitration clause in special economic zone development agreements between private entities and government authorities for the settlement of future disputes.[51] Similarly, the Federal Public Procurement Rules 2004 (FPP Rules)[52] are the most significant example of primary legislation. The FPP Rules require disputes between parties to a public procurement contract to be settled by arbitration.[53] The FPP Rules have been made under sections 26 and 27 of the Public Procurement Regulatory Authority Ordinance 2002,[54] which is an Act of Parliament that regulates all procurement of goods, services, and works in the public sector. The SEZA does not provide any details on the arbitration rules to be followed or the applicable law. However, the FPP Rules specifically require the procuring agencies to provide a method of arbitration in procurement contracts, consistent with the laws of Pakistan.[55]

Other notable examples of primary legislation giving general consent of public authorities to arbitrate future disputes include the rules made by the federal government,[56] and provincial governments of Baluchistan,[57] Khyber

[49] See eg *Khawaja Muhammad Usaf v North-West Frontier Province* (PLD 1955 (Peshawar) 72) (Justice Muhammad Shafi). This is one of the oldest reported cases where a Pakistani court validated arbitration in a public-private agreement.

[50] Special Economic Zones Act (XX of 2012).

[51] ibid ss 21(2)(iii) and 39.

[52] Federal Public Procurement Rules 2004 (9 June 2004) SRO432(I)/2004. A ditto copy of these rules, which apply to public procurement by the federal authorities, has been adopted in the province of Punjab as Punjab Public Procurement Rules 2009 (No MD.PPRA/1-1/2009). The province of Sindh has adopted the same with slight variation as the Sindh Public Procurement Rules 2010 (No SORI(SGA&CD)2-30/2010). The Balochistan Public Procurement Rules 2014 (No FD-SO (Mont:)1-31/BPPRA/2014/3725-3940/), however, do not include a detailed provision on arbitration but still refer to arbitration to resolve unsettled claims (See r 55 (C)). On the other hand, the Khyber Pakhtunkhwa Public Procurement of Goods, Works and Services Rules (2014) do not refer to arbitration at all.

[53] Federal Public Procurement Rules 2004 (n 52) rs 45(2) and 49.

[54] Public Procurement Regulatory Authority Ordinance (XXII of 2002).

[55] Federal Public Procurement Rules 2004 (n 52) r 49(2).

[56] Pakistan Mining Concession Rules 1949, r 80, cls (1), (5), and (6); Pakistan Mining Concession Rules 1960, r 77(6).

[57] The Balochistan Mineral Rules (No SO(MR)4-6/2002) of 2002, r 94.

Pakhtunkhwa,[58] and Punjab,[59] under the Regulation of Mines and Oil Fields and Mineral Development (Government Control) Act 1948.[60] These provincial and federal rules give a general consent of government authorities to arbitrate disputes relating to agreements between mining companies and government authorities. These rules require arbitration proceedings to be governed by domestic law and conducted in Pakistan.

The general consent given in these primary legislations eliminates the need for a separate arbitration agreement, or inclusion of arbitration clauses in every agreement between private entities and public authorities. Such pre-existing consent to arbitration is arguably intended to send positive signals to private entities that future disputes will be settled outside of the local courts. However, the pre-existing consent can also be seen as a preordained compulsion. The entire idea of pre-existing consent to arbitration is open to two crucial critiques. On the one hand, it has been argued that arbitration primarily operates in a 'private mode' of dispute resolution where interests of private entities can be preferred over public interests. Allowing private-public disputes to be resolved by arbitration leads to public interest being both unaccounted for and unprotected.[61] On the other hand, when public authorities give licences to, or conclude commercial contracts with, private entities, preordained arbitration—either in primary legislation, as a mandatory clause in licences, or a precondition in private-public contracts—can be viewed as unjust because it deprives private parties of enforcing their fundamental rights and constitutional protections against possible misuse of public authority through a court.[62]

Interestingly, the Mining Concession Rules 2002 of the Province of Sindh do not have arbitration provisions.[63] It is unclear why the Sindh authorities would not require arbitration when all other provinces and the federal government have required arbitration for the resolution of disputes with mining contractors. There is no indication that the government of Sindh has a general policy to exclude arbitration in private-public contracts. Perhaps the idea is to leave the matter to negotiation of individual contracts, which seems to be a better policy that counters the criticisms brought against the pre-existing consent to arbitration.

There is a more frequent practice of arbitration provisions in private-public contracts as a matter of public policy even though it is not required by primary legislation. This 'contract-based' practice of private-public arbitration is present in a variety of public governance sectors. An overview of the cases decided by Pakistani courts

[58] North-West Frontier Province Mining Concession Rules (No SOIV/M/3-143/03(Rules)/1807) of 2005, r 77.

[59] Punjab Mining Concession Rules (No V(I&MD)3-21/95 VOL-II) of 2002, r 78.

[60] See s 2 of the Regulation of Mines and Oil Fields and Mineral Development (Government Control) Act (XXIV of 1948).

[61] Stavros Brekoulakis and Margaret B Devaney, 'Public-Private Arbitration and the Public Interest Under English Law' (2017) 80(1) MLR 22.

[62] There is a growing body of literature in the United States examining the legal and moral implications of mandatory arbitration imposed through unilaterally drafted contracts. See eg Jean R Sternlight, 'Creeping Mandatory Arbitration: Is It Just?' (2005) 57(5) Stan L Rev 1631; Victor D Quintanilla and Alexander B Avtgis, 'The Public Believes Predispute Binding Arbitration Clauses Are Unjust: Ethical Implications for Dispute-System Design in the Time of Vanishing Trials' (2017) 85 Fordham L Rev 2119. See also discussion in section VI below.

[63] Sindh Mining Concession Rules (No SC(Tech)/M&MD/3-9/2002) of 2002.

suggests that the most prominent use of private-public arbitration has been in public procurement contracts, government concessions, leases and licenses, infrastructure and development contracts, and private-public partnership agreements.[64]

Despite the well-established practice of including arbitration clauses in private-public contracts, the development of private-public arbitration has experienced some drawbacks as well. In 1975 the government passed legislation called the Capital Development Authority (Abatement of Arbitration Proceedings) Act (CDA-AAP).[65] The CDA-AAP annulled all arbitration agreements and pending arbitration proceedings between the Capital Development Authority (CDA) and private contractors. These contracts were mostly concluded for the execution of development projects or the supply of goods or services to CDA. The preamble of the CDA-AAP states that the references made to arbitration in such contracts had failed to achieve their objectives, which presumably were the speedy disposal of disputes. The government, as a matter of public interest, wanted to assert more administrative control to ensure timely and effective implementation of those contracts hampered by the repeated arbitration requests made by private contractors. Although the CDA-AAP was limited only to the contracts concluded by the CDA, it could have been viewed as a general policy against the inclusion of arbitration in private-public contracts. However, the courts have interpreted the CDA-AAP as a one-off law to block arbitration proceedings and annul arbitration contracts concluded by the CDA prior to the passing of the CDA-AAP. The courts have also clarified that the prohibition was inapplicable to arbitration agreements concluded by the CDA after the CDA-AAP was passed. Furthermore, the courts have also held that the prohibition contained in the CDA-AAP was applicable only to the CDA and did not affect arbitration agreements concluded by any other public entity.[66]

Arbitration is explicitly or impliedly allowed by major commercial laws in Pakistan without making specific distinction between private-private arbitration and private-public arbitration. For example, the Partnership Act 1932 gives an implied authority to a partner acting on behalf of the firm to refer any dispute to arbitration.[67] The Companies Act 2017 allows companies to refer their present and future disputes to arbitration by a written agreement.[68] Interestingly, the Companies Act 2017 requires the application of AA 1940 to all arbitrations agreed to by companies.[69] This is potentially problematic when foreign companies have registered their subsidiaries in Pakistan but may not want their arbitration agreements with local companies or public entities to be governed by Pakistani law. The Companies Act 2017 also allows a liquidator to resolve any dispute with the company's shareholders over the share price through arbitration.[70] The limitation that arbitration agreements in these important areas of

[64] See discussion in section IV below.

[65] Capital Development Authority (Abatement of Arbitration Proceedings) Act (XXVII of 1975).

[66] *Capital Development Authority v RM Gulistan Engineers and Contractors (Pvt) Ltd* (2015 CLC 734) (Athar Minallah, and Aamer Farooq, JJ); *Capital Development Authority v Muhammad Ahsan* (2009 MLD 451) (Dr Sajid Qureshi J).

[67] The Partnership Act (IX of 1932) s 19(2)(a).

[68] Companies Act (XIX of 2017) s 278.

[69] ibid s 278(3).

[70] ibid s 356(3)(b).

commercial activity are governed by the AA 1940 has implications for those private-public arbitration agreements where contracting parties have agreed to decide their disputes at international forums outside Pakistan. In such cases, the AA 1940 would remain the law governing the arbitration agreement although parties may have agreed to a foreign law as applicable to their main contract.

As regards the possible theoretical foundations, although the Pakistani Constitution suggests a fair balance between private rights and regulatory interests, the AA 1940 provides detailed provisions on arbitration, and the major commercial laws allow arbitration as an alternative to litigation in the courts; these legal provisions, individually or taken together, do not offer a unified theory of private-private or private-public arbitration.

B. Judicial Recognition of Private-Public Arbitration

The new legislation implementing the NYC and the ICSID Convention has brought much-needed certainty on the enforcement of international arbitration agreements and awards in Pakistan. The courts are now more willing to enforce private-private international arbitration agreements and awards.[71] However, the courts have continued with their cautious approach on arbitration in cases of private-public disputes involving important issues of public interest. This cautious approach has not developed because the courts do not recognize, as a matter of principle, the right of public authorities to enter into arbitration agreements. The courts' reasonings in three prominent cases, namely *Hubco*, *SGS*, and *Tethyan*,[72] suggest that private-public arbitration will not be enforced only when important public interests are at stake.

In *Hubco*, the private claimant requested the court to refer its dispute over the performance of a power purchase agreement (PPA) with a public authority (the Water and Power Development Authority (WAPDA)) to arbitration under the terms of their contract. WAPDA opposed this request, alleging that the dispute was not arbitrable because it involved serious allegations of corruption, fraud, and mala fide acts on the part of the government officials in the formation of the PPA. The matter was heard by a five-member bench of the Supreme Court, where WAPDA's contention was upheld by a majority decision. The majority drew a clear line between arbitrable commercial matters and non-arbitrable matters involving the public interest. The majority observed that the allegations levelled by WAPDA were not commercial in nature as they raised very serious public policy questions.[73] The courts in the *SGS* and *Tethyan* cases also prevented the enforcement of private-public arbitration agreements due

[71] See eg *Lakhra* (n 25); Ghouri (n 11).

[72] See *The Hub Power Company Ltd (Hubco) v Pakistan WAPDA* (PLD 2000 Supreme Court 841) (Muhammad Bashir Jehangiri, Actg CJ, Sh Ijaz Nisar, Abdur Rehman Khan, Sh Riaz Ahmed and Munir A Sheikh, JJ); *SGS* (n 28); *Tethyan* (otherwise known in Pakistan as the *Maulana Abdul Haque Baloch* case) (n 31).

[73] *Hubco* (n 72). See also Mr Justice Mian Saqib Nisar, 'International Arbitration in the Context of Globalization: A Pakistani Perspective' (Speech on 50th year celebration of the Supreme Court of Pakistan, Islamabad, August 2006).

to similar allegations of corruption by public officials in the formation of underlying contracts.

This principled stance by Pakistani courts is tenable. For, regardless of the presence of an arbitration agreement, private-public disputes involving issues of corruption by public officials have no possibility to be decided by arbitration as a matter of domestic, international, and transnational public policy.[74] Matters that are against public interest are most likely to be considered as against public policy with regards to the recognition and enforcement of arbitration agreements and awards. This was recently illustrated by Justice Ayesha Malik in *Orient Power.*[75]

In *Orient Power*, a two-member bench of the Lahore High Court, exercising its appellate jurisdiction, was asked to determine, among other things, whether the award of compensation under the 'take-or-pay' clause of a gas supply agreement (GSA) between private-public disputants was unjust and therefore against the public policy of Pakistan.[76] The 'take-or-pay' clause in the GSA required the purchaser (a private entity) to pay for the quantity of gas it had agreed to take within a prescribed time frame, even if it was not actually taken by the purchaser. 'Take-or-pay' clauses are commonly found in the energy sector, where overhead costs are high, and are meant to guarantee the agreed upon payment to sellers or suppliers if the buyers fail to buy the agreed amount of goods. The arbitration tribunal had awarded a large amount of compensation to the supplier (a public entity) under the 'take-or-pay' clause for the quantity of gas the purchaser had failed to take within the agreed time frame. However, according to the purchaser, the gas produced for the purchaser was in fact sold to other purchasers and the purchaser's failure to take the same had caused no actual financial loss to the supplier.[77]

The purchaser primarily argued that the court should protect the fundamental notions of justice, fairness, and morality, and that anything done in contravention of the same would offend public policy.[78] This argument was further strengthened by the purchaser arguing that: (1) a party should not be permitted to recover more than what it has actually lost; (2) a public sector entity should not be allowed to unjustly enrich itself at the expense of a private person; (3) that unjust enrichment offends the principles of economic justice as embodied in the Constitution; (4) that section 74 of the Contract Act[79] does not permit the supplier to recover more than reasonable compensation; and (5) that the supplier can, at best, only recover losses that it has actually incurred.[80] On the other hand, the supplier primarily argued that the amount awarded in compensation was in fact based on the price of gas supplied. The supplier further argued that the purchaser's arguments based on public policy were flawed because public policy exception could be triggered where there was an element of injury

[74] See eg Emmanuel Gaillard, 'The Emergence of Transnational Responses to Corruption in International Arbitration' (2019) 35(1) Arb Int'l 1.
[75] *Orient Power Company (Private) Limited v Sui Northern Gas Pipelines Limited* (2019 PLD (Lahore) 607) Ayesha A Malik, and Shahid Jamil Khan, JJ.
[76] ibid para 22.
[77] ibid para 23.
[78] ibid para 28.
[79] See n 8 above.
[80] *Orient Power* (n 75).

to the public or public interest, or where the enforcement of the award was not possible because it violated the laws of Pakistan.[81]

Justice Malik began her analysis with an observation that public policy, in the sense of Article V of the NYC as incorporated in Pakistan,[82] included moral, social, or economic principles that were sacrosanct and required protection without any restriction.[83] She observed that the notion of public policy under Article V of the NYC was kept fluid and adaptive, and could be invoked in cases of patent illegality or matters that were fundamental for a state. Justice Malik further opined that the public policy exception allowed a state to safeguard its core values and fundamental notions of morality and justice, which may change over time. She concluded that an arbitration award could be set aside when its enforcement offended these fundamentals.[84]

However, Justice Malik eventually decided to enforce the award on the basis of a factual finding that the compensation awarded was in fact based on moneys owed by the purchaser for the gas actually supplied. The co-presiding Justice Shahid Jamil Khan agreed with the decision but disagreed with the reasoning of the arbitrator with regard to the domestic court's ability to set aside an award when the contract is found to be null and void, inoperative, or incapable of being performed under Article II(3) of the NYC.[85] Justice Khan struggled with the arbitrator's observation that there were lacunae in Pakistani law regarding the concept of the 'take-or-pay' clause. In other words, Justice Khan could have declined to enforce the award had the 'take-or-pay' clause been affected by any of the components of Article II(3) of the NYC.

It appears from the reasoning of Justice Malik that she was not prepared to refuse enforcement of the award even though the factual finding had not favoured the supplier. She was inclined to enforce contractual obligations under the 'take-or-pay' clause of the GSA, which were considered as freely acquired by contracting parties regardless of the power imbalances between a government entity and a private party at the time of negotiation and conclusion of the contract. On the other hand, it appears that both presiding judges would have enforced the award regardless of whether a part of the awarded compensation had represented the unsupplied gas under the terms of the 'take-or-pay' clause. Justice Malik seemed to have been equally unpersuaded by the arguments based on unjust enrichment and economic injustice despite her own observation regarding the importance of morality and justice as necessary ingredients of domestic public policy.[86] Justice Khan did not comment on this issue in his concurring opinion.

Justice Malik's clarification of public policy as 'moral, social or economic principles', 'patent illegality or matters fundamental for a state', and 'core values and fundamental notions of morality and justice' clarifies the types of public interests covered by the notion of public policy. The reasonings of both justices indicate that, although they were prepared to take the public policy arguments very seriously, they were not inclined to refuse the enforcement of a freely agreed upon arbitration agreement and

[81] ibid para 33.
[82] See n 18 above.
[83] *Orient Power* (n 75) para 42.
[84] ibid para 57.
[85] ibid, separate note by Justice Shahid Jamil Khan, which is part of this judgment.
[86] ibid paras 58–60.

the resulting award merely because it was financially more favourable to one of the contracting parties. Furthermore, both justices did not consider the inequality between private parties and public entities with regard to bargaining power in the negotiation and conclusion of contracts as economic injustice, and as contravening the notion of public interest.

In other cases, while dealing with disputes related to private-public contracts, Pakistani High Courts and the Supreme Court have rather frequently addressed the question of arbitrability using their original jurisdiction under Articles 199 and 184(3) of the 1973 Constitution. The original jurisdiction of Pakistani superior courts, commonly referred to as writ jurisdiction when exercised by the High Courts, is meant to facilitate greater protection of constitutional rights and accountability for misuse of public power.[87] The courts in such cases have, although not very consistently, taken a similar approach to maintaining the *jure gestionis* and *jure imperii* distinctions,[88] and have distinguished the breach of contract cases from the cases of illegal exercise of administrative authority.[89] In the former category of cases, the courts have swayed the parties to resort to arbitration, whereas in the latter category, the courts have not enforced arbitration clauses in private-public contracts, declaring that they are not ordinary commercial contracts.[90] This means that, although courts have rendered arbitration as primarily a private law subject, they have separated the public law cases from private law cases when enforcing arbitration clauses in private-public contracts. These aspects are elaborated in more detail in the next section, which discusses the scope of judicial review in private-public disputes.

IV. Judicial Review of Private-Public Arbitration

Pakistani courts have never affirmed the strict doctrines of ouster of jurisdiction and non-arbitrability.[91] Unlike the earlier stance of courts in the United States,[92] and some other jurisdictions,[93] Pakistani courts have always been open to the idea

[87] Melissa Crouch, 'The Prerogative Writs as Constitutional Transfer' (2018) 38 OJLS 653, 664.

[88] For discussion on the distinction between *jure gestionis* and *jure imperii*, see Gus Van Harten, 'The Public-Private Distinction in the International Arbitration of Individual Claims against the State' (2007) 56 ICLQ 371.

[89] More detailed discussion on this is in section IV below.

[90] *Messrs Airport Support Services v The Airport Manager, Quaid-E-Azam International Airport, Karachi* (1998 SCMR 2268) (Saiduzzaman Siddiqui, Raja Afrasiab Khan, and Wajihuddin Ahmed, JJ) para (e).

[91] cf ibid. The classical position of the US courts is explained by Robert Braucher, 'Arbitration under Government Contracts' (1952) 17 LCP 473. The use of arbitration to settle administrative disputes in the US has come a long way from being categorized by the courts as an ouster of jurisdiction and non-arbitrable to an opposite view allowing complete freedom to administrative agencies to resolve their disputes with private parties through arbitration. See eg Bruff (n 2); Rebecca Hanner White, 'Arbitration and the Administrative State' (2003) 38 Wake Forest L Rev 1283.

[92] Rutledge (n 42) 16.

[93] See eg Andrey Kalimanov, 'Non-Arbitrability of Disputes Arising Out of Government Contracts in Russia' (*CIS Arbitration Forum*, 18 July 2014) <www.cisarbitration.com/2014/07/18/non-arbitrability-of-disputes-arising-out-of-government-contracts-in-russia/> accessed 6 January 2025; Gavin Margetson and Vanina Sucharitkul, 'Thai Government Lifts Total Ban on Arbitration Clauses in State Contracts' (*Herbert Smith Freehills*, 25 November 2015) <http://hsfnotes.com/arbitration/2015/11/25/thai-government-lifts-total-ban-on-arbitration-clauses-in-state-contracts/> accessed 6 January 2025.

of settlement of private-public disputes by arbitration. For example, in one of the earliest cases involving the enforceability of an arbitration agreement between a government functionary and a private supplier, the Peshawar High Court enforced the arbitration agreement.[94] Likewise, in *Messrs M Esmailjee & Sons*,[95] a mining lease had been granted by the federal government to a private entity and a dispute arose out of an alleged default by the lessee to pay rent and a royalty to the government. A blanket clause in the Pakistan Mining Concession Rules 1949 (PMCR) applicable to all leases and licenses required the settlement of disputes by arbitration.[96] The federal government argued that matters between a public authority and a private entity should not be referred to arbitration, in the interests of national security and sovereignty. However, Justice Wahiduddin Ahmed ruled that the dispute was primarily private and commercial in nature, and no risk to national security or sovereignty was involved. He ordered the government to participate in the arbitration proceedings that the lessee had initiated.

A. Balancing Party Autonomy Against Public Interest

The analysis of decided cases reveals that Pakistani courts have given precedence to the protection of the public interest over the enforcement of a party's right to arbitration when issues of public interest, such as the protection of constitutional rights and accountability for misuse of public power, arise from a private-public contract. For this, the courts have distinguished a simple breach of contract from a breach of contract involving arbitrary and unlawful action on the part of a public authority. The courts have declared the latter category of breach as being subject to judicial review regardless of whether the contract contained an arbitration clause. In such cases, the courts have granted relief to disputing parties themselves instead of referring the dispute to arbitration under the terms of their contract.

A leading case in this regard is *Messrs Airport Support Services*.[97] The dispute in this case was related to a licence awarded by a public authority to a private entity to provide passenger facilitation and assistant services at the Quaid-e-Azam International Airport in Karachi. The public authority had cancelled the licence and confiscated a security deposit, alleging that the licensee was carrying out unauthorized money exchange business at the airport. The private entity filed a writ petition under Article 199 of the 1973 Constitution, where a two-member bench of the Karachi High Court was required to review whether the cancellation of the licence by the public authority was arbitrary and against the petitioner's constitutional rights. Justice Abdul Majid Khanzada and Justice Abdul Latif Qureshi referred the petitioner to the arbitration clause contained in the licence. Declaring that a breach of contract by the government authority did not, by itself, constitute a breach of constitutional rights requiring

[94] *Khawaja Muhammad Usaf* (n 49).

[95] *Messrs M Esmailjee & Sons v The Federation of Pakistan* (PLD 1959 (Karachi) 87).

[96] See nn 57 and 60 above.

[97] *Messrs Airport Support Services v The Airport Manager, Civil Aviation Authority, Karachi* (1997 CLC (Karachi) 1212).

judicial review, the court directed the petitioner to resort to arbitration in accordance with the terms of licence.[98]

On appeal, however, the Supreme Court reversed the decision, holding that the High Court had failed to take into consideration the public interest involved.[99] A three-member bench of the Supreme Court, composed of Justice Saiduzzaman Siddiqui, Justice Raja Afrasiab Khan, and Justice Wajihuddin Ahmed,[100] held that, regardless of an arbitration clause in a contract, the court's discretion in a constitutional petition under Articles 199 or 184(3) may give way to judicial review to protect public interests and public goods where a public authority has exceeded its power and wilfully or wantonly trampled upon vested private or public rights.[101] However, the Supreme Court refused any relief to the petitioner because it concluded that the petitioner was in fact carrying out the unauthorized money exchange business.

This line of reasoning by the Supreme Court means that the principled stance taken by Pakistani courts to enforce arbitration in private-public disputes does not undermine the legitimate exercise of regulatory powers by public authorities. Pakistani courts have considered a public authority's action as legitimate exercise of regulatory power when such action was taken in the broader public interest, or when it came within the domain of government's regulatory power and not within the category of commercial activity. In such cases, the courts have refused to enforce arbitration in private-public contracts although the government's regulatory action has negatively affected the interests of the private parties to such contracts. The courts, therefore, have maintained a distinction between non-arbitrable private-public disputes that relate to the legitimate exercise of regulatory power and arbitrable disputes relating to the breach of contracts.

Inpaktech Industries is another illuminating example that further clarifies the basis of such judicial intervention in private-public disputes.[102] In this case, Justice Sheikh Amjad Ali of the Lahore High Court was required to review the provincial government's decision to exempt certain items from the goods exit tax. The Zila Council, which is a district-level layer of the provincial government, had awarded the petitioner a contract for the collection of goods exit tax. However, the government's decision to exempt taxable goods had caused loss of profit to the contractor/petitioner. A provision in the Punjab Zila Council (Export Tax) Rules 1990 required the disputes arising from such contracts to be referred to arbitration. Ironically, instead of arguing that changes in the tax regime are a prerogative of the provincial government and do not amount to breach of contract, the respondent Zila Council argued that the matter be referred to arbitration in accordance with the Export Tax Rules. However, the court meticulously held that the petitioner had not challenged the contract or claimed any relief against Zila Council, but had in fact challenged the authority of the provincial government to regulate the tax regime. The court concluded that changing the tax regime was within the legitimate exercise of the government's regulatory

[98] ibid.

[99] *Messrs Airport Support Services* (n 90).

[100] ibid para (e), relying on *Anjuman-e-Ahmadlya Sergodha v Deputy Commissioner, Sargodha* (PLD 1966 SC 639) and *Muhammad Ashraf Ali v Muhammad Naseer* (1986 SCMR 1096).

[101] ibid.

[102] *Messrs Inpaktech Industries (Pvt) Ltd v Government of Punjab* (1998 MLD 1383).

power and could not be referred to arbitration although it may have negatively affected the interests of a private party to a private-public contract.[103]

Messrs Airport Support Services and *Inpaktech Industries* brought much-needed clarity to the question of arbitrability of disputes related to private-public contracts. In these two cases, the courts have shown a clear approach to ensuring a right balance between the protection of public interest and the legitimate exercise of the government's regulatory powers, on the one hand, and the enforcement of arbitration clauses contained in private-public contracts, on the other. These two cases explicitly distinguished the types of issues involved in private-public disputes where arbitration will or will not be enforced.

The subsequent explanation in *Wak Orient Power* further clarified that the public interest requiring protection can either be in the form of a public authority overstepping its powers and violating constitutional rights of an individual or an entity, or it can be a wider public interest in the form of a public good.[104] The dispute in *Wak Orient Power* resulted from the defendant public authority's termination of a contract for the production and supply of electricity by the petitioner. A three-member bench of Lahore High Court, consisting of Justice Malik Muhammad Qayyum, Justice Muhammad Asif Jan, and Justice Mian Saeed-ur-Rehman Farrukhin, first reaffirmed the basic requirement that private-public contracts can be subject to judicial review only when relief against an arbitrary and unlawful action on the part of a public authority is sought. Second, the Court emphasized that the public authority had acted against the public interest by terminating the contract for unjustifiable reasons in the face of an acute shortage of electricity in the country. Importantly, the Court emphasized that the arbitration agreement would have remained enforceable had the dispute related only to the breach of contract. However, the Court held that judicial review was a more effective remedy in this case as the dispute related to the legality of the administrative action terminating the contract.[105]

The *Wak Orient Power* court further clarified conditions upon which a relief by way of judicial review may be refused to a private entity seeking enforcement of a contract, or its arbitration clause, against a public authority. Those conditions include when:[106] (1) the national interest is thereby likely to be endangered; and (2) the contract is shown to be unconscionable, mala fide, unreasonable, or against public policy. These two conditions essentially showcase the wider spectrum of public interests that the courts are inclined to protect in private-public disputes. The reference to 'national interest' in the first condition is more appropriately described as 'national security interest' in contemporary vocabulary. The second condition is likely to apply to cases involving corruption by public officials.

Based on the reasoning of these three cases, it can be concluded that arbitration in a private-public dispute is possible, subject to the following three conditions: (1) the public authority's action does not fall in the category of the legitimate exercise of

[103] ibid para (b).
[104] *Messrs Wak Orient Power and Light Ltd v Government of Pakistan, Ministry of Water and Power* (1998 CLC 1178).
[105] ibid para 12.
[106] ibid para 23.

regulatory power; (2) the public authority's action does not violate the public interest understood narrowly as the constitutional rights of individuals to be treated with fairness and justice; and (3) the public authority's action does not violate the public interest understood broadly as the interests of public at large.

1 Challenges with *Jure Gestionis*- and *Jure Imperii*-Based Distinctions

Messrs Airport Support Services, *Inpaktech Industries*, and *Wak Orient Power* have undoubtedly provided a set of clear principles for the consideration of public interests in the enforcement of arbitration in private-public contracts. However, the subsequent *Pharmax* case decided by the Lahore High Court used a different line of reasoning.[107] The *Pharmax* dispute related to the terms and conditions of a partnership contract between a private entity and a public authority for the establishment of pharmacies in public hospitals. The court took up the question whether the contract was concluded by the public authority acting in an administrative capacity or as a commercial entity. Justice Syed Najum-ul-Hassan Kazmi divided private-public contracts into two categories, namely:[108] (1) 'private contracts', which are not mandated by primary legislation; and (2) 'statutory contracts', which are mandated by primary legislation. The court found that the private-public partnership was a private contract and not a statutory contract. It referred the parties to arbitration, declaring that such contracts do not fall within the purview of judicial review.[109]

The *Pharmax* court's distinction of *jure gestionis* and *jure imperii* is based on whether or not the public authority had a statutory mandate to conclude a private-public contract rather than acting in a commercial or administrative capacity. This line of reasoning essentially means that any private-public contract concluded to fulfil the requirements of primary legislation falls under the *jure imperii* category and, therefore, disputes arising out of such contacts are non-arbitrable. This position is untenable, however, when legislation has by itself required arbitration for the resolution of disputes related to private-public contracts. For example, according to the *Pharmax* court's distinction, public procurement contracts concluded under the FPP Rules[110] would fall under the *jure imperii* category; however, the FPP Rules themselves prescribe that any disputes over such contracts will be resolved by arbitration.

In principle, the *Pharmax* court should have ruled that the scope of judicial review was limited to *jure imperii* administrative actions and did not include cases of breaches of *jure gestionis* contracts that are concluded by a public authority acting merely as a commercial enterprise. This would have provided a more logical ground to compel arbitration in private-public contracts, to contrast and complement the highly sophisticated expositions for the exercise of judicial review based on various aspects of public interest given by the courts in *Messrs Airport Support Services*, *Inpaktech Industries*, and *Wak Orient Power*. The courts in these three cases have established clear rules for the exercise of their constitutional jurisdiction to review cases

107 *Messrs Pharmax Pakistan (Pvt) Ltd v Government of Pakistan through Secretary, Ministry of Health* (2000 CLC 628).
108 ibid paras (a) and (7).
109 ibid para 6.
110 Federal Public Procurement Rules 2004 (n 52).

involving public interests instead of referring them to arbitration. Similar to the public interests involved in these three cases—such as the provision of public services at an airport, the increase in government's revenue by collection of taxes, and the provision of electricity to the public—in *Pharmax*, too, the primary purpose of opening pharmacies in public hospitals on the basis of a private-public partnership was to provide affordable medicine to the public.[111]

As a matter of fact, it is highly unlikely to completely rule out the question of public interest in any private-public contract. Public authorities may have concluded contracts with private entities specifically to meet public needs. However, if the primary intention of private parties to such contracts is to make legitimate profit, these contracts should be treated as commercial transactions. In cases involving such private-public contracts, whether or not they are statutory or private according to the *Pharmax* court's distinction, courts should not exercise judicial review and refer the dispute to arbitration, subject, of course, to the three conditions summarized above, namely: (1) the public authority's action does not fall in the category of the legitimate exercise of regulatory power; (2) the public authority's action does not violate the public interest understood narrowly as the constitutional rights of individuals to be treated with fairness and justice; and (3) the public authority's action does not violate the public interest understood broadly as the interests of public at large.

Additionally, the *Pharmax* court's division of private and statutory contracts obliterates the government's policy to include mandatory arbitration in private-public contracts. If the inclusion of mandatory arbitration in recent and primary legislations, such as the SEZA[112] and the FPP Rules,[113] is meant to prefer arbitration over litigation as a matter of policy for certain types of private-public contracts, the courts need to make a clearer distinction between commercial and administrative actions of public authorities based on *jure gestionis* and *jure imperii* principles. Just as the courts have clearly identified cases requiring judicial intervention where constitutional rights and public interests need protection, the courts need to develop clear and consistent rules for cases involving breaches of commercial contracts that should be referred to arbitration.

Subsequently, in *Toyota Frontier Motors*,[114] the court used a much stronger and clearer tone while refusing to interfere in disputes involving breaches of private-public contracts where the public authority was acting *jure gestionis*.[115] In that case, the petitioner company challenged the termination of a contract by a public authority, related to the supply of vehicles. The contract included an arbitration clause. The petitioner had neither alleged any mala fide action on the part of the public authority's termination of contract nor disputed the flaws identified in the supplied vehicles by a technical committee. Justice Waqar Ahmad Seth and Justice Musarrat Hilali Such were convinced that they should not interfere in such private-public contracts by exercising their constitutional jurisdiction. They opined that routine contractual disputes

[111] ibid para 2.
[112] See n 50 above.
[113] See n 52 above.
[114] *Toyota Frontier Motors (Pvt) Ltd v Government of Khyber Pakhtunkhwa through Chief Secretary, KPK* (2016 YLR Peshawar 1631).
[115] See section IV above.

between private parties and public authorities were not open to scrutiny under constitutional jurisdiction when there was no allegation of ill will or mala fide conduct of the public authority. The court clarified that questions over whether a private-public contract was just, fair, transparent, and reasonable could come under its constitutional jurisdiction when there was an element of public interest involved. This further strengthens the view that the *Pharmax* court's distinction between private and statutory contracts is not tenable. The appropriate way to distinguish ordinary private-public contracts concluded in a commercial capacity from contracts concluded in the exercise of a public authority's administrative capacity is based on *jure gestionis* and *jure imperii* principles.

V. Procedural Structure and Support for Private-Public Arbitration

There is a frequent practice to use arbitration clauses in private-public contracts, and Pakistani courts have never objected per se to the arbitrability of disputes related to private-public contracts. The courts have reviewed private-public contracts to ensure the protection of public interest and the constitutional rights of citizens but not as a means to block the resolution of disputes through arbitration. This applies not only to private-public contracts providing for resolution of disputes through domestic arbitration, such as in *Messrs Airport Support Services*[116]and *Wak Orient Power*,[117] but also to those that provided for international arbitration, such as in *SGS*, *Lakhra*, and *Tethyan*.[118] Likewise, Pakistani courts have neither prevented government executives from giving consent to arbitration in government contracts with private parties, such as in *Khawaja Muhammad Usaf*,[119] nor have they objected to such consent given in primary legislation, such as in *Messrs M Esmailjee & Sons*.[120] Additionally, Pakistani courts have enforced arbitration agreements concluded by a public authority acting as a commercial entity, such as in *Pharmax*.[121] The courts have, however, objected to public authorities' consent to arbitration given in a treaty when such treaty has not attained the force of law through domestic legislation, such as in *SGS*.[122]

In principle, therefore, there is no legal obstacle for a private-public dispute to be decided by arbitration. This is true for both domestic and international arbitration. Many laws and statutory enactments, such as the SEZA and the FPP Rules, require private-public disputes to be settled by domestic arbitration.[123] The FPP Rules require the procuring public agencies to provide a detailed method of arbitration in the procurement contract.[124] As there is no special procedure applicable to private-public

[116] See n 90 above.
[117] See n 104 above.
[118] See nn 25, 28, and 31 above.
[119] *Khawaja Muhammad Usaf* (n 49).
[120] *Messrs M Esmailjee* (n 95).
[121] *Messrs Pharmax Pakistan Ltd* (n 107).
[122] *SGS* (n 28).
[123] See nn 51–53 above.
[124] Federal Public Procurement Rules 2004 (n 52) r 49.

arbitration, the general arbitration law set out in the AA 1940 applies to all types of domestic arbitrations. This essentially means that private-public arbitration is also conducted just as arbitration between private parties. There is no specific public record of private-public disputes decided by arbitration, but the evidence of this practice is well found in the court cases where the resulting awards are presented for enforcement. The following discussions explain the general arbitration procedures prescribed by the AA 1940 for arbitrations conducted in Pakistan, highlighting if they are suitable for private-public disputes.

A. Submission of a Private-Public Dispute to Arbitration

As there is no special law providing for the procedure to submit private-public disputes to arbitration, the provisions of the AA 1940 will apply. In fact, most of the arbitration clauses included in private-public contracts state that the arbitration will be governed by the AA 1940 provisions.[125] The AA 1940 provides for three classes or routes of arbitration: (1) arbitration without intervention of the court;[126] (2) arbitration with intervention of the court where there is no suit pending;[127] and (3) arbitration in suits.[128]

The first class of arbitration is applicable where parties have concluded an arbitration agreement and, on accrual of a dispute, are willing to submit their dispute to arbitration in accordance with their arbitration agreement. The courts should normally have a limited role in this class of arbitration, that is, only to assist the parties to carry through the terms of their agreement.[129] As such, there is no apparent legal obstacle if a private-public dispute is submitted to arbitration without a court's intervention.[130] However, Pakistani courts have not hesitated to intervene in private-public disputes even when both of the disputing parties were willing to arbitrate. In *Lakhra*, for example, both the public authority and the private party were willing to submit to arbitration. However, the court held that the public authority's consent was marred with allegations of corruption by its officials brought to light by a *suo moto* case taken up by the Supreme Court.[131]

Additionally, in private-public disputes, the courts have taken very serious note of all types of conceding statements made by public officials incurring liability to the

[125] See eg the Standard Form of Contract for Engineering Consultancy Services (art 9 of the contract for smaller projects, art 8.2 of the larger contracts of time-based assignment, and art 7.2 for larger contracts of lump sum assignments) (11 June 2007) available on the Pakistan Engineering Council's (PEC) website (<www.pec.org.pk≥) accessed 6 January 2025. The drafts specifically mention that the standard contract is harmonized with the PPRA Rules.

[126] AA 1940 (n 7) ch II, ss 3–19.

[127] ibid ch III, ss 20.

[128] ibid ch IV, ss 21–25.

[129] *Haji Abdul Rashid Arif v Aziz Rehman and others* (2010 CLC 1014).

[130] See eg *Government of Balochistan v Enterprise and Development Consulting (Pvt) Ltd* (2015 CLD 1743).

[131] *Lakhra* (n 25) para 5. The Supreme Court in Pakistan has in the past taken many *suo moto* actions under Article 184(3) of the Constitution to review contracts concluded by public authorities where allegations of kickbacks and large-scale corruption by public officials have surfaced in the local media.

government.[132] To avoid such complications, public officials do not normally prefer to submit a dispute having implications for the public purse to arbitration without a court's intervention. The private parties to a private-public arbitration agreement are, of course, not restricted by such implications. However, the public authorities are likely to challenge the referral of a dispute to arbitration by courts in disputes having public interest implications. In practice, therefore, a private-public arbitration will most likely be ordered and assisted by a court. This means that the AA 1940's three classes or routes of arbitration are less significant for private-public disputes, although this limitation to private-public arbitration might not apply to international arbitration, where domestic courts have no control over the arbitration proceedings.

B. Establishment of the Arbitral Tribunal and Organization of the Proceedings

There is no express provision in the AA 1940 on the procedure of establishment of an arbitral tribunal. However, the implied sense is that a tribunal may be established by the disputing parties in accordance with their arbitration agreement. If the arbitration agreement is silent on the mode of appointment or the number of arbitrators, the AA 1940 provides implied conditions requiring the appointment of sole arbitrator.[133] It is also an implied condition that if the arbitration agreement provides for an even number of arbitrators, the arbitrators shall appoint an 'umpire' not later than one month from the latest date of their respective appointments.[134] Parties may also agree that a tribunal be appointed by a third person or by a designated public office.[135] The AA 1940 also authorizes the Civil Court to appoint an arbitral tribunal in certain circumstances, namely: (1) when the parties fail to agree to the appointment of arbitrators in accordance with the terms of their arbitration agreement; (2) when the umpire neglects or refuses to act, or is incapable of acting, or dies and the parties' agreement is silent on the appointment of a replacement arbitrator; and (3) when the contract requires parties or arbitrators to appoint an umpire and they fail to do so.[136] The AA 1940 further provides that the authority of an appointed arbitrator or umpire shall not be revocable except with the leave of court unless a contrary intention is expressed in the arbitration agreement.[137]

There is no special provision in the AA 1940 for the establishment of a tribunal for private-public arbitration. There is nothing in the administrative or constitutional law either that would require public entities to follow a particular method for the appointment of a tribunal. The assumption is that the private-public agreement having an arbitration clause would also provide the procedure for the appointment of the arbitral tribunal. The FPP Rules, for example, state that 'the procuring agencies shall provide

[132] See eg *Ch Qaiser Mehmood v Province of Punjab through Secretary, Government Communication and Works* (2012 SCMR Supreme Court 1606) (Nasir-ul-Mulk and Amir Hani Muslim, JJ).
[133] AA 1940 (n 7) s 3 and 1st sch, item 1.
[134] ibid s 3 and 1st sch, item 1.
[135] ibid s 4.
[136] ibid s 8.
[137] ibid s 5.

for a method of arbitration in the procurement contract, not inconsistent with the laws of Pakistan'.[138]

Giving leverage to public authorities to prescribe arbitration procedures in private-public arbitrations in a practical sense means that the principle of equality of parties and free consent is undermined. This is particularly evident, for example, from those private-public contracts where the public authority is allowed to appoint a sole arbitrator by itself or designate its own official as a sole arbitrator. This was the case in *Haji Naimatullah*, where the Karachi High Court did not find anything wrong with the appointment of a sole arbitrator by the public authority in accordance with an express provision in the private-public contract.[139] Likewise, the law does not provide a special procedure for the appointment of counsel representing public authorities in arbitrations. Although the law gives freedom to parties to negotiate procedural aspects of arbitration in their contracts, clearly defined procedures laid down in the law will reduce the burden on the negotiating parties to devise such procedures by agreement.

Where the parties to a private-public agreement have not provided for the detailed procedure for the appointment of arbitrators, the default provisions set out in the First Schedule of the AA 1940 would apply.[140] The First Schedule provides a list of implied conditions for arbitration agreements, which are applicable unless the parties have agreed otherwise. It requires, among other things, that the tribunal will consist of a sole arbitrator unless an arbitration agreement expressly provides otherwise.[141]

C. Powers, Duties, and Jurisdiction of the Arbitral Tribunal

The general powers of an arbitral tribunal are provided for by the AA 1940 as follows:[142]

a) administer oath to the parties and witnesses;
b) state a special case for the opinion of the court on any question of law involved, or state the award, wholly or in part, in the form of a special case of such question for the opinion of the court;
c) make the award conditional or in the alternative;
d) correct any clerical mistake or error in an award arising from any accidental slip or omission;
e) administer to any party to the arbitration such interrogatories as may be necessary in the opinion of the arbitrators or umpire.

However, all these powers are subject to the terms agreed by the parties in their arbitration agreement.[143] A tribunal also has the power to make an interim award.[144]

[138] Federal Public Procurement Rules 2004 (n 52).
[139] *Haji Naimatullah v Federation of Pakistan Through Secretary Ministry of Defence* (2013 PLD (Sindh) 406) (Nadeem Akhtar, J).
[140] AA 1940 (n 7) s 3 and 1st sch, item 1.
[141] ibid.
[142] ibid s 13.
[143] ibid.
[144] ibid s 27.

In the absence of any special provisions, all these powers will presumably apply to a private-public arbitration as well.

Regarding the competence of a private-public arbitration tribunal, again the law is no different from the general law applicable to all types of arbitrations. The courts in Pakistan have partially adopted the automatic waiver principle; that is, if the question of proper constitution of an arbitral tribunal was not raised before the tribunal itself, this would constitute a waiver of the right to object to the enforcement of the arbitral award in a court. For example, in *Karachi Dock Labour Board*, the court held that where the appointment of an arbitrator was not made in compliance with the terms of the arbitration agreement, the parties may amend the terms of their arbitration agreement by way of waiver.[145] However, the court clarified that the automatic waiver principle had no application where the appointment of arbitrators was made in contravention of the provisions of the AA 1940.[146] Likewise, the AA 1940 gives arbitration tribunals ample authority to require parties to submit any type or form of evidence to be examined by the arbitrators.[147]

D. Control by Domestic Courts

As discussed above, Pakistani courts have abundant control of the arbitration proceedings, which are in most cases either ordered or assisted by the courts.[148] In addition to the general powers to appoint and remove arbitrators,[149] the courts may modify the award in certain circumstances:[150]

a) where it appears that a part of the award addresses a matter not referred to arbitration and such part can be separated from the other parts and does not affect the decision on the matter referred; or
b) where the award is imperfect in form, or contains any obvious error which can be amended without effecting such decision; or
c) where the award contains clerical mistakes or errors arising from an accidental slip or omission.

The courts also have the power to remit the award to an arbitral tribunal for correction and reconsideration;[151] are able to pass interim orders to preserve the enforcement of the award;[152] and are also empowered to annul arbitration where the award becomes void or is set aside.[153] These general powers of the courts would naturally be exercisable in cases of private-public arbitration as well.

145 ibid para (k).
146 *Karachi Dock Labour Board v Quality Builders LTD* (2016 PLD Supreme Court 121) (Mian Saqib Nisar, Ijaz Ahmed Chaudhry and Qazi Faez Isa, JJ).
147 AA 1940 (n 7) s 3 and 1st sch, item 6.
148 See sections VI.A and B above.
149 AA 1940 (n 5) ss 8 to 12.
150 ibid s 15.
151 ibid s 17.
152 ibid s 18.
153 ibid ss 19 and 30.

In terms of the standard of review applied by the courts in reviewing arbitral awards rendered in private-public arbitrations, the courts are likely to follow the standards they have adopted to review private-public arbitration agreements. Pakistani courts have consistently declined to enforce arbitration agreements involving questions of corruption by government officials.[154] The courts are, therefore, unlikely to enforce an arbitral award that involves similar questions. Likewise, the courts have suspected the involvement of corruption and have declined to enforce arbitral awards where tribunals have based their findings against a public authority solely on statements made by the public officials admitting liability on behalf of a public authority.[155]

E. Recognition and Enforcement of Awards

Although Pakistan was one of the earliest signatories, it only implemented the NYC in 2011.[156] The implementing statute was first promulgated as a presidential ordinance in 2005,[157] which was reissued intermittently until it was finally passed as an implementing legislation by the parliament in 2011.[158] Prior to this, the recognition and enforcement of foreign arbitral awards was governed by the Arbitration (Protocol and Convention) Act 1937,[159] which gave effect to the Geneva Protocol 1923[160] and the Geneva Convention 1927.[161] Pakistan also implemented the ICSID Convention in 2011.[162] Since 2011, the courts have shown willingness to enforce foreign arbitral awards.[163] However, there are still cases where courts refuse to enforce foreign arbitration agreements.[164] Despite some inconsistent decisions regarding the enforceability of private-public arbitration agreements, discussed in section III above, there is a degree of clarity as to the kind of intervention courts are prepared to make in the enforcement of awards resulting from private-public arbitration. Overall, the trend is pro-enforcement.[165] As regards international investment arbitration, Pakistani courts have not strictly taken a pro-enforcement stance even after the domestic implementation of the ICSID Convention.[166]

There is no special procedure required when a public authority approaches courts for the enforcement of an international arbitration award against a private entity.

[154] *Hubco* (n 72).

[155] *Ch Qaiser Mehmood* (n 132).

[156] See n 19 above.

[157] Recognition and Enforcement (Arbitration Agreements and Foreign Arbitral Awards) Ordinance 2005.

[158] Under Article 89 of the Constitution of Pakistan 1973, the President of Pakistan has the power to make emergency legislation valid only for 120 days, which is referred to as an ordinance. An ordinance may be reissued by the President as many times as required.

[159] Arbitration (Protocol and Convention) Act (n 20).

[160] Protocol on Arbitration Clauses (n 21).

[161] Convention on the Execution of Foreign Arbitral Awards (n 22).

[162] See n 27 above.

[163] See eg *Abdullah* (n 24) (Munib Akhtar J); *Fal Oil Company Ltd* n 24 (Munib Akhtar J).

[164] *Lakhra* (n 25).

[165] *Abdullah* (n 24); *Retex Global (Pvt) Ltd v Export Processing Zones Authority* (2009 CLD 814) (Amir Hani Muslim, J).

[166] *Maulana Abdul Haque Baloch* case (n 31) (Iftikhar Muhammad Chaudhry, Gulzar Ahmed, and Sh Azmat Saeed, JJ).

In *Sabah Shipyard*,[167] the Ministry of Water and Power brought a petition before the Karachi High Court through the managing director of the Private Power and Infrastructure Board (PPIB) as a creditor to enforce an International Chamber of Commerce award against the respondent Saba Shipyard, which was a private entity. The award specifically stated itself to be in favour of the Ministry of Water and Power, Islamic Republic of Pakistan, and did not specifically name PPIB as a creditor. The respondent argued that because the award was in favour of the Islamic Republic of Pakistan, the enforcement proceedings had to be specifically authorized by the President of Pakistan, being the head of the state. However, the court held that the PPIB in its capacity as a representing public authority for the Ministry of Water and Power, Islamic Republic of Pakistan, was the rightful petitioner and there was no need to refer the matter to the President.

Likewise, Pakistani courts have readily enforced domestic arbitration awards made both for and against public authorities. In *Sh M Riaz Shahid*, the Supreme Court of Pakistan made it very clear that a public authority will not be treated differently as compared with a private person when it comes to the enforcement of an arbitration award against it.[168] The Supreme Court did, however, reiterate one important concern raised in earlier decisions; that is, that the public authorities could have the possibility to connive with private persons for illicit considerations to let them have a favourable arbitral award causing loss to the public exchequer. The Supreme Court, in fact, suggested that the government should review this practice.[169]

Corruption of public officials has always raised concerns for the courts when it comes to any type of out-of-court settlement of a private-public dispute where the courts lose their oversight of the matter. This remains a serious impediment to the development of arbitration as a true alternative to litigation in private-public disputes. Where the overall direction of the Pakistani government's and the judicial policy appear to favour the settlement of private-public disputes by arbitration, it would be a good idea to have a well-defined set of procedural rules specifically for this type of arbitration. This would bring legal certainty and develop a coherent practice of private-public arbitration in Pakistan. It would also increase the credibility of private-public arbitration as a reliable dispute resolution alternative to the courts, giving confidence to public officials to use it more frequently in their dealings with private entities.

VI. Challenges Posed to Private-Public Arbitration

The frequency of including arbitration in private-public contracts shows that it has become a significant feature of public governance in Pakistan.[170] This view is further strengthened when Pakistani courts have repeatedly upheld the arbitrability of private-public disputes. The courts have even validated private-public arbitration

[167] *Islamic Republic of Pakistan v Messrs Sabah Shipyard (Pakistan) Ltd* (2009 CLD 999) (Nadeem Azhar Siddiqi, J).

[168] *Province of Punjab v Sh M Riaz Shahid* (2005 SCMR 1435) (Khalil-ur-Rehman Ramday and Falak Sher, JJ).

[169] ibid para 9.

[170] See eg *Pakistan Steel Mills Corporation Ltd v Messrs Mustafa Sons (Pvt) Ltd* (2003 YLR 1560).

agreements that designate a public official as an arbitrator.[171] Likewise, private-public arbitration has been mandated by the government through several primary legislations, portraying it as an important feature of public governance policy. Arbitration has, therefore, been silently serving Pakistani society—below the surface layer of the judiciary and bureaucracy—not only as a dispute settlement system but also as a governance mechanism for private-public contracts through which many important aspects of public policy and public interests are implemented. However, a more sophisticated contribution of private-public arbitration is yet to come whereby arbitrators and their decision-making develop a body of administrative law that impacts on how private-public relations are structured and governed.

This is largely because arbitration as an independent and systemic institution has not yet been developed through legislation. Some private arbitration institutions have emerged.[172] Despite their own inherent limitations, they may eventually develop a body of arbitral jurisprudence steering the governance of private-public relations. However, for the development of private-public arbitration as a real, coherent, and consistent public governance system, fundamental questions regarding its democratic legitimacy and implications for the rule of law and human rights must be considered. It is important to comprehend and address these critical questions to fully appreciate the possible governance functions that private-public arbitration can play in Pakistan.

In principle, arbitration stems from the mutual agreement of contracting parties. Because an arbitration agreement restricts the jurisdiction of otherwise competent courts, it is fair only if both parties have given free consent to such an agreement.[173] However, in private-public arbitration where contracting parties do not have equal bargaining power, consent can be viewed as compelled rather than free. This weakness is obvious in private-public arbitration originating from primary legislation, as well as where it is included as a prerequisite in leases, licences, and concessions granted by public authorities to private entities. The democratic legitimacy of compelled arbitration, either based on legislation or unilaterally drafted private-public contracts, has been called into question because it gives public authorities additional control over private conduct.[174] In the United States, for example, the preclusion of access to a court in compelled arbitration where the enforcement of public rights can be at stake has been viewed as 'an unconstitutional evisceration of statutory and common law rights'.[175] Likewise, it has been argued in the United States that compelled arbitration undermines both the legitimacy of arbitration and the functions of courts by precluding the public from 'assessing the qualities of what gains the force of law and debating what law ought to require'.[176] Although Pakistani courts have carefully guarded against the exploitation of public interests, both in the sense of an

[171] See eg *Province of Punjab v Shafsal Enterprises, Government Contractor* (1994 SCMR 1993); *Naimatullah* (n 139).

[172] Centre for International Investment and Commercial Arbitration (n 39) and National Centre for Dispute Resolution (n 40).

[173] New York Convention (n 19) arts II(1), (2), and V.

[174] Richard C Reuben, 'Democracy and Dispute Resolution: The Problem of Arbitration' (2004) 67 LCP 279, 280.

[175] Judith Resnik, 'Diffusing Disputes: The Public in the Private of Arbitration, the Private in Courts, and the Erasure of Rights' (2015) 124 Yale LJ 2804.

[176] ibid.

individual's fundamental rights and the broader societal interests, a lack of clear legislative and policy guidelines make these criticisms equally relevant to the practice of private-public arbitration in Pakistan.

Likewise, there is a vigorous and diverse criticism of arbitration based on its rule-of-law shortcomings. There has been serious contestation surrounding the basic conception of the rule of law in the context of arbitration. Sornarajah, for example, has argued that the rule-of-law doctrine, which basically means equality before the law, has been misused in the context of private-public arbitration based on investment agreements and BITs. He argues that, under the pretext of the rule of law, foreign investors are entitled to a preferential treatment as compared with local entrepreneurs. Foreign investors have access to international arbitration and the substantive rights granted in investment agreements, both of which are not available to local entrepreneurs.[177]

Sornarajah's main argument is placed in the historical development of international investment law and arbitration. It emphasises that this subversion of the rule of law is specifically designed to protect the interests of developed countries and their multinational corporations, thus undermining the interests of developing countries and their populations. However, Fathi has provokingly argued that developing countries have also connived in this subversion.[178] With specific examples, Fathi demonstrates how undemocratic and corrupt regimes benefit from embracing international arbitration, allowing them to maintain control by obviating the need to create independent domestic courts. This view has been affirmed in Pakistan by the dicta of Justice Munib Akhtar in *Lakhra*, where he refused to enforce an international arbitration agreement, suggesting that taking the dispute to international arbitration was a manoeuvre to cover up corruption by public officials.[179]

Although these criticisms are specifically directed at international arbitration, they equally apply to compelled domestic arbitration where corrupt public officials would want to avoid scrutiny of their contracts by domestic courts. Likewise, compelled private-public arbitration can violate the rule of law by causing unjust inequalities at the domestic level.[180] Using Lord Bingham's exposition on the rule of law, Lord Neuberger has elaborated the following eight most significant strands of the rule of law that have implications for arbitration:[181]

I. The law must be accessible, intelligible, clear, and predictable;
II. Issues should be resolved by law, not discretion;
III. Laws should apply equally to all;
IV. The law must protect fundamental human rights;

[177] M Sornarajah, 'The Case Against a Regime on International Investment Law' in Leon E Trakman and Nicola W Ranieri (eds), *Regionalism in International Investment Law* (OUP 2013) 489.

[178] Mark Fathi Massoud, 'International Arbitration and Judicial Politics in Authoritarian States' (2014) 39 L & Soc Inquiry 1.

[179] *Lakhra* (n 25) para 5.

[180] See eg David S Schwartz, 'If You Love Arbitration, Set it Free: How "Mandatory" Undermines "Arbitration"' (2007) 8 Nevada LJ 400.

[181] Lord Neuberger, 'Arbitration and the Rule of Law' (Chartered Institute of Arbitrators Centenary Celebration, Hong Kong, 20 March 2015) <https://uk-supremecourt.co.uk/uploads/speech_150320_0c5f8a0471.pdf> accessed 6 January 2025.

V. Disputes must be resolved economically and fast;
VI. Public powers must be exercised reasonably, *bona fide*, and appropriately;
VII. Adjudicative procedures provided by the state should be fair;
VIII. The state must comply with its obligations in international law.

Although Lord Neuberger offered this list in the context of arbitration generally, most of these implications are essentially relevant to private-public arbitration as well. In the context of Pakistani practice, for example, can a government official designated as an arbitrator in a compelled private-public contract be trusted to ensure the rule of law instead of exercising discretion? Can procedural equality be maintained in compelled private-public arbitration where public authorities have control over the arbitration process?

These concerns have not been directly raised or considered in Pakistan, as the entire idea of private-public arbitration has evolved without any cautious effort or measured policy. The civil society, public institutions, and Pakistani courts have taken it as given by the dictates of British India common law. However, Pakistani courts have readily scrutinized the private-public arbitration in order to review the fairness and validity of actions by public officials as against fundamental rights and public interests.[182] Courts can, therefore, mitigate the negative consequences of private-public arbitration, pushing aside the question of its democratic legitimacy and the rule of law. In fact, as discussed in section IV above, Pakistani courts have ensured a right balance between the protection of public interests and the legitimate exercise of the government's regulatory powers, on the one hand, and the enforcement of arbitration clauses contained in private-public contracts, on the other. Fortunately, Pakistani courts have the constitutional jurisdiction to review private-public contracts including arbitration clauses. The courts have symptomatically exercised this power, upholding public interests and public goods where a public authority has exceeded its power and wilfully or wantonly trampled upon vested private or public rights. However, the courts have also repeatedly called for legislative interventions to develop the systemic rules for private-public arbitration. There is indeed a serious need for legislation on private-public arbitration to develop it as a predictable and impartial system of public governance, and to prevent malpractices and corruption.

However, despite the calls for legislation, there are certain aspects of private-public arbitration that are likely to remain open to judicial interpretation. The fundamental rights and rule-of-law debates in arbitration are principally linked to the public policy compliance requirements.[183] For an arbitral award to be enforceable in a domestic court it must be in accordance with the public policy of the country where enforcement is sought. This is clearly set out in Article V of the NYC, and domestic courts can refuse to enforce an arbitral award that is contrary to domestic public policy.[184] However, the notion of public interest or policy is necessarily open-textured.[185] It primarily requires a balance between the respect for party autonomy and the wider need to respect principles of human rights recognized internationally.[186] The *travaux*

182 See section IV above.
183 Lord Neuberger (n 181) para 12.
184 New York Convention (n 19) art V(2)(b).
185 See eg *Orient Power* (n 75).
186 Lord Neuberger (n 181) para 12.

préparatoires of the NYC also portray public policy as a wider concept equivalent to 'fundamental notions and principles of justice'.[187] The public policy exception under the NYC is incorporated into arbitration laws in many countries, including Pakistan.[188] However, because of its open-textured nature, it will be extremely difficult to capture every aspect of public policy in a piece of legislation. It is therefore likely that the contracting parties will continue to approach courts with questions related to public policy for the recognition and enforcement of arbitration agreements and awards.

The AA 1940, being pre-NYC legislation, does not include public policy as a test for the validity and enforcement of an arbitration award. However, the newly passed REFA requires recognition and enforcement of foreign arbitral awards in accordance with Article V of the NYC.[189] Pakistani courts have traditionally required an award to satisfy the requirements of natural justice,[190] and have ruled that an arbitral award can be set aside if it violates domestic public policy.[191] In *Nan Fung Textiles*, Justice Rasheed A Razvi of the Karachi High Court ruled that the court was competent to refuse the enforcement of an award on 'any ground' contrary or violative of fundamental rights and other laws of Pakistan.[192] The recent *Orient Power* decision demonstrates that private-public contracts that include arbitration clauses are by no means an exception to this requirement.[193] In fact, Pakistani courts are likely to continue to test private-public contracts on the public policy parameters due to their susceptibility to corruption, nepotism, and other similar malpractices.[194]

In other words, although the concerns regarding the democratic legitimacy, the rule of law, and the human rights implications provide serious challenges to the development of private-public arbitration as a just and fair practice, Pakistani courts have meticulously guarded against such challenges. They have sought to ensure the correct balance between the rightful exercise of public authorities' administrative capacity and protection of public interests and public goods. However, the practice of designating public officials as arbitrators in private-public contracts should be discouraged to safeguard impartial and fair resolution of private-public disputes through arbitration and enhance public trust and confidence in this practice. This, along with the development of special procedural rules for private-public arbitration, can be done by legislation.

[187] ibid.

[188] See eg s 103(3) of the UK's Arbitration Act 1996; ss 1053(a) and 1059(2)(b) of the German Code of Civil Procedure 1887; ss 34, 47, and 57 of the Indian Arbitration and Conciliation Act (XXVI of 1996).

[189] REFA (n 18) s 7.

[190] *Dar Okaz Printing and Publishing Ltd v Printing Corporation of Pakistan (Pvt) Ltd* (2003 PLD Supreme Court 808) (Iftikhar Muhammad Chaudhry, Rana Bhagwandas and Faqir Muhammad Khokhar JJ).

[191] *A Meredith Jones & Co v Usman Textile Mills Ltd* (2002 CLD (Karachi) 1121) (Mushir Alam J); *Hubco* (n 72).

[192] *Nan Fung Textiles Ltd v Nichimen & Co (Pakistan)* (1999 YLR 2226).

[193] *Orient Power* (n 75).

[194] See eg Suo Motu Case No 18 of 2010 (2014 SCMR 585) (Iftikhar Muhammad Chaudhry, Jawwad S Khawaja, and Amir Hani Muslim JJ).

VII. Conclusion

Private-public arbitration exists in different forms in Pakistan. It is often sanctioned by primary legislation and also regularly included in private-public contracts. Pakistani courts have neither prevented public authorities from giving consent to arbitration in private-public contracts nor have they objected to such consent being given in primary legislation. Likewise, Pakistani courts have never objected to the arbitrability of disputes related to private-public contracts, but they have often reviewed such contracts to ensure the protection of public interest and the constitutional rights of citizens.

Pakistani courts have treated private-public contracts as distinct from ordinary contracts between private parties. This distinction has enabled courts to review private-public contracts by exercising their constitutional powers or writ jurisdiction, which is meant to facilitate greater protection of constitutional rights and accountability of public authorities. Pakistani courts have exercised judicial review to redress breaches of private-public contracts by public authorities when such breaches amount to abuse of public authority. Additionally, the courts have distinguished the private law cases of breach of contract from the public law cases of illegal exercise of administrative authority. In the former category of cases, the courts have persuaded the parties to resort to arbitration, whereas in the latter category, the courts have declined to enforce private-public arbitration. The courts have also exercised judicial review and prevented the enforcement of rights of private parties to a private-public contract, including their right to arbitration, when the private parties have failed to abide by the terms of their contract or when the formation or performance of such contract was marred with corruption of public officials.

Where a public authority's action was taken in the public interest or came within its regulatory domain, courts have considered such action as a legitimate exercise of regulatory power, even if it amounted to a breach of a private-public contract or negatively affected the rights of a private party to such contract. In such cases of the legitimate exercise of regulatory power, the courts have refused to enforce private-public arbitration agreements and awards and denied any relief to private parties.

Pakistani courts have enforced arbitration in private-public contracts when such contracts were concluded by public authorities acting as commercial entities. However, more clarity is needed on the rules to distinguish between commercial and regulatory actions of public authorities. The courts should use the *jure gestionis* and *jure imperii* distinction to bring further clarity to this important aspect of private-public contracts. Where a private-public contract amounts to actions *jure gestionis*, the courts should enforce arbitration for the resolution of disputes arising out of such contract, whereas in cases of actions *jure imperii*, the courts should continue to exercise their constitutional powers to ensure a right balance between the legitimate exercise of public authority and the protection of fundamental rights and public interests.

Yet, there is no special law on private-public arbitration in Pakistan. The general law of arbitration—the AA 1940—also governs private-public arbitration. The AA 1940 provides clear rules on the submission of a dispute to arbitration and the procedure and powers of an arbitration tribunal. The AA 1940 also gives ample powers to courts to interfere in arbitration proceedings and even modify arbitral awards. The courts have exercised those powers frequently. They have declined to enforce private-public arbitration agreements in appropriate cases where public interests were in question, even though both parties were willing to submit their dispute to arbitration. In other cases of private-public arbitration where no public interest was at stake, the courts have clarified that public authorities should not be treated differently from their private counterparts, and have enforced arbitration agreements, corrected defects in the constitution of arbitration tribunals at the request of parties, and enforced arbitral awards against public authorities.

The frequent use of arbitration in private-public contracts proves that arbitration has an important place in the Pakistani public governance system. However, the overall arbitration practice in Pakistan remains uninstitutionalized. There are no government-backed formal arbitration institutions in Pakistan. This is one of the reasons that arbitration in general has not been able to develop its own independent and consistent body of law. The ad hoc nature of arbitration has also led to the lack of a significant contribution of arbitral decisions to the development of arbitral jurisprudence. For the same reasons, private-public arbitration has not produced any distinct principle of public governance policy despite its frequent use by public authorities. This has also resulted in the lack of a development of a distinct body of arbitral jurisprudence applicable to private-public contracts.

As regards potential challenges posed to private-public arbitration, particularly when it is included in compelled contracts, Pakistani courts have successfully guarded their adherence to the rule of law and the protection of fundamental human rights. Fortunately, Pakistani courts have the constitutional jurisdiction to review private-public contracts containing arbitration clauses, which the courts have symptomatically exercised, upholding public interest and public good where a public authority has exceeded its power and wilfully or wantonly trampled upon vested private or public rights. Overall, Pakistani courts have ensured the right balance between the protection of public interest and the legitimate exercise of public authorities' regulatory powers, on the one hand, and the enforcement of arbitration in private-public disputes, on the other.

In terms of opportunities, there is a huge potential for the development of localized arbitration institutions that satisfy the commercial needs of society and also serve as an effective tool for private-public dispute management and public governance. Such institutions will likely produce a body of law bringing substantive and procedural constancy and predictability. There are also opportunities for legislative intervention to provide procedural rules and guidelines for public authorities for the inclusion of arbitration clauses in private-public contracts. There is also an opportunity for the government to intervene and change the practice of designating public officials as sole arbitrators in private-public contracts. This will ensure fairness and improve the public trust and confidence in private-public arbitration. As the overall direction of the Pakistani government's policy appears to be to promote the settlement of private-public disputes by arbitration, it would be better to have a well-defined set of procedural rules specifically for this type of arbitration. These policy and legislative interventions will bring legal certainty and develop a coherent practice of private-public arbitration in Pakistan. They will also increase the credibility of private-public arbitration as a reliable dispute resolution alternative to the courts, giving confidence to public officials to use it more frequently in their dealings with private entities.

Select Materials

Bibliography

Ali Saleem, Raja M, 'The Special Parliamentary Committee on Constitutional Reforms and the Concurrent List' (*The Forum for Federations*, January 2010)

Almeida, Cyril, 'Are You Current With the Concurrent List!' (*The Dawn News*, 8 April 2010)

Born, Gary B, 'Keynote Address: Arbitration and Freedom to Associate' (2009) 38 Ga J Int'l & Comp L 7

Brekoulakis, Stavros and Margaret B Devaney, 'Public-Private Arbitration and the Public Interest Under English Law' (2017) 80(1) MLR 22

Crouch, Melissa, 'The Prerogative Writs as Constitutional Transfer' (2018) 38 OJLS 653

Fathi Massoud, Mark, 'International Arbitration and Judicial Politics in Authoritarian States' (2014) 39 L & Soc Inquiry 1

Freeman, Jody, 'The Private Role in Public Governance' (2000) 75 NYU L Rev 543

Gaillard, Emmanuel, 'The Emergence of Transnational Responses to Corruption in International Arbitration' (2019) 35(1) Arb Int'l 1

Ghouri, Ahmad, *Law and Practice of Foreign Arbitration and Enforcement of Foreign Arbitral Awards in Pakistan* (Springer 2012)

Hanner White, Rebecca, 'Arbitration and the Administrative State' (2003) 38 Wake Forest L Rev 1283

Jaffer, Mahomed J and Sarmad J Osmany, 'National Report – Pakistan' in Pieter Sanders (ed), *Yearbook Commercial Arbitration* (Kluwer Law International 1982)

Karamat Bhandari, Uzair and others, 'Pakistan' in Michael J Moser and John Choong (eds), *Asia Arbitration Handbook* (OUP 2011) ch 20

Landau, Toby T, 'International Arbitration and Pakistan's State Responsibility: Redefining the Role of the Court' (Speech on 50th year celebration of the Supreme Court of Pakistan, Islamabad, August 2006)

Neuberger, Lord, 'Arbitration and the Rule of Law' (Chartered Institute of Arbitrators Centenary Celebration, Hong Kong, 20 March 2015) <https://uk-supremecourt.co.uk/uploads/speech_150320_0c5f8a0471.pdf> accessed 6 January 2025

Nisar, Justice Mian Saqib, 'International Arbitration in the Context of Globalization: A Pakistani Perspective' (Speech on 50th year celebration of the Supreme Court of Pakistan, Islamabad, August 2006)

Resnik, Judith, 'Diffusing Disputes: The Public in the Private of Arbitration, the Private in Courts, and the Erasure of Rights' (2015) 124 Yale LJ 2804

Rizwan, Muhammad and others, 'Revitalization of Parliamentary Democracy in Pakistan under 18th Amendment' (2014) 19(2) IOSR-JHSS 149

Rutledge, Peter B, *Arbitration and the Constitution* (CUP 2012)

Van Harten, Gus, 'The Public-Private Distinction in the International Arbitration of Individual Claims against the State' (2007) 56 ICLQ 371
Sornarajah, M, 'The Case Against a Regime on International Investment Law' in Leon E Trakman and Nicola W Ranieri (eds), *Regionalism in International Investment* Law (OUP 2013)

Legislation

Arbitration Bill (2009)
Balochistan Public Procurement Rules (2014)
Capital Development Authority (Abatement of Arbitration Proceedings) Act (XXVII of 1975)
Companies Act (XIX of 2017)
Contract Act (IX of 1872)
Federal Public Procurement Rules (2004)
Indian Arbitration and Conciliation Act (XXVI of 1996)
Indian Independence Act (10 & 11 Geo 6, c 30 of 1947)
Khyber Pakhtunkhwa Public Procurement of Goods, Works and Services Rules (2014)
North-West Frontier Province Mining Concession Rules (2005)
Pakistan Mining Concession Rules (1949)
Pakistan Mining Concession Rules (1960)
Public Procurement Regulatory Authority Ordinance (XXII of 2002)
Punjab Mining Concession Rules (2002)
Punjab Public Procurement Rules (2009)
Recognition and Enforcement (Arbitration Agreements and Foreign Arbitral Awards) Act (XVII of 2011)
Recognition and Enforcement (Arbitration Agreements and Foreign Arbitral Awards) Ordinance (2005)
Regulation of Mines and Oilfields and Mineral Development (Government Control) Act (XXIV of 1948)
Sindh Mining Concession Rules (2002)
Sindh Public Procurement Rules (2010)
Special Economic Zones Act (XX of 2012)
The Arbitration (Protocol and Convention) Act (VI of 1937)
The Arbitration Act (X of 1940)
The Balochistan Mineral Rules (2002)
The Constitution (Eighteenth Amendment) Act (X of 2010)
The Constitution of Pakistan (1973)
The Partnership Act (IX of 1932).

Cases

A Meredith Jones & Co v Usman Textile Mills Ltd (2002 CLD (Karachi) 1121)
Abdullah v CNAN Group SPA through Chief Executive/Managing Director (2014 PLD 349)

Abdullah v Messrs CNAN Group SPA (2014 PLD (Karachi) 349)
Messrs Airport Support Services v The Airport Manager, Civil Aviation Authority, Karachi (1997 CLC (Karachi) 1212)
Alleged Corruption in Rental Power Plants; Fraud in Payment of Rental Power Plants Detected by NEPRA (2012 SCMR 273)
Anjuman-e-Ahmadlya Sergodha v Deputy Commissioner, Sargodha (PLD 1966 SC 639)
Capital Development Authority v Muhammad Ahsan (2009 MLD 451)
Capital Development Authority v RM Gulistan Engineers and Contractors (Pvt) Ltd (2015 CLC 734)
Ch Qaiser Mehmood v Province of Punjab through Secretary, Government Communication and Works (2012 SCMR Supreme Court 1606)
Dallah Real Estate and Tourism Holding Company v The Ministry of Religious Affairs, Government of Pakistan [2010] UKSC 46
Dar Okaz Printing and Publishing Ltd v Printing Corporation of Pakistan (Pvt) Ltd (2003 PLD Supreme Court 808)
Fal Oil Company Ltd v Pakistan State Oil Company Ltd (2014 PLD (Karachi) 427)
Government of Balochistan v Enterprise and Development Consulting (Pvt) Ltd (2015 CLD 1743)
Haji Abdul Rashid Arif v Aziz Rehman and others (2010 CLC 1014)
Haji Naimatullah v Federation of Pakistan Through Secretary Ministry of Defence (PLD 2013 Sindh 406)
Islamic Republic of Pakistan v Messrs Sabah Shipyard (Pakistan) Ltd (2009 CLD 999)
Karachi Dock Labour Board v Quality Builders LTD (2016 PLD Supreme Court 121)
Karkey Karadeniz Elektrik Uretim AS v Islamic Republic of Pakistan, ICSID Case No ARB/ 13/1, Award (22 August 2017)
Khawaja Muhammad Usaf v North-West Frontier Province (PLD 1955 (Peshawar) 72)
Lakhra Power Generation Company Limited (LPGCL) v Karadeniz Powership Kaya Bey (2014 CLD (Karachi) 337)
Maulana Abdul Haque Baloch v Government of Balochistan (2013 PLD (Supreme Court) 641) and (2012 SCMR 402)
Messrs Airport Support Services v The Airport Manager, Quaid-E-Azam International Airport, Karachi (1998 SCMR 2268)
Messrs Inpaktech Industries (Pvt) Ltd v Government of Punjab (1998 MLD 1383)
Messrs M Esmailjee & Sons v The Federation of Pakistan (PLD 1959 (Karachi) 87)
Messrs Pharmax Pakistan (Pvt) Ltd v Government of Pakistan through Secretary, Ministry of Health (2000 CLC 628)
Messrs Wak Orient Power and Light Ltd v Government of Pakistan, Ministry of Water and Power (1998 CLC 1178)
Muhammad Ashraf Ali v Muhammad Naseer (1986 SCMR 1096)
Nan Fung Textiles Ltd v Nichimen & Co (Pakistan) (1999 YLR 2226)
Orient Power Company (Private) Limited v Sui Northern Gas Pipelines Limited (2019 PLD (Lahore) 607)
Pakistan Steel Mills Corporation Ltd v Messrs Mustafa Sons (Pvt) Ltd (2003 YLR 1560)
Province of Punjab v Sh M Riaz Shahid (2005 SCMR 1435)
Province of Punjab v Shafsal Enterprises, Government Contractor (1994 SCMR 1993)
Retex Global (Pvt) Ltd v Export Processing Zones Authority (2009 CLD 814)

Société Générale de Surveillance SA v Pakistan (2002 SCMR 1694)
Suo Motu Case No 18 of 2010 (2014 SCMR 585)
Tethyan (reported in Pakistan as *Maulana Abdul Haque Baloch v Government of Balochistan* (2013 PLD (Supreme Court) 641) and (2012 SCMR 402))
Tethyan Copper Company Pty Limited v Islamic Republic of Pakistan, ICSID Case No ARB/12/1, Award (13 July 2019)
The Hub Power Company (Ltd) v Pakistan WAPDA (PLD 2000 (Supreme Court) 841)
The Hub Power Company Ltd (Hubco) v Pakistan WAPDA (PLD 2000 Supreme Court 841)
Toyota Frontier Motors (Pvt) Ltd v Government of Khyber Pakhtunkhwa through Chief Secretary, KPK (2016 YLR Peshawar 1631)

16

China's Bifurcated Attitudes towards Private-Public Arbitration

*Manjiao Chi**

I. Introduction

Arbitration between public and private parties (PPA), especially investor-state arbitration (ISA), is getting increasingly popular, despite the absence of a uniform definition thereof. PPA is different from inter-state and commercial arbitration because of the difference in the disputants and of the nature of the disputes;[1] it is also different from litigation as arbitration is a form of 'privatized' adjudication. PPA allows private arbitrators to scrutinize states' regulatory measures; thus, it may give rise to concerns over states' regulatory space and the effectiveness of other international legal regimes.[2] For such reason, it has been suggested that ISA should be deemed not only a dispute settlement mechanism, but also 'a method of public law adjudication' that may 'solve regulatory disputes between individuals and the state as opposed to reciprocal disputes between private parties or between states'.[3]

In China, PPA can be roughly divided into two types, depending on their legal basis. The major type of PPA is ISA based on international investment agreements (IIAs); the other is PPA based on Chinese national law, referring to arbitration of commercial disputes between private and public parties (typically government organs).

This chapter is organized as follows: sections II and III focus on the two types of PPA in China; section IV addresses the enforcement of PPA awards against public parties in China; and section V observes that both types of PPA are allowed in China, but face heavy legal and practical restraints. Although such restraints make it difficult to initiate PPA and to enforce PPA awards in China, they are helpful in reserving state regulatory power.

II. Private-Public Arbitration under Chinese National Law

Chinese arbitration law does not draw a clear line between private arbitration and public arbitration. While in Chinese arbitration law and practice, the most distinct

* The author would like to extent special thanks are due to Mr Zongyao Li for his kind assistance. The opinions and possible errors in this chapter are the author's.

[1] See M Sornarajah, *The Settlement of Foreign Investment Disputes* (Kluwer Law International 2000) 159–60; Robert Y Jennings, 'State Contract in International Law' (1961) 37 BYBIL 156, 164; FA Mann, 'State Contracts and International Arbitration' (1967) 42 BYBIL 1, 6.

[2] See Stephan W Schill (ed), *International Investment Law and Comparative Public Law* (OUP 2010) 77.

[3] Gus Van Harten, *Investment Treaty Arbitration and Public Law* (OUP 2008) 4.

Manjiao Chi, *China's Bifurcated Attitudes towards Private-Public Arbitration* In: *The Comparative Constitutional Foundations of Private-Public Arbitration*. Edited by: Stephan W. Schill, Oxford University Press.
 DOI: 10.1093/9780191987960.003.0016

and important feature is the separation of foreign-related and international ('purely foreign') arbitration and domestic arbitration, clear definitions of these types of arbitration are not provided in Chinese national law. The implied test of dividing these types of arbitration lies in the relevant Supreme People's Court (SPC) judicial interpretation in relation to foreign-related civil legal relations.[4] Roughly speaking, a civil and commercial legal relation is 'foreign-related' if: (1) one of or both parties are foreign nationals, stateless persons, or foreign companies or organizations; or (2) the legal actions leading to the formation, amendment, or termination of a legal relationship occurred in a foreign country; or (3) the subject matter is located in a foreign country (Hong Kong Special Administrative Region, Macau Special Administrative Region, and Taiwan Region are deemed as 'foreign' in China's arbitration and judicial practice).

While following the above 'three-element test', if one of the elements of a dispute is in foreign territory, the arbitration of this dispute is a foreign-related one; if all three elements are in China, the arbitration is a domestic arbitration; and if all of these elements are in a foreign country, the arbitration is deemed as a foreign or international arbitration. China adopts a 'dual-track' system in treating these three different types of arbitration, especially in the stage of award enforcement: while domestic arbitrations are subject to Chinese national law, foreign-related and international arbitrations are subject to the New York Convention regime.[5] The division of foreign-related, international, and domestic arbitration is the most fundamental feature of Chinese arbitration law and practice.

Historically, arbitration in China was almost an imitation of civil litigation proceedings where the parties' autonomy and the arbitrators' discretion were heavily limited.[6] Chinese arbitration law had not been modernized until the Arbitration Law of the People's Republic of China (CAL) was adopted in 1994, which recognizes the principles of modern arbitration, such as the principle of party autonomy.[7] The CAL in general is deemed supportive of arbitration.[8] Despite the popularization of arbitration in China in recent years, arbitration is primarily developed and perceived as a mechanism for settling civil and commercial disputes between private parties. China remains reluctant to allow privately appointed arbitrators to adjudicate the state's administrative acts, which is deemed an erosion of the state's judicial sovereignty.

[4] The SPC Opinions Regarding Various Issues Arising from the Application of the Civil Procedural Law of 1991 (adopted on 14 July 1992).

[5] See generally Manjiao Chi, 'Drinking Poison to Quench Thirst: The Discriminatory Arbitral Award Enforcement Regime under Chinese Arbitration Law' (2009) 39(2) Hong Kong LJ 541.

[6] See generally Wang Wenying, 'Distinct Features of Arbitration in China: An Historical Perspective' (2006) 23(1) J Int'l Arb 49.

[7] Adopted by the 9th Session of the Standing Committee of the 8th National People's Congress of China on 31 August 1994.

[8] Friven Yeoh and Yu Fu, 'The People's Court and Arbitration: A Snapshot of Recent Judicial Attitudes in Arbitrability and Enforcement' (2007) 24 (6) J Int'l Arb 635, 635–36.

A. Can a Public Party Be a Party to Arbitration under Chinese Law?

China has a legal tradition of prioritizing state and state interest over individuals and private interests. This tradition has not fundamentally changed and the Chinese legal system remains highly state-centric and lacks a clear public-private division.[9] China's state-centric legal tradition and the private nature of arbitration therefore often appear incompatible.

Chinese arbitration law neither contains rules that expressly define the term 'public party' nor provides operable criteria to draw the private/public division for dispute settlement purposes. According to the CAL, not all parties have access to arbitration. Article 2 of the CAL confines the parties with access to arbitration to 'citizens, legal persons and other organizations as equal subjects of law', without further explanation. Thus, for state and government organs to be a party to arbitration under Chinese law, they should be 'legal persons' or 'other organizations' and 'equal subjects of law' (ie with citizens and legal persons).

As the CAL contains no explanation of these terms, reference needs to be made to other relevant laws. According to the General Principles of Civil Law of China (GPCL),[10] China's civil code, 'legal person' is a concept with a broad coverage.[11] It refers to any institution established in accordance with law which has its own property, name, organizational structure, and premise, and can independently undertake civil liabilities.[12] As held by China's leading scholars, the term 'legal person' includes both enterprises and non-enterprise entities, and the latter include state organs, social institutions, and social organizations.[13] The SPC Opinions Concerning Certain Questions on the Application of the Civil Procedural Law clarify that 'other organization' refers to an institution established in accordance with law, which has its own property and organizational structure but does not meet the other requirements of 'legal person', such as some foreign enterprises and social organizations.[14] In light of these provisions, it seems that state and government organs can be 'legal persons' or 'other organizations' under Chinese law.

Further, as required by Article 2 of the CAL, a state or government organ must also be an 'equal subject of law' with its counterparty (citizens and legal persons) in arbitration. No Chinese law provides a definition of the term 'equal subjects of law' or a method to assess the equality of parties in arbitration or litigation, and there is no case law in this regard. The Constitution of the People's Republic of China provides that 'all state organs, the armed forces, all political parties and public organizations and all enterprises and institutions in the country must take the Constitution as the basic standard of conduct',[15] and that 'all Chinese nationals are equal before law'.[16] It seems

[9] See eg Xingzhong Yu, 'State Legalism and the Public/Private Divide in Chinese Legal Development' (2014) 15(1) Theo Inq L 28.

[10] Adopted by the 4th Session of the 6th National People's Congress of China on 12 April 1986.

[11] See ch III (Legal Persons) of the GPCL.

[12] ibid, art 36.

[13] See eg Jiang Ping (ed), *Civil Law* (2nd edn, CUPL Press 2011) 76.

[14] SPC Opinions Concerning Certain Questions on the Application of the Civil Procedural Law (adopted at the 528th meeting of the Judicial Committee of the Supreme People's Court on 14 July 1992) Fa Fa No 22 (1992), art 40.

[15] Constitution of China, preamble.

[16] ibid, art 33.

reasonable to say that state and government organs should be 'equal subjects of law' in relation to citizens, legal persons, and other organizations, and that they should be equally bound by law and liable for violation of law. In this sense, the restrictions of the CAL with regard to the suitability of disputants do not necessarily bar state or government organs from participating in arbitration.

B. The Special Case of Chinese SOEs

One of the reasons for the confusion of the character of arbitration in China is caused by the vague legal status of China's state-owned and state-controlled enterprises (referred to collectively as SOEs). Arbitration involving China's SOEs could have a profound impact on China given that China has a large number of SOEs, and that the SOEs are playing a predominant role in China's economic development. In practice, the legal status of China's SOEs is often disputed. Such disputes typically relate to whether China's SOEs should be considered as private parties or public parties. The main reason for this is that Chinese SOEs lack sufficient independence from the state of China and often do not function like other market (private) actors.[17]

China has no specialized law on SOEs. China's SOEs are regulated by different branches of law, largely depending on their form of incorporation and source of capital. Most SOEs are incorporated as companies of limited liability, companies limited by shares, or wholly state-owned companies; thus, they fall under the scope of application of the Company Law of China (CCL).[18] According to the CCL, companies incorporated in China, including SOEs, 'shall have independent property rights as a legal person' and 'shall take responsibility for their debts with all properties'.[19] As this provision does not draw a distinction between SOEs and private companies, it confirms by implication that SOEs possess independent legal personality.

In reality, however, Chinese SOEs often enjoy more favourable treatment and are subject to stricter control, *de jure* or de facto, compared with many private enterprises. For instance, some SOEs are legally entitled to monopolize certain profitable industries, such as the oil, gas, and electricity industries, and enjoy financial and regulatory advantages that are unavailable to private enterprises.[20] Many large-scale SOEs are under the direct supervision of the central government (State Council) and their high-ranking managerial personnel are directly appointed by the government.[21] In addition, China has tightened its control of SOEs in recent years.[22]

[17] See Shen Hong and Zhao Nong, *China's State-Owned Enterprises: Nature, Performance and Reform* (World Scientific Publishing 2013) 279–81.

[18] Adopted by the 5th Session of the Standing Committee of the 8th National People's Congress of China on 29 December 1993, last amended by the 5th Session of the Standing Committee of the 12th National People's Congress of China on 28 December 2013.

[19] CCL, art 2.

[20] See generally Ming Du, 'China's State Capitalism and World Trade' (2014) 63(2) ICLQ 409, 422–26.

[21] A list of these SOEs is available at <http://www.sasac.gov.cn/n2588045/n27271785/n27271792/c14159097/content.html> accessed 10 January 2025 (original in Chinese).

[22] SASAC, 'Enhancing the Roots and Soul of SOEs: Leading the High-Quality Development of SOEs through Strengthening Party Building', available at <http://www.sasac.gov.cn/n2588025/n2641611/n4518437/c9842863/content.html> accessed 10 January 2025 (original in Chinese).

That China treats its SOEs and private enterprises differently in the marketplace often gives rise to the doubt whether Chinese SOEs should be deemed as 'equal subjects of law' with private parties. It has therefore been suggested that the boundary between SOEs and government organs in China is not sufficiently clear.[23] The Constitution of China provides that the 'state-owned economy is the leading force in the national economy. The state ensures the consolidation and growth of the state-owned economy.'[24] Although the Constitution does not make clear what a 'state-owned economy' is, it is suggested that such economy is represented by SOEs and should be differentiated from 'private economy' and 'foreign-invested economy', which only play a supplementary role in China's national economy.[25] In practice, such understanding is often deemed as the legal basis to justify the 'prioritized status' of SOEs in China.

Notwithstanding the debates over the legal status of SOEs and the preferential treatment SOEs are granted, there is insufficient empirical evidence to show that SOEs are treated as public parties (state and government organs) in arbitration and domestic litigation in China. On the contrary, it is often seen that Chinese SOEs are parties involved in domestic or transnational arbitration with individuals or private companies.

C. Can Public-Private Disputes Be Arbitrated under Chinese Law?

Arbitrability is a key requirement under Chinese law for a dispute to be legally submitted to arbitration. The existing arbitrability requirements in Chinese arbitration law are composed of a positive list and a negative list, mainly through confining the nature of disputes.

Article 2 of the CAL provides a positive list, allowing 'disputes over contracts and disputes over property rights and interests' to be arbitrated. Although Chinese law provides no clear definition of these terms, a typical and practical understanding is that such disputes should be 'commercial' in nature. Yet, Chinese law does not contain a clear definition of this term. Here, it is helpful to mention China's 'commercial reservation' of the Convention on Recognition and Enforcement of Foreign Arbitral Awards of 1958 (New York Convention), according to which only foreign arbitral awards 'concerning disputes arising from contractual and non-contractual commercial legal relationships' can be enforced in China.[26] The SPC Notice on the Enforcement of the Convention on the Recognition and Enforcement of Foreign Arbitral Awards provides a descriptive definition of 'contractual and non-contractual

[23] See eg Yan Ruosen and Li Linshan, 'The Strategic Highlights for Reconstruction and Governance of Chinese SOEs' available at <www.sasac.gov.cn/n1180/n1271/n20515/n2697175/16075029.html> accessed 30 January 2017 (original in Chinese).

[24] Constitution of China, art 7.

[25] See eg Song Fangmin, 'The Deepening of SOE Reform Requires Construction of Socialist State-Owned Economy Governance System with Chinese Characteristics' available at <http://theory.people.com.cn/n/2014/1215/c143844-26207189.html> accessed 1 June 2015.

[26] The current status of the New York Convention is available at <www.uncitral.org/uncitral/de/uncitral_texts/arbitration/NYConvention.html> accessed 30 January 2017.

commercial legal relationship' as 'the economic rights and obligations resulted from contract, infringement or arising according to law ... and it does not include the dispute between foreign investors and the host government'.[27]

Further clarification can be found in various SPC judicial interpretations and other relevant documents. Typically, according to the *SPC Interpretation Concerning Certain Issues on Application of the Arbitration Law of China*, 'contractual disputes' refers to 'the disputes arising out of formation, effectiveness, modification, assignment, performance, liabilities for breach, interpretation and termination of a contract'.[28] According to a non-binding explanation issued by the Office of Legal Affairs of the State Council, the term 'other disputes over property rights and interests' refers to disputes over torts, often seen in the fields of maritime, real estate, product liability, and intellectual property rights.[29] In light of such descriptions, it is advisable that the term 'commercial' should be broadly understood. Consequently, if private-public relations qualify as commercial—for example, if they are based on a commercial contract—arbitrations are possible for resulting disputes under Chinese law.

As can be seen, notwithstanding the positive list, Chinese law seems to focus only on the nature or characteristics of disputes in order to determine arbitrability. It provides no clear answer as to whether disputes relating to or arising out of administrative (regulatory) acts of public parties can be submitted to arbitration. The answer should be explored in light of the negative list enshrined principally in Article 3 of the CAL. Under this provision, two major types of disputes are excluded from arbitration in China: 'disputes over marriage, adoption, guardianship, family maintenance and inheritance' and 'administrative disputes falling within the jurisdiction of the relevant administrative organs according to law'.

In light of the above explanation, one may find that the key test in determining whether a dispute concerning the exercise of state regulatory authority is admissible for PPA under Chinese law is whether the dispute is an administrative one in nature. The CAL contains no definition of 'administrative dispute'. This term is defined in Article 2 of the Administrative Litigation Law of People's Republic of China (CAPL),[30] according to which the term 'administrative dispute' refers to a dispute between citizens, legal persons, or other organizations, on the one side, and state administrative organs or their personnel, on the other, arising out of the infringement of the private party's lawful rights or interests by administrative acts.[31] The CAPL has no explicit definition of 'administrative acts' but provides a list of actionable and a list of non-actionable administrative disputes.[32] As these two lists are pertinent to the current study, it is necessary to reproduce them in brief.

[27] Notice Issued by the SPC on 10 April 1987, art 3, available at <www.people.com.cn/zixun/flfgk/item/dwjjf/falv/9/9-1-7-1.html> accessed 10 June 2015 (original in Chinese).

[28] SPC Interpretation Concerning Certain Issues on Application of the Arbitration Law of the People's Republic of China (adopted at the 1375th meeting of the Judicial Committee of the Supreme People's Court on 26 December 2005) Fa Shi No 7 (2006), art 2.

[29] See the Office of Legal Affairs of the State Council of China, *Explanation and Supplementation to the Arbitration Law of the People's Republic of China* (China Fazhi Press 2008) 3.

[30] Adopted by the 2nd Session of the 7th National People's Congress of China on 4 April 1989, last amendment adopted 11th Session of the Standing Committee of the 12th National People's Congress of China on 1 November 2014.

[31] CAPL, art 2.

[32] ibid, arts 12 and 13.

Actionable 'administrative disputes' include the following:

(1) An administrative punishment, such as administrative detention, suspension, or revocation of a licence or permit, ordered suspension of production or business, confiscation of illegal income, confiscation of illegal property, fine, or warning.
(2) An administrative compulsory measure, such as restriction of personal freedom or seizure, impoundment, freezing of property, or administrative enforcement measure.
(3) An administrative organ's denial of an application for administrative licence or other administrative decisions, or failure to respond to such application within the statutory period.
(4) An administrative organ's decision to confirm the ownership or the right to use any natural resource, such as land, mineral resources, water, forest, hill, grassland, wasteland, tidal flat, or sea area.
(5) A decision on expropriation or requisition or a decision on compensation for expropriation or requisition.
(6) An administrative organ's refusal to perform, or failure to respond to an application for the administrative agency to perform, its statutory duties and responsibilities in respect of protecting personal rights, property rights, and other lawful rights and interests.
(7) An administrative organ has infringed upon the plaintiff's autonomy in business management, right in the contractual operations on rural land, or right in operations on rural land.
(8) A claim that an administrative organ has abused its administrative power to preclude or restrict competition.
(9) A claim that an administrative organ has illegally raised funds or apportioned expenses or illegally required performance of other obligations.
(10) A claim that an administrative organ has failed to pay consolation money, minimum subsistence, or social insurance benefits according to the law.
(11) A claim that an administrative organ has failed to perform according to the law or as agreed upon, or illegally modified or rescinded an agreement, such as a government concession agreement or a land and building expropriation compensation agreement.
(12) A claim that an administrative organ has infringed upon personal rights, property rights, or other lawful rights and interests.

In addition to the situations set out in the preceding list, the people's courts shall accept administrative disputes which may be filed as prescribed by laws and regulations.[33]

Non-actionable administrative disputes includes the following:

(1) Disputes concerning national defence and foreign affairs.

[33] ibid, art 12.

(2) Administrative regulations and decrees and decisions or orders with general application that are promulgated and issued by administrative organs.
(3) Decisions of administrative organs on award, punishment, appointment, or removal of their personnel.
(4) Administrative acts that shall be finally decided by administrative organs according to the relevant law.[34]

As can be seen, although the list of administrative disputes is not exhaustive, almost all listed disputes concern the taking of regulatory acts by Chinese government organs. In reality, the majority of public-private disputes in China concern the legality and consequences of regulatory acts of government organs. Therefore, Article 3 of the CAPL, by only allowing the listed disputes to be settled through litigation, constitutes a hidden ban on PPA in China for covered subject matters. Furthermore, although there is no explicit prohibition in law, only administrative acts per se are actionable before administrative courts, while laws, regulations, and rules that violate the Constitution cannot be challenged by individuals through litigation and arbitration. They can only be corrected through legislative avenues. This is a fundamental defect of Chinese administrative law and a contradiction to China's efforts in becoming a rule-of-law country. As a consequence, PPA related to these issues is not possible either.

Admittedly, not all public-private disputes are administrative in nature. Some can be deemed commercial in nature. For instance, a sales contract between a government body and a company for the purchase of commodities is a commercial contract. Disputes arising out of the performance of such a contract should not be deemed administrative and can be settled through arbitration as a commercial contract. Such PPA often occurs in China. For example, the China International Economic and Trade Arbitration Commission (CIETAC) clarifies that government organs can be a proper party to arbitration just like any private party as long as the disputes are commercial and trade-related but not administrative in nature.[35] Although not binding legally, this pronouncement carries practical significance in guiding CIETAC's arbitration practice. In *Bureau v Nuoya*, a local Land and Resource Bureau refused to perform its contractual obligation, relying on a State Council regulation provision. The tribunal of the Ji'nan Arbitration Commission found that this provision is not mandatory and ruled that the Bureau's non-performance constituted a breach of contract. This award was later enforced by the court.[36] This case shows that private-public disputes can in fact be settled through domestic arbitration, although in reality such cases are not frequently seen.

[34] ibid, art 13.

[35] See CIETAC, Frequently Asked Questions, available at <http://cn.cietac.org/shiwu/read_ &ptitle=%B shiwu.asp?ptype=43%CC%D0%F2%D6%B8%C4%CF&stitle=%B3%A3%BC%FB%CE%CA%CC%E2> accessed 10 June 2015.

[36] *Bureau of Land and Resource of Yazhou District of Jining Municipality v Jiangsu Nuoya Investment Development Co Ltd*, Judgment, Intermediate People's Court of Ji'nan Municipality, Doc No (2014) Ji Zhong Li Chu Zi Di 31 Hao, available at <www.pkulaw.cn/fulltext_form.aspx?Db=pfnl&Gid=120663325&keyword=&EncodingName=help/help/JavaScript/showDialog.js&Search_Mode> accessed 30 January 2017.

To conclude, to properly understand PPA in China, the key point is to ascertain the nature and characteristics of the dispute. China has no law and legal tradition of clearly defining 'public' or 'private'. Judicial and administrative practice suggest that the public nature of a legal relation is often judged by whether one or all of the parties thereto are state government (administrative) organs, disregarding whether the legal relation involves the public interest. Still, public-private commercial disputes can be arbitrated and are subject to Chinese arbitration law. Chinese law has no special rules dealing with such arbitration, however, either as regards substance or procedure. This implies that public parties and private parties shall be treated as equal parties to the extent their dispute is arbitrable. Public-private administrative disputes, by contrast, can only be settled through administrative litigation.

III. Investor-State Arbitration under China's Investment Agreements

ISA relying on Chinese IIAs has become a frequent phenomenon in recent years. Up to 2019, China had concluded 145 bilateral investment treaties (BITs), one trilateral investment treaty (TIT), and over twenty free trade agreements (FTAs) with investment chapters.[37] China has also acceded to some relevant international treaties, including the New York Convention and the 1965 Convention on the Settlement of Investment Disputes between States and Nationals of Other States (ICSID Convention).[38]

Roughly speaking, all of these treaties, and BITs in particular, form a legal framework that is friendly towards ISA. With a few exceptions, most Chinese IIAs allow foreign investors to resort to ICSID or ad hoc arbitration (typically under UNCITRAL Arbitration Rules).[39] Chinese BITs can be roughly divided into three generations.[40] The evolution of the ISA clauses of the different generations of BITs also suggests that China's attitude towards ISA is getting friendlier. China has progressively and gradually expanded the scope of consent to ISA in its IIAs, meaning that a broader range of disputes is allowed to be arbitrated.[41] Almost all recent BITs and TIT, such as the China–Canada BIT[42] and the China–Japan–Korea TIT, generally allow 'investment disputes' or 'legal disputes relating to an investment' to be submitted to ISA.[43] Earlier

[37] A list of China's BITs, FTAs, and other IIAs is available at <https://investmentpolicy.unctad.org/international-investment-agreements/countries/42/china> accessed 30 October 2019.

[38] The current status of the ICSID Convention is available at <https://icsid.worldbank.org/ICSID/FrontServlet?requestType=ICSIDDocRH&actionVal=ContractingStates&ReqFrom=Main> accessed 15 October 2014.

[39] There are three Chinese BITs that have no provision of ISA. They are the China–Thailand BIT (1985), the China–Romania BIT (1994), and the China–Turkmenistan BIT (1992).

[40] See eg Elodie Dulac, 'The Emerging Third Generation of Chinese Investment Treaties' (2007) 7 TDM 1, 1–31; Norah Gallagher and Wenhua Shan, *Chinese Investment Treaties: Policies and Practice* (OUP 2009) 1, 1–14.

[41] See generally Manjiao Chi and Xi Wang, 'The Evolution of ISA Clauses in Chinese IIAs and Its Implications: The Admissibility of Disputes for Investor-State Arbitration' (2015) 16(5–6) JWIT 862, 863–91.

[42] China–Canada BIT, arts 20 and 21.

[43] China–Japan–Korea TIT, art 15.

IIAs, by contrast, restricted dispute settlement to 'disputes relating to the amount of compensation of expropriation'.[44]

The ISA-friendliness of Chinese IIAs can be understood from a historical perspective. China's IIA programme was initiated in the early 1980s, shortly after the start of its economic reforms. Concluding BITs, especially with Western countries, was an important strategy to help attract foreign direct investment to boost China's national economy.[45] Because foreign investors often had concerns over China's legal environment and the independence of Chinese courts, access to ISA to solve potential investment disputes was a priority of China's BIT-making.

Since the new millennium, there have been some reported ISA cases relying on Chinese BITs, initiated by Chinese investors against foreign states or by foreign investors against China.[46] The first IIA case relying on a Chinese BIT, *Tza Yap Shum v Peru*, is a milestone. In this case, the dispute settlement clause of the applicable BIT, the China–Peru BIT 1994, provides in relevant part that 'a dispute involving the amount of compensation for expropriation' can be submitted to ISA.[47] The ICSID tribunal interpreted this provision as granting it jurisdiction not only to address questions relating to the amount of compensation due but also to decide the issue of the existence and lawfulness of the alleged expropriation:

> [T]he words 'involving the amount of compensation for expropriation' includes not only the mere determination of the amount but also any other issues normally inherent to an expropriation, including whether the property was actually expropriated in accordance with the BIT provisions and requirements, as well as the determination of the amount of compensation due, if any.[48]

Such an 'expansive' interpretation of the narrowly designed ISA clause in China's first-generation BITs, in *Tza Yap Shum v Peru*, has been criticized by some Chinese scholars, who worry that such interpretation, together with the broad ISA clauses in China's second- and third-generation BITs, may harm China's regulatory power and national interest.[49] Following the jurisdictional decision in *Tza Yap Shum v Peru*,[50]

[44] See generally Chi and Wang (n 41) 863–91.

[45] As can be seen from the MOFCOM BIT List, the majority of China's early BITs were concluded with European countries.

[46] There are seven publicly reported ISA cases based on Chinese BITs. These cases are, listed chronologically: (1) *Tza Yap Shum v The Republic of Peru*, ICSID Case No ARB/07/6; (2) *China Heilongjiang International Economic & Technical Cooperative Corp, Beijing Shougang Mining Investment Company Ltd and Qinhuangdaoshi Qinlong International Industrial Co Ltd v Mongolia*, PCA Case No 2010-20 (UNCITRAL); (3) *Ekran Berhad v People's Republic of China*, ICSID Case No ARB/11/15; (4) *Ping An Life Insurance Company of China, Limited and Ping An Insurance (Group) Company of China, Ltd v Kingdom of Belgium*, ICSID Case No ARB/12/29; (5) *Beijing Urban Construction Group Co Ltd v Republic of Yemen*, ICSID Case No ARB/14/30; (6) *Ansung Housing Co, Ltd v People's Republic of China*, ICSID Case No ARB/14/25; and (7) *Sanum Investments Ltd v Lao People's Democratic Republic*, PCA Case No 2013-13 (UNCITRAL).

[47] China–Peru BIT, art 8.3.

[48] See *Tza Yap Shum v The Republic of Peru* (n 46) Decision on Jurisdiction and Competence (20 January 2017) para 188.

[49] See eg An Chen, 'Should the Four Great Safeguards in Sino-Foreign BITS Be Hastily Dismantled? Comments on Provisions Concerning Dispute Settlement in Model US and Canadian BITs' (2006) 7(6) JWIT 899.

[50] See eg An Chen, 'Queries to the Recent ICSID Decision on Jurisdiction Upon the Case of Tza Yap Shum v Republic of Peru: Should China-Peru BIT 1994 Be Applied to Hong Kong SAR under the "One

and compounded by the fear that China might also be dragged into a huge number of cases like Argentina if the ISA clauses are made broad,[51] the call for a halt to negotiating broad ISA clauses in China's BITs has grown increasingly strong.

Admittedly, one of the possible consequences of the broad ISA clauses in Chinese IIAs is that, as foreign investors can increasingly easily initiate arbitration against China, China's regulatory autonomy may face an increasing challenge. Especially given China's large number of IIAs and its active engagement in international investment activities, more ISA cases relying on Chinese IIAs are likely to appear in the future. This would make it more difficult for China to protect its public interest in foreign investment governance. China's IIA negotiators seemed to have been aware of this situation. While recognizing that broad ISA clauses in IIAs may help protect Chinese overseas investors and their investments, they acknowledge that China should pay more attention to the development and reform of the ISDS system in its future IIA-making.[52] Thus, it may be expected that ISA clauses in China's future IIAs will be made more balanced.

IV. Enforcement of PPA Awards in China

Private parties may apply to Chinese courts for recognition and enforcement of PPA awards against public parties under the ICSID Convention (ICSID awards), the New York Convention, or Chinese national law (non-ICSID PPA awards). In different legal frameworks, the private parties may encounter different difficulties. It is likely that an award will not be enforced by a Chinese court for public interest considerations, especially under the New York Convention.

Country Two Systems" Policy' (2009) 10 JWIT 829; Manjiao Chi, 'Preliminary Study on Application of Law in International Mixed Arbitration: The Application of Law in Tza Yap Shum v Peru by the ICSID Tribunal' (2010) 17(3) Chin JIEL 122 (original in Chinese); Nils Eliasson, 'Investor-State Arbitration and Chinese Investors: Recent Developments in Light of the Decision on Jurisdiction in the Case *Mr Tza Yap Shum v the Republic of Peru*' (2009) 2 Contemp Asia Arb J 347; Golden Smith, 'Chinese Bilateral Investment Treaties: Restrictions on International Arbitration' (2010) 76 Arb 58; Jane Y Willems, 'The Settlement of Investor State Disputes and China New Developments on ICSID Jurisdiction' (2011) 8 S Carolina J Int'l L & Bus 1; Wei Shen, 'The Good, the Bad or the Ugly? A Critique of the Decision on Jurisdiction and Competence in Tza Yap Shum v The Republic of Peru' (2011) 10 Chin J Int'l L 55.

51 See eg Wei Yanru, 'On the Impropriety of China's Recent Complete Acceptance of ICSID Jurisdiction' (2006) 13(1) Chin JIEL 109 (original in Chinese); Wang Hailang, 'Falling Behind or Going Far beyond the Limit? – China's Consent to the Jurisdiction of ICSID' (2006) 13(1) Chin JIEL 145 (original in Chinese); Cai Congyan, 'Loosening Jurisdiction Imprudently, A Tidal Wave of Litigations Arising out of Argentina's Imprudent Attitude towards investment Disputes Jurisdiction and Its Serious Lessons' (2006) 13(1) Chin JIEL 207 (original in Chinese).

52 See eg Yongjie Li, 'Factors to Be Considered for China's Future Investment Treaties' in Wenhua Shan (ed), *China and International Investment Law* (Brill 2014) 173, 173–79.

A. Enforcement of ICSID Awards in China

The ICSID Convention requires Contracting States to 'recognize an award rendered pursuant to this Convention as binding and enforce the pecuniary obligations imposed by that award within its territories as if it were a final judgment of a court in that state'.[53] While Chinese IIAs generally allow ICSID arbitration, almost none contain a clear provision with regard to the enforcement of ICSID awards except for the statement that 'the award shall be final'.

The mere existence of these provisions cannot guarantee the enforcement of ICSID awards in China. First, the ICSID Convention requires the Contracting States to take 'necessary legislative or other measures' for making its provisions effective in their territories.[54] Yet, no publicly available evidence shows that China has taken such measures. For instance, it is unclear which courts (or level of courts or other state organs) in China are charged to enforce ICSID awards and what procedures should be followed. Second, Article 54(1) of the ICSID Convention provides that ICSID awards are deemed as 'a final judgment of a court in that state'. However, according to the CPL, even a 'final judgment' of a Chinese court may still be further 'appealed' through judicial supervision proceedings, although this is not commonly seen. This means that a final judgment may still be reheard upon the decision of the judicial committee of the issuing court or the decision of the SPC, though such cases are rarely seen.[55] The non-finality of final judgments in China may give rise to profound concerns over whether ICSID awards will be reviewed by Chinese courts and whether such review would negatively impact the enforcement of ICSID awards in China.[56]

Consequently, although China has an obligation to enforce ICSID awards, it lacks supportive national law to satisfactorily fulfil that obligation. One explanation is that China has not considered itself a likely target of ISA. Thus, the Chinese legislator has not adopted laws on the enforcement of ICSID awards.[57] Up to the present, China has not been requested to enforce any ICSID awards,[58] but it should be prepared for the enforcement of ICSID awards in the future.

B. Enforcement of Non-ICSID PPA Awards in China

As to non-ICSID ISA awards (such as those rendered by arbitration institutions other than ICSID or by ad hoc arbitral tribunals) and other foreign PPA awards, they normally will be covered by the New York Convention. Though the New York Convention

[53] ICSID Convention, art 54(1).

[54] ibid, art 69.

[55] CPL, ch 16 (Judicial Supervision Proceedings).

[56] Xiao Fang, 'Recognition and Enforcement of International Investment Arbitration Award in China' (2011) 6 The Jurist 94, 101 (original in Chinese).

[57] Julian Ku, 'Enforcement of ICSID Awards in the People's Republic of China' (2013) 6(1) Contemp Asia Arb J 31, 44.

[58] Up to the present, there have been only two ISA cases against China and relying on China's BITs. The first case is *Ekran v China*, which has been discontinued according to the ICSID Arbitration Rule. The second case is *Ansung v China*, which is still pending.

is silent on the enforcement of arbitral awards against states, its *travaux préparatoires* imply that awards against states should not be excluded from its ambit of application.[59] Yet, it should be noted that China has made a 'commercial reservation' to the New York Convention which explicitly excludes ISA awards from the scope of application of the Convention in China. Thus, ISA awards cannot be enforced under the New York Convention. Such awards should be enforced in accordance with Chinese national law.

Turning to the national law of China, both the CAL and the CPL have provisions on the recognition and enforcement of foreign arbitral awards in general. According to the CAL, if the award debtor fails to voluntarily execute an award, the award creditor may apply to a court for enforcement in accordance with the CPL.[60] According to the CPL, Chinese courts shall enforce such an award in accordance with the pertinent international treaties to which China is a party or, absent such treaties, the principle of reciprocity.[61] From a practical perspective, the pertinent treaties under the CPL essentially refer to the New York Convention and the ICSID Convention. As mentioned, because China has made a commercial reservation to the New York Convention, no such 'pertinent treaties' are available for non-ICSID ISA awards. Thus, such awards can only be enforced in China according to the reciprocity principle as set forth in the CPL. Up to the present, this principle has never been elaborated on in Chinese law or applied by any Chinese courts. It is unclear how this principle will be applied and what impacts it will have on the enforcement of PPA awards in China.

C. State Immunity and Enforcement of PPA Awards in China

Compared with commercial arbitration, a unique issue relating to PPA is that the enforcement of PPA awards would involve state immunity (from execution). Neither the ICSID Convention nor the New York Convention explicitly address the immunity issue. According to the former, enforcement of an ICSID award shall not be deemed 'as derogating from the law in force in any contracting state relating to immunity of that state or of any foreign state from execution'.[62] According to the latter, any 'contracting state shall recognize arbitral awards as binding and enforce them in accordance with the rules of procedure of the territory where the award is relied upon'.[63] Therefore, under both conventions, the immunity issue is to be decided in accordance with the national law of the forum state.

Under Chinese law, insurmountable difficulties may arise when enforcing PPA awards. First, a legislative lacuna exists with regard to foreign state immunity in Chinese law which makes the enforcement of PPA awards in China extremely uncertain. The CAL and CPL provisions regarding enforcement of foreign arbitral awards are silent on the immunity issue. Up to the present, China has not enacted national

[59] Albert Jan van den Berg, 'The New York Convention and State Immunity' in Karl-Heinz Böckstiegel (ed), *Acts of State and Arbitration* (Carl Heymanns 1997) 41, 43–44.
[60] CAL, art 62.
[61] CPL, art 283.
[62] ICSID Convention, art 55.
[63] New York Convention, art III.

law on foreign state immunity and the existing rules are insufficient and unclear.[64] The only exception is the 2005 Law of Immunity of Assets of Foreign Central Banks of the People's Republic of China (Foreign Bank Immunity Law).[65] According to this law, assets of foreign central banks located in China shall be immune from judicial execution and property preservation unless these banks or their governments waive such immunity in writing or designate the assets for execution or preservation purposes.[66]

Second, China's strong adherence to the doctrine of absolute immunity likely implies a ban on the enforcement of PPA awards in China.[67] Despite the fact that China has signed the United Nations Convention on Jurisdictional Immunities of States and Their Property,[68] China has not ratified this Convention. In practice, China still adheres to absolute immunity. This position can be seen from the above Foreign Bank Immunity Law provision. It has also been reiterated in two letters sent to the Hong Kong courts by the Office of the Commissioner of the Chinese Ministry of Foreign Affairs in Hong Kong in the high-profile case of *Democratic Republic of the Congo and others v FG Hemisphere Associates LLC* in 2011.[69]

Third, as a matter of fact, Chinese courts have never exercised jurisdiction over acts of foreign states, nor have they enforced any decisions involving public property of foreign states.[70] Such practical inexperience of Chinese courts could make it difficult to predict whether and how PPA awards can be enforced in China.

Given China's legislative lacuna, adherence to the absolute immunity doctrine, and the lack of previous cases in Chinese courts, it seems natural to conclude that no PPA awards can be enforced by Chinese courts unless the award-debtor state waives its immunity.[71]

V. Conclusion

Two major conclusions can be drawn from the above. First and foremost, although China generally allows PPA of two types—domestic PPA (based on national law) and ISA (based on IIAs)—its overall attitude towards PPA cannot be said to be

[64] See generally Dahai Qi, 'State Immunity, China and Its Shifting Position' (2008) 7(2) Chin J Int'l L 307.

[65] Adopted at the 18th Meeting of the Standing Committee of the 10th National People's Congress of China on 25 October 2005, available at <www.china.com.cn/chinese/PI-c/1010926.htm> accessed 20 May 2017 (original in Chinese).

[66] Foreign Bank Immunity Law, art 1.

[67] See eg JV Feinerman, 'Sovereign Immunity in the Chinese Case and Its Implications for the Future International Law' in R St J Macdonald (ed), *Essays in Honour of Wang Tieya* (Martinus Nijhoff 1994) 269; James Crawford, *Brownlie's Principles of Public International Law* (8th edn, OUP 2012) 505.

[68] See 'United Nations Convention on Jurisdictional Immunities of States and Their Property' available at <https://treaties.un.org/Pages/ShowMTDSGDetails.aspx?src=UNTSONLINE&tabid=2&mtdsg_no=III-13&chapter=3&lang=en> accessed 20 May 2017.

[69] The decisions are (2009) 1 HKLRD 410 (Court of First Instance) (2010) 2 HKLRD 66 (Court of Appeal), and FACV 5, 6 & 7/2010 (Court of Final Appeal). These decisions are available at <www.judiciary.gov.hk/en/legal_ref/judgments.htm> accessed 10 February 2015. The relevant paragraphs of the two letters are reproduced in FACV 5, 6 & 7/2010 (Court of Final Appeal) para 461.

[70] Xue Hanqin, 'Chinese Contemporary Perspective on International Law: History, Culture and International Law' (2011) 355 RdC 41, 100–01.

[71] See generally Manjiao Chi, 'The Impeding Effects of the Immunity Plea on International Arbitration: China's Position Revisited' (2016) 12 Asian Int'l Arb J 21, 21–39.

sufficiently friendly. On the one hand, only commercial disputes can be arbitrated in domestic PPA, while administrative disputes are excluded from PPA. On the other hand, although ISA is allowed in the majority of China's existing IIAs, the enforcement of ISA awards in China is still subject to a high level of uncertainty, which is due chiefly to China's legislative lacuna and adherence to the absolute immunity doctrine.

Second, notwithstanding China's overall unfriendliness towards PPA, China's attitudes towards PPA under national law and under IIAs seem bifurcated. More specifically, while China impliedly bans PPA in its national laws, it allows ISA through IIAs. The consequence of such bifurcated attitudes would be that, while China allows foreign investors to challenge its regulatory measures through arbitration, it does not allow Chinese citizens and enterprises to do the same. Chinese citizens will have to resort to administrative litigation to defend their interests against Chinese government bodies. China does not provide a reason to justify these bifurcated and discriminatory attitudes. Besides, it seems that such bifurcated attitudes could not help protect public interest or preserve state regulatory autonomy. A reasonable explanation seems to be that, given China's state-centric legal tradition, the pro-ISA bias of Chinese IIAs represents a response to the external pressure from foreign investors and their home states, while in the national plane, China seems to sense little pressure as the implied ban on PPA under Chinese national law principally affects Chinese citizens and enterprises.

In short, though PPA is allowed under both Chinese national law and IIAs, private parties may face profound difficulty in initiating PPA or enforcing PPA awards in China. This not only shows that the role of arbitration in settling public-private disputes in China is extremely limited but also suggests that China's 'friendly' attitudes towards ISA in its IIAs should not be deemed as a shift of its generally 'unfriendly' attitude towards PPA more generally.

Select Materials

Bibliography

Chen, An, 'Should the Four Great Safeguards in Sino-Foreign BITS Be Hastily Dismantled? Comments on Provisions Concerning Dispute Settlement in Model US and Canadian BITs' (2006) 7(6) J World Inv & Trade 899

Chi, Manjiao, 'Drinking Poison to Quench Thirst: The Discriminatory Arbitral Award Enforcement Regime under Chinese Arbitration Law' (2009) 39(2) Hong Kong LJ 541

Chi, Manjiao, 'The Impeding Effects of the Immunity Plea on International Arbitration: China's Position Revisited' (2016) 12 Asian Int'l Arb J 21

Chi, Manjiao and Xi Wang, 'The Evolution of ISA Clauses in Chinese IIAs and Its Implications: The Admissibility of Disputes for Investor-State Arbitration' (2015) 16 (5–6) J World Inv & Trade 862

Crawford, James, *Brownlie's Principles of Public International Law* (8th edn, OUP 2012)

Du, Ming, 'China's State Capitalism and World Trade' (2014) 63(2) ICLQ 409

Dulac, Elodie, 'The Emerging Third Generation of Chinese Investment Treaties' (2007) 7 TDM 1

Feinerman, JV, 'Sovereign Immunity in the Chinese Case and Its Implications for the Future International Law' in R St J Macdonald (ed), *Essays in Honour of Wang Tieya* (Martinus Nijhoff 1994)

Gallagher, Norah and Wenhua Shan, *Chinese Investment Treaties: Policies and Practice* (OUP 2009)

Hanqin, Xue, *Chinese Contemporary Perspective on International Law: History, Culture and International Law* (2011) 355 Recueil des Cours 41

Hong, Shen and Zhao Nong, *China's State-Owned Enterprises: Nature, Performance and Reform* (World Scientific Publishing 2013)

Jennings, RY, 'State Contract in International Law' (1961) 37 BYBIL 156

Ku, Julian, 'Enforcement of ICSID Awards in the People's Republic of China' (2013) 6(1) Contemp Asia Arb J 31

Li, Yongjie, 'Factors to be Considered for China's Future Investment Treaties' in Wenhua Shan (ed), *China and International Investment Law* (Brill 2014)

Mann, FA, 'State Contracts and International Arbitration' (1967) 42 BYBIL 1

Qi, Dahai, 'State Immunity, China and Its Shifting Position' (2008) 7(2) Chinese J Int'l L 307

Schill, Stephan W (ed), *International Investment Law and Comparative Public Law* (OUP 2010)

Sornarajah, M, *The Settlement of Foreign Investment Disputes* (Kluwer Law International 2000)

van den Berg, Albert Jan, 'The New York Convention and State Immunity' in Karl-Heinz Böckstiegel (ed), *Acts of State and Arbitration* (Carl Heymanns 1997) 41

Van Harten, Gus, *Investment Treaty Arbitration and Public Law* (OUP 2008)

Wenying, Wang, 'Distinct Features of Arbitration in China: An Historical Perspective' (2006) 23(1) J Int'l Arb 49

Yeoh, Friven and Yu Fu, 'The People's Court and Arbitration: A Snapshot of Recent Judicial Attitudes in Arbitrability and Enforcement' (2007) 24(6) J Int'l Arb 635

Yu, Xingzhong, 'State Legalism and the Public/Private Divide in Chinese Legal Development' (2014) 15(1) Theo Inq L 28

Legislation

Administrative Litigation Law of People's Republic of China, adopted by the 2nd Session of the 7th National People's Congress of China on 4 April 1989, last amendment adopted 11th Session of the Standing Committee of the 12th National People's Congress of China on 1 November 2014

Arbitration Law of the People's Republic of China, adopted by the 9th Session of the Standing Committee of the 8th National People's Congress of China on 31 August 1994

Company Law of the People's Republic of China, adopted by the 5th Session of the Standing Committee of the 8th National People's Congress of China on 29 December

1993, last amended by the 5th Session of the Standing Committee of the 12th National People's Congress of China on 28 December 2013
General Principles of Civil Law of People's Republic of China, adopted by the 4th Session of the 6th National People's Congress of China on 12 April 1986
Law of Immunity of Assets of Foreign Central Banks of the People's Republic of China, adopted at the 18th Meeting of the Standing Committee of the 10th National People's Congress of China on 25 October 2005

Cases

Bureau of Land and Resource of Yazhou District of Jining Municipality v Jiangsu Nuoya Investment Development Co Ltd, Judgment of the Intermediate People's Court of Ji'nan Municipality, Doc. No.: (2014) Ji Zhong Li Chu Zi Di 31 Hao
Democratic Republic of the Congo and others v FG Hemisphere Associates LLC [2009] 1 HKLRD 410 (Court of First Instance) [2010] 2 HKLRD 66 (Court of Appeal) and FACV 5, 6 & 7/2010 (Court of Final Appeal)
Tza Yap Shum v The Republic of Peru, ICSID Case No ARB/07/6, Decision on Jurisdiction and Competence (19 June 2009)

17

Public Policy Dimensions of Public-Private Arbitration

Recent Development and New Systemic Awareness in Korea

Jaemin Lee

I. Introduction

Investor-state dispute settlement (ISDS) proceedings under international investment agreements (IIAs) have received a great deal of attention recently. Various concerns have been raised with regard to ISDS.[1] Robust discussions for reform are currently under way.

The current ISDS reform discussion aims to strike a balance between a host state's legitimate regulatory authority, on the one hand, and the protection of foreign investors, on the other. More specifically, the discussion purports to deal with the following items: (1) inconsistency in arbitral decisions; (2) limited mechanisms to ensure the correctness of arbitral decisions; (3) lack of predictability; 4) appointment of arbitrators by the parties; (5) the impact of party appointment on the impartiality and independence of arbitrators; (6) lack of transparency; and (7) increasing duration and costs of procedure.[2]

ISDS proceedings based on IIAs, where the respondent is a government and the subject matter relates to governmental regulation, have already drawn much attention in Korea as they arguably touch upon the outer parameters of the government's legitimate regulatory authority.[3] Debates have been intensifying in Korea regarding ISDS proceedings during the past decade due to the fact that international 'arbitration' somehow determines an essentially 'public law' issue which would otherwise fall under the jurisdiction of Korean courts.

A new trend, however, is now burgeoning: some contract-based public-private arbitration appears to raise similar concerns and problems as ISDS proceedings do. Contract-based arbitrations often proceed ad hoc, conducted between a foreign business entity and a host state government agency, but implicate 'regulatory space' in the same

[1] See UNCITRAL, 'Possible Future Work in the Field of Dispute Settlement: Reforms of Investor-State Dispute Settlement (ISDS)' UN Doc A/CN.9/917 (3–21 July 2017) paras 11–12; UNCITRAL, 'Possible Reform of Investor-State Dispute Settlement (ISDS)' UN Doc A/CN.9/WG.III/WP.142 (18 September 2017).

[2] See UNCITRAL, 'Possible Future Work' (n 1).

[3] See eg Heejun Kim, 'Study on the Major Issues of ISDS between Lone Star Fund and the Republic of Korea' (2019) 12(2) Contemp Asia Arb J 207, 226–27; Jaemin Lee, 'Two Bites at the Same Apple? "Derivative" ISDS Proceedings in the Revised Korea-US FTA' (2019) 12(1) J E Asia and Int L 107, 114.

Jaemin Lee, *Public Policy Dimensions of Public-Private Arbitration* In: *The Comparative Constitutional Foundations of Private-Public Arbitration*. Edited by: Stephan W. Schill, Oxford University Press.
DOI: 10.1093/9780191987960.003.0017

manner as ISDS proceedings under IIAs do. Contract-based arbitrations arising from public-private partnership (PPP) projects provide a vivid example. Disputes referred to public-private arbitration arguably involve 'public interest' dimensions, but they elude the safety net that domestic dispute settlement systems provide for public interest issues.

Korea is also experiencing this new phenomenon. Generally speaking, contract-based arbitration involving international disputes has been steadily increasing in Korea over recent years.[4] Amid this trend, contract-based arbitrations to resolve international disputes taking place in Korea or relating to Korean entities increasingly involve government agencies as parties. In other words, one party to a dispute is a government agency (either Korean or foreign) and the other party is a private entity. A governing contract stipulates that any dispute arising from the contract is subject to contract-based arbitration. It seems that both the government agency and the other private party have realized and enjoy the benefit of resorting to contract-based arbitration as opposed to a lengthy court proceeding.

Nonetheless, few discussions have taken place in Korea to address the unique issues arising from public-private contract-based arbitration. In principle, the rules, procedures, and jurisprudence governing private-private contract-based arbitration also apply to public-private contract-based arbitration. This is contrasted with domestic court proceedings in Korea, where a separate set of rules and jurisprudence are applied to disputes involving public law issues between a private entity, on the one hand, and a government agency, on the other. In Korea, administrative law and related case law regulate this particular issue. Thus, one may argue that a similar consideration is indeed appropriate or even required with respect to public-private contract-based arbitration when the core issue relates to public law matters that affect the public interest. Viewed from this perspective, public-private contract-based arbitration offers a new occasion to look into different facets of contract-based arbitration in Korea.

With this in mind, this chapter aims to examine how this particular issue has been observed and discussed in Korea, and looks into possible implications flowing from this new development. This chapter purports to address new aspects of contract-based arbitration. It argues that public-private contract-based arbitration, in particular concerning PPP projects, shares certain core traits with ISDS proceedings under IIAs, and thus stands to raise similar concerns in the long run. The term public-private arbitration is used in this chapter within the specific context of PPP projects that can lead to contract-based arbitration. Arguably, this is still a novel issue in Korea, with many aspects remaining in an inchoate state. Scholars and experts in Korea are paying close attention to the developments in other countries relating to this new awareness and concern.

The rest of this chapter is structured as follows. Section II explains the increasing trend of public-private contract-based arbitration in Korea, focusing on high-profile

[4] See the Annual Reports of the Korean Commercial Arbitration Board available on its website at <http://www.kcabinternational.or.kr/publications/annual_report.do> accessed 25 February 2025; Sue Hyun Lim, 'Innovation in Progress – Developments in Korea after the Launch of KCAB International' in Global Arbitration Review (ed), *The Asia-Pacific Arbitration Review 2021* (GAR 2020) 18. As the volume of trade has increased, the number of commercial arbitrations in Korea has steadily increased over the years.

PPP projects, and explores similarities of concerns being raised over such contract-based arbitration and ISDS proceedings. The statutory framework under the Korean law relating to public-private contract-based arbitration is then discussed in section III. Section IV argues that public-private contract-based arbitration falling under this category poses a risk to Korean public law, setting forth specific issues to be dealt with in future discussions in Korea, and possibly in other countries. Section V concludes.

II. Increase of Public-Private Contract-Based Arbitration in Korea

Contract-based arbitration involving state agencies has been on the rise globally.[5] In 2019, 20 per cent of the new cases registered with the International Chamber of Commerce (ICC) involved a state or state entities.[6] This issue is not confined to disputes arising from contracts to which a government agency and a foreign business entity are parties. It also covers situations where a government-affiliated business entity enters into a contract with a foreign counterpart: the former is regarded as exercising regulatory authority or otherwise serving governmental objectives. State-owned enterprises (SOEs) operate actively in many countries,[7] in particular in the field of national infrastructure, where PPP projects are prominent.[8] As a consequence, they have become one of the controversial issues in international economic law, and international contract-based arbitration involving these SOEs' PPP projects stands to raise similar concerns. Thus, the public policy dimension of such contract-based arbitrations could be more far-reaching than it seems.

The increasing trend of contract-based arbitration is also visible in Korea.[9] The table below presenting statistics compiled by the Korean Commercial Arbitration Board (KCAB) indicates this steady trend.

The table only concerns KCAB arbitration. It should be noted that there are other arbitral institutions administering contract-based arbitrations involving Korean parties, as well as cases that are not officially reported or disclosed due to confidentiality agreements.[10] Once all of these cases are accounted for, it is believed that an upward trend will be more visible.[11] The duration of arbitral proceedings administered by KCAB was, on average, 263 days in 2020 (236 days for 372 domestic arbitrations and 398 days for 77 international arbitrations), and it is this speedy process that is

[5] See Kaj Hobér, 'Arbitration Involving States' in Lawrence W Newman and Richard D Hill (eds), *The Leading Arbitrators' Guide to International Arbitration* (3rd edn, Juris 2014) 929.

[6] See International Chamber of Commerce (ICC), 'ICC Dispute Resolution 2019 Statistics' (2019) 4 <https://iccwbo.org/publication/icc-dispute-resolution-statistics/> accessed 25 February 2025.

[7] See Przemyslaw Kowalski and others, 'State-Owned Enterprises: Trade Effects and Policy Implications' OECD Trade Policy Paper No 147 (2013) 21, Tables 3 and 4.

[8] ibid 28.

[9] See Kim Bae and LLC Lee, *Arbitration Law of Korea: Practice and Procedure* (Juris 2012) 71; Korean Commercial Arbitration Board (KCAB), '2015 Annual Report' (2015) 5 <www.kcab.or.kr> accessed 25 February 2025.

[10] See Bae and Lee (n 9) 130.

[11] ibid; KCAB (n 9) 7.

Table 17.1 KCAB Domestic and International Case Filings, 2007–19

	2007	2008	2009	2010	2011	2012	2013	2014	2015	2016	2017	2018	2019
International	59	47	78	52	77	85	77	87	74	62	78	62	70
Domestic	174	215	240	264	246	275	261	295	339	319	307	331	373
Total	233	262	318	316	323	360	338	382	413	381	385	393	443

Source: KCAB, 'Annual Reports' (2013–19) and 'Claims Statistics' (2007–12), available via <www.kcabinternational.or.kr> accessed 25 February 2025 (all documents originally in Korean).

reportedly one of the main reasons why participants, at least those from Korea, are generally satisfied.[12]

Contract-based arbitration in Korea follows the basic features and formats of contract-based arbitration as understood and implemented in other countries. Over the years, Korea has adopted many of the applicable model laws (such as those developed by the United Nations Commission on International Trade Law (UNCITRAL)) and general practice of the international community relating to contract-based arbitration. It can be said that Korea has consistently pursued a policy of incorporating, encouraging, and facilitating contract-based arbitration within its jurisdiction as a means to settle various kinds of contractual disputes.

A. Public-Private Arbitration—PPP Projects

Contracts concluded between foreign corporations or individuals and Korean government agencies usually contain arbitration clauses. Foreign counterparties tend to feel more familiar and comfortable with international arbitration than Korean domestic court proceedings.[13] The three main areas of public-private arbitration in Korea concern construction, trade, and procurement.[14] Large construction projects commissioned by government agencies, both at the central and local levels, are particularly common candidates for contract-based arbitration, and many of them are pursued as PPP projects.

In recent years, several high-profile public-private contract-based arbitrations involving PPP projects have drawn keen national attention. Interestingly, this attention did not so much focus on the terms of the contracts involved, but rather the fact that government agencies, and with them the public policies they pursue, are being brought before international arbitral tribunals. These arbitral proceedings have also been highlighted in Korea as a new type of foreign/international regulatory oversight over governmental policies. These proceedings also show the long-term repercussions

[12] See Korean Commercial Arbitration Board (KCAB), '2014 Arbitration Award Cases' (2014) 33, 38 <www.kcab.or.kr/servlet/kcab_kor/data/4422?seq=53&clsf=3&pageno=1&search_word_kind=titl&search_word=> accessed 25 February 2025.

[13] ibid 141.

[14] ibid 31.

that a government agency's international contract and the ensuing contract-based arbitration may have, as well as their implications for the 'public interest'. This section discusses five exemplary cases. Note that the last two had not proceeded to arbitration as of the time of this writing, but they are included as they show similar factual patterns and trends in this regard.

1 The *Yongin City Light Train* Case

In February 2011, the Yongin Rapid Transit Corporation, a private consortium controlled by the Canadian investor Bombardier, Inc, initiated an ICC arbitration.[15] Yongin City, located to the south of Seoul, had adopted a light train project in 1996, but while the construction was under way, the city government cancelled the contract citing abnormalities surrounding the contract negotiations. The foreign investors initiated arbitral proceedings against the city government claiming construction expenses and losses due to the delayed start of the operation.[16] The arbitration was the largest arbitration in 2011 in Asia, and it was also the first international case arising from a construction project of a local government in Korea.[17] The arbitral tribunal awarded the payment of KRW 779 billion (USD 692 million) to the consortium.[18]

2 The *Incheon Grand Bridge* Case

Another contract-based ICC arbitration between a consortium (Macquarie and Incheon Bridge Co, Ltd. (IBC)) and a Korean government entity (the Ministry of Land, Infrastructure and Transport (MOLIT)) occured over the construction of the Incheon Grand Bridge.[19] Although IBC has a concession to operate and manage the bridge until 23 October 2039, Incheon City wanted a new competing road. IBC, fearing a reduction in profit, raised a claim based on a non-compete provision, and initiated an ICC arbitration in April 2018.[20] In its award of June 2020,[21] the arbitral tribunal ruled that a newly constructed competing road was subject to the non-compete provision, and therefore the MOLIT has an obligation to compensate IBC for the loss arising from it.[22]

[15] See Yooil Bae and Yu-Min Joo, 'Pathways to Meet Critical Success Factors for Local PPPs: The Cases of Urban Transport Infrastructure in Korean Cities' (2016) 53 Cities 35, 38.

[16] ibid.

[17] ibid.

[18] See Export-Import Bank of Korea, '2016/17 KSP Policy Consultation III: Public-Private Partnership for Urban Transportation Infrastructure in Colombia' (2016); World Bank, 'The Municipal Public-Private Partnership Framework' (2019) 8–9; Bae and Joo (n 15) 39.

[19] See Macquarie Korea Infrastructure Fund, '2020 Full Year Results Presentation' (29 January 2021) <https://www.mkif.com/assets/mkif/en/investor-centre/public-filings-and-reports/2021/2101-ir-general-presentation-4q-2020-eng.pdf> accessed 25 February 2025.

[20] See Macquarie Korea Infrastructure Fund, 'Incheon Bridge Co, Ltd Submits a Request for Arbitration to the International Chamber of Commerce' (20 April 2018) <https://www.mkif.com/assets/mkif/en/investor-centre/public-filings-and-reports/2018/ir-release-1804-ibc-to-submit-icc-arbitration-eng.pdf> accessed 25 February 2025.

[21] See ibid.

[22] See Macquarie Korea Infrastructure Fund, 'Incheon Bridge Co, Ltd Receives the Final Award for Arbitration from the International Chamber of Commerce' (25 June 2020) <https://www.mkif.com/assets/mkif/en/investor-centre/public-filings-and-reports/2020/IR-Release-2006-IBC-Arbitration-Result-Eng.pdf> accessed 25 February 2025.

3 The *Machang Bridge* Case

In 2014, Machang Bridge Co, Ltd. (MCB) filed an arbitration at the ICC regarding KRW 13.1 billion worth of overdue payments from the Provincial Government of Gyeongsangnamdo (PGG).[23] According to the underlying concession agreement, Macquarie Korea Infrastructure Fund (MKIF) owned 70 per cent of equity (KRW 33.9 billion) and 50 per cent of subordinated debt (KRW 79.0 billion) in the concessionaire MCB.[24] To reduce burdensome Minimum Revenue Guarantee (MRG), PGG requested refinancing and restructuring of MCB, but the parties could not reach an agreement.[25] PGG then considered a measure under a public interest provision (Article 47 of Act on Public-Private Partnerships in Infrastructure),[26] causing a dispute with MCB and MKIF. The ICC award confirmed that PGG had an obligation to make financial support payments in accordance with the concession agreement.[27] After the proceeding, a new memorandum of understanding was concluded between PGG and MKIF in December 2016 regarding the refinancing.[28]

4 The *Seoul Metro Line 9* Case

Yet another example concerns the construction of a subway line in the city of Seoul. Metro Line Number 9 Co, Ltd. (Metro 9) held a concession to operate the newly constructed subway line No 9 for thirty years.[29] MKIF's equity interest in Metro 9 was 24.5 per cent and the city of Seoul was obliged to compensate Metro 9 with MRG under the contract.[30] Due to financial pressure, however, Seoul City pursued the exclusion of the MRG clause or a reduction of the coverage rate from 8.9 per cent to 5 per cent.[31] MKIF filed a lawsuit at the Seoul Administrative Court in May 2012.[32] The

[23] See Macquarie Korea Infrastructure Fund, 'Machang Bridge Receives An Award by Consent from the Arbitral Tribunal of the International Chamber of Commerce' (6 April 2015) <https://www.mkif.com/assets/mkif/en/investor-centre/public-filings-and-reports/2015/2015-04-06-mcb-award-eng.pdf> accessed 25 February 2025.

[24] See Macquarie Korea Infrastructure Fund, 'Machang Bridge to Submit a Request for Arbitration to the International Chamber of Commerce' (Media Release, 18 September 2014) <https://www.mkif.com/assets/mkif/en/investor-centre/public-filings-and-reports/2014/2014-09-18-mcb-icc-arbitration-eng.pdf> accessed 25 February 2025.

[25] See Maekyung Media Group, 'Would Disposition for Public Interest in the Case of MRG over Machang Bridge Enter into International Arbitration?' (30 April 2014) <www.mk.co.kr/news/stock/view/2014/04/675029/> accessed 25 February 2025.

[26] Act on Public-Private Partnerships in Infrastructure (21 March 2017) art 47 (stipulating the discretion of the government agency in adjusting conditions of operation where public interest so demands).

[27] See Macquarie Korea Infrastructure Fund (n 23).

[28] See Macquarie Korea Infrastructure Fund, 'Project Restructuring of Machang Bridge' (2 January 2017) <https://www.mkif.com/assets/mkif/en/investor-centre/public-filings-and-reports/2017/20170102_mcb_restructuring_eng.pdf> accessed 25 February 2025.

[29] See Macquarie Korea Infrastructure Fund, 'Seoul Subway Line 9, Section 1 – Open to Passengers' (Media Release, 24 July 2009) <https://www.mkif.com/assets/mkif/en/investor-centre/public-filings-and-reports/2009/ir-release-0906-subway-9-opening-to-traffic-en.pdf> accessed 25 February 2025.

[30] See Business Korea, 'Withdrawal from Investment: How Much Did Macquarie Make On Subway Line 9?' (12 August 2013) <https://www.businesskorea.co.kr/news/articleView.html?idxno=1249> accessed 25 February 2025.

[31] See Money Today, 'Macquarie Considering a Withdrawal from the Line 9 Project' (20 March 2013) <https://news.mt.co.kr/mtview.php?no=2013032107378293962> accessed 25 February 2025.

[32] See Hankyung, 'Seoul Metropolitan City-Macquarie, a Year-Long Dispute over Seoul Metro Line 9 over MRG Adjustment' (5 June 2013) <https://www.hankyung.com/article/2013060462391>. See Hankyoreh, 'Macquarie Korea Expected to Pull Out of Seoul Subway Line 9' (8 August 2013) <http://english.hani.co.kr/arti/english_edition/e_international/598812.html> both accessed 25 February 2025.

court ruled against MKIF in 2013[33] and Seoul City further sought a revision of the MRG provision.[34] Consequently, MKIF pulled its investment from Seoul Metro Line 9[35] and sold its shares to a consortium of three local finance companies.[36] This was the first case of a private infrastructure provider's withdrawal in Seoul, and this incident sparked debates on MRG in PPP contracts in the area of key infrastructure construction projects.[37] How to accommodate elements of public interest in PPP projects was one of the main issues. While the dispute did not proceed to arbitration and was settled after domestic court proceedings, it has become known as a signature dispute of PPP projects.

5 The *Uijeongbu Light Rail* Case

Uijeongbu City's U Line Project was selected as a PPP project by the Ministry of Strategy and Finance in 1998, and Uijeongbu Light Rail Transit Co Ltd. (ULRT) was established as its operating company.[38] The city, located to the north of Seoul, signed a concession agreement with a consortium, comprising various domestic and foreign entities such as GS Engineering & Construction and Siemens, which participated in ULRT.[39] The local government adopted an MRG clause promising the city's compensation for the loss when the number of passengers fell short of 50 per cent of the target level.[40] In 2013, ULRT's debt increased sharply as only 18 per cent of the targeted passenger volume was reached.[41] The figure stagnated in 2014 with just 30 per cent.[42] Unable to overcome its financial difficulties, ULRT ultimately filed for bankruptcy in 2017.[43] This was the first case of bankruptcy resulting from a PPP project.[44] Following the bankruptcy filing, the concession agreement was terminated. Public interest considerations were an important factor in the termination decision. The question was then raised whether the city had to pay an early termination fee as stipulated by the contract. The dispute proceeded to the Korean domestic courts. In October 2019, a

[33] See Seoul Administrative Court Case, 2012GuHap15029 (30 May 2013); Bae and Joo (n 15) 6.

[34] See Business Korea, 'How Much Did Macquarie Make on Subway Line 9?' (12 August 2013) <https://www.businesskorea.co.kr/news/articleView.html?idxno=1249#google_vignette> accessed 25 February 2025.

[35] See Hankyung, 'Macquarie Pulled Out from Seoul Metro Line 9 and 11 Financial Companies Become Shareholders' (23 October 2013) <http://news.hankyung.com/article/2013102364491>; 'Macquarie Kicked Out of Korea' *Korea Times* (Seoul, 25 October 2013) <http://koreatimes.co.kr/www/nation/2020/04/113_144944.html>; Macquarie Korea Infrastructure Fund, 'Divestment of Stake in Seoul Metro Line 9' (23 October 2013) <https://www.mkif.com/assets/mkif/en/investor-centre/public-filings-and-reports/2013/2013-10-23-sm9-eng.pdf> all accessed 25 February 2025.

[36] See Hankyung, 'Macquarie Pulled Out from Seoul Metro Line 9 and Eleven Financial Companies Become Shareholders' (23 October 2013) <https://www.hankyung.com/article/2013102364491> accessed 25 February 2025.

[37] See Hankyoreh (n 32).

[38] See Jinyoung Park and Jinsu Mun, *Korea's Railway PPP (Public-Private Partnership) Projects* (The Korea Transportation Institute 2014) 68–69.

[39] See Chosun Daily, 'Uijeongbu Light RailUijeongbu Light Rail Transit to Break Ground 14 Years After Its Launch' (26 February 2007) <https://www.chosun.com/site/data/html_dir/2007/02/26/2007022601059.html> accessed 28 February 2021.

[40] See The JoongAng, 'Uijeongbu Light Rail Company Goes Bankrupt' (26 May 2017) <https://www.joongang.co.kr/article/21612042> accessed 25 February 2025.

[41] See MBC News, 'Uijeongbu Light Rail Transit The More You Run, the More You Lose' (1 April 2013) <https://imnews.imbc.com/replay/2013/nw1800/article/3259220_30737.html> accessed 25 February 2025.

[42] See Korea Joongang Daily (n 40).

[43] See Sisain, 'Uijeongbu Light Rail Goes Bankrupt by Exaggerated Numbers' (15 June 2017) <www.sisain.co.kr/?mod=news&act=articleView&idxno=29340> accessed 25 February 2025.

[44] ibid.

district court ruled for the termination fee to be paid, awarding ULRT a total of KRW 115.3 billion (USD 96 million). The city appealed the lower court's judgment, but it ultimately lost.[45] Even though the dispute did not proceed to international arbitration, it still highlights the relevant concerns of public interest that are embedded in PPP projects, as well as the ensuing legal problems.

B. ISDS Proceedings against Korea

In addition to contract-based arbitration, Korea has also recently been facing an increasing number of treaty-based ISDS proceedings under IIAs. Domestic concerns have been raised in this regard because of the impact international investment arbitration may have on the state's regulatory space. Considerations regarding the state's regulatory authority are also now permeating into public-private arbitration of PPP projects. As a matter of fact, contract-based arbitration and ISDS proceedings have structural similarities. For instance, an international tribunal's jurisdiction may also be based on an investment contract providing for ISDS.[46] Likewise, when domestic courts delay or refuse the enforcement of contract-based arbitrations, denial of justice claims under applicable IIAs may be raised.[47] Furthermore, via umbrella clauses in IIAs, contractual obligations are elevated to treaty claims.[48] In addition, when corporations' actions are attributable to the state, ISDS proceedings can be initiated.[49] Contract-based public-private arbitration of PPP projects involves similar entities

[45] See Yeonhap, 'Supreme Court: "Uijeongbu City to Return 10.8 Billion Won to Investors of Past Bankrupt Light Rail Project"' (2 December 2023) <https://www.yna.co.kr/view/AKR20231201141400004> accessed 25 February 2025.

[46] See Convention on the Settlement of Investment Disputes between States and Nationals of other States (adopted 18 March 1965, entered into force 14 October 1966) 575 UNTS 159 (ICSID Convention) art 25(1) (providing jurisdiction of ICSID to 'any legal dispute arising directly out of an investment', between a contracting state and a national of another contracting state). For recent cases, see eg *Lighthouse Corporation Pty Ltd and Lighthouse Corporation Ltd, IBC v Democratic Republic of Timor-Leste*, ICSID Case No ARB/15/2, Award (22 December 2017); *Standard Chartered Bank (Hong Kong) Limited v Tanzania*, ICSID Case No ARB/15/41, Award (11 October 2019). In the fiscal year 2020, ie between 1 July 2019 and 30 June 2020, forty new cases were registered with ICSID, five of which were based on investment contracts instead of IIAs. See ICSID, '2020 Annual Report' (2020) 21 <https://icsid.worldbank.org/resources/publications/icsid-annual-report> accessed 25 February 2025.

[47] See eg *Desert Line Projects LLC v Yemen*, ICSID Case No ARB/05/17, Award (6 February 2008); *ATA Construction, Industrial and Trading Company v Jordan*, ICSID Case No ARB/08/2, Award (18 May 2010); *Saipem SpA v Bangladesh*, ICSID Case No ARB/05/07, Award (30 June 2009); *White Industries Australia Limited v India*, UNCITRAL, Final Award (30 November 2011).

[48] See eg *SGS Société Générale de Surveillance SA v Pakistan*, ICSID Case No ARB/01/13, Decision on Jurisdiction (3 August 2003); *SGS Société Générale de Surveillance SA v Philippines*, ICSID Case No ARB/02/6, Decision on Jurisdiction (29 January 2004); *Joy Mining Machinery Limited v Egypt*, ICSID Case No ARB/03/11, Decision on Jurisdiction (30 July 2004); *Sempra Energy v Argentina*, ICSID Case No ARB/02/16, Decision on Annulment (29 June 2010); *Toto Costruzioni Generali SpA v Lebanon*, ICSID Case No ARB/07/12, Decision on Jurisdiction (11 September 2009). As for Korea, umbrella clauses appear in BITs with Kyrgyzstan (2007), Mauritius (2007), the Dominican Republic (2006), Vietnam (2003), Saudi Arabia (2002), and Belarus (1997).

[49] See eg *Mohammad Reza Dayyani and others v The Republic of Korea*, PCA Case No 2015-38 (UNCITRAL), Award (6 June 2018); *Jan de Nul NV and Dredging International NV v Egypt*, ICSID Case No ARB/04/13, Award (6 November 2008); *Salini Costruttori SpA and Italstrade SpA v Morocco*, ICSID Case No ARB/00/4, Decision on Jurisdiction (31 July 2001).

and similar issues but does not proceed to ISDS. The structural link between the two advises us to follow the developments in ISDS proceedings in assessing the public interest dimensions of public-private arbitrations more generally.

As of the time of writing, the first investment arbitration involving Korea as respondent, a case brought by Lone Star on 22 November 2012 under the 2007 Korea–Belgium Bilateral Investment Treaty (BIT), was rendered in favor of the investor at ICSID.[50] Being the first ISDS case against Korea, the arbitral tribunal's award is expected to gain much attention from the general public. Not long after the registration of the above-mentioned case, two further proceedings were initiated against the Korean government in 2015: one by a Dutch company called Hanocal under the 2003 Korea–Netherlands BIT,[51] and another by an Iranian electronics company under the 1998 Korea–Iran BIT.[52] Interestingly, the contested measure in the latter dispute involves a Korean public corporation, Korea Asset Management Corporation (KAMCO), which is not a government agency but an entity of which the government owns controlling shareholdings.

The Korea–United States Free Trade Agreement (KORUS FTA) was also invoked in a few ISDS proceedings. For example, on 1 May 2018, Elliott Management Corporation, an affiliate of a hedge fund from the United States, lodged a claim under the 2007 KORUS FTA for their alleged damages from Park Geun-Hye administration's intervention during the merger of Samsung C&T and Cheil Industries.[53] The case was decided by the arbitral tribunal in 2023 in favor of the foreign investor, but is still pending before a national court in a set-aside proceeding. The case revolved around alleged violations of fair and equitable treatment and minimum standard of treatment, including claims of denial of justice.[54] In September 2018, another US-registered hedge fund filed a notice of arbitration over the aforementioned merger between Samsung C&T and Cheil Industries.[55] The claimants invoke a violation of fair and equitable treatment, full protection and security, and national treatment over an undervalued merger.[56] The alleged breaches in this high profile ICSID case are still being discussed for the upcoming arbitration award.

Another investor-state claim loomed over Korea in July 2018, but it was dismissed by the arbitral tribunal, which sustained Korea's preliminary objection for lack of jurisdiction. A former Korean citizen who later became a naturalized US citizen initiated an ISDS proceeding against Korea under the KORUS FTA,[57] demanding

[50] See *LSF-KEB Holdings SCA and others v Republic of Korea*, ICSID Case No ARB/12/37 (registered 10 December 2012).

[51] See *Hanocal Holding BV and IPIC International BV v Republic of Korea*, ICSID Case No ARB/15/17 (discontinued 5 October 2016).

[52] See *Dayyani and others v Republic of Korea* (n 49).

[53] *Elliott Associates, LP v Republic of Korea*, PCA Case No 2018-51 (UNCITRAL) (registered 12 July 2018).

[54] See Luke Eric Peterson, 'Elliott Hedge Fund BIT Claims: US Hedge Fund Threatens Korea, as Its Separate BIT Case Against Poland Nears Conclusion, and Compliance with Adverse Costs Award in a Third BIT Case Remains a Mystery' (*IA Reporter*, 1 May 2018).

[55] See *Mason Capital LP and Mason Management LLC v Republic of Korea*, PCA No 2018-55 (UNCITRAL) (registered 13 September 2018).

[56] See Jarrod Hepburn, 'Korea Investment Treaty Arbitrations: A Round-Up of Recent Developments' (*IAReporter*, 24 September 2018).

[57] See *Jin-Hye Seo and the Government of the Republic of Korea*, HKIAC Case No 18117 (UNCITRAL), Final Award (24 September 2019) paras 22–23.

compensation for the alleged direct expropriation of her estate property located in Seoul.[58] However, the claimant's investment was found by the arbitral tribunal not to qualify as a covered investment under the FTA.[59] In yet another instance, in June 2019, Gale Investment Company LLC, a property developer based in New York, submitted a notice of intent over the Songdo International Business District development project with POSCO Engineering & Construction Co Ltd, under the KORUS FTA.[60] The claim involves the alleged expropriation of Gale's investment by the Korean government, and is seeking more than USD 2 billion in damages.[61]

There are other cases involving a variety of foreign firms. Schindler Holding AG, a Swiss-based elevator maker, filed a USD 264 million claim against Korea before ICSID.[62] The Schindler Group, the second-largest shareholder of Korea's Hyundai Elevator company, objected to the government's approval of Hyundai Elevator's share capital increase and other measures, which caused serious impairment to the claimant's participation rights.[63] As of the time of writing, the case is still pending, involving inter alia the standards of minimum and fair and equitable treatment as well as denial of justice. In addition, on 23 May 2019 two Canadian investors notified the Korean Ministry of Justice of their intent to initiate arbitral proceedings based on an alleged expropriation of their commercial property.[64] In the claimants' view, the government's actions lacked public purpose and compensation was far below the fair market value.[65]

ISDS proceedings were also triggered by some investors from Asian countries. Berjaya Group's notice of intent to initiate arbitral proceedings under the Korea–Malaysia BIT was disclosed on 10 July 2019.[66] The claimants alleged that their investments had been harmed by acts and omissions of the Jeju Free International City Development Centre and the Korean courts, but the case was withdrawn following a settlement agreement providing for the payment of compensation by the Korean

[58] See ibid paras 33–55; Yonhap News Agency, 'S. Korea Wins Int'l Arbitration against Korean-American in Property Dispute' (30 September 2019) <https://en.yna.co.kr/view/AEN20190930013100325> accessed 25 February 2025.

[59] See *Seo v Korea* (n 57) paras 57–61, 168–69; Damien Charlotin, 'Analysis: Newly-Published Award in Seo v Korea Case Finds that Property Acquired as a Private Residence and Later Rented Out Does Not Qualify as an Investment under the Korea-US FTA' (*IAReporter*, 4 November 2019).

[60] *Gale Investments Company LLC v Republic of Korea*, Notice of Intent (9 June 2019). See Beomsu Kim, Young Suk Park, and Jae Hyuk Chang, 'Korea' (*Global Arbitration Review*, 11 June 2020); Peter Grant, 'Developer Feuds With Korean Partner Over Busted "Smart" City' *Wall Street Journal* (New York, 11 June 2019).

[61] See Business Korea, 'Gale International Files Arbitration Seeking $2 Bil in Damages against Korean Government' (13 June 2019) <www.businesskorea.co.kr/news/articleView.html?idxno=32836> accessed 25 February 2025.

[62] See *Schindler Holding AG v Republic of Korea*, PCA Case No 2019-44 (UNCITRAL) (registered 10 October 2018).

[63] See 'An UNCITRAL Tribunal is in Place in First Known Arbitration Under the EFTA-Korea FTA' (*IAReporter*, 24 March 2020).

[64] See Damien Charlotin, 'Canadian Investor Puts South Korea on Notice of Real Estate Dispute' (*IAReporter*, 4 June 2019).

[65] See Damien Charlotin, 'South Korea Round-Up: Revised Submissions, a Claim Averted, and New Developments in Lone Star's ICSID Case' (*IAReporter*, 24 July 2020).

[66] See *Berjaya Land Berhad v Republic of Korea*, Notice of Intent (10 July 2019) <https://jusmundi.com/en/document/pdf/other/en-berjaya-land-berhad-v-republic-of-korea-notice-of-intent-wednesday-10th-july-2019> accessed 25 February 2025.

government.[67] In August 2020, Mr. Min from China claimed that South Korea had expropriated his investment, and embarked on legal proceedings based on the breach of the fair and equal treatment standard under the 2007 China–Korea BIT and denial of justice claims.[68] When Mr. Min had failed to repay loans,[69] Woori Bank had seized the collateral and sold it. Mr. Min was found guilty of embezzlement and fraud in 2017.[70]

These investment disputes constitute new examples of public-private arbitrations; although they are not contract-based, they largely involve public law issues in Korea with various government agencies as parties to the arbitrations. The increasing trend of ISDS proceedings against Korea arguably indicates that the country is likely to face more investment disputes in the future, possibly touching upon a variety of public law issues. The sudden advent and surge of investment arbitration in Korea for the past decade seems to signal that public-private arbitration will become a more important and controversial issue in the coming years, be it investment arbitration or contract-based arbitration.

It should also be noted that, at least in Korea, the general public does not necessarily seem to distinguish between contract-based arbitration and investment arbitration. There are apparent commonalities. They both involve: (1) disputes between foreign corporations and Korean government agencies; (2) foreign arbitrators instead of the Korean judiciary; and (3) public interest- or public policy-related issues. As such, the conventional concerns over ISDS proceedings may well soon spill over to contract-based arbitration over PPP projects. If so, current debates and discussions on ISDS reform, or at least some of them, may reappear *mutatis mutandis* in the context of contract-based arbitration.

III. The Statutory Framework of Public-Private Arbitration

Following the general overview of the practice of public-private arbitration in Korea in section II, this section examines the statutory framework regarding public-private contract-based arbitration in Korea, which includes, most notably, PPP projects. It first discusses the Arbitration Act of Korea, followed by the Administrative Law and Administrative Procedures Act of Korea.

First of all, in Korea, contracts concluded by state agencies are regulated by the State Contract Act (SCA).[71] Accordingly, government agencies' contracts with foreign entities for PPP projects are also covered by the SCA. In principle, these contracts are considered to have the same legal status as private contracts.[72] When a government

[67] See Hankyoreh, 'Organization in Charge of Jeju Yerae Residential Resort Complex to Pay over US$100 Million to Malaysia's Berjaya Group' (4 July 2020) <http://english.hani.co.kr/arti/english_edition/e_business/952233.html> accessed 25 February 2025; Cosmo Sanderson, 'South Korea Averts Treaty Claim over Island Resort' (*Global Arbitration Review*, 9 July 2020).

[68] See *Fengzhen Min v Republic of Korea*, ICSID Case No ARB/20/26 (registered 3 August 2020).

[69] See Cosmo Sanderson, 'Imprisoned Chinese Businessman Files Claims against South Korea' (*Global Arbitration Review*, 30 July 2020).

[70] See Damien Charlotin, 'Imprisoned Chinese Investor Files Arbitration Against South Korea' (*IAReporter*, 30 July 2020).

[71] See State Contract Act (SCA) (2012) art 2.

[72] See Supreme Court Decision 2001Da33604 (11 December 2001) [Provisional Injunction for the Preservation of Position]; Supreme Court Decision 95Da11436 (26 April 1996).

agency's contractual action is closely related to an applicable statutory law, however, it may be the case that such action is regarded as a governmental measure amenable to court proceedings under administrative law.[73] In these instances, public traits of an agency action are underscored.[74]

A. The Arbitration Act

The Arbitration Act is Korea's stand-alone legislation regulating contract-based arbitration. The Arbitration Act was first approved by the National Assembly on 31 December 1965, and entered into force on 16 March 1966.[75] The provisions of the 1965 Arbitration Act were modelled after the arbitration provisions found in the German Code of Civil Procedure of 1877.[76] Three decades later, in December 1998, a subcommittee under the Korean Ministry of Justice initiated discussions to amend the Arbitration Act, incorporating the UNCITRAL Model Law of 1985.[77] The amended Arbitration Act was approved by the National Assembly on 2 December 1999, and entered into force on 31 December of the same year. At that time, Korea was the first country in East Asia to adopt the UNCITRAL Model Law.[78] Key features of the Act are set forth below.

1 Territorial Application

The Arbitration Act regulates the conducting of contract-based arbitration seated in Korea,[79] regardless of the nature of the dispute or the parties' identities. As such, the Arbitration Act applies to both international and domestic arbitration, as well as both private-private and public-private arbitration.[80] In other words, in principle, the Act equally applies to all contract-based arbitration, even if the party opposing the government agency is a private party from another country. The Act also applies to cases that involve issues of public interest or aspects relating to public law.

2 Arbitrability

The Arbitration Act defines arbitrability in broad terms, adopting a 'negative list' approach. Stated differently, all matters are deemed to be arbitrable except for those that are excluded from arbitration by other statutes of Korea. In this respect, Article 2(2) of the Act provides:

[73] See Supreme Court Decision 2015Da215526 (9 November 2017).
[74] ibid.
[75] See Bae and Lee (n 9) 11; Sean (Sungwoo) Lim, 'Proposed Amendments to the Korean Arbitration Act' (2015) 5 Korean Arb Rev 4.
[76] Lim (n 75).
[77] BC Yoon and Joel Richardson, 'Key Provisions of the 2015 Amendments to the KCAB International Arbitration Rules' (2015) 5 Korean Arb Rev 11, 17.
[78] ibid.
[79] See Arbitration Act, art 2(1).
[80] ibid. See also Kevin Kim, 'Arbitration Guide. IBA Arbitration Committee: South Korea' (2012) 3 <https://www.ibanet.org/document?id=South-Korea-country-guide-arbitration> accessed 25 February 2025; Ho Won Lee, *Issues on Arbitration Law* (Parkyoungsa 2020) 76 (original in Korean); Ho Won Lee, 'Important Issues of 2016 Revision of the Korean Arbitration Act' (2020) 30(1) J Arb Stud 3, 8 (original in Korean).

> Article 2 (Scope of Application)
> (2) This Act shall not affect any other act by virtue of which certain disputes may not be referred to arbitration or may be referred to arbitration only according to provisions of such other act, nor does this Act affect those treaties which come into force for the Republic of Korea.

The provision stipulates that the Arbitration Act does not affect the validity of any other law or treaty in force. Thus, if any other Act or treaty contains a provision relating to arbitration or arbitrability, that Act or treaty shall prevail. This reflects Article 1(5) of the UNCITRAL Model Law on International Commercial Arbitration.[81] In turn, Article 36 of the Arbitration Act further provides that 'recourse against an arbitral award may be raised only by an action for setting aside such arbitral award to a court', and an arbitral award may be set aside by the court only under certain conditions. The provision stipulates that, other than in situations of defect in agreement requiring its nullification (such as coercion or duress) or contravention of the public order, a reviewing court is authorized to set an arbitral award aside when 'the subject-matter of the dispute is not capable of settlement by arbitration under the law of [Korea]'. If arbitrability is determined by provisions of laws other than the Arbitration Act, the relevant provision follows the same rationale as Article 2(2) of the Arbitration Act.

Thus, the scope of contract-based arbitration in Korea is basically determined not by the Arbitration Act but by provisions of other statutes that may determine the arbitrability or non-arbitrability of a particular dispute. As of the time of writing, such other statutes that specifically regulate public-private arbitration in Korea have not been identified or found. This absence implies that the collective operation of Articles 2(2) and 36(2) of the Arbitration Act indicates that public-private arbitration has not been, and is not, excluded from the application of the Act, nor is there a sign that public-private arbitration should be treated differently. This understanding would then lead to the conclusion that public-private contract-based arbitration, just as private-private contract-based arbitration, falls under the jurisdiction of the Arbitration Act. This has been the prevailing view in Korea when it comes to contract-based arbitration generally.

That being said, however, there are other provisions in the Arbitration Act that arguably indicate, or can be interpreted to indicate, that public-private contract-based arbitration involving matters of public law fall outside of its scope of application. In this regard, Article 1 of the Arbitration Act provides with respect to its object and purpose:

> Article 1 (Purpose)
> The purpose of this Act is to ensure the appropriate, impartial and prompt settlement of disputes in private laws by arbitration.

Accordingly, one could argue that the disputes to be settled by arbitration are limited to subject matters of private law, thus excluding disputes involving public law matters.

[81] See Kwang Hyun Suk, *Essays in International Commercial Arbitration Law* (Parkyoungsa 2007) vol 1, 63 (original in Korean); art 1(5) of the UNCITRAL Model Law on International Commercial Arbitration.

A similar reference is also found in Article 3(1) of the Arbitration Act, which also defines arbitration within the meaning of the Act as relating to the settlement of any dispute under private law.[82] Article 3(1) provides:

> Article 3 (Definitions)
> The term 'arbitration' means a procedure to settle any dispute in *private laws*, not by the judgment of a court, but by the decision of an arbitrator, as agreed by the parties (emphasis added).

In interpreting these provisions, the Supreme Court of Korea opined that these are disputes 'which have arisen or which may arise between the parties out of or in connection with private legal relationships'.[83] The Court underscored the 'private legal relationship', in contrast to 'public legal relationship', for the purpose of defining contract-based arbitration within the ambit of the Arbitration Act. Likewise, the prevalent academic view in Korea concerning this provision is that 'private legal relationship' should be interpreted as a property rights-related legal relationship.[84] This jurisprudence arguably stands for the proposition that public-private arbitration should be distinguished from ordinary private-private arbitration.

This new awareness in scholarship has yet to rise to the level of an official reinterpretation of the scope of the Arbitration Act in such a way as to exclude public-private arbitration. Today, the prevailing view is still that public-private arbitration is a 'commercial arbitration' involving property rights of parties even if one of the parties happens to be a government agency. Commentators of the prevailing view in Korea have argued that it is possible to arbitrate public law disputes as well.[85] This view underscores that public law issues are sometimes embedded in, or mixed with, private law issues, and that distinguishing between the two is thus impractical. For example, in cases where the validity of patent rights is disputed, an arbitrator could arbitrate that question as a matter of prior decision, even if it involves a public law issue. In addition, if the parties have agreed to submit their dispute to arbitration, such agreement should be respected, be it a private or a public law issue. Likewise, a situation where an issue of public law is merely raised as an incidental matter should be distinguished from a situation where such issue is the subject matter of the proceeding. In the former situation, it can still be argued that the dispute is deemed to involve private law matters.

3 Applicable Law

When necessary, Korean law is adopted as applicable law in contract-based arbitration. For instance, contracts involving government agencies or state-owned banks often provide for Korean law as the substantive law to be applied in contract-based arbitration, even though the place of arbitration is located outside Korea.[86]

[82] See Suk (n 81); Kim (n 80) 7.
[83] See Supreme Court Decision 2003Da318 (22 August 2003) [Affirmation of Absence of Liability].
[84] See Suk (n 81) 64; Lee, *Issues on Arbitration Law* (n 80) 73–74; Kwang Hyun Suk, *Essays in International Commercial Arbitration Law* (Parkyoungsa 2019) vol 2, 97 (original in Korean).
[85] Donghee Kim, *Administrative Law* (20th edn, Parkyoungsa 2014) 104 (original in Korean).
[86] See Ministry of Justice, Republic of Korea, 'A Guide to International Commercial Arbitration for Companies' (2013) 142 (original in Korean).

Furthermore, in contract-based arbitration, parties are free to agree on the procedure. If the parties fail to reach an agreement, the tribunal may conduct the arbitration in such a manner as it considers appropriate.[87] This party autonomy is also regarded as one of the cornerstones of arbitration in Korea.[88]

However, within the broad ambit of party autonomy, parties should not diverge from the mandatory provisions of the Arbitration Act, such as due process or independence and impartiality of arbitrators.[89] This jurisprudence also stands for the proposition that contract-based arbitration involving public law issues merits a careful treatment since it may be subject to other legal provisions in Korea.

B. Administrative Law

Other than the Arbitration Act, there are also other domestic legal schemes in Korea that regulate public-private arbitration. In the context of public-private arbitration, the discussion of administrative law is crucial as it regulates the relationship between a government agency and private entities affected by government action. Korean administrative law is premised on the recognition of the 'public interest' of acts of government, as opposed to mere transactions between private entities. The dimension of the 'public interest' connected to administrative actions permeates the entire discussion of administrative law and related disputes in Korea, and this logic can be applied to contract-based public-private arbitration as well.

As with any other country, Korea allows an entity or an individual who has been adversely affected by a decision or action (called 'disposition' in Korean administrative law) of an administrative agency to bring a case before the Administrative Court. In principle, only the entity or individual who holds a direct and concrete legal interest from the prospective revocation of the administrative disposition in question may bring the action before the court. In other words, if the interest to be vindicated is either indirect or abstract, such legal action is not permitted.[90] As noted above, the Administrative Court is a special court with jurisdiction over actions of administrative agencies of the Korean government. This court, composed of approximately fifty judges, is located only in Seoul, the capital. In other regions, the respective District Courts will perform the functions of an administrative court until separate (regional) administrative court are established.[91]

In the past, the exhaustion of administrative remedies was a prerequisite for initiating a judicial review proceeding at the court. Since the establishment of the Administrative Court, however, a judicial review proceeding may be initiated without first resorting to administrative remedies unless otherwise provided by law.[92]

[87] See art 20 of the Arbitration Act; Bae and Lee (n 9) 170; Kim (n 80) 1.

[88] See Bae and Lee (n 9) 170.

[89] ibid.

[90] See Supreme Court of Korea, 'The Judiciary – Proceedings: Administrative' (2021) <https://eng.scourt.go.kr/eng/judiciary/proceedings/administrative.jsp> accessed 25 February 2025.

[91] See Supreme Court of Korea, 'The Judiciary – Organization and Composition: Courts' (2021) <https://eng.scourt.go.kr/eng/judiciary/organization/courts.jsp> accessed 25 February 2025.

[92] ibid.

Instances that require the exhaustion of remedies as a prerequisite to filing an action before the court include challenges of tax assessments, or a local police agency's suspension or revocation of a person's driver's license.[93]

At the same time, the Administrative Litigation Act currently in force in Korea requires that, for an agency action to be eligible for judicial review, the administering agency should issue an 'administrative disposition' first.[94] Administrative disposition, in turn, means that the administrative action in question should *dispose* of the rights of private entities in a way that infringes upon the said rights. Thus, judicial review in this context means a judicial proceeding initiated for the purpose of annulling or modifying an underlying administrative disposition because of its alleged illegality or illegitimacy, which has resulted in the breach of the right of an aggrieved private entity.

Administrative judicial proceedings are similar to civil proceedings with respect to the procedure to be followed. A significant difference is, however, that a judge presiding over a proceeding at the Administrative Court may intervene, *ex officio*, in the proceeding more actively than a judge presiding over a civil proceeding may do. In administrative judicial proceedings, the reviewing court may examine evidence *ex officio* and consider the facts not averred by the parties, even though the burden of proof in principle still lies with the party invoking a right.[95] This practice and jurisprudence reflect the public interest dimension embedded in the administrative action. Arguably, similar consideration should equally apply to public-private arbitration.

The focus of the review by the Administrative Court is to determine whether the disputed administrative action is reasonable. If the action is found to be so, it will then be upheld even if the court might have a different opinion. In other words, the reviewing judge would not conduct a *de novo* review of the agency action: the judge merely determines whether the agency action at issue is reasonable given the factual circumstances and within the legal parameters, that is, statutes and regulations. This jurisprudence is the reflection of the principle that the judge hearing a judicial review case of agency determination would defer to the expertise of the agency in charge. Thus, in borderline cases where the judge may have a different opinion from the administrative agency, the judge will probably uphold the agency's determination: unless the plaintiff has evidence to the contrary, the court will favour the defendant government. This deference for agency discretion, however, does not rise to the level of the prohibition of *de novo* review.[96] It is still possible that a judge in a particular case does not agree with and overturns the agency's determination. This is contrasted with the practice of some countries, where a reviewing judge is prohibited from conducting a *de novo* review in a particular case.[97]

[93] ibid.

[94] ibid. See also Yongwoo Lee, 'A Legal-Doctrine Investigation into the Application of ADR to Administrative Cases' (2004) 13(2) J Arb Cases 459, 461 (original in Korean).

[95] See Supreme Court of Korea, 'Proceedings – Administrative' (2021) <https://eng.scourt.go.kr/eng/judiciary/proceedings/administrative.jsp> accessed 25 February 2025.

[96] See Seoul Administrative Court, Case 2008 Guhab 43805 (10 March 2009).

[97] For instance, the United States Court of International Trade is prohibited from conducting a *de novo* review. See *Am Spring Wire Corp v United States*, 8 CIT 20, 22, 590 F Supp 1273, 1276 (1984).

If, on the other hand, an applicable statute sets forth precise requirements with respect to the disputed action, the agency would have to follow such requirements. In such a case, the judge will overturn any administrative action that disregards such statutory requirements. Decisions by the Administrative Court may be appealed to the High Court and then to the Supreme Court. With respect to the format of the judicial proceeding, generally, all hearings and the pronouncements of judgments should be open to the public. Exceptions may apply where there are compelling reasons, for example concerning national security, public order, and public morals. If the court finds the concerns to be legitimate, it may order the hearing to be closed to the public. Nonetheless, the pronouncement of the judgment should still be public.

Special and deferential treatment by the Korean judiciary towards agency discretion would also stand for the proposition that contract-based arbitration involving a government agency should be accorded similar treatment. In devising a new path applicable for public-private arbitration, if need be, this existing practice and jurisprudence would operate as or offer useful guidelines in the process.

C. The Administrative Procedures Act

The Administrative Procedures Act of Korea reflects the public interest concern regarding disputes involving government agencies' disposition of public law-related issues. The purpose of this Act is to ensure fairness, transparency, and credibility in administrative agencies' operations and the protection of the citizens' rights and interests. It is meant to give affected individuals a better access to administrative procedure.[98] This Act mainly sets forth procedures concerning the exercise of public authority and the challenges by private entities of such exercise, or any other corresponding administrative action by administrative agencies in the course of applying laws and regulations to particular instances.[99] The notion of 'administrative agency' in terms of the Act encompasses the following entities: (a) an agency of a central or local government that issues an administrative decision; (b) any other public organization or its related entity; or (c) a private individual with administrative authority vested, delegated, or entrusted by an agency of a government in accordance with relevant Acts or subordinate decrees.[100]

The scope of the application is provided in Article 3 of the Act as follows:

> Article 3 (Scope of Application)
> (1) The procedures for dispositions, reports, administrative pre-announcement of legislation, pre-announcement of dispositions, and administrative guidance . . . shall be governed by this Act . . .
> (2) This Act shall not apply to any of the following matters:

[98] See art 1 of the Administrative Procedures Act.

[99] This type of action is termed as 'disposition' in this Act. See art 2(2) of the Administrative Procedures Act.

[100] See ibid art 2(3).

1. Matters implemented by resolution or with the assent or approval of the National Assembly . . . ;
2. Matters implemented based on judgments of courts . . . ;
3. Matters implemented through decisions by the Constitutional Court;
4. Matters implemented through resolution by . . . Election Commissions;
5. Matters implemented by the Board of Audit and Inspection . . . ;
6. Matters implemented in accordance with the Acts . . . on criminal . . . measures;
7. Matters concerning national security, national defense, diplomacy . . . ;
8. Matters relating to the procedures for requests for review . . . tax trials, patent trials, administrative appeals . . . ;
9. Matters prescribed by Presidential Decree as being impossible or deemed unnecessary to complete administrative procedures.

The provision indicates the wide variety of decisions by administrative agencies that may invite special consideration when they are referred to an adjudicative proceeding due to the public interest dimension of the dispute. Similar considerations may equally apply to contract-based arbitration between government agencies and private entities in Korea.

D. The Status of Public-Private Arbitration in Korea

In sum, the current Arbitration Act does not contain a specific provision regulating arbitrability. Within the current framework it may be argued that public-private arbitration is accorded the same treatment as private-private arbitration, which has been the prevailing view in Korea for a long time. An examination of other provisions of the Arbitration Act, however, arguably indicates that the Act is designed to address primarily 'private law' disputes in Korea. This understanding, triggered by recent concerns over the unique characteristics of public-private arbitration, would then lead to a conclusion that public law disputes are presumably not covered by the Act. An argument can be made that certain public-private arbitrations involving public law matters are not covered by the Act and by extension are not suitable for ordinary contract-based arbitration. If, on the other hand, public-private arbitration involves private law matters such as contractual transactions and related issues, this should still be considered to fall within the area of private law which is undoubtedly suitable for contract-based arbitration under the Arbitration Act.

IV. Contract-Based Public-Private Arbitration as a Risk to Public Law

The analysis of the current legal framework and jurisprudence in Korea in sections II and III above shows that Korea does not yet have a specific statutory scheme for contract-based public-private arbitration. This section discusses the risks such a void poses for public law in Korea. The risks can be categorized into three groups. The first is a risk of structural mismatch. Basically, the private law framework is applied to what are essentially public law issues. Secondly, putting too much emphasis on the public interest may create an imbalance over the interest of the other private party that poses another risk. Finding an appropriate balance would be critical. Thirdly, there is a risk that the fast development in the area of reform of treaty-based ISDS proceedings creates a new gap between treaty-based and contract-based public-private arbitration. Each issue is discussed in turn below.

A. Structural Mismatch: Applying a Private Law Framework to Public Law Issues

In the absence of a specific statutory scheme in Korea regulating contract-based public-private arbitration, a government agency is largely authorized to choose—or at least is not prohibited from choosing—contract-based arbitration as a means to resolve disputes with private entities.[101] In other words, when it comes to choosing a mode of dispute settlement for a dispute resulting from a government agency's discharge of 'public' authority, the agency possesses wide discretion regardless of whether the subject matter at issue involves, in essence, public law or private law.[102] That said, once the agency in question exercises its wide discretion and chooses contract-based arbitration, the current statutory framework and jurisprudence then require the arbitration to be confined to matters of 'private' laws. In short, if the agency somehow decides to resolve an essentially 'public law' issue through arbitration (for which it has discretion), inevitable tensions emerge as arbitration in turn has to be restricted to resolving 'private law' issues. Stated differently, what happens in this instance is a type of a structural mismatch: 'public law' issues are forced into a 'private law' framework. This structural mismatch arguably raises a continuing tension for contract-based public-private arbitration, which becomes visible in the following three aspects.

1 The Application of Private Law to Public Law Relations

In Korea, public law relations are basically regulated by administrative law, under the umbrella of the Constitution. When there is a loophole or a gap in the applicable public law regime, principles of private law can be 'borrowed' and applied *mutatis mutandis*.[103] Certainly, some challenge the appropriateness of importing private law principles into the law governing public law issues,[104] as private law and public law constitute two distinct legal regimes and their mixture would be questionable.[105] But others support such borrowing to fill the inevitable loopholes in public law relations. A compromise is accepted in Korea: the application of private law principles to public

[101] This discretionary latitude mainly stems from Article 20 of the Arbitration Act, which stipulates party autonomy in choosing arbitration as a means to settle disputes between parties. Thus, the government and its agencies preserve in principle full capacity to enter into arbitration agreements and participate in arbitration proceedings as they see fit. See Bae and Lee (n 9) 77 and 170.

[102] See Kyunsung Park, *Lecture on Administrative Law* (12th edn, Parkyoungsa 2015) 59 (original in Korean).

[103] See Kim (n 85) 104.

[104] See Erk Volkmar Heyen (ed), *Otto Mayer. Kleine Schriften zum öffentlichen Recht* (Duncker & Humblot 1981) vol 1, 3–61 (whose argument is cited in the discussion of scholars in Korea).

[105] See Kim (n 85) 104–05.

law relations is at least partially recognized depending on the specific contents and nature of the private law to be applied by analogy.[106]

Granted, there are instances in which private law should apply to the conduct of an administrative body, namely in the event that the state and its private counterpart stand on an equal footing, as in the case of a commercial transaction. For example, when an administrative agency acts in the same capacity as a private individual—for example, in the purchase of goods—in the conclusion of delivery contracts, the sale of property, issuance of cheques, and lending and borrowing of funds, it is private law that should apply.[107] Private law remains inevitably applicable to these kinds of commercial transactions even when the transactions involve government agencies. Accordingly, disputes arising from such transactions should fall under the jurisdiction of civil law and civil procedure.[108] There is special legislation applicable to certain financial transactions of government agencies, such as the Act on Contracts to Which the State Is a Party, the State Property Act, and the Commodity Management Act. Nonetheless, these statutes are considered to regulate private law relations rather than public law relations, even though they take into account the unique status of government agencies. An agency's choice of contract-based public-private arbitration would hardly raise public interest considerations in these instances.

In the areas of public activities of an agency, a more careful approach is warranted. Legal principles that should apply to the activities of government agencies in the realm of public law include the principles of equality, proportionality, continuance of public service, and obligation of assurance of basic rights, etc. These principles of public law should arguably be maintained for the public activities of agencies.[109] In conducting such activities, it may be the case that government agencies should not be permitted to 'escape to private law'.[110] If anything, private law principles may not be amenable to addressing these situations properly. Thus, arguably there are areas in public law that are not to be covered by private law.

As it currently stands, public-private arbitration of PPP projects in Korea does not seem to have a reliable framework in place so as to reflect the public law elements of the dispute adequately and appropriately. According to public law-related Acts, arbitration is widely permitted and sometimes even encouraged for the activities of government agencies, including those involving public law elements, and yet according to arbitration-related Acts, arbitration (regardless of the identity of disputing parties) is reserved to private law matters. As a consequence, there arguably exits an inherent mismatch in the web of statutory schemes in this regard that poses a structural risk.

2 Agency Commercial Contracts Implicating the Public Interest

Another aspect of a structural mismatch concerns government agencies' commercial contracts. As noted above, the contracts of central and local governments with private

[106] ibid 105.

[107] See Park (n 102) 58.

[108] ibid 10. A similar view is found in Supreme Court, Judgment 2012Da15696 (27 December 2012).

[109] See Rainer Pitschas, Haeryong Kim, and Seungpil Choi (tr), 'Mediation im Verwaltungsverfahren- und Verwaltungsprozess' (2009) 33(1) HUFS Law Rev 1, 42 (original in German and translated into Korean).

[110] See Park (n 102) 59.

entities for commercial transactions, negotiated and concluded on an equal footing, would not generally raise public law issues. These contracts, in principle, are regulated by civil law.

There is a caveat, however. It is still possible that commercial contracts of agencies might trigger public law elements. One of the examples concerns the procedures and formalities of how such contracts are negotiated and concluded. In other words, the content (ie substance) of a contract may be commercial but the process of bidding and awarding it may not. For instance, the Act on Contracts to Which the State Is a Party applies to all contracts involving government agencies, be they commercial or non-commercial. The Act stipulates detailed aspects of concluding contracts, supervising performance, and regulating qualifications of participants in tenders.[111] These provisions aim to ensure fairness, transparency, and equality, which are arguably all public law virtues. Accordingly, it is still possible that commercial contracts (even without public law elements) entered into by government agencies in Korea and concluded on an equal footing with private counterparts still raise public law issues because of the procedural aspects of contract negotiation, conclusion, and implementation.[112] As with substantive issues, these contracts also arguably warrant special consideration in contemplating dispute settlement involving activities of government agencies.

The apparent lack (or insufficiency) of the consideration of these procedural aspects of contracts in the course of public-private arbitration raises a further question as to the appropriateness of resorting to this type of dispute settlement in the area of public law matters such as PPP projects, without fine-tuning or adjusting the dispute settlement proceeding for these matters. Arbitration proceedings have evolved from the perspective of two equal parties' commercial contracts for private transactions. PPP projects certainly do not fit this conventional profile, and yet the same procedures still apply here without distinction. Thus, the structural mismatch may run deeper than it seems; it is being observed not only from substantive issues but also procedural ones relating to government contracts for public law matters, most notably PPP projects.

3 Application of ADR in Administrative Law Disputes

Increasing reliance on alternative dispute resolution (ADR) methods in Korea in order to deal with administrative law issues also raises another feature of the structural mismatch. To put it simply, often ADR in this context is pursued in the vacuum of public law consideration; ADR is geared toward resolving outstanding disputes efficiently by finding a compromising ground as opposed to contemplating long-term implications on various stakeholders (who may not necessarily be parties) in the society, which is arguably a public law-aspect consideration.

[111] See Kim (n 85) 227. The relevant provisions of the Act on Contracts to Which the State is a Party are Articles 7 (method of contracting), 13 (Supervision), and 27 (limitation on qualifications of unjust businessmen to participate in tender). Those provisions are for fairness.

[112] See Kim (n 85) 228. For instance, in light of the Constitutional Court and Supreme Court cases, public law provisions apply to sales contracts when these contracts are for public law performance. See Supreme Court, Judgment 98Da60422 (22 August 2000); Constitutional Court, 6-1 KCCR 38, 92Hun-Ka15, etc (24 February 1994) [Repurchase Period Limitation Case].

As a matter of fact, the popularity of ADR in dealing with administrative law issues is not just confined to Korea. In the United States, for example, with the adoption of several pieces of legislation in the 1990s, ADR began to be actively used in administrative proceedings.[113] Korea's approach to ADR in this area is rather unique: officially, utilization of ADR is constrained, but in practice it is widely used.

In principle, administrative decisions and official dispositions of agencies are generally regarded as not suitable for ADR. The prevailing view has been that administrative decisions are not amenable to 'judicial conciliation' or 'judicial mediation', which are the most common forms of ADR in Korea, in light of Article 8(2) of the Administrative Procedure Act.[114] In fact, Article 1 of the Judicial Conciliation of Civil Disputes Act stipulates that conciliation is applied to 'civil' disputes.[115] This provision apparently prohibits the application of ADR to administrative proceedings generally.[116]

However, in practice, de facto conciliation or de facto settlement has been pursued.[117] This means that, for the process of informal settlement of disputes between a government agency in question and a private entity, neither an official statutory framework nor an official third-party facilitator or adjudicator exists. Nonetheless, this de facto procedure has been gaining a foothold: in 2010, more than 15 per cent of the total of 7,703 administrative cases/disputes have reportedly been settled through de facto conciliation.[118] Efficiency and convenience might explain the trend.

Some criticize de facto conciliation or mediation in administrative cases as possibly harming the rule of law in administrative proceedings.[119] It has been argued that in administrative law cases involving public law matters, a decision may well affect, directly or indirectly, the interest of third parties or the general public.[120] The best outcome for the parties may not necessarily guarantee the best outcome for the public at large, which is in many cases the core objective of government regulation. This realization raises a critical question as to the appropriateness and limitations of using ADR in administrative law issues and disputes.[121]

[113] See Heekon Kim, 'Administration Cases and ADR' (2008) 26 Chonbuk NatUniv L Rev 61, 68 (original in Korean).

[114] ibid.

[115] Article 1 of the Judicial Conciliation of Civil Procedure Act provides: 'The purpose of this Act is to settle civil disputes according to a simple procedure based on the mutual concession between the parties, common sense and actual circumstances.'

[116] See Sang-Tae Kim, 'A Study on Admissibility of ADR in Administrative Law' (2009) 35 Korean L Assoc L Rev 46, 61 (original in Korean).

[117] See Kim (n 113) 71–73; Inyoung Cheong, 'A Study on Dispute Resolution by Administrative Agencies from a Public Law Perspective' (Master's thesis, Seoul National University 2018) 38–40.

[118] See Law Times, '"Faster the Better"... Increasing Cases of Medication in Administrative Proceedings' (18 July 2011) <https://www.lawtimes.co.kr/news/58466> accessed 25 February 2025 (original in Korean).

[119] See Youngjoo Ham, 'Systematic Approach to Mass Dispute (Social Conflict) Resolution by ADR: As a New System to Overcome Process Disregarding Trends' (2010) 121 The Justice 676, 695 (original in Korean); Kim (n 116) 58; Yoo-Hwan Kim, 'Administrative Dispute Resolution through Public Participation' (2004) 81 The Justice 40, 68; Kim (n 113) 73–74; Jeong-Soon Kim, 'A Study on Alternative Dispute Resolution in Administrative Law' (Korea Legislation Research Institute Report 2006) 20–21.

[120] See Sang-Tae Kim (n 116) 60–61; Yoo-Hwan Kim (n 119) 69.

[121] See eg Sang-Tae Kim (n 116) 60–61; Supreme Court, Judgment 2012Du22911 (23 July 2015). This case deals not only with related interests of the disputing parties but also with those of the third party. In a

The norm–reality gap being observed in ADR in administrative issues would be equally applicable to contract-based public-private arbitration. In this unique type of arbitration, mere efficiency and convenience should not be a determinative factor. To the extent that the statutory hurdle contained in the Administrative Procedures Act is based on the realization that the exercise of government authority is not generally suitable for ADR, the rationale should be equally applicable to public-private arbitration involving public interest matters, as seen in PPP projects. Contract-based public-private arbitrations at present do not reflect this aspect. They are adopted and applied without careful consideration of what has been similarly raised in the general ADR framework. When viewed from the discussions and jurisprudence on ADR generally, public-private arbitration in Korea suggests a structural mismatch.

A fundamental question in this regard seems to be how one could justify a dispute settlement mechanism through which a private entity and an administrative body settle their dispute autonomously on their own accord.[122] A plausible argument can be made that ADR in administrative law matters should be applied sparingly and cautiously, though not necessarily confined to exceptional cases, even if its benefits are recognized.[123] The same may also be true of public-private arbitration.

Thus, as the statutory framework has not been adjusted to address this unique aspect of public-private arbitrations, and instead treats them like any other contract-based arbitration, Korea is observing a structural mismatch of 'public law' issues in 'private law' clothes.

B. Striking a Balance: Protection of the Private Party

At the same time, a counterweight is also important. Putting too much emphasis on public interest and 'sacrificing' the interest of a private party may also pose a problem. After all, the protection of private interests which deserve such protection may also serve the public interest in the long run. As such, private entities' interests should be duly protected as well. What is needed here is a balancing exercise between the two sets of interests.

Korean arbitration laws and practice are based on the assumption that private entities in public-private arbitrations meet with their government agency counterparts on an equal footing. It may be the case, however, that quite often a government agency, possessing the regulatory authority and discretion, tends to have an upper hand vis-à-vis a private entity.[124] This imbalance may well affect the performance of PPP contracts, and ensuing disputes through public-private arbitration. Thus, a blanket assumption that the parties stand on an equal footing and engage in ordinary commercial dealings to maximize their separate interests may not always be pertinent.

lot of cases involving the Act on Acquisition of and Compensation for Land, etc for Public Works Projects, the third party's interests are concerned.

[122] See Kim (n 116) 73.

[123] See Ham (n 119) 695; Ji-Won Park and Gap-Rae Ha, 'A Study on the Legal Nature of Public Disputes and the Resolutions Thereon' (2011) 9(1) Disp Res Stud Rev 95, 119 (original in Korean).

[124] See Park and Ha (n 123) 120; Lee (n 94) 472.

Private entities are well versed in the benefits and shortcomings of arbitration. According to a KCAB survey, many respondents listed expediency as one of the main reasons for their satisfaction with arbitration.[125] On the other hand, enforcement of arbitral awards and absence of appellate review were referred to as its shortcomings.[126] Arbitration with foreign government agencies may bring another benefit: private entities may value the possibility to avoid sovereign immunity. It should be noted that the logic goes both ways: applying to both foreign government agencies in Korean courts[127] and Korean government agencies in foreign courts. Moreover, sovereign immunity provides a protective layer for a foreign government not only in the merits phase but also in the enforcement phase.[128] On balance, arbitration would be one way to address this uncertainty.[129] This being the case, private entities agreeing to and participating in public-private arbitration are keen to preserve their commercial interests stemming from the projects in question. One might argue that any viable public-private arbitration should reflect the commercial interest of a private party properly.

In fact, contract-based public-private arbitration is a double-edged sword. As for Korea, it may involve a dispute between a Korean government agency and a foreign company regarding a PPP project in Korea. It may also involve a dispute between a foreign government agency and a Korean company for a PPP project in the foreign country. In terms of a systemic point of view, therefore, states may have common interests in striving to preserve the interests of private entities to the extent reasonable and equitable. This notion of balancing has yet to come; conventional arbitration is premised upon private laws and private interest matters, while the awareness of the new dimensions of public-private arbitration focuses on preserving public interests. A solution would have to be found somewhere between the two ends of the spectrum. The non-existence of a balancing scale appears to pose a long-term risk to public-private arbitration.

C. Minding a New Gap: ISDS Reform's Stride for New Experiments

Robust discussions for ISDS reform are currently introducing and exploring new schemes for international investment arbitration. With ISDS reform moving forward at a fast pace, the gap between investment arbitration and contract-based public-private arbitration is growing; the public interest is increasingly addressed in investment arbitration but not in public-private arbitration, so a rift between the two is being created and then widened. As the general public tends to view the

[125] See KCAB (n 12) 38.

[126] ibid 38–43.

[127] See Bae and Lee (n 9) 77.

[128] See Suk (n 81) 325. For example, the Supreme Court decided that only when a foreign country has explicitly consented to compulsory execution is the court empowered to exercise a jurisdiction to issue an order for seizure and collection. See Supreme Court Decision, 2009Da16766 (13 December 2011) [Collection on Debt].

[129] See Taehyun Choi, 'A Study on Jurisdiction by Domestic Courts over the Disputes between Foreign States and Private Entities, with Special Reference to Restriction of State Immunity' (Doctoral thesis, Seoul National University 1991) 58.

two as being similar or sharing close commonalities, the growing gap between the two may stand to pose a critical question for the lagging behind of public-private arbitration.

By way of example, consider transparency requirements. On the one hand, investment arbitration is now expanding its transparency requirements. According to ICSID Rules Article 48(4), the Centre should promptly include in its publications excerpts of the legal reasoning of the tribunal.[130] The UNCITRAL Rules on Transparency in Treaty-based Investor-State Arbitration, which became effective on 1 April 2014, provide for a wide range of obligations including the disclosure of written documents and the opening of hearings to the public.[131] In the case of Korea, its recent IIAs adopt similar transparency requirements.[132]

On the other hand, contract-based private-public arbitrations are still subject to strict confidentiality requirements.[133] As a matter of fact, one of the major benefits and characteristics of contract-based private-public arbitration is said to lie in its strict confidentiality.[134] The requirements of confidentiality apply with full force to public-private contract-based arbitration.[135] Thus, the confidentiality requirements applicable to contract-based public-private arbitration and transparency requirements applicable to investment arbitration seem to collide. This results in a rather interesting situation: even if the same or similar government agencies are involved, they will be subject to two diametrically opposed rules depending on whether a dispute is settled on the basis of contract or under an IIA. Suppose key information and materials are not disclosed to, or easily accessible by, the general public in public-private arbitration, which is often the case because of the confidentiality requirement. Realizing that similar information and materials are disclosed and remain accessible in investment arbitration, one might question the legitimacy or appropriateness of non-disclosure in public-private arbitration.[136]

As new attempts are being made on the ISDS front, the gap between investment treaty arbitration and contract-based public-private arbitration may expand. This poses another risk to public-private arbitration. Mindful of the increasing PPP project disputes involving foreign corporations, it is expected that this will be an issue to be discussed and elaborated in Korea in the near future.

[130] See ICSID Administrative and Financial Regulation, art 22(1).

[131] See United Nations Commission on International Trade Law Rules on Transparency in Treaty-based Investor-State Arbitration and Arbitration Rules (adopted 16 December 2013, entered into force 1 April 2014) art 3(1) ('Publication of Documents') (UNCITRAL Transparency Rules) <https://uncitral.un.org/en/texts/arbitration/contractualtexts/transparency> accessed 25 February 2025.

[132] See Korea–United States FTA (signed 30 June 2007, entered into force 15 March 2012) art 7.6.

[133] See Bae and Lee (n 9) 130; art 52 of the KCAB's International Rules.

[134] See Bae and Lee (n 9) 130–31.

[135] ibid.

[136] See Judith Resnik, 'Diffusing Disputes: The Public in the Private of Arbitration, the Private in Courts, and the Erasure of Rights' (2015) 24 Yale LJ 2804, 2895–97.

V. Concluding Thoughts—Two Faces of Public-Private Arbitration

Given the current trend, private-public arbitrations in Korea, whether contract-based or treaty-based, will continue to increase over time. The increase in treaty-based ISDS has been well-documented and thoroughly followed in Korea. What are drawing new attention are contract-based arbitrations between government agencies and private entities. Contract-based public-private arbitration has been on the rise. When combined with PPP projects, the arbitration arguably shares key commonalities with investment arbitration. As a result, the general public has begun to express concerns over this particular type of dispute settlement. Reminiscent of the concerns raised by treaty-based investment arbitration, many are wary of contract-based public-private arbitrations for their potential impact on the regulatory authority of the government.

At the same time, academic discussion in Korea has started to take note of the unique traits of contract-based public-private arbitration compared with private-private arbitration.[137] From the perspective of Korean administrative law and the Korean principles of arbitration law, the prevailing view is that contract-based arbitration is suitable for private law matters but not necessarily for public law issues. This view is based on the understanding that public law matters are not always amenable to ordinary ADR mechanisms due to the public interests involved. This realization notwithstanding, the statutory framework does not account for this critical distinction, and it treats private-private and public-private arbitration in the same manner. In short, in public-private arbitration, public law issues are forced into a private law framework, creating a structural mismatch. This structural mismatch causes a tension both in terms of legal and political aspects. It stands to pose a critical risk to contract-based public-private arbitration in terms of getting public support and recognition as an efficient vehicle of resolving import disputes.

The new attention that is being paid to public-private arbitration arguably underscores that the current ISDS reform discussion may also affect, and be affected by, contract-based private-public arbitration that is unrelated to investment matters. As far as the preservation of public interests is concerned, the two types of arbitration are regarded by many to be in the same (or a closely related) category. In some respects, such contract-based arbitration would also have to be brought into the overall discussion on ISDS reform.[138] Therefore, it is time to be aware of the 'two faces' that public-private arbitration possesses: on the one hand, it expedites dispute resolution with high efficiency; on the other hand, it may blur the line between party autonomy and matters of public interest.[139] The advent of high-profile PPP projects in Korea signals that the larger impact of public-private arbitration should be carefully calibrated, and that statutory schemes should be adjusted accordingly.

[137] See Rui Cunha Marques, 'Is Arbitration the Right Way to Settle Conflicts in PPP Arrangements?' (2018) 34(1) J Manage Eng 1.

[138] See generally UNCITRAL Secretariat, 'Possible Future Work in the Field of Dispute Settlement: Reforms of Investor-State Dispute Settlement (ISDS)' UN Doc A/CN.9/917 (2017). In many respects, these concerns would arguably apply to commercial arbitration of PPP projects.

[139] See Marques (n 137) 2, 6.

Select Materials

Bibliography

Bae, Kim and Lee, LLC, *Arbitration Law of Korea: Practice and Procedure* (Juris 2012)
Bae, Yooil and Yu-Min Joo, 'Pathways to Meet Critical Success Factors for Local PPPs: The Cases of Urban Transport Infrastructure in Korean Cities' (2016) 53 Cities 35
Kim, Donghee, *Administrative Law* (20th edn, Parkyoungsa 2014) (original in Korean)
Kim, Heejun, 'Study on the Major Issues of ISDS between Lone Star Fund and the Republic of Korea' (2019) 12(2) Contemp Asia Arb J 207
Kim, Jeong-Soon, 'A Study on Alternative Dispute Resolution in Administrative Law' (Korea Legislation Research Institute 2006)
Kim, Kevin, 'Arbitration Guide. IBA Arbitration Committee: South Korea' (2012) <https://www.ibanet.org/document?id=South-Korea-country-guide-arbitration> accessed 25 February 2025
Lee, Ho Won, *Issues on Arbitration Law* (Parkyoungsa 2020) (original in Korean)
Lee, Ho Won, 'Important Issues of 2016 Revision of the Korean Arbitration Act' (2020) 30(1) J Arb Stud 3 (original in Korean)
Lee, Jaemin, 'Two Bites at the Same Apple? "Derivative" ISDS Proceedings in the Revised Korea-US FTA' (2019) 12(1) J E Asia and Int Law 107
Lim, Sean (Sungwoo), 'Proposed Amendments to the Korean Arbitration Act' (2015) 5 Korean Arb Rev 4
Park, Ji-Won and Gap-Rae Ha, 'A Study on the Legal Nature of Public Disputes and the Resolutions Thereon' (2011) 9(1) Disp Res Stud Rev 95 (original in Korean)
Park, Jinyoung and Jinsu Mun, *Korea's Railway PPP (Public–Private Partnership) Projects* (The Korea Transportation Institute 2014)
Park, Kyunsung, *Lecture on Administrative Law* (12th edn, Parkyoungsa 2015) (original in Korean)
Suk, Kwang Hyun, *Essays in International Commercial Arbitration Law* (Parkyoungsa 2007 and 2019) vols 1 and 2 (original in Korean)

Legislation

Act on Contracts to Which the State is a Party
Act on Public-Private Partnerships in Infrastructure
Administrative Procedures Act.
Arbitration Act
State Contract Act

Cases

Constitutional Court, 6-1 KCCR 38, 92Hun-Ka15, etc (24 February 1994)
Supreme Court, Decision 95Da11436 (26 April 1996)
Supreme Court, Judgment 98Da60422 (22 August 2000)

Supreme Court, Decision 2001Da33604 (11 December 2001)
Supreme Court, Decision 2003Da318 (22 August 2003)
Supreme Court, Judgment 2012Da15696 (27 December 2012)
Supreme Court, Judgment 2012Du22911 (23 July 2015)
Supreme Court, Decision 2015Da215526 (9 November 2017)
Mohammad Reza Dayyani and others v The Republic of Korea, PCA Case No 2015-38 (UNCITRAL), Award (6 June 2018)
Jin-Hye Seo and the Government of the Republic of Korea, HKIAC Case No 18117 (UNCITRAL), Final Award (24 September 2019)

18

The Constitutional and Public Interest Foundations of Public-Private Arbitration in Ghana

*Dominic Npoanlari Dagbanja**

I. Introduction

The practice of public-private arbitration at the international plane, especially investor-state dispute settlement (ISDS) by arbitration, reveals systemic and endemic deficiencies in the regime.[1] The United Nations Conference on International Trade and Development (UNCTAD) has summarized the issues as 'a perceived deficit of legitimacy and transparency; contradictions between arbitral awards; difficulties in correcting erroneous arbitral decisions; questions about the independence and impartiality of arbitrators, and concerns relating to the costs and time of arbitral procedures'.[2] Public-private arbitration in the international plane has also become a very powerful tool that multinational business entities use to challenge measures adopted by states in the public interest. More than 70 per cent of the 2013 investor-state claims concerned investments in the services sector, where public interest regulation is important, such as the supply of electricity or gas, telecommunications, construction, tourism, banking, real estate services, water, media, and advertising.[3] This should be of concern to Ghana, the constitution of which accords the state authority and policy space to 'take all necessary action to ensure that the national economy is managed in such a manner as to maximize the rate of economic development and to secure the maximum welfare, freedom and happiness of every person in Ghana and to provide adequate means of livelihood and suitable employment and public assistance to the needy'.[4]

In view of the limitations that public-private arbitration places on states' regulatory autonomy, legal scholarship has focused mainly on the implications of treaty-based arbitration for public interest regulation and the strategies to address these.[5] The

* I am most grateful to Stephan Schill, Violetta Sefkow-Werner and copyeditors for their critical reading and feedback. All errors remain mine. The legislation and case law are current as of January 2025.

[1] United Nations Commission on International Trade and Development (UNCTAD), 'Reform of Investor-State Dispute Settlement: In Search of a Roadmap' (IIA Issue Note No 2, June 2013) 2.

[2] ibid 1; Leon E Trakman, 'Investor State Arbitration or Local Courts: Will Australia Set a New Trend?' (2012) 46(1) JWIT 83, 100–08.

[3] UNCTAD, 'Investor-State Dispute Settlement: A Sequel' (United Nations 2014) <https://unctad.org/en/PublicationsLibrary/diaeia2013d2_en.pdf> accessed 19 January 2025.

[4] Constitution of the Republic of Ghana 1992, art 36(1).

[5] See eg David Schneiderman, *Resisting Economic Globalization: Critical Theory and International Investment Law* (Palgrave Macmillan 2013); David Schneiderman, *Constitutionalizing Economic Globalization: Investment Rules and Democracy's Promise* (CUP 2008).

Dominic Npoanlari Dagbanja, *The Constitutional and Public Interest Foundations of Public-Private Arbitration in Ghana* In: *The Comparative Constitutional Foundations of Private-Public Arbitration*. Edited by: Stephan W. Schill, Oxford University Press. © Stephan W. Schill 2025. DOI: 10.1093/9780191987960.003.0018

scholarship can be grouped, first, into those scholars supporting transnational investment and trade regimes (including international arbitration) because of their abiding belief in the good of these global regimes for national development and the need for free trade and investment therein.[6] Second, there are also scholars who are sceptical about the role of private capital in national development and are therefore critical of the regimes' ability to limit what states need to do in order to advance the very development objective that is used to justify these regimes.[7] There is also a third group of scholars who argue that it is possible to have 'a nuanced system of international private law, sensitive to both the sovereign state's public values and the private rights and interests of foreign investors whose protection is central to the object and purpose of the regime'.[8]

Ghana is a party to twenty-seven investment treaties, nine of which are in force. These investment treaties provide for substantive standards of investment protection as well as for ISDS.[9] Domestic legislation also provides for public-private arbitration. A number of conclusions can be made about public-private arbitration in Ghana. The first point is that the Alternative Dispute Resolution Act 2010 (Act 798) (ADRA),[10] the primary legislation governing arbitration in Ghana, insulates the public interest from both domestic arbitration and international arbitration by providing that certain matters of the public interest, including the interpretation of the Constitution of the Republic of Ghana 1992 (the Constitution) and matters relating to the environment and human rights, are not arbitrable.

The position of ADRA on arbitrability is influenced by the constitutional assignment of exclusive or original jurisdiction to the Supreme Court of Ghana and the High Court when it comes to interpreting the Constitution and enforcing fundamental human rights. This limitation ensures that certain functions inherent in the nature of government cannot be assigned to private arbitrators. While these ideals can easily be achieved in domestic arbitration, this is not the case in international arbitration, where issues involving constitutionality of international business transactions and the original jurisdiction of the Supreme Court of Ghana have been entertained by tribunals. To safeguard the public interest in public-private arbitration, ADRA also provides for a monitoring role of the courts in arbitration proceedings while ensuring that the integrity of the arbitral proceeding is not jeopardized by the involvement of the courts. The involvement of the courts, whether in the course of an arbitration or in the enforcement of a final award, ensures that both the public and private interests are protected and that the role of the state in the protection of both the public and private

[6] Leon E Trakman, 'The Case for Investment Liberalization' in Leon Trakman and Nicola Ranieri (eds), *Regionalism in International Investment Law* (OUP 2013) 499.

[7] M Sornarajah, 'The Case Against a Regime on International Investment Law' in Leon Trakman and Nicola Ranieri (eds), *Regionalism in International Investment Law* (OUP 2013) 475.

[8] Julian Arato, 'Toward a Private Law Theory of International Investment Law' (submitted in partial fulfilment of the requirements for the degree of Doctor of the Science of Law in the School of Law, Columbia University 2016) 1.

[9] UNCTAD, 'Investment Policy Hub: IIAs by Economy' <https://investmentpolicy.unctad.org/international-investment-agreements/by-economy> accessed 19 January 2025.

[10] For a broader analysis of the Alternative Dispute Resolution Act 2010 (Act 798) (ADRA) see Emilia Onyema, 'The New Ghana ADR Act 2010: A Critical Overview' (2012) 28(1) Arb Int'l 101.

individuals, whether foreign or domestic, is not left entirely in the hands of private actors.[11]

The second point is that Ghana's legal system does not make a difference between public-private arbitration and private-private arbitration when it comes to arbitrability of certain issues. Domestic arbitration is conducted in accordance with ADRA and the procedures to which the state and the private parties agree. Therefore, contract-based arbitration involving a domestic private party and the state is conducted in accordance with ADRA and any agreement between the state and the private party. Treaty-based arbitrations between a foreign party and the state are conducted in accordance with the applicable convention and any agreement between the parties and will be enforced in accordance with ADRA and the applicable convention. ADRA accords a lot of respect for party autonomy. Thus, if the subject matter is capable of arbitration it can be resolved in a forum, and in accordance with the terms and procedures, specified by the parties.

The third point is that ADRA is silent on what happens in arbitration involving a private company exercising a public function. In international commercial and investment arbitrations the actions of such a company might be attributable to the state to the extent that it exercises public functions despite being private. However, public companies that are independent of government control will be treated as separate from the state and their actions will not be attributable to the state even if they perform a public function. In such a case, only those companies can be sued directly and not the state.[12] The common law is part of Ghana's legal system under Article 11(1) and (2) of the Constitution. Thus, it might be argued that the state can, under the common law, delegate its functions to a private company, and that if it does so, the same considerations that apply to public-private arbitration will apply to arbitration involving such a company. However, as argued by Professor Kojo Yelpaala, the principle of constitutional law and administrative law is that:

> [T]he State itself is an instrument of its citizenry that is given certain functions and responsibilities which would tend to limit the powers of the State to delegate. The State cannot therefore authorize its agents and instrumentalities to do those things that the State itself is not authorized to do or prohibited from doing.[13]

The principle that the state cannot delegate its responsibilities particularly works in the case of constitutional functions of the state. For example, the constitutional functions of the courts and the executive cannot be assigned to a different institution or person unless the Constitution is amended to allow that to happen. More specifically, it is provided for in Article 130(1)(a) of the Constitution of Ghana that the Supreme Court has original jurisdiction in matters that centre on constitutional interpretation. This is the reason for the removal of an issue such as constitutional interpretation from being a subject matter of arbitration. Thus, the question of a private company

[11] ADRA (n 10) ss 6–7, 26, 39, and 58.

[12] *Gustav FW Hamester GmbH & Co KG v Ghana*, ICSID Case No ARB/07/24, Award (18 June 2010).

[13] Kojo Yelpaala, 'Fundamentalism in Public Health and Safety in Bilateral Investment Treaties [Part II]' (2008) 3(2) AJWH 465, 468.

exercising a public function independently does not seem to be one that will arise in Ghana, given the constitutional and administrative laws of Ghana.

The fourth and final, but not least, point is that arbitration in Ghana is a governance system. ADRA specifically establishes the legal and institutional framework for arbitration. Under the Ghana Investment Promotion Centre Act 2013 (Act 865) (GPICA) and Ghana's investment treaty framework, the promotion and protection of investment is primarily aimed at meeting the development objectives of the state. The substantive protection of investments under this legislation and these investment treaties and accompanying public-private arbitration is aimed at providing a secure and stable environment for business in the hope that foreign business will bring development. The development focus of domestic legislation on investment and investment treaties is consistent with the duties of the Government under the Constitution. A relevant provision of the Constitution is Article 1(1), which requires the Government to exercise the powers of government in the name, and for the welfare, of the people of Ghana.

Arbitration in Ghana is promoted not only in the interest of private business interests but the public interest as well. Therefore, constitutional law plays an important role in the system for private-public arbitration in Ghana because it sets the framework governing the role of the state in protecting the public interest and bringing about development and the role of the private sector therein. Trade, commercial and investment agreements, and arbitration are part of important policy measures that the state adopts to meet its development objectives.

The role of the Constitution in Ghana's arbitration system is also reflected in the fact that the Constitution stipulates the treaty-making powers of the executive in Article 75. The powers of the state to agree to treaties with clauses on arbitration and the constitutionality of such agreements are all governed by the Constitution and the values relating to the public interest, including the protection of the environment and fundamental human rights it preserves. Arbitration in Ghana draws inspiration from both municipal law (for example, the Constitution, ADRA, and the Ghana Investment Promotion Centre Act (GIPCA)) and international law (for example, international investment treaties and international commercial agreements and contracts), based on the idea that trade and investment, or business generally, lead to development. There would, therefore, be a natural expectation that, given the public interest and private interest elements of arbitration in Ghana, arbitrators will contribute to law-making that is sensitive not only to the interests of the private parties to arbitration but also those of the state and the public interest it represents. The role of arbitrators in this manner has not engaged national debate in Ghana and has only attracted limited scholarly analysis.[14]

[14] Dominic Dagbanja, *The Investment Treaty Regime and Public Interest Regulation in Africa* (OUP 2022); Dominic Dagbanja, *The Investment Treaty Regime and Public Interest Regulation in Ghana: Perspectives in Constitutionalism and General International Law* (PhD thesis, University of Auckland 2015); Dominic Dagbanja, 'Constitutionalism and Local Remedies Rule as Limitations on Investor-State Arbitration: Perspectives from Ghana' (2017) 17(1) OUCLJ 1; Richard Oppong Frimpong, 'Recognition and Enforcement of Foreign Judgments in Ghana: A Second Look at a Colonial Inheritance' (2005) 31(4) CLB 19; Richard Oppong Frimpong, *The Government of Ghana and International Arbitration* (Wildy, Simmonds and Hill Publishing 2017).

This chapter argues that the right to regulate in the public interest is constitutionally entrenched in Ghana, as reflected in the state's constitutional duty to exercise its powers to promote the welfare of the people. This chapter also argues that the protection of the public interest through the promotion of development is a primary objective of public-private arbitration in Ghana. The development objective underlies domestic legislation on foreign direct investment and public-private arbitration and is reflected in constitutional provisions for the protection of private business.

Constitutional and statutory provisions carve out certain areas of the public interest, such as constitutional interpretation and environmental and human rights issues, from being the subject matters of public-private arbitration. Constitutional requirements in Ghana apply to both contractual arbitration and investment treaty arbitration. However, recent arbitral cases demonstrate that arbitral tribunals have ignored or vacated decisions made by even the Supreme Court of Ghana on a matter such as the interpretation of the Constitution of Ghana. This trend threatens constitutionalism, judicial independence, and the protection of the public interest using domestic institutions. There is the danger of arbitration undermining constitutional principles and values in Ghana, and indeed arbitration has undermined these principles and values as reflected in the arbitral cases analysed below. Public-private arbitration can be justified within the terms of the Constitution only if constitutional principles and values are respected and upheld in the making of international business and economic transactions. The development objective underlying domestic legislation and international agreements on the protection of private business in which provision is made for public-private arbitration must also inform the interpretation and enforcement of the respective legislation and international agreements.

II. History, Foundations, and Coverage of Public-Private Arbitration Legislation in Ghana

A. The History of Public-Private Arbitration in Ghana

This section reviews briefly the history of arbitration in Ghana post-colonialization and establishes that arbitration has been part of Ghana's legal system since colonial times. The post-independence arbitration legislation protected the autonomy of the arbitral process, but it also limited arbitral power by providing that an arbitrator must not make an award that in effect amounted to a judgment in rem. Arbitral power was limited to making awards that affected property only as between the parties to the dispute.[15] The most recent arbitration legislation specially exempts certain constitutional and public interest matters from being the subject of arbitration.[16] In this sense, arbitration in Ghana has always been designed to operate within the limits of specific constitutional and public interest considerations so that the protection of private interests is not done at the expense of the public interest. This is consistent with the entrenchment of the right to regulate and constitutionalism in Ghana. However, as

[15] Arbitration Act 1961 (Act 38).
[16] Alternative Dispute Resolution Act 2010 (Act 798).

established in subsequent analysis, constitutionalism and public interest are under threat by the unrestrained exercise of arbitral power today.

Arbitration is consensual in nature in the sense of being based on an agreement by the parties to resolve disputes through a third party nominated or selected by the parties rather than having the dispute litigated before a court.[17] In that sense, Professor Cindy Buys is right when she states that arbitration 'is about choice', because the parties choose to arbitrate their disputes and decide who the arbitrators will be, the place of arbitration, and procedures to be applied.[18]

The public-private character of public-private arbitration is reflected in the involvement of a state and its organs as fiduciaries[19] of the people in public-private agreements to arbitrate, and in the actual participation of public actors in arbitration with private businesses and individuals, whether foreign or domestic. The public-private nature of public-private arbitration is also reflected in the use of public money and resources to arbitrate and to pay the costs, fees, and awards,[20] as well as in the implications of arbitration for public interest regulation.[21] Before the emergence of arbitration mechanisms, state–private business disputes were resolved through direct state–private party dialogue, in the municipal courts, or through diplomatic espousal (by which a foreign business entity would convince its home country to exercise diplomatic protection), and sometimes by the threat or use of military force.[22] For example, investor-state arbitration as a form of public-private arbitration became popular in particular with the establishment of the International Centre for Settlement of Investment Disputes

[17] Law Reform Commission, 'Arbitration' (Report No 20, 1991) 90 <http://www.lawcom.govt.nz/sites/default/files/projectAvailableFormats/NZLC%20R20.pdf> accessed 19 January 2025.

[18] Cindy G Buys, 'The Arbitrators' Duty to Respect the Parties' Choice of Law in Commercial Arbitration' (2005) 79 St John's LR 59.

[19] Evan Fox-Decent, *Sovereignty's Promise: The State as Fiduciary* (OUP 2011); Evan Criddle and Evan Fox-Decent, 'A Fiduciary Theory of Jus Cogens' (2009) 34 Yale J Int'l Law 331.

[20] On whether arbitration reduces cost in Ghana see Kofi Poku and Akua Adu-Gyamfi, 'Effectiveness of Alternative Dispute Resolution in International Business Dispute Resolution: A Case Study of Selected Companies in Ghana' (2014) 11(2) IJBP 135.

[21] On the public-private nature of arbitration and implications of arbitration for public interest regulation see Gus Van Harten, 'The Public-Private Distinction in the International Arbitration of Individual Claims Against the State' (2007) 56 ICLQ 371; Gus Van Harten, *Investment Treaty Arbitration and Public Law* (OUP 2007); Gus Van Harten, *Sovereign Choices and Sovereign Constraints: Judicial Restraint in Investment Treaty Arbitration* (OUP 2013); Santiago Montt, *State Liability in Investment Treaty Arbitration: Global Constitutional and Administrative Law in the BIT Generation* (Hart 2009); Jane Kelsey, 'Global Economic Policy-Making: A New Constitutionalism?' (1999–2000) 9 OLR 535; David Schneiderman, *Constitutionalizing Economic Globalization* (n 5); M Sornarajah, *Resistance and Change in the International Law on Foreign Investment* (CUP 2015); M Sornarajah, *The International Law on Foreign Investment* (3rd edn, CUP 2010); M Sornarajah, 'A Law for Need or a Law for Greed? Restoring the Lost Law in the International Law of Foreign Investment' (2006) Int Env'l Agreements 329; Stephan W Schill, 'International Investment Law and Comparative Public Law' in Stephan W Schill (ed), *International Investment Law and Comparative Public Law* (OUP 2010) 3; Stephan W Schill and Benedict Kingsbury, 'Public Law Concepts to Balance Investors' Rights with State Regulatory Actions in the Public Interest – The Concept of Proportionality' in Stephan W Schill (ed), *International Investment Law and Comparative Public Law* (OUP 2010) 75; Stephan W Schill, 'Public or Private Dispute Settlement? The Culture Clash in Investment Treaty Arbitration and its Impact on the Role of the Arbitrator' in Todd Weiler and Freya Baetens (eds), *New Directions in International Economic Law: In Memoriam Thomas Wälde* (Martinus Nijhoff 2011) 23.

[22] Edwin Borchard, *The Diplomatic Protection of Citizens Abroad* (Banks Pub 1919); M Sornarajah, *The Pursuit of Nationalized Property* (Martinus Nijhoff 1986); Jeswald W Salacuse, *The Law of Investment Treaties* (OUP 2010); Christopher Dugan and others, *Investor-State Arbitration* (OUP 2008).

(ICSID) in 1966 and the making of the UNCITRAL Arbitration Rules in 1976.[23] States started to include arbitration clauses in investment treaties in the 1960s. By the 1990s it had become the standard in investment treaties.[24]

The Convention on the Settlement of Investment Disputes between States and Nationals of Other States (ICSID Convention) states that, while investment disputes between states and foreign investors 'would usually be subject to national legal processes, international methods of settlement may be appropriate in certain cases'.[25] The 'creation of an institution designed to facilitate the settlement of disputes between States and foreign investors can be a major step toward promoting an atmosphere of mutual confidence and thus stimulating a larger flow of private international capital into those countries which wish to attract it'.[26] Ghana gave notification of its ratification of the ICSID Convention on 13 July 1966 with the Convention taking effect for Ghana three months later, on 14 October 1966, the very day the Convention came into effect.[27]

According to UNCTAD, arbitration was designed to 'create a forum that would offer investors a fair hearing before an independent, neutral and qualified tribunal. It was seen as a mechanism for rendering final and enforceable decisions through a swift, cheap, and flexible process'.[28] The provision for arbitration under domestic law and in investment treaties and other international contractual and commercial agreements demonstrates the importance states attach to this mechanism as a guarantee that disputes that arise between them and private business parties will be settled in a supposedly neutral forum. Such a guarantee, it is claimed, is necessary to attract foreign trade and investment.[29]

The foregoing ideals about the role of public-private arbitration in investment and international business attraction, and for development, are reflected in the legal and institutional framework for alternative dispute resolution in Ghana. Indeed, in the case of the African continent in general, Professor Samuel Asante rightly argued that 'compelling requirements of international trade, investment and finance have induced many African countries to subscribe to international arbitration through various mechanisms'.[30] Specifically in relation to Ghana, the first post-colonial legislation on arbitration is the Arbitration Act 1961 (Act 38). This Act built on the colonial arbitration legislation it repealed, namely the Arbitration Ordinance 1928

[23] Convention on the Settlement of Investment Disputes between States and Nationals of Other States (adopted 18 March 1965, entered into force 14 October 1966) 575 UNTS 159 (ICSID Convention); United Nations Commission on International Trade Law, UNCITRAL Arbitration Rules, UNGA Res 31/98 (Adopted by the General Assembly on 15 December 1976) UN Doc A/RES/31/98 as revised by UNGA Res 65/22 (6 December 2010) UN Doc A/RES/65/22.

[24] UNCTAD (n 3) 24.

[25] ICSID Convention (n 23) preamble para 3.

[26] International Bank for Reconstruction and Development, 'Report of the Executive Directors on the Convention on the Settlement of Investment Disputes Between States and Nationals of Other States' (18 March 1965) para 9 <http://icsidfiles.worldbank.org/icsid/ICSID/StaticFiles/basicdoc/partB.htm> accessed 19 January 2025.

[27] ICSID, 'Database of ICSID Member States' <https://icsid.worldbank.org/en/Pages/about/Database-of-Member-States.aspx> accessed 19 January 2025.

[28] UNCTAD (n 1) 2.

[29] M Sornarajah, *The International Law on Foreign Investment* (n 21) 48–49.

[30] Samuel Asante, 'The Perspectives of African Countries on International Commercial Arbitration' (1993) 6(2) LJIL 331, 336. Dr Asante rightly points out: 'It is trite that the attainment of political

(Cap 16) and the Arbitration (Foreign Awards) Ordinance 1928 (Cap 17). Act 38 largely reflected the English Arbitration Act of 1950.

Ghana acceded to the United Nations Convention on the Recognition and Enforcement of Foreign Arbitral Awards (New York Convention)[31] on 9 April 1968 and it entered into force for Ghana on 8 July 1968. The New York Convention was set out in the schedule to the 1961 Arbitration Act, manifesting the incorporation of the Convention into domestic law. Section 39 of the Arbitration Act empowered the High Court to refuse to enforce a foreign award if the agreement to arbitrate was not valid under the governing law or under the law of the country where the award was made. Section 39 of the Arbitration Act also allowed the refusal to recognize and enforce an arbitral award if the subject matter of the difference between the parties was not capable of settlement by arbitration or where recognition or enforcement of the award would be contrary to the public policy of Ghana. Section 39 of the Arbitration Act thus gave effect to Article V of the New York Convention. Thus, right from the first post-independence legislation, Ghana subscribed to a system of arbitration (public-private or private-private) that allowed for public policy considerations, including for example the constitutionality of an agreement to arbitrate, to be taken into account in recognizing and enforcing arbitral awards. Indeed, section 5 of the Arbitration Act defined an agreement to arbitrate in terms that accommodated broader public interest considerations and limited the powers of arbitrators accordingly. According to Section 5(1) and (2):

> An arbitration agreement is a contract in writing to refer present or future differences to arbitration, whether an arbitrator is named in the contract or not.
>
> An arbitration agreement may relate to an issue arising between the parties to it which is capable of being the subject of a civil action, but an arbitrator is not entitled to make an award in the nature of a judgment *in rem*, that is, a decision affecting the status of a person or thing or determining an interest in property except as between the parties themselves.

independence in Africa and elsewhere did not mean insulation from the international economic system. Indeed, independence has highlighted the hard fact of international economic interdependence. The internationalization of production and services is a salient feature of the modern world economy, and international transactions, whether they are of a bilateral or multilateral variety, whether they are with foreign governments, international institutions or transnational enterprises, whether they are for trade, investments, technology, finance, debt rescheduling, or for procurement of goods and services, are now essential aspects of the dynamics of international commercial intercourse. More importantly, African countries, like other developing countries, appreciate that these transactions are inescapable for the implementation of their economic and social programmes. African governments and private parties involved in negotiating international business transactions such as loan agreements, petroleum and mining agreements, industrial joint ventures, management agreements, international procurement contracts, international supply contracts, bilateral or international trade agreements and bilateral investment agreements have come to the realization that foreign parties to these transactions, ie, foreign governments, transnational corporations, international banks, foreign investors, international suppliers and contractors, all insist on an appropriate dispute settlement mechanism, which is invariably international arbitration' (ibid 331–32).

[31] United Nations Convention on the Recognition and Enforcement of Foreign Arbitral Awards (adopted 10 June 1958, entered into force 7 June 1959) 330 UNTS 38 (New York Convention).

The 1961 Arbitration Act was repealed by the current legislation, the Alternative Dispute Resolution Act (ADRA), in 2010.[32] ADRA, according to legislative history, was intended to 'harmonise the law governing arbitration with international conventions, rules and practices in arbitration, mediation and customary arbitration'.[33]

B. The Coverage of Public-Private Arbitration Laws in Ghana

The ADRA applies to both domestic and international arbitration. The enforcement of awards arising from arbitration held outside Ghana is also subject to the Act. The Act unambiguously removes certain matters of public interest from being the subject matter of arbitration. Section 1 states that ADRA does not apply to matters related to the national or public interest, the environment, the enforcement and interpretation of the Constitution, and any other matter that by law cannot be settled by an alternative dispute resolution method. This provision is an important safeguard for public interest regulation as well as for reserving matters of constitutional interpretation to the Supreme Court, which, according to Article 130(1)(a) of the Constitution, has original jurisdiction to interpret the Constitution.

The coverage of ADRA is also reflected in its title 'alternative dispute resolution', which is defined in section 135 as 'the collective description of methods of resolving disputes otherwise than through the normal trial process'. Thus, ADRA regulates methods of dispute resolution such as arbitration ('the voluntary submission of a dispute to one or more impartial persons for a final and binding determination'), conciliation ('the submission by the parties of a dispute which is the subject of an arbitration during the cause of the arbitration to an impartial person who is not the arbitrator to facilitate the resolution of the dispute between the parties'), customary arbitration ('the voluntary submission of a dispute, whether or not relating to a written agreement, for a final binding determination'), and mediation ('a nonbinding process ... in which the parties discuss their dispute with an impartial person who assists them to reach a resolution').[34]

The ADRA establishes the Alternative Dispute Resolution Centre (ADRC) under sections 114 and 115 to facilitate the practice of alternative dispute resolution, including through arbitration in Ghana. According to section 5 of ADRA, a party to a dispute based on an arbitration agreement may refer the dispute to any person or institution for arbitration. Alternatively, a party may refer the dispute to the ADRC established under the Act to facilitate arbitration. Where reference is made to a person or an arbitral institution, the procedure and rules shall be as determined by the parties and arbitrators. If a party chooses to refer the dispute to the ADRC then the rules of the Centre will apply to the arbitration. In this sense, the ADRC provides for public

[32] For details see Parliament of Ghana, 'Parliamentary Debates' (9 December 2009) <www.parliament.gh/epanel/docs/pb/9dec2009.pdf#viewer.action=download> accessed 19 January 2025.
[33] ibid.
[34] All as defined in ADRA (n 10) s 135.

institutional arbitration. The parties are at liberty to appoint arbitrators and may use a list of registered arbitrators to do so.[35]

To attain the object of the ADRC to facilitate alternative dispute resolution, the ADRC has statutory duties under section 115 of ADRA, such as:

(a) providing facilities for the settlement of disputes;
(b) exercising any power for alternative dispute resolution conferred on it by the parties (though it shall not be involved in the actual resolution of the dispute);
(c) keeping a register of arbitrators and mediators and providing the list to persons who request for the services of arbitrators and mediators;
(d) providing guidelines on fees;
(e) arranging for the provision of assistance to persons who may need such assistance relating to arbitration;
(f) examining the rules of arbitration and mediation and recommending changes; and
(g) conducting research, educating and issuing specialized publications on all forms of alternative dispute resolution.

The object and functions of the ADRC (a public institution) regarding arbitration support the argument that arbitration in Ghana is conceived as a governance system: not only does the state make the law on arbitration but it is also directly involved in the administration and facilitation of arbitration practice through the ADRC, which is funded with public money.

The legal regime for public-private arbitration extends to the GIPCA and investment treaties to which Ghana is a party. The GIPCA protects foreign investment in terms of substantive legal protection (for example, prohibition of expropriation without due process and compensation), investment incentives, and dispute settlement. GIPCA states in section 33(1) that an 'effort shall be made through mutual discussion to reach an amicable settlement' where a dispute arises between a foreign investor and the government. Section 33(2) of GIPCA provides that a dispute 'which is not amicably settled through mutual discussions within six months may be submitted at the option of the aggrieved party to arbitration'. Under Section 33(3) of GIPCA, where there is no agreement to arbitrate for the settlement of investment disputes in a contract or investment agreement, and the parties disagree on the mode of dispute resolution, the dispute is to be resolved through mediation under ADRA.

Similarly, under Ghana's bilateral investment treaties (BITs), investment disputes are to be settled by ISDS if they are not resolved through mutual discussion within the specified time after the written notification of a claim. The institutions specified include the Arbitration Institute of the Stockholm Chamber of Commerce, ICSID, and ad hoc arbitration under UNCITRAL Arbitration Rules or pursuant to a special agreement between the parties.[36] By providing for ISDS, GIPCA and investment treaties have internationalized the settlement of investment disputes.

[35] ibid s 14.

[36] Agreement between the Government of the United Kingdom of Great Britain and Northern Ireland and the Government of the Republic of Ghana for the Promotion and Protection of Investments (signed 22 March 1989, entered into force 25 October 1991) (Ghana–UK Investment Treaty) art 10; Agreement

There are variations between BITs. The Ghana–China BIT limits an investor-state dispute to '[a]ny dispute . . . concerning the amount of compensation for expropriation',[37] while the Ghana–Malaysia, Ghana–Denmark, Ghana–Netherlands, and Ghana–United Kingdom BITs provide for arbitration in respect of disputes 'concerning an obligation . . . in relation to an investment'.[38] The broad scope of the latter means, for example, that BIT disputes concerning the implementation of human rights norms that affect the value of foreign investment still have to be settled, pursuant to the BIT in question, through arbitration.

The GIPCA and investment treaties thus provide for three ways to resolve investment disputes: first, mutual discussion for an amicable settlement; second, arbitration, if an amicable settlement cannot be reached; and third, mediation, if the parties did not agree to arbitration and subsequently disagreed on the mode of dispute settlement. The specification of these modes indicates that the courts are to have nothing to do with the settlement of investment disputes in substance, unless perhaps the parties mutually agree to submit to the jurisdiction of these courts. In fact, the requirement in section 33(3) of GIPCA that, where there is no agreement to arbitrate, a dispute is to be resolved through mediation under ADRA lends further support to the proposition that the provision for ISDS in GIPCA and Ghana's investment treaties is aimed at ensuring that investment disputes do not have to be settled in the courts.

Party autonomy under ADRA is reflected in the right of the parties to a written agreement to provide that a dispute arising under the agreement be resolved by arbitration.[39] ADRA provides in section 2(2) that a provision to submit a dispute to arbitration 'may be in the form of an arbitration clause in the agreement or in the form of a separate agreement'. Thus, ADRA will be applicable to international commercial arbitration and international investment arbitration to the extent that the commercial agreement or investment contract contains an arbitration clause.

However, where a state is a party to an agreement for the promotion and protection of investments in which the state parties have agreed to investment arbitration, the provisions of the investment treaty on where and how arbitral proceedings are to be conducted may arguably take precedence over the provisions of ADRA, on the theory that the treaty constitutes international law while the Act is municipal law.[40] There is,

on Encouragement and Reciprocal Protection of Investments between the Kingdom of the Netherlands and the Republic of Ghana (signed 31 March 1989, entered into force 1 July 1991) (Ghana–Netherlands Investment Treaty) art 9; Agreement between the Government of the Kingdom of Denmark and the Government of the Republic of Ghana Concerning the Promotion and Protection of Investments (signed 13 January 1992, entered into force 6 January 1995) (Ghana–Denmark Investment Treaty) art 10; Agreement between the Government of the Republic of Ghana and the Government of Malaysia for the Promotion and Protection of Investments (signed on 8 November 1996, entered into force18 April 1997) (Ghana–Malaysia Investment Treaty) art 7; Agreement between the Government of the People's Republic of China and the Government of the Republic of Ghana Concerning the Encouragement and Reciprocal Protection of Investments (signed 12 October 1989, entered into force on 22 November 1991) (Ghana–China Investment Treaty) art 10.

[37] Ghana–China Investment Treaty (n 36) art 10(1).

[38] Ghana–Malaysia Investment Treaty (n 36) art 7(1); Ghana–Denmark Investment Treaty (n 36) art 10(1); Ghana–Netherlands Investment Treaty (n 36) art 9(1); Ghana–UK Investment Treaty (n 36) art 10(1).

[39] ADRA (n 10) s 2(1).

[40] Malcolm Shaw, *International Law* (6th edn, CUP 2008) 129–94.

therefore, the potential for conflict between municipal arbitration law and investment treaty law and arbitration. If, however, the parties agree that the governing law to the arbitration proceedings should be the municipal law of a specified country, knowing very well that they have a right of arbitration under an investment treaty, they should be treated as excluding their investment treaty right to arbitration. By agreeing on the governing municipal law, the parties mean to exclude all other possibly applicable laws, including investment treaties.[41]

The state has an obligation under Article 36(2)(c) of the Constitution to establish a sound and healthy economy; that is, an economy that, among other things, ensures that the private sector has a role to play in the national and social life of the country through, for example, contribution to the development of Ghana. It can be argued that promoting access to public-private arbitration is one way to fulfil this constitutional duty. The challenge is how to ensure that the public interest underlying the state's participation in arbitration is not squeezed out of, or sacrificed in, the actual practice of public-private arbitration.

C. The Private Business Foundation of Public-Private Arbitration in Ghana

The constitutional framework for the involvement of the private sector in national development makes a case for an effective dispute resolution mechanism for private businesses, but this does mean that forum must be only public-private arbitration. Public-private arbitration that respects constitutional boundaries can be justified on the basis of such constitutional framework for the promotion and protection of private business interests in Ghana.

The Constitution recognizes that there are private sector interests and concerns that need recognition and protection in Ghana. This constitutional recognition, presumably, was deliberate on the part of the framers of the Constitution to ensure that public policy concerns accommodate private sector interests. There are provisions in the Constitution that seek to promote and protect private activities and business concerns. Under the Constitution, the principles that must guide the state in taking necessary steps to establish 'a sound and healthy economy' include: (1) affording ample opportunity for individual initiative and creativity in economic activities; (2) fostering an enabling environment for a pronounced role of the private sector in the economy; and (3) ensuring that the private sector bears its fair share of social and national responsibilities, including the responsibility to contribute to the overall development of Ghana.[42] It is significant to state that all actions or policies to promote private sector activities, including the promotion of business, must include steps necessary and geared towards the establishment of a sound and health economy, that is, an economy that promotes the welfare of the people of Ghana.

[41] Dominic Npoanlari Dagbanja, 'The Scope and Legal Effect of Choice of Law in International Arbitration' (2019) IV(1) Cambridge LR 59.

[42] Constitution of Ghana, art 36(2)(b) and (c).

The Constitution thus laid down the parameters within which public and private interests can be promoted and protected in Ghana. In this sense, public-private arbitration could help promote these constitutional goals because, with this form of arbitration, businesses out to do genuine business can be assured that when they have a dispute with the state of Ghana they will have a choice as to the forum for dispute resolution. The crucial issue then, as appropriately stated by Professor Emmanuel Benneh, is:[43]

> In truth, foreign investors will always seek protection under the most effective legal framework – domestic or international. Host-States desirous of attracting foreign investment will always strive to provide the necessary legal protections; they will also expect that their national sovereignty be recognized and be accorded the right to adopt measures in pursuance of public policy. Herein, the problem of how and where the respective limits should be established and a proper balance struck between investor protection, on the one hand, and national sovereign prerogatives, on the other hand.

The constitutional protections regarding the right of the private sector to carry out private business activities, and the corresponding duty of the state to design policies and develop legal frameworks that promote private business, are fulfilled in a sense in the enactment of ADRA, which provides for various forms of alternative dispute resolution, including state-private party dispute settlement by arbitration. However, this right and the corresponding duty have to be exercised or carried out within constitutional limits. The relevant constitutional provision, namely Article 36(2)(b), which imposes a duty on the state to afford ample opportunity for individual initiative and creativity in economic activities, requires that duty to be performed because the Constitution considers the promotion of business as important in the establishment of a sound and healthy economy. An economy cannot be sound and healthy if it promotes private business interests (domestic or international) at the expense of the public interest. The constitutional framework connects the promotion and protection of business to the broader public interest, and this is reflected in the constitutional responsibilities of the private sector to contribute to the overall development of Ghana.

The Constitution states in Article 36(4) that foreign investment 'shall be encouraged within Ghana, subject to any law for the time being in force regulating foreign investment in Ghana'. Those laws include the Constitution and GIPCA, the primary legislation on investment promotion and protection. The Constitution states in Article 1(1) that the sovereignty of Ghana resides in the people and that the powers of government must be exercised in the name of the people and for their welfare and within constitutional limits.[44] GIPCA links the duty to promote and protect investment to the role that investment will play in national development. GIPCA states in

[43] Emmanuel Yaw Benneh, 'International Law, Sovereign Rights and Foreign Direct Investment: Directions from the Jurisprudence of International Arbitral Tribunals' (2000–2002) 21 U Ghana LJ 1, 88–89.

[44] For an analysis of this provision see Dominic N Dagbanja, 'The Conflict of Legal Norms and Interests in International Investment Law: Towards the Constitutional-General International Law Imperatives Theory' (2015) 6(3–4) Trans'l Legal Theory 518, 527, and 543–46.

section 3(a) that the object of the Ghana Investment Promotion Centre 'is to create an enhanced, transparent and responsive environment for investment and the development of the Ghanaian economy through investment'.

Therefore, private businesses have a responsibility to ensure that their activities bring a public benefit. Given the constitutional imperative for the private sector to contribute to the development of Ghana, public-private arbitration can only be justified in constitutional terms if its public benefits, and the need for domestic policy space, are not overshadowed by private business interests in such arbitration. In this respect, public-private arbitration cannot be constitutionally justified on the simple argument that the investor cannot trust domestic courts. If investors take the benefits of state regulatory and administrative support to make profit, they should take the direct and incidental risks inherent in regulatory and administrative actions. And if arbitration cannot be used to protect the interests of the state then the government has no business, given its constitutional mandate to exercise its powers to promote the welfare of the people, making the state a party to public-private arbitration. The government cannot protect investment or commercial business at the expense of the public for whose welfare the state has to promote and protect business in the first place.

D. The Public Interest Foundations of Public-Private Arbitration in Ghana

Public-private arbitration is about resolving disputes between a private party and a state or a government entity. These disputes raise public interest and public policy considerations. Indeed, most private-public disputes also raise public policy considerations because public money and public time are spent defending claims against the states. Public money is used to pay awards. It would be expected, then, that public-private arbitration would accommodate legitimate public interests and public considerations just as it operates to protect private business interests. However, the extent to which public interests can be accommodated and protected in public-private arbitration depends on how the parties' underlying agreement and the arbitration legislation make room for public interests to be protected.

With regard to safeguarding the public interest in arbitration, arbitration under ADRA does not seem to pose unsurmountable challenges to public interest regulation, unlike investment treaty law and arbitration, which poses a challenge to the right to regulate. Section 1 of ADRA provides that the Act 'applies to matters other than those that relate to (a) the national or public interest; (b) the environment; (c) the enforcement and interpretation of the Constitution; or (d) any other matter that by law cannot be settled by an alternative dispute resolution method'. These matters are not capable of settlement by arbitration. Section 116 of ADRA, which deals with the independence of the ADRC, provides that, '[s]ubject to the Constitution and unless otherwise provided in this Act, and any other enactment, the Centre shall not be under the direction or control of any person or authority in the performance of its functions.' This provision ensures that the operation of the ADRC is subject to constitutional constraints. This means, for example, that the ADRC may not entertain settling disputes relating to the interpretation of the Constitution and the enforcement of fundamental human rights and freedoms because the Supreme Court and the High Court have original jurisdiction over these matters according to Articles 33 and 130 of the Constitution.

The concept of the public interest is not defined in ADRA. Professor Barry Mitnick has stated that the public interest 'has been the subject of a voluminous literature in political theory, and there remains no accepted definition of the phrase, much less an accepted operational definition offering indicators that we may use to determine empirically whether something is in the public interest'.[45] Professor Arthur Miller also notes that the concept of public interest has variously been defined by reference to the exercise of governmental powers for the common good, and the need for 'responsible government, for accountability of those who wield governmental power, both with respect to decisions that directly affect the value position of individuals and to decisions that affect society generally'.[46]

The public interest is often used in relation to the political order because, in political life, governments, as agents of the people, act in the name and on behalf of all of the members of the society, and their actions apply to and affect all.[47] The public interest is used to express evaluations of public policies, governmental decisions, and legislative and administrative actions. It requires an assessment of the consequences of policies and governmental actions and decisions for the members of the public.[48]

The public interest is very important for determining justifiable and acceptable governmental policy in the face of conflict and diversity of interests.[49] It consists of e interests which all members of a community have in common[50] or the 'commonality or common characteristic between and among citizens'.[51] These interests include health and welfare, jobs, income, housing, a monetary system, the protection of individual rights, constitutional heritage, and a variety of other civic, social, economic, and religious values.[52]

According to Professor Norton Long, '[t]he bottom line of the appraisal of a policy's being in the public interest is its impact on the important dimensions of the lives of the individuals who make up the relevant public'.[53] This is consistent with the constitutional definition of the public interest in Ghana as 'any right or advantage which enures or is intended to enure to the benefit generally of the whole of the people of Ghana'.[54] In this regard, by section 1 of ADRA, environmental and human rights disputes—or issues that substantially affect them—as well as matters of constitutional

[45] Barry M Mitnick, 'A Typology of Conceptions of the Public Interest' (1976) 8 Adm Soc 5.
[46] Arthur Miller, 'Foreword: The Public Interest Undefined' (1961) 10 JPL 184, 201.
[47] Mitnick (n 45) 5.
[48] ibid 8–9.
[49] ibid 13.
[50] ibid 9.
[51] Stephen M King and others, 'Reflections on Defining the Public Interest' (2010) 41(8) Adm Soc 954, 957.
[52] Richard E Flathman, *The Public Interest: An Essay Concerning the Normative Discourse of Politics* (John Wiley 1966) 99; King and others (n 51).
[53] Norton E Long, 'Conceptual Notes on the Public Interest for Public Administration and Policy Analysts' (1990) 22(2) Adm Soc 170, 179.
[54] Constitution of Ghana, art 295(1).

interpretation, do not fall within the jurisdiction of arbitral tribunals. In *Dey v The Republic*, Justice Forster decided the public interest 'connotes those rights or advantages in things that are public *juris* and therefore considered as vested in the public, the entire State or community and not restricted to the dominion of a particular private person'.[55] Justice Forster conceived of such public interest as consisting of 'a clean environment, the unfettered right to enjoy the beaches and the greenery'. Accordingly, he concluded that various offences including 'dumping of toxic matter' were 'clearly offences committed against the public interest'.[56]

Another safeguard for the public interest in public-private arbitration in Ghana relates to the right to challenge the jurisdiction of an arbitral tribunal. ADRA gives effect to the competence-competence principle in international arbitration, which allows tribunals to determine questions concerning their jurisdiction. Thus, section 24 of the Act says that:

> [un]less otherwise agreed by the parties, the arbitral tribunal may rule on its own jurisdiction particularly in respect of (a) the existence, scope or validity of the arbitration agreement; (b) the existence or validity of the agreement to which the arbitration agreement relates; (c) whether the matters submitted to arbitration are in accordance with the arbitration agreement.

Thus, if an objection is made to the jurisdiction of a tribunal in respect of the matters that cannot be the subject of arbitration, then the arbitral tribunal has jurisdiction to decide whether the subject matter is capable of arbitration. Section 25(1) of ADRA states that a party intending to make a jurisdictional objection 'shall do so before taking the first step in the proceedings to contest the case on its merits'. Further to the tribunal's ruling on jurisdiction, a dissatisfied party can appeal to the High Court. According to section 26 of ADRA, a party dissatisfied with the arbitrator's ruling on jurisdiction may apply to the appointing authority[57] or the High Court for a determination of the arbitrator's jurisdiction. Unless the parties otherwise agreed to a stay of proceedings, an application challenging an arbitral decision on jurisdiction cannot give rise to a stay of the arbitral proceedings.[58]

It is also possible under section 40 of ADRA to raise a jurisdictional objection on a point of law, particularly if the basis of the objection comes up after commencement of arbitration proceedings. According to section 40, unless otherwise agreed by the parties, the High Court may, on an application by a party to an arbitral proceeding, 'determine any question of law that arises in the course of the proceedings if the Court is satisfied that the question substantially affects the rights of the other party'.[59] It is also possible under this provision to raise a point of law relevant for the protection of the public interest. The party making the application must identify the question of

[55] *Dey v The Republic* [1997–1998] 2 GLR 919, 927.
[56] ibid.
[57] ADRA (n 10) s 135 defines an appointing authority as any person or authority in whom parties to an arbitration agreement vest power to take any action for or on behalf of the parties in relation to the arbitration.
[58] ibid s 26(4).
[59] ibid s 40(1).

law to be determined and state the grounds which require that the question should be decided by the Court.[60] Again, like in an objection to jurisdiction, '[u]nless otherwise agreed by the parties, the arbitrator may continue the arbitral proceedings and make an award while the application to the Court . . . is pending.' An appeal to the Court of Appeal, with leave of the High Court, may be made from the decision of the High Court on the question of law. An appeal requires the leave of the High Court and leave shall not be given unless the question 'is one of importance or is one which for some other special reason should be considered by the Court of Appeal.'[61]

Thus, it can be said that ADRA contains a number of safeguards for the protection of the public interest and the private rights of the parties to an agreement. The fact that certain subject matters are not capable of settlement by arbitration safeguards and secures the protection of the relevant public interests. This is strengthened by the right to raise an objection in court to the jurisdiction of a tribunal. However, to safeguard the sacredness of the parties' agreement to arbitrate and the arbitral proceedings founded on it, ADRA provides that arbitral proceedings shall continue while court proceedings are ongoing unless the parties have agreed otherwise. It is significant to note that ADRA subjects the continuance of arbitral proceedings, while the court is exercising jurisdiction over a matter in relation to which arbitral proceedings are pending, to an agreement made by parties, not to the discretion of the court. The court process will help safeguard the rights of the party applying to court, while continuing the arbitral proceedings will safeguard the integrity of arbitral proceedings and the rights of the parties under the arbitration agreement.

The ADRA also shows respect for party autonomy by making any stay of arbitral proceedings subject to an agreement between the parties. In fact, to safeguard the right to arbitration, section 54(2) of ADRA states that '[a] party's right to arbitration is not waived because the party has initiated judicial proceedings in relation to the subject matter of the arbitration.' Clearly, therefore, judicial proceedings on a matter in relation to which arbitral proceedings are pending are not intended to jeopardize the rights of the parties to arbitral proceedings but to safeguard them. In fact, it has been noted that there 'is a balance to be struck between allowing the courts adequate powers to support arbitral proceedings on the one hand, and avoiding excessive court interference on the other', and that 'limited court intervention in arbitral proceedings is widely recognised as a central underlying principle of arbitration law.'[62]

Further legislative safeguards of the public interest and of private rights are reflected in the finality and binding effect of an arbitral award and the right of a party to request the set- aside of an award on specified grounds. Thus, section 52 of ADRA states that, '[s]ubject to the right of a party to set aside an award . . . an arbitration award is final and binding as between the parties and any person claiming through or under them.' An award may be enforced in the same manner as a judgment or order of

[60] ibid s 40(2).
[61] ibid s 40(3).
[62] Kwadwo Sarkodie, 'Arbitration in Ghana – The Alternative Dispute Resolution Act 2010' (*Mayer Brown*, November 2011) 5 < https://www.mayerbrown.com/-/media/files/news/2011/10/arbitration-in-ghana--the-alternative-dispute-reso/files/artsarkodieoct11arbitrationinghanapdf/fileattachment/art_sarkodie_oct11_arbitration-in-ghana.pdf> accessed 19 January 2024.

the High Court, subject to the leave of the Court,[63] and where leave is given, the judgment may be entered in accordance with the terms of an award.[64] However, leave to enforce an award 'shall not be given where . . . the arbitrator lacked substantive jurisdiction to make the award'.[65] These provisions are intended to give effect to an arbitral award subject to relevant limitations on the grant of leave to enforce an award.

The limitation on the grant of leave is an important safeguard for both the parties, whether in respect of public or private rights. ADRA is very clear that certain matters cannot be the subject matter of arbitration. On the one hand, ADRA safeguards arbitral proceedings by saying that, even when an arbitral process is challenged in court, arbitral proceedings shall continue unless the parties otherwise agree. On the other hand, the limitation on granting leave if an arbitral tribunal lacks jurisdiction is intended to ensure that the prohibition against arbitral tribunals entertaining jurisdiction over the specified subject matters which are not capable of settlement by arbitration is not rendered useless by leave to enforce an award. The provision therefore puts the parties on notice to ensure that arbitral tribunals entertain jurisdiction over matters they have jurisdiction over.

ADRA covers the enforcement of foreign arbitral awards and awards made under ADRA itself. In the case of an award subject to ADRA, leave of the High Court is required, and once leave is granted the Court will enforce the award. However, the enforcement of the award may be challenged in court. Under section 58(1) of ADRA, an arbitral award may be set aside and not enforced by the High Court on an application by a party to arbitration. The award may be set aside only where the applicant satisfies the Court on any of the following:[66]

(a) where a party to the arbitration was under some disability or incapacity;
(b) where the law applicable to the arbitration agreement is not valid;
(c) if a party was not given notice of the appointment of the arbitrator or of the proceedings;
(d) if a party was unable to present the applicant's case (presumably if the failure was not due to the applicant's fault);
(e) if the award deals with a dispute not within the scope of the arbitration agreement;
(f) if the award deals with a dispute outside the agreement (but the Court must not set aside any part of the award that falls within the agreement);
(g) if there has been failure to conform to the agreed procedure by the parties;
(h) if the arbitrator has an interest in the subject matter of arbitration which the arbitrator failed to disclose; or
(i) where the subject matter of the dispute is incapable of being settled by arbitration or the arbitral award was induced by fraud or corruption.

Foreign awards[67] are enforceable in the High Court, provided that:[68]

[63] ADRA (n 10) s 57(1).
[64] ibid s 57(2).
[65] ibid s 57(3).
[66] ibid s (58)(2) and (3).
[67] ibid s 59(1)(a). A foreign arbitral award is an award made by a competent authority under the laws of another country.
[68] ibid s 59(1).

(a) the award was made by a competent authority under the laws of the country in which the award was made;
(b) a reciprocal arrangement exists between Ghana and the country in which the award was made (or the award was made under the Convention on the Recognition and Enforcement of Foreign Arbitral Awards (New York Convention)[69] or under any other international convention on arbitration ratified by the Parliament of Ghana);
(c) the party that seeks to enforce the award has produced the original authenticated award and the agreement pursuant to which the award was made; and
(d) no appeal is pending against the award in any court under the law applicable to the arbitration.

These requirements on the setting aside of arbitral awards and the enforceability of foreign awards, including the requirements that an award is not enforceable either if the subject matter of the dispute is incapable of being settled by arbitration or if the award was induced by fraud or corruption, serve to protect both public interests and private rights. The requirements on setting aside arbitral awards are about good governance, and good governance is good for the private sector just as it is for the public.

E. Public Policy, the Constitution, and International Agreements in Ghana

In respect of the enforcement of an award arising from an unconstitutional international business and economic transaction, the Supreme Court of Ghana held in *Amidu v The Attorney General* that:[70]

> there should be less room to award a restitutionary remedy where . . . breach is of a constitutional provision. A contract which breaches article 181(5) of the Constitution is null and void and therefore creates no rights. It should not be legitimate to evade this nullity by the grant of a restitutionary remedy. Although one accepts the cogency of the argument that there is need to avoid unjust enrichment to the State through its receipt of benefits it has not paid for, there is the higher order countervailing argument that the enforcement of the Constitution should not be undermined by allowing the State and its partners an avenue or opportunity for doing indirectly what it is constitutionally prohibited from doing directly. The supremacy of the Constitution in the hierarchy of legal norms in the legal system has to be preserved and jealously guarded.

The position of the Supreme Court on the unenforceability of awards founded on unconstitutional agreements is consistent with the New York Convention and the Vienna Convention on the Law of Treaties (VCLT).[71] Under Article V(2)(b) of the New York

[69] New York Convention (n 31).
[70] *Amidu v The Attorney*-General, Writ No JI/15/2012, Judgment (14 June 2013) 24.
[71] Vienna Convention on the Law of Treaties (adopted 22 May 1969, entered into force 27 January 1980) 1155 UNTS 331 (VCLT).

Convention, the recognition and enforcement of an arbitral award may be refused if the competent authority in the country where recognition and enforcement is sought finds that the subject matter of the legal dispute is not capable of settlement by arbitration under the law of that country, or recognition or enforcement of the award would be contrary to the public policy of that country. The New York Convention also recognizes in Article II(3) that the courts of a state which has agreed to arbitration have the competence to make a finding that an agreement to arbitrate 'is null and void, inoperative or incapable of being performed'. In *The Republic v High Court: Ex Parte; Attorney-General*,[72] the Supreme Court held that 'there is no obligation to enforce a foreign judgment which offends the local public policy of the forum state'.[73]

Where an investment treaty is not ratified by Parliament, the state might challenge the enforcement of an arbitral award made under the investment treaty by arguing that the treaty was entered into contrary to Article 75 of the Constitution, which requires parliamentary ratification of treaties. The private party to a public-private dispute would have a case, arguing under Article 46 of the VCLT, that violation of the Constitution must be manifest. However, the discretion under the New York Convention[74] for a state not to recognize or enforce an award if the subject matter is not capable of arbitration or is contrary to public policy is not predicated on whether the basis of the violation of internal law of fundamental importance or public policy was manifest.

The Supreme Court has held in *The Republic v High Court: Ex Parte; Attorney-General* that 'the independence of Ghanaian courts is subject to the received common law rules on conflict of laws relating to foreign judgments'.[75] These international conventions, in addition to statute, require the recognition of foreign judgments and thus 'allow for the application of the principle of *res judicata* for the purpose of proceedings properly brought in a Ghanaian court in which issues determined in a foreign court arise'.[76] Thus, the private party in a public-private dispute could also argue that the state is estopped from relitigating the lack of constitutionality of arbitration agreements or awards in Ghanaian courts. However, one of the requirements of issue estoppel is that 'the foreign court must be a court of competent jurisdiction; and its decision must have been final and conclusive'.[77] As the constitutionality of agreements is not capable of settlement by arbitration, arbitral tribunals are not competent to make decisions on constitutionality of the main contract and arbitration agreement.

Therefore, arbitral tribunals' decisions on the constitutionality of either the underlying contract or the arbitration clause cannot be final and conclusive. The state is entitled to raise the issue of constitutionality of an arbitration agreement both in an arbitral proceeding and in court. As constitutionality is a public policy issue, the state is entitled to argue against the enforceability of awards founded on a substantive contract or an arbitration agreement that is found to be unconstitutional or contrary to public policy under the Constitution, the VCLT, or New York Convention. Private

[72] *The Republic v High Court: Ex Parte; Attorney-General*, Case No J5/10/2013 (20 June 2013).
[73] ibid 23.
[74] New York Convention (n 31)
[75] *Republic v High Court* (n 72) 15.
[76] ibid.
[77] ibid 18.

parties must not, by public-private contracts or private-private agreements to arbitrate, evade the jurisdiction of the courts over issues that the Constitution says are not arbitrable or can be entertained only in the courts.

III. Constitutionalism and Public-Private Arbitration in Ghana

In this section, this chapter discusses how constitutionalism and the role of the courts to protect that constitutionalism, and the national interest at large, are at the mercy of public private-arbitration based on actual arbitral cases in which arbitral tribunals were engaged in constitutional interpretation. One arbitral case has shown respect and deferred to the judgment of the Supreme Court of Ghana in a dispute that concerned constitutional interpretation. In other cases, however, the decisions of the Supreme Court interpreting the applicable constitutional provisions were ignored by arbitral tribunals, which turned to adopt their own interpretations of the Constitution of Ghana without proving that the Supreme Court was wrong in any way.

The principles of constitutional supremacy and constitutionalism are entrenched in the Constitution of Ghana. Article 1(1) states that the Constitution is 'the supreme law of Ghana and any other law found to be inconsistent with any provision of this Constitution shall, to the extent of the inconsistency, be void'. The preamble shows that the Constitution was enacted by the people of Ghana in the exercise of their 'natural and inalienable right to establish a framework of government which shall secure for [themselves] and posterity the blessings of liberty, equality of opportunity and prosperity'. The people, then, are the source of the legal validity of the Constitution of Ghana, and the Government of Ghana must work to advance the interests of the people and act within the limits laid down in the Constitution. In the celebrated case of *Tuffuor v Attorney-General*, the Supreme Court of Ghana, per Justice Sowah, underscored the supremacy and importance of the Constitution, stating that:

> A written Constitution . . . is not an ordinary Act of Parliament. It embodies the will of a people. It also mirrors their history. Account, therefore, needs to be taken of it as a landmark in a people's search for progress. It contains within it their aspirations and their hopes for a better and fuller life . . . It is the fountainhead for the authority which each of the three arms of government possesses and exercises. It is a source of strength. It is a source of power. The executive, the legislature and the judiciary are created by the Constitution. Their authority is derived from the Constitution. Their sustenance is derived from the Constitution.

The conflict of public-private arbitration with the jurisdiction of domestic courts,[78] and with associated constitutional principles and values, is well illustrated by the

[78] See eg *The Loewen Group, Inc and Raymond L Loewen v United States of America*, ICSID Case No ARB(AF)/98/3, Decision on Hearing of Respondent's Objection to Competence and Jurisdiction (5 January 2001) and Award (26 June 2003); *Chevron Corporation v Republic of Ecuador*, PCA Case No 2009-23 (UNCITRAL), Fourth Interim Award on Interim Measures (7 February 2013); *Ambiente Ufficio SpA v Argentine*, ICSID Case No ARB/08/9, Decision on Jurisdiction and Admissibility (8 February 2013).

following arbitral cases challenging decisions reached by the courts of Ghana. These cases demonstrate how tribunals can disregard the decisions of domestic courts and thereby render them ineffectual. The implication is that issues of constitutional interpretation, which the Constitution has specifically assigned to the Supreme Court, and which ADRA has specified as not arbitrable, have come up in arbitration involving Ghana and private parties.

According to Article 125(1) of the Constitution, justice 'emanates from the people and shall be administered in the name of the Republic by the Judiciary which shall be independent and subject only to this Constitution'. Consequently, Article 125(2) of the Constitution vests the judicial power of Ghana in the judiciary, which by Article 125(5) 'shall have jurisdiction in all matters civil and criminal'. The independence of the judiciary is clearly protected in Article 127(1) of the Constitution, which states that the judiciary 'is subject to only this Constitution and shall not be subject to the control or direction of any person or authority'. Under Article 130(1) of the Constitution, the Supreme Court has 'exclusive original jurisdiction in . . . all matters relating to the enforcement or interpretation' of the Constitution. The Supreme Court, by Article 129(1) of the Constitution, is also the 'final court of appeal'. Persons who are aggrieved by the Court's decision may only seek a review in accordance with Article 133 of the Constitution, which provides that the Supreme Court 'may review any decision made or given by it on such grounds and subject to such conditions as may be prescribed by the rules of court'. Thus, the decision of the Supreme Court can be reviewed only within the terms of the Constitution and by the Court itself. These constitutional principles have not been respected by arbitral tribunals adjudicating disputes between Ghana and private business parties.

A. Second-guessing Domestic Judicial Decisions

The first case to consider is *Balkan Energy Limited (Ghana) v The Republic of Ghana* (*BELG v Ghana*), which was brought under a power purchase agreement (PPA).[79] BELG was a limited liability company incorporated under the laws of Ghana. Its sole shareholder was Balkan Energy Limited (incorporated in the United Kingdom), which was in turn wholly owned by Balkan Energy LLC of the United States. BELG entered into the PPA with Ghana in 2007 for the refurbishment and commissioning of a dual-fired (diesel and gas) barge and associated facilities. The PPA provided for the settlement of disputes by arbitration. BELG alleged that the state had 'failed to provide adequate site electricity' and 'connection to the national grid through a proper transmission line' and 'to comply with its obligation to facilitate the importation of equipment and the acquisition of all necessary permits, approvals, and visas', and owed it tolling fees totalling over USD 50 million.[80]

In December 2009, BELG instituted arbitration proceedings against the state, seeking 'a declaration that Ghana had breached the PPA' and 'an order that Ghana pay

[79] *Balkan Energy Limited (Ghana) v Republic of Ghana*, PCA Case No 2010-7 (UNCITRAL), Interim Award (22 December 2010).

[80] ibid para 4.

the tolling fees' and damages for the breaches.[81] After the appointment of the tribunal to decide on a jurisdictional challenge raised by Ghana, Ghana applied to the High Court of Ghana for an interlocutory injunction against the continuance of arbitral proceedings. The High Court issued an injunction restraining BELG from proceeding with arbitration pending the determination of the enforceability of the arbitration clause and the PPA under Article 181(5) of the Constitution, which requires that an international business or economic transaction be ratified by Parliament to have legal effect.[82] Ghana objected to the jurisdiction of the tribunal, arguing 'that both the PPA and the arbitration clause were void because the PPA did not receive Parliamentary approval as required by [Article 181(5) of] the Constitution'.[83] Ghana argued that the determination of the validity of either the PPA or the arbitration clause involved questions of interpretation of the Constitution, and was therefore non-arbitrable.

In spite of the High Court's injunction, the tribunal proceeded to entertain the suit and held that it was competent to decide on the validity of the arbitration agreement and had jurisdiction to entertain the substantive suit under the competence-competence and separability principles in international arbitration. These principles allow tribunals to determine questions concerning their jurisdiction and the substantive validity of the arbitration clause, respectively.[84] According to the tribunal, the arbitration clause was valid because all the formalities for its validity had been met.[85] The tribunal held that the law applicable to the arbitration agreement was the law of the seat of arbitration, namely that of the Netherlands.[86] It reasoned that the constitutional interpretation issue fell outside the public policy exception in The Netherlands. According to the tribunal, if the constitutional interpretation issue fell within the public policy restriction, any challenge of the constitutionality of arbitration agreements or contracts would oust arbitral tribunals of their jurisdiction.[87] By doing so, the tribunal not only ignored the decision of Ghana's High Court but also assumed jurisdiction over a matter that was exclusively within the jurisdiction of the Ghanaian courts under the Constitution of Ghana.

In the Award on the Merits,[88] the issue was whether the PPA was an international business or economic transaction and therefore needed parliamentary approval in accordance with Article 181(1), (2), and (5) of the Constitution. The Supreme Court, which has original jurisdiction on matters relating to the interpretation of the Constitution of Ghana, held in *The Attorney-General v Balkan Energy Ghana Ltd & Ors*[89] (*AG v BELG*) that the PPA constituted 'an international business transaction within the meaning of Article 181(5) of the Constitution'.[90] The court held that a business or economic transaction was international if it is 'major' with a 'significant' foreign element or the parties to the transaction have a foreign nationality or reside in

[81] ibid para 7.
[82] ibid paras 8, 45.
[83] ibid para 9.
[84] ibid paras 99, 152–53, 167.
[85] ibid para 147.
[86] ibid para 152.
[87] ibid para 144.
[88] ibid Award on the Merits (1 April 2014).
[89] *The Attorney-General v Balkan Energy Ghana Ltd & Ors*, Writ No J6/1/2012, Judgment (16 May 2012).
[90] ibid 41.

different countries or, in the case of companies, the place of their central management and control is outside Ghana.[91]

The court held that the analysis of Article 181(5) of the Constitution should focus on the substance of the transaction, not its form.[92] In relation to the PPA, the court observed that the transaction for the refurbishment of the barge involved a foreign investment by a US company in a power generation project for the supply of energy to Ghana that involved negotiations with the Government of Ghana. Although BELG was incorporated under the laws of Ghana, it was wholly owned by a US company. The directors were foreign, and the control and central management of the company were in foreign hands. The PPA not only provided for arbitration but some of its clauses, such as the waiver of sovereign immunity, were usually contained in foreign investment transactions.[93] The Court had previously stated in *The Attorney-General v Faroe Atlantic Co Ltd*[94] (*AG v FACL*) that international business or economic transactions to which the government is a party require parliamentary approval. Any such transaction that has not been approved 'cannot take effect'.[95] These decisions of the court on what constitutes an international business or economic transaction were made within its jurisdiction under the Constitution and were not against any rule of international law. One would expect that such decisions are respected and upheld domestically and internationally.

The tribunal in *BELG v Ghana*, however, disagreed with the decision and reasoning of the Supreme Court of Ghana. It held that BELG had reasonable expectations that Ghana had accepted the validity of the PPA, and it was, therefore, entitled to rely on it and to expect that the state would fulfil its obligations thereunder.[96] The tribunal said the court's interpretation of Article 181(5) of the Constitution was 'plausible but it is only one possible alternative'.[97] It admitted that the court had made an affirmative finding that the PPA constituted an international business transaction under Article 181(5).[98] It agreed with the reasoning of the court that the PPA embodied the existence of significant foreign components and contained several international components, such as the nature of the business and the related investments made, and the waiver of sovereign immunity.[99] The tribunal admitted that the court:

> rightly considered the provisions of paragraph 5 in the context of Article 181 as a whole, the main concern of which . . . is that an agreement entered into by the Government for the granting of a loan out of public funds or public accounts must be authorized by Parliament.[100]

[91] ibid 34, 37.
[92] ibid 31.
[93] ibid 39–40.
[94] *The Attorney-General v Faroe Atlantic Co Ltd* [2005–2006] SCGLR 271 (SC).
[95] ibid 305.
[96] *BELG v Ghana*, Award on the Merits (n 88) para 397.
[97] ibid para 387.
[98] ibid para 376.
[99] ibid para 380.
[100] ibid para 380.

Yet, when confronted with the question of whether the PPA constituted an international business transaction within the meaning of Article 181(5) of the Constitution, the tribunal determined that it was not. The Court had emphasized substance over form in determining whether a transaction was international and needed parliamentary approval. The tribunal insisted on form over substance, holding that, although the PPA involved foreign components as found by the Court, it was entered into by a company registered in Ghana which had its principal place of business in Ghana. It held further that the production envisaged under the PPA was to supply the domestic electricity market and payments were to be made in Ghana, which suggested that 'performance under the PPA was entirely a domestic business'.[101] Disregarding the criteria specified by the Supreme Court, the tribunal upheld BELG's arguments that it 'was organized as a Ghanaian company in compliance with the applicable legislation . . . and thus the foreign ownership of the company or the foreign nationality of its executives should not necessarily be an obstacle to concluding'[102] that it was not an international business transaction.

The tribunal further reasoned that, since the Attorney-General had advised on the constitutionality of the PPA before it was executed, Ghana could not 'be heard . . . to argue the contrary'.[103] Yet, the Supreme Court had held in *AG v BELG* that the certification of the Attorney-General as to whether a transaction constituted an international business or economic transaction 'cannot be conclusive',[104] since such certification has to be made 'before a dispute has arisen between the Government and any party'.[105]

It can be concluded from this analysis that the tribunal was predisposed to making a decision in favour of BELG without a demonstration that the Supreme Court was legally wrong or had failed to administer justice. The tribunal was, therefore, usurping the constitutional jurisdictional powers of the Supreme Court of Ghana.

Bankswitch Ghana Ltd (Ghana) v The Republic of Ghana[106] concerned the constitutional validity of the Ghana Customs, Excise and Preventive Service Secure Document Management System Agreement entered into between Bankswitch and Ghana in 2012 (the Agreement). Under this Agreement, Bankswitch was to provide the state with intelligent price evaluation software to assist customs officers in price evaluation and to provide an electronic data interchange system which was required for the purpose of securing data interchange among various parties, including customs, importers, and carriers.[107]

One legal issue considered by the tribunal was whether the Agreement was valid and enforceable under the laws of Ghana, specifically whether it was an international business or economic agreement within the meaning of Article 181(5) of the Constitution. Ghana argued that pursuant to Article 181(1) and (2) of the

101 ibid para 388.
102 ibid para 380.
103 ibid para 392.
104 *AG v BELG* (n 89) 37.
105 ibid.
106 *Bankswitch Ghana Ltd (Ghana) v The Republic of Ghana*, PCA Case No 118294 (UNCITRAL), Award Save as to Costs (11 April 2014).
107 ibid para 6.1.

Constitution, the Agreement could not come into operation unless and until it was approved by Parliament. As the resolution was never passed, Ghana argued, the Agreement was void and of no effect.[108]

The tribunal applied the Supreme Court's decision in *AG v FACL* to determine whether the Agreement fell under the ambit of an international business or economic transaction that required the approval of Parliament.[109] The tribunal found that Bankswitch was significantly owned by foreign shareholders and the Agreement provided for the development of a national customs system dealing with imports to Ghana which had numerous international elements. On the basis of these factors, the tribunal concluded that the Agreement was an international business or economic transaction under Article 181(5) of the Constitution as interpreted by the Supreme Court in *AG v BELG*.[110] The tribunal then considered whether Ghana was estopped from relying on this provision in defending its position.

The tribunal observed that Ghanaian law adopts the doctrine of incorporation (dualism) and concluded that the principles of customary international law were part of the laws of Ghana.[111] Therefore, the government's conduct must be measured 'against international standards and . . . principles of customary international law'.[112] Accordingly, the tribunal concluded that Ghana 'cannot rely on its own Constitution to avoid the customary international law rule that a host State must act in good faith and in a manner that is consistent with international law principles when dealing with a foreign investor'.[113]

The tribunal's decision on whether internal law could be invoked to excuse the performance of an obligation under international law was made *per incuriam* because it did not consider the current position of international law on the subject. The two cases[114] the tribunal relied on to come to the conclusion that a state may not rely on its municipal law to evade an obligation in international law were decided in 1932 and 1957, when the Vienna Convention on the Law of Treaties (VCLT)[115] had not come into force. Article 46(1) of the VCLT permits a state to invoke the fact that its consent to be bound by a treaty was 'expressed in violation of a provision of its internal law regarding competence to conclude treaties as invalidating its consent' if the 'violation was manifest and concerned a rule of its internal law of fundamental importance'. In 2002, the International Court of Justice (ICJ) in *Land and Maritime Boundary between Cameroon and Nigeria (Cameroon v Nigeria)* recognized a constitution as an 'internal law of fundamental importance' which a state may be able to invoke to excuse the performance of treaty obligations.[116] In the same way, a state should be able

[108] ibid para 9.11.6.
[109] ibid paras 11.25–11.27.
[110] ibid paras 11.29–11.34.
[111] ibid paras 11.36–11.50, 11.62–11.63.
[112] ibid para 11.57.
[113] ibid para 11.59.
[114] *Treatment of Polish Nationals and Other Persons of Polish Origin or Speech in the Danzig Territory* (Advisory Opinion) PCIJ Series A/B No 44; *Case of Certain Norwegian Loans (France v Norway)* (Separate Opinion of Judge Lauterpacht) [1957] ICJ Rep 9, 34.
[115] VCLT (n 71).
[116] *Land and Maritime Boundary Between Cameroon and Nigeria (Cameroon v Nigeria)* [2002] ICJ Rep 303, paras 265 and 258–66.

to argue that an international business transaction agreement or an international law obligation is unconstitutional if the expression of consent to be bound by the agreement or obligation was done in violation of the constitution of the country.

Although the tribunal agreed with the decision of the Supreme Court of Ghana on the elements of an international business or economic transaction, its ultimate position renders otiose the decision of the Court that estoppel cannot validate or override an unconstitutional contract or agreement and that damages cannot flow from breach of such an unconstitutional contract or unconstitutional agreement.[117] For the tribunal, while 'Ghanaian law may not allow for a party to plead estoppel in relation to a constitutional question, there is no such prohibition in international law'.[118] If Ghana had to comply with the decision of the tribunal, it meant that the Supreme Court's decision that an agreement reached in violation of the Constitution cannot bind Ghana would have no legal effect, as that decision has to give way to the decision of the tribunal.

The issue in *Bankswitch v Ghana* was whether the Agreement constituted an international economic or business transaction within the meaning of Article 181 of the Constitution and was invalid for lack of parliamentary approval. That determination had to be made under municipal law and not the Agreement itself or any other principles of international law. Therefore, it was inaccurate for the tribunal to hold that the arguments Ghana advanced about the invalidity of the agreement under the Constitution were intended to enable Ghana to evade its international obligations under the agreement. The tribunal ultimately resolved the issue of whether the agreement was an international economic or business transaction by relying on the decisions of the Supreme Court which were made based on the Constitution. The issue was not one of conflict between an international obligation and a municipal legal obligation for which the former had to take precedence over the latter. As the Constitution was the only basis for determining the validity of the Agreement, it is not accurate to say that Ghana was invoking internal law to evade a treaty obligation.

B. The Need to Respect and Uphold Domestic Judicial Decisions

The two arbitral cases involving Ghana discussed above highlight the fact that international arbitration can render the decisions of national courts ineffectual, no matter what the subject matter of the legal dispute between the state and a foreign business entity is. If decisions of national courts can be rendered ineffectual by arbitral decisions then a case of conflict between international arbitration and the constitutional function of the national courts arises. Such a conflict can adversely affect the right of citizens and the nation itself to effective justice before municipal courts. Pursuant to Article 35(3) of the Constitution, the 'State shall promote just and reasonable access by all citizens to public facilities and services'. To assure open and transparent administration of justice, Article 126(1) of the Constitution provides that 'the proceedings

[117] *AG v FACL* (n 94) 298–99, 302, 310, and 311.
[118] *Bankswitch v Ghana* (n 106) para 11.75.

of every court shall be held in public' except 'in the interest of public morality, public safety or public order'.

The only case in which an arbitral tribunal deferred to the decision of the Supreme Court on similar issues as in the above two cases is *Waterville Holdings Limited v Republic of Ghana*. In 2006, the Government of Ghana and Waterville Holdings (BVI) Ltd (Waterville) entered into a Contract for the Rehabilitation of the Ohene Djan Sports Stadium and the El Wak Stadium in Accra, Republic of Ghana and a Contract for the Rehabilitation of the Baba Yara Sports Stadium in Kumasi, Republic of Ghana (the stadia contracts). The two contracts were governed by Ghanaian law, as agreed by the parties, and each contained an agreement to arbitrate. Waterville carried out some works. The Government repudiated the contracts sometime after work commenced. These works were independently valued and the Government agreed, under a settlement agreement reached in October 2010, to pay 25 million euros to Waterville. The sums were subsequently paid.[119]

In June 2012, Martin Amidu, a former Attorney-General and Minister for Justice, commenced action in the Supreme Court of Ghana for a declaration that payments made to Waterville pursuant to the stadia contracts and the settlement agreement were unlawful because these contracts and the ensuing settlement agreement were international economic business transactions which had to be approved by Parliament in accordance with Article 181(5) of the Constitution. Since the stadia contracts and the settlement agreement were not approved, they were invalid and could not give rise to the payment of the agreed sum to Waterville.[120]

A year later, in June 2013, the Supreme Court indeed held that the stadia contracts and the settlement agreement were invalid for want of parliamentary approval in accordance with Article 181(5) of the Constitution of Ghana. The court ordered Waterville to repay the amount it received from the Government.[121] In July 2013, the Attorney-General commenced proceedings in the High Court (based on the Supreme Court's decision) to recover the sum of 47,365,624.40 euros paid to Waterville.[122] Waterville sought a stay of judicial proceedings in the High Court to allow for arbitration. In November 2013, the High Court dismissed the application for a stay of proceedings, reasoning that the contracts Waterville sought to rely on to stay the proceedings did not exist because the Supreme Court had found them null and void because of their inconsistency with the Constitution.

The High Court reasoned that, once the 'highest court of the land has pronounced on them and held them to be null and void, it is not open to any other court to determine them valid and accord either party the benefits of any of the said contracts'.[123] The High Court also held the arbitration agreement to be part and parcel of the main contract.[124] Waterville appealed to the Court of Appeal against the decision of the High Court. The Court of Appeal dismissed the appeal. Waterville then commenced

[119] *Waterville Holdings (BVI) Limited v The Republic of Ghana*, ICC Case No 205.61/TO, Partial Award on Jurisdiction (20 March 2017) paras 1–3.
[120] ibid paras 4–5.
[121] ibid paras 4 and 67–69.
[122] ibid para 4.
[123] ibid para 72.
[124] ibid.

International Chamber of Commerce arbitration, seeking, among other reliefs, a declaration that that the stadia contracts and the settlement agreement pursuant to the agreements to arbitrate contained in the stadia contracts were valid.[125]

The Government of Ghana opposed the arbitration proceedings. It argued that the governing law to the stadia contracts was Ghanaian law and that this same law governed the arbitration agreements contained in the two stadia contracts. The arbitration agreements were not autonomous as they drew their lives from the main contracts. Therefore, the arbitration agreements were not severable from the main contracts by virtue of Article 181 of the Constitution.[126] The Government argued that the issue as to the validity of the main contracts was exclusively within the jurisdiction of the Supreme Court, which had already decided on the matter. The tribunal did not have appellate jurisdiction over decisions of the Supreme Court.[127] The Government also argued that Waterville had waived its right to arbitrate by participating in the proceedings before the Supreme Court without objecting to the jurisdiction of the court and without requesting a stay of proceedings to commence arbitration.[128] Waterville argued that the governing law was the closest law (namely the law of the seat of arbitration) and that the arbitration agreements were severable based on the separability principle.[129]

Based on an application of English conflict-of-law rules, the law of the seat of arbitration being in London, the tribunal held that the arbitration agreements were governed by the law of Ghana.[130] Since the parties had not made an express choice of law in the arbitration agreements, it was 'reasonable to assume that the parties intended their entire relationship to be governed by the same system of law. If they had intended otherwise, they could have easily provided so.'[131] The choice of the seat of arbitration did not overcome this presumption.[132] The tribunal came to the conclusion that:[133]

> while the arbitration proceedings are subject to the English Arbitration Act 1996 as the law of the seat (to the extent the provisions are mandatory), the law governing the Arbitration Agreements is the law of Ghana. This means that such matters as the validity and enforceability of the Arbitration Agreements, including whether a particular dispute is arbitrable, will fall to be determined by the relevant provisions of Ghan[a]ian law.

The tribunal also held that the separability principle was part of Ghanaian common law and section 3 of ADRA and section 7 of the English Arbitration Act 1996.[134] The tribunal came to the conclusion that the arbitration agreements were 'valid, binding and separable under the laws of Ghana and are not extinguished by the alleged

125 ibid para 74
126 ibid paras 82–84.
127 ibid para 107.
128 ibid para 85.
129 ibid paras 87–89.
130 ibid paras 92–93.
131 ibid para 96.
132 ibid para 97.
133 ibid para 98.
134 ibid para 100.

invalidity of the Stadia Contracts or the Settlement Agreement'.[135] The tribunal also reasoned that the Supreme Court of Ghana had not made a decision on the constitutionality of an agreement to arbitrate.[136]

The decision of the tribunal to apply the separability principle and to hold the arbitration agreement valid is legally absurd. The tribunal found that the law of Ghana governed the main contracts, the settlement agreement, and the arbitration agreements, and 'determined . . . the validity and enforceability of the Arbitration Agreements'.[137] Therefore, it is not clear why the application of the separability principle was necessary in deciding the validity of the same arbitration agreements. Since the law governing the validity and enforceability of the main agreements and the arbitration agreements had already been determined by the tribunal, it was no longer necessary for the same tribunal to use the separability principle to determine which law determined the validity of the arbitration agreements in each of the main contracts, unless the object of doing so was to avoid invalidating the arbitration agreements based on the governing Ghanaian law. Moreover, the common law and statutory law which govern the separability principle are subject to the Constitution of Ghana as the supreme law of the land.

An agreement to arbitrate contained in the main contract is a term of that contract just like any other term of that contract. Therefore, the Supreme Court's decision that affects the validity of the entire contract affects an agreement to arbitrate contained in that main contract. For example, if an agreement to arbitrate contained in the contract sought to oust the Supreme Court of its jurisdiction over the interpretation and enforcement of the Constitution of Ghana, such an agreement would be inconsistent with Article 130 of the Constitution. It cannot be said that such an agreement is constitutionally valid by virtue of the separability principle. Constitutionally, therefore, any decision of the Supreme Court that affects the validity of the main contract affects or should affect the validity of the agreement to arbitrate embedded in it. The separability principle which would otherwise apply to give legal effect to an arbitration agreement embedded in the main contract is a principle of the common law and therefore subject to the supreme law of the land. If this were not so, arbitration agreements saved under the separability principle could be used to defeat the object of constitutional principles on which the main contract would have been declared invalid, when the merits and legitimacy of those constitutional principles may not be denied in relation to the main contract.

The tribunal also concluded that Waterville's right to commence the arbitration had not been extinguished by the settlement agreement because the settlement agreement did not revoke the agreements to arbitrate. The arbitration dispute arose out of, and in connection with, the stadia contracts and a party could commence more than one dispute settlement procedure under the arbitration agreements.[138] The tribunal also held that Waterville's participation in proceedings before the Supreme Court did

[135] ibid para 105.
[136] ibid para 101.
[137] ibid para 98.
[138] ibid para 103.

not waive its right to arbitrate because the Court's proceedings were not commenced by a party to the arbitration agreements.[139]

On the request of Waterville to the tribunal to declare the stadia contracts and settlement agreement valid, the tribunal held that it did not have jurisdiction to so declare. In the opinion of the tribunal, this was a public interest and interpretive issue that was within the exclusive jurisdiction of the Supreme Court of Ghana pursuant to Articles 2 and 130(1) of the Constitution of Ghana. Therefore, Waterville had an obligation to repay as directed by the court.[140] The tribunal, however, said it had the jurisdiction over the parties' disagreement as to the amount to be repaid.[141] The tribunal reasoned that the Supreme Court of Ghana was 'vested with exclusive jurisdiction to deal with constitutional or "public interest" matters' and '[s]uch matters, therefore, would be beyond the jurisdiction of this Tribunal'.[142] Accordingly, only '[o]ther aspects of the Parties' disputes which do not involve an issue of interpretation of the . . . Constitution would be arbitrable.'[143]

The tribunal's decision on its jurisdiction over the dispute on the quantum to be repaid is erroneous and problematic. As it decided it did not have jurisdiction to determine the validity of the main contracts and settlement agreement out of which the dispute over the quantum to be repaid arose, it is unclear how its jurisdiction over the amount to be repaid could be justified. The amount to be repaid was not independent of the validity of the underlying agreements over which the tribunal rightly decided it did not have jurisdiction. Indeed, the amount paid to Waterville was the foundation and reason for the public interest litigation to recover this amount and any interest that accrued on it. It was the same Supreme Court that the tribunal found had exclusive jurisdiction over the dispute over the validity of the main contracts and the settlement agreement that had decided on the amount to be repaid. The amount to be repaid was a public interest issue, just as the issue as to the constitutionality of the main contract and settlement agreement which gave rise to the determination of the amount to repay was. So how could it be that the amount to be repaid, which the Supreme Court had already determined in any case, was not within the exclusive jurisdiction of the same court? Such an issue fell within the jurisdiction of the Supreme Court and the investor had the constitutional right to seek a review of the decision in the Supreme Court over the amount if there was a genuine dispute.

The tribunal unjustifiably severed the exclusive jurisdiction of the Supreme Court over matters that are inseparable and thereby gave itself jurisdiction where it did not obviously exist in light of its own finding on the exclusive jurisdiction of the court. By assuming jurisdiction, the tribunal usurped the jurisdiction of the Supreme Court and, therefore, could impose on Waterville the obligation to repay an amount that would not have been in the contemplation of the Supreme Court had it exercised jurisdiction itself.

[139] ibid para 104.
[140] ibid paras 110 and 112–15.
[141] ibid para 115.
[142] Ibid para 110
[143] ibid.

Balkan Energy (Ghana) Limited v Ghana, *Bankswitch v Ghana*, and *Waterville Holdings Limited v Republic of Ghana* allow the point to be made that the international arbitration system is predisposed to give foreign investors and businesses absolute remedies and to find remedies for them where they do not or should not exist, even when the public interest objectives and constitutional issues underlying states' actions are at stake. This should not be so. In particular, where a state and a private business entity agree that the underlying agreement governing their business relationship shall be governed by the domestic law of a state, which includes the constitutional framework and judicial decisions made under it, then arbitral decisions must respect and uphold that legal framework voluntarily chosen by the parties.

IV. Conclusion

Public-private arbitration of commercial and other business disputes is promoted on the basis that it provides the neutrality and efficiency that cannot be found in domestic courts. The case for such a system is made uniquely attractive and almost irresistible by the claim that an arbitral system is necessary to attract multinational business entities whose business activities can bring about development, especially to the developing world. These ideals inspired public-private arbitration in Ghana. Public-private arbitration is promoted in Ghana not only to provide private actors dealing with the state with an alternative dispute resolution forum, but, more importantly, to serve as a mechanism that will attract multinational business entities interested in doing business in Ghana. It gives such businesses the assurance that their disputes with the state will be resolved in a forum that is neutral and efficient.

The ADRA, which governs public-private arbitration, establishes the legal and institutional framework for the domestic resolution of disputes by methods other than court trial processes, such as arbitration. It applies to both domestic and international arbitrations. It provides for the recognition and enforcement of foreign arbitral awards. GIPCA, which is the primary legislation on foreign direct investment, provides for the resolution of investment disputes between the state and private parties by arbitration in accordance with international arbitration conventions and before foreign arbitral bodies.

The analysis of the arbitral system in Ghana reveals that there are safeguards to protect the public interest, especially under the Constitution and ADRA. The Act removes certain matters of the public interest from being capable of settlement by arbitration. The Act also allows for arbitral tribunals' exercise of jurisdiction over matters not capable of settlement by arbitration to be challenged in the law courts. Another safeguard for the protection of the public interest is in the provision for the intervention of the High Court on application by a party to arbitral proceedings to challenge a step taken by the arbitral tribunal or even to challenge the enforcement of a final arbitral award. To guarantee the efficiency and efficacy of arbitral proceedings, a court process cannot stay arbitral proceedings unless the parties have agreed such a stay.

The constitutional safeguards analysed in this chapter were intended to ensure that the functions reserved for public institutions in the public interest must not be performed by arbitral tribunals. The original and exclusive jurisdiction of the courts over matters of the public interest under the Constitution also helps to ensure that the courts can intervene in the arbitral process where the public interest so requires, or in fact to ensure that the performance of functions inherent in government such as the protection of fundamental human and labour rights and the environment and other constitutional and political values are not left in the hands of private actors. These safeguards are not only contained in domestic law but also in international conventions such as the New York Convention. Under the New York Convention, a domestic court may refuse the enforcement of an award on grounds of public policy. Under the VCLT, an expression of consent to be bound by a treaty in manifest violation of internal law of fundamental importance is not binding on the state. These international conventions serve to preserve constitutional values and the public interest to achieve a balance in the protection of competing interests.

However, the experience of Ghana with public-private arbitration shows that international arbitral tribunals are often prepared to exercise their jurisdiction irrespective of constitutional and even international law limitations on their powers. Arbitral tribunals' exercise of jurisdiction over issues of constitutional interpretation, and in deliberate disregard of, and lack of deference to, the Supreme Court and the finality of its decisions makes a mockery of judicial independence and the finality of judicial decisions under the Constitution. The enforcement of final arbitral awards can always be refused on grounds of public policy and on matters of constitutional law and within the context of relevant principles of international law. Nevertheless, it should be stated that if final decisions of the courts cannot be respected, upheld, and followed by arbitral tribunals even when the state and the private actor have chosen municipal law as the governing law to their dispute, then the safeguards for the protection of the public interest in the arbitral system in Ghana can be seriously and completely eroded. Thus, it is time to rethink and debate the necessity of arbitration in Ghana.

Select Materials

Bibliography

Benneh, Emmanuel Yaw, 'International Law, Sovereign Rights and Foreign Direct Investment: Directions from the Jurisprudence of International Arbitral Tribunals' (2000–2002) 21 U Ghana LJ 1

Dagbanja, Dominic, 'The Conflict of Legal Norms and Interests in International Investment Law: Towards The Constitutional-General International Law Imperatives Theory' (2015) 6(3–4) Trans'l Legal Theory 518

Dagbanja, Dominic, 'Constitutionalism and Local Remedies Rule as Limitations on Investor-State Arbitration: Perspectives from Ghana' (2017) 17(1) OUCLJ 1

Dagbanja, Dominic N, 'The Investment Treaty Regime and Public Interest Regulation in Ghana: Perspectives in Constitutionalism and General International Law' (PhD thesis, University of Auckland 2015)

Dagbanja, Dominic Npoanlari, 'The Scope and Legal Effect of Choice of Law in International Arbitration' (2019) IV(1) Cambridge LR 59

Frimpong, Richard Oppong, 'Recognition and Enforcement of Foreign Judgments in Ghana: A Second Look at a Colonial Inheritance' (2005) 31(4) CLB 19

Frimpong, Richard Oppong, *The Government of Ghana and International Arbitration* (Wildy, Simmonds and Hill Publishing 2017)

Onyema, Emilia, 'The New Ghana ADR Act 2010: A Critical Overview' (2012) 28(1) Arb Int'l 101

Legislation

Alternative Dispute Resolution Act 2010 (Act 798)
Arbitration Act 1961 (Act 38)
Arbitration Ordinance 1928 (Cap 16)
Arbitration (Foreign Awards) Ordinance 1928 (Cap 17)
Constitution of the Republic of Ghana 1992
English Arbitration Act 1950
Ghana Investment Promotion Centre Act 2013 (Act 865)

Cases

Amidu v The Attorney-General, Writ No JI/15/2012, Judgment (14 June 2013)

Balkan Energy Limited (Ghana) v Ghana, PCA Case No 2010-7 (UNCITRAL), Interim Award (22 December 2010)

Balkan Energy (Ghana) Limited v The Republic of Ghana, UNCITRAL, PCA Case No 2010-7, Award on the Merits (1 April 2014)

Bankswitch Ghana Ltd (Ghana) v The Republic of Ghana, PCA Case No 118294 (UNCITRAL), Award Save as to Costs (11 April 2014)

Dey v The Republic [1997–1998] 2 GLR 919

Gustav FW Hamester GmbH & Co KG v Ghana, ICSID Case No ARB/07/24, Award (18 June 2010)

The Attorney-General v Faroe Atlantic Co Ltd [2005–2006] SCGLR 271

The Attorney-General v Balkan Energy Ghana Ltd & Ors, Writ No J6/1/2012, Supreme Court of Ghana, Judgment of 16 May 2012

The Republic v High Court: Ex Parte; Attorney-General, Case No J5/10/2013 (20 June 2013)

Waterville Holdings (BVI) Limited v The Republic of Ghana, ICC Arbitration Case No 205.61/TO, Partial Award on Jurisdiction (20 March 2017)

19

The Dichotomy of Arbitration with the State in South Africa

*Engela C. Schlemmer**

I. Introduction

In general, and across jurisdictions, whether one talks about private or international arbitration, the privacy of arbitration is considered one of its core qualities, especially in comparison with dispute resolution by courts. Parties are only involved in an arbitration if they agree to it: disputing parties, rather than the state, appoint the arbitrator(s); disputing parties determine the procedure to be followed, and they also determine whether the arbitrator should decide the dispute on the basis of legal principles and, if so, which law should be applied.[1] At the same time, the limited state supervision over arbitrators may raise questions about the legitimacy of the arbitration process, particularly where a state is involved as a disputing party.

South Africa is no different. Notwithstanding the lack of government oversight over arbitrators, until fairly recently the South African state (or public bodies more generally) regularly agreed to investor-state arbitration as a means of resolving disputes in bilateral investment treaties (BITs), and the state (or public bodies more generally) continues to include arbitration clauses in contractual agreements, while certain statutes even provide for mandatory arbitration as a means of dispute resolution.

More recently, the South African government has revisited its policy on arbitration as a dispute settlement mechanism especially where foreign investments are concerned and promulgate d the Protection of Investment Act, which no longer allows investor-state arbitration unless it is still available under an existing BIT. Dispute settlement for the foreign investor is now limited to mediation, and litigation in the domestic courts. After the exhaustion of domestic remedies, if the South African government consents, international arbitration with the home state of the foreign investor may take place.[2] However, the same does not apply to international commercial transactions[3] or domestic transactions involving the state: here, arbitration remains possible as a mechanism for settling private-public disputes.[4] The resulting situation

* Since completing this chapter, the Expropriation Bill was signed into law on 23 January 2025. The Expropriation Act No. 13 of 2024 is not operational yet. See <https://pmg.org.za/files/1/51964_24-1-2025_Expropriation_Act13_2024.pdf> accessed 20 February 2025. Any further developments since 2020 could not be taken into account.

[1] See Ralf Michaels, 'International Arbitration as Private or Public Good', Duke Law School Public Law & Legal Theory Series No 2017-57 (2017) <https://ssrn.com/abstract=3019557> accessed 6 January 2025.

[2] See the Protection of Investment Act 22 of 2015.

[3] See s 5 of the International Commercial Arbitration Act 15 of 2017 and the discussion below in section III.B.4.

[4] Arbitration Act 42 of 1965 dealing with domestic arbitrations, which provides in s 39 that the state is bound by the legislation.

Engela C. Schlemmer, *The Dichotomy of Arbitration with the State in South Africa* In: *The Comparative Constitutional Foundations of Private-Public Arbitration*. Edited by: Stephan W. Schill, Oxford University Press.
 DOI: 10.1093/9780191987960.003.0019

has created a dichotomy between the treatment of contractual and other partners in their relations with the South African government.

What has caused this change when state involvement is not based on an arms-length contractual engagement, but is, rather, based on a treaty provision commonly found in international investment treaties? After all, the state parties to the treaty consciously provided foreign investors with the option of resolving disputes by way of arbitration. How does international commercial arbitration involving the state differ from international investment arbitration involving the state? Are different policy issues at stake? The South African government appears not to have taken a negative policy stance on international commercial arbitration, other than ensuring (in the new International Arbitration Act) that arbitration involving a public body usually takes place in public unless the arbitrators decide otherwise.[5] At the domestic level a number of questions also arise: why would certain statutes require arbitration as the means of resolving some disputes to which the state can be a party but not investment disputes?

The state is bound by both the Arbitration Act and the International Arbitration Act. However, it is compelled not to subject its investment-related disputes to arbitration at both the international and domestic levels, but may submit disputes to arbitration in relation to both domestic[6] and international[7] commercial disputes.

It appears that treaty-based international investment disputes are founded on a different basis: the consensus to use arbitration is based both on the agreement between the state parties and the investor's choice to use this mechanism. The state parties agree to grant standing to foreign investors before an international arbitration tribunal to address claims for a host state's breaches or violations of treaty provisions, if the investor decides to choose this cause of action. The resolution of the dispute is therefore grounded in international law rather than in an arms-length transaction.[8] By agreeing to investor-state arbitration in an investment treaty, a state agrees to have sovereign or regulatory actions evaluated by international arbitration tribunals, thus potentially allowing arbitrators as 'private entities [to] construct law without sovereign authorization'.[9]

Furthermore, the state can also be a party to arbitration proceedings when service level agreements or public-private partnerships contain arbitration clauses. Even in these contracts the parties may not necessarily be contracting at arm's length, since the state (or a public body) acts as a public law organ which may have stronger bargaining power.[10] In these public law contracts the usual private (commercial) law

[5] International Commercial Arbitration Act, s 11.

[6] See n 4 above.

[7] International Commercial Arbitration Act, s 7.

[8] In instances where umbrella clauses are found in treaties, what is dealt with before an international investment tribunal is an international law violation and not a private law matter, since the breach of a contract that exists between the host state and the investor, for example, would amount to a breach of the host state's obligations in terms of the treaty.

[9] See Gus Van Harten, 'The Public-Private Distinction in the International Arbitration of Individual Claims Against the State' (2007) 56(2) ICLQ 371. I say 'potentially' due to the fact that arbitral awards are, as a rule, not published and tribunals are not bound to follow earlier decisions, unlike in a system of precedent. It would thus be hard to 'construct law', as Van Harten puts it.

[10] This is the case when one looks at the South African position.

principles may be supplemented by additional legal principles of administrative law which determine the capacity of the public body to conclude agreements. Also, the activities of the public body are subject to constitutional scrutiny due to the provisions of section 33 of the Constitution of the Republic of South Africa, 1996 that relate to just administrative action, and which may render the public body's actions ultra vires and thereby null and void.

Both these instances of government involvement in arbitrations may potentially have a bearing on aspects of public policy, yet arbitration is allowed in the one instance and not in the other, thus creating a dichotomy. This contribution investigates these issues to determine the extent to which private-public arbitration in South Africa is allowed.[11] Section II focuses on state contractual capacity and its arbitrability in light of administrative law principles, as well as the arbitrability of government's actions or conduct which amounts to administrative action. Section III deals with the arbitration laws in South Africa, the role of the Constitution, and arbitrability in terms of the arbitration legislation; focus is also placed on investor-state disputes and international commercial arbitration involving the state. Both the confidentiality of arbitrations and public policy are considered in section IV, linking them with the accountability of public bodies and the right to information. Section V concludes the chapter.

II. State Contractual Capacity

This section gives an overview of the impact of constitutional values and provisions on the capacity of the government to conclude contracts. It considers the unresolved issue of whether the constitutionality of government conduct may be scrutinized by arbitrators or only by the courts. This would impact on the government's ability to agree to arbitration as a means of dispute settlement. This is particularly important to those parties who enter into contractual relations with the state.

A. The Constitutionalization of State Contracting

The Constitution is central to all actions involving the state,[12] and any law or conduct that is inconsistent with it is invalid.[13] Furthermore, the National Assembly must:[14] (a) create mechanisms which render all executive state organs in the national sphere of government accountable to it (the National Assembly); and (b) oversee (i) the exercise of national executive authority, including the implementation of legislation, and (ii) any organ of state.[15] The implication is thus that all government activities

[11] As will be seen in section III.B.3 below, arbitration is not allowed in terms of the Protection of Investment Act, but in other instances there is no prohibition on the state to be involved in arbitration and sometimes it is even required to arbitrate rather than settle disputes in domestic courts.

[12] See s 55(2) of the Constitution.

[13] See s 2 of the Constitution.

[14] The South African Parliament consists of a National Assembly and a National Council of Provinces: see s 42 of the Constitution.

[15] See s 55(2) of the Constitution.

should be subject to scrutiny by the National Assembly in terms of the Constitution. However, public officials cannot be held responsible if a contractual dispute is not in the public domain, which may be the case if such disputes are resolved through arbitrations.

In *Goodman Brothers (Pty) Ltd v Transnet Ltd*,[16] Judge Blieden held that a government organ or public body cannot be treated as a normal contracting party because, in addition to all the 'normal' legal principles and requirements, state conduct must be 'fair, equitable, transparent, competitive and cost-effective',[17] due to the provisions of section 217[18] of the Constitution:

> the Constitution has had a profound effect on the relationship which every organ of State, such as the respondent, has in its dealings with other persons or bodies and in the manner in which it conducts its business activities. Section 217 read together with ss 32(1) and 33 [dealing with administrative acts] makes it plain that in addition to his common-law rights, any person dealing with a State organ such as the respondent, is entitled to expect fairness, openness and equitable conduct from it in all its actions.[19]

One could thus say that government contracting in South Africa has been 'constitutionalized'.[20] This implies that, in addition to contractual rights and remedies, the private contracting party potentially also has administrative law remedies on the basis of the state's conduct, both prior to and after concluding the contract.

The constitutionalization of the government's contracting capacity affects the procedures to be followed prior to the conclusion of the contract, particularly relating to government procurement, which must be fair, equitable, transparent, competitive, and cost-effective.[21] Framework legislation[22] regulates public procurement at all levels of government.[23] Legislation exists that govern the provision of services by

[16] 1998 (4) SA 989 (W).

[17] ibid 996E-F. S 217 of the Constitution of South Africa, 1996 broadly deals with public procurement. For a detailed discussion, see Glenn Penfold and Pippa Reyburn, 'Public Procurement' in *Constitutional Law of South Africa* (looseleaf, 2nd edn, 2014) (Original Service March 2012) ch 25-8; Phoebe Bolton, *The Law of Government Procurement in South Africa* (LexisNexis 2007).

[18] s 217 of the Constitution provides that, 'when an organ of state in the national, provincial or local sphere of government, or any other institution identified in national legislation, contracts for goods or services, it must do so in accordance with a system which is *fair, equitable, transparent, competitive and cost-effective*' (emphasis added).

[19] *Goodman Brothers (Pty) Ltd v Transnet Ltd* (n 16) 997A-B.

[20] See Phoebe Bolton, 'An Analysis of the Criteria Used to Evaluate and Award Public Tenders' [2014] SJ 1, 2; JC Sonnekus, 'Procurement Contracts and Underlying Principles of the Law – No Special Dispensation for Organs of State (Part 1 – the Principles)' [2014] Tydskrif vir die Suid-Afrikaanse Reg/J South Afr L 320, 328 ff.

[21] See the Preferential Procurement Policy Framework Act 5 of 2000, promulgated to give effect to the requirement of a preferential procurement policy in s 217(2) of the Constitution.

[22] See the Public Finance Management Act 1 of 1999, prescribing the general system for procurement that must be followed by national and provincial governments and certain prescribed public entities; and the Local Government: Municipal Finance Management Act 56 of 2003, which regulates procurement on the local government level.

[23] See generally on the South African public procurement system, Phoebe Bolton, 'The Regulatory Framework for Public Procurement in South Africa' in Geo Quinot and Sure Arrowsmith (eds), *Public Procurement Regulation in Africa* (LexisNexis 2013) 178; Bolton (n 17); Stephanus Petrus Le Roux De

public-private partnerships, and the conclusion of such service delivery agreements, that occur on national, provincial, and local government level.[24]

The coming into operation of the Constitution removed what was considered a 'clear divide' between private law (ie the law governing the relations between the state and its contractual counterparties when participating in normal commercial activities) and public law (ie those aspects governed by principles of administrative law) which existed prior to its coming into operation.[25] Sonnekus explains it as follows:

> The power or capacity of an organ of state to enter into a contract is governed not merely by the norms of contract law but also by the constitutional and other statutory qualifications of the power. The state's capacity or ability to contract is without doubt not exclusively founded on its common law 'powers' or 'prerogatives'.[26]

Thus, any aspect of public administration which does not comply with the constitutional or statutory requirements will be subject to judicial review.[27] The constitutional principle of legality guarantees a minimum level of justification in the realm of non-administrative action. In those instances where the acts of a government department do not fall under what is defined as an administrative action,[28] the action must nevertheless comply with the legality principle. One author argues that, in considering the commercial actions of the government:

> Two types of challenges to state commercial activity should be distinguished... Firstly, there are challenges on strict legality grounds, which may indicate that the particular public authority acted beyond its power or grossly abused its power in taking the commercial decision under scrutiny. In this type of case invalidity should in principle be a competent remedy, because here the function of judicial review as a constitutional control over the exercise of state power outweighs efficiency and certainty concerns. A party should thus be able to pursue judicial review to invalidate state commercial decisions in such cases. Secondly, there are challenges that may indicate that while the authority was objectively authorised to take the decision at issue it adopted an irregular process. In this second type of case, however, review should in principle not be able to result in invalidity. It is submitted that in these cases efficiency and certainty generally favour the continued factual validity of the

la Harpe, 'Public Procurement Law: A Comparative Analysis' (LLD thesis, University of South Africa 2009) ch 5.

[24] This framework legislation does not prescribe the content of contracts concluded by the government with private companies or individuals. There exist, however, standardized provisions for public-private partnerships that give an indication as to what the government would prefer to be contained in a public-private partnership agreement. These provisions are not prescriptive and it seems that the principle of party autonomy still applies.

[25] See Geo Quinot, 'Towards Effective Judicial Review of State Commercial Activity' [2009] Tydskrif vir die Suid-Afrikaanse Reg/J South Afr L 436; Bolton (n 17) 74 (stating that 'its power to conclude contracts is limited'). See also ibid 75–98.

[26] Sonnekus (n 20) 331 and the sources cited therein. See also Cora Hoexter, *Administrative Law in South Africa* (Juta 2012) 36.

[27] Sonnekus (n 20) 328.

[28] See s 1 of the Promotion of Administrative Justice Act 3 of 2000, which defines 'administrative action'.

commercial conduct. Such an approach will not offend against the basic rule of law justification for judicial review.[29]

The fact that constitutional values permeate every sphere of activity has particular ramifications for parties who contract with the government,[30] and for the contents of these contracts. These implications are not confined to issues of party autonomy but include the resolution of contractual disputes, and, particularly, whether they may be resolved by arbitration.[31] Dispute resolution under private-public contracts must also conform to constitutional law and constitutional values. This, in turn, raises questions about the confidentiality of arbitration, specifically when issues of public policy are at stake.[32]

B. The Impact of Administrative Law on Contracts with Public Bodies

Contractual relations with the government and state-related enterprises are generally distinguished from arm's-length commercial contracts because of the state's position of authority and potentially stronger bargaining power vis-à-vis a private contracting party. As a result, these contracts are often referred to as public law contracts which may be subject to rules and principles that differ from regular commercial contracts between private parties.[33] Whether the basic private law principles, like *pacta sunt servanda*, should be applied to agreements with the state remains the subject of an ongoing debate.[34]

In determining the applicability of elements of public law, and in particular administrative law, it is crucial to decide whether the public body, in concluding a contract, is engaged in administrative action. This will have an effect on how the public body exercises its rights and also on the judicial scrutiny that can be used to evaluate the exercise of those rights.[35] State conduct which amounts to an administrative action

[29] Quinot (n 25) 444; also quoted in Sonnekus (n 20) 328.

[30] In relation to government procurement, see s 217 of the Constitution. For a detailed discussion, see Penfold and Reyburn (n 17) ch 25; Bolton (n 17); Quinot (n 25); De la Harpe (n 23). See also the Broad-Based Black Economic Empowerment Act 53 of 2003 and the codes published in terms of the Act.

[31] See n 24 above.

[32] See s 32 of the Constitution, which deals with access to information.

[33] See also Cora Hoexter, 'Contracts in Administrative Law: Life after Formalism?' [2004] S African Law Journal 595, 596; Tjakie Naude, 'The Consumer's "Right to Fair, Reasonable and Just Terms" under the New Consumer Protection Act in Comparative Perspective' [2009] SALJ 505; Deeksha Bhana, 'Constitutionalising Contract Law: Ideology, Judicial Method and Contractual Autonomy' (PhD thesis, University of the Witwatersrand 2013). See also Jonathan Klaaren and Glen Penfold, 'Just Administrative Action' in *Constitutional Law of South Africa* (n 17) (Original Service August 2008) chs 63, 49 ff.

[34] See for instance Thomas Floyd, 'Die Owerheidsooreenkoms – 'n Administratiefregtelike Ondersoek' (LLD thesis, University of South Africa 1994); Yvonne Burns, 'Government Contracts and the Public/Private Divide' [1998] SA Public Law 234, 236; Geo Quinot, 'The Judicial Regulation of State Commercial Activity' (LLD thesis, Stellenbosch University 2007); Phoebe Bolton, 'Government Contracts and the Fettering of Discretion – A Question of Validity' [2004] SA Public Law 90, 109.

[35] See Klaaren and Penfold (n 33) 49. It is important to remember, however, that if such a contract contains an arbitration clause to deal with a contractual dispute, the issue of taking an administrative act of the one contracting party on review does not boil down to dispute resolution but to the accountability of the public body to the public in general.

can only be judicially reviewed under the Promotion of Administrative Justice Act by South African courts[36] and not by private arbitrators.

It is, therefore, crucial to establish whether the contract that is concluded and/or the conduct complained about falls within the ambit of an administrative action in order to judge whether such action is subject to judicial review proceedings, or whether it could be dealt with in terms of private law, which would in principle include the possibility of settling resulting disputes by arbitration.

There are different views on whether the public body's actions or conduct amount to conduct that should be dealt with purely in terms of contract law or whether they fall under the determination of administrative action to be dealt with in terms of administrative law. The classification of the conduct as either administrative action or not will determine whether the dispute could be referred to arbitration or not. Acting Judge of Appeal Rogers recently stated in his minority judgment[37] that:

> it may be that the 'final word has yet to be spoken' on the interplay between contract law and administrative law and that the decisions of this court [ie the Supreme Court of Appeal] are not entirely harmonious. What can, however, be deduced from this court's decisions, as a minimum proposition, is that the exercise of a contractual power by an organ of state does not constitute the exercise of a public power (a) where the contractual power does not mirror a statutory power; and (b) where, additionally, the contract is of the kind explained by Cameron JA[[38] in *Logbro*.[39]

The determination of the nature of the conduct determines the appropriate remedy:

> In the present case neither SanParks nor MTO contends that, in their relationship inter se, there is any element of public power. If MTO were to regard a refusal of consent in terms of clause 10.5 as unreasonable, its remedy would be private arbitration, not judicial review.[40]

The contract in *South African National Parks v MTO Foresty (Pty) Ltd* was concluded between a public body (South African National Parks (SanParks)) and a private party (MTO Forestry) and included an arbitration clause. SanParks agreed to MTO's request to vary the tree-felling schedule. A third party, Parkscape, an association concerned with preserving the plantation area, instituted proceedings to review

[36] See further section II.C below. South Africa does not have a specialized court similar to the German Verwaltungsgericht that deals with administrative law-related issues. In terms of s 6 of the Promotion of Administrative Justice Act 2 of 2000, an administrative act may be reviewed by 'a court or, where appropriate, an independent and impartial tribunal' in accordance with s 33(3) of the Constitution. See n 46 below.

[37] While a minority judgment does not have any binding value, sometimes some of its arguments are indeed more correct than that of the majority. It may then be used to argue that the majority's decision was wrong. It is then often quoted in academic literature. The same holds true when the minority judgment deals with an aspect that does not form the *ratio decidendi* of the majority's decision.

[38] *Logbro Properties CC v Bedderson NO* 2003 (2) SA 460 (SCA) para 10.

[39] *South African National Parks v MTO Foresty (Pty) Ltd* 2018 (5) SA 177 (SCA) 199C-D (referring to *Logbro* (n 38)).

[40] *South African National Parks* (n 39) 199F.

the amended tree-felling schedule. The High Court found that SanParks' decision amounted to administrative action, which was procedurally unfair because no prior notice had been given to Parkscape.[41]

SanParks appealed to the Supreme Court of Appeal. They reasoned that the variation of the felling schedule was purely a contractual matter which did not amount to administrative action.[42] The majority of the Supreme Court of Appeal held that 'the conclusion of the lease agreement and the exercise of powers pursuant to it were clearly an exercise of public power'.[43] It must be noted that, in this instance, the conduct of the public body was aimed at its co-contracting party (MTO) but yet the party who was complaining about the effect of the conduct was a third party who had no contractual link with the public body. In determining the nature of SanParks' conduct, the court considered both the conduct at the time of agreement and the contents of the agreement, holding that SanParks' action amounted to administrative action as defined in the Promotion to Administrative Justice Act, and set aside the variation because 'Parkscape and its members had a legitimate expectation to be consulted before the decision to vary the lease was made'.[44]

The minority, however, held that the action did not amount to administrative action because, once the lease was concluded, a commercial contract came into existence and the 'exercise of its contractual rights was . . . a private matter'. Acting Judge of Appeal Rogers also stated that:

> while accelerated felling might require SanParks to consult with the public concerning consequential changes to SanParks' post-lease management of the land, SanParks was not obliged to consult with the public about how it exercised and performed its contractual rights and obligations. The question of reasonableness, in the context of clause 10.5, is a contractual standard in a bilateral commercial contract. The time limits which clause 10.5 imposes, and the fact that disputes as to reasonableness are to be determined by private arbitration, are quite inconsistent to my mind with the characterisation of clause 10.5 as a source of public power.[45]

In the present author's view, the minority decision provides a more accurate assessment of the legal situation. This discussion has shown that it may be difficult to determine whether the actions of a public body amount to administrative action or the exercise of a contractual right. The following section will consider the arbitrability of administrative action.

[41] ibid 202C–D (stating that, '[i]n the present case, it is argued that SanParks should have consulted with members of the public because, if the lease came to an end sooner, SanParks' post-termination management of the land might yield less satisfactory shady recreational areas than would otherwise have been the case').

[42] ibid 186A–187A. See also *Cape Metro Council v Metro Inspection Services (Western Cape) CC* 2001 (3) SA 1013 (SCA).

[43] *South African National Parks* (n 39) 188C.

[44] ibid 191D–E.

[45] ibid 201C.

C. Arbitrability of Administrative Action?

Conduct of a public body which amounts to an administrative action[46] must be lawful, reasonable, procedurally fair, and comply with the provisions of section 33 of the Constitution; if it is not, it would be reviewable under the Promotion of Administrative Justice Act.[47] The purpose of this statute (section 6) is to 'provide for the review of administrative action by a court or, where appropriate, an independent and impartial tribunal' in accordance with section 33(3) of the Constitution. Just administrative action is a constitutional issue and unconstitutional actions by public bodies may be set aside. However, only courts of law may declare legislation or conduct unconstitutional.[48]

The Promotion of Administrative Justice Act defines a 'tribunal' as being 'established by national legislation for the purpose of judicially reviewing an administrative action in terms of this Act'. This reference to 'tribunal' has never been considered to include arbitration tribunals but only statutory tribunals. Arbitration tribunals which are created by agreement would therefore be precluded from reviewing administrative action.[49] The focus is thus always on judicial review of administrative action, which has three important functions, namely 'the achievement of accountability,[50] the promotion of good administration and safeguarding the rights of individuals against the abuse of power'.[51] As the Constitutional Court held:

> There can be no doubt that the separation of powers attributes responsibility to the courts for ensuring that unconstitutional conduct is declared invalid and that constitutionally mandated remedies are afforded for violations of the Constitution. This

[46] 'Administrative action' is defined in s 1 of the Promotion of Administrative Justice Act 3 of 2000. For a detailed discussion, see Hoexter (n 26) 171–252.

[47] Judicial review 'refers ... to the power of the courts to scrutinise and set aside administrative decisions or rules (delegated legislation) on the basis of certain grounds of review': see Hoexter (n 26) 113. For a detailed discussion of the topic, see ibid 107–70. S 6 of the Promotion of Administrative Justice Act provides for the review of administrative action by 'a court or, where appropriate, an independent and impartial tribunal' (see also s 33(3) of the Constitution). Pursuant to s 1 of the Promotion of Administrative Justice Act, 'court' means: '(a) the Constitutional Court acting in terms of section 167 (6) (a) of the Constitution; or (b) (i) a High Court or another court of similar status; or (ii) a Magistrate's Court for any district or for any regional division established by the Minister for the purposes of adjudicating civil disputes in terms of section 2 of the Magistrates' Courts Act, 1944 (Act 32 of 1944), either generally or in respect of a specified class of administrative actions, designated by the Minister by notice in the Gazette and presided over by a magistrate, an additional magistrate or a magistrate of a regional division established for the purposes of adjudicating civil disputes, as the case may be, designated in terms of section 9A; within whose area of jurisdiction the administrative action occurred or the administrator has his or her or its principal place of administration or the party whose rights have been affected is domiciled or ordinarily resident or the adverse effect of the administrative action was, is or will be experienced.' 'Tribunal' is defined as 'any independent and impartial tribunal established by national legislation for the purpose of judicially reviewing an administrative action in terms of this Act' (ibid).

[48] See generally Matthew Chaskalson, Gilbert Marcus, and Michael Bishop, 'Constitutional Litigation' in *Constitutional Law of South Africa* (n 17) (Original Service July 2011) chs 3, 4.

[49] But see Cora Hoexter, 'The Transformation of South African Administrative Law since 1994 with Particular Reference to the Promotion of Administrative Justice Act 3 of 2000' (PhD thesis, University of the Witwatersrand 2009) 113.

[50] Arbitral awards, unless they are not confidential, cannot be used in holding a public body accountable. See the discussion in section IV below.

[51] Hoexter (n 49) 191.

> means that the court must provide effective relief for infringements of constitutional rights.[52]

The proper approach for a remedy for violations of a constitutional right (ie a public law remedy which may result in disciplinary proceedings against the responsible official which can lead to dismissal and/or damages) has also been decided upon by the Constitutional Court in *Steenkamp NO v Provincial Tender Board, Eastern Cape*:

> It goes without saying that every improper performance of an administrative function would implicate the Constitution and entitle the aggrieved party to appropriate relief. In each case the remedy must fit the injury. The remedy must be fair to those affected by it and yet vindicate effectively the right violated. It must be just and equitable in the light of the facts, the implicated constitutional principles, if any, and the controlling law. It is nonetheless appropriate to note that ordinarily a breach of administrative justice attracts public-law remedies and not private-law remedies. The purpose of a public-law remedy is to pre-empt or correct or reverse an improper administrative function . . . Ultimately the purpose of a public remedy is to afford the prejudiced party administrative justice, to advance efficient and effective public administration compelled by constitutional precepts and at a broader level, to entrench the rule of law.[53]

In determining whether a particular act is unconstitutional, the nature of the act must be considered, because that influences both the appropriate remedies and the adjudicator. Only the courts (excluding the magistrate's courts)[54] have jurisdiction to determine unconstitutional conduct,[55] and if such a matter were to arise in an arbitration, the arbitration tribunal would not have the jurisdiction to finally determine the constitutionality of conduct, although it may draw on the provisions of the Constitution.

Section 7(4) of the Promotion of Administrative Justice Act provides that 'all proceedings for judicial review under this Act must be instituted in a High Court or another court having jurisdiction'. Acting Judge Vally held in *Airports Company South Africa Ltd v ISO Leisure OR Tambi (Pty) Ltd*[56] that:

> s 7(4) of PAJA [Promotion of Administrative Justice Act] precludes any forum, apart from the High Court and the Constitutional Court, to adjudicate over claims brought in terms of PAJA. The parties cannot, in my view, confer jurisdiction upon a private arbitrator to decide a claim brought in terms of PAJA. To allow such would

[52] *AllPay Consolidated Investment Holdings (Pty) Ltd v CEO, South African Social Security Agency* 2014 (4) SA 179 (CC) 191H.

[53] *Steenkamp NO v Provincial Tender Board, Eastern Cape* 2007 (3) SA 121 (CC) 134E–135A.

[54] The judicial system in South Africa consists of the Constitutional Court, the Supreme Court of Appeal, the High Court of South Africa, the Magistrate's Courts, and any other court established or recognized in terms of an Act of Parliament. Magistrate's Courts are of a status lower than the High Court of South Africa and may not enquire into or rule on the constitutionality of any legislation or any conduct of the President: see s 170 of the Constitution.

[55] See s 172 of the Constitution.

[56] 2011 (4) SA 642 (GSJ).

> be to allow parties to privatise constitutional disputes, and this bears the risk of allowing a parallel constitutional jurisprudence to develop in this country—one that is separate and independent from that developed by the Constitutional Court. Such a development goes against the entire grain of our constitutional system, which is based on recognising the Constitutional Court as the highest and, in some respects, the only court that can make pronouncements on constitutional matters. The privatisation of disputes involving constitutional matters is anathema to our Constitution, and rightly so, in my view.[57]

To summarize: the determination of whether an administrative action was just can only be done by way of judicial review—it is not a matter that is arbitrable. The following section considers South Africa's arbitration legislation, the role of the Constitution, and arbitrability in terms of the arbitration legislation; focus is also placed on investor-state disputes and international commercial arbitration involving the state.

III. South Africa's Arbitration Laws

A. Introduction

Although the history of arbitration in South Africa can be traced to Roman and Roman Dutch law, English law has been more influential, because the legislation adopted in three of the former colonies (that became provinces of the Union of South Africa in 1910) in the late 1800s was based on the English Arbitration Act of 1889.[58] The current Arbitration Act,[59] which repealed the colonial statutes, has also been extensively influenced by the English Arbitration Act of 1960. However, 'the South African courts right from the outset adopted a substantially less interventionist approach than their English counterparts in applying virtually the same legislation'.[60]

After the implementation of the Arbitration Act in 1965, a number of important changes took place. South Africa became a constitutional democracy in 1994 with a Bill of Rights in its Constitution. At the international level, after returning to the international arena after years of isolation, the country signed a number of BITs providing

[57] ibid 663B–E; see also Grégor Wolter and others, 'South Africa' in Damian Taylor (ed), *The Dispute Resolution Review* (10th edn, The Law Reviews 2018) 420, 435.

[58] See s 42 of the Arbitration Act 42 of 1965 that repealed the Cape Arbitration Act 29 of 1898; the Natal Arbitration Act 24 of 1898; and the Transvaal Ordinance 24 of 1904. See FDJ Brand, 'Judicial Review of Arbitration Awards' (2014) 2 SLR 247, 250 with reference to RH Christie, 'Arbitration: Party Autonomy or Curial Intervention – The Historical Background' (1994) 111 SALJ 143, 144; DW Butler and E Finsen, *Arbitration in South Africa – Law and Practice* (Juta 1993) 4 ff, for the history of arbitration and the sources they refer to; Jeremy Gauntlett, 'The Legal System of South Africa and Its Approach to Arbitration' (2007) 20(2) Adv 28 ff. See also Ditaba Petrus Rantsane, 'Consumer Arbitration in South Africa and its Effect on the Consumer's Right to Redress and Enforcement' (LLD thesis, University of Pretoria 2017) 19 ff and the sources cited therein.

[59] Act 42 of 1965.

[60] See Brand (n 58) 250.

for investor-state arbitration.[61] It became a member of the World Trade Organization and concluded a number of free trade agreements.[62] At the international level, investor-state disputes flourished and criticism of the system increased as governments realized the potential impact of arbitral awards.[63] Voices questioning the legitimacy of the system, and to a lesser extent questioning whether arbitration tribunals are not bringing a new form of governance to the fore, grew more prominent. In particular, resistance to investor-state arbitration was stimulated by questions over the legitimacy of arbitration tribunals—the new 'governance system'—which are immune to state scrutiny and democratic accountability, but nevertheless make findings about the validity of the sovereign actions of governments.[64]

Academic voices in South Africa remained silent on this issue, perhaps as a result of the country's initial isolation and because of an initial inability to appreciate the potential impact of investor-state arbitration on the government. Only after South Africa's involvement in two investor-state disputes, which ended to the detriment of the state, did awareness grow and research deepen;[65] it is not unknown that the loser in a major sporting event also tends to blame the impartial referee for the unvictorious

[61] See Engela C Schlemmer, 'An Overview of South Africa's Bilateral Investment Treaties and Investment Policy' (2016) 31(1) ICSID Review–FILJ 167. See the Government's Position Paper, 'Bilateral Investment Policy Framework Review' General Notice 961, in Government Gazette 32386 (7 July 2009) 14, where it is stated that there was 'no legal or economic analysis of the risk associated with the conclusion of BITs' and that there was 'a lack of understanding regarding the real nature and consequences of BITs at that time. Cabinet was not fully apprised of the dangers inherent in BITs.' Poulsen's research confirms the statement cited from the government's position paper: see Lauge N Skovgaard Poulsen, 'Sacrificing Sovereignty by Chance: Investment Treaties, Developing Countries, and Bounded Rationality' (PhD thesis, London School of Economics and Political Science 2011) 257–300.

[62] See eg the Treaty of the Southern African Development Community (adopted 17 August 1992, entered into force 30 September 1993) <https://treaties.dirco.gov.za/dbtw-wpd/images/19920817SADCDeclarationTreatyandProtocol.pdf> to which South Africa acceded on 29 August 1994. The Protocol on Trade (in terms of art 22 of the Treaty) (adopted 1 August 1996, entered into force on 25 January 2000) <https://treaties.dirco.gov.za/dbtw-wpd/images/19960824SADCProtocolTrade.pdf> has as one of its objectives the creation of a Free Trade Area (art 2), which was to a large extent achieved by the year 2008: see SADC Secretariat, *Summary of the SADC Revised Regional Indicative Strategic Development Plan 2015–2020* (SADC 2017) 5. Most recent is the Agreement Establishing the Continental Free Trade Area (adopted 21 March 2018, entered into force 30 May 2019) <https://treaties.dirco.gov.za/dbtw-wpd/images/20180321%20Agreement%20establishing%20the%20AfCFTA.pdf> all accessed 6 January 2025.

[63] For eg Susan D Franck, 'The Legitimacy Crisis in Investment Treaty Arbitration: Privatizing Public International Law Through Inconsistent Decisions' (2005) 73(4) Fordham LR 1521.

[64] See in general Benedict Kingsbury and Stephan W Schill, 'Investor-State Arbitration as Governance: Fair and Equitable Treatment, Proportionality, and the Emerging Global Administrative Law' in Albert Jan van den Berg (ed), *50 Years of the New York Convention* (Kluwer 2009) 5; Gus Van Harten and Martin Loughlin, 'Investment Treaty Arbitration as a Species of Global Administrative Law' (2006)17 EJIL 121; Stephan W Schill, 'Crafting the International Economic Order: The Public Function of Investment Treaty Arbitration and its Significance for the Role of the Arbitrator' (2010) 23 Leiden JIL 401. See also Javier Robalino-Orellana and Jaime Rodríguez-Arana Muñoz (eds), *Global Administrative Law: Towards a* Lex Administrativa (Cameron May 2010); Valentina Vadi, 'Global Cultural Governance by Investment Arbitral Tribunals: The Making of *lex administrativa culturalis*' (2015) 33 Boston Univ ILJ 457; Walter Mattli and Thomas Dietz (eds), *International Arbitration and Global Governance: Contending Theories and Evidence* (OUP 2014).

[65] Jason Brickhill and Max du Plessis, 'Two's Company, Three's a Crowd: Public Interest Intervention in Investor-State Arbitration (*Piero Foresti v South Africa*)' (2011) 27(1) SAJHR 152; Nicole Yazbek, 'Bilateral Investment Treaties: The Foreclosure of Domestic Policy Space' (2010) 17 SAJIA 103; Tania Steenkamp, *South Africa's New Bilateral Investment Treaty Policy: A Reasonable Response to a Flawed Regime?* (LLM thesis, University of British Columbia 2014); David Schneiderman, 'Promoting Equality, Black Economic Empowerment, and the Future of Investment Rules' (2009) 25(2) SAJHR 246.

outcome. This led to a review of the government's policies in relation to BITs.[66] These events added impetus to earlier calls for a renewal of the arbitration landscape in anticipation of the growth in arbitration and the possibility of South Africa becoming an arbitration centre of choice.[67]

The following sections will investigate the developments in South Africa's arbitration regime, both at the investor-state level and in relation to international commercial arbitration.

B. Developments in South African Arbitration Law

Arbitration in South Africa takes on different forms depending on the agreement between the parties or whether it is prescribed by legislation or merely regulated or governed by legislation or international treaty. It is either consensual (private arbitration) or compulsory (formal arbitration) when it is prescribed by legislation.[68] What the present book terms 'private-public arbitration', involving the state as a party, has not attracted separate attention in South Africa except in relation to investor-state arbitration. This may be due to the potential impact of private-public arbitrations not yet being considered in the same depth as compulsory or private arbitration. Neglected issues include the constitutionality of the system or whether arbitration itself is considered to be similar to administrative action (as was found by the Constitutional Court in relation to awards of the Commission for Conciliation, Mediation and Arbitration)[69] and the types of disputes which may be subjected to arbitration.

Whether arbitration constitutes a new form of governance has also not been considered, although the impact of arbitral awards in investor-state arbitration involving South Africa has led government to comment that the obligations contained in BITs limit its 'right to regulate'.[70] The impact of private-public arbitration on public administration has not been considered at all and the involvement of the state or public bodies in arbitration is not treated uniformly. The following subsections focus on the impact of the Constitution on arbitration, the arbitrability of disputes, investor-state disputes, and international commercial arbitration.

1 Arbitration and the Constitution

South African courts tend to support arbitration rather than to interfere with it. In *Telcordia Technologies Inc v Telkom SA Ltd*,[71] the Supreme Court of

[66] See South African Law Commission, *Discussion Paper 69, Project 94: Arbitration: A Draft International Arbitration Act for South Africa* (South African Law Commission 1996) para 1.1.

[67] See Stephan Wilske and Jade G Ewers, 'Why South Africa Should Update its International Arbitration Legislation. An Appeal from the International Arbitration Community for Legal Reform in South Africa' (2011) 28(1) J Int'l Arb 1, 2, and 5 ff; David Butler, 'South African Arbitration Legislation – The Need for Reform' (1994) 27 Comp Int'l LJ Southern Afr 118; Peter Ramsden (assisted by Kelly Ramsden), *The Law of Arbitration: South African & International Arbitration* (Juta 2009) 18–19.

[68] Formal or compulsory arbitration is required under s 33 of the Labour Relations Act 66 of 1995.

[69] This relates to compulsory arbitration in terms of the Labour Relations Act, which also binds the state (see s 209).

[70] See the Government Position Paper (n 61).

[71] 2007 (3) SA 266 (SCA).

Appeal[72] reversed a finding of a High Court judge, who, it found:

> disregarded the principle of party autonomy in arbitration proceedings and failed to give due deference to an arbitral award, something our courts have consistently done since the early part of the 19th century. This approach is not peculiar to us; it is indeed part of a worldwide tradition ... And the 'concerns of international comity, respect for the capacities of foreign and transnational tribunals, and sensitivity to the need of the international commercial system for predictability in the resolution of disputes' [*Mitsubishi Motors Corporation v Soler Chrysler-Plymouth Inc* 473 50 US 614 (1985) per Blackmun J at 629] have given rise in other jurisdictions to the adoption of a 'standard which seeks to preserve the autonomy of the forum selected by the parties and to minimise judicial intervention when reviewing international commercial arbitration awards'.[73]

The Constitutional Court in *Lufuno Mphaphuli & Associates (Pty) Ltd v Andrews*[74] emphasized the consensual and private nature of arbitration and considered whether section 34 of the Constitution, which provides that 'everyone has the right to have any dispute that can be resolved by the application of law decided in a fair public hearing before a court or, where appropriate, another independent and impartial tribunal or forum', applies to private arbitration.[75] It held that section 34 was not directly applicable to private arbitration,[76] but that parties who choose arbitration as a dispute resolution mechanism 'have instead chosen not to exercise their right under s 34'.[77] The Court regarded the obligation of fairness in section 34 as applying to the arbitration agreement itself and an arbitration agreement which expressly provides for a procedure that is unfair would be *contra bonos mores*.[78] It thus confirmed that the use of arbitration was not in violation of the rights guaranteed in the Bill of Rights.

However, whether an arbitration agreement is contrary to public policy must be decided 'in the light of the values of the Constitution'.[79] Public policy is now rooted in the Constitution and other fundamental values which include 'human dignity, the achievement of equality and the advancement of human rights and freedoms, non-racialism and non-sexism'.[80] Moreover, according to *Afrox Healthcare Bpk v Strydom*,[81] the unequal bargaining power of parties to a contract may, together with other factors, play a role in determining whether a contractual provision that is to the benefit of the 'stronger party' would offend public policy.[82] Thus, if a contractant

[72] Which used to be the highest court in all matters except constitutional matters – this position changed in August 2013 with the coming into force of the Constitution 17th Amendment Act, which made the Constitutional Court the highest court in all matters.

[73] *Telcordia Technologies Inc* (n 71) 278I–279C.

[74] 2009 (4) SA 529 (CC).

[75] s 34 provides that 'everyone has the right to have any dispute that can be resolved by the application of law decided in a fair public hearing before a court or, where appropriate, another independent and impartial tribunal or forum'.

[76] See *Lufuno Mphaphuli & Associates* (n 74) 591E–H.

[77] ibid 592A.

[78] Per Acting Deputy Chief Justice O'Regan in ibid 594A.

[79] ibid 592F–G.

[80] Per Judge of Appeal Cameron in *Brisley v Drotsky* 2002 (4) SA 1 (SCA) 34G–35A.

[81] 2002 (6) SA 21 (SCA).

[82] This was confirmed by the Constitutional Court in *Barkhuizen v Napier* 2007 (5) SA 323 (CC).

argues that, due to their weaker bargaining power, they were 'forced' to submit to an arbitration agreement, this unequal bargaining position may be considered in establishing that the arbitration agreement is against public policy and therefore void.

Since there is no general impediment on the South African government's ability to participate in normal commercial activities it is also considered bound by its contractual agreements, including agreements to use arbitration as a mechanism of dispute resolution where the dispute is arbitrable.[83] The Arbitration Act and the International Arbitration Act—albeit subject to the provisions of the Protection of Investment Act—bind the state and public bodies, thus allowing the use of arbitration in dealings with the government and public bodies, subject to the arbitrability of the disputes.[84]

2 Arbitrability of Disputes

Questions concerning the arbitrability of public acts have not been investigated in depth and it is not something that the South African arbitration community has pondered upon to any extent.[85] The Arbitration Act and other statutes exclude certain topics from arbitration[86] but, on the whole, the issue is largely ignored.[87]

Section 2 of the Arbitration Act provides that:

> Matters not subject to arbitration
> A reference to arbitration shall not be permissible in respect of –
> (a) any matrimonial cause or any matter incidental to any such cause; or
> (b) any matter relating to status.[88]

[83] In *Minister for Justice and Constitutional Development v Nyathi* 2010 (4) SA 567 (CC), the Constitutional Court found that the provision in the State Liability Act 20 of 1957 preventing execution against, or the attachment of, state assets is unconstitutional. This provision has now been amended, allowing parties to attach government assets when satisfaction of a judgment is not forthcoming.

[84] See s 39 of the Arbitration Act and s 5 of the International Arbitration Act.

[85] Marna Lourens, 'The Issue of Arbitrability in the Context of International Commercial Arbitration' (1999) 11 SA Merc LJ 363, 364 (pt 1); and Marna Lourens, 'The Issue of Arbitrability in the Context of International Commercial Arbitration' (1999) 11 SA Merc LJ 439 (pt 2). See Carla Mrotzek, 'The Development of Concept of Arbitrability – An International Comparison' (LLM thesis, University of Cape Town 2017) 4, 37. Criminal matters are not arbitrable in terms of the South African common law (see Johannes Voet, *Commentarius ad Pandectas Tomus Primus* Liber 4 Titulus 8 para 10 (Apud Fratres de Tournes (1778)); Butler and Finsen (n 58) 55). S 35(3)(c) of the Constitution now guarantees a right to a fair public trial, thus excluding by implication arbitration.

[86] Such as the Promotion of Administrative Justice Act: see section II.C of this chapter.

[87] See also Mrotzek (n 85) 44 ff. See South African Law Commission (n 66) para 1.1.

[88] But see the developments to have informal arbitrations in family matters, being advocated by the Law Society of South Africa: see Susan Abro, 'Arbitration in Family Law Paper to Be Presented at the Annual General Meeting of the Law Society of South Africa: 2 April 2016' <www.lssa.org.za/upload/LSSA%20AGM%202016%20Susan%20Abro%20Paper%20on%20ARBITRATION%20IN%20FAMILY%20LAW.pdf> accessed 25 September 2020. The members of the Law Society of South Africa's Family Law Committee, together with the Family Law Arbitration Foundation of South Africa, submitted a proposal for the amendment of the Arbitration Act 42 of 1965 to remove the prohibition against arbitration in domestic matters to the relevant ministry, but there has not been any legislative amendment done yet: see Law Society of South Africa, *Annual Report April 2017 to March 2018* (2018) 40; Law Society of South Africa, *Annual Report April 2018 to March 2019* (2019) 35.

The International Arbitration Act, in turn, provides that:

> 7.(1) For the purposes of this Chapter, any international commercial dispute which the parties have agreed to submit to arbitration under an arbitration agreement and which relates to a matter which the parties are entitled to dispose of by agreement may be determined by arbitration, unless—
>
> (*a*) such a dispute is not capable of determination by arbitration under any law of the Republic; or
>
> (*b*) the arbitration agreement is contrary to the public policy of the Republic.
>
> (2) Arbitration may not be excluded solely on the ground that an enactment confers jurisdiction on a court or other tribunal to determine a matter falling within the terms of an arbitration agreement.

Thus, if agreed upon by the parties, and if not considered to be unarbitrable, international commercial disputes may be subjected to international commercial arbitration.

The arbitrability of disputes involving the state and public policy, and some of the issues which the current study raises, were not considered in the South African Law Reform Commission's investigation into the modernization of the Arbitration Act which resulted in the International Arbitration Act.[89] This investigation by the Commission created an ideal platform to debate and address issues in domestic and international arbitration, such as the constitutionality of arbitration, the role of public policy, the arbitrability of disputes, and the role of the state in arbitration. These issues were not canvassed in detail, but the Commission recommended that the UNCITRAL Model Law on International Commercial Arbitration be adopted for purposes of international commercial arbitrations[90] and that the Arbitration Act[91] (as it is) be retained for domestic arbitrations.[92] Its recommendation that South Africa become a party to the Washington Convention[93] was not taken up by the government.

There was no discussion of the role of the state in arbitration[94] and very little on the impact of the Constitution on arbitration to which the state is a party. The Commission's Report on Domestic Arbitration states that:

[89] See eg Research Unit, Parliament of the Republic of South Africa, 'The International Arbitration Bill [B10-2017]' (13 June 2017) 1 <pmg-assets.s3-website-eu-west-1.amazonaws.com/171101researcher.pdf> accessed 6 January 2025.

[90] See section III.B.4 below.

[91] A second report containing recommendations for legislative amendments to domestic arbitration was published in 2001: see South African Law Commission, 'Project 94: Domestic Arbitration Report' (May 2001) <www.justice.gov.za/salrc/reports/r_prj94_dom2001.pdf>. It has not been submitted to parliament yet. See Justice and Constitutional Development Portfolio Committee, 'Meeting Report' (25 September 2002) app 1 <https://pmg.org.za/committee-meeting/1837/> all accessed 6 January 2025.

[92] See, for criticism on this position, WG Schulze, 'Of Arbitration, Politics and the Price of Neglect – South African International Arbitration Legislation Continues to Lag Behind: *Bidoli v Bidoli*' (2011) 23 SA Merc LJ 291, 293. See also Jacqui Pile, 'Arbitration in the Dock' (*Financial Mail*, 11 March 2005).

[93] Convention on the Settlement of Investment Disputes between States and Nationals of Other States (adopted 18 March 1965, entered into force 14 October 1966) 575 UNTS 159.

[94] Apart from repeating that the state is bound by the Arbitration Act unless otherwise provided for in other legislation.

> S 5(2) [of the Domestic Arbitration Bill][95] makes it clear that s 5 does not define comprehensively what disputes are arbitrable and that another law can therefore impose restrictions on arbitrability. In terms of s 5(3), this result is not achieved merely by conferring jurisdiction on a court or other tribunal to determine any matter. An interesting example, because of its constitutional implications, is the possible interaction between s 5(3) and the Promotion of Administrative Justice Act 3 of 2000, which empowers the High Court and certain Magistrates' Courts to review administrative action. On the wording of s 5(3), this would not by itself preclude the entity whose administrative action is challenged and the party whose rights were affected by such action from agreeing that the validity or invalidity of the action should be determined by arbitration. Public policy considerations however may arguably require a different interpretation [fn 149: It could be argued that the public interest in an open democracy precludes arbitration because arbitration hearings are normally regarded as private and the results of an arbitration as confidential. This objection could however be met by the public interest exception to the principle of confidentiality.].[96]

The report does not consider this aspect any further, but in light of the earlier discussion and the Constitutional Court decisions referred to,[97] an arbitral tribunal is not competent to deal with the validity of administrative actions. Public policy considerations would arguably also point to these issues not being arbitrable.[98]

With respect to local government and public-private partnerships specifically, the National Treasury, after a lengthy inclusive consultation process, published a number of standardized provisions that should be included in a public-private partnership that is governed by the Public Finance Management Act of 1999.[99] The provisions include a preference for the use of independent experts to resolve disputes of a technical nature, and that—and this is clearly stated—arbitration is not considered sustainable for the following reasons:

> 86.1.3 . . . arbitration is not necessarily quicker or cheaper than litigation through the courts. The rules of court permit the appointment of technical and financial experts to assist judges in regard to matters that require expert consideration. The private negotiated selection of arbitrators does not ensure the selection of the most able persons for such appointments and, in so far as such selection is not an open process or otherwise subject to the regulatory checks inherent in the process of

[95] The bill is attached to the Discussion Paper of the South African Law Commission (n 66).

[96] South African Law Commission (n 91) para 3.32. See also ibid para 3.180.

[97] See sections II.B and II.C above.

[98] See section II.C above. See also *Gray Moodliar Inc v Nelson Mandela Bay Metropolitan Municipality and Another* 2019 (10) BLLR 1163, para 23.

[99] See n 22 above. 'The *National Treasury's PPP Manual* and *Standardised PPP Provisions* are founded on the PFMA [Public Finance Management Act] and Treasury Regulation 16, and have been produced for national and provincial departments, constitutional institutions, and public entities listed or required to be listed in schedules 3A, 3B, 3C and 3D of the PFMA, and any subsidiaries of such public entities.' The standardized provisions were issued by the National Treasury in accordance with s 76(4)(g) of the Public Finance Management Act as National Treasury PPP Practice Note Number 01 of 2004 after a lengthy inclusive consultative process (see Covering letter issued on the publication of the standardized PPP provisions dated 13 April 2004 (on file with author)).

> judicial selection, may even be tainted by claims of nepotism. But the most compelling reason for the preference for curial adjudication over arbitration is the need to build up a substantial legal precedent base for the interpretation and enforcement of PPP Agreements, to provide the courts with the opportunity to grow the expertise required to deal with the complexities of PPP Agreements and to promote a measure of transparency regarding the interpretation and enforcement of PPP Agreements.
>
> 86.1.4 Accordingly, the prescribed approach for disputes arising in connection with PPP Agreements is for these to be settled ultimately through the courts, except in the case of any specific categories of dispute requiring fast-track dispute resolution by expert adjudicators. Further, alternative forms of dispute resolution processes such as informal conciliation must first be attempted.[100]

For these reasons, it seems that the government is reluctant to agree to arbitration for disputes arising under public-private partnerships. However, in March 2018, the South African Local Government Association (SALGA) entered into an agreement with the Arbitration Foundation of Southern Africa (AFSA), a private institution in the form of a non-profit organization, to provide dispute resolution services to the municipalities in South Africa. AFSA states in its official newsletter that '[l]ocal government is at the coalface of service delivery in this country and arbitration and other forms of dispute resolution, unlike litigation, offers disputants a mechanism which is fast, cost-effective and flexible.'[101] Thus, apart from the limitation placed by the Local Government: Municipal Systems Act, which prohibits a municipality from submitting to arbitration a 'matter involving a decision on its status, powers or duties or the validity of its actions or by-laws',[102] disputes between private service suppliers and local governments may be submitted to arbitration.[103]

Hitherto there has been no litigation on arbitrations in public-private partnerships, but the confidential nature of arbitrations means that the existence of such arbitrations would not be generally known. It is, however, clear, and has been confirmed by the public-private partnership unit situated in the national Treasury,[104] that public-private partnership agreements often contain deviations from the standardized provisions and that the Treasury does not consider them to be problematic, especially where the preferred mode of dispute resolution was not inserted into the agreement but arbitration was nevertheless chosen.[105] It thus seems clear that, in purely

[100] 'National Treasury Standardised PPP Provisions: First Issue' (11 March 2004) paras 86.1.3 and 86.1.4.

[101] See Arbitration Foundation of Southern Africa (AFSA), 'AFSA Signs Agreement with SALGA on Municipal Disputes' [May/June 2018] AFSA @ Work 4; Shantalie Hewavisenti, 'SALGA Signs Memorandum of Understanding' [2018] Voice of Local Govt 35, 36 (regarding the appointment of a panel of independent arbitrators for this purpose).

[102] See s 109 of the Local Government: Municipal Systems Act.

[103] This was confirmed in *Gray Moodliar Inc* (n 98). See also Nico Steytler and Jaap de Visser, *Local Government Law of South Africa* (Issue 13, LexisNexis 2020) para 12.2, stating that '[i]n the case of disputes with a private sector supplier, the usual legal remedies are available. The municipality may, however, "compromise or compound any action claim or proceedings, and may submit to arbitration any matter"', with a qualification added that 'any matter "involving a decision on [a municipality's] status, powers or duties or the validity of its actions or bylaws" may not be submitted to arbitration' (para 8.6.4).

[104] Email confirmation on this practice is on file with author.

[105] In terms of r 16.5.1 of Treasury Regulation 16 (n 99), '[p]rior to the issuing of any procurement documentation for a PPP to any prospective bidders, the institution must obtain approval from the relevant treasury for the procurement documentation, including the draft PPP agreement.' The National Treasury

contractual matters, government does not oppose arbitration as a dispute settlement mechanism.[106]

However, other statutes, common law, and public policy also point to other issues which are considered unarbitrable.[107] For example, the Patent Act[108] provides that 'no tribunal shall have jurisdiction in the first instance ... relating to matters under the Patent Act'; and the former Insurance Act granted exclusive jurisdiction to the courts,[109] and thus excluded arbitration for the determination of general disputes.[110] This has been omitted from the Short-term Insurance Act[111] and the Long-term Insurance Act,[112] but in terms of the Policyholder Protection Rules (Short-term Insurance) of 2017, published in terms of section 55 of the Short-term Insurance Act,[113] any provision requiring mandatory arbitration is void.[114] Voluntary arbitration can, however, be agreed upon but only after a dispute has arisen.[115]

A number of statutes also allow or even require arbitration as a means of dispute resolution with the government, including: section 22 of the Extension of Security of Tenure Act;[116] the National Environmental Management Act,[117] which provides for conciliation and arbitration of conflicts;[118] section 21 of the Water Services Act;[119]

gives approval at three stages of the process (initially to commence a feasibility study (r 16.4)); at the procurement stage just mentioned (r 16.5); as well as after conclusion of the procurement process but before the PPP agreement is concluded (r 16.6)). All PPP agreements in existence, which include arbitration provisions, went through the approval process as well, and confirm that irrespective of the standardized provisions which do not prefer arbitration, the National Treasury nevertheless approved the agreements.

[106] Issues concerning confidentiality of the proceedings and the award remain, and it is submitted that due to public policy reasons and for purposes of democratic accountability, such arbitrations should not be confidential. This seems to be confirmed in s 11 of the new International Arbitration Act. See also EC Schlemmer, 'Regsaard van arbitrasieverrigtinge – geen verabsolutering van vertroulikheid nie' [2011] Tydskrif vir die Suid-Afrikaanse Reg/J South Afr L 741 ff; EC Schlemmer, 'Vertroulikheid en deursigtigheid in beleggingsarbitrasie – die staat versus die belegger (en dalk ook die eie belastingbetaler?)' [2012] Tydskrif vir die Suid-Afrikaanse Reg/J South Afr L 160–71; EC Schlemmer, 'The Interaction Between Public Policy, Constitutional Rights and Public-Private Arbitration' [2016] Tydskrif vir die Suid-Afrikaanse Reg/J South Afr L 500–18 and 660–79.

[107] See Mrotzek (n 85) 38 (referring to Nicholas Taitz, *Arbitration Procedures in South Africa* (2016) para 4). The law reports contain numerous cases dealing with arbitrations that took place between public bodies and their contracting parties: see eg *Indwe Aviation (Pty) Ltd v Petroleum Oil and Gas Corporation of South Africa (Pty) Ltd (No 1)* 2012 (6) SA 96 (WCC) 106A–B; *Ntshangase v MEC for Finance, Kwazulu-Natal* 2010 (3) SA 201 (SCA) 209C–F; or references in cases to arbitrations that have taken place, eg in *Waenhuiskrans Arniston Ratepayers Association v Verreweide Eiendomsontwikkeling (Edms) Bpk* 2011 (3) SA 434 (WCC) 446C.

[108] Act 57 of 1978, s 18(1).

[109] Act 27 of 1943, s 63.

[110] See ibid s 63(1).

[111] Act 53 of 1998.

[112] Act 52 of 1998.

[113] GN 1433 in Government Gazette 41329 of 15 December 2017. These rules have not yet been before a South African court.

[114] See r 7.1(d) of the Policyholder Protection Rules (Short-term Insurance) of 2017 published in terms of s 55 of the Short-term Insurance Act as GN 1433 in Government Gazette 41329 of 15 December 2017 with effect from 1 January 2018.

[115] See ibid r 7.2.

[116] Extension of Security of Tenure Act 62 of 1997, s 22.

[117] Act 107 of 1998.

[118] See National Environmental Management Act, s 19.

[119] Act 108 of 1997. See also Malcolm Langford, Richard Stacey, and Danwood Chirwa, 'Water' in *Constitutional Law of South Africa* (n 17) ch 56B-40.

section 14 of the Expropriation Act (to determine the amount of compensation);[120] the Nuclear Energy Act;[121] and the Local Government: Municipal Systems Act.[122]

These disparate provisions in statutes do not illustrate a consistent government policy on the use of arbitration involving the state but, rather, confirm the existence of a dichotomy in the government's approach to the arbitrability of disputes involving the government: in some instances, arbitration is required; in others, arbitration is prohibited.

However, it could be argued that public policy considerations should play an important role in considering the arbitrability of disputes involving the state or public bodies. Investigations of so-called state capture in South Africa[123] strongly point to the need for transparency and public accountability in the dealings between the public bodies and private enterprises or individuals. In these instances, arbitration, which entails confidential processes and outcomes, may not be suitable.

Public policy could also be the reason for the government's change of attitude on the use of arbitration in investment disputes, in addition to its argument that BITs limit its rights to regulate.

3 Investor-State Disputes

When South Africa signed on to investment treaties, it barely considered[124] how these obligations would affect its constitutional commitments[125] and the authority of its domestic courts.[126] But the consequences of its first two treaty-based investment arbitrations[127] moved South Africa from avidly entering into BITs to opposing the conclusion of BITs in the absence of compelling economic and political motivations.[128]

[120] Expropriation Act 63 of 1975, s 14.

[121] Nuclear Energy Act 46 of 1999, s 44.

[122] Local Government: Municipal Systems Act 32 of 2000, s 109(2).

[123] See Public Protector of South Africa, 'State of Capture' Report No 6 of 2016/17 (2017) 3 <http://saflii.org/images/329756472-State-of-Capture.pdf> accessed 6 January 2025 (stating that '[t]his report relates to an investigation into complaints of alleged improper and unethical conduct by the President and other State functionaries relating to alleged improper relationships and involvement of the Gupta family in the removal and appointment of ministers and directors of State Owned Entities (SOEs) resulting in improper and possibly corrupt award of state contracts and benefits to the Gupta family's businesses.').

[124] See the Government Position Paper (n 61) 14, where it is stated that there was 'no legal or economic analysis of the risk associated with the conclusion of BITs' and that there was 'a lack of understanding regarding the real nature and consequences of BITs at that time. Cabinet was not fully apprised of the dangers inherent in BITs.'

[125] Regarding the lack of understanding concerning the role and importance of BITs, see ibid. This is confirmed by Poulsen (n 61) ch 9.

[126] See Poulsen (n 61) 332, indicating that, in his interviews with South African government officials—negotiators as well as legal advisors—it never crossed their minds that there could be any ramifications or problems arising from the conclusion of BITs.

[127] See Schlemmer (n 61) 173, 186 ff; Luke Peterson, 'Swiss Investor Prevailed in 2003 in Confidential BIT Arbitration over South Africa Land Dispute; Award Remains Unpublished, But IA Reporter Investigation Unearths Significant Details About Arbitration Outcome' (*Investment Arbitration Reporter*, 22 October 2008); see also Peter Leon, 'Balancing Investor Certainty and SA's Legitimate Interests' (*Business Day*, 16 September 2009) 13; *Piero Foresti, Laura de Carli and others v Republic of South Africa*, ICSID Case No ARB(AF)/07/1, Award (4 August 2010).

[128] See 'Speech delivered by the Minister of Trade and Industry Dr Rob Davies at the South African launch of the United Nations Conference on Trade and Development (UNCTAD) Investment Policy Framework for Sustainable Development at the University of the Witwatersrand' (26 July 2012) < https://www.gov.za/news/speeches/speech-delivered-minister-trade-and-industry-dr-rob-davies-south-african-launch > accessed 20 January 2025; Schlemmer (n 61) 190.

The best-known investment treaty case against South Africa considered whether the amendments to its mineral law, implemented as part of the socio-economic reforms related to South Africa's Broad-Based Black Economic Empowerment policies, were compatible with its BIT commitments.[129] The arbitral award demonstrated that government policy (and government conduct) and constitutional prerogatives could be scrutinized by an international arbitration tribunal, in addition to being subjected to judicial review in domestic courts, if there was a complaint of unjust administrative action. The government's policies on their own are deemed not justiciable before the courts.[130]

However, arbitration takes place within the framework of a BIT and not within the constitutional parameters that would bind a municipal court. Arbitrators' decisions on the international responsibility of a host state are based on the state's treaty commitments relating to investments[131] and the dispute does not fall within the realm of municipal law.[132] The acts of the defendant state are measured against its international law obligations and not against its own constitutional or municipal prerogatives. Consequently, an arbitration tribunal could hold a government accountable in international law even though, within its municipal borders, its actions are justifiable and valid. Essentially, the arbitration tribunal has stronger powers than municipal courts. This was the hard lesson learnt by the South African government.

The fact that an arbitration tribunal can adjudicate on matters of public interest, and can interpret the constitutional duties of the government to determine whether actions taken under its constitutional duty to correct the injustices of the past amount to a breach of a BIT, situates such a dispute in the public law realm (even though it deals with international law obligations). However, because investment arbitrations have traditionally not been accessible to the public,[133] the finding that the governmental action breached a BIT is not, and often may not be, communicated to the government at large or to the public.

As a result of the confidentiality of investment arbitrations, the government's conduct can continue, with detrimental effects on the state coffers—especially if damages or legal costs have been awarded against the government. Similarly, the public is not able to hold the government accountable at the next elections if the awards remain

[129] *Foresti and others v South Africa* (n 127). See Schlemmer (n 61). See also Peter Leon, 'Creeping Expropriation of Mining Investments: An African Perspective' (2009) 27 J Energy Nat Resources L 597.

[130] See *Helen Suzman Foundation v President of the RSA* 2015 (2) SA 1 (CC), where it was held by Chief Justice Mogoeng that '[s]eparation of powers requires that the judiciary refrain from being unnecessarily prescriptive to both the executive and parliament' (at 32C); *Glenister v President of the RSA* 2011 (3) SA 347 (CC). See also the statement by Judge of Appeal Nugent: 'The more a decision is to be driven by considerations of executive policy the further it moves from being reviewable under PAJA and vice versa. That seems to me to be consistent with *SARFU [President of the Republic of South Africa v South African Rugby Football Union* 2000 1 SA 1 (CC)], in which it was said that one of the considerations to be taken into account in determining what constitutes administrative action is "how closely it is related ... to policy matters, which are not administrative"' *(Minister of Home Affairs v Scalabrini Centre* 2013 (6) SA 421 (SCA) 438B–C).

[131] This is in contrast to commercial arbitration or public-private arbitration, where the arbitrator deals with the parties' contractual or legal rights and obligations.

[132] Even when umbrella clauses play a role, the breach of contract will be considered a treaty breach and thus also falls within the international law ambit.

[133] See eg the first investment arbitration where South Africa was a defendant (see Poulsen (n 61)).

confidential. There is, thus, a real need for access to these awards. Government may well dispute the arbitrators' interpretation of its constitutional duties and argue that the finding is against public policy, but in order to address these issues in a transparent manner, publicity needs to be given to the processes and awards.

The South African government's reaction to the investment arbitrations was to reconsider its BIT and investor-state arbitration policy so as to ensure, among other things, the primacy of its constitutional commitments.[134] The development of a domestic legal framework for the promotion and protection of investment was initiated and a draft Promotion and Protection of Investment Bill was published for comment in late 2013. The purpose of the draft bill was aimed to achieve a balance between the rights and obligations of investors and those of the government.[135] It tried to prevent challenges of the government's decisions on beneficiation[136] and black economic empowerment before foreign or international tribunals as encroaching on or expropriating[137] investments of foreign investors, thus balancing the protection of investors' rights and the government's regulatory space, to give effect to its constitutional obligations without having to answer to international tribunals or pay damages for actions which were fully in line with its own internal policies and aimed to redress the inequalities of the past, but which could nevertheless be found to constitute violations of BIT obligations.

The Protection of Investment Act[138] was promulgated in 2015 and came into operation on 13 July 2018.[139] The Act applies to all investors irrespective of nationality and includes South African investors.[140] Investment, in turn, is defined in very broad terms in section 2 of the Act and the definition could be interpreted that it may, for all practical purposes, include normal contractual relations, even with the state.[141] The

[134] This happened shortly after the government's decision not to conclude any new BITs.

[135] The concern related to the fact that the investors had no obligations in a BIT framework but only rights (and these rights were more comprehensive than that of local investors), and that all the obligations were placed on the home state.

[136] Beneficiation is defined in s 1 of the Mineral and Petroleum Development Act 28 of 2002 in relation to any mineral resource, to mean the following: '(a) primary stage, which includes any process of the winning, recovering, extracting, concentrating, refining, calcining, classifying, crushing, screening, washing, reduction, smelting or gasification thereof; (b) secondary stage, which includes any action of converting a concentrate or mineral resource into an intermediate product; (c) tertiary stage, which includes any action of further converting that product into a refined product suitable for purchase by minerals-based industries and enterprises; and (d) final stage, which is the action of producing properly processed, cut, polished or manufactured products or articles from minerals accepted in the industry and trade as fully and finally processed or manufactured and value added products or articles'.

[137] The provisions on expropriation that were contained in the 2013 draft did not reappear in the following drafts or the final Act. However, a Draft Expropriation Bill has been published since (Government Gazette 42127 of 21 December 2018). Furthermore, even though s 10 of the Protection of Investment Act 22 of 2015 deals with the '[l]egal protection of investment' by providing that '[i]nvestors have the right to property in terms of section 25 of the Constitution', a decision was made by parliament to amend the Constitution to make provision for expropriation with the possibility of paying no compensation at all. A draft bill (Constitution Eighteenth Amendment Bill) to this effect was published on 13 December 2019. See <http://pmg-assets.s3-website-eu-west-1.amazonaws.com/191203Draft_advertised.pdf> accessed 25 September 2020. See also Government Gazette 42902 of 13 December 2019.

[138] Protection of Investment Act 22 of 2015.

[139] GN 395 in Government Gazette 41766 of 13 July 2018.

[140] An 'investor' is defined as 'an enterprise making an investment in the Republic regardless of nationality': s 1 of the Protection of Investment Act.

[141] See s 2(2)(e), Protection of Investment Act and the discussion under section II.B.4 of this chapter in the text at n 152.

only limitation to potential interaction with the state is found in the definition of dispute, which limits it to claims that the investor has that the government has allegedly breached the protection provided for in this Act.

The Act has several other noteworthy features: first, it omits the investor-state dispute resolution mechanisms provided for in South Africa's BITs. For all practical purposes, mediation is the preferred avenue of dispute resolution,[142] although an investor 'is not precluded from approaching any competent court, independent tribunal or statutory body within the Republic for the resolution of a dispute relating to an investment'.[143] Second, it significantly restricts the availability of international arbitration[144] by allowing it only after exhaustion of domestic remedies, if the government consents, and only 'between [South Africa] and the home state of the applicable investor'.[145]

The Act thus effectively precludes future investors from taking any investment-related dispute with the government to arbitration.[146] This also creates a dichotomy because, in terms of section 15(2), 'any investments made after the termination of such treaties, but before promulgation of this Act, will be governed by the general South African law'. There is no provision in 'general South African law' which would prevent an investor from proposing arbitration as a means of dispute resolution in a dispute with the government or public body. And, as is discussed in the next subsection, international commercial disputes may be subjected to international commercial arbitration even if the other party to the agreement is a public body or an organ of state.

4 International Commercial Disputes

The International Arbitration Act,[147] which, inter alia, adopts the UNCITRAL Model Law on International Commercial Arbitration, came into operation on 20 December 2017. Section 7 sets out the scope of international commercial arbitration,[148] and the provisions of the Model Law apply if South Africa is the juridical seat of the arbitration.

Furthermore, the Act binds 'public bodies',[149] 'subject to the provisions of section 13 of the Protection of Investment Act, 2015 ... and applies to any international commercial arbitration in terms of an arbitration agreement to which a public body is

[142] See s 13(1)–(3) Protection of Investment Act and the Mediation Rules, 2018 RGN 712/41767/19 (13 July 2018).

[143] See s 13(4) of the Protection of Investment Act.

[144] The initial bill contained the possibility of domestic arbitration, but this was removed completely from the Protection of Investment Act.

[145] See s 13(5) of the Protection of Investment Act.

[146] No such provision applies to other forms of international commercial arbitration: see s 5 of the International Arbitration Act. The arbitration route still exists for those investors whose investments are protected by BITs that are still in force, and in terms of the survival clauses of the BITs that have been (and will be) terminated: see Engela C Schlemmer, 'Dispute Settlement in Investment-Related Matters: South Africa and the BRICS' as part of the 'Symposium on the BRICS Approach to the Investment Treaty System' in (2018) 112 AJIL Unbound 212–16; Engela C Schlemmer 'Investor Protection in South Africa – Eroded Bit by Bit' in Congyan Cai, Huiping Chen, and Yifei Wang (eds), *The BRICS in the New International Legal Order on Investment: Reformers or Disruptors* (Brill Nijhoff 2020) 113, 154–55.

[147] Act 15 of 2017, Government Gazette 41347 of 20 December 2017.

[148] The objective of the Act, briefly stated, is the incorporation of the Model Law on International Commercial Arbitration, as adopted by the United Nations Commission on International Trade Law, into South African law, and to provide anew for the recognition and enforcement of foreign arbitral awards.

[149] See s 1 of International Arbitration Act for the definition of 'public body'.

a party'.[150] The implication is that investment-related disputes arising out of investments made after 13 July 2018 which involve the state or public bodies are excluded from the scope of the International Arbitration Act. This limitation does not apply, however, to 'any investments made after the termination of [BITs] ... but before promulgation of this Act'; those investments are 'governed by the general South African law'.[151] This would mean that those latter investment disputes can be subjected to arbitration as there is no general prohibition on the arbitrability of investment disputes in general South African law. By contrast, a dispute that arises in a contractual agreement between the state or a public body and a party in relation to an agreement (which may amount to an investment) concluded after 13 July 2018—the date when the Promotion of Investment Act entered into force—which may fall under the scope of application of that Act cannot be subjected to international commercial arbitration. If, however, the dispute relates to a matter that does not fall within the ambit of the Protection of Investment Act, such a dispute may be resolved through international commercial arbitration or, for that matter, domestic arbitration, as there is no prohibition on the state or public bodies to participate in domestic arbitration.

It is, therefore, relevant to briefly consider the scope of the Protection of Investment Act. Section 1 provides that '"dispute" means a claim by an investor, instituted in accordance with section 13, that the government has allegedly breached the protection provided for in this Act'.[152] An 'investment', in turn, is defined in section 2 as follows:

> (1) For the purpose of this Act, an investment is—
> (a) any lawful enterprise established, acquired or expanded by an investor in accordance with the laws of the Republic, committing resources of economic value over a reasonable period of time, in anticipation of profit;
> (b) the holding or acquisition of shares, debentures or other ownership instruments of such an enterprise; or
> (c) the holding, acquisition or merger by such an enterprise with another enterprise outside the Republic to the extent that such holding, acquisition or merger with another enterprise outside the Republic, has an effect on an investment contemplated by paragraphs (a) and (b) in the Republic;
> (2) For the purposes of the definition of 'investment', an enterprise may possess assets such as, amongst others—
> (a) shares as defined by the Companies Act, 2008 (Act No. 71 of 2008), stocks, debentures, securities as defined in the Financial Markets Act, 2012

[150] See s 5 of International Arbitration Act.

[151] See s 15 of the Protection of Investment Act.

[152] The Protection of Investment Act, in s 13(1), provides that '[a]n investor that has a dispute in respect of action taken by the government, which action affected an investment of such foreign investor, may within six months of becoming aware of the dispute request the Department to facilitate the resolution of such dispute by appointing a mediator.' It is obvious that the action complained about must relate to a breach of the provisions of this Act (see ibid s 13(3)(d)). It is hypothetically possible (similar to instances of actions covered by umbrella clauses in BITs) that the actions of the government which amount to a breach of the Act could also amount to a breach of contract which could, had it not been for the Act, have been resolved by an arbitration tribunal.

(Act No. 19 of 2012), or other equity instruments of the enterprise or another enterprise;
(b) a debt security of another enterprise;
(c) loans to an enterprise;
(d) movable or immovable property or other property rights such as mortgages, liens or pledges;
(e) claims to money or to any performance under contract having a financial value;
(f) copyrights, know how, goodwill, or intellectual property rights such as patents, trademarks, industrial designs and trade names, to the extent that they are recognised under the law of South Africa;
(g) returns such as profits, dividends, royalties or income yielded by an investment; or
(h) rights or concessions conferred by law or under contract, including licenses to cultivate, extract or exploit natural resources.

Without an in-depth analysis, it can be pointed out that 'claims to money or to any performance under contract having a financial value' are simply claims arising from a contract. For example, a claim for contractual performance arising from a government party's action or omission would be based on the government's breach of a contract which would, in terms of the Protection of Investment Act, be considered an investment. Without the provisions of the Protection of Investment Act and the International Arbitration Act, this would have been a normal contractual dispute which could have been resolved through arbitration. Therefore, even disputes involving international commercial transactions and those involving government or public bodies could have been resolved by arbitration. The nature of the government or public body's act does not determine whether the act amounts to a breach of contract or not, and would thus not have an impact on the arbitrability of the dispute.[153]

As a result of the enactment of the Promotion of Investment Act, there is thus a marked distinction in the way in which international investors and international business people (or investments and international commercial transactions) are treated in relation to the resolution of disputes. Furthermore, the date on which the transaction was concluded can also play a significant role.

There is no clear policy reason for this difference but it may be the consequence of the two Acts having been introduced by different government departments. Be that as it may, the implications of the distinction between an investment, on the one hand, and an international commercial transaction, on the other, have not been carefully considered. It may be quite possible, in light of the different definitions that are generally used for describing 'investment', and what is considered an 'investment' for purposes of a treaty (or the Protection of Investment Act), that the same transaction ('an investment') may also be considered as an international commercial transaction for purposes of the application of the Model Law and thus the International Arbitration Act. Falling within the ambit of the Protection of Investment Act will

[153] See again the discussion above at sections II.C and III.B.2.

remove the option for arbitration and remove such a transaction from the ambit of the International Arbitration Act, which may arguably not bode well for foreigners doing business with and investing in South Africa. On the one hand, an arbitration tribunal is allowed to adjudicate a matter involving an act of a state organ or public body; on the other hand, arbitration is prohibited if it involves a dispute between a foreign investor and the state—such investor would have to exhaust local remedies and then resort to their home state for assistance.

A field for further investigation is to determine whether the potential exists for businesses to consider structuring business interactions with organs of state or public bodies in South Africa (and phrasing the dispute) in a way that avoids falling under the Protection of Investment Act, thus allowing them to choose international commercial arbitration when a dispute arises.

IV. Confidentiality of Arbitration: Public Policy and Accountability

A. Confidentiality

One of the reasons the South African government is not in favour of the use of arbitration in public-private partnership agreements is the need to build up a substantial legal precedent base and to promote a measure of transparency[154] in the interpretation of these agreements. This cannot be done unless arbitral awards are publicized. If arbitrations and awards are not publicized, public interest cannot be protected and government accountability cannot be ensured.

If all these issues were considered when the review of the BIT practice took place and the International Arbitration Act and the Protection of Investment Act were formulated and discussed, the rationale underlying the different approaches to arbitration with public bodies followed in the two Acts, and in the law generally, remain obscure. The current position in South Africa concerning the confidentiality of disputes involving the government or public bodies (whether in arbitration or mediation) also contains a dichotomy, as will be indicated.

There is no definitive obligation on parties in South Africa to keep an arbitration confidential.[155] Very little academic writing has addressed this aspect of arbitration. Although the privacy of arbitration is a generally accepted principle,[156] it is not contained in legislation or any common law source.[157] In *Replication Technology Group v Gallo Africa Ltd*,[158] the first case dealing with confidentiality, Judge Malan held that 'it seems to follow that the Arbitration Act does not treat arbitration proceedings as being inherently confidential. There is nothing in the Arbitration Act that suggests

[154] See n 99 above and accompanying text.

[155] See Schlemmer, 'Regsaard van arbitrasieverrigtinge' (n 106) 741 ff and the sources referred to therein.

[156] See also IM Rautenbach, 'Private arbitrasie en die handves van regte' [2010] Tydskrif vir die Suid-Afrikaanse Reg/J South Afr L 185, 190 ff.

[157] See *Replication Technology Group v Gallo Africa Ltd* 2009 (5) SA 531 (GSJ) 546H. See also Butler and Finsen (n 58) 213–14.

[158] *Replication Technology Group v Gallo Africa Ltd* (n 157) 546H.

that arbitration proceedings are confidential.'[159] There is, thus, no general obligation of confidentiality unless the parties have agreed to it.

In the light of the topic under discussion, the importance of public arbitrations and arbitral awards being made public, particularly those concerning issues of public policy, cannot be stressed enough. Publication would encourage legal certainty, aid the development of legal rules in that particular field, and ensure transparency and accountability, especially when the state is involved. It is noteworthy that, during the discussions of the International Arbitration Bill in the Justice and Correctional Services Committee meeting of the National Assembly, the Department of Justice and Constitutional Development answered a question on arbitration between private parties and the state as follows:

> [A]rbitration between private parties would be private to protect their trade secrets. Arbitration between private parties and the state would be public. This is because the public interest in transparency overrides any concerns of confidentiality which the state may have in keeping such arbitration confidential.[160]

Accordingly, section 11 of the International Arbitration Act provides that:

> (1) Arbitration proceedings to which a public body is a party are held in public, unless for compelling reasons, the arbitral tribunal directs otherwise.
> (2) Where the arbitration is held in private, the award and all documents created for the arbitration which are not otherwise in the public domain must be kept confidential by the parties and tribunal, except to the extent that the disclosure of such documents may be required by reason of a legal duty or to protect or enforce a legal right.

However, the Arbitration Act, which deals with domestic arbitrations and also binds the state, contains no similar provision. The legislature had foregone the opportunity to harmonise the approaches to issues of public policy and confidentiality

[159] ibid 547C–D; see also *MV Alina II, Transnet Ltd v MV Alina II* 2013 (6) SA 556 (WCC). This is also the position taken by the Commercial Rules for Domestic Arbitration of the Arbitration Foundation of South Africa (AFSA), which specifically deal with the question of confidentiality (available at <https://arbitration.co.za/domestic-arbitration/commercial-rules/> accessed 6 January 2025). Article 21.2.2 provides that, 'save as is required by law, or for the exercise of a party's rights in a court of law, the Secretariat and the Registrar shall, unless the parties in writing notify the Secretariat otherwise, maintain confidentiality in regard to any matter being dealt with or dealt with by the Foundation'. See also *Replication Technology Group* (n 157) 548A (stating that '[a]rbitrations under the rules of AFSA are to be private, not necessarily confidential'). The AFSA rules provide in Article 21.2.1 that 'the arbitration proceedings shall be conducted in private, and a party shall be entitled to require the arbitrator to exclude therefrom any person whose presence is not reasonably required by another party'.

[160] See Justice and Correctional Services, 'Protected Disclosures Amendment Bill: NCOP Amendments; International Arbitration Bill: Briefing' (14 June 2017) <https://pmg.org.za/committee-meeting/24601/> accessed 6 January 2025. In terms of rr 12 and 19 of the Regulations on Mediation Rules of 2018 (GenN 395 in Government Gazette 41766 of 13 July 2018), mediation proceedings are confidential with there being an 'obligation to maintain the confidential nature of the mediation proceedings and or information disclosed therein' but an exemption exists inter alia 'if disclosure is compelled by law'. Whether the same arguments that are raised concerning accountability and transparency in relation to arbitration do also apply in the case of mediation is only doubtworthy if one were to consider that the purpose of mediation is to come to an agreement.

in the two statutes. There is no logical reason for the different approaches. Also, in cases involving investor-state arbitrations, there is no obligation on the parties to have the arbitration in public or to have the award published. This is in stark contrast to the international development with the United Nations Convention on Transparency in Treaty-based Investor-State Arbitration[161] and the UNCITRAL Rules on Transparency in Treaty-based Investor-State Arbitration,[162] which provide for transparency and accessibility to the treaty-based investor-state arbitrations. Also, the Regulations on Mediation Rules of 2018,[163] made in terms of section 14 of the Protection of Investment Act, do not make provision for transparency.[164] Regulation 19(2) provides that:

> The obligation to maintain the confidential nature of the mediation proceedings and or information disclosed therein may be dispensed with-
> (a) if disclosure is compelled by law;
> (b) to the extent necessary to give effect to any agreement which the parties to the dispute may reach during these proceedings or to enforce any agreement to settle or resolve the whole or any part of the dispute; or
> (c) if the parties to the mediation agree in writing to the disclosure of confidential information.

This contrasts with international commercial arbitration involving a public body, in which public arbitrations are now the norm, 'unless for compelling reasons, the arbitral tribunal directs otherwise'. Mediation and domestic arbitrations (also investment-related domestic arbitrations) have no similar requirement.

The privacy of arbitration is recognized by the South African courts, with the Supreme Court of Appeal holding that parties who choose arbitration waive their right to a public hearing.[165] The Constitutional Court, taking a different angle, held that by choosing arbitration, parties merely choose not to exercise their right of access to court enshrined in section 34[166] of the Constitution.[167] Because private (consensual) arbitration is normally confidential, section 34 does not apply.[168] However, that does not mean that the right to access to court no longer exists. Some authors argue that the Constitutional Court's approach on this issue should be reconsidered

161 United Nations Convention on Transparency in Treaty-based Investor-State Arbitration (adopted 10 December 2014, entered into force 18 October 2017) A/RES/69/119, Annex (Mauritius Convention).

162 Effective as of 1 April 2014, available at <https://uncitral.un.org/sites/uncitral.un.org/files/media-documents/uncitral/en/rules-on-transparency-e.pdf> accessed 6 January 2025.

163 GN R712 of 2018 Government Gazette 41767 of 13 July 2018.

164 reg 19.

165 *Telcordia Technologies* (n 71) 291A.

166 See s 34 of the Constitution, which provides that '[e]veryone has the right to have any dispute that can be resolved by the application of law decided in a fair public hearing before a court or, where appropriate, another independent and impartial tribunal or forum.'

167 *Lufuno Mphaphuli & Associates* (n 74) 599D–E. For a detailed discussion see Rautenbach (n 156) 185 ff. See also Schlemmer, 'The Interaction' (n 106) 666 ff.

168 *Lufuno Mphaphuli & Associates* (n 74) 591A–C and 592 B–C.

in light of the guarantee contained in section 34.[169] Due to the exponential growth in arbitrations and its implications for legal development (or the lack thereof if awards are not published), a change in the general approach to the confidentiality of arbitrations might be necessary from both a constitutional law and global governance perspective, especially when a public body is involved.

B. Accountability of Organs of State

It is important to note, especially in relation to the confidentiality of arbitration proceedings and awards, that the National Assembly has an obligation to provide mechanisms to maintain oversight of any organ of state in terms of s 55(2) of the Constitution.[170]

Government departments and public bodies which are financially affected by arbitral awards are accountable to the National Assembly. The National Assembly also has a constitutional duty to hold government officials and public bodies accountable for actions causing disputes (whether relating to BITs or merely contracts) which impact on the government's budget. Arguably, section 55(2) of the Constitution can be interpreted to mean that if arbitration (and mediation) proceedings involving public bodies and their awards are not disclosed to the National Assembly,[171] and in the absence of procedures to ensure disclosure, the National Assembly would be in violation of its constitutional obligations.[172]

In order to foster a culture of transparency and accountability in public (and private) bodies, effect has been given to the right of access to information in the Promotion of Access to Information Act,[173] in terms of which the public can request access to records if they comply with the requirements of the Act.[174] However, one must first be aware of the existence of the arbitration and its award before one could consider relying on this Act, which reinforces the point that when the public interest or public policy is at stake, confidentiality should only be allowed in exceptional instances.[175]

[169] See Rautenbach (n 156) 192.

[170] See also nn 14–16 above and accompanying text.

[171] ie if there are no mechanisms in place to ensure that arbitral proceedings and awards are notified to it.

[172] The same arguments can apply to a potential referral for investigation of state conduct to the Public Protector, who has the power 'to investigate any conduct in state affairs, or in the public administration in any sphere of government, that is alleged or suspected to be improper or to have resulted in any impropriety or prejudice, to report on that conduct and to take appropriate remedial action, in order to strengthen and support constitutional democracy in the Republic': see the preamble to the Public Protector Act 23 of 1994.

[173] Act 2 of 2000.

[174] See eg the discussion in De la Harpe (n 23) 91, in relation to tender documents and tender processes, and the sources cited therein.

[175] The provisions of s 42 of the Promotion of Access to Information Act address the ground allowing the information officer of a public body to refuse a request for access to a record of the body if the record inter alia concerns the commercial activities of public bodies and if disclosure would harm the commercial interests of the public body or prejudice a public body in commercial competition.

V. Concluding Remarks

The South African approach to arbitration to which the state is a party is not uniform. In some instances arbitration with a public body is allowed, in others it is not, and no clear reasons can be established for the divergent approaches.

An investment that is not protected under a BIT no longer entitles the investor to use arbitration to resolve disputes with a public body, if such an investment was made after the coming into operation of the Protection of Investment Act. If the investment was made prior to the coming into operation of the Act, such an investor may potentially be able to use arbitration if the government or public body agrees to it.

Other investors who can still rely on investor-state arbitration clauses in a BIT (or on the sunset clause of a terminated BIT) may still make use of international investment arbitration with the state.

If a person is not classified as an investor, and their business activities fall within the ambit of the International Arbitration Act and the UNCITRAL Model Law, international commercial arbitration with the state or public bodies is possible. If, however, the transaction is not classified as an international commercial transaction (hence qualifying for international commercial arbitration) or as an investment (and thus disqualified from using arbitration), domestic arbitration in terms of the Arbitration Act may be possible. As discussed, there is no prohibition on the use of arbitration for normal commercial transactions between private and public actors. For purposes of the determination of compensation after expropriation, for the time being at least, arbitration is prescribed.[176]

Arbitration between the state, public bodies, and individuals is mandated by a number of statutes and, apart from the review of administrative action and the Protection of Investment Act, there is no prohibition on the use of arbitration when dealing with the state. Arbitration is allowed for the purposes of certain types of business-related transactions (international commercial transactions) but not for others (investments). Arbitration with the state is sometimes prescribed, but in instances relating to investments it is prohibited. No clear-cut public policy reasons are provided for this dichotomy.

The existence of this dichotomy, however, makes it possible for potential investors to carefully consider the different provisions in the respective Acts and to draft their agreements or craft their business plans in such a way that they either do or do not fall within the ambit of the International Arbitration Act or the Protection of Investment Act, depending on whether or not they want arbitration as a means of dispute settlement. This creates the opportunity for forum shopping.

Allowing the state or public entities to resolve disputes through arbitration can assist in finding quicker solutions to disputes, but it can also impede transparency and accountability, especially where it relates to public bodies. The legislature took this into account when the International Arbitration Act was drafted and it was provided that, in matters involving public bodies, the arbitration should be public. This is a step in the right direction which should be followed when the current Arbitration Act is amended or replaced. That publicity should be given to disputes involving public

[176] See n 136 above.

bodies was, however, not considered when the Regulations on Mediation Rules of 2018 were drafted, again providing for a dichotomy, but this time in the approach to the transparency of proceedings that involve public bodies. Again, no clear policy reasons could be found for the contrasting approach.

Nevertheless, due to the importance of transparency and accountability where public bodies are concerned, it is submitted that arbitration in matters relating to the validity of government actions or those of a public body is not ideal. The first Chief Justice of South Africa after 1994, Justice Chaskalson, said the following:

> Whilst there is no bright line between public and private law, administrative law, which forms the core of public law, occupies a special place in our jurisprudence. It is an incident of the separation of powers under which courts regulate and control the exercise of public power by the other branches of government. It is built on constitutional principles which define the authority of each branch of government, their inter-relationship and the boundaries between them.[177]

It is thus the responsibility of the courts to ensure that unconstitutional conduct is declared invalid.[178] Using arbitral tribunals to determine disputes relating to constitutionality and public policy should not be permitted.

Select Materials

Bibliography

Bolton, Phoebe, *The Law of Government Procurement in South Africa* (LexisNexis 2007)

Brand, FDJ, 'Judicial Review of Arbitration Awards' (2014) 2 SLR 247

Brickhill, Jason and Max du Plessis, 'Two's Company, Three's a Crowd: Public Interest Intervention in Investor-State Arbitration (*Piero Foresti v South Africa*)' (2011) 27(1) SAJHR 152

Butler, David, 'South African Arbitration Legislation – The Need for Reform' (1994) 27 Comp Int'l LJ Southern Afr 118

Butler, DW and E Finsen, *Arbitration in South Africa – Law and Practice* (Juta 1993)

Gauntlett, Jeremy, 'The Legal System of South Africa and Its Approach to Arbitration' (2007) 20(2) Adv 28

Hoexter, Cora, *Administrative Law in South Africa* (Juta 2012)

Lourens, Marna, 'The Issue of Arbitrability in the Context of International Commercial Arbitration' (1999) 11 SA Merc LJ 363 and 439

Penfold, Glenn and Pippa Reyburn, 'Public Procurement' in *Constitutional Law of South Africa* (looseleaf, 2nd edn, 2014) (Original Service March 2012) ch 25–8

Ramsden, Peter (assisted by Kelly Ramsden), *The Law of Arbitration: South African & International Arbitration* (Juta 2009)

[177] *Pharmaceutical Manufacturers Association of SA: In re Ex parte President of the RSA* 2000 (2) SA 674 (CC) 696C–I (also quoted in *Transnet Ltd v Goodman Brothers (Pty) Ltd* 2001 (1) SA 853 (SCA) 865B–C).

[178] See also *AllPay Consolidated Investment Holdings* (n 52).

Schlemmer, Engela C, 'An Overview of South Africa's Bilateral Investment Treaties and Investment Policy' (2016) 31(1) ICSID Review–FILJ 167

Schlemmer, Engela C, 'The Interaction Between Public Policy, Constitutional Rights and Public-Private Arbitration' [2016] Tydskrif vir die Suid-Afrikaanse Reg/J South Afr L 500–18 and 660–79

Schlemmer, Engela C, 'Investor Protection in South Africa – Eroded Bit by Bit' in Congyan Cai, Huiping Chen, and Yifei Wang (eds), *The BRICS in the New International Legal Order on Investment. Reformers or Disruptors* (Brill Nijhoff 2020) 113

Schneiderman, David, 'Promoting Equality, Black Economic Empowerment, and the Future of Investment Rules' (2009) 25(2) SAJHR 246

Schulze, WG, 'Of Arbitration, Politics and the Price of Neglect – South African International Arbitration Legislation Continues to Lag Behind: *Bidoli v Bidoli*' (2011) 23 SA Merc LJ 291

Sonnekus, JC, 'Procurement Contracts and Underlying Principles of the Law – No Special Dispensation for Organs of State (Part 1 – the Principles)' [2014] Tydskrif vir die Suid-Afrikaanse Reg/J South Afr L 320

Taitz, Nicholas, *Arbitration Procedures in South Africa* (2016)

Wilske, Stephan and Jade G Ewers, 'Why South Africa Should Update its International Arbitration Legislation. An Appeal from the International Arbitration Community for Legal Reform in South Africa' (2011) 28(1) J Int'l Arb 1

Yazbek, Nicole, 'Bilateral Investment Treaties: The Foreclosure of Domestic Policy Space' (2010) 17 SAJ IA 103

Legislation

Arbitration Act 42 of 1965
Constitution of the Republic of South Africa 1996
Expropriation Act 63 of 1975
Extension of Security of Tenure Act 62 of 1997
International Commercial Arbitration Act 15 of 2017
Labour Relations Act 66 of 1995
Local Government: Municipal Systems Act 32 of 2000
Municipal Finance Management Act 56 of 2003
National Environmental Management Act 107 of 1998
Nuclear Energy Act 46 of 1999
Patent Act 57 of 1978
Preferential Procurement Policy Framework Act 5 of 2000
Promotion of Administrative Justice Act 3 of 2000
Protection of Investment Act 11 of 2015
Public Finance Management Act 1 of 1999
Water Services Act 108 of 1997

Cases

Afrox Healthcare Bpk v Strydom 2002 (6) SA 21 (SCA)
Airports Company South Africa Ltd v ISO Leisure OR Tambi (Pty) Ltd 2011 (4) SA 642 (GSJ)
Barkhuizen v Napier 2007 (5) SA 323 (CC)
Brisley v Drotsky 2002 (4) SA 1 (SCA)
Cape Metro Council v Metro Inspection Services (Western Cape) CC 2001 (3) SA 1013 (SCA)
Goodman Brothers (Pty) Ltd v Transnet Ltd 1998 (4) SA 989 (W)
Gray Moodliar Inc v Nelson Mandela Bay Metropolitan Municipality and Another 2019 (10) BLLR 1163
Indwe Aviation (Pty) Ltd v Petroleum Oil and Gas Corporation of South Africa (Pty) Ltd (No 1) 2012 (6) SA 96 (WCC)
Logbro Properties CC v Bedderson NO 2003 (2) SA 460 (SCA)
Lufuno Mphaphuli & Associates (Pty) Ltd v Andrews 2009 (4) SA 529 (CC)
MV Alina II, Transnet Ltd v MV Alina II 2013 (6) SA 556 (WCC)
Ntshangase v MEC for Finance, Kwazulu-Natal 2010 (3) SA 201 (SCA)
Pharmaceutical Manufacturers Association of SA: In re Ex parte President of the RSA 2000 (2) SA 674 (CC)
Piero Foresti, Laura de Carli and others v Republic of South Africa, ICSID Case No ARB(AF)/07/1, Award (4 August 2010)
Replication Technology Group v Gallo Africa Ltd 2009 (5) SA 531 (GSJ)
South African National Parks v MTO Foresty (Pty) Ltd 2018 (5) SA 177 (SCA)
Telcordia Technologies Inc v Telkom SA Ltd 2007 (3) SA 266 (SCA)
Transnet Ltd v Goodman Brothers (Pty) Ltd 2001 (1) SA 853 (SCA)
Waenhuiskrans Arniston Ratepayers Association v Verreweide Eiendomsontwikkeling (Edms) Bpk 2011 (3) SA 434 (WCC)

Reports

Government Position Paper, 'Bilateral Investment Policy Framework Review' General Notice 961, in Government Gazette 32386 (7 July 2009)
Law Society of South Africa, *Annual Report April 2017 to March 2018* (2018)
Law Society of South Africa, *Annual Report April 2018 to March 2019* (2019)
Research Unit, Parliament of the Republic of South Africa, 'The International Arbitration Bill [B10-2017]' (13 June 2017) <pmg-assets.s3-website-eu-west-1.amazonaws.com/171101researcher.pdf>
South African Law Commission, D*iscussion Paper 69, Project 94: Arbitration: A Draft International Arbitration Act for South Africa* (South African Law Commission 1996) <www.justice.gov.za/salrc/dpapers/dp69.pdf>
South African Law Commission, 'Project 94: Domestic Arbitration Report' (May 2001) <www.justice.gov.za/salrc/reports/r_prj94_dom2001.pdf>

20

Private-Public Arbitration in Australia

Public Law Concerns, Private Law Responses

Caroline Henckels[*]

I. Introduction

This chapter analyses the disjuncture between the law regulating private-public arbitration in Australia and principles of Australian public law. Public debate about the merits of investment treaty arbitration ignited when Philip Morris Asia brought an investment claim against Australia's tobacco plain packaging legislation, [1] However, the issue of other arbitrations taking place between governments and private actors attracted comparatively scant attention until 2020, when a state government legislated to nullify an arbitral award made against it in favour of a mining company owned by a prominent Australian. The legislation's effect was to prevent the company and its owner from recovering billions of dollars from the government and to retroactively remove any right to claim damages for any breaches of the agreement.[2] Yet despite the significant media attention raised by the award and the legislation, the question of the aptness of using arbitration to resolve disputes under government contracts remains underexplored.

Section II of this chapter discusses the significance of private-public arbitration in Australia both on the basis of investment treaties and pursuant to contracts. Section III examines several points of tension that arise between Australian public law and arbitration law: the less rigorous test for arbitrator impartiality than for judges and administrative tribunal members, the absence of transparency and participation mechanisms in the law governing contract-based arbitrations, and the limited ability for courts to exercise supervisory functions over arbitral tribunals vis-à-vis administrative tribunals and lower courts. This section discusses the way that Australian law regulates government contracting and private-public arbitration, noting that governments largely enjoy freedom to contract like any other person or body, and that public law places few controls on government contracting and the contracting parties' conduct in relation to third parties. Section IV analyses some as-yet-unresolved constitutional law questions relating to Australia's arbitration legislation: whether the law might lack constitutional validity for undermining the courts' integrity by enlisting

* The author wishes to thank the Hon Robert French AC, as well as Janina Boughey, Lisa Burton Crawford, Patrick Emerton, Graeme Hodge, Luke Nottage, and Stephan Schill, for helpful discussions.

[1] *Philip Morris Asia Ltd v Commonwealth of Australia*, PCA Case No 2012-12 (UNCITRAL), Award on Jurisdiction and Admissibility (17 December 2015).

[2] The law survived a constitutional challenge and is now the subject of an investor-state dispute brought by the Australian company's Singaporean subsidiary (pending at the time of writing): *Zeph Investments Pte. Ltd v The Commonwealth of Australia*, PCA Case No 2023-40 (UNCITRAL).

Caroline Henckels, *Private-Public Arbitration in Australia* In: *The Comparative Constitutional Foundations of Private-Public Arbitration*. Edited by: Stephan W. Schill, Oxford University Press. © Stephan W. Schill 2025.
DOI: 10.1093/9780191987960.003.0020

courts in the enforcement of arbitral awards and/or for impermissibly vesting arbitrators with federal judicial power, and whether legislative authorization is required for governmental decisions to enter into treaties containing an arbitration mechanism.

II. Private-Public Arbitration in the Spotlight

A. Investment Treaty Arbitration

The issue of investment treaty arbitration attracted little political or scholarly attention in Australia until 2010, when the Australian Productivity Commission[3] released a research report on trade agreements. The report concluded (among other findings) that the economic rationale for entering treaties containing an investor-state dispute settlement mechanism was weak, and that Australia risked incursions into its regulatory autonomy and public finances by entering into such agreements.[4] The Commission recommended that the Australian government should seek to avoid including investor-state dispute settlement provisions in trade and investment treaties where the treaty's substantive obligations would grant greater substantive or procedural rights to foreign investors over their Australian counterparts.[5]

The former Labor-led (centre-left) coalition government's response to the report's findings, the Gillard Government Trade Policy Statement, announced the government's intention to discontinue the practice of including investor-state arbitration clauses in future investment treaties on the basis that the government did not support treaty provisions that would have the effect of hampering Australia's ability to regulate and take other actions to promote public welfare.[6] Of particular concern to the government were the planned plain tobacco packaging law and ensuring that the government would be able to continue to subsidize pharmaceuticals to consumers—a long-standing domestic political issue that had previously resulted in the programme being the subject of a carve-out in the Australia–United States Free Trade Agreement.[7]

Immediately after coming into force, the Tobacco Plain Packaging Act 2011 (Cth) and associated regulations became the subject of an investor-state arbitration under the Australia–Hong Kong Bilateral Investment Treaty.[8] Although decided in Australia's favour, the investment claim attracted negative public attention, and Australian scholars, like others, were concerned that an adverse tribunal decision (or the threat of such a decision) could have a chilling effect on governments' willingness

[3] The Australian Productivity Commission is an independent advisory body to government.

[4] See Australian Productivity Commission, 'Bilateral and Regional Trade Agreements' Research Report (2010) iv, xxxvi <www.pc.gov.au/inquiries/completed/trade-agreements/report/trade-agreements-report.pdf> accessed 28 January 2025.

[5] ibid xxxviii.

[6] Australian Government, Department of Foreign Affairs and Trade, 'Gillard Government Trade Policy Statement: Trading Our Way to More Jobs and Prosperity' (2011) <https://webarchive.nla.gov.au/awa/20110502020942/http://pandora.nla.gov.au/pan/126547/20110502-1209/www.dfat.gov.au/publications/trade/trading-our-way-to-more-jobs-and-prosperity.html> accessed 28 January 2025.

[7] Australia–US Free Trade Agreement (2004) Annex 2-C.

[8] *Philip Morris Asia v Australia* (n 1).

to enact public welfare measures,[9] and were concerned about the regime's lack of transparency and the prospect that tribunal decisions would not be made public.[10]

The policy of eschewing investor-state arbitration changed during the Liberal–National (conservative) administration from 2013 to 2022. The government determined that it would include investor-state arbitration provisions in trade and investment agreements on a case-by-case basis, but would not enter treaties that would 'restrict Australia's capacity to govern in the public interest'.[11] The election of the Labor government in 2022 resulted in a return to the approach of the previous Labor-led government, with the trade minister announcing that 'we will not include investor-state dispute settlement in any new trade agreement',[12] and the government embarking on a review of all of its treaties containing investor-state arbitration with a view to possible reform.[13]

B. Contract-Based Private-Public Arbitration

Although the relationship between government contracting and public law has attracted some scholarly attention,[14] far less attention has been paid to the use of arbitration under these contracts.

The federal government and the state and territory governments are party to several different types of contracts, each of which may contain an arbitration clause: procurement contracts, contracts for the provision of public services, resource extraction contracts, and public-private partnerships contracts (contracts for the construction, and sometimes operation, of public assets such as toll roads and prisons).[15] No empirical data is available that would give a complete picture of the prevalence of private-public contracts containing an arbitration clause, but publicly available information suggests that aside from contracts for resource extraction, there has been only a modest uptake of these types of agreements, which might explain their relative

[9] For example, Kyla Tienhaara, 'Regulatory Chill and the Threat of Arbitration: A View from Political Science' in Chester Brown and Kate Miles (eds), *Evolution in Investment Treaty Law and Arbitration* (CUP 2011) 606; Jonathan Bonnitcha, *Substantive Protection under Investment Treaties* (CUP 2014) 113–32.

[10] For example, Thomas Faunce, 'Australia's Embrace of Investor State Dispute Settlement: A Challenge to the Social Contract Ideal?' (2015) 69 Australian J Int'l Affairs 595.

[11] Australian Government, Department of Foreign Affairs and Trade, 'Investor-State Dispute Settlement' (2014), quoted in Lexology, 'It's Official – The Australian Government's Position on Investor-State Dispute Settlement'(2014) <https://www.lexology.com/library/detail.aspx?g=b3ccc9b6-fccb-4b5e-a0e2-b53843a5e11b>, accessed 28 January 2025. Labor maintained its previous stance of rejecting investor-state dispute settlement during this period: Australian Labor Party, 'Generating Jobs Through Trade and Investment' (2016) <https://parlinfo.aph.gov.au/parlInfo/download/library/partypol/4632700/upload_binary/4632700.pdf;fileType=application%2Fpdf#search=%22library/partypol/4632700%22> accessed 28 January 2025.

[12] Senator Don Farrell, 'Trading our way to greater prosperity and security: Albanese Government Trade and Investment Agenda' (14 November 2022) <https://www.trademinister.gov.au/minister/don-farrell/speech/trading-our-way-greater-prosperity-and-security> accessed 28 January 2025.

[13] See Australian Government, Department of Foreign Affairs and Trade, 'Review of Australia's Bilateral Investment Treaties' (2020) <https://www.dfat.gov.au/sites/default/files/review-australia-bilateral-investment-treaties.pdf> accessed 28 January 2025.

[14] See eg Nick Seddon, 'The Interaction of Contract and Executive Power' (2003) 31 FL Rev 541; KM Hayne, 'Government Contracts and Public Law' (2017) 41 MULR 155.

[15] See Hayne (n 14).

insulation from the political environment. The federal government, for example, generally eschews arbitration in contracts for the provision of goods and services.[16] State and territory governments sometimes provide for arbitration in their contracts, but frequently favour legal proceedings.[17] There are no legal constraints on governments that would prevent them in the future from entering into contracts that contain an arbitration clause.

When a government is acting in the exercise of its contractual rights—which would ordinarily be regarded as an exercise of a private law power—its actions may well have a public interest dimension. The involvement of taxpayers' money and governments' special responsibility to promote the public good in undertaking its activities distinguishes private-public contracts from purely private contracts.[18] By applying domestic law to exercises of power by public bodies, arbitrators contribute to the governance of those bodies. Yet, government accountability in relation to contracting decisions—including the decision to rely on arbitration rather than legal proceedings—has traditionally been understood as a political rather than legal issue.[19]

Australian arbitration law has few mechanisms in place to ensure that the public interest is not compromised where a public body agrees with a private entity to resort to arbitration in the event of a dispute, rather than having the dispute dealt with through ordinary court processes. There are no limitations or principles concerning in which cases, under which circumstances, and in relation to which subject matter any actor (including government) can enter into an arbitration agreement.[20] The parties are free to agree on a procedure for appointing arbitrators.[21] No special qualifications are required to conduct an arbitration, nor are there special rules that regulate, for example, the procedure for appointment of counsel or permissible communication between counsel and arbitrator. Arbitrators have the power to rule on the validity

[16] Australian Government, Department of Finance, 'Commonwealth Contract Terms' (2022) <https://www.finance.gov.au/sites/default/files/2022 08/Commonwealth_Contract_Terms_v7.0_5_September_2022.pdf> accessed 28 January 2025 (providing for mediation followed by legal proceedings).

[17] See eg Government of Victoria, Victorian Government Purchasing Board, 'Goods and Services Standard Contract Templates' (2024) <https://www.buyingfor.vic.gov.au/goods-and-services-standard-contract-templates> and 'Construction Standard Form Contracts' (2024) <https://www.buyingfor.vic.gov.au/construction-standard-form-contracts> (providing for mediation followed by arbitration); Northern Territory Government, 'Conditions of Contract – Quotation – Works' (2019) <https://nt.gov.au/__data/assets/pdf_file/0008/746225/v5.4-conditions-of-contract-quotation-works.pdf> (providing for mediation followed by legal proceedings) and 'Conditions of Contract – Supply of Goods Period Contract' (2019) <https://nt.gov.au/__data/assets/pdf_file/0004/746428/v5.4-conditions-of-contract-supply-of-goods-period-contract.pdf> (providing for mediation followed by 'independent expert determination'); Queensland Government, 'General Contract Conditions for General Goods and Services' (2024) <https://www.forgov.qld.gov.au/__data/assets/pdf_file/0025/187702/ggs-general-contract-conditions.pdf> (providing for negotiation followed by legal proceedings), all accessed 28 January 2025. Information is not readily available for all Australian jurisdictions.

[18] See Nicholas Seddon, *Government Contracts: Federal, State and Local* (7th edn, Federation Press 2023) 2-3.

[19] See eg Hayne (n 14) 165, 177.

[20] See eg Commercial Arbitration Act 2010 (NSW) s 7, Model Law art 7. The parties to any 'defined legal relationship' (be it contractual or otherwise) can make an arbitration agreement in which the parties agree to submit some or all disputes between them to arbitration.

[21] Failing which, a party can request the court's assistance in the appointment process: see eg Commercial Arbitration Act 2010 (NSW) s 11; Model Law art 11.

of the arbitration agreement and the extent of their own jurisdiction.[22] Moreover, the government is subject to arbitral awards in all cases and cannot claim immunity from their execution.[23] As section III demonstrates, the phenomenon of public-private arbitration appears not to have been contemplated by the framers of Australian arbitration legislation.

III. The Regulation of Private-Public Arbitration and Government Contracting

Commercial arbitration in Australia is regulated by state and territory legislation (domestic commercial arbitration) and by federal legislation (international commercial arbitration). All Australian states and territories have enacted uniform legislation based on the United Nations Commission on International Trade Law (UNCITRAL) Model Law on International Commercial Arbitration (Model Law),[24] while federal legislation (the International Arbitration Act 1974 (Cth)) governs international commercial arbitration.[25]

A. Tensions Between Arbitration Law and Principles of Australian Public Law

There are several areas in which Australian arbitration law and Australian public law are in tension with one another. The hallmarks of the judicial system include impartiality, proceedings conducted in public, participation of affected persons, and the opportunity for review or appeal of decisions made at first instance. Arbitration prioritizes party autonomy, confidentiality, finality, and enforceability of decisions, which, while unproblematic in the sphere of ordinary commercial arbitration between private parties, raises questions of suitability when government is a party to a dispute.

1 Arbitrator Impartiality

Arbitrators are appointed by the parties and are not expected to be fully independent of them. Under both the domestic and international commercial arbitration regimes, persons approached to serve as arbitrators must disclose 'any circumstances likely to give rise to justifiable doubts as to the person's impartiality or independence', and

[22] Model Law art 16.

[23] Commercial Arbitration Act 2010 (NSW) s 40; International Arbitration Act 1974 (Cth) s 2B.

[24] Commercial Arbitration Act 2010 (NSW); Commercial Arbitration Act 2011 (VIC); Commercial Arbitration Act 2011 (SA); Commercial Arbitration (National Uniform Legislation) Act 2011 (NT); Commercial Arbitration Act 2011 (Tas); Commercial Arbitration Act 2013 (Qld); Commercial Arbitration Act 2012 (WA); Commercial Arbitration Act 2017 (ACT) (not yet in force). The provisions referred to in this chapter are to the New South Wales legislation.

[25] This Act implements the Model Law as well as the Convention on the Settlement of Investment Disputes between States and Nationals of other States ('ICSID Convention') and the Convention on the Recognition and Enforcement of Foreign Arbitral Awards ('New York Convention').

must disclose any such circumstances that arise throughout the proceeding. The legal test for disqualification is met by establishing that there is 'a real danger' of bias on the part of the arbitrator.[26]

The test for bias in Australian administrative law, by comparison, requires a higher standard of impartiality by judges and administrative tribunal members.[27] A judge (whether hearing a private law or public law matter) or administrative tribunal member may be disqualified where a fair-minded and reasonably well-informed observer might conclude that the decision-maker might not bring an impartial or unprejudiced mind to the issues.[28] The 'real danger' test, which still governs arbitration, was abandoned in Australian administrative law in 1994 on the basis that to assess bias from the perspective of the court and not the perspective of members of the public (ie those who are subject to judicial and administrative decisions)[29] does not conform with a fundamental principle underpinning the impartiality doctrine: that justice must not only be done, but must also be *seen* to be done.[30]

The justification for the less strict 'real danger' test in the arbitration legislation is that arbitrators are providers of a commercial service and may well have business relationships or other professional connections with the parties.[31] Whether this rationale of service provision rings true in relation to private-public arbitrations is at least questionable, particularly given the importance that the High Court places upon the independence and impartiality of the judiciary.[32] It might be argued that private-public arbitrations, at the very least, demand a higher level of arbitral impartiality and independence than for ordinary commercial arbitrations—an issue that has long attracted concern in the literature on investor–state arbitration.[33]

2 Transparency and Participation

Unlike court proceedings involving contracts, arbitral proceedings are private under both the domestic and international commercial arbitration regimes, and neither the existence nor the outcome of proceedings is on the public record.[34] Rather, the law imposes a duty of confidence on the parties and the arbitral tribunal unless an

[26] Commercial Arbitration Act 2010 (NSW) s 12, Model Law art 12 (as well as the additional ground that 'the arbitrator does not possess the qualifications agreed to by the parties').

[27] Apparent bias. The test for actual bias requires proof that the decision-maker had prejudged the issue or had a closed mind: something that is very difficult to prove, requiring an assessment of the actual state of mind of a decision-maker. See Mark Aronson, Matthew Groves, and Greg Weeks, *Judicial Review of Administrative Action and Government Liability* (7th edn, Thomson 2017) 617–19.

[28] This is regarded as a question of possibility rather than probability: see *Ebner v Official Trustee in Bankruptcy, Clenae Pty Ltd v Australia and New Zealand Banking Group Ltd* (2000) 205 CLR 337, 343, 345.

[29] See *Webb v The Queen* (1994) 181 CLR 41, 50–51.

[30] See (explaining similar developments in English law) Mark Elliott, *Beatson, Matthews and Elliott's Administrative Law* (4th edn, OUP 2011) 309.

[31] Sam Luttrell, *Bias Challenges in International Commercial Arbitration: The Need for a 'Real Danger' Test* (Kluwer 2009) 4; Doug Jones, *Commercial Arbitration in Australia* (2nd edn, Thomson Reuters 2013) 143.

[32] That said, it seems unlikely that the prospect of public-private arbitrations was at the forefront of legislators' minds.

[33] See generally Gus Van Harten, *Investment Treaty Arbitration and Public Law* (OUP 2007).

[34] See Jones (n 31) 356–57 (with further references).

exception to the duty applies or both parties agree to opt out of the duty.[35] There is no statutory exception that would permit unilateral disclosure in the public interest, although under both regimes, a tribunal may exercise its discretion to permit the disclosure of confidential information on request of one of the parties after giving each party an opportunity to be heard.[36] Any such decision is subject to appeal to the Federal Court, which must balance the public interest in favour of disclosure against the party's interest in favour of preserving the confidentiality of the information.[37]

Although there are no cases directly on point, in the High Court case of *Esso Australia Resources Ltd v Plowman* (decided under previous provisions of the commercial arbitration legislation that did not oblige confidentiality), Mason CJ opined that 'governmental secrets' ought to be viewed differently from 'personal and commercial secrets'.[38] In Mason CJ's view, there should be a presumption in favour of disclosure of governmental information in the public interest because 'there may be circumstances, in which third parties and the public have a legitimate interest in knowing what has transpired in an arbitration'.[39] Other members of the High Court in this case similarly recognized that there would be an exception to any duty of confidentiality for governmental information on the basis of the desirability of transparency about governmental activities.[40] The extent to which these *obiter dicta* will be influential remains to be seen, but given that the presumption in favour of confidentiality may be overridden in the public interest, Mason CJ's judgment may well be persuasive. Still, unlike court proceedings, disclosure of the proceedings is far from automatic, and only a party to the arbitration could demand disclosure—it may well be that both government and contractor prefer confidentiality.

The legislation also does not provide any procedural safeguards that would ensure the representation of the public interest in private-public arbitrations or provide other ways for tribunals to inform themselves on relevant issues not raised by the parties. Again, we see a disjuncture between private-public arbitration and public law: in Australian courts, there is the possibility for third-party participation in litigation as an intervener[41] (including by the Attorney-General in relation to constitutional law issues)[42] and as amicus curiae (including by the Australian Human Rights Commission in matters raising human rights issues).[43] Third-party participation aims to prevent courts from deciding important issues without full argument. Given the absence of

[35] Commercial Arbitration Act 2010 (NSW) ss 27E–27I; International Arbitration Act 1974 (Cth) ss 23C–23D.

[36] Commercial Arbitration Act 2010 (NSW) s 26G; International Arbitration Act 1974 (Cth) s 23E. The legislation does not stipulate criteria upon which such a decision would be based.

[37] Commercial Arbitration Act 2010 (NSW) ss 27H–27I; International Arbitration Act 1974 (Cth) ss 23F and 23G.

[38] *Esso Australia Resources Ltd v Plowman* (1995) 183 CLR 10, 31 (Mason CJ).

[39] ibid.

[40] ibid 36 (Brennan J); 48 (Toohey J).

[41] Administrative Decisions (Judicial Review) Act 1977 (Cth) s 12.

[42] The federal and state Attorneys-General have rights to intervene in proceedings in any court which 'relate to a matter arising under the Constitution or involving its interpretation' (Judiciary Act 1903 (Cth) s 78A).

[43] Australian Human Rights Commission Act 1986 (Cth) s 46PV(1)(a) (where the Commissioner thinks that the orders sought, or likely to be sought, may affect to a significant extent the human rights of persons who are not parties to the proceedings).

any restrictions on the subject matter of government contracting, to the extent that arbitrators decide cases that raise broader issues of public interest, it might be proper for them to permit intervention or amici, as has taken place in the realm of investor-state arbitration.

3 Judicial Oversight

Consistently with the purpose of arbitration—expeditious, confidential, and final dispute resolution—opportunity for judicial oversight of arbitral awards by the courts is significantly circumscribed compared with the courts' power to review or determine appeals from the decisions of tribunals or lower courts as a matter of public law. Where the conduct of government or the exercise of public power is at issue, one might expect not only that decisions pertaining to governmental powers ought to be made in accordance with democratically produced legal rules and standards but that there should be a greater degree of judicial supervision of erroneous decisions than the current law permits.[44]

(a) Appeal

The international commercial arbitration legislation does not permit appeals. Appeals from arbitral tribunal decisions under the domestic commercial arbitration legislation are possible, but only where both of the parties agree that an application may be made, and with leave of the court.[45] This provision is modelled on the UK legislation.[46] An appeal is only possible in respect of an error of law: the applicant must satisfy the court firstly that the decision on the question was 'obviously wrong' (ie obvious and readily apparent)[47] or that the question of law is one of 'general public importance' and is open to 'at least serious doubt', and secondly that, despite the agreement of the parties to resolve the matter by arbitration, it would be 'just and proper' for the court to determine the question of law asked.[48] There are no cases involving private-public arbitration or others that shed light on the issue of 'general public importance', although the previous legislation expressed this concept as where 'the determination of the question may add, or may be likely to add, substantially to the certainty of commercial law' rather than other broader issues of public interest.[49]

(b) Subject Matter of Dispute Not Arbitrable

Under both the domestic and international commercial arbitration regimes, an award can be set aside where the subject matter of the dispute was not capable of settlement by arbitration.[50]

[44] By way of comparison, the Federal Court and High Court have supervisory jurisdiction over administrative tribunals and lower courts.

[45] Commercial Arbitration Act 2010 (NSW) s 34A.

[46] See Jones (n 31) 494, 503.

[47] ibid 504.

[48] Commercial Arbitration Act 2010 (NSW) s 34A.

[49] See Jones (n 31) 504.

[50] Model Law art 34(2)(b)(i) (incorporated into Australian law by virtue of the International Arbitration Act 1974 (Cth) s 16); Commercial Arbitration Act 2010 (NSW) s 34(2)(b)(i).

Under the domestic arbitration legislation, Australian courts have generally taken a liberal approach to arbitrability, but have held that some issues are unsuitable for arbitration where they raise an issue of policy that is more suitable for determination by the courts, or the interests of third parties are affected by the dispute.[51] These cases have involved questions of one of the disputing parties' compliance with legislative regimes, such as competition law,[52] the granting of intellectual property rights,[53] tax law,[54] corporations law,[55] insolvency law,[56] and the law pertaining to industrial relations.[57]

The situation is less clear in relation to the international commercial arbitration legislation, although there are some intriguing hints by some federal judges as to the limits of arbitrability. In the international arbitration case of *Comandate Marine Corp v Pan Australia Shipping Pty Ltd*, one of the Federal Court judges stated that the notion of non-arbitrability rested on a 'sufficient element of legitimate public interest in [the] subject matters' that made arbitration 'inappropriate', and that 'the identification and control of these subjects was the legitimate domain of national legislatures and courts'.[58] In the earlier case of *Tanning Research Laboratories Inc v O'Brien*, two members of the High Court held that arbitrability was contingent upon the dispute 'perhaps . . . relating to rights which are not required to be determined exclusively by the exercise of judicial power', which hardly sheds much light on the issue.[59] There is no case law in this area in relation to private-public arbitrations, but this could be a potential entry point in the future for arguments of non-arbitrability to be raised (ie where the subject matter of the dispute gave rise to public interest concerns). Still, only a party to the arbitration could make such an application, and commentators take the view that it would be only in 'extremely limited circumstances' that a matter that the parties had agreed would be resolved by arbitration will be held to be non-arbitrable.[60]

(c) Award Contrary to Public Policy

Both the domestic and international commercial arbitration statutes permit recourse against an award where its enforcement would be contrary to public policy.[61] The international commercial arbitration legislation clarifies that an award would be contrary to the public policy of Australia in the event that its making 'was induced or

[51] See Jones (n 31) 161–62, 487. See further *Larkden Pty Ltd v Lloyd Energy Systems Pty Ltd* (2011) 279 ALR 772, paras 62–65.

[52] Jones (n 31) 162–66.

[53] ibid 167–68.

[54] ibid 168.

[55] ibid 169.

[56] ibid 169–70.

[57] ibid 170.

[58] *Comandate Marine Corp v Pan Australia Shipping Pty Ltd* [2006] FCAFC 192, para 200 (Allsop J). See further James Morrison and Luke Nottage, '2014 Australia Report' in Simon Greenberg, Christopher Kee, and Romesh Weeramantry (eds), *International Commercial Arbitration: An Asia Pacific Perspective* (2nd edn, Kluwer 2021).

[59] (1990) 169 CLR 332, para 14 (Deane and Gaudron JJ).

[60] John Hockley and others, *Australian Commercial Arbitration* (LexisNexis Butterworths 2015) 201.

[61] Model Law art 34(2)(b)(ii) (incorporated into Australian law by virtue of the International Arbitration Act 1974 (Cth) s 16); Commercial Arbitration Act 2010 (NSW) s 34(2)(b)(ii).

affected by fraud or corruption' or 'a breach of the rules of natural justice occurred in connection with the making of the . . . award'.[62] The domestic commercial arbitration law does not define the term 'public policy', but the *travaux préparatoires* for the Model Law make it clear that the term intends to capture circumstances such as corruption on the part of the arbitrators or where the award was based on misleading evidence.[63] It has also been suggested that this ground would, like the international commercial arbitration legislation, cover situations where the award was rendered in breach of the rules of procedural fairness.[64]

It appears that the courts will continue to exercise a high degree of restraint consistently with courts in other jurisdictions that are parties to the New York Convention, if the issue was to arise in relation to a private-public arbitration award. In the international commercial arbitration case of *TCL Air Conditioner v Castel Electronics*, the Federal Court stated that it would not engage in an evaluation of the fact-finding process (to determine, for example, whether probative evidence supported the factual findings of the arbitrator) as this would cause 'a grave danger that the international commercial arbitral system will be undermined by judicial review . . . in circumstances where the hearing or reference has been conducted regularly and fairly'.[65] In order for an award to be set aside for being contrary to public policy, a plaintiff would need to demonstrate that there had been 'real unfairness or real practical injustice' in the conduct of the proceedings or the making of the award.[66] The concern is that to engage in review of the merits of an arbitration award, even in this limited context, would undermine the principle of judicial non-intervention in arbitral procedure that supports the finality of awards. It appears that, bar fraud or corruption, the conflict with public policy would have to be very significant for an award to be set aside.

This decision raises another point of departure from Australian administrative law: administrative law cases that concern procedural fairness are concerned not with whether the decision-making process had reached a certain ('real') threshold of injustice or unfairness, but rather with the instrumental reason of ensuring that the person affected by the proposed decision had the opportunity to be heard so that the decision-maker had access to all relevant information upon which to base their decision. In other words, a decision of a governmental officer, tribunal, or lower court may be more readily subject to judicial control on this basis than decisions of arbitrators in this respect.

(d) Enforcement

Under both the domestic and international commercial arbitration regimes, an award (including awards made under the ICSID Convention)[67] may be enforced with leave

[62] International Arbitration Act 1974 (Cth) s 19.

[63] Reproduced in Harold M Holtzmann and Joseph E Neuhaus, *A Guide to the UNCITRAL Model Law on International Commercial Arbitration: Legislative History and Commentary* (Kluwer 1989) 923–1003.

[64] Jones (n 31) 489–90 (also suggesting that this ground would be engaged where an award seeks to give effect to an illegal contract, which would also go to the question of arbitrability).

[65] *TCL Air Conditioner (Zhongshan) Co Ltd v Castel Electronics Pty Ltd* (2014) 311 ALR 387, para 54.

[66] ibid para 111.

[67] See International Arbitration Act 1974 (Cth) s 35.

of the court as though the award was a judgment or order of that court.[68] The substantive grounds for resisting recognition and enforcement of an award are the same as the grounds for having the award set aside under these statutes (with the exception of ICSID Convention awards), namely where the subject matter of the dispute is not capable of settlement by arbitration, or if the enforcement of the award would be contrary to public policy.[69] However, the international commercial arbitration legislation is particularly pro-enforcement, stating that when a court is considering whether to enforce or refuse to enforce an award (including in relation to whether it would be contrary to public policy to do so) the court must have regard to 'the objects of the Act' (which include 'to facilitate the recognition and enforcement of arbitral awards') and to the fact that 'arbitration is an . . . enforceable and timely method by which to resolve commercial disputes' and that 'awards are intended to provide certainty and finality'.[70] Accordingly, it is difficult to resist enforcement and the prospect of public interest considerations playing much of a role in this context seems rather slim.

B. Controls on Governments' Power to Contract

The issues highlighted above must be seen in the light of the lacuna in public law accountability for decisions made by government and its contractors. The choice of arbitration as the dispute resolution mechanism can operate to even further insulate exercises of public power from the already limited prospect of judicial scrutiny.

In Australia, the relationship between government and contractor is governed almost exclusively by contract law. Governments can sue and be sued for breach of contract in the same way as any other contracting party and must comply with the law of contract (formation, avoidance, performance, etc). However, governments enjoy certain modifications to contract law on account of their unique role. Parliaments can enact legislation to override an existing contract or class of contracts,[71] and a government may be able to rely on the doctrine of executive necessity to break a contract without paying damages, although the circumstances in which this may take place are not entirely clear and are likely to be narrow.[72] In practice, the utility of these tools is limited due to their potentially adverse impact on Australia's credit rating and reputation for potential investors.[73] And where there is an arbitration clause in the contract, it will be the arbitrator rather than a court that determines any disputes arising from such a decision.

Still, there are some legal restrictions on governments' ability to enter contracts. A government cannot contract out of pre-existing statutory obligations or fetter

[68] Commercial Arbitration Act 2010 (NSW) s 35; International Arbitration Act 1974 (Cth) s 8 (by the Federal Court or by a state Supreme Court).

[69] Commercial Arbitration Act 2010 (NSW) s 36(b); Model Law art 36.

[70] International Arbitration Act 1974 (Cth) s 39(2).

[71] Seddon (n 18) 294-301.

[72] Ibid 273-77. Additionally, some government contracts contain a termination for convenience clause, permitting government to unilaterally terminate the contract in the event of a change of government policy or related governmental exigencies, obliging the government to compensate the contractor up to the point of termination but not for loss of future profits (ibid 277–78).

[73] Seddon (n 14) 547.

its future use of a power or discretion conferred by pre-existing legislation.[74] Nor can a government, by contract, fetter its future exercise of executive[75] or legislative[76] power. In two related cases (*Williams v Commonwealth (No 1)* and *Williams v Commonwealth (No 2)*), the High Court held that the federal government could not enter into contracts that obliged the expenditure of public funds without legislative authorization, with the exception of routine expenditure for the administration of government departments.[77] Nor can the federal government enter into contracts in relation to areas of law where the states have exclusive legislative competence or that are otherwise outside of the scope of federal legislative power.[78]

Post-*Williams*, it appears that parliamentary authority by way of legislative appropriation of public funds is required for the performance of all federal government contracts (apart from those relating to routine governmental expenditure), even where liability is on a contingent basis—which would include all contracts that contain an arbitration clause.[79] *Williams* does mean that the federal parliament has some oversight of the fact that contracts will be entered into by the federal executive. The executive branch commands a majority of the House of Representatives but not necessarily in the Senate, meaning that the Senate may refuse to pass, or may effectively force amendments to, proposed legislation. However, legislation authorizing expenditure can be expressed in general terms,[80] and parliament is unlikely to be appraised of the details of contracts themselves, including the nature of the dispute resolution mechanism. As such, the extent to which democratic input might assuage concerns about government contracting, including contracts involving arbitration to resolve disputes, is likely to be limited.

It is unclear whether the rule in *Williams* would also apply to state and territory governments, which would permit some democratic input into these governments' decisions to enter contracts containing an arbitration clause. On one view, the states and territories have plenary power to enter contracts without legislative authorization.[81] Still, it might be that the principle in *Williams* will in the future be extended to the states, as the decision was partly based on the Westminster constitutional principle of responsible government—that the executive branch is accountable to the

[74] Seddon (n 18) 284–89.

[75] ibid 289–292 (with further references).

[76] ibid 292–94 (with further references).

[77] *Williams v Commonwealth (No 1)* (2012) 248 CLR 156.

[78] Such as in a manner inconsistent with the express and implied limitations on federal legislative power: *Williams v Commonwealth (No 2)* (2014) 252 CLR 416.

[79] Former High Court Justice Kenneth Hayne suggests that the relevant question is whether the contract is or may be politically contentious: Hayne (n 14). Australian law permits legislation with retrospective effect, ie to retrospectively validate existing contracts where the contract has already been signed.

[80] In *Combet v Commonwealth* (2005) 224 CLR 494, the High Court held (at 523, para 6 (Gleeson CJ), 577, para 161 (Gummow, Hayne, Callinan, and Heydon JJ)) that appropriation legislation need not be especially specific.

[81] On the basis that the executive branch of a state government has complete freedom of contract as a legal person: the states are regarded as having inherited their power to contract from the British Crown at the point of Australian federation. As to the British position, see Carol Harlow and Richard Rawlings, *Law and Administration* (3rd edn, CUP 2009) 341–42.

legislature.[82] Should this be the case, there would be the opportunity for greater democratic oversight of decisions to contract, but as noted above, a legislature is unlikely to be informed of the contractual terms themselves, including the arbitration mechanism.[83]

The requirements of legislative authorization of expenditure are the only substantive limits on the scope of governments' contracting powers, and therefore the scope of the types of agreements that can be arbitrable. That is to say, there are no real restrictions on government contracting that could function as a means of ensuring that arbitration does not undermine the public interest, namely by permitting arbitration only in relation to particular disputes (such as disputes of a wholly commercial nature), apart from the currently rather nebulous restrictions on arbitrability that can be distilled from the case law to date.[84]

C. Public Law Controls on Contractual Decisions

The extent to which governments and contractors may be held accountable for their actions to third parties is limited. As the doctrine of privity prevents a person who is not party to the contract from enforcing it, those receiving outsourced services or who are otherwise affected by the actions of government or a contractor would need to seek redress as a matter of public law.[85] Yet, prevailing judicial interpretations of applicable constitutional and statutory provisions also largely exclude judicial control of governments' or contractors' conduct under the contract as a matter of public law, leaving a potentially significant gap in government accountability.

The Federal Court has statutory jurisdiction to undertake judicial review of the legality of a decision[86] only in relation to 'decisions of an administrative character . . . made under an enactment' or 'conduct for the purpose of making [such] a decision'.[87] The courts have interpreted the term 'under an enactment' very narrowly;[88] most decisions made by private bodies exercising public functions would not come within this definition. Successive governments have not adopted recommendations to reform the legislation to give the courts jurisdiction over non-statutory decisions made by the federal government.[89] Moreover, the High Court's constitutionally

[82] Lisa Burton Crawford, Patrick Emerton, and Emmanuel Laryea, 'Investor-State Dispute Settlement and the Australian Constitutional Framework' in Colin Picker, Heng Wang, and Weihuan Zhou (eds), *The China–Australia Free Trade Agreement: A 21st-Century Model* (Hart 2017) 259, 273–74.

[83] States have fewer restrictions on the areas of law they may legislate for compared with the federal parliament, and in particular, state statutes need not be connected with a head of power.

[84] Discussed in section III.A.3(b) above.

[85] Seddon (n 18) 53–55.

[86] Federal courts do not, due to the constitutional separation of federal judicial power, undertake so-called 'merits review' of administrative decisions, that is, reconsidering decisions taking into account facts, law, policy, and discretion. Instead, dedicated administrative tribunals undertake this role, and courts only determine the 'legality' of government action: whether the decision-maker has acted for an authorized purpose, has considered irrelevant matters or failed to consider relevant matters, has afforded procedural fairness, and so on.

[87] Administrative Decisions (Judicial Review) Act 1977 (Cth) ss 3, 5, 6.

[88] See *Griffith University v Tang* (2005) 221 CLR 99; *Neat Domestic Trading Pty Ltd v AWB Ltd* (2003) 216 CLR 277.

[89] See Australian Government, Administrative Review Council, Report No 32, 'Review of the Administrative Decisions (Judicial Review) Act: The Ambit of the Act' (1989) and Administrative Review

entrenched jurisdiction to review jurisdictional errors made by the Commonwealth and its officers[90] has not yet been interpreted in such a way as to include contractors exercising public power on behalf of government, although the High Court has signalled that it is aware of the issue and will confront it in an appropriate case.[91]

Australian courts have generally declined to subject government contracting (whether the decision to contract or the actions of either government or the contractor under contract) to public law judicial review in the same way as exercise of statutory or other governmental powers. A decision by government to enter into a contract will be amenable to administrative law review only where the particular contracting action is made 'under an enactment', and constitutional review where the contracting decision is made by an 'officer of the Commonwealth'. There are relatively few instances of such cases, but those challenges that have been brought concern alleged failure to afford procedural fairness in the process of awarding contracts.[92]

The High Court has not yet had the occasion to directly confront the question whether it has jurisdiction to review non-statutory exercises of governmental power by private bodies (the United Kingdom *Datafin*[93] principle), and the courts have been inconsistent in their approach to the issue.[94] There is some support in Australian law for the United Kingdom case of *Aga Khan*:[95] that a decision made by a private body in relation to a contract cannot be subject to administrative law review even where the body is involved in some regulatory activity or the decision otherwise raises public law issues. The case of *Plaintiff M68/2015 v Minister for Immigration*[96] demonstrates the difficulties involved in holding government accountable as a matter of public law where it outsources public services.[97] The High Court held that, by entering into an agreement with the government of Nauru and by contracting a private company to provide an 'offshore processing facility' for asylum seekers, the Australian government was not involved, as a matter of law, in the detention of the plaintiff. This in turn

Council, Report No 50, 'Federal Judicial Review in Australia' (2012), both at <https://webarchive.nla.gov.au/awa/20190808004201/https://www.arc.ag.gov.au/Publications/Reports/Pages/default.aspx> accessed 28 January 2025. The Administrative Review Council was formerly an advisory body to the Attorney-General on matters of administrative law.

[90] Constitution ss 75(iii) and (v). Legislation permits the Federal Court to exercise largely the same powers: Judiciary Act 1903 (Cth) s 39B.

[91] In *Plaintiff M61/2010E v Commonwealth* (2010) 243 CLR 319, paras 51, 68, 69, the Court held that processing of asylum claims by private contractors pursuant to a contract with the federal government could be set aside for error of law or failure to afford procedural fairness, because the immigration minister was the statutory repository of the power to determine applications and the role of the contractor was regarded as advisory in nature. The High Court said that it would leave for a future case the question whether a contractor would fall within the definition of 'officer of the Commonwealth' in circumstances where the contractor was acting without other governmental involvement.

[92] See Denis O'Brien, 'Administrative Law Dimensions of Commonwealth Tendering and Contracting' (2004) 40 AIAL Forum 40, 42 (with further references).

[93] *R v Panel on Take-overs and Mergers; ex parte Datafin plc* [1986] EWCA Civ 8; [1987] QB 815.

[94] See Janina Boughey and Greg Weeks, '"Officers of the Commonwealth" in the Private Sector: Can the High Court Review Outsourced Exercises of Power?' (2013) 36 Uni NSW LJ 316; Emilios Kryou, 'Judicial Review of Decisions of Non-Governmental Bodies Exercising Governmental Powers: Is *Datafin* Part of Australian Law?' (2012) 86 Australian LJ 20; Aronson, Groves, and Weeks (n 27) 201–2.

[95] *R v Jockey Club Disciplinary Committee, ex parte Aga Khan* [1993] 2 All ER 853.

[96] (2016) 257 CLR 42.

[97] These contracts do not contain an arbitration clause.

meant that the legality of the plaintiff's detention under the Constitution could not be ruled upon. This decision also highlights the incentives that governments have to contract out contentious programmes in order to minimize judicial scrutiny.

The states and territories appear to be in the same position as the United Kingdom in relation to decisions made by private bodies vis-à-vis third parties, namely that decisions made under contract cannot be subject to administrative law controls, even where the power exercised appears to be public in nature (*Aga Khan*, discussed above).[98] An argument can also be made that to permit judicial review of decisions made under contract would infringe a constitutional principle that prevents state courts from acting in a way that is incompatible with their institutional integrity.[99] It might be seen as incompatible with the role of a state court to engage in the policing of government power exercised pursuant to contracts, rather than their traditional role in reviewing exercises of statutory power and non-statutory prerogative power. This would leave states and territories in a roughly equivalent position to federal law, namely that decisions made under or pursuant to private-public contracts are regarded as a matter of private law.

Still, the question is not free from doubt, as state courts have on a number of occasions reviewed the actions of private bodies that exercise only quasi-public powers, albeit only on the limited basis of failure to observe procedural fairness in decision-making.[100] State administrative law might therefore extend to permit review of the exercise of non-statutory public power by government in relation to contractors and the exercise of public power by contractors in relation to third parties, which would create a potentially greater scope for judicial review than the position at federal law.

IV. Constitutional Law Issues Arising from Private-Public Arbitration

There are three other potential issues of incompatibility between Australia's arbitration law and its Constitution. Two of these issues arise from the strict separation of judicial power in the Constitution as interpreted by the High Court. These are whether arbitration is a type of 'judicial power'—a power which is exclusively reserved to courts exercising federal jurisdiction—and whether the courts' role in enforcing arbitral awards undermines their integrity. The third issue arises as a consequence of the financial control on the federal governments' power to contract (discussed in section III.B above) and whether this principle extends to require legislative authorization of the government's entry into treaties that provide for investor-state arbitration.[101]

[98] State and territory Supreme Courts enjoy common law judicial review jurisdiction, which does not have the same constraints as federal law in terms of limiting jurisdiction to reviewing decisions made under statutory authority and/or by a governmental officer. Like federal law, some states and territory statutes only permit judicial review of decisions made under an enactment, but other decisions can be reviewed using the common law mechanism.

[99] As courts that exercise federal judicial power: *Kable v Director of Public Prosecutions for New South Wales* (1996) 189 CLR 51. This issue is discussed more generally in section IV.B of this chapter.

[100] See Aronson, Groves, and Weeks (n 27) 491–96.

[101] Discussed extensively by Burton Crawford, Emerton, and Laryea (n 82).

A. Whether Arbitration Infringes the Constitutional Separation of Judicial Power

The separation of judicial power from other types of governmental power in the Constitution has resulted in the development of a jurisprudence that has sought to define and delimit the concept of 'judicial power'. The High Court has the power to invalidate federal and state laws that do not comply with express and implied constitutional limitations on legislative power. One such limitation is that legislation will be invalid if it is contrary to Chapter III of the Constitution, which vests federal judicial power exclusively in the High Court and certain other courts. In other words, the High Court has held that the Constitution impliedly prohibits (with limited exceptions) the exercise of 'judicial power' by any person or body other than a court with federal jurisdiction—such as, for example, an arbitrator or arbitral tribunal.[102]

Another limitation arising from the constitutional separation of judicial power is that these courts must only exercise judicial power (or power that is ancillary or incidental to judicial power).[103] Moreover, any power that is exercised by a court must be 'compatible with the essential character of a court as an institution that is, and is seen to be, both impartial between the parties and independent of the parties and of other branches of government in the exercise of the decision-making functions conferred on it'.[104] Courts must not, for example, act at the behest of the other arms of government or another non-judicial body, such as parties to a contract or arbitrators.

In *TCL Air Conditioner (Zhongshan) Co Ltd v The Judges of the Federal Court of Australia*,[105] a party to an arbitration sought to resist the enforcement of two awards made against it, arguing that the legislation impermissibly vested federal judicial power in arbitral tribunals by making their awards binding and conclusive. The High Court rejected this argument. Distinguishing arbitral from judicial power, the Court observed that the finality of an arbitral award merely reflected the outcome of the parties' consensual decision to submit their dispute to arbitration and, in any event, the binding effect of an award relied on the court's power of enforcement.[106] Unlike arbitrators, courts exercise jurisdiction independently of the consent of those whose rights and obligations are at issue.[107]

Although the matter concerned two private actors, the principles enunciated by the High Court might well extend to private-public arbitrations: that by entering a contract or an investment treaty containing an arbitration clause, government does not (unlawfully) invest arbitral tribunals with federal judicial power.[108] Arbitrators do not interpret the Constitution or decide whether actions taken by governments are within constitutional limitations on their respective powers, but rather determine

[102] Constitution s 71 (namely other federal courts created by the parliament and state courts invested with federal jurisdiction).

[103] *R v Kirby; Ex parte Boilermakers' Society of Australia* (1956) 94 CLR 254.

[104] ibid.

[105] *TCL Air Conditioner (Zhongshan) Co Ltd v The Judges of the Federal Court of Australia* [2013] HCA 5.

[106] ibid paras 106–09 (Hayne, Crennan, Kiefel, and Bell JJ), citing *Construction, Forestry, Mining and Energy Union v Australian Industrial Relations Commission* (2001) 203 CLR 645, 658, para 31.

[107] *TCL Air Conditioner v Federal Court* (n 105) para 28 (French CJ and Gageler J); 108 (Hayne, Crennan, Kiefel, and Bell JJ).

[108] Burton Crawford, Emerton, and Laryea (n 82) 279.

compliance with the contractual terms or the norms in the relevant investment treaty. And despite the enforceability of damages awards (and potential chilling effects on future government conduct), an unfavourable arbitral decision does not affect the legal validity of government action.[109]

Still, this issue highlights the broader question of the appropriate role of arbitrators in conducting private-public arbitrations. As Australia's former Chief Justice Robert French has observed, adjudication by courts 'serves larger purposes than the efficiencies, economic benefits and party autonomy served by the arbitral process'.[110] Unlike judges, arbitrators need not heed the implications of their decision-making for third parties or the legal system in general, and as distinct from arbitrators, 'courts have a special and constitutional role in publicly maintaining and affirming the rule of law as they make their decisions'.[111] The insulation of arbitral decision-making from the broader context might be seen as especially problematic where arbitrators in private-public arbitrations determine whether a public body has conducted itself in accordance with domestic law. By applying domestic law to exercises of power by public bodies, arbitrators contribute to the governance of those bodies, yet the fact that they need not conduct themselves in the same way as courts, in terms of impartiality, transparency, and so on, should be cause for concern.[112] The same can be said where an award of damages in the event of a breach has the effect of restricting the state's ability to use such money for other government expenditure, or of chilling future government conduct.[113]

B. Whether Enforcement of Arbitral Awards by the Courts Undermines the Integrity of the Courts

Another issue that arose in *TCL Air Conditioner* was the question whether the enforcement of arbitral awards could undermine the courts' integrity on the basis that courts were enlisted in the enforcement of arbitral awards, including potentially those made in legal error. According to the plaintiff, the independence of the court was distorted because, when determining an application for enforcement, the Court would have no opportunity to engage in substantive review of an award allegedly containing an error of law, thereby giving the arbitral tribunal the last word on legal questions.

[109] Even if the ratification of such treaties was found to be unlawful as a matter of constitutional law, Australia would still be bound by its act of ratification at international law and could not rely on constitutional constrains to evade its obligations.

[110] Chief Justice of the High Court of Australia Robert French AC, 'ISDS – Litigating the Judiciary' (Chartered Institute of Arbitrators Centenary Conference, Hong Kong, 21 March 2015); Robert French, 'Arbitration and Public Policy' (Goff Lecture, Hong Kong, 18 April 2016).

[111] French, 'Arbitration and Public Policy' (n 110), but see Alec Stone Sweet and Florian Grisel, *The Evolution of International Arbitration: Judicialization, Governance, Legitimacy* (OUP 2017) 28: arbitrators owe duties not only to the parties but also to the arbitral 'system' and, more broadly, the community in which they exist (be it domestic or transnational), including the arbitration house, the rules, and the supervision of the domestic courts.

[112] That is, arbitrators need not adhere to the same strict standards of independence as judges, their decisions are confidential, there is only a limited prospect of third-party participation, and there are extremely limited prospects of substantive review by the courts.

[113] Burton Crawford, Emerton, and Laryea (n 82).

The High Court also rejected this argument. Again emphasizing the consensual nature of arbitration, the court held that its role in an application for enforcement of an arbitral award was to enforce 'the binding result of the agreement of the parties to submit their dispute to arbitration' rather than to enforce 'any disputed right submitted to arbitration'.[114] The powers given to the court under the international commercial arbitration legislation to refuse to enforce an award or to set aside an award in certain circumstances were protective of the institutional integrity of the courts, and judicial independence was not distorted on account of the absence of a specific power to review the decision for error of law.[115] This point is also relevant to private-public arbitration to the extent that the High Court has taken a strong stance in favour of enforceability of awards and a dim view of the argument that the legislation enlisted the court in exercising a power incompatible with its judicial role.[116]

C. The Power to Enter Investment Treaties without Legislative Authorization

Another potential issue of constitutional law arising from the High Court's decision in *Williams* that governmental expenditure must be authorized by the legislature (discussed in section III.B above), namely whether this requirement might also restrict the power of the federal government to enter into international treaties providing for investor-state arbitration.

As a starting point, the executive branch of the federal government has the power to enter treaties without parliamentary ratification.[117] However, post-*Williams*,[118] an argument can be made that parliament's approval is needed to enter into any treaty that provides for the payment of damages in the event of a breach of the obligations therein. The argument from *Williams* is that the ratification of the treaty is analogous to a contract in the sense that the government has made a binding and enforceable commitment that Australia will abide by the obligations contained in the treaty, including paying any compensation or damages that an arbitral tribunal may award in the event of a breach.[119] If the principle in *Williams* was extended by the court to treaties in the future, parliament would need to enact legislation approving Australia's membership of treaties that include an investor-state arbitration mechanism.

Yet, it is not entirely clear whether *Williams* would apply in this situation. As noted above, the case concerned the power of the executive to enter into contracts and not its power to enter into international treaties; each power may well be subject to different types of inherent limitations.[120] Yet, one of the rationales underlying *Williams* is

[114] *TCL Air Conditioner v Federal Court* (n 105) paras 28–29, 34 (French CJ and Gageler J); 76–78, 81, 101, 106–09 (Hayne, Crennan, Kiefel, and Bell JJ).

[115] ibid paras 104–05 (Hayne, Crennan, Kiefel, and Bell JJ).

[116] See Burton Crawford, Emerton, and Laryea (n 82).

[117] Although the incorporation of a treaty into domestic law requires the passage of implementing legislation by the parliament.

[118] See section III.B above.

[119] Burton Crawford, Emerton, and Laryea (n 82).

[120] ibid.

equally applicable to the investment treaty context: that, according to the principle of responsible government, the executive branch of government is accountable to the legislature, including by means of parliamentary supervision of governmental expenditure. Should the *Williams* principle be extended to treaties that contain a contingent promise to spend public moneys, parliament would debate the merits of this aspect of the proposed treaty, meaning there could be potential for meaningful deliberation on the benefits of investor-state arbitration. The opportunity for parliamentary ventilation of the issues might, in turn, address some of the criticisms of Australia's entry into treaties providing for investor-state arbitration in the sense that, currently, it is the executive alone that decides whether to bind Australia as a matter of international law by entering into a treaty.[121] The omission of investor-state dispute settlement from the Australia–United States FTA arose in part from the Senate's threatened refusal to approve the tariff reduction legislation that was needed before Australia could ratify the treaty, and the Senate could refuse to pass legislation providing for investor-state arbitration if it was so inclined.

V. Conclusion

This chapter has analysed the disjuncture between private-public arbitration and principles of public law in Australia. It is clear that Australian contract law, arbitration law, constitutional law, and administrative law frameworks do not adequately account for the public interest concerns that may arise in relation to private-public arbitration. Decisions taken under contract are a matter of private law, and there are no real restrictions on governments entering contracts providing for arbitration other than budgetary control by the legislature. Although there are some entry points for the public interest under the domestic and international commercial arbitration statutes (the courts' power to disclose confidential information, the limited prospect of appeal under the domestic scheme, and recourse against awards for non-arbitrability or where the decision was contrary to public policy), these regimes are characterized by far less transparency and accountability than proceedings in domestic courts. While this may not be seen as problematic for private commercial arbitration, the participation of government raises issues that the current regulatory framework does not adequately address.

The phenomenon of private-public arbitration compounds the existing lacuna in Australian administrative law for government accountability in relation to private-public contracts. Judicial review of exercises of public power by and in relation to contractors is generally precluded, as the courts have taken a narrow approach to when a decision is 'made under an enactment' for the purpose of the federal judicial review legislation, and have thus far not found that a private body is an 'officer of the Commonwealth' so as to enliven constitutional review by the High Court. Courts have tended to view the existence of a contract between a public body and a private entity

[121] ibid. In *Williams (No 1)* (n 77), Crennan J noted the importance of both responsible government and the need for 'the ventilation, accommodation and effective authorization of political decisions' by parliament (at para 516).

as a matter of private law—and arbitrators as providers of a private, consent-based dispute resolution service. These factors combine to restrict the extent to which public law can inform and influence the current paradigm of private-public arbitration. There appears to be no appetite among members of the High Court to depart from the orthodox view of the arbitration regime (one based on consent and party autonomy) and to make arbitral decision-making in private-public arbitrations subject to a more expansive form of judicial scrutiny—although such a case has yet to come before it.

This chapter has also discussed some unresolved issues of constitutional interpretation: (1) whether state and territory governments may enter into contracts (including those that provide for investor-state arbitration) without statutory authorization; (2) whether the executive branch of the federal government may enter into investment treaties that contain an arbitration clause without legislative authority; (3) whether contract-based arbitrators would impermissibly exercise de facto judicial power in relation to decisions involving a public body given that their decision-making may raise questions of public law and the public interest; and (4) whether it would impair the integrity of the judiciary for a court to enforce an arbitral award containing a legal error against a public body. Even if these issues do not turn out to be fatal to the validity of certain provisions of the domestic and international commercial arbitration statutes or to the powers of the executive branch of federal and state and territory governments—and some are more strongly arguable than others—they nevertheless highlight rule-of-law concerns where privately contracted government services are subject to private dispute resolution and avoid public law accountability.

In 2016, Chief Justice Robert French observed that 'evolving applications of arbitration may enliven debates about its proper scope and the criteria for its legislative support'.[122] Time will tell whether the mining dispute referred to in the Introduction to this chapter will galvanize legislative reform to better protect the public interest in relation to dispute settlement under government contracts, such as by enacting special provisions applicable to private-public arbitration.

Select Materials

Bibliography

Aronson, Mark, Matthew Groves, and Greg Weeks, *Judicial Review of Administrative Action and Government Liability* (7th edn, Thomson 2022)

Bonnitcha, Jonathan, *Substantive Protection under Investment Treaties* (CUP 2014)

Boughey, Janina and Greg Weeks, '"Officers of the Commonwealth" in the Private Sector: Can the High Court Review Outsourced Exercises of Power?' (2013) 36 Uni NSW L J 316

Burton Crawford, Lisa, Patrick Emerton, and Emmanuel Laryea, 'Investor-State Dispute Settlement and the Australian Constitutional Framework' in Colin Picker, Heng Wang,

[122] French, 'Arbitration and Public Policy' (n 110).

and Weihuan Zhou (eds), *The China–Australia Free Trade Agreement: A 21st-Century Model* (Hart Publishing 2017)
Elliott, Mark, *Beatson, Matthews and Elliott's Administrative Law* (4th edn, OUP 2011)
Faunce, Thomas, 'Australia's Embrace of Investor State Dispute Settlement: A Challenge to the Social Contract Ideal?' (2015) 69 Australian J Int'l Affairs 595
French, Robert, 'ISDS – Litigating the Judiciary', Chartered Institute of Arbitrators Centenary Conference, Hong Kong, 21 March 2015
French, Robert, 'Arbitration and Public Policy', Goff Lecture, Hong Kong, 18 April 2016
Harlow, Carol and Richard Rawlings, *Law and Administration* (3rd edn, CUP 2009)
Hayne, KM, 'Government Contracts and Public Law' (2017) 41 MULR 155
Hockley, John and others, *Australian Commercial Arbitration* (LexisNexis Butterworths 2015)
Holtzmann, Harold M and Joseph E Neuhaus, *A Guide to the UNCITRAL Model Law on International Commercial Arbitration: Legislative History and Commentary* (Kluwer 1989)
Jones, Doug, *Commercial Arbitration in Australia* (2nd edn, Thomson Reuters 2013)
Kryou, Emilios, 'Judicial Review of Decisions of Non-Governmental Bodies Exercising Governmental Powers: Is *Datafin* Part of Australian Law?' (2012) 86 Australian LJ 20
Luttrell, Sam, *Bias Challenges in International Commercial Arbitration: The Need for a 'Real Danger' Test* (Kluwer 2009)
Morrison, James and Luke Nottage, 'Australia' in Simon Greenberg, Christopher Kee, and Romesh Weeramantry, *International Commercial Arbitration: An Asia-Pacific Perspective* (2nd ed, Kluwer 2021
Nottage, Luke and Richard Garnett (eds), *International Arbitration in Australia* (Federation Press 2010)
O'Brien, Denis, 'Administrative Law Dimensions of Commonwealth Tendering and Contracting' (2004) 40 AIAL Forum 40
Seddon, Nicholas, *Government Contracts: Federal, State and Local* (7th edn, Federation Press 2023)
Seddon, Nick, 'The Interaction of Contract and Executive Power' (2003) 31 FL Rev 541
Stewart, Daniel, 'Statutory Authority to Contract and the Role of Judicial Review' (2014) 33 UQLJ 43
Stone Sweet, Alec and Florian Grisel, *The Evolution of International Arbitration: Judicialization, Governance, Legitimacy* (OUP 2017)
Tienhaara, Kyla, 'Regulatory Chill and the Threat of Arbitration: A View from Political Science' in Chester Brown and Kate Miles (eds), *Evolution in Investment Treaty Law and Arbitration* (CUP 2011) 606
Van Harten, Gus, *Investment Treaty Arbitration and Public Law* (OUP 2007).

Reports

Australian Government, Department of Foreign Affairs and Trade, 'Gillard Government Trade Policy Statement: Trading Our Way to More Jobs and Prosperity' (2011)
Australian Productivity Commission, 'Bilateral and Regional Trade Agreements' (2010)

Legislation

Commercial Arbitration Act 2010 (NSW)
International Arbitration Act 1974 (Cth)

Cases

Comandate Marine Corp v Pan Australia Shipping Pty Ltd [2006] FCAFC 192
Ebner v Official Trustee in Bankruptcy, Clenae Pty Ltd v Australia and New Zealand Banking Group Ltd (2000) 205 CLR 337
Esso Australia Resources Ltd v Plowman (1995) 183 CLR 10
Larkden Pty Ltd v Lloyd Energy Systems Pty Ltd (2011) 279 ALR 772
Philip Morris Asia Limited v The Commonwealth of Australia, PCA Case No 2012-12 (UNCITRAL), Award on Jurisdiction and Admissibility, 17 December 2015
TCL Air Conditioner (Zhongshan) Co Ltd v Castel Electronics Pty Ltd (2014) 311 ALR 387
TCL Air Conditioner (Zhongshan) Co Ltd v The Judges of the Federal Court of Australia [2013] HCA 5
Webb v The Queen (1994) 181 CLR 41

Annex: Author Questionnaire

Note: The following reproduces the text of the questionnaire contributors to the present book were provided with as a guideline to prepare their chapters for the book. The introductory note of the text has undergone minor edits for the purposes of the present publication.

The following questionnaire is not thought to be the basis of classical country reports that stick slavishly to the questionnaire and answer the questions in it in a dry and mechanical fashion, but rather as a checklist for the issues to be included in a chapter that develops a thesis about how the constitutional legal system or systems dealt with looks at private-public arbitration. The questionnaire is therefore merely intended to provide a skeleton or checklist concerning the doctrinal structure that should be covered in the chapter, while the chapter itself should be an intellectual endeavour that probes the relationship between arbitration (domestic and international) and constitutional/administrative law.

The questionnaire is organized in three parts: 1. Context; 2. Arbitration as Dispute Resolution; and 3. Arbitration as Governance. Parts 1 and 2 contain a number of key questions the contribution should aim to answer. These questions are broad and allow for a degree of abstraction. Parts 1 and 2 also contain a series of guiding questions. These questions are meant as an inspiration as to topics that might be relevant to deal with in the contribution. Some of the guiding questions relate to the existence of provisions regulating certain aspects of arbitration in your legal system(s). When providing answers to these questions please include provisions and principles that refer directly to arbitration as well as provisions and principles that only implicitly, or as a result of interpretation by domestic courts, or in doctrine, influence arbitration. Should there be no provision or principle dealing either directly or indirectly with the relevant aspect of arbitration, please also consider what this absence signifies. Part 3 turns to the working assumption that arbitration is not only a dispute settlement mechanism, but also a governance mechanism in the context of which arbitrators and their decision-making develop a body of law that impacts how private-public relations are structured.

Some definitions are in order: for purposes of this project, we understand arbitration as 'an adjudicatory process resulting in a final and binding resolution of a dispute based on law or equity'. A private-public arbitration is an arbitration between a private actor and a public actor. Public actors encompass the state itself; state organs; sub-state entities, such as regions or municipalities; instrumentalities of the state, including state enterprises, to the extent they are organized in accordance with public law, as well as entities organized under private law to the extent they exercise public authority or public functions. The legal basis of the dispute, that is, whether it is based on a treaty or contract, whether it involves a purely commercial relationship between private and public actors, or whether the relationship is one subjected to public law, is irrelevant for purposes of the research envisioned here. Equally, it does not matter whether the arbitration is between a public actor and a foreign private entity. Instead, the project is interested both in purely domestic settings and transborder contexts.

1. Context

Please provide the relevant context for how private-public arbitration and constitutional law interrelate in your legal system(s). This encompasses the practical importance of private-public arbitration in your legal system(s), such as the frequency with which arbitration agreements are included in contracts between private and public actors, whether there are specific areas in which arbitration agreements in private-public relations are primarily used, how often arbitration is used to resolve disputes between private and public actors, etc. Similarly, we are interested in the theoretical and academic context in which private-public arbitration has to be seen in your legal system. Is it a topic addressed in doctrinal writing and academic debate? Of which legal discipline, if any, is it considered part? Furthermore, we are interested in the relevant constitutional and statutory provisions that govern the involvement of public actors in private-public arbitration and would like to gain a better understanding of where the ideas on private-public arbitration and the norms relating to it came from in your legal system(s) and what impact your legal system may have beyond the respective state's territory in the context of private-public arbitration.

A. Private-Public Arbitration as a Practical and Theoretical Discipline

1.1. What is the current practical importance of private-public arbitration in your legal system(s)? In which circumstances is private-public arbitration used to settle disputes? Why is arbitration chosen over dispute settlement in courts?

1.2. How has private-public arbitration developed historically in your legal system(s)?

1.3. How is private-public arbitration conceptualized in your legal system(s)? Is it part of private or public law? Is it seen as part of commercial arbitration, of civil procedure, as part of the organization of the adjudicative system, etc? Is private-public arbitration analogized to private-private arbitration and/or public law litigation in domestic courts?

1.4. To what extent is private-public arbitration addressed in academia in your legal system(s)? Which discipline within the legal sciences deals with private-public arbitration?

B. Constitutional Norms and Applicable Legislation

1.5. What are the provisions of the Constitution, if any, that refer to arbitration generally or to arbitration with a public actor?

1.6. What are the constitutional principles or norms, if any, that influence arbitration with a public actor independent of any express mention?

1.7. What perceived conflicts with constitutional principles and norms could private-public arbitration give rise to?

1.8. What are the legislative provisions, if any, that apply to arbitration generally or to arbitration with a public actor?

1.9. What are the principles or norms, if any, that influence arbitration with a public actor?

1.10. What are the provisions of the domestic legislation regulating arbitration? Do these provisions distinguish between private-private arbitration, private-public arbitration, and other forms of arbitration?

C. Origin of Ideas and Concepts

The following questions aim at understanding whether the arbitration law, as well as administrative and constitutional law, in your legal system(s) have developed in relative independence or isolation from other systems, or whether they have been influenced and borrowed from other legal systems, whether domestic or international. Likewise, as part of a mapping exercise, we are interested in which other domestic legal systems or international legal regimes were influenced by the arbitration, administrative, or constitutional law of the legal system(s) your chapter covers.

1.11. Have the basic legal concepts, ideas, and principles of the arbitration law, administrative law, or constitutional law in your legal system(s) developed autonomously or are they, even if only partly, influenced by foreign legal systems and/or international law (such as model laws etc)?
   i. If so, which foreign legal system(s) or which international legal regime(s) have served as inspiration in developing the basic legal concepts of your legal system(s) in respect of arbitration, administrative law, and constitutional law?
   ii. From where does the influence stem and in which way has it materialized and/or been crystallized in your legal system(s)? What changes occurred in adapting the rules from another legal system?
   iii. Are there specific reasons (legal, political, cultural) accounting for the influence of this/these particular foreign legal system(s) and/or international law on your legal system(s)?

1.12. Are there any foreign legal systems that are, or have been, even if partly, influenced by the basic legal concepts, ideas, or principles of your legal system(s) in respect of arbitration, administrative, and/or constitutional law?
   i. If so, which foreign legal systems have been subject to such influence?
   ii. In which way has the influence of your system(s) materialized in the foreign legal systems in question? What changes occurred?
   iii. Are there any specific reasons (legal, historical, cultural) accounting for the influence of your legal system(s) on the foreign legal system in question?

1.13. When developing new laws/rules, interpreting existing laws/rules, or filling lacunae, are foreign legal systems and/or international rules and mechanisms looked at by your legal system(s) for ideas on how to provide solutions to the problem in question in respect of arbitration, administrative law, and constitutional law?
   i. If so, which legal systems or international rules and mechanisms often serve as inspiration?
   ii. What is the rationale behind seeking inspiration from the particular foreign legal system in question and/or relevant rules of international law?

2. Arbitration as Dispute Resolution

This Part turns to the technical rules and principles relating to private-public arbitration as a dispute settlement mechanism. It is structured along the lines of the key issues dealt with in relation to any arbitration proceeding, starting from the agreement to arbitrate up to the enforcement of arbitral awards.

Guiding questions for this Part are the following: is private-public arbitration allowed under your legal system(s) and if so under which conditions? How is it ensured in your legal system(s) that the public interest is not negatively affected by private-public arbitrations? To which extent is private-public arbitration treated differently from private-private (commercial) arbitration?

A. Submission to Arbitration

2.1. Are there any provisions or principles (of constitutional, procedural, administrative, or other law) that govern when, in which cases, and under which circumstances a public actor can enter into an arbitration agreement?

2.2. Do public actors have the capacity to submit to arbitration?
2.3. What subject matters are arbitrable in arbitrations with a public actor? Is the sphere of arbitrable subject matters in relation to arbitration with a public actor different from arbitrable subject matters in private-private arbitration, and if so, in which way?
2.4. Are there any areas in which arbitration is used as the primary mechanism through which to solve disputes between a private party and a public actor? If so, is arbitration the primary mechanism of dispute resolution by law or through a practice of submitting to arbitration in certain contracts?
2.5. What are the provisions or principles of domestic law, if any, that govern the procedure by which a public actor may submit to arbitration?
2.6. What are the provisions or principles of domestic law, if any, that regulate when and to what extent a public actor has to disclose to the public that it has submitted or intends to submit to arbitration?
2.7. Are there any provisions or principles of domestic law that require that public hearings be held or other participatory mechanisms be employed before a public actor may submit to arbitration? Is a specific permission, for example by a superior agency or ministry, necessary?

B. Establishment of the Arbitral Tribunal and Organization of the Proceedings

Appointment of Arbitrators

2.8. What is the procedure for appointment of arbitrators in an arbitration with a public actor? Is the procedure for appointment of arbitrators in an arbitration with a public actor different from that in other forms of arbitration, and if so, in which way?
2.9. What are the rules regarding arbitrator independence and impartiality?
2.10. Do arbitrators in private-public arbitration have to have a certain expertise or qualification?
2.11. Is the scope of circumstances that must be disclosed because they could lead to doubts as to the arbitrators' impartiality and independence regulated in domestic law and, if so, does the scope vary depending on whether the arbitration involves only private parties or includes a public actor?

Appointment of Counsel

2.12. What are the provisions or principles of domestic law, if any, that regulate the procedure for appointment of counsel representing a public actor in arbitrations? Is this procedure different from the one required when appointing counsel to represent a public actor in litigation in domestic courts?
2.13. What are the rules for communication between counsel and arbitrators, in particular the party-appointed arbitrator? Are *ex parte* communications permissible?

C. Powers, Duties, and Jurisdiction of the Arbitral Tribunal

Jurisdiction

2.14. Do arbitrators in arbitrations involving a public actor have the ability to rule on the validity of the arbitration agreement and the extent of their own jurisdiction? If so, does the extent to which arbitrators have the power to rule on their own competence to hear certain disputes diverge from the extent of this power conferred upon arbitrators in private-private arbitrations?

Conducting Arbitral Proceedings

2.15. In conducting the proceedings, do arbitrators in arbitrations involving a public actor have any additional or special procedural abilities to steer the proceedings and/or secure that decisions are made on a sufficiently informed basis? Do they have *suo motu* powers in requesting evidence, or are they entirely dependent on the parties' submissions without the power to assume a more active role?

2.16. For purposes of comparison with domestic litigation, in conducting litigation proceedings involving a public actor in domestic courts, do the judges of these courts have any additional or special procedural abilities to steer the proceedings and/or secure that decisions are made on a sufficiently informed basis as compared to litigation involving only private parties?

Transparency and Confidentiality

2.17. What are the provisions or principles of domestic law, if any, that regulate if and to what extent the existence, content, and/or result of arbitral proceedings involving a public actor have to be made accessible to the public?

2.18. What are the provisions or principles of domestic law, if any, that regulate the degree of transparency that arbitrations, including oral hearings, involving a public actor are subject to?

2.19. What are the provisions or principles of domestic law, if any, that regulate the existence and scope of a duty of confidentiality and the persons and entities bound by such duty in arbitrations involving a public actor? Is there any difference between the existence, scope, and/or extent of the duty of confidentiality in arbitrations involving a public actor and other forms of arbitration?

Protecting Public Interests

2.20. Are there any special procedural safeguards securing that the public interest in arbitrations with a public actor is properly and sufficiently represented?

2.21. For purposes of comparison with domestic litigation, are there any special procedural safeguards securing that the public interest is properly and sufficiently represented in litigation in domestic courts between a private party and a public actor?

2.22. Are third parties allowed to intervene in arbitrations between a private party and a public actor? If so, to what extent and under which conditions?

D. Control by Domestic Courts

2.23. What are the grounds for challenging an award made in a private-public arbitration? Are these grounds different from the grounds for which an award rendered in a private-private arbitration may be challenged?

2.24. What parts of the arbitral award are subject to review by the domestic courts when the award is rendered in a private-public arbitration? Is the scope of the parts that are reviewable different from the scope of the parts that are reviewable in private-private arbitrations, and if so, in which way?

2.25. What is the standard of review that domestic courts must apply in reviewing arbitral awards rendered in private-public arbitrations? Is the standard of review different from the one domestic courts are required to apply in private-private arbitrations, and if so, in which way?

2.26. Is there any provision in domestic legislation allowing the parties to an arbitration to exclude review by the domestic courts of any award rendered in the arbitration? If so, does this provision also apply to private-public arbitrations?

E. Recognition and Enforcement of Awards

2.27. What are the grounds for refusing recognition/enforcement of an award rendered in a private-public arbitration? Are these grounds different from the grounds for which recognition/enforcement of an award rendered in a private-private arbitration can be refused or are they interpreted/applied differently?

2.28. If enforcement of an award can be refused on the ground that the award is contrary to the public policy of your legal system, is the concept of public policy interpreted differently depending on whether the award is rendered in a private-public or private-private arbitration? Is there a difference whether the award concerned an international arbitration as compared to a domestic arbitration?

2.29. When, if at all, can a state claim immunity from execution of an arbitral award rendered in an arbitration involving a public actor of that state in your legal system?

3. Arbitration as Governance

To a large extent, the technical rules governing private-public arbitrations as dispute settlement addressed in Part 2 will help to find answers relating to the conditions under which private-public arbitration is permissible, and how domestic legal systems try to ensure that the public interest is not compromised by public actors agreeing to arbitrate disputes with private actors rather than litigating them in domestic courts. In this Part, we want to take a step further and ask you to consider whether the assessment of private-public arbitration, in particular from the perspective of the constitutional principles of democracy, the protection of fundamental and human rights, and governance under the rule of law changes if private-public arbitration is not only a form to settle individual disputes but also has the function of actively crafting and further developing the law governing private-public relations. In fact, at least in certain areas of private-public interaction, arbitration may even replace domestic courts as institutions that settle disputes but also control the other branches of government; in such cases, arbitration tribunals may also have the effect of further developing the governing law.

This can create problems for constitutional principles, such as the principle of democracy, human rights, and the rule of law, because arbitration is a decentralized one-off structure that is not embedded in a separation-of-powers framework as we know it from the state court system. These problems are the background to the questions formulated in this Part. They focus on the extent to which your domestic legal system(s), and in particular its constitutional principles, contain, or can be interpreted to contain, requirements that constitutional principles establish for the functioning of arbitration as a governance mechanism. Do your constitutional provisions share the concerns sketched out below? What requirements are set up by your constitutional legal system(s) in order to control that arbitration as a governance mechanism does not compromise the public interest?

A. Democracy Problems with Private-Public Arbitration

What democracy means is notoriously difficult to define. In addition, different constitutional systems have different understandings of what democracy means and entails. As a crude definition, for the purposes of defining potential problems that private-public arbitration may create for the principle of democracy, we follow here the ideas set out in Abraham Lincoln's Gettysburg Address that democracy is 'government of the people, by the people, for the people'.[1] Against this background, private-public arbitration as governance could be a problem because arbitrators have a status different from judges in domestic courts and because arbitrators as a group have a relationship to domestic legislators different from domestic courts. More concretely, private-public arbitration as governance could create problems for the principle of democracy in respect of the following considerations:

Status and Appointment of Arbitrators

3.1. If democracy means government of the people by the people, and if one accepts that public-private arbitral tribunals exercise governance functions in controlling government conduct and in contributing to making the law governing private-public relations, is it a democracy problem that at least one arbitrator is appointed by a private party that is not accountable to the public, or that the mode of appointment is agreed upon by the public and private party? Is it problematic that the (direct or indirect) control of government conduct is exercised by someone who is not a public official?

Law Application by Arbitrators

3.2. If democracy is government for the people, does this suggests that the outcome of arbitration must be in conformity with legal standards made by the public or standards with which the public agrees? Does it become a problem for the principle of democracy if the outcomes diverge from the outcome of the identical or essentially similar dispute in a domestic court? Does the principle of democracy mandate a certain level or control of arbitrator decision-making?

3.3. Does the principle of democracy require a restriction on the remedies available to arbitral tribunals? Does the principle of democracy allow arbitrators to order specific performance, for example the revocation of an act by the executive, declaring a legislative act illegal, etc?

Lawmaking by Arbitrators

3.4. If arbitral tribunals not only settle disputes but also further develop the law applicable to private-public relations, and therefore become lawmakers, does the principle of democracy require specific democratic control mechanisms? Does the delegation of lawmaking powers raise problems for the principle of democracy?

Openness and Transparency

3.5. In order to control whether arbitrators properly apply the governing law, but also whether the law made by arbitral tribunals is in line with the public interest, is it a problem from the perspective of the principle of democracy if proceedings in private-public arbitrations are confidential and not open to the public?

[1] Abraham Lincoln, 'The Gettysburg Address' (19 November 1863) Abraham Lincoln Online <www.abrahamlincolnonline.org/lincoln/speeches/gettysburg.htm> accessed 2 February 2023.

3.6. Does the principle of democracy require participation of actors other than the parties in the arbitration (eg affected third parties or institutions representing the public interests, whether NGOs or specific public actors, such as Advocate Generals, etc)?

B. Rule-of-Law Problems with Private-Public Arbitration

Similar to the principle of democracy, there are different and partly diverging definitions of the concept of rule of law. Notwithstanding these differences, there are core components around which the concept of the rule of law converges. Still, there are differences between what one can call 'thin' versions of the rule of law—that is, notions that have a primarily formal/procedural understanding of the rule of law—and 'thick' versions of the rule of law that encompass a yardstick for measuring the outcome of certain decisions. Such a thick version of the rule of law is supported, for example, in a report by the United Nations Secretary General which states:

> the rule of law as a principle of governance in which all persons, institutions and entities, public and private, including the State itself, are accountable to laws that are publicly promulgated, equally enforced and independently adjudicated, and which are consistent with international human rights norms and standards. It requires, as well, measures to ensure adherence to the principles of supremacy of law, equality before the law, accountability to the law, fairness in the application of the law, separation of powers, participation in decisionmaking, legal certainty, avoidance of arbitrariness, and procedural and legal transparency.[2]

Under this definition, there are several aspects of private-public arbitration that can be analysed as problems for the concept of the rule of law:

Rule of Law and Independence and Impartiality of Arbitrators

3.7. Does the concept of the rule of law impose requirements concerning the independence and impartiality of arbitrators? Is the lack of tenure of arbitrators a problem from the perspective of the concept of the rule of law? What challenge and control procedures does the concept of the rule of law demand in regard to arbitrator independence and impartiality?

Rule of Law and Arbitral Procedure

3.8. Does the concept of the rule of law, in particular its due process component, contain requirements for how private-public arbitrations are to be conducted? Are there specific principles or procedural maxims that the concept of the rule of law demands private-public arbitration to conform to? Are these principles or maxims different from private-private arbitrations?

Rule of Law and Separation of Powers

3.9. Given that the function of domestic courts in private-public disputes is also to review whether public actors conduct themselves in accordance with the applicable law (ie ensuring accountability and responsibility of public actors), is it a problem from the perspective of the rule of law if arbitrators do not fulfil this function in the same way as courts? Does the concept of the rule of law require that private-public

[2] United Nations, 'Delivering Justice: Programme of Action to Strengthen the Rule of Law at the National and International Levels, Report of the Secretary General' (UN GAOR, 66th Session, Agenda Item 83, UN Doc A/66/749, 16 March 2012) para 2.

arbitrations provide the same extent of 'judicial review' of government conduct as domestic courts? Does the concept of the rule of law require that arbitrators be knowledgeable in the applicable law?

3.10. What about the impact of the concept of the rule of law in ensuring that arbitrators conduct themselves in accordance with the applicable procedural and substantive law? Does the rule of law mandate specific standards of review for domestic court supervision of arbitral tribunals? Does the rule of law require the application of specific standards concerning recognition and enforcement of arbitral awards?

Rule of Law and Legal Certainty/Predictability in Decision-Making

3.11. Are inconsistent or incoherent decisions a problem for the concept of the rule of law? What, if any, consequences does the concept of the rule of law demand in dealing with, or avoiding, inconsistent decisions?

C. Human/Fundamental Rights Problems with Private-Public Arbitration

Finally, problems may arise when disputes between private and public actors are arbitrated instead of litigated also in light of various considerations relating to the protection of fundamental or human rights. In this context, the following problems may exist from the perspective of constitutional law:

3.12. Do due process rights as the individual rights dimension of procedural rights impose certain requirements in respect of the procedure applied by arbitral tribunals or as regards the standard of review supervising courts apply to private-public arbitrations?

3.13. Is it, and if so under which circumstances, an access-to-justice problem if disputes with public actors are arbitrated instead of litigated? Does an agreement to arbitrate deprive private actors of constitutionally guaranteed rights to access to justice? Or is access to arbitration a form of access to justice from the perspective of constitutional law?

3.14. Is it a problem from the perspective of human/fundamental rights if arbitral tribunals rebalance competing rights through their lawmaking activities? What accountability and control mechanisms do human/fundamental rights require in regard to private-public arbitration?